Professional Resources

- **Document/Work Product Templates:** If you need examples of the format and content of software engineering work products, they are provided for you to download.

- **Software Engineering Checklists:** When you conduct a review or assess software engineering work products, it is a good idea to have a checklist to guide your evaluation. A wide variety of checklists are provided, and links to additional checklists are also included.

- **Tiny Tools:** There are lots of little things that lead to success in software engineering work. This collection of simple software engineering tools will help you with some of them.

- **Professional Tools (CASE):** "What is the best CASE tool for our situation?" is a commonly asked question. The SEPA, 7/e website provides you with links to hundreds of CASE tools and more than a few comparisons of these tools.

- **Software Engineering Resources:** If you need to do some research or take an online tutorial, the SEPA, 7/e website contains over 900 pointers to a broad array of software engineering topics.

- **Adaptable Process Model:** The adaptable process model is a comprehensive process template that can be tuned to your organization's needs.

- **Distance Learning:** An Internet-based curriculum, designed for use by individuals, teams, and entire software organizations, is available to supplement SEPA, 7/e. Information about this product is available at the website.

- **Industry Commentary:** A collection of short essays, extracted from a number of industry sources, is provided to help spur thoughtful debate.

Stu[dent Resources]

- **Study Guide:** Need a quick review during exam time? The Study Guide can help by summarizing the key points presented within each SEPA, 7/e chapter.

- **Self-Tests:** Have you learned the key points as you've read a chapter? Multiple-choice self-tests enable you to test your knowledge of chapter content and tell you where to look for the right answer.

- **Solved Problems:** Do you want to reinforce your understanding of key topics? SEPA, 7/e presents well over 300 problems for you to solve, and provides solutions for many of them.

- **Web-based Resources:** Need to learn a bit more about a software engineering topic? The SEPA, 7/e website contains over 900 pointers, organized by chapter, to a broad array of software engineering topics.

- **Case Study:** Would you like examples of software engineering work products? The case study provides running examples of all important software engineering work products.

- **Reference Library:** Have you been assigned some in-depth research? The SEPA, 7/e website provides access to over 500 downloadable papers on a broad array of software engineering topics.

- **Supplementary Content:** Need even more information? The site contains a collection of supplementary materials that expand on topics presented with the book.

- **Message Board:** Want to talk [with] other readers? The message bo[ard] promotes Q&A among stude[nts,] others, and provides a usef[ul] for informal communicati[on.]

Software Engineering

A PRACTITIONER'S APPROACH

SEVENTH EDITION

Roger S. Pressman, Ph.D.

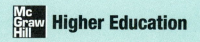 **Higher Education**

Boston   Burr Ridge, IL   Dubuque, IA   New York   San Francisco   St. Louis
Bangkok   Bogotá   Caracas   Kuala Lumpur   Lisbon   London   Madrid   Mexico City
Milan   Montreal   New Delhi   Santiago   Seoul   Singapore   Sydney   Taipei   Toronto

The McGraw-Hill Companies

Higher Education

SOFTWARE ENGINEERING: A PRACTITIONER'S APPROACH, SEVENTH EDITION

ISBN 978–0–07–337597–7
MHID 0–07–337597–7

Global Publisher: *Raghothaman Srinivasan*
Director of Development: *Kristine Tibbetts*
Senior Marketing Manager: *Curt Reynolds*
Senior Managing Editor: *Faye M. Schilling*
Lead Production Supervisor: *Sandy Ludovissy*
Senior Media Project Manager: *Sandra M. Schnee*
Associate Design Coordinator: *Brenda A. Rolwes*
Cover Designer: *Studio Montage, St. Louis, Missouri*
(USE) Cover Image: © *The Studio Dog/Getty Images*
Compositor: *Macmillan Publishing Solutions*
Typeface: *8.5/13.5 Leawood*
Printer: *R. R. Donnelley Crawfordsville, IN*

Library of Congress Cataloging-in-Publication Data

Pressman, Roger S.
  Software engineering : a practitioner's approach / Roger S. Pressman. — 7th ed.
      p. cm.
  Includes index.
  ISBN 978–0–07–337597–7 — ISBN 0–07–337597–7 (hard copy : alk. paper)
  1. Software engineering. I. Title.
QA76.758.P75   2010
005.1—dc22

                                                                          2008048802

In loving memory of my father who lived 94 years and taught me, above all, that honesty and integrity were the best guides for my journey through life.

Roger S. Pressman is an internationally recognized authority in software process improvement and software engineering technologies. For almost four decades, he has worked as a software engineer, a manager, a professor, an author, and a consultant, focusing on software engineering issues.

As an industry practitioner and manager, Dr. Pressman worked on the development of CAD/CAM systems for advanced engineering and manufacturing applications. He has also held positions with responsibility for scientific and systems programming.

After receiving a Ph.D. in engineering from the University of Connecticut, Dr. Pressman moved to academia where he became Bullard Associate Professor of Computer Engineering at the University of Bridgeport and director of the university's Computer-Aided Design and Manufacturing Center.

Dr. Pressman is currently president of R.S. Pressman & Associates, Inc., a consulting firm specializing in software engineering methods and training. He serves as principal consultant and has designed and developed *Essential Software Engineering,* a complete video curriculum in software engineering, and *Process Advisor,* a self-directed system for software process improvement. Both products are used by thousands of companies worldwide. More recently, he has worked in collaboration with *EdistaLearning* in India to develop comprehensive Internet-based training in software engineering.

Dr. Pressman has written many technical papers, is a regular contributor to industry periodicals, and is author of seven technical books. In addition to *Software Engineering: A Practitioner's Approach,* he has co-authored *Web Engineering* (McGraw-Hill), one of the first books to apply a tailored set of software engineering principles and practices to the development of Web-based systems and applications. He has also written the award-winning *A Manager's Guide to Software Engineering* (McGraw-Hill); *Making Software Engineering Happen* (Prentice Hall), the first book to address the critical management problems associated with software process improvement; and *Software Shock* (Dorset House), a treatment that focuses on software and its impact on business and society. Dr. Pressman has been on the editorial boards of a number of industry journals, and for many years, was editor of the "Manager" column in *IEEE Software.*

Dr. Pressman is a well-known speaker, keynoting a number of major industry conferences. He is a member of the IEEE, and Tau Beta Pi, Phi Kappa Phi, Eta Kappa Nu, and Pi Tau Sigma.

On the personal side, Dr. Pressman lives in South Florida with his wife, Barbara. An athlete for most of his life, he remains a serious tennis player (NTRP 4.5) and a single-digit handicap golfer. In his spare time, he has written two novels, The *Aymara Bridge* and *The Puppeteer,* and plans to begin work on another.

Contents at a Glance

TABLE OF CONTENTS

CHAPTER 6   REQUIREMENTS MODELING: SCENARIOS, INFORMATION, AND ANALYSIS CLASSES   148

CHAPTER 7   REQUIREMENTS MODELING: FLOW, BEHAVIOR, PATTERNS, AND WEBAPPS   186

CHAPTER 8   DESIGN CONCEPTS   215

CHAPTER 18   TESTING CONVENTIONAL APPLICATIONS   481

CHAPTER 19   TESTING OBJECT-ORIENTED APPLICATIONS   511

CHAPTER 20   TESTING WEB APPLICATIONS   529

When computer software succeeds—when it meets the needs of the people who use it, when it performs flawlessly over a long period of time, when it is easy to modify and even easier to use—it can and does change things for the better. But when software fails—when its users are dissatisfied, when it is error prone, when it is difficult to change and even harder to use—bad things can and do happen. We all want to build software that makes things better, avoiding the bad things that lurk in the shadow of failed efforts. To succeed, we need discipline when software is designed and built. We need an engineering approach.

It has been almost three decades since the first edition of this book was written. During that time, software engineering has evolved from an obscure idea practiced by a relatively small number of zealots to a legitimate engineering discipline. Today, it is recognized as a subject worthy of serious research, conscientious study, and tumultuous debate. Throughout the industry, software engineer has replaced programmer as the job title of preference. Software process models, software engineering methods, and software tools have been adopted successfully across a broad spectrum of industry segments.

Although managers and practitioners alike recognize the need for a more disciplined approach to software, they continue to debate the manner in which discipline is to be applied. Many individuals and companies still develop software haphazardly, even as they build systems to service today's most advanced technologies. Many professionals and students are unaware of modern methods. And as a result, the quality of the software that we produce suffers, and bad things happen. In addition, debate and controversy about the true nature of the software engineering approach continue. The status of software engineering is a study in contrasts. Attitudes have changed, progress has been made, but much remains to be done before the discipline reaches full maturity.

The seventh edition of *Software Engineering: A Practitioner's Approach* is intended to serve as a guide to a maturing engineering discipline. Like the six editions that preceded it, the seventh edition is intended for both students and practitioners, retaining its appeal as a guide to the industry professional and a comprehensive introduction to the student at the upper-level undergraduate or first-year graduate level.

The seventh edition is considerably more than a simple update. The book has been revised and restructured to improve pedagogical flow and emphasize new and important software engineering processes and practices. In addition, a revised and updated "support system," illustrated in the figure, provides a comprehensive set of student, instructor, and professional resources to complement the content of the book. These resources are presented as part of a website (www.mhhe.com/ pressman) specifically designed for *Software Engineering: A Practitioner's Approach*.

The Seventh Edition. The 32 chapters of the seventh edition have been reorganized into five parts. This organization, which differs considerably from the sixth edition, has been done to better compartmentalize topics and assist instructors who may not have the time to complete the entire book in one term.

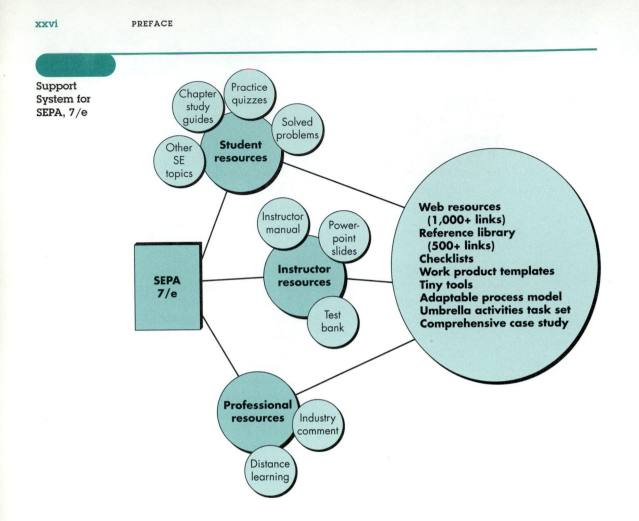

Part 1, *The Process,* presents a variety of different views of software process, considering all important process models and addressing the debate between prescriptive and agile process philosophies. Part 2, *Modeling,* presents analysis and design methods with an emphasis on object-oriented techniques and UML modeling. Pattern-based design and design for Web applications are also considered. Part 3, *Quality Management,* presents the concepts, procedures, techniques, and methods that enable a software team to assess software quality, review software engineering work products, conduct SQA procedures, and apply an effective testing strategy and tactics. In addition, formal modeling and verification methods are also considered. Part 4, *Managing Software Projects,* presents topics that are relevant to those who plan, manage, and control a software development project. Part 5, *Advanced Topics,* considers software process improvement and software engineering trends. Continuing in the tradition of past editions, a series of sidebars is used throughout the book to present the trials and tribulations of a (fictional) software team and to provide supplementary materials about methods and tools that are relevant to chapter topics. Two new appendices provide brief tutorials on UML and object-oriented thinking for those who may be unfamiliar with these important topics.

The five-part organization of the seventh edition enables an instructor to "cluster" topics based on available time and student need. An entire one-term course can be built around one or more of the five parts. A software engineering survey course would select chapters from all five parts. A software engineering course that emphasizes analysis and design would select topics from Parts 1 and 2. A testing-oriented software engineering course would select topics from Parts 1 and 3, with a brief foray into Part 2. A "management course" would stress Parts 1 and 4. By organizing the seventh edition in this way, I have attempted to provide an instructor with a number of teaching options. In every case, the content of the seventh edition is complemented by the following elements of the *SEPA, 7/e Support System*.

Student Resources. A wide variety of student resources includes an extensive online learning center encompassing chapter-by-chapter study guides, practice quizzes, problem solutions, and a variety of Web-based resources including software engineering checklists, an evolving collection of "tiny tools," a comprehensive case study, work product templates, and many other resources. In addition, over 1000 categorized *Web References* allow a student to explore software engineering in greater detail and a *Reference Library* with links to over 500 downloadable papers provides an in-depth source of advanced software engineering information.

Instructor Resources. A broad array of instructor resources has been developed to supplement the seventh edition. These include a complete online *Instructor's Guide* (also downloadable) and supplementary teaching materials including a complete set of over 700 *PowerPoint Slides* that may be used for lectures, and a test bank. Of course, all resources available for students (e.g., tiny tools, the Web References, the downloadable Reference Library) and professionals are also available.

The *Instructor's Guide for Software Engineering: A Practitioner's Approach* presents suggestions for conducting various types of software engineering courses, recommendations for a variety of software projects to be conducted in conjunction with a course, solutions to selected problems, and a number of useful teaching aids.

Professional Resources. A collection of resources available to industry practitioners (as well as students and faculty) includes outlines and samples of software engineering documents and other work products, a useful set of software engineering checklists, a catalog of software engineering (CASE) tools, a comprehensive collection of Web-based resources, and an "adaptable process model" that provides a detailed task breakdown of the software engineering process.

When coupled with its online support system, the seventh edition of *Software Engineering: A Practitioner's Approach,* provides flexibility and depth of content that cannot be achieved by a textbook alone.

Acknowledgments. My work on the seven editions of *Software Engineering: A Practitioner's Approach* has been the longest continuing technical project of my life. Even when the writing stops, information extracted from the technical literature continues to be assimilated and organized, and criticism and suggestions from readers worldwide is evaluated and cataloged. For this reason, my thanks to the many authors of books, papers, and articles (in both hardcopy and electronic media) who have provided me with additional insight, ideas, and commentary over nearly 30 years.

Special thanks go to Tim Lethbridge of the University of Ottawa, who assisted me in the development of UML and OCL examples and developed the case study that accompanies this book, and Dale Skrien of Colby College, who developed the UML tutorial in

Appendix 1. Their assistance and comments were invaluable. Special thanks also go to Bruce Maxim of the University of Michigan–Dearborn, who assisted me in developing much of the pedagogical website content that accompanies this book. Finally, I wish to thank the reviewers of the seventh edition: Their in-depth comments and thoughtful criticism have been invaluable.

Osman Balci,
  Virginia Tech University
Max Fomitchev,
  Penn State University
Jerry (Zeyu) Gao,
  San Jose State University
Guillermo Garcia,
  Universidad Alfonso X Madrid
Pablo Gervas,
  Universidad Complutense de Madrid

SK Jain,
  National Institute of Technology Hamirpur
Saeed Monemi,
  Cal Poly Pomona
Ahmed Salem,
  California State University
Vasudeva Varma,
  IIIT Hyderabad

The content of the seventh edition of *Software Engineering: A Practitioner's Approach* has been shaped by industry professionals, university professors, and students who have used earlier editions of the book and have taken the time to communicate their suggestions, criticisms, and ideas. My thanks to each of you. In addition, my personal thanks go to our many industry clients worldwide, who certainly have taught me as much or more than I could ever teach them.

As the editions of this book have evolved, my sons, Mathew and Michael, have grown from boys to men. Their maturity, character, and success in the real world have been an inspiration to me. Nothing has filled me with more pride. And finally, to Barbara, my love and thanks for tolerating the many, many hours in the office and encouraging still another edition of "the book."

Roger S. Pressman

SOFTWARE AND
SOFTWARE ENGINEERING

He had the classic look of a senior executive for a major software company—mid-40s, slightly graying at the temples, trim and athletic, with eyes that penetrated the listener as he spoke. But what he said shocked me. "Software is *dead*."

I blinked with surprise and then smiled. "You're joking, right? The world is driven by software and your company has profited handsomely because of it. It isn't dead! It's alive and growing."

He shook his head emphatically. "No, it's dead . . . at least as we once knew it."

I leaned forward. "Go on."

He spoke while tapping the table for emphasis. "The old-school view of software—you buy it, you own it, and it's your job to manage it—that's coming to an end. Today, with Web 2.0 and pervasive computing coming on strong, we're going to be seeing a completely different generation of software. It'll be delivered via the Internet and will look exactly like it's residing on each user's computing device . . . but it'll reside on a far-away server."

QUICK LOOK

What is it? Computer software is the product that software professionals build and then support over the long term. It encompasses programs that execute within a computer of any size and architecture, content that is presented as the computer programs execute, and descriptive information in both hard copy and virtual forms that encompass virtually any electronic media. Software engineering encompasses a process, a collection of methods (practice) and an array of tools that allow professionals to build high-quality computer software.

Who does it? Software engineers build and support software, and virtually everyone in the industrialized world uses it either directly or indirectly.

Why is it important? Software is important because it affects nearly every aspect of our lives and has become pervasive in our commerce, our culture, and our everyday activities.

Software engineering is important because it enables us to build complex systems in a timely manner and with high quality.

What are the steps? You build computer software like you build any successful product, by applying an agile, adaptable process that leads to a high-quality result that meets the needs of the people who will use the product. You apply a software engineering approach.

What is the work product? From the point of view of a software engineer, the work product is the set of programs, content (data), and other work products that are computer software. But from the user's viewpoint, the work product is the resultant information that somehow makes the user's world better.

How do I ensure that I've done it right? Read the remainder of this book, select those ideas that are applicable to the software that you build, and apply them to your work.

I had to agree. "So, your life will be much simpler. You guys won't have to worry about five different versions of the same App in use across tens of thousands of users."

He smiled. "Absolutely. Only the most current version residing on our servers. When we make a change or a correction, we supply updated functionality and content to every user. Everyone has it instantly!"

I grimaced. "But if you make a mistake, everyone has that instantly as well."

He chuckled. "True, that's why we're redoubling our efforts to do even better software engineering. Problem is, we have to do it 'fast' because the market has accelerated in every application area."

I leaned back and put my hands behind my head. "You know what they say, . . . you can have it fast, you can have it right, or you can have it cheap. Pick two!"

"I'll take it fast and right," he said as he began to get up.

I stood as well. "Then you really do need software engineering."

"I know that," he said as he began to move away. "The problem is, we've got to convince still another generation of techies that it's true!"

Is software *really* dead? If it was, you wouldn't be reading this book!

Computer software continues to be the single most important technology on the world stage. And it's also a prime example of the law of unintended consequences. Fifty years ago no one could have predicted that software would become an indispensable technology for business, science, and engineering; that software would enable the creation of new technologies (e.g., genetic engineering and nanotechnology), the extension of existing technologies (e.g., telecommunications), and the radical change in older technologies (e.g., the printing industry); that software would be the driving force behind the personal computer revolution; that shrink-wrapped software products would be purchased by consumers in neighborhood malls; that software would slowly evolve from a product to a service as "on-demand" software companies deliver just-in-time functionality via a Web browser; that a software company would become larger and more influential than almost all industrial-era companies; that a vast software-driven network called the Internet would evolve and change everything from library research to consumer shopping to political discourse to the dating habits of young (and not so young) adults.

No one could foresee that software would become embedded in systems of all kinds: transportation, medical, telecommunications, military, industrial, entertainment, office machines, . . . the list is almost endless. And if you believe the law of unintended consequences, there are many effects that we cannot yet predict.

No one could predict that millions of computer programs would have to be corrected, adapted, and enhanced as time passed. The burden of performing these "maintenance" activities would absorb more people and more resources than all work applied to the creation of new software.

As software's importance has grown, the software community has continually attempted to develop technologies that will make it easier, faster, and less expensive

Quote:

"Ideas and technological discoveries are the driving engines of economic growth."

Wall Street Journal

to build and maintain high-quality computer programs. Some of these technologies are targeted at a specific application domain (e.g., website design and implementation); others focus on a technology domain (e.g., object-oriented systems or aspect-oriented programming); and still others are broad-based (e.g., operating systems such as Linux). However, we have yet to develop a software technology that does it all, and the likelihood of one arising in the future is small. And yet, people bet their jobs, their comforts, their safety, their entertainment, their decisions, and their very lives on computer software. It better be right.

This book presents a framework that can be used by those who build computer software—people who must get it right. The framework encompasses a process, a set of methods, and an array of tools that we call *software engineering*.

1.1 THE NATURE OF SOFTWARE

KEY POINT

Software is both a product and a vehicle that delivers a product.

Today, software takes on a dual role. It is a product, and at the same time, the vehicle for delivering a product. As a product, it delivers the computing potential embodied by computer hardware or more broadly, by a network of computers that are accessible by local hardware. Whether it resides within a mobile phone or operates inside a mainframe computer, software is an information transformer—producing, managing, acquiring, modifying, displaying, or transmitting information that can be as simple as a single bit or as complex as a multimedia presentation derived from data acquired from dozens of independent sources. As the vehicle used to deliver the product, software acts as the basis for the control of the computer (operating systems), the communication of information (networks), and the creation and control of other programs (software tools and environments).

Software delivers the most important product of our time—*information*. It transforms personal data (e.g., an individual's financial transactions) so that the data can be more useful in a local context; it manages business information to enhance competitiveness; it provides a gateway to worldwide information networks (e.g., the Internet), and provides the means for acquiring information in all of its forms.

The role of computer software has undergone significant change over the last half-century. Dramatic improvements in hardware performance, profound changes in computing architectures, vast increases in memory and storage capacity, and a wide variety of exotic input and output options, have all precipitated more sophisticated and complex computer-based systems. Sophistication and complexity can produce dazzling results when a system succeeds, but they can also pose huge problems for those who must build complex systems.

uote:

"Software is a place where dreams are planted and nightmares harvested, an abstract, mystical swamp where terrible demons compete with magical panaceas, a world of werewolves and silver bullets."

Brad J. Cox

Today, a huge software industry has become a dominant factor in the economies of the industrialized world. Teams of software specialists, each focusing on one part of the technology required to deliver a complex application, have replaced the lone programmer of an earlier era. And yet, the questions that were asked of the lone programmer are the same questions that are asked when modern computer-based systems are built:[1]

- Why does it take so long to get software finished?
- Why are development costs so high?
- Why can't we find all errors before we give the software to our customers?
- Why do we spend so much time and effort maintaining existing programs?
- Why do we continue to have difficulty in measuring progress as software is being developed and maintained?

These, and many other questions, are a manifestation of the concern about software and the manner in which it is developed—a concern that has lead to the adoption of software engineering practice.

1.1.1   Defining Software

Today, most professionals and many members of the public at large feel that they understand software. But do they?

A textbook description of software might take the following form:

How should we define software?

> Software is: (1) instructions (computer programs) that when executed provide desired features, function, and performance; (2) data structures that enable the programs to adequately manipulate information, and (3) descriptive information in both hard copy and virtual forms that describes the operation and use of the programs.

There is no question that other more complete definitions could be offered.

But a more formal definition probably won't measurably improve your understanding. To accomplish that, it's important to examine the characteristics of software that make it different from other things that human beings build. Software is a logical rather than a physical system element. Therefore, software has characteristics that are considerably different than those of hardware:

KEY POINT

Software is engineered, not manufactured.

1. *Software is developed or engineered; it is not manufactured in the classical sense.*

   Although some similarities exist between software development and hardware manufacturing, the two activities are fundamentally different. In both activities, high quality is achieved through good design, but the manufacturing phase for hardware can introduce quality problems that are nonexistent

---

1   In an excellent book of essays on the software business, Tom DeMarco [DeM95] argues the counterpoint. He states: "Instead of asking why software costs so much, we need to begin asking 'What have we done to make it possible for today's software to cost so little?' The answer to that question will help us continue the extraordinary level of achievement that has always distinguished the software industry."

FIGURE 1.1

Failure curve
for hardware

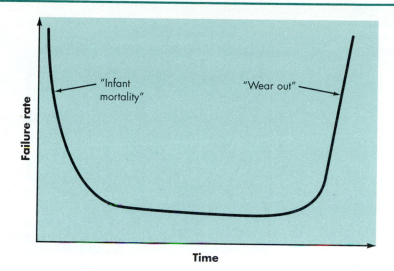

(or easily corrected) for software. Both activities are dependent on people, but the relationship between people applied and work accomplished is entirely different (see Chapter 24). Both activities require the construction of a "product," but the approaches are different. Software costs are concentrated in engineering. This means that software projects cannot be managed as if they were manufacturing projects.

2. *Software doesn't "wear out."*

KEY POINT

Software doesn't wear
out, but it does
deteriorate.

Figure 1.1 depicts failure rate as a function of time for hardware. The relationship, often called the "bathtub curve," indicates that hardware exhibits relatively high failure rates early in its life (these failures are often attributable to design or manufacturing defects); defects are corrected and the failure rate drops to a steady-state level (hopefully, quite low) for some period of time. As time passes, however, the failure rate rises again as hardware components suffer from the cumulative effects of dust, vibration, abuse, temperature extremes, and many other environmental maladies. Stated simply, the hardware begins to *wear out.*

ADVICE

*If you want to reduce
software deterioration,
you'll have to do
better software design
(Chapters 8 to 13).*

Software is not susceptible to the environmental maladies that cause hardware to wear out. In theory, therefore, the failure rate curve for software should take the form of the "idealized curve" shown in Figure 1.2. Undiscovered defects will cause high failure rates early in the life of a program. However, these are corrected and the curve flattens as shown. The idealized curve is a gross oversimplification of actual failure models for software. However, the implication is clear—software doesn't wear out. But it does *deteriorate!*

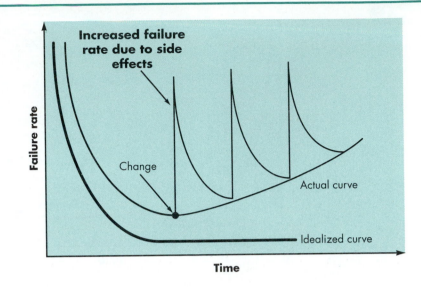

Increased failure rate due to side effects

Failure rate

Change

Actual curve

Idealized curve

Time

This seeming contradiction can best be explained by considering the actual curve in Figure 1.2. During its life,[2] software will undergo change. As changes are made, it is likely that errors will be introduced, causing the failure rate curve to spike as shown in the "actual curve" (Figure 1.2). Before the curve can return to the original steady-state failure rate, another change is requested, causing the curve to spike again. Slowly, the minimum failure rate level begins to rise—the software is deteriorating due to change.

Another aspect of wear illustrates the difference between hardware and software. When a hardware component wears out, it is replaced by a spare part. There are no software spare parts. Every software failure indicates an error in design or in the process through which design was translated into machine executable code. Therefore, the software maintenance tasks that accommodate requests for change involve considerably more complexity than hardware maintenance.

3. *Although the industry is moving toward component-based construction, most software continues to be custom built.*

As an engineering discipline evolves, a collection of standard design components is created. Standard screws and off-the-shelf integrated circuits are only two of thousands of standard components that are used by mechanical and electrical engineers as they design new systems. The reusable components have been created so that the engineer can concentrate on the truly innovative elements of a design, that is, the parts of the design that represent

2   In fact, from the moment that development begins and long before the first version is delivered, changes may be requested by a variety of different stakeholders.

something new. In the hardware world, component reuse is a natural part of the engineering process. In the software world, it is something that has only begun to be achieved on a broad scale.

A software component should be designed and implemented so that it can be reused in many different programs. Modern reusable components encapsulate both data and the processing that is applied to the data, enabling the software engineer to create new applications from reusable parts.[3] For example, today's interactive user interfaces are built with reusable components that enable the creation of graphics windows, pull-down menus, and a wide variety of interaction mechanisms. The data structures and processing detail required to build the interface are contained within a library of reusable components for interface construction.

1.1.2 Software Application Domains

Today, seven broad categories of computer software present continuing challenges for software engineers:

System software—a collection of programs written to service other programs. Some system software (e.g., compilers, editors, and file management utilities) processes complex, but determinate,[4] information structures. Other systems applications (e.g., operating system components, drivers, networking software, telecommunications processors) process largely indeterminate data. In either case, the systems software area is characterized by heavy interaction with computer hardware; heavy usage by multiple users; concurrent operation that requires scheduling, resource sharing, and sophisticated process management; complex data structures; and multiple external interfaces.

WebRef

One of the most comprehensive libraries of shareware/ freeware can be found at **shareware.cnet .com**

Application software—stand-alone programs that solve a specific business need. Applications in this area process business or technical data in a way that facilitates business operations or management/technical decision making. In addition to conventional data processing applications, application software is used to control business functions in real time (e.g., point-of-sale transaction processing, real-time manufacturing process control).

Engineering/scientific software—has been characterized by "number crunching" algorithms. Applications range from astronomy to volcanology, from automotive stress analysis to space shuttle orbital dynamics, and from molecular biology to automated manufacturing. However, modern applications within the engineering/scientific area are moving away from

---

3 Component-based development is discussed in Chapter 10.

4 Software is *determinate* if the order and timing of inputs, processing, and outputs is predictable. Software is *indeterminate* if the order and timing of inputs, processing, and outputs cannot be predicted in advance.

conventional numerical algorithms. Computer-aided design, system simulation, and other interactive applications have begun to take on real-time and even system software characteristics.

Embedded software—resides within a product or system and is used to implement and control features and functions for the end user and for the system itself. Embedded software can perform limited and esoteric functions (e.g., key pad control for a microwave oven) or provide significant function and control capability (e.g., digital functions in an automobile such as fuel control, dashboard displays, and braking systems).

Product-line software—designed to provide a specific capability for use by many different customers. Product-line software can focus on a limited and esoteric marketplace (e.g., inventory control products) or address mass consumer markets (e.g., word processing, spreadsheets, computer graphics, multimedia, entertainment, database management, and personal and business financial applications).

Web applications—called "WebApps," this network-centric software category spans a wide array of applications. In their simplest form, WebApps can be little more than a set of linked hypertext files that present information using text and limited graphics. However, as Web 2.0 emerges, WebApps are evolving into sophisticated computing environments that not only provide stand-alone features, computing functions, and content to the end user, but also are integrated with corporate databases and business applications.

Artificial intelligence software—makes use of nonnumerical algorithms to solve complex problems that are not amenable to computation or straightforward analysis. Applications within this area include robotics, expert systems, pattern recognition (image and voice), artificial neural networks, theorem proving, and game playing.

Quote:

"There is no computer that has common sense."

Marvin Minsky

Millions of software engineers worldwide are hard at work on software projects in one or more of these categories. In some cases, new systems are being built, but in many others, existing applications are being corrected, adapted, and enhanced. It is not uncommon for a young software engineer to work a program that is older than she is! Past generations of software people have left a legacy in each of the categories I have discussed. Hopefully, the legacy to be left behind by this generation will ease the burden of future software engineers. And yet, new challenges (Chapter 31) have appeared on the horizon:

Open-world computing—the rapid growth of wireless networking may soon lead to true pervasive, distributed computing. The challenge for software engineers will be to develop systems and application software that will allow mobile devices, personal computers, and enterprise systems to communicate across vast networks.

Netsourcing—the World Wide Web is rapidly becoming a computing engine as well as a content provider. The challenge for software engineers is to architect simple (e.g., personal financial planning) and sophisticated applications that provide a benefit to targeted end-user markets worldwide.

Open source—a growing trend that results in distribution of source code for systems applications (e.g., operating systems, database, and development environments) so that many people can contribute to its development. The challenge for software engineers is to build source code that is self-descriptive, but more importantly, to develop techniques that will enable both customers and developers to know what changes have been made and how those changes manifest themselves within the software.

uote:

"You can't always predict, but you can always prepare."

Anonymous

Each of these new challenges will undoubtedly obey the law of unintended consequences and have effects (for businesspeople, software engineers, and end users) that cannot be predicted today. However, software engineers can prepare by instantiating a process that is agile and adaptable enough to accommodate dramatic changes in technology and to business rules that are sure to come over the next decade.

1.1.3 Legacy Software

Hundreds of thousands of computer programs fall into one of the seven broad application domains discussed in the preceding subsection. Some of these are state-of-the-art software—just released to individuals, industry, and government. But other programs are older, in some cases *much* older.

These older programs—often referred to as *legacy software*—have been the focus of continuous attention and concern since the 1960s. Dayani-Fard and his colleagues [Day99] describe legacy software in the following way:

> Legacy software systems . . . were developed decades ago and have been continually modified to meet changes in business requirements and computing platforms. The proliferation of such systems is causing headaches for large organizations who find them costly to maintain and risky to evolve.

Liu and his colleagues [Liu98] extend this description by noting that "many legacy systems remain supportive to core business functions and are 'indispensable' to the business." Hence, legacy software is characterized by longevity and business criticality.

? What do I do if I encounter a legacy system that exhibits poor quality?

Unfortunately, there is sometimes one additional characteristic that is present in legacy software—*poor quality*.[5] Legacy systems sometimes have inextensible designs, convoluted code, poor or nonexistent documentation, test cases and results

---

5 In this case, quality is judged based on modern software engineering thinking—a somewhat unfair criterion since some modern software engineering concepts and principles may not have been well understood at the time that the legacy software was developed.

that were never archived, a poorly managed change history—the list can be quite long. And yet, these systems support "core business functions and are indispensable to the business." What to do?

The only reasonable answer may be: *Do nothing,* at least until the legacy system must undergo some significant change. If the legacy software meets the needs of its users and runs reliably, it isn't broken and does not need to be fixed. However, as time passes, legacy systems often evolve for one or more of the following reasons:

What types of changes are made to legacy systems?

- The software must be adapted to meet the needs of new computing environments or technology.

- The software must be enhanced to implement new business requirements.

- The software must be extended to make it interoperable with other more modern systems or databases.

- The software must be re-architected to make it viable within a network environment.

ADVICE

Every software engineer must recognize that change is natural. Don't try to fight it.

When these modes of evolution occur, a legacy system must be reengineered (Chapter 29) so that it remains viable into the future. The goal of modern software engineering is to "devise methodologies that are founded on the notion of evolution"; that is, the notion that software systems continually change, new software systems are built from the old ones, and . . . all must interoperate and cooperate with each other" [Day99].

1.2   THE UNIQUE NATURE OF WEBAPPS

Quote:

"By the time we see any sort of stabilization, the Web will have turned into something completely different."

Louis Monier

In the early days of the World Wide Web (circa 1990 to 1995), *websites* consisted of little more than a set of linked hypertext files that presented information using text and limited graphics. As time passed, the augmentation of HTML by development tools (e.g., XML, Java) enabled Web engineers to provide computing capability along with informational content. *Web-based systems and applications*[6] (I refer to these collectively as *WebApps*) were born. Today, WebApps have evolved into sophisticated computing tools that not only provide stand-alone function to the end user, but also have been integrated with corporate databases and business applications.

As noted in Section 1.1.2, WebApps are one of a number of distinct software categories. And yet, it can be argued that WebApps are different. Powell [Pow98] suggests that Web-based systems and applications "involve a mixture between print publishing and software development, between marketing and computing, between

---

6   In the context of this book, the term *Web application* (WebApp) encompasses everything from a simple Web page that might help a consumer compute an automobile lease payment to a comprehensive website that provides complete travel services for businesspeople and vacationers. Included within this category are complete websites, specialized functionality within websites, and information processing applications that reside on the Internet or on an Intranet or Extranet.

internal communications and external relations, and between art and technology." The following attributes are encountered in the vast majority of WebApps.

? What characteristic differentiates WebApps from other software?

Network intensiveness.   A WebApp resides on a network and must serve the needs of a diverse community of clients. The network may enable world-wide access and communication (i.e., the Internet) or more limited access and communication (e.g., a corporate Intranet).

Concurrency.   A large number of users may access the WebApp at one time. In many cases, the patterns of usage among end users will vary greatly.

Unpredictable load.   The number of users of the WebApp may vary by orders of magnitude from day to day. One hundred users may show up on Monday; 10,000 may use the system on Thursday.

Performance.   If a WebApp user must wait too long (for access, for server-side processing, for client-side formatting and display), he or she may decide to go elsewhere.

Availability.   Although expectation of 100 percent availability is unreasonable, users of popular WebApps often demand access on a 24/7/365 basis. Users in Australia or Asia might demand access during times when traditional domestic software applications in North America might be taken off-line for maintenance.

Data driven.   The primary function of many WebApps is to use hypermedia to present text, graphics, audio, and video content to the end user. In addition, WebApps are commonly used to access information that exists on databases that are not an integral part of the Web-based environment (e.g., e-commerce or financial applications).

Content sensitive.   The quality and aesthetic nature of content remains an important determinant of the quality of a WebApp.

Continuous evolution.   Unlike conventional application software that evolves over a series of planned, chronologically spaced releases, Web applications evolve continuously. It is not unusual for some WebApps (specifically, their content) to be updated on a minute-by-minute schedule or for content to be independently computed for each request.

Immediacy.   Although *immediacy*—the compelling need to get software to market quickly—is a characteristic of many application domains, WebApps often exhibit a time-to-market that can be a matter of a few days or weeks.[7]

Security.   Because WebApps are available via network access, it is difficult, if not impossible, to limit the population of end users who may access the application. In order to protect sensitive content and provide secure modes

---

7   With modern tools, sophisticated Web pages can be produced in only a few hours.

of data transmission, strong security measures must be implemented throughout the infrastructure that supports a WebApp and within the application itself.

Aesthetics.   An undeniable part of the appeal of a WebApp is its look and feel. When an application has been designed to market or sell products or ideas, aesthetics may have as much to do with success as technical design.

It can be argued that other application categories discussed in Section 1.1.2 can exhibit some of the attributes noted. However, WebApps almost always exhibit all of them.

1.3   SOFTWARE ENGINEERING

In order to build software that is ready to meet the challenges of the twenty-first century, you must recognize a few simple realities:

Understand the problem before you build a solution.

- Software has become deeply embedded in virtually every aspect of our lives, and as a consequence, the number of people who have an interest in the features and functions provided by a specific application[8] has grown dramatically. When a new application or embedded system is to be built, many voices must be heard. And it sometimes seems that each of them has a slightly different idea of what software features and functions should be delivered. *It follows that a concerted effort should be made to understand the problem before a software solution is developed.*

Design is a pivotal software engineering activity.

- The information technology requirements demanded by individuals, businesses, and governments grow increasing complex with each passing year. Large teams of people now create computer programs that were once built by a single individual. Sophisticated software that was once implemented in a predictable, self-contained, computing environment is now embedded inside everything from consumer electronics to medical devices to weapons systems. The complexity of these new computer-based systems and products demands careful attention to the interactions of all system elements. *It follows that design becomes a pivotal activity.*

Both quality and maintainability are an outgrowth of good design.

- Individuals, businesses, and governments increasingly rely on software for strategic and tactical decision making as well as day-to-day operations and control. If the software fails, people and major enterprises can experience anything from minor inconvenience to catastrophic failures. *It follows that software should exhibit high quality.*

- As the perceived value of a specific application grows, the likelihood is that its user base and longevity will also grow. As its user base and time-in-use

---

8   I will call these people "stakeholders" later in this book.

increase, demands for adaptation and enhancement will also grow. *It follows that software should be maintainable.*

These simple realities lead to one conclusion: *software in all of its forms and across all of its application domains should be engineered.* And that leads us to the topic of this book—*software engineering.*

Although hundreds of authors have developed personal definitions of software engineering, a definition proposed by Fritz Bauer [Nau69] at the seminal conference on the subject still serves as a basis for discussion:

> [Software engineering is] the establishment and use of sound engineering principles in order to obtain economically software that is reliable and works efficiently on real machines.

You will be tempted to add to this definition.[9] It says little about the technical aspects of software quality; it does not directly address the need for customer satisfaction or timely product delivery; it omits mention of the importance of measurement and metrics; it does not state the importance of an effective process. And yet, Bauer's definition provides us with a baseline. What are the "sound engineering principles" that can be applied to computer software development? How do we "economically" build software so that it is "reliable"? What is required to create computer programs that work "efficiently" on not one but many different "real machines"? These are the questions that continue to challenge software engineers.

The IEEE [IEE93a] has developed a more comprehensive definition when it states:

How do we define software engineering?

> Software Engineering: (1) The application of a systematic, disciplined, quantifiable approach to the development, operation, and maintenance of software; that is, the application of engineering to software. (2) The study of approaches as in (1).

And yet, a "systematic, disciplined, and quantifiable" approach applied by one software team may be burdensome to another. We need discipline, but we also need adaptability and agility.

Software engineering is a layered technology. Referring to Figure 1.3, any engineering approach (including software engineering) must rest on an organizational commitment to quality. Total quality management, Six Sigma, and similar philosophies[10] foster a continuous process improvement culture, and it is this culture that ultimately leads to the development of increasingly more effective approaches to software engineering. The bedrock that supports software engineering is a quality focus.

KEY POINT

Software engineering encompasses a process, methods for managing and engineering software, and tools.

The foundation for software engineering is the *process* layer. The software engineering process is the glue that holds the technology layers together and enables rational and timely development of computer software. Process defines a framework

---

9 For numerous additional definitions of *software engineering,* see www.answers.com/topic/software-engineering#wp-_note-13.

10 Quality management and related approaches are discussed in Chapter 14 and throughout Part 3 of this book.

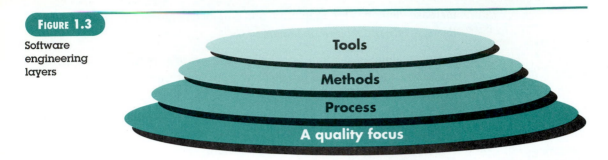

that must be established for effective delivery of software engineering technology. The software process forms the basis for management control of software projects and establishes the context in which technical methods are applied, work products (models, documents, data, reports, forms, etc.) are produced, milestones are established, quality is ensured, and change is properly managed.

Software engineering *methods* provide the technical how-to's for building software. Methods encompass a broad array of tasks that include communication, requirements analysis, design modeling, program construction, testing, and support. Software engineering methods rely on a set of basic principles that govern each area of the technology and include modeling activities and other descriptive techniques.

Software engineering *tools* provide automated or semiautomated support for the process and the methods. When tools are integrated so that information created by one tool can be used by another, a system for the support of software development, called *computer-aided software engineering*, is established.

1.4   THE SOFTWARE PROCESS

A *process* is a collection of activities, actions, and tasks that are performed when some work product is to be created. An *activity* strives to achieve a broad objective (e.g., communication with stakeholders) and is applied regardless of the application domain, size of the project, complexity of the effort, or degree of rigor with which software engineering is to be applied. An *action* (e.g., architectural design) encompasses a set of tasks that produce a major work product (e.g., an architectural design model). A *task* focuses on a small, but well-defined objective (e.g., conducting a unit test) that produces a tangible outcome.

In the context of software engineering, a process is *not* a rigid prescription for how to build computer software. Rather, it is an adaptable approach that enables the people doing the work (the software team) to pick and choose the appropriate set of work actions and tasks. The intent is always to deliver software in a timely manner and with sufficient quality to satisfy those who have sponsored its creation and those who will use it.

A *process framework* establishes the foundation for a complete software engineering process by identifying a small number of *framework activities* that are applicable to all software projects, regardless of their size or complexity. In addition, the process framework encompasses a set of *umbrella activities* that are applicable across the entire software process. A generic process framework for software engineering encompasses five activities:

? **What are the five generic process framework activities?**

Communication. Before any technical work can commence, it is critically important to communicate and collaborate with the customer (and other stakeholders[11] The intent is to understand stakeholders' objectives for the project and to gather requirements that help define software features and functions.

Planning. Any complicated journey can be simplified if a map exists. A software project is a complicated journey, and the planning activity creates a "map" that helps guide the team as it makes the journey. The map—called a *software project plan*—defines the software engineering work by describing the technical tasks to be conducted, the risks that are likely, the resources that will be required, the work products to be produced, and a work schedule.

Modeling. Whether you're a landscaper, a bridge builder, an aeronautical engineer, a carpenter, or an architect, you work with models every day. You create a "sketch" of the thing so that you'll understand the big picture—what it will look like architecturally, how the constituent parts fit together, and many other characteristics. If required, you refine the sketch into greater and greater detail in an effort to better understand the problem and how you're going to solve it. A software engineer does the same thing by creating models to better understand software requirements and the design that will achieve those requirements.

Construction. This activity combines code generation (either manual or automated) and the testing that is required to uncover errors in the code.

Deployment. The software (as a complete entity or as a partially completed increment) is delivered to the customer who evaluates the delivered product and provides feedback based on the evaluation.

> **uote:**
>
> "Einstein argued that there must be a simplified explanation of nature, because God is not capricious or arbitrary. No such faith comforts the software engineer. Much of the complexity that he must master is arbitrary complexity."
>
> **Fred Brooks**

These five generic framework activities can be used during the development of small, simple programs, the creation of large Web applications, and for the engineering of large, complex computer-based systems. The details of the software process will be quite different in each case, but the framework activities remain the same.

---

11 A *stakeholder* is anyone who has a stake in the successful outcome of the project—business managers, end users, software engineers, support people, etc. Rob Thomsett jokes that, "a stakeholder is a person holding a large and sharp stake. . . . If you don't look after your stakeholders, you know where the stake will end up.").

For many software projects, framework activities are applied iteratively as a project progresses. That is, **communication, planning, modeling, construction,** and **deployment** are applied repeatedly through a number of project iterations. Each project iteration produces a *software increment* that provides stakeholders with a subset of overall software features and functionality. As each increment is produced, the software becomes more and more complete.

Software engineering process framework activities are complemented by a number of *umbrella activities.* In general, umbrella activities are applied throughout a software project and help a software team manage and control progress, quality, change, and risk. Typical umbrella activities include:

Software project tracking and control—allows the software team to assess progress against the project plan and take any necessary action to maintain the schedule.

Risk management—assesses risks that may affect the outcome of the project or the quality of the product.

Software quality assurance—defines and conducts the activities required to ensure software quality.

Technical reviews—assesses software engineering work products in an effort to uncover and remove errors before they are propagated to the next activity.

Measurement—defines and collects process, project, and product measures that assist the team in delivering software that meets stakeholders' needs; can be used in conjunction with all other framework and umbrella activities.

Software configuration management—manages the effects of change throughout the software process.

Reusability management—defines criteria for work product reuse (including software components) and establishes mechanisms to achieve reusable components.

Work product preparation and production—encompasses the activities required to create work products such as models, documents, logs, forms, and lists.

Each of these umbrella activities is discussed in detail later in this book.

Earlier in this section, I noted that the software engineering process is not a rigid prescription that must be followed dogmatically by a software team. Rather, it should be agile and adaptable (to the problem, to the project, to the team, and to the organizational culture). Therefore, a process adopted for one project might be significantly different than a process adopted for another project. Among the differences are

? How do process models differ from one another?

- Overall flow of activities, actions, and tasks and the interdependencies among them
- Degree to which actions and tasks are defined within each framework activity
- Degree to which work products are identified and required

- Manner in which quality assurance activities are applied
- Manner in which project tracking and control activities are applied
- Overall degree of detail and rigor with which the process is described
- Degree to which the customer and other stakeholders are involved with the project
- Level of autonomy given to the software team
- Degree to which team organization and roles are prescribed

In Part 1 of this book, I'll examine software process in considerable detail. *Prescriptive process models* (Chapter 2) stress detailed definition, identification, and application of process activities and tasks. Their intent is to improve system quality, make projects more manageable, make delivery dates and costs more predictable, and guide teams of software engineers as they perform the work required to build a system. Unfortunately, there have been times when these objectives were not achieved. If prescriptive models are applied dogmatically and without adaptation, they can increase the level of bureaucracy associated with building computer-based systems and inadvertently create difficulty for all stakeholders.

 What characterizes an "agile" process?

Agile process models (Chapter 3) emphasize project "agility" and follow a set of principles that lead to a more informal (but, proponents argue, no less effective) approach to software process. These process models are generally characterized as "agile" because they emphasize maneuverability and adaptability. They are appropriate for many types of projects and are particularly useful when Web applications are engineered.

1.5 SOFTWARE ENGINEERING PRACTICE

In Section 1.4, I introduced a generic software process model composed of a set of activities that establish a framework for software engineering practice. Generic framework activities—**communication, planning, modeling, construction,** and **deployment**—and umbrella activities establish a skeleton architecture for software engineering work. But how does the practice of software engineering fit in? In the sections that follow, you'll gain a basic understanding of the generic concepts and principles that apply to framework activities.[12]

1.5.1 The Essence of Practice

In a classic book, *How to Solve It,* written before modern computers existed, George Polya [Pol45] outlined the essence of problem solving, and consequently, the essence of software engineering practice:

1. *Understand the problem* (communication and analysis).
2. *Plan a solution* (modeling and software design).

---

12 You should revisit relevant sections within this chapter as specific software engineering methods and umbrella activities are discussed later in this book.

3. *Carry out the plan* (code generation).

4. *Examine the result for accuracy* (testing and quality assurance).

In the context of software engineering, these commonsense steps lead to a series of essential questions [adapted from Pol45]:

Understand the problem.   It's sometimes difficult to admit, but most of us suffer from hubris when we're presented with a problem. We listen for a few seconds and then think, *Oh yeah, I understand, let's get on with solving this thing.* Unfortunately, understanding isn't always that easy. It's worth spending a little time answering a few simple questions:

- *Who has a stake in the solution to the problem?* That is, who are the stake-holders?

- *What are the unknowns?* What data, functions, and features are required to properly solve the problem?

- *Can the problem be compartmentalized?* Is it possible to represent smaller problems that may be easier to understand?

- *Can the problem be represented graphically?* Can an analysis model be created?

Plan the solution.   Now you understand the problem (or so you think) and you can't wait to begin coding. Before you do, slow down just a bit and do a little design:

- *Have you seen similar problems before?* Are there patterns that are recognizable in a potential solution? Is there existing software that implements the data, functions, and features that are required?

- *Has a similar problem been solved?* If so, are elements of the solution reusable?

- *Can subproblems be defined?* If so, are solutions readily apparent for the subproblems?

- *Can you represent a solution in a manner that leads to effective implementation?* Can a design model be created?

Carry out the plan.   The design you've created serves as a road map for the system you want to build. There may be unexpected detours, and it's possible that you'll discover an even better route as you go, but the "plan" will allow you to proceed without getting lost.

- *Does the solution conform to the plan?* Is source code traceable to the design model?

- *Is each component part of the solution provably correct?* Have the design and code been reviewed, or better, have correctness proofs been applied to the algorithm?

Examine the result.   You can't be sure that your solution is perfect, but you can be sure that you've designed a sufficient number of tests to uncover as many errors as possible.

- *Is it possible to test each component part of the solution?* Has a reasonable testing strategy been implemented?
- *Does the solution produce results that conform to the data, functions, and features that are required?* Has the software been validated against all stakeholder requirements?

It shouldn't surprise you that much of this approach is common sense. In fact, it's reasonable to state that a commonsense approach to software engineering will never lead you astray.

1.5.2 General Principles

The dictionary defines the word *principle* as "an important underlying law or assumption required in a system of thought." Throughout this book I'll discuss principles at many different levels of abstraction. Some focus on software engineering as a whole, others consider a specific generic framework activity (e.g., **communication**), and still others focus on software engineering actions (e.g., architectural design) or technical tasks (e.g., write a usage scenario). Regardless of their level of focus, principles help you establish a mind-set for solid software engineering practice. They are important for that reason.

David Hooker [Hoo96] has proposed seven principles that focus on software engineering practice as a whole. They are reproduced in the following paragraphs:[13]

Before beginning a software project, be sure the software has a business purpose and that users perceive value in it.

The First Principle: *The Reason It All Exists*

A software system exists for one reason: *to provide value to its users*. All decisions should be made with this in mind. Before specifying a system requirement, before noting a piece of system functionality, before determining the hardware platforms or development processes, ask yourself questions such as: "Does this add real value to the system?" If the answer is "no," don't do it. All other principles support this one.

The Second Principle: *KISS (Keep It Simple, Stupid!)*

Software design is not a haphazard process. There are many factors to consider in any design effort. *All design should be as simple as possible, but no simpler.* This facilitates having a more easily understood and easily maintained system. This is

---

13 Reproduced with permission of the author [Hoo96]. Hooker defines patterns for these principles at http://c2.com/cgi/wiki?SevenPrinciplesOfSoftwareDevelopment.

not to say that features, even internal features, should be discarded in the name of simplicity. Indeed, the more elegant designs are usually the more simple ones. Simple also does not mean "quick and dirty." In fact, it often takes a lot of thought and work over multiple iterations to simplify. The payoff is software that is more maintainable and less error-prone.

The Third Principle: *Maintain the Vision*

A clear vision is essential to the success of a software project. Without one, a project almost unfailingly ends up being "of two [or more] minds" about itself. Without conceptual integrity, a system threatens to become a patchwork of incompatible designs, held together by the wrong kind of screws. . . . Compromising the architectural vision of a software system weakens and will eventually break even the well-designed systems. Having an empowered architect who can hold the vision and enforce compliance helps ensure a very successful software project.

The Fourth Principle: *What You Produce, Others Will Consume*

Seldom is an industrial-strength software system constructed and used in a vacuum. In some way or other, someone else will use, maintain, document, or otherwise depend on being able to understand your system. So, *always specify, design, and implement knowing someone else will have to understand what you are doing.* The audience for any product of software development is potentially large. Specify with an eye to the users. Design, keeping the implementers in mind. Code with concern for those that must maintain and extend the system. Someone may have to debug the code you write, and that makes them a user of your code. Making their job easier adds value to the system.

The Fifth Principle: *Be Open to the Future*

A system with a long lifetime has more value. In today's computing environments, where specifications change on a moment's notice and hardware platforms are obsolete just a few months old, software lifetimes are typically measured in months instead of years. However, true "industrial-strength" software systems must endure far longer. To do this successfully, these systems must be ready to adapt to these and other changes. Systems that do this successfully are those that have been designed this way from the start. *Never design yourself into a corner.* Always ask "what if," and prepare for all possible answers by creating systems that solve the general problem, not just the specific one.[14] This could very possibly lead to the reuse of an entire system.

---

14 This advice can be dangerous if it is taken to extremes. Designing for the "general problem" sometimes requires performance compromises and can make specific solutions inefficient.

The Sixth Principle: *Plan Ahead for Reuse*

Reuse saves time and effort.[15] Achieving a high level of reuse is arguably the hardest goal to accomplish in developing a software system. The reuse of code and designs has been proclaimed as a major benefit of using object-oriented technologies. However, the return on this investment is not automatic. To leverage the reuse possibilities that object-oriented [or conventional] programming provides requires forethought and planning. There are many techniques to realize reuse at every level of the system development process. . . . *Planning ahead for reuse reduces the cost and increases the value of both the reusable components and the systems into which they are incorporated.*

The Seventh principle: *Think!*

This last principle is probably the most overlooked. *Placing clear, complete thought before action almost always produces better results.* When you think about something, you are more likely to do it right. You also gain knowledge about how to do it right again. If you do think about something and still do it wrong, it becomes a valuable experience. A side effect of thinking is learning to recognize when you don't know something, at which point you can research the answer. When clear thought has gone into a system, value comes out. Applying the first six principles requires intense thought, for which the potential rewards are enormous.

If every software engineer and every software team simply followed Hooker's seven principles, many of the difficulties we experience in building complex computer-based systems would be eliminated.

1.6   SOFTWARE MYTHS

Quote:

"In the absence of meaningful standards, a new industry like software comes to depend instead on folklore."

Tom DeMarco

Software myths—erroneous beliefs about software and the process that is used to build it—can be traced to the earliest days of computing. Myths have a number of attributes that make them insidious. For instance, they appear to be reasonable statements of fact (sometimes containing elements of truth), they have an intuitive feel, and they are often promulgated by experienced practitioners who "know the score."

Today, most knowledgeable software engineering professionals recognize myths for what they are—misleading attitudes that have caused serious problems for managers and practitioners alike. However, old attitudes and habits are difficult to modify, and remnants of software myths remain.

---

15 Although this is true for those who reuse the software on future projects, reuse can be expensive for those who must design and build reusable components. Studies indicate that designing and building reusable components can cost between 25 to 200 percent more than targeted software. In some cases, the cost differential cannot be justified.

WebRef

The Software Project Managers Network at **www.spmn.com** can help you dispel these and other myths.

Management myths. Managers with software responsibility, like managers in most disciplines, are often under pressure to maintain budgets, keep schedules from slipping, and improve quality. Like a drowning person who grasps at a straw, a software manager often grasps at belief in a software myth, if that belief will lessen the pressure (even temporarily).

Myth: *We already have a book that's full of standards and procedures for building software. Won't that provide my people with everything they need to know?*

Reality: The book of standards may very well exist, but is it used? Are software practitioners aware of its existence? Does it reflect modern software engineering practice? Is it complete? Is it adaptable? Is it streamlined to improve time-to-delivery while still maintaining a focus on quality? In many cases, the answer to all of these questions is "no."

Myth: *If we get behind schedule, we can add more programmers and catch up (sometimes called the "Mongolian horde" concept).*

Reality: Software development is not a mechanistic process like manufacturing. In the words of Brooks [Bro95]: "adding people to a late software project makes it later." At first, this statement may seem counterintuitive. However, as new people are added, people who were working must spend time educating the newcomers, thereby reducing the amount of time spent on productive development effort. People can be added but only in a planned and well-coordinated manner.

Myth: *If I decide to outsource the software project to a third party, I can just relax and let that firm build it.*

Reality: If an organization does not understand how to manage and control software projects internally, it will invariably struggle when it outsources software projects.

Customer myths. A customer who requests computer software may be a person at the next desk, a technical group down the hall, the marketing/sales department, or an outside company that has requested software under contract. In many cases, the customer believes myths about software because software managers and practitioners do little to correct misinformation. Myths lead to false expectations (by the customer) and, ultimately, dissatisfaction with the developer.

ADVICE

Work very hard to understand what you have to do before you start. You may not be able to develop every detail, but the more you know, the less risk you take.

Myth: *A general statement of objectives is sufficient to begin writing programs—we can fill in the details later.*

Reality: Although a comprehensive and stable statement of requirements is not always possible, an ambiguous "statement of objectives" is a recipe for disaster. Unambiguous requirements (usually derived iteratively) are developed only through effective and continuous communication between customer and developer.

Myth: *Software requirements continually change, but change can be easily accommodated because software is flexible.*

Reality: It is true that software requirements change, but the impact of change varies with the time at which it is introduced. When requirements changes are requested early (before design or code has been started), the cost impact is relatively small.[16] However, as time passes, the cost impact grows rapidly—resources have been committed, a design framework has been established, and change can cause upheaval that requires additional resources and major design modification.

ADVICE

Whenever you think, we don't have time for software engineering, ask yourself, "Will we have time to do it over again?"

Practitioner's myths.   Myths that are still believed by software practitioners have been fostered by over 50 years of programming culture. During the early days, programming was viewed as an art form. Old ways and attitudes die hard.

Myth: *Once we write the program and get it to work, our job is done.*

Reality: Someone once said that "the sooner you begin 'writing code,' the longer it'll take you to get done." Industry data indicate that between 60 and 80 percent of all effort expended on software will be expended after it is delivered to the customer for the first time.

Myth: *Until I get the program "running" I have no way of assessing its quality.*

Reality: One of the most effective software quality assurance mechanisms can be applied from the inception of a project—*the technical review.* Software reviews (described in Chapter 15) are a "quality filter" that have been found to be more effective than testing for finding certain classes of software defects.

Myth: *The only deliverable work product for a successful project is the working program.*

Reality: A working program is only one part of a software configuration that includes many elements. A variety of work products (e.g., models, documents, plans) provide a foundation for successful engineering and, more important, guidance for software support.

Myth: *Software engineering will make us create voluminous and unnecessary documentation and will invariably slow us down.*

Reality: Software engineering is not about creating documents. It is about creating a quality product. Better quality leads to reduced rework. And reduced rework results in faster delivery times.

---

16 Many software engineers have adopted an "agile" approach that accommodates change incrementally, thereby controlling its impact and cost. Agile methods are discussed in Chapter 3.

Many software professionals recognize the fallacy of the myths just described. Regrettably, habitual attitudes and methods foster poor management and technical practices, even when reality dictates a better approach. Recognition of software realities is the first step toward formulation of practical solutions for software engineering.

1.7 How It All Starts

Every software project is precipitated by some business need—the need to correct a defect in an existing application; the need to adapt a "legacy system" to a changing business environment; the need to extend the functions and features of an existing application; or the need to create a new product, service, or system.

At the beginning of a software project, the business need is often expressed informally as part of a simple conversation. The conversation presented in the sidebar is typical.

SafeHome[17]

How a Project Starts

The scene: Meeting room at CPI Corporation, a (fictional) company that makes consumer products for home and commercial use.

The players: Mal Golden, senior manager, product development; Lisa Perez, marketing manager; Lee Warren, engineering manager; Joe Camalleri, executive VP, business development

The conversation:

Joe: Okay, Lee, what's this I hear about your folks developing a what? A generic universal wireless box?

Lee: It's pretty cool . . . about the size of a small matchbook . . . we can attach it to sensors of all kinds, a digital camera, just about anything. Using the 802.11g wireless protocol. It allows us to access the device's output without wires. We think it'll lead to a whole new generation of products.

Joe: You agree, Mal?

Mal: I do. In fact, with sales as flat as they've been this year, we need something new. Lisa and I have been doing a little market research, and we think we've got a line of products that could be big.

Joe: How big . . . bottom line big?

Mal (avoiding a direct commitment): Tell him about our idea, Lisa.

Lisa: It's a whole new generation of what we call "home management products." We call 'em SafeHome. They use the new wireless interface, provide homeowners or small-business people with a system that's controlled by their PC—home security, home surveillance, appliance and device control—you know, turn down the home air conditioner while you're driving home, that sort of thing.

Lee (jumping in): Engineering's done a technical feasibility study of this idea, Joe. It's doable at low manufacturing cost. Most hardware is off-the-shelf. Software is an issue, but it's nothing that we can't do.

Joe: Interesting. Now, I asked about the bottom line.

Mal: PCs have penetrated over 70 percent of all households in the USA. If we could price this thing right, it could be a killer-App. Nobody else has our wireless box . . . it's proprietary. We'll have a 2-year jump on the competition. Revenue? Maybe as much as 30 to 40 million dollars in the second year.

Joe (smiling): Let's take this to the next level. I'm interested.

---

17 The *SafeHome* project will be used throughout this book to illustrate the inner workings of a project team as it builds a software product. The company, the project, and the people are purely fictitious, but the situations and problems are real.

With the exception of a passing reference, software was hardly mentioned as part of the conversation. And yet, software will make or break the *SafeHome* product line. The engineering effort will succeed only if *SafeHome* software succeeds. The market will accept the product only if the software embedded within it properly meets the customer's (as yet unstated) needs. We'll follow the progression of *SafeHome* software engineering in many of the chapters that follow.

1.8 SUMMARY

Software is the key element in the evolution of computer-based systems and products and one of the most important technologies on the world stage. Over the past 50 years, software has evolved from a specialized problem solving and information analysis tool to an industry in itself. Yet we still have trouble developing high-quality software on time and within budget.

Software—programs, data, and descriptive information—addresses a wide array of technology and application areas. Legacy software continues to present special challenges to those who must maintain it.

Web-based systems and applications have evolved from simple collections of information content to sophisticated systems that present complex functionality and multimedia content. Although these WebApps have unique features and requirements, they are software nonetheless.

Software engineering encompasses process, methods, and tools that enable complex computer-based systems to be built in a timely manner with quality. The software process incorporates five framework activities—communication, planning, modeling, construction, and deployment—that are applicable to all software projects. Software engineering practice is a problem solving activity that follows a set of core principles.

A wide array of software myths continue to lead managers and practitioners astray, even as our collective knowledge of software and the technologies required to build it grows. As you learn more about software engineering, you'll begin to understand why these myths should be debunked whenever they are encountered.

PROBLEMS AND POINTS TO PONDER

1.1. Provide at least five additional examples of how the law of unintended consequences applies to computer software.

1.2. Provide a number of examples (both positive and negative) that indicate the impact of software on our society.

1.3. Develop your own answers to the five questions asked at the beginning of Section 1.1. Discuss them with your fellow students.

1.4. Many modern applications change frequently—before they are presented to the end user and then after the first version has been put into use. Suggest a few ways to build software to stop deterioration due to change.

1.5. Consider the seven software categories presented in Section 1.1.2. Do you think that the same approach to software engineering can be applied for each? Explain your answer.

1.6. Figure 1.3 places the three software engineering layers on top of a layer entitled "a quality focus." This implies an organizational quality program such as total quality management. Do a bit of research and develop an outline of the key tenets of a total quality management program.

1.7. Is software engineering applicable when WebApps are built? If so, how might it be modified to accommodate the unique characteristics of WebApps?

1.8. As software becomes more pervasive, risks to the public (due to faulty programs) become an increasingly significant concern. Develop a doomsday but realistic scenario in which the failure of a computer program could do great harm (either economic or human).

1.9. Describe a process framework in your own words. When we say that framework activities are applicable to all projects, does this mean that the same work tasks are applied for all projects, regardless of size and complexity? Explain.

1.10. Umbrella activities occur throughout the software process. Do you think they are applied evenly across the process, or are some concentrated in one or more framework activities.

1.11. Add two additional myths to the list presented in Section 1.6. Also state the reality that accompanies the myth.

FURTHER READINGS AND INFORMATION SOURCES[18]

There are literally thousands of books written about computer software. The vast majority discuss programming languages or software applications, but a few discuss software itself. Pressman and Herron (*Software Shock*, Dorset House, 1991) presented an early discussion (directed at the layperson) of software and the way professionals build it. Negroponte's best-selling book (*Being Digital*, Alfred A. Knopf, Inc., 1995) provides a view of computing and its overall impact in the twenty-first century. DeMarco (*Why Does Software Cost So Much?* Dorset House, 1995) has produced a collection of amusing and insightful essays on software and the process through which it is developed.

Minasi (*The Software Conspiracy: Why Software Companies Put out Faulty Products, How They Can Hurt You, and What You Can Do,* McGraw-Hill, 2000) argues that the "modern scourge" of software bugs can be eliminated and suggests ways to accomplish this. Compaine (*Digital Divide: Facing a Crisis or Creating a Myth,* MIT Press, 2001) argues that the "divide" between those who have access to information resources (e.g., the Web) and those that do not is narrowing as we move into the first decade of this century. Books by Greenfield (*Everyware: The Dawning Age of Ubiquitous Computing,* New Riders Publishing, 2006) and Loke (*Context-Aware Pervasive Systems: Architectures for a New Breed of Applications,* Auerbach, 2006) introduce the concept of "open-world" software and predict a wireless environment in which software must adapt to requirements that emerge in real time.

The current state of the software engineering and the software process can best be determined from publications such as *IEEE Software, IEEE Computer, CrossTalk,* and *IEEE Transactions on Software Engineering.* Industry periodicals such as *Application Development Trends* and *Cutter*

---

18 The *Further Reading and Information Sources* section presented at the conclusion of each chapter presents a brief overview of print sources that can help to expand your understanding of the major topics presented in the chapter. I have created a comprehensive website to support *Software Engineering: A Practitioner's Approach* at **www.mhhe.com/compsci/pressman**. Among the many topics addressed within the website are chapter-by-chapter software engineering resources to Web-based information that can complement the material presented in each chapter. An Amazon.com link to every book noted in this section is contained within these resources.

IT Journal often contain articles on software engineering topics. The discipline is "summarized" every year in the *Proceeding of the International Conference on Software Engineering,* sponsored by the IEEE and ACM, and is discussed in depth in journals such as *ACM Transactions on Software Engineering and Methodology, ACM Software Engineering Notes,* and *Annals of Software Engineering.* Tens of thousands of websites are dedicated to software engineering and the software process.

Many books addressing the software process and software engineering have been published in recent years. Some present an overview of the entire process, while others delve into a few important topics to the exclusion of others. Among the more popular offerings (in addition to this book!) are

Abran, A., and J. Moore, *SWEBOK: Guide to the Software Engineering Body of Knowledge,* IEEE, 2002.

Andersson, E., et al., *Software Engineering for Internet Applications,* The MIT Press, 2006.

Christensen, M., and R. Thayer, *A Project Manager's Guide to Software Engineering Best Practices,* IEEE-CS Press (Wiley), 2002.

Glass, R., *Fact and Fallacies of Software Engineering,* Addison-Wesley, 2002.

Jacobson, I., *Object-Oriented Software Engineering: A Use Case Driven Approach,* 2d ed., Addison-Wesley, 2008.

Jalote, P., *An Integrated Approach to Software Engineering,* Springer, 2006.

Pfleeger, S., *Software Engineering: Theory and Practice,* 3d ed., Prentice-Hall, 2005.

Schach, S., *Object-Oriented and Classical Software Engineering,* 7th ed., McGraw-Hill, 2006.

Sommerville, I., *Software Engineering,* 8th ed., Addison-Wesley, 2006.

Tsui, F., and O. Karam, *Essentials of Software Engineering,* Jones & Bartlett Publishers, 2006.

Many software engineering standards have been published by the IEEE, ISO, and their standards organizations over the past few decades. Moore (*The Road Map to Software Engineering: A Standards-Based Guide,* Wiley-IEEE Computer Society Press, 2006) provides a useful survey of relevant standards and how they apply to real projects.

A wide variety of information sources on software engineering and the software process are available on the Internet. An up-to-date list of World Wide Web references that are relevant to the software process can be found at the SEPA website: **www.mhhe.com/engcs/compsci/ pressman/professional/olc/ser.htm.**

One

THE SOFTWARE PROCESS

In this part of *Software Engineering: A Practitioner's Approach* you'll learn about the process that provides a framework for software engineering practice. These questions are addressed in the chapters that follow:

- What is a software process?
- What are the generic framework activities that are present in every software process?
- How are processes modeled and what are process patterns?
- What are the prescriptive process models and what are their strengths and weaknesses?
- Why is *agility* a watchword in modern software engineering work?
- What is agile software development and how does it differ from more traditional process models?

Once these questions are answered you'll be better prepared to understand the context in which software engineering practice is applied.

PROCESS MODELS

In a fascinating book that provides an economist's view of software and software engineering, Howard Baetjer, Jr. [Bae98], comments on the software process:

> Because software, like all capital, is embodied knowledge, and because that knowledge is initially dispersed, tacit, latent, and incomplete in large measure, software development is a social learning process. The process is a dialogue in which the knowledge that must become the software is brought together and embodied in the software. The process provides interaction between users and designers, between users and evolving tools, and between designers and evolving tools [technology]. It is an iterative process in which the evolving tool itself serves as the medium for communication, with each new round of the dialogue eliciting more useful knowledge from the people involved.

Indeed, building computer software is an iterative social learning process, and the outcome, something that Baetjer would call "software capital," is an embodiment of knowledge collected, distilled, and organized as the process is conducted.

QUICK LOOK

What is it? When you work to build a product or system, it's important to go through a series of predictable steps—a road map that helps you create a timely, high-quality result. The road map that you follow is called a "software process."

Who does it? Software engineers and their managers adapt the process to their needs and then follow it. In addition, the people who have requested the software have a role to play in the process of defining, building, and testing it.

Why is it important? Because it provides stability, control, and organization to an activity that can, if left uncontrolled, become quite chaotic. However, a modern software engineering approach must be "agile." It must demand only those activities, controls, and work products that are appropriate for the project team and the product that is to be produced.

What are the steps? At a detailed level, the process that you adopt depends on the software that you're building. One process might be appropriate for creating software for an aircraft avionics system, while an entirely different process would be indicated for the creation of a website.

What is the work product? From the point of view of a software engineer, the work products are the programs, documents, and data that are produced as a consequence of the activities and tasks defined by the process.

How do I ensure that I've done it right? There are a number of software process assessment mechanisms that enable organizations to determine the "maturity" of their software process. However, the quality, timeliness, and long-term viability of the product you build are the best indicators of the efficacy of the process that you use.

But what exactly is a software process from a technical point of view? Within the context of this book, I define a *software process* as a framework for the activities, actions, and tasks that are required to build high-quality software. Is "process" synonymous with software engineering? The answer is "yes and no." A software process defines the approach that is taken as software is engineered. But software engineering also encompasses technologies that populate the process—technical methods and automated tools.

More important, software engineering is performed by creative, knowledgeable people who should adapt a mature software process so that it is appropriate for the products that they build and the demands of their marketplace.

2.1 A Generic Process Model

In Chapter 1, a process was defined as a collection of work activities, actions, and tasks that are performed when some work product is to be created. Each of these activities, actions, and tasks reside within a framework or model that defines their relationship with the process and with one another.

The software process is represented schematically in Figure 2.1. Referring to the figure, each framework activity is populated by a set of software engineering actions. Each software engineering action is defined by a *task set* that identifies the work tasks that are to be completed, the work products that will be produced, the quality assurance points that will be required, and the milestones that will be used to indicate progress.

As I discussed in Chapter 1, a generic process framework for software engineering defines five framework activities—**communication, planning, modeling, construction,** and **deployment.** In addition, a set of umbrella activities—project tracking and control, risk management, quality assurance, configuration management, technical reviews, and others—are applied throughout the process.

You should note that one important aspect of the software process has not yet been discussed. This aspect—called *process flow*—describes how the framework activities and the actions and tasks that occur within each framework activity are organized with respect to sequence and time and is illustrated in Figure 2.2.

A *linear process flow* executes each of the five framework activities in sequence, beginning with communication and culminating with deployment (Figure 2.2a). An *iterative process flow* repeats one or more of the activities before proceeding to the next (Figure 2.2b). An *evolutionary process flow* executes the activities in a "circular" manner. Each circuit through the five activities leads to a more complete version of the software (Figure 2.2c). A *parallel process flow* (Figure 2.2d) executes one or more activities in parallel with other activities (e.g., modeling for one aspect of the software might be executed in parallel with construction of another aspect of the software).

POINT

The hierarchy of technical work within the software process is activities, encompassing actions, populated by tasks.

uote:

"We think that software developers are missing a vital truth: most organizations don't know what they do. They think they know, but they don't know."

Tom DeMarco

FIGURE 2.1

A software
process
framework

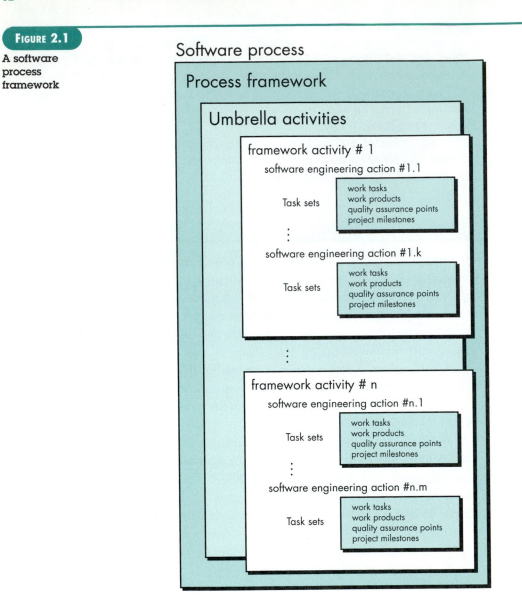

2.1.1   Defining a Framework Activity

Although I have described five framework activities and provided a basic definition of each in Chapter 1, a software team would need significantly more information before it could properly execute any one of these activities as part of the software process. Therefore, you are faced with a key question: *What actions are appropriate for a framework activity, given the nature of the problem to be solved, the characteristics of the people doing the work, and the stakeholders who are sponsoring the project?*

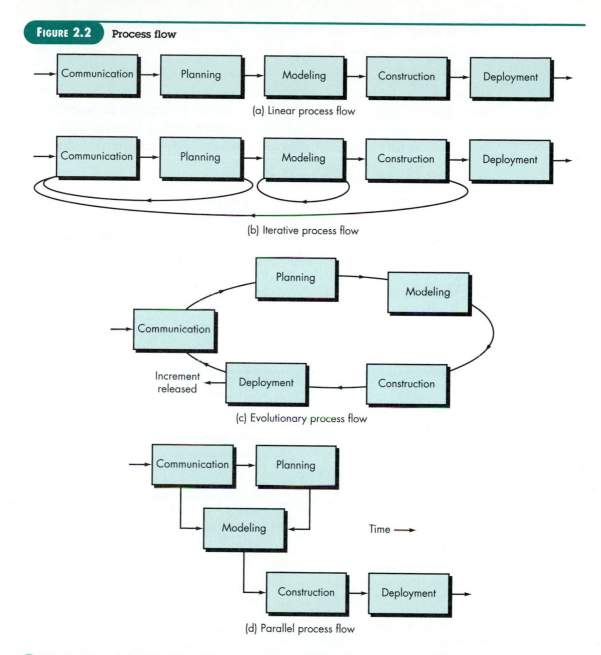

FIGURE 2.2 Process flow

(a) Linear process flow

(b) Iterative process flow

(c) Evolutionary process flow

(d) Parallel process flow

How does a framework activity change as the nature of the project changes?

For a small software project requested by one person (at a remote location) with simple, straightforward requirements, the communication activity might encompass little more than a phone call with the appropriate stakeholder. Therefore, the only necessary action is *phone conversation,* and the work tasks (the *task set*) that this action encompasses are:

1. Make contact with stakeholder via telephone.

2. Discuss requirements and take notes.

3. Organize notes into a brief written statement of requirements.

4. E-mail to stakeholder for review and approval.

If the project was considerably more complex with many stakeholders, each with a different set of (sometime conflicting) requirements, the communication activity might have six distinct actions (described in Chapter 5): *inception, elicitation, elaboration, negotiation, specification,* and *validation.* Each of these software engineering actions would have many work tasks and a number of distinct work products.

2.1.2   Identifying a Task Set

Referring again to Figure 2.1, each software engineering action (e.g., *elicitation,* an action associated with the communication activity) can be represented by a number of different *task sets*—each a collection of software engineering work tasks, related work products, quality assurance points, and project milestones. You should choose a task set that best accommodates the needs of the project and the characteristics of your team. This implies that a software engineering action can be adapted to the specific needs of the software project and the characteristics of the project team.

Task Set

A task set defines the actual work to be done to accomplish the objectives of a software engineering action. For example, *elicitation* (more commonly called "requirements gathering") is an important software engineering action that occurs during the communication activity. The goal of requirements gathering is to understand what various stakeholders want from the software that is to be built.

For a small, relatively simple project, the task set for requirements gathering might look like this:

1. Make a list of stakeholders for the project.
2. Invite all stakeholders to an informal meeting.
3. Ask each stakeholder to make a list of features and functions required.
4. Discuss requirements and build a final list.
5. Prioritize requirements.
6. Note areas of uncertainty.

For a larger, more complex software project, a different task set would be required. It might encompass the following work tasks:

1. Make a list of stakeholders for the project.
2. Interview each stakeholder separately to determine overall wants and needs.

3. Build a preliminary list of functions and features based on stakeholder input.
4. Schedule a series of facilitated application specification meetings.
5. Conduct meetings.
6. Produce informal user scenarios as part of each meeting.
7. Refine user scenarios based on stakeholder feedback.
8. Build a revised list of stakeholder requirements.
9. Use quality function deployment techniques to prioritize requirements.
10. Package requirements so that they can be delivered incrementally.
11. Note constraints and restrictions that will be placed on the system.
12. Discuss methods for validating the system.

Both of these task sets achieve "requirements gathering," but they are quite different in their depth and formality. The software team chooses the task set that will allow it to achieve the goal of each action and still maintain quality and agility.

2.1.3 Process Patterns

Every software team encounters problems as it moves through the software process. It would be useful if proven solutions to these problems were readily available to the team so that the problems could be addressed and resolved quickly. A *process pattern*[1] describes a process-related problem that is encountered during software engineering work, identifies the environment in which the problem has been encountered, and suggests one or more proven solutions to the problem. Stated in more general terms, a process pattern provides you with a template [Amb98]—a consistent method for describing problem solutions within the context of the software process. By combining patterns, a software team can solve problems and construct a process that best meets the needs of a project.

Patterns can be defined at any level of abstraction.[2] In some cases, a pattern might be used to describe a problem (and solution) associated with a complete process model (e.g., prototyping). In other situations, patterns can be used to describe a problem (and solution) associated with a framework activity (e.g., **planning**) or an action within a framework activity (e.g., project estimating).

Ambler [Amb98] has proposed a template for describing a process pattern:

> **Pattern Name.** The pattern is given a meaningful name describing it within the context of the software process (e.g., **TechnicalReviews**).
>
> **Forces.** The environment in which the pattern is encountered and the issues that make the problem visible and may affect its solution.
>
> **Type.** The pattern type is specified. Ambler [Amb98] suggests three types:
>
> 1. *Stage pattern*—defines a problem associated with a framework activity for the process. Since a framework activity encompasses multiple actions and work tasks, a stage pattern incorporates multiple task patterns (see the following) that are relevant to the stage (framework activity). An example of a stage pattern might be **EstablishingCommunication.** This pattern would incorporate the task pattern **RequirementsGathering** and others.
>
> 2. *Task pattern*—defines a problem associated with a software engineering action or work task and relevant to successful software engineering practice (e.g., **RequirementsGathering** is a task pattern).
>
> 3. *Phase pattern*—define the sequence of framework activities that occurs within the process, even when the overall flow of activities is iterative in nature. An example of a phase pattern might be **SpiralModel** or **Prototyping.**[3]

---

1 A detailed discussion of patterns is presented in Chapter 12.

2 Patterns are applicable to many software engineering activities. Analysis, design, and testing patterns are discussed in Chapters 7, 9, 10, 12, and 14. Patterns and "antipatterns" for project management activities are discussed in Part 4 of this book.

3 These phase patterns are discussed in Section 2.3.3.

Initial context.   Describes the conditions under which the pattern applies. Prior to the initiation of the pattern: (1) What organizational or team-related activities have already occurred? (2) What is the entry state for the process? (3) What software engineering information or project information already exists?

For example, the **Planning** pattern (a stage pattern) requires that (1) customers and software engineers have established a collaborative communication; (2) successful completion of a number of task patterns [specified] for the **Communication** pattern has occurred; and (3) the project scope, basic business requirements, and project constraints are known.

Problem.   The specific problem to be solved by the pattern.

Solution.   Describes how to implement the pattern successfully. This section describes how the initial state of the process (that exists before the pattern is implemented) is modified as a consequence of the initiation of the pattern. It also describes how software engineering information or project information that is available before the initiation of the pattern is transformed as a consequence of the successful execution of the pattern.

Resulting Context.   Describes the conditions that will result once the pattern has been successfully implemented. Upon completion of the pattern: (1) What organizational or team-related activities must have occurred? (2) What is the exit state for the process? (3) What software engineering information or project information has been developed?

Related Patterns.   Provide a list of all process patterns that are directly related to this one. This may be represented as a hierarchy or in some other diagrammatic form. For example, the stage pattern **Communication** encompasses the task patterns: **ProjectTeam, CollaborativeGuidelines, ScopeIsolation, RequirementsGathering, ConstraintDescription,** and **ScenarioCreation.**

Known Uses and Examples.   Indicate the specific instances in which the pattern is applicable. For example, **Communication** is mandatory at the beginning of every software project, is recommended throughout the software project, and is mandatory once the deployment activity is under way.

WebRef

Comprehensive resources on process patterns can be found at **www. ambysoft.com/ processPatternsPage .html**.

Process patterns provide an effective mechanism for addressing problems associated with any software process. The patterns enable you to develop a hierarchical process description that begins at a high level of abstraction (a phase pattern). The description is then refined into a set of stage patterns that describe framework activities and are further refined in a hierarchical fashion into more detailed task patterns for each stage pattern. Once process patterns have been developed, they can be reused for the definition of process variants—that is, a customized process model can be defined by a software team using the patterns as building blocks for the process model.

An Example Process Pattern

The following abbreviated process pattern describes an approach that may be applicable when stakeholders have a general idea of what must be done but are unsure of specific software requirements.

Pattern name. RequirementsUnclear

Intent. This pattern describes an approach for building a model (a prototype) that can be assessed iteratively by stakeholders in an effort to identify or solidify software requirements.

Type. Phase pattern.

Initial context. The following conditions must be met prior to the initiation of this pattern: (1) stakeholders have been identified; (2) a mode of communication between stakeholders and the software team has been established; (3) the overriding software problem to be solved has been identified by stakeholders; (4) an initial understanding of project scope, basic business requirements, and project constraints has been developed.

Problem. Requirements are hazy or nonexistent, yet there is clear recognition that there is a problem to be solved, and the problem must be addressed with a software solution. Stakeholders are unsure of what they want; that is, they cannot describe software requirements in any detail.

Solution. A description of the prototyping process would be presented here and is described later in Section 2.3.3.

Resulting context. A software prototype that identifies basic requirements (e.g., modes of interaction, computational features, processing functions) is approved by stakeholders. Following this, (1) the prototype may evolve through a series of increments to become the production software or (2) the prototype may be discarded and the production software built using some other process pattern.

Related patterns. The following patterns are related to this pattern: **CustomerCommunication, IterativeDesign, IterativeDevelopment, CustomerAssessment, RequirementExtraction.**

Known uses and examples. Prototyping is recommended when requirements are uncertain.

2.2 PROCESS ASSESSMENT AND IMPROVEMENT

KEY POINT

Assessment attempts to understand the current state of the software process with the intent of improving it.

? **What formal techniques are available for assessing the software process?**

The existence of a software process is no guarantee that software will be delivered on time, that it will meet the customer's needs, or that it will exhibit the technical characteristics that will lead to long-term quality characteristics (Chapters 14 and 16). Process patterns must be coupled with solid software engineering practice (Part 2 of this book). In addition, the process itself can be assessed to ensure that it meets a set of basic process criteria that have been shown to be essential for a successful software engineering.[4]

A number of different approaches to software process assessment and improvement have been proposed over the past few decades:

Standard CMMI Assessment Method for Process Improvement (SCAMPI)—provides a five-step process assessment model that incorporates five phases: initiating, diagnosing, establishing, acting, and learning. The SCAMPI method uses the SEI CMMI as the basis for assessment [SEI00].

---

4 The SEI's CMMI [CMM07] describes the characteristics of a software process and the criteria for a successful process in voluminous detail.

CMM-Based Appraisal for Internal Process Improvement (CBA IPI)—provides a diagnostic technique for assessing the relative maturity of a software organization; uses the SEI CMM as the basis for the assessment [Dun01].

SPICE (ISO/IEC15504)—a standard that defines a set of requirements for software process assessment. The intent of the standard is to assist organizations in developing an objective evaluation of the efficacy of any defined software process [ISO08].

ISO 9001:2000 for Software—a generic standard that applies to any organization that wants to improve the overall quality of the products, systems, or services that it provides. Therefore, the standard is directly applicable to software organizations and companies [Ant06].

A more detailed discussion of software assessment and process improvement methods is presented in Chapter 30.

2.3   PRESCRIPTIVE PROCESS MODELS

Prescriptive process models were originally proposed to bring order to the chaos of software development. History has indicated that these traditional models have brought a certain amount of useful structure to software engineering work and have provided a reasonably effective road map for software teams. However, software engineering work and the product that it produces remain on "the edge of chaos."

In an intriguing paper on the strange relationship between order and chaos in the software world, Nogueira and his colleagues [Nog00] state

The edge of chaos is defined as "a natural state between order and chaos, a grand compromise between structure and surprise" [Kau95]. The edge of chaos can be visualized as an unstable, partially structured state. . . . It is unstable because it is constantly attracted to chaos or to absolute order.

We have the tendency to think that order is the ideal state of nature. This could be a mistake. Research . . . supports the theory that operation away from equilibrium generates creativity, self-organized processes, and increasing returns [Roo96]. Absolute order means the absence of variability, which could be an advantage under unpredictable environments. Change occurs when there is some structure so that the change can be organized, but not so rigid that it cannot occur. Too much chaos, on the other hand, can make coordination and coherence impossible. Lack of structure does not always mean disorder.

The philosophical implications of this argument are significant for software engineering. If prescriptive process models[5] strive for structure and order, are they inappropriate for a software world that thrives on change? Yet, if we reject traditional process

---

5   Prescriptive process models are sometimes referred to as "traditional" process models.

POINT

Prescriptive process models define a prescribed set of process elements and a predictable process work flow.

models (and the order they imply) and replace them with something less structured, do we make it impossible to achieve coordination and coherence in software work?

There are no easy answers to these questions, but there are alternatives available to software engineers. In the sections that follow, I examine the prescriptive process approach in which order and project consistency are dominant issues. I call them "prescriptive" because they prescribe a set of process elements—framework activities, software engineering actions, tasks, work products, quality assurance, and change control mechanisms for each project. Each process model also prescribes a process flow (also called a *work flow*)—that is, the manner in which the process elements are interrelated to one another.

All software process models can accommodate the generic framework activities described in Chapter 1, but each applies a different emphasis to these activities and defines a process flow that invokes each framework activity (as well as software engineering actions and tasks) in a different manner.

2.3.1 The Waterfall Model

There are times when the requirements for a problem are well understood—when work flows from **communication** through **deployment** in a reasonably linear fashion. This situation is sometimes encountered when well-defined adaptations or enhancements to an existing system must be made (e.g., an adaptation to accounting software that has been mandated because of changes to government regulations). It may also occur in a limited number of new development efforts, but only when requirements are well defined and reasonably stable.

The *waterfall model,* sometimes called the *classic life cycle,* suggests a systematic, sequential approach[6] to software development that begins with customer specification of requirements and progresses through planning, modeling, construction, and deployment, culminating in ongoing support of the completed software (Figure 2.3).

A variation in the representation of the waterfall model is called the *V-model.* Represented in Figure 2.4, the V-model [Buc99] depicts the relationship of quality

FIGURE 2.3   The waterfall model

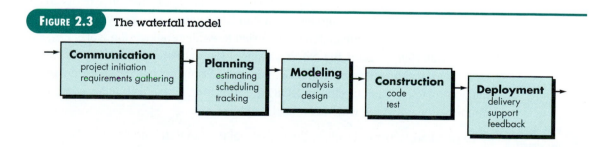

___

6   Although the original waterfall model proposed by Winston Royce [Roy70] made provision for "feedback loops," the vast majority of organizations that apply this process model treat it as if it were strictly linear.

FIGURE 2.4

The V-model

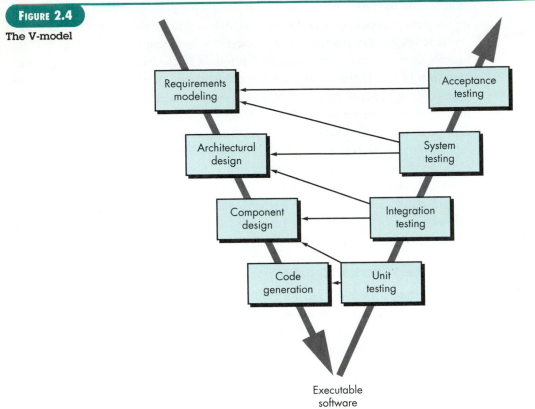

KEY POINT

The V-model illustrates how verification and validation actions are associated with earlier engineering actions.

assurance actions to the actions associated with communication, modeling, and early construction activities. As a software team moves down the left side of the V, basic problem requirements are refined into progressively more detailed and technical representations of the problem and its solution. Once code has been generated, the team moves up the right side of the V, essentially performing a series of tests (quality assurance actions) that validate each of the models created as the team moved down the left side.[7] In reality, there is no fundamental difference between the classic life cycle and the V-model. The V-model provides a way of visualizing how verification and validation actions are applied to earlier engineering work.

The waterfall model is the oldest paradigm for software engineering. However, over the past three decades, criticism of this process model has caused even ardent supporters to question its efficacy [Han95]. Among the problems that are sometimes encountered when the waterfall model is applied are:

? Why does the waterfall model sometimes fail?

1. Real projects rarely follow the sequential flow that the model proposes. Although the linear model can accommodate iteration, it does so indirectly. As a result, changes can cause confusion as the project team proceeds.

---

7   A detailed discussion of quality assurance actions is presented in Part 3 of this book.

2. It is often difficult for the customer to state all requirements explicitly. The waterfall model requires this and has difficulty accommodating the natural uncertainty that exists at the beginning of many projects.

3. The customer must have patience. A working version of the program(s) will not be available until late in the project time span. A major blunder, if undetected until the working program is reviewed, can be disastrous.

In an interesting analysis of actual projects, Bradac [Bra94] found that the linear nature of the classic life cycle leads to "blocking states" in which some project team members must wait for other members of the team to complete dependent tasks. In fact, the time spent waiting can exceed the time spent on productive work! The blocking states tend to be more prevalent at the beginning and end of a linear sequential process.

Today, software work is fast-paced and subject to a never-ending stream of changes (to features, functions, and information content). The waterfall model is often inappropriate for such work. However, it can serve as a useful process model in situations where requirements are fixed and work is to proceed to completion in a linear manner.

2.3.2 Incremental Process Models

There are many situations in which initial software requirements are reasonably well defined, but the overall scope of the development effort precludes a purely linear process. In addition, there may be a compelling need to provide a limited set of software functionality to users quickly and then refine and expand on that functionality in later software releases. In such cases, you can choose a process model that is designed to produce the software in increments.

The *incremental* model combines elements of linear and parallel process flows discussed in Section 2.1. Referring to Figure 2.5, the incremental model applies linear sequences in a staggered fashion as calendar time progresses. Each linear sequence produces deliverable "increments" of the software [McD93] in a manner that is similar to the increments produced by an evolutionary process flow (Section 2.3.3).

For example, word-processing software developed using the incremental paradigm might deliver basic file management, editing, and document production functions in the first increment; more sophisticated editing and document production capabilities in the second increment; spelling and grammar checking in the third increment; and advanced page layout capability in the fourth increment. It should be noted that the process flow for any increment can incorporate the prototyping paradigm.

When an incremental model is used, the first increment is often a *core product*. That is, basic requirements are addressed but many supplementary features (some known, others unknown) remain undelivered. The core product is used by the customer (or undergoes detailed evaluation). As a result of use and/or evaluation, a

KEY POINT

The incremental model delivers a series of releases, called increments, that provide progressively more functionality for the customer as each increment is delivered.

ADVICE

Your customer demands delivery by a date that is impossible to meet. Suggest delivering one or more increments by that date and the rest of the software (additional increments) later.

FIGURE 2.5

The
incremental
model

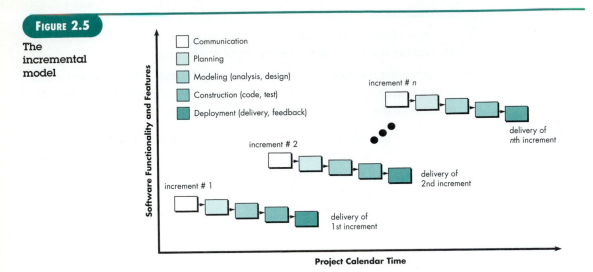

plan is developed for the next increment. The plan addresses the modification of the core product to better meet the needs of the customer and the delivery of additional features and functionality. This process is repeated following the delivery of each increment, until the complete product is produced.

The incremental process model focuses on the delivery of an operational product with each increment. Early increments are stripped-down versions of the final product, but they do provide capability that serves the user and also provide a platform for evaluation by the user.[8]

Incremental development is particularly useful when staffing is unavailable for a complete implementation by the business deadline that has been established for the project. Early increments can be implemented with fewer people. If the core product is well received, then additional staff (if required) can be added to implement the next increment. In addition, increments can be planned to manage technical risks. For example, a major system might require the availability of new hardware that is under development and whose delivery date is uncertain. It might be possible to plan early increments in a way that avoids the use of this hardware, thereby enabling partial functionality to be delivered to end users without inordinate delay.

2.3.3 Evolutionary Process Models

Software, like all complex systems, evolves over a period of time. Business and product requirements often change as development proceeds, making a straight line path to an end product unrealistic; tight market deadlines make completion of a comprehensive software product impossible, but a limited version must be introduced to

KEY POINT

Evolutionary process models produce an increasingly more complete version of the software with each iteration.

---

8   It is important to note that an incremental philosophy is also used for all "agile" process models discussed in Chapter 3.

meet competitive or business pressure; a set of core product or system requirements is well understood, but the details of product or system extensions have yet to be defined. In these and similar situations, you need a process model that has been explicitly designed to accommodate a product that evolves over time.

Evolutionary models are iterative. They are characterized in a manner that enables you to develop increasingly more complete versions of the software. In the paragraphs that follow, I present two common evolutionary process models.

Quote:

"Plan to throw one away. You will do that, anyway. Your only choice is whether to try to sell the throwaway to customers."

Frederick P. Brooks

Prototyping.   Often, a customer defines a set of general objectives for software, but does not identify detailed requirements for functions and features. In other cases, the developer may be unsure of the efficiency of an algorithm, the adaptability of an operating system, or the form that human-machine interaction should take. In these, and many other situations, a *prototyping paradigm* may offer the best approach.

Although prototyping can be used as a stand-alone process model, it is more commonly used as a technique that can be implemented within the context of any one of the process models noted in this chapter. Regardless of the manner in which it is applied, the prototyping paradigm assists you and other stakeholders to better understand what is to be built when requirements are fuzzy.

ADVICE

When your customer has a legitimate need, but is clueless about the details, develop a prototype as a first step.

The prototyping paradigm (Figure 2.6) begins with communication. You meet with other stakeholders to define the overall objectives for the software, identify whatever requirements are known, and outline areas where further definition is mandatory. A prototyping iteration is planned quickly, and modeling (in the form of a "quick design") occurs. A quick design focuses on a representation of those aspects of the software that will be visible to end users (e.g., human interface layout or output display

---

FIGURE 2.6

The prototyping paradigm

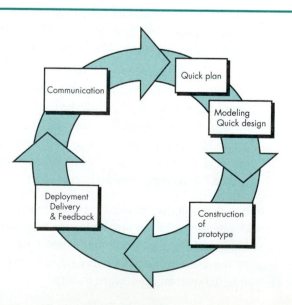

formats). The quick design leads to the construction of a prototype. The prototype is deployed and evaluated by stakeholders, who provide feedback that is used to further refine requirements. Iteration occurs as the prototype is tuned to satisfy the needs of various stakeholders, while at the same time enabling you to better understand what needs to be done.

Ideally, the prototype serves as a mechanism for identifying software requirements. If a working prototype is to be built, you can make use of existing program fragments or apply tools (e.g., report generators and window managers) that enable working programs to be generated quickly.

But what do you do with the prototype when it has served the purpose described earlier? Brooks [Bro95] provides one answer:

> In most projects, the first system built is barely usable. It may be too slow, too big, awkward in use or all three. There is no alternative but to start again, smarting but smarter, and build a redesigned version in which these problems are solved.

The prototype can serve as "the first system." The one that Brooks recommends you throw away. But this may be an idealized view. Although some prototypes are built as "throwaways," others are evolutionary in the sense that the prototype slowly evolves into the actual system.

Both stakeholders and software engineers like the prototyping paradigm. Users get a feel for the actual system, and developers get to build something immediately. Yet, prototyping can be problematic for the following reasons:

Resist pressure to extend a rough prototype into a production product. Quality almost always suffers as a result.

1. Stakeholders see what appears to be a working version of the software, unaware that the prototype is held together haphazardly, unaware that in the rush to get it working you haven't considered overall software quality or long-term maintainability. When informed that the product must be rebuilt so that high levels of quality can be maintained, stakeholders cry foul and demand that "a few fixes" be applied to make the prototype a working product. Too often, software development management relents.

2. As a software engineer, you often make implementation compromises in order to get a prototype working quickly. An inappropriate operating system or programming language may be used simply because it is available and known; an inefficient algorithm may be implemented simply to demonstrate capability. After a time, you may become comfortable with these choices and forget all the reasons why they were inappropriate. The less-than-ideal choice has now become an integral part of the system.

Although problems can occur, prototyping can be an effective paradigm for software engineering. The key is to define the rules of the game at the beginning; that is, all stakeholders should agree that the prototype is built to serve as a mechanism for defining requirements. It is then discarded (at least in part), and the actual software is engineered with an eye toward quality.

SAFEHOME

Selecting a Process Model, Part 1

The scene: Meeting room for the software engineering group at CPI Corporation, a (fictional) company that makes consumer products for home and commercial use.

The players: Lee Warren, engineering manager; Doug Miller, software engineering manager; Jamie Lazar, software team member; Vinod Raman, software team member; and Ed Robbins, software team member.

The conversation:

Lee: So let's recapitulate. I've spent some time discussing the *SafeHome* product line as we see it at the moment. No doubt, we've got a lot of work to do to simply define the thing, but I'd like you guys to begin thinking about how you're going to approach the software part of this project.

Doug: Seems like we've been pretty disorganized in our approach to software in the past.

Ed: I don't know, Doug, we always got product out the door.

Doug: True, but not without a lot of grief, and this project looks like it's bigger and more complex than anything we've done in the past.

Jamie: Doesn't look that hard, but I agree . . . our ad hoc approach to past projects won't work here, particularly if we have a very tight time line.

Doug (smiling): I want to be a bit more professional in our approach. I went to a short course last week and learned a lot about software engineering . . . good stuff. We need a process here.

Jamie (with a frown): My job is to build computer programs, not push paper around.

Doug: Give it a chance before you go negative on me. Here's what I mean. [Doug proceeds to describe the process framework described in this chapter and the prescriptive process models presented to this point.]

Doug: So anyway, it seems to me that a linear model is not for us . . . assumes we have all requirements up front and, knowing this place, that's not likely.

Vinod: Yeah, and it sounds way too IT-oriented . . . probably good for building an inventory control system or something, but it's just not right for *SafeHome*.

Doug: I agree.

Ed: That prototyping approach seems OK. A lot like what we do here anyway.

Vinod: That's a problem. I'm worried that it doesn't provide us with enough structure.

Doug: Not to worry. We've got plenty of other options, and I want you guys to pick what's best for the team and best for the project.

The Spiral Model.   Originally proposed by Barry Boehm [Boe88], the *spiral model* is an evolutionary software process model that couples the iterative nature of prototyping with the controlled and systematic aspects of the waterfall model. It provides the potential for rapid development of increasingly more complete versions of the software. Boehm [Boe01a] describes the model in the following manner:

> The spiral development model is a *risk*-driven *process model* generator that is used to guide multi-stakeholder concurrent engineering of software intensive systems. It has two main distinguishing features. One is a *cyclic* approach for incrementally growing a system's degree of definition and implementation while decreasing its degree of risk. The other is a set of *anchor point milestones* for ensuring stakeholder commitment to feasible and mutually satisfactory system solutions.

Using the spiral model, software is developed in a series of evolutionary releases. During early iterations, the release might be a model or prototype. During later iterations, increasingly more complete versions of the engineered system are produced.

FIGURE 2.7

A typical
spiral model

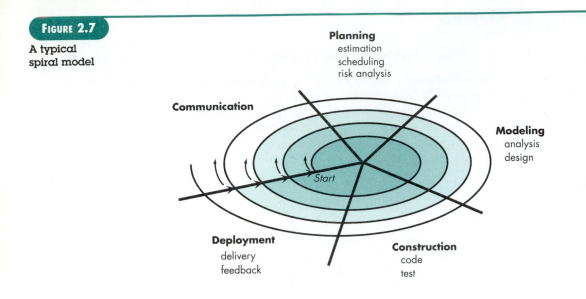

A spiral model is divided into a set of framework activities defined by the software engineering team. For illustrative purposes, I use the generic framework activities discussed earlier.[9] Each of the framework activities represent one segment of the spiral path illustrated in Figure 2.7. As this evolutionary process begins, the software team performs activities that are implied by a circuit around the spiral in a clockwise direction, beginning at the center. Risk (Chapter 28) is considered as each revolution is made. *Anchor point milestones*—a combination of work products and conditions that are attained along the path of the spiral—are noted for each evolutionary pass.

The first circuit around the spiral might result in the development of a product specification; subsequent passes around the spiral might be used to develop a prototype and then progressively more sophisticated versions of the software. Each pass through the planning region results in adjustments to the project plan. Cost and schedule are adjusted based on feedback derived from the customer after delivery. In addition, the project manager adjusts the planned number of iterations required to complete the software.

Unlike other process models that end when software is delivered, the spiral model can be adapted to apply throughout the life of the computer software. Therefore, the first circuit around the spiral might represent a "concept development project" that starts at the core of the spiral and continues for multiple iterations[10] until concept

---

9   The spiral model discussed in this section is a variation on the model proposed by Boehm. For further information on the original spiral model, see [Boe88]. More recent discussion of Boehm's spiral model can be found in [Boe98].

10 The arrows pointing inward along the axis separating the **deployment** region from the **communication** region indicate a potential for local iteration along the same spiral path.

If your management demands fixed-budget development (generally a bad idea), the spiral can be a problem. As each circuit is completed, project cost is revisited and revised.

development is complete. If the concept is to be developed into an actual product, the process proceeds outward on the spiral and a "new product development project" commences. The new product will evolve through a number of iterations around the spiral. Later, a circuit around the spiral might be used to represent a "product enhancement project." In essence, the spiral, when characterized in this way, remains operative until the software is retired. There are times when the process is dormant, but whenever a change is initiated, the process starts at the appropriate entry point (e.g., product enhancement).

The spiral model is a realistic approach to the development of large-scale systems and software. Because software evolves as the process progresses, the developer and customer better understand and react to risks at each evolutionary level. The spiral model uses prototyping as a risk reduction mechanism but, more important, enables you to apply the prototyping approach at any stage in the evolution of the product. It maintains the systematic stepwise approach suggested by the classic life cycle but incorporates it into an iterative framework that more realistically reflects the real world. The spiral model demands a direct consideration of technical risks at all stages of the project and, if properly applied, should reduce risks before they become problematic.

"I'm only this far and only tomorrow leads my way."

Dave Matthews Band

But like other paradigms, the spiral model is not a panacea. It may be difficult to convince customers (particularly in contract situations) that the evolutionary approach is controllable. It demands considerable risk assessment expertise and relies on this expertise for success. If a major risk is not uncovered and managed, problems will undoubtedly occur.

SAFEHOME

Selecting a Process Model, Part 2

The scene: Meeting room for the software engineering group at CPI Corporation, a company that makes consumer products for home and commercial use.

The players: Lee Warren, engineering manager; Doug Miller, software engineering manager; Vinod and Jamie, members of the software engineering team.

The conversation: [Doug describes evolutionary process options.]

Jamie: Now I see something I like. An incremental approach makes sense, and I really like the flow of that spiral model thing. That's keepin' it real.

Vinod: I agree. We deliver an increment, learn from customer feedback, replan, and then deliver another increment. It also fits into the nature of the product. We

can have something on the market fast and then add functionality with each version, er, increment.

Lee: Wait a minute. Did you say that we regenerate the plan with each tour around the spiral, Doug? That's not so great; we need one plan, one schedule, and we've got to stick to it.

Doug: That's old-school thinking, Lee. Like the guys said, we've got to keep it real. I submit that it's better to tweak the plan as we learn more and as changes are requested. It's way more realistic. What's the point of a plan if it doesn't reflect reality?

Lee (frowning): I suppose so, but . . . senior management's not going to like this . . . they want a fixed plan.

Doug (smiling): Then you'll have to reeducate them, buddy.

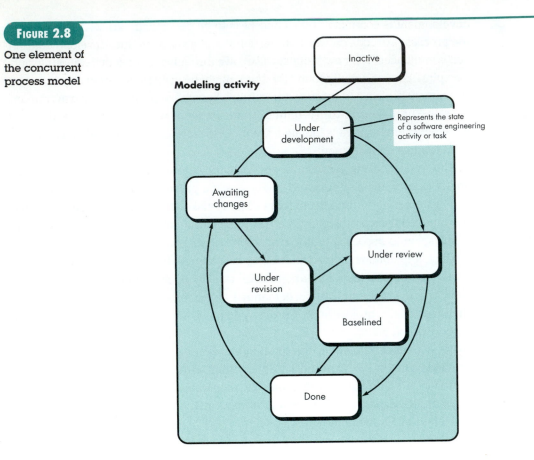

2.3.4   Concurrent Models

The *concurrent development model,* sometimes called *concurrent engineering,* allows a software team to represent iterative and concurrent elements of any of the process models described in this chapter. For example, the modeling activity defined for the spiral model is accomplished by invoking one or more of the following software engineering actions: prototyping, analysis, and design.[11]

Figure 2.8 provides a schematic representation of one software engineering activity within the modeling activity using a concurrent modeling approach. The activity—**modeling**—may be in any one of the states[12] noted at any given time. Similarly, other activities, actions, or tasks (e.g., **communication** or **construction**) can be represented in an analogous manner. All software engineering activities exist concurrently but reside in different states.

---

11 It should be noted that analysis and design are complex tasks that require substantial discussion. Part 2 of this book considers these topics in detail.

12 A *state* is some externally observable mode of behavior.

For example, early in a project the communication activity (not shown in the figure) has completed its first iteration and exists in the **awaiting changes** state. The modeling activity (which existed in the **inactive** state while initial communication was completed, now makes a transition into the **under development** state. If, however, the customer indicates that changes in requirements must be made, the modeling activity moves from the **under development** state into the **awaiting changes** state.

Concurrent modeling defines a series of events that will trigger transitions from state to state for each of the software engineering activities, actions, or tasks. For example, during early stages of design (a major software engineering action that occurs during the modeling activity), an inconsistency in the requirements model is uncovered. This generates the event *analysis model correction,* which will trigger the requirements analysis action from the **done** state into the **awaiting changes** state.

Concurrent modeling is applicable to all types of software development and provides an accurate picture of the current state of a project. Rather than confining software engineering activities, actions, and tasks to a sequence of events, it defines a process network. Each activity, action, or task on the network exists simultaneously with other activities, actions, or tasks. Events generated at one point in the process network trigger transitions among the states.

2.3.5 A Final Word on Evolutionary Processes

I have already noted that modern computer software is characterized by continual change, by very tight time lines, and by an emphatic need for customer–user satisfaction. In many cases, time-to-market is the most important management requirement. If a market window is missed, the software project itself may be meaningless.[13]

Evolutionary process models were conceived to address these issues, and yet, as a general class of process models, they too have weaknesses. These are summarized by Nogueira and his colleagues [Nog00] :

> Despite the unquestionable benefits of evolutionary software processes, we have some concerns. The first concern is that prototyping [and other more sophisticated evolutionary processes] poses a problem to project planning because of the uncertain number of cycles required to construct the product. Most project management and estimation techniques are based on linear layouts of activities, so they do not fit completely.
>
> Second, evolutionary software processes do not establish the maximum speed of the evolution. If the evolutions occur too fast, without a period of relaxation, it is certain that the process will fall into chaos. On the other hand if the speed is too slow then productivity could be affected . . .

---

13 It is important to note, however, that being the first to reach a market is no guarantee of success. In fact, many very successful software products have been second or even third to reach the market (learning from the mistakes of their predecessors).

Third, software processes should be focused on flexibility and extensibility rather than on high quality. This assertion sounds scary. However, we should prioritize the speed of the development over zero defects. Extending the development in order to reach high quality could result in a late delivery of the product, when the opportunity niche has disappeared. This paradigm shift is imposed by the competition on the edge of chaos.

Indeed, a software process that focuses on flexibility, extensibility, and speed of development over high quality does sound scary. And yet, this idea has been proposed by a number of well-respected software engineering experts (e.g., [You95], [Bac97]).

The intent of evolutionary models is to develop high-quality software[14] in an iterative or incremental manner. However, it is possible to use an evolutionary process to emphasize flexibility, extensibility, and speed of development. The challenge for software teams and their managers is to establish a proper balance between these critical project and product parameters and customer satisfaction (the ultimate arbiter of software quality).

2.4   SPECIALIZED PROCESS MODELS

Specialized process models take on many of the characteristics of one or more of the traditional models presented in the preceding sections. However, these models tend to be applied when a specialized or narrowly defined software engineering approach is chosen.[15]

2.4.1   Component-Based Development

WebRef

Useful information on component-based development can be obtained at: **www .cbd-hq.com**.

Commercial off-the-shelf (COTS) software components, developed by vendors who offer them as products, provide targeted functionality with well-defined interfaces that enable the component to be integrated into the software that is to be built. The *component-based development model* incorporates many of the characteristics of the spiral model. It is evolutionary in nature [Nie92], demanding an iterative approach to the creation of software. However, the component-based development model constructs applications from prepackaged software components.

Modeling and construction activities begin with the identification of candidate components. These components can be designed as either conventional software modules or object-oriented classes or packages[16] of classes. Regardless of the

---

14 In this context software quality is defined quite broadly to encompass not only customer satisfaction, but also a variety of technical criteria discussed in Chapters 14 and 16.

15 In some cases, these specialized process models might better be characterized as a collection of techniques or a "methodology" for accomplishing a specific software development goal. However, they do imply a process.

16 Object-oriented concepts are discussed in Appendix 2 and are used throughout Part 2 of this book. In this context, a class encompasses a set of data and the procedures that process the data. A package of classes is a collection of related classes that work together to achieve some end result.

technology that is used to create the components, the component-based development model incorporates the following steps (implemented using an evolutionary approach):

1. Available component-based products are researched and evaluated for the application domain in question.

2. Component integration issues are considered.

3. A software architecture is designed to accommodate the components.

4. Components are integrated into the architecture.

5. Comprehensive testing is conducted to ensure proper functionality.

The component-based development model leads to software reuse, and reusability provides software engineers with a number of measurable benefits. Your software engineering team can achieve a reduction in development cycle time as well as a reduction in project cost if component reuse becomes part of your culture. Component-based development is discussed in more detail in Chapter 10.

2.4.2 The Formal Methods Model

The *formal methods model* encompasses a set of activities that leads to formal mathematical specification of computer software. Formal methods enable you to specify, develop, and verify a computer-based system by applying a rigorous, mathematical notation. A variation on this approach, called *cleanroom software engineering* [Mil87, Dye92], is currently applied by some software development organizations.

When formal methods (Chapter 21) are used during development, they provide a mechanism for eliminating many of the problems that are difficult to overcome using other software engineering paradigms. Ambiguity, incompleteness, and inconsistency can be discovered and corrected more easily—not through ad hoc review, but through the application of mathematical analysis. When formal methods are used during design, they serve as a basis for program verification and therefore enable you to discover and correct errors that might otherwise go undetected.

Although not a mainstream approach, the formal methods model offers the promise of defect-free software. Yet, concern about its applicability in a business environment has been voiced:

> **?** **If formal methods can demonstrate software correctness, why is it they are not widely used?**

- The development of formal models is currently quite time consuming and expensive.

- Because few software developers have the necessary background to apply formal methods, extensive training is required.

- It is difficult to use the models as a communication mechanism for technically unsophisticated customers.

These concerns notwithstanding, the formal methods approach has gained adherents among software developers who must build safety-critical software (e.g., developers of aircraft avionics and medical devices) and among developers that would suffer severe economic hardship should software errors occur.

2.4.3   Aspect-Oriented Software Development

Regardless of the software process that is chosen, the builders of complex software invariably implement a set of localized features, functions, and information content. These localized software characteristics are modeled as components (e.g., object-oriented classes) and then constructed within the context of a system architecture. As modern computer-based systems become more sophisticated (and complex), certain *concerns*—customer required properties or areas of technical interest—span the entire architecture. Some concerns are high-level properties of a system (e.g., security, fault tolerance). Other concerns affect functions (e.g., the application of business rules), while others are systemic (e.g., task synchronization or memory management).

POINT

AOSD defines "aspects" that express customer concerns that cut across multiple system functions, features, and information.

When concerns cut across multiple system functions, features, and information, they are often referred to as *crosscutting concerns. Aspectual requirements* define those crosscutting concerns that have an impact across the software architecture. *Aspect-oriented software development* (AOSD), often referred to as *aspect-oriented programming* (AOP), is a relatively new software engineering paradigm that provides a process and methodological approach for defining, specifying, designing, and constructing *aspects*—"mechanisms beyond subroutines and inheritance for localizing the expression of a crosscutting concern" [Elr01].

Grundy [Gru02] provides further discussion of aspects in the context of what he calls *aspect-oriented component engineering* (AOCE):

> AOCE uses a concept of horizontal slices through vertically-decomposed software components, called "aspects," to characterize cross-cutting functional and non-functional properties of components. Common, systemic aspects include user interfaces, collaborative work, distribution, persistency, memory management, transaction processing, security, integrity and so on. Components may provide or require one or more "aspect details" relating to a particular aspect, such as a viewing mechanism, extensible affordance and interface kind (user interface aspects); event generation, transport and receiving (distribution aspects); data store/retrieve and indexing (persistency aspects); authentication, encoding and access rights (security aspects); transaction atomicity, concurrency control and logging strategy (transaction aspects); and so on. Each aspect detail has a number of properties, relating to functional and/or non-functional characteristics of the aspect detail.

A distinct aspect-oriented process has not yet matured. However, it is likely that such a process will adopt characteristics of both evolutionary and concurrent process models. The evolutionary model is appropriate as aspects are identified and then constructed. The parallel nature of concurrent development is essential because aspects are engineered independently of localized software components and yet, aspects have a direct impact on these components. Hence, it is essential to instantiate asynchronous communication between the software process activities applied to the engineering and construction of aspects and components.

A detailed discussion of aspect-oriented software development is best left to books dedicated to the subject. If you have further interest, see [Saf08], [Cla05], [Jac04], and [Gra03].

SOFTWARE TOOLS

Process Management

Objective: To assist in the definition, execution, and management of prescriptive process models.

Mechanics: Process management tools allow a software organization or team to define a complete software process model (framework activities, actions, tasks, QA checkpoints, milestones, and work products). In addition, the tools provide a road map as software engineers do technical work and a template for managers who must track and control the software process.

Representative Tools:[17]

GDPA, a research process definition tool suite, developed at Bremen University in Germany (**www.informatik** **.uni-bremen.de/uniform/gdpa/home.htm**), provides a wide array of process modeling and management functions.

SpeeDev, developed by SpeeDev Corporation (**www.speedev.com**) encompasses a suite of tools for process definition, requirements management, issue resolution, project planning, and tracking.

ProVision BPMx, developed by Proforma (**www.proformacorp.com**), is representative of many tools that assist in process definition and workflow automation.

A worthwhile listing of many different tools associated with the software process can be found at **www .processwave.net/Links/tool_links.htm**.

2.5   THE UNIFIED PROCESS

In their seminal book on the *Unified Process,* Ivar Jacobson, Grady Booch, and James Rumbaugh [Jac99] discuss the need for a "use case driven, architecture-centric, iterative and incremental" software process when they state:

> Today, the trend in software is toward bigger, more complex systems. That is due in part to the fact that computers become more powerful every year, leading users to expect more from them. This trend has also been influenced by the expanding use of the Internet for exchanging all kinds of information. . . . Our appetite for ever-more sophisticated software grows as we learn from one product release to the next how the product could be improved. We want software that is better adapted to our needs, but that, in turn, merely makes the software more complex. In short, we want more.

In some ways the Unified Process is an attempt to draw on the best features and characteristics of traditional software process models, but characterize them in a way that implements many of the best principles of agile software development

---

17 Tools noted here do not represent an endorsement, but rather a sampling of tools in this category. In most cases, tool names are trademarked by their respective developers.

(Chapter 3). The Unified Process recognizes the importance of customer communi-cation and streamlined methods for describing the customer's view of a system (the use case[18]). It emphasizes the important role of software architecture and "helps the architect focus on the right goals, such as understandability, reliance to future changes, and reuse" [Jac99]. It suggests a process flow that is iterative and incremental, providing the evolutionary feel that is essential in modern software development.

2.5.1   A Brief History

During the early 1990s James Rumbaugh [Rum91], Grady Booch [Boo94], and Ivar Jacobson [Jac92] began working on a "unified method" that would combine the best features of each of their individual object-oriented analysis and design methods and adopt additional features proposed by other experts (e.g., [Wir90]) in object-oriented modeling. The result was UML—a *unified modeling language* that contains a robust notation for the modeling and development of object-oriented systems. By 1997, UML became a de facto industry standard for object-oriented software development.

UML is used throughout Part 2 of this book to represent both requirements and design models. Appendix 1 presents an introductory tutorial for those who are unfa-miliar with basic UML notation and modeling rules. A comprehensive presentation of UML is best left to textbooks dedicated to the subject. Recommended books are listed in Appendix 1.

UML provided the necessary technology to support object-oriented software engi-neering practice, but it did not provide the process framework to guide project teams in their application of the technology. Over the next few years, Jacobson, Rumbaugh, and Booch developed the *Unified Process,* a framework for object-oriented software engineering using UML. Today, the Unified Process (UP) and UML are widely used on object-oriented projects of all kinds. The iterative, incremental model proposed by the UP can and should be adapted to meet specific project needs.

2.5.2   Phases of the Unified Process[19]

Earlier in this chapter, I discussed five generic framework activities and argued that they may be used to describe any software process model. The Unified Process is no exception. Figure 2.9 depicts the "phases" of the UP and relates them to the generic activities that have been discussed in Chapter 1 and earlier in this chapter.

---

18 A *use case* (Chapter 5) is a text narrative or template that describes a system function or feature from the user's point of view. A use case is written by the user and serves as a basis for the creation of a more comprehensive requirements model.

19 The Unified Process is sometimes called the *Rational Unified Process* (RUP) after the Rational Cor-poration (subsequently acquired by IBM), an early contributor to the development and refinement of the UP and a builder of complete environments (tools and technology) that support the process.

FIGURE 2.9

The Unified
Process

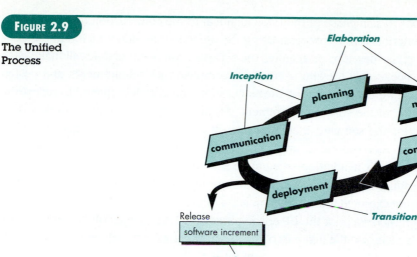

UP *phases* are similar
in intent to the generic
framework activities
defined in this book.

The *inception phase* of the UP encompasses both customer communication and planning activities. By collaborating with stakeholders, business requirements for the software are identified; a rough architecture for the system is proposed; and a plan for the iterative, incremental nature of the ensuing project is developed. Fundamental business requirements are described through a set of preliminary use cases (Chapter 5) that describe which features and functions each major class of users desires. Architecture at this point is nothing more than a tentative outline of major subsystems and the function and features that populate them. Later, the architecture will be refined and expanded into a set of models that will represent different views of the system. Planning identifies resources, assesses major risks, defines a schedule, and establishes a basis for the phases that are to be applied as the software increment is developed.

The *elaboration phase* encompasses the communication and modeling activities of the generic process model (Figure 2.9). Elaboration refines and expands the preliminary use cases that were developed as part of the inception phase and expands the architectural representation to include five different views of the software—the use case model, the requirements model, the design model, the implementation model, and the deployment model. In some cases, elaboration creates an "executable architectural baseline" [Arl02] that represents a "first cut" executable system.[20] The architectural baseline demonstrates the viability of the architecture but does not provide all features and functions required to use the system. In addition, the plan is carefully reviewed at the culmination of the elaboration phase to ensure that scope, risks, and delivery dates remain reasonable. Modifications to the plan are often made at this time.

---

20 It is important to note that the architectural baseline is not a prototype in that it is not thrown away. Rather, the baseline is fleshed out during the next UP phase.

WebRef

An interesting discussion of the UP in the context of agile development can be found at **www.ambysoft .com/ unifiedprocess/ agileUP.html**.

The *construction phase* of the UP is identical to the construction activity defined for the generic software process. Using the architectural model as input, the construction phase develops or acquires the software components that will make each use case operational for end users. To accomplish this, requirements and design models that were started during the elaboration phase are completed to reflect the final version of the software increment. All necessary and required features and functions for the software increment (i.e., the release) are then implemented in source code. As components are being implemented, unit tests[21] are designed and executed for each. In addition, integration activities (component assembly and integration testing) are conducted. Use cases are used to derive a suite of acceptance tests that are executed prior to the initiation of the next UP phase.

The *transition phase* of the UP encompasses the latter stages of the generic construction activity and the first part of the generic deployment (delivery and feedback) activity. Software is given to end users for beta testing and user feedback reports both defects and necessary changes. In addition, the software team creates the necessary support information (e.g., user manuals, troubleshooting guides, installation procedures) that is required for the release. At the conclusion of the transition phase, the software increment becomes a usable software release.

The *production phase* of the UP coincides with the deployment activity of the generic process. During this phase, the ongoing use of the software is monitored, support for the operating environment (infrastructure) is provided, and defect reports and requests for changes are submitted and evaluated.

It is likely that at the same time the construction, transition, and production phases are being conducted, work may have already begun on the next software increment. This means that the five UP phases do not occur in a sequence, but rather with staggered concurrency.

A software engineering workflow is distributed across all UP phases. In the context of UP, a *workflow* is analogous to a task set (described earlier in this chapter). That is, a workflow identifies the tasks required to accomplish an important software engineering action and the work products that are produced as a consequence of successfully completing the tasks. It should be noted that not every task identified for a UP workflow is conducted for every software project. The team adapts the process (actions, tasks, subtasks, and work products) to meet its needs.

2.6 PERSONAL AND TEAM PROCESS MODELS

The best software process is one that is close to the people who will be doing the work. If a software process model has been developed at a corporate or organizational level, it can be effective only if it is amenable to significant adaptation to meet

---

21 A comprehensive discussion of software testing (including *unit tests*) is presented in Chapters 17 through 20.

the needs of the project team that is actually doing software engineering work. In an ideal setting, you would create a process that best fits your needs, and at the same time, meets the broader needs of the team and the organization. Alternatively, the team itself can create its own process, and at the same time meet the narrower needs of individuals and the broader needs of the organization. Watts Humphrey ([Hum97] and [Hum00]) argues that it is possible to create a "personal software process" and/or a "team software process." Both require hard work, training, and coordination, but both are achievable.[22]

2.6.1 Personal Software Process (PSP)

Every developer uses some process to build computer software. The process may be haphazard or ad hoc; may change on a daily basis; may not be efficient, effective, or even successful; but a "process" does exist. Watts Humphrey [Hum97] suggests that in order to change an ineffective personal process, an individual must move through four phases, each requiring training and careful instrumentation. The *Personal Software Process* (PSP) emphasizes personal measurement of both the work product that is produced and the resultant quality of the work product. In addition PSP makes the practitioner responsible for project planning (e.g., estimating and scheduling) and empowers the practitioner to control the quality of all software work products that are developed. The PSP model defines five framework activities:

Planning.   This activity isolates requirements and develops both size and resource estimates. In addition, a defect estimate (the number of defects projected for the work) is made. All metrics are recorded on worksheets or templates. Finally, development tasks are identified and a project schedule is created.

High-level design.   External specifications for each component to be constructed are developed and a component design is created. Prototypes are built when uncertainty exists. All issues are recorded and tracked.

High-level design review.   Formal verification methods (Chapter 21) are applied to uncover errors in the design. Metrics are maintained for all important tasks and work results.

Development.   The component-level design is refined and reviewed. Code is generated, reviewed, compiled, and tested. Metrics are maintained for all important tasks and work results.

Postmortem.   Using the measures and metrics collected (this is a substantial amount of data that should be analyzed statistically), the effectiveness of the process is determined. Measures and metrics should provide guidance for modifying the process to improve its effectiveness.

---

22 It's worth noting the proponents of agile software development (Chapter 3) also argue that the process should remain close to the team. They propose an alternative method for achieving this.

PSP emphasizes the need to record and analyze the types of errors you make, so that you can develop strategies to eliminate them.

PSP stresses the need to identify errors early and, just as important, to understand the types of errors that you are likely to make. This is accomplished through a rigorous assessment activity performed on all work products you produce.

PSP represents a disciplined, metrics-based approach to software engineering that may lead to culture shock for many practitioners. However, when PSP is properly introduced to software engineers [Hum96], the resulting improvement in software engineering productivity and software quality are significant [Fer97]. However, PSP has not been widely adopted throughout the industry. The reasons, sadly, have more to do with human nature and organizational inertia than they do with the strengths and weaknesses of the PSP approach. PSP is intellectually challenging and demands a level of commitment (by practitioners and their managers) that is not always possible to obtain. Training is relatively lengthy, and training costs are high. The required level of measurement is culturally difficult for many software people.

Can PSP be used as an effective software process at a personal level? The answer is an unequivocal "yes." But even if PSP is not adopted in its entirely, many of the personal process improvement concepts that it introduces are well worth learning.

2.6.2   Team Software Process (TSP)

WebRef

Information on building high-performance teams using TSP and PSP can be obtained at:
www.sei.cmu .edu/tsp/.

Because many industry-grade software projects are addressed by a team of practitioners, Watts Humphrey extended the lessons learned from the introduction of PSP and proposed a *Team Software Process* (TSP). The goal of TSP is to build a "self-directed" project team that organizes itself to produce high-quality software. Humphrey [Hum98] defines the following objectives for TSP:

- Build self-directed teams that plan and track their work, establish goals, and own their processes and plans. These can be pure software teams or integrated product teams (IPTs) of 3 to about 20 engineers.
- Show managers how to coach and motivate their teams and how to help them sustain peak performance.
- Accelerate software process improvement by making CMM[23] Level 5 behavior normal and expected.
- Provide improvement guidance to high-maturity organizations.
- Facilitate university teaching of industrial-grade team skills.

ADVICE

To form a self-directed team, you must collaborate well internally and communicate well externally.

A self-directed team has a consistent understanding of its overall goals and objectives; defines roles and responsibilities for each team member; tracks quantitative project data (about productivity and quality); identifies a team process that is appropriate for the project and a strategy for implementing the process; defines local standards that are applicable to the team's software engineering work; continually assesses risk and reacts to it; and tracks, manages, and reports project status.

---

23 The Capability Maturity Model (CMM), a measure of the effectiveness of a software process, is discussed in Chapter 30.

TSP defines the following framework activities: **project launch, high-level design, implementation, integration and test,** and **postmortem.** Like their counterparts in PSP (note that terminology is somewhat different), these activities enable the team to plan, design, and construct software in a disciplined manner while at the same time quantitatively measuring the process and the product. The postmortem sets the stage for process improvements.

TSP makes use of a wide variety of scripts, forms, and standards that serve to guide team members in their work. "Scripts" define specific process activities (i.e., project launch, design, implementation, integration and system testing, postmortem) and other more detailed work functions (e.g., development planning, requirements development, software configuration management, unit test) that are part of the team process.

KEY POINT

TSP scripts define elements of the team process and activities that occur within the process.

TSP recognizes that the best software teams are self-directed.[24] Team members set project objectives, adapt the process to meet their needs, control the project schedule, and through measurement and analysis of the metrics collected, work continually to improve the team's approach to software engineering.

Like PSP, TSP is a rigorous approach to software engineering that provides distinct and quantifiable benefits in productivity and quality. The team must make a full commitment to the process and must undergo thorough training to ensure that the approach is properly applied.

2.7   PROCESS TECHNOLOGY

One or more of the process models discussed in the preceding sections must be adapted for use by a software team. To accomplish this, *process technology tools* have been developed to help software organizations analyze their current process, organize work tasks, control and monitor progress, and manage technical quality.

Process technology tools allow a software organization to build an automated model of the process framework, task sets, and umbrella activities discussed in Section 2.1. The model, normally represented as a network, can then be analyzed to determine typical workflow and examine alternative process structures that might lead to reduced development time or cost.

Once an acceptable process has been created, other process technology tools can be used to allocate, monitor, and even control all software engineering activities, actions, and tasks defined as part of the process model. Each member of a software team can use such tools to develop a checklist of work tasks to be performed, work products to be produced, and quality assurance activities to be conducted. The process technology tool can also be used to coordinate the use of other software engineering tools that are appropriate for a particular work task.

---

24 In Chapter 3 I discuss the importance of "self-organizing" teams as a key element in agile software development.

Process Modeling Tools

Objective: If an organization works to improve a business (or software) process, it must first understand it. Process modeling tools (also called *process technology* or *process management* tools) are used to represent the key elements of a process so that it can be better understood. Such tools can also provide links to process descriptions that help those involved in the process to understand the actions and work tasks that are required to perform it. Process modeling tools provide links to other tools that provide support to defined process activities.

Mechanics: Tools in this category allow a team to define the elements of a unique process model (actions, tasks, work products, QA points), provide detailed guidance on the content or description of each process element, and then manage the process as it is conducted. In some cases, the process technology tools incorporate standard project management tasks such as estimating, scheduling, tracking, and control.

Representative Tools:[25]

Igrafx Process Tools—tools that enable a team to map, measure, and model the software process (**www.micrografx.com**)

Adeptia BPM Server—designed to manage, automate, and optimize business processes (**www.adeptia.com**)

SpeedDev Suite—a collection of six tools with a heavy emphasis on the management of communication and modeling activities (**www.speedev.com**)

2.8   PRODUCT AND PROCESS

If the process is weak, the end product will undoubtedly suffer. But an obsessive over-reliance on process is also dangerous. In a brief essay written many years ago, Margaret Davis [Dav95a] makes timeless comments on the duality of product and process:

> About every ten years give or take five, the software community redefines "the problem" by shifting its focus from product issues to process issues. Thus, we have embraced structured programming languages (product) followed by structured analysis methods (process) followed by data encapsulation (product) followed by the current emphasis on the Software Engineering Institute's Software Development Capability Maturity Model (process) [followed by object-oriented methods, followed by agile software development].
>
> While the natural tendency of a pendulum is to come to rest at a point midway between two extremes, the software community's focus constantly shifts because new force is applied when the last swing fails. These swings are harmful in and of themselves because they confuse the average software practitioner by radically changing what it means to perform the job let alone perform it well. The swings also do not solve "the problem" for they are doomed to fail as long as product and process are treated as forming a dichotomy instead of a duality.
>
> There is precedence in the scientific community to advance notions of duality when contradictions in observations cannot be fully explained by one competing theory or another. The dual nature of light, which seems to be simultaneously particle and wave, has been accepted since the 1920s when Louis de Broglie proposed it. I believe that the

---

25 Tools noted here do not represent an endorsement, but rather a sampling of tools in this category. In most cases, tool names are trademarked by their respective developers.

observations we can make on the artifacts of software and its development demonstrate a fundamental duality between product and process. You can never derive or understand the full artifact, its context, use, meaning, and worth if you view it as only a process or only a product . . .

All of human activity may be a process, but each of us derives a sense of self-worth from those activities that result in a representation or instance that can be used or appreciated either by more than one person, used over and over, or used in some other context not considered. That is, we derive feelings of satisfaction from reuse of our products by ourselves or others.

Thus, while the rapid assimilation of reuse goals into software development potentially increases the satisfaction software practitioners derive from their work, it also increases the urgency for acceptance of the duality of product and process. Thinking of a reusable artifact as only product or only process either obscures the context and ways to use it or obscures the fact that each use results in product that will, in turn, be used as input to some other software development activity. Taking one view over the other dramatically reduces the opportunities for reuse and, hence, loses the opportunity for increasing job satisfaction.

People derive as much (or more) satisfaction from the creative process as they do from the end product. An artist enjoys the brush strokes as much as the framed result. A writer enjoys the search for the proper metaphor as much as the finished book. As creative software professional, you should also derive as much satisfaction from the process as the end product. The duality of product and process is one important element in keeping creative people engaged as software engineering continues to evolve.

2.9 SUMMARY

A generic process model for software engineering encompasses a set of framework and umbrella activities, actions, and work tasks. Each of a variety of process models can be described by a different process flow—a description of how the framework activities, actions, and tasks are organized sequentially and chronologically. Process patterns can be used to solve common problems that are encountered as part of the software process.

Prescriptive process models have been applied for many years in an effort to bring order and structure to software development. Each of these models suggests a somewhat different process flow, but all perform the same set of generic framework activities: communication, planning, modeling, construction, and deployment.

Sequential process models, such as the waterfall and V models, are the oldest software engineering paradigms. They suggest a linear process flow that is often inconsistent with modern realities (e.g., continuous change, evolving systems, tight time lines) in the software world. They do, however, have applicability in situations where requirements are well defined and stable.

Incremental process models are iterative in nature and produce working versions of software quite rapidly. Evolutionary process models recognize the iterative, incremental nature of most software engineering projects and are designed to accommodate change. Evolutionary models, such as prototyping and the spiral model, produce incremental work products (or working versions of the software) quickly. These models can be adopted to apply across all software engineering activities—from concept development to long-term system maintenance.

The concurrent process model allows a software team to represent iterative and concurrent elements of any process model. Specialized models include the component-based model that emphasizes component reuse and assembly; the formal methods model that encourages a mathematically based approach to software development and verification; and the aspect-oriented model that accommodates crosscutting concerns spanning the entire system architecture. The Unified Process is a "use case driven, architecture-centric, iterative and incremental" software process designed as a framework for UML methods and tools.

Personal and team models for the software process have been proposed. Both emphasize measurement, planning, and self-direction as key ingredients for a successful software process.

PROBLEMS AND POINTS TO PONDER

2.1. In the introduction to this chapter Baetjer notes: "The process provides interaction between users and designers, between users and evolving tools, and between designers and evolving tools [technology]." List five questions that (a) designers should ask users, (b) users should ask designers, (c) users should ask themselves about the software product that is to be built, (d) designers should ask themselves about the software product that is to be built and the process that will be used to build it.

2.2. Try to develop a set of actions for the communication activity. Select one action and define a task set for it.

2.3. A common problem during **communication** occurs when you encounter two stakeholders who have conflicting ideas about what the software should be. That is, you have mutually conflicting requirements. Develop a process pattern (this would be a stage pattern) using the template presented in Section 2.1.3 that addresses this problem and suggest an effective approach to it.

2.4. Do some research on PSP and present a brief presentation that describes the types of measurements that an individual software engineer is asked to make and how those measurement can be used to improve personal effectiveness.

2.5. The use of "scripts" (a required mechanism in TSP) is not universally praised within the software community. Make a list of pros and cons regarding scripts and suggest at least two situations in which they would be useful and another two situations where they might provide less benefit.

2.6. Read [Nog00] and write a two- or three-page paper that discusses the impact of "chaos" on software engineering.

2.7. Provide three examples of software projects that would be amenable to the waterfall model. Be specific.

2.8. Provide three examples of software projects that would be amenable to the prototyping model. Be specific.

2.9. What process adaptations are required if the prototype will evolve into a deliverable system or product?

2.10. Provide three examples of software projects that would be amenable to the incremental model. Be specific.

2.11. As you move outward along the spiral process flow, what can you say about the software that is being developed or maintained?

2.12. Is it possible to combine process models? If so, provide an example.

2.13. The concurrent process model defines a set of "states." Describe what these states represent in your own words, and then indicate how they come into play within the concurrent process model.

2.14. What are the advantages and disadvantages of developing software in which quality is "good enough"? That is, what happens when we emphasize development speed over product quality?

2.15. Provide three examples of software projects that would be amenable to the component-based model. Be specific.

2.16. It is possible to prove that a software component and even an entire program is correct. So why doesn't everyone do this?

2.17. Are the Unified Process and UML the same thing? Explain your answer.

FURTHER READINGS AND INFORMATION SOURCES

Most software engineering textbooks consider traditional process models in some detail. Books by Sommerville (*Software Engineering,* 8th ed., Addison-Wesley, 2006), Pfleeger and Atlee (*Software Engineering,* 3d ed., Prentice-Hall, 2005), and Schach (*Object-Oriented and Classical Software Engineering,* 7th ed., McGraw-Hill, 2006) consider traditional paradigms and discuss their strengths and weaknesses. Glass (*Facts and Fallacies of Software Engineering,* Prentice-Hall, 2002) provides an unvarnished, pragmatic view of the software engineering process. Although not specifically dedicated to process, Brooks (*The Mythical Man-Month,* 2d ed., Addison-Wesley, 1995) presents age-old project wisdom that has everything to do with process.

Firesmith and Henderson-Sellers (*The OPEN Process Framework: An Introduction,* Addison-Wesley, 2001) present a general template for creating "flexible, yet discipline software processes" and discuss process attributes and objectives. Madachy (*Software Process Dynamics,* Wiley-IEEE, 2008) discusses modeling techniques that allow the interrelated technical and social elements of the software process to be analyzed. Sharpe and McDermott (*Workflow Modeling: Tools for Process Improvement and Application Development,* Artech House, 2001) present tools for modeling both software and business processes.

Lim (*Managing Software Reuse,* Prentice Hall, 2004) discusses reuse from a manager's perspective. Ezran, Morisio, and Tully (*Practical Software Reuse,* Springer, 2002) and Jacobson, Griss, and Jonsson (*Software Reuse,* Addison-Wesley, 1997) present much useful information on component-based development. Heineman and Council (*Component-Based Software Engineering,* Addison-Wesley, 2001) describe the process required to implement component-based systems. Kenett and Baker (*Software Process Quality: Management and Control,* Marcel Dekker, 1999) consider how quality management and process design are intimately connected to one another.

Nygard (*Release It!: Design and Deploy Production-Ready Software,* Pragmatic Bookshelf, 2007) and Richardson and Gwaltney (*Ship it! A Practical Guide to Successful Software Projects,* Pragmatic Bookshelf, 2005) present a broad collection of useful guidelines that are applicable to the deployment activity.

In addition to Jacobson, Rumbaugh, and Booch's seminal book on the Unified Process [Jac99], books by Arlow and Neustadt (*UML 2 and the Unified Process,* Addison-Wesley, 2005), Kroll and Kruchten (*The Rational Unified Process Made Easy,* Addison-Wesley, 2003), and Farve (*UML and the Unified Process,* IRM Press, 2003) provide excellent complementary information. Gibbs (*Project Management with the IBM Rational Unified Process,* IBM Press, 2006) discusses project management within the context of the UP.

A wide variety of information sources on software engineering and the software process are available on the Internet. An up-to-date list of World Wide Web references that are relevant to the software process can be found at the SEPA website: **www.mhhe.com/engcs/compsci/ pressman/professional/olc/ser.htm**.

AGILE DEVELOPMENT

In 2001, Kent Beck and 16 other noted software developers, writers, and consultants [Bec01a] (referred to as the "Agile Alliance") signed the "Manifesto for Agile Software Development." It stated:

We are uncovering better ways of developing software by doing it and helping others do it. Through this work we have come to value:

Individuals and interactions over processes and tools

Working software over comprehensive documentation

Customer collaboration over contract negotiation

Responding to change over following a plan

That is, while there is value in the items on the right, we value the items on the left more.

QUICK LOOK

What is it? Agile software engineering combines a philosophy and a set of development guidelines. The philosophy encourages customer satisfaction and early incremental delivery of software; small, highly motivated project teams; informal methods; minimal software engineering work products; and overall development simplicity. The development guidelines stress delivery over analysis and design (although these activities are not discouraged), and active and continuous communication between developers and customers.

Who does it? Software engineers and other project stakeholders (managers, customers, end users) work together on an agile team—a team that is self-organizing and in control of its own destiny. An agile team fosters communication and collaboration among all who serve on it.

Why is it important? The modern business environment that spawns computer-based systems and software products is fast-paced and ever-changing. Agile software engineering represents a reasonable alternative to conventional software engineering for certain classes of software and certain types of software projects. It has been demonstrated to deliver successful systems quickly.

What are the steps? Agile development might best be termed "software engineering lite." The basic framework activities—communication, planning, modeling, construction, and deployment—remain. But they morph into a minimal task set that pushes the project team toward construction and delivery (some would argue that this is done at the expense of problem analysis and solution design).

What is the work product? Both the customer and the software engineer have the same view—the only really important work product is an operational "software increment" that is delivered to the customer on the appropriate commitment date.

How do I ensure that I've done it right? If the agile team agrees that the process works, and the team produces deliverable software increments that satisfy the customer, you've done it right.

A manifesto is normally associated with an emerging political movement—one that attacks the old guard and suggests revolutionary change (hopefully for the better). In some ways, that's exactly what agile development is all about.

Although the underlying ideas that guide agile development have been with us for many years, it has been less than two decades since these ideas have crystallized into a "movement." In essence, agile[1] methods were developed in an effort to overcome perceived and actual weaknesses in conventional software engineering. Agile development can provide important benefits, but it is not applicable to all projects, all products, all people, and all situations. It is also *not* antithetical to solid software engineering practice and can be applied as an overriding philosophy for all software work.

In the modern economy, it is often difficult or impossible to predict how a computer-based system (e.g., a Web-based application) will evolve as time passes. Market conditions change rapidly, end-user needs evolve, and new competitive threats emerge without warning. In many situations, you won't be able to define requirements fully before the project begins. You must be agile enough to respond to a fluid business environment.

Fluidity implies change, and change is expensive. Particularly if it is uncontrolled or poorly managed. One of the most compelling characteristics of the agile approach is its ability to reduce the costs of change throughout the software process.

Does this mean that a recognition of challenges posed by modern realities causes you to discard valuable software engineering principles, concepts, methods, and tools? Absolutely not! Like all engineering disciplines, software engineering continues to evolve. It can be adapted easily to meet the challenges posed by a demand for agility.

In a thought-provoking book on agile software development, Alistair Cockburn [Coc02] argues that the prescriptive process models introduced in Chapter 2 have a major failing: *they forget the frailties of the people who build computer software.* Software engineers are not robots. They exhibit great variation in working styles; significant differences in skill level, creativity, orderliness, consistency, and spontaneity. Some communicate well in written form, others do not. Cockburn argues that process models can "deal with people's common weaknesses with [either] discipline or tolerance" and that most prescriptive process models choose discipline. He states: "Because consistency in action is a human weakness, high discipline methodologies are fragile."

If process models are to work, they must provide a realistic mechanism for encouraging the discipline that is necessary, or they must be characterized in a manner that shows "tolerance" for the people who do software engineering work. Invariably, tolerant practices are easier for software people to adopt and sustain, but (as Cockburn admits) they may be less productive. Like most things in life, trade-offs must be considered.

> uote:
>
> "Agility: 1,
> everything else: 0."
>
> **Tom DeMarco**

---

1   Agile methods are sometimes referred to as *light methods* or *lean methods*.

3.1 WHAT IS AGILITY?

Just what is agility in the context of software engineering work? Ivar Jacobson [Jac02a] provides a useful discussion:

> *Agility* has become today's buzzword when describing a modern software process. Everyone is agile. An agile team is a nimble team able to appropriately respond to changes. Change is what software development is very much about. Changes in the software being built, changes to the team members, changes because of new technology, changes of all kinds that may have an impact on the product they build or the project that creates the product. Support for changes should be built-in everything we do in software, something we embrace because it is the heart and soul of software. An agile team recognizes that software is developed by individuals working in teams and that the skills of these people, their ability to collaborate is at the core for the success of the project.

In Jacobson's view, the pervasiveness of change is the primary driver for agility. Software engineers must be quick on their feet if they are to accommodate the rapid changes that Jacobson describes.

Don't make the mistake of assuming that agility gives you license to hack out solutions. A process is required and discipline is essential.

But agility is more than an effective response to change. It also encompasses the philosophy espoused in the manifesto noted at the beginning of this chapter. It encourages team structures and attitudes that make communication (among team members, between technologists and business people, between software engineers and their managers) more facile. It emphasizes rapid delivery of operational software and de-emphasizes the importance of intermediate work products (not always a good thing); it adopts the customer as a part of the development team and works to eliminate the "us and them" attitude that continues to pervade many software projects; it recognizes that planning in an uncertain world has its limits and that a project plan must be flexible.

Agility can be applied to any software process. However, to accomplish this, it is essential that the process be designed in a way that allows the project team to adapt tasks and to streamline them, conduct planning in a way that understands the fluidity of an agile development approach, eliminate all but the most essential work products and keep them lean, and emphasize an incremental delivery strategy that gets working software to the customer as rapidly as feasible for the product type and operational environment.

3.2 AGILITY AND THE COST OF CHANGE

The conventional wisdom in software development (supported by decades of experience) is that the cost of change increases nonlinearly as a project progresses (Figure 3.1, solid black curve). It is relatively easy to accommodate a change when a software team is gathering requirements (early in a project). A usage scenario might have to be modified, a list of functions may be extended, or a written specification can be edited. The costs of doing this work are minimal, and the time required will

FIGURE 3.1

Change costs
as a function
of time in
development

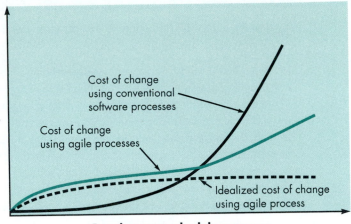

uote:

"Agility is dynamic, content specific, aggressively change embracing, and growth oriented."

—Steven Goldman et al.

An agile process reduces the cost of change because software is released in increments and change can be better controlled within an increment.

not adversely affect the outcome of the project. But what if we fast-forward a number of months? The team is in the middle of validation testing (something that occurs relatively late in the project), and an important stakeholder is requesting a major functional change. The change requires a modification to the architectural design of the software, the design and construction of three new components, modifications to another five components, the design of new tests, and so on. Costs escalate quickly, and the time and cost required to ensure that the change is made without unintended side effects is nontrivial.

Proponents of agility (e.g., [Bec00], [Amb04]) argue that a well-designed agile process "flattens" the cost of change curve (Figure 3.1, shaded, solid curve), allowing a software team to accommodate changes late in a software project without dramatic cost and time impact. You've already learned that the agile process encompasses incremental delivery. When incremental delivery is coupled with other agile practices such as continuous unit testing and pair programming (discussed later in this chapter), the cost of making a change is attenuated. Although debate about the degree to which the cost curve flattens is ongoing, there is evidence [Coc01a] to suggest that a significant reduction in the cost of change can be achieved.

3.3   What Is an Agile Process?

Any agile software process is characterized in a manner that addresses a number of key assumptions [Fow02] about the majority of software projects:

1. It is difficult to predict in advance which software requirements will persist and which will change. It is equally difficult to predict how customer priorities will change as the project proceeds.

2. For many types of software, design and construction are interleaved. That is, both activities should be performed in tandem so that design models are proven as they are created. It is difficult to predict how much design is necessary before construction is used to prove the design.

3. Analysis, design, construction, and testing are not as predictable (from a planning point of view) as we might like.

Given these three assumptions, an important question arises: How do we create a process that can manage *unpredictability?* The answer, as I have already noted, lies in process adaptability (to rapidly changing project and technical conditions). An agile process, therefore, must be *adaptable.*

But continual adaptation without forward progress accomplishes little. Therefore, an agile software process must adapt *incrementally.* To accomplish incremental adaptation, an agile team requires customer feedback (so that the appropriate adaptations can be made). An effective catalyst for customer feedback is an operational prototype or a portion of an operational system. Hence, an *incremental development strategy* should be instituted. *Software increments* (executable prototypes or portions of an operational system) must be delivered in short time periods so that adaptation keeps pace with change (unpredictability). This iterative approach enables the customer to evaluate the software increment regularly, provide necessary feedback to the software team, and influence the process adaptations that are made to accommodate the feedback.

3.3.1 Agility Principles

KEY POINT

Although agile processes embrace change, it is still important to examine the reasons for change.

The Agile Alliance (see [Agi03], [Fow01]) defines 12 agility principles for those who want to achieve agility:

1. Our highest priority is to satisfy the customer through early and continuous delivery of valuable software.

2. Welcome changing requirements, even late in development. Agile processes harness change for the customer's competitive advantage.

3. Deliver working software frequently, from a couple of weeks to a couple of months, with a preference to the shorter timescale.

4. Business people and developers must work together daily throughout the project.

ADVICE

Working software is important, but don't forget that it must also exhibit a variety of quality attributes including reliability, usability, and maintainability.

5. Build projects around motivated individuals. Give them the environment and support they need, and trust them to get the job done.

6. The most efficient and effective method of conveying information to and within a development team is face-to-face conversation.

7. Working software is the primary measure of progress.

8. Agile processes promote sustainable development. The sponsors, developers, and users should be able to maintain a constant pace indefinitely.

9. Continuous attention to technical excellence and good design enhances agility.

10. Simplicity—the art of maximizing the amount of work not done—is essential.

11. The best architectures, requirements, and designs emerge from self–organizing teams.

12. At regular intervals, the team reflects on how to become more effective, then tunes and adjusts its behavior accordingly.

Not every agile process model applies these 12 principles with equal weight, and some models choose to ignore (or at least downplay) the importance of one or more of the principles. However, the principles define an *agile spirit* that is maintained in each of the process models presented in this chapter.

3.3.2 The Politics of Agile Development

There is considerable debate (sometimes strident) about the benefits and applicability of agile software development as opposed to more conventional software engineering processes. Jim Highsmith [Hig02a] (facetiously) states the extremes when he characterizes the feeling of the pro-agility camp ("agilists"). "Traditional methodologists are a bunch of stick-in-the-muds who'd rather produce flawless documentation than a working system that meets business needs." As a counterpoint, he states (again, facetiously) the position of the traditional software engineering camp: "Lightweight, er, 'agile' methodologists are a bunch of glorified hackers who are going to be in for a heck of a surprise when they try to scale up their toys into enterprise-wide software."

You don't have to choose between agility and software engineering. Rather, define a software engineering approach that is agile.

Like all software technology arguments, this methodology debate risks degenerating into a religious war. If warfare breaks out, rational thought disappears and beliefs rather than facts guide decision making.

No one is against agility. The real question is: What is the best way to achieve it? As important, how do you build software that meets customers' needs today and exhibits the quality characteristics that will enable it to be extended and scaled to meet customers' needs over the long term?

There are no absolute answers to either of these questions. Even within the agile school itself, there are many proposed process models (Section 3.4), each with a subtly different approach to the agility problem. Within each model there is a set of "ideas" (agilists are loath to call them "work tasks") that represent a significant departure from traditional software engineering. And yet, many agile concepts are simply adaptations of good software engineering concepts. Bottom line: there is much that can be gained by considering the best of both schools and virtually nothing to be gained by denigrating either approach.

If you have further interest, see [Hig01], [Hig02a], and [DeM02] for an entertaining summary of other important technical and political issues.

3.3.3   Human Factors

Proponents of agile software development take great pains to emphasize the importance of "people factors." As Cockburn and Highsmith [Coc01a] state, "Agile development focuses on the talents and skills of individuals, molding the process to specific people and teams." The key point in this statement is that *the process molds to the needs of the people and team,* not the other way around.[2]

If members of the software team are to drive the characteristics of the process that is applied to build software, a number of key traits must exist among the people on an agile team and the team itself:

Competence.   In an agile development (as well as software engineering) context, "competence" encompasses innate talent, specific software-related skills, and overall knowledge of the process that the team has chosen to apply. Skill and knowledge of process can and should be taught to all people who serve as agile team members.

Common focus.   Although members of the agile team may perform different tasks and bring different skills to the project, all should be focused on one goal—to deliver a working software increment to the customer within the time promised. To achieve this goal, the team will also focus on continual adaptations (small and large) that will make the process fit the needs of the team.

Collaboration.   Software engineering (regardless of process) is about assessing, analyzing, and using information that is communicated to the software team; creating information that will help all stakeholders understand the work of the team; and building information (computer software and relevant databases) that provides business value for the customer. To accomplish these tasks, team members must collaborate—with one another and all other stakeholders.

Decision-making ability.   Any good software team (including agile teams) must be allowed the freedom to control its own destiny. This implies that the team is given autonomy—decision-making authority for both technical and project issues.

Fuzzy problem-solving ability.   Software managers must recognize that the agile team will continually have to deal with ambiguity and will continually be buffeted by change. In some cases, the team must accept the fact that the problem they are solving today may not be the problem that needs to be solved tomorrow. However, lessons learned from any problem-solving

? What key traits must exist among the people on an effective software team?

---

2   Successful software engineering organizations recognize this reality regardless of the process model they choose.

activity (including those that solve the wrong problem) may be of benefit to the team later in the project.

Mutual trust and respect.   The agile team must become what DeMarco and Lister [DeM98] call a "jelled" team (Chapter 24). A jelled team exhibits the trust and respect that are necessary to make them "so strongly knit that the whole is greater than the sum of the parts." [DeM98]

Self-organization.   In the context of agile development, self-organization implies three things: (1) the agile team organizes itself for the work to be done, (2) the team organizes the process to best accommodate its local environment, (3) the team organizes the work schedule to best achieve delivery of the software increment. Self-organization has a number of technical benefits, but more importantly, it serves to improve collaboration and boost team morale. In essence, the team serves as its own management. Ken Schwaber [Sch02] addresses these issues when he writes: "The team selects how much work it believes it can perform within the iteration, and the team commits to the work. Nothing demotivates a team as much as someone else making commitments for it. Nothing motivates a team as much as accepting the responsibility for fulfilling commitments that it made itself."

KEY POINT

A self-organizing team is in control of the work it performs. The team makes its own commitments and defines plans to achieve them.

3.4   EXTREME PROGRAMMING (XP)

In order to illustrate an agile process in a bit more detail, I'll provide you with an overview of *Extreme Programming* (XP), the most widely used approach to agile software development. Although early work on the ideas and methods associated with XP occurred during the late 1980s, the seminal work on the subject has been written by Kent Beck [Bec04a]. More recently, a variant of XP, called *Industrial XP* (IXP) has been proposed [Ker05]. IXP refines XP and targets the agile process specifically for use within large organizations.

3.4.1   XP Values

Beck [Bec04a] defines a set of five *values* that establish a foundation for all work performed as part of XP—communication, simplicity, feedback, courage, and respect. Each of these values is used as a driver for specific XP activities, actions, and tasks.

In order to achieve effective *communication* between software engineers and other stakeholders (e.g., to establish required features and functions for the software), XP emphasizes close, yet informal (verbal) collaboration between customers and developers, the establishment of effective metaphors[3] for communicating important concepts, continuous feedback, and the avoidance of voluminous documentation as a communication medium.

---

3   In the XP context, a *metaphor* is "a story that everyone—customers, programmers, and managers— can tell about how the system works" [Bec04a].

Keep it simple whenever you can, but recognize that continual "refactoring" can absorb significant time and resources.

To achieve *simplicity,* XP restricts developers to design only for immediate needs, rather than consider future needs. The intent is to create a simple design that can be easily implemented in code). If the design must be improved, it can be *refactored*[4] at a later time.

Feedback is derived from three sources: the implemented software itself, the customer, and other software team members. By designing and implementing an effective testing strategy (Chapters 17 through 20), the software (via test results) provides the agile team with feedback. XP makes use of the *unit test* as its primary testing tactic. As each class is developed, the team develops a unit test to exercise each operation according to its specified functionality. As an increment is delivered to a customer, the *user stories* or *use cases* (Chapter 5) that are implemented by the increment are used as a basis for acceptance tests. The degree to which the software implements the output, function, and behavior of the use case is a form of feedback. Finally, as new requirements are derived as part of iterative planning, the team provides the customer with rapid feedback regarding cost and schedule impact.

Beck [Bec04a] argues that strict adherence to certain XP practices demands *courage.* A better word might be *discipline.* For example, there is often significant pressure to design for future requirements. Most software teams succumb, arguing that "designing for tomorrow" will save time and effort in the long run. An agile XP team must have the discipline (courage) to design for today, recognizing that future requirements may change dramatically, thereby demanding substantial rework of the design and implemented code.

"XP is the answer to the question, 'How little can we do and still build great software?'"

Anonymous

By following each of these values, the agile team inculcates *respect* among it members, between other stakeholders and team members, and indirectly, for the software itself. As they achieve successful delivery of software increments, the team develops growing respect for the XP process.

3.4.2 The XP Process

WebRef

An excellent overview of "rules" for XP can be found at **www .extremeprogramm ing.org/rules.html.**

Extreme Programming uses an object-oriented approach (Appendix 2) as its preferred development paradigm and encompasses a set of rules and practices that occur within the context of four framework activities: planning, design, coding, and testing. Figure 3.2 illustrates the XP process and notes some of the key ideas and tasks that are associated with each framework activity. Key XP activities are summarized in the paragraphs that follow.

Planning. The planning activity (also called *the planning game*) begins with *listening*—a requirements gathering activity that enables the technical members of the XP team to understand the business context for the software and to get a broad

---

4 Refactoring allows a software engineer to improve the internal structure of a design (or source code) without changing its external functionality or behavior. In essence, refactoring can be used to improve the efficiency, readability, or performance of a design or the code that implements a design.

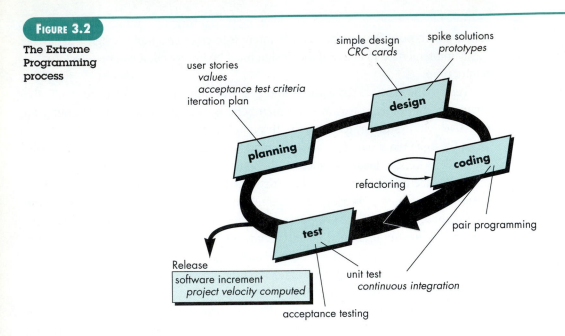

FIGURE 3.2

The Extreme
Programming
process

feel for required output and major features and functionality. Listening leads to the creation of a set of "stories" (also called *user stories*) that describe required output, features, and functionality for software to be built. Each *story* (similar to use cases described in Chapter 5) is written by the customer and is placed on an index card. The customer assigns a *value* (i.e., a priority) to the story based on the overall business value of the feature or function.[5] Members of the XP team then assess each story and assign a *cost*—measured in development weeks—to it. If the story is estimated to require more than three development weeks, the customer is asked to split the story into smaller stories and the assignment of value and cost occurs again. It is important to note that new stories can be written at any time.

Customers and developers work together to decide how to group stories into the next release (the next software increment) to be developed by the XP team. Once a basic *commitment* (agreement on stories to be included, delivery date, and other project matters) is made for a release, the XP team orders the stories that will be developed in one of three ways: (1) all stories will be implemented immediately (within a few weeks), (2) the stories with highest value will be moved up in the schedule and implemented first, or (3) the riskiest stories will be moved up in the schedule and implemented first.

After the first project release (also called a software increment) has been delivered, the XP team computes project velocity. Stated simply, *project velocity* is the

**What is an
XP "story"?**

WebRef

A worthwhile XP
"planning game" can
be found at:
**c2.com/cgi/
wiki?planningGame**.

---

5   The value of a story may also be dependent on the presence of another story.

number of customer stories implemented during the first release. Project velocity can then be used to (1) help estimate delivery dates and schedule for subsequent releases and (2) determine whether an overcommitment has been made for all stories across the entire development project. If an overcommitment occurs, the content of releases is modified or end delivery dates are changed.

As development work proceeds, the customer can add stories, change the value of an existing story, split stories, or eliminate them. The XP team then reconsiders all remaining releases and modifies its plans accordingly.

Design. XP design rigorously follows the KIS (keep it simple) principle. A simple design is always preferred over a more complex representation. In addition, the design provides implementation guidance for a story as it is written—nothing less, nothing more. The design of extra functionality (because the developer assumes it will be required later) is discouraged.[6]

XP encourages the use of CRC cards (Chapter 7) as an effective mechanism for thinking about the software in an object-oriented context. CRC (class-responsibility-collaborator) cards identify and organize the object-oriented classes[7] that are relevant to the current software increment. The XP team conducts the design exercise using a process similar to the one described in Chapter 8. The CRC cards are the only design work product produced as part of the XP process.

If a difficult design problem is encountered as part of the design of a story, XP recommends the immediate creation of an operational prototype of that portion of the design. Called a *spike solution*, the design prototype is implemented and evaluated. The intent is to lower risk when true implementation starts and to validate the original estimates for the story containing the design problem.

In the preceding section, we noted that XP encourages *refactoring*—a construction technique that is also a method for design optimization. Fowler [Fow00] describes refactoring in the following manner:

> Refactoring is the process of changing a software system in such a way that it does not alter the external behavior of the code yet improves the internal structure. It is a disciplined way to clean up code [and modify/simplify the internal design] that minimizes the chances of introducing bugs. In essence, when you refactor you are improving the design of the code after it has been written.

Because XP design uses virtually no notation and produces few, if any, work products other than CRC cards and spike solutions, design is viewed as a transient artifact that can and should be continually modified as construction proceeds. The intent of refactoring is to control these modifications by suggesting small design changes

---

6 These design guidelines should be followed in every software engineering method, although there are times when sophisticated design notation and terminology may get in the way of simplicity.

7 Object-oriented classes are discussed in Appendix 2, in Chapter 8, and throughout Part 2 of this book.

Refactoring improves the internal structure of a design (or source code) without changing its external functionality or behavior.

Useful information on XP can be obtained at **www .xprogramming. com.**

What is pair programming?

Many software teams are populated by individualists. You'll have to work to change that culture if pair programming is to work effectively.

How are unit tests used in XP?

that "can radically improve the design" [Fow00]. It should be noted, however, that the effort required for refactoring can grow dramatically as the size of an application grows.

A central notion in XP is that design occurs both before *and after* coding commences. Refactoring means that design occurs continuously as the system is constructed. In fact, the construction activity itself will provide the XP team with guidance on how to improve the design.

Coding.   After stories are developed and preliminary design work is done, the team does *not* move to code, but rather develops a series of unit tests that will exercise each of the stories that is to be included in the current release (software increment).[8] Once the unit test[9] has been created, the developer is better able to focus on what must be implemented to pass the test. Nothing extraneous is added (KIS). Once the code is complete, it can be unit-tested immediately, thereby providing instantaneous feedback to the developers.

A key concept during the coding activity (and one of the most talked about aspects of XP) is *pair programming*. XP recommends that two people work together at one computer workstation to create code for a story. This provides a mechanism for real-time problem solving (two heads are often better than one) and real-time quality assurance (the code is reviewed as it is created). It also keeps the developers focused on the problem at hand. In practice, each person takes on a slightly different role. For example, one person might think about the coding details of a particular portion of the design while the other ensures that coding standards (a required part of XP) are being followed or that the code for the story will satisfy the unit test that has been developed to validate the code against the story.

As pair programmers complete their work, the code they develop is integrated with the work of others. In some cases this is performed on a daily basis by an integration team. In other cases, the pair programmers have integration responsibility. This "continuous integration" strategy helps to avoid compatibility and interfacing problems and provides a "smoke testing" environment (Chapter 17) that helps to uncover errors early.

Testing.   I have already noted that the creation of unit tests before coding commences is a key element of the XP approach. The unit tests that are created should be implemented using a framework that enables them to be automated (hence, they can be executed easily and repeatedly). This encourages a regression testing strategy (Chapter 17) whenever code is modified (which is often, given the XP refactoring philosophy).

---

8   This approach is analogous to knowing the exam questions before you begin to study. It makes studying much easier by focusing attention only on the questions that will be asked.

9   Unit testing, discussed in detail in Chapter 17, focuses on an individual software component, exercising the component's interface, data structures, and functionality in an effort to uncover errors that are local to the component.

As the individual unit tests are organized into a "universal testing suite" [Wel99], integration and validation testing of the system can occur on a daily basis. This provides the XP team with a continual indication of progress and also can raise warning flags early if things go awry. Wells [Wel99] states: "Fixing small problems every few hours takes less time than fixing huge problems just before the deadline."

XP *acceptance tests*, also called *customer tests,* are specified by the customer and focus on overall system features and functionality that are visible and reviewable by the customer. Acceptance tests are derived from user stories that have been implemented as part of a software release.

3.4.3 Industrial XP

Joshua Kerievsky [Ker05] describes *Industrial Extreme Programming* (IXP) in the following manner: "IXP is an organic evolution of XP. It is imbued with XP's minimalist, customer-centric, test-driven spirit. IXP differs most from the original XP in its greater inclusion of management, its expanded role for customers, and its upgraded technical practices." IXP incorporates six new practices that are designed to help ensure that an XP project works successfully for significant projects within a large organization.

? **What new practices are appended to XP to create IXP?**

Readiness assessment. Prior to the initiation of an IXP project, the organization should conduct a *readiness assessment.* The assessment ascertains whether (1) an appropriate development environment exists to support IXP, (2) the team will be populated by the proper set of stakeholders, (3) the organization has a distinct quality program and supports continuous improvement, (4) the organizational culture will support the new values of an agile team, and (5) the broader project community will be populated appropriately.

Project community. Classic XP suggests that the right people be used to populate the agile team to ensure success. The implication is that people on the team must be well-trained, adaptable and skilled, and have the proper temperament to contribute to a self-organizing team. When XP is to be applied for a significant project in a large organization, the concept of the "team" should morph into that of a *community.* A community may have a technologist and customers who are central to the success of a project as well as many other stakeholders (e.g., legal staff, quality auditors, manufacturing or sales types) who "are often at the periphery of an IXP project yet they may play important roles on the project" [Ker05]. In IXP, the community members and their roles should be explicitly defined and mechanisms for communication and coordination between community members should be established.

Project chartering. The IXP team assesses the project itself to determine whether an appropriate business justification for the project exists and whether the project will further the overall goals and objectives of the organization. Chartering also examines the context of the project to determine how it complements, extends, or replaces existing systems or processes.

Test-driven management.   An IXP project requires measurable criteria for assessing the state of the project and the progress that has been made to date. Test-driven management establishes a series of measurable "destinations" [Ker05] and then defines mechanisms for determining whether or not these destinations have been reached.

Retrospectives.   An IXP team conducts a specialized technical review (Chapter 15) after a software increment is delivered. Called a *retrospective,* the review examines "issues, events, and lessons-learned" [Ker05] across a software increment and/or the entire software release. The intent is to improve the IXP process.

Continuous learning.   Because learning is a vital part of continuous process improvement, members of the XP team are encouraged (and possibly, incented) to learn new methods and techniques that can lead to a higher-quality product.

In addition to the six new practices discussed, IXP modifies a number of existing XP practices. *Story-driven development* (SDD) insists that stories for acceptance tests be written before a single line of code is generated. *Domain-driven design* (DDD) is an improvement on the "system metaphor" concept used in XP. DDD [Eva03] suggests the evolutionary creation of a domain model that "accurately represents how domain experts think about their subject" [Ker05]. *Pairing* extends the XP pair-programming concept to include managers and other stakeholders. The intent is to improve knowledge sharing among XP team members who may not be directly involved in technical development. *Iterative usability* discourages front-loaded interface design in favor of usability design that evolves as software increments are delivered and users' interaction with the software is studied.

IXP makes smaller modifications to other XP practices and redefines certain roles and responsibilities to make them more amenable to significant projects for large organizations. For further discussion of IXP, visit **http://industrialxp.org**.

3.4.4   The XP Debate

All new process models and methods spur worthwhile discussion and in some instances heated debate. Extreme Programming has done both. In an interesting book that examines the efficacy of XP, Stephens and Rosenberg [Ste03] argue that many XP practices are worthwhile, but others have been overhyped, and a few are problematic. The authors suggest that the codependent nature of XP practices are both its strength and its weakness. Because many organizations adopt only a subset of XP practices, they weaken the efficacy of the entire process. Proponents counter that XP is continuously evolving and that many of the issues raised by critics have been addressed as XP practice matures. Among the issues that continue to trouble some critics of XP are:[10]

? **What are some of the issues that lead to an XP debate?**

- *Requirements volatility.* Because the customer is an active member of the XP team, changes to requirements are requested informally. As a consequence, the scope of the project can change and earlier work may have to be modified to accommodate current needs. Proponents argue that this happens regardless of the process that is applied and that XP provides mechanisms for controlling scope creep.

- *Conflicting customer needs.* Many projects have multiple customers, each with his own set of needs. In XP, the team itself is tasked with assimilating the needs of different customers, a job that may be beyond their scope of authority.

- *Requirements are expressed informally.* User stories and acceptance tests are the only explicit manifestation of requirements in XP. Critics argue that a more formal model or specification is often needed to ensure that omissions, inconsistencies, and errors are uncovered before the system is built. Proponents counter that the changing nature of requirements makes such models and specification obsolete almost as soon as they are developed.

- *Lack of formal design.* XP deemphasizes the need for architectural design and in many instances, suggests that design of all kinds should be relatively informal. Critics argue that when complex systems are built, design must be emphasized to ensure that the overall structure of the software will exhibit quality and maintainability. XP proponents suggest that the incremental nature of the XP process limits complexity (simplicity is a core value) and therefore reduces the need for extensive design.

You should note that every software process has flaws and that many software organizations have used XP successfully. The key is to recognize where a process may have weaknesses and to adapt it to the specific needs of your organization.

SafeHome

Considering Agile Software Development

The scene: Doug Miller's office.

The Players: Doug Miller, software engineering manager; Jamie Lazar, software team member; Vinod Raman, software team member.

The conversation:

(A knock on the door, Jamie and Vinod enter Doug's office)

Jamie: Doug, you got a minute?

---

10 For a detailed look at some thoughtful criticism that has been leveled at XP, visit www.softwarereality.com/ExtremeProgramming.jsp.

Doug: Sure Jamie, what's up?

Jamie: We've been thinking about our process discussion yesterday . . . you know, what process we're going to choose for this new *SafeHome* project.

Doug: And?

Vinod: I was talking to a friend at another company, and he was telling me about Extreme Programming. It's an agile process model . . . heard of it?

Doug: Yeah, some good, some bad.

Jamie: Well, it sounds pretty good to us. Lets you develop software really fast, uses something called pair programming to do real-time quality checks . . . it's pretty cool, I think.

Doug: It does have a lot of really good ideas. I like the pair-programming concept, for instance, and the idea that stakeholders should be part of the team.

Jamie: Huh? You mean that marketing will work on the project team with us?

Doug (nodding): They're a stakeholder, aren't they?

Jamie: Jeez . . . they'll be requesting changes every five minutes.

Vinod: Not necessarily. My friend said that there are ways to "embrace" changes during an XP project.

Doug: So you guys think we should use XP?

Jamie: It's definitely worth considering.

Doug: I agree. And even if we choose an incremental model as our approach, there's no reason why we can't incorporate much of what XP has to offer.

Vinod: Doug, before you said "some good, some bad." What was the "bad"?

Doug: The thing I don't like is the way XP downplays analysis and design . . . sort of says that writing code is where the action is . . .

(The team members look at one another and smile.)

Doug: So you agree with the XP approach?

Jamie (speaking for both): Writing code is what we do, Boss!

Doug (laughing): True, but I'd like to see you spend a little less time coding and then recoding and a little more time analyzing what has to be done and designing a solution that works.

Vinod: Maybe we can have it both ways, agility with a little discipline.

Doug: I think we can, Vinod. In fact, I'm sure of it.

3.5   OTHER AGILE PROCESS MODELS

The history of software engineering is littered with dozens of obsolete process descriptions and methodologies, modeling methods and notations, tools, and technology. Each flared in notoriety and was then eclipsed by something new and (purportedly) better. With the introduction of a wide array of agile process models—each contending for acceptance within the software development community—the agile movement is following the same historical path.[11]

As I noted in the last section, the most widely used of all agile process models is Extreme Programming (XP). But many other agile process models have been proposed and are in use across the industry. Among the most common are:

- Adaptive Software Development (ASD)

- Scrum

- Dynamic Systems Development Method (DSDM)

---

11 This is not a bad thing. Before one or more models or methods are accepted as a de facto standard, all must contend for the hearts and minds of software engineers. The "winners" evolve into best practice, while the "losers" either disappear or merge with the winning models.

- Crystal
- Feature Drive Development (FDD)
- Lean Software Development (LSD)
- Agile Modeling (AM)
- Agile Unified Process (AUP)

In the sections that follow, I present a very brief overview of each of these agile process models. It is important to note that *all* agile process models conform (to a greater or lesser degree) to the *Manifesto for Agile Software Development* and the principles noted in Section 3.3.1. For additional detail, refer to the references noted in each subsection or for a survey, examine the "agile software development" entry in Wikipedia.[12]

3.5.1 Adaptive Software Development (ASD)

Adaptive Software Development (ASD) has been proposed by Jim Highsmith [Hig00] as a technique for building complex software and systems. The philosophical underpinnings of ASD focus on human collaboration and team self-organization.

Highsmith argues that an agile, adaptive development approach based on collaboration is "as much a source of *order* in our complex interactions as discipline and engineering." He defines an ASD "life cycle" (Figure 3.3) that incorporates three phases, speculation, collaboration, and learning.

FIGURE 3.3

Adaptive software development

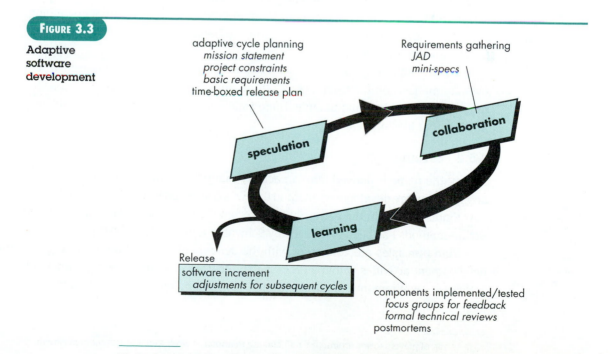

12 See http://en.wikipedia.org/wiki/Agile_software_development#Agile_methods.

During *speculation,* the project is initiated and *adaptive cycle planning* is conducted. Adaptive cycle planning uses project initiation information—the customer's mission statement, project constraints (e.g., delivery dates or user descriptions), and basic requirements—to define the set of release cycles (software increments) that will be required for the project.

No matter how complete and farsighted the cycle plan, it will invariably change. Based on information obtained at the completion of the first cycle, the plan is reviewed and adjusted so that planned work better fits the reality in which an ASD team is working.

Motivated people use *collaboration* in a way that multiplies their talent and creative output beyond their absolute numbers. This approach is a recurring theme in all agile methods. But collaboration is not easy. It encompasses communication and teamwork, but it also emphasizes individualism, because individual creativity plays an important role in collaborative thinking. It is, above all, a matter of trust. People working together must trust one another to (1) criticize without animosity, (2) assist without resentment, (3) work as hard as or harder than they do, (4) have the skill set to contribute to the work at hand, and (5) communicate problems or concerns in a way that leads to effective action.

As members of an ASD team begin to develop the components that are part of an adaptive cycle, the emphasis is on "learning" as much as it is on progress toward a completed cycle. In fact, Highsmith [Hig00] argues that software developers often overestimate their own understanding (of the technology, the process, and the project) and that learning will help them to improve their level of real understanding. ASD teams learn in three ways: focus groups (Chapter 5), technical reviews (Chapter 14), and project postmortems.

The ASD philosophy has merit regardless of the process model that is used. ASD's overall emphasis on the dynamics of self-organizing teams, interpersonal collaboration, and individual and team learning yield software project teams that have a much higher likelihood of success.

3.5.2 Scrum

Scrum (the name is derived from an activity that occurs during a rugby match[13]) is an agile software development method that was conceived by Jeff Sutherland and his development team in the early 1990s. In recent years, further development on the Scrum methods has been performed by Schwaber and Beedle [Sch01a].

Scrum principles are consistent with the agile manifesto and are used to guide development activities within a process that incorporates the following framework activities: requirements, analysis, design, evolution, and delivery. Within each

ADVICE

Effective collaboration with your customer will only occur if you jettison any "us and them" attitudes.

KEY POINT

ASD emphasizes learning as a key element in achieving a "self-organizing" team.

WebRef

Useful Scrum information and resources can be found at **www .controlchaos.com**.

---

13 A group of players forms around the ball and the teammates work together (sometimes violently!) to move the ball downfield.

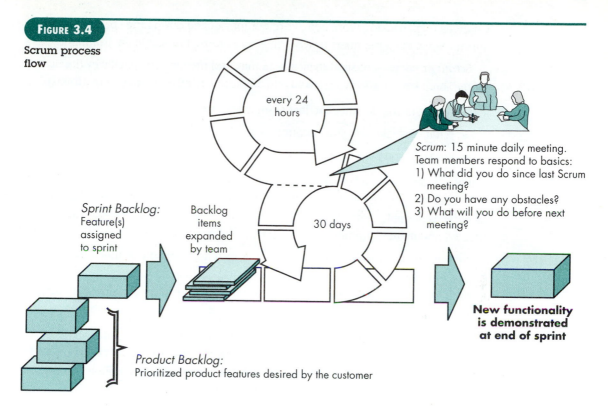

FIGURE 3.4

Scrum process flow

every 24 hours

Scrum: 15 minute daily meeting. Team members respond to basics:
1) What did you do since last Scrum meeting?
2) Do you have any obstacles?
3) What will you do before next meeting?

30 days

Sprint Backlog: Feature(s) assigned to sprint

Backlog items expanded by team

New functionality is demonstrated at end of sprint

Product Backlog: Prioritized product features desired by the customer

framework activity, work tasks occur within a process pattern (discussed in the following paragraph) called a *sprint*. The work conducted within a sprint (the number of sprints required for each framework activity will vary depending on product complexity and size) is adapted to the problem at hand and is defined and often modified in real time by the Scrum team. The overall flow of the Scrum process is illustrated in Figure 3.4.

Scrum emphasizes the use of a set of software process patterns [Noy02] that have proven effective for projects with tight timelines, changing requirements, and business criticality. Each of these process patterns defines a set of development actions:

Backlog—a prioritized list of project requirements or features that provide business value for the customer. Items can be added to the backlog at any time (this is how changes are introduced). The product manager assesses the backlog and updates priorities as required.

Sprints—consist of work units that are required to achieve a requirement defined in the backlog that must be fit into a predefined time-box[14] (typically 30 days).

POINT

Scrum incorporates a set of process patterns that emphasize project priorities, compartmentalized work units, communication, and frequent customer feedback.

---

14 A *time-box* is a project management term (see Part 4 of this book) that indicates a period of time that has been allocated to accomplish some task.

Changes (e.g., backlog work items) are not introduced during the sprint. Hence, the sprint allows team members to work in a short-term, but stable environment.

Scrum meetings—are short (typically 15 minutes) meetings held daily by the Scrum team. Three key questions are asked and answered by all team members [Noy02]:

- What did you do since the last team meeting?
- What obstacles are you encountering?
- What do you plan to accomplish by the next team meeting?

A team leader, called a *Scrum master,* leads the meeting and assesses the responses from each person. The Scrum meeting helps the team to uncover potential problems as early as possible. Also, these daily meetings lead to "knowledge socialization" [Bee99] and thereby promote a self-organizing team structure.

Demos—deliver the software increment to the customer so that functionality that has been implemented can be demonstrated and evaluated by the customer. It is important to note that the demo may not contain all planned functionality, but rather those functions that can be delivered within the time-box that was established.

Beedle and his colleagues [Bee99] present a comprehensive discussion of these patterns in which they state: "Scrum assumes up-front the existence of chaos. . . . " The Scrum process patterns enable a software team to work successfully in a world where the elimination of uncertainty is impossible.

3.5.3   Dynamic Systems Development Method (DSDM)

WebRef

Useful resources for DSSD can be found at **www.dsdm.org**.

The *Dynamic Systems Development Method* (DSDM) [Sta97] is an agile software development approach that "provides a framework for building and maintaining systems which meet tight time constraints through the use of incremental prototyping in a controlled project environment" [CCS02]. The DSDM philosophy is borrowed from a modified version of the Pareto principle—80 percent of an application can be delivered in 20 percent of the time it would take to deliver the complete (100 percent) application.

DSDM is an iterative software process in which each iteration follows the 80 percent rule. That is, only enough work is required for each increment to facilitate movement to the next increment. The remaining detail can be completed later when more business requirements are known or changes have been requested and accommodated.

The DSDM Consortium (**www.dsdm.org**) is a worldwide group of member companies that collectively take on the role of "keeper" of the method. The consortium has defined an agile process model, called the *DSDM life cycle* that defines three different iterative cycles, preceded by two additional life cycle activities:

Feasibility study—establishes the basic business requirements and constraints associated with the application to be built and then assesses whether the application is a viable candidate for the DSDM process.

Business study—establishes the functional and information requirements that will allow the application to provide business value; also, defines the basic application architecture and identifies the maintainability requirements for the application.

Functional model iteration—produces a set of incremental prototypes that demonstrate functionality for the customer. (Note: All DSDM prototypes are intended to evolve into the deliverable application.) The intent during this iterative cycle is to gather additional requirements by eliciting feedback from users as they exercise the prototype.

Design and build iteration—revisits prototypes built during *functional model iteration* to ensure that each has been engineered in a manner that will enable it to provide operational business value for end users. In some cases, *functional model iteration* and *design and build iteration* occur concurrently.

Implementation—places the latest software increment (an "operationalized" prototype) into the operational environment. It should be noted that (1) the increment may not be 100 percent complete or (2) changes may be requested as the increment is put into place. In either case, DSDM development work continues by returning to the functional model iteration activity.

DSDM can be combined with XP (Section 3.4) to provide a combination approach that defines a solid process model (the DSDM life cycle) with the nuts and bolts practices (XP) that are required to build software increments. In addition, the ASD concepts of collaboration and self-organizing teams can be adapted to a combined process model.

3.5.4 Crystal

Alistair Cockburn [Coc05] and Jim Highsmith [Hig02b] created the *Crystal family of agile methods*[15] in order to achieve a software development approach that puts a premium on "maneuverability" during what Cockburn characterizes as "a resource-limited, cooperative game of invention and communication, with a primary goal of delivering useful, working software and a secondary goal of setting up for the next game" [Coc02].

To achieve maneuverability, Cockburn and Highsmith have defined a set of methodologies, each with core elements that are common to all, and roles, process patterns, work products, and practice that are unique to each. The Crystal family is actually a set of example agile processes that have been proven effective for different types of projects. The intent is to allow agile teams to select the member of the crystal family that is most appropriate for their project and environment.

---

15 The name "crystal" is derived from the characteristics of geological crystals, each with its own color, shape, and hardness.

3.5.5 Feature Driven Development (FDD)

Feature Driven Development (FDD) was originally conceived by Peter Coad and his colleagues [Coa99] as a practical process model for object-oriented software engineering. Stephen Palmer and John Felsing [Pal02] have extended and improved Coad's work, describing an adaptive, agile process that can be applied to moderately sized and larger software projects.

WebRef

A wide variety of articles and presentations on FDD can be found at: **www.featuredrive ndevelopment .com/**.

Like other agile approaches, FDD adopts a philosophy that (1) emphasizes collaboration among people on an FDD team; (2) manages problem and project complexity using feature-based decomposition followed by the integration of software increments, and (3) communication of technical detail using verbal, graphical, and text-based means. FDD emphasizes software quality assurance activities by encouraging an incremental development strategy, the use of design and code inspections, the application of software quality assurance audits (Chapter 16), the collection of metrics, and the use of patterns (for analysis, design, and construction).

In the context of FDD, a *feature* "is a client-valued function that can be implemented in two weeks or less" [Coa99]. The emphasis on the definition of features provides the following benefits:

- Because features are small blocks of deliverable functionality, users can describe them more easily; understand how they relate to one another more readily; and better review them for ambiguity, error, or omissions.
- Features can be organized into a hierarchical business-related grouping.
- Since a feature is the FDD deliverable software increment, the team develops operational features every two weeks.
- Because features are small, their design and code representations are easier to inspect effectively.
- Project planning, scheduling, and tracking are driven by the feature hierarchy, rather than an arbitrarily adopted software engineering task set.

Coad and his colleagues [Coa99] suggest the following template for defining a feature:

<**action**> the <**result**> <**by** | **for** | **of** | **to**> a(n) <**object**>

where an <**object**> is "a person, place, or thing (including roles, moments in time or intervals of time, or catalog-entry-like descriptions)." Examples of features for an e-commerce application might be:

Add the product to shopping cart

Display the technical-specifications of the product

Store the shipping-information for the customer

FIGURE 3.5

Feature Driven Development [Coa99] (with permission)

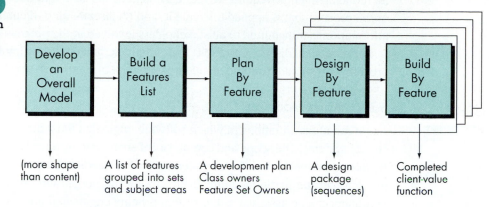

Develop an Overall Model	Build a Features List	Plan By Feature	Design By Feature	Build By Feature

(more shape than content) — A list of features grouped into sets and subject areas — A development plan Class owners Feature Set Owners — A design package (sequences) — Completed client-value function

A feature set groups related features into business-related categories and is defined [Coa99] as:

<action><-ing> a(n) **<object>**

For example: *Making a product sale* is a feature set that would encompass the features noted earlier and others.

The FDD approach defines five "collaborating" [Coa99] framework activities (in FDD these are called "processes") as shown in Figure 3.5.

FDD provides greater emphasis on project management guidelines and techniques than many other agile methods. As projects grow in size and complexity, ad hoc project management is often inadequate. It is essential for developers, their managers, and other stakeholders to understand project status—what accomplishments have been made and problems have been encountered. If deadline pressure is significant, it is critical to determine if software increments (features) are properly scheduled. To accomplish this, FDD defines six milestones during the design and implementation of a feature: "design walkthrough, design, design inspection, code, code inspection, promote to build" [Coa99].

3.5.6   Lean Software Development (LSD)

Lean Software Development (LSD) has adapted the principles of lean manufacturing to the world of software engineering. The lean principles that inspire the LSD process can be summarized ([Pop03], [Pop06a]) as *eliminate waste, build quality in, create knowledge, defer commitment, deliver fast, respect people,* and *optimize the whole.*

Each of these principles can be adapted to the software process. For example, *eliminate waste* within the context of an agile software project can be interpreted to mean [Das05]: (1) adding no extraneous features or functions, (2) assessing the cost and schedule impact of any newly requested requirement, (3) removing any superfluous process steps, (4) establishing mechanisms to improve the way team members find information, (5) ensuring the testing finds as many errors as possible,

(6) reducing the time required to request and get a decision that affects the software or the process that is applied to create it, and (7) streamlining the manner in which information is transmitted to all stakeholders involved in the process.

For a detailed discussion of LSD and pragmatic guidelines for implementing the process, you should examine [Pop06a] and [Pop06b].

3.5.7   Agile Modeling (AM)

WebRef

Comprehensive information on agile modeling can be found at: **www .agilemodeling.com**.

There are many situations in which software engineers must build large, business-critical systems. The scope and complexity of such systems must be modeled so that (1) all constituencies can better understand what needs to be accomplished, (2) the problem can be partitioned effectively among the people who must solve it, and (3) quality can be assessed as the system is being engineered and built.

Over the past 30 years, a wide variety of software engineering modeling methods and notation have been proposed for analysis and design (both architectural and component-level). These methods have merit, but they have proven to be difficult to apply and challenging to sustain (over many projects). Part of the problem is the "weight" of these modeling methods. By this I mean the volume of notation required, the degree of formalism suggested, the sheer size of the models for large projects, and the difficulty in maintaining the model(s) as changes occur. Yet analysis and design modeling have substantial benefit for large projects—if for no other reason than to make these projects intellectually manageable. Is there an agile approach to software engineering modeling that might provide an alternative?

At "The Official Agile Modeling Site," Scott Ambler [Amb02a] describes *agile modeling* (AM) in the following manner:

> Agile Modeling (AM) is a practice-based methodology for effective modeling and documentation of software-based systems. Simply put, Agile Modeling (AM) is a collection of values, principles, and practices for modeling software that can be applied on a software development project in an effective and light-weight manner. Agile models are more effective than traditional models because they are just barely good, they don't have to be perfect.

uote:

"I was in the drug store the other day trying to get a cold medication . . . not easy. There's an entire wall of products you need. You stand there going, Well, this one is quick acting but this is long lasting. . . . Which is more important, the present or the future?"

Jerry Seinfeld

Agile modeling adopts all of the values that are consistent with the agile manifesto. The agile modeling philosophy recognizes that an agile team must have the courage to make decisions that may cause it to reject a design and refactor. The team must also have the humility to recognize that technologists do not have all the answers and that business experts and other stakeholders should be respected and embraced.

Although AM suggests a wide array of "core" and "supplementary" modeling principles, those that make AM unique are [Amb02a]:

Model with a purpose.   A developer who uses AM should have a specific goal (e.g., to communicate information to the customer or to help better understand some aspect of the software) in mind before creating the model. Once the goal for the model is identified, the type of notation to be used and level of detail required will be more obvious.

Use multiple models.   There are many different models and notations that can be used to describe software. Only a small subset is essential for most projects. AM suggests that to provide needed insight, each model should present a different aspect of the system and only those models that provide value to their intended audience should be used.

"Traveling light" is an appropriate philosophy for all software engineering work. Build only those models that provide value ... no more, no less.

Travel light.   As software engineering work proceeds, keep only those models that will provide long-term value and jettison the rest. Every work product that is kept must be maintained as changes occur. This represents work that slows the team down. Ambler [Amb02a] notes that "Every time you decide to keep a model you trade-off agility for the convenience of having that information available to your team in an abstract manner (hence potentially enhancing communication within your team as well as with project stakeholders)."

Content is more important than representation.   Modeling should impart information to its intended audience. A syntactically perfect model that imparts little useful content is not as valuable as a model with flawed notation that nevertheless provides valuable content for its audience.

Know the models and the tools you use to create them.   Understand the strengths and weaknesses of each model and the tools that are used to create it.

Adapt locally.   The modeling approach should be adapted to the needs of the agile team.

A major segment of the software engineering community has adopted the Unified Modeling Language (UML)[16] as the preferred method for representing analysis and design models. The Unified Process (Chapter 2) has been developed to provide a framework for the application of UML. Scott Ambler [Amb06] has developed a simplified version of the UP that integrates his agile modeling philosophy.

3.5.8   Agile Unified Process (AUP)

The *Agile Unified Process* (AUP) adopts a "serial in the large" and "iterative in the small" [Amb06] philosophy for building computer-based systems. By adopting the classic UP phased activities—*inception, elaboration, construction,* and *transition*—AUP provides a serial overlay (i.e., a linear sequence of software engineering activities) that enables a team to visualize the overall process flow for a software project. However, within each of the activities, the team iterates to achieve agility and to deliver meaningful software increments to end users as rapidly as possible. Each AUP iteration addresses the following activities [Amb06]:

- *Modeling.* UML representations of the business and problem domains are created. However, to stay agile, these models should be "just barely good enough" [Amb06] to allow the team to proceed.

---

16 A brief tutorial on UML is presented in Appendix 1.

- *Implementation.* Models are translated into source code.

- *Testing.* Like XP, the team designs and executes a series of tests to uncover errors and ensure that the source code meets its requirements.

- *Deployment.* Like the generic process activity discussed in Chapters 1 and 2, deployment in this context focuses on the delivery of a software increment and the acquisition of feedback from end users.

- *Configuration and project management.* In the context of AUP, configuration management (Chapter 22) addresses change management, risk management, and the control of any persistent work products[17] that are produced by the team. Project management tracks and controls the progress of the team and coordinates team activities.

- *Environment management.* Environment management coordinates a process infrastructure that includes standards, tools, and other support technology available to the team.

Although the AUP has historical and technical connections to the Unified Modeling Language, it is important to note that UML modeling can be using in conjunction with any of the agile process models described in Section 3.5.

Agile Development

Objective: The objective of agile development tools is to assist in one or more aspects of agile development with an emphasis on facilitating the rapid generation of operational software. These tools can also be used when prescriptive process models (Chapter 2) are applied.

Mechanics: Tool mechanics vary. In general, agile tool sets encompass automated support for project planning, use case development and requirements gathering, rapid design, code generation, and testing.

Representative Tools:[18]
Note: Because agile development is a hot topic, most software tools vendors purport to sell tools that support

the agile approach. The tools noted here have characteristics that make them particularly useful for agile projects.

OnTime, developed by Axosoft (**www.axosoft.com**), provides agile process management support for various technical activities within the process.

Ideogramic UML, developed by Ideogramic (**www.ideogramic.com**) is a UML tool set specifically developed for use within an agile process.

Together Tool Set, distributed by Borland (**www.borland.com**), provides a tools suite that supports many technical activities within XP and other agile processes.

---

17 A *persistent work product* is a model or document or test case produced by the team that will be kept for an indeterminate period of time. It will *not* be discarded once the software increment is delivered.

18 Tools noted here do not represent an endorsement, but rather a sampling of tools in this category. In most cases, tool names are trademarked by their respective developers.

3.6   A Tool Set for the Agile Process

Some proponents of the agile philosophy argue that automated software tools (e.g., design tools) should be viewed as a minor supplement to the team's activities, and not at all pivotal to the success of the team. However, Alistair Cockburn [Coc04] suggests that tools can have a benefit and that "agile teams stress using tools that permit the rapid flow of understanding. Some of those tools are social, starting even at the hiring stage. Some tools are technological, helping distributed teams simulate being physically present. Many tools are physical, allowing people to manipulate them in workshops."

Because acquiring the right people (hiring), team collaboration, stakeholder communication, and indirect management are key elements in virtually all agile process models, Cockburn argues that "tools" that address these issues are critical success factors for agility. For example, a hiring "tool" might be the requirement to have a prospective team member spend a few hours pair programming with an existing member of the team. The "fit" can be assessed immediately.

Collaborative and communication "tools" are generally low tech and incorporate any mechanism ("physical proximity, whiteboards, poster sheets, index cards, and sticky notes" [Coc04]) that provides information and coordination among agile developers. Active communication is achieved via the team dynamics (e.g., pair programming), while passive communication is achieved by "information radiators" (e.g., a flat panel display that presents the overall status of different components of an increment). Project management tools deemphasize the Gantt chart and replace it with earned value charts or "graphs of tests created versus passed . . . other agile tools are used to optimize the environment in which the agile team works (e.g., more efficient meeting areas), improve the team culture by nurturing social interactions (e.g., collocated teams), physical devices (e.g., electronic whiteboards), and process enhancement (e.g., pair programming or time-boxing)" [Coc04].

Are any of these things really tools? They are, if they facilitate the work performed by an agile team member and enhance the quality of the end product.

3.7   Summary

In a modern economy, market conditions change rapidly, customer and end-user needs evolve, and new competitive threats emerge without warning. Practitioners must approach software engineering in a manner that allows them to remain agile—to define maneuverable, adaptive, lean processes that can accommodate the needs of modern business.

An agile philosophy for software engineering stresses four key issues: the importance of self-organizing teams that have control over the work they perform, communication and collaboration between team members and between practitioners and their customers, a recognition that change represents an opportunity, and an emphasis on rapid delivery of software that satisfies the customer. Agile process models have been designed to address each of these issues.

Extreme programming (XP) is the most widely used agile process. Organized as four framework activities—planning, design, coding, and testing—XP suggests a number of innovative and powerful techniques that allow an agile team to create frequent software releases that deliver features and functionality that have been described and then prioritized by stakeholders.

Other agile process models also stress human collaboration and team self-organization, but define their own framework activities and select different points of emphasis. For example, ASD uses an iterative process that incorporates adaptive cycle planning, relatively rigorous requirement gathering methods, and an iterative development cycle that incorporates customer focus groups and formal technical reviews as real-time feedback mechanisms. Scrum emphasizes the use of a set of software process patterns that have proven effective for projects with tight time lines, changing requirements, and business criticality. Each process pattern defines a set of development tasks and allows the Scrum team to construct a process that is adapted to the needs of the project. The Dynamic Systems Development Method (DSDM) advocates the use of time-box scheduling and suggests that only enough work is required for each software increment to facilitate movement to the next increment. Crystal is a family of agile process models that can be adopted to the specific characteristics of a project.

Feature Driven Development (FDD) is somewhat more "formal" than other agile methods, but still maintains agility by focusing the project team on the development of features—a client-valued function that can be implemented in two weeks or less. Lean Software Development (LSD) has adapted the principles of lean manufacturing to the world of software engineering. Agile modeling (AM) suggests that modeling is essential for all systems, but that the complexity, type, and size of the model must be tuned to the software to be built. The Agile Unified Process (AUP) adopts a "serial in the large" and "iterative in the small" philosophy for building software.

PROBLEMS AND POINTS TO PONDER

3.1. Reread "The Manifesto for Agile Software Development" at the beginning of this chapter. Can you think of a situation in which one or more of the four "values" could get a software team into trouble?

3.2. Describe agility (for software projects) in your own words.

3.3. Why does an iterative process make it easier to manage change? Is every agile process discussed in this chapter iterative? Is it possible to complete a project in just one iteration and still be agile? Explain your answers.

3.4. Could each of the agile processes be described using the generic framework activities noted in Chapter 2? Build a table that maps the generic activities into the activities defined for each agile process.

3.5. Try to come up with one more "agility principle" that would help a software engineering team become even more maneuverable.

3.6. Select one agility principle noted in Section 3.3.1 and try to determine whether each of the process models presented in this chapter exhibits the principle. [Note: I have presented an overview of these process models only, so it may not be possible to determine whether a principle has been addressed by one or more of the models, unless you do additional research (which is not required for this problem).]

3.7. Why do requirements change so much? After all, don't people know what they want?

3.8. Most agile process models recommend face-to-face communication. Yet today, members of a software team and their customers may be geographically separated from one another. Do you think this implies that geographical separation is something to avoid? Can you think of ways to overcome this problem?

3.9. Write an XP user story that describes the "favorite places" or "bookmarks" feature available on most Web browsers.

3.10. What is a spike solution in XP?

3.11. Describe the XP concepts of refactoring and pair programming in your own words.

3.12. Do a bit more reading and describe what a time-box is. How does this assist an ASD team in delivering software increments in a short time period?

3.13. Do the 80 percent rule in DSDM and the time-boxing approach defined for ASD achieve the same result?

3.14. Using the process pattern template presented in Chapter 2, develop a process pattern for any one of the Scrum patterns presented in Section 3.5.2.

3.15. Why is Crystal called a family of agile methods?

3.16. Using the FDD feature template described in Section 3.5.5, define a feature set for a Web browser. Now develop a set of features for the feature set.

3.17. Visit the Official Agile Modeling Site and make a complete list of all core and supplementary AM principles.

3.18. The tool set proposed in Section 3.6 supports many of the "soft" aspects of agile methods. Since communication is so important, recommend an actual tool set that might be used to enhance communication among stakeholders on an agile team.

FURTHER READINGS AND INFORMATION SOURCES

The overall philosophy and underlying principles of agile software development are considered in depth in many of the books referenced in the body of this chapter. In addition, books by Shaw and Warden (*The Art of Agile Development,* O'Reilly Media, Inc., 2008), Hunt (*Agile Software Construction,* Springer, 2005), and Carmichael and Haywood (*Better Software Faster,* Prentice-Hall, 2002) present useful discussions of the subject. Aguanno (*Managing Agile Projects,* Multi-Media Publications, 2005), Highsmith (*Agile Project Management: Creating Innovative Products,* Addison-Wesley, 2004), and Larman (*Agile and Iterative Development: A Manager's Guide,* Addison-Wesley, 2003) present a management overview and consider project management issues. Highsmith (*Agile Software Development Ecosystems,* Addison-Wesley, 2002) presents a survey of agile principles, processes, and practices. A worthwhile discussion of the delicate balance between agility and discipline is presented by Booch and his colleagues (*Balancing Agility and Discipline,* Addison-Wesley, 2004).

Martin (*Clean Code: A Handbook of Agile Software Craftsmanship,* Prentice-Hall, 2009) presents the principles, patterns, and practices required to develop "clean code" in an agile software engineering environment. Leffingwell (*Scaling Software Agility: Best Practices for Large Enterprises,* Addison-Wesley, 2007) discusses strategies for scaling up agile practices for large projects. Lippert and Rook (*Refactoring in Large Software Projects: Performing Complex Restructurings Successfully,* Wiley, 2006) discuss the use of refactoring when applied in large, complex systems.

Stamelos and Sfetsos (*Agile Software Development Quality Assurance,* IGI Global, 2007) discuss SQA techniques that conform to the agile philosophy.

Dozens of books have been written about Extreme Programming over the past decade. Beck (*Extreme Programming Explained: Embrace Change,* 2d ed., Addison-Wesley, 2004) remains the definitive treatment of the subject. In addition, Jeffries and his colleagues (*Extreme Programming Installed,* Addison-Wesley, 2000), Succi and Marchesi (*Extreme Programming Examined,* Addison-Wesley, 2001), Newkirk and Martin (*Extreme Programming in Practice,* Addison-Wesley, 2001), and Auer and his colleagues (*Extreme Programming Applied: Play to Win,* Addison-Wesley, 2001) provide a nuts-and-bolts discussion of XP along with guidance on how best to apply it. McBreen (*Questioning Extreme Programming,* Addison-Wesley, 2003) takes a critical look at XP, defining when and where it is appropriate. An in-depth consideration of pair programming is presented by McBreen (*Pair Programming Illuminated,* Addison-Wesley, 2003).

ASD is addressed in depth by Highsmith [Hig00]. Schwaber (*The Enterprise and Scrum,* Microsoft Press, 2007) discusses the use of Scrum for projects that have a major business impact. The nuts and bolts of Scrum are discussed by Schwaber and Beedle (*Agile Software Development with SCRUM,* Prentice-Hall, 2001). Worthwhile treatments of DSDM have been written by the DSDM Consortium (*DSDM: Business Focused Development,* 2d ed., Pearson Education, 2003) and Stapleton (*DSDM: The Method in Practice,* Addison-Wesley, 1997). Cockburn (*Crystal Clear,* Addison-Wesley, 2005) presents an excellent overview of the Crystal family of processes. Palmer and Felsing [Pal02] present a detailed treatment of FDD. Carmichael and Haywood (*Better Software Faster,* Prentice-Hall, 2002) provides another useful treatment of FDD that includes a step-by-step journey through the mechanics of the process. Poppendieck and Poppendieck (*Lean Development: An Agile Toolkit for Software Development Managers,* Addison-Wesley, 2003) provide guidelines for managing and controlling agile projects. Ambler and Jeffries (*Agile Modeling,* Wiley, 2002) discuss AM in some depth.

A wide variety of information sources on agile software development are available on the Internet. An up-to-date list of World Wide Web references that are relevant to the agile process can be found at the SEPA website: **www.mhhe.com/engcs/compsci/pressman/professional/olc/ser.htm**.

In this part of *Software Engineering: A Practitioner's Approach* you'll learn about the principles, concepts, and methods that are used to create high-quality requirements and design models. These questions are addressed in the chapters that follow:

- What concepts and principles guide software engineering practice?

- What is requirements engineering and what are the underlying concepts that lead to good requirements analysis?

- How is the requirements model created and what are its elements?

- What are the elements of a good design?

- How does architectural design establish a framework for all other design actions and what models are used?

- How do we design high-quality software components?

- What concepts, models, and methods are applied as a user interface is designed?

- What is pattern-based design?

- What specialized strategies and methods are used to design WebApps?

Once these questions are answered you'll be better prepared to apply software engineering practice.

4

PRINCIPLES THAT GUIDE PRACTICE

In a book that explores the lives and thoughts of software engineers, Ellen Ullman [Ull97] depicts a slice of life as she relates the thoughts of practitioner under pressure:

I have no idea what time it is. There are no windows in this office and no clock, only the blinking red LED display of a microwave, which flashes 12:00, 12:00, 12:00, 12:00. Joel and I have been programming for days. We have a bug, a stubborn demon of a bug. So the red pulse no-time feels right, like a read-out of our brains, which have somehow synchronized themselves at the same blink rate . . .

What are we working on? . . . The details escape me just now. We may be helping poor sick people or tuning a set of low-level routines to verify bits on a distributed database protocol—I don't care. I should care; in another part of my being—later, perhaps when we emerge from this room full of computers—I will care very much why and for whom and for what purpose I am writing software. But just now: no. I have passed through a membrane where the real world and its uses no longer matter. I am a software engineer. . . .

QUICK LOOK

What is it? Software engineering practice is a broad array of principles, concepts, methods, and tools that you must consider as software is planned and developed. Principles that guide practice establish a foundation from which software engineering is conducted.

Who does it? Practitioners (software engineers) and their managers conduct a variety of software engineering tasks.

Why is it important? The software process provides everyone involved in the creation of a computer-based system or product with a road map for getting to a successful destination. Practice provides you with the detail you'll need to drive along the road. It tells you where the bridges, the roadblocks, and the forks are located. It helps you understand the concepts and principles that must be understood and followed to drive safely and rapidly. It instructs you on how to drive, where to slow down, and where to speed up. In the context of software engineering,

practice is what you do day in and day out as software evolves from an idea to a reality.

What are the steps? Three elements of practice apply regardless of the process model that is chosen. They are: principles, concepts, and methods. A fourth element of practice—tools—supports the application of methods.

What is the work product? Practice encompasses the technical activities that produce all work products that are defined by the software process model that has been chosen.

How do I ensure that I've done it right? First, have a firm understanding of the principles that apply to the work (e.g., design) that you're doing at the moment. Then, be certain that you've chosen an appropriate method for the work, be sure that you understand how to apply the method, use automated tools when they're appropriate for the task, and be adamant about the need for techniques to ensure the quality of work products that are produced.

A dark image of software engineering practice to be sure, but upon reflection, many of the readers of this book will be able to relate to it.

People who create computer software practice the art or craft or discipline[1] that is software engineering. But what is software engineering "practice"? In a generic sense, *practice* is a collection of concepts, principles, methods, and tools that a software engineer calls upon on a daily basis. Practice allows managers to manage software projects and software engineers to build computer programs. Practice populates a software process model with the necessary technical and management how-to's to get the job done. Practice transforms a haphazard unfocused approach into something that is more organized, more effective, and more likely to achieve success.

Various aspects of software engineering practice will be examined throughout the remainder of this book. In this chapter, my focus is on principles and concepts that guide software engineering practice in general.

4.1 SOFTWARE ENGINEERING KNOWLEDGE

In an editorial published in *IEEE Software* a decade ago, Steve McConnell [McC99] made the following comment:

> Many software practitioners think of software engineering knowledge almost exclusively as knowledge of specific technologies: Java, Perl, html, C++, Linux, Windows NT, and so on. Knowledge of specific technology details is necessary to perform computer programming. If someone assigns you to write a program in C++, you have to know something about C++ to get your program to work.
>
> You often hear people say that software development knowledge has a 3-year half-life: half of what you need to know today will be obsolete within 3 years. In the domain of technology-related knowledge, that's probably about right. But there is another kind of software development knowledge—a kind that I think of as "software engineering principles"—that does not have a three-year half-life. These software engineering principles are likely to serve a professional programmer throughout his or her career.

McConnell goes on to argue that the body of software engineering knowledge (circa the year 2000) had evolved to a "stable core" that he estimated represented about "75 percent of the knowledge needed to develop a complex system." But what resides within this stable core?

As McConnell indicates, core principles—the elemental ideas that guide software engineers in the work that they do—now provide a foundation from which software engineering models, methods, and tools can be applied and evaluated.

---

1 Some writers argue for one of these terms to the exclusion of the others. In reality, software engineering is all three.

4.2   CORE PRINCIPLES

Software engineering is guided by a collection of core principles that help in the application of a meaningful software process and the execution of effective software engineering methods. At the process level, core principles establish a philosophical foundation that guides a software team as it performs framework and umbrella activities, navigates the process flow, and produces a set of software engineering work products. At the level of practice, core principles establish a collection of values and rules that serve as a guide as you analyze a problem, design a solution, implement and test the solution, and ultimately deploy the software in the user community.

In Chapter 1, I identified a set of general principles that span software engineering process and practice: (1) provide value to end users, (2) keep it simple, (3) maintain the vision (of the product and the project), (4) recognize that others consume (and must understand) what you produce, (5) be open to the future, (6) plan ahead for reuse, and (7) think! Although these general principles are important, they are characterized at such a high level of abstraction that they are sometimes difficult to translate into day-to-day software engineering practice. In the subsections that follow, I take a more detailed look at the core principles that guide process and practice.

4.2.1   Principles That Guide Process

In Part 1 of this book I discussed the importance of the software process and described the many different process models that have been proposed for software engineering work. Regardless of whether a model is linear or iterative, prescriptive or agile, it can be characterized using the generic process framework that is applicable for all process models. The following set of core principles can be applied to the framework, and by extension, to every software process.

Principle 1. *Be agile.* Whether the process model you choose is prescriptive or agile, the basic tenets of agile development should govern your approach. Every aspect of the work you do should emphasize economy of action—keep your technical approach as simple as possible, keep the work products you produce as concise as possible, and make decisions locally whenever possible.

Principle 2. *Focus on quality at every step.* The exit condition for every process activity, action, and task should focus on the quality of the work product that has been produced.

Principle 3. *Be ready to adapt.* Process is not a religious experience, and dogma has no place in it. When necessary, adapt your approach to constraints imposed by the problem, the people, and the project itself.

Principle 4. *Build an effective team.* Software engineering process and practice are important, but the bottom line is people. Build a self-organizing team that has mutual trust and respect.

Principle 5. *Establish mechanisms for communication and coordination.* Projects fail because important information falls into the cracks and/or stakeholders fail to coordinate their efforts to create a successful end product. These are management issues and they must be addressed.

Principle 6. *Manage change.* The approach may be either formal or informal, but mechanisms must be established to manage the way changes are requested, assessed, approved, and implemented.

Principle 7. *Assess risk.* Lots of things can go wrong as software is being developed. It's essential that you establish contingency plans.

Principle 8. *Create work products that provide value for others.* Create only those work products that provide value for other process activities, actions, or tasks. Every work product that is produced as part of software engineering practice will be passed on to someone else. A list of required functions and features will be passed along to the person (people) who will develop a design, the design will be passed along to those who generate code, and so on. Be sure that the work product imparts the necessary information without ambiguity or omission.

Part 4 of this book focuses on project and process management issues and considers various aspects of each of these principles in some detail.

4.2.2 Principles That Guide Practice

Software engineering practice has a single overriding goal—to deliver on-time, high-quality, operational software that contains functions and features that meet the needs of all stakeholders. To achieve this goal, you should adopt a set of core principles that guide your technical work. These principles have merit regardless of the analysis and design methods that you apply, the construction techniques (e.g., programming language, automated tools) that you use, or the verification and validation approach that you choose. The following set of core principles are fundamental to the practice of software engineering:

Principle 1. *Divide and conquer.* Stated in a more technical manner, analysis and design should always emphasize *separation of concerns* (SoC). A large problem is easier to solve if it is subdivided into a collection of elements (or *concerns*). Ideally, each concern delivers distinct functionality that can be developed, and in some cases validated, independently of other concerns.

Principle 2. *Understand the use of abstraction.* At its core, an abstraction is a simplification of some complex element of a system used to communicate meaning in a single phrase. When I use the abstraction *spreadsheet*, it is assumed that you understand what a spreadsheet is, the general structure of content that a spreadsheet presents, and the typical functions that can be applied to it. In software engineering practice, you use many different levels

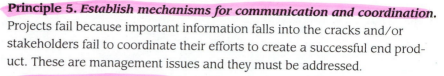

of abstraction, each imparting or implying meaning that must be communicated. In analysis and design work, a software team normally begins with models that represent high levels of abstraction (e.g., a spreadsheet) and slowly refines those models into lower levels of abstraction (e.g., a *column* or the *SUM* function).

Joel Spolsky [Spo02] suggests that "all non-trivial abstractions, to some degree, are leaky." The intent of an abstraction is to eliminate the need to communicate details. But sometimes, problematic effects precipitated by these details "leak" through. Without an understanding of the details, the cause of a problem cannot be easily diagnosed.

Principle 3. Strive for consistency.   Whether it's creating a requirements model, developing a software design, generating source code, or creating test cases, the principle of consistency suggests that a familiar context makes software easier to use. As an example, consider the design of a user interface for a WebApp. Consistent placement of menu options, the use of a consistent color scheme, and the consistent use of recognizable icons all help to make the interface ergonomically sound.

Principle 4. *Focus on the transfer of information.*   Software is about information transfer—from a database to an end user, from a legacy system to a WebApp, from an end user into a graphic user interface (GUI), from an operating system to an application, from one software component to another—the list is almost endless. In every case, information flows across an interface, and as a consequence, there are opportunities for error, or omission, or ambiguity. The implication of this principle is that you must pay special attention to the analysis, design, construction, and testing of interfaces.

Principle 5. *Build software that exhibits effective modularity.*
Separation of concerns (Principle 1) establishes a philosophy for software. *Modularity* provides a mechanism for realizing the philosophy. Any complex system can be divided into modules (components), but good software engineering practice demands more. Modularity must be *effective*. That is, each module should focus exclusively on one well-constrained aspect of the system—it should be cohesive in its function and/or constrained in the content it represents. Additionally, modules should be interconnected in a relatively simple manner—each module should exhibit low coupling to other modules, to data sources, and to other environmental aspects.

Use patterns (Chapter 12) to capture knowledge and experience for future generations of software engineers.

Principle 6. *Look for patterns.*   Brad Appleton [App00] suggests that:

> The goal of patterns within the software community is to create a body of literature to help software developers resolve recurring problems encountered throughout all of software development. Patterns help create a shared language for communicating insight and experience about these problems and their solutions. Formally codifying these solutions and their relationships lets us successfully capture the

body of knowledge which defines our understanding of good architectures that meet the needs of their users.

Principle 7. *When possible, represent the problem and its solution from a number of different perspectives.* When a problem and its solution are examined from a number of different perspectives, it is more likely that greater insight will be achieved and that errors and omissions will be uncovered. For example, a requirements model can be represented using a data-oriented viewpoint, a function-oriented viewpoint, or a behavioral viewpoint (Chapters 6 and 7). Each provides a different view of the problem and its requirements.

Principle 8. *Remember that someone will maintain the software.* Over the long term, software will be corrected as defects are uncovered, adapted as its environment changes, and enhanced as stakeholders request more capabilities. These maintenance activities can be facilitated if solid software engineering practice is applied throughout the software process.

These principles are not all you'll need to build high-quality software, but they do establish a foundation for every software engineering method discussed in this book.

4.3 PRINCIPLES THAT GUIDE EACH FRAMEWORK ACTIVITY

In the sections that follow I consider principles that have a strong bearing on the success of each generic framework activity defined as part of the software process. In many cases, the principles that are discussed for each of the framework activities are a refinement of the principles presented in Section 4.2. They are simply core principles stated at a lower level of abstraction.

4.3.1 Communication Principles

Before customer requirements can be analyzed, modeled, or specified they must be gathered through the communication activity. A customer has a problem that may be amenable to a computer-based solution. You respond to the customer's request for help. Communication has begun. But the road from communication to understanding is often full of potholes.

Effective communication (among technical peers, with the customer and other stakeholders, and with project managers) is among the most challenging activities that you will confront. In this context, I discuss communication principles as they apply to customer communication. However, many of the principles apply equally to all forms of communication that occur within a software project.

Principle 1. *Listen.* Try to focus on the speaker's words, rather than formulating your response to those words. Ask for clarification if something is unclear, but avoid constant interruptions. *Never* become contentious in your words or actions (e.g., rolling your eyes or shaking your head) as a person is talking.

Principle 2. *Prepare before you communicate.* Spend the time to understand the problem before you meet with others. If necessary, do some research to understand business domain jargon. If you have responsibility for conducting a meeting, prepare an agenda in advance of the meeting.

Principle 3. *Someone should facilitate the activity.* Every communication meeting should have a leader (a facilitator) to keep the conversation moving in a productive direction, (2) to mediate any conflict that does occur, and (3) to ensure than other principles are followed.

Principle 4. *Face-to-face communication is best.* But it usually works better when some other representation of the relevant information is present. For example, a participant may create a drawing or a "strawman" document that serves as a focus for discussion.

Principle 5. *Take notes and document decisions.* Things have a way of falling into the cracks. Someone participating in the communication should serve as a "recorder" and write down all important points and decisions.

Principle 6. *Strive for collaboration.* Collaboration and consensus occur when the collective knowledge of members of the team is used to describe product or system functions or features. Each small collaboration serves to build trust among team members and creates a common goal for the team.

Principle 7. *Stay focused; modularize your discussion.* The more people involved in any communication, the more likely that discussion will bounce from one topic to the next. The facilitator should keep the conversation modular, leaving one topic only after it has been resolved (however, see Principle 9).

Principle 8. *If something is unclear, draw a picture.* Verbal communication goes only so far. A sketch or drawing can often provide clarity when words fail to do the job.

Principle 9. *(a) Once you agree to something, move on. (b) If you can't agree to something, move on. (c) If a feature or function is unclear and cannot be clarified at the moment, move on.* Communication, like any software engineering activity, takes time. Rather than iterating endlessly, the people who participate should recognize that many topics require discussion (see Principle 2) and that "moving on" is sometimes the best way to achieve communication agility.

Principle 10. *Negotiation is not a contest or a game. It works best when both parties win.* There are many instances in which you and other stakeholders must negotiate functions and features, priorities, and delivery dates. If the team has collaborated well, all parties have a common goal. Still, negotiation will demand compromise from all parties.

? **What happens if I can't come to an agreement with the customer on some project-related issue?**

The Difference Between Customers and End Users

Software engineers communicate with many different stakeholders, but customers and end users have the most significant impact on the technical work that follows. In some cases the customer and the end user are one and the same, but for many projects, the customer and the end user are different people, working for different managers, in different business organizations.

A *customer* is the person or group who (1) originally requested the software to be built, (2) defines overall business objectives for the software, (3) provides basic product requirements, and (4) coordinates funding for the project. In a product or system business, the customer is often the marketing department. In an information technology (IT) environment, the customer might be a business component or department.

An *end user* is the person or group who (1) will actually use the software that is built to achieve some business purpose and (2) will define operational details of the software so the business purpose can be achieved.

SafeHome

Communication Mistakes

The scene: Software engineering team workspace

The players: Jamie Lazar, software team member; Vinod Raman, software team member; Ed Robbins, software team member.

The conversation:

Ed: "What have you heard about this *SafeHome* project?"

Vinod: "The kick-off meeting is scheduled for next week."

Jamie: "I've already done a little bit of investigation, but it didn't go well."

Ed: "What do you mean?"

Jamie: "Well, I gave Lisa Perez a call. She's the marketing honcho on this thing."

Vinod: "And . . . ?"

Jamie: "I wanted her to tell me about *SafeHome* features and functions . . . that sort of thing. Instead, she began asking me questions about security systems, surveillance systems . . . I'm no expert."

Vinod: "What does that tell you?"

(Jamie shrugs.)

Vinod: "That marketing will need us to act as consultants and that we'd better do some homework on this product area before our kick-off meeting. Doug said that he wanted us to 'collaborate' with our customer, so we'd better learn how to do that."

Ed: "Probably would have been better to stop by her office. Phone calls just don't work as well for this sort of thing."

Jamie: "You're both right. We've got to get our act together or our early communications will be a struggle."

Vinod: "I saw Doug reading a book on 'requirements engineering.' I'll bet that lists some principles of good communication. I'm going to borrow it from him."

Jamie: "Good idea . . . then you can teach us."

Vinod (smiling): "Yeah, right."

4.3.2 Planning Principles

The communication activity helps you to define your overall goals and objectives (subject, of course, to change as time passes). However, understanding these goals and objectives is not the same as defining a plan for getting there. The planning activity encompasses a set of management and technical practices that enable the software team to define a road map as it travels toward its strategic goal and tactical objectives.

Try as we might, it's impossible to predict exactly how a software project will evolve. There is no easy way to determine what unforeseen technical problems will be encountered, what important information will remain undiscovered until late in the project, what misunderstandings will occur, or what business issues will change. And yet, a good software team must plan its approach.

There are many different planning philosophies.[2] Some people are "minimalists," arguing that change often obviates the need for a detailed plan. Others are "traditionalists," arguing that the plan provides an effective road map and the more detail it has, the less likely the team will become lost. Still others are "agilists," arguing that a quick "planning game" may be necessary, but that the road map will emerge as "real work" on the software begins.

What to do? On many projects, overplanning is time consuming and fruitless (too many things change), but underplanning is a recipe for chaos. Like most things in life, planning should be conducted in moderation, enough to provide useful guidance for the team—no more, no less. Regardless of the rigor with which planning is conducted, the following principles always apply:

Principle 1. *Understand the scope of the project.* It's impossible to use a road map if you don't know where you're going. Scope provides the software team with a destination.

Principle 2. *Involve stakeholders in the planning activity.* Stakeholders define priorities and establish project constraints. To accommodate these realities, software engineers must often negotiate order of delivery, time lines, and other project-related issues.

Principle 3. *Recognize that planning is iterative.* A project plan is never engraved in stone. As work begins, it is very likely that things will change. As a consequence, the plan must be adjusted to accommodate these changes. In addition, iterative, incremental process models dictate replanning after the delivery of each software increment based on feedback received from users.

Principle 4. *Estimate based on what you know.* The intent of estimation is to provide an indication of effort, cost, and task duration, based on the team's current understanding of the work to be done. If information is vague or unreliable, estimates will be equally unreliable.

Principle 5. *Consider risk as you define the plan.* If you have identified risks that have high impact and high probability, contingency planning is necessary. In addition, the project plan (including the schedule) should be adjusted to accommodate the likelihood that one or more of these risks will occur.

---

2   A detailed discussion of software project planning and management is presented in Part 4 of this book.

Principle 6. Be realistic. People don't work 100 percent of every day. Noise always enters into any human communication. Omissions and ambiguity are facts of life. Change will occur. Even the best software engineers make mistakes. These and other realities should be considered as a project plan is established.

Principle 7. Adjust granularity as you define the plan. *Granularity* refers to the level of detail that is introduced as a project plan is developed. A "high-granularity" plan provides significant work task detail that is planned over relatively short time increments (so that tracking and control occur frequently). A "low-granularity" plan provides broader work tasks that are planned over longer time periods. In general, granularity moves from high to low as the project time line moves away from the current date. Over the next few weeks or months, the project can be planned in significant detail. Activities that won't occur for many months do not require high granularity (too much can change).

Principle 8. Define how you intend to ensure quality. The plan should identify how the software team intends to ensure quality. If technical reviews[3] are to be conducted, they should be scheduled. If pair programming (Chapter 3) is to be used during construction, it should be explicitly defined within the plan.

Principle 9. Describe how you intend to accommodate change. Even the best planning can be obviated by uncontrolled change. You should identify how changes are to be accommodated as software engineering work proceeds. For example, can the customer request a change at any time? If a change is requested, is the team obliged to implement it immediately? How is the impact and cost of the change assessed?

Principle 10. Track the plan frequently and make adjustments as required. Software projects fall behind schedule one day at a time. Therefore, it makes sense to track progress on a daily basis, looking for problem areas and situations in which scheduled work does not conform to actual work conducted. When slippage is encountered, the plan is adjusted accordingly.

To be most effective, everyone on the software team should participate in the planning activity. Only then will team members "sign up" to the plan.

4.3.3 Modeling Principles

We create models to gain a better understanding of the actual entity to be built. When the entity is a physical thing (e.g., a building, a plane, a machine), we can build a model that is identical in form and shape but smaller in scale. However, when the

KEY POINT

The term *granularity* refers to the detail with which some element of planning is represented or conducted.

---

3 Technical reviews are discussed in Chapter 15.

entity to be built is software, our model must take a different form. It must be capable of representing the information that software transforms, the architecture and functions that enable the transformation to occur, the features that users desire, and the behavior of the system as the transformation is taking place. Models must accomplish these objectives at different levels of abstraction—first depicting the software from the customer's viewpoint and later representing the software at a more technical level.

KEY POINT

Requirements models represent customer requirements. Design models provide a concrete specification for the construction of the software.

In software engineering work, two classes of models can be created: requirements models and design models. *Requirements models* (also called *analysis models*) represent customer requirements by depicting the software in three different domains: the information domain, the functional domain, and the behavioral domain. *Design models* represent characteristics of the software that help practitioners to construct it effectively: the architecture, the user interface, and component-level detail.

In their book on agile modeling, Scott Ambler and Ron Jeffries [Amb02b] define a set of modeling principles[4] that are intended for those who use the agile process model (Chapter 3) but are appropriate for all software engineers who perform modeling actions and tasks:

Principle 1. *The primary goal of the software team is to build software, not create models.*   Agility means getting software to the customer in the fastest possible time. Models that make this happen are worth creating, but models that slow the process down or provide little new insight should be avoided.

Principle 2. *Travel light—don't create more models than you need.* Every model that is created must be kept up-to-date as changes occur. More importantly, every new model takes time that might otherwise be spent on construction (coding and testing). Therefore, create only those models that make it easier and faster to construct the software.

Principle 3. *Strive to produce the simplest model that will describe the problem or the software.*   Don't overbuild the software [Amb02b]. By keeping models simple, the resultant software will also be simple. The result is software that is easier to integrate, easier to test, and easier to maintain (to change). In addition, simple models are easier for members of the software team to understand and critique, resulting in an ongoing form of feedback that optimizes the end result.

Principle 4. *Build models in a way that makes them amenable to change.* Assume that your models will change, but in making this assumption don't

ADVICE

The intent of any model is to communicate information. To accomplish this, use a consistent format. Assume that you won't be there to explain the model. It should stand on its own.

---

4   The principles noted in this section have been abbreviated and rephrased for the purposes of this book.

get sloppy. For example, since requirements will change, there is a tendency to give requirements models short shrift. Why? Because you know that they'll change anyway. The problem with this attitude is that without a reasonably complete requirements model, you'll create a design (design model) that will invariably miss important functions and features.

Principle 5. *Be able to state an explicit purpose for each model that is created.* Every time you create a model, ask yourself why you're doing so. If you can't provide solid justification for the existence of the model, don't spend time on it.

Principle 6. *Adapt the models you develop to the system at hand.* It may be necessary to adapt model notation or rules to the application; for example, a video game application might require a different modeling technique than real-time, embedded software that controls an automobile engine.

Principle 7. *Try to build useful models, but forget about building perfect models.* When building requirements and design models, a software engineer reaches a point of diminishing returns. That is, the effort required to make the model absolutely complete and internally consistent is not worth the benefits of these properties. Am I suggesting that modeling should be sloppy or low quality? The answer is "no." But modeling should be conducted with an eye to the next software engineering steps. Iterating endlessly to make a model "perfect" does not serve the need for agility.

Principle 8. *Don't become dogmatic about the syntax of the model. If it communicates content successfully, representation is secondary.* Although everyone on a software team should try to use consistent notation during modeling, the most important characteristic of the model is to communicate information that enables the next software engineering task. If a model does this successfully, incorrect syntax can be forgiven.

Principle 9. *If your instincts tell you a model isn't right even though it seems okay on paper, you probably have reason to be concerned.* If you are an experienced software engineer, trust your instincts. Software work teaches many lessons—some of them on a subconscious level. If something tells you that a design model is doomed to fail (even though you can't prove it explicitly), you have reason to spend additional time examining the model or developing a different one.

Principle 10. *Get feedback as soon as you can.* Every model should be reviewed by members of the software team. The intent of these reviews is to provide feedback that can be used to correct modeling mistakes, change misinterpretations, and add features or functions that were inadvertently omitted.

Requirements modeling principles. Over the past three decades, a large number of requirements modeling methods have been developed. Investigators have identified requirements analysis problems and their causes and have developed a variety of modeling notations and corresponding sets of heuristics to overcome them. Each analysis method has a unique point of view. However, all analysis methods are related by a set of operational principles:

Principle 1. *The information domain of a problem must be represented and understood.* The *information domain* encompasses the data that flow into the system (from end users, other systems, or external devices), the data that flow out of the system (via the user interface, network interfaces, reports, graphics, and other means), and the data stores that collect and organize persistent data objects (i.e., data that are maintained permanently).

Principle 2. *The functions that the software performs must be defined.* Software functions provide direct benefit to end users and also provide internal support for those features that are user visible. Some functions transform data that flow into the system. In other cases, functions effect some level of control over internal software processing or external system elements. Functions can be described at many different levels of abstraction, ranging from a general statement of purpose to a detailed description of the processing elements that must be invoked.

Principle 3. *The behavior of the software (as a consequence of external events) must be represented.* The behavior of computer software is driven by its interaction with the external environment. Input provided by end users, control data provided by an external system, or monitoring data collected over a network all cause the software to behave in a specific way.

Principle 4. *The models that depict information, function, and behavior must be partitioned in a manner that uncovers detail in a layered (or hierarchical) fashion.* Requirements modeling is the first step in software engineering problem solving. It allows you to better understand the problem and establishes a basis for the solution (design). Complex problems are difficult to solve in their entirety. For this reason, you should use a divide-and-conquer strategy. A large, complex problem is divided into subproblems until each subproblem is relatively easy to understand. This concept is called *partitioning* or *separation of concerns,* and it is a key strategy in requirements modeling.

Principle 5. *The analysis task should move from essential information toward implementation detail.* Requirements modeling begins by describing the problem from the end-user's perspective. The "essence" of the problem is described without any consideration of how a solution will be implemented. For example, a video game requires that the player "instruct" its protagonist on what direction to proceed as she moves into a dangerous maze. That is the essence of the problem. Implementation detail (normally described as part of the design model) indicates how the essence will be implemented. For the video game, voice input might be used. Alternatively,

KEY POINT

Analysis modeling focuses on three attributes of software: information to be processed, function to be delivered, and behavior to be exhibited.

Quote:

"The engineer's first problem in any design situation is to discover what the problem really is."

Author unknown

a keyboard command might be typed, a joystick (or mouse) might be pointed in a specific direction, or a motion-sensitive device might be waved in the air.

By applying these principles, a software engineer approaches a problem systematically. But how are these principles applied in practice? This question will be answered in Chapters 5 through 7.

Design Modeling Principles.   The software design model is analogous to an architect's plans for a house. It begins by representing the totality of the thing to be built (e.g., a three-dimensional rendering of the house) and slowly refines the thing to provide guidance for constructing each detail (e.g., the plumbing layout). Similarly, the design model that is created for software provides a variety of different views of the system.

There is no shortage of methods for deriving the various elements of a software design. Some methods are data driven, allowing the data structure to dictate the program architecture and the resultant processing components. Others are pattern driven, using information about the problem domain (the requirements model) to develop architectural styles and processing patterns. Still others are object oriented, using problem domain objects as the driver for the creation of data structures and the methods that manipulate them. Yet all embrace a set of design principles that can be applied regardless of the method that is used:

Principle 1. *Design should be traceable to the requirements model.* The requirements model describes the information domain of the problem, user-visible functions, system behavior, and a set of requirements classes that package business objects with the methods that service them. The design model translates this information into an architecture, a set of subsystems that implement major functions, and a set of components that are the realization of requirements classes. The elements of the design model should be traceable to the requirements model.

Principle 2. *Always consider the architecture of the system to be built.* Software architecture (Chapter 9) is the skeleton of the system to be built. It affects interfaces, data structures, program control flow and behavior, the manner in which testing can be conducted, the maintainability of the resultant system, and much more. For all of these reasons, design should start with architectural considerations. Only after the architecture has been established should component-level issues be considered.

Principle 3. *Design of data is as important as design of processing functions.*   Data design is an essential element of architectural design. The manner in which data objects are realized within the design cannot be left to chance. A well-structured data design helps to simplify program flow, makes the design and implementation of software components easier, and makes overall processing more efficient.

Quote:

"See first that the design is wise and just: that ascertained, pursue it resolutely; do not for one repulse forego the purpose that you resolved to effect."

William Shakespeare

WebRef

Insightful comments on the design process, along with a discussion of design aesthetics, can be found at **cs.wwc.edu/~aabyan/Design/**.

Principle 4. Interfaces (both internal and external) must be designed with care. The manner in which data flows between the components of a system has much to do with processing efficiency, error propagation, and design simplicity. A well-designed interface makes integration easier and assists the tester in validating component functions.

Principle 5. User interface design should be tuned to the needs of the end user. However, in every case, it should stress ease of use. The user interface is the visible manifestation of the software. No matter how sophisticated its internal functions, no matter how comprehensive its data structures, no matter how well designed its architecture, a poor interface design often leads to the perception that the software is "bad."

Principle 6. Component-level design should be functionally independent. Functional independence is a measure of the "single-mindedness" of a software component. The functionality that is delivered by a component should be cohesive—that is, it should focus on one and only one function or subfunction.[5]

Principle 7. Components should be loosely coupled to one another and to the external environment. Coupling is achieved in many ways—via a component interface, by messaging, through global data. As the level of coupling increases, the likelihood of error propagation also increases and the overall maintainability of the software decreases. Therefore, component coupling should be kept as low as is reasonable.

Principle 8. Design representations (models) should be easily understandable. The purpose of design is to communicate information to practitioners who will generate code, to those who will test the software, and to others who may maintain the software in the future. If the design is difficult to understand, it will not serve as an effective communication medium.

Principle 9. The design should be developed iteratively. With each iteration, the designer should strive for greater simplicity. Like almost all creative activities, design occurs iteratively. The first iterations work to refine the design and correct errors, but later iterations should strive to make the design as simple as is possible.

When these design principles are properly applied, you create a design that exhibits both external and internal quality factors [Mye78]. *External quality factors* are those properties of the software that can be readily observed by users (e.g., speed, reliability, correctness, usability). *Internal quality factors* are of importance to software engineers. They lead to a high-quality design from the technical perspective. To achieve internal quality factors, the designer must understand basic design concepts (Chapter 8).

---

5   Additional discussion of cohesion can be found in Chapter 8.

4.3.4 Construction Principles

The construction activity encompasses a set of coding and testing tasks that lead to operational software that is ready for delivery to the customer or end user. In modern software engineering work, coding may be (**1**) the direct creation of programming language source code (e.g., Java), (**2**) the automatic generation of source code using an intermediate design-like representation of the component to be built, or (**3**) the automatic generation of executable code using a "fourth-generation programming language" (e.g., Visual C++).

The initial focus of testing is at the component level, often called *unit testing.* Other levels of testing include (1) *integration testing* (conducted as the system is constructed), *validation testing* that assesses whether requirements have been met for the complete system (or software increment), and (3) *acceptance testing* that is conducted by the customer in an effort to exercise all required features and functions. The following set of fundamental principles and concepts are applicable to coding and testing:

Coding Principles.   The principles that guide the coding task are closely aligned with programming style, programming languages, and programming methods. However, there are a number of fundamental principles that can be stated:

Preparation principles: *Before you write one line of code, be sure you*

- Understand of the problem you're trying to solve.
- Understand basic design principles and concepts.
- Pick a programming language that meets the needs of the software to be built and the environment in which it will operate.
- Select a programming environment that provides tools that will make your work easier.
- Create a set of unit tests that will be applied once the component you code is completed.

Programming principles: *As you begin writing code, be sure you*

- Constrain your algorithms by following structured programming [Boh00] practice.
- Consider the use of pair programming.
- Select data structures that will meet the needs of the design.
- Understand the software architecture and create interfaces that are consistent with it.
- Keep conditional logic as simple as possible.
- Create nested loops in a way that makes them easily testable.
- Select meaningful variable names and follow other local coding standards.

- Write code that is self-documenting.
- Create a visual layout (e.g., indentation and blank lines) that aids understanding.

Validation Principles: *After you've completed your first coding pass, be sure you*

- Conduct a code walkthrough when appropriate.
- Perform unit tests and correct errors you've uncovered.
- Refactor the code.

WebRef

A wide variety of links to coding standards can be found at **www .literateprogramm ing.com/fpstyle .html**.

More books have been written about programming (coding) and the principles and concepts that guide it than about any other topic in the software process. Books on the subject include early works on programming style [Ker78], practical software construction [McC04], programming pearls [Ben99], the art of programming [Knu98], pragmatic programming issues [Hun99], and many, many other subjects. A comprehensive discussion of these principles and concepts is beyond the scope of this book. If you have further interest, examine one or more of the references noted.

Testing Principles.   In a classic book on software testing, Glen Myers [Mye79] states a number of rules that can serve well as testing objectives:

What are the objectives of software testing?

- Testing is a process of executing a program with the intent of finding an error.
- A good test case is one that has a high probability of finding an as-yet-undiscovered error.
- A successful test is one that uncovers an as-yet-undiscovered error.

ADVICE

In a broader software design context, recall that you begin "in the large" by focusing on software architecture and end "in the small" focusing on components. For testing, you simply reverse the focus and test your way out.

These objectives imply a dramatic change in viewpoint for some software developers. They move counter to the commonly held view that a successful test is one in which no errors are found. Your objective is to design tests that systematically uncover different classes of errors and to do so with a minimum amount of time and effort.

If testing is conducted successfully (according to the objectives stated previously), it will uncover errors in the software. As a secondary benefit, testing demonstrates that software functions appear to be working according to specification, and that behavioral and performance requirements appear to have been met. In addition, the data collected as testing is conducted provide a good indication of software reliability and some indication of software quality as a whole. But testing cannot show the absence of errors and defects; it can show only that software errors and defects are present. It is important to keep this (rather gloomy) statement in mind as testing is being conducted.

Davis [Dav95b] suggests a set of testing principles[6] that have been adapted for use in this book:

Principle 1. *All tests should be traceable to customer requirements.*[7] The objective of software testing is to uncover errors. It follows that the most severe defects (from the customer's point of view) are those that cause the program to fail to meet its requirements.

Principle 2. *Tests should be planned long before testing begins.* Test planning (Chapter 17) can begin as soon as the requirements model is complete. Detailed definition of test cases can begin as soon as the design model has been solidified. Therefore, all tests can be planned and designed before any code has been generated.

Principle 3. *The Pareto principle applies to software testing.* In this context the Pareto principle implies that 80 percent of all errors uncovered during testing will likely be traceable to 20 percent of all program components. The problem, of course, is to isolate these suspect components and to thoroughly test them.

Principle 4. *Testing should begin "in the small" and progress toward testing "in the large."* The first tests planned and executed generally focus on individual components. As testing progresses, focus shifts in an attempt to find errors in integrated clusters of components and ultimately in the entire system.

Principle 5. *Exhaustive testing is not possible.* The number of path permutations for even a moderately sized program is exceptionally large. For this reason, it is impossible to execute every combination of paths during testing. It is possible, however, to adequately cover program logic and to ensure that all conditions in the component-level design have been exercised.

4.3.5 Deployment Principles

As I noted earlier in Part 1 of this book, the deployment activity encompasses three actions: delivery, support, and feedback. Because modern software process models are evolutionary or incremental in nature, deployment happens not once, but a number of times as software moves toward completion. Each delivery cycle provides the customer and end users with an operational software increment that provides usable functions and features. Each support cycle provides documentation and human assistance for all functions and features introduced during all deployment cycles to

---

6 Only a small subset of Davis's testing principles are noted here. For more information, see [Dav95b].

7 This principle refers to *functional tests*, i.e., tests that focus on requirements. *Structural tests* (tests that focus on architectural or logical detail) may not address specific requirements directly.

date. Each feedback cycle provides the software team with important guidance that results in modifications to the functions, features, and approach taken for the next increment.

The delivery of a software increment represents an important milestone for any software project. A number of key principles should be followed as the team prepares to deliver an increment:

ADVICE

Be sure that your customer knows what to expect before a software increment is delivered. Otherwise, you can bet the customer will expect more than you deliver.

Principle 1. *Customer expectations for the software must be managed.* Too often, the customer expects more than the team has promised to deliver, and disappointment occurs immediately. This results in feedback that is not productive and ruins team morale. In her book on managing expectations, Naomi Karten [Kar94] states: "The starting point for managing expectations is to become more conscientious about what you communicate and how." She suggests that a software engineer must be careful about sending the customer conflicting messages (e.g., promising more than you can reasonably deliver in the time frame provided or delivering more than you promise for one software increment and then less than promised for the next).

Principle 2. *A complete delivery package should be assembled and tested.* A CD-ROM or other media (including Web-based downloads) containing all executable software, support data files, support documents, and other relevant information should be assembled and thoroughly beta-tested with actual users. All installation scripts and other operational features should be thoroughly exercised in as many different computing configurations (i.e., hardware, operating systems, peripheral devices, networking arrangements) as possible.

Principle 3. *A support regime must be established before the software is delivered.* An end user expects responsiveness and accurate information when a question or problem arises. If support is ad hoc, or worse, nonexistent, the customer will become dissatisfied immediately. Support should be planned, support materials should be prepared, and appropriate record-keeping mechanisms should be established so that the software team can conduct a categorical assessment of the kinds of support requested.

Principle 4. *Appropriate instructional materials must be provided to end users.* The software team delivers more than the software itself. Appropriate training aids (if required) should be developed; troubleshooting guidelines should be provided, and when necessary, a "what's different about this software increment" description should be published.[8]

---

8   During the communication activity, the software team should determine what types of help materials users want.

Principle 5. *Buggy software should be fixed first, delivered later.* Under time pressure, some software organizations deliver low-quality increments with a warning to the customer that bugs "will be fixed in the next release." This is a mistake. There's a saying in the software business: "Customers will forget you delivered a high-quality product a few days late, but they will never forget the problems that a low-quality product caused them. The software reminds them every day."

The delivered software provides benefit for the end user, but it also provides useful feedback for the software team. As the increment is put into use, end users should be encouraged to comment on features and functions, ease of use, reliability, and any other characteristics that are appropriate.

4.4 SUMMARY

Software engineering practice encompasses principles, concepts, methods, and tools that software engineers apply throughout the software process. Every software engineering project is different. Yet, a set of generic principles apply to the process as a whole and to the practice of each framework activity regardless of the project or the product.

A set of core principles help in the application of a meaningful software process and the execution of effective software engineering methods. At the process level, core principles establish a philosophical foundation that guides a software team as it navigates through the software process. At the level of practice, core principles establish a collection of values and rules that serve as a guide as you analyze a problem, design a solution, implement and test the solution, and ultimately deploy the software in the user community.

Communication principles focus on the need to reduce noise and improve bandwidth as the conversation between developer and customer progresses. Both parties must collaborate for the best communication to occur.

Planning principles provide guidelines for constructing the best map for the journey to a completed system or product. The plan may be designed solely for a single software increment, or it may be defined for the entire project. Regardless, it must address what will be done, who will do it, and when the work will be completed.

Modeling encompasses both analysis and design, describing representations of the software that progressively become more detailed. The intent of the models is to solidify understanding of the work to be done and to provide technical guidance to those who will implement the software. Modeling principles serve as a foundation for the methods and notation that are used to create representations of the software.

Construction incorporates a coding and testing cycle in which source code for a component is generated and tested. Coding principles define generic actions that should occur before code is written, while it is being created, and after it has been completed. Although there are many testing principles, only one is dominant: testing is a process of executing a program with the intent of finding an error.

Deployment occurs as each software increment is presented to the customer and encompasses delivery, support, and feedback. Key principles for delivery consider managing customer expectations and providing the customer with appropriate support information for the software. Support demands advance preparation. Feedback allows the customer to suggest changes that have business value and provide the developer with input for the next iterative software engineering cycle.

PROBLEMS AND POINTS TO PONDER

4.1. Since a focus on quality demands resources and time, is it possible to be agile and still maintain a quality focus?

4.2. Of the eight core principles that guide process (discussed in Section 4.2.1), which do you believe is most important?

4.3. Describe the concept of *separation of concerns* in your own words.

4.4. An important communication principle states "prepare before you communicate." How should this preparation manifest itself in the early work that you do? What work products might result as a consequence of early preparation?

4.5. Do some research on "facilitation" for the communication activity (use the references provided or others) and prepare a set of guidelines that focus solely on facilitation.

4.6. How does agile communication differ from traditional software engineering communication? How is it similar?

4.7. Why is it necessary to "move on"?

4.8. Do some research on "negotiation" for the communication activity and prepare a set of guidelines that focus solely on negotiation.

4.9. Describe what *granularity* means in the context of a project schedule.

4.10. Why are models important in software engineering work? Are they always necessary? Are there qualifiers to your answer about necessity?

4.11. What three "domains" are considered during requirements modeling?

4.12. Try to add one additional principle to those stated for coding in Section 4.3.4.

4.13. What is a successful test?

4.14. Do you agree or disagree with the following statement: "Since we deliver multiple increments to the customer, why should we be concerned about quality in the early increments—we can fix problems in later iterations." Explain your answer.

4.15. Why is feedback important to the software team?

FURTHER READINGS AND INFORMATION SOURCES

Customer communication is a critically important activity in software engineering, yet few practitioners spend any time reading about it. Withall (*Software Requirements Patterns,* Microsoft Press, 2007) presents a variety of useful patterns that address communications problems. Sutliff

(*User-Centred Requirements Engineering,* Springer, 2002) focuses heavily on communications-related challenges. Books by Weigers (*Software Requirements,* 2d ed., Microsoft Press, 2003), Pardee (*To Satisfy and Delight Your Customer,* Dorset House, 1996), and Karten [Kar94] provide much insight into methods for effective customer interaction. Although their book does not focus on software, Hooks and Farry (*Customer Centered Products,* American Management Association, 2000) present useful generic guidelines for customer communication. Young (*Effective Requirements Practices,* Addison-Wesley, 2001) emphasizes a "joint team" of customers and developers who develop requirements collaboratively. Somerville and Kotonya (*Requirements Engineering: Processes and Techniques,* Wiley, 1998) discuss "elicitation" concepts and techniques and other requirements engineering principles.

Communication and planning concepts and principles are considered in many project management books. Useful project management offerings include books by Bechtold (*Essentials of Software Project Management,* 2d ed., Management Concepts, 2007), Wysocki (*Effective Project Management: Traditional, Adaptive, Extreme,* 4th ed., Wiley, 2006), Leach (*Lean Project Management: Eight Principles for Success,* BookSurge Publishing, 2006), Hughes (*Software Project Management,* McGraw-Hill, 2005), and Stellman and Greene (*Applied Software Project Management,* O'Reilly Media, Inc., 2005).

Davis [Dav95] has compiled an excellent collection of software engineering principles. In addition, virtually every book on software engineering contains a useful discussion of concepts and principles for analysis, design, and testing. Among the most widely used offerings (in addition to this book!) are:

Abran, A., and J. Moore, *SWEBOK: Guide to the Software Engineering Body of Knowledge,* IEEE, 2002.

Christensen, M., and R. Thayer, *A Project Manager's Guide to Software Engineering Best Practices,* IEEE-CS Press (Wiley), 2002.

Jalote, P., *An Integrated Approach to Software Engineering,* Springer, 2006.

Pfleeger, S., *Software Engineering: Theory and Practice,* 3d ed., Prentice-Hall, 2005.

Schach, S., *Object-Oriented and Classical Software Engineering,* McGraw-Hill, 7th ed., 2006.

Sommerville, I., *Software Engineering,* 8th ed., Addison-Wesley, 2006.

These books also present detailed discussion of modeling and construction principles.

Modeling principles are considered in many books dedicated to requirements analysis and/or software design. Books by Lieberman (*The Art of Software Modeling,* Auerbach, 2007), Rosenberg and Stephens (*Use Case Driven Object Modeling with UML: Theory and Practice,* Apress, 2007), Roques (*UML in Practice,* Wiley, 2004), Penker and Eriksson (*Business Modeling with UML: Business Patterns at Work,* Wiley, 2001) discuss modeling principles and methods.

Norman's (*The Design of Everyday Things,* Currency/Doubleday, 1990) is must reading for every software engineer who intends to do design work. Winograd and his colleagues (*Bringing Design to Software,* Addison-Wesley, 1996) have edited an excellent collection of essays that address practical issues for software design. Constantine and Lockwood (*Software for Use,* Addison-Wesley, 1999) present the concepts associated with "user centered design." Tognazzini (*Tog on Software Design,* Addison-Wesley, 1995) presents a worthwhile philosophical discussion of the nature of design and the impact of decisions on quality and a team's ability to produce software that provides great value to its customer. Stahl and his colleagues (*Model-Driven Software Development: Technology, Engineering,* Wiley, 2006) discuss the principles of model-driven development.

Hundreds of books address one or more elements of the construction activity. Kernighan and Plauger [Ker78] have written a classic text on programming style, McConnell [McC93] presents pragmatic guidelines for practical software construction, Bentley [Ben99] suggests a wide variety of programming pearls, Knuth [Knu99] has written a classic three-volume series on the art of programming, and Hunt [Hun99] suggests pragmatic programming guidelines.

Myers and his colleagues (*The Art of Software Testing,* 2d ed., Wiley, 2004) have developed a major revision of his classic text and discuss many important testing principles. Books by Perry

(*Effective Methods for Software Testing,* 3d ed., Wiley, 2006), Whittaker (*How to Break Software,* Addison-Wesley, 2002), Kaner and his colleagues (*Lessons Learned in Software Testing,* Wiley, 2001), and Marick (*The Craft of Software Testing,* Prentice-Hall, 1997) each present important testing concepts and principles and much pragmatic guidance.

A wide variety of information sources on software engineering practice are available on the Internet. An up-to-date list of World Wide Web references that are relevant to software engineering practice can be found at the SEPA website: **www.mhhe.com/engcs/compsci/pressman/professional/olc/ser.htm**.

UNDERSTANDING REQUIREMENTS

Understanding the requirements of a problem is among the most difficult tasks that face a software engineer. When you first think about it, developing a clear understanding of requirements doesn't seem that hard. After all, doesn't the customer know what is required? Shouldn't the end users have a good understanding of the features and functions that will provide benefit? Surprisingly, in many instances the answer to these questions is "no." And even if customers and end-users are explicit in their needs, those needs will change throughout the project.

In the forward to a book by Ralph Young [You01] on effective requirements practices, I wrote:

It's your worst nightmare. A customer walks into your office, sits down, looks you straight in the eye, and says, "I know you think you understand what I said, but what you don't understand is what I said is not what I meant." Invariably, this happens late

QUICK LOOK

What is it? Before you begin any technical work, it's a good idea to apply a set of requirements engineering tasks. These tasks lead to an understanding of what the business impact of the software will be, what the customer wants, and how end users will interact with the software.

Who does it? Software engineers (sometimes referred to as system engineers or "analysts" in the IT world) and other project stakeholders (managers, customers, end users) all participate in requirements engineering.

Why is it important? Designing and building an elegant computer program that solves the wrong problem serves no one's needs. That's why it's important to understand what the customer wants before you begin to design and build a computer-based system.

What are the steps? Requirements engineering begins with inception—a task that defines the scope and nature of the problem to be solved. It moves onwards to elicitation—a task that helps stakeholders define what is required, and then

elaboration—where basic requirements are refined and modified. As stakeholders define the problem, negotiation occurs—what are the priorities, what is essential, when is it required? Finally, the problem is specified in some manner and then reviewed or validated to ensure that your understanding of the problem and the stakeholders' understanding of the problem coincide.

What is the work product? The intent of requirements engineering is to provide all parties with a written understanding of the problem. This can be achieved though a number of work products: usage scenarios, functions and features lists, requirements models, or a specification.

How do I ensure that I've done it right? Requirements engineering work products are reviewed with stakeholders to ensure that what you have learned is what they really meant. A word of warning: even after all parties agree, things will change, and they will continue to change throughout the project.

in the project, after deadline commitments have been made, reputations are on the line, and serious money is at stake.

All of us who have worked in the systems and software business for more than a few years have lived this nightmare, and yet, few of us have learned to make it go away. We struggle when we try to elicit requirements from our customers. We have trouble understanding the information that we do acquire. We often record requirements in a disorganized manner, and we spend far too little time verifying what we do record. We allow change to control us, rather than establishing mechanisms to control change. In short, we fail to establish a solid foundation for the system or software. Each of these problems is challenging. When they are combined, the outlook is daunting for even the most experienced managers and practitioners. But solutions do exist.

It's reasonable to argue that the techniques I'll discuss in this chapter are not a true "solution" to the challenges just noted. But they do provide a solid approach for addressing these challenges.

5.1   REQUIREMENTS ENGINEERING

uote:

"The hardest single part of building a software system is deciding what to build. No part of the work so cripples the resulting system if done wrong. No other part is more difficult to rectify later."

Fred Brooks

POINT

Requirements engineering establishes a solid base for design and construction. Without it, the resulting software has a high probability of not meeting customer's needs.

Designing and building computer software is challenging, creative, and just plain fun. In fact, building software is so compelling that many software developers want to jump right in before they have a clear understanding of what is needed. They argue that things will become clear as they build, that project stakeholders will be able to understand need only after examining early iterations of the software, that things change so rapidly that any attempt to understand requirements in detail is a waste of time, that the bottom line is producing a working program and all else is secondary. What makes these arguments seductive is that they contain elements of truth.[1] But each is flawed and can lead to a failed software project.

The broad spectrum of tasks and techniques that lead to an understanding of requirements is called *requirements engineering*. From a software process perspective, requirements engineering is a major software engineering action that begins during the communication activity and continues into the modeling activity. It must be adapted to the needs of the process, the project, the product, and the people doing the work.

Requirements engineering builds a bridge to design and construction. But where does the bridge originate? One could argue that it begins at the feet of the project stakeholders (e.g., managers, customers, end users), where business need is defined, user scenarios are described, functions and features are delineated, and project constraints are identified. Others might suggest that it begins with a broader system definition, where software is but one component of the larger system domain. But regardless of the starting point, the journey across the bridge takes you

---

1   This is particularly true for small projects (less than one month) and smaller, relatively simple software efforts. As software grows in size and complexity, these arguments begin to break down.

high above the project, allowing you to examine the context of the software work to be performed; the specific needs that design and construction must address; the priorities that guide the order in which work is to be completed; and the information, functions, and behaviors that will have a profound impact on the resultant design.

Requirements engineering provides the appropriate mechanism for understanding what the customer wants, analyzing need, assessing feasibility, negotiating a reasonable solution, specifying the solution unambiguously, validating the specification, and managing the requirements as they are transformed into an operational system [Tha97]. It encompasses seven distinct tasks: inception, elicitation, elaboration, negotiation, specification, validation, and management. It is important to note that some of these tasks occur in parallel and all are adapted to the needs of the project.

Inception.   How does a software project get started? Is there a single event that becomes the catalyst for a new computer-based system or product, or does the need evolve over time? There are no definitive answers to these questions. In some cases, a casual conversation is all that is needed to precipitate a major software engineering effort. But in general, most projects begin when a business need is identified or a potential new market or service is discovered. Stakeholders from the business community (e.g., business managers, marketing people, product managers) define a business case for the idea, try to identify the breadth and depth of the market, do a rough feasibility analysis, and identify a working description of the project's scope. All of this information is subject to change, but it is sufficient to precipitate discussions with the software engineering organization.[2]

At project inception,[3] you establish a basic understanding of the problem, the people who want a solution, the nature of the solution that is desired, and the effectiveness of preliminary communication and collaboration between the other stakeholders and the software team.

Elicitation.   It certainly seems simple enough—ask the customer, the users, and others what the objectives for the system or product are, what is to be accomplished, how the system or product fits into the needs of the business, and finally, how the system or product is to be used on a day-to-day basis. But it isn't simple—it's very hard.

Christel and Kang [Cri92] identify a number of problems that are encountered as elicitation occurs.

- **Problems of scope.** The boundary of the system is ill-defined or the customers/users specify unnecessary technical detail that may confuse, rather than clarify, overall system objectives.

---

2   If a computer-based system is to be developed, discussions begin within the context of a system engineering process. For a detailed discussion of system engineering, visit the website that accompanies this book.

3   Recall that the Unified Process (Chapter 2) defines a more comprehensive "inception phase" that encompasses the inception, elicitation, and elaboration tasks discussed in this chapter.

- **Problems of understanding.** The customers/users are not completely sure of what is needed, have a poor understanding of the capabilities and limitations of their computing environment, don't have a full understanding of the problem domain, have trouble communicating needs to the system engineer, omit information that is believed to be "obvious," specify requirements that conflict with the needs of other customers/users, or specify requirements that are ambiguous or untestable.

- **Problems of volatility.** The requirements change over time.

To help overcome these problems, you must approach requirements gathering in an organized manner.

Elaboration is a good thing, but you have to know when to stop. The key is to describe the problem in a way that establishes a firm base for design. If you work beyond that point, you're doing design.

Elaboration.   The information obtained from the customer during inception and elicitation is expanded and refined during elaboration. This task focuses on developing a refined requirements model (Chapters 6 and 7) that identifies various aspects of software function, behavior, and information.

Elaboration is driven by the creation and refinement of user scenarios that describe how the end user (and other actors) will interact with the system. Each user scenario is parsed to extract analysis classes—business domain entities that are visible to the end user. The attributes of each analysis class are defined, and the services[4] that are required by each class are identified. The relationships and collaboration between classes are identified, and a variety of supplementary diagrams are produced.

There should be no winner and no loser in an effective negotiation. Both sides win, because a "deal" that both can live with is solidified.

Negotiation.   It isn't unusual for customers and users to ask for more than can be achieved, given limited business resources. It's also relatively common for different customers or users to propose conflicting requirements, arguing that their version is "essential for our special needs."

You have to reconcile these conflicts through a process of negotiation. Customers, users, and other stakeholders are asked to rank requirements and then discuss conflicts in priority. Using an iterative approach that prioritizes requirements, assesses their cost and risk, and addresses internal conflicts, requirements are eliminated, combined, and/or modified so that each party achieves some measure of satisfaction.

Specification.   In the context of computer-based systems (and software), the term *specification* means different things to different people. A specification can be a written document, a set of graphical models, a formal mathematical model, a collection of usage scenarios, a prototype, or any combination of these.

Some suggest that a "standard template" [Som97] should be developed and used for a specification, arguing that this leads to requirements that are presented in a

---

4   A *service* manipulates the data encapsulated by the class. The terms *operation* and *method* are also used. If you are unfamiliar with object-oriented concepts, a basic introduction is presented in Appendix 2.

KEY POINT

The formality and format of a specification varies with the size and the complexity of the software to be built.

consistent and therefore more understandable manner. However, it is sometimes necessary to remain flexible when a specification is to be developed. For large systems, a written document, combining natural language descriptions and graphical models may be the best approach. However, usage scenarios may be all that are required for smaller products or systems that reside within well-understood technical environments.

INFO

Software Requirements Specification Template

A *software requirements specification* (SRS) is a document that is created when a detailed description of all aspects of the software to be built must be specified before the project is to commence. It is important to note that a formal SRS is not always written. In fact, there are many instances in which effort expended on an SRS might be better spent in other software engineering activities. However, when software is to be developed by a third party, when a lack of specification would create severe business issues, or when a system is extremely complex or business critical, an SRS may be justified.

Karl Wiegers [Wie03] of Process Impact Inc. has developed a worthwhile template (available at **www.processimpact.com/process_assets/srs_template.doc**) that can serve as a guideline for those who must create a complete SRS. A topic outline follows:

Table of Contents
Revision History

1.   Introduction
1.1   Purpose
1.2   Document Conventions
1.3   Intended Audience and Reading Suggestions
1.4   Project Scope
1.5   References

2.   Overall Description
2.1   Product Perspective

2.2   Product Features
2.3   User Classes and Characteristics
2.4   Operating Environment
2.5   Design and Implementation Constraints
2.6   User Documentation
2.7   Assumptions and Dependencies

3.   System Features
3.1   System Feature 1
3.2   System Feature 2 (and so on)

4.   External Interface Requirements
4.1   User Interfaces
4.2   Hardware Interfaces
4.3   Software Interfaces
4.4   Communications Interfaces

5.   Other Nonfunctional Requirements
5.1   Performance Requirements
5.2   Safety Requirements
5.3   Security Requirements
5.4   Software Quality Attributes

6.   Other Requirements

Appendix A: Glossary
Appendix B: Analysis Models
Appendix C: Issues List

A detailed description of each SRS topic can be obtained by downloading the SRS template at the URL noted earlier in this sidebar.

Validation. The work products produced as a consequence of requirements engineering are assessed for quality during a validation step. Requirements validation examines the specification[5] to ensure that all software requirements have been

---

5   Recall that the nature of the specification will vary with each project. In some cases, the "specification" is a collection of user scenarios and little else. In others, the specification may be a document that contains scenarios, models, and written descriptions.

stated unambiguously; that inconsistencies, omissions, and errors have been detected and corrected; and that the work products conform to the standards established for the process, the project, and the product.

The primary requirements validation mechanism is the technical review (Chapter 15). The review team that validates requirements includes software engineers, customers, users, and other stakeholders who examine the specification looking for errors in content or interpretation, areas where clarification may be required, missing information, inconsistencies (a major problem when large products or systems are engineered), conflicting requirements, or unrealistic (unachievable) requirements.

INFO

Requirements Validation Checklist

It is often useful to examine each requirement against a set of checklist questions. Here is a small subset of those that might be asked:

- Are requirements stated clearly? Can they be misinterpreted?
- Is the source (e.g., a person, a regulation, a document) of the requirement identified? Has the final statement of the requirement been examined by or against the original source?
- Is the requirement bounded in quantitative terms?
- What other requirements relate to this requirement? Are they clearly noted via a cross-reference matrix or other mechanism?

- Does the requirement violate any system domain constraints?
- Is the requirement testable? If so, can we specify tests (sometimes called validation criteria) to exercise the requirement?
- Is the requirement traceable to any system model that has been created?
- Is the requirement traceable to overall system/product objectives?
- Is the specification structured in a way that leads to easy understanding, easy reference, and easy translation into more technical work products?
- Has an index for the specification been created?
- Have requirements associated with performance, behavior, and operational characteristics been clearly stated? What requirements appear to be implicit?

Requirements management. Requirements for computer-based systems change, and the desire to change requirements persists throughout the life of the system. Requirements management is a set of activities that help the project team identify, control, and track requirements and changes to requirements at any time as the project proceeds.[6] Many of these activities are identical to the software configuration management (SCM) techniques discussed in Chapter 22.

---

6 Formal requirements management is initiated only for large projects that have hundreds of identifiable requirements. For small projects, this requirements engineering action is considerably less formal.

5.2 ESTABLISHING THE GROUNDWORK

In an ideal setting, stakeholders and software engineers work together on the same team.[8] In such cases, requirements engineering is simply a matter of conducting meaningful conversations with colleagues who are well-known members of the team. But reality is often quite different.

Customer(s) or end users may be located in a different city or country, may have only a vague idea of what is required, may have conflicting opinions about the system to be built, may have limited technical knowledge, and may have limited time to interact with the requirements engineer. None of these things are desirable, but all are fairly common, and you are often forced to work within the constraints imposed by this situation.

In the sections that follow, I discuss the steps required to establish the groundwork for an understanding of software requirements—to get the project started in a way that will keep it moving forward toward a successful solution.

KEY POINT

A *stakeholder* is anyone who has a direct interest in or benefits from the system that is to be developed.

5.2.1 Identifying Stakeholders

Sommerville and Sawyer [Som97] define a stakeholder as "anyone who benefits in a direct or indirect way from the system which is being developed." I have already

---

7   Tools noted here do not represent an endorsement, but rather a sampling of tools in this category. In most cases, tool names are trademarked by their respective developers.

8   This approach is strongly recommended for projects that adopt an agile software development philosophy.

identified the usual suspects: business operations managers, product managers, marketing people, internal and external customers, end users, consultants, product engineers, software engineers, support and maintenance engineers, and others. Each stakeholder has a different view of the system, achieves different benefits when the system is successfully developed, and is open to different risks if the development effort should fail.

At inception, you should create a list of people who will contribute input as requirements are elicited (Section 5.3). The initial list will grow as stakeholders are contacted because every stakeholder will be asked: "Whom else do you think I should talk to?"

5.2.2 Recognizing Multiple Viewpoints

Because many different stakeholders exist, the requirements of the system will be explored from many different points of view. For example, the marketing group is interested in functions and features that will excite the potential market, making the new system easy to sell. Business managers are interested in a feature set that can be built within budget and that will be ready to meet defined market windows. End users may want features that are familiar to them and that are easy to learn and use. Software engineers may be concerned with functions that are invisible to nontechnical stakeholders but that enable an infrastructure that supports more marketable functions and features. Support engineers may focus on the maintainability of the software.

Each of these constituencies (and others) will contribute information to the requirements engineering process. As information from multiple viewpoints is collected, emerging requirements may be inconsistent or may conflict with one another. You should categorize all stakeholder information (including inconsistent and conflicting requirements) in a way that will allow decision makers to choose an internally consistent set of requirements for the system.

5.2.3 Working toward Collaboration

If five stakeholders are involved in a software project, you may have five (or more) different opinions about the proper set of requirements. Throughout earlier chapters, I have noted that customers (and other stakeholders) must collaborate among themselves (avoiding petty turf battles) and with software engineering practitioners if a successful system is to result. But how is this collaboration accomplished?

The job of a requirements engineer is to identify areas of commonality (i.e., requirements on which all stakeholders agree) and areas of conflict or inconsistency (i.e., requirements that are desired by one stakeholder but conflict with the needs of another stakeholder). It is, of course, the latter category that presents a challenge.

Using "Priority Points"

One way of resolving conflicting requirements and at the same time better understanding the relative importance of all requirements is to use a "voting" scheme based on *priority points*. All stakeholders are provided with some number of priority points that can be "spent" on any number of requirements. A list of requirements is presented, and each stakeholder indicates the relative importance of

each (from his or her viewpoint) by spending one or more priority points on it. Points spent cannot be reused. Once a stakeholder's priority points are exhausted, no further action on requirements can be taken by that person. Overall points spent on each requirement by all stakeholders provide an indication of the overall importance of each requirement.

Collaboration does not necessarily mean that requirements are defined by committee. In many cases, stakeholders collaborate by providing their view of requirements, but a strong "project champion"(e.g., a business manager or a senior technologist) may make the final decision about which requirements make the cut.

5.2.4   Asking the First Questions

Questions asked at the inception of the project should be "context free" [Gau89]. The first set of context-free questions focuses on the customer and other stakeholders, the overall project goals and benefits. For example, you might ask:

- Who is behind the request for this work?
- Who will use the solution?
- What will be the economic benefit of a successful solution?
- Is there another source for the solution that you need?

These questions help to identify all stakeholders who will have interest in the software to be built. In addition, the questions identify the measurable benefit of a successful implementation and possible alternatives to custom software development.

The next set of questions enables you to gain a better understanding of the problem and allows the customer to voice his or her perceptions about a solution:

? **What questions will help you gain a preliminary understanding of the problem?**

- How would you characterize "good" output that would be generated by a successful solution?
- What problem(s) will this solution address?
- Can you show me (or describe) the business environment in which the solution will be used?
- Will special performance issues or constraints affect the way the solution is approached?

The final set of questions focuses on the effectiveness of the communication activity itself. Gause and Weinberg [Gau89] call these "meta-questions" and propose the following (abbreviated) list:

- Are you the right person to answer these questions? Are your answers "official"?
- Are my questions relevant to the problem that you have?
- Am I asking too many questions?
- Can anyone else provide additional information?
- Should I be asking you anything else?

These questions (and others) will help to "break the ice" and initiate the communication that is essential to successful elicitation. But a question-and-answer meeting format is not an approach that has been overwhelmingly successful. In fact, the Q&A session should be used for the first encounter only and then replaced by a requirements elicitation format that combines elements of problem solving, negotiation, and specification. An approach of this type is presented in Section 5.3.

5.3   ELICITING REQUIREMENTS

Requirements elicitation (also called *requirements gathering*) combines elements of problem solving, elaboration, negotiation, and specification. In order to encourage a collaborative, team-oriented approach to requirements gathering, stakeholders work together to identify the problem, propose elements of the solution, negotiate different approaches and specify a preliminary set of solution requirements [Zah90].[9]

5.3.1   Collaborative Requirements Gathering

Many different approaches to collaborative requirements gathering have been proposed. Each makes use of a slightly different scenario, but all apply some variation on the following basic guidelines:

? What are the basic guidelines for conducting a collaborative requirements gathering meeting?

- Meetings are conducted and attended by both software engineers and other stakeholders.
- Rules for preparation and participation are established.
- An agenda is suggested that is formal enough to cover all important points but informal enough to encourage the free flow of ideas.
- A "facilitator" (can be a customer, a developer, or an outsider) controls the meeting.
- A "definition mechanism" (can be work sheets, flip charts, or wall stickers or an electronic bulletin board, chat room, or virtual forum) is used.

---

9   This approach is sometimes called a *facilitated application specification technique* (FAST).

The goal is to identify the problem, propose elements of the solution, negotiate different approaches, and specify a preliminary set of solution requirements in an atmosphere that is conducive to the accomplishment of the goal. To better understand the flow of events as they occur, I present a brief scenario that outlines the sequence of events that lead up to the requirements gathering meeting, occur during the meeting, and follow the meeting.

During inception (Section 5.2) basic questions and answers establish the scope of the problem and the overall perception of a solution. Out of these initial meetings, the developer and customers write a one- or two-page "product request."

A meeting place, time, and date are selected; a facilitator is chosen; and attendees from the software team and other stakeholder organizations are invited to participate. The product request is distributed to all attendees before the meeting date.

As an example,[10] consider an excerpt from a product request written by a marketing person involved in the *SafeHome* project. This person writes the following narrative about the home security function that is to be part of *SafeHome:*

> Our research indicates that the market for home management systems is growing at a rate of 40 percent per year. The first *SafeHome* function we bring to market should be the home security function. Most people are familiar with "alarm systems" so this would be an easy sell.
>
> The home security function would protect against and/or recognize a variety of undesirable "situations" such as illegal entry, fire, flooding, carbon monoxide levels, and others. It'll use our wireless sensors to detect each situation. It can be programmed by the homeowner, and will automatically telephone a monitoring agency when a situation is detected.

In reality, others would contribute to this narrative during the requirements gathering meeting and considerably more information would be available. But even with additional information, ambiguity would be present, omissions would likely exist, and errors might occur. For now, the preceding "functional description" will suffice.

While reviewing the product request in the days before the meeting, each attendee is asked to make a list of objects that are part of the environment that surrounds the system, other objects that are to be produced by the system, and objects that are used by the system to perform its functions. In addition, each attendee is asked to make another list of services (processes or functions) that manipulate or interact with the objects. Finally, lists of constraints (e.g., cost, size, business rules) and performance criteria (e.g., speed, accuracy) are also developed. The attendees are informed that the lists are not expected to be exhaustive but are expected to reflect each person's perception of the system.

---

10 This example (with extensions and variations) is used to illustrate important software engineering methods in many of the chapters that follow. As an exercise, it would be worthwhile to conduct your own requirements gathering meeting and develop a set of lists for it.

Objects described for *SafeHome* might include the control panel, smoke detectors, window and door sensors, motion detectors, an alarm, an event (a sensor has been activated), a display, a PC, telephone numbers, a telephone call, and so on. The list of services might include *configuring* the system, *setting* the alarm, *monitoring* the sensors, *dialing* the phone, *programming* the control panel, and *reading* the display (note that services act on objects). In a similar fashion, each attendee will develop lists of constraints (e.g., the system must recognize when sensors are not operating, must be user-friendly, must interface directly to a standard phone line) and performance criteria (e.g., a sensor event should be recognized within one second, and an event priority scheme should be implemented).

The lists of objects can be pinned to the walls of the room using large sheets of paper, stuck to the walls using adhesive-backed sheets, or written on a wall board. Alternatively, the lists may have been posted on an electronic bulletin board, at an internal website, or posed in a chat room environment for review prior to the meeting. Ideally, each listed entry should be capable of being manipulated separately so that lists can be combined, entries can be modified, and additions can be made. At this stage, critique and debate are strictly prohibited.

After individual lists are presented in one topic area, the group creates a combined list by eliminating redundant entries, adding any new ideas that come up during the discussion, but not deleting anything. After you create combined lists for all topic areas, discussion—coordinated by the facilitator—ensues. The combined list is shortened, lengthened, or reworded to properly reflect the product/system to be developed. The objective is to develop a consensus list of objects, services, constraints, and performance for the system to be built.

In many cases, an object or service described on a list will require further explanation. To accomplish this, stakeholders develop *mini-specifications* for entries on the lists.[11] Each mini-specification is an elaboration of an object or service. For example, the mini-spec for the *SafeHome* object **Control Panel** might be:

> The control panel is a wall-mounted unit that is approximately 9 × 5 inches in size. The control panel has wireless connectivity to sensors and a PC. User interaction occurs through a keypad containing 12 keys. A 3 × 3 inch LCD color display provides user feedback. Software provides interactive prompts, echo, and similar functions.

The mini-specs are presented to all stakeholders for discussion. Additions, deletions, and further elaboration are made. In some cases, the development of mini-specs will uncover new objects, services, constraints, or performance requirements that will be added to the original lists. During all discussions, the team may raise an issue that cannot be resolved during the meeting. An *issues list* is maintained so that these ideas will be acted on later.

---

11 Rather than creating a mini-specification, many software teams elect to develop user scenarios called *use cases*. These are considered in detail in Section 5.4 and in Chapter 6.

SafeHome

Conducting a Requirements Gathering Meeting

The scene: A meeting room. The first requirements gathering meeting is in progress.

The players: Jamie Lazar, software team member; Vinod Raman, software team member; Ed Robbins, software team member; Doug Miller, software engineering manager; three members of marketing; a product engineering representative; and a facilitator.

The conversation:

Facilitator (pointing at whiteboard): So that's the current list of objects and services for the home security function.

Marketing person: That about covers it from our point of view.

Vinod: Didn't someone mention that they wanted all *SafeHome* functionality to be accessible via the Internet? That would include the home security function, no?

Marketing person: Yes, that's right . . . we'll have to add that functionality and the appropriate objects.

Facilitator: Does that also add some constraints?

Jamie: It does, both technical and legal.

Production rep: Meaning?

Jamie: We better make sure an outsider can't hack into the system, disarm it, and rob the place or worse. Heavy liability on our part.

Doug: Very true.

Marketing: But we still need that . . . just be sure to stop an outsider from getting in.

Ed: That's easier said than done and . . .

Facilitator (interrupting): I don't want to debate this issue now. Let's note it as an action item and proceed.

(Doug, serving as the recorder for the meeting, makes an appropriate note.)

Facilitator: I have a feeling there's still more to consider here.

(The group spends the next 20 minutes refining and expanding the details of the home security function.)

5.3.2 Quality Function Deployment

Quality function deployment (QFD) is a quality management technique that translates the needs of the customer into technical requirements for software. QFD "concentrates on maximizing customer satisfaction from the software engineering process" [Zul92]. To accomplish this, QFD emphasizes an understanding of what is valuable to the customer and then deploys these values throughout the engineering process. QFD identifies three types of requirements [Zul92]:

KEY POINT

QFD defines requirements in a way that maximizes customer satisfaction.

Normal requirements. The objectives and goals that are stated for a product or system during meetings with the customer. If these requirements are present, the customer is satisfied. Examples of normal requirements might be requested types of graphical displays, specific system functions, and defined levels of performance.

ADVICE

Everyone wants to implement lots of exciting requirements, but be careful. That's how "requirements creep" sets in. On the other hand, exciting requirements lead to a breakthrough product!

Expected requirements. These requirements are implicit to the product or system and may be so fundamental that the customer does not explicitly state them. Their absence will be a cause for significant dissatisfaction. Examples of expected requirements are: ease of human/machine interaction, overall operational correctness and reliability, and ease of software installation.

Exciting requirements. These features go beyond the customer's expectations and prove to be very satisfying when present. For example, software for a new mobile phone comes with standard features, but is coupled with a set of unexpected capabilities (e.g., multitouch screen, visual voice mail) that delight every user of the product.

WebRef

Useful information on QFD can be obtained at **www.qfdi.org**.

Although QFD concepts can be applied across the entire software process [Par96a], specific QFD techniques are applicable to the requirements elicitation activity. QFD uses customer interviews and observation, surveys, and examination of historical data (e.g., problem reports) as raw data for the requirements gathering activity. These data are then translated into a table of requirements—called the *customer voice table*—that is reviewed with the customer and other stakeholders. A variety of diagrams, matrices, and evaluation methods are then used to extract expected requirements and to attempt to derive exciting requirements [Aka04].

5.3.3 Usage Scenarios

As requirements are gathered, an overall vision of system functions and features begins to materialize. However, it is difficult to move into more technical software engineering activities until you understand how these functions and features will be used by different classes of end users. To accomplish this, developers and users can create a set of scenarios that identify a thread of usage for the system to be constructed. The scenarios, often called *use cases* [Jac92], provide a description of how the system will be used. Use cases are discussed in greater detail in Section 5.4.

SAFEHOME

Developing a Preliminary User Scenario

The scene: A meeting room, continuing the first requirements gathering meeting.

The players: Jamie Lazar, software team member; Vinod Raman, software team member; Ed Robbins, software team member; Doug Miller, software engineering manager; three members of marketing; a product engineering representative; and a facilitator.

The conversation:

Facilitator: We've been talking about security for access to *SafeHome* functionality that will be accessible via the Internet. I'd like to try something. Let's develop a usage scenario for access to the home security function.

Jamie: How?

Facilitator: We can do it a couple of different ways, but for now, I'd like to keep things really informal. Tell us (he points at a marketing person) how you envision accessing the system.

Marketing person: Um . . . well, this is the kind of thing I'd do if I was away from home and I had to let someone into the house, say a housekeeper or repair guy, who didn't have the security code.

Facilitator (smiling): That's the reason you'd do it . . . tell me how you'd actually do this.

Marketing person: Um . . . the first thing I'd need is a PC. I'd log on to a website we'd maintain for all users of *SafeHome*. I'd provide my user id and . . .

Vinod (interrupting): The Web page would have to be secure, encrypted, to guarantee that we're safe and . . .

Facilitator (interrupting): That's good information, Vinod, but it's technical. Let's just focus on how the end user will use this capability. OK?

Vinod: No problem.

Marketing person: So as I was saying, I'd log on to a website and provide my user ID and two levels of passwords.

Jamie: What if I forget my password?

Facilitator (interrupting): Good point, Jamie, but let's not address that now. We'll make a note of that and call it an *exception*. I'm sure there'll be others.

Marketing person: After I enter the passwords, a screen representing all *SafeHome* functions will appear. I'd select the home security function. The system might request that I verify who I am, say, by asking for my address or phone number or something. It would then display a picture of the security system control panel

along with a list of functions that I can perform—arm the system, disarm the system, disarm one or more sensors. I suppose it might also allow me to reconfigure security zones and other things like that, but I'm not sure.

(As the marketing person continues talking, Doug takes copious notes; these form the basis for the first informal usage scenario. Alternatively, the marketing person could have been asked to write the scenario, but this would be done outside the meeting.)

5.3.4   Elicitation Work Products

The work products produced as a consequence of requirements elicitation will vary depending on the size of the system or product to be built. For most systems, the work products include

? What information is produced as a consequence of requirements gathering?

- A statement of need and feasibility.
- A bounded statement of scope for the system or product.
- A list of customers, users, and other stakeholders who participated in requirements elicitation.
- A description of the system's technical environment.
- A list of requirements (preferably organized by function) and the domain constraints that apply to each.
- A set of usage scenarios that provide insight into the use of the system or product under different operating conditions.
- Any prototypes developed to better define requirements.

Each of these work products is reviewed by all people who have participated in requirements elicitation.

5.4   DEVELOPING USE CASES

In a book that discusses how to write effective use cases, Alistair Cockburn [Coc01b] notes that "a use case captures a contract ... [that] describes the system's behavior under various conditions as the system responds to a request from one of its stakeholders ..." In essence, a use case tells a stylized story about how an end user (playing one of a number of possible roles) interacts with the system under a specific set of circumstances. The story may be narrative text, an outline of tasks or interactions, a template-based description, or a diagrammatic representation. Regardless of its form, a use case depicts the software or system from the end user's point of view.

POINT

Use cases are defined from an actor's point of view. An actor is a role that people (users) or devices play as they interact with the software.

The first step in writing a use case is to define the set of "actors" that will be involved in the story. *Actors* are the different people (or devices) that use the system or product within the context of the function and behavior that is to be described. Actors represent the roles that people (or devices) play as the system operates. Defined somewhat more formally, an actor is anything that communicates with the system or product and that is external to the system itself. Every actor has one or more goals when using the system.

It is important to note that an actor and an end user are not necessarily the same thing. A typical user may play a number of different roles when using a system, whereas an actor represents a class of external entities (often, but not always, people) that play just one role in the context of the use case. As an example, consider a machine operator (a user) who interacts with the control computer for a manufacturing cell that contains a number of robots and numerically controlled machines. After careful review of requirements, the software for the control computer requires four different modes (roles) for interaction: programming mode, test mode, monitoring mode, and troubleshooting mode. Therefore, four actors can be defined: programmer, tester, monitor, and troubleshooter. In some cases, the machine operator can play all of these roles. In others, different people may play the role of each actor.

Because requirements elicitation is an evolutionary activity, not all actors are identified during the first iteration. It is possible to identify primary actors [Jac92] during the first iteration and secondary actors as more is learned about the system. *Primary actors* interact to achieve required system function and derive the intended benefit from the system. They work directly and frequently with the software. *Secondary actors* support the system so that primary actors can do their work.

Once actors have been identified, use cases can be developed. Jacobson [Jac92] suggests a number of questions[12] that should be answered by a use case:

WebRef

An excellent paper on use cases can be downloaded from **www.ibm.com/ developerworks/ webservices/ library/ codesign7.html**.

? **What do I need to know in order to develop an effective use case?**

- Who is the primary actor, the secondary actor(s)?
- What are the actor's goals?
- What preconditions should exist before the story begins?
- What main tasks or functions are performed by the actor?
- What exceptions might be considered as the story is described?
- What variations in the actor's interaction are possible?
- What system information will the actor acquire, produce, or change?
- Will the actor have to inform the system about changes in the external environment?
- What information does the actor desire from the system?
- Does the actor wish to be informed about unexpected changes?

---

12 Jacobson's questions have been extended to provide a more complete view of use-case content.

Recalling basic *SafeHome* requirements, we define four actors: **homeowner** (a user), **setup manager** (likely the same person as **homeowner,** but playing a different role), **sensors** (devices attached to the system), and the **monitoring and response subsystem** (the central station that monitors the *SafeHome* home security function). For the purposes of this example, we consider only the **homeowner** actor. The **homeowner** actor interacts with the home security function in a number of different ways using either the alarm control panel or a PC:

- Enters a password to allow all other interactions.
- Inquires about the status of a security zone.
- Inquires about the status of a sensor.
- Presses the panic button in an emergency.
- Activates/deactivates the security system.

Considering the situation in which the homeowner uses the control panel, the basic use case for system activation follows:[13]

1. The homeowner observes the *SafeHome* control panel (Figure 5.1) to determine if the system is ready for input. If the system is not ready, a *not ready* message is displayed on the LCD display, and the homeowner must physically close windows or doors so that the *not ready* message disappears. [A *not ready* message implies that a sensor is open; i.e., that a door or window is open.]

FIGURE 5.1

SafeHome control panel

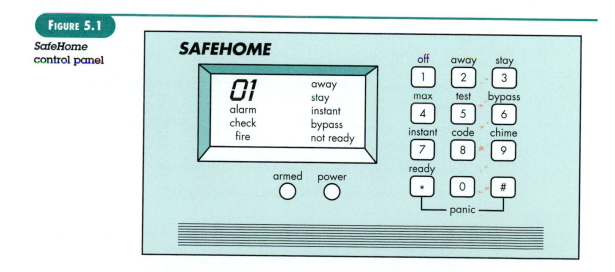

---

13 Note that this use case differs from the situation in which the system is accessed via the Internet. In this case, interaction occurs via the control panel, not the graphical user interface (GUI) provided when a PC is used.

2. The homeowner uses the keypad to key in a four-digit password. The password is compared with the valid password stored in the system. If the password is incorrect, the control panel will beep once and reset itself for additional input. If the password is correct, the control panel awaits further action.

3. The homeowner selects and keys in *stay* or *away* (see Figure 5.1) to activate the system. *Stay* activates only perimeter sensors (inside motion detecting sensors are deactivated). *Away* activates all sensors.

4. When activation occurs, a red alarm light can be observed by the homeowner.

The basic use case presents a high-level story that describes the interaction between the actor and the system.

In many instances, uses cases are further elaborated to provide considerably more detail about the interaction. For example, Cockburn [Coc01b] suggests the following template for detailed descriptions of use cases:

Use cases are often written informally. However, use the template shown here to ensure that you've addressed all key issues.

Use case:	*InitiateMonitoring*
Primary actor:	Homeowner.
Goal in context:	To set the system to monitor sensors when the homeowner leaves the house or remains inside.
Preconditions:	System has been programmed for a password and to recognize various sensors.
Trigger:	The homeowner decides to "set" the system, i.e., to turn on the alarm functions.

Scenario:

1. Homeowner: observes control panel

2. Homeowner: enters password

3. Homeowner: selects "stay" or "away"

4. Homeowner: observes read alarm light to indicate that *SafeHome* has been armed

Exceptions:

1. Control panel is *not ready:* homeowner checks all sensors to determine which are open; closes them.

2. Password is incorrect (control panel beeps once): homeowner reenters correct password.

3. Password not recognized: monitoring and response subsystem must be contacted to reprogram password.

4. *Stay* is selected: control panel beeps twice and a *stay* light is lit; perimeter sensors are activated.

5. *Away* is selected: control panel beeps three times and an *away* light is lit; all sensors are activated.

Priority:	Essential, must be implemented
When available:	First increment

Frequency of use:	Many times per day
Channel to actor:	Via control panel interface
Secondary actors:	Support technician, sensors

Channels to secondary actors:

Support technician: phone line

Sensors: hardwired and radio frequency interfaces

Open issues:

1. Should there be a way to activate the system without the use of a password or with an abbreviated password?

2. Should the control panel display additional text messages?

3. How much time does the homeowner have to enter the password from the time the first key is pressed?

4. Is there a way to deactivate the system before it actually activates?

Use cases for other **homeowner** interactions would be developed in a similar manner. It is important to review each use case with care. If some element of the interaction is ambiguous, it is likely that a review of the use case will indicate a problem.

SafeHome

Developing a High-Level Use-Case Diagram

The scene: A meeting room, continuing the requirements gathering meeting

The players: Jamie Lazar, software team member; Vinod Raman, software team member; Ed Robbins, software team member; Doug Miller, software engineering manager; three members of marketing; a product engineering representative; and a facilitator.

The conversation:

Facilitator: We've spent a fair amount of time talking about *SafeHome* home security functionality. During the break I sketched a use case diagram to summarize the important scenarios that are part of this function. Take a look.

(All attendees look at Figure 5.2.)

Jamie: I'm just beginning to learn UML notation.[14] So the home security function is represented by the big box with the ovals inside it? And the ovals represent use cases that we've written in text?

Facilitator: Yep. And the stick figures represent actors— the people or things that interact with the system as described by the use case . . . oh, I use the labeled square to represent an actor that's not a person . . . in this case, sensors.

Doug: Is that legal in UML?

Facilitator: Legality isn't the issue. The point is to communicate information. I view the use of a humanlike stick figure for representing a device to be misleading. So I've adapted things a bit. I don't think it creates a problem.

Vinod: Okay, so we have use-case narratives for each of the ovals. Do we need to develop the more detailed template-based narratives I've read about?

Facilitator: Probably, but that can wait until we've considered other *SafeHome* functions.

Marketing person: Wait, I've been looking at this diagram and all of a sudden I realize we missed something.

Facilitator: Oh really. Tell me what we've missed.

(The meeting continues.)

---

14 A brief UML tutorial is presented in Appendix 1 for those who are unfamiliar with the notation.

FIGURE 5.2

UML use case
diagram for
SafeHome
home security
function

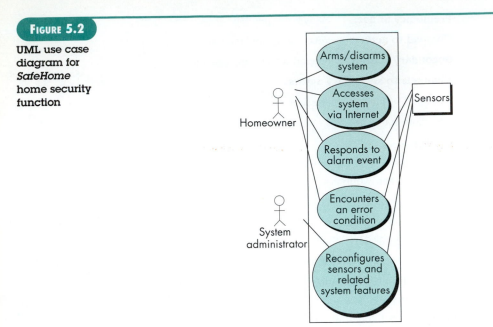

SOFTWARE TOOLS

Use-Case Development

Objective: Assist in the development of
use cases by providing automated templates
and mechanisms for assessing clarity and consistency.

Mechanics: Tool mechanics vary. In general, use-case
tools provide fill-in-the-blank templates for creating effective
use cases. Most use-case functionality is embedded into a
set of broader requirements engineering functions.

Representative Tools:[15]
The vast majority of UML-based analysis modeling tools
provide both text and graphical support for use-case
development and modeling.
Objects by Design
(**www.objectsbydesign.com/tools/
umltools_byCompany.html**) provides
comprehensive links to tools of this type.

5.5 BUILDING THE REQUIREMENTS MODEL[16]

The intent of the analysis model is to provide a description of the required informational,
functional, and behavioral domains for a computer-based system. The model changes
dynamically as you learn more about the system to be built, and other stakeholders understand more about what they really require. For that reason, the analysis model is a
snapshot of requirements at any given time. You should expect it to change.

15 Tools noted here do not represent an endorsement, but rather a sampling of tools in this category.
   In most cases, tool names are trademarked by their respective developers.
16 Throughout this book, I use the terms *analysis model* and *requirements model* synonymously. Both
   refer to representations of the information, functional, and behavioral domains that describe problem requirements.

As the requirements model evolves, certain elements will become relatively stable, providing a solid foundation for the design tasks that follow. However, other elements of the model may be more volatile, indicating that stakeholders do not yet fully understand requirements for the system. The analysis model and the methods that are used to build it are presented in detail in Chapters 6 and 7. I present a brief overview in the sections that follow.

5.5.1 Elements of the Requirements Model

There are many different ways to look at the requirements for a computer-based system. Some software people argue that it's best to select one mode of representation (e.g., the use case) and apply it to the exclusion of all other modes. Other practitioners believe that it's worthwhile to use a number of different modes of representation to depict the requirements model. Different modes of representation force you to consider requirements from different viewpoints—an approach that has a higher probability of uncovering omissions, inconsistencies, and ambiguity.

The specific elements of the requirements model are dictated by the analysis modeling method (Chapters 6 and 7) that is to be used. However, a set of generic elements is common to most requirements models.

It is always a good idea to get stakeholders involved. One of the best ways to do this is to have each stakeholder write use cases that describe how the software will be used.

Scenario-based elements. The system is described from the user's point of view using a scenario-based approach. For example, basic use cases (Section 5.4) and their corresponding use-case diagrams (Figure 5.2) evolve into more elaborate template-based use cases. Scenario-based elements of the requirements model are often the first part of the model that is developed. As such, they serve as input for the creation of other modeling elements. Figure 5.3 depicts a UML activity diagram[17] for eliciting requirements and representing them using use cases. Three levels of elaboration are shown, culminating in a scenario-based representation.

One way to isolate classes is to look for descriptive nouns in a use-case script. At least some of the nouns will be candidate classes. More on this in the Chapter 8.

Class-based elements. Each usage scenario implies a set of objects that are manipulated as an actor interacts with the system. These objects are categorized into classes—a collection of things that have similar attributes and common behaviors. For example, a UML class diagram can be used to depict a **Sensor** class for the *SafeHome* security function (Figure 5.4). Note that the diagram lists the attributes of sensors (e.g., name, type) and the operations (e.g., *identify, enable*) that can be applied to modify these attributes. In addition to class diagrams, other analysis modeling elements depict the manner in which classes collaborate with one another and the relationships and interactions between classes. These are discussed in more detail in Chapter 7.

Behavioral elements. The behavior of a computer-based system can have a profound effect on the design that is chosen and the implementation approach that is applied. Therefore, the requirements model must provide modeling elements that depict behavior.

17 A brief UML tutorial is presented in Appendix 1 for those who are unfamiliar with the notation.

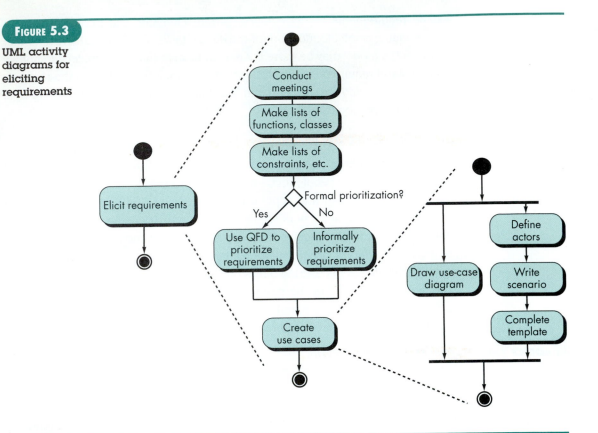

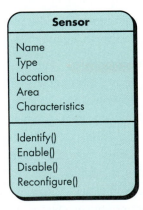

The *state diagram* is one method for representing the behavior of a system by de-picting its states and the events that cause the system to change state. A *state* is any externally observable mode of behavior. In addition, the state diagram indicates actions (e.g., process activation) taken as a consequence of a particular event.

To illustrate the use of a state diagram, consider software embedded within the *SafeHome* control panel that is responsible for reading user input. A simplified UML state diagram is shown in Figure 5.5.

FIGURE 5.5

UML state
diagram
notation

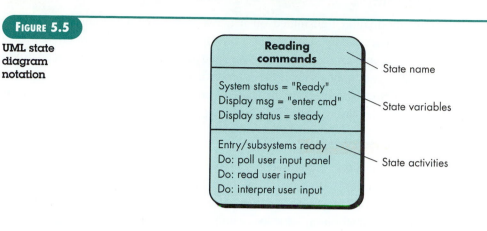

In addition to behavioral representations of the system as a whole, the behavior of individual classes can also be modeled. Further discussion of behavioral modeling is presented in Chapter 7.

SafeHome

Preliminary Behavioral Modeling

The scene: A meeting room, continuing the requirements meeting.

The players: Jamie Lazar, software team member; Vinod Raman, software team member; Ed Robbins, software team member; Doug Miller, software engineering manager; three members of marketing; a product engineering representative; and a facilitator.

The conversation:

Facilitator: We've just about finished talking about *SafeHome* home security functionality. But before we do, I want to discuss the behavior of the function.

Marketing person: I don't understand what you mean by behavior.

Ed (smiling): That's when you give the product a "timeout" if it misbehaves.

Facilitator: Not exactly. Let me explain.

(The facilitator explains the basics of behavioral modeling to the requirements gathering team.)

Marketing person: This seems a little technical. I'm not sure I can help here.

Facilitator: Sure you can. What behavior do you observe from the user's point of view?

Marketing person: Uh . . . well, the system will be *monitoring* the sensors. It'll be *reading commands* from the homeowner. It'll be *displaying* its status.

Facilitator: See, you can do it.

Jamie: It'll also be *polling* the PC to determine if there is any input from it, for example, Internet-based access or configuration information.

Vinod: Yeah, in fact, *configuring the system* is a state in its own right.

Doug: You guys are rolling. Let's give this a bit more thought . . . is there a way to diagram this stuff?

Facilitator: There is, but let's postpone that until after the meeting.

Flow-oriented elements. Information is transformed as it flows through a computer-based system. The system accepts input in a variety of forms, applies functions to transform it, and produces output in a variety of forms. Input may be a control signal transmitted by a transducer, a series of numbers typed by a human operator, a packet of information transmitted on a network link, or a voluminous data file retrieved from secondary storage. The transform(s) may comprise a single logical comparison, a complex numerical algorithm, or a rule-inference approach of an expert system. Output may light a single LED or produce a 200-page report. In effect, we can create a flow model for any computer-based system, regardless of size and complexity. A more detailed discussion of flow modeling is presented in Chapter 7.

5.5.2 Analysis Patterns

Anyone who has done requirements engineering on more than a few software projects begins to notice that certain problems reoccur across all projects within a specific application domain.[18] These *analysis patterns* [Fow97] suggest solutions (e.g., a class, a function, a behavior) within the application domain that can be reused when modeling many applications.

Geyer-Schulz and Hahsler [Gey01] suggest two benefits that can be associated with the use of analysis patterns:

> First, analysis patterns speed up the development of abstract analysis models that capture the main requirements of the concrete problem by providing reusable analysis models with examples as well as a description of advantages and limitations. Second, analysis patterns facilitate the transformation of the analysis model into a design model by suggesting design patterns and reliable solutions for common problems.

Analysis patterns are integrated into the analysis model by reference to the pattern name. They are also stored in a repository so that requirements engineers can use search facilities to find and apply them. Information about an analysis pattern (and other types of patterns) is presented in a standard template [Gey01][19] that is discussed in more detail in Chapter 12. Examples of analysis patterns and further discussion of this topic are presented in Chapter 7.

5.6 NEGOTIATING REQUIREMENTS

In an ideal requirements engineering context, the inception, elicitation, and elaboration tasks determine customer requirements in sufficient detail to proceed to subsequent software engineering activities. Unfortunately, this rarely happens. In reality, you may have to enter into a negotiation with one or more stakeholders. In most cases, stakeholders are asked to balance functionality, performance, and other product or system characteristics against cost and time-to-market. The intent of this negotiation is to develop a project plan that meets stakeholder needs while at the

---

18 In some cases, problems reoccur regardless of the application domain. For example, the features and functions used to solve user interface problems are common regardless of the application domain under consideration.

19 A variety of patterns templates have been proposed in the literature. If you have interest, see [Fow97], [Gam95], [Yac03], and [Bus07] among many sources.

same time reflecting the real-world constraints (e.g., time, people, budget) that have been placed on the software team.

The best negotiations strive for a "win-win" result.[20] That is, stakeholders win by getting the system or product that satisfies the majority of their needs and you (as a member of the software team) win by working to realistic and achievable budgets and deadlines.

WebRef

A brief paper on negotiation for software requirements can be downloaded from **www.alexander-egyed.com/ publications/ Software_ Requirements_ Negotiation-Some_Lessons_ Learned.html**.

Boehm [Boe98] defines a set of negotiation activities at the beginning of each software process iteration. Rather than a single customer communication activity, the following activities are defined:

1. Identification of the system or subsystem's key stakeholders.

2. Determination of the stakeholders' "win conditions."

3. Negotiation of the stakeholders' win conditions to reconcile them into a set of win-win conditions for all concerned (including the software team).

Successful completion of these initial steps achieves a win-win result, which becomes the key criterion for proceeding to subsequent software engineering activities.

The Art of Negotiation

INFO

Learning how to negotiate effectively can serve you well throughout your personal and technical life. The following guidelines are well worth considering:

1. *Recognize that it's not a competition.* To be successful, both parties have to feel they've won or achieved something. Both will have to compromise.

2. *Map out a strategy.* Decide what you'd like to achieve; what the other party wants to achieve, and how you'll go about making both happen.

3. *Listen actively.* Don't work on formulating your response while the other party is talking. Listen to her. It's likely you'll gain knowledge that will help you to better negotiate your position.

4. *Focus on the other party's interests.* Don't take hard positions if you want to avoid conflict.

5. *Don't let it get personal.* Focus on the problem that needs to be solved.

6. *Be creative.* Don't be afraid to think out of the box if you're at an impasse.

7. *Be ready to commit.* Once an agreement has been reached, don't waffle; commit to it and move on.

SafeHome

The Start of a Negotiation

The scene: Lisa Perez's office, after the first requirements gathering meeting.

The players: Doug Miller, software engineering manager and Lisa Perez, marketing manager.

The conversation:

Lisa: So, I hear the first meeting went really well.

Doug: Actually, it did. You sent some good people to the meeting . . . they really contributed.

---

20 Dozens of books have been written on negotiating skills (e.g., [Lew06], [Rai06], [Fis06]). It is one of the more important skills that you can learn. Read one.

Lisa (smiling): Yeah, they actually told me they got into it and it wasn't a "propeller head activity."

Doug (laughing): I'll be sure to take off my techie beanie the next time I visit . . . Look, Lisa, I think we may have a problem with getting all of the functionality for the home security system out by the dates your management is talking about. It's early, I know, but I've already been doing a little back-of-the-envelope planning and . . .

Lisa (frowning): We've got to have it by that date, Doug. What functionality are you talking about?

Doug: I figure we can get full home security functionality out by the drop-dead date, but we'll have to delay Internet access 'til the second release.

Lisa: Doug, it's the Internet access that gives *SafeHome* "gee whiz" appeal. We're going to build our entire marketing campaign around it. We've gotta have it!

Doug: I understand your situation, I really do. The problem is that in order to give you Internet access, we'll have to have a fully secure website up and running. That takes time and people. We'll also have to build a lot of additional functionality into the first release . . . I don't think we can do it with the resources we've got.

Lisa (still frowning): I see, but you've got to figure out a way to get it done. It's pivotal to home security functions and to other functions as well . . . those can wait until the next releases . . . I'll agree to that.

Lisa and Doug appear to be at an impasse, and yet they must negotiate a solution to this problem. Can they both "win" here? Playing the role of a mediator, what would you suggest?

5.7   VALIDATING REQUIREMENTS

As each element of the requirements model is created, it is examined for inconsistency, omissions, and ambiguity. The requirements represented by the model are prioritized by the stakeholders and grouped within requirements packages that will be implemented as software increments. A review of the requirements model addresses the following questions:

? When I review requirements, what questions should I ask?

- Is each requirement consistent with the overall objectives for the system/product?

- Have all requirements been specified at the proper level of abstraction? That is, do some requirements provide a level of technical detail that is inappropriate at this stage?

- Is the requirement really necessary or does it represent an add-on feature that may not be essential to the objective of the system?

- Is each requirement bounded and unambiguous?

- Does each requirement have attribution? That is, is a source (generally, a specific individual) noted for each requirement?

- Do any requirements conflict with other requirements?

- Is each requirement achievable in the technical environment that will house the system or product?

- Is each requirement testable, once implemented?

- Does the requirements model properly reflect the information, function, and behavior of the system to be built?

● Has the requirements model been "partitioned" in a way that exposes progressively more detailed information about the system?

● Have requirements patterns been used to simplify the requirements model? Have all patterns been properly validated? Are all patterns consistent with customer requirements?

These and other questions should be asked and answered to ensure that the requirements model is an accurate reflection of stakeholder needs and that it provides a solid foundation for design.

5.8 SUMMARY

Requirements engineering tasks are conducted to establish a solid foundation for design and construction. Requirements engineering occurs during the communication and modeling activities that have been defined for the generic software process. Seven distinct requirements engineering functions—inception, elicitation, elaboration, negotiation, specification, validation, and management—are conducted by members of the software team.

At project inception, stakeholders establish basic problem requirements, define overriding project constraints, and address major features and functions that must be present for the system to meet its objectives. This information is refined and expanded during elicitation—a requirements gathering activity that makes use of facilitated meetings, QFD, and the development of usage scenarios.

Elaboration further expands requirements in a model—a collection of scenario-based, class-based, behavioral, and flow-oriented elements. The model may reference analysis patterns, solutions for analysis problems that have been seen to reoccur across different applications.

As requirements are identified and the requirements model is being created, the software team and other project stakeholders negotiate the priority, availability, and relative cost of each requirement. The intent of this negotiation is to develop a realistic project plan. In addition, each requirement and the requirements model as a whole are validated against customer need to ensure that the right system is to be built.

PROBLEMS AND POINTS TO PONDER

5.1. Why is it that many software developers don't pay enough attention to requirements engineering? Are there ever circumstances where you can skip it?

5.2. You have been given the responsibility to elicit requirements from a customer who tells you he is too busy to meet with you. What should you do?

5.3. Discuss some of the problems that occur when requirements must be elicited from three or four different customers.

5.4. Why do we say that the requirements model represents a snapshot of a system in time?

5.5. Let's assume that you've convinced the customer (you're a very good salesperson) to agree to every demand that you have as a developer. Does that make you a master negotiator? Why?

5.6. Develop at least three additional "context-free questions" that you might ask a stakeholder during inception.

5.7. Develop a requirements gathering "kit." The kit should include a set of guidelines for conducting a requirements gathering meeting and materials that can be used to facilitate the creation of lists and any other items that might help in defining requirements.

5.8. Your instructor will divide the class into groups of four to six students. Half of the group will play the role of the marketing department and half will take on the role of software engineering. Your job is to define requirements for the *SafeHome* security function described in this chapter. Conduct a requirements gathering meeting using the guidelines presented in this chapter.

5.9. Develop a complete use case for one of the following activities:

    a. Making a withdrawal at an ATM
    b. Using your charge card for a meal at a restaurant
    c. Buying a stock using an on-line brokerage account
    d. Searching for books (on a specific topic) using an on-line bookstore
    e. An activity specified by your instructor.

5.10. What do use case "exceptions" represent?

5.11. Describe what an *analysis pattern* is in your own words.

5.12. Using the template presented in Section 5.5.2, suggest one or more analysis pattern for the following application domains:

    a. Accounting software
    b. E-mail software
    c. Internet browsers
    d. Word-processing software
    e. Website creation software
    f. An application domain specified by your instructor

5.13. What does *win-win* mean in the context of negotiation during the requirements engineering activity?

5.14. What do you think happens when requirement validation uncovers an error? Who is involved in correcting the error?

FURTHER READINGS AND INFORMATION SOURCES

Because it is pivotal to the successful creation of any complex computer-based system, requirements engineering is discussed in a wide array of books. Hood and his colleagues (*Requirements Management,* Springer, 2007) discuss a variety of requirements engineering issues that span both systems and software engineering. Young (*The Requirements Engineering Handbook,* Artech House Publishers, 2007) presents an in-depth discussion of requirements engineering tasks. Wiegers (*More About Software Requirements,* Microsoft Press, 2006) provides many practical techniques for requirements gathering and management. Hull and her colleagues (*Requirements Engineering,* 2d ed., Springer-Verlag, 2004), Bray (*An Introduction to Requirements Engineering,* Addison-Wesley, 2002), Arlow (*Requirements Engineering,* Addison-Wesley, 2001), Gilb (*Requirements Engineering,* Addison-Wesley, 2000), Graham (*Requirements Engineering and Rapid Development,* Addison-Wesley, 1999), and Sommerville and Kotonya (*Requirement Engineering: Processes and Techniques,* Wiley, 1998) are but a few of many books dedicated to the subject. Gottesdiener (*Requirements by Collaboration: Workshops for Defining*

Needs, Addison-Wesley, 2002) provides useful guidance for those who must establish a collaborative requirements gathering environment with stakeholders.

Lauesen (*Software Requirements: Styles and Techniques,* Addison-Wesley, 2002) presents a comprehensive survey of requirement analysis methods and notation. Weigers (*Software Requirements,* Microsoft Press, 1999) and Leffingwell and his colleagues (*Managing Software Requirements: A Use Case Approach,* 2d ed., Addison-Wesley, 2003) present a useful collection of requirement best practices and suggest pragmatic guidelines for most aspects of the requirements engineering process.

A patterns-based view of requirements engineering is described by Withall (*Software Requirement Patterns,* Microsoft Press, 2007). Ploesch (*Assertions, Scenarios and Prototypes,* Springer-Verlag, 2003) discusses advanced techniques for developing software requirements. Windle and Abreo (*Software Requirements Using the Unified Process,* Prentice-Hall, 2002) discuss requirements engineering within the context of the Unified Process and UML notation. Alexander and Steven (*Writing Better Requirements,* Addison-Wesley, 2002) present a brief set of guidelines for writing clear requirements, representing them as scenarios, and reviewing the end result.

Use-case modeling is often the driver for the creation of all other aspects of the analysis model. The subject is discussed at length by Rosenberg and Stephens (*Use Case Driven Object Modeling with UML: Theory and Practice,* Apress, 2007), Denny (*Succeeding with Use Cases: Working Smart to Deliver Quality,* Addison-Wesley, 2005), Alexander and Maiden (eds.) (*Scenarios, Stories, Use Cases: Through the Systems Development Life-Cycle,* Wiley, 2004), Leffingwell and his colleagues (*Managing Software Requirements: A Use Case Approach,* 2d ed., Addison-Wesley, 2003) present a useful collection of requirement best practices. Bittner and Spence (*Use Case Modeling,* Addison-Wesley, 2002), Cockburn [Coc01], Armour and Miller (*Advanced Use Case Modeling: Software Systems,* Addison-Wesley, 2000), and Kulak and his colleagues (*Use Cases: Requirements in Context,* Addison-Wesley, 2000) discuss requirements gathering with an emphasis on use-case modeling.

A wide variety of information sources on requirements engineering and analysis is available on the Internet. An up-to-date list of World Wide Web references that are relevant to requirements engineering and analysis can be found at the SEPA website: **www.mhhe.com/engcs/ compsci/pressman/professional/olc/ser.htm**.

REQUIREMENTS MODELING: SCENARIOS, INFORMATION, AND ANALYSIS CLASSES

At a technical level, software engineering begins with a series of modeling tasks that lead to a specification of requirements and a design representation for the software to be built. The requirements model[1]— actually a set of models—is the first technical representation of a system.

In a seminal book on requirements modeling methods, Tom DeMarco [DeM79] describes the process in this way:

> Looking back over the recognized problems and failings of the analysis phase, I suggest that we need to make the following additions to our set of analysis phase goals. The products of analysis must be highly maintainable. This applies particularly to the

QUICK LOOK

What is it? The written word is a wonderful vehicle for communication, but it is not necessarily the best way to represent the requirements for computer software. Requirements modeling uses a combination of text and diagrammatic forms to depict requirements in a way that is relatively easy to understand, and more important, straightforward to review for correctness, completeness, and consistency.

Who does it? A software engineer (sometimes called an "analyst") builds the model using requirements elicited from the customer.

Why is it important? To validate software requirements, you need to examine them from a number of different points of view. In this chapter you'll consider requirements modeling from three different perspectives: scenario-based models, data (information) models, and class-based models. Each represents requirements in a different "dimension," thereby increasing the probability that errors will be found, that inconsistency will surface, and that omissions will be uncovered.

What are the steps? Scenario-based modeling represents the system from the user's point of view. Data modeling represents the information space and depicts the data objects that the software will manipulate and the relationships among them. Class-based modeling defines objects, attributes, and relationships. Once preliminary models are created, they are refined and analyzed to assess their clarity, completeness, and consistency. In Chapter 7, we extend the modeling dimensions noted here with additional representations, providing a more robust view of requirements.

What is the work product? A wide array of text-based and diagrammatic forms may be chosen for the requirements model. Each of these representations provides a view of one or more of the model elements.

How do I ensure that I've done it right? Requirements modeling work products must be reviewed for correctness, completeness, and consistency. They must reflect the needs of all stakeholders and establish a foundation from which design can be conducted.

---

1   In past editions of this book, I used the term *analysis model,* rather than *requirements model.* In this edition, I've decided to use both phrases to represent the modeling activity that defines various aspects of the problem to be solved. *Analysis* is the action that occurs as *requirements* are derived.

Target Document [software requirements specification]. Problems of size must be dealt with using an effective method of partitioning. The Victorian novel specification is out. Graphics have to be used whenever possible. We have to differentiate between logical [essential] and physical [implementation] considerations.... At the very least, we need.... Something to help us partition our requirements and document that partitioning before specification.... Some means of keeping track of and evaluating interfaces.... New tools to describe logic and policy, something better than narrative text.

Although DeMarco wrote about the attributes of analysis modeling more than a quarter century ago, his comments still apply to modern requirements modeling methods and notation.

6.1   REQUIREMENTS ANALYSIS

Requirements analysis results in the specification of software's operational characteristics, indicates software's interface with other system elements, and establishes constraints that software must meet. Requirements analysis allows you (regardless of whether you're called a *software engineer,* an *analyst,* or a *modeler*) to elaborate on basic requirements established during the inception, elicitation, and negotiation tasks that are part of requirements engineering (Chapter 5).

The requirements modeling action results in one or more of the following types of models:

uote:

"Any one 'view'
of requirements
is insufficient
to understand
or describe the
desired behavior of
a complex system."

Alan M. Davis

- *Scenario-based models* of requirements from the point of view of various system "actors"

- *Data models* that depict the information domain for the problem

- *Class-oriented models* that represent object-oriented classes (attributes and operations) and the manner in which classes collaborate to achieve system requirements

- *Flow-oriented models* that represent the functional elements of the system and how they transform data as it moves through the system

- *Behavioral models* that depict how the software behaves as a consequence of external "events"

POINT

The analysis model
and requirements
specification provide
a means for assessing
quality once the
software is built.

These models provide a software designer with information that can be translated to architectural, interface, and component-level designs. Finally, the requirements model (and the software requirements specification) provides the developer and the customer with the means to assess quality once software is built.

In this chapter, I focus on *scenario-based modeling*—a technique that is growing increasingly popular throughout the software engineering community; *data modeling*—a more specialized technique that is particularly appropriate when an application must create or manipulate a complex information space; and *class*

FIGURE 6.1

The
requirements
model as
a bridge
between the
system
description
and the design
model

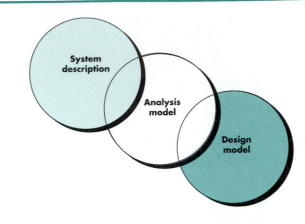

modeling—a representation of the object-oriented classes and the resultant collaborations that allow a system to function. Flow-oriented models, behavioral models, pattern-based modeling, and WebApp models are discussed in Chapter 7.

6.1.1   Overall Objectives and Philosophy

Throughout requirements modeling, your primary focus is on *what,* not *how.* What user interaction occurs in a particular circumstance, what objects does the system manipulate, what functions must the system perform, what behaviors does the system exhibit, what interfaces are defined, and what constraints apply?[2]

In earlier chapters, I noted that complete specification of requirements may not be possible at this stage. The customer may be unsure of precisely what is required for certain aspects of the system. The developer may be unsure that a specific approach will properly accomplish function and performance. These realities mitigate in favor of an iterative approach to requirements analysis and modeling. The analyst should model what is known and use that model as the basis for design of the software increment.[3]

The requirements model must achieve three primary objectives: (1) to describe what the customer requires, (2) to establish a basis for the creation of a software design, and (3) to define a set of requirements that can be validated once the software is built. The analysis model bridges the gap between a system-level description that describes overall system or business functionality as it is achieved by applying software, hardware, data, human, and other system elements and a software design (Chapters 8 through 13) that describes the software's application architecture, user interface, and component-level structure. This relationship is illustrated in Figure 6.1.

---

2   It should be noted that as customers become more technologically sophisticated, there is a trend toward the specification of *how* as well as *what.* However, the primary focus should remain on *what.*

3   Alternatively, the software team may choose to create a prototype (Chapter 2) in an effort to better understand requirements for the system.

It is important to note that all elements of the requirements model will be directly traceable to parts of the design model. A clear division of analysis and design tasks between these two important modeling activities is not always possible. Some design invariably occurs as part of analysis, and some analysis will be conducted during design.

6.1.2 Analysis Rules of Thumb

Arlow and Neustadt [Arl02] suggest a number of worthwhile rules of thumb that should be followed when creating the analysis model:

Are there basic guidelines that can help us as we do requirements analysis work?

- *The model should focus on requirements that are visible within the problem or business domain. The level of abstraction should be relatively high.* "Don't get bogged down in details" [Arl02] that try to explain how the system will work.

- *Each element of the requirements model should add to an overall understanding of software requirements and provide insight into the information domain, function, and behavior of the system.*

- *Delay consideration of infrastructure and other nonfunctional models until design.* That is, a database may be required, but the classes necessary to implement it, the functions required to access it, and the behavior that will be exhibited as it is used should be considered only after problem domain analysis has been completed.

- *Minimize coupling throughout the system.* It is important to represent relationships between classes and functions. However, if the level of "interconnectedness" is extremely high, effort should be made to reduce it.

- *Be certain that the requirements model provides value to all stakeholders.* Each constituency has its own use for the model. For example, business stakeholders should use the model to validate requirements; designers should use the model as a basis for design; QA people should use the model to help plan acceptance tests.

- *Keep the model as simple as it can be.* Don't create additional diagrams when they add no new information. Don't use complex notational forms, when a simple list will do.

Quote:

"Problems worthy of attack, prove their worth by hitting back."

Piet Hein

6.1.3 Domain Analysis

WebRef

Many useful resources for domain analysis can be found at **www.iturls .com/English/ Software Engineering/ SE_mod5.asp**.

In the discussion of requirements engineering (Chapter 5), I noted that analysis patterns often reoccur across many applications within a specific business domain. If these patterns are defined and categorized in a manner that allows you to recognize and apply them to solve common problems, the creation of the analysis model is expedited. More important, the likelihood of applying design patterns and executable software components grows dramatically. This improves time-to-market and reduces development costs.

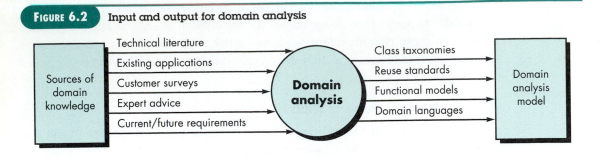

FIGURE 6.2 Input and output for domain analysis

But how are analysis patterns and classes recognized in the first place? Who defines them, categorizes them, and readies them for use on subsequent projects? The answers to these questions lie in *domain analysis.* Firesmith [Fir93] describes domain analysis in the following way:

> Software domain analysis is the identification, analysis, and specification of common requirements from a specific application domain, typically for reuse on multiple projects within that application domain. . . . [Object-oriented domain analysis is] the identification, analysis, and specification of common, reusable capabilities within a specific application domain, in terms of common objects, classes, subassemblies, and frameworks.

KEY POINT

Domain analysis doesn't look at a specific application, but rather at the domain in which the application resides. The intent is to identify common problem solving elements that are applicable to all applications within the domain.

The "specific application domain" can range from avionics to banking, from multimedia video games to software embedded within medical devices. The goal of domain analysis is straightforward: to find or create those analysis classes and/or analysis patterns that are broadly applicable so that they may be reused.[4]

Using terminology that was introduced earlier in this book, domain analysis may be viewed as an umbrella activity for the software process. By this I mean that domain analysis is an ongoing software engineering activity that is not connected to any one software project. In a way, the role of a domain analyst is similar to the role of a master toolsmith in a heavy manufacturing environment. The job of the toolsmith is to design and build tools that may be used by many people doing similar but not necessarily the same jobs. The role of the domain analyst[5] is to discover and define analysis patterns, analysis classes, and related information that may be used by many people working on similar but not necessarily the same applications.

Figure 6.2 [Ara89] illustrates key inputs and outputs for the domain analysis process. Sources of domain knowledge are surveyed in an attempt to identify objects that can be reused across the domain.

---

4   A complementary view of domain analysis "involves modeling the domain so that software engineers and other stakeholders can better learn about it . . . not all domain classes necessarily result in the development of reusable classes . . ." [Let03a].

5   Do not make the assumption that because a domain analyst is at work, a software engineer need not understand the application domain. Every member of a software team should have some understanding of the domain in which the software is to be placed.

Domain Analysis

The scene: Doug Miller's office, after a meeting with marketing.

The players: Doug Miller, software engineering manager, and Vinod Raman, a member of the software engineering team.

The conversation:

Doug: I need you for a special project, Vinod. I'm going to pull you out of the requirements gathering meetings.

Vinod (frowning): Too bad. That format actually works . . . I was getting something out of it. What's up?

Doug: Jamie and Ed will cover for you. Anyway, marketing insists that we deliver the Internet capability along with the home security function in the first release of *SafeHome*. We're under the gun on this . . . not enough time or people, so we've got to solve both problems—the PC interface and the Web interface—at once.

Vinod (looking confused): I didn't know the plan was set . . . we're not even finished with requirements gathering.

Doug (a wan smile): I know, but the time lines are so short that I decided to begin strategizing with marketing right now . . . anyhow, we'll revisit any tentative plan once we have the info from all of the requirements gathering meetings.

Vinod: Okay, what's up? What do you want me to do?

Doug: Do you know what "domain analysis" is?

Vinod: Sort of. You look for similar patterns in Apps that do the same kinds of things as the App you're building. If possible, you then steal the patterns and reuse them in your work.

Doug: Not sure I like the word *steal*, but basically you have it right. What I'd like you to do is to begin researching existing user interfaces for systems that control something like *SafeHome*. I want you to propose a set of patterns and analysis classes that can be common to both the PC-based interface that'll sit in the house and the browser-based interface that is accessible via the Internet.

Vinod: We can save time by making them the same . . . why don't we just do that?

Doug: Ah . . . it's nice to have people who think like you do. That's the whole point—we can save time and effort if both interfaces are nearly identical, implemented with the same code, blah, blah, that marketing insists on.

Vinod: So you want, what—classes, analysis patterns, design patterns?

Doug: All of 'em. Nothing formal at this point. I just want to get a head start on our internal analysis and design work.

Vinod: I'll go to our class library and see what we've got. I'll also use a patterns template I saw in a book I was reading a few months back.

Doug: Good. Go to work.

6.1.4 Requirements Modeling Approaches

One view of requirements modeling, called *structured analysis,* considers data and the processes that transform the data as separate entities. Data objects are modeled in a way that defines their attributes and relationships. Processes that manipulate data objects are modeled in a manner that shows how they transform data as data objects flow through the system.

A second approach to analysis modeling, called *object-oriented analysis,* focuses on the definition of classes and the manner in which they collaborate with one another to effect customer requirements. UML and the Unified Process (Chapter 2) are predominantly object oriented.

Although the requirements model proposed in this book combines features of both approaches, software teams often choose one approach and exclude all representations from the other. The question is not which is best, but rather, what

FIGURE 6.3

Elements of
the analysis
model

? What
different
points of view
can be used to
describe the
requirements
model?

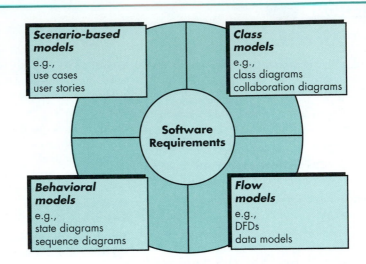

Quote:

"Why should we
build models? Why
not just build the
system itself? The
answer is that we
can construct
models in such a
way as to highlight,
or emphasize,
certain critical
features of a
system, while
simultaneously
de-emphasizing
other aspects of
the system."

Ed Yourdon

combination of representations will provide stakeholders with the best model of
software requirements and the most effective bridge to software design.

Each element of the requirements model (Figure 6.3) presents the problem from
a different point of view. Scenario-based elements depict how the user interacts with
the system and the specific sequence of activities that occur as the software is used.
Class-based elements model the objects that the system will manipulate, the operations that will be applied to the objects to effect the manipulation, relationships
(some hierarchical) between the objects, and the collaborations that occur between
the classes that are defined. Behavioral elements depict how external events change
the state of the system or the classes that reside within it. Finally, flow-oriented elements represent the system as an information transform, depicting how data objects
are transformed as they flow through various system functions.

Analysis modeling leads to the derivation of each of these modeling elements.
However, the specific content of each element (i.e., the diagrams that are used to
construct the element and the model) may differ from project to project. As we have
noted a number of times in this book, the software team must work to keep it simple. Only those modeling elements that add value to the model should be used.

6.2   SCENARIO-BASED MODELING

Although the success of a computer-based system or product is measured in many
ways, user satisfaction resides at the top of the list. If you understand how end users
(and other actors) want to interact with a system, your software team will be better
able to properly characterize requirements and build meaningful analysis and design

models. Hence, requirements modeling with UML[6] begins with the creation of scenarios in the form of use cases, activity diagrams, and swimlane diagrams.

6.2.1 Creating a Preliminary Use Case

Alistair Cockburn characterizes a use case as a "contract for behavior" [Coc01b]. As we discussed in Chapter 5, the "contract" defines the way in which an actor[7] uses a computer-based system to accomplish some goal. In essence, a use case captures the interactions that occur between producers and consumers of information and the system itself. In this section, I examine how use cases are developed as part of the requirements modeling activity.[8]

In Chapter 5, I noted that a use case describes a specific usage scenario in straightforward language from the point of view of a defined actor. But how do you know (1) what to write about, (2) how much to write about it, (3) how detailed to make your description, and (4) how to organize the description? These are the questions that must be answered if use cases are to provide value as a requirements modeling tool.

What to write about?   The first two requirements engineering tasks—inception and elicitation—provide you with the information you'll need to begin writing use cases. Requirements gathering meetings, QFD, and other requirements engineering mechanisms are used to identify stakeholders, define the scope of the problem, specify overall operational goals, establish priorities, outline all known functional requirements, and describe the things (objects) that will be manipulated by the system.

To begin developing a set of use cases, list the functions or activities performed by a specific actor. You can obtain these from a list of required system functions, through conversations with stakeholders, or by an evaluation of activity diagrams (Section 6.3.1) developed as part of requirements modeling.

SafeHome

Developing Another Preliminary User Scenario

The scene: A meeting room, during the second requirements gathering meeting.

The players: Jamie Lazar, software team member; Ed Robbins, software team member; Doug Miller, software engineering manager; three members of marketing; a product engineering representative; and a facilitator.

The conversation:

Facilitator: It's time that we begin talking about the *SafeHome* surveillance function. Let's develop a user scenario for access to the surveillance function.

Jamie: Who plays the role of the actor on this?

---

6 UML will be used as the modeling notation throughout this book. Appendix 1 provides a brief tutorial for those readers who may be unfamiliar with basic UML notation.

7 An actor is not a specific person, but rather a role that a person (or a device) plays within a specific context. An actor "calls on the system to deliver one of its services" [Coc01b].

8 Use cases are a particularly important part of analysis modeling for user interfaces. Interface analysis is discussed in detail in Chapter 11.

Facilitator: I think Meredith (a marketing person) has been working on that functionality. Why don't you play the role?

Meredith: You want to do it the same way we did it last time, right?

Facilitator: Right . . . same way.

Meredith: Well, obviously the reason for surveillance is to allow the homeowner to check out the house while he or she is away, to record and play back video that is captured . . . that sort of thing.

Ed: Will we use compression to store the video?

Facilitator: Good question, Ed, but let's postpone implementation issues for now. Meredith?

Meredith: Okay, so basically there are two parts to the surveillance function . . . the first configures the system including laying out a floor plan—we have to have tools to help the homeowner do this—and the second part is the actual surveillance function itself. Since the layout is part of the configuration activity, I'll focus on the surveillance function.

Facilitator (smiling): Took the words right out of my mouth.

Meredith: Um . . . I want to gain access to the surveillance function either via the PC or via the Internet. My feeling is that the Internet access would be more frequently used. Anyway, I want to be able to display camera views on a PC and control pan and zoom for a specific camera. I specify the camera by selecting it from the house floor plan. I want to selectively record camera output and replay camera output. I also want to be able to block access to one or more cameras with a specific password. I also want the option of seeing small windows that show views from all cameras and then be able to pick the one I want enlarged.

Jamie: Those are called thumbnail views.

Meredith: Okay, then I want thumbnail views of all the cameras. I also want the interface for the surveillance function to have the same look and feel as all other *SafeHome* interfaces. I want it to be intuitive, meaning I don't want to have to read a manual to use it.

Facilitator: Good job. Now, let's go into this function in a bit more detail . . .

The *SafeHome* home surveillance function (subsystem) discussed in the sidebar identifies the following functions (an abbreviated list) that are performed by the **homeowner** actor:

- Select camera to view.
- Request thumbnails from all cameras.
- Display camera views in a PC window.
- Control pan and zoom for a specific camera.
- Selectively record camera output.
- Replay camera output.
- Access camera surveillance via the Internet.

As further conversations with the stakeholder (who plays the role of a homeowner) progress, the requirements gathering team develops use cases for each of the functions noted. In general, use cases are written first in an informal narrative fashion. If more formality is required, the same use case is rewritten using a structured format similar to the one proposed in Chapter 5 and reproduced later in this section as a sidebar.

To illustrate, consider the function *access camera surveillance via the Internet—display camera views* **(ACS-DCV).** The stakeholder who takes on the role of the **homeowner** actor might write the following narrative:

Use case: Access camera surveillance via the Internet—display camera views (ACS-DCV)

Actor: homeowner

If I'm at a remote location, I can use any PC with appropriate browser software to log on to the *SafeHome Products* website. I enter my user ID and two levels of passwords and once I'm validated, I have access to all functionality for my installed *SafeHome* system. To access a specific camera view, I select "surveillance" from the major function buttons displayed. I then select "pick a camera" and the floor plan of the house is displayed. I then select the camera that I'm interested in. Alternatively, I can look at thumbnail snapshots from all cameras simultaneously by selecting "all cameras" as my viewing choice. Once I choose a camera, I select "view" and a one-frame-per-second view appears in a viewing window that is identified by the camera ID. If I want to switch cameras, I select "pick a camera" and the original viewing window disappears and the floor plan of the house is displayed again. I then select the camera that I'm interested in. A new viewing window appears.

A variation of a narrative use case presents the interaction as an ordered sequence of user actions. Each action is represented as a declarative sentence. Revisiting the **ACS-DCV** function, you would write:

Use case: Access camera surveillance via the Internet—display camera views (ACS-DCV)

Actor: homeowner

1. The homeowner logs onto the *SafeHome Products* website.

2. The homeowner enters his or her user ID.

3. The homeowner enters two passwords (each at least eight characters in length).

4. The system displays all major function buttons.

5. The homeowner selects the "surveillance" from the major function buttons.

6. The homeowner selects "pick a camera."

7. The system displays the floor plan of the house.

8. The homeowner selects a camera icon from the floor plan.

9. The homeowner selects the "view" button.

10. The system displays a viewing window that is identified by the camera ID.

11. The system displays video output within the viewing window at one frame per second.

It is important to note that this sequential presentation does not consider any alternative interactions (the narrative is more free-flowing and did represent a few alternatives). Use cases of this type are sometimes referred to as *primary scenarios* [Sch98a].

6.2.2   Refining a Preliminary Use Case

A description of alternative interactions is essential for a complete understanding of the function that is being described by a use case. Therefore, each step in the primary scenario is evaluated by asking the following questions [Sch98a]:

? How do I examine alternative courses of action when I develop a use case?

- *Can the actor take some other action at this point?*
- *Is it possible that the actor will encounter some error condition at this point?* If so, what might it be?
- *Is it possible that the actor will encounter some other behavior at this point (e.g., behavior that is invoked by some event outside the actor's control)?* If so, what might it be?

Answers to these questions result in the creation of a set of *secondary scenarios* that are part of the original use case but represent alternative behavior. For example, consider steps 6 and 7 in the primary scenario presented earlier:

6. The homeowner selects "pick a camera."

7. The system displays the floor plan of the house.

Can the actor take some other action at this point? The answer is "yes." Referring to the free-flowing narrative, the actor may choose to view thumbnail snapshots of all cameras simultaneously. Hence, one secondary scenario might be "View thumbnail snapshots for all cameras."

Is it possible that the actor will encounter some error condition at this point? Any number of error conditions can occur as a computer-based system operates. In this context, we consider only error conditions that are likely as a direct result of the action described in step 6 or step 7. Again the answer to the question is "yes." A floor plan with camera icons may have never been configured. Hence, selecting "pick a camera" results in an error condition: "No floor plan configured for this house."[9] This error condition becomes a secondary scenario.

Is it possible that the actor will encounter some other behavior at this point? Again the answer to the question is "yes." As steps 6 and 7 occur, the system may encounter an alarm condition. This would result in the system displaying a special alarm notification (type, location, system action) and providing the actor with a number of options relevant to the nature of the alarm. Because this secondary scenario can occur at any time for virtually all interactions, it will not become part of the **ACS-DCV** use case. Rather, a separate use case—**Alarm condition encountered**—would be developed and referenced from other use cases as required.

---

9   In this case, another actor, the **system administrator,** would have to configure the floor plan, install and initialize (e.g., assign an equipment ID) all cameras, and test each camera to be certain that it is accessible via the system and through the floor plan.

Each of the situations described in the preceding paragraphs is characterized as a use-case exception. An *exception* describes a situation (either a failure condition or an alternative chosen by the actor) that causes the system to exhibit somewhat different behavior.

Cockburn [Coc01b] recommends using a "brainstorming" session to derive a reasonably complete set of exceptions for each use case. In addition to the three generic questions suggested earlier in this section, the following issues should also be explored:

- *Are there cases in which some "validation function" occurs during this use case?* This implies that validation function is invoked and a potential error condition might occur.

- *Are there cases in which a supporting function (or actor) will fail to respond appropriately?* For example, a user action awaits a response but the function that is to respond times out.

- *Can poor system performance result in unexpected or improper user actions?* For example, a Web-based interface responds too slowly, resulting in a user making multiple selects on a processing button. These selects queue inappropriately and ultimately generate an error condition.

The list of extensions developed as a consequence of asking and answering these questions should be "rationalized" [Co01b] using the following criteria: an exception should be noted within the use case if the software can detect the condition described and then handle the condition once it has been detected. In some cases, an exception will precipitate the development of another use case (to handle the condition noted).

6.2.3 Writing a Formal Use Case

The informal use cases presented in Section 6.2.1 are sometimes sufficient for requirements modeling. However, when a use case involves a critical activity or describes a complex set of steps with a significant number of exceptions, a more formal approach may be desirable.

The **ACS-DCV** use case shown in the sidebar follows a typical outline for formal use cases. The *goal in context* identifies the overall scope of the use case. The *precondition* describes what is known to be true before the use case is initiated. The *trigger* identifies the event or condition that "gets the use case started" [Coc01b]. The *scenario* lists the specific actions that are required by the actor and the appropriate system responses. *Exceptions* identify the situations uncovered as the preliminary use case is refined (Section 6.2.2). Additional headings may or may not be included and are reasonably self-explanatory.

SafeHome

Use Case Template for Surveillance

Use case: Access camera surveillance via the Internet—display camera views (ACS-DCV)

Iteration: 2, last modification: January 14 by V. Raman.

Primary actor: Homeowner.

Goal in context: To view output of camera placed throughout the house from any remote location via the Internet.

Preconditions: System must be fully configured; appropriate user ID and passwords must be obtained.

Trigger: The homeowner decides to take a look inside the house while away.

Scenario:

1. The homeowner logs onto the *SafeHome Products* website.
2. The homeowner enters his or her user ID.
3. The homeowner enters two passwords (each at least eight characters in length).
4. The system displays all major function buttons.
5. The homeowner selects the "surveillance" from the major function buttons.
6. The homeowner selects "pick a camera."
7. The system displays the floor plan of the house.
8. The homeowner selects a camera icon from the floor plan.
9. The homeowner selects the "view" button.
10. The system displays a viewing window that is identified by the camera ID.
11. The system displays video output within the viewing window at one frame per second.

Exceptions:

1. ID or passwords are incorrect or not recognized— see use case **Validate ID and passwords.**
2. Surveillance function not configured for this system—system displays appropriate error message; see use case **Configure surveillance function.**
3. Homeowner selects "View thumbnail snapshots for all camera"—see use case **View thumbnail snapshots for all cameras.**
4. A floor plan is not available or has not been configured—display appropriate error message and see use case **Configure floor plan.**
5. An alarm condition is encountered—see use case **Alarm condition encountered.**

Priority: Moderate priority, to be implemented after basic functions.

When available: Third increment.

Frequency of use: Moderate frequency.

Channel to actor: Via PC-based browser and Internet connection.

Secondary actors: System administrator, cameras.

Channels to secondary actors:

1. System administrator: PC-based system.
2. Cameras: wireless connectivity.

Open issues:

1. What mechanisms protect unauthorized use of this capability by employees of *SafeHome Products*?
2. Is security sufficient? Hacking into this feature would represent a major invasion of privacy.
3. Will system response via the Internet be acceptable given the bandwidth required for camera views?
4. Will we develop a capability to provide video at a higher frames-per-second rate when high-bandwidth connections are available?

WebRef

When are you finished writing use cases? For a worthwhile discussion of this topic, see ootips.org/use-cases-done.html.

In many cases, there is no need to create a graphical representation of a usage scenario. However, diagrammatic representation can facilitate understanding, particularly when the scenario is complex. As we noted earlier in this book, UML does provide use-case diagramming capability. Figure 6.4 depicts a preliminary use-case diagram for the *SafeHome* product. Each use case is represented by an oval. Only the **ACS-DCV** use case has been discussed in this section.

FIGURE 6.4

Preliminary
use-case
diagram for
the *SafeHome*
system

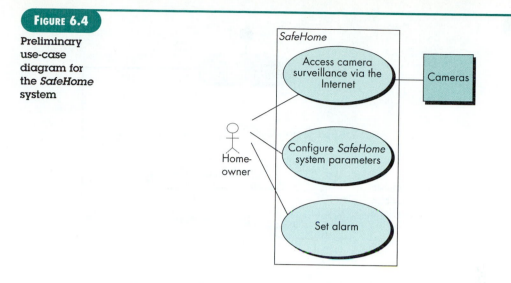

Every modeling notation has limitations, and the use case is no exception. Like any other form of written description, a use case is only as good as its author(s). If the description is unclear, the use case can be misleading or ambiguous. A use case focuses on functional and behavioral requirements and is generally inappropriate for nonfunctional requirements. For situations in which the requirements model must have significant detail and precision (e.g., safety critical systems), a use case may not be sufficient.

However, scenario-based modeling is appropriate for a significant majority of all situations that you will encounter as a software engineer. If developed properly, the use case can provide substantial benefit as a modeling tool.

6.3   UML MODELS THAT SUPPLEMENT THE USE CASE

There are many requirements modeling situations in which a text-based model—even one as simple as a use case—may not impart information in a clear and concise manner. In such cases, you can choose from a broad array of UML graphical models.

A UML activity diagram
represents the actions
and decisions that
occur as some function
is performed.

6.3.1   Developing an Activity Diagram

The UML activity diagram supplements the use case by providing a graphical representation of the flow of interaction within a specific scenario. Similar to the flowchart, an activity diagram uses rounded rectangles to imply a specific system function, arrows to represent flow through the system, decision diamonds to depict a branching decision (each arrow emanating from the diamond is labeled), and solid horizontal lines to indicate that parallel activities are occurring. An activity diagram for the **ACS-DCV** use case is shown in Figure 6.5. It should be noted that the activity diagram adds additional detail not directly mentioned (but implied) by the use case.

FIGURE 6.5

Activity
diagram for
Access
camera
surveillance
via the
Internet—
display
camera views
function.

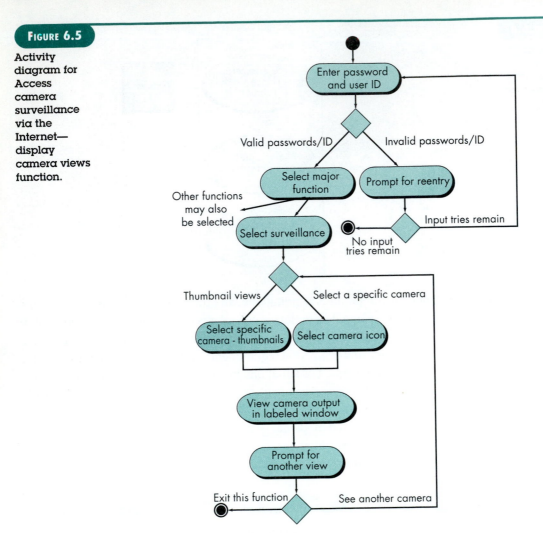

For example, a user may only attempt to enter **userID** and **password** a limited number of times. This is represented by a decision diamond below "Prompt for reentry."

6.3.2 Swimlane Diagrams

The UML *swimlane diagram* is a useful variation of the activity diagram and allows you to represent the flow of activities described by the use case and at the same time indicate which actor (if there are multiple actors involved in a specific use case) or analysis class (discussed later in this chapter) has responsibility for the action described by an activity rectangle. Responsibilities are represented as parallel segments that divide the diagram vertically, like the lanes in a swimming pool.

Three analysis classes—**Homeowner, Camera,** and **Interface**—have direct or indirect responsibilities in the context of the activity diagram represented in Figure 6.5.

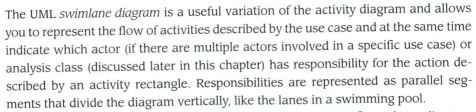

A UML swimlane
diagram represents the
flow of actions and
decisions and indicates
which actors perform
each.

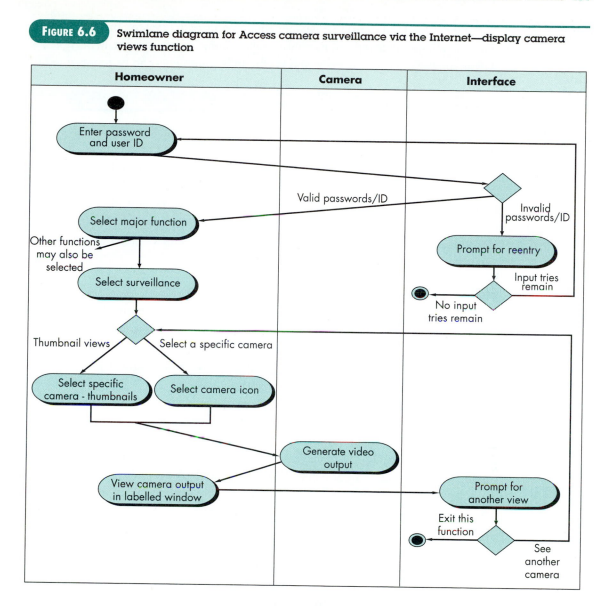

FIGURE 6.6   Swimlane diagram for Access camera surveillance via the Internet—display camera views function

Referring to Figure 6.6, the activity diagram is rearranged so that activities associated with a particular analysis class fall inside the swimlane for that class. For example, the **Interface** class represents the user interface as seen by the homeowner. The activity diagram notes two prompts that are the responsibility of the interface—"prompt for reentry" and "prompt for another view." These prompts and the decisions associated with them fall within the **Interface** swimlane. However, arrows lead from that swimlane back to the **Homeowner** swimlane, where homeowner actions occur.

Use cases, along with the activity and swimlane diagrams, are procedurally oriented. They represent the manner in which various actors invoke specific functions

uote:

"A good model guides your thinking, a bad one warps it."

Brian Marick

(or other procedural steps) to meet the requirements of the system. But a procedural view of requirements represents only a single dimension of a system. In Section 6.4, I examine the information space and how data requirements can be represented.

6.4   DATA MODELING CONCEPTS

WebRef

Useful information on data modeling can be found at **www .datamodel.org**.

If software requirements include the need to create, extend, or interface with a data-base or if complex data structures must be constructed and manipulated, the software team may choose to create a *data model* as part of overall requirements modeling. A software engineer or analyst defines all data objects that are processed within the system, the relationships between the data objects, and other information that is pertinent to the relationships. The *entity-relationship diagram* (ERD) addresses these issues and represents all data objects that are entered, stored, transformed, and produced within an application.

6.4.1   Data Objects

? How does a data object manifest itself within the context of an application?

A *data object* is a representation of composite information that must be understood by software. By *composite information,* I mean something that has a number of different properties or attributes. Therefore, width (a single value) would not be a valid data object, but **dimensions** (incorporating height, width, and depth) could be defined as an object.

A data object can be an external entity (e.g., anything that produces or consumes information), a thing (e.g., a report or a display), an occurrence (e.g., a telephone call) or event (e.g., an alarm), a role (e.g., salesperson), an organizational unit (e.g., accounting department), a place (e.g., a warehouse), or a structure (e.g., a file). For example, a **person** or a **car** can be viewed as a data object in the sense that either can be defined in terms of a set of attributes. The description of the data object incorporates the data object and all of its attributes.

A data object is a representation of any composite information that is processed by software.

A data object encapsulates data only—there is no reference within a data object to operations that act on the data.[10] Therefore, the data object can be represented as a table as shown in Figure 6.7. The headings in the table reflect attributes of the object. In this case, a car is defined in terms of **make, model, ID number, body type, color,** and **owner**. The body of the table represents specific instances of the data object. For example, a Chevy Corvette is an instance of the data object **car.**

6.4.2   Data Attributes

Attributes name a data object, describe its characteristics, and in some cases, make reference to another object.

Data attributes define the properties of a data object and take on one of three different characteristics. They can be used to (1) name an instance of the data object, (2) describe the instance, or (3) make reference to another instance in another table. In addition, one or more of the attributes must be defined as an identifier—that is, the identifier

---

10 This distinction separates the data object from the class or object defined as part of the object-oriented approach (Appendix 2).

FIGURE 6.7

Tabular
representation
of data objects

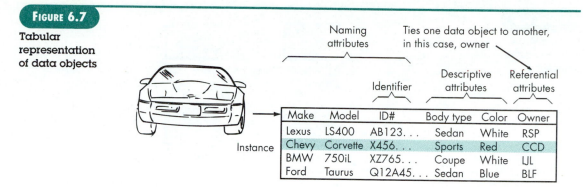

attribute becomes a "key" when we want to find an instance of the data object. In some cases, values for the identifier(s) are unique, although this is not a requirement. Referring to the data object **car,** a reasonable identifier might be the **ID number.**

The set of attributes that is appropriate for a given data object is determined through an understanding of the problem context. The attributes for **car** might serve well for an application that would be used by a department of motor vehicles, but these attributes would be useless for an automobile company that needs manufacturing control software. In the latter case, the attributes for **car** might also include **ID number, body type,** and **color,** but many additional attributes (e.g., **interior code, drive train type, trim package designator, transmission type**) would have to be added to make **car** a meaningful object in the manufacturing control context.

WebRef

A concept called "normalization" is important to those who intend to do thorough data modeling. A useful introduction can be found at **www .datamodel.org.**

INFO

Data Objects and Object-Oriented Classes—Are They the Same Thing?

A common question occurs when data objects are discussed: Is a data object the same thing as an object-oriented[11] class? The answer is "no."

A data object defines a composite data item; that is, it incorporates a collection of individual data items (attributes) and gives the collection of items a name (the name of the data object).

An object-oriented class encapsulates data attributes but also incorporates the operations (methods) that manipulate the data implied by those attributes. In addition, the definition of classes implies a comprehensive infrastructure that is part of the object-oriented software engineering approach. Classes communicate with one another via messages, they can be organized into hierarchies, and they provide inheritance characteristics for objects that are an instance of a class.

6.4.3 Relationships

Data objects are connected to one another in different ways. Consider the two data objects, **person** and **car.** These objects can be represented using the simple notation

---

11 Readers who are unfamiliar with object-oriented concepts and terminology should refer to the brief tutorial presented in Appendix 2.

FIGURE 6.8

Relationships
between data
objects

(a) A basic connection between data
objects

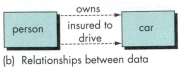

(b) Relationships between data
objects

KEY POINT

Relationships indicate
the manner in which
data objects are
connected to one
another.

illustrated in Figure 6.8a. A connection is established between **person** and **car**
because the two objects are related. But what are the relationships? To determine the
answer, you should understand the role of people (owners, in this case) and cars
within the context of the software to be built. You can establish a set of object/
relationship pairs that define the relevant relationships. For example,

- A person *owns* a car.

- A person *is insured to drive* a car.

The relationships *owns* and *insured to drive* define the relevant connections between
person and **car.** Figure 6.8b illustrates these object-relationship pairs graphically.
The arrows noted in Figure 6.8b provide important information about the directionality of the relationship and often reduce ambiguity or misinterpretations.

INFO

Entity-Relationship Diagrams

The object-relationship pair is the cornerstone
of the data model. These pairs can be
represented graphically using the entity-relationship
diagram (ERD).[12] The ERD was originally proposed by
Peter Chen [Che77] for the design of relational database
systems and has been extended by others. A set of
primary components is identified for the ERD: data objects,
attributes, relationships, and various type indicators. The
primary purpose of the ERD is to represent data objects
and their relationships.

Rudimentary ERD notation has already been
introduced. Data objects are represented by a labeled
rectangle. Relationships are indicated with a labeled line
connecting objects. In some variations of the ERD, the
connecting line contains a diamond that is labeled with the
relationship. Connections between data objects and
relationships are established using a variety of special
symbols that indicate cardinality and modality.[13] If you
desire further information about data modeling and the
entity-relationship diagram, see [Hob06] or [Sim05].

---

12 Although the ERD is still used in some database design applications, UML notation (Appendix 1)
can now be used for data design.
13 The *cardinality* of an object-relationship pair specifies "the number of occurrences of one [object]
that can be related to the number of occurrences of another [object]" [Til93]. The *modality* of a relationship is 0 if there is no explicit need for the relationship to occur or the relationship is optional.
The modality is 1 if an occurrence of the relationship is mandatory.

Data Modeling

Objective: Data modeling tools provide a software engineer with the ability to represent data objects, their characteristics, and their relationships. Used primarily for large database applications and other information systems projects, data modeling tools provide an automated means for creating comprehensive entity-relation diagrams, data object dictionaries, and related models.

Mechanics: Tools in this category enable the user to describe data objects and their relationships. In some cases, the tools use ERD notation. In others, the tools model relations using some other mechanism. Tools in this category are often used as part of database design and enable the creation of a database model by generating a database schema for common database management systems (DBMS).

Representative Tools:[14]

AllFusion ERWin, developed by Computer Associates (**www3.ca.com**), assists in the design of data objects, proper structure, and key elements for databases.

ER/Studio, developed by Embarcadero Software (**www.embarcadero.com**), supports entity-relationship modeling.

Oracle Designer, developed by Oracle Systems (**www.oracle.com**), "models business processes, data entities and relationships [that] are transformed into designs from which complete applications and databases are generated."

Visible Analyst, developed by Visible Systems (**www.visible.com**), supports a variety of analysis modeling functions including data modeling.

6.5   CLASS-BASED MODELING

Class-based modeling represents the objects that the system will manipulate, the operations (also called methods or services) that will be applied to the objects to effect the manipulation, relationships (some hierarchical) between the objects, and the collaborations that occur between the classes that are defined. The elements of a class-based model include classes and objects, attributes, operations, class-responsibility-collaborator (CRC) models, collaboration diagrams, and packages. The sections that follow present a series of informal guidelines that will assist in their identification and representation.

6.5.1   Identifying Analysis Classes

If you look around a room, there is a set of physical objects that can be easily identified, classified, and defined (in terms of attributes and operations). But when you "look around" the problem space of a software application, the classes (and objects) may be more difficult to comprehend.

We can begin to identify classes by examining the usage scenarios developed as part of the requirements model and performing a "grammatical parse" [Abb83] on the use cases developed for the system to be built. Classes are determined by underlining each noun or noun phrase and entering it into a simple table. Synonyms should be noted. If the class (noun) is required to implement a solution, then it is part of the solution space; otherwise, if a class is necessary only to describe a solution, it is part of the problem space.

---

14 Tools noted here do not represent an endorsement, but rather a sampling of tools in this category. In most cases, tool names are trademarked by their respective developers.

But what should we look for once all of the nouns have been isolated? *Analysis classes* manifest themselves in one of the following ways:

? **How do analysis classes manifest themselves as elements of the solution space?**

- *External entities* (e.g., other systems, devices, people) that produce or consume information to be used by a computer-based system.

- *Things* (e.g., reports, displays, letters, signals) that are part of the information domain for the problem.

- *Occurrences or events* (e.g., a property transfer or the completion of a series of robot movements) that occur within the context of system operation.

- *Roles* (e.g., manager, engineer, salesperson) played by people who interact with the system.

- *Organizational units* (e.g., division, group, team) that are relevant to an application.

- *Places* (e.g., manufacturing floor or loading dock) that establish the context of the problem and the overall function of the system.

- *Structures* (e.g., sensors, four-wheeled vehicles, or computers) that define a class of objects or related classes of objects.

This categorization is but one of many that have been proposed in the literature.[15] For example, Budd [Bud96] suggests a taxonomy of classes that includes *producers* (sources) and *consumers* (sinks) of data, *data managers, view* or *observer classes*, and *helper classes*.

It is also important to note what classes or objects are not. In general, a class should never have an "imperative procedural name" [Cas89]. For example, if the developers of software for a medical imaging system defined an object with the name **InvertImage** or even **ImageInversion,** they would be making a subtle mistake. The **Image** obtained from the software could, of course, be a class (it is a thing that is part of the information domain). Inversion of the image is an operation that is applied to the object. It is likely that inversion would be defined as an operation for the object **Image,** but it would not be defined as a separate class to connote "image inversion." As Cashman [Cas89] states: "the intent of object-orientation is to encapsulate, but still keep separate, data and operations on the data."

To illustrate how analysis classes might be defined during the early stages of modeling, consider a grammatical parse (nouns are underlined, verbs italicized) for a processing narrative[16] for the *SafeHome* security function.

---

15 Another important categorization, defining entity, boundary, and controller classes, is discussed in Section 6.5.4.

16 A processing narrative is similar to the use case in style but somewhat different in purpose. The processing narrative provides an overall description of the function to be developed. It is not a scenario written from one actor's point of view. It is important to note, however, that a grammatical parse can also be used for every use case developed as part of requirements gathering (elicitation).

The <u>SafeHome security function</u> *enables* the <u>homeowner</u> to *configure* the <u>security system</u> when it is *installed, monitors* all <u>sensors</u> *connected* to the security system, and *interacts* with the homeowner through the <u>Internet</u>, a <u>PC</u>, or a <u>control panel</u>.

During <u>installation</u>, the SafeHome PC is used to *program* and *configure* the <u>system</u>. Each sensor is assigned a <u>number</u> and <u>type</u>, a <u>master password</u> is programmed for *arming* and *disarming* the system, and <u>telephone number(s)</u> are *input* for *dialing* when a <u>sensor event</u> occurs.

When a sensor event is *recognized,* the software *invokes* an <u>audible alarm</u> attached to the system. After a <u>delay time</u> that is *specified* by the homeowner during system configuration activities, the software dials a telephone number of a <u>monitoring service</u>, *provides* <u>information</u> about the <u>location</u>, *reporting* the nature of the event that has been detected. The telephone number will be *redialed* every 20 seconds until <u>telephone connection</u> is *obtained.*

The homeowner *receives* <u>security information</u> via a control panel, the PC, or a browser, collectively called an <u>interface</u>. The interface *displays* <u>prompting messages</u> and <u>system status information</u> on the control panel, the PC ,or the browser window. Homeowner interaction takes the following form . . .

Extracting the nouns, we can propose a number of potential classes:

Potential Class	General Classification
homeowner	role or external entity
sensor	external entity
control panel	external entity
installation	occurrence
system (alias security system)	thing
number, type	not objects, attributes of sensor
master password	thing
telephone number	thing
sensor event	occurrence
audible alarm	external entity
monitoring service	organizational unit or external entity

The list would be continued until all nouns in the processing narrative have been considered. Note that I call each entry in the list a potential object. You must consider each further before a final decision is made.

Coad and Yourdon [Coa91] suggest six selection characteristics that should be used as you consider each potential class for inclusion in the analysis model:

1. *Retained information.* The potential class will be useful during analysis only if information about it must be remembered so that the system can function.

2. *Needed services.* The potential class must have a set of identifiable operations that can change the value of its attributes in some way.

ADVICE

The grammatical parse is not foolproof, but it can provide you with an excellent jump start, if you're struggling to define data objects and the transforms that operate on them.

? **How do I determine whether a potential class should, in fact, become an analysis class?**

3. *Multiple attributes.* During requirement analysis, the focus should be on "major" information; a class with a single attribute may, in fact, be useful during design, but is probably better represented as an attribute of another class during the analysis activity.

4. *Common attributes.* A set of attributes can be defined for the potential class and these attributes apply to all instances of the class.

5. *Common operations.* A set of operations can be defined for the potential class and these operations apply to all instances of the class.

6. *Essential requirements.* External entities that appear in the problem space and produce or consume information essential to the operation of any solution for the system will almost always be defined as classes in the requirements model.

To be considered a legitimate class for inclusion in the requirements model, a potential object should satisfy all (or almost all) of these characteristics. The decision for inclusion of potential classes in the analysis model is somewhat subjective, and later evaluation may cause an object to be discarded or reinstated. However, the first step of class-based modeling is the definition of classes, and decisions (even subjective ones) must be made. With this in mind, you should apply the selection characteristics to the list of potential *SafeHome* classes:

uote:

"Classes struggle, some classes triumph, others are eliminated."

Mao Zedong

Potential Class	Characteristic Number That Applies
homeowner	rejected: 1, 2 fail even though 6 applies
sensor	accepted: all apply
control panel	accepted: all apply
installation	rejected
system (alias security function)	accepted: all apply
number, type	rejected: 3 fails, attributes of sensor
master password	rejected: 3 fails
telephone number	rejected: 3 fails
sensor event	accepted: all apply
audible alarm	accepted: 2, 3, 4, 5, 6 apply
monitoring service	rejected: 1, 2 fail even though 6 applies

It should be noted that (1) the preceding list is not all-inclusive, additional classes would have to be added to complete the model; (2) some of the rejected potential classes will become attributes for those classes that were accepted (e.g., **number** and **type** are attributes of **Sensor,** and **master password** and **telephone number** may become attributes of **System**); (3) different statements of the problem might cause different "accept or reject" decisions to be made (e.g., if each homeowner had an individual password or was identified by voice print, the **Homeowner** class would satisfy characteristics 1 and 2 and would have been accepted).

6.5.2 Specifying Attributes

Attributes describe a class that has been selected for inclusion in the requirements model. In essence, it is the attributes that define the class—that clarify what is meant by the class in the context of the problem space. For example, if we were to build a system that tracks baseball statistics for professional baseball players, the attributes of the class **Player** would be quite different than the attributes of the same class when it is used in the context of the professional baseball pension system. In the former, attributes such as name, position, batting average, fielding percentage, years played, and games played might be relevant. For the latter, some of these attributes would be meaningful, but others would be replaced (or augmented) by attributes like average salary, credit toward full vesting, pension plan options chosen, mailing address, and the like.

To develop a meaningful set of attributes for an analysis class, you should study each use case and select those "things" that reasonably "belong" to the class. In addition, the following question should be answered for each class: "What data items (composite and/or elementary) fully define this class in the context of the problem at hand?"

To illustrate, we consider the **System** class defined for *SafeHome*. A homeowner can configure the security function to reflect sensor information, alarm response information, activation/deactivation information, identification information, and so forth. We can represent these composite data items in the following manner:

identification information = system ID + verification phone number + system status

alarm response information = delay time + telephone number

activation/deactivation information = master password + number of allowable tries + temporary password

Each of the data items to the right of the equal sign could be further defined to an elementary level, but for our purposes, they constitute a reasonable list of attributes for the **System** class (shaded portion of Figure 6.9).

Sensors are part of the overall *SafeHome* system, and yet they are not listed as data items or as attributes in Figure 6.9. **Sensor** has already been defined as a class, and multiple **Sensor** objects will be associated with the **System** class. In general, we avoid defining an item as an attribute if more than one of the items is to be associated with the class.

6.5.3 Defining Operations

Operations define the behavior of an object. Although many different types of operations exist, they can generally be divided into four broad categories: (1) operations that manipulate data in some way (e.g., adding, deleting, reformatting, selecting), (2) operations that perform a computation, (3) operations that inquire about the state

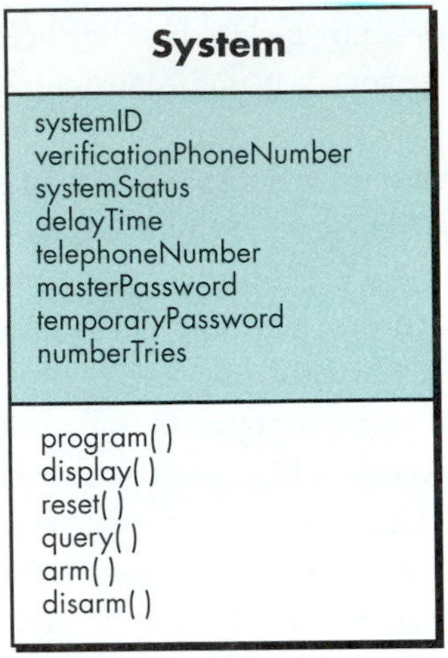

FIGURE 6.9

Class diagram
for the system
class

of an object, and (4) operations that monitor an object for the occurrence of a con-trolling event. These functions are accomplished by operating on attributes and/or associations (Section 6.5.5). Therefore, an operation must have "knowledge" of the nature of the class' attributes and associations.

As a first iteration at deriving a set of operations for an analysis class, you can again study a processing narrative (or use case) and select those operations that rea-sonably belong to the class. To accomplish this, the grammatical parse is again stud-ied and verbs are isolated. Some of these verbs will be legitimate operations and can be easily connected to a specific class. For example, from the *SafeHome* processing narrative presented earlier in this chapter, we see that "sensor is *assigned* a number and type" or "a master password is *programmed* for *arming and disarming* the system." These phrases indicate a number of things:

- That an *assign()* operation is relevant for the **Sensor** class.
- That a *program()* operation will be applied to the **System** class.
- That *arm()* and *disarm()* are operations that apply to **System** class.

Upon further investigation, it is likely that the operation *program()* will be divided into a number of more specific suboperations required to configure the system. For ex-ample, *program()* implies specifying phone numbers, configuring system character-istics (e.g., creating the sensor table, entering alarm characteristics), and entering password(s). But for now, we specify *program()* as a single operation.

In addition to the grammatical parse, you can gain additional insight into other operations by considering the communication that occurs between objects. Objects communicate by passing messages to one another. Before continuing with the spec-ification of operations, I explore this matter in a bit more detail.

SafeHome

Class Models

The scene: Ed's cubicle, as requirements modeling begins.

The players: Jamie, Vinod, and Ed—all members of the *SafeHome* software engineering team.

The conversation:

[Ed has been working to extract classes from the use case template for ACS-DCV (presented in an earlier sidebar in this chapter) and is presenting the classes he has extracted to his colleagues.]

Ed: So when the homeowner wants to pick a camera, he or she has to pick it from a floor plan. I've defined a **FloorPlan** class. Here's the diagram.

(They look at Figure 6.10.)

Jamie: So **FloorPlan** is an object that is put together with walls, doors, windows, and cameras. That's what those labeled lines mean, right?

Ed: Yeah, they're called "associations." One class is associated with another according to the associations I've shown. [Associations are discussed in Section 6.5.5.]

Vinod: So the actual floor plan is made up of walls and contains cameras and sensors that are placed within those walls. How does the floor plan know where to put those objects?

Ed: It doesn't, but the other classes do. See the attributes under, say, **WallSegment,** which is used to build a wall. The wall segment has start and stop coordinates and the *draw()* operation does the rest.

Jamie: And the same goes for windows and doors. Looks like camera has a few extra attributes.

Ed: Yeah, I need them to provide pan and zoom info.

Vinod: I have a question. Why does the camera have an ID but the others don't? I notice you have an attribute called **nextWall.** How will **WallSegment** know what the next wall will be?

Ed: Good question, but as they say, that's a design decision, so I'm going to delay that until . . .

Jamie: Give me a break . . . I'll bet you've already figured it out.

Ed (smiling sheepishly): True, I'm gonna use a list structure which I'll model when we get to design. If you get religious about separating analysis and design, the level of detail I have right here could be suspect.

Jamie: Looks pretty good to me, but I have a few more questions.

(Jamie asks questions which result in minor modifications)

Vinod: Do you have CRC cards for each of the objects? If so, we ought to role-play through them, just to make sure nothing has been omitted.

Ed: I'm not quite sure how to do them.

Vinod: It's not hard and they really pay off. I'll show you.

6.5.4   Class-Responsibility-Collaborator (CRC) Modeling

Class-responsibility-collaborator (CRC) modeling [Wir90] provides a simple means for identifying and organizing the classes that are relevant to system or product requirements. Ambler [Amb95] describes CRC modeling in the following way:

> A CRC model is really a collection of standard index cards that represent classes. The cards are divided into three sections. Along the top of the card you write the name of the class. In the body of the card you list the class responsibilities on the left and the collaborators on the right.

In reality, the CRC model may make use of actual or virtual index cards. The intent is to develop an organized representation of classes. *Responsibilities* are the attributes and operations that are relevant for the class. Stated simply, a responsibility is "anything the class knows or does" [Amb95]. *Collaborators* are those classes that are

FIGURE 6.10

Class diagram
for FloorPlan
(see sidebar
discussion)

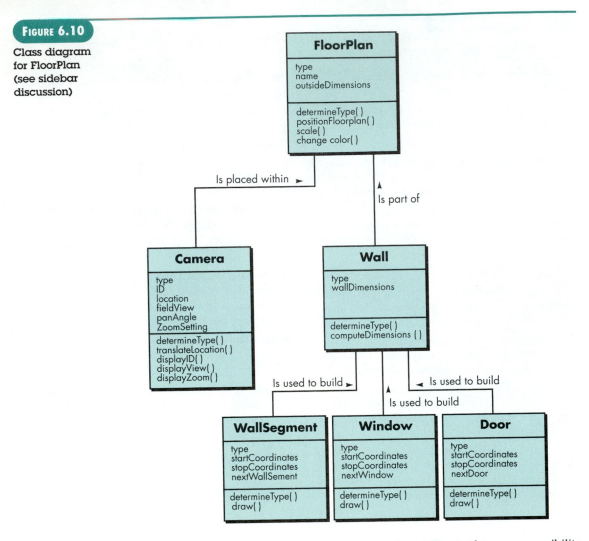

required to provide a class with the information needed to complete a responsibility. In general, a *collaboration* implies either a request for information or a request for some action.

A simple CRC index card for the **FloorPlan** class is illustrated in Figure 6.11. The list of responsibilities shown on the CRC card is preliminary and subject to additions or modification. The classes **Wall** and **Camera** are noted next to the responsibility that will require their collaboration.

WebRef

An excellent discussion
of these class types
can be found at
**www.theumlcafe
.com/a0079.htm**.

Classes.   Basic guidelines for identifying classes and objects were presented earlier in this chapter. The taxonomy of class types presented in Section 6.5.1 can be extended by considering the following categories:

- *Entity classes*, also called *model* or *business* classes, are extracted directly from the statement of the problem (e.g., **FloorPlan** and **Sensor**). These

FIGURE 6.11

A CRC model
index card

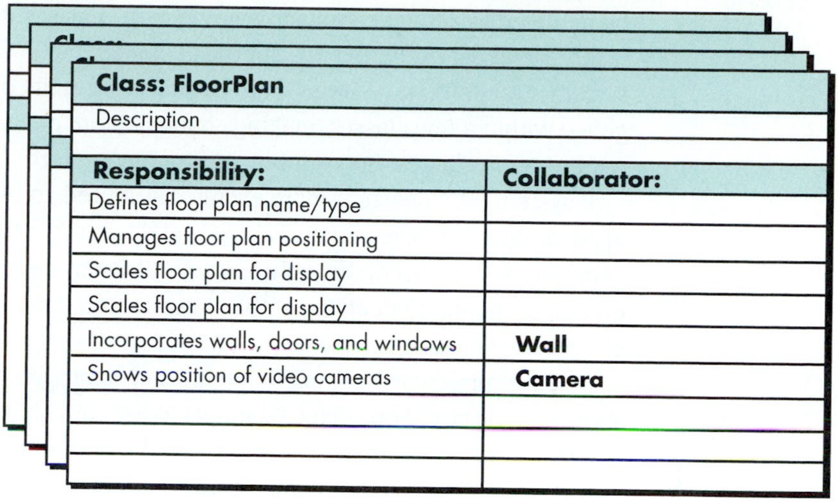

Class: FloorPlan

Description

Responsibility:	Collaborator:
Defines floor plan name/type	
Manages floor plan positioning	
Scales floor plan for display	
Scales floor plan for display	
Incorporates walls, doors, and windows	**Wall**
Shows position of video cameras	**Camera**

uote:

"Objects can be
classified
scientifically into
three major
categories: those
that don't work,
those that break
down, and those
that get lost."

Russell Baker

classes typically represent things that are to be stored in a database and persist throughout the duration of the application (unless they are specifically deleted).

- *Boundary classes* are used to create the interface (e.g., interactive screen or printed reports) that the user sees and interacts with as the software is used. Entity objects contain information that is important to users, but they do not display themselves. Boundary classes are designed with the responsibility of managing the way entity objects are represented to users. For example, a boundary class called **CameraWindow** would have the responsibility of displaying surveillance camera output for the *SafeHome* system.

- *Controller classes* manage a "unit of work" [UML03] from start to finish. That is, controller classes can be designed to manage (1) the creation or update of entity objects, (2) the instantiation of boundary objects as they obtain information from entity objects, (3) complex communication between sets of objects, (4) validation of data communicated between objects or between the user and the application. In general, controller classes are not considered until the design activity has begun.

What
guidelines
can be applied
for allocating
responsibilities
to classes?

Responsibilities.   Basic guidelines for identifying responsibilities (attributes and operations) have been presented in Sections 6.5.2 and 6.5.3. Wirfs-Brock and her colleagues [Wir90] suggest five guidelines for allocating responsibilities to classes:

1. **System intelligence should be distributed across classes to best address the needs of the problem.** Every application encompasses a certain degree of intelligence; that is, what the system knows and what it can do. This intelligence can be distributed across classes in a number of

different ways. "Dumb" classes (those that have few responsibilities) can be modeled to act as servants to a few "smart" classes (those having many responsibilities). Although this approach makes the flow of control in a system straightforward, it has a few disadvantages: it concentrates all intelligence within a few classes, making changes more difficult, and it tends to require more classes, hence more development effort.

If system intelligence is more evenly distributed across the classes in an application, each object knows about and does only a few things (that are generally well focused), the cohesiveness of the system is improved.[17] This enhances the maintainability of the software and reduces the impact of side effects due to change.

To determine whether system intelligence is properly distributed, the responsibilities noted on each CRC model index card should be evaluated to determine if any class has an extraordinarily long list of responsibilities. This indicates a concentration of intelligence.[18] In addition, the responsibilities for each class should exhibit the same level of abstraction. For example, among the operations listed for an aggregate class called **CheckingAccount** a reviewer notes two responsibilities: *balance-the-account* and *check-off-cleared-checks.* The first operation (responsibility) implies a complex mathematical and logical procedure. The second is a simple clerical activity. Since these two operations are not at the same level of abstraction, *check-off-cleared-checks* should be placed within the responsibilities of **CheckEntry,** a class that is encompassed by the aggregate class **CheckingAccount.**

2. **Each responsibility should be stated as generally as possible.** This guideline implies that general responsibilities (both attributes and operations) should reside high in the class hierarchy (because they are generic, they will apply to all subclasses).

3. **Information and the behavior related to it should reside within the same class.** This achieves the object-oriented principle called *encapsulation*. Data and the processes that manipulate the data should be packaged as a cohesive unit.

4. **Information about one thing should be localized with a single class, not distributed across multiple classes.** A single class should take on the responsibility for storing and manipulating a specific type of information. This responsibility should not, in general, be shared across a number of classes. If information is distributed, software becomes more difficult to maintain and more challenging to test.

---

17 Cohesiveness is a design concept that is discussed in Chapter 8.
18 In such cases, it may be necessary to spit the class into multiple classes or complete subsystems in order to distribute intelligence more effectively.

5. **Responsibilities should be shared among related classes, when appropriate.** There are many cases in which a variety of related objects must all exhibit the same behavior at the same time. As an example, consider a video game that must display the following classes: **Player, PlayerBody, PlayerArms, PlayerLegs, PlayerHead.** Each of these classes has its own attributes (e.g., position, orientation, color, speed) and all must be updated and displayed as the user manipulates a joystick. The responsibilities *update()* and *display()* must therefore be shared by each of the objects noted. **Player** knows when something has changed and *update()* is required. It collaborates with the other objects to achieve a new position or orientation, but each object controls its own display.

Collaborations. Classes fulfill their responsibilities in one of two ways: (1) A class can use its own operations to manipulate its own attributes, thereby fulfilling a particular responsibility, or (2) a class can collaborate with other classes. Wirfs-Brock and her colleagues [Wir90] define collaborations in the following way:

> Collaborations represent requests from a client to a server in fulfillment of a client responsibility. A collaboration is the embodiment of the contract between the client and the server. . . . We say that an object collaborates with another object if, to fulfill a responsibility, it needs to send the other object any messages. A single collaboration flows in one direction—representing a request from the client to the server. From the client's point of view, each of its collaborations is associated with a particular responsibility implemented by the server.

Collaborations are identified by determining whether a class can fulfill each responsibility itself. If it cannot, then it needs to interact with another class. Hence, a collaboration.

As an example, consider the *SafeHome* security function. As part of the activation procedure, the **ControlPanel** object must determine whether any sensors are open. A responsibility named *determine-sensor-status()* is defined. If sensors are open, **ControlPanel** must set a status attribute to "not ready." Sensor information can be acquired from each **Sensor** object. Therefore, the responsibility *determine-sensor-status()* can be fulfilled only if **ControlPanel** works in collaboration with **Sensor.**

To help in the identification of collaborators, you can examine three different generic relationships between classes [Wir90]: (1) the *is-part-of* relationship, (2) the *has-knowledge-of* relationship, and (3) the *depends-upon* relationship. Each of the three generic relationships is considered briefly in the paragraphs that follow.

All classes that are part of an aggregate class are connected to the aggregate class via an *is-part-of* relationship. Consider the classes defined for the video game noted earlier, the class **PlayerBody** *is-part-of* **Player,** as are **PlayerArms, PlayerLegs,** and **PlayerHead.** In UML, these relationships are represented as the aggregation shown in Figure 6.12.

FIGURE 6.12

A composite
aggregate
class

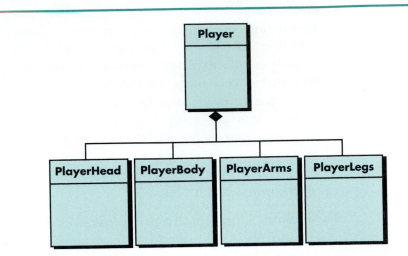

When one class must acquire information from another class, the *has-knowledge-of* relationship is established. The *determine-sensor-status()* responsibility noted earlier is an example of a *has-knowledge-of* relationship.

The *depends-upon* relationship implies that two classes have a dependency that is not achieved by *has-knowledge-of* or *is-part-of.* For example, **PlayerHead** must always be connected to **PlayerBody** (unless the video game is particularly violent), yet each object could exist without direct knowledge of the other. An attribute of the **PlayerHead** object called center-position is determined from the center position of **PlayerBody.** This information is obtained via a third object, **Player,** that acquires it from **PlayerBody.** Hence, **PlayerHead** *depends-upon* **PlayerBody.**

In all cases, the collaborator class name is recorded on the CRC model index card next to the responsibility that has spawned the collaboration. Therefore, the index card contains a list of responsibilities and the corresponding collaborations that enable the responsibilities to be fulfilled (Figure 6.11).

When a complete CRC model has been developed, stakeholders can review the model using the following approach [Amb95]:

1. All participants in the review (of the CRC model) are given a subset of the CRC model index cards. Cards that collaborate should be separated (i.e., no reviewer should have two cards that collaborate).

2. All use-case scenarios (and corresponding use-case diagrams) should be organized into categories.

3. The review leader reads the use case deliberately. As the review leader comes to a named object, she passes a token to the person holding the corresponding class index card. For example, a use case for *SafeHome* contains the following narrative:

The homeowner observes the *SafeHome* control panel to determine if the system is ready for input. If the system is not ready, the homeowner must physically close windows/doors so that the ready indicator is present. [A not-ready indicator implies that a sensor is open, i.e., that a door or window is open.]

When the review leader comes to "control panel," in the use case narrative, the token is passed to the person holding the **ControlPanel** index card. The phrase "implies that a sensor is open" requires that the index card contains a responsibility that will validate this implication (the responsibility *determine-sensor-status()* accomplishes this). Next to the responsibility on the index card is the collaborator **Sensor.** The token is then passed to the **Sensor** object.

4. When the token is passed, the holder of the **Sensor** card is asked to describe the responsibilities noted on the card. The group determines whether one (or more) of the responsibilities satisfies the use-case requirement.

5. If the responsibilities and collaborations noted on the index cards cannot accommodate the use case, modifications are made to the cards. This may include the definition of new classes (and corresponding CRC index cards) or the specification of new or revised responsibilities or collaborations on existing cards.

This modus operandi continues until the use case is finished. When all use cases have been reviewed, requirements modeling continues.

SafeHome

CRC Models

The scene: Ed's cubicle, as requirements modeling begins.

The players: Vinod and Ed—members of the *SafeHome* software engineering team.

The conversation:

[Vinod has decided to show Ed how to develop CRC cards by showing him an example.]

Vinod: While you've been working on surveillance and Jamie has been tied up with security, I've been working on the home management function.

Ed: What's the status of that? Marketing kept changing its mind.

Vinod: Here's the first-cut use case for the whole function . . . we've refined it a bit, but it should give you an overall view . . .

Use case: *SafeHome* home management function.

Narrative: We want to use the home management interface on a PC or an Internet connection to control electronic devices that have wireless interface controllers.

The system should allow me to turn specific lights on and off, to control appliances that are connected to a wireless interface, to set my heating and air conditioning system to temperatures that I define. To do this, I want to select the devices from a floor plan of the house. Each device must be identified on the floor plan. As an optional feature, I want to control all audiovisual devices—audio, television, DVD, digital recorders, and so forth.

With a single selection, I want to be able to set the entire house for various situations. One is *home*, another is *away*, a third is *overnight travel*, and a fourth is *extended travel*. All of these situations will have settings that will be applied to all devices. In the *overnight travel* and *extended travel* states, the system should turn lights on and off at random intervals (to make it look like someone is home) and control the heating and air conditioning system. I should be able to override these setting via the Internet with appropriate password protection . . .

Ed: The hardware guys have got all the wireless interfacing figured out?

Vinod (smiling): They're working on it; say it's no problem. Anyway, I extracted a bunch of classes for home management and we can use one as an example. Let's use the **HomeManagementInterface** class.

Ed: Okay . . . so the responsibilities are what . . . the attributes and operations for the class and the collaborations are the classes that the responsibilities point to.

Vinod: I thought you didn't understand CRC.

Ed: Maybe a little, but go ahead.

Vinod: So here's my class definition for **HomeManagementInterface.**

Attributes:

optionsPanel—contains info on buttons that enable user to select functionality.

situationPanel—contains info on buttons that enable user to select situation.

floorplan—same as surveillance object but this one displays devices.

deviceIcons—info on icons representing lights, appliances, HVAC, etc.

devicePanels—simulation of appliance or device control panel; allows control.

Operations:

displayControl(), selectControl(), displaySituation(), select situation(), accessFloorplan(), selectDeviceIcon(), displayDevicePanel(), accessDevicePanel(), . . .

Class: HomeManagementInterface

Responsibility	**Collaborator**
displayControl()	**OptionsPanel** (class)
selectControl()	**OptionsPanel** (class)
displaySituation()	**SituationPanel** (class)
selectSituation()	**SituationPanel** (class)
accessFloorplan()	**FloorPlan** (class) . . .

. . .

Ed: So when the operation *accessFloorplan()* is invoked, it collaborates with the **FloorPlan** object just like the one we developed for surveillance. Wait, I have a description of it here. (They look at Figure 6.10.)

Vinod: Exactly. And if we wanted to review the entire class model, we could start with this index card, then go to the collaborator's index card, and from there to one of the collaborator's collaborators, and so on.

Ed: Good way to find omissions or errors.

Vinod: Yep.

6.5.5   Associations and Dependencies

> **KEY POINT**
>
> An association defines a relationship between classes. Multiplicity defines how many of one class are related to how many of another class.

In many instances, two analysis classes are related to one another in some fashion, much like two data objects may be related to one another (Section 6.4.3). In UML these relationships are called *associations*. Referring back to Figure 6.10, the **FloorPlan** class is defined by identifying a set of associations between **FloorPlan** and two other classes, **Camera** and **Wall.** The class **Wall** is associated with three classes that allow a wall to be constructed, **WallSegment, Window,** and **Door.**

In some cases, an association may be further defined by indicating *multiplicity*. Referring to Figure 6.10, a **Wall** object is constructed from one or more **WallSegment** objects. In addition, the **Wall** object may contain 0 or more **Window** objects and 0 or more **Door** objects. These multiplicity constraints are illustrated in Figure 6.13, where "one or more" is represented using 1. .*, and "0 or more" by 0 . .*. In UML, the asterisk indicates an unlimited upper bound on the range.[19]

---

19 Other multiplicity relations—one to one, one to many, many to many, one to a specified range with lower and upper limits, and others—may be indicated as part of an association.

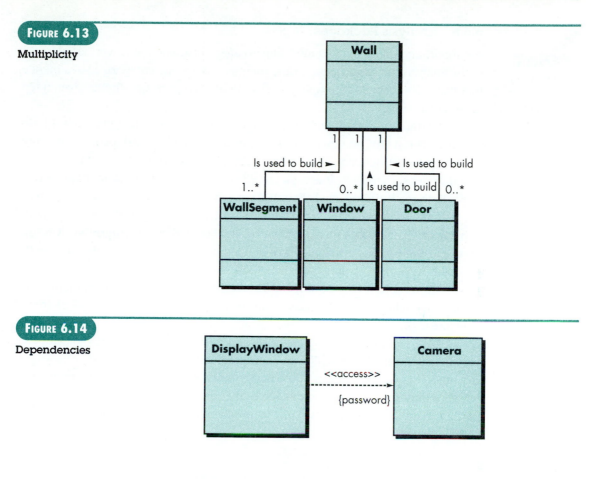

FIGURE 6.13

Multiplicity

FIGURE 6.14

Dependencies

? What is a stereotype?

In many instances, a client-server relationship exists between two analysis classes. In such cases, a client class depends on the server class in some way and a *dependency relationship* is established. Dependencies are defined by a stereotype. A *stereotype* is an "extensibility mechanism" [Arl02] within UML that allows you to define a special modeling element whose semantics are custom defined. In UML stereotypes are represented in double angle brackets (e.g., <<stereotype>>).

As an illustration of a simple dependency within the *SafeHome* surveillance system, a **Camera** object (in this case, the server class) provides a video image to a **DisplayWindow** object (in this case, the client class). The relationship between these two objects is not a simple association, yet a dependency association does exist. In a use case written for surveillance (not shown), you learn that a special password must be provided in order to view specific camera locations. One way to achieve this is to have **Camera** request a password and then grant permission to the **DisplayWindow** to produce the video display. This can be represented as shown in Figure 6.14 where <<access>> implies that the use of the camera output is controlled by a special password.

6.5.6   Analysis Packages

An important part of analysis modeling is categorization. That is, various elements of the analysis model (e.g., use cases, analysis classes) are categorized in a manner that packages them as a grouping—called an *analysis package*—that is given a representative name.

To illustrate the use of analysis packages, consider the video game that I introduced earlier. As the analysis model for the video game is developed, a large number of classes are derived. Some focus on the game environment—the visual scenes that the user sees as the game is played. Classes such as **Tree, Landscape, Road, Wall, Bridge, Building,** and **VisualEffect** might fall within this category. Others focus on the characters within the game, describing their physical features, actions, and constraints. Classes such as **Player** (described earlier), **Protagonist, Antagonist,** and **SupportingRoles** might be defined. Still others describe the rules of the game—how a player navigates through the environment. Classes such as **RulesOfMovement** and **ConstraintsOnAction** are candidates here. Many other categories might exist. These classes can be grouped in analysis packages as shown in Figure 6.15.

The plus sign preceding the analysis class name in each package indicates that the classes have public visibility and are therefore accessible from other packages. Although they are not shown in the figure, other symbols can precede an element within a package. A minus sign indicates that an element is hidden from all other packages and a # symbol indicates that an element is accessible only to packages contained within a given package.

FIGURE 6.15

Packages

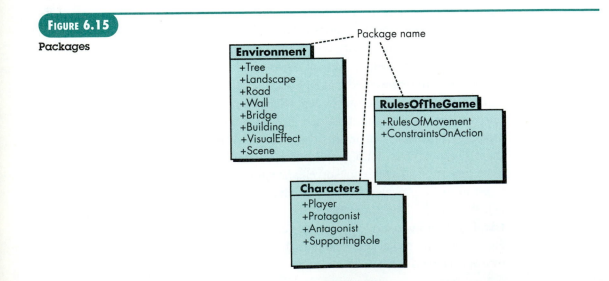

6.6 SUMMARY

The objective of requirements modeling is to create a variety of representations that describe what the customer requires, establish a basis for the creation of a software design, and define a set of requirements that can be validated once the software is built. The requirements model bridges the gap between a system-level representation that describes overall system and business functionality and a software design that describes the software's application architecture, user interface, and component-level structure.

Scenario-based models depict software requirements from the user's point of view. The use case—a narrative or template-driven description of an interaction between an actor and the software—is the primary modeling element. Derived during requirements elicitation, the use case defines the keys steps for a specific function or interaction. The degree of use-case formality and detail varies, but the end result provides necessary input to all other analysis modeling activities. Scenarios can also be described using an activity diagram—a flowchart-like graphical representation that depicts the processing flow within a specific scenario. Swim-lane diagrams illustrate how the processing flow is allocated to various actors or classes.

Data modeling is used to describe the information space that will be constructed or manipulated by the software. Data modeling begins by representing data objects—composite information that must be understood by the software. The attributes of each data object are identified and relationships between data objects are described.

Class-based modeling uses information derived from scenario-based and data modeling elements to identify analysis classes. A grammatical parse may be used to extract candidate classes, attributes, and operations from text-based narratives. Criteria for the definition of a class are defined. A set of class-responsibility-collaborator index cards can be used to define relationships between classes. In addition, a variety of UML modeling notation can be applied to define hierarchies, relationships, associations, aggregations, and dependencies among classes. Analysis packages are used to categorize and group classes in a manner that makes them more manageable for large systems.

PROBLEMS AND POINTS TO PONDER

6.1. Is it possible to begin coding immediately after an analysis model has been created? Explain your answer and then argue the counterpoint.

6.2. An analysis rule of thumb is that the model "should focus on requirements that are visible within the problem or business domain." What types of requirements are *not* visible in these domains? Provide a few examples.

6.3. What is the purpose of domain analysis? How is it related to the concept of requirements patterns?

6.4. Is it possible to develop an effective analysis model without developing all four elements shown in Figure 6.3? Explain.

6.5. You have been asked to build one of the following systems:

a. a network-based course registration system for your university.
b. a Web-based order-processing system for a computer store.
c. a simple invoicing system for a small business.
d. an Internet-based cookbook that is built into an electric range or microwave.

Select the system that is of interest to you and develop an entity-relationship diagram that describes data objects, relationships, and attributes.

6.6. The department of public works for a large city has decided to develop a Web-based pothole tracking and repair system (PHTRS). A description follows:

Citizens can log onto a website and report the location and severity of potholes. As potholes are reported they are logged within a "public works department repair system" and are assigned an identifying number, stored by street address, size (on a scale of 1 to 10), location (middle, curb, etc.), district (determined from street address), and repair priority (determined from the size of the pothole). Work order data are associated with each pothole and include pothole location and size, repair crew identifying number, number of people on crew, equipment assigned, hours applied to repair, hole status (work in progress, repaired, temporary repair, not repaired), amount of filler material used, and cost of repair (computed from hours applied, number of people, material and equipment used). Finally, a damage file is created to hold information about reported damage due to the pothole and includes citizen's name, address, phone number, type of damage, and dollar amount of damage. PHTRS is an online system; all queries are to be made interactively.

a. Draw a UML use case diagram for the PHTRS system. You'll have to make a number of assumptions about the manner in which a user interacts with this system.
b. Develop a class model for the PHTRS system.

6.7. Write a template-based use case for the *SafeHome* home management system described informally in the sidebar following Section 6.5.4.

6.8. Develop a complete set of CRC model index cards on the product or system you chose as part of Problem 6.5.

6.9. Conduct a review of the CRC index cards with your colleagues. How many additional classes, responsibilities, and collaborators were added as a consequence of the review?

6.10. What is an analysis package and how might it be used?

FURTHER READINGS AND INFORMATION SOURCES

Use cases can serve as the foundation for all requirements modeling approaches. The subject is discussed at length by Rosenberg and Stephens (*Use Case Driven Object Modeling with UML: Theory and Practice*, Apress, 2007), Denny (*Succeeding with Use Cases: Working Smart to Deliver Quality*, Addison-Wesley, 2005), Alexander and Maiden (eds.) (*Scenarios, Stories, Use Cases: Through the Systems Development Life-Cycle*, Wiley, 2004), Bittner and Spence (*Use Case Modeling*, Addison-Wesley, 2002), Cockburn [Coc01b], and other references noted in both Chapters 5 and 6.

Data modeling presents a useful method for examining the information space. Books by Hoberman [Hob06] and Simsion and Witt [Sim05] provide reasonably comprehensive treatments. In addition, Allen and Terry (*Beginning Relational Data Modeling*, 2d ed., Apress, 2005), Allen (*Data Modeling for Everyone*, Wrox Press, 2002), Teorey and his colleagues (*Database Modeling and Design: Logical Design*, 4th ed., Morgan Kaufmann, 2005), and Carlis and Maguire (*Mastering Data Modeling*, Addison-Wesley, 2000) present detailed tutorials for creating industry-quality data models. An interesting book by Hay (*Data Modeling Patterns,* Dorset House, 1995) presents typical data model patterns that are encountered in many different businesses.

UML modeling techniques that can be applied for both analysis and design are discussed by O'Docherty (*Object-Oriented Analysis and Design: Understanding System Development with UML 2.0,* Wiley, 2005), Arlow and Neustadt (*UML 2 and the Unified Process,* 2d ed., Addison-Wesley, 2005), Roques (*UML in Practice,* Wiley, 2004), Dennis and his colleagues (*Systems Analysis and Design with UML Version 2.0,* Wiley, 2004), Larman (*Applying UML and Patterns,* 2d ed., Prentice-Hall, 2001), and Rosenberg and Scott (*Use Case Driven Object Modeling with UML,* Addison-Wesley, 1999).

A wide variety of information sources on requirements modeling are available on the Internet. An up-to-date list of World Wide Web references that are relevant to analysis modeling can be found at the SEPA website: **www.mhhe.com/engcs/compsci/pressman/ professional/olc/ser.htm**.

REQUIREMENTS MODELING: FLOW, BEHAVIOR, PATTERNS, AND WEBAPPS

After my discussion of use cases, data modeling, and class-based models in Chapter 6, it's reasonable to ask, "Aren't those requirements modeling representations enough?"

The only reasonable answer is, "That depends."

For some types of software, the use case may be the only requirements modeling representation that is required. For others, an object-oriented approach is chosen and class-based models may be developed. But in other situations, complex application requirements may demand an examination of how data objects are transformed as they move through a system; how an application behaves as a consequence of external events; whether existing domain knowledge can be adapted to the current problem; or in the case of Web-based systems and applications, how content and functionality meld to provide an end user with the ability to successfully navigate a WebApp to achieve usage goals.

7.1 REQUIREMENTS MODELING STRATEGIES

One view of requirements modeling, called *structured analysis,* considers data and the processes that transform the data as separate entities. Data objects are modeled in a way that defines their attributes and relationships. Processes that manipulate data objects are modeled in a manner that shows how they transform data as data objects flow through the system. A second approach to analysis

What are the steps? Flow-oriented modeling provides an indication of how data objects are transformed by processing functions. Behavioral modeling depicts the states of the system and its classes and the impact of events on these states. Pattern-based modeling makes use of existing domain knowledge to facilitate requirements analysis. WebApp requirements models are especially adapted for the representation of content, interaction, function, and configuration-related requirements.

What is the work product? A wide array of text-based and diagrammatic forms may be chosen for the requirements model. Each of these representations provides a view of one or more of the model elements.

How do I ensure that I've done it right? Requirements modeling work products must be reviewed for correctness, completeness, and consistency. They must reflect the needs of all stakeholders and establish a foundation from which design can be conducted.

modeled, called *object-oriented analysis,* focuses on the definition of classes and the manner in which they collaborate with one another to effect customer requirements.

Although the analysis model that we propose in this book combines features of both approaches, software teams often choose one approach and exclude all representations from the other. The question is not which is best, but rather, what combination of representations will provide stakeholders with the best model of software requirements and the most effective bridge to software design.

7.2 FLOW-ORIENTED MODELING

Although data flow-oriented modeling is perceived as an outdated technique by some software engineers, it continues to be one of the most widely used requirements analysis notations in use today.[1] Although the *data flow diagram* (DFD) and related diagrams and information are not a formal part of UML, they can be used to complement UML diagrams and provide additional insight into system requirements and flow.

Some will suggest that the DFD is old-school and it has no place in modern practice. That's a view that excludes a potentially useful mode of representation at the analysis level. If it can help, use the DFD.

The DFD takes an input-process-output view of a system. That is, data objects flow into the software, are transformed by processing elements, and resultant data objects flow out of the software. Data objects are represented by labeled arrows, and transformations are represented by circles (also called bubbles). The DFD is presented in a hierarchical fashion. That is, the first data flow model (sometimes called a level 0 DFD or *context diagram*) represents the system as a whole. Subsequent data flow diagrams refine the context diagram, providing increasing detail with each subsequent level.

---

1   Data flow modeling is a core modeling activity in *structured analysis.*

FIGURE 7.1

Context-level
DFD for the
SafeHome
security
function

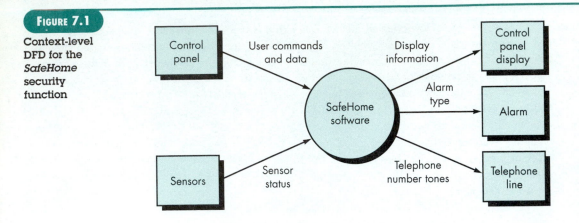

7.2.1   Creating a Data Flow Model

The data flow diagram enables you to develop models of the information domain and functional domain. As the DFD is refined into greater levels of detail, you perform an implicit functional decomposition of the system. At the same time, the DFD refinement results in a corresponding refinement of data as it moves through the processes that embody the application.

A few simple guidelines can aid immeasurably during the derivation of a data flow diagram: (1) the level 0 data flow diagram should depict the software/system as a single bubble; (2) primary input and output should be carefully noted; (3) refinement should begin by isolating candidate processes, data objects, and data stores to be represented at the next level; (4) all arrows and bubbles should be labeled with meaningful names; (5) *information flow continuity* must be maintained from level to level,[2] and (6) one bubble at a time should be refined. There is a natural tendency to overcomplicate the data flow diagram. This occurs when you attempt to show too much detail too early or represent procedural aspects of the software in lieu of information flow.

To illustrate the use of the DFD and related notation, we again consider the *SafeHome* security function. A level 0 DFD for the security function is shown in Figure 7.1. The primary *external entities* (boxes) produce information for use by the system and consume information generated by the system. The labeled arrows represent data objects or data object hierarchies. For example, **user commands and data** encompasses all configuration commands, all activation/deactivation commands, all miscellaneous interactions, and all data that are entered to qualify or expand a command.

The level 0 DFD must now be expanded into a level 1 data flow model. But how do we proceed? Following an approach suggested in Chapter 6, you should apply a

KEY POINT

Information flow continuity must be maintained as each DFD level is refined. This means that input and output at one level must be the same as input and output at a refined level.

---

2   That is, the data objects that flow into the system or into any transformation at one level must be the same data objects (or their constituent parts) that flow into the transformation at a more refined level.

"grammatical parse" [Abb83] to the use case narrative that describes the context-level bubble. That is, we isolate all nouns (and noun phrases) and verbs (and verb phrases) in a *SafeHome* processing narrative derived during the first requirements gathering meeting. Recalling the parsed processing narrative text presented in Section 6.5.1:

The grammatical parse is not foolproof, but it can provide you with an excellent jump start, if you're struggling to define data objects and the transforms that operate on them.

> The SafeHome security function *enables* the homeowner to *configure* the security system when it is *installed, monitors* all sensors *connected* to the security system, and *interacts* with the homeowner through the Internet, a PC, or a control panel.
>
> During installation, the *SafeHome* PC is used to *program* and *configure* the system. Each sensor is assigned a number and type, a master password is programmed for *arming* and *disarming* the system, and telephone number(s) are *input* for *dialing* when a sensor event occurs.
>
> When a sensor event is *recognized,* the software *invokes* an audible alarm attached to the system. After a delay time that is specified by the homeowner during system configuration activities, the software dials a telephone number of a monitoring service, *provides* information about the location, *reporting* the nature of the event that has been detected. The telephone number will be *redialed* every 20 seconds until telephone connection is *obtained.*
>
> The homeowner *receives* security information via a control panel, the PC, or a browser, collectively called an interface. The interface *displays* prompting messages and system status information on the control panel, the PC, or the browser window. Homeowner interaction takes the following form . . .

Be certain that the processing narrative you intend to parse is written at the same level of abstraction throughout.

Referring to the grammatical parse, verbs are *SafeHome* processes and can be represented as bubbles in a subsequent DFD. Nouns are either external entities (boxes), data or control objects (arrows), or data stores (double lines). From the discussion in Chapter 6, recall that nouns and verbs can be associated with one another (e.g., each sensor is assigned a number and type; therefore **number** and **type** are attributes of the data object **sensor**). Therefore, by performing a grammatical parse on the processing narrative for a bubble at any DFD level, you can generate much useful information about how to proceed with the refinement to the next level. Using this information, a level 1 DFD is shown in Figure 7.2. The context level process shown in Figure 7.1 has been expanded into six processes derived from an examination of the grammatical parse. Similarly, the information flow between processes at level 1 has been derived from the parse. In addition, information flow continuity is maintained between levels 0 and 1.

The processes represented at DFD level 1 can be further refined into lower levels. For example, the process *monitor sensors* can be refined into a level 2 DFD as shown in Figure 7.3. Note once again that information flow continuity has been maintained between levels.

The refinement of DFDs continues until each bubble performs a simple function. That is, until the process represented by the bubble performs a function that would be easily implemented as a program component. In Chapter 8, I discuss a concept, called *cohesion,* that can be used to assess the processing focus of a given function. For now, we strive to refine DFDs until each bubble is "single-minded."

FIGURE 7.2

Level 1 DFD for *SafeHome* security function

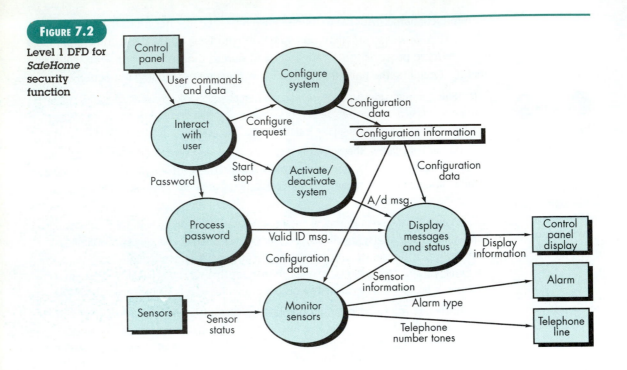

FIGURE 7.3

Level 2 DFD that refines the *monitor sensors* process

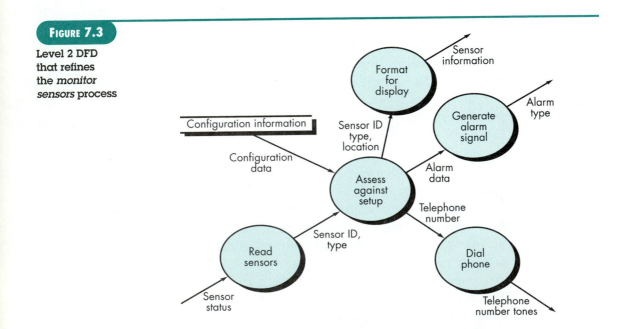

7.2.2 Creating a Control Flow Model

For some types of applications, the data model and the data flow diagram are all that is necessary to obtain meaningful insight into software requirements. As I have already noted, however, a large class of applications are "driven" by events rather than data, produce control information rather than reports or displays, and process information with heavy concern for time and performance. Such applications require the use of *control flow modeling* in addition to data flow modeling.

I have already noted that an event or control item is implemented as a Boolean value (e.g., true or false, on or off, 1 or 0) or a discrete list of conditions (e.g., empty, jammed, full). To select potential candidate events, the following guidelines are suggested:

> **How do I select potential events for a control flow diagram, state diagram, or CSPEC?**

- List all sensors that are "read" by the software.

- List all interrupt conditions.

- List all "switches" that are actuated by an operator.

- List all data conditions.

- Recalling the noun/verb parse that was applied to the processing narrative, review all "control items" as possible control specification inputs/outputs.

- Describe the behavior of a system by identifying its states, identify how each state is reached, and define the transitions between states.

- Focus on possible omissions—a very common error in specifying control; for example, ask: "Is there any other way I can get to this state or exit from it?"

Among the many events and control items that are part of *SafeHome* software are **sensor event** (i.e., a sensor has been tripped), **blink flag** (a signal to blink the display), and **start/stop switch** (a signal to turn the system on or off).

7.2.3 The Control Specification

A *control specification* (CSPEC) represents the behavior of the system (at the level from which it has been referenced) in two different ways.[3] The CSPEC contains a state diagram that is a sequential specification of behavior. It can also contain a program activation table—a combinatorial specification of behavior.

Figure 7.4 depicts a preliminary state diagram[4] for the level 1 control flow model for *SafeHome*. The diagram indicates how the system responds to events as it traverses the four states defined at this level. By reviewing the state diagram, you can determine the behavior of the system and, more important, ascertain whether there are "holes" in the specified behavior.

For example, the state diagram (Figure 7.4) indicates that the transitions from the **Idle** state can occur if the system is reset, activated, or powered off. If the system is

---

3 Additional behavioral modeling notation is presented in Section 7.3.
4 The state diagram notation used here conforms to UML notation. A "state transition diagram" is available in structured analysis, but the UML format is superior in information content and representation.

FIGURE 7.4   State diagram for *SafeHome* security function

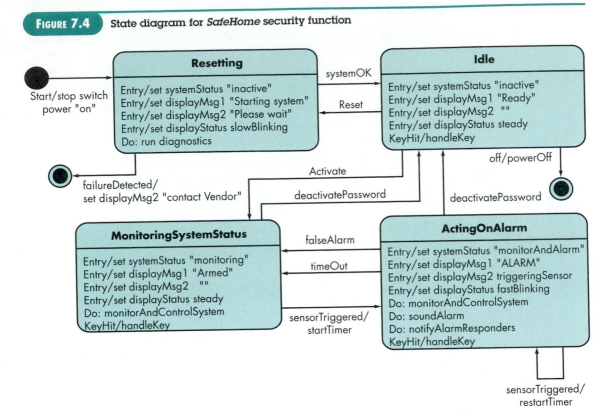

activated (i.e., alarm system is turned on), a transition to the **Monitoring-SystemStatus** state occurs, display messages are changed as shown, and the process *monitorAndControlSystem* is invoked. Two transitions occur out of the **MonitoringSystemStatus** state—(1) when the system is deactivated, a transition occurs back to the **Idle** state; (2) when a sensor is triggered into the **ActingOnAlarm** state. All transitions and the content of all states are considered during the review.

A somewhat different mode of behavioral representation is the process activation table. The PAT represents information contained in the state diagram in the context of processes, not states. That is, the table indicates which processes (bubbles) in the flow model will be invoked when an event occurs. The PAT can be used as a guide for a designer who must build an executive that controls the processes represented at this level. A PAT for the level 1 flow model of *SafeHome* software is shown in Figure 7.5.

The CSPEC describes the behavior of the system, but it gives us no information about the inner working of the processes that are activated as a result of this behavior. The modeling notation that provides this information is discussed in Section 7.2.4.

7.2.4   The Process Specification

The *process specification* (PSPEC) is used to describe all flow model processes that appear at the final level of refinement. The content of the process specification can

FIGURE 7.5

Process activation table for *SafeHome* security function

input events						
sensor event	0	0	0	0	1	0
blink flag	0	0	1	1	0	0
start stop switch	0	1	0	0	0	0
display action status complete	0	0	0	1	0	0
in-progress	0	0	1	0	0	0
time out	0	0	0	0	0	1
output						
alarm signal	0	0	0	0	1	0
process activation						
monitor and control system	0	1	0	0	1	1
activate/deactivate system	0	1	0	0	0	0
display messages and status	1	0	1	1	1	1
interact with user	1	0	0	1	0	1

SafeHome

Data Flow Modeling

The scene: Jamie's cubicle, after the last requirements gathering meeting has concluded.

The players: Jamie, Vinod, and Ed—all members of the *SafeHome* software engineering team.

The conversation:

(Jamie has sketched out the models shown in Figures 7.1 through 7.5 and is showing them to Ed and Vinod.)

Jamie: I took a software engineering course in college, and they taught us this stuff. The Prof said it's a bit old-fashioned, but you know what, it helps me to clarify things.

Ed: That's cool. But I don't see any classes or objects here.

Jamie: No . . . this is just a flow model with a little behavioral stuff thrown in.

Vinod: So these DFDs represent an I-P-O view of the software, right.

Ed: I-P-O?

Vinod: Input-process-output. The DFDs are actually pretty intuitive . . . if you look at 'em for a moment, they show how data objects flow through the system and get transformed as they go.

Ed: Looks like we could convert every bubble into an executable component . . . at least at the lowest level of the DFD.

Jamie: That's the cool part, you can. In fact, there's a way to translate the DFDs into an design architecture.

Ed: Really?

Jamie: Yeah, but first we've got to develop a complete requirements model and this isn't it.

Vinod: Well, it's a first step, but we're going to have to address class-based elements and also behavioral aspects, although the state diagram and PAT does some of that.

Ed: We've got a lot work to do and not much time to do it.

(Doug—the software engineering manager—walks into the cubical.)

Doug: So the next few days will be spent developing the requirements model, huh?

Jamie (looking proud): We've already begun.

Doug: Good, we've got a lot of work to do and not much time to do it.

(The three software engineers look at one another and smile.)

KEY POINT

The PSPEC is a "mini-specification" for each transform at the lowest refined level of a DFD.

include narrative text, a program design language (PDL) description[5] of the process algorithm, mathematical equations, tables, or UML activity diagrams. By providing a PSPEC to accompany each bubble in the flow model, you can create a "mini-spec" that serves as a guide for design of the software component that will implement the bubble.

To illustrate the use of the PSPEC, consider the *process password* transform represented in the flow model for *SafeHome* (Figure 7.2). The PSPEC for this function might take the form:

> **PSPEC: process password (at control panel).** The *process password* transform performs password validation at the control panel for the *SafeHome* security function. *Process password* receives a four-digit password from the *interact with user* function. The password is first compared to the master password stored within the system. If the master password matches, <valid id message = true> is passed to the *message and status display* function. If the master password does not match, the four digits are compared to a table of secondary passwords (these may be assigned to house guests and/or workers who require entry to the home when the owner is not present). If the password matches an entry within the table, <valid id message = true> is passed to the *message and status display function*. If there is no match, <valid id message = false> is passed to the message and status display function.

If additional algorithmic detail is desired at this stage, a program design language representation may also be included as part of the PSPEC. However, many believe that the PDL version should be postponed until component design commences.

SOFTWARE TOOLS

Structured Analysis

Objective: Structured analysis tools allow a software engineer to create data models, flow models, and behavioral models in a manner that enables consistency and continuity checking and easy editing and extension. Models created using these tools provide the software engineer with insight into the analysis representation and help to eliminate errors before they propagate into design, or worse, into implementation itself.

Mechanics: Tools in this category use a "data dictionary" as the central database for the description of all data objects. Once entries in the dictionary are defined, entity-relationship diagrams can be created and object hierarchies can be developed. Data flow diagramming features allow easy creation of this graphical model and also provide features for the creation of PSPECs and CSPECs. Analysis tools also enable the software

engineer to create behavioral models using the state diagram as the operative notation.

Representative Tools:[6]

MacA&D, WinA&D, developed by Excel software (**www.excelsoftware.com**), provides a set of simple and inexpensive analysis and design tools for Macs and Windows machines.

MetaCASE Workbench, developed by MetaCase Consulting (**www.metacase.com**), is a metatool used to define an analysis or design method (including structured analysis) and its concepts, rules, notations, and generators.

System Architect, developed by Popkin Software (**www.popkin.com**) provides a broad range of analysis and design tools including tools for data modeling and structured analysis.

---

5   Program design language (PDL) mixes programming language syntax with narrative text to provide procedural design detail. PDL is discussed briefly in Chapter 10.

6   Tools noted here do not represent an endorsement, but rather a sampling of tools in this category. In most cases, tool names are trademarked by their respective developers.

7.3 CREATING A BEHAVIORAL MODEL

? How do I
model the
software's
reaction to some
external event?

The modeling notation that I have discussed to this point represents static elements of the requirements model. It is now time to make a transition to the dynamic behavior of the system or product. To accomplish this, you can represent the behavior of the system as a function of specific events and time.

The *behavioral model* indicates how software will respond to external events or stimuli. To create the model, you should perform the following steps:

1. Evaluate all use cases to fully understand the sequence of interaction within the system.

2. Identify events that drive the interaction sequence and understand how these events relate to specific objects.

3. Create a sequence for each use case.

4. Build a state diagram for the system.

5. Review the behavioral model to verify accuracy and consistency.

Each of these steps is discussed in the sections that follow.

7.3.1 Identifying Events with the Use Case

In Chapter 6 you learned that the use case represents a sequence of activities that involves actors and the system. In general, an event occurs whenever the system and an actor exchange information. In Section 7.2.3, I indicated that an event is *not* the information that has been exchanged, but rather the fact that information has been exchanged.

A use case is examined for points of information exchange. To illustrate, we reconsider the use case for a portion of the *SafeHome* security function.

The homeowner uses the keypad to key in a four-digit password. The password is compared with the valid password stored in the system. If the password is incorrect, the control panel will beep once and reset itself for additional input. If the password is correct, the control panel awaits further action.

The underlined portions of the use case scenario indicate events. An actor should be identified for each event; the information that is exchanged should be noted, and any conditions or constraints should be listed.

As an example of a typical event, consider the underlined use case phrase "homeowner uses the keypad to key in a four-digit password." In the context of the requirements model, the object, **Homeowner,**[7] transmits an event to the object **ControlPanel.** The event might be called *password entered.* The information

---

7 In this example, we assume that each user (homeowner) that interacts with *SafeHome* has an identifying password and is therefore a legitimate object.

transferred is the four digits that constitute the password, but this is not an essential part of the behavioral model. It is important to note that some events have an explicit impact on the flow of control of the use case, while others have no direct impact on the flow of control. For example, the event *password entered* does not explicitly change the flow of control of the use case, but the results of the event *password compared* (derived from the interaction "password is compared with the valid password stored in the system") will have an explicit impact on the information and control flow of the *SafeHome* software.

Once all events have been identified, they are allocated to the objects involved. Objects can be responsible for generating events (e.g., **Homeowner** generates the *password entered* event) or recognizing events that have occurred elsewhere (e.g., **ControlPanel** recognizes the binary result of the *password compared* event).

7.3.2   State Representations

In the context of behavioral modeling, two different characterizations of states must be considered: (1) the state of each class as the system performs its function and (2) the state of the system as observed from the outside as the system performs its function.[8]

KEY POINT

The system has states that represent specific externally observable behavior; a class has states that represent its behavior as the system performs its functions.

The state of a class takes on both passive and active characteristics [Cha93]. A *passive state* is simply the current status of all of an object's attributes. For example, the passive state of the class **Player** (in the video game application discussed in Chapter 6) would include the current **position** and **orientation** attributes of **Player** as well as other features of **Player** that are relevant to the game (e.g., an attribute that indicates **magic wishes remaining**). The *active state* of an object indicates the current status of the object as it undergoes a continuing transformation or processing. The class **Player** might have the following active states: *moving, at rest, injured, being cured; trapped, lost,* and so forth. An event (sometimes called a *trigger*) must occur to force an object to make a transition from one active state to another.

Two different behavioral representations are discussed in the paragraphs that follow. The first indicates how an individual class changes state based on external events and the second shows the behavior of the software as a function of time.

State diagrams for analysis classes. One component of a behavioral model is a UML state diagram[9] that represents active states for each class and the events (triggers) that cause changes between these active states. Figure 7.6 illustrates a state diagram for the **ControlPanel** object in the *SafeHome* security function.

Each arrow shown in Figure 7.6 represents a transition from one active state of an object to another. The labels shown for each arrow represent the event that

---

8   The state diagrams presented in Chapter 6 and in Section 7.3.2 depict the state of the system. Our discussion in this section will focus on the state of each class within the analysis model.

9   If you are unfamiliar with UML, a brief introduction to this important modeling notation is presented in Appendix 1.

FIGURE 7.6

State diagram
for the
ControlPanel
class

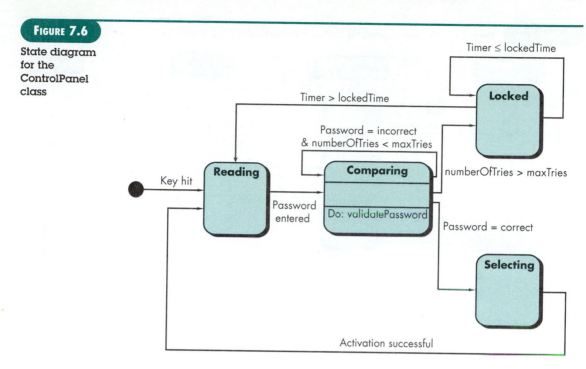

triggers the transition. Although the active state model provides useful insight into the "life history" of an object, it is possible to specify additional information to provide more depth in understanding the behavior of an object. In addition to specifying the event that causes the transition to occur, you can specify a guard and an action [Cha93]. A *guard* is a Boolean condition that must be satisfied in order for the transition to occur. For example, the guard for the transition from the "reading" state to the "comparing" state in Figure 7.6 can be determined by examining the use case:

> if (password input = 4 digits) then compare to stored password

In general, the guard for a transition usually depends upon the value of one or more attributes of an object. In other words, the guard depends on the passive state of the object.

An *action* occurs concurrently with the state transition or as a consequence of it and generally involves one or more operations (responsibilities) of the object. For example, the action connected to the *password entered* event (Figure 7.6) is an operation named *validatePassword()* that accesses a **password** object and performs a digit-by-digit comparison to validate the entered password.

Sequence diagrams.   The second type of behavioral representation, called a *sequence diagram* in UML, indicates how events cause transitions from object to object. Once events have been identified by examining a use case, the modeler

FIGURE 7.7 Sequence diagram (partial) for the *SafeHome* security function

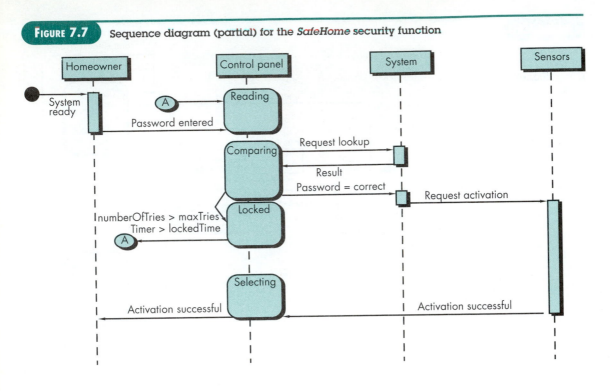

creates a sequence diagram—a representation of how events cause flow from one object to another as a function of time. In essence, the sequence diagram is a shorthand version of the use case. It represents key classes and the events that cause behavior to flow from class to class.

Figure 7.7 illustrates a partial sequence diagram for the *SafeHome* security function. Each of the arrows represents an event (derived from a use case) and indicates how the event channels behavior between *SafeHome* objects. Time is measured vertically (downward), and the narrow vertical rectangles represent time spent in processing an activity. States may be shown along a vertical time line.

The first event, *system ready*, is derived from the external environment and channels behavior to the **Homeowner** object. The homeowner enters a password. A *request lookup* event is passed to **System,** which looks up the password in a simple database and returns a *result* (*found* or *not found*) to **ControlPanel** (now in the *comparing* state). A valid password results in a *password=correct* event to **System,** which activates **Sensors** with a *request activation* event. Ultimately, control is passed back to the homeowner with the *activation successful* event.

Once a complete sequence diagram has been developed, all of the events that cause transitions between system objects can be collated into a set of input events and output events (from an object). This information is useful in the creation of an effective design for the system to be built.

KEY POINT

Unlike a state diagram that represents behavior without noting the classes involved, a sequence diagram represents behavior, by describing how classes move from state to state.

Generalized Analysis Modeling in UML

Objective: Analysis modeling tools provide the capability to develop scenario-based models, class-based models, and behavioral models using UML notation.

Mechanics: Tools in this category support the full range of UML diagrams required to build an analysis model (these tools also support design modeling). In addition to diagramming, tools in this category (1) perform consistency and correctness checks for all UML diagrams, (2) provide links for design and code generation, (3) build a database that enables the management and assessment of large UML models required for complex systems.

Representative Tools:[10]
The following tools support a full range of UML diagrams required for analysis modeling:

ArgoUML is an open source tool available at **argouml.tigris.org**.
Enterprise Architect, developed by Sparx Systems (**www.sparxsystems.com.au**).
PowerDesigner, developed by Sybase (**www.sybase.com**).
Rational Rose, developed by IBM (Rational) (**www01.ibm.com/software/rational/**).
System Architect, developed by Popkin Software (**www.popkin.com**).
UML Studio, developed by Pragsoft Corporation (**www.pragsoft.com**).
Visio, developed by Microsoft (**www.microsoft.com**).
Visual UML, developed by Visual Object Modelers (**www.visualuml.com**).

7.4 PATTERNS FOR REQUIREMENTS MODELING

Software patterns are a mechanism for capturing domain knowledge in a way that allows it to be reapplied when a new problem is encountered. In some cases, the domain knowledge is applied to a new problem within the same application domain. In other cases, the domain knowledge captured by a pattern can be applied by analogy to a completely different application domain.

The original author of an analysis pattern does not "create" the pattern, but, rather, *discovers* it as requirements engineering work is being conducted. Once the pattern has been discovered, it is documented by describing "explicitly the general problem to which the pattern is applicable, the prescribed solution, assumptions and constraints of using the pattern in practice, and often some other information about the pattern, such as the motivation and driving forces for using the pattern, discussion of the pattern's advantages and disadvantages, and references to some known examples of using that pattern in practical applications" [Dev01].

In Chapter 5, I introduced the concept of analysis patterns and indicated that these patterns represent a solution that often incorporates a class, a function, or a behavior within the application domain. The pattern can be reused when performing requirements modeling for an application within a domain.[11] Analysis patterns are stored in a repository so that members of the software team can use search facilities to find and reuse them. Once an appropriate pattern is selected, it is integrated into the requirements model by reference to the pattern name.

---

10 Tools noted here do not represent an endorsement, but rather a sampling of tools in this category. In most cases, tool names are trademarked by their respective developers.
11 An in-depth discussion of the use of patterns during software design is presented in Chapter 12.

7.4.1   Discovering Analysis Patterns

The requirements model is comprised of a wide variety of elements: scenario-based (use cases), data-oriented (the data model), class-based, flow-oriented, and behavioral. Each of these elements examines the problem from a different perspective, and each provides an opportunity to discover patterns that may occur throughout an application domain, or by analogy, across different application domains.

The most basic element in the description of a requirements model is the use case. In the context of this discussion, a coherent set of use cases may serve as the basis for discovering one or more analysis patterns. A *semantic analysis pattern* (SAP) "is a pattern that describes a small set of coherent use cases that together describe a basic generic application" [Fer00].

Consider the following preliminary use case for software required to control and monitor a real-view camera and proximity sensor for an automobile:

> **Use case: *Monitor reverse motion***
>
> **Description:** When the vehicle is placed in *reverse* gear, the control software enables a video feed from a rear-placed video camera to the dashboard display. The control software superimposes a variety of distance and orientation lines on the dashboard display so that the vehicle operator can maintain orientation as the vehicle moves in reverse. The control software also monitors a proximity sensor to determine whether an object is inside 10 feet of the rear of the vehicle. It will automatically break the vehicle if the proximity sensor indicates an object within x feet of the rear of the vehicle, where x is determined based on the speed of the vehicle.

This use case implies a variety of functionality that would be refined and elaborated (into a coherent set of use cases) during requirements gathering and modeling. Regardless of how much elaboration is accomplished, the use cases suggest a simple, yet widely applicable SAP—the software-based monitoring and control of sensors and actuators in a physical system. In this case, the "sensors" provide information about proximity and video information. The "actuator" is the breaking system of the vehicle (invoked if an object is very close to the vehicle). But in a more general case, a widely applicable pattern is discovered.

Software in many different application domains is required to monitor sensors and control physical actuators. It follows that an analysis pattern that describes generic requirements for this capability could be used widely. The pattern, called **Actuator-Sensor,** would be applicable as part of the requirements model for *SafeHome* and is discussed in Section 7.4.2, which follows.

7.4.2   A Requirements Pattern Example: Actuator-Sensor[12]

One of the requirements of the *SafeHome* security function is the ability to monitory security sensors (e.g., break-in sensors, fire, smoke or CO sensors, water sensors).

---

12 This section has been adapted from [Kon02] with the permission of the authors.

Internet-based extensions to *SafeHome* will require the ability to control the movement (e.g., pan, zoom) of a security camera within a residence. The implication—*SafeHome* software must manage various sensors and "actuators" (e.g., camera control mechanisms).

Konrad and Cheng [Kon02] have suggested a requirements pattern named **Actuator-Sensor** that provides useful guidance for modeling this requirement within *SafeHome* software. An abbreviated version of the **Actuator-Sensor** pattern, originally developed for automotive applications, follows.

Pattern Name.   **Actuator-Sensor**

Intent.   Specify various kinds of sensors and actuators in an embedded system.

Motivation.   Embedded systems usually have various kinds of sensors and actuators. These sensors and actuators are all either directly or indirectly connected to a control unit. Although many of the sensors and actuators look quite different, their behavior is similar enough to structure them into a pattern. The pattern shows how to specify the sensors and actuators for a system, including attributes and operations. The **Actuator-Sensor** pattern uses a *pull* mechanism (explicit request for information) for **PassiveSensors** and a *push* mechanism (broadcast of information) for the **ActiveSensors.**

Constraints

- Each passive sensor must have some method to read sensor input and attributes that represent the sensor value.

- Each active sensor must have capabilities to broadcast update messages when its value changes.

- Each active sensor should send a *life tick*, a status message issued within a specified time frame, to detect malfunctions.

- Each actuator must have some method to invoke the appropriate response determined by the **ComputingComponent.**

- Each sensor and actuator should have a function implemented to check its own operation state.

- Each sensor and actuator should be able to test the validity of the values received or sent and set its operation state if the values are outside of the specifications.

Applicability.   Useful in any system in which multiple sensors and actuators are present.

Structure.   A UML class diagram for the **Actuator-Sensor** pattern is shown in Figure 7.8. **Actuator, PassiveSensor,** and **ActiveSensor** are abstract classes and denoted in italics. There are four different types of sensors and actuators in this pattern.

FIGURE 7.8   UML sequence diagram for the Actuator-Sensor pattern. *Source:* Adapted from [Kon02] with permission.

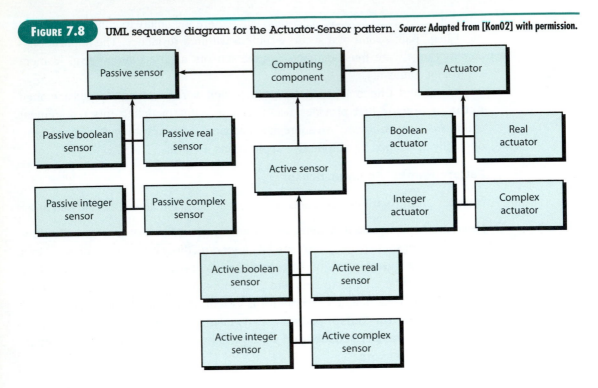

The **Boolean, Integer,** and **Real** classes represent the most common types of sensors and actuators. The complex classes are sensors or actuators that use values that cannot be easily represented in terms of primitive data types, such as a radar device. Nonetheless, these devices should still inherit the interface from the abstract classes since they should have basic functionalities such as querying the operation states.

Behavior. Figure 7.9 presents a UML sequence diagram for an example of the **Actuator-Sensor** pattern as it might be applied for the *SafeHome* function that controls the positioning (e.g., pan, zoom) of a security camera. Here, the **ControlPanel**[13] queries a sensor (a passive position sensor) and an actuator (pan control) to check the operation state for diagnostic purposes before reading or setting a value. The messages *Set Physical Value* and *Get Physical Value* are not messages between objects. Instead, they describe the interaction between the physical devices of the system and their software counterparts. In the lower part of the diagram, below the horizontal line, the **PositionSensor** reports that the operation state is zero. The **ComputingComponent** (represented as **ControlPanel**) then sends the error code for a position sensor failure to the **FaultHandler** that will decide how this error affects the system and what actions are required. It gets the data from the sensors and computes the required response for the actuators.

---

13 The original pattern uses the generic phrase **ComputingComponent.**

FIGURE 7.9 UML Class diagram for the Actuator-Sensor pattern. *Source:* Reprinted from [Kon02] with permission.

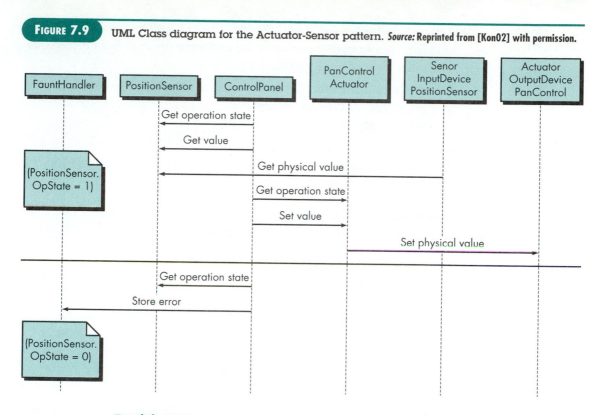

Participants. This section of the patterns description "itemizes the classes/objects that are included in the requirements pattern" [Kon02] and describes the responsibilities of each class/object (Figure 7.8). An abbreviated list follows:

- **PassiveSensor abstract:** Defines an interface for passive sensors.
- **PassiveBooleanSensor:** Defines passive Boolean sensors.
- **PassiveIntegerSensor:** Defines passive integer sensors.
- **PassiveRealSensor:** Defines passive real sensors.
- **ActiveSensor abstract:** Defines an interface for active sensors.
- **ActiveBooleanSensor:** Defines active Boolean sensors.
- **ActiveIntegerSensor:** Defines active integer sensors.
- **ActiveRealSensor:** Defines active real sensors.
- **Actuator abstract:** Defines an interface for actuators.
- **BooleanActuator:** Defines Boolean actuators.
- **IntegerActuator:** Defines integer actuators.
- **RealActuator:** Defines real actuators.
- **ComputingComponent:** The central part of the controller; it gets the data from the sensors and computes the required response for the actuators.

- **ActiveComplexSensor:** Complex active sensors have the basic functionality of the abstract **ActiveSensor** class, but additional, more elaborate, methods and attributes need to be specified.

- **PassiveComplexSensor:** Complex passive sensors have the basic functionality of the abstract **PassiveSensor** class, but additional, more elaborate, methods and attributes need to be specified.

- **ComplexActuator:** Complex actuators also have the base functionality of the abstract **Actuator** class, but additional, more elaborate methods and attributes need to be specified.

Collaborations.   This section describes how objects and classes interact with one another and how each carries out its responsibilities.

- When the **ComputingComponent** needs to update the value of a **PassiveSensor,** it queries the sensors, requesting the value by sending the appropriate message.

- **ActiveSensors** are not queried. They initiate the transmission of sensor values to the computing unit, using the appropriate method to set the value in the **ComputingComponent.** They send a life tick at least once during a specified time frame in order to update their timestamps with the system clock's time.

- When the **ComputingComponent** needs to set the value of an actuator, it sends the value to the actuator.

- The **ComputingComponent** can query and set the operation state of the sensors and actuators using the appropriate methods. If an operation state is found to be zero, then the error is sent to the **FaultHandler,** a class that contains methods for handling error messages, such as starting a more elaborate recovery mechanism or a backup device. If no recovery is possible, then the system can only use the last known value for the sensor or the default value.

- The **ActiveSensors** offer methods to add or remove the addresses or address ranges of the components that want to receive the messages in case of a value change.

Consequences

1. Sensor and actuator classes have a common interface.
2. Class attributes can only be accessed through messages, and the class decides whether or not to accept the message. For example, if a value of an actuator is set above a maximum value, then the actuator class may not accept the message, or it might use a default maximum value.
3. The complexity of the system is potentially reduced because of the uniformity of interfaces for actuators and sensors.

The requirements pattern description might also provide references to other related requirements and design patterns.

7.5   REQUIREMENTS MODELING FOR WEBAPPS[14]

Web developers are often skeptical when the idea of requirements analysis for WebApps is suggested. "After all," they argue, "the Web development process must be agile, and analysis is time consuming. It'll slow us down just when we need to be designing and building the WebApp."

Requirements analysis does take time, but solving the wrong problem takes even more time. The question for every WebApp developer is simple—are you sure you understand the requirements of the problem? If the answer is an unequivocal "yes," then it may be possible to skip requirements modeling, but if the answer is "no," then requirements modeling should be performed.

7.5.1   How Much Analysis Is Enough?

The degree to which requirements modeling for WebApps is emphasized depends on the following factors:

- Size and complexity of WebApp increment.
- Number of stakeholders (analysis can help to identify conflicting requirements coming from different sources).
- Size of the WebApp team.
- Degree to which members of the WebApp team have worked together before (analysis can help develop a common understanding of the project).
- Degree to which the organization's success is directly dependent on the success of the WebApp.

The converse of the preceding points is that as the project becomes smaller, the number of stakeholders fewer, the development team more cohesive, and the application less critical, it is reasonable to apply a more lightweight analysis approach.

Although it is a good idea to analyze the problem *before* beginning design, it is not true that *all* analysis must precede *all* design. In fact, the design of a specific part of the WebApp only demands an analysis of those requirements that affect only that part of the WebApp. As an example from *SafeHome*, you could validly design the overall website aesthetics (layouts, color schemes, etc.) without having analyzed the functional requirements for e-commerce capabilities. You only need to analyze that part of the problem that is relevant to the design work for the increment to be delivered.

---

14 This section has been adapted from Pressman and Lowe [Pre08] with permission.

7.5.2   Requirements Modeling Input

An agile version of the generic software process discussed in Chapter 2 can be applied when WebApps are engineered. The process incorporates a communication activity that identifies stakeholders and user categories, the business context, defined informational and applicative goals, general WebApp requirements, and usage scenarios—information that becomes input to requirements modeling. This information is represented in the form of natural language descriptions, rough outlines, sketches, and other informal representations.

Analysis takes this information, structures it using a formally defined representation scheme (where appropriate), and then produces more rigorous models as an output. The requirements model provides a detailed indication of the true structure of the problem and provides insight into the shape of the solution.

The *SafeHome* **ACS-DCV** (camera surveillance) function was introduced in Chapter 6. When it was introduced, this function seemed relatively clear and was described in some detail as part of a use case (Section 6.2.1). However, a reexamination of the use case might uncover information that is missing, ambiguous, or unclear.

Some aspects of this missing information would naturally emerge during the design. Examples might include the specific layout of the function buttons, their aesthetic look and feel, the size of snapshot views, the placement of camera views and the house floor plan, or even minutiae such as the maximum and minimum length of passwords. Some of these aspects are design decisions (such as the layout of the buttons) and others are requirements (such as the length of the passwords) that don't fundamentally influence early design work.

But some missing information might actually influence the overall design itself and relate more to an actual understanding of the requirements. For example:

Q_1:   What output video resolution is provided by *SafeHome* cameras?

Q_2:   What occurs if an alarm condition is encountered while the camera is being monitored?

Q_3:   How does the system handle cameras that can be panned and zoomed?

Q_4:   What information should be provided along with the camera view? (For example, location? time/date? last previous access?)

None of these questions were identified or considered in the initial development of the use case, and yet, the answers could have a substantial effect on different aspects of the design.

Therefore, it is reasonable to conclude that although the communication activity provides a good foundation for understanding, requirements analysis refines this understanding by providing additional interpretation. As the problem structure is delineated as part of the requirements model, questions invariably arise. It is these questions that fill in the gaps—or in some cases, actually help us to find the gaps in the first place.

To summarize, the inputs to the requirements model will be the information collected during the communication activity—anything from an informal e-mail to a detailed project brief complete with comprehensive usage scenarios and product specifications.

7.5.3   Requirements Modeling Output

Requirements analysis provides a disciplined mechanism for representing and evaluating WebApp content and function, the modes of interaction that users will encounter, and the environment and infrastructure in which the WebApp resides.

Each of these characteristics can be represented as a set of models that allow the WebApp requirements to be analyzed in a structured manner. While the specific models depend largely upon the nature of the WebApp, there are five main classes of models:

- **Content model**—identifies the full spectrum of content to be provided by the WebApp. Content includes text, graphics and images, video, and audio data.

- **Interaction model**—describes the manner in which users interact with the WebApp.

- **Functional model**—defines the operations that will be applied to WebApp content and describes other processing functions that are independent of content but necessary to the end user.

- **Navigation model**—defines the overall navigation strategy for the WebApp.

- **Configuration model**—describes the environment and infrastructure in which the WebApp resides.

You can develop each of these models using a representation scheme (often called a "language") that allows its intent and structure to be communicated and evaluated easily among members of the Web engineering team and other stakeholders. As a consequence, a list of key issues (e.g., errors, omissions, inconsistencies, suggestions for enhancement or modification, points of clarification) are identified and acted upon.

7.5.4   Content Model for WebApps

The content model contains structural elements that provide an important view of content requirements for a WebApp. These structural elements encompass content objects and all analysis classes—user-visible entities that are created or manipulated as a user interacts with the WebApp.[15]

Content can be developed prior to the implementation of the WebApp, while the WebApp is being built, or long after the WebApp is operational. In every case, it is

---

15 Analysis classes were discussed in Chapter 6.

incorporated via navigational reference into the overall WebApp structure. A *content object* might be a textual description of a product, an article describing a news event, an action photograph taken at a sporting event, a user's response on a discussion forum, an animated representation of a corporate logo, a short video of a speech, or an audio overlay for a collection of presentation slides. The content objects might be stored as separate files, embedded directly into Web pages, or obtained dynamically from a database. In other words, a content object is any item of cohesive information that is to be presented to an end user.

Content objects can be determined directly from use cases by examining the scenario description for direct and indirect references to content. For example, a WebApp that supports *SafeHome* is established at **SafeHomeAssured.com.** A use case, *Purchasing Select SafeHome Components,* describes the scenario required to purchase a *SafeHome* component and contains the sentence:

> I will be able to get descriptive and pricing information for each product component.

The content model must be capable of describing the content object **Component.** In many instances, a simple list of content objects, coupled with a brief description of each object, is sufficient to define the requirements for content that must be designed and implemented. However, in some cases, the content model may benefit from a richer analysis that graphically illustrates the relationships among content objects and/or the hierarchy of content maintained by a WebApp.

For example, consider the *data tree* [Sri01] created for a **SafeHomeAssured.com** component shown in Figure 7.10. The tree represents a hierarchy of information that is used to describe a component. Simple or composite data items (one or more data

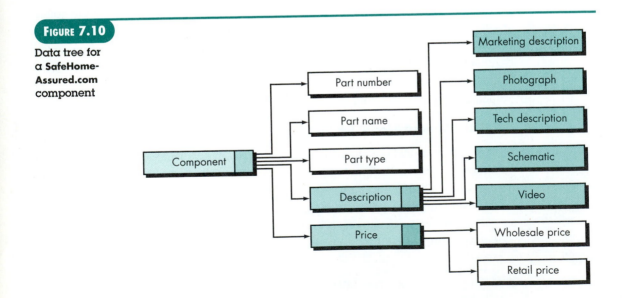

FIGURE 7.10

Data tree for a SafeHome-Assured.com component

values) are represented as unshaded rectangles. Content objects are represented as shaded rectangles. In the figure, **description** is defined by five content objects (the shaded rectangles). In some cases, one or more of these objects would be further refined as the data tree expands.

A data tree can be created for any content that is composed of multiple content objects and data items. The data tree is developed in an effort to define hierarchical relationships among content objects and to provide a means for reviewing content so that omissions and inconsistencies are uncovered before design commences. In addition, the data tree serves as the basis for content design.

7.5.5   Interaction Model for WebApps

The vast majority of WebApps enable a "conversation" between an end user and application functionality, content, and behavior. This conversation can be described using an *interaction* model that can be composed of one or more of the following elements: (1) use cases, (2) sequence diagrams, (3) state diagrams,[16] and/or (4) user interface prototypes.

In many instances, a set of use cases is sufficient to describe the interaction at an analysis level (further refinement and detail will be introduced during design). However, when the sequence of interaction is complex and involves multiple analysis classes or many tasks, it is sometimes worthwhile to depict it using a more rigorous diagrammatic form.

The layout of the user interface, the content it presents, the interaction mechanisms it implements, and the overall aesthetic of the user-WebApp connections have much to do with user satisfaction and the overall success of the WebApp. Although it can be argued that the creation of a user interface prototype is a design activity, it is a good idea to perform it during the creation of the analysis model. The sooner that a physical representation of a user interface can be reviewed, the higher the likelihood that end users will get what they want. The design of user interfaces is discussed in detail in Chapter 11.

Because WebApp construction tools are plentiful, relatively inexpensive, and functionally powerful, it is best to create the interface prototype using such tools. The prototype should implement the major navigational links and represent the overall screen layout in much the same way that it will be constructed. For example, if five major system functions are to be provided to the end user, the prototype should represent them as the user will see them upon first entering the WebApp. Will graphical links be provided? Where will the navigation menu be displayed? What other information will the user see? Questions like these should be answered by the prototype.

---

16 Sequence diagrams and state diagrams are modeled using UML notation. State diagrams are described in Section 7.3. See Appendix 1 for additional detail.

7.5.6 Functional Model for WebApps

Many WebApps deliver a broad array of computational and manipulative functions that can be associated directly with content (either using it or producing it) and that are often a major goal of user-WebApp interaction. For this reason, functional requirements must be analyzed, and when necessary, modeled.

The *functional model* addresses two processing elements of the WebApp, each representing a different level of procedural abstraction: (1) user-observable functionality that is delivered by the WebApp to end users, and (2) the operations contained within analysis classes that implement behaviors associated with the class.

User-observable functionality encompasses any processing functions that are initiated directly by the user. For example, a financial WebApp might implement a variety of financial functions (e.g., a college tuition savings calculator or a retirement savings calculator). These functions may actually be implemented using operations within analysis classes, but from the point of view of the end user, the function (more correctly, the data provided by the function) is the visible outcome.

At a lower level of procedural abstraction, the requirements model describes the processing to be performed by analysis class operations. These operations manipulate class attributes and are involved as classes collaborate with one another to accomplish some required behavior.

Regardless of the level of procedural abstraction, the UML activity diagram can be used to represent processing details. At the analysis level, activity diagrams should be used only where the functionality is relatively complex. Much of the complexity of many WebApps occurs not in the functionality provided, but rather with the nature of the information that can be accessed and the ways in which this can be manipulated.

An example of relatively complex functionality for **SafeHomeAssured.com** is addressed by a use case entitled *Get recommendations for sensor layout for my space.* The user has already developed a layout for the space to be monitored, and in this use case, selects that layout and requests recommended locations for sensors within the layout. **SafeHomeAssured.com** responds with a graphical representation of the layout with additional information on the recommended locations for sensors. The interaction is quite simple, the content is somewhat more complex, but the underlying functionality it very sophisticated. The system must undertake a relatively complex analysis of the floor layout in order to determine the optimal set of sensors. It must examine room dimensions, the location of doors and windows, and coordinate these with sensor capabilities and specifications. No small task! A set of activity diagrams can be used to describe processing for this use case.

The second example is the use case *Control cameras.* In this use case, the interaction is relatively simple, but there is the potential for complex functionality, given that this "simple" operation requires complex communication with devices located remotely and accessible across the Internet. A further possible complication relates

FIGURE 7.11

Activity
diagram
for the
*takeControlOf-
Camera()*
operation

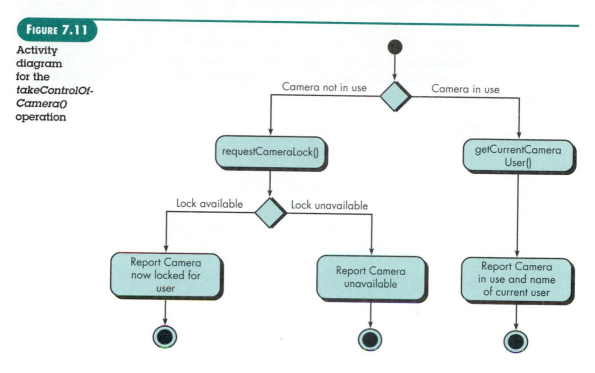

to negotiation of control when multiple authorized people attempt to monitor
and/or control a single sensor at the same time.

Figure 7.11 depicts an activity diagram for the *takeControlOfCamera()* operation
that is part of the **Camera** analysis class used within the *Control cameras* use case.
It should be noted that two additional operations are invoked with the procedural
flow: *requestCameraLock(),* which tries to lock the camera for this user, and
getCurrentCameraUser(), which retrieves the name of the user who is currently controlling the camera. The construction details indicating how these operations are invoked and the interface details for each operation are not considered until WebApp
design commences.

7.5.7   Configuration Models for WebApps

In some cases, the configuration model is nothing more than a list of server-side
and client-side attributes. However, for more complex WebApps, a variety of configuration complexities (e.g., distributing load among multiple servers, caching
architectures, remote databases, multiple servers serving various objects on the
same Web page) may have an impact on analysis and design. The UML *deployment
diagram* can be used in situations in which complex configuration architectures
must be considered.

For **SafeHomeAssured.com** the public content and functionality should be
specified to be accessible across all major Web clients (i.e., those with more than

1 percent market share or greater[17]). Conversely, it may be acceptable to restrict the more complex control and monitoring functionality (which is only accessible to **Homeowner** users) to a smaller set of clients. The configuration model for **SafeHomeAssured.com** will also specify interoperability with existing product databases and monitoring applications.

7.5.8 Navigation Modeling

Navigation modeling considers how each user category will navigate from one WebApp element (e.g., content object) to another. The mechanics of navigation are defined as part of design. At this stage, you should focus on overall navigation requirements. The following questions should be considered:

- Should certain elements be easier to reach (require fewer navigation steps) than others? What is the priority for presentation?
- Should certain elements be emphasized to force users to navigate in their direction?
- How should navigation errors be handled?
- Should navigation to related groups of elements be given priority over navigation to a specific element?
- Should navigation be accomplished via links, via search-based access, or by some other means?
- Should certain elements be presented to users based on the context of previous navigation actions?
- Should a navigation log be maintained for users?
- Should a full navigation map or menu (as opposed to a single "back" link or directed pointer) be available at every point in a user's interaction?
- Should navigation design be driven by the most commonly expected user behaviors or by the perceived importance of the defined WebApp elements?
- Can a user "store" his previous navigation through the WebApp to expedite future usage?
- For which user category should optimal navigation be designed?
- How should links external to the WebApp be handled? Overlaying the existing browser window? As a new browser window? As a separate frame?

These and many other questions should be asked and answered as part of navigation analysis.

---

17 Determining market share for browsers is notoriously problematic and varies depending on which survey is used. Nevertheless, at the time of writing, Internet Explorer and Firefox are the only browsers that were reported in excess of 30 percent, and Mozilla, Opera, and Safari the only other ones consistently above 1 percent.

You and other stakeholders must also determine overall requirements for navigation. For example, will a "site map" be provided to give users an overview of the entire WebApp structure? Can a user take a "guided tour" that will highlight the most important elements (content objects and functions) that are available? Will a user be able to access content objects or functions based on defined attributes of those elements (e.g., a user might want to access all photographs of a specific building or all functions that allow computation of weight)?

7.6   SUMMARY

Flow-oriented models focus on the flow of data objects as they are transformed by processing functions. Derived from structured analysis, flow-oriented models use the data flow diagram, a modeling notation that depicts how input is transformed into output as data objects move through a system. Each software function that transforms data is described by a process specification or narrative. In addition to data flow, this modeling element also depicts control flow—a representation that illustrates how events affect the behavior of a system.

Behavioral modeling depicts dynamic behavior. The behavioral model uses input from scenario-based, flow-oriented, and class-based elements to represent the states of analysis classes and the system as a whole. To accomplish this, states are identified, the events that cause a class (or the system) to make a transition from one state to another are defined, and the actions that occur as transition is accomplished are also identified. State diagrams and sequence diagrams are the notation used for behavioral modeling.

Analysis patterns enable a software engineer to use existing domain knowledge to facilitate the creation of a requirements model. An analysis pattern describes a specific software feature or function that can be described by a coherent set of use cases. It specifies the intent of the pattern, the motivation for its use, constraints that limit its use, its applicability in various problem domains, the overall structure of the pattern, its behavior and collaborations, and other supplementary information.

Requirements modeling for WebApps can use most, if not all, of the modeling elements discussed in this book. However, these elements are applied within a set of specialized models that address content, interaction, function, navigation, and the client-server configuration in which the WebApp resides.

PROBLEMS AND POINTS TO PONDER

7.1. What is the fundamental difference between the structured analysis and object-oriented strategies for requirements analysis?

7.2. In a data flow diagram, does an arrow represent a flow of control or something else?

7.3. What is "information flow continuity" and how is it applied as a data flow diagram is refined?

7.4. How is a grammatical parse used in the creation of a DFD?

7.5. What is a control specification?

7.6. Are a PSPEC and a use case the same thing? If not, explain the differences.

7.7. There are two different types of "states" that behavioral models can represent. What are they?

7.8. How does a sequence diagram differ from a state diagram. How are they similar?

7.9. Suggest three requirements patterns for a modern mobile phone and write a brief description of each. Could these patterns be used for other devices. Provide an example.

7.10. Select one of the patterns you developed in Problem 7.9 and develop a reasonably complete pattern description similar in content and style to the one presented in Section 7.4.2.

7.11. How much analysis modeling do you think would be required for **SafeHomeAssured .com?** Would each of the model types described in Section 7.5.3 be required?

7.12. What is the purpose of the interaction model for a WebApp?

7.13. It could be argued that a WebApp functional model should be delayed until design. Present pros and cons for this argument.

7.14. What is the purpose of a configuration model?

7.15. How does the navigation model differ from the interaction model?

FURTHER READINGS AND INFORMATION SOURCES

Dozens of books have been published on structured analysis. All cover the subject adequately, but only a few do a truly excellent job. DeMarco and Plauger (*Structured Analysis and System Specification,* Pearson, 1985) is a classic that remains a good introduction to the basic notation. Books by Kendall and Kendall (*Systems Analysis and Design*, 5th ed., Prentice-Hall, 2002), Hoffer et al. (*Modern Systems Analysis and Design,* Addison-Wesley, 3d ed., 2001), Davis and Yen (*The Information System Consultant's Handbook: Systems Analysis and Design,* CRC Press, 1998), and Modell (*A Professional's Guide to Systems Analysis,* 2d ed., McGraw-Hill, 1996) are worthwhile references. Yourdon's book (*Modern Structured Analysis,* Yourdon-Press, 1989) on the subject remains among the most comprehensive coverage published to date.

Behavioral modeling presents an important dynamic view of system behavior. Books by Wagner and his colleagues (*Modeling Software with Finite State Machines: A Practical Approach,* Auerbach, 2006) and Boerger and Staerk (*Abstract State Machines,* Springer, 2003) present thorough discussion of state diagrams and other behavioral representations.

The majority of books written about software patterns focus on software design. However, books by Evans (*Domain-Driven Design,* Addison-Wesley, 2003) and Fowler ([Fow03] and [Fow97]) address analysis patterns specifically.

An in-depth treatment of analysis modeling for WebApps is presented by Pressman and Lowe [Pre08]. Papers contained within an anthology edited by Murugesan and Desphande (*Web Engineering: Managing Diversity and Complexity of Web Application Development,* Springer, 2001) treat various aspects of WebApp requirements. In addition, the annual *Proceedings of the International Conference on Web Engineering* regularly addresses requirements modeling issues.

A wide variety of information sources on requirements modeling are available on the Internet. An up-to-date list of World Wide Web references that are relevant to analysis modeling can be found at the SEPA website: **www.mhhe.com/engcs/compsci/pressman/ professional/olc/ser.htm.**

DESIGN CONCEPTS

Software design encompasses the set of principles, concepts, and practices that lead to the development of a high-quality system or product. Design principles establish an overriding philosophy that guides you in the design work you must perform. Design concepts must be understood before the mechanics of design practice are applied, and design practice itself leads to the creation of various representations of the software that serve as a guide for the construction activity that follows.

Design is pivotal to successful software engineering. In the early 1990s Mitch Kapor, the creator of Lotus 1-2-3, presented a "software design manifesto" in *Dr. Dobbs Journal.* He said:

> What is design? It's where you stand with a foot in two worlds—the world of technology and the world of people and human purposes—and you try to bring the two together. . . .

QUICK LOOK

What is it? Design is what almost every engineer wants to do. It is the place where creativity rules—where stakeholder requirements, business needs, and technical considerations all come together in the formulation of a product or system. Design creates a representation or model of the software, but unlike the requirements model (that focuses on describing required data, function, and behavior), the design model provides detail about software architecture, data structures, interfaces, and components that are necessary to implement the system.

Who does it? Software engineers conduct each of the design tasks.

Why is it important? Design allows you to model the system or product that is to be built. This model can be assessed for quality and improved before code is generated, tests are conducted, and end users become involved in large numbers. Design is the place where software quality is established.

What are the steps? Design depicts the software in a number of different ways. First, the architecture of the system or product must be represented. Then, the interfaces that connect the software to end users, to other systems and devices, and to its own constituent components are modeled. Finally, the software components that are used to construct the system are designed. Each of these views represents a different design action, but all must conform to a set of basic design concepts that guide software design work.

What is the work product? A design model that encompasses architectural, interface, component-level, and deployment representations is the primary work product that is produced during software design.

How do I ensure that I've done it right? The design model is assessed by the software team in an effort to determine whether it contains errors, inconsistencies, or omissions; whether better alternatives exist; and whether the model can be implemented within the constraints, schedule, and cost that have been established.

The Roman architecture critic Vitruvius advanced the notion that well-designed build-ings were those which exhibited firmness, commodity, and delight. The same might be said of good software. *Firmness:* A program should not have any bugs that inhibit its func-tion. *Commodity:* A program should be suitable for the purposes for which it was in-tended. *Delight:* The experience of using the program should be a pleasurable one. Here we have the beginnings of a theory of design for software.

The goal of design is to produce a model or representation that exhibits firmness, commodity, and delight. To accomplish this, you must practice diversification and then convergence. Belady [Bel81] states that "diversification is the acquisition of a repertoire of alternatives, the raw material of design: components, component solu-tions, and knowledge, all contained in catalogs, textbooks, and the mind." Once this diverse set of information is assembled, you must pick and choose elements from the repertoire that meet the requirements defined by requirements engineering and the analysis model (Chapters 5 through 7). As this occurs, alternatives are considered and rejected and you converge on "one particular configuration of components, and thus the creation of the final product" [Bel81].

Diversification and convergence combine intuition and judgment based on expe-rience in building similar entities, a set of principles and/or heuristics that guide the way in which the model evolves, a set of criteria that enables quality to be judged, and a process of iteration that ultimately leads to a final design representation.

Software design changes continually as new methods, better analysis, and broader understanding evolve.[1] Even today, most software design methodologies lack the depth, flexibility, and quantitative nature that are normally associated with more clas-sical engineering design disciplines. However, methods for software design do exist, criteria for design quality are available, and design notation can be applied. In this chapter, I explore the fundamental concepts and principles that are applicable to all software design, the elements of the design model, and the impact of patterns on the design process. In Chapters 9 through 13 I'll present a variety of software design methods as they are applied to architectural, interface, and component-level design as well as pattern-based and Web-oriented design approaches.

8.1   DESIGN WITHIN THE CONTEXT OF SOFTWARE ENGINEERING

Software design sits at the technical kernel of software engineering and is applied regardless of the software process model that is used. Beginning once software re-quirements have been analyzed and modeled, software design is the last software engineering action within the modeling activity and sets the stage for **construction** (code generation and testing).

---

1   Those readers with further interest in the philosophy of software design might have interest in Philippe Kruchen's intriguing discussion of "post-modern" design [Kru05a].

FIGURE 8.1

FIGURE 8.1   Translating the requirements model into the design model

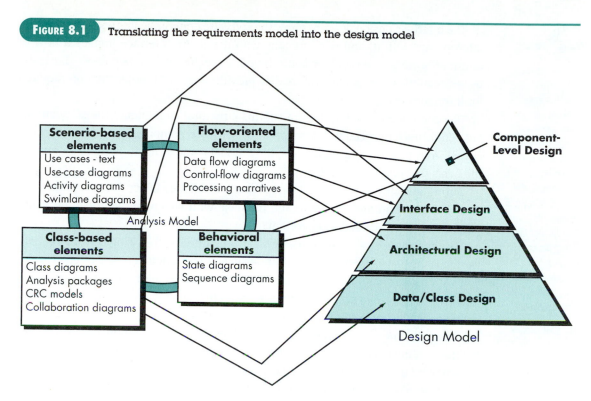

Each of the elements of the requirements model (Chapters 6 and 7) provides information that is necessary to create the four design models required for a complete specification of design. The flow of information during software design is illustrated in Figure 8.1. The requirements model, manifested by scenario-based, class-based, flow-oriented, and behavioral elements, feed the design task. Using design notation and design methods discussed in later chapters, design produces a data/class design, an architectural design, an interface design, and a component design.

The data/class design transforms class models (Chapter 6) into design class realizations and the requisite data structures required to implement the software. The objects and relationships defined in the CRC diagram and the detailed data content depicted by class attributes and other notation provide the basis for the data design action. Part of class design may occur in conjunction with the design of software architecture. More detailed class design occurs as each software component is designed.

The architectural design defines the relationship between major structural elements of the software, the architectural styles and design patterns that can be used to achieve the requirements defined for the system, and the constraints that affect the way in which architecture can be implemented [Sha96]. The architectural design representation—the framework of a computer-based system—is derived from the requirements model.

ADVICE

Software design should always begin with a consideration of data—the foundation for all other elements of the design. After the foundation is laid, the architecture must be derived. Only then should you perform other design tasks.

The interface design describes how the software communicates with systems that interoperate with it, and with humans who use it. An interface implies a flow of information (e.g., data and/or control) and a specific type of behavior. Therefore, usage scenarios and behavioral models provide much of the information required for interface design.

The component-level design transforms structural elements of the software architecture into a procedural description of software components. Information obtained from the class-based models, flow models, and behavioral models serve as the basis for component design.

During design you make decisions that will ultimately affect the success of software construction and, as important, the ease with which software can be maintained. But why is design so important?

The importance of software design can be stated with a single word—*quality*. Design is the place where quality is fostered in software engineering. Design provides you with representations of software that can be assessed for quality. Design is the only way that you can accurately translate stakeholder's requirements into a finished software product or system. Software design serves as the foundation for all the software engineering and software support activities that follow. Without design, you risk building an unstable system—one that will fail when small changes are made; one that may be difficult to test; one whose quality cannot be assessed until late in the software process, when time is short and many dollars have already been spent.

SAFEHOME

Design versus Coding

The scene: Jamie's cubicle, as the team prepares to translate requirements into design.

The players: Jamie, Vinod, and Ed—all members of the *SafeHome* software engineering team.

The conversation:

Jamie: You know, Doug [the team manager] is obsessed with design. I gotta be honest, what I really love doing is coding. Give me C++ or Java, and I'm happy.

Ed: Nah . . . you like to design.

Jamie: You're not listening; coding is where it's at.

Vinod: I think what Ed means is you don't really like coding; you like to design and express it in code. Code is the language you use to represent the design.

Jamie: And what's wrong with that?

Vinod: Level of abstraction.

Jamie: Huh?

Ed: A programming language is good for representing details like data structures and algorithms, but it's not so good for representing architecture or component-to-component collaboration . . . stuff like that.

Vinod: And a screwed-up architecture can ruin even the best code.

Jamie (thinking for a minute): So, you're saying that I can't represent architecture in code . . . that's not true.

Vinod: You can certainly imply architecture in code, but in most programming languages, it's pretty difficult to get a quick, big-picture read on architecture by examining the code.

Ed: And that's what we want before we begin coding.

Jamie: Okay, maybe design and coding are different, but I still like coding better.

8.2 THE DESIGN PROCESS

Software design is an iterative process through which requirements are translated into a "blueprint" for constructing the software. Initially, the blueprint depicts a holistic view of software. That is, the design is represented at a high level of abstraction—a level that can be directly traced to the specific system objective and more detailed data, functional, and behavioral requirements. As design iterations occur, subsequent refinement leads to design representations at much lower levels of abstraction. These can still be traced to requirements, but the connection is more subtle.

8.2.1 Software Quality Guidelines and Attributes

Throughout the design process, the quality of the evolving design is assessed with a series of technical reviews discussed in Chapter 15. McGlaughlin [McG91] suggests three characteristics that serve as a guide for the evaluation of a good design:

uote:

". . . writing a clever piece of code that works is one thing; designing something that can support a long-lasting business is quite another."

C. Ferguson

- The design must implement all of the explicit requirements contained in the requirements model, and it must accommodate all of the implicit requirements desired by stakeholders.

- The design must be a readable, understandable guide for those who generate code and for those who test and subsequently support the software.

- The design should provide a complete picture of the software, addressing the data, functional, and behavioral domains from an implementation perspective.

Each of these characteristics is actually a goal of the design process. But how is each of these goals achieved?

Quality Guidelines. In order to evaluate the quality of a design representation, you and other members of the software team must establish technical criteria for good design. In Section 8.3, I discuss design concepts that also serve as software quality criteria. For the time being, consider the following guidelines:

? **What are the characteristics of a good design?**

1. A design should exhibit an architecture that (1) has been created using recognizable architectural styles or patterns, (2) is composed of components that exhibit good design characteristics (these are discussed later in this chapter), and (3) can be implemented in an evolutionary fashion,[2] thereby facilitating implementation and testing.

2. A design should be modular; that is, the software should be logically partitioned into elements or subsystems.

3. A design should contain distinct representations of data, architecture, interfaces, and components.

---

2 For smaller systems, design can sometimes be developed linearly.

4. A design should lead to data structures that are appropriate for the classes to be implemented and are drawn from recognizable data patterns.

5. A design should lead to components that exhibit independent functional characteristics.

6. A design should lead to interfaces that reduce the complexity of connections between components and with the external environment.

7. A design should be derived using a repeatable method that is driven by information obtained during software requirements analysis.

8. A design should be represented using a notation that effectively communicates its meaning.

These design guidelines are not achieved by chance. They are achieved through the application of fundamental design principles, systematic methodology, and thorough review.

INFO

Assessing Design Quality—The Technical Review

Design is important because it allows a software team to assess the quality[3] of the software before it is implemented—at a time when errors, omissions, or inconsistencies are easy and inexpensive to correct. But how do we assess quality during design? The software can't be tested, because there is no executable software to test. What to do?

During design, quality is assessed by conducting a series of technical reviews (TRs). TRs are discussed in detail in Chapter 15,[4] but it's worth providing a summary of the technique at this point. A technical review is a meeting conducted by members of the software team. Usually two, three, or four people participate depending on the scope of the design information to be reviewed. Each person plays

a role: the *review leader* plans the meeting, sets an agenda, and runs the meeting; the *recorder* takes notes so that nothing is missed; the *producer* is the person whose work product (e.g., the design of a software component) is being reviewed. Prior to the meeting, each person on the review team is given a copy of the design work product and is asked to read it, looking for errors, omissions, or ambiguity. When the meeting commences, the intent is to note all problems with the work product so that they can be corrected before implementation begins. The TR typically lasts between 90 minutes and 2 hours. At the conclusion of the TR, the review team determines whether further actions are required on the part of the producer before the design work product can be approved as part of the final design model.

---

uote:

"Quality isn't something you lay on top of subjects and objects like tinsel on a Christmas tree."

Robert Pirsig

Quality Attributes. Hewlett-Packard [Gra87] developed a set of software quality attributes that has been given the acronym FURPS—functionality, usability, reliability, performance, and supportability. The FURPS quality attributes represent a target for all software design:

- *Functionality* is assessed by evaluating the feature set and capabilities of the program, the generality of the functions that are delivered, and the security of the overall system.

---

3   The quality factors discussed in Chapter 23 can assist the review team as it assesses quality.
4   You might consider reviewing Chapter 15 at this time. Technical reviews are a critical part of the design process and are an important mechanism for achieving design quality.

- *Usability* is assessed by considering human factors (Chapter 11), overall aesthetics, consistency, and documentation.

- *Reliability* is evaluated by measuring the frequency and severity of failure, the accuracy of output results, the mean-time-to-failure (MTTF), the ability to recover from failure, and the predictability of the program.

- *Performance* is measured by considering processing speed, response time, resource consumption, throughput, and efficiency.

- *Supportability* combines the ability to extend the program (extensibility), adaptability, serviceability—these three attributes represent a more common term, *maintainability*—and in addition, testability, compatibility, configurability (the ability to organize and control elements of the software configuration, Chapter 22), the ease with which a system can be installed, and the ease with which problems can be localized.

Not every software quality attribute is weighted equally as the software design is developed. One application may stress functionality with a special emphasis on security. Another may demand performance with particular emphasis on processing speed. A third might focus on reliability. Regardless of the weighting, it is important to note that these quality attributes must be considered as design commences, *not* after the design is complete and construction has begun.

8.2.2 The Evolution of Software Design

The evolution of software design is a continuing process that has now spanned almost six decades. Early design work concentrated on criteria for the development of modular programs [Den73] and methods for refining software structures in a top-down manner [Wir71]. Procedural aspects of design definition evolved into a philosophy called *structured programming* [Dah72], [Mil72]. Later work proposed methods for the translation of data flow [Ste74] or data structure (e.g., [Jac75], [War74]) into a design definition. Newer design approaches (e.g., [Jac92], [Gam95]) proposed an object-oriented approach to design derivation. More recent emphasis in software design has been on software architecture [Kru06] and the design patterns that can be used to implement software architectures and lower levels of design abstractions (e.g., [Hol06] [Sha05]). Growing emphasis on aspect-oriented methods (e.g., [Cla05], [Jac04]), model-driven development [Sch06], and test-driven development [Ast04] emphasize techniques for achieving more effective modularity and architectural structure in the designs that are created.

A number of design methods, growing out of the work just noted, are being applied throughout the industry. Like the analysis methods presented in Chapters 6 and 7, each software design method introduces unique heuristics and notation, as well as a somewhat parochial view of what characterizes design quality. Yet, all of these methods have a number of common characteristics: (1) a mechanism for the translation of the requirements model into a design representation, (2) a notation for representing functional components and their interfaces, (3) heuristics for refinement and partitioning, and (4) guidelines for quality assessment.

Regardless of the design method that is used, you should apply a set of basic concepts to data, architectural, interface, and component-level design. These concepts are considered in the sections that follow.

TASK SET

Generic Task Set for Design

1. Examine the information domain model, and design appropriate data structures for data objects and their attributes.
2. Using the analysis model, select an architectural style that is appropriate for the software.
3. Partition the analysis model into design subsystems and allocate these subsystems within the architecture:
   Be certain that each subsystem is functionally cohesive.
   Design subsystem interfaces.
   Allocate analysis classes or functions to each subsystem.
4. Create a set of design classes or components:
   Translate analysis class description into a design class.
   Check each design class against design criteria; consider inheritance issues.
   Define methods and messages associated with each design class.

Evaluate and select design patterns for a design class or a subsystem.
Review design classes and revise as required.
5. Design any interface required with external systems or devices.
6. Design the user interface:
   Review results of task analysis.
   Specify action sequence based on user scenarios.
   Create behavioral model of the interface.
   Define interface objects, control mechanisms.
   Review the interface design and revise as required.
7. Conduct component-level design.
   Specify all algorithms at a relatively low level of abstraction.
   Refine the interface of each component.
   Define component-level data structures.
   Review each component and correct all errors uncovered.
8. Develop a deployment model.

8.3   DESIGN CONCEPTS

A set of fundamental software design concepts has evolved over the history of software engineering. Although the degree of interest in each concept has varied over the years, each has stood the test of time. Each provides the software designer with a foundation from which more sophisticated design methods can be applied. Each helps you answer the following questions:

- What criteria can be used to partition software into individual components?
- How is function or data structure detail separated from a conceptual representation of the software?
- What uniform criteria define the technical quality of a software design?

M. A. Jackson [Jac75] once said: "The beginning of wisdom for a [software engineer] is to recognize the difference between getting a program to work, and getting it right." Fundamental software design concepts provide the necessary framework for "getting it right."

In the sections that follow, I present a brief overview of important software design concepts that span both traditional and object-oriented software development.

8.3.1 Abstraction

When you consider a modular solution to any problem, many levels of abstraction can be posed. At the highest level of abstraction, a solution is stated in broad terms using the language of the problem environment. At lower levels of abstraction, a more detailed description of the solution is provided. Problem-oriented terminology is coupled with implementation-oriented terminology in an effort to state a solution. Finally, at the lowest level of abstraction, the solution is stated in a manner that can be directly implemented.

As different levels of abstraction are developed, you work to create both procedural and data abstractions. A *procedural abstraction* refers to a sequence of instructions that have a specific and limited function. The name of a procedural abstraction implies these functions, but specific details are suppressed. An example of a procedural abstraction would be the word *open* for a door. *Open* implies a long sequence of procedural steps (e.g., walk to the door, reach out and grasp knob, turn knob and pull door, step away from moving door, etc.).[5]

A *data abstraction* is a named collection of data that describes a data object. In the context of the procedural abstraction *open,* we can define a data abstraction called **door.** Like any data object, the data abstraction for **door** would encompass a set of attributes that describe the door (e.g., door type, swing direction, opening mechanism, weight, dimensions). It follows that the procedural abstraction *open* would make use of information contained in the attributes of the data abstraction **door.**

8.3.2 Architecture

Software architecture alludes to "the overall structure of the software and the ways in which that structure provides conceptual integrity for a system" [Sha95a]. In its simplest form, architecture is the structure or organization of program components (modules), the manner in which these components interact, and the structure of data that are used by the components. In a broader sense, however, components can be generalized to represent major system elements and their interactions.

One goal of software design is to derive an architectural rendering of a system. This rendering serves as a framework from which more detailed design activities are conducted. A set of architectural patterns enables a software engineer to solve common design problems.

---

5 It should be noted, however, that one set of operations can be replaced with another, as long as the function implied by the procedural abstraction remains the same. Therefore, the steps required to implement *open* would change dramatically if the door were automatic and attached to a sensor.

Shaw and Garlan [Sha95a] describe a set of properties that should be specified as part of an architectural design:

Structural properties. This aspect of the architectural design representation defines the components of a system (e.g., modules, objects, filters) and the manner in which those components are packaged and interact with one another. For example, objects are packaged to encapsulate both data and the processing that manipulates the data and interact via the invocation of methods.

Extra-functional properties. The architectural design description should address how the design architecture achieves requirements for performance, capacity, reliability, security, adaptability, and other system characteristics.

Families of related systems. The architectural design should draw upon repeatable patterns that are commonly encountered in the design of families of similar systems. In essence, the design should have the ability to reuse architectural building blocks.

Given the specification of these properties, the architectural design can be represented using one or more of a number of different models [Gar95]. *Structural models* represent architecture as an organized collection of program components. *Framework models* increase the level of design abstraction by attempting to identify repeatable architectural design frameworks that are encountered in similar types of applications. *Dynamic models* address the behavioral aspects of the program architecture, indicating how the structure or system configuration may change as a function of external events. *Process models* focus on the design of the business or technical process that the system must accommodate. Finally, *functional models* can be used to represent the functional hierarchy of a system.

A number of different *architectural description languages* (ADLs) have been developed to represent these models [Sha95b]. Although many different ADLs have been proposed, the majority provide mechanisms for describing system components and the manner in which they are connected to one another.

You should note that there is some debate about the role of architecture in design. Some researchers argue that the derivation of software architecture should be separated from design and occurs between requirements engineering actions and more conventional design actions. Others believe that the derivation of architecture is an integral part of the design process. The manner in which software architecture is characterized and its role in design are discussed in Chapter 9.

8.3.3 Patterns

Brad Appleton defines a *design pattern* in the following manner: "A pattern is a named nugget of insight which conveys the essence of a proven solution to a recurring problem within a certain context amidst competing concerns" [App00]. Stated in another way, a design pattern describes a design structure that solves a particular design problem within a specific context and amid "forces" that may have an impact on the manner in which the pattern is applied and used.

The intent of each design pattern is to provide a description that enables a designer to determine (1) whether the pattern is applicable to the current work, (2) whether the pattern can be reused (hence, saving design time), and (3) whether the pattern can serve as a guide for developing a similar, but functionally or structurally different pattern. Design patterns are discussed in detail in Chapter 12.

8.3.4 Separation of Concerns

Separation of concerns is a design concept [Dij82] that suggests that any complex problem can be more easily handled if it is subdivided into pieces that can each be solved and/or optimized independently. A *concern* is a feature or behavior that is specified as part of the requirements model for the software. By separating concerns into smaller, and therefore more manageable pieces, a problem takes less effort and time to solve.

The argument for separation of concerns can be taken too far. If you divide a problem into an inordinate number of very small problems, solving each will be easy, but putting the solution together—integration—may be very difficult.

For two problems, p_1 and p_2, if the perceived complexity of p_1 is greater than the perceived complexity of p_2, it follows that the effort required to solve p_1 is greater than the effort required to solve p_2. As a general case, this result is intuitively obvious. It does take more time to solve a difficult problem.

It also follows that the perceived complexity of two problems when they are combined is often greater than the sum of the perceived complexity when each is taken separately. This leads to a divide-and-conquer strategy—it's easier to solve a complex problem when you break it into manageable pieces. This has important implications with regard to software modularity.

Separation of concerns is manifested in other related design concepts: modularity, aspects, functional independence, and refinement. Each will be discussed in the subsections that follow.

8.3.5 Modularity

Modularity is the most common manifestation of separation of concerns. Software is divided into separately named and addressable components, sometimes called *modules,* that are integrated to satisfy problem requirements.

It has been stated that "modularity is the single attribute of software that allows a program to be intellectually manageable" [Mye78]. Monolithic software (i.e., a large program composed of a single module) cannot be easily grasped by a software engineer. The number of control paths, span of reference, number of variables, and overall complexity would make understanding close to impossible. In almost all instances, you should break the design into many modules, hoping to make understanding easier and, as a consequence, reduce the cost required to build the software.

Recalling my discussion of separation of concerns, it is possible to conclude that if you subdivide software indefinitely the effort required to develop it will become negligibly small! Unfortunately, other forces come into play, causing this conclusion to be (sadly) invalid. Referring to Figure 8.2, the effort (cost) to develop an individual software module does decrease as the total number of modules increases. Given the

FIGURE 8.2

Modularity
and software
cost

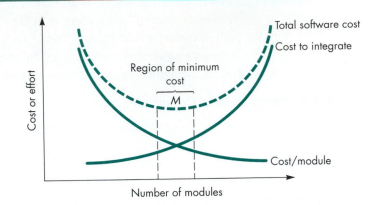

same set of requirements, more modules means smaller individual size. However, as the number of modules grows, the effort (cost) associated with integrating the modules also grows. These characteristics lead to a total cost or effort curve shown in the figure. There is a number, M, of modules that would result in minimum development cost, but we do not have the necessary sophistication to predict M with assurance.

The curves shown in Figure 8.2 do provide useful qualitative guidance when modularity is considered. You should modularize, but care should be taken to stay in the vicinity of M. Undermodularity or overmodularity should be avoided. But how do you know the vicinity of M? How modular should you make software? The answers to these questions require an understanding of other design concepts considered later in this chapter.

 What is the right number of modules for a given system?

You modularize a design (and the resulting program) so that development can be more easily planned; software increments can be defined and delivered; changes can be more easily accommodated; testing and debugging can be conducted more efficiently, and long-term maintenance can be conducted without serious side effects.

8.3.6   Information Hiding

The concept of modularity leads you to a fundamental question: "How do I decompose a software solution to obtain the best set of modules?" The principle of information hiding [Par72] suggests that modules be "characterized by design decisions that (each) hides from all others." In other words, modules should be specified and designed so that information (algorithms and data) contained within a module is inaccessible to other modules that have no need for such information.

KEY POINT

The intent of information hiding is to hide the details of data structures and procedural processing behind a module interface. Knowledge of the details need not be known by users of the module.

Hiding implies that effective modularity can be achieved by defining a set of independent modules that communicate with one another only that information necessary to achieve software function. Abstraction helps to define the procedural (or informational) entities that make up the software. Hiding defines and enforces access constraints to both procedural detail within a module and any local data structure used by the module [Ros75].

The use of information hiding as a design criterion for modular systems provides the greatest benefits when modifications are required during testing and later during software maintenance. Because most data and procedural detail are hidden from other parts of the software, inadvertent errors introduced during modification are less likely to propagate to other locations within the software.

8.3.7 Functional Independence

The concept of functional independence is a direct outgrowth of separation of concerns, modularity, and the concepts of abstraction and information hiding. In landmark papers on software design, Wirth [Wir71] and Parnas [Par72] allude to refinement techniques that enhance module independence. Later work by Stevens, Myers, and Constantine [Ste74] solidified the concept.

Functional independence is achieved by developing modules with "single-minded" function and an "aversion" to excessive interaction with other modules. Stated another way, you should design software so that each module addresses a specific subset of requirements and has a simple interface when viewed from other parts of the program structure. It is fair to ask why independence is important.

Why should you strive to create independent modules?

Software with effective modularity, that is, independent modules, is easier to develop because function can be compartmentalized and interfaces are simplified (consider the ramifications when development is conducted by a team). Independent modules are easier to maintain (and test) because secondary effects caused by design or code modification are limited, error propagation is reduced, and reusable modules are possible. To summarize, functional independence is a key to good design, and design is the key to software quality.

Independence is assessed using two qualitative criteria: cohesion and coupling. *Cohesion* is an indication of the relative functional strength of a module. *Coupling* is an indication of the relative interdependence among modules.

KEY POINT

Cohesion is a qualitative indication of the degree to which a module focuses on just one thing.

Cohesion is a natural extension of the information-hiding concept described in Section 8.3.6. A cohesive module performs a single task, requiring little interaction with other components in other parts of a program. Stated simply, a cohesive module should (ideally) do just one thing. Although you should always strive for high cohesion (i.e., single-mindedness), it is often necessary and advisable to have a software component perform multiple functions. However, "schizophrenic" components (modules that perform many unrelated functions) are to be avoided if a good design is to be achieved.

KEY POINT

Coupling is a qualitative indication of the degree to which a module is connected to other modules and to the outside world.

Coupling is an indication of interconnection among modules in a software structure. Coupling depends on the interface complexity between modules, the point at which entry or reference is made to a module, and what data pass across the interface. In software design, you should strive for the lowest possible coupling. Simple connectivity among modules results in software that is easier to understand and less prone to a "ripple effect" [Ste74], caused when errors occur at one location and propagate throughout a system.

8.3.8 Refinement

Stepwise refinement is a top-down design strategy originally proposed by Niklaus Wirth [Wir71]. A program is developed by successively refining levels of procedural detail. A hierarchy is developed by decomposing a macroscopic statement of function (a procedural abstraction) in a stepwise fashion until programming language statements are reached.

Refinement is actually a process of *elaboration*. You begin with a statement of function (or description of information) that is defined at a high level of abstraction. That is, the statement describes function or information conceptually but provides no information about the internal workings of the function or the internal structure of the information. You then elaborate on the original statement, providing more and more detail as each successive refinement (elaboration) occurs.

Abstraction and refinement are complementary concepts. Abstraction enables you to specify procedure and data internally but suppress the need for "outsiders" to have knowledge of low-level details. Refinement helps you to reveal low-level details as design progresses. Both concepts allow you to create a complete design model as the design evolves.

8.3.9 Aspects

As requirements analysis occurs, a set of "concerns" is uncovered. These concerns "include requirements, use cases, features, data structures, quality-of-service issues, variants, intellectual property boundaries, collaborations, patterns and contracts" [AOS07]. Ideally, a requirements model can be organized in a way that allows you to isolate each concern (requirement) so that it can be considered independently. In practice, however, some of these concerns span the entire system and cannot be easily compartmentalized.

As design begins, requirements are refined into a modular design representation. Consider two requirements, *A* and *B*. Requirement *A* *crosscuts* requirement *B* "if a software decomposition [refinement] has been chosen in which *B* cannot be satisfied without taking *A* into account" [Ros04].

For example, consider two requirements for the **SafeHomeAssured.com** WebApp. Requirement *A* is described via the **ACS-DCV** use case discussed in Chapter 6. A design refinement would focus on those modules that would enable a registered user to access video from cameras placed throughout a space. Requirement *B* is a generic security requirement that states that *a registered user must be validated prior to using* **SafeHomeAssured.com.** This requirement is applicable for all functions that are available to registered *SafeHome* users. As design refinement occurs, *A** is a design representation for requirement *A* and *B** is a design representation for requirement *B*. Therefore, *A** and *B** are representations of concerns, and *B** *crosscuts A**.

An *aspect* is a representation of a crosscutting concern. Therefore, the design representation, *B**, of the requirement *a registered user must be validated prior to using* **SafeHomeAssured.com,** is an aspect of the *SafeHome* WebApp. It is important to identify aspects so that the design can properly accommodate them as refinement and modularization occur. In an ideal context, an aspect is implemented as a separate module (component) rather than as software fragments that are "scattered" or "tangled" throughout many components [Ban06]. To accomplish this, the design architecture should support a mechanism for defining an aspect—a module that enables the concern to be implemented across all other concerns that it crosscuts.

8.3.10   Refactoring

WebRef

Excellent resources for refactoring can be found at **www .refactoring.com**.

An important design activity suggested for many agile methods (Chapter 3), *refactoring* is a reorganization technique that simplifies the design (or code) of a component without changing its function or behavior. Fowler [Fow00] defines refactoring in the following manner: "Refactoring is the process of changing a software system in such a way that it does not alter the external behavior of the code [design] yet improves its internal structure."

WebRef

A variety of refactoring patterns can be found at **http://c2.com/cgi/ wiki?Refactoring Patterns**.

When software is refactored, the existing design is examined for redundancy, unused design elements, inefficient or unnecessary algorithms, poorly constructed or inappropriate data structures, or any other design failure that can be corrected to yield a better design. For example, a first design iteration might yield a component that exhibits low cohesion (i.e., it performs three functions that have only limited relationship to one another). After careful consideration, you may decide that the component should be refactored into three separate components, each exhibiting high cohesion.

SAFEHOME

Design Concepts

The scene: Vinod's cubicle, as design modeling begins.

The players: Vinod, Jamie, and Ed—members of the *SafeHome* software engineering team. Also, Shakira, a new member of the team.

The conversation:

[All four team members have just returned from a morning seminar entitled "Applying Basic Design Concepts," offered by a local computer science professor.]

Vinod: Did you get anything out of the seminar?

Ed: Knew most of the stuff, but it's not a bad idea to hear it again, I suppose.

Jamie: When I was an undergrad CS major, I never really understood why information hiding was as important as they say it is.

Vinod: Because . . . bottom line . . . it's a technique for reducing error propagation in a program. Actually, functional independence also accomplishes the same thing.

Shakira: I wasn't a CS grad, so a lot of the stuff the instructor mentioned is new to me. I can generate good code and fast. I don't see why this stuff is so important.

Jamie: I've seen your work, Shak, and you know what, you do a lot of this stuff naturally . . . that's why your designs and code work.

Shakira (smiling): Well, I always do try to partition the code, keep it focused on one thing, keep interfaces simple and constrained, reuse code whenever I can . . . that sort of thing.

Ed: Modularity, functional independence, hiding, patterns . . . see.

Jamie: I still remember the very first programming course I took . . . they taught us to refine the code iteratively.

Vinod: Same thing can be applied to design, you know.

Vinod: The only concepts I hadn't heard of before were "aspects" and "refactoring."

The result will be software that is easier to integrate, easier to test, and easier to maintain.

8.3.11   Object-Oriented Design Concepts

The object-oriented (OO) paradigm is widely used in modern software engineering. Appendix 2 has been provided for those readers who may be unfamiliar with OO design concepts such as classes and objects, inheritance, messages, and polymorphism, among others.

8.3.12   Design Classes

The requirements model defines a set of analysis classes (Chapter 6). Each describes some element of the problem domain, focusing on aspects of the problem that are user visible. The level of abstraction of an analysis class is relatively high.

As the design model evolves, you will define a set of *design classes* that refine the analysis classes by providing design detail that will enable the classes to be implemented, and implement a software infrastructure that supports the business solution. Five different types of design classes, each representing a different layer of the design architecture, can be developed [Amb01]:

? **What types of classes does the designer create?**

- *User interface classes* define all abstractions that are necessary for human-computer interaction (HCI). In many cases, HCI occurs within the context of a *metaphor* (e.g., a checkbook, an order form, a fax machine), and the design classes for the interface may be visual representations of the elements of the metaphor.

- *Business domain classes* are often refinements of the analysis classes defined earlier. The classes identify the attributes and services (methods) that are required to implement some element of the business domain.

- *Process classes* implement lower-level business abstractions required to fully manage the business domain classes.

- *Persistent classes* represent data stores (e.g., a database) that will persist beyond the execution of the software.

- *System classes* implement software management and control functions that enable the system to operate and communicate within its computing environment and with the outside world.

As the architecture forms, the level of abstraction is reduced as each analysis class is transformed into a design representation. That is, analysis classes represent data objects (and associated services that are applied to them) using the jargon of the business domain. Design classes present significantly more technical detail as a guide for implementation.

Arlow and Neustadt [Arl02] suggest that each design class be reviewed to ensure that it is "well-formed." They define four characteristics of a well-formed design class:

? **What is a "well-formed" design class?**

Complete and sufficient. A design class should be the complete encapsulation of all attributes and methods that can reasonably be expected (based on a knowledgeable interpretation of the class name) to exist for the class. For example, the class **Scene** defined for video-editing software is complete only if it contains all attributes and methods that can reasonably be associated with the creation of a video scene. Sufficiency ensures that the design class contains only those methods that are sufficient to achieve the intent of the class, no more and no less.

Primitiveness. Methods associated with a design class should be focused on accomplishing one service for the class. Once the service has been implemented with a method, the class should not provide another way to accomplish the same thing. For example, the class **VideoClip** for video-editing software might have attributes start-point and end-point to indicate the start and end points of the clip (note that the raw video loaded into the system may be longer than the clip that is used). The methods, *setStartPoint()* and *setEndPoint()*, provide the only means for establishing start and end points for the clip.

High cohesion. A cohesive design class has a small, focused set of responsibilities and single-mindedly applies attributes and methods to implement those responsibilities. For example, the class **VideoClip** might contain a set of methods for editing the video clip. As long as each method focuses solely on attributes associated with the video clip, cohesion is maintained.

Low coupling. Within the design model, it is necessary for design classes to collaborate with one another. However, collaboration should be kept to an acceptable minimum. If a design model is highly coupled (all design classes collaborate with all other design classes), the system is difficult to implement, to test, and to maintain over time. In general, design classes within a subsystem should have only limited knowledge of other classes. This restriction, called the *Law of Demeter* [Lie03], suggests that a method should only send messages to methods in neighboring classes.[6]

---

6 A less formal way of stating the Law of Demeter is "Each unit should only talk to its friends; Don't talk to strangers."

SafeHome

Refining an Analysis Class into a Design Class

The scene: Ed's cubicle, as design modeling begins.

The players: Vinod and Ed—members of the *SafeHome* software engineering team.

The conversation:

[Ed is working on the **FloorPlan** class (see sidebar discussion in Section 6.5.3 and Figure 6.10) and has refined it for the design model.]

Ed: So you remember the **FloorPlan** class, right? It's used as part of the surveillance and home management functions.

Vinod (nodding): Yeah, I seem to recall that we used it as part of our CRC discussions for home management.

Ed: We did. Anyway, I'm refining it for design. Want to show how we'll actually implement the **FloorPlan** class. My idea is to implement it as a set of linked lists [a specific data structure] So . . . I had to refine the analysis class **FloorPlan** (Figure 6.10) and actually, sort of simplify it.

Vinod: The analysis class showed only things in the problem domain, well, actually on the computer screen, that were visible to the end user, right?

Ed: Yep, but for the **FloorPlan** design class, I've got to add some things that are implementation specific. I needed to show that **FloorPlan** is an aggregation of segments—hence the **Segment** class—and that the **Segment** class is composed of lists for wall segments, windows, doors, and so on. The class **Camera** collaborates with **FloorPlan,** and obviously, there can be many cameras in the floor plan.

Vinod: Phew, let's see a picture of this new **FloorPlan** design class.

[Ed shows Vinod the drawing shown in Figure 8.3.]

Vinod: Okay, I see what you're trying to do. This allows you to modify the floor plan easily because new items can be added to or deleted from the list—the aggregation—without any problems.

Ed (nodding): Yeah, I think it'll work.
Vinod: So do I.

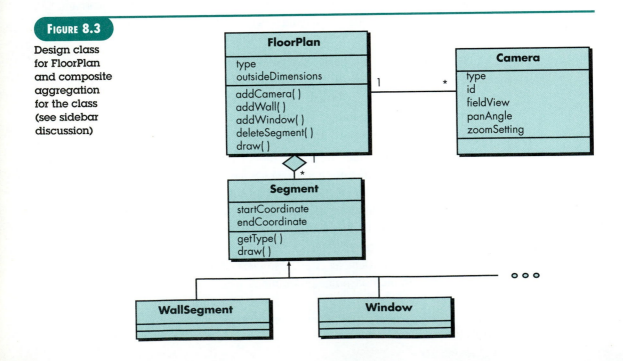

FIGURE 8.3

Design class
for FloorPlan
and composite
aggregation
for the class
(see sidebar
discussion)

8.4 THE DESIGN MODEL

The design model can be viewed in two different dimensions as illustrated in Figure 8.4. The *process dimension* indicates the evolution of the design model as design tasks are executed as part of the software process. The *abstraction dimension* represents the level of detail as each element of the analysis model is transformed into a design equivalent and then refined iteratively. Referring to Figure 8.4, the dashed line indicates the boundary between the analysis and design models. In some cases, a clear distinction between the analysis and design models is possible. In other cases, the analysis model slowly blends into the design and a clear distinction is less obvious.

The elements of the design model use many of the same UML diagrams[7] that were used in the analysis model. The difference is that these diagrams are refined and elaborated as part of design; more implementation-specific detail is provided, and architectural structure and style, components that reside within the architecture, and interfaces between the components and with the outside world are all emphasized.

KEY POINT

The design model has four major elements: data, architecture, components, and interface.

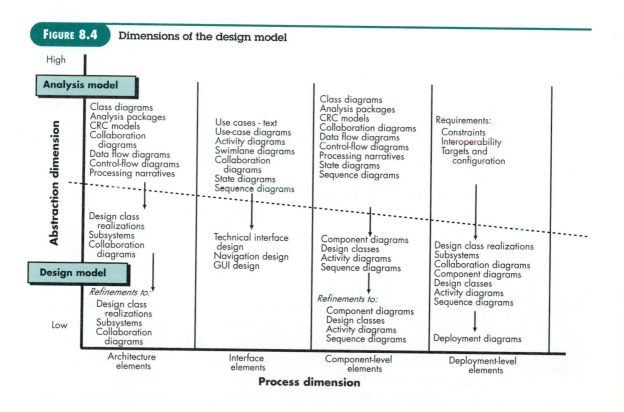

| **FIGURE 8.4** | Dimensions of the design model |

Process dimension

7 Appendix 1 provides a tutorial on basic UML concepts and notation.

You should note, however, that model elements indicated along the horizontal axis are not always developed in a sequential fashion. In most cases preliminary architectural design sets the stage and is followed by interface design and component-level design, which often occur in parallel. The deployment model is usually delayed until the design has been fully developed.

You can apply design patterns (Chapter 12) at any point during design. These patterns enable you to apply design knowledge to domain-specific problems that have been encountered and solved by others.

8.4.1 Data Design Elements

Like other software engineering activities, data design (sometimes referred to as *data architecting*) creates a model of data and/or information that is represented at a high level of abstraction (the customer/user's view of data). This data model is then refined into progressively more implementation-specific representations that can be processed by the computer-based system. In many software applications, the architecture of the data will have a profound influence on the architecture of the software that must process it.

The structure of data has always been an important part of software design. At the program component level, the design of data structures and the associated algorithms required to manipulate them is essential to the creation of high-quality applications. At the application level, the translation of a data model (derived as part of requirements engineering) into a database is pivotal to achieving the business objectives of a system. At the business level, the collection of information stored in disparate databases and reorganized into a "data warehouse" enables data mining or knowledge discovery that can have an impact on the success of the business itself. In every case, data design plays an important role. Data design is discussed in more detail in Chapter 9.

8.4.2 Architectural Design Elements

The *architectural design* for software is the equivalent to the floor plan of a house. The floor plan depicts the overall layout of the rooms; their size, shape, and relationship to one another; and the doors and windows that allow movement into and out of the rooms. The floor plan gives us an overall view of the house. Architectural design elements give us an overall view of the software.

The architectural model [Sha96] is derived from three sources: (1) information about the application domain for the software to be built; (2) specific requirements model elements such as data flow diagrams or analysis classes, their relationships and collaborations for the problem at hand; and (3) the availability of architectural styles (Chapter 9) and patterns (Chapter 12).

The architectural design element is usually depicted as a set of interconnected subsystems, often derived from analysis packages within the requirements model. Each subsystem may have it's own architecture (e.g., a graphical user interface might be structured according to a preexisting architectural style for user interfaces). Techniques for deriving specific elements of the architectural model are presented in Chapter 9.

8.4.3 Interface Design Elements

The interface design for software is analogous to a set of detailed drawings (and specifications) for the doors, windows, and external utilities of a house. These drawings depict the size and shape of doors and windows, the manner in which they operate, the way in which utility connections (e.g., water, electrical, gas, telephone) come into the house and are distributed among the rooms depicted in the floor plan. They tell us where the doorbell is located, whether an intercom is to be used to announce a visitor's presence, and how a security system is to be installed. In essence, the detailed drawings (and specifications) for the doors, windows, and external utilities tell us how things and information flow into and out of the house and within the rooms that are part of the floor plan. The interface design elements for software depict information flows into and out of the system and how it is communicated among the components defined as part of the architecture.

There are three important elements of interface design: (1) the user interface (UI); (2) external interfaces to other systems, devices, networks, or other producers or consumers of information; and (3) internal interfaces between various design components. These interface design elements allow the software to communicate externally and enable internal communication and collaboration among the components that populate the software architecture.

UI design (increasingly called *usability design*) is a major software engineering action and is considered in detail in Chapter 11. Usability design incorporates aesthetic elements (e.g., layout, color, graphics, interaction mechanisms), ergonomic elements (e.g., information layout and placement, metaphors, UI navigation), and technical elements (e.g., UI patterns, reusable components). In general, the UI is a unique subsystem within the overall application architecture.

The design of external interfaces requires definitive information about the entity to which information is sent or received. In every case, this information should be collected during requirements engineering (Chapter 5) and verified once the interface design commences.[8] The design of external interfaces should incorporate error checking and (when necessary) appropriate security features.

The design of internal interfaces is closely aligned with component-level design (Chapter 10). Design realizations of analysis classes represent all operations and the messaging schemes required to enable communication and collaboration between operations in various classes. Each message must be designed to accommodate the requisite information transfer and the specific functional requirements of the

---

8 Interface characteristics can change with time. Therefore, a designer should ensure that the specification for the interface is accurate and complete.

operation that has been requested. If the classic input-process-output approach to design is chosen, the interface of each software component is designed based on data flow representations and the functionality described in a processing narrative.

In some cases, an interface is modeled in much the same way as a class. In UML, an interface is defined in the following manner [OMG03a]: "An interface is a specifier for the externally-visible [public] operations of a class, component, or other classifier (including subsystems) without specification of internal structure." Stated more simply, an interface is a set of operations that describes some part of the behavior of a class and provides access to these operations.

For example, the *SafeHome* security function makes use of a control panel that allows a homeowner to control certain aspects of the security function. In an advanced version of the system, control panel functions may be implemented via a wireless PDA or mobile phone.

The **ControlPanel** class (Figure 8.5) provides the behavior associated with a keypad, and therefore, it must implement the operations *readKeyStroke ()* and *decodeKey ()*. If these operations are to be provided to other classes (in this case, **WirelessPDA** and **MobilePhone**), it is useful to define an interface as shown in the figure. The interface, named **KeyPad**, is shown as an <<interface>> stereotype or as a small, labeled circle connected to the class with a line. The interface is defined with no attributes and the set of operations that are necessary to achieve the behavior of a keypad.

The dashed line with an open triangle at its end (Figure 8.5) indicates that the **ControlPanel** class provides **KeyPad** operations as part of its behavior. In UML, this

uote:

"A common mistake that people make when trying to design something completely foolproof was to underestimate the ingenuity of complete fools."

Douglas Adams

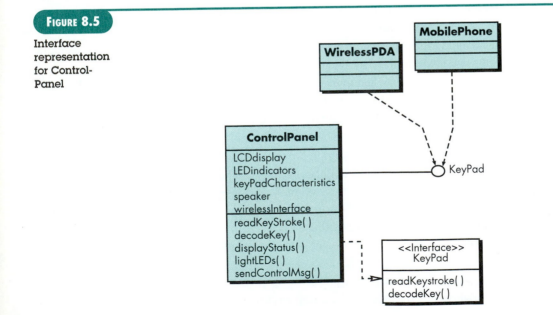

FIGURE 8.5

Interface representation for Control-Panel

is characterized as a *realization.* That is, part of the behavior of **ControlPanel** will be implemented by realizing **KeyPad** operations. These operations will be provided to other classes that access the interface.

8.4.4 Component-Level Design Elements

The component-level design for software is the equivalent to a set of detailed drawings (and specifications) for each room in a house. These drawings depict wiring and plumbing within each room, the location of electrical receptacles and wall switches, faucets, sinks, showers, tubs, drains, cabinets, and closets. They also describe the flooring to be used, the moldings to be applied, and every other detail associated with a room. The component-level design for software fully describes the internal detail of each software component. To accomplish this, the component-level design defines data structures for all local data objects and algorithmic detail for all processing that occurs within a component and an interface that allows access to all component operations (behaviors).

Within the context of object-oriented software engineering, a component is represented in UML diagrammatic form as shown in Figure 8.6. In this figure, a component named **SensorManagement** (part of the *SafeHome* security function) is represented. A dashed arrow connects the component to a class named **Sensor** that is assigned to it. The **SensorManagement** component performs all functions associated with *SafeHome* sensors including monitoring and configuring them. Further discussion of component diagrams is presented in Chapter 10.

The design details of a component can be modeled at many different levels of abstraction. A UML activity diagram can be used to represent processing logic. Detailed procedural flow for a component can be represented using either pseudocode (a programming language-like representation described in Chapter 10) or some other diagrammatic form (e.g., flowchart or box diagram). Algorithmic structure follows the rules established for structured programming (i.e., a set of constrained procedural constructs). Data structures, selected based on the nature of the data objects to be processed, are usually modeled using pseudocode or the programming language to be used for implementation.

8.4.5 Deployment-Level Design Elements

Deployment-level design elements indicate how software functionality and subsystems will be allocated within the physical computing environment that will support

FIGURE 8.6

A UML component diagram

FIGURE 8.7

A UML
deployment
diagram

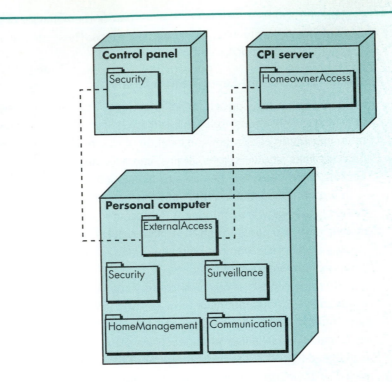

the software. For example, the elements of the *SafeHome* product are configured
to operate within three primary computing environments—a home-based PC, the
SafeHome control panel, and a server housed at CPI Corp. (providing Internet-based
access to the system).

During design, a UML deployment diagram is developed and then refined as
shown in Figure 8.7. In the figure, three computing environments are shown (in
actuality, there would be more including sensors, cameras, and others). The subsystems (functionality) housed within each computing element are indicated. For
example, the personal computer houses subsystems that implement security, surveillance, home management, and communications features. In addition, an external access subsystem has been designed to manage all attempts to access the
SafeHome system from an external source. Each subsystem would be elaborated to
indicate the components that it implements.

The diagram shown in Figure 8.7 is in *descriptor form.* This means that the deployment diagram shows the computing environment but does not explicitly indicate
configuration details. For example, the "personal computer" is not further identified.
It could be a Mac or a Windows-based PC, a Sun workstation, or a Linux-box. These
details are provided when the deployment diagram is revisited in *instance form*
during the latter stages of design or as construction begins. Each instance of the
deployment (a specific, named hardware configuration) is identified.

8.5 SUMMARY

Software design commences as the first iteration of requirements engineering comes to a conclusion. The intent of software design is to apply a set of principles, concepts, and practices that lead to the development of a high-quality system or product. The goal of design is to create a model of software that will implement all customer requirements correctly and bring delight to those who use it. Software designers must sift through many design alternatives and converge on a solution that best suits the needs of project stakeholders.

The design process moves from a "big picture" view of software to a more narrow view that defines the detail required to implement a system. The process begins by focusing on architecture. Subsystems are defined; communication mechanisms among subsystems are established; components are identified, and a detailed description of each component is developed. In addition, external, internal, and user interfaces are designed.

Design concepts have evolved over the first 60 years of software engineering work. They describe attributes of computer software that should be present regardless of the software engineering process that is chosen, the design methods that are applied, or the programming languages that are used. In essence, design concepts emphasize the need for abstraction as a mechanism for creating reusable software components; the importance of architecture as a way to better understand the overall structure of a system; the benefits of pattern-based engineering as a technique for designing software with proven capabilities; the value of separation of concerns and effective modularity as a way to make software more understandable, more testable, and more maintainable; the consequences of information hiding as a mechanism for reducing the propagation of side effects when errors do occur; the impact of functional independence as a criterion for building effective modules; the use of refinement as a design mechanism; a consideration of aspects that crosscut system requirements; the application of refactoring for optimizing the design that is derived; and the importance of object-oriented classes and the characteristics that are related to them.

The design model encompasses four different elements. As each of these elements is developed, a more complete view of the design evolves. The architectural element uses information derived from the application domain, the requirements model, and available catalogs for patterns and styles to derive a complete structural representation of the software, its subsystems, and components. Interface design elements model external and internal interfaces and the user interface. Component-level elements define each of the modules (components) that populate the architecture. Finally, deployment-level design elements allocate the architecture, its components, and the interfaces to the physical configuration that will house the software.

PROBLEMS AND POINTS TO PONDER

8.1. Do you design software when you "write" a program? What makes software design different from coding?

8.2. If a software design is not a program (and it isn't), then what is it?

8.3. How do we assess the quality of a software design?

8.4. Examine the task set presented for design. Where is quality assessed within the task set? How is this accomplished? How are the quality attributes discussed in Section 8.2.1 achieved?

8.5. Provide examples of three data abstractions and the procedural abstractions that can be used to manipulate them.

8.6. Describe software architecture in your own words.

8.7. Suggest a design pattern that you encounter in a category of everyday things (e.g., consumer electronics, automobiles, appliances). Briefly describe the pattern.

8.8. Describe separation of concerns in your own words. Is there a case when a divide-and-conquer strategy may not be appropriate? How might such a case affect the argument for modularity?

8.9. When should a modular design be implemented as monolithic software? How can this be accomplished? Is performance the only justification for implementation of monolithic software?

8.10. Discuss the relationship between the concept of information hiding as an attribute of effective modularity and the concept of module independence.

8.11. How are the concepts of coupling and software portability related? Provide examples to support your discussion.

8.12. Apply a "stepwise refinement approach" to develop three different levels of procedural abstractions for one or more of the following programs: (a) Develop a check writer that, given a numeric dollar amount, will print the amount in words normally required on a check. (b) Iteratively solve for the roots of a transcendental equation. (c) Develop a simple task scheduling algorithm for an operating system.

8.13. Consider the software required to implement a full navigation capability (using GPS) in a mobile, handheld communication device. Describe two or three crosscutting concerns that would be present. Discuss how you would represent one of these concerns as an aspect.

8.14. Does "refactoring" mean that you modify the entire design iteratively? If not, what does it mean?

8.15. Briefly describe each of the four elements of the design model.

FURTHER READINGS AND INFORMATION SOURCES

Donald Norman has written two books (*The Design of Everyday Things,* Doubleday, 1990, and *The Psychology of Everyday Things,* Harpercollins, 1988) that have become classics in the design literature and "must" reading for anyone who designs anything that humans use. Adams (*Conceptual Blockbusting,* 3d ed., Addison-Wesley, 1986) has written a book that is essential reading for designers who want to broaden their way of thinking. Finally, a classic text by Polya (*How to Solve It,* 2d ed., Princeton University Press, 1988) provides a generic problem-solving process that can help software designers when they are faced with complex problems.

Following in the same tradition, Winograd et al. (*Bringing Design to Software,* Addison-Wesley, 1996) discusses software designs that work, those that don't, and why. A fascinating book edited by Wixon and Ramsey (*Field Methods Casebook for Software Design,* Wiley, 1996) suggests field research methods (much like those used by anthropologists) to understand how end users do the work they do and then design software that meets their needs. Beyer and Holtzblatt (*Contextual Design: A Customer-Centered Approach to Systems Designs,* Academic Press, 1997) offer another view of software design that integrates the customer/user into every aspect of the software design process. Bain (*Emergent Design,* Addison-Wesley, 2008) couples patterns, refactoring, and test-driven development into an effective design approach.

Comprehensive treatment of design in the context of software engineering is presented by Fox (*Introduction to Software Engineering Design,* Addison-Wesley, 2006) and Zhu (*Software Design Methodology,* Butterworth-Heinemann, 2005). McConnell (*Code Complete,* 2d ed., Microsoft Press, 2004) presents an excellent discussion of the practical aspects of designing high-quality computer software. Robertson (*Simple Program Design,* 3d ed., Boyd and Fraser Publishing, 1999) presents an introductory discussion of software design that is useful for those beginning their study of the subject. Budgen (*Software Design,* 2d ed., Addison-Wesley, 2004) introduces a variety of popular design methods, comparing and contrasting each. Fowler and his colleagues (*Refactoring: Improving the Design of Existing Code,* Addison-Wesley, 1999) discusses techniques for the incremental optimization of software designs. Rosenberg and Stevens (*Use Case Driven Object Modeling with UML,* Apress, 2007) discuss the development of object-oriented designs using use cases as a foundation.

An excellent historical survey of software design is contained in an anthology edited by Freeman and Wasserman (*Software Design Techniques,* 4th ed., IEEE, 1983). This tutorial reprints many of the classic papers that have formed the basis for current trends in software design. Measures of design quality, presented from both the technical and management perspectives, are considered by Card and Glass (*Measuring Software Design Quality,* Prentice-Hall, 1990).

A wide variety of information sources on software design are available on the Internet. An up-to-date list of World Wide Web references that are relevant to software design and design engineering can be found at the SEPA website: **www.mhhe.com/engcs/compsci/ pressman/professional/olc/ser.htm**.

Design has been described as a multistep process in which representations of data and program structure, interface characteristics, and procedural detail are synthesized from information requirements. This description is extended by Freeman [Fre80]:

> [D]esign is an activity concerned with making major decisions, often of a structural nature. It shares with programming a concern for abstracting information representation and processing sequences, but the level of detail is quite different at the extremes. Design builds coherent, well-planned representations of programs that concentrate on the interrelationships of parts at the higher level and the logical operations involved at the lower levels.

As I noted in Chapter 8, design is information driven. Software design methods are derived from consideration of each of the three domains of the analysis model. The data, functional, and behavioral domains serve as a guide for the creation of the software design.

Methods required to create "coherent, well-planned representations" of the data and architectural layers of the design model are presented in this chapter. The objective is to provide a systematic approach for the derivation of the architectural design—the preliminary blueprint from which software is constructed.

QUICK LOOK

What is it? Architectural design represents the structure of data and program components that are required to build a computer-based system. It considers the architectural style that the system will take, the structure and properties of the components that constitute the system, and the interrelationships that occur among all architectural components of a system.

Who does it? Although a software engineer can design both data and architecture, the job is often allocated to specialists when large, complex systems are to be built. A database or data warehouse designer creates the data architecture for a system. The "system architect" selects an appropriate architectural style from the requirements derived during software requirements analysis.

Why is it important? You wouldn't attempt to build a house without a blueprint, would you? You also wouldn't begin drawing blueprints by sketching the plumbing layout for the house. You'd need to look at the big picture—the house itself—before you worry about details. That's what architectural design does—it provides you with the big picture and ensures that you've got it right.

What are the steps? Architectural design begins with data design and then proceeds to the derivation of one or more representations of the architectural structure of the system. Alternative architectural styles or patterns are analyzed to derive the structure that is best suited to customer requirements and quality attributes. Once an alternative has been selected, the architecture is elaborated using an architectural design method.

What is the work product? An architecture model encompassing data architecture and program structure is created during architectural design. In addition, component properties and relationships (interactions) are described.

How do I ensure that I've done it right? At each stage, software design work products are reviewed for clarity, correctness, completeness, and consistency with requirements and with one another.

9.1   SOFTWARE ARCHITECTURE

In their landmark book on the subject, Shaw and Garlan [Sha96] discuss software architecture in the following manner:

> Ever since the first program was divided into modules, software systems have had architectures, and programmers have been responsible for the interactions among the modules and the global properties of the assemblage. Historically, architectures have been implicit—accidents of implementation, or legacy systems of the past. Good software developers have often adopted one or several architectural patterns as strategies for system organization, but they use these patterns informally and have no means to make them explicit in the resulting system.

Today, effective software architecture and its explicit representation and design have become dominant themes in software engineering.

9.1.1   What Is Architecture?

> **uote:**
>
> "The architecture of a system is a comprehensive framework that describes its form and structure—its components and how they fit together."
>
> **Jerrold Grochow**

When you consider the architecture of a building, many different attributes come to mind. At the most simplistic level, you think about the overall shape of the physical structure. But in reality, architecture is much more. It is the manner in which the various components of the building are integrated to form a cohesive whole. It is the way in which the building fits into its environment and meshes with other buildings in its vicinity. It is the degree to which the building meets its stated purpose and satisfies the needs of its owner. It is the aesthetic feel of the structure—the visual impact of the building—and the way textures, colors, and materials are combined to create the external facade and the internal "living environment." It is small details—the design of lighting fixtures, the type of flooring, the placement of wall hangings, the list is almost endless. And finally, it is art.

But architecture is also something else. It is "thousands of decisions, both big and small" [Tyr05]. Some of these decisions are made early in design and can have a profound impact on all other design actions. Others are delayed until later, thereby eliminating overly restrictive constraints that would lead to a poor implementation of the architectural style.

But what about software architecture? Bass, Clements, and Kazman [Bas03] define this elusive term in the following way:

> The software architecture of a program or computing system is the structure or structures of the system, which comprise software components, the externally visible properties of those components, and the relationships among them.

The architecture is not the operational software. Rather, it is a representation that enables you to (1) analyze the effectiveness of the design in meeting its stated requirements, (2) consider architectural alternatives at a stage when making design changes is still relatively easy, and (3) reduce the risks associated with the construction of the software.

This definition emphasizes the role of "software components" in any architectural representation. In the context of architectural design, a software component can be something as simple as a program module or an object-oriented class, but it can also be extended to include databases and "middleware" that enable the configuration of a network of clients and servers. The properties of components are those characteristics that are necessary for an understanding of how the components interact with other components. At the architectural level, internal properties (e.g., details of an algorithm) are not specified. The relationships between components can be as simple as a procedure call from one module to another or as complex as a database access protocol.

Some members of the software engineering community (e.g., [Kaz03]) make a distinction between the actions associated with the derivation of a software architecture (what I call "architectural design") and the actions that are applied to derive the software design. As one reviewer of this edition noted:

> There is a distinct difference between the terms architecture and design. A *design* is an instance of an *architecture* similar to an object being an instance of a class. For example, consider the client-server architecture. I can design a network-centric software system in many different ways from this architecture using either the Java platform (Java EE) or Microsoft platform (.NET framework). So, there is one architecture, but many designs can be created based on that architecture. Therefore, you cannot mix "architecture" and "design" with each other.

Although I agree that a software design is an instance of a specific software architecture, the elements and structures that are defined as part of an architecture are the root of every design that evolves from them. Design begins with a consideration of architecture.

In this book the design of software architecture considers two levels of the design pyramid (Figure 8.1)—data design and architectural design. In the context of the preceding discussion, data design enables you to represent the data component of the architecture in conventional systems and class definitions (encompassing attributes and operations) in object-oriented systems. Architectural design focuses on the representation of the structure of software components, their properties, and interactions.

9.1.2 Why Is Architecture Important?

In a book dedicated to software architecture, Bass and his colleagues [Bas03] identify three key reasons that software architecture is important:

- Representations of software architecture are an enabler for communication between all parties (stakeholders) interested in the development of a computer-based system.

- The architecture highlights early design decisions that will have a profound impact on all software engineering work that follows and, as important, on the ultimate success of the system as an operational entity.

- Architecture "constitutes a relatively small, intellectually graspable model of how the system is structured and how its components work together" [Bas03].

The architectural design model and the architectural patterns contained within it are transferable. That is, architecture genres, styles, and patterns (Sections 9.2 through 9.4) can be applied to the design of other systems and represent a set of abstractions that enable software engineers to describe architecture in predictable ways.

9.1.3 Architectural Descriptions

Each of us has a mental image of what the word *architecture* means. In reality, however, it means different things to different people. The implication is that different stakeholders will see an architecture from different viewpoints that are driven by different sets of concerns. This implies that an architectural description is actually a set of work products that reflect different views of the system.

For example, the architect of a major office building must work with a variety of different stakeholders. The primary concern of the owner of the building (one stakeholder) is to ensure that it is aesthetically pleasing and that it provides sufficient office space and infrastructure to ensure its profitability. Therefore, the architect must develop a description using views of the building that address the owner's concerns. The viewpoints used are a three-dimensional drawings of the building (to illustrate the aesthetic view) and a set of two-dimensional floor plans to address this stakeholder's concern for office space and infrastructure.

But the office building has many other stakeholders, including the structural steel fabricator who will provide steel for the building skeleton. The structural steel fabricator needs detailed architectural information about the structural steel that will support the building, including types of I-beams, their dimensions, connectivity, materials, and many other details. These concerns are addressed by different work products that represent different views of the architecture. Specialized drawings

KEY POINT

The architectural model provides a Gestalt view of the system, allowing the software engineer to examine it as a whole.

ADVICE

Your effort should focus on architectural representations that will guide all other aspects of design. Spend the time to carefully review the architecture. A mistake here will have a long-term negative impact.

(another viewpoint) of the structural steel skeleton of the building focus on only one of many of the fabricator's concerns.

An architectural description of a software-based system must exhibit characteristics that are analogous to those noted for the office building. Tyree and Akerman [Tyr05] note this when they write: "Developers want clear, decisive guidance on how to proceed with design. Customers want a clear understanding on the environmental changes that must occur and assurances that the architecture will meet their business needs. Other architects want a clear, salient understanding of the architecture's key aspects." Each of these "wants" is reflected in a different view represented using a different viewpoint.

The IEEE Computer Society has proposed IEEE-Std-1471-2000, *Recommended Practice for Architectural Description of Software-Intensive Systems,* [IEE00], with the following objectives: (1) to establish a conceptual framework and vocabulary for use during the design of software architecture, (2) to provide detailed guidelines for representing an architectural description, and (3) to encourage sound architectural design practices.

The IEEE standard defines an *architectural description* (AD) as "a collection of products to document an architecture." The description itself is represented using multiple views, where each *view* is "a representation of a whole system from the perpective of a related set of [stakeholder] concerns." A *view* is created according to rules and conventions defined in a *viewpoint*—"a specification of the conventions for constructing and using a view" [IEE00]. A number of different work products that are used to develop different views of the software architecture are discussed later in this chapter.

9.1.4 Architectural Decisions

Each view developed as part of an architectural description addresses a specific stakeholder concern. To develop each view (and the architectural description as a whole) the system architect considers a variety of alternatives and ultimately decides on the specific architectural features that best meet the concern. Therefore, architectural decisions themselves can be considered to be one view of the architecture. The reasons that decisions were made provide insight into the structure of a system and its conformance to stakeholder concerns.

As a system architect, you can use the template suggested in the sidebar to document each major decision. By doing this, you provide a rationale for your work and establish an historical record that can be useful when design modifications must be made.

9.2 ARCHITECTURAL GENRES

Although the underlying principles of architectural design apply to all types of architecture, the architectural *genre* will often dictate the specific architectural approach to the structure that must be built. In the context of architectural design, *genre* implies a

Architecture Decision Description Template

Each major architectural decision can be documented for later review by stakeholders who want to understand the architecture description that has been proposed. The template presented in this sidebar is an adapted and abbreviated version of a template proposed by Tyree and Ackerman [Tyr05].

Design issue: Describe the architectural design issues that are to be addressed.

Resolution: State the approach you've chosen to address the design issue.

Category: Specify the design category that the issue and resolution address (e.g., data design, content structure, component structure, integration, presentation).

Assumptions: Indicate any assumptions that helped shape the decision.

Constraints: Specify any environmental constraints that helped shape the decision (e.g., technology standards, available patterns, project-related issues).

Alternatives: Briefly describe the architectural design alternatives that were considered and why they were rejected.

Argument: State why you chose the resolution over other alternatives.

Implications: Indicate the design consequences of making the decision. How will the resolution affect other architectural design issues? Will the resolution constrain the design in any way?

Related decisions: What other documented decisions are related to this decision?

Related concerns: What other requirements are related to this decision?

Work products: Indicate where this decision will be reflected in the architecture description.

Notes: Reference any team notes or other documentation that was used to make the decision.

KEY POINT

A number of different architectural styles may be applicable to a specific genre (also called an application domain).

specific category within the overall software domain. Within each category, you encounter a number of subcategories. For example, within the genre of *buildings*, you would encounter the following general styles: houses, condos, apartment buildings, office buildings, industrial building, warehouses, and so on. Within each general style, more specific styles might apply (Section 9.3). Each style would have a structure that can be described using a set of predictable patterns.

In his evolving *Handbook of Software Architecture* [Boo08], Grady Booch suggests the following architectural genres for software-based systems:

- **Artificial intelligence**—Systems that simulate or augment human cognition, locomotion, or other organic processes.

- **Commercial and nonprofit**—Systems that are fundamental to the operation of a business enterprise.

- **Communications**—Systems that provide the infrastructure for transferring and managing data, for connecting users of that data, or for presenting data at the edge of an infrastructure.

- **Content authoring**—Systems that are used to create or manipulate textual or multimedia artifacts.

- **Devices**—Systems that interact with the physical world to provide some point service for an individual.
- **Entertainment and sports**—Systems that manage public events or that provide a large group entertainment experience.
- **Financial**—Systems that provide the infrastructure for transferring and managing money and other securities.
- **Games**—Systems that provide an entertainment experience for individuals or groups.
- **Government**—Systems that support the conduct and operations of a local, state, federal, global, or other political entity.
- **Industrial**—Systems that simulate or control physical processes.
- **Legal**—Systems that support the legal industry.
- **Medical**—Systems that diagnose or heal or that contribute to medical research.
- **Military**—Systems for consultation, communications, command, control, and intelligence (C4I) as well as offensive and defensive weapons.
- **Operating systems**—Systems that sit just above hardware to provide basic software services.
- **Platforms**—Systems that sit just above operating systems to provide advanced services.
- **Scientific**—Systems that are used for scientific research and applications.
- **Tools**—Systems that are used to develop other systems.
- **Transportation**—Systems that control water, ground, air, or space vehicles.
- **Utilities**—Systems that interact with other software to provide some point service.

From the standpoint of architectural design, each genre represents a unique challenge. As an example, consider the software architecture for a game system. Game systems, sometimes called *immersive interactive applications,* require the computation of intensive algorithms, sophisticated computer graphics, streaming multimedia data sources, real-time interactivity via conventional and unconventional inputs, and a variety of other specialized concerns.

Alexandre Francois [Fra03] suggests a software architecture for *Immersipresence*[1] that can be applied for a gaming environment. He describes the architecture in the following manner:

> SAI (Software Architecture for Immersipresence) is a new software architecture model for designing, analyzing and implementing applications performing distributed,

---

1   Francois uses the term *immersipresence* for immersive, interactive applications.

asynchronous parallel processing of generic data streams. The goal of SAI is to provide a universal framework for the distributed implementation of algorithms and their easy integration into complex systems. . . . The underlying extensible data model and hybrid (shared repository and message-passing) distributed asynchronous parallel processing model allow natural and efficient manipulation of generic data streams, using existing libraries or native code alike. The modularity of the style facilitates distributed code development, testing, and reuse, as well as fast system design and integration, maintenance and evolution.

A detailed discussion of SAI is beyond the scope of this book. However, it is important to recognize that the gaming system genre can be addressed with an architectural style (Section 9.3) that has been specifically designed to address gaming system concerns. If you have further interest, see [Fra03].

9.3 ARCHITECTURAL STYLES

? **What is an architectural style?**

When a builder uses the phrase "center hall colonial" to describe a house, most people familiar with houses in the United States will be able to conjure a general image of what the house will look like and what the floor plan is likely to be. The builder has used an *architectural style* as a descriptive mechanism to differentiate the house from other styles (e.g., A-frame, raised ranch, Cape Cod). But more important, the architectural style is also a template for construction. Further details of the house must be defined, its final dimensions must be specified, customized features may be added, building materials are to be determined, but the style—a "center hall colonial"—guides the builder in his work.

The software that is built for computer-based systems also exhibits one of many architectural styles. Each style describes a system category that encompasses (1) a set of components (e.g., a database, computational modules) that perform a function required by a system; (2) a set of connectors that enable "communication, coordination and cooperation" among components; (3) constraints that define how components can be integrated to form the system; and (4) semantic models that enable a designer to understand the overall properties of a system by analyzing the known properties of its constituent parts [Bas03].

An architectural style is a transformation that is imposed on the design of an entire system. The intent is to establish a structure for all components of the system. In the case where an existing architecture is to be reengineered (Chapter 29), the imposition of an architectural style will result in fundamental changes to the structure of the software including a reassignment of the functionality of components [Bos00].

An architectural pattern, like an architectural style, imposes a transformation on the design of an architecture. However, a pattern differs from a style in a number of fundamental ways: (1) the scope of a pattern is less broad, focusing on one aspect of the architecture rather than the architecture in its entirety; (2) a pattern imposes a rule on the architecture, describing how the software will handle some aspect of its functionality at the infrastructure level (e.g., concurrency) [Bos00]; (3) architectural patterns (Section 9.4) tend to address specific behavioral issues within the context of the architecture (e.g., how real-time applications handle synchronization or interrupts). Patterns can be used in conjunction with an architectural style to shape the overall structure of a system. In Section 9.3.1, I consider commonly used architectural styles and patterns for software.

Canonical Architectural Structures

In essence, software architecture represents a structure in which some collection of entities (often called *components*) is connected by a set of defined relationships (often called *connectors*). Both components and connectors are associated with a set of *properties* that allow the designer to differentiate the types of components and connectors that can be used. But what kinds of structures (components, connectors, and properties) can be used to describe an architecture? Bass and Kazman [Bas03] suggest five canonical or foundation architectural structures:

Functional structure. Components represent function or processing entities. Connectors represent interfaces that provide the ability to "use" or "pass data to" a component. Properties describe the nature of the components and the organization of the interfaces.

Implementation structure. "Components can be packages, classes, objects, procedures, functions, methods, etc., all of which are vehicles for packaging functionality at various levels of abstraction" [Bas03]. Connectors include the ability to pass data and control, share data, "use", and "is-an-instance-of." Properties

focus on quality characteristics (e.g., maintainability, reusability) that result when the structure is implemented.

Concurrency structure. Components represent "units of concurrency" that are organized as parallel tasks or threads. "Relations [connectors] include synchronizes-with, is-higher-priority-than, sends-data-to, can't-run-without, and can't-run-with. Properties relevant to this structure include priority, preemptability, and execution time" [Bas03].

Physical structure. This structure is similar to the deployment model developed as part of design. The components are the physical hardware on which software resides. Connectors are the interfaces between hardware components, and properties address capacity, bandwidth, performance, and other attributes.

Developmental structure. This structure defines the components, work products, and other information sources that are required as software engineering proceeds. Connectors represent the relationships among work products, and properties identify the characteristics of each item.

Each of these structures presents a different view of software architecture, exposing information that is useful to the software team as modeling and construction proceed.

9.3.1   A Brief Taxonomy of Architectural Styles

Although millions of computer-based systems have been created over the past 60 years, the vast majority can be categorized into one of a relatively small number of architectural styles:

Data-centered architectures. A data store (e.g., a file or database) resides at the center of this architecture and is accessed frequently by other components that update, add, delete, or otherwise modify data within the store. Figure 9.1 illustrates a typical data-centered style. Client software accesses a central repository. In some cases the data repository is passive. That is, client software accesses the data independent of any changes to the data or the actions of other client software. A variation on this approach transforms the repository into a "blackboard"

FIGURE 9.1

Data-centered
architecture

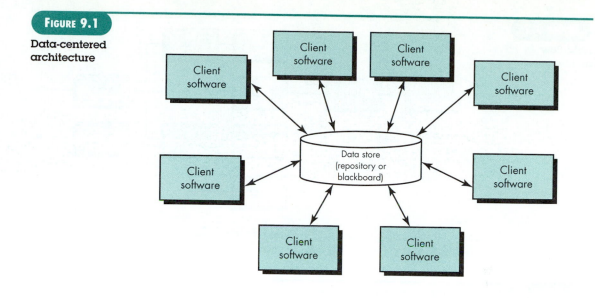

FIGURE 9.1

Data-centered
architecture

that sends notifications to client software when data of interest to the client changes.

Data-centered architectures promote *integrability* [Bas03]. That is, existing components can be changed and new client components added to the architecture without concern about other clients (because the client components operate independently). In addition, data can be passed among clients using the blackboard mechanism (i.e., the blackboard component serves to coordinate the transfer of information between clients). Client components independently execute processes.

Data-flow architectures. This architecture is applied when input data are to be transformed through a series of computational or manipulative components into output data. A pipe-and-filter pattern (Figure 9.2) has a set of components, called *filters*, connected by *pipes* that transmit data from one component to the next. Each filter works independently of those components upstream and downstream, is designed to expect data input of a certain form, and produces data output (to the next filter) of a specified form. However, the filter does not require knowledge of the workings of its neighboring filters.

If the data flow degenerates into a single line of transforms, it is termed batch sequential. This structure accepts a batch of data and then applies a series of sequential components (filters) to transform it.

Call and return architectures. This architectural style enables you to achieve a program structure that is relatively easy to modify and scale. A number of substyles [Bas03] exist within this category:

- *Main program/subprogram architectures.* This classic program structure decomposes function into a control hierarchy where a "main" program

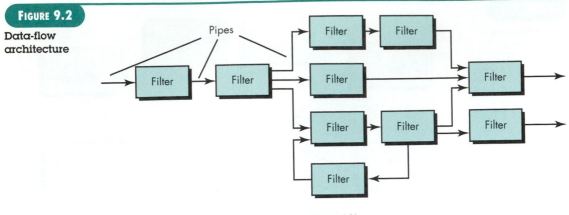

FIGURE 9.2

Data-flow
architecture

Pipes and filters

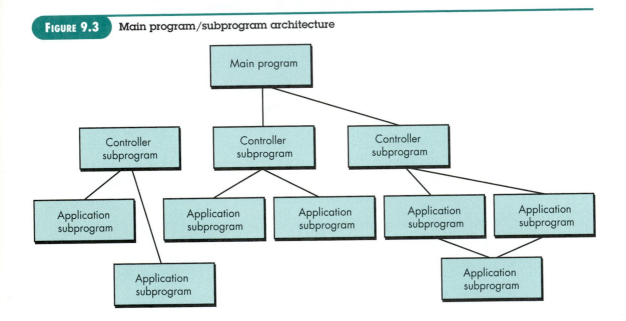

FIGURE 9.3   Main program/subprogram architecture

invokes a number of program components that in turn may invoke still other
components. Figure 9.3 illustrates an architecture of this type.

- *Remote procedure call architectures.* The components of a main
  program/subprogram architecture are distributed across multiple computers
  on a network.

Object-oriented architectures. The components of a system encapsulate data
and the operations that must be applied to manipulate the data. Communication and
coordination between components are accomplished via message passing.

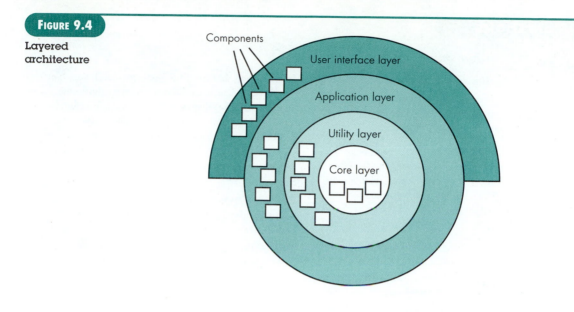

FIGURE 9.4

Layered architecture

Layered architectures. The basic structure of a layered architecture is illustrated in Figure 9.4. A number of different layers are defined, each accomplishing operations that progressively become closer to the machine instruction set. At the outer layer, components service user interface operations. At the inner layer, components perform operating system interfacing. Intermediate layers provide utility services and application software functions.

These architectural styles are only a small subset of those available.[2] Once requirements engineering uncovers the characteristics and constraints of the system to be built, the architectural style and/or combination of patterns that best fits those characteristics and constraints can be chosen. In many cases, more than one pattern might be appropriate and alternative architectural styles can be designed and evaluated. For example, a layered style (appropriate for most systems) can be combined with a data-centered architecture in many database applications.

9.3.2 Architectural Patterns

As the requirements model is developed, you'll notice that the software must address a number of broad problems that span the entire application. For example, the requirements model for virtually every e-commerce application is faced with the following problem: *How do we offer a broad array of goods to a broad array of customers and allow those customers to purchase our goods online?*

---

2   See [Bus07], [Gor06], [Roz05], [Bas03], [Bos00], or [Hof00] for a detailed discussion of architectural styles and patterns.

SafeHome

Choosing an Architectural Style

The scene: Jamie's cubicle, as design modeling begins.

The players: Jamie and Ed—members of the SafeHome software engineering team.

The conversation:

Ed (frowning): We've been modeling the security function using UML . . . you know classes, relationships, that sort of stuff. So I guess the object-oriented architecture[3] is the right way to go.

Jamie: But . . .?

Ed: But . . . I have trouble visualizing what an object-oriented architecture is. I get the call and return architecture, sort of a conventional process hierarchy, but OO . . . I don't know, it seems sort of amorphous.

Jamie (smiling): Amorphous, huh?

Ed: Yeah . . . what I mean is I can't visualize a real structure, just design classes floating in space.

Jamie: Well, that's not true. There are class hierarchies . . . think of the hierarchy (aggregation) we did for the **FloorPlan** object [Figure 8.3]. An OO architecture is a combination of that structure and the interconnections— you know, collaborations—between the classes. We can show it by fully describing the attributes and operations, the messaging that goes on, and the structure of the classes.

Ed: I'm going to spend an hour mapping out a call and return architecture; then I'll go back and consider an OO architecture.

Jamie: Doug'll have no problem with that. He said that we should consider architectural alternatives. By the way, there's absolutely no reason why both of these architectures couldn't be used in combination with one another.

Ed: Good. I'm on it.

The requirements model also defines a context in which this question must be answered. For example, an e-commerce business that sells golf equipment to consumers will operate in a different context than an e-commerce business that sells high-priced industrial equipment to medium and large corporations. In addition, a set of limitations and constraints may affect the way in which you address the problem to be solved.

Architectural patterns address an application-specific problem within a specific context and under a set of limitations and constraints. The pattern proposes an architectural solution that can serve as the basis for architectural design.

Earlier in this chapter, I noted that most applications fit within a specific domain or genre and that one or more architectural styles may be appropriate for that genre. For example, the overall architectural style for an application might be call-and-return or object-oriented. But within that style, you will encounter a set of common problems that might best be addressed with specific architectural patterns. Some of these problems and a more complete discussion of architectural patterns are presented in Chapter 12.

---

3   It can be argued that the *SafeHome* architecture should be considered at a higher level than the architecture noted. *SafeHome* has a variety of subsystems—home monitoring functionality, the company's monitoring site, and the subsystem running on the owner's PC. Within subsystems, concurrent processes (e.g., those monitoring sensors) and event handling are prevalent. Some architectural decisions at this level are made during product engineering, but architectural design within software engineering may very well have to consider these issues.

9.3.3   Organization and Refinement

Because the design process often leaves you with a number of architectural alternatives, it is important to establish a set of design criteria that can be used to assess an architectural design that is derived. The following questions [Bas03] provide insight into an architectural style:

How do I assess an architectural style that has been derived?

Control. How is control managed within the architecture? Does a distinct control hierarchy exist, and if so, what is the role of components within this control hierarchy? How do components transfer control within the system? How is control shared among components? What is the control topology (i.e., the geometric form that the control takes)? Is control synchronized or do components operate asynchronously?

Data. How are data communicated between components? Is the flow of data continuous, or are data objects passed to the system sporadically? What is the mode of data transfer (i.e., are data passed from one component to another or are data available globally to be shared among system components)? Do data components (e.g., a blackboard or repository) exist, and if so, what is their role? How do functional components interact with data components? Are data components passive or active (i.e., does the data component actively interact with other components in the system)? How do data and control interact within the system?

These questions provide the designer with an early assessment of design quality and lay the foundation for more detailed analysis of the architecture.

9.4   ARCHITECTURAL DESIGN

Quote:

"A doctor can bury his mistakes, but an architect can only advise his client to plant vines."

Frank Lloyd Wright

As architectural design begins, the software to be developed must be put into context—that is, the design should define the external entities (other systems, devices, people) that the software interacts with and the nature of the interaction. This information can generally be acquired from the requirements model and all other information gathered during requirements engineering. Once context is modeled and all external software interfaces have been described, you can identify a set of architectural archetypes. An *archetype* is an abstraction (similar to a class) that represents one element of system behavior. The set of archetypes provides a collection of abstractions that must be modeled architecturally if the system is to be constructed, but the archetypes themselves do not provide enough implementation detail. Therefore, the designer specifies the structure of the system by defining and refining software components that implement each archetype. This process continues iteratively until a complete architectural structure has been derived. In the sections that follow we examine each of these architectural design tasks in a bit more detail.

9.4.1   Representing the System in Context

At the architectural design level, a software architect uses an *architectural context diagram* (ACD) to model the manner in which software interacts with entities external to its boundaries. The generic structure of the architectural context diagram is illustrated in Figure 9.5.

Referring to the figure, systems that interoperate with the *target system* (the system for which an architectural design is to be developed) are represented as

- *Superordinate systems*—those systems that use the target system as part of some higher-level processing scheme.

- *Subordinate systems*—those systems that are used by the target system and provide data or processing that are necessary to complete target system functionality.

- *Peer-level systems*—those systems that interact on a peer-to-peer basis (i.e., information is either produced or consumed by the peers and the target system.

- *Actors*—entities (people, devices) that interact with the target system by producing or consuming information that is necessary for requisite processing.

Each of these external entities communicates with the target system through an interface (the small shaded rectangles).

To illustrate the use of the ACD, consider the home security function of the *SafeHome* product. The overall *SafeHome* product controller and the Internet-based system are both superordinate to the security function and are shown above the

? How do systems interoperate with one another?

FIGURE 9.5

Architectural context diagram
Source: Adapted from [Bos00].

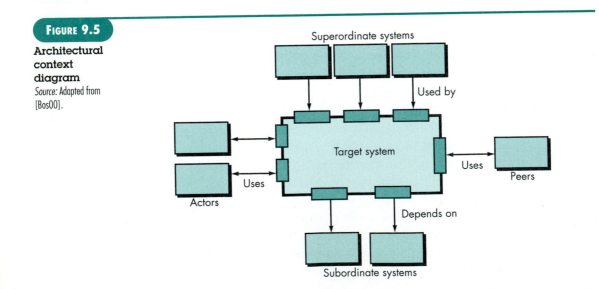

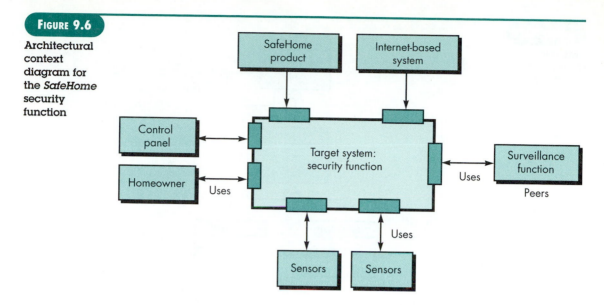

FIGURE 9.6

Architectural context diagram for the *SafeHome* security function

function in Figure 9.6. The surveillance function is a *peer system* and uses (is used by) the home security function in later versions of the product. The homeowner and control panels are actors that are both producers and consumers of information used/produced by the security software. Finally, sensors are used by the security software and are shown as subordinate to it.

As part of the architectural design, the details of each interface shown in Figure 9.6 would have to be specified. All data that flow into and out of the target system must be identified at this stage.

9.4.2   Defining Archetypes

Archetypes are the abstract building blocks of an architectural design.

An *archetype* is a class or pattern that represents a core abstraction that is critical to the design of an architecture for the target system. In general, a relatively small set of archetypes is required to design even relatively complex systems. The target system architecture is composed of these archetypes, which represent stable elements of the architecture but may be instantiated many different ways based on the behavior of the system.

In many cases, archetypes can be derived by examining the analysis classes defined as part of the requirements model. Continuing the discussion of the *SafeHome* home security function, you might define the following archetypes:

- **Node.** Represents a cohesive collection of input and output elements of the home security function. For example a node might be comprised of (1) various sensors and (2) a variety of alarm (output) indicators.

- **Detector.** An abstraction that encompasses all sensing equipment that feeds information into the target system.

FIGURE 9.7

UML relation-
ships for
SafeHome
security
function
archetypes
Source: Adapted from
[Bos00].

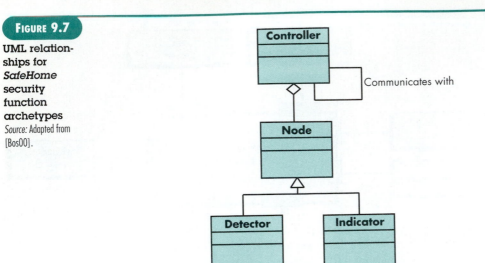

- **Indicator.** An abstraction that represents all mechanisms (e.g., alarm siren, flashing lights, bell) for indicating that an alarm condition is occurring.

- **Controller.** An abstraction that depicts the mechanism that allows the arming or disarming of a node. If controllers reside on a network, they have the ability to communicate with one another.

Each of these archetypes is depicted using UML notation as shown in Figure 9.7. Recall that the archetypes form the basis for the architecture but are abstractions that must be further refined as architectural design proceeds. For example, **Detector** might be refined into a class hierarchy of sensors.

9.4.3   Refining the Architecture into Components

As the software architecture is refined into components, the structure of the system begins to emerge. But how are these components chosen? In order to answer this question, you begin with the classes that were described as part of the requirements model.[4] These analysis classes represent entities within the application (business) domain that must be addressed within the software architecture. Hence, the application domain is one source for the derivation and refinement of components. Another source is the infrastructure domain. The architecture must accommodate many infrastructure components that enable application components but have no business connection to the application domain. For example, memory management components, communication components, database components, and task management components are often integrated into the software architecture.

---

4   If a conventional (non-object-oriented) approach is chosen, components are derived from the data flow model. I discuss this approach briefly in Section 9.6.

The interfaces depicted in the architecture context diagram (Section 9.4.1) imply one or more specialized components that process the data that flows across the interface. In some cases (e.g., a graphical user interface), a complete subsystem architecture with many components must be designed.

Continuing the *SafeHome* home security function example, you might define the set of top-level components that address the following functionality:

- *External communication management*—coordinates communication of the security function with external entities such as other Internet-based systems and external alarm notification.

- *Control panel processing*—manages all control panel functionality.

- *Detector management*—coordinates access to all detectors attached to the system.

- *Alarm processing*—verifies and acts on all alarm conditions.

Each of these top-level components would have to be elaborated iteratively and then positioned within the overall *SafeHome* architecture. Design classes (with appropriate attributes and operations) would be defined for each. It is important to note, however, that the design details of all attributes and operations would not be specified until component-level design (Chapter 10).

The overall architectural structure (represented as a UML component diagram) is illustrated in Figure 9.8. Transactions are acquired by *external communication management* as they move in from components that process the *SafeHome* GUI and the

FIGURE 9.8 Overall architectural structure for *SafeHome* with top-level components

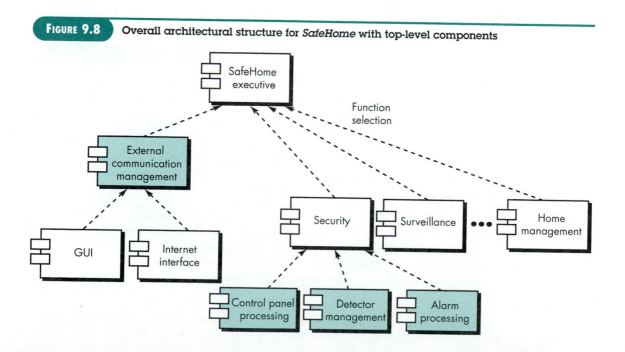

Internet interface. This information is managed by a *SafeHome* executive component that selects the appropriate product function (in this case security). The *control panel processing* component interacts with the homeowner to arm/disarm the security function. The *detector management* component polls sensors to detect an alarm condition, and the *alarm processing* component produces output when an alarm is detected.

9.4.4 Describing Instantiations of the System

The architectural design that has been modeled to this point is still relatively high level. The context of the system has been represented, archetypes that indicate the important abstractions within the problem domain have been defined, the overall structure of the system is apparent, and the major software components have been identified. However, further refinement (recall that all design is iterative) is still necessary.

To accomplish this, an actual instantiation of the architecture is developed. By this I mean that the architecture is applied to a specific problem with the intent of demonstrating that the structure and components are appropriate.

Figure 9.9 illustrates an instantiation of the *SafeHome* architecture for the security system. Components shown in Figure 9.8 are elaborated to show additional detail. For example, the *detector management* component interacts with a *scheduler* infrastructure component that implements polling of each *sensor* object used by the security system. Similar elaboration is performed for each of the components represented in Figure 9.8.

5   Tools noted here do not represent an endorsement, but rather a sampling of tools in this category. In most cases, tool names are trademarked by their respective developers.

FIGURE 9.9   **An instantiation of the security function with component elaboration**

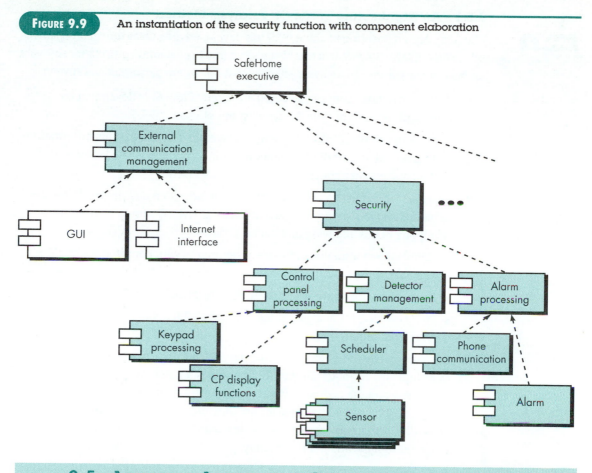

9.5   ASSESSING ALTERNATIVE ARCHITECTURAL DESIGNS

In their book on the evaluation of software architectures, Clements and his colleagues [Cle03] state:

> To put it bluntly, an architecture is a bet, a wager on the success of a system. Wouldn't it be nice to know in advance if you've placed your bet on a winner, as opposed to waiting until the system is mostly completed before knowing whether it will meet its requirements or not? If you're buying a system or paying for its development, wouldn't you like to have some assurance that it's started off down the right path? If you're the architect yourself, wouldn't you like to have a good way to validate your intuitions and experience, so that you can sleep at night knowing that the trust placed in your design is well founded?

Indeed, answers to these questions would have value. Design results in a number of architectural alternatives that are each assessed to determine which is the most appropriate for the problem to be solved. In the sections that follow, I present two different approaches for the assessment of alternative architectural designs. The first method uses an iterative method to assess design trade-offs. The second approach applies a pseudo-quantitative technique for assessing design quality.

9.5.1   An Architecture Trade-Off Analysis Method

The Software Engineering Institute (SEI) has developed an *architecture trade-off analysis method* (ATAM) [Kaz98] that establishes an iterative evaluation process for software architectures. The design analysis activities that follow are performed iteratively:

1. *Collect scenarios.* A set of use cases (Chapters 5 and 6) is developed to represent the system from the user's point of view.

2. *Elicit requirements, constraints, and environment description.* This information is determined as part of requirements engineering and is used to be certain that all stakeholder concerns have been addressed.

3. *Describe the architectural styles/patterns that have been chosen to address the scenarios and requirements.* The architectural style(s) should be described using one of the following architectural views:

   - *Module view* for analysis of work assignments with components and the degree to which information hiding has been achieved.

   - *Process view* for analysis of system performance.

   - *Data flow view* for analysis of the degree to which the architecture meets functional requirements.

4. *Evaluate quality attributes by considering each attribute in isolation.* The number of quality attributes chosen for analysis is a function of the time available for review and the degree to which quality attributes are relevant to the system at hand. Quality attributes for architectural design assessment include reliability, performance, security, maintainability, flexibility, testability, portability, reusability, and interoperability.

5. *Identify the sensitivity of quality attributes to various architectural attributes for a specific architectural style.* This can be accomplished by making small changes in the architecture and determining how sensitive a quality attribute, say performance, is to the change. Any attributes that are significantly affected by variation in the architecture are termed *sensitivity points.*

6. *Critique candidate architectures (developed in step 3) using the sensitivity analysis conducted in step 5.* The SEI describes this approach in the following manner [Kaz98]:

   > Once the architectural sensitivity points have been determined, finding trade-off points is simply the identification of architectural elements to which multiple attributes are sensitive. For example, the performance of a client-server architecture might be highly sensitive to the number of servers (performance increases, within some range, by increasing the number of servers). . . . The number of servers, then, is a trade-off point with respect to this architecture.

These six steps represent the first ATAM iteration. Based on the results of steps 5 and 6, some architecture alternatives may be eliminated, one or more of the remaining architectures may be modified and represented in more detail, and then the ATAM steps are reapplied.[6]

SafeHome

Architecture Assessment

The scene: Doug Miller's office as architectural design modeling proceeds.

The players: Vinod, Jamie, and Ed—members of the *SafeHome* software engineering team and Doug Miller, manager of the software engineering group.

The conversation:

Doug: I know you guys are deriving a couple of different architectures for the *SafeHome* product, and that's a good thing. I guess my question is, how are we going to choose the one that's best?

Ed: I'm working on a call and return style and then either Jamie or I are going to derive an OO architecture.

Doug: Okay, and how do we choose?

Jamie: I took a CS course in design in my senior year, and I remember that there are a number of ways to do it.

Vinod: There are, but they're a bit academic. Look, I think we can do our assessment and choose the right one using use cases and scenarios.

Doug: Isn't that the same thing?

Vinod: Not when you're talking about architectural assessment. We already have a complete set of use cases. So we apply each to both architectures and see how the system reacts, how components and connectors work in the use case context.

Ed: That's a good idea. Makes sure we didn't leave anything out.

Vinod: True, but it also tells us whether the architectural design is convoluted, whether the system has to twist itself into a pretzel to get the job done.

Jamie: Scenarios aren't just another name for use cases.

Vinod: No, in this case a scenario implies something different.

Doug: You're talking about a quality scenario or a change scenario, right?

Vinod: Yes. What we do is go back to the stakeholders and ask them how *SafeHome* is likely to change over the next, say, three years. You know, new versions, features, that sort of thing. We build a set of change scenarios. We also develop a set of quality scenarios that define the attributes we'd like to see in the software architecture.

Jamie: And we apply them to the alternatives.

Vinod: Exactly. The style that handles the use cases and scenarios best is the one we choose.

9.5.2 Architectural Complexity

A useful technique for assessing the overall complexity of a proposed architecture is to consider dependencies between components within the architecture. These dependencies are driven by information/control flow within the system. Zhao [Zha98] suggests three types of dependencies:

Sharing dependencies represent dependence relationships among consumers who use the same resource or producers who produce for the same consumers. For example, for two components u and v, if u and v refer to the same global data, then there exists a shared dependence relationship between u and v.

Flow dependencies represent dependence relationships between producers and consumers of resources. For example, for two components u and v, if u must complete before

---

6   The *Software Architecture Analysis Method* (SAAM) is an alternative to ATAM and is well-worth examining by those readers interested in architectural analysis. A paper on SAAM can be downloaded from www.sei.cmu.edu/publications/articles/saam-metho-propert-sas.html.

control flows into **v** (prerequisite), or if **u** communicates with **v** by parameters, then there exists a flow dependence relationship between **u** and **v.**

Constrained dependencies represent constraints on the relative flow of control among a set of activities. For example, for two components **u** and **v**, **u** and **v** cannot execute at the same time (mutual exclusion), then there exists a constrained dependence relationship between **u** and **v.**

The sharing and flow dependencies noted by Zhao are similar to the concept of coupling discussed in Chapter 8. Coupling is an important design concept that is applicable at the architectural level and at the component level. Simple metrics for evaluating coupling are discussed in Chapter 23.

9.5.3 Architectural Description Languages

The architect of a house has a set of standardized tools and notation that allow the design to be represented in an unambiguous, understandable fashion. Although the software architect can draw on UML notation, other diagrammatic forms, and a few related tools, there is a need for a more formal approach to the specification of an architectural design.

Architectural description language (ADL) provides a semantics and syntax for describing a software architecture. Hofmann and his colleagues [Hof01] suggest that an ADL should provide the designer with the ability to decompose architectural components, compose individual components into larger architectural blocks, and represent interfaces (connection mechanisms) between components. Once descriptive, language-based techniques for architectural design have been established, it is more likely that effective assessment methods for architectures will be established as the design evolves.

Architectural Description Languages

The following summary of a number of important ADLs was prepared by Rickard Land [Lan02] and is reprinted with the author's permission. It should be noted that the first five ADLs listed have been developed for research purposes and are not commercial products.

Rapide (http://poset.stanford.edu/rapide/) builds on the notion of partial ordered sets, and thus introduces quite new (but seemingly powerful) programming constructs.

UniCon (www.cs.cmu.edu/~UniCon) is "an architectural description language intended to aid designers in defining software architectures in terms of abstractions that they find useful."

Aesop (www.cs.cmu.edu/~able/aesop/) addresses the problem of style reuse. With Aesop, it is possible to define styles and use them when constructing an actual system.

Wright (www.cs.cmu.edu/~able/wright/) is a formal language including the following elements: *components* with *ports*, *connectors* with *roles*, and *glue* to attach roles to ports. Architectural styles can be formalized in the language with predicates, thus allowing for static checks to determine the consistency and completeness of an architecture.

Acme (www.cs.cmu.edu/~acme/) can be seen as a second-generation ADL, in that its intention is to identify a kind of least common denominator for ADLs.

UML (www.uml.org/) includes many of the artifacts needed for architectural descriptions—processes, nodes, views, etc. For informal descriptions, UML is well suited just because it is a widely understood standard. It, however, lacks the full strength needed for an adequate architectural description.

9.6 Architectural Mapping Using Data Flow

The architectural styles discussed in Section 9.3.1 represent radically different architectures. So it should come as no surprise that a comprehensive mapping that accomplishes the transition from the requirements model to a variety of architectural styles does not exist. In fact, there is no practical mapping for some architectural styles, and the designer must approach the translation of requirements to design for these styles in using the techniques discussed in Section 9.4.

To illustrate one approach to architectural mapping, consider the call and return architecture—an extremely common structure for many types of systems. The call and return architecture can reside within other more sophisticated architectures discussed earlier in this chapter. For example, the architecture of one or more components of a client-server architecture might be call and return.

A mapping technique, called *structured design* [You79], is often characterized as a data flow-oriented design method because it provides a convenient transition from a data flow diagram (Chapter 7) to software architecture.[7] The transition from information flow (represented as a DFD) to program structure is accomplished as part of a six-step process: (1) the type of information flow is established, (2) flow boundaries are indicated, (3) the DFD is mapped into the program structure, (4) control hierarchy is defined, (5) the resultant structure is refined using design measures and heuristics, and (6) the architectural description is refined and elaborated.

As a brief example of data flow mapping, I present a step-by-step "transform" mapping for a small part of the *SafeHome* security function.[8] In order to perform the mapping, the type of information flow must be determined. One type of information flow is called *transform flow* and exhibits a linear quality. Data flows into the system along an *incoming flow path* where it is transformed from an external world representation into internalized form. Once it has been internalized, it is processed at a *transform center*. Finally, it flows out of the system along an *outgoing flow path* that transforms the data into external world form.[9]

9.6.1 Transform Mapping

Transform mapping is a set of design steps that allows a DFD with transform flow characteristics to be mapped into a specific architectural style. To illustrate this approach, we again consider the *SafeHome* security function.[10] One element of the analysis model is a set of data flow diagrams that describe information flow within

---

7   It should be noted that other elements of the requirements model are also used during the mapping method.

8   A more detailed discussion of structured design is presented within the website that accompanies this book.

9   Another important type of information flow, *transaction flow,* is not considered in this example, but is addressed in the structured design example presented within the website that accompanies this book.

10 We consider only the portion of the *SafeHome* security function that uses the control panel. Other features discussed throughout this book are not considered here.

the security function. To map these data flow diagrams into a software architecture, you would initiate the following design steps:

Step 1. Review the fundamental system model.   The fundamental system model or context diagram depicts the security function as a single transformation, representing the external producers and consumers of data that flow into and out of the function. Figure 9.10 depicts a level 0 context model, and Figure 9.11 shows refined data flow for the security function.

FIGURE 9.10

Context-level DFD for the *SafeHome* security function

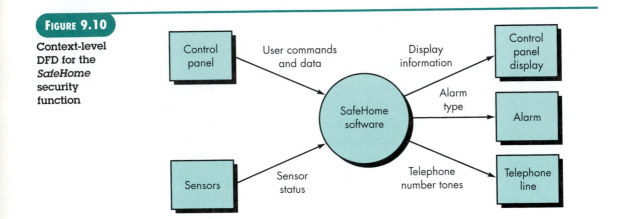

FIGURE 9.11

Level 1 DFD for the *SafeHome* security function

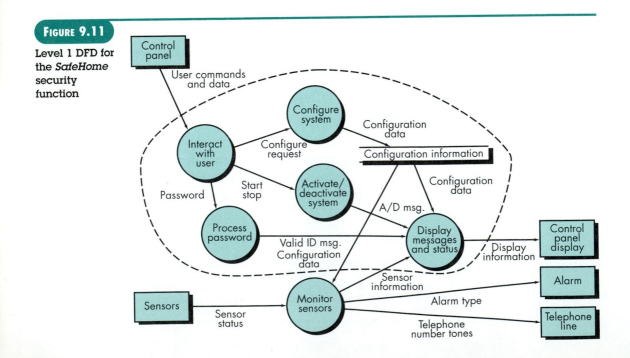

If the DFD is refined further at this time, strive to derive bubbles that exhibit high cohesion.

Step 2. Review and refine data flow diagrams for the software. Information obtained from the requirements model is refined to produce greater detail. For example, the level 2 DFD for *monitor sensors* (Figure 9.12) is examined, and a level 3 data flow diagram is derived as shown in Figure 9.13. At level 3, each transform in

FIGURE 9.12

Level 2 DFD that refines the *monitor sensors* transform

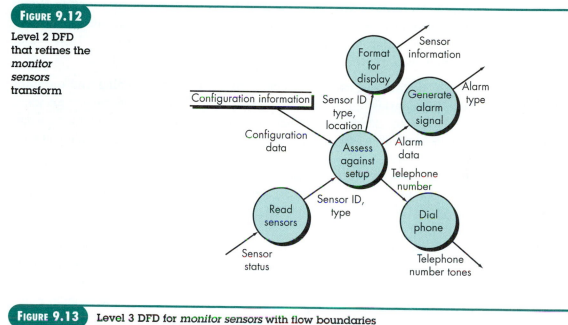

FIGURE 9.13 Level 3 DFD for *monitor sensors* with flow boundaries

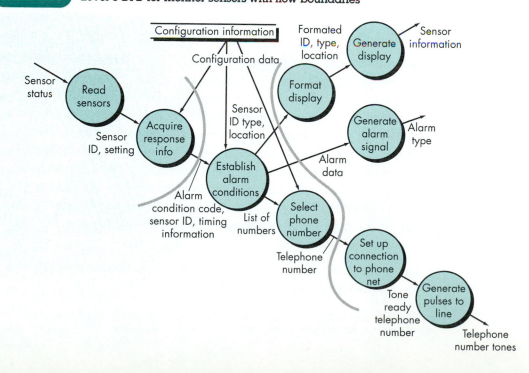

the data flow diagram exhibits relatively high cohesion (Chapter 8). That is, the process implied by a transform performs a single, distinct function that can be implemented as a component in the *SafeHome* software. Therefore, the DFD in Figure 9.13 contains sufficient detail for a "first cut" at the design of architecture for the *monitor sensors* subsystem, and we proceed without further refinement.

Step 3. Determine whether the DFD has transform or transaction flow[11] characteristics.   Evaluating the DFD (Figure 9.13), we see data entering the software along one incoming path and exiting along three outgoing paths. Therefore, an overall transform characteristic will be assumed for information flow.

Step 4. Isolate the transform center by specifying incoming and outgoing flow boundaries.   Incoming data flows along a path in which information is converted from external to internal form; outgoing flow converts internalized data to external form. Incoming and outgoing flow boundaries are open to interpretation. That is, different designers may select slightly different points in the flow as boundary locations. In fact, alternative design solutions can be derived by varying the placement of flow boundaries. Although care should be taken when boundaries are selected, a variance of one bubble along a flow path will generally have little impact on the final program structure.

Flow boundaries for the example are illustrated as shaded curves running vertically through the flow in Figure 9.13. The transforms (bubbles) that constitute the transform center lie within the two shaded boundaries that run from top to bottom in the figure. An argument can be made to readjust a boundary (e.g., an incoming flow boundary separating *read sensors* and *acquire response info* could be proposed). The emphasis in this design step should be on selecting reasonable boundaries, rather than lengthy iteration on placement of divisions.

Step 5. Perform "first-level factoring."   The program architecture derived using this mapping results in a top-down distribution of control. *Factoring* leads to a program structure in which top-level components perform decision making and low-level components perform most input, computation, and output work. Middle-level components perform some control and do moderate amounts of work.

When transform flow is encountered, a DFD is mapped to a specific structure (a call and return architecture) that provides control for incoming, transform, and outgoing information processing. This first-level factoring for the *monitor sensors* subsystem is illustrated in Figure 9.14. A main controller (called *monitor sensors executive*) resides at the top of the program structure and coordinates the following subordinate control functions:

- An incoming information processing controller, called *sensor input controller*, coordinates receipt of all incoming data.

---

11 In transaction flow, a single data item, called a *transaction,* causes the data flow to branch along one of a number of flow paths defined by the nature of the transaction.

FIGURE 9.14

First-level
factoring for
monitor
sensors

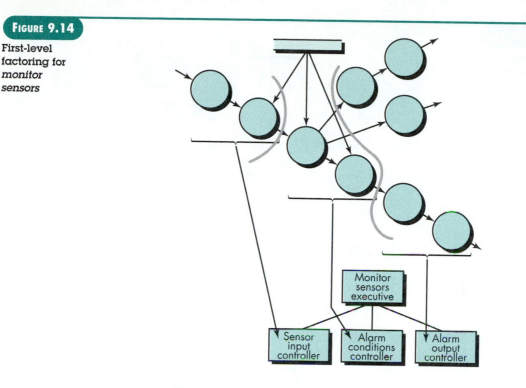

- A transform flow controller, called *alarm conditions controller*, supervises all operations on data in internalized form (e.g., a module that invokes various data transformation procedures).

- An outgoing information processing controller, called *alarm output controller*, coordinates production of output information.

Although a three-pronged structure is implied by Figure 9.14, complex flows in large systems may dictate two or more control modules for each of the generic control functions described previously. The number of modules at the first level should be limited to the minimum that can accomplish control functions and still maintain good functional independence characteristics.

Step 6. Perform "second-level factoring." Second-level factoring is accomplished by mapping individual transforms (bubbles) of a DFD into appropriate modules within the architecture. Beginning at the transform center boundary and moving outward along incoming and then outgoing paths, transforms are mapped into subordinate levels of the software structure. The general approach to second-level factoring is illustrated in Figure 9.15.

Although Figure 9.15 illustrates a one-to-one mapping between DFD transforms and software modules, different mappings frequently occur. Two or even three bubbles can be combined and represented as one component, or a single bubble may be expanded to two or more components. Practical considerations and measures

FIGURE 9.15

Second-level
factoring for
monitor
sensors

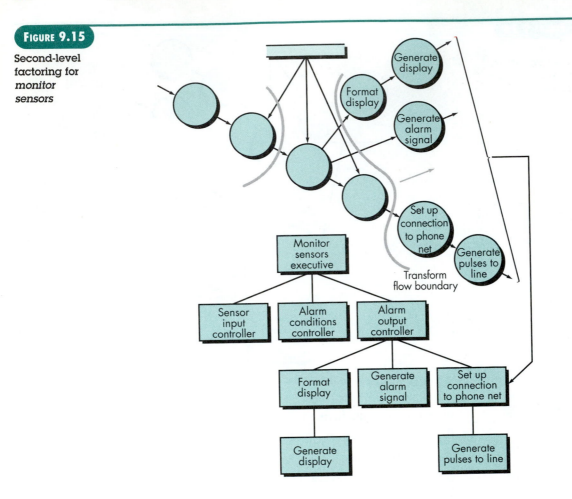

of design quality dictate the outcome of second-level factoring. Review and refinement may lead to changes in this structure, but it can serve as a "first-iteration" design.

Second-level factoring for incoming flow follows in the same manner. Factoring is again accomplished by moving outward from the transform center boundary on the incoming flow side. The transform center of *monitor sensors* subsystem software is mapped somewhat differently. Each of the data conversion or calculation transforms of the transform portion of the DFD is mapped into a module subordinate to the transform controller. A completed first-iteration architecture is shown in Figure 9.16.

The components mapped in the preceding manner and shown in Figure 9.16 represent an initial design of software architecture. Although components are named in a manner that implies function, a brief processing narrative (adapted from the process specification developed for a data transformation created during requirements modeling) should be written for each. The narrative describes the

ADVICE

Keep "worker" modules low in the program structure. This will lead to an architecture that is easier to maintain.

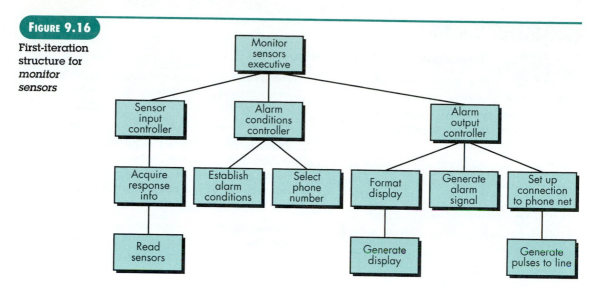

FIGURE 9.16

First-iteration
structure for
monitor
sensors

component interface, internal data structures, a functional narrative, and a brief
discussion of restrictions and special features (e.g., file input-output, hardware-
dependent characteristics, special timing requirements).

**Step 7. Refine the first-iteration architecture using design heuristics for
improved software quality.**   A first-iteration architecture can always be refined by
applying concepts of functional independence (Chapter 8). Components are exploded
or imploded to produce sensible factoring, separation of concerns, good cohesion,
minimal coupling, and most important, a structure that can be implemented without
difficulty, tested without confusion, and maintained without grief.

Refinements are dictated by the analysis and assessment methods described
briefly in Section 9.5, as well as practical considerations and common sense. There
are times, for example, when the controller for incoming data flow is totally unnecessary, when some input processing is required in a component that is subordinate to the transform controller, when high coupling due to global data cannot be
avoided, or when optimal structural characteristics cannot be achieved. Software
requirements coupled with human judgment is the final arbiter.

The objective of the preceding seven steps is to develop an architectural representation of software. That is, once structure is defined, we can evaluate and refine
software architecture by viewing it as a whole. Modifications made at this time
require little additional work, yet can have a profound impact on software quality.

You should pause for a moment and consider the difference between the design
approach described and the process of "writing programs." If code is the only representation of software, you and your colleagues will have great difficulty evaluating
or refining at a global or holistic level and will, in fact, have difficulty "seeing the
forest for the trees."

uote:

"Make it as simple
as possible. But no
simpler."

Albert Einstein

FIGURE 9.17

Refined program structure for *monitor sensors*

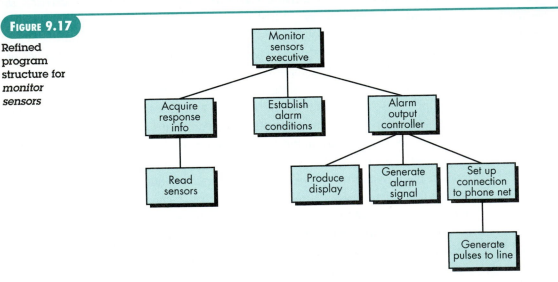

9.6.2   Refining the Architectural Design

Any discussion of design refinement should be prefaced with the following comment: "Remember that an 'optimal design' that doesn't work has questionable merit." You should be concerned with developing a representation of software that will meet all functional and performance requirements and merit acceptance based on design measures and heuristics.

? **What happens after the architecture has been created?**

Refinement of software architecture during early stages of design is to be encouraged. As I discussed earlier in this chapter, alternative architectural styles may be derived, refined, and evaluated for the "best" approach. This approach to optimization is one of the true benefits derived by developing a representation of software architecture.

It is important to note that structural simplicity often reflects both elegance and efficiency. Design refinement should strive for the smallest number of components that is consistent with effective modularity and the least complex data structure that adequately serves information requirements.

9.7 SUMMARY

Software architecture provides a holistic view of the system to be built. It depicts the structure and organization of software components, their properties, and the connections between them. Software components include program modules and the various data representations that are manipulated by the program. Therefore, data design is an integral part of the derivation of the software architecture. Architecture highlights early design decisions and provides a mechanism for considering the benefits of alternative system structures.

A number of different architectural styles and patterns are available to the software engineer and may be applied within a given architectural genre. Each style describes a system category that encompasses a set of components that perform a function required by a system; a set of connectors that enable communication, coordination, and cooperation among components; constraints that define how components can be integrated to form the system; and semantic models that enable a designer to understand the overall properties of a system.

In a general sense, architectural design is accomplished using four distinct steps. First, the system must be represented in context. That is, the designer should define the external entities that the software interacts with and the nature of the interaction. Once context has been specified, the designer should identify a set of top-level abstractions, called archetypes, that represent pivotal elements of the system's behavior or function. After abstractions have been defined, the design begins to move closer to the implementation domain. Components are identified and represented within the context of an architecture that supports them. Finally, specific instantiations of the architecture are developed to "prove" the design in a real-world context.

As a simple example of architectural design, the mapping method presented in this chapter uses data flow characteristics to derive a commonly used architectural style. A data flow diagram is mapped into program structure using a transform mapping approach. Transform mapping is applied to an information flow that exhibits distinct boundaries between incoming and outgoing data. The DFD is mapped into a structure that allocates control to input, processing, and output along three separately factored module hierarchies. Once an architecture has been derived, it is elaborated and then analyzed using quality criteria.

PROBLEMS AND POINTS TO PONDER

9.1. Using the architecture of a house or building as a metaphor, draw comparisons with software architecture. How are the disciplines of classical architecture and the software architecture similar? How do they differ?

9.2. Present two or three examples of applications for each of the architectural styles noted in Section 9.3.1.

9.3. Some of the architectural styles noted in Section 9.3.1 are hierarchical in nature and others are not. Make a list of each type. How would the architectural styles that are not hierarchical be implemented?

9.4. The terms *architectural style, architectural pattern,* and *framework* (not discussed in this book) are often encountered in discussions of software architecture. Do some research and describe how each of these terms differs from its counterparts.

9.5. Select an application with which you are familiar. Answer each of the questions posed for control and data in Section 9.3.3.

9.6. Research the ATAM (using [Kaz98]) and present a detailed discussion of the six steps presented in Section 9.5.1.

9.7. If you haven't done so, complete Problem 6.6. Use the design methods described in this chapter to develop a software architecture for the PHTRS.

9.8. Using a data flow diagram and a processing narrative, describe a computer-based system that has distinct transform flow characteristics. Define flow boundaries and map the DFD into a software architecture using the technique described in Section 9.6.1.

FURTHER READINGS AND INFORMATION SOURCES

The literature on software architecture has exploded over the past decade. Books by Gorton (*Essential Software Architecture,* Springer, 2006), Reekie and McAdam (*A Software Architecture Primer,* Angophora Press, 2006), Albin (*The Art of Software Architecture,* Wiley, 2003), and Bass and his colleagues (*Software Architecture in Practice,* 2d ed., Addison-Wesley, 2002) present worthwhile introductions to an intellectually challenging topic area.

Buschman and his colleagues (*Pattern-Oriented Software Architecture,* Wiley, 2007) and Kuchana (*Software Architecture Design Patterns in Java,* Auerbach, 2004) discuss pattern-oriented aspects of architectural design. Rozanski and Woods (*Software Systems Architecture,* Addison-Wesley, 2005), Fowler (*Patterns of Enterprise Application Architecture,* Addison-Wesley, 2003), Clements and his colleagues (*Documenting Software Architecture: View and Beyond,* Addison-Wesley, 2002), Bosch [Bos00], and Hofmeister and his colleagues [Hof00] provide in-depth treatments of software architecture.

Hennesey and Patterson (*Computer Architecture,* 4th ed., Morgan-Kaufmann, 2007) take a distinctly quantitative view of software architectural design issues. Clements and his colleagues (*Evaluating Software Architectures,* Addison-Wesley, 2002) consider the issues associated with the assessment of architectural alternatives and the selection of the best architecture for a given problem domain.

Implementation-specific books on architecture address architectural design within a specific development environment or technology. Marks and Bell (*Service-Oriented Architecture,* Wiley, 2006) discuss a design approach that links business and computational resources with the requirements defined by customers. Stahl and his colleagues (*Model-Driven Software Development,* Wiley, 2006) discuss architecture within the context of domain-specific modeling approaches. Radaideh and Al-ameed (*Architecture of Reliable Web Applications Software,* GI Global, 2007) consider architectures that are appropriate for WebApps. Clements and Northrop (*Software Product Lines: Practices and Patterns,* Addison-Wesley, 2001) address the design of architectures that support software product lines. Shanley (*Protected Mode Software Architecture,* Addison-Wesley, 1996) provides architectural design guidance for anyone designing PC-based real-time operating systems, multitask operating systems, or device drivers.

Current software architecture research is documented yearly in the *Proceedings of the International Workshop on Software Architecture,* sponsored by the ACM and other computing organizations, and the *Proceedings of the International Conference on Software Engineering.*

A wide variety of information sources on architectural design are available on the Internet. An up-to-date list of World Wide Web references that are relevant to architectural design can be found at the SEPA website: **www.mhhe.com/engcs/compsci/pressman/professional/olc/ser.htm**.

10

COMPONENT-LEVEL DESIGN

omponent-level design occurs after the first iteration of architectural design has been completed. At this stage, the overall data and program structure of the software has been established. The intent is to translate the design model into operational software. But the level of abstraction of the existing design model is relatively high, and the abstraction level of the operational program is low. The translation can be challenging, opening the door to the introduction of subtle errors that are difficult to find and correct in later stages of the software process. In a famous lecture, Edsgar Dijkstra, a major contributor to our understanding of software design, stated [Dij72]:

> Software seems to be different from many other products, where as a rule higher quality implies a higher price. Those who want really reliable software will discover that they must find a means of avoiding the majority of bugs to start with, and as a result,

QUICK LOOK

What is it? A complete set of software components is defined during architectural design. But the internal data structures and processing details of each component are not represented at a level of abstraction that is close to code. Component-level design defines the data structures, algorithms, interface characteristics, and communication mechanisms allocated to each software component.

Who does it? A software engineer performs component-level design.

Why is it important? You have to be able to determine whether the software will work before you build it. The component-level design represents the software in a way that allows you to review the details of the design for correctness and consistency with other design representations (i.e., the data, architectural, and interface designs). It provides a means for assessing whether data structures, interfaces, and algorithms will work.

What are the steps? Design representations of data, architecture, and interfaces form the foundation for component-level design. The class definition or processing narrative for each component is translated into a detailed design that makes use of diagrammatic or text-based forms that specify internal data structures, local interface detail, and processing logic. Design notation encompasses UML diagrams and supplementary forms. Procedural design is specified using a set of structured programming constructs. It is often possible to acquire existing reusable software components rather than building new ones.

What is the work product? The design for each component, represented in graphical, tabular, or text-based notation, is the primary work product produced during component-level design.

How do I ensure that I've done it right? A design review is conducted. The design is examined to determine whether data structures, interfaces, processing sequences, and logical conditions are correct and will produce the appropriate data or control transformation allocated to the component during earlier design steps.

the programming process will become cheaper . . . effective programmers . . . should not waste their time debugging—they should not introduce bugs to start with.

Although these words were spoken many years ago, they remain true today. As you translate the design model into source code, you should follow a set of design principles that not only perform the translation but also do not "introduce bugs to start with."

It is possible to represent the component-level design using a programming language. In essence, the program is created using the architectural design model as a guide. An alternative approach is to represent the component-level design using some intermediate (e.g., graphical, tabular, or text-based) representation that can be translated easily into source code. Regardless of the mechanism that is used to represent the component-level design, the data structures, interfaces, and algorithms defined should conform to a variety of well-established design guidelines that help you to avoid errors as the procedural design evolves. In this chapter, I examine these design guidelines and the methods available for achieving them.

10.1   WHAT IS A COMPONENT?

A *component* is a modular building block for computer software. More formally, the *OMG Unified Modeling Language Specification* [OMG03a] defines a component as ". . . a modular, deployable, and replaceable part of a system that encapsulates implementation and exposes a set of interfaces."

As we discussed in Chapter 9, components populate the software architecture and, as a consequence, play a role in achieving the objectives and requirements of the system to be built. Because components reside within the software architecture, they must communicate and collaborate with other components and with entities (e.g., other systems, devices, people) that exist outside the boundaries of the software.

The true meaning of the term *component* will differ depending on the point of view of the software engineer who uses it. In the sections that follow, I examine three important views of what a component is and how it is used as design modeling proceeds.

10.1.1   An Object-Oriented View

KEY POINT

From an object-oriented viewpoint, a component is a set of collaborating classes.

In the context of object-oriented software engineering, a component contains a set of collaborating classes.[1] Each class within a component has been fully elaborated to include all attributes and operations that are relevant to its implementation. As part of the design elaboration, all interfaces that enable the classes to communicate and collaborate with other design classes must also be defined. To accomplish this, you begin with the requirements model and elaborate analysis classes (for components that relate to the problem domain) and infrastructure classes (for components that provide support services for the problem domain).

---

1   In some cases, a component may contain a single class.

FIGURE 10.1

Elaboration of
a design
component

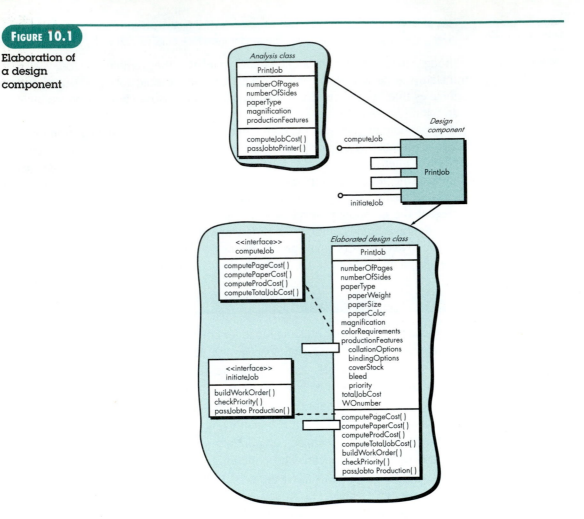

To illustrate this process of design elaboration, consider software to be built for a sophisticated print shop. The overall intent of the software is to collect the customer's requirements at the front counter, cost a print job, and then pass the job on to an automated production facility. During requirements engineering, an analysis class called **PrintJob** was derived. The attributes and operations defined during analysis are noted at the top of Figure 10.1. During architectural design, **PrintJob** is defined as a component within the software architecture and is represented using the shorthand UML notation[2] shown in the middle right of the figure. Note that **PrintJob** has two interfaces, *computeJob*, which provides job costing capability, and *initiateJob*, which passes the job along to the production facility. These are represented using the "lollipop" symbols shown to the left of the component box.

---

2 Readers who are unfamiliar with UML notation should refer to Appendix 1.

Component-level design begins at this point. The details of the component **PrintJob** must be elaborated to provide sufficient information to guide implementation. The original analysis class is elaborated to flesh out all attributes and operations required to implement the class as the component **PrintJob.** Referring to the lower right portion of Figure 10.1, the elaborated design class **PrintJob** contains more detailed attribute information as well as an expanded description of operations required to implement the component. The interfaces *computeJob* and *initiateJob* imply communication and collaboration with other components (not shown here). For example, the operation *computePageCost()* (part of the *computeJob* interface) might collaborate with a **PricingTable** component that contains job pricing information. The *checkPriority()* operation (part of the *initiateJob* interface) might collaborate with a **JobQueue** component to determine the types and priorities of jobs currently awaiting production.

This elaboration activity is applied to every component defined as part of the architectural design. Once it is completed, further elaboration is applied to each attribute, operation, and interface. The data structures appropriate for each attribute must be specified. In addition, the algorithmic detail required to implement the processing logic associated with each operation is designed. This procedural design activity is discussed later in this chapter. Finally, the mechanisms required to implement the interface are designed. For object-oriented software, this may encompass the description of all messaging that is required to effect communication between objects within the system.

10.1.2   The Traditional View

In the context of traditional software engineering, a component is a functional element of a program that incorporates processing logic, the internal data structures that are required to implement the processing logic, and an interface that enables the component to be invoked and data to be passed to it. A traditional component, also called a *module,* resides within the software architecture and serves one of three important roles: (1) a *control component* that coordinates the invocation of all other problem domain components, (2) a *problem domain component* that implements a complete or partial function that is required by the customer, or (3) an *infrastructure component* that is responsible for functions that support the processing required in the problem domain.

Like object-oriented components, traditional software components are derived from the analysis model. In this case, however, the data flow-oriented element of the analysis model serves as the basis for the derivation. Each transform (bubble) represented at the lowest levels of the data flow diagram is mapped (Section 9.6) into a module hierarchy. Control components (modules) reside near the top of the hierarchy (program architecture), and problem domain components tend to reside toward the bottom of the hierarchy. To achieve effective modularity, design concepts like functional independence (Chapter 8) are applied as components are elaborated.

To illustrate this process of design elaboration for traditional components, again consider software to be built for a sophisticated print shop. A set of data flow diagrams

FIGURE 10.2

Structure chart for a traditional system

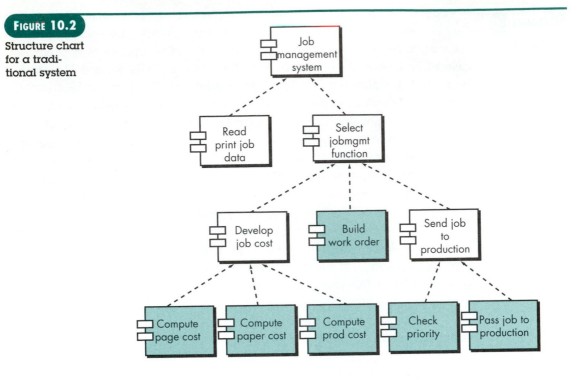

would be derived during requirements modeling. Assume that these are mapped into an architecture shown in Figure 10.2. Each box represents a software component. Note that the shaded boxes are equivalent in function to the operations defined for the **PrintJob** class discussed in Section 10.1.1. In this case, however, each operation is represented as a separate module that is invoked as shown in the figure. Other modules are used to control processing and are therefore control components.

During component-level design, each module in Figure 10.2 is elaborated. The module interface is defined explicitly. That is, each data or control object that flows across the interface is represented. The data structures that are used internal to the module are defined. The algorithm that allows the module to accomplish its intended function is designed using the stepwise refinement approach discussed in Chapter 8. The behavior of the module is sometimes represented using a state diagram.

To illustrate this process, consider the module *ComputePageCost*. The intent of this module is to compute the printing cost per page based on specifications provided by the customer. Data required to perform this function are: **number of pages in the document, total number of documents to be produced, one- or two-side printing, color requirements**, and **size requirements.** These data are passed to *ComputePageCost* via the module's interface. *ComputePageCost* uses these data to determine a page cost that is based on the size and complexity of the job—a function of all data passed to the module via the interface. Page cost is inversely proportional to the size of the job and directly proportional to the complexity of the job.

As the design for each software component is elaborated, the focus shifts to the design of specific data structures and procedural design to manipulate the data structures. However, don't forget the architecture that must house the components or the global data structures that may serve many components.

FIGURE 10.3   Component-level design for *ComputePageCost*

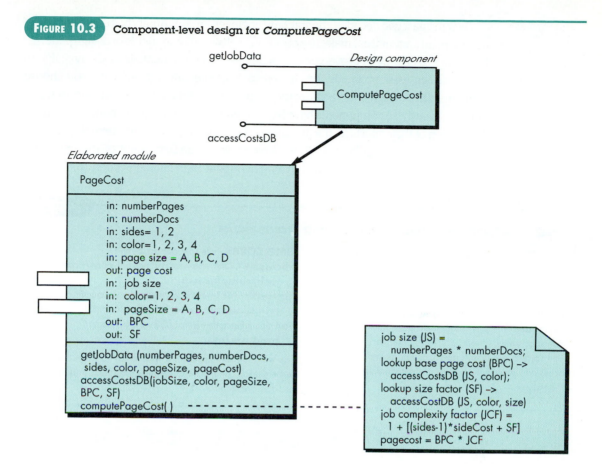

Figure 10.3 represents the component-level design using a modified UML notation. The *ComputePageCost* module accesses data by invoking the module *getJobData*, which allows all relevant data to be passed to the component, and a database interface, *accessCostsDB*, which enables the module to access a database that contains all printing costs. As design continues, the *ComputePageCost* module is elaborated to provide algorithm detail and interface detail (Figure 10.3). Algorithm detail can be represented using the pseudocode text shown in the figure or with a UML activity diagram. The interfaces are represented as a collection of input and output data objects or items. Design elaboration continues until sufficient detail is provided to guide construction of the component.

10.1.3   A Process-Related View

The object-oriented and traditional views of component-level design presented in Sections 10.1.1 and 10.1.2 assume that the component is being designed from scratch. That is, you have to create a new component based on specifications derived from the requirements model. There is, of course, another approach.

Over the past two decades, the software engineering community has emphasized the need to build systems that make use of existing software components or design patterns. In essence, a catalog of proven design or code-level components is made available to you as design work proceeds. As the software architecture is developed, you choose components or design patterns from the catalog and use them to populate the architecture. Because these components have been created with reusability in mind, a complete description of their interface, the function(s) they perform, and the communication and collaboration they require are all available to you. I discuss some of the important aspects of component-based software engineering (CBSE) later in Section 10.6.

10.2   DESIGNING CLASS-BASED COMPONENTS

As I have already noted, component-level design draws on information developed as part of the requirements model (Chapters 6 and 7) and represented as part of the architectural model (Chapter 9). When an object-oriented software engineering approach is chosen, component-level design focuses on the elaboration of problem domain specific classes and the definition and refinement of infrastructure classes contained in the requirements model. The detailed description of the attributes, operations, and interfaces used by these classes is the design detail required as a precursor to the construction activity.

10.2.1   Basic Design Principles

Four basic design principles are applicable to component-level design and have been widely adopted when object-oriented software engineering is applied. The underlying motivation for the application of these principles is to create designs that are more amenable to change and to reduce the propagation of side effects when changes do occur. You can use these principles as a guide as each software component is developed.

The Open-Closed Principle (OCP). *"A module [component] should be open for extension but closed for modification"* [Mar00]. This statement seems to be a

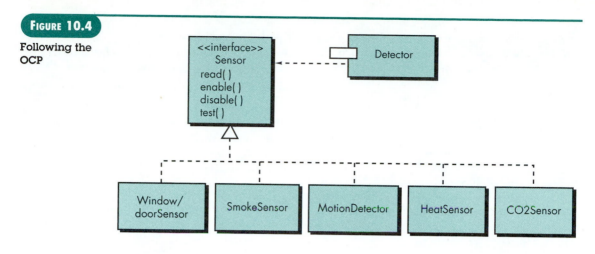

FIGURE 10.4

Following the OCP

contradiction, but it represents one of the most important characteristics of a good component-level design. Stated simply, you should specify the component in a way that allows it to be extended (within the functional domain that it addresses) without the need to make internal (code or logic-level) modifications to the component itself. To accomplish this, you create abstractions that serve as a buffer between the functionality that is likely to be extended and the design class itself.

For example, assume that the *SafeHome* security function makes use of a **Detector** class that must check the status of each type of security sensor. It is likely that as time passes, the number and types of security sensors will grow. If internal processing logic is implemented as a sequence of if-then-else constructs, each addressing a different sensor type, the addition of a new sensor type will require additional internal processing logic (still another if-then-else). This is a violation of OCP.

One way to accomplish OCP for the **Detector** class is illustrated in Figure 10.4. The *sensor* interface presents a consistent view of sensors to the detector component. If a new type of sensor is added no change is required for the **Detector** class (component). The OCP is preserved.

SAFEHOME

The OCP in Action

The scene: Vinod's cubicle.

The players: Vinod and Shakira—members of the *SafeHome* software engineering team.

The conversation:

Vinod: I just got a call from Doug [the team manager]. He says marketing wants to add a new sensor.

Shakira (smirking): Not again, jeez!

Vinod: Yeah . . . and you're not going to believe what these guys have come up with.

Shakira: Amaze me.

Vinod (laughing): They call it a doggie angst sensor.

Shakira: Say what?

Vinod: It's for people who leave their pets home in apartments or condos or houses that are close to one another. The dog starts to bark. The neighbor gets angry and complains. With this sensor, if the dog barks for more than, say, a minute, the sensor sets a special alarm mode that calls the owner on his or her cell phone.

Shakira: You're kidding me, right?

Vinod: Nope. Doug wants to know how much time it's going to take to add it to the security function.

Shakira (thinking a moment): Not much . . . look. [She shows Vinod Figure 10.4] We've isolated the actual sensor classes behind the **sensor** interface. As long as we have specs for the doggie sensor, adding it should be a piece of cake. Only thing I'll have to do is create an appropriate component . . . uh, class, for it. No change to the **Detector** component at all.

Vinod: So I'll tell Doug it's no big deal.

Shakira: Knowing Doug, he'll keep us focused and not deliver the doggie thing until the next release.

Vinod: That's not a bad thing, but you can implement now if he wants you to?

Shakira: Yeah, the way we designed the interface lets me do it with no hassle.

Vinod (thinking a moment): Have you ever heard of the open-closed principle?

Shakira (shrugging): Never heard of it.

Vinod (smiling): Not a problem.

The Liskov Substitution Principle (LSP). *"Subclasses should be substitutable for their base classes"* [Mar00]. This design principle, originally proposed by Barbara Liskov [Lis88], suggests that a component that uses a base class should continue to function properly if a class derived from the base class is passed to the component instead. LSP demands that any class derived from a base class must honor any implied contract between the base class and the components that use it. In the context of this discussion, a "contract" is a *precondition* that must be true before the component uses a base class and a *postcondition* that should be true after the component uses a base class. When you create derived classes, be sure they conform to the pre- and postconditions.

If you dispense with design and hack out code, just remember that code is the ultimate "concretion." You're violating DIP.

Dependency Inversion Principle (DIP). *"Depend on abstractions. Do not depend on concretions"* [Mar00]. As we have seen in the discussion of the OCP, abstractions are the place where a design can be extended without great complication. The more a component depends on other concrete components (rather than on abstractions such as an interface), the more difficult it will be to extend.

The Interface Segregation Principle (ISP). *"Many client-specific interfaces are better than one general purpose interface"* [Mar00]. There are many instances in which multiple client components use the operations provided by a server class. ISP suggests that you should create a specialized interface to serve each major category of clients. Only those operations that are relevant to a particular category of clients should be specified in the interface for that client. If multiple clients require the same operations, it should be specified in each of the specialized interfaces.

As an example, consider the **FloorPlan** class that is used for the *SafeHome* security and surveillance functions (Chapter 6). For the security functions, **FloorPlan** is used only during configuration activities and uses the operations *placeDevice()*, *showDevice()*, *groupDevice()*, and *removeDevice()* to place, show, group, and remove sensors from the floor plan. The *SafeHome* surveillance function uses the four operations noted for security, but also requires special operations to manage cameras: *showFOV()* and *showDeviceID()*. Hence, the ISP suggests that client components from the two *SafeHome* functions have specialized interfaces defined for them. The interface for security would encompass only the operations *placeDevice()*, *showDevice()*, *groupDevice()*, and *removeDevice()*. The interface for surveillance would incorporate the operations *placeDevice()*, *showDevice()*, *groupDevice()*, and *removeDevice()*, along with *showFOV()* and *showDeviceID()*.

Although component-level design principles provide useful guidance, components themselves do not exist in a vacuum. In many cases, individual components or classes are organized into subsystems or packages. It is reasonable to ask how this packaging activity should occur. Exactly how should components be organized as the design proceeds? Martin [Mar00] suggests additional packaging principles that are applicable to component-level design:

The Release Reuse Equivalency Principle (REP). *"The granule of reuse is the granule of release"* [Mar00]. When classes or components are designed for reuse, there is an implicit contract that is established between the developer of the reusable entity and the people who will use it. The developer commits to establish a release control system that supports and maintains older versions of the entity while the users slowly upgrade to the most current version. Rather than addressing each class individually, it is often advisable to group reusable classes into packages that can be managed and controlled as newer versions evolve.

The Common Closure Principle (CCP). *"Classes that change together belong together."* [Mar00]. Classes should be packaged cohesively. That is, when classes are packaged as part of a design, they should address the same functional or behavioral area. When some characteristic of that area must change, it is likely that only those classes within the package will require modification. This leads to more effective change control and release management.

The Common Reuse Principle (CRP). *"Classes that aren't reused together should not be grouped together"* [Mar00]. When one or more classes within a package changes, the release number of the package changes. All other classes or packages that rely on the package that has been changed must now update to the most recent release of the package and be tested to ensure that the new release operates without incident. If classes are not grouped cohesively, it is possible that a class with no relationship to other classes within a package is changed. This will precipitate unnecessary integration and testing. For this reason, only classes that are reused together should be included within a package.

10.2.2   Component-Level Design Guidelines

In addition to the principles discussed in Section 10.2.1, a set of pragmatic design guidelines can be applied as component-level design proceeds. These guidelines apply to components, their interfaces, and the dependencies and inheritance characteristics that have an impact on the resultant design. Ambler [Amb02b] suggests the following guidelines:

? **What should we consider when we name components?**

Components.   Naming conventions should be established for components that are specified as part of the architectural model and then refined and elaborated as part of the component-level model. Architectural component names should be drawn from the problem domain and should have meaning to all stakeholders who view the architectural model. For example, the class name **FloorPlan** is meaningful to everyone reading it regardless of technical background. On the other hand, infrastructure components or elaborated component-level classes should be named to reflect implementation-specific meaning. If a linked list is to be managed as part of the **FloorPlan** implementation, the operation *manageList()* is appropriate, even if a nontechnical person might misinterpret it.[3]

You can choose to use stereotypes to help identify the nature of components at the detailed design level. For example, <<infrastructure>> might be used to identify an infrastructure component, <<database>> could be used to identify a database that services one or more design classes or the entire system; <<table>> can be used to identify a table within a database.

Interfaces.   Interfaces provide important information about communication and collaboration (as well as helping us to achieve the OCP). However, unfettered representation of interfaces tends to complicate component diagrams. Ambler [Amb02c] recommends that (1) lollipop representation of an interface should be used in lieu of the more formal UML box and dashed arrow approach, when diagrams grow complex; (2) for consistency, interfaces should flow from the left-hand side of the component box; (3) only those interfaces that are relevant to the component under consideration should be shown, even if other interfaces are available. These recommendations are intended to simplify the visual nature of UML component diagrams.

Dependencies and Inheritance.   For improved readability, it is a good idea to model dependencies from left to right and inheritance from bottom (derived classes) to top (base classes). In addition, component interdependencies should be represented via interfaces, rather than by representation of a component-to-component dependency. Following the philosophy of the OCP, this will help to make the system more maintainable.

10.2.3 Cohesion

In Chapter 8, I described cohesion as the "single-mindedness" of a component. Within the context of component-level design for object-oriented systems, *cohesion*

---

3 It is unlikely that someone from marketing or the customer organization (a nontechnical type) would examine detailed design information.

FIGURE 10.5

Layer cohesion

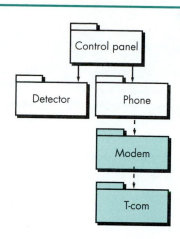

implies that a component or class encapsulates only attributes and operations that are closely related to one another and to the class or component itself. Lethbridge and Laganiére [Let01] define a number of different types of cohesion (listed in order of the level of the cohesion[4]):

Functional. Exhibited primarily by operations, this level of cohesion occurs when a component performs a targeted computation and then returns a result.

Although an understanding of the various levels of cohesion is instructive, it is more important to be aware of the general concept as you design components. Keep cohesion as high as is possible.

Layer. Exhibited by packages, components, and classes, this type of cohesion occurs when a higher layer accesses the services of a lower layer, but lower layers do not access higher layers. Consider, for example, the *SafeHome* security function requirement to make an outgoing phone call if an alarm is sensed. It might be possible to define a set of layered packages as shown in Figure 10.5. The shaded packages contain infrastructure components. Access is from the control panel package downward.

Communicational. All operations that access the same data are defined within one class. In general, such classes focus solely on the data in question, accessing and storing it.

Classes and components that exhibit functional, layer, and communicational cohesion are relatively easy to implement, test, and maintain. You should strive to achieve these levels of cohesion whenever possible. It is important to note, however, that pragmatic design and implementation issues sometimes force you to opt for lower levels of cohesion.

---

4   In general, the higher the level of cohesion, the easier the component is to implement, test, and maintain.)

SafeHome

Cohesion in Action

The scene: Jamie's cubicle.

The players: Jamie and Ed—members of the *SafeHome* software engineering team who are working on the surveillance function.

The conversation:

Ed: I have a first-cut design of the **camera** component.

Jamie: Wanna do a quick review?

Ed: I guess . . . but really, I'd like your input on something.

(Jamie gestures for him to continue.)

Ed: We originally defined five operations for **camera**. Look . . .

  determineType() tells me the type of camera.

  translateLocation() allows me to move the camera around the floor plan.

  displayID() gets the camera ID and displays it near the camera icon.

  displayView() shows me the field of view of the camera graphically.

  displayZoom() shows me the magnification of the camera graphically.

Ed: I've designed each separately, and they're pretty simple operations. So I thought it might be a good idea to combine all of the display operations into just one that's called *displayCamera()*—it'll show the ID, the view, and the zoom. Whaddaya think?

Jamie (grimacing): Not sure that's such a good idea.

Ed (frowning): Why, all of these little ops can cause headaches.

Jamie: The problem with combining them is we lose cohesion, you know, the *displayCamera()* op won't be single-minded.

Ed (mildly exasperated): So what? The whole thing will be less than 100 source lines, max. It'll be easier to implement, I think.

Jamie: And what if marketing decides to change the way that we represent the view field?

Ed: I just jump into the *displayCamera()* op and make the mod.

Jamie: What about side effects?

Ed: Whaddaya mean?

Jamie: Well, say you make the change but inadvertently create a problem with the ID display.

Ed: I wouldn't be that sloppy.

Jamie: Maybe not, but what if some support person two years from now has to make the mod. He might not understand the op as well as you do, and, who knows, he might be sloppy.

Ed: So you're against it?

Jamie: You're the designer . . . it's your decision . . . just be sure you understand the consequences of low cohesion.

Ed (thinking a moment): Maybe we'll go with separate display ops.

Jamie: Good decision.

10.2.4 Coupling

In earlier discussions of analysis and design, I noted that communication and collaboration are essential elements of any object-oriented system. There is, however, a darker side to this important (and necessary) characteristic. As the amount of communication and collaboration increases (i.e., as the degree of "connectedness" between classes increases), the complexity of the system also increases. And as complexity increases, the difficulty of implementing, testing, and maintaining software grows.

Coupling is a qualitative measure of the degree to which classes are connected to one another. As classes (and components) become more interdependent, coupling increases. An important objective in component-level design is to keep coupling as low as is possible.

Class coupling can manifest itself in a variety of ways. Lethbridge and Laganiére [Let01] define the following coupling categories:

Content coupling. Occurs when one component "surreptitiously modifies data that is internal to another component" [Let01]. This violates information hiding—a basic design concept.

Common coupling. Occurs when a number of components all make use of a global variable. Although this is sometimes necessary (e.g., for establishing default values that are applicable throughout an application), common coupling can lead to uncontrolled error propagation and unforeseen side effects when changes are made.

Control coupling. Occurs when operation *A()* invokes operation *B()* and passes a control flag to *B*. The control flag then "directs" logical flow within *B*. The problem with this form of coupling is that an unrelated change in *B* can result in the necessity to change the meaning of the control flag that *A* passes. If this is overlooked, an error will result.

Stamp coupling. Occurs when **ClassB** is declared as a type for an argument of an operation of **ClassA**. Because **ClassB** is now a part of the definition of **ClassA**, modifying the system becomes more complex.

Data coupling. Occurs when operations pass long strings of data arguments. The "bandwidth" of communication between classes and components grows and the complexity of the interface increases. Testing and maintenance are more difficult.

Routine call coupling. Occurs when one operation invokes another. This level of coupling is common and is often quite necessary. However, it does increase the connectedness of a system.

Type use coupling. Occurs when component **A** uses a data type defined in component **B** (e.g., this occurs whenever "a class declares an instance variable or a local variable as having another class for its type" [Let01]). If the type definition changes, every component that uses the definition must also change.

Inclusion or import coupling. Occurs when component **A** imports or includes a package or the content of component **B**.

External coupling. Occurs when a component communicates or collaborates with infrastructure components (e.g., operating system functions, database capability, telecommunication functions). Although this type of coupling is necessary, it should be limited to a small number of components or classes within a system.

Software must communicate internally and externally. Therefore, coupling is a fact of life. However, the designer should work to reduce coupling whenever possible and understand the ramifications of high coupling when it cannot be avoided.

SafeHome

Coupling in Action

The scene: Shakira's cubicle.

The players: Vinod and Shakira—members of the *SafeHome* software team who are working on the security function.

The conversation:

Shakira: I had what I thought was a great idea . . . then I thought about it a little, and it seemed like a not so great idea. I finally rejected it, but I just thought I'd run it by you.

Vinod: Sure. What's the idea?

Shakira: Well, each of the sensors recognizes an alarm condition of some kind, right?

Vinod (smiling): That's why we call them sensors, Shakira.

Shakira (exasperated): Sarcasm, Vinod, you've got to work on your interpersonal skills.

Vinod: You were saying?

Shakira: Okay, anyway, I figured . . . why not create an operation within each sensor object called *makeCall()* that

would collaborate directly with the **OutgoingCall** component, well, with an interface to the **OutgoingCall** component.

Vinod (pensive): You mean rather than having that collaboration occur out of a component like **ControlPanel** or something?

Shakira: Yeah . . . but then I said to myself, that means that every sensor object will be connected to the **OutgoingCall** component, and that means that its indirectly coupled to the outside world and . . . well, I just thought it made things complicated.

Vinod: I agree. In this case, it's a better idea to let the sensor interface pass info to the **ControlPanel** and let it initiate the outgoing call. Besides, different sensors might result in different phone numbers. You don't want the senor to store that information because if it changes . . .

Shakira: It just didn't feel right.

Vinod: Design heuristics for coupling tell us it's not right.

Shakira: Whatever . . .

10.3   CONDUCTING COMPONENT-LEVEL DESIGN

Quote:

"If I had more time, I would have written a shorter letter."

Blaise Pascal

If you're working in a non-OO environment, the first three steps focus on refinement of data objects and processing functions (transforms) identified as part of the requirements model.

Earlier in this chapter I noted that component-level design is elaborative in nature. You must transform information from requirements and architectural models into a design representation that provides sufficient detail to guide the construction (coding and testing) activity. The following steps represent a typical task set for component-level design, when it is applied for an object-oriented system.

Step 1. Identify all design classes that correspond to the problem domain. Using the requirements and architectural model, each analysis class and architectural component is elaborated as described in Section 10.1.1.

Step 2. Identify all design classes that correspond to the infrastructure domain.   These classes are not described in the requirements model and are often missing from the architecture model, but they must be described at this point. As we have noted earlier, classes and components in this category include GUI components (often available as reusable components), operating system components, and object and data management components.

Step 3. Elaborate all design classes that are not acquired as reusable components.   Elaboration requires that all interfaces, attributes, and operations

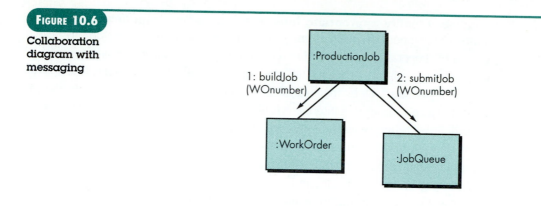

FIGURE 10.6

Collaboration
diagram with
messaging

necessary to implement the class be described in detail. Design heuristics (e.g., component cohesion and coupling) must be considered as this task is conducted.

Step 3a. Specify message details when classes or components collaborate.

The requirements model makes use of a collaboration diagram to show how analysis classes collaborate with one another. As component-level design proceeds, it is sometimes useful to show the details of these collaborations by specifying the structure of messages that are passed between objects within a system. Although this design activity is optional, it can be used as a precursor to the specification of interfaces that show how components within the system communicate and collaborate.

Figure 10.6 illustrates a simple collaboration diagram for the printing system discussed earlier. Three objects, **ProductionJob, WorkOrder,** and **JobQueue,** collaborate to prepare a print job for submission to the production stream. Messages are passed between objects as illustrated by the arrows in the figure. During requirements modeling the messages are specified as shown in the figure. However, as design proceeds, each message is elaborated by expanding its syntax in the following manner [Ben02]:

> [guard condition] sequence expression (return value) :=
> message name (argument list)

where a **[guard condition]** is written in Object Constraint Language (OCL)[5] and specifies any set of conditions that must be met before the message can be sent; **sequence expression** is an integer value (or other ordering indicator, e.g., 3.1.2) that indicates the sequential order in which a message is sent; **(return value)** is the name of the information that is returned by the operation invoked by the message; **message name** identifies the operation that is to be invoked, and **(argument list)** is the list of attributes that are passed to the operation.

---

5   OCL is discussed briefly in Appendix 1.

Step 3b. Identify appropriate interfaces for each component. Within the context of component-level design, a UML interface is "a group of externally visible (i.e., public) operations. The interface contains no internal structure, it has no attributes, no associations . . ." [Ben02]. Stated more formally, an interface is the equivalent of an abstract class that provides a controlled connection between design classes. The elaboration of interfaces is illustrated in Figure 10.1. In essence, operations defined for the design class are categorized into one or more abstract classes. Every operation within the abstract class (the interface) should be cohesive; that is, it should exhibit processing that focuses on one limited function or subfunction.

Referring to Figure 10.1, it can be argued that the interface *initiateJob* does not exhibit sufficient cohesion. In actuality, it performs three different subfunctions—building a work order, checking job priority, and passing a job to production. The interface design should be refactored. One approach might be to reexamine the design classes and define a new class **WorkOrder** that would take care of all activities associated with the assembly of a work order. The operation *buildWorkOrder()* becomes a part of that class. Similarly, we might define a class **JobQueue** that would incorporate the operation *checkPriority()*. A class **ProductionJob** would encompass all information associated with a production job to be passed to the production facility. The interface *initiateJob* would then take the form shown in Figure 10.7. The interface *initiateJob* is now cohesive, focusing on one function. The interfaces associated with **ProductionJob, WorkOrder,** and **JobQueue** are similarly single-minded.

Step 3c. Elaborate attributes and define data types and data structures required to implement them. In general, data structures and types used to define attributes are defined within the context of the programming language that is to be

---

FIGURE 10.7   Refactoring interfaces and class definitions for PrintJob

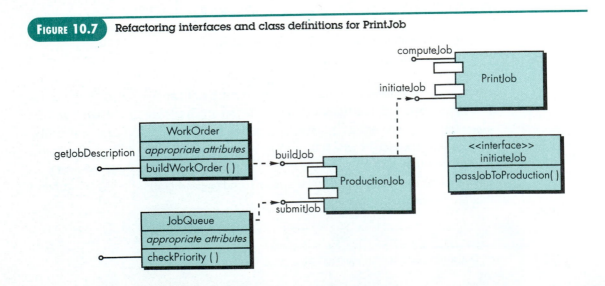

used for implementation. UML defines an attribute's data type using the following syntax:

name : type-expression = initial-value {property string}

where **name** is the attribute name, **type expression** is the data type, **initial value** is the value that the attribute takes when an object is created, and **property-string** defines a property or characteristic of the attribute.

During the first component-level design iteration, attributes are normally described by name. Referring once again to Figure 10.1, the attribute list for **PrintJob** lists only the names of the attributes. However, as design elaboration proceeds, each attribute is defined using the UML attribute format noted. For example, **paperType-weight** is defined in the following manner:

paperType-weight: string = "A" { contains 1 of 4 values - A, B, C, or D}

which defines **paperType-weight** as a string variable initialized to the value A that can take on one of four values from the set {A,B,C, D}.

If an attribute appears repeatedly across a number of design classes, and it has a relatively complex structure, it is best to create a separate class to accommodate the attribute.

Step 3d. Describe processing flow within each operation in detail.

This may be accomplished using a programming language-based pseudocode or with a UML activity diagram. Each software component is elaborated through a number of iterations that apply the stepwise refinement concept (Chapter 8).

The first iteration defines each operation as part of the design class. In every case, the operation should be characterized in a way that ensures high cohesion; that is, the operation should perform a single targeted function or subfunction. The next iteration does little more than expand the operation name. For example, the operation *computePaperCost()* noted in Figure 10.1 can be expanded in the following manner:

computePaperCost (weight, size, color): numeric

This indicates that *computePaperCost()* requires the attributes **weight, size,** and **color** as input and returns a value that is numeric (actually a dollar value) as output.

If the algorithm required to implement *computePaperCost()* is simple and widely understood, no further design elaboration may be necessary. The software engineer who does the coding will provide the detail necessary to implement the operation. However, if the algorithm is more complex or arcane, further design elaboration is required at this stage. Figure 10.8 depicts a UML activity diagram for *computePaperCost()*. When activity diagrams are used for component-level design specification, they are generally represented at a level of abstraction that is somewhat higher than source code. An alternative approach—the use of pseudocode for design specification—is discussed in Section 10.5.3.

Use stepwise elaboration as you refine the component design. Always ask, "Is there a way this can be simplified and yet still accomplish the same result?"

FIGURE 10.8

UML activity
diagram for
compute-
PaperCost()

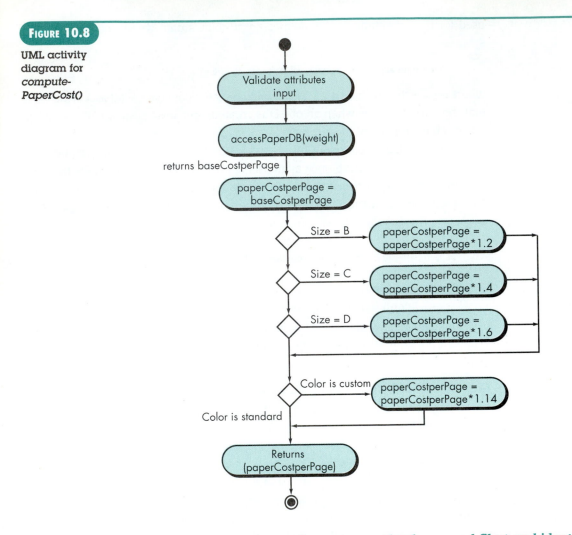

Step 4. Describe persistent data sources (databases and files) and identify the classes required to manage them. Databases and files normally transcend the design description of an individual component. In most cases, these persistent data stores are initially specified as part of architectural design. However, as design elaboration proceeds, it is often useful to provide additional detail about the structure and organization of these persistent data sources.

Step 5. Develop and elaborate behavioral representations for a class or component. UML state diagrams were used as part of the requirements model to represent the externally observable behavior of the system and the more localized behavior of individual analysis classes. During component-level design, it is sometimes necessary to model the behavior of a design class.

The dynamic behavior of an object (an instantiation of a design class as the program executes) is affected by events that are external to it and the current state

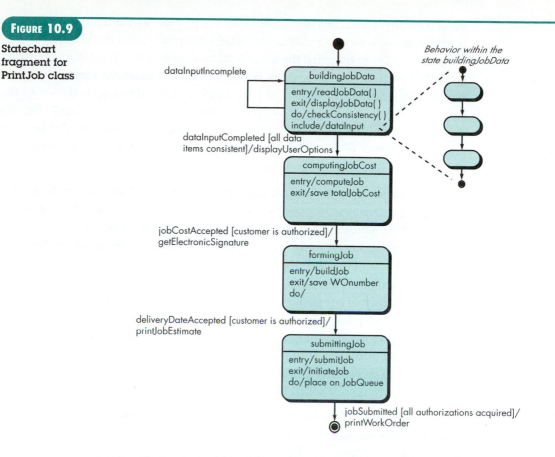

FIGURE 10.9

Statechart
fragment for
PrintJob class

(mode of behavior) of the object. To understand the dynamic behavior of an object, you should examine all use cases that are relevant to the design class throughout its life. These use cases provide information that helps you to delineate the events that affect the object and the states in which the object resides as time passes and events occur. The transitions between states (driven by events) are represented using a UML statechart [Ben02] as illustrated in Figure 10.9.

The transition from one state (represented by a rectangle with rounded corners) to another occurs as a consequence of an event that takes the form:

Event-name (parameter-list) [guard-condition] / action expression

where **event-name** identifies the event, **parameter-list** incorporates data that are associated with the event, **guard-condition** is written in Object Constraint Language (OCL) and specifies a condition that must be met before the event can occur, and **action expression** defines an action that occurs as the transition takes place.

Referring to Figure 10.9, each state may define *entry/* and *exit/* actions that occur as transition into the state occurs and as transition out of the state occurs, respectively. In most cases, these actions correspond to operations that are relevant to the class that is being modeled. The *do/* indicator provides a mechanism for indicating activities that occur while in the state, and the *include/* indicator provides a means for elaborating the behavior by embedding more statechart detail within the definition of a state.

It is important to note that the behavioral model often contains information that is not immediately obvious in other design models. For example, careful examination of the statechart in Figure 10.9 indicates that the dynamic behavior of the **PrintJob** class is contingent upon two customer approvals as costs and schedule data for the print job are derived. Without approvals (the guard condition ensures that the customer is authorized to approve) the print job cannot be submitted because there is no way to reach the *submittingJob* state.

Step 6. Elaborate deployment diagrams to provide additional implementation detail. Deployment diagrams (Chapter 8) are used as part of architectural design and are represented in descriptor form. In this form, major system functions (often represented as subsystems) are represented within the context of the computing environment that will house them.

During component-level design, deployment diagrams can be elaborated to represent the location of key packages of components. However, components generally are not represented individually within a component diagram. The reason for this is to avoid diagrammatic complexity. In some cases, deployment diagrams are elaborated into instance form at this time. This means that the specific hardware and operating system environment(s) that will be used is (are) specified and the location of component packages within this environment is indicated.

Step 7. Refactor every component-level design representation and always consider alternatives. Throughout this book, I have emphasized that design is an iterative process. The first component-level model you create will not be as complete, consistent, or accurate as the *n*th iteration you apply to the model. It is essential to refactor as design work is conducted.

In addition, you should not suffer from tunnel vision. There are always alternative design solutions, and the best designers consider all (or most) of them before settling on the final design model. Develop alternatives and consider each carefully, using the design principles and concepts presented in Chapter 8 and in this chapter.

10.4   COMPONENT-LEVEL DESIGN FOR WEBAPPS

The boundary between content and function is often blurred when Web-based systems and applications (WebApps) are considered. Therefore, it is reasonable to ask: What is a WebApp component?

In the context of this chapter, a WebApp component is (1) a well-defined cohesive function that manipulates content or provides computational or data processing for an end user or (2) a cohesive package of content and functionality that provides the end user with some required capability. Therefore, component-level design for WebApps often incorporates elements of content design and functional design.

10.4.1   Content Design at the Component Level

Content design at the component level focuses on content objects and the manner in which they may be packaged for presentation to a WebApp end user. As an example, consider a Web-based video surveillance capability within **SafeHomeAssured.com**. Among many capabilities, the user can select and control any of the cameras represented as part of a floor plan, require video-capture thumbnail images from all the cameras, and display streaming video from any one camera. In addition, the user can control pan and zoom for a camera using appropriate control icons.

A number of potential content components can be defined for the video surveillance capability: (1) the content objects that represent the space layout (the floor plan) with additional icons representing the location of sensors and video cameras, (2) the collection of thumbnail video captures (each a separate data object), and (3) the streaming video window for a specific camera. Each of these components can be separately named and manipulated as a package.

Consider a floor plan that depicts four cameras placed strategically throughout a house. Upon user request, a video frame is captured from each camera and is identified as a dynamically generated content object, **VideoCaptureN**, where N identifies cameras 1 to 4. A content component, named **Thumbnail-Images**, combines all four **VideoCaptureN** content objects and displays them on the video surveillance page.

The formality of content design at the component level should be tuned to the characteristics of the WebApp to be built. In many cases, content objects need not be organized as components and can be manipulated individually. However, as the size and complexity (of the WebApp, content objects, and their interrelationships) grows, it may be necessary to organize content in a way that allows easier reference and design manipulation.[6] In addition, if content is highly dynamic (e.g., the content for an online auction site), it becomes important to establish a clear structural model that incorporates content components.

10.4.2   Functional Design at the Component Level

Modern Web applications deliver increasingly sophisticated processing functions that (1) perform localized processing to generate content and navigation capability in a dynamic fashion, (2) provide computation or data processing capability that is appropriate for the WebApp's business domain, (3) provide sophisticated database query and access, or (4) establish data interfaces with external corporate systems. To

---

6   Content components can also be reused in other WebApps.

achieve these (and many other) capabilities, you will design and construct WebApp functional components that are similar in form to software components for conventional software.

WebApp functionality is delivered as a series of components developed in parallel with the information architecture to ensure that they are consistent. In essence you begin by considering both the requirements model and the initial information architecture and then examining how functionality affects the user's interaction with the application, the information that is presented, and the user tasks that are conducted.

During architectural design, WebApp content and functionality are combined to create a functional architecture. A *functional architecture* is a representation of the functional domain of the WebApp and describes the key functional components in the WebApp and how these components interact with each other.

For example, the pan and zoom functions for the **SafeHomeAssured.com** video surveillance capability are implemented as part of a **CameraControl** component. Alternatively, pan and zoom can be implemented as the operations, *pan()* and *zoom()*, which are part of a **Camera** class. In either case, the functionality implied by pan and zoom must be implemented as modules within **SafeHomeAssured.com**.

10.5   DESIGNING TRADITIONAL COMPONENTS

POINT

Structured programming is a design technique that constrains logic flow to three constructs: sequence, condition, and repetition.

The foundations of component-level design for traditional software components[7] were formed in the early 1960s and were solidified with the work of Edsger Dijkstra and his colleagues ([Boh66], [Dij65], [Dij76b]). In the late 1960s, Dijkstra and others proposed the use of a set of constrained logical constructs from which any program could be formed. The constructs emphasized "maintenance of functional domain." That is, each construct had a predictable logical structure and was entered at the top and exited at the bottom, enabling a reader to follow procedural flow more easily.

The constructs are sequence, condition, and repetition. *Sequence* implements processing steps that are essential in the specification of any algorithm. *Condition* provides the facility for selected processing based on some logical occurrence, and *repetition* allows for looping. These three constructs are fundamental to *structured programming*—an important component-level design technique.

The structured constructs were proposed to limit the procedural design of software to a small number of predictable logical structures. Complexity metrics (Chapter 23) indicate that the use of the structured constructs reduces program complexity and thereby enhances readability, testability, and maintainability. The use of

---

7   A traditional software component implements an element of processing that addresses a function or subfunction in the problem domain or some capability in the infrastructure domain. Often called modules, procedures, or subroutines, traditional components do not encapsulate data in the same way that object-oriented components do.

a limited number of logical constructs also contributes to a human understanding process that psychologists call *chunking*. To understand this process, consider the way in which you are reading this page. You do not read individual letters but rather recognize patterns or chunks of letters that form words or phrases. The structured constructs are logical chunks that allow a reader to recognize procedural elements of a module, rather than reading the design or code line by line. Understanding is enhanced when readily recognizable logical patterns are encountered.

Any program, regardless of application area or technical complexity, can be designed and implemented using only the three structured constructs. It should be noted, however, that dogmatic use of only these constructs can sometimes cause practical difficulties. Section 10.5.1 considers this issue in further detail.

10.5.1   Graphical Design Notation

"A picture is worth a thousand words," but it's rather important to know which picture and which 1000 words. There is no question that graphical tools, such as the UML activity diagram or the flowchart, provide useful pictorial patterns that readily depict procedural detail. However, if graphical tools are misused, the wrong picture may lead to the wrong software.

The activity diagram allows you to represent sequence, condition, and repetition—all elements of structured programming—and is a descendent of an earlier pictorial design representation (still used widely) called a *flowchart*. A flowchart, like an activity diagram, is quite simple pictorially. A box is used to indicate a processing step. A diamond represents a logical condition, and arrows show the flow of control. Figure 10.10 illustrates three structured constructs. The *sequence* is

FIGURE 10.10

Flowchart constructs

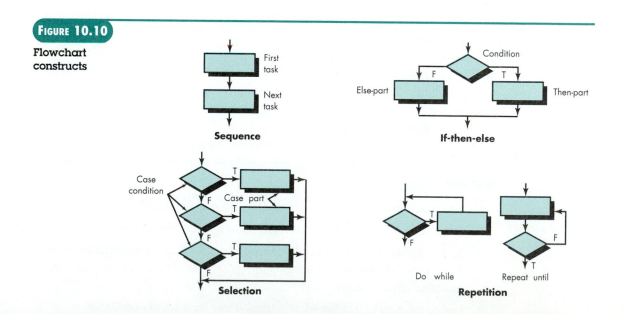

represented as two processing boxes connected by a line (arrow) of control. *Condition,* also called *if-then-else,* is depicted as a decision diamond that, if true, causes *then-part* processing to occur, and if false, invokes *else-part* processing. *Repetition* is represented using two slightly different forms. The *do while* tests a condition and executes a loop task repetitively as long as the condition holds true. A *repeat until* executes the loop task first and then tests a condition and repeats the task until the condition fails. The *selection* (or *select-case*) construct shown in the figure is actually an extension of the *if-then-else.* A parameter is tested by successive decisions until a true condition occurs and a *case part* processing path is executed.

In general, the dogmatic use of only the structured constructs can introduce inefficiency when an escape from a set of nested loops or nested conditions is required. More important, additional complication of all logical tests along the path of escape can cloud software control flow, increase the possibility of error, and have a negative impact on readability and maintainability. What can you do?

You're left with two options: (1) The procedural representation is redesigned so that the "escape branch" is not required at a nested location in the flow of control or (2) the structured constructs are violated in a controlled manner; that is, a constrained branch out of the nested flow is designed. Option 1 is obviously the ideal approach, but option 2 can be accommodated without violating the spirit of structured programming.

10.5.2 Tabular Design Notation

Use a decision table when a complex set of conditions and actions are encountered within a component.

In many software applications, a module may be required to evaluate a complex combination of conditions and select appropriate actions based on these conditions. *Decision tables* [Hur83] provide a notation that translates actions and conditions (described in a processing narrative or a use case) into a tabular form. The table is difficult to misinterpret and may even be used as a machine-readable input to a table-driven algorithm.

Decision table organization is illustrated in Figure 10.11. Referring to the figure, the table is divided into four sections. The upper left-hand quadrant contains a list of all conditions. The lower left-hand quadrant contains a list of all actions that are possible based on combinations of conditions. The right-hand quadrants form a matrix that indicates condition combinations and the corresponding actions that will occur for a specific combination. Therefore, each column of the matrix may be interpreted as a *processing rule.* The following steps are applied to develop a decision table:

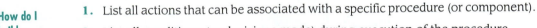

1. List all actions that can be associated with a specific procedure (or component).

2. List all conditions (or decisions made) during execution of the procedure.

3. Associate specific sets of conditions with specific actions, eliminating impossible combinations of conditions; alternatively, develop every possible permutation of conditions.

4. Define rules by indicating what actions occur for a set of conditions.

FIGURE 10.11

Decision table
nomenclature

		Rules					
Conditions		1	2	3	4	5	6
Regular customer		T	T				
Silver customer				T	T		
Gold customer						T	T
Special discount		F	T	F	T	F	T
Actions							
No discount		✓					
Apply 8 percent discount				✓	✓		
Apply 15 percent discount						✓	✓
Apply additional x percent discount			✓		✓		✓

To illustrate the use of a decision table, consider the following excerpt from an informal use case that has just been proposed for the print shop system:

> Three types of customers are defined: a regular customer, a silver customer, and a gold customer (these types are assigned by the amount of business the customer does with the print shop over a 12 month period). A regular customer receives normal print rates and delivery. A silver customer gets an 8 percent discount on all quotes and is placed ahead of all regular customers in the job queue. A gold customer gets a 15 percent reduction in quoted prices and is placed ahead of both regular and silver customers in the job queue. A special discount of x percent in addition to other discounts can be applied to any customer's quote at the discretion of management.

Figure 10.11 illustrates a decision table representation of the preceding informal use case. Each of the six rules indicates one of six viable conditions. As a general rule, the decision table can be used effectively to supplement other procedural design notation.

10.5.3 Program Design Language

Program design language (PDL), also called *structured English* or *pseudocode,* incorporates the logical structure of a programming language with the free-form expressive ability of a natural language (e.g., English). Narrative text (e.g., English) is embedded within a programming language-like syntax. Automated tools (e.g., [Cai03]) can be used to enhance the application of PDL.

A basic PDL syntax should include constructs for component definition, interface description, data declaration, block structuring, condition constructs, repetition constructs, and input-output (I/O) constructs. It should be noted that PDL can be extended to include keywords for multitasking and/or concurrent processing, interrupt handling, interprocess synchronization, and many other features. The application design for which PDL is to be used should dictate the final form for the design language. The format and semantics for some of these PDL constructs are presented in the example that follows.

To illustrate the use of PDL, consider a procedural design for the *SafeHome* security function discussed in earlier chapters. The system monitors alarms for fire, smoke, burglar, water, and temperature (e.g., the heating system fails while the homeowner is away during winter) and produces an alarm bell and calls a monitoring service, generating a voice-synthesized message.

Recall that PDL is *not* a programming language. You can adapt as required without worry about syntax errors. However, the design for the monitoring software would have to be reviewed (do you see any problems?) and further refined before code could be written. The following PDL[8] provides an elaboration of the procedural design for an early version of an alarm management component.

```
component alarmManagement;
The intent of this component is to manage control panel switches and input from sensors by
type and to act on any alarm condition that is encountered.
    set default values for systemStatus (returned value), all data items
    initialize all system ports and reset all hardware
    check controlPanelSwitches (cps)
        if cps = "test" then invoke alarm set to "on"
        if cps = "alarmOff" then invoke alarm set to "off"
        if cps = "newBoundingValue" then invoke keyboardInput
        if cps = "burglarAlarmOff" invoke deactivateAlarm;

        •

        •

        •

        default for cps = none
    reset all signalValues and switches
    do for all sensors
        invoke checkSensor procedure returning signalValue
        if signalValue > bound [alarmType]
            then phoneMessage = message [alarmType]
                set alarmBell to "on" for alarmTimeSeconds
                set system status = "alarmCondition"
                parbegin
                    invoke alarm procedure with "on", alarmTimeSeconds;
                    invoke phone procedure set to alarmType, phoneNumber
                endpar
            else skip
        endif
    enddofor
end alarmManagement
```

---

8   The level of detail represented by the PDL is defined locally. Some people prefer a more natural language-oriented description, while others prefer something that is close to code.

Note that the designer for the **alarmManagement** component has used the construct **parbegin ... parend** that specifies a parallel block. All tasks specified within the **parbegin** block are executed in parallel. In this case, implementation details are not considered.

10.6 COMPONENT-BASED DEVELOPMENT

In the software engineering context, reuse is an idea both old and new. Programmers have reused ideas, abstractions, and processes since the earliest days of computing, but the early approach to reuse was ad hoc. Today, complex, high-quality computer-based systems must be built in very short time periods and demand a more organized approach to reuse.

Component-based software engineering (CBSE) is a process that emphasizes the design and construction of computer-based systems using reusable software "components." Clements [Cle95] describes CBSE in the following way:

> [CBSE] embodies the "buy, don't build" philosophy espoused by Fred Brooks and others. In the same way that early subroutines liberated the programmer from thinking about details, [CBSE] shifts the emphasis from programming software to composing software systems. Implementation has given way to integration as the focus.

But a number of questions arise. Is it possible to construct complex systems by assembling them from a catalog of reusable software components? Can this be accomplished in a cost- and time-effective manner? Can appropriate incentives be established to encourage software engineers to reuse rather than reinvent? Is management willing to incur the added expense associated with creating reusable software components? Can the library of components necessary to accomplish reuse be created in a way that makes it accessible to those who need it? Can components that do exist be found by those who need them?

Increasingly, the answer to each of these questions is "yes." In the rest of this section, I examine some of the issues that must be considered to make CBSE successful within a software engineering organization.

uote:

"Domain engineering is about finding commonalities among systems to identify components that can be applied to many systems . . ."

Paul Clements

10.6.1 Domain Engineering

The intent of *domain engineering* is to identify, construct, catalog, and disseminate a set of software components that have applicability to existing and future software in a particular application domain.[9] The overall goal is to establish mechanisms that enable software engineers to share these components—to reuse them—during work on new and existing systems. Domain engineering includes three major activities—analysis, construction, and dissemination.

---

9 In Chapter 9 we referred to architectural genres that identify specific application domains.

ADVICE

The analysis process we discuss in this section focuses on reusable components. However, the analysis of complete COTS systems (e.g., e-commerce Apps, sales force automation Apps) can also be a part of domain analysis.

The overall approach to *domain analysis* is often characterized within the context of object-oriented software engineering. The steps in the process are defined as:

1. Define the domain to be investigated.
2. Categorize the items extracted from the domain.
3. Collect a representative sample of applications in the domain.
4. Analyze each application in the sample and define analysis classes.
5. Develop a requirements model for the classes.

It is important to note that domain analysis is applicable to any software engineering paradigm and may be applied for conventional as well as object-oriented development.

10.6.2   Component Qualification, Adaptation, and Composition

Domain engineering provides the library of reusable components that are required for component-based software engineering. Some of these reusable components are developed in-house, others can be extracted from existing applications, and still others may be acquired from third parties.

Unfortunately, the existence of reusable components does not guarantee that these components can be integrated easily or effectively into the architecture chosen for a new application. It is for this reason that a sequence of component-based development actions is applied when a component is proposed for use.

Component Qualification.   Component qualification ensures that a candidate component will perform the function required, will properly "fit" into the architectural style (Chapter 9) specified for the system, and will exhibit the quality characteristics (e.g., performance, reliability, usability) that are required for the application.

An interface description provides useful information about the operation and use of a software component, but it does not provide all of the information required to determine if a proposed component can, in fact, be reused effectively in a new application. Among the many factors considered during component qualification are [Bro96]:

? What factors are considered during component qualification?

- Application programming interface (API).
- Development and integration tools required by the component.
- Run-time requirements, including resource usage (e.g., memory or storage), timing or speed, and network protocol.
- Service requirements, including operating system interfaces and support from other components.
- Security features, including access controls and authentication protocol.
- Embedded design assumptions, including the use of specific numerical or nonnumerical algorithms.
- Exception handling.

Each of these factors is relatively easy to assess when reusable components that have been developed in-house are proposed. If good software engineering practices were applied during the development of a component, answers to the questions implied by the list can be developed. However, it is much more difficult to determine the internal workings of commercial off-the-shelf (COTS) or third-party components because the only available information may be the interface specification itself.

Component Adaptation. In an ideal setting, domain engineering creates a library of components that can be easily integrated into an application architecture. The implication of "easy integration" is that (1) consistent methods of resource management have been implemented for all components in the library, (2) common activities such as data management exist for all components, and (3) interfaces within the architecture and with the external environment have been implemented in a consistent manner.

In addition to assessing whether the cost of adaptation for reuse is justified, you should also assess whether achieving required functionality and performance can be done cost effectively.

In reality, even after a component has been qualified for use within an application architecture, conflicts may occur in one or more of the areas just noted. To avoid these conflicts, an adaptation technique called *component wrapping* [Bro96] is sometimes used. When a software team has full access to the internal design and code for a component (often not the case unless open-source COTS components are used), *white-box wrapping* is applied. Like its counterpart in software testing (Chapter 18), white-box wrapping examines the internal processing details of the component and makes code-level modifications to remove any conflict. *Gray-box wrapping* is applied when the component library provides a component extension language or API that enables conflicts to be removed or masked. *Black-box wrapping* requires the introduction of pre- and postprocessing at the component interface to remove or mask conflicts. You must determine whether the effort required to adequately wrap a component is justified or whether a custom component (designed to eliminate the conflicts encountered) should be engineered instead.

Component Composition. The component composition task assembles qualified, adapted, and engineered components to populate the architecture established for an application. To accomplish this, an infrastructure must be established to bind the components into an operational system. The infrastructure (usually a library of specialized components) provides a model for the coordination of components and specific services that enable components to coordinate with one another and perform common tasks.

Because the potential impact of reuse and CBSE on the software industry is enormous, a number of major companies and industry consortia have proposed standards for component software.[10]

---

10 Greg Olsen [Ols06] provides an excellent discussion of past and present industry efforts to make CBSE a reality.

WebRef

The latest information on CORBA can be obtained at **www.omg.org**.

WebRef

The latest information on COM and .NET can be obtained at **www.microsoft .com/COM** and **msdn2.microsoft .com/en-us/ netframework default.aspx**.

WebRef

The latest information on JavaBeans can be obtained at **java.sun.com/ products/ javabeans/docs/**.

OMG/CORBA. The Object Management Group has published a *common object request broker architecture* (OMG/CORBA). An object request broker (ORB) provides a variety of services that enable reusable components (objects) to communicate with other components, regardless of their location within a system.

Microsoft COM and .NET. Microsoft has developed a *component object model* (COM) that provides a specification for using components produced by various vendors within a single application running under the Windows operating system. From the point of view of the application, "the focus is not on how [COM objects are] implemented, only on the fact that the object has an interface that it registers with the system, and that it uses the component system to communicate with other COM objects" [Har98a]. The Microsoft .NET framework encompasses COM and provides a reusable class library that covers a wide array of application domains.

Sun JavaBeans Components. The JavaBeans component system is a portable, platform-independent CBSE infrastructure developed using the Java programming language. The JavaBeans component system encompasses a set of tools, called the *Bean Development Kit* (BDK), that allows developers to (1) analyze how existing Beans (components) work, (2) customize their behavior and appearance, (3) establish mechanisms for coordination and communication, (4) develop custom Beans for use in a specific application, and (5) test and evaluate Bean behavior.

None of these standards dominate the industry. Although many developers have standardized on one, it is likely that large software organizations may choose to use a standard based on the application categories and platforms that are chosen.

10.6.3 Analysis and Design for Reuse

Although the CBSE process encourages the use of existing software components, there are times when new software components must be developed and integrated with existing COTS and in-house components. Because these new components become members of the in-house library of reusable components, they should be engineered for reuse.

Design concepts such as abstraction, hiding, functional independence, refinement, and structured programming, along with object-oriented methods, testing, software quality assurance (SQA), and correctness verification methods (Chapter 21), all contribute to the creation of software components that are reusable. In this subsection, I consider the reuse-specific issues that are complementary to solid software engineering practices.

The requirements model is analyzed to determine those elements that point to existing reusable components. Elements of the requirements model are compared to descriptions of reusable components in a process that is sometimes referred to as "specification matching" [Bel95]. If specification matching points to an existing component that fits the needs of the current application, you can extract the component from a reuse library (repository) and use it in the design of a new system. If components cannot be found (i.e., there is no match), a new component is created. It is at this point—when you begin to create a new component—that *design for reuse* (DFR) should be considered.

As we have already noted, DFR requires that you apply solid software design concepts and principles (Chapter 8). But the characteristics of the application domain must also be considered. Binder [Bin93] suggests a number of key issues[11] that form a basis for design for reuse:

DFR can be quite difficult when components must be interfaced or integrated with legacy systems or with multiple systems whose architecture and interfacing protocols are inconsistent.

Standard data. The application domain should be investigated and standard global data structures (e.g., file structures or a complete database) should be identified. All design components can then be characterized to make use of these standard data structures.

Standard interface protocols. Three levels of interface protocol should be established: the nature of intramodular interfaces, the design of external technical (nonhuman) interfaces, and the human-computer interface.

Program templates. An architectural style (Chapter 9) is chosen and can serve as a template for the architectural design of a new software.

Once standard data, interfaces, and program templates have been established, you have a framework in which to create the design. New components that conform to this framework have a higher probability for subsequent reuse.

10.6.4 Classifying and Retrieving Components

Consider a large university library. Hundreds of thousands of books, periodicals, and other information resources are available for use. But to access these resources, a categorization scheme must be developed. To navigate this large volume of information, librarians have defined a classification scheme that includes a Library of Congress classification code, keywords, author names, and other index entries. All enable the user to find the needed resource quickly and easily.

Now, consider a large component repository. Tens of thousands of reusable software components reside in it. But how do you find the one that you need? To answer this question, another question arises: How do we describe software components in unambiguous, classifiable terms? These are difficult questions, and no definitive answer has yet been developed. In this section I explore current directions that will enable future software engineers to navigate reuse libraries.

---

11 In general, DFR preparations should be undertaken as part of domain engineering.

A reusable software component can be described in many ways, but an ideal description encompasses what Tracz [Tra95] has called the *3C model*—concept, content, and context. The *concept* of a software component is "a description of what the component does" [Whi95]. The interface to the component is fully described and the semantics—represented within the context of pre- and postconditions—is identified. The concept should communicate the intent of the component. The *content* of a component describes how the concept is realized. In essence, the content is information that is hidden from casual users and need be known only to those who intend to modify or test the component. The *context* places a reusable software component within its domain of applicability. That is, by specifying conceptual, operational, and implementation features, the context enables a software engineer to find the appropriate component to meet application requirements.

To be of use in a pragmatic setting, concept, content, and context must be translated into a concrete specification scheme. Dozens of papers and articles have been written about classification schemes for reusable software components (e.g., see [Cec06] for an overview of current trends).

Classification enables you to find and retrieve candidate reusable components, but a reuse environment must exist to integrate these components effectively. A reuse environment exhibits the following characteristics:

? What are the key characteristics of a component reuse environment?

- A component database capable of storing software components and the classification information necessary to retrieve them.
- A library management system that provides access to the database.
- A software component retrieval system (e.g., an object request broker) that enables a client application to retrieve components and services from the library server.
- CBSE tools that support the integration of reused components into a new design or implementation.

Each of these functions interact with or is embodied within the confines of a reuse library.

The *reuse library* is one element of a larger software repository (Chapter 22) and provides facilities for the storage of software components and a wide variety of reusable work products (e.g., specifications, designs, patterns, frameworks, code fragments, test cases, user guides). The library encompasses a database and the tools that are necessary to query the database and retrieve components from it. The component classification scheme serves as the basis for library queries.

Queries are often characterized using the context element of the 3C model described earlier in this section. If an initial query results in a voluminous list of candidate components, the query is refined to narrow the list. Concept and content information are then extracted (after candidate components are found) to assist you in selecting the proper component.

WebRef

A comprehensive collection of resources on CBSE can be found at www.cbd-hq .com/.

10.7 SUMMARY

The component-level design process encompasses a sequence of activities that slowly reduces the level of abstraction with which software is represented. Component-level design ultimately depicts the software at a level of abstraction that is close to code.

Three different views of component-level design may be taken, depending on the nature of the software to be developed. The object-oriented view focuses on the elaboration of design classes that come from both the problem and infrastructure domain. The traditional view refines three different types of components or modules: control modules, problem domain modules, and infrastructure modules. In both cases, basic design principles and concepts that lead to high-quality software are applied. When considered from a process viewpoint, component-level design draws on reusable software components and design patterns that are pivotal elements of component-based software engineering.

A number of important principles and concepts guide the designer as classes are elaborated. Ideas encompassed in the Open-Closed Principle and the Dependency Inversion Principle and concepts such as coupling and cohesion guide the software engineer in building testable, implementable, and maintainable software components. To conduct component-level design in this context, classes are elaborated by specifying messaging details, identifying appropriate interfaces, elaborating attributes and defining data structures to implement them, describing processing flow

---

12 Tools noted here do not represent an endorsement, but rather a sampling of tools in this category. In most cases, tool names are trademarked by their respective developers.

within each operation, and representing behavior at a class or component level. In every case, design iteration (refactoring) is an essential activity.

Traditional component-level design requires the representation of data structures, interfaces, and algorithms for a program module in sufficient detail to guide in the generation of programming language source code. To accomplish this, the designer uses one of a number of design notations that represent component-level detail in either graphical, tabular, or text-based formats.

Component-level design for WebApps considers both content and functionality as it is delivered by a Web-based system. Content design at the component level focuses on content objects and the manner in which they may be packaged for presentation to a WebApp end user. Functional design for WebApps focuses on processing functions that manipulate content, perform computations, query and access a database, and establish interfaces with other systems. All component-level design principles and guidelines apply.

Structured programming is a procedural design philosophy that constrains the number and type of logical constructs used to represent algorithmic detail. The intent of structured programming is to assist the designer in defining algorithms that are less complex and therefore easier to read, test, and maintain.

Component-based software engineering identifies, constructs, catalogs, and disseminates a set of software components in a particular application domain. These components are then qualified, adapted, and integrated for use in a new system. Reusable components should be designed within an environment that establishes standard data structures, interface protocols, and program architectures for each application domain.

PROBLEMS AND POINTS TO PONDER

10.1. The term *component* is sometimes a difficult one to define. First provide a generic definition, and then provide more explicit definitions for object-oriented and traditional software. Finally, pick three programming languages with which you are familiar and illustrate how each defines a component.

10.2. Why are control components necessary in traditional software and generally not required in object-oriented software?

10.3. Describe the OCP in your own words. Why is it important to create abstractions that serve as an interface between components?

10.4. Describe the DIP in your own words. What might happen if a designer depends too heavily on concretions?

10.5. Select three components that you have developed recently and assess the types of cohesion that each exhibits. If you had to define the primary benefit of high cohesion, what would it be?

10.6. Select three components that you have developed recently and assess the types of coupling that each exhibits. If you had to define the primary benefit of low coupling, what would it be?

10.7. Is it reasonable to say that problem domain components should never exhibit external coupling? If you agree, what types of component would exhibit external coupling?

10.8. Develop (1) an elaborated design class, (2) interface descriptions, (3) an activity diagram for one of the operations within the class, and (4) a detailed statechart diagram for one of the *SafeHome* classes that we have discussed in earlier chapters.

10.9. Are stepwise refinement and refactoring the same thing? If not, how do they differ?

10.10. What is a WebApp component?

10.11. Select a small portion of an existing program (approximately 50 to 75 source lines). Isolate the structured programming constructs by drawing boxes around them in the source code. Does the program excerpt have constructs that violate the structured programming philosophy? If so, redesign the code to make it conform to structured programming constructs. If not, what do you notice about the boxes that you've drawn?

10.12. All modern programming languages implement the structured programming constructs. Provide examples from three programming languages.

10.13. Select a small coded component and represent it using (1) an activity diagram, (2) a flowchart, (3) a decision table, and (4) PDL.

10.14. Why is "chunking" important during the component-level design review process?

FURTHER READINGS AND INFORMATION SOURCES

Many books on component-based development and component reuse have been published in recent years. Apperly and his colleagues (*Service- and Component-Based Development*, Addison-Wesley, 2003), Heineman and Councill (*Component Based Software Engineering*, Addison-Wesley, 2001), Brown (*Large Scale Component-Based Development*, Prentice-Hall, 2000), Allen (*Realizing e-Business with Components*, Addison-Wesley, 2000), Herzum and Sims (*Business Component Factory*, Wiley, 1999), Allen, Frost, and Yourdon (*Component-Based Development for Enterprise Systems: Applying the Select Perspective*, Cambridge University Press, 1998) cover all important aspects of the CBSE process. Cheesman and Daniels (*UML Components*, Addison-Wesley, 2000) discuss CBSE with a UML emphasis.

Gao and his colleagues (*Testing and Quality Assurance for Component-Based Software*, Artech House, 2006) and Gross (*Component-Based Software Testing with UML*, Springer, 2005) discuss testing and SQA issues for component-based systems.

Dozens of books describing the industry's component-based standards have been published in recent years. These address the inner workings of the standards themselves but also consider many important CBSE topics.

The work of Linger, Mills, and Witt (*Structured Programming—Theory and Practice*, Addison-Wesley, 1979) remains a definitive treatment of the subject. The text contains a good PDL as well as detailed discussions of the ramifications of structured programming. Other books that focus on procedural design issues for traditional systems include those by Robertson (*Simple Program Design*, 3d ed., Course Technology, 2000), Farrell (*A Guide to Programming Logic and Design*, Course Technology, 1999), Bentley (*Programming Pearls*, 2d ed., Addison-Wesley, 1999), and Dahl (*Structured Programming*, Academic Press, 1997).

Relatively few recent books have been dedicated solely to component-level design. In general, programming language books address procedural design in some detail but always in the context of the language that is introduced by the book. Hundreds of titles are available.

A wide variety of information sources on component-level design are available on the Internet. An up-to-date list of World Wide Web references that are relevant to component-level design can be found at the SEPA website: **www.mhhe.com/engcs/compsci/pressman/ professional/olc/ser.htm**.

We live in a world of high-technology products, and virtually all of them—consumer electronics, industrial equipment, corporate systems, military systems, personal computer software, and WebApps—require human interaction. If a product is to be successful, it must exhibit good *usability*—a qualitative measure of the ease and efficiency with which a human can employ the functions and features offered by the high-technology product.

Whether an interface has been designed for a digital music player or the weapons control system for a fighter aircraft, usability matters. If interface mechanisms have been well designed, the user glides through the interaction using a smooth rhythm that allows work to be accomplished effortlessly. But if the interface is poorly conceived, the user moves in fits and starts, and the end result is frustration and poor work efficiency.

For the first three decades of the computing era, usability was not a dominant concern among those who built software. In his classic book on design, Donald Norman [Nor88] argued that it was time for a change in attitude:

> To make technology that fits human beings, it is necessary to study human beings. But now we tend to study only the technology. As a result, people are required to conform to technology. It is time to reverse this trend, time to make technology that conforms to people.

QUICK LOOK

What is it? User interface design creates an effective communication medium between a human and a computer. Following a set of interface design principles, design identifies interface objects and actions and then creates a screen layout that forms the basis for a user interface prototype.

Who does it? A software engineer designs the user interface by applying an iterative process that draws on predefined design principles.

Why is it important? If software is difficult to use, if it forces you into mistakes, or if it frustrates your efforts to accomplish your goals, you won't like it, regardless of the computational power it exhibits, the content it delivers, or the functionality it offers. The interface has to be right because it molds a user's perception of the software.

What are the steps? User interface design begins with the identification of user, task, and environ-mental requirements. Once user tasks have been identified, user scenarios are created and ana-lyzed to define a set of interface objects and actions. These form the basis for the creation of screen layout that depicts graphical design and placement of icons, definition of descriptive screen text, specification and titling for windows, and specification of major and minor menu items. Tools are used to prototype and ultimately implement the design model, and the result is evaluated for quality.

What is the work product? User scenarios are created and screen layouts are generated. An interface prototype is developed and modified in an iterative fashion.

How do I ensure that I've done it right? An in-terface prototype is "test driven" by the users, and feedback from the test drive is used for the next iterative modification of the prototype.

As technologists studied human interaction, two dominant issues arose. First, a set of *golden rules* (discussed in Section 11.1) were identified. These applied to all human interaction with technology products. Second, a set of *interaction mechanisms* were defined to enable software designers to build systems that properly implemented the golden rules. These interaction mechanisms, collectively called the *graphical user interface* (GUI), have eliminated some of the most egregious problems associated with human interfaces. But even in a "Windows world," we all have encountered user interfaces that are difficult to learn, difficult to use, confusing, counterintuitive, unforgiving, and in many cases, totally frustrating. Yet, someone spent time and energy building each of these interfaces, and it is not likely that the builder created these problems purposely.

11.1   THE GOLDEN RULES

In his book on interface design, Theo Mandel [Man97] coins three *golden rules:*

1. Place the user in control.

2. Reduce the user's memory load.

3. Make the interface consistent.

These golden rules actually form the basis for a set of user interface design principles that guide this important aspect of software design.

11.1.1 Place the User in Control

During a requirements-gathering session for a major new information system, a key user was asked about the attributes of the window-oriented graphical interface.

"What I really would like," said the user solemnly, "is a system that reads my mind. It knows what I want to do before I need to do it and makes it very easy for me to get it done. That's all, just that."

My first reaction was to shake my head and smile, but I paused for a moment. There was absolutely nothing wrong with the user's request. She wanted a system that reacted to her needs and helped her get things done. She wanted to control the computer, not have the computer control her.

Most interface constraints and restrictions that are imposed by a designer are intended to simplify the mode of interaction. But for whom?

As a designer, you may be tempted to introduce constraints and limitations to simplify the implementation of the interface. The result may be an interface that is easy to build, but frustrating to use. Mandel [Man97] defines a number of design principles that allow the user to maintain control:

Define interaction modes in a way that does not force a user into unnecessary or undesired actions. An interaction mode is the current state of the interface. For example, if *spell check* is selected in a word-processor menu, the software moves to a spell-checking mode. There is no reason to force the user to remain in spell-checking mode if the user desires to make a small text edit along the way. The user should be able to enter and exit the mode with little or no effort.

Provide for flexible interaction.   Because different users have different interaction preferences, choices should be provided. For example, software might allow a user to interact via keyboard commands, mouse movement, a digitizer pen, a multitouch screen, or voice recognition commands. But every action is not amenable to every interaction mechanism. Consider, for example, the difficulty of using keyboard command (or voice input) to draw a complex shape.

Allow user interaction to be interruptible and undoable.   Even when involved in a sequence of actions, the user should be able to interrupt the sequence to do something else (without losing the work that had been done). The user should also be able to "undo" any action.

Streamline interaction as skill levels advance and allow the interaction to be customized.   Users often find that they perform the same sequence of interactions repeatedly. It is worthwhile to design a "macro" mechanism that enables an advanced user to customize the interface to facilitate interaction.

Hide technical internals from the casual user.   The user interface should move the user into the virtual world of the application. The user should not be aware of the operating system, file management functions, or other arcane computing technology. In essence, the interface should never require that the user interact at a level that is "inside" the machine (e.g., a user should never be required to type operating system commands from within application software).

Design for direct interaction with objects that appear on the screen.   The user feels a sense of control when able to manipulate the objects that are necessary to perform a task in a manner similar to what would occur if the object were a physical thing. For example, an application interface that allows a user to "stretch" an object (scale it in size) is an implementation of direct manipulation.

11.1.2 Reduce the User's Memory Load

The more a user has to remember, the more error-prone the interaction with the system will be. It is for this reason that a well-designed user interface does not tax the user's memory. Whenever possible, the system should "remember" pertinent information and assist the user with an interaction scenario that assists recall. Mandel [Man97] defines design principles that enable an interface to reduce the user's memory load:

Reduce demand on short-term memory.   When users are involved in complex tasks, the demand on short-term memory can be significant. The interface should be designed to reduce the requirement to remember past actions, inputs, and results.

This can be accomplished by providing visual cues that enable a user to recognize past actions, rather than having to recall them.

Establish meaningful defaults. The initial set of defaults should make sense for the average user, but a user should be able to specify individual preferences. However, a "reset" option should be available, enabling the redefinition of original default values.

Define shortcuts that are intuitive. When mnemonics are used to accomplish a system function (e.g., alt-P to invoke the print function), the mnemonic should be tied to the action in a way that is easy to remember (e.g., first letter of the task to be invoked).

The visual layout of the interface should be based on a real-world metaphor. For example, a bill payment system should use a checkbook and check register metaphor to guide the user through the bill paying process. This enables the user to rely on well-understood visual cues, rather than memorizing an arcane interaction sequence.

Disclose information in a progressive fashion. The interface should be organized hierarchically. That is, information about a task, an object, or some behavior should be presented first at a high level of abstraction. More detail should be presented after the user indicates interest with a mouse pick. An example, common to many word-processing applications, is the underlining function. The function itself is one of a number of functions under a *text style* menu. However, every underlining capability is not listed. The user must pick underlining; then all underlining options (e.g., single underline, double underline, dashed underline) are presented.

SafeHome

Violating a UI Golden Rule

The scene: Vinod's cubicle, as user interface design begins.

The players: Vinod and Jamie, members of the *SafeHome* software engineering team.

The conversation:

Jamie: I've been thinking about the surveillance function interface.

Vinod (smiling): Thinking is good.

Jamie: I think maybe we can simplify matters some.

Vinod: Meaning?

Jamie: Well, what if we eliminate the floor plan entirely. It's flashy, but it's going to take serious development effort. Instead we just ask the user to specify the camera he wants to see and then display the video in a video window.

Vinod: How does the homeowner remember how many cameras are set up and where they are?

Jamie (mildly irritated): He's the homeowner; he should know.

Vinod: But what if he doesn't?

Jamie: He should.

Vinod: That's not the point . . . what if he forgets?

Jamie: Uh, we could provide a list of operational cameras and their locations.

Vinod: That's possible, but why should he have to ask for a list?

Jamie: Okay, we provide the list whether he asks or not.

Vinod: Better. At least he doesn't have to remember stuff that we can give him.

Jamie (thinking for a moment): But you like the floor plan, don't you?

Vinod: Uh huh.

Jamie: Which one will marketing like, do you think?

Vinod: You're kidding, right?

Jamie: No.

Vinod: Duh . . . the one with the flash . . . they love sexy product features . . . they're not interested in which is easier to build.

Jamie (sighing): Okay, maybe I'll prototype both.

Vinod: Good idea . . . then we let the customer decide.

11.1.3 Make the Interface Consistent

The interface should present and acquire information in a consistent fashion. This implies that (1) all visual information is organized according to design rules that are maintained throughout all screen displays, (2) input mechanisms are constrained to a limited set that is used consistently throughout the application, and (3) mechanisms for navigating from task to task are consistently defined and implemented. Mandel [Man97] defines a set of design principles that help make the interface consistent:

uote:

"Things that look different should act different. Things that look the same should act the same."

Larry Marine

Allow the user to put the current task into a meaningful context.   Many interfaces implement complex layers of interactions with dozens of screen images. It is important to provide indicators (e.g., window titles, graphical icons, consistent color coding) that enable the user to know the context of the work at hand. In addition, the user should be able to determine where he has come from and what alternatives exist for a transition to a new task.

Maintain consistency across a family of applications.   A set of applications (or products) should all implement the same design rules so that consistency is maintained for all interaction.

If past interactive models have created user expectations, do not make changes unless there is a compelling reason to do so.   Once a particular interactive sequence has become a de facto standard (e.g., the use of alt-S to save a file), the user expects this in every application he encounters. A change (e.g., using alt-S to invoke scaling) will cause confusion.

The interface design principles discussed in this and the preceding sections provide you with basic guidance. In the sections that follow, you'll learn about the interface design process itself.

Usability

In an insightful paper on usability, Larry Constantine [Con95] asks a question that has significant bearing on the subject: "What do users want, anyway?" He answers this way:

> What users really want are good tools. All software systems, from operating systems and languages to data entry and decision support applications, are just tools. End users want from the tools we engineer for them much the same as we expect from the tools we use. They want systems that are easy to learn and that help them do their work. They want software that doesn't slow them down, that doesn't trick or confuse them, that doesn't make it easier to make mistakes or harder to finish the job.

Constantine argues that usability is not derived from aesthetics, state-of-the-art interaction mechanisms, or built-in interface intelligence. Rather, it occurs when the architecture of the interface fits the needs of the people who will be using it.

A formal definition of usability is somewhat illusive. Donahue and his colleagues [Don99] define it in the following manner: "Usability is a measure of how well a computer system . . . facilitates learning; helps learners remember what they've learned; reduces the likelihood of errors; enables them to be efficient, and makes them satisfied with the system."

The only way to determine whether "usability" exists within a system you are building is to conduct usability assessment or testing. Watch users interact with the system and answer the following questions [Con95]:

- Is the system usable without continual help or instruction?
- Do the rules of interaction help a knowledgeable user to work efficiently?
- Do interaction mechanisms become more flexible as users become more knowledgeable?
- Has the system been tuned to the physical and social environment in which it will be used?
- Is the user aware of the state of the system? Does the user know where she is at all times?
- Is the interface structured in a logical and consistent manner?
- Are interaction mechanisms, icons, and procedures consistent across the interface?
- Does the interaction anticipate errors and help the user correct them?
- Is the interface tolerant of errors that are made?
- Is the interaction simple?

If each of these questions is answered "yes," it is likely that usability has been achieved.

Among the many measurable benefits derived from a usable system are [Don99]: increased sales and customer satisfaction, competitive advantage, better reviews in the media, better word of mouth, reduced support costs, improved end-user productivity, reduced training costs, reduced documentation costs, reduced likelihood of litigation from unhappy customers.

11.2   USER INTERFACE ANALYSIS AND DESIGN

WebRef

An excellent source of UI design information can be found at **www.useit.com**.

The overall process for analyzing and designing a user interface begins with the creation of different models of system function (as perceived from the outside). You begin by delineating the human- and computer-oriented tasks that are required to achieve system function and then considering the design issues that apply to all interface designs. Tools are used to prototype and ultimately implement the design model, and the result is evaluated by end users for quality.

11.2.1   Interface Analysis and Design Models

Four different models come into play when a user interface is to be analyzed and designed. A human engineer (or the software engineer) establishes a *user model*, the software engineer creates a *design model,* the end user develops a mental image that is often called the user's *mental model* or the *system perception,* and the implementers of the system create an *implementation model*. Unfortunately, each of these models may differ significantly. Your role, as an interface designer, is to reconcile these differences and derive a consistent representation of the interface.

The user model establishes the profile of end users of the system. In his introductory column on "user-centric design," Jeff Patton [Pat07] notes:

> The truth is, designers and developers—myself included—often think about users. However, in the absence of a strong mental model of specific users, we self-substitute. Self-substitution isn't user centric—it's self-centric.

To build an effective user interface, "all design should begin with an understanding of the intended users, including profiles of their age, gender, physical abilities, education, cultural or ethnic background, motivation, goals and personality" [Shn04]. In addition, users can be categorized as:

Even a novice user wants shortcuts; even knowledgeable, frequent users sometimes need guidance. Give them what they need.

Novices. No syntactic knowledge[1] of the system and little semantic knowledge[2] of the application or computer usage in general.

Knowledgeable, intermittent users. Reasonable semantic knowledge of the application but relatively low recall of syntactic information necessary to use the interface.

Knowledgeable, frequent users. Good semantic and syntactic knowledge that often leads to the "power-user syndrome"; that is, individuals who look for shortcuts and abbreviated modes of interaction.

The user's mental model shapes how the user perceives the interface and whether the UI meets the user's needs.

The user's *mental model* (system perception) is the image of the system that end users carry in their heads. For example, if the user of a particular word processor were asked to describe its operation, the system perception would guide the response. The accuracy of the description will depend upon the user's profile (e.g., novices would provide a sketchy response at best) and overall familiarity with software in the application domain. A user who understands word processors fully but has worked with the specific word processor only once might actually be able to provide a more complete description of its function than the novice who has spent weeks trying to learn the system.

The *implementation model* combines the outward manifestation of the computer-based system (the look and feel of the interface), coupled with all supporting information (books, manuals, videotapes, help files) that describes interface syntax and semantics. When the implementation model and the user's mental model are coincident, users generally feel comfortable with the software and use it effectively. To accomplish this "melding" of the models, the design model must have been

---

1   In this context, *syntactic knowledge* refers to the mechanics of interaction that are required to use the interface effectively.
2   Sema*ntic knowledge* refers to the underlying sense of the application—an understanding of the functions that are performed, the meaning of input and output, and the goals and objectives of the system.

developed to accommodate the information contained in the user model, and the implementation model must accurately reflect syntactic and semantic information about the interface.

The models described in this section are "abstractions of what the user is doing or thinks he is doing or what somebody else thinks he ought to be doing when he uses an interactive system" [Mon84]. In essence, these models enable the interface designer to satisfy a key element of the most important principle of user interface design: "Know the user, know the tasks."

11.2.2   The Process

The analysis and design process for user interfaces is iterative and can be represented using a spiral model similar to the one discussed in Chapter 2. Referring to Figure 11.1, the user interface analysis and design process begins at the interior of the spiral and encompasses four distinct framework activities [Man97]: (1) interface analysis and modeling, (2) interface design, (3) interface construction, and (4) interface validation. The spiral shown in Figure 11.1 implies that each of these tasks will occur more than once, with each pass around the spiral representing additional elaboration of requirements and the resultant design. In most cases, the construction activity involves prototyping—the only practical way to validate what has been designed.

Interface analysis focuses on the profile of the users who will interact with the system. Skill level, business understanding, and general receptiveness to the new system are recorded; and different user categories are defined. For each user category, requirements are elicited. In essence, you work to understand the system perception (Section 11.2.1) for each class of users.

Once general requirements have been defined, a more detailed *task analysis* is conducted. Those tasks that the user performs to accomplish the goals of the system

FIGURE 11.1

The user interface design process

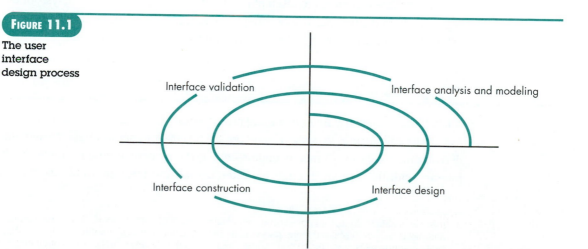

Interface validation

Interface analysis and modeling

Interface construction

Interface design

are identified, described, and elaborated (over a number of iterative passes through the spiral). Task analysis is discussed in more detail in Section 11.3. Finally, analysis of the user environment focuses on the physical work environment. Among the questions to be asked are

? What do we need to know about the environment as we begin UI design?

- Where will the interface be located physically?
- Will the user be sitting, standing, or performing other tasks unrelated to the interface?
- Does the interface hardware accommodate space, light, or noise constraints?
- Are there special human factors considerations driven by environmental factors?

The information gathered as part of the analysis action is used to create an analysis model for the interface. Using this model as a basis, the design action commences.

The goal of *interface design* is to define a set of interface objects and actions (and their screen representations) that enable a user to perform all defined tasks in a manner that meets every usability goal defined for the system. Interface design is discussed in more detail in Section 11.4.

Interface construction normally begins with the creation of a prototype that enables usage scenarios to be evaluated. As the iterative design process continues, a user interface tool kit (Section 11.5) may be used to complete the construction of the interface.

Interface validation focuses on (1) the ability of the interface to implement every user task correctly, to accommodate all task variations, and to achieve all general user requirements; (2) the degree to which the interface is easy to use and easy to learn, and (3) the users' acceptance of the interface as a useful tool in their work.

As I have already noted, the activities described in this section occur iteratively. Therefore, there is no need to attempt to specify every detail (for the analysis or design model) on the first pass. Subsequent passes through the process elaborate task detail, design information, and the operational features of the interface.

11.3   INTERFACE ANALYSIS[3]

A key tenet of all software engineering process models is this: *understand the problem before you attempt to design a solution.* In the case of user interface design, understanding the problem means understanding (1) the people (end users) who will interact with the system through the interface, (2) the tasks that end users must

---

3   It is reasonable to argue that this section should be placed in Chapter 5, 6, or 7, since requirements analysis issues are discussed there. It has been positioned here because interface analysis and design are intimately connected to one another, and the boundary between the two is often fuzzy.

perform to do their work, (3) the content that is presented as part of the interface, and (4) the environment in which these tasks will be conducted. In the sections that follow, I examine each of these elements of interface analysis with the intent of establishing a solid foundation for the design tasks that follow.

11.3.1 User Analysis

The phrase "user interface" is probably all the justification needed to spend some time understanding the user before worrying about technical matters. Earlier I noted that each user has a mental image of the software that may be different from the mental image developed by other users. In addition, the user's mental image may be vastly different from the software engineer's design model. The only way that you can get the mental image and the design model to converge is to work to understand the users themselves as well as how these people will use the system. Information from a broad array of sources can be used to accomplish this:

How do we learn what the user wants from the UI?

User Interviews. The most direct approach, members of the software team meet with end users to better understand their needs, motivations, work culture, and a myriad of other issues. This can be accomplished in one-on-one meetings or through focus groups.

Sales input. Sales people meet with users on a regular basis and can gather information that will help the software team to categorize users and better understand their requirements.

Marketing input. Market analysis can be invaluable in the definition of market segments and an understanding of how each segment might use the software in subtly different ways.

Support input. Support staff talks with users on a daily basis. They are the most likely source of information on what works and what doesn't, what users like and what they dislike, what features generate questions and what features are easy to use.

Above all, spend time talking to actual users, but be careful. One strong opinion doesn't necessarily mean that the majority of users will agree.

The following set of questions (adapted from [Hac98]) will help you to better understand the users of a system:

How do we learn about the demographics and characteristics of end users?

- Are users trained professionals, technicians, clerical, or manufacturing workers?
- What level of formal education does the average user have?
- Are the users capable of learning from written materials or have they expressed a desire for classroom training?
- Are users expert typists or keyboard phobic?
- What is the age range of the user community?
- Will the users be represented predominately by one gender?
- How are users compensated for the work they perform?

- Do users work normal office hours or do they work until the job is done?
- Is the software to be an integral part of the work users do or will it be used only occasionally?
- What is the primary spoken language among users?
- What are the consequences if a user makes a mistake using the system?
- Are users experts in the subject matter that is addressed by the system?
- Do users want to know about the technology that sits behind the interface?

Once these questions are answered, you'll know who the end users are, what is likely to motivate and please them, how they can be grouped into different user classes or profiles, what their mental models of the system are, and how the user interface must be characterized to meet their needs.

11.3.2   Task Analysis and Modeling

The goal of task analysis is to answer the following questions:

- What work will the user perform in specific circumstances?
- What tasks and subtasks will be performed as the user does the work?
- What specific problem domain objects will the user manipulate as work is performed?
- What is the sequence of work tasks—the workflow?
- What is the hierarchy of tasks?

KEY POINT

The user's goal is to accomplish one or more tasks via the UI. To accomplish this, the UI must provide mechanisms that allow the user to achieve her goal.

To answer these questions, you must draw upon techniques that I have discussed earlier in this book, but in this instance, these techniques are applied to the user interface.

Use cases.   In earlier chapters you learned that the use case describes the manner in which an actor (in the context of user interface design, an actor is always a person) interacts with a system. When used as part of task analysis, the use case is developed to show how an end user performs some specific work-related task. In most instances, the use case is written in an informal style (a simple paragraph) in the first-person. For example, assume that a small software company wants to build a computer-aided design system explicitly for interior designers. To get a better understanding of how they do their work, actual interior designers are asked to describe a specific design function. When asked: "How do you decide where to put furniture in a room?" an interior designer writes the following informal use case:

> I begin by sketching the floor plan of the room, the dimensions and the location of windows and doors. I'm very concerned about light as it enters the room, about the view out of the windows (if it's beautiful, I want to draw attention to it), about the running length of an unobstructed wall, about the flow of movement through the room. I then look at the list of furniture my customer and I have chosen—tables, chairs, sofa, cabinets, the list of

accents—lamps, rugs, paintings, sculpture, plants, smaller pieces, and my notes on any desires my customer has for placement. I then draw each item from my lists using a template that is scaled to the floor plan. I label each item I draw and use pencil because I always move things. I consider a number of alternative placements and decide on the one I like best. Then, I draw a rendering (a 3-D picture) of the room to give my customer a feel for what it'll look like.

This use case provides a basic description of one important work task for the computer-aided design system. From it, you can extract tasks, objects, and the overall flow of the interaction. In addition, other features of the system that would please the interior designer might also be conceived. For example, a digital photo could be taken looking out each window in a room. When the room is rendered, the actual outside view could be represented through each window.

SafeHome

Use Cases for UI Design

The scene: Vinod's cubicle, as user interface design continues.

The players: Vinod and Jamie, members of the *SafeHome* software engineering team.

The conversation:

Jamie: I pinned down our marketing contact and had her write a use case for the surveillance interface.

Vinod: From whose point of view?

Jamie: The homeowner, who else is there?

Vinod: There's also the system administrator role, even if it's the homeowner playing the role, it's a different point of view. The "administrator" sets the system up, configures stuff, lays out the floor plan, places the cameras . . .

Jamie: All I had her do was play the role of the homeowner when he wants to see video.

Vinod: That's okay. It's one of the major behaviors of the surveillance function interface. But we're going to have to examine the system administration behavior as well.

Jamie (irritated): You're right.

[Jamie leaves to find the marketing person. She returns a few hours later.]

Jamie: I was lucky, I found her and we worked through the administrator use case together. Basically, we're going to define "administration" as one function that's applicable to all other *SafeHome* functions. Here's what we came up with.

[Jamie shows the informal use case to Vinod.]

Informal use case: I want to be able to set or edit the system layout at any time. When I set up the system, I select an administration function. It asks me whether I want to do a new setup or whether I want to edit an existing setup. If I select a new setup, the system displays a drawing screen that will enable me to draw the floor plan onto a grid. There will be icons for walls, windows, and doors so that drawing is easy. I just stretch the icons to their appropriate lengths. The system will display the lengths in feet or meters (I can select the measurement system). I can select from a library of sensors and cameras and place them on the floor plan. I get to label each, or the system will do automatic labeling. I can establish settings for sensors and cameras from appropriate menus. If I select edit, I can move sensors or cameras, add new ones or delete existing ones, edit the floor plan, and edit the settings for cameras and sensors. In every case, I expect the system to do consistency checking and to help me avoid mistakes.

Vinod (after reading the scenario): Okay, there are probably some useful design patterns [Chapter 12] or reusable components for GUIs for drawing programs. I'll betcha 50 bucks we can implement some or most of the administrator interface using them.

Jamie: Agreed. I'll check it out.

Task elaboration.   In Chapter 8, I discussed stepwise elaboration (also called functional decomposition or stepwise refinement) as a mechanism for refining the processing tasks that are required for software to accomplish some desired function. Task analysis for interface design uses an elaborative approach to assist in understanding the human activities the user interface must accommodate.

Task analysis can be applied in two ways. As I have already noted, an interactive, computer-based system is often used to replace a manual or semimanual activity. To understand the tasks that must be performed to accomplish the goal of the activity, you must understand the tasks that people currently perform (when using a manual approach) and then map these into a similar (but not necessarily identical) set of tasks that are implemented in the context of the user interface. Alternatively, you can study an existing specification for a computer-based solution and derive a set of user tasks that will accommodate the user model, the design model, and the system perception.

Regardless of the overall approach to task analysis, you must first define and classify tasks. I have already noted that one approach is stepwise elaboration. For example, let's reconsider the computer-aided design system for interior designers discussed earlier. By observing an interior designer at work, you notice that interior design comprises a number of major activities: furniture layout (note the use case discussed earlier), fabric and material selection, wall and window coverings selection, presentation (to the customer), costing, and shopping. Each of these major tasks can be elaborated into subtasks. For example, using information contained in the use case, furniture layout can be refined into the following tasks: (1) draw a floor plan based on room dimensions, (2) place windows and doors at appropriate locations, (3a) use furniture templates to draw scaled furniture outlines on the floor plan, (3b) use accents templates to draw scaled accents on the floor plan, (4) move furniture outlines and accent outlines to get the best placement, (5) label all furniture and accent outlines, (6) draw dimensions to show location, and (7) draw a perspective-rendering view for the customer. A similar approach could be used for each of the other major tasks.

Subtasks 1 to 7 can each be refined further. Subtasks 1 to 6 will be performed by manipulating information and performing actions within the user interface. On the other hand, subtask 7 can be performed automatically in software and will result in little direct user interaction.[4] The design model of the interface should accommodate each of these tasks in a way that is consistent with the user model (the profile of a "typical" interior designer) and system perception (what the interior designer expects from an automated system).

Object elaboration.   Rather than focusing on the tasks that a user must perform, you can examine the use case and other information obtained from the user and extract the physical objects that are used by the interior designer. These objects can

---

4   However, this may not be the case. The interior designer might want to specify the perspective to be drawn, the scaling, the use of color, and other information. The use case related to drawing perspective renderings would provide the information you need to address this task.

be categorized into classes. Attributes of each class are defined, and an evaluation of the actions applied to each object provide a list of operations. For example, the furniture template might translate into a class called **Furniture** with attributes that might include **size, shape, location,** and others. The interior designer would *select* the object from the **Furniture** class, *move* it to a position on the floor plan (another object in this context), *draw* the furniture outline, and so forth. The tasks *select, move,* and *draw* are operations. The user interface analysis model would not provide a literal implementation for each of these operations. However, as the design is elaborated, the details of each operation are defined.

Workflow analysis.   When a number of different users, each playing different roles, makes use of a user interface, it is sometimes necessary to go beyond task analysis and object elaboration and apply *workflow analysis.* This technique allows you to understand how a work process is completed when several people (and roles) are involved. Consider a company that intends to fully automate the process of prescribing and delivering prescription drugs. The entire process[5] will revolve around a Web-based application that is accessible by physicians (or their assistants), pharmacists, and patients. Workflow can be represented effectively with a UML swimlane diagram (a variation on the activity diagram).

We consider only a small part of the work process: the situation that occurs when a patient asks for a refill. Figure 11.2 presents a swimlane diagram that indicates the tasks and decisions for each of the three roles noted earlier. This information may have been elicited via interview or from use cases written by each actor. Regardless, the flow of events (shown in the figure) enables you to recognize a number of key interface characteristics:

1. Each user implements different tasks via the interface; therefore, the look and feel of the interface designed for the patient will be different than the one defined for pharmacists or physicians.

2. The interface design for pharmacists and physicians must accommodate access to and display of information from secondary information sources (e.g., access to inventory for the pharmacist and access to information about alternative medications for the physician).

3. Many of the activities noted in the swimlane diagram can be further elaborated using task analysis and/or object elaboration (e.g., *Fills prescription* could imply a mail-order delivery, a visit to a pharmacy, or a visit to a special drug distribution center).

Hierarchical representation.   A process of elaboration occurs as you begin to analyze the interface. Once workflow has been established, a task hierarchy can be defined for each user type. The hierarchy is derived by a stepwise elaboration of

---

5   This example has been adapted from [Hac98].

FIGURE 11.2   Swimlane diagram for prescription refill function

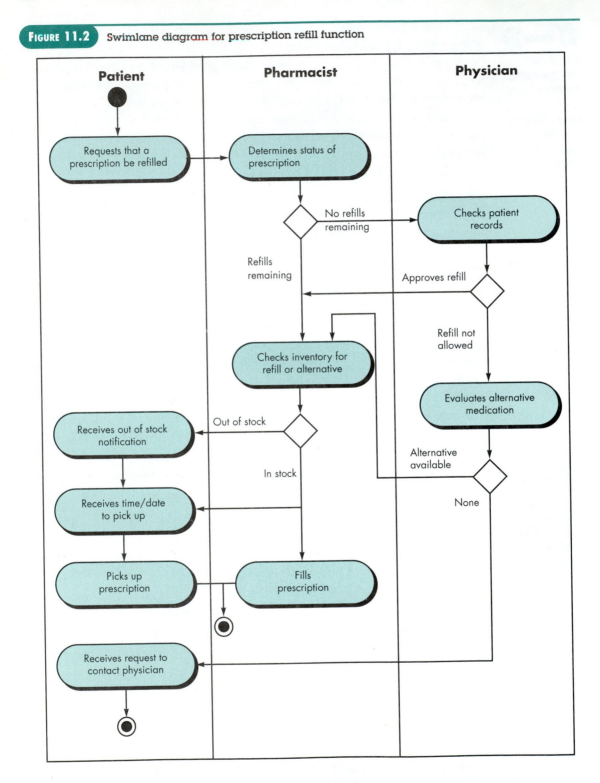

each task identified for the user. For example, consider the following user task and subtask hierarchy.

> **User task: *Requests that a prescription be refilled***
>
> - *Provide identifying information.*
>   - *Specify name.*
>   - *Specify userid.*
>   - *Specify PIN and password.*
> - *Specify prescription number.*
> - *Specify date refill is required.*

To complete the task, three subtasks are defined. One of these subtasks, *provide identifying information,* is further elaborated in three additional sub-subtasks.

11.3.3   Analysis of Display Content

The user tasks identified in Section 11.3.2 lead to the presentation of a variety of different types of content. For modern applications, display content can range from character-based reports (e.g., a spreadsheet), graphical displays (e.g., a histogram, a 3-D model, a picture of a person), or specialized information (e.g., audio or video files). The analysis modeling techniques discussed in Chapters 6 and 7 identify the output data objects that are produced by an application. These data objects may be (1) generated by components (unrelated to the interface) in other parts of an application, (2) acquired from data stored in a database that is accessible from the application, or (3) transmitted from systems external to the application in question.

During this interface analysis step, the format and aesthetics of the content (as it is displayed by the interface) are considered. Among the questions that are asked and answered are:

> **? How do we determine the format and aesthetics of content displayed as part of the UI?**

- Are different types of data assigned to consistent geographic locations on the screen (e.g., photos always appear in the upper right-hand corner)?
- Can the user customize the screen location for content?
- Is proper on-screen identification assigned to all content?
- If a large report is to be presented, how should it be partitioned for ease of understanding?
- Will mechanisms be available for moving directly to summary information for large collections of data?
- Will graphical output be scaled to fit within the bounds of the display device that is used?
- How will color be used to enhance understanding?
- How will error messages and warnings be presented to the user?

The answers to these (and other) questions will help you to establish requirements for content presentation.

11.3.4 Analysis of the Work Environment

Hackos and Redish [Hac98] discuss the importance of work environment analysis when they state:

> People do not perform their work in isolation. They are influenced by the activity around them, the physical characteristics of the workplace, the type of equipment they are using, and the work relationships they have with other people. If the products you design do not fit into the environment, they may be difficult or frustrating to use.

In some applications the user interface for a computer-based system is placed in a "user-friendly location" (e.g., proper lighting, good display height, easy keyboard access), but in others (e.g., a factory floor or an airplane cockpit), lighting may be suboptimal, noise may be a factor, a keyboard or mouse may not be an option, display placement may be less than ideal. The interface designer may be constrained by factors that mitigate against ease of use.

In addition to physical environmental factors, the workplace culture also comes into play. Will system interaction be measured in some manner (e.g., time per transaction or accuracy of a transaction)? Will two or more people have to share information before an input can be provided? How will support be provided to users of the system? These and many related questions should be answered before the interface design commences.

11.4 INTERFACE DESIGN STEPS

Quote:

"Interactive design [is] a seamless blend of graphic arts, technology, and psychology."

Brad Wieners

Once interface analysis has been completed, all tasks (or objects and actions) required by the end user have been identified in detail and the interface design activity commences. Interface design, like all software engineering design, is an iterative process. Each user interface design step occurs a number of times, elaborating and refining information developed in the preceding step.

Although many different user interface design models (e.g., [Nor86], [Nie00]) have been proposed, all suggest some combination of the following steps:

1. Using information developed during interface analysis (Section 11.3), define interface objects and actions (operations).

2. Define events (user actions) that will cause the state of the user interface to change. Model this behavior.

3. Depict each interface state as it will actually look to the end user.

4. Indicate how the user interprets the state of the system from information provided through the interface.

In some cases, you can begin with sketches of each interface state (i.e., what the user interface looks like under various circumstances) and then work backward to define objects, actions, and other important design information. Regardless of the sequence of design tasks, you should (1) always follow the golden rules discussed in Section 11.1, (2) model how the interface will be implemented, and (3) consider the environment (e.g., display technology, operating system, development tools) that will be used.

11.4.1   Applying Interface Design Steps

The definition of interface objects and the actions that are applied to them is an important step in interface design. To accomplish this, user scenarios are parsed in much the same way as described in Chapter 6. That is, a use case is written. Nouns (objects) and verbs (actions) are isolated to create a list of objects and actions.

Once the objects and actions have been defined and elaborated iteratively, they are categorized by type. Target, source, and application objects are identified. A *source object* (e.g., a report icon) is dragged and dropped onto a *target object* (e.g., a printer icon). The implication of this action is to create a hard-copy report. An *application object* represents application-specific data that are not directly manipulated as part of screen interaction. For example, a mailing list is used to store names for a mailing. The list itself might be sorted, merged, or purged (menu-based actions), but it is not dragged and dropped via user interaction.

When you are satisfied that all important objects and actions have been defined (for one design iteration), screen layout is performed. Like other interface design activities, screen layout is an interactive process in which graphical design and placement of icons, definition of descriptive screen text, specification and titling for windows, and definition of major and minor menu items are conducted. If a real-world metaphor is appropriate for the application, it is specified at this time, and the layout is organized in a manner that complements the metaphor.

To provide a brief illustration of the design steps noted previously, consider a user scenario for the *SafeHome* system (discussed in earlier chapters). A preliminary use case (written by the homeowner) for the interface follows:

Preliminary use case: I want to gain access to my *SafeHome* system from any remote location via the Internet. Using browser software operating on my notebook computer (while I'm at work or traveling), I can determine the status of the alarm system, arm or disarm the system, reconfigure security zones, and view different rooms within the house via preinstalled video cameras.

To access *SafeHome* from a remote location, I provide an identifier and a password. These define levels of access (e.g., all users may not be able to reconfigure the system) and provide security. Once validated, I can check the status of the system and change the status by arming or disarming *SafeHome*. I can reconfigure the system by displaying a floor plan of the house, viewing each of the security sensors, displaying each currently configured zone, and modifying zones as required. I can view the interior of the house via strategically placed video cameras. I can pan and zoom each camera to provide different views of the interior.

Based on this use case, the following homeowner tasks, objects, and data items are identified:

- *accesses* the *SafeHome* system
- *enters* an **ID** and **password** to allow remote access
- *checks* **system status**
- *arms* or *disarms SafeHome* system
- *displays* **floor plan** and **sensor locations**
- *displays* **zones** on floor plan
- *changes* **zones** on floor plan
- *displays* **video camera locations** on floor plan
- *selects* **video camera** for viewing
- *views* **video images** (four frames per second)
- *pans* or *zooms* the **video camera**

Objects (boldface) and actions (italics) are extracted from this list of homeowner tasks. The majority of objects noted are application objects. However, **video camera location** (a source object) is dragged and dropped onto **video camera** (a target object) to create a **video image** (a window with video display).

A preliminary sketch of the screen layout for video monitoring is created (Figure 11.3).[6] To invoke the video image, a video camera location icon, *C*, located in the floor plan displayed in the monitoring window is selected. In this case a camera location in the living room (LR) is then dragged and dropped onto the video camera icon in the upper left-hand portion of the screen. The video image window appears, displaying streaming video from the camera located in the LR. The zoom and pan control slides are used to control the magnification and direction of the video image. To select a view from another camera, the user simply drags and drops a different camera location icon into the camera icon in the upper left-hand corner of the screen.

The layout sketch shown would have to be supplemented with an expansion of each menu item within the menu bar, indicating what actions are available for the video monitoring mode (state). A complete set of sketches for each homeowner task noted in the user scenario would be created during the interface design.

Although automated tools can be useful in developing layout prototypes, sometimes a pencil and paper are all that are needed.

11.4.2 User Interface Design Patterns

Graphical user interfaces have become so common that a wide variety of user interface design patterns has emerged. As I noted earlier in this book, a design pattern is

---

6   Note that this differs somewhat from the implementation of these features in earlier chapters. This might be considered a first draft design and represents one alternative that might be considered.

FIGURE 11.3

Preliminary
screen layout

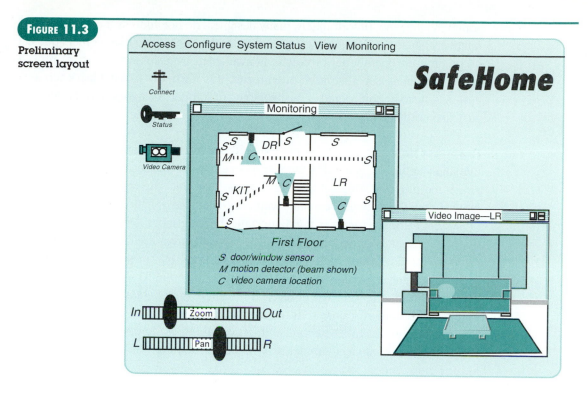

an abstraction that prescribes a design solution to a specific, well-bounded design problem.

As an example of a commonly encountered interface design problem, consider a situation in which a user must enter one or more calendar dates, sometimes months in advance. There are many possible solutions to this simple problem, and a number of different patterns that might be proposed. Laakso [Laa00] suggests a pattern called **CalendarStrip** that produces a continuous, scrollable calendar in which the current date is highlighted and future dates may be selected by picking them from the calendar. The calendar metaphor is well known to every user and provides an effective mechanism for placing a future date in context.

A vast array of interface design patterns has been proposed over the past decade. A more detailed discussion of user interface design patterns is presented in Chapter 12. In addition, Erickson [Eri08] provides pointers to many Web-based collections.

11.4.3   Design Issues

As the design of a user interface evolves, four common design issues almost always surface: system response time, user help facilities, error information handling, and

WebRef

A wide variety of UI
design patterns has
been proposed. For
pointers to a variety of
patterns sites, visit
**www.hcipatterns
.org**.

command labeling. Unfortunately, many designers do not address these issues until relatively late in the design process (sometimes the first inkling of a problem doesn't occur until an operational prototype is available). Unnecessary iteration, project delays, and end-user frustration often result. It is far better to establish each as a design issue to be considered at the beginning of software design, when changes are easy and costs are low.

Response time.   System response time is the primary complaint for many interactive applications. In general, system response time is measured from the point at which the user performs some control action (e.g., hits the return key or clicks a mouse) until the software responds with desired output or action.

System response time has two important characteristics: length and variability. If system response is too long, user frustration and stress are inevitable. *Variability* refers to the deviation from average response time, and in many ways, it is the most important response time characteristic. Low variability enables the user to establish an interaction rhythm, even if response time is relatively long. For example, a 1-second response to a command will often be preferable to a response that varies from 0.1 to 2.5 seconds. When variability is significant, the user is always off balance, always wondering whether something "different" has occurred behind the scenes.

Help facilities.   Almost every user of an interactive, computer-based system requires help now and then. In some cases, a simple question addressed to a knowledgeable colleague can do the trick. In others, detailed research in a multivolume set of "user manuals" may be the only option. In most cases, however, modern software provides online help facilities that enable a user to get a question answered or resolve a problem without leaving the interface.

A number of design issues [Rub88] must be addressed when a help facility is considered:

- Will help be available for all system functions and at all times during system interaction? Options include help for only a subset of all functions and actions or help for all functions.

- How will the user request help? Options include a help menu, a special function key, or a HELP command.

- How will help be represented? Options include a separate window, a reference to a printed document (less than ideal), or a one- or two-line suggestion produced in a fixed screen location.

- How will the user return to normal interaction? Options include a return button displayed on the screen, a function key, or control sequence.

• How will help information be structured? Options include a "flat" structure in which all information is accessed through a keyword, a layered hierarchy of information that provides increasing detail as the user proceeds into the structure, or the use of hypertext.

Error handling.   Error messages and warnings are "bad news" delivered to users of interactive systems when something has gone awry. At their worst, error messages and warnings impart useless or misleading information and serve only to increase user frustration. There are few computer users who have not encountered an error of the form: *"Application XXX has been forced to quit because an error of type 1023 has been encountered."* Somewhere, an explanation for error 1023 must exist; otherwise, why would the designers have added the identification? Yet, the error message provides no real indication of what went wrong or where to look to get additional information. An error message presented in this manner does nothing to assuage user anxiety or to help correct the problem.

In general, every error message or warning produced by an interactive system should have the following characteristics:

• The message should describe the problem in jargon that the user can understand.

• The message should provide constructive advice for recovering from the error.

• The message should indicate any negative consequences of the error (e.g., potentially corrupted data files) so that the user can check to ensure that they have not occurred (or correct them if they have).

• The message should be accompanied by an audible or visual cue. That is, a beep might be generated to accompany the display of the message, or the message might flash momentarily or be displayed in a color that is easily recognizable as the "error color."

• The message should be "nonjudgmental." That is, the wording should never place blame on the user.

Because no one really likes bad news, few users will like an error message no matter how well designed. But an effective error message philosophy can do much to improve the quality of an interactive system and will significantly reduce user frustration when problems do occur.

Menu and command labeling.   The typed command was once the most common mode of interaction between user and system software and was commonly used for applications of every type. Today, the use of window-oriented, point-and-pick interfaces has reduced reliance on typed commands, but some power-users continue to prefer a command-oriented mode of interaction. A number of design

? **What characteristics should a "good'" error message have?**

issues arise when typed commands or menu labels are provided as a mode of interaction:

- Will every menu option have a corresponding command?
- What form will commands take? Options include a control sequence (e.g., alt-P), function keys, or a typed word.
- How difficult will it be to learn and remember the commands? What can be done if a command is forgotten?
- Can commands be customized or abbreviated by the user?
- Are menu labels self-explanatory within the context of the interface?
- Are submenus consistent with the function implied by a master menu item?

As I noted earlier in this chapter, conventions for command usage should be established across all applications. It is confusing and often error-prone for a user to type alt-D when a graphics object is to be duplicated in one application and alt-D when a graphics object is to be deleted in another. The potential for error is obvious.

WebRef

Guidelines for developing accessible software can be found at **www3.ibm.com/ able/guidelines/ software/ accesssoftware .html**.

Application accessibility. As computing applications become ubiquitous, software engineers must ensure that interface design encompasses mechanisms that enable easy access for those with special needs. *Accessibility* for users (and software engineers) who may be physically challenged is an imperative for ethical, legal, and business reasons. A variety of accessibility guidelines (e.g., [W3C03])—many designed for Web applications but often applicable to all types of software—provide detailed suggestions for designing interfaces that achieve varying levels of accessibility. Others (e.g., [App08], [Mic08]) provide specific guidelines for "assistive technology" that addresses the needs of those with visual, hearing, mobility, speech, and learning impairments.

Internationalization. Software engineers and their managers invariably underestimate the effort and skills required to create user interfaces that accommodate the needs of different locales and languages. Too often, interfaces are designed for one locale and language and then jury-rigged to work in other countries. The challenge for interface designers is to create "globalized" software. That is, user interfaces should be designed to accommodate a generic core of functionality that can be delivered to all who use the software. *Localization* features enable the interface to be customized for a specific market.

A variety of internationalization guidelines (e.g., [IBM03]) are available to software engineers. These guidelines address broad design issues (e.g., screen layouts may differ in various markets) and discrete implementation issues (e.g., different alphabets may create specialized labeling and spacing requirements). The *Unicode* standard [Uni03] has been developed to address the daunting challenge of managing dozens of natural languages with hundreds of characters and symbols.

SOFTWARE TOOLS

User Interface Development

Objective: These tools enable a software engineer to create a sophisticated GUI with relatively little custom software development. The tools provide access to reusable components and make the creation of an interface a matter of selecting from predefined capabilities that are assembled using the tool.

Mechanics: Modern user interfaces are constructed using a set of reusable components that are coupled with some custom components developed to provide specialized features. Most user interface development tools enable a software engineer to create an interface using "drag and drop" capability. That is, the developer selects from many predefined capabilities (e.g., forms builders, interaction mechanisms, command processing capability) and places these capabilities within the content of the interface to be created.

Representative Tools:[7]

LegaSuite GUI, developed by Seagull Software (**www.seagullsoftware.com**), enabled the creation of browser-based GUIs and provide facilities for reengineering antiquated interfaces.

Motif Common Desktop Environment, developed by The Open Group (**www.osf.org/tech/desktop/cde/**), is an integrated graphical user interface for open systems desktop computing. It delivers a single, standard graphical interface for the management of data and files (the graphical desktop) and applications.

Altia Design 8.0, developed by Altia (**www.altia.com**), is a tool for creating GUIs on a variety of different platforms (e.g., automotive, handheld, industrial).

11.5   WebApp Interface Design

Every user interface—whether it is designed for a WebApp, a traditional software application, a consumer product, or an industrial device—should exhibit the usability characteristics that were discussed earlier in this chapter. Dix [Dix99] argues that you should design a WebApp interface so that it answers three primary questions for the end user:

If it is likely that users may enter your WebApp at various locations and levels in the content hierarchy, be sure to design every page with navigation features that will lead the user to other points of interest.

Where am I? The interface should (1) provide an indication of the WebApp that has been accessed[8] and (2) inform the user of her location in the content hierarchy.

What can I do now? The interface should always help the user understand his current options—what functions are available, what links are live, what content is relevant?

Where have I been, where am I going? The interface must facilitate navigation. Hence, it must provide a "map" (implemented in a way that is easy to understand) of where the user has been and what paths may be taken to move elsewhere within the WebApp.

An effective WebApp interface must provide answers for each of these questions as the end user navigates through content and functionality.

---

7 Tools noted here do not represent an endorsement, but rather a sampling of tools in this category.
8 Each of us has bookmarked a Web page, only to revisit it later and have no indication of the website or the context for the page (as well as no way to move to another location within the site).

11.5.1   Interface Design Principles and Guidelines

The user interface of a WebApp is its "first impression." Regardless of the value of its content, the sophistication of its processing capabilities and services, and the overall benefit of the WebApp itself, a poorly designed interface will disappoint the potential user and may, in fact, cause the user to go elsewhere. Because of the sheer volume of competing WebApps in virtually every subject area, the interface must "grab" a potential user immediately.

Bruce Tognozzi [Tog01] defines a set of fundamental characteristics that all interfaces should exhibit and in doing so, establishes a philosophy that should be followed by every WebApp interface designer:

> Effective interfaces are visually apparent and forgiving, instilling in their users a sense of control. Users quickly see the breadth of their options, grasp how to achieve their goals, and do their work.
>
> Effective interfaces do not concern the user with the inner workings of the system. Work is carefully and continuously saved, with full option for the user to undo any activity at any time.
>
> Effective applications and services perform a maximum of work, while requiring a minimum of information from users.

KEY POINT

A good WebApp interface is understandable and forgiving, providing the user with a sense of control.

In order to design WebApp interfaces that exhibit these characteristics, Tognozzi [Tog01] identifies a set of overriding design principles:[9]

? Is there a set of basic principles that can be applied as you design a GUI?

Anticipation. *A WebApp should be designed so that it anticipates the user's next move.* For example, consider a customer support WebApp developed by a manufacturer of computer printers. A user has requested a content object that presents information about a printer driver for a newly released operating system. The designer of the WebApp should anticipate that the user might request a download of the driver and should provide navigation facilities that allow this to happen without requiring the user to search for this capability.

Communication. *The interface should communicate the status of any activity initiated by the user.* Communication can be obvious (e.g., a text message) or subtle (e.g., an image of a sheet of paper moving through a printer to indicate that printing is under way). The interface should also communicate user status (e.g., the user's identification) and her location within the WebApp content hierarchy.

Consistency. *The use of navigation controls, menus, icons, and aesthetics (e.g., color, shape, layout) should be consistent throughout the WebApp.* For example, if underlined blue text implies a navigation link, content should never incorporate blue underlined text that does not imply a link. In addition, an object, say a yellow triangle, used to

---

9   Tognozzi's original principles have been adapted and extended for use this book. See [Tog01] for further discussion of these principles.

indicate a caution message before the user invokes a particular function or action, should not be used for other purposes elsewhere in the WebApp. Finally, every feature of the interface should respond in a manner that is consistent with user expectations.[10]

Controlled autonomy. *The interface should facilitate user movement throughout the WebApp, but it should do so in a manner that enforces navigation conventions that have been established for the application.* For example, navigation to secure portions of the WebApp should be controlled by userID and password, and there should be no navigation mechanism that enables a user to circumvent these controls.

Efficiency. *The design of the WebApp and its interface should optimize the user's work efficiency, not the efficiency of the developer who designs and builds it or the client-server environment that executes it.* Tognozzi [Tog01] discusses this when he writes: "This simple truth is why it is so important for everyone involved in a software project to appreciate the importance of making user productivity goal one and to understand the vital difference between building an efficient system and empowering an efficient user."

Flexibility. *The interface should be flexible enough to enable some users to accomplish tasks directly and others to explore the WebApp in a somewhat random fashion.* In every case, it should enable the user to understand where he is and provide the user with functionality that can undo mistakes and retrace poorly chosen navigation paths.

Focus. *The WebApp interface (and the content it presents) should stay focused on the user task(s) at hand.* In all hypermedia there is a tendency to route the user to loosely related content. Why? Because it's very easy to do! The problem is that the user can rapidly become lost in many layers of supporting information and lose sight of the original content that she wanted in the first place.

Fitt's law. *"The time to acquire a target is a function of the distance to and size of the target"* [Tog01]. Based on a study conducted in the 1950s [Fit54], Fitt's law "is an effective method of modeling rapid, aimed movements, where one appendage (like a hand) starts at rest at a specific start position, and moves to rest within a target area" [Zha02]. If a sequence of selections or standardized inputs (with many different options within the sequence) is defined by a user task, the first selection (e.g., mouse pick) should be physically close to the next selection. For example, consider a WebApp home page interface at an e-commerce site that sells consumer electronics.

Each user option implies a set of follow-on user choices or actions. For example, the "buy a product" option requires that the user enter a product category followed by the product name. The product category (e.g., audio equipment, televisions, DVD

---

10 Tognozzi [Tog01] notes that the only way to be sure that user expectations are properly understood is through comprehensive user testing (Chapter 20).

players) appears as a pull-down menu as soon as "buy a product" is picked. There-fore, the next choice is immediately obvious (it is nearby) and the time to acquire it is negligible. If, on the other hand, the choice appeared on a menu that was located on the other side of the screen, the time for the user to acquire it (and then make the choice) would be far too long.

Human interface objects.   *A vast library of reusable human interface objects has been developed for WebApps. Use them.* Any interface object that can be "seen, heard, touched or otherwise perceived" [Tog01] by an end user can be acquired from any one of a number of object libraries.

Latency reduction.   *Rather than making the user wait for some internal operation to complete (e.g., downloading a complex graphical image), the WebApp should use multitasking in a way that lets the user proceed with work as if the operation has been completed.* In addition to reducing latency, delays must be acknowledged so that the user understands what is happening. This includes (1) providing audio feedback when a selection does not result in an immediate action by the WebApp, (2) displaying an animated clock or progress bar to indicate that processing is under way, and (3) providing some entertainment (e.g., an animation or text presentation) while lengthy processing occurs.

Learnability.   *A WebApp interface should be designed to minimize learning time, and once learned, to minimize relearning required when the WebApp is revisited.* In general the interface should emphasize a simple, intuitive design that organizes content and functionality into categories that are obvious to the user.

Metaphors are an excellent idea because they mirror real-world experience. Just be sure that the metaphor you choose is well known to end users.

Metaphors.   *An interface that uses an interaction metaphor is easier to learn and easier to use, as long as the metaphor is appropriate for the application and the user.* A metaphor should call on images and concepts from the user's experience, but it does not need to be an exact reproduction of a real-world experience. For example, an e-commerce site that implements automated bill paying for a financial institution, uses a checkbook metaphor (not surprisingly) to assist the user in specifying and scheduling bill payments. However, when a user "writes" a check, he need not enter the complete payee name but can pick from a list of payees or have the system select based on the first few typed letters. The metaphor remains intact, but the user gets an assist from the WebApp.

Maintain work product integrity.   *A work product (e.g., a form completed by the user, a user-specified list) must be automatically saved so that it will not be lost if an error occurs.* Each of us has experienced the frustration associated with completing a lengthy WebApp form only to have the content lost because of an error (made by us, by the WebApp, or in transmission from client to server). To avoid this, a WebApp should be designed to autosave all user-specified data. The interface should support this function and provide the user with an easy mechanism for recovering "lost" information.

Readability.   *All information presented through the interface should be readable by young and old.* The interface designer should emphasize readable type styles, font sizes, and color background choices that enhance contrast.

Track state.   *When appropriate, the state of the user interaction should be tracked and stored so that a user can logoff and return later to pick up where she left off.* In general, cookies can be designed to store state information. However, cookies are a controversial technology, and other design solutions may be more palatable for some users.

Visible navigation.   *A well-designed WebApp interface provides "the illusion that users are in the same place, with the work brought to them"* [Tog01]. When this approach is used, navigation is not a user concern. Rather, the user retrieves content objects and selects functions that are displayed and executed through the interface.

SAFEHOME

Interface Design Review

The scene: Doug Miller's office.

The players: Doug Miller (manager of the *SafeHome* software engineering group) and Vinod Raman, a member of the *SafeHome* product software engineering team.

The conversation:

Doug: Vinod, have you and the team had a chance to review the **SafeHomeAssured.com** e-commerce interface prototype?

Vinod: Yeah . . . we all went through it from a technical point of view, and I have a bunch of notes. I e-mailed 'em to Sharon [manager of the WebApp team for the outsourcing vendor for the *SafeHome* e-commerce website] yesterday.

Doug: You and Sharon can get together and discuss the small stuff . . . give me a summary of the important issues.

Vinod: Overall, they've done a good job, nothing ground breaking, but it's a typical e-commerce interface, decent aesthetics, reasonable layout, they've hit all the important functions . . .

Doug (smiling ruefully): But?

Vinod: Well, there are a few things . . . .

Doug: Such as . . .

Vinod (showing Doug a sequence of storyboards for the interface prototype): Here's the major functions menu that's displayed on the home page:

   Learn about *SafeHome*.

   Describe your home.

   Get *SafeHome* component recommendations.

   Purchase a *SafeHome* system.

   Get technical support.

The problem isn't with these functions. They're all okay, but the level of abstraction isn't right.

Doug: They're all major functions, aren't they?

Vinod: They are, but here's the thing . . . you can purchase a system by inputting a list of components . . . no real need to describe the house if you don't want to. I'd suggest only four menu options on the home page:

   Learn about *SafeHome*.

   Specify the *SafeHome* system you need.

   Purchase a *SafeHome* system.

   Get technical support.

When you select **Specify the *SafeHome* system you need**, you'll then have the following options:

   Select *SafeHome* components.

   Get *SafeHome* component recommendations.

If you're a knowledgeable user, you'll select components from a set of categorized pull-down menus for sensors, cameras, control panels, etc. If you need help, you'll ask for a recommendation and that will require that you describe your house. I think it's a bit more logical.

Doug: I agree. Have you talked with Sharon about this?

Vinod: No, I want to discuss this with marketing first; then I'll give her a call.

Nielsen and Wagner [Nie96] suggest a few pragmatic interface design guidelines (based on their redesign of a major WebApp) that provide a nice complement to the principles suggested earlier in this section:

- Reading speed on a computer monitor is approximately 25 percent slower than reading speed for hardcopy. Therefore, do not force the user to read voluminous amounts of text, particularly when the text explains the operation of the WebApp or assists in navigation.

- Avoid "under construction" signs—an unnecessary link is sure to disappoint.

- Users prefer not to scroll. Important information should be placed within the dimensions of a typical browser window.

- Navigation menus and head bars should be designed consistently and should be available on all pages that are available to the user. The design should not rely on browser functions to assist in navigation.

- Aesthetics should never supersede functionality. For example, a simple button might be a better navigation option than an aesthetically pleasing, but vague image or icon whose intent is unclear.

- Navigation options should be obvious, even to the casual user. The user should not have to search the screen to determine how to link to other content or services.

A well-designed interface improves the user's perception of the content or services provided by the site. It need not necessarily be flashy, but it should always be well structured and ergonomically sound.

11.5.2 Interface Design Workflow for WebApps

Earlier in this chapter I noted that user interface design begins with the identification of user, task, and environmental requirements. Once user tasks have been identified, user scenarios (use cases) are created and analyzed to define a set of interface objects and actions.

Information contained within the requirements model forms the basis for the creation of a screen layout that depicts graphical design and placement of icons, definition of descriptive screen text, specification and titling for windows, and specification of major and minor menu items. Tools are then used to prototype and ultimately implement the interface design model. The following tasks represent a rudimentary workflow for WebApp interface design:

1. **Review information contained in the requirements model and refine as required.**

2. **Develop a rough sketch of the WebApp interface layout.** An interface prototype (including the layout) may have been developed as part of the requirements modeling activity. If the layout already exists, it should be reviewed and refined as required. If the interface layout has not been

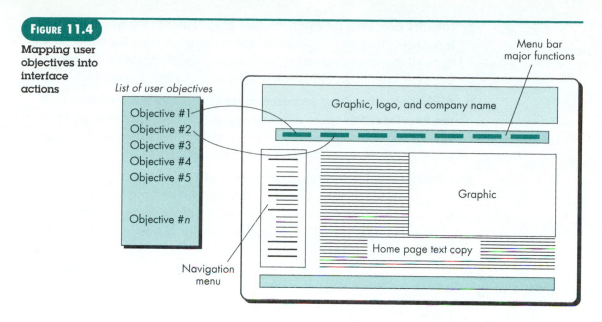

FIGURE 11.4

Mapping user
objectives into
interface
actions

developed, you should work with stakeholders to develop it at this time. A
schematic first-cut layout sketch is shown in Figure 11.4.

3. **Map user objectives into specific interface actions.** For the vast majority of WebApps, the user will have a relatively small set of primary objectives.
   These should be mapped into specific interface actions as shown in Figure 11.4.
   In essence, you must answer the following question: "How does the interface
   enable the user to accomplish each objective?"

4. **Define a set of user tasks that are associated with each action.** Each
   interface action (e.g., "buy a product") is associated with a set of user tasks.
   These tasks have been identified during requirements modeling. During design, they must be mapped into specific interactions that encompass navigation issues, content objects, and WebApp functions.

5. **Storyboard screen images for each interface action.** As each action is
   considered, a sequence of storyboard images (screen images) should be created
   to depict how the interface responds to user interaction. Content objects should
   be identified (even if they have not yet been designed and developed), WebApp
   functionality should be shown, and navigation links should be indicated.

6. **Refine interface layout and storyboards using input from aesthetic
   design.** In most cases, you'll be responsible for rough layout and story-
   boarding, but the aesthetic look and feel for a major commercial site is
   often developed by artistic, rather than technical, professionals. Aesthetic
   design (Chapter 13) is integrated with the work performed by the interface
   designer.

7. **Identify user interface objects that are required to implement the interface.** This task may require a search through an existing object library to find those reusable objects (classes) that are appropriate for the WebApp interface. In addition, any custom classes are specified at this time.

8. **Develop a procedural representation of the user's interaction with the interface.** This optional task uses UML sequence diagrams and/or activity diagrams (Appendix 1) to depict the flow of activities (and decisions) that occur as the user interacts with the WebApp.

9. **Develop a behavioral representation of the interface.** This optional task makes use of UML state diagrams (Appendix 1) to represent state transitions and the events that cause them. Control mechanisms (i.e., the objects and actions available to the user to alter a WebApp state) are defined.

10. **Describe the interface layout for each state.** Using design information developed in Tasks 2 and 5, associate a specific layout or screen image with each WebApp state described in Task 8.

11. **Refine and review the interface design model.** Review of the interface should focus on usability.

It is important to note that the final task set you choose should be adapted to the special requirements of the application that is to be built.

11.6   DESIGN EVALUATION

Once you create an operational user interface prototype, it must be evaluated to determine whether it meets the needs of the user. Evaluation can span a formality spectrum that ranges from an informal "test drive," in which a user provides impromptu feedback to a formally designed study that uses statistical methods for the evaluation of questionnaires completed by a population of end users.

The user interface evaluation cycle takes the form shown in Figure 11.5. After the design model has been completed, a first-level prototype is created. The prototype is evaluated by the user,[11] who provides you with direct comments about the efficacy of the interface. In addition, if formal evaluation techniques are used (e.g., questionnaires, rating sheets), you can extract information from these data (e.g., 80 percent of all users did not like the mechanism for saving data files). Design modifications are made based on user input, and the next level prototype is created. The evaluation cycle continues until no further modifications to the interface design are necessary.

---

11 It is important to note that experts in ergonomics and interface design may also conduct reviews of the interface. These reviews are called *heuristic evaluations* or *cognitive walkthroughs*.

FIGURE 11.5

The interface
design evalua-
tion cycle

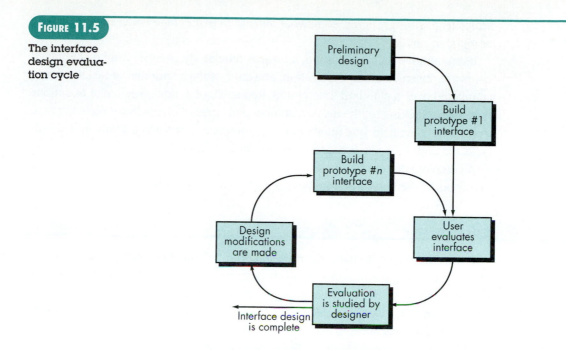

The prototyping approach is effective, but is it possible to evaluate the quality of a user interface before a prototype is built? If you identify and correct potential problems early, the number of loops through the evaluation cycle will be reduced and development time will shorten. If a design model of the interface has been created, a number of evaluation criteria [Mor81] can be applied during early design reviews:

1. The length and complexity of the requirements model or written specification of the system and its interface provide an indication of the amount of learning required by users of the system.

2. The number of user tasks specified and the average number of actions per task provide an indication of interaction time and the overall efficiency of the system.

3. The number of actions, tasks, and system states indicated by the design model imply the memory load on users of the system.

4. Interface style, help facilities, and error handling protocol provide a general indication of the complexity of the interface and the degree to which it will be accepted by the user.

Once the first prototype is built, you can collect a variety of qualitative and quantitative data that will assist in evaluating the interface. To collect qualitative data, questionnaires can be distributed to users of the prototype. Questions can be: (1) simple yes/no response, (2) numeric response, (3) scaled (subjective) response, (4) Likert scales (e.g., strongly agree, somewhat agree), (5) percentage (subjective) response, or (6) open-ended.

If quantitative data are desired, a form of time-study analysis can be conducted. Users are observed during interaction, and data—such as number of tasks correctly completed over a standard time period, frequency of actions, sequence of actions, time spent "looking" at the display, number and types of errors, error recovery time, time spent using help, and number of help references per standard time period—are collected and used as a guide for interface modification.

A complete discussion of user interface evaluation methods is beyond the scope of this book. For further information, see [Hac98] and [Sto05].

11.7 SUMMARY

The user interface is arguably the most important element of a computer-based system or product. If the interface is poorly designed, the user's ability to tap the computational power and informational content of an application may be severely hindered. In fact, a weak interface may cause an otherwise well-designed and solidly implemented application to fail.

Three important principles guide the design of effective user interfaces: (1) place the user in control, (2) reduce the user's memory load, and (3) make the interface consistent. To achieve an interface that abides by these principles, an organized design process must be conducted.

The development of a user interface begins with a series of analysis tasks. User analysis defines the profiles of various end users and is gathered from a variety of business and technical sources. Task analysis defines user tasks and actions using either an elaborative or object-oriented approach, applying use cases, task and object elaboration, workflow analysis, and hierarchical task representations to fully understand the human-computer interaction. Environmental analysis identifies the physical and social structures in which the interface must operate.

Once tasks have been identified, user scenarios are created and analyzed to define a set of interface objects and actions. This provides a basis for the creation of a screen layout that depicts graphical design and placement of icons, definition of descriptive screen text, specification and titling for windows, and specification of major and minor menu items. Design issues such as response time, command and action structure, error handling, and help facilities are considered as the design model is refined. A variety of implementation tools are used to build a prototype for evaluation by the user.

Like interface design for conventional software, the design of WebApp interfaces describes the structure and organization of the user interface and includes a representation of screen layout, a definition of the modes of interaction, and a description of navigation mechanisms. A set of interface design principles and an interface design workflow guide a WebApp designer when layout and interface control mechanisms are designed.

The user interface is the window into the software. In many cases, the interface molds a user's perception of the quality of the system. If the "window" is smudged, wavy, or broken, the user may reject an otherwise powerful computer-based system.

PROBLEMS AND POINTS TO PONDER

11.1. Describe the worst interface that you have ever worked with and critique it relative to the concepts introduced in this chapter. Describe the best interface that you have ever worked with and critique it relative to the concepts introduced in this chapter.

11.2. Develop two additional design principles that "place the user in control."

11.3. Develop two additional design principles that "reduce the user's memory load."

11.4. Develop two additional design principles that "make the interface consistent."

11.5. Consider one of the following interactive applications (or an application assigned by your instructor):

    a. A desktop publishing system
    b. A computer-aided design system
    c. An interior design system (as described in Section 11.3.2)
    d. An automated course registration system for a university
    e. A library management system
    f. An Internet-based polling booth for public elections
    g. A home banking system
    h. An interactive application assigned by your instructor

Develop a user model, design model, mental model, and an implementation model, for any one of these systems.

11.6. Perform a detailed task analysis for any one of the systems listed in Problem 11.5 Use either an elaborative or object-oriented approach.

11.7. Add at least five additional questions to the list developed for content analysis in Section 11.3.3.

11.8. Continuing Problem 11.5, define interface objects and actions for the application you have chosen. Identify each object type.

11.9. Develop a set of screen layouts with a definition of major and minor menu items for the system you chose in Problem 11.5.

11.10. Develop a set of screen layouts with a definition of major and minor menu items for the *SafeHome* system. You may elect to take a different approach than the one shown for the screen layout in Figure 11.3.

11.11. Describe your approach to user help facilities for the task analysis design model and task analysis you have performed as part of Problems 11.5 through 11.8.

11.12. Provide a few examples that illustrate why response time variability can be an issue.

11.13. Develop an approach that would automatically integrate error messages and a user help facility. That is, the system would automatically recognize the error type and provide a help window with suggestions for correcting it. Perform a reasonably complete software design that considers appropriate data structures and algorithms.

11.14. Develop an interface evaluation questionnaire that contains 20 generic questions that would apply to most interfaces. Have 10 classmates complete the questionnaire for an interactive system that you all use. Summarize the results and report them to your class.

FURTHER READINGS AND INFORMATION SOURCES

Although his book is not specifically about human-computer interfaces, much of what Donald Norman (*The Design of Everyday Things,* reissue edition, Currency/Doubleday, 1990) has to say about the psychology of effective design applies to the user interface. It is recommended reading for anyone who is serious about doing high-quality interface design.

Graphical user interfaces are ubiquitous in the modern world of computing. Whether it's an ATM, a mobile phone, an electronic dashboard in an automobile, a website, or a business application, the user interface provides a window into the software. It is for this reason that books addressing interface design abound. Butow (*User Interface Design for Mere Mortals,* Addison-Wesley, 2007), Galitz (*The Essential Guide to User Interface Design,* 3d ed., Wiley, 2007), Lehikonen and his colleagues (*Personal Content Experience: Managing Digital Life in the Mobile Age,* Wiley-Interscience, 2007), Cooper and his colleagues (*About Face 3: The Essentials of Interaction Design,* 3d ed., Wiley, 2007), Ballard *(Designing the Mobile User Experience,* Wiley, 2007), Nielsen (*Coordinating User Interfaces for Consistency,* Morgan-Kaufmann, 2006), Lauesen (*User Interface Design: A Software Engineering Perspective,* Addison-Wesley, 2005), Barfield (*The User Interface: Concepts and Design,* Bosko Books, 2004) all discuss usability, user interface concepts, principles, and design techniques and contain many useful examples.

Older books by Beyer and Holtzblatt (*Contextual Design: A Customer Centered Approach to Systems Design,* Morgan-Kaufmann, 2002), Raskin (*The Humane Interface,* Addison-Wesley, 2000), Constantine and Lockwood (*Software for Use,* ACM Press, 1999), and Mayhew (*The Usability Engineering Lifecycle,* Morgan-Kaufmann, 1999) present treatments that provide additional design guidelines and principles as well as suggestions for interface requirements elicitation, design modeling, implementation, and testing.

Johnson (*GUI Bloopers: Don'ts and Do's for Software Developers and Web Designers,* Morgan-Kaufmann, 2000) provides useful guidance for those that learn more effectively by examining counterexamples. An enjoyable book by Cooper (*The Inmates Are Running the Asylum,* Sams Publishing, 1999) discusses why high-tech products drive us crazy and how to design ones that don't.

A wide variety of information sources on user interface design are available on the Internet. An up-to-date list of World Wide Web references that are relevant to user interface design can be found at the SEPA website: **www.mhhe.com/engcs/compsci/pressman/professional/olc/ser.htm**.

PATTERN-BASED DESIGN

Each of us has encountered a design problem and silently thought: *I wonder if anyone has developed a solution for this?* The answer is almost always— *yes!* The problem is finding the solution; ensuring that it does, in fact, fit the problem you've encountered; understanding the constraints that may restrict the manner in which the solution is applied; and finally, translating the proposed solution into your design environment.

But what if the solution were codified in some manner? What if there was a standard way of describing a problem (so you could look it up), and an organized method for representing the solution to the problem? It turns out that software problems have been codified and described using a standardized template, and solutions to them (along with constraints) have been proposed. Called *design patterns,*

QUICK LOOK

What is it? Pattern-based design creates a new application by finding a set of proven solutions to a clearly delineated set of problems. Each problem and its solution is described by a design pattern that has been cataloged and vetted by other software engineers who have encountered the problem and implemented the solution while designing other applications. Each design pattern provides you with a proven approach to one part of the problem to be solved.

Who does it? A software engineer examines each problem encountered for a new application and then attempts to find a relevant solution by searching one or more patterns repositories.

Why is it important? Have you ever heard the phrase "reinventing the wheel"? It happens all the time in software development, and it's a waste of time and energy. By using existing design patterns, you can acquire a proven solution for a specific problem. As each pattern is applied, solutions are integrated and the application to be built moves closer to a complete design.

What are the steps? The requirements model is examined in order to isolate the hierarchical set of problems to be solved. The problem space is partitioned so that subsets of problems associated with specific software functions and features can be identified. Problems can also be organized by type: architectural, component-level, algorithmic, user interface, etc. Once a subset of problems is defined, one or more pattern repositories are searched to determine if an existing design pattern, represented at an appropriate level of abstraction, exists. Patterns that are applicable are adapted to the specific needs of the software to be built. Custom problem solving is applied in situations for which no patterns can be found.

What is the work product? A design model that depicts the architectural structure, user interface, and component-level detail is developed.

How do I ensure that I've done it right? As each design pattern is translated into some element of the design model, work products are reviewed for clarity, correctness, completeness, and consistency with requirements and with one another.

this codified method for describing problems and their solution allows the software engineering community to capture design knowledge in a way that enables it to be reused.

The early history of software patterns begins not with a computer scientist but a building architect, Christopher Alexander, who recognized that a recurring set of problems were encountered whenever a building was designed. He characterized these recurring problems and their solutions as *patterns,* describing them in the following manner [Ale77]:

> Each pattern describes a problem that occurs over and over again in our environment and then describes the core of the solution to that problem in such a way that you can use the solution a million times over without ever doing it the same way twice.

Alexander's ideas were first translated into the software world in books by Gamma [Gam95], Buschmann [Bus96], and their many colleagues.[1] Today, dozens of pattern repositories exist, and pattern-based design can be applied in many different application domains.

12.1   DESIGN PATTERNS

KEY POINT

Forces are those characteristics of the problem and attributes of the solution that constrain the way in which the design can be developed.

A *design pattern* can be characterized as "a three-part rule which expresses a relation between a certain context, a problem, and a solution" [Ale79]. For software design, *context* allows the reader to understand the environment in which the problem resides and what solution might be appropriate within that environment. A set of requirements, including limitations and constraints, acts as a *system of forces* that influences how the problem can be interpreted within its context and how the solution can be effectively applied.

To better understand these concepts, consider a situation[2] in which a person must travel between New York and Los Angeles. In this context, travel will occur within an industrialized country (the United States), using an existing transportation infrastructure (e.g., roads, airlines, railways). The system of forces that will affect the way in which the travel problem is solved will include: how quickly the person wants to get from New York to LA, whether the trip will include site-seeing or stopovers, how much money the person can spend, whether the trip is intended to accomplish a specific purpose, and the personal vehicles the person has at her disposal. Given these forces, the problem (traveling from New York to LA) can be better defined. For example, investigation (requirements gathering) indicates that the person has very little money, owns only a bicycle (and is an avid cyclist), wants to make the trip to raise money for her favorite charity, and has plenty of time to spare. The solution to the problem, given the context and the system of forces, might be a cross-country

---

1   Earlier discussions of software patterns do exist, but these two classic books were the first cohesive treatments of the subject.
2   This example has been adapted from [Cor98].

bike trip. If the forces were different (e.g., travel time must be minimized and the purpose of the trip is a business meeting), another solution might be more appropriate.

It is reasonable to argue that most problems have multiple solutions, but that a solution is effective only if it is appropriate within the context of the existing problem. It is the system of forces that causes a designer to choose a specific solution. The intent is to provide a solution that best satisfies the system of forces, even when these forces are contradictory. Finally, every solution has consequences that may have an impact on other aspects of the software and may themselves become part of the system of forces for other problems to be solved within the larger system.

Coplien [Cop05] characterizes an effective design pattern in the following way:

- *It solves a problem*: Patterns capture solutions, not just abstract principles or strategies.

- *It is a proven concept*: Patterns capture solutions with a track record, not theories or speculation.

- *The solution isn't obvious*: Many problem-solving techniques (such as software design paradigms or methods) try to derive solutions from first principles. The best patterns *generate* a solution to a problem indirectly—a necessary approach for the most difficult problems of design.

- *It describes a relationship*: Patterns don't just describe modules, but describe deeper system structures and mechanisms.

- *The pattern has a significant human component (minimize human intervention).* All software serves human comfort or quality of life; the best patterns explicitly appeal to aesthetics and utility.

Stated even more pragmatically, a good design pattern captures hard-earned, pragmatic design knowledge in a way that enables others to reuse that knowledge "a million times over without ever doing it the same way twice." A design pattern saves you from "reinventing the wheel," or worse, inventing a "new wheel" that is slightly out of round, too small for its intended use, and too narrow for the ground it will roll over. Design patterns, if used effectively, will invariably make you a better software designer.

12.1.1 Kinds of Patterns

One of the reasons that software engineers are interested in (and intrigued by) design patterns is that human beings are inherently good at pattern recognition. If we weren't, we'd be frozen in space and time—unable to learn from past experience, unwilling to venture forward because of our inability to recognize situations that might lead to high risk, unhinged by a world that seems to have no regularity or logical consistency. Luckily, none of this occurs because we do recognize patterns in virtually every aspect of our lives.

In the real world, the patterns we recognize are learned over a lifetime of experience. We recognize them instantly and inherently understand what they mean and how they might be used. Some of these patterns provide us with insight into recurring phenomenon. For example, you're on your way home from work on the interstate when your navigation system (or car radio) informs you that a serious accident has occurred on the interstate in the opposing direction. You're 4 miles from the accident, but already you begin to see traffic slowing, recognizing a pattern that we'll call **RubberNecking.** People in the travel lanes moving in your direction are slowing at the sight of the accident to get a better view of what happened on the opposite side of the highway. The **RubberNecking** pattern yields remarkably predictable results (a traffic jam), but it does nothing more than describe a phenomenon. In patterns jargon, it might be called a *nongenerative* pattern because it describes a context and a problem but it does not provide any clear-cut solution.

When software design patterns are considered, we strive to identify and document *generative* patterns. That is, we identify a pattern that describes an important and repeatable aspect of a system and that provides us with a way to build that aspect within a system of forces that are unique to a given context. In an ideal setting, a collection of generative design patterns could be used to "generate" an application or computer-based system whose architecture enables it to adapt to change. Sometimes called *generativity,* "the successive application of several patterns, each encapsulating its own problem and forces, unfolds a larger solution which emerges indirectly as a result of the smaller solutions" [App00].

Design patterns span a broad spectrum of abstraction and application. *Architectural patterns* describe broad-based design problems that are solved using a structural approach. *Data patterns* describe recurring data-oriented problems and the data modeling solutions that can be used to solve them. *Component patterns* (also referred to as *design patterns*) address problems associated with the development of subsystems and components, the manner in which they communicate with one another, and their placement within a larger architecture. *Interface design patterns* describe common user interface problems and their solution with a system of forces that includes the specific characteristics of end users. *WebApp patterns* address a problem set that is encountered when building WebApps and often incorporates many of the other patterns categories just mentioned. At a lower level of abstraction, *idioms* describe how to implement all or part of a specific algorithm or data structure for a software component within the context of a specific programming language.

In their seminal book on design patterns, Gamma and his colleagues[3] [Gam95] focus on three types of patterns that are particularly relevant to object-oriented design: creational patterns, structural patterns, and behavioral patterns.

Creational patterns focus on the "creation, composition, and representation" of objects. Gamma and his colleagues [Gam95] note that creational patterns "encapsulate knowledge about which concrete classes the system uses" but at the same time "hide how instances of these classes are created and put together." Creational patterns provide mechanisms that make the instantiation of objects

KEY POINT

A "generative" pattern describes the problem, a context, and forces, but it also describes a pragmatic solution to the problem.

? **Is there a way to categorize pattern types?**

---

3   Gamma and his colleagues [Gam95] are often referred to as the "Gang of Four" (GoF) in patterns literature.

easier within a system and enforce "constraints on the type and number of objects that can be created within a system" [Maa07].

Structural patterns focus on problems and solutions associated with how classes and objects are organized and integrated to build a larger structure. In essence, they help to establish relationships between entities within a system. For example, structural patterns that focus on class-oriented issues might provide inheritance mechanisms that lead to more effective program interfaces. Structural patterns that focus on objects suggest techniques for combining objects within other objects or integrating objects into a larger structure.

Behavioral patterns address problems associated with the assignment of responsibility between objects and the manner in which communication is effected between objects.

INFO

Creational, Structural, and Behavioral Patterns

A wide variety of design patterns that fit into creational, structural, and behavioral categories have been proposed and can be found on the Web. Wikipedia (**www.wikipedia.org**) notes the following sampling:

Creational Patterns

- **Abstract factory pattern:** centralize decision of what factory to instantiate.
- **Factory method pattern:** centralize creation of an object of a specific type choosing one of several implementations.
- **Builder pattern:** separate the construction of a complex object from its representation so that the same construction process can create different representations.
- **Prototype pattern:** used when the inherent cost of creating a new object in the standard way (e.g., using the "new" keyword) is prohibitively expensive for a given application.
- **Singleton pattern:** restrict instantiation of a class to one object.

Structural Patterns

- **Adapter pattern:** "adapts" one interface for a class into one that a client expects.
- **Aggregate pattern:** a version of the composite pattern with methods for aggregation of children.
- **Bridge pattern:** decouple an abstraction from its implementation so that the two can vary independently.
- **Composite pattern:** a tree structure of objects where every object has the same interface.

- **Container pattern:** create objects for the sole purpose of holding other objects and managing them.
- **Proxy pattern:** a class functioning as an interface to another thing.
- **Pipes and filters:** a chain of processes where the output of each process is the input of the next.

Behavioral Patterns

- **Chain of responsibility pattern:** Command objects are handled or passed on to other objects by logic-containing processing objects.
- **Command pattern:** Command objects encapsulate an action and its parameters.
- **Event listener:** Data are distributed to objects that are registered to receive them.
- **Interpreter pattern:** Implement a specialized computer language to rapidly solve a specific set of problems.
- **Iterator pattern:** Iterators are used to access the elements of an aggregate object sequentially without exposing its underlying representation.
- **Mediator pattern:** Provides a unified interface to a set of interfaces in a subsystem.
- **Visitor pattern:** A way to separate an algorithm from an object.
- **Single-serving visitor pattern:** Optimize the implementation of a visitor that is allocated, used only once, and then deleted.
- **Hierarchical visitor pattern:** Provide a way to visit every node in a hierarchical data structure such as a tree.

Comprehensive descriptions of each of these patterns can be obtained via links at **www.wikipedia.org**.

12.1.2   Frameworks

Patterns themselves may not be sufficient to develop a complete design. In some cases it may be necessary to provide an implementation-specific skeletal infrastructure, called a *framework,* for design work. That is, you can select a *"reusable mini-architecture* that provides the generic structure and behavior for a family of software abstractions, along with a context . . . which specifies their collaboration and use within a given domain"* [Amb98].

A framework is not an architectural pattern, but rather a skeleton with a collection of "plug points" (also called *hooks* and *slots*) that enable it to be adapted to a specific problem domain. The plug points enable you to integrate problem-specific classes or functionality within the skeleton. In an object-oriented context, a framework is a collection of cooperating classes.

Gamma and his colleagues [Gam95] describe the differences between design patterns and frameworks in the following manner:

1. *Design patterns are more abstract than frameworks.* Frameworks can be embodied in code, but only *examples* of patterns can be embodied in code. A strength of frameworks is that they can be written down in programming languages and not only studied but executed and reused directly. . . .

2. *Design patterns are smaller architectural elements than frameworks.* A typical framework contains several design patterns but the reverse is never true.

3. *Design patterns are less specialized than frameworks.* Frameworks always have a particular application domain. In contrast, design patterns can be used in nearly any kind of application. While more specialized design patterns are certainly possible, even these wouldn't dictate an application architecture.

In essence, the designer of a framework will argue that one reusable mini-architecture is applicable to all software to be developed within a limited domain of application. To be most effective, frameworks are applied with no changes. Additional design elements may be added, but only via the plug points that allow the designer to flesh out the framework skeleton.

12.1.3   Describing a Pattern

Pattern-based design begins with the recognition of patterns within the application you intend to build, continues with a search to determine whether others have addressed the pattern, and concludes with the application of an appropriate pattern to the problem at hand. The second of these three tasks is often the most difficult. How do you find patterns that fit your needs?

An answer to this question must rely on effective communication of the problem the pattern addresses, the context in which the pattern resides, the system of forces that mold the context, and the solution that is proposed. To communicate this information unambiguously, a standard form or template for pattern descriptions is required. Although a number of different pattern templates have been proposed, almost all contain a major subset of the content suggested by Gamma and his colleagues [Gam95]. A simplified pattern template is shown in the sidebar.

INFO

Design Pattern Template

Pattern name—describes the essence of the pattern in a short but expressive name
Problem—describes the problem that the pattern addresses
Motivation—provides an example of the problem
Context—describes the environment in which the problem resides including the application domain
Forces—lists the system of forces that affect the manner in which the problem must be solved; includes a discussion of limitations and constraints that must be considered
Solution—provides a detailed description of the solution proposed for the problem

Intent—describes the pattern and what it does
Collaborations—describes how other patterns contribute to the solution
Consequences—describes the potential trade-offs that must be considered when the pattern is implemented and the consequences of using the pattern
Implementation—identifies special issues that should be considered when implementing the pattern
Known uses—provides examples of actual uses of the design pattern in real applications
Related patterns—cross-references related design patterns

Quote:

"Patterns are half-baked—meaning you always have to finish them yourself and adapt them to your own environment."

Martin Fowler

The names of design patterns should be chosen with care. One of the key technical problems in pattern-based design is the inability to find existing patterns when hundreds or thousands of candidate patterns exist. The search for the "right" pattern is aided immeasurably by a meaningful pattern name.

A pattern template provides a standardized means for describing a design pattern. Each of the template entries represents characteristics of the design pattern that can be searched (e.g., via a database) so that the appropriate pattern can be found.

12.1.4   Pattern Languages and Repositories

When we use the term *language,* the first thing that comes to mind is either a natural language (e.g., English, Spanish, Chinese) or a programming language (e.g., C++, Java). In both cases the language has a syntax and semantics that are used to communicate ideas or procedural instructions in an effective manner.

When the term *language* is used in the context of design patterns, it takes on a slightly different meaning. A *pattern language* encompasses a collection of patterns, each described using a standardized template (Section 12.1.3) and interrelated to show how these patterns collaborate to solve problems across an application domain.[4]

In a natural language, words are organized into sentences that impart meaning. The structure of sentences is described by the language's syntax. In a pattern language, design patterns are organized in a way that provides a "structured method of describing good design practices within a particular domain."[5]

---

4   Christopher Alexander originally proposed pattern languages for building architecture and urban planning. Today, pattern languages have been developed for everything from the social sciences to the software engineering process.

5   This Wikipedia description can be found at http://en.wikipedia.org/wiki/Pattern_language.

ADVICE

If you can't find a
pattern language that
addresses your
problem domain, look
for analogies in
another set of
patterns.

WebRef

For a listing of useful
patterns languages
see **c2.com/ppr/
titles.html**.
Additional information
can be obtained at
**hillside.net/
patterns/**.

In a way, a pattern language is analogous to a hypertext instruction manual for problem solving in a specific application domain. The problem domain under consideration is first described hierarchically, beginning with broad design problems associated with the domain and then refining each of the broad problems into lower levels of abstraction. In a software context, broad design problems tend to be architectural in nature and address the overall structure of the application and the data or content that serve it. Architectural problems are refined to lower levels of abstraction, leading to design patterns that solve subproblems and collaborate with one another at the component (or class) level. Rather than a sequential list of patterns, a pattern language represents an interconnected collection in which the user can begin with a broad design problem and "burrow down" to uncover specific problems and their solutions.

Dozens of pattern languages have been proposed for software design [Hil08]. In most cases, the design patterns that are part of pattern language are stored in a Web-accessible patterns repository (e.g., [Boo08], [Cha03], [HPR02]). The repository provides an index of all design patterns and contains hypermedia links that enable the user to understand the collaborations between patterns.

12.2   PATTERN-BASED SOFTWARE DESIGN

The best designers in any field have an uncanny ability to see patterns that characterize a problem and corresponding patterns that can be combined to create a solution. The software developers at Microsoft [Mic04] discuss this when they write:

> While pattern-based design is relatively new in the field of software development, industrial technology has used pattern-based design for decades, perhaps even centuries. Catalogs of mechanisms and standard configurations provide design elements that are used to engineer automobiles, aircraft, machine tools, and robots. Applying pattern-based design to software development promises the same benefits to software as it does to industrial technology: predictability, risk mitigation, and increased productivity.

Throughout the design process, you should look for every opportunity to apply existing design patterns (when they meet the needs of the design) rather than creating new ones.

12.2.1   Pattern-Based Design in Context

Pattern-based design is not used in a vacuum. The concepts and techniques discussed for architectural, component-level, and user interface design (Chapters 9 through 11) are all used in conjunction with a pattern-based approach.

In Chapter 8, I noted that a set of quality guidelines and attributes serve as the basis for all software design decisions. The decisions themselves are influenced by a set of fundamental design concepts (e.g., separation of concerns, stepwise refinement, functional independence) that are achieved using heuristics that have evolved over many decades, and best practices (e.g., techniques, modeling notation) that

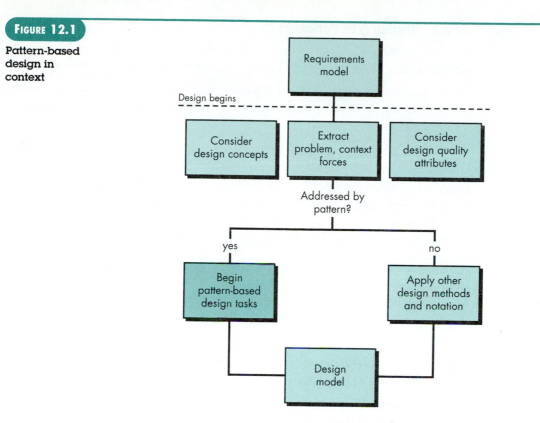

have been proposed to make design easier to perform and more effective as a basis for construction.

The role of pattern-based design in all of this is illustrated in Figure 12.1. A software designer begins with a requirements model (either explicit or implied) that presents an abstract representation of the system. The requirements model describes the problem set, establishes the context, and identifies the system of forces that hold sway. It may imply the design in an abstract manner, but the requirements model does little to represent the design explicitly.

As you begin your work as a designer, it's always important to keep quality attributes in mind. These attributes (e.g., a design must implement all explicit requirements addressed in the requirements model) establish a way to assess software quality but do little to help you actually achieve it. The design you create should exhibit the fundamental design concepts discussed in Chapter 8. Therefore, you should apply proven techniques for translating the abstractions contained in the requirements model into a more concrete form that is the software design. To accomplish this, you'll use the methods and modeling tools available for architectural, component-level, and interface design. But only when you're faced with a problem, context, and system of forces that have not been solved before. If a solution already exists, use it! And that means applying a pattern-based design approach.

12.2.2   Thinking in Patterns

In an excellent book on pattern-based design, Shalloway and Trott [Sha05] comment on a "new way of thinking" when one uses patterns as part of the design activity:

> I had to open my mind to a new way of thinking. And when I did so, I heard [Christopher] Alexander say that "good software design cannot be achieved simply by adding together performing parts."

Good design begins by considering context—the big picture. As context is evaluated, you extract a hierarchy of problems that must be solved. Some of these problems will be global in nature, while others will address specific features and functions of the software. All will be affected by a system of forces that will influence the nature of the solution that is proposed.

Shalloway and Trott [Sha05] suggest the following approach[6] that enables a designer to think in patterns:

> **Pattern-based design looks interesting for the problem I have to solve. How do I get started?**

1. Be sure you understand the big picture—the context in which the software to be built resides. The requirements model should communicate this to you.

2. Examining the big picture, extract the patterns that are present at that level of abstraction.

3. Begin your design with "big picture" patterns that establish a context or skeleton for further design work.

4. "Work inward from the context" [Sha05] looking for patterns at lower levels of abstraction that contribute to the design solution.

5. Repeat steps 1 to 4 until the complete design is fleshed out.

6. Refine the design by adapting each pattern to the specifics of the software you're trying to build.

It's important to note that patterns are not independent entities. Design patterns that are present at a high level of abstraction will invariably influence the manner in which other patterns are applied at lower levels of abstraction. In addition, patterns often collaborate with one another. The implication—when you select an architectural pattern, it may very well influence the component-level design patterns you choose. Likewise, when you select a specific interface design pattern, you are sometimes forced to use other patterns that collaborate with it.

To illustrate, consider the **SafeHomeAssured.com** WebApp. If you consider the big picture, the WebApp must address a number of fundamental problems such as:

- How to provide information about *SafeHome* products and services
- How to sell *SafeHome* products and services to customers
- How to establish Internet-based monitoring and control of an installed security system

---

6   Based on the work of Christopher Alexander [Ale79].

Each of these fundamental problems can be further refined into a set of subproblems. For example *How to sell via the Internet* implies an **E-commerce** pattern that itself implies a large number of patterns at lower levels of abstraction. The **E-commerce** pattern (likely, an architectural pattern) implies mechanisms for setting up a customer account, displaying the products to be sold, selecting products for purchase, and so forth. Hence, if you think in patterns, it is important to determine whether a pattern for setting up an account exists. If **SetUpAccount** is available as a viable pattern for the problem context, it may collaborate with other patterns such as **BuildInputForm, ManageFormsInput,** and **Validate-FormsEntry.** Each of these patterns delineates problems to be solved and solutions that may be applied.

12.2.3   Design Tasks

The following design tasks are applied when a pattern-based design philosophy is used:

? **What are the tasks required to create a pattern-based design?**

1. **Examine the requirements model and develop a problem hierarchy.** Describe each problem and subproblem by isolating the problem, the context, and the system of forces that apply. Work from broad problems (high level of abstraction) to smaller subproblems (at lower levels of abstraction).

2. **Determine if a reliable pattern language has been developed for the problem domain.** As I noted in Section 12.1.4, a pattern language addresses problems associated with a specific application domain. The *SafeHome* software team would look for a pattern language developed specifically for home security products. If that level of pattern language specificity could not be found, the team would partition the *SafeHome* software problem into a series of generic problem domains (e.g., digital device monitoring problems, user interface problems, digital video management problems) and search for appropriate pattern languages.

3. **Beginning with a broad problem, determine whether one or more architectural patterns is available for it.** If an architectural pattern is available, be certain to examine all collaborating patterns. If the pattern is appropriate, adapt the design solution proposed and build a design model element that adequately represents it. As I noted in Section 12.2.2, a broad problem for the **SafeHomeAssured.com** WebApp is addressed with an **E-commerce** pattern. This pattern will suggest a specific architecture for addressing e-commerce requirements.

4. **Using the collaborations provided for the architectural pattern, examine subsystem or component-level problems and search for appropriate patterns to address them.** It may be necessary to search through other pattern repositories as well as the list of patterns that corresponds to the architectural solution. If an appropriate pattern is found, adapt

the design solution proposed and build a design model element that adequately represents it. Be certain to apply step 7.

5. **Repeat steps 2 through 5 until all broad problems have been addressed.** The implication is to begin with the big picture and elaborate to solve problems at increasingly more detailed levels.

6. **If user interface design problems have been isolated (this is almost always the case), search the many user interface design pattern repositories for appropriate patterns.** Proceed in a manner similar to steps 3, 4, and 5.

7. **Regardless of its level of abstraction, if a pattern language and/or patterns repository or individual pattern shows promise, compare the problem to be solved against the existing pattern(s) presented.** Be certain to examine context and forces to ensure that the pattern does, in fact, provide a solution that is amenable to the problem.

8. **Be certain to refine the design as it is derived from patterns using design quality criteria as a guide.**

Although this design approach is top-down, real-life design solutions are sometimes more complex. Gillis [Gil06] comments on this when he writes:

> Design patterns in software engineering are meant to be used in a deductive, rationalistic fashion. So you have this general problem or requirement, X, design pattern Y solves X, therefore use Y. Now, when I reflect on my own process—and I've got reason to believe that I'm not alone here—I find that it's more organic than that, more inductive than deductive, more bottom-up than top-down.
>
> Obviously, there's a balance to be achieved. When a project is in the initial bootstrap phase and I'm trying to make the jump from abstract requirements to a concrete design solution, I'll often perform a sort of breadth-first search . . . I've found design patterns to be helpful, allowing me to quickly frame up the design problem in concrete terms.

In addition, the pattern-based approach must be used in conjunction with other software design concepts and techniques.

12.2.4   Building a Pattern-Organizing Table

As pattern-based design proceeds, you may encounter trouble organizing and categorizing candidate patterns from multiple pattern languages and repositories. To help organize your evaluation of candidate patterns, Microsoft [Mic04] suggests the creation of a *pattern-organizing table* that takes the general form shown in Figure 12.2.

A pattern-organizing table can be implemented as a spreadsheet model using the form shown in the figure. An abbreviated list of problem statements, organized by data/content, architecture, component-level, and user interface issues, is presented in the left-hand (shaded) column. Four pattern types—database, application,

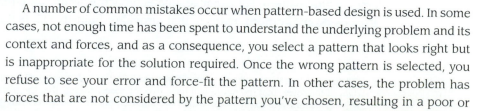

FIGURE 12.2

A pattern-organizing table

Source: Adapted from [Mic04].

	Database	Application	Implementation	Infrastructure
Data/Content				
Problem statement ...	PatternName(s)		PatternName(s)	
Problem statement ...		PatternName(s)		PatternName(s)
Problem statement ...	PatternName(s)			PatternName(s)
Architecture				
Problem statement ...		PatternName(s)		
Problem statement ...		PatternName(s)		PatternName(s)
Problem statement ...				
Component-level				
Problem statement ...		PatternName(s)	PatternName(s)	
Problem statement ...				PatternName(s)
Problem statement ...		PatternName(s)	PatternName(s)	
User interface				
Problem statement ...		PatternName(s)	PatternName(s)	
Problem statement ...		PatternName(s)	PatternName(s)	
Problem statement ...		PatternName(s)	PatternName(s)	

implementation, and infrastructure—are listed across the top row. The names of candidate patterns are noted in the cells of the table.

To provide entries for the organizing table, you'll search through pattern languages and repositories for patterns that address a particular problem statement. When one or more candidate patterns is found, it is entered in the row corresponding to the problem statement and the column that corresponds to the pattern type. The name of the pattern is entered as a hyperlink to the URL of the Web address that contains a complete description of the pattern.

12.2.5 Common Design Mistakes

Pattern-based design can make you a better software designer, but it is *not* a panacea. Like all design methods, you must begin with first principles, emphasizing software quality fundamentals and ensuring that the design does, in fact, address the needs expressed by the requirements model.

Don't force a pattern, even if it addresses the problem at hand. If the context and forces are wrong, look for another pattern.

A number of common mistakes occur when pattern-based design is used. In some cases, not enough time has been spent to understand the underlying problem and its context and forces, and as a consequence, you select a pattern that looks right but is inappropriate for the solution required. Once the wrong pattern is selected, you refuse to see your error and force-fit the pattern. In other cases, the problem has forces that are not considered by the pattern you've chosen, resulting in a poor or erroneous fit. Sometimes a pattern is applied too literally and the required adaptations for your problem space are not implemented.

Can these mistakes be avoided? In most cases the answer is "yes." Every good designer looks for a second opinion and welcomes review of her work. The review techniques discussed in Chapter 15 can help to ensure that the pattern-based design you've developed will result in a high-quality solution for the software problem to be solved.

12.3 ARCHITECTURAL PATTERNS

If a house builder decides to construct a center-hall colonial, there is a single architectural style that can be applied. The details of the style (e.g., number of fireplaces, façade of the house, placement of doors and windows) can vary considerably, but once the decision on the overall architecture of the house is made, the style is imposed on the design.[7]

Architectural patterns are a bit different. For example, every house (and every architectural style for houses) employs a **Kitchen** pattern. The **Kitchen** pattern and patterns it collaborates with address problems associated with the storage and preparation of food, the tools required to accomplish these tasks, and rules for placement of these tools relative to workflow in the room. In addition, the pattern might address problems associated with countertops, lighting, wall switches, a central island, flooring, and so on. Obviously, there is more than a single design for a kitchen, often dictated by the context and system of forces. But every design can be conceived within the context of the "solution" suggested by the **Kitchen** pattern.

As I have already noted, architectural patterns for software define a specific approach for handling some characteristic of the system. Bosch [Bos00] and Booch [Boo08] define a number of architectural pattern domains. Representative examples are provided in the paragraphs that follow:

? What are some typical architectural pattern domains?

Access control.   There are many situations in which access to data, features, and functionality delivered by an application is limited to specifically defined end users. From an architectural point of view, access to some portion of the software architecture must be controlled rigorously.

Concurrency.   Many applications must handle multiple tasks in a manner that simulates parallelism (i.e., this occurs whenever multiple "parallel" tasks or components are managed by a single processor). There are a number of different ways in which an application can handle concurrency, and each can be presented by a different architectural pattern. For example, one approach is to use an **OperatingSystemProcessManagement** pattern that provides built-in OS features that allow

---

7   This implies that there will be a central foyer and hallway, that rooms will be placed to the left and right of the foyer, that the house will have two (or more) stories, that the bedrooms of the house will be upstairs, and so on. These "rules" are imposed once the decision is made to use the center-hall colonial style.

components to execute concurrently. The pattern also incorporates OS functionality that manages communication between processes, scheduling, and other capabilities required to achieve concurrency. Another approach might be to define a task scheduler at the application level. A **TaskScheduler** pattern contains a set of active objects that each contains a *tick()* operation [Bos00]. The scheduler periodically invokes *tick()* for each object, which then performs the functions it must perform before returning control back to the scheduler which then invokes the *tick()* operation for the next concurrent object.

Distribution.   The distribution problem addresses the manner in which systems or components within systems communicate with one another in a distributed environment. Two subproblems are considered: (1) the way in which entities connect to one another, and (2) the nature of the communication that occurs. The most common architectural pattern established to address the distribution problem is the **Broker** pattern. A broker acts as a "middleman" between the client component and a server component. The client sends a message to the broker (containing all appropriate information for the communication to be effected) and the broker completes the connection.

Persistence.   Data persists if it survives past the execution of the process that created it. Persistent data are stored in a database or file and may be read or modified by other processes at a later time. In object-oriented environments, the idea of a persistent object extends the persistence concept a bit further. The values of all of the object's attributes, the general state of the object, and other supplementary information are stored for future retrieval and use. In general, two architectural patterns are used to achieve persistence—a **DatabaseManagementSystem** pattern that applies the storage and retrieval capability of a DBMS to the application architecture or an **Application Level-Persistence** pattern that builds persistence features into the application architecture (e.g., word processing software that manages its own document structure).

Before any one of the representative architectural patterns noted in the preceding paragraphs can be chosen, it must be assessed for its appropriateness for the application and the overall architectural style, as well as the context and system of forces that it specifies.

Bibliographic reference to hundreds of architectural and component design patterns

UI Patterns Collections
UI/HCI Patterns
  www.hcipatterns.org/patterns.html
Jennifer Tidwell's UI patterns
  www.time-tripper.com/uipatterns/
Mobile UI Design Patterns
  http://patterns.littlespringsdesign.com/
  wikka.php?wakka=Mobile

Patterns
Pattern Language for UI Design
  www.maplefish.com/todd/papers/
  Experiences.html
Interaction Design Library for Games
  www.eelke.com/research/usability.html

UI Design Patterns
  www.cs.helsinki.fi/u/salaakso/patterns/

Specialized Design Patterns:
Aircraft Avionics
  http://g.oswego.edu/dl/acs/acs/acs.html
Business Information Systems
  www.objectarchitects.de/arcus/cookbook/
Distributed Processing
  www.cs.wustl.edu/~schmidt/
IBM Patterns for e-Business **www128.ibm.com/**
  developerworks/patterns/
Yahoo! Design Pattern Library
  http://developer.yahoo.com/ypatterns/
WebPatterns.org **http://webpatterns.org/**

12.4   COMPONENT-LEVEL DESIGN PATTERNS

Component-level design patterns provide you with proven solutions that address one or more subproblems extracted from the requirements model. In many cases, design patterns of this type focus on some functional element of a system. For example, the **SafeHomeAssured.com** application must address the following design subproblem: *How can we get product specifications and related information for any SafeHome device?*

Having enunciated the subproblem that must be solved, you should now consider context and the system of forces that affect the solution. Examining the appropriate requirements model use case, you learn that the consumer uses the specification for a *SafeHome* device (e.g., a security sensor or camera) for informational purposes. However, other information that is related to the specification (e.g., pricing) may be used when e-commerce functionality is selected.

The solution to the subproblem involves a search. Since searching is a very common problem, it should come as no surprise that there are many search-related patterns. Looking through a number of patterns repositories, you find the following patterns, along with the problem that each solves:

AdvancedSearch.   Users must find a specific item in a large collection of items.

HelpWizard.   Users need help on a certain topic related to the website or when they need to find a specific page within the site.

SearchArea.   Users must find a page.

SearchTips.   Users need to know how to control the search engine.

SearchResults.   Users have to process a list of search results.

SearchBox.   Users have to find an item or specific information.

For **SafeHomeAssured.com** the number of products is not particularly large, and each has a relatively simple categorization, so **AdvancedSearch** and **HelpWizard** are probably not necessary. Similarly, the search is simple enough not to require **SearchTips**. The description of **SearchBox**, however, is given (in part) as:

Search Box

(Adapted from www.welie.com/patterns/showPattern.php?patternID=search.)

Problem: The users need to find an item or specific information.

Motivation: Any situation in which a keyword search is applied across a collection of content objects organized as Web pages.

Context: Rather than using navigation to acquire information or content, the user wants to do a direct search through content contained on multiple Web pages. Any website that already has primary navigation. User may want to search for an item in a category. User might want to further specify a query.

Forces: The website already has primary navigation. Users may want to search for an item in a category. Users might want to further specify a query using simple Boolean operators.

Solution: Offer search functionality consisting of a search label, a keyword field, a filter if applicable, and a "go" button. Pressing the return key has the same function as selecting the go button. Also provide Search Tips and examples in a separate page. A link to that page is placed next to the search functionality. The edit box for the search term is large enough to accommodate three typical user queries (typically around 20 characters). If the number of filters is more than 2, use a combo box for filters selection, otherwise a radio button.

The search results are presented on a new page with a clear label containing at least "Search results" or similar. The search function is repeated in the top part of the page with the entered keywords, so that the users know what the keywords were.

The pattern description continues with other entries as described in Section 12.1.3.

The pattern goes on to describe how the search results are accessed, presented, matched, and so on. Based on this, the **SafeHomeAssured.com** team can design the components required to implement the search or (more likely) acquire existing reusable components.

SAFEHOME

Applying Patterns

The scene: Informal discussion during the design of a software increment that implements sensor control via the Internet for **SafeHomeAssured.com.**

The players: Jamie (responsible for design) and Vinod (**SafeHomeAssured.com** chief system architect).

The conversation:

Vinod: So how is the design of the camera control interface coming along?

Jamie: Not too bad. I've designed most of the capability to connect to the actual sensors without too many problems. I've also started thinking about the interface for the users to actually move, pan, and zoom the cameras from a remote Web page, but I'm not sure I've got it right yet.

Vinod: What have you come up with?

Jamie: Well, the requirements are that the camera control needs to be highly interactive—as the user moves the control, the camera should move as soon as possible. So, I was thinking of having a set of buttons laid out like a normal camera, but when the user clicks them, it controls the camera.

Vinod: Hmmm. Yeah, that would work, but I'm not sure it's right—for each click of a control you need to wait for the whole client-server communication to occur, and so you won't get a good sense of quick feedback.

Jamie: That's what I thought—and why I wasn't very happy with the approach, but I'm not sure how else I might do it.

Vinod: Well, why not just use the **InteractiveDeviceControl** pattern!

Jamie: Uhmmm—what's that? I haven't heard of it?

Vinod: It's basically a pattern for exactly the problem you are describing. The solution it proposes is basically to create a control connection to the server with the device, through which control commands can be sent. That way you don't need to send normal HTTP requests. And the pattern even shows how you can implement this using some simple AJAX techniques. You have some simple client-side JavaScript that communicates directly with the server and sends the commands as soon as the user does anything.

Jamie: Cool! That's just what I needed to solve this thing. Where do I find it?

Vinod: It's available in an online repository. Here's the URL.

Jamie: I'll go check it out.

Vinod: Yep—but remember to check the consequences field for the pattern. I seem to remember that there was something in there about needing to be careful about issues of security. I think it might be because you are creating a separate control channel and so bypassing the normal Web security mechanisms.

Jamie: Good point. I probably wouldn't have thought of that! Thanks.

12.5   USER INTERFACE DESIGN PATTERNS

Hundreds of user interface (UI) patterns have been proposed in recent years. Most fall within one of the following 10 categories of patterns (discussed with a representative example[8]) as described by Tidwell [Tid02] and vanWelie [Wel01]:

Whole UI.   Provide design guidance for top-level structure and navigation throughout the entire interface.

> **Pattern: TopLevelNavigation**
>
> **Brief description:** Used when a site or application implements a number of major functions. Provides a top-level menu, often coupled with a logo or

---

8   An abbreviated pattern template is used here. Full pattern descriptions (along with dozens of other patterns) can be found at [Tid02] and [Wel01].

identifying graphic, that enables direct navigation to any of the system's major functions.

Details: Major functions (generally limited to between four and seven function names) are listed across the top of the display (vertical column formats are also possible) in a horizontal line of text. Each name provides a link to the appropriate function or information source. Often used with the **BreadCrumbs** pattern discussed later.

Navigation elements: Each function/content name represents a link to the appropriate function or content.

Page layout.   Address the general organization of pages (for websites) or distinct screen displays (for interactive applications).

Pattern: CardStack

Brief description: Used when a number of specific subfunctions or content categories related to a feature or function must be selected in random order. Provides the appearance of a stack of tabbed cards, each selectable with a mouse click and each representing specific subfunctions or content categories.

Details: Tabbed cards are a well-understood metaphor and are easy for the user to manipulate. Each tabbed card (divider) may have a slightly different format. Some may require input and have buttons or other navigation mechanisms; others may be informational. May be combined with other patterns such as **DropDownList**, **Fill-in-the-Blanks,** and others.

Navigation elements: A mouse click on a tab causes the appropriate card to appear. Navigation features within the card may also be present, but in general, these should initiate a function that is related to card data, not cause an actual link to some other display.

Forms and input.   Consider a variety of design techniques for completing form-level input.

Pattern: Fill-in-the-Blanks

Brief description: Allow alphanumeric data to be entered in a "text box."

Details: Data may be entered within a text box. In general, the data are validated and processed after some text or graphic indicator (e.g., a button containing "go," "submit," "next") is picked. In many cases this pattern can be combined with drop-down list or other patterns (e.g., SEARCH *<drop down list>* FOR *<fill-in-the-blanks text box>*).

Navigation elements: A text or graphic indicator that initiates validation and processing.

Tables.   Provide design guidance for creating and manipulating tabular data of all kinds.

Pattern: SortableTable

Brief description: Display a long list of records that can be sorted by selecting a toggle mechanism for any column label.

Details: Each row in the table represents a complete record. Each column represents one field in the record. Each column header is actually a selectable button that can be toggled to initiate an ascending or descending sort on the field associated with the column for all records displayed. The table is generally resizable and may have a scrolling mechanism if the number of records is larger than available window space.

Navigation elements: Each column header initiates a sort on all records. No other navigation is provided, although in some cases, each record may itself contain navigation links to other content or functionality.

Direct data manipulation.   Address data editing, modification, and transformation.

Pattern: BreadCrumbs

Brief description: Provides a full navigation path when the user is working with a complex hierarchy of pages or display screens.

Details: Each page or display screen is given a unique identifier. The navigation path to the current location is specified in a predefined location for every display. The path takes the form: **home>major topic page>subtopic page> specific page>current page.**

Navigation elements: Any of the entries within the bread crumbs display can be used as a pointer to link back to a higher level of the hierarchy.

Navigation.   Assist the user in navigating through hierarchical menus, Web pages, and interactive display screens.

Pattern: EditInPlace

Brief description: Provide simple text editing capability for certain types of content in the location that it is displayed. No need for the user to enter a text editing function or mode explicitly.

Details: The user sees content on the display that must be changed. A mouse double click on the content indicates to the system that editing is desired. The content is highlighted to signify that editing mode is available and the user makes appropriate changes.

Navigation elements: None.

Searching.   Enable content-specific searches through information maintained within a website or contained by persistent data stores that are accessible via an interactive application.

Pattern: SimpleSearch

Brief description: Provides the ability to search a website or persistent data source for a simple data item described by an alphanumeric string.

Details: Provides the ability to search either locally (one page or one file) or globally (entire site or complete database) for the search string. Generates a list of "hits" in order of their probability of meeting the user's needs. Does not provide multiple item searches or special Boolean operations (see *advanced search pattern*).

Navigation elements: Each entry in the list of hits represents a navigation link to the data referenced by the entry.

Page elements. Implement specific elements of a Web page or display screen.

Pattern: Wizard

Brief description: Takes the user through a complex task one step at a time, providing guidance for the completion of the task through a series of simple window displays.

Details: Classic example is a registration process that contains four steps. The wizard pattern generates a window for each step, requesting specific information from the user one step at a time.

Navigation elements: Forward and back navigation allows the user to revisit each step in the wizard process.

E-commerce. Specific to websites, these patterns implement recurring elements of e-commerce applications.

Pattern: ShoppingCart

Brief description: Provides a list of items selected for purchase.

Details: Lists item, quantity, product code, availability (in stock, out of stock), price, delivery information, shipping costs, and other relevant purchase information. Also provides ability to edit (e.g., remove, change quantity).

Navigation elements: Contains ability to proceed with shopping or go to checkout.

Miscellaneous. Patterns that do not easily fit into one of the preceding categories. In some cases, these patterns are domain dependent or occur only for specific classes of users.

Pattern: ProgressIndicator

Brief description: Provides an indication of progress when an operation takes longer than n seconds.

Details: Represented as an animated icon or a message box that contains some visual indication (e.g., a rotating "barber pole," a slider with a percent complete indicator) that processing is under way. May also contain a text content indication of the status of processing.

Navigation elements: Often contains a button that allows the user to pause or cancel processing.

Each of the preceding example patterns (and all patterns within each category) would also have a complete component-level design, including design classes, attributes, operations, and interfaces.

A comprehensive discussion of user interface patterns is beyond the scope of this book. If you have further interest, see [Duy02], [Bor01], [Tid02], and [Wel01] for further information.

12.6 WEBAPP DESIGN PATTERNS

Throughout this chapter you've learned that there are different types of patterns and many different ways they can be categorized. When you consider the design problems that must be solved when a WebApp is to be built, it's worth considering pattern categories by focusing on two dimensions: the design focus of the pattern and its level of granularity. *Design focus* identifies which aspect of the design model is relevant (e.g., information architecture, navigation, interaction). *Granularity* identifies the level of abstraction that is being considered (e.g., does the pattern apply to the entire WebApp, to a single Web page, to a subsystem, or an individual WebApp component?).

12.6.1 Design Focus

KEY POINT

Your focus becomes "narrower" the further you move into design.

In earlier chapters I emphasized a design progression that begins by considering architecture, component-level issues, and user interface representations. At each step, the problems you consider and the solutions you propose begin at a high level of abstraction and slowly become more detailed and specific. Stated another way, design focus becomes "narrower" as you move further into design. The problems (and solutions) you will encounter when designing an information architecture for a WebApp are different from the problems (and solutions) that are encountered when performing interface design. Therefore, it should come as no surprise that patterns for WebApp design can be developed for different levels of design focus, so that you can address the unique problems (and related solutions) that are encountered at each level. WebApp patterns can be categorized using the following levels of design focus:

- **Information architecture patterns** relate to the overall structure of the information space, and the ways in which users will interact with the information.

- **Navigation patterns** define navigation link structures, such as hierarchies, rings, tours, and so on.

- **Interaction patterns** contribute to the design of the user interface. Patterns in this category address how the interface informs the user of the consequences of a specific action, how a user expands content based on usage context and user desires, how to best describe the destination that is implied by a link, how to inform the user about the status of an ongoing interaction, and interface-related issues.

- **Presentation patterns** assist in the presentation of content as it is presented to the user via the interface. Patterns in this category address how to organize user interface control functions for better usability, how to show the relationship between an interface action and the content objects it affects, and how to establish effective content hierarchies.

- **Functional patterns** define the workflows, behaviors, processing, communication, and other algorithmic elements within a WebApp.

In most cases, it would be fruitless to explore the collection of information architecture patterns when a problem in interaction design is encountered. You would examine interaction patterns, because that is the design focus that is relevant to the work being performed.

12.6.2   Design Granularity

When a problem involves "big picture" issues, you should attempt to develop solutions (and use relevant patterns) that focus on the big picture. Conversely, when the focus is very narrow (e.g., uniquely selecting one item from a small set of five or fewer items), the solution (and the corresponding pattern) is targeted quite narrowly. In terms of the level of granularity, patterns can be described at the following levels:

- **Architectural patterns.** This level of abstraction will typically relate to patterns that define the overall structure of the WebApp, indicate the relationships among different components or increments, and define the rules for specifying relationships among the elements (pages, packages, components, subsystems) of the architecture.

- **Design patterns.** These address a specific element of the design such as an aggregation of components to solve some design problem, relationships among elements on a page, or the mechanisms for effecting component-to-component communication. An example might be the **Broadsheet** pattern for the layout of a WebApp home page.

- **Component patterns.** This level of abstraction relates to individual small-scale elements of a WebApp. Examples include individual interaction elements (e.g., radio buttons), navigation items (e.g., how might you format links?) or functional elements (e.g., specific algorithms).

It is also possible to define the relevance of different patterns to different classes of applications or domains. For example, a collection of patterns (at different levels of design focus and granularity) might be particularly relevant to e-business.

Hypermedia Design Patterns Repositories

The IAWiki website (**http://iawiki.net/ WebsitePatterns**), a collaborative discussion space for information architects, contains many useful resources. Among them are links to a number of useful hypermedia patterns catalogs and repositories. Hundreds of design patterns are represented:

Hypermedia Design Patterns Repository
www.designpattern.lu.unisi.ch/
InteractionPatterns by Tom Erickson
www.pliant.org/personal/Tom_Erickson/ InteractionPatterns.html
Web Design Patterns by Martijn vanWelie
www.welie.com/patterns/
Web Patterns for UI Design
http://harbinger.sims.berkeley.edu/ ui_designpatterns/webpatterns2/ webpatterns/home.php

Patterns for Personal Websites
www.rdrop.com/%7Ehalf/Creations/Writin gs/Web.patterns/index.html
Improving Web Information Systems with Navigational Patterns **http://www8.org/w8-papers/ 5b-hypertext- media/improving/ improving.html**
An HTML 2.0 Pattern Language
www.anamorph.com/docs/patterns/ default.html
Common Ground—A Pattern Language for HCI Design
www.mit.edu/~jtidwell/interaction_patterns .html
Patterns for Personal Websites **www.rdrop.com/ ~half/Creations/Writings/Web.patterns/ index.html**
Indexing Pattern Language **www.cs.brown.edu/ ~rms/InformationStructures/Indexing/ Overview.html**

12.7 SUMMARY

Design patterns provide a codified mechanism for describing problems and their solution in a way that allows the software engineering community to capture design knowledge for reuse. A pattern describes a problem, indicates the context enabling the user to understand the environment in which the problem resides, and lists a system of forces that indicate how the problem can be interpreted within its context and how the solution can be applied. In software engineering work, we identify and document generative patterns that describe an important and repeatable aspect of a system and then provide us with a way to build that aspect within a system of forces that is unique to a given context.

Architectural patterns describe broad-based design problems that are solved using a structural approach. Data patterns describe recurring data-oriented problems and the data modeling solutions that can be used to solve them. Component patterns (also referred to as design patterns) address problems associated with the development of subsystems and components, the manner in which they communicate with one another, and their placement within a larger architecture. Interface design patterns describe common user interface problems and their solution with a system of forces that includes the specific characteristics of end users. WebApp patterns address a problem set that is encountered when building WebApps and often incorporates many of the other patterns categories just mentioned. A framework provides an infrastructure in which patterns may reside and idioms describe programming language–specific implementation detail for all or part of a specific algorithm or data structure. A standard form or template is used for pattern descriptions. A pattern language encompasses a collection of patterns, each described using a standardized template and interrelated to show how these patterns collaborate to solve problems across an application domain.

Pattern-based design is used in conjunction with architectural, component-level, and user interface design methods. The design approach begins with an examination of the requirements model to isolate problems, define context, and describe the system of forces. Next, pattern languages for the problem domain are searched to determine if patterns exist for the problems that have been isolated. Once appropriate patterns have been found, they are used as a design guide.

PROBLEMS AND POINTS TO PONDER

12.1. Discuss the three "parts" of a design pattern and provide a concrete example of each from some field other than software.

12.2. What is the difference between a nongenerative and a generative pattern?

12.3. How do architectural patterns differ from component patterns?

12.4. What is a framework and how does it differ from a pattern? What is an idiom and how does it differ from a pattern?

12.5. Using the design pattern template presented in Section 12.1.3, develop a complete pattern description for a pattern suggested by your instructor.

12.6. Develop a skeletal pattern language for a sport with which you are familiar. You can begin by addressing the context, the system of forces, and the broad problems that a coach and team must solve. You need only specify pattern names and provide a one-sentence description for each pattern.

12.7. Find five patterns repositories and present an abbreviated description of the types of patterns contained in each.

12.8. When Christopher Alexander says "good design cannot be achieved simply by adding together performing parts," what do you think he means?

12.9. Using the pattern-based design tasks noted in Section 12.2.3, develop a skeletal design for the "interior design system" described in Section 11.3.2.

12.10. Build a pattern-organizing table for the patterns you used in Problem 12.9.

12.11. Using the design pattern template presented in Section 12.1.3, develop a complete pattern description for the **Kitchen** pattern mentioned in Section 12.3.

12.12. The gang of four [Gam95] have proposed a variety of component patterns that are applicable to object-oriented systems. Select one (these are available on the Web) and discuss it.

12.13. Find three patterns repositories for user interface patterns. Select one pattern from each and present an abbreviated description of it.

12.14. Find three patterns repositories for WebApp patterns. Select one pattern from each and present an abbreviated description of it.

FURTHER READING AND INFORMATION SOURCES

Over the past decade, many books on pattern-based design have been written for software engineers. Gamma and his colleagues [Gam95] have written the seminal book on the subject. More recent contributions include books by Lasater (*Design Patterns,* Wordware Publishing, Inc., 2007), Holzner (*Design Patterns for Dummies,* For Dummies, 2006), Freeman and her colleagues (*Head First Design Patterns,* O'Reilly Media, Inc., 2005), and Shalloway and Trott (*Design Patterns Explained,* 2d. ed., Addison-Wesley, 2004). A special issues of *IEEE Software* (July/August, 2007) discusses a wide variety of software patterns topics. Kent Beck (*Implementation Patterns,* Addison-Wesley, 2008) addresses patterns for coding and implementation issues that are encountered during the construction activity.

Other books focus on design patterns as they are supplied in specific application development and language environments. Contributions in this area include: Bowers (*Pro CSS and HTML Design Patterns,* Apress, 2007), Tropashko and Burleson (*SQL Design Patterns: Expert Guide to SQL Programming,* Rampant Techpress, 2007), Mahemoff (*Ajax Design Patterns,* O'Reilly Media, Inc., 2006), Metsker and Wake (*Design Patterns in Java,* Addison-Wesley, 2006), Nilsson (*Applying Domain-Driven Design and Patterns: With Examples in C# and .NET,* Addison-Wesley, 2006), Sweat (*PHPArchitect's Guide to PHP Design Patterns,* Marco Tabini & Associates, Inc., 2005), Metsker (*Design Patterns C#,* Addison-Wesley, 2004), Grand and Merrill (*Visual Basic .NET Design Patterns,* Wiley, 2003), Crawford and Kaplan (*J2EE Design Patterns,* O'Reilly Media, Inc., 2003), Juric et al. (*J2EE Design Patterns Applied,* Wrox Press, 2002), and Marinescu and Roman (*EJB Design Patterns,* Wiley, 2002).

Still other books address specific application domains. These include contributions by Kuchana (*Software Architecture Design Patterns in Java,* Auerbach, 2004), Joshi (*C++ Design Patterns and Derivatives Pricing,* Cambridge University Press, 2004), Douglass (*Real-Time Design Patterns,* Addison-Wesley, 2002), and Schmidt and Rising (*Design Patterns in Communication Software,* Cambridge University Press, 2001).

Classic books by the architect Christopher Alexander (*Notes on the Synthesis of Form,* Harvard University Press, 1964, and *A Pattern Language: Towns, Buildings, Construction,* Oxford University Press, 1977) are worthwhile reading for a software designer who intends to fully understand design patterns.

A wide variety of information sources on pattern-based design are available on the Internet. An up-to-date list of World Wide Web references that are relevant to pattern-based design can be found at the SEPA website: **www.mhhe.com/engcs/compsci/pressman/professional/olc/ser.htm**.

WebApp Design

13

In his authoritative book on Web design, Jakob Nielsen [Nie00] states: "There are essentially two basic approaches to design: the artistic ideal of expressing yourself and the engineering ideal of solving a problem for a customer." During the first decade of Web development, the artistic idea was the approach that many developers chose. Design occurred in an ad hoc manner and was usually conducted as HTML was generated. Design evolved out of an artistic vision that evolved as WebApp construction occurred.

Even today, many Web developers use WebApps as poster children for "limited design." They argue that WebApp immediacy and volatility mitigate against formal design; that design evolves as an application is built (coded), and that relatively little time should be spent on creating a detailed design model. This argument has merit, but only for relatively simple WebApps. When content and

Quick Look

What is it? Design for WebApps encompasses technical and nontechnical activities that include: establishing the look and feel of the WebApp, creating the aesthetic layout of the user interface, defining the overall architectural structure, developing the content and functionality that reside within the architecture, and planning the navigation that occurs within the WebApp.

Who does it? Web engineers, graphic designers, content developers, and other stakeholders all participate in the creation of a WebApp design model.

Why is it important? Design allows you to create a model that can be assessed for quality and improved before content and code are generated, tests are conducted, and end users become involved in large numbers. Design is the place where WebApp quality is established.

What are the steps? WebApp design encompasses six major steps that are driven by information obtained during requirements modeling. Content design uses the content model (developed during analysis) as the basis for establishing the design of content objects. Aesthetic design (also called graphic design) establishes the look and feel that the end user sees. Architectural design focuses on the overall hypermedia structure of all content objects and functions. Interface design establishes the layout and interaction mechanisms that define the user interface. Navigation design defines how the end user navigates through the hypermedia structure, and component design represents the detailed internal structure of functional elements of the WebApp.

What is the work product? A design model that encompasses content, aesthetics, architecture, interface, navigation, and component-level design issues is the primary work product that is produced during WebApp design.

How do I ensure that I've done it right? Each element of the design model is reviewed in an effort to uncover errors, inconsistencies, or omissions. In addition, alternative solutions are considered, and the degree to which the current design model will lead to an effective implementation is also assessed.

function are complex; when the size of the WebApp encompasses hundreds or thousands of content objects, functions, and analysis classes; and when the success of the WebApp will have a direct impact on the success of the business, design cannot and should not be taken lightly.

This reality leads us to Nielsen's second approach—"the engineering ideal of solving a problem for a customer." Web engineering[1] adopts this philosophy, and a more rigorous approach to WebApp design enables developers to achieve it.

13.1   WEBAPP DESIGN QUALITY

Design is the engineering activity that leads to a high-quality product. This leads us to a recurring question that is encountered in all engineering disciplines: What is quality? In this section I'll examine the answer within the context of WebApp development.

Every person who has surfed the Web or used a corporate Intranet has an opinion about what makes a "good" WebApp. Individual viewpoints vary widely. Some users enjoy flashy graphics; others want simple text. Some demand copious information; others desire an abbreviated presentation. Some like sophisticated analytical tools or database access; others like to keep it simple. In fact, the user's perception of "goodness" (and the resultant acceptance or rejection of the WebApp as a consequence) might be more important than any technical discussion of WebApp quality.

But how is WebApp quality perceived? What attributes must be exhibited to achieve goodness in the eyes of end users and at the same time exhibit the technical characteristics of quality that will enable you to correct, adapt, enhance, and support the application over the long term?

In reality, all of the technical characteristics of design quality discussed in Chapter 8 and the generic quality attributes presented in Chapter 14 apply to WebApps. However, the most relevant of these generic attributes—usability, functionality, reliability, efficiency, and maintainability—provide a useful basis for assessing the quality of Web-based systems.

Olsina and his colleagues [Ols99] have prepared a "quality requirement tree" that identifies a set of technical attributes—usability, functionality, reliability, efficiency, and maintainability—that lead to high-quality WebApps.[2] Figure 13.1 summarizes their work. The criteria noted in the figure are of particular interest if you design, build, and maintain WebApps over the long term.

uote:

"If products are designed to better fit the natural tendencies of human behavior, then people will be more satisfied, more fulfilled, and more productive."

Susan
Weinschenk

---

1   *Web engineering* [Pre08] is an adapted version of the software engineering approach that is presented throughout this book. It proposes an agile, yet disciplined framework for building industry-quality Web-based systems and applications.

2   These quality attributes are quite similar to those presented in Chapters 8 and 14. The implication: quality characteristics are universal for all software.

FIGURE 13.1

**Quality
requirements
tree.**
Source: [Ols99].

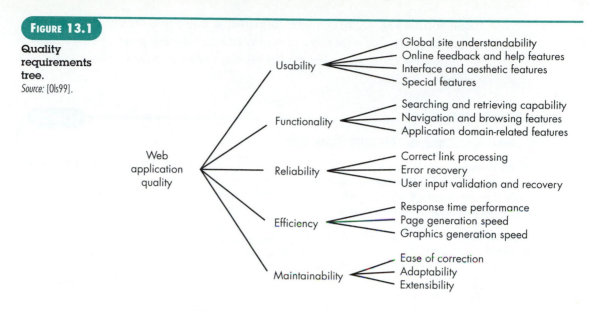

Offutt [Off02] extends the five major quality attributes noted in Figure 13.1 by adding the following attributes:

> **?** **What are
> the major
> attributes of
> quality for
> WebApps?**

Security.   WebApps have become heavily integrated with critical corporate and government databases. E-commerce applications extract and then store sensitive customer information. For these and many other reasons, WebApp security is paramount in many situations. The key measure of security is the ability of the WebApp and its server environment to rebuff unauthorized access and/or thwart an outright malevolent attack. A detailed discussion of WebApp security is beyond the scope of this book. If you have further interest, see [Vac06], [Kiz05], or [Kal03].

Availability.   Even the best WebApp will not meet users' needs if it is unavailable. In a technical sense, availability is the measure of the percentage of time that a WebApp is available for use. The typical end user expects WebApps to be available 24/7/365. Anything less is deemed unacceptable.[3] But "up-time" is not the only indicator of availability. Offutt [Off02] suggests that "using features available on only one browser or one platform" makes the WebApp unavailable to those with a different browser/platform configuration. The user will invariably go elsewhere.

Scalability.   Can the WebApp and its server environment be scaled to handle 100, 1000, 10,000, or 100,000 users? Will the WebApp and the systems with which it is interfaced handle significant variation in volume or will responsiveness drop dramatically (or cease altogether)? It is not enough to build a WebApp that is successful. It is equally important to build a WebApp that can accommodate the burden of success (significantly more end users) and become even more successful.

---

3   This expectation is, of course, unrealistic. Major WebApps must schedule "downtime" for fixes and upgrades.

Time-to-market. Although time-to-market is not a true quality attribute in the technical sense, it is a measure of quality from a business point of view. The first WebApp to address a specific market segment often captures a disproportionate number of end users.

WebApp Design—Quality Checklist

The following checklist, adapted from information presented at **Webreference.com**, provides a set of questions that will help both Web designers and end users assess overall WebApp quality:

- Can content and/or function and/or navigation options be tailored to the user's preferences?
- Can content and/or functionality be customized to the bandwidth at which the user communicates?
- Have graphics and other nontext media been used appropriately? Are graphics file sizes optimized for display efficiency?

- Are tables organized and sized in a manner that makes them understandable and displayed efficiently?
- Is HTML optimized to eliminate inefficiencies?
- Is the overall page design easy to read and navigate?
- Do all pointers provide links to information that is of interest to users?
- Is it likely that most links have persistence on the Web?
- Is the WebApp instrumented with site management utilities that include tools for usage tracking, link testing, local searching, and security?

Billions of Web pages are available for those in search of information. Even well-targeted Web searches result in an avalanche of content. With so many sources of information to choose from, how does the user assess the quality (e.g., veracity, accuracy, completeness, timeliness) of the content that is presented within a WebApp? Tillman [Til00] suggests a useful set of criteria for assessing the quality of content:

? What should we consider when assessing content quality?

- Can the scope and depth of content be easily determined to ensure that it meets the user's needs?
- Can the background and authority of the content's authors be easily identified?
- Is it possible to determine the currency of the content, the last update, and what was updated?
- Are the content and its location stable (i.e., will they remain at the referenced URL)?

In addition to these content-related questions, the following might be added:

- Is content credible?
- Is content unique? That is, does the WebApp provide some unique benefit to those who use it?
- Is content valuable to the targeted user community?
- Is content well organized? Indexed? Easily accessible?

The checklists noted in this section represent only a small sampling of the issues that should be addressed as the design of a WebApp evolves.

13.2 DESIGN GOALS

In her regular column on Web design, Jean Kaiser [Kai02] suggests a set of design goals that are applicable to virtually every WebApp regardless of application domain, size, or complexity:

Simplicity.   Although it may seem old-fashioned, the aphorism "all things in moderation" applies to WebApps. There is a tendency among some designers to provide the end user with "too much"—exhaustive content, extreme visuals, intrusive animation, enormous Web pages, the list is long. Better to strive for moderation and simplicity.

Content should be informative but succinct and should use a delivery mode (e.g., text, graphics, video, audio) that is appropriate to the information that is being delivered. Aesthetics should be pleasing, but not overwhelming (e.g., too many colors tend to distract the user rather than enhancing the interaction). Architecture should achieve WebApp objectives in the simplest possible manner. Navigation should be straightforward and navigation mechanisms should be intuitively obvious to the end user. Functions should be easy to use and easier to understand.

Consistency.   This design goal applies to virtually every element of the design model. Content should be constructed consistently (e.g., text formatting and font styles should be the same across all text documents; graphic art should have a consistent look, color scheme, and style). Graphic design (aesthetics) should present a consistent look across all parts of the WebApp. Architectural design should establish templates that lead to a consistent hypermedia structure. Interface design should define consistent modes of interaction, navigation, and content display. Navigation mechanisms should be used consistently across all WebApp elements. As Kaiser [Kai02] notes: "Remember that to a visitor, a Web site is a physical place. It is confusing if pages within a site are not consistent in design."

Identity.   The aesthetic, interface, and navigational design of a WebApp must be consistent with the application domain for which it is to be built. A website for a hip-hop group will undoubtedly have a different look and feel than a WebApp designed for a financial services company. The WebApp architecture will be entirely different, interfaces will be constructed to accommodate different categories of users; navigation will be organized to accomplish different objectives. You (and other design contributors) should work to establish an identity for the WebApp through the design.

Robustness.   Based on the identity that has been established, a WebApp often makes an implicit "promise" to a user. The user expects robust content and functions that are relevant to the user's needs. If these elements are missing or insufficient, it is likely that the WebApp will fail.

Navigability.   I have already noted that navigation should be simple and consistent. It should also be designed in a manner that is intuitive and predictable. That is, the user should understand how to move about the WebApp without having to search for navigation links or instructions. For example, if a field of graphic icons or images contains selected icons or images that will be used as navigation mechanisms, these must be identified visually. Nothing is more frustrating than trying to find the appropriate live link among many graphical images.

It is also important to position links to major WebApp content and functions in a predictable location on every Web page. If page scrolling is required (and this is often the case), links at the top and bottom of the page make the user's navigation tasks easier.

Visual Appeal.   Of all software categories, Web applications are unquestionably the most visual, the most dynamic, and the most unapologetically aesthetic. Beauty (visual appeal) is undoubtedly in the eye of the beholder, but many design characteristics (e.g., the look and feel of content; interface layout; color coordination; the balance of text, graphics, and other media; navigation mechanisms) do contribute to visual appeal.

Compatibility.   A WebApp will be used in a variety of environments (e.g., different hardware, Internet connection types, operating systems, browsers) and must be designed to be compatible with each.

13.3   A DESIGN PYRAMID FOR WEBAPPS

> **Quote:**
>
> "If a site is perfectly usable but it lacks an elegant and appropriate design style, it will fail."
>
> **Curt Cloninger**

What is WebApp design? This simple question is more difficult to answer than one might believe. In our book [Pre08] on Web engineering, David Lowe and I discuss this when we write:

> The creation of an effective design will typically require a diverse set of skills. Sometimes, for small projects, a single developer may need to be multi-skilled. For larger projects, it may be advisable and/or feasible to draw on the expertise of specialists: Web engineers, graphic designers, content developers, programmers, database specialists, information architects, network engineers, security experts, and testers. Drawing on these diverse skills allows the creation of a model that can be assessed for quality and improved *before* content and code are generated, tests are conducted, and end-users become involved in large numbers. If analysis is where *WebApp quality is established,* then design is where the *quality is truly embedded.*

The appropriate mix of design skills will vary depending upon the nature of the WebApp. Figure 13.2 depicts a design pyramid for WebApps. Each level of the pyramid represents a design action that is described in the sections that follow.

13.4   WEBAPP INTERFACE DESIGN

When a user interacts with a computer-based system, a set of fundamental principles and overriding design guidelines apply. These have been discussed in

FIGURE 13.2

A design
pyramid for
WebApps

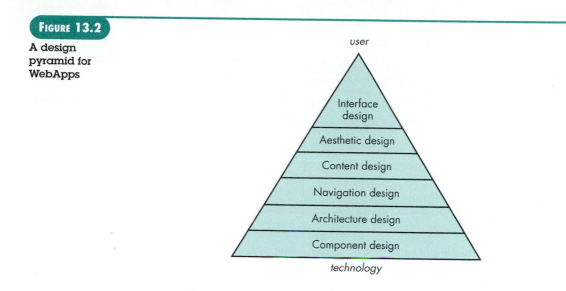

Chapter 11.[4] Although WebApps present a few special user interface design challenges, the basic principles and guidelines are applicable.

One of the challenges of interface design for WebApps is the indeterminate nature of the user's entry point. That is, the user may enter the WebApp at a "home" location (e.g., the home page) or may be linked into some lower level of the WebApp architecture. In some cases, the WebApp can be designed in a way that reroutes the user to a home location, but if this is undesirable, the WebApp design must provide interface navigation features that accompany all content objects and are available regardless of how the user enters the system.

The objectives of a WebApp interface are to: (1) establish a consistent window into the content and functionality provided by the interface, (2) guide the user through a series of interactions with the WebApp, and (3) organize the navigation options and content available to the user. To achieve a consistent interface, you should first use aesthetic design (Section 13.5) to establish a coherent "look." This encompasses many characteristics, but must emphasize the layout and form of navigation mechanisms. To guide user interaction, you may draw on an appropriate metaphor[5] that enables the user to gain an intuitive understanding of the interface. To implement navigation options, you can select from one of a number of interaction mechanisms:

- *Navigation menus*—keyword menus (organized vertically or horizontally) that list key content and/or functionality. These menus may be implemented so

---

4   Section 11.5 is dedicated to WebApp interface design. If you have not already done so, read it at this time.
5   In this context, a *metaphor* is a representation (drawn from the user's real-world experience) that can be modeled within the context of the interface. A simple example might be a slider switch that is used to control the auditory volume of an .mpg file.

What interaction mechanisms are available to WebApp designers?

that the user can choose from a hierarchy of subtopics that is displayed when the primary menu option is selected.

- *Graphic icons*—button, switches, and similar graphical images that enable the user to select some property or specify a decision.
- *Graphic images*—some graphical representation that is selectable by the user and implements a link to a content object or WebApp functionality.

It is important to note that one or more of these control mechanisms should be provided at every level of the content hierarchy.

13.5   AESTHETIC DESIGN

Not every Web engineer (or software engineer) has artistic (aesthetic) talent. If you fall into this category, hire an experienced graphic designer for aesthetic design work.

Aesthetic design, also called *graphic design,* is an artistic endeavor that complements the technical aspects of WebApp design. Without it, a WebApp may be functional, but unappealing. With it, a WebApp draws its users into a world that embraces them on a visceral, as well as an intellectual level.

But what is aesthetic? There is an old saying, "beauty exists in the eye of the beholder." This is particularly appropriate when aesthetic design for WebApps is considered. To perform effective aesthetic design, return to the user hierarchy developed as part of the requirements model (Chapter 5) and ask, *Who are the WebApp's users and what "look" do they desire?*

13.5.1   Layout Issues

Every Web page has a limited amount of "real estate" that can be used to support nonfunctional aesthetics, navigation features, informational content, and user-directed functionality. The development of this real estate is planned during aesthetic design.

Like all aesthetic issues, there are no absolute rules when screen layout is designed. However, a number of general layout guidelines are worth considering:

uote:

"We find that people quickly evaluate a site by visual design alone."

Stanford Guidelines for Web Credibility

Don't be afraid of white space.   It is inadvisable to pack every square inch of a Web page with information. The resulting clutter makes it difficult for the user to identify needed information or features and create visual chaos that is not pleasing to the eye.

Emphasize content.   After all, that's the reason the user is there. Nielsen [Nie00] suggests that the typical Web page should be 80 percent content with the remaining real estate dedicated to navigation and other features.

Organize layout elements from top-left to bottom-right.   The vast majority of users will scan a Web page in much the same way as they scan the page of a book—top-left to bottom-right.[6] If layout elements have specific

---

6   There are exceptions that are cultural and language-based, but this rule does hold for most users.

priorities, high-priority elements should be placed in the upper-left portion of the page real estate.

Group navigation, content, and function geographically within the page. Humans look for patterns in virtually all things. If there are no discernable patterns within a Web page, user frustration is likely to increase (due to unnecessary searching for needed information).

Don't extend your real estate with the scrolling bar. Although scrolling is often necessary, most studies indicate that users would prefer not to scroll. It is better to reduce page content or to present necessary content on multiple pages.

Consider resolution and browser window size when designing layout. Rather than defining fixed sizes within a layout, the design should specify all layout items as a percentage of available space [Nie00].

Users tend to tolerate vertical scrolling more readily than horizontal scrolling. Avoid wide page formats.

13.5.2 Graphic Design Issues

Graphic design considers every aspect of the look and feel of a WebApp. The graphic design process begins with layout (Section 13.5.1) and proceeds into a consideration of global color schemes; text types, sizes, and styles; the use of supplementary media (e.g., audio, video, animation); and all other aesthetic elements of an application.

A comprehensive discussion of graphic design issues for WebApps is beyond the scope of this book. You can obtain design tips and guidelines from many websites that are dedicated to the subject (e.g., **www.graphic-design.com**, **www.grantasticdesigns .com**, **www.wpdfd.com**) or from one or more print resources (e.g., [Roc06] and [Gor02]).

13.6   CONTENT DESIGN

Content design focuses on two different design tasks, each addressed by individuals with different skill sets. First, a design representation for content objects and the mechanisms required to establish their relationship to one another is developed. In addition, the information within a specific content object is created. The latter task may be conducted by copywriters, graphic designers, and others who generate the content to be used within a WebApp.

13.6.1   Content Objects

The relationship between content objects defined as part of a requirements model for the WebApp and design objects representing content is analogous to the relationship between analysis classes and design components described in earlier chapters. In the context of WebApp design, a content object is more closely aligned with a data object for traditional software. A content object has attributes that include content-specific information (normally defined during WebApp requirements modeling) and implementation-specific attributes that are specified as part of design.

As an example, consider an analysis class, **ProductComponent,** developed for the *SafeHome* e-commerce system. The analysis class attribute, description, is represented as a design class named **CompDescription** composed of five content objects: **MarketingDescription, Photograph, TechDescription, Schematic,** and **Video** shown as shaded objects noted in Figure 13.3. Information contained within the content object is noted as attributes. For example, **Photograph** (a .jpg image) has the attributes horizontal dimension, vertical dimension, and border style.

UML association and an aggregation[7] may be used to represent relationships between content objects. For example, the UML association shown in Figure 13.3 indicates that one **CompDescription** is used for each instance of the **ProductComponent** class. **CompDescription** is composed on the five content objects shown. However, the multiplicity notation shown indicates that **Schematic** and **Video** are optional (0 occurrences are possible), one **MarketingDescription** and one **TechDescription** are required, and one or more instances of **Photograph** are used.

13.6.2   Content Design Issues

Once all content objects are modeled, the information that each object is to deliver must be authored and then formatted to best meet the customer's needs. Content authoring is the job of specialists in the relevant area who design the content object by providing an outline of information to be delivered and an indication of the types of generic content objects (e.g., descriptive text, graphic images, photographs) that will be used to deliver the information. Aesthetic design (Section 13.5) may also be applied to represent the proper look and feel for the content.

---

7   Both of these representations are discussed in Appendix 1.

FIGURE 13.3

Design representation of content objects

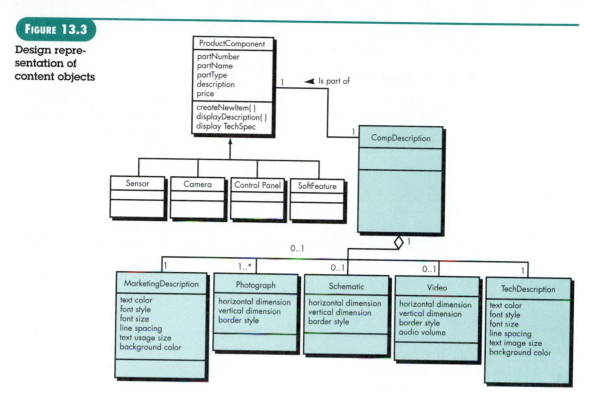

As content objects are designed, they are "chunked" [Pow02] to form WebApp pages. The number of content objects incorporated into a single page is a function of user needs, constraints imposed by download speed of the Internet connection, and restrictions imposed by the amount of scrolling that the user will tolerate.

13.7   ARCHITECTURE DESIGN

Architecture design is tied to the goals established for a WebApp, the content to be presented, the users who will visit, and the navigation philosophy that has been established. As an architectural designer, you must identify content architecture and WebApp architecture. *Content architecture*[8] focuses on the manner in which content objects (or composite objects such as Web pages) are structured for presentation and navigation. *WebApp architecture* addresses the manner in which the application is structured to manage user interaction, handle internal processing tasks, effect navigation, and present content.

In most cases, architecture design is conducted in parallel with interface design, aesthetic design, and content design. Because the WebApp architecture may have a

---

8   The term *information architecture* is also used to connote structures that lead to better organization, labeling, navigation, and searching of content objects.

strong influence on navigation, the decisions made during this design action will influence work conducted during navigation design.

13.7.1   Content Architecture

The design of content architecture focuses on the definition of the overall hypermedia structure of the WebApp. Although custom architectures are sometimes created, you always have the option of choosing from four different content structures [Pow00]:

Linear structures (Figure 13.4) are encountered when a predictable sequence of interactions (with some variation or diversion) is common. A classic example might be a tutorial presentation in which pages of information along with related graphics, short videos, or audio are presented only after prerequisite information has been presented. The sequence of content presentation is predefined and generally linear. Another example might be a product order entry sequence in which specific information must be specified in a specific order. In such cases, the structures shown in Figure 13.4 are appropriate. As content and processing become more complex, the purely linear flow shown on the left of the figure gives way to more sophisticated linear structures in which alternative content may be invoked or a diversion to acquire complementary content (structure shown on the right side of Figure 13.4) occurs.

Grid structures (Figure 13.5) are an architectural option that you can apply when WebApp content can be organized categorically in two (or more) dimensions. For example, consider a situation in which an e-commerce site sells golf clubs. The horizontal dimension of the grid represents the type of club to be sold (e.g., woods, irons, wedges, putters). The vertical dimension represents the offerings provided by various golf club manufacturers. Hence, a user might navigate the grid horizontally to find the putters column and then vertically to examine the offerings provided by

? What types of content architectures are commonly encountered?

Figure 13.4

Linear structures

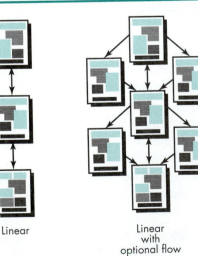

Linear

Linear
with
optional flow

Linear
with
diversions

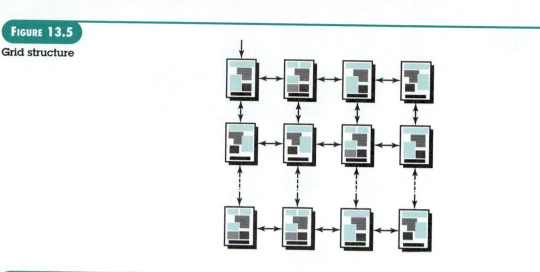

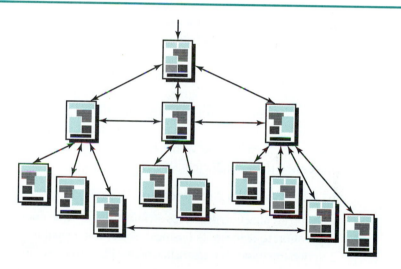

those manufacturers that sell putters. This WebApp architecture is useful only when highly regular content is encountered [Pow00].

Hierarchical structures (Figure 13.6) are undoubtedly the most common WebApp architecture. Unlike the partitioned software hierarchies discussed in Chapter 9 that encourage flow of control only along vertical branches of the hierarchy, a WebApp hierarchical structure can be designed in a manner that enables (via hypertext branching) flow of control horizontally across vertical branches of the structure. Hence, content presented on the far left-hand branch of the hierarchy can have hypertext links that lead directly to content that exists in the middle or right-hand branch of the structure. It should be noted, however, that although such branching allows rapid navigation across WebApp content, it can lead to confusion on the part of the user.

A *networked* or *"pure web"* structure (Figure 13.7) is similar in many ways to the architecture that evolves for object-oriented systems. Architectural components

(in this case, Web pages) are designed so that they may pass control (via hypertext links) to virtually every other component in the system. This approach allows considerable navigation flexibility, but at the same time, can be confusing to a user.

The architectural structures discussed in the preceding paragraphs can be combined to form *composite structures*. The overall architecture of a WebApp may be hierarchical, but part of the structure may exhibit linear characteristics, while another part of the architecture may be networked. Your goal as an architectural designer is to match the WebApp structure to the content to be presented and the processing to be conducted.

13.7.2   WebApp Architecture

WebApp architecture describes an infrastructure that enables a Web-based system or application to achieve its business objectives. Jacyntho and his colleagues [Jac02b] describe the basic characteristics of this infrastructure in the following manner:

> Applications should be built using layers in which different concerns are taken into account; in particular, application data should be separated from the page's contents (navigation nodes) and these contents, in turn, should be clearly separated from the interface look-and-feel (pages).

The authors suggest a three-layer design architecture that decouples interface from navigation and from application behavior. They argue that keeping interface, application, and navigation separate simplifies implementation and enhances reuse.

The *Model-View-Controller* (MVC) architecture [Kra88][9] is one of a number of suggested WebApp infrastructure models that decouple the user interface from the

---

9   It should be noted that MVC is actually an architectural design pattern developed for the Smalltalk environment (see **www.cetus-links.org/oo_smalltalk.html**) and can be used for any interactive application.

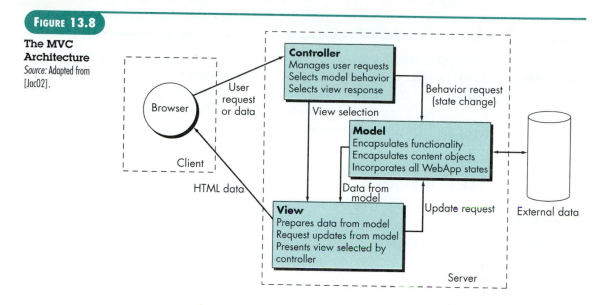

FIGURE 13.8

The MVC Architecture
Source: Adapted from [Jac02].

The MVC architecture decouples the user interface from WebApp functionality and information content.

WebApp functionality and informational content. The *model* (sometimes referred to as the "model object") contains all application-specific content and processing logic, including all content objects, access to external data/information sources, and all processing functionality that is application specific. The *view* contains all interface-specific functions and enables the presentation of content and processing logic, including all content objects, access to external data/information sources, and all processing functionality required by the end user. The *controller* manages access to the model and the view and coordinates the flow of data between them. In a WebApp, "the view is updated by the controller with data from the model based on user input" [WMT02]. A schematic representation of the MVC architecture is shown in Figure 13.8.

Referring to the figure, user requests or data are handled by the controller. The controller also selects the view object that is applicable based on the user request. Once the type of request is determined, a behavior request is transmitted to the model, which implements the functionality or retrieves the content required to accommodate the request. The model object can access data stored in a corporate database, as part of a local data store, or as a collection of independent files. The data developed by the model must be formatted and organized by the appropriate view object and then transmitted from the application server back to the client-based browser for display on the customer's machine.

In many cases, WebApp architecture is defined within the context of the development environment in which the application is to be implemented. If you have further interest, see [Fow03] for a discussion of development environments and their role in the design of Web application architectures.

13.8   NAVIGATION DESIGN

Once the WebApp architecture has been established and the components (pages, scripts, applets, and other processing functions) of the architecture have been identified, you must define navigation pathways that enable users to access WebApp content and functions. To accomplish this, you should (1) identify the semantics of navigation for different users of the site, and (2) define the mechanics (syntax) of achieving the navigation.

13.8.1   Navigation Semantics

Like many WebApp design actions, navigation design begins with a consideration of the user hierarchy and related use cases (Chapter 5) developed for each category of user (actor). Each actor may use the WebApp somewhat differently and therefore have different navigation requirements. In addition, the use cases developed for each actor will define a set of classes that encompass one or more content objects or WebApp functions. As each user interacts with the WebApp, she encounters a series of *navigation semantic units* (NSUs)—"a set of information and related navigation structures that collaborate in the fulfillment of a subset of related user requirements" [Cac02].

An NSU describes the navigation requirements for each use case. In essence, the NSU shows how an actor moves between content objects or WebApp functions.

An NSU is composed of a set of navigation elements called *ways of navigating* (WoN) [Gna99]. A WoN represents the best navigation pathway to achieve a navigational goal for a specific type of user. Each WoN is organized as a set of *navigational nodes* (NN) that are connected by navigational links. In some cases, a navigational link may be another NSU. Therefore, the overall navigation structure for a WebApp may be organized as a hierarchy of NSUs.

To illustrate the development of an NSU, consider the use case **Select SafeHome Components**:

Use Case: Select SafeHome Components

The WebApp will recommend <u>product components</u> (e.g., control panels, sensors, cameras) and other features (e.g., PC-based functionality implemented in software) for each <u>room</u> and <u>exterior entrance</u>. If I request alternatives, the WebApp will provide them, if they exist. I will be able to get <u>descriptive and pricing information</u> for each product component. The WebApp will create and display a <u>bill-of-materials</u> as I select various components. I'll be able to give the bill-of-materials a name and save it for future reference (see use case **Save Configuration**).

The underlined items in the use-case description represent classes and content objects that will be incorporated into one or more NSUs that will enable a new customer to perform the scenario described in the **Select SafeHome Components** use case.

Figure 13.9 depicts a partial semantic analysis of the navigation implied by the **Select SafeHome Components** use case. Using the terminology introduced earlier, the figure also represents a way of navigating (WoN) for the

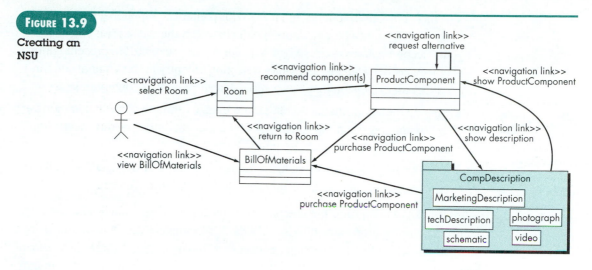

FIGURE 13.9

Creating an NSU

SafeHomeAssured.com WebApp. Important problem domain classes are shown along with selected content objects (in this case the package of content objects named **CompDescription,** an attribute of the **ProductComponent** class). These items are navigation nodes. Each of the arrows represents a navigation link[10] and is labeled with the user-initiated action that causes the link to occur.

You can create an NSU for each use case associated with each user role. For example, a **new customer** for **SafeHomeAssured.com** may have three different use cases, all resulting in access to different information and WebApp functions. An NSU is created for each goal.

During the initial stages of navigation design, the WebApp content architecture is assessed to determine one or more WoN for each use case. As noted earlier, a WoN identifies navigation nodes (e.g., content) and then links that enable navigation between them. The WoN are then organized into NSUs.

13.8.2   Navigation Syntax

As design proceeds, your next task is to define the mechanics of navigation. A number of options are available as you develop an approach for implementing each NSU:

In most situations, choose either horizontal or vertical navigation mechanisms, but not both.

- *Individual navigation link*—includes text-based links, icons, buttons and switches, and graphical metaphors. You must choose navigation links that are appropriate for the content and consistent with the heuristics that lead to high-quality interface design.

- *Horizontal navigation bar*—lists major content or functional categories in a bar containing appropriate links. In general, between four and seven categories are listed.

10 These are sometimes referred to as *navigation semantic links* (NSL) [Cac02].

- *Vertical navigation column*—(1) lists major content or functional categories, or (2) lists virtually all major content objects within the WebApp. If you choose the second option, such navigation columns can "expand" to present content objects as part of a hierarchy (i.e., selecting an entry in the original column causes an expansion that lists a second layer of related content objects).

- *Tabs*—a metaphor that is nothing more than a variation of the navigation bar or column, representing content or functional categories as tab sheets that are selected when a link is required.

- *Site maps*—provide an all-inclusive table of contents for navigation to all content objects and functionality contained within the WebApp.

The site map should be accessible from every page. The map itself should be organized so that the structure of WebApp information is readily apparent.

In addition to choosing the mechanics of navigation, you should also establish appropriate navigation conventions and aids. For example, icons and graphical links should look "clickable" by beveling the edges to give the image a three-dimensional look. Audio or visual feedback should be designed to provide the user with an indication that a navigation option has been chosen. For text-based navigation, color should be used to indicate navigation links and to provide an indication of links already traveled. These are but a few of dozens of design conventions that make navigation user-friendly.

13.9   COMPONENT-LEVEL DESIGN

Modern WebApps deliver increasingly sophisticated processing functions that (1) perform localized processing to generate content and navigation capability in a dynamic fashion, (2) provide computation or data processing capability that are appropriate for the WebApp's business domain, (3) provide sophisticated database query and access, and (4) establish data interfaces with external corporate systems. To achieve these (and many other) capabilities, you must design and construct program components that are identical in form to software components for traditional software.

The design methods discussed in Chapter 10 apply to WebApp components with little, if any, modification. The implementation environment, programming languages, and design patterns, frameworks, and software may vary somewhat, but the overall design approach remains the same.

13.10   OBJECT-ORIENTED HYPERMEDIA DESIGN METHOD (OOHDM)

A number of design methods for Web applications have been proposed over the past decade. To date, no single method has achieved dominance.[11] In this section I present a brief overview of one of the most widely discussed WebApp design methods—OOHDM.

---

11 In fact, relatively few Web developers use a specific method when designing a WebApp. Hopefully, this ad hoc approach to design will change as time passes.

FIGURE 13.10   **Summary of the OOHDM method.**
Source: Adapted from [Sch95].

	Conceptual design	Navigational design	Abstract interface design	Implementation
Work products	Classes, subsystems, relationships, attributes	Nodes links, access structures, navigational contexts, navigational transformations	Abstract interface objects, responses to external events, transformations	Executable WebApp
Design mechanisms	Classification, composition, aggregation, generalization specialization	Mapping between conceptual and navigation objects	Mapping between navigation and perceptible objects	Resource provided by target environment
Design concerns	Modeling semantics of the application domain	Takes into account user profile and task. Emphasis on cognitive aspects.	Modeling perceptible objects, implementing chosen metaphors. Describe interface for navigational objects.	Correctness; application performance; completeness

Daniel Schwabe and his colleagues [Sch95, Sch98b] originally proposed the *Object-Oriented Hypermedia Design Method* (OOHDM), which is composed of four different design activities: conceptual design, navigational design, abstract interface design, and implementation. A summary of these design activities is shown in Figure 13.10 and discussed briefly in the sections that follow.

13.10.1   Conceptual Design for OOHDM

OOHDM *conceptual design* creates a representation of the subsystems, classes, and relationships that define the application domain for the WebApp. UML may be used[12] to create appropriate class diagrams, aggregations, and composite class representations, collaboration diagrams, and other information that describes the application domain.

As a simple example of OOHDM conceptual design, consider the **SafeHomeAssured .com** e-commerce application. A partial "conceptual schema" is shown in Figure 13.11. The class diagrams, aggregations, and related information developed as part of WebApp analysis are reused during conceptual design to represent relationships between classes.

13.10.2   Navigational Design for OOHDM

Navigational design identifies a set of "objects" that are derived from the classes defined in conceptual design. A series of "navigational classes" or "nodes" are

---

12 OOHDM does not prescribe a specific notation; however, the use of UML is common when this method is applied.

FIGURE 13.11   Partial conceptual schema for SafeHomeAssured.com

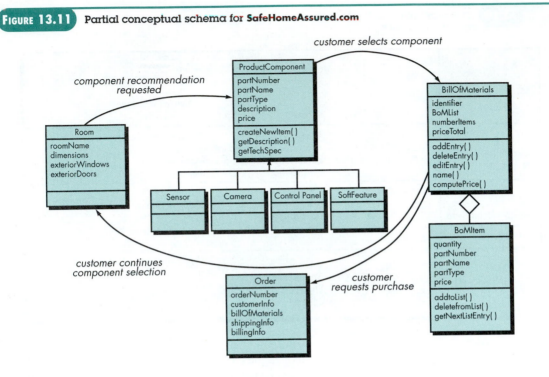

defined to encapsulate these objects. UML may be used to create appropriate use cases, state charts, and sequence diagrams—all representations that assist you in better understanding navigational requirements. In addition, design patterns for navigational design may be used as the design is developed. OOHDM uses a predefined set of navigation classes—nodes, links, anchors, and access structures [Sch98b]. Access structures are more elaborate and include mechanisms such as a WebApp index, a site map, or a guided tour.

Once navigation classes are defined, OOHDM "structures the navigation space by grouping navigation objects into sets called contexts" [Sch98b]. A *context* includes a description of the local navigation structure, restriction imposed on the access of content objects, and methods (operations) required to effect access of content objects. A context template (analogous to CRC cards discussed in Chapter 6) is developed and may be used to track the navigation requirements of each category of user through the various contexts defined in OOHDM. Doing this, specific navigation paths (what we called WoN in Section 13.8.1) emerge.

13.10.3   Abstract Interface Design and Implementation

The *abstract interface design* action specifies the interface objects that the user sees as WebApp interaction occurs. A formal model of interface objects, called an *abstract data view* (ADV), is used to represent the relationship between interface objects and navigation objects, and the behavioral characteristics of interface objects.

The ADV model defines a "static layout" [Sch98b] that represents the interface metaphor and includes a representation of navigation objects within the interface and the specification of the interface objects (e.g., menus, buttons, icons) that assist in navigation and interaction. In addition, the ADV model contains a behavioral component (similar to the UML state diagram) that indicates how external events "trigger navigation and which interface transformations occur when the user interacts with the application" [Sch01a].

The OOHDM *implementation* activity represents a design iteration that is specific to the environment in which the WebApp will operate. Classes, navigation, and the interface are each characterized in a manner that can be constructed for the client-server environment, operating systems, support software, programming languages, and other environmental characteristics that are relevant to the problem.

13.11   SUMMARY

The quality of a WebApp—defined in terms of usability, functionality, reliability, efficiency, maintainability, security, scalability, and time-to-market—is introduced during design. To achieve these quality attributes, a good WebApp design should exhibit the following characteristics: simplicity, consistency, identity, robustness, navigability, and visual appeal. To achieve these characteristics, the WebApp design activity focuses on six different elements of the design.

Interface design describes the structure and organization of the user interface and includes a representation of screen layout, a definition of the modes of interaction, and a description of navigation mechanisms. A set of interface design principles and an interface design workflow guide you when layout and interface control mechanisms are designed.

Aesthetic design, also called graphic design, describes the "look and feel" of the WebApp and includes color schemes; geometric layout; text size, font, and placement; the use of graphics; and related aesthetic decisions. A set of graphic design guidelines provides the basis for a design approach.

Content design defines the layout, structure, and outline for all content that is presented as part of the WebApp and establishes the relationships between content objects. Content design begins with the representation of content objects, their associations, and relationships. A set of browsing primitives establishes the basis for navigation design.

Architecture design identifies the overall hypermedia structure for the WebApp and encompasses both content architecture and WebApp architecture. Architectural styles for content include linear, grid, hierarchical, and network structures. WebApp architecture describes an infrastructure that enables a Web-based system or application to achieve its business objectives.

Navigation design represents the navigational flow between content objects and for all WebApp functions. Navigation semantics are defined by describing a set of navigation semantic units. Each unit is composed of ways of navigating and navigational links and nodes. Navigation syntax depicts the mechanisms used for effecting the navigation described as part of the semantics.

Component design develops the detailed processing logic required to implement functional components that implement a complete WebApp function. Design techniques described in Chapter 10 are applicable for the engineering of WebApp components.

The Object-Oriented Hypermedia Design Method (OOHDM) is one of a number of methods proposed for WebApp design. OOHDM suggests a design process that includes conceptual design, navigational design, abstract interface design, and implementation.

PROBLEMS AND POINTS TO PONDER

13.1. Why is the "artistic ideal" an insufficient design philosophy when modern WebApps are built? Is there ever a case in which the artistic ideal is the philosophy to follow?

13.2. In this chapter we select a broad array of quality attributes for WebApps. Select the three that you believe are most important, and make an argument that explains why each should be emphasized in WebApp design work.

13.3. Add at least five additional questions to the WebApp Design—Quality Checklist presented in Section 13.1.

13.4. You are a WebApp designer for *FutureLearning Corporation*, a distance learning company. You intend to implement an Internet-based "learning engine" that will enable you to deliver course content to a student. The learning engine provides the basic infrastructure for delivering learning content on any subject (content designers will prepare appropriate content). Develop a prototype interface design for the learning engine.

13.5. What is the most aesthetically pleasing website you have ever visited and why?

13.6. Consider the content object **Order,** generated once a user of **SafeHomeAssured.com** has completed the selection of all components and is ready to finalize his purchase. Develop a UML description for **Order** along with all appropriate design representations.

13.7. What is the difference between content architecture and WebApp architecture?

13.8. Reconsidering the *FutureLearning* "learning engine" described in Problem 13.4, select a content architecture that would be appropriate for the WebApp. Discuss why you made the choice.

13.9. Use UML to develop three or four design representations for content objects that would be encountered as the "learning engine" described in Problem 13.4 is designed.

13.10. Do a bit of additional research on the MVC architecture and decide whether it would be an appropriate WebApp architecture for the "learning engine" discussed in Problem 13.4.

13.11. What is the difference between navigation syntax and navigation semantics?

13.12. Define two or three NSUs for the **SafeHomeAssured.com** WebApp. Describe each in some detail.

13.13. Write a brief paper on a hypermedia design method other than OOHDM.

FURTHER READINGS AND INFORMATION SOURCES

Van Duyne and his colleagues (*The Design of Sites,* 2d ed., Prentice Hall, 2007) have written a comprehensive book that covers most important aspects of the WebApp design process. Design process models and design patterns are covered in detail. Wodtke (*Information Architecture,* New Riders Publishing, 2003), Rosenfeld and Morville (*Information Architecture for the World Wide Web,* O'Reilly & Associates, 2002), and Reiss (*Practical Information Architecture,* Addison-Wesley, 2000) address content architecture and other topics.

Although hundreds of books have been written on "Web design," very few of these discuss any meaningful technical methods for doing design work. At best, a variety of useful guidelines for WebApp design is presented, worthwhile examples of Web pages and Java programming are shown, and the technical details important for implementing modern WebApps are discussed. Among the many offerings in this category are books by Sklar (*Principles of Web Design,* 4th ed., Course Technology, 2008), McIntire (*Visual Design for the Modern Web,* New Riders Press, 2007), Niederst (*Web Design in a Nutshell,* 3d ed., O-Reilly, 2006), Eccher (*Advanced Professional Web Design,* Charles River Media, 2006), Cederholm (*Bulletproof Web Design,* New Riders Press, 2005), and Shelly and his colleagues (*Web Design,* 2d ed., Course Technology, 2005). Powell's [Pow02] encyclopedic discussion and Nielsen's [Nie00] in-depth discussion of design are also worthwhile additions to any library.

Books by Beaird (*The Principles of Beautiful Web Design,* SitePoint, 2007), Clarke and Holzschlag (*Transcending CSS: The Fine Art of Web Design,* New Riders Press, 2006), and Golbeck (*Art Theory for Web Design,* Addison Wesley, 2005) emphasize aesthetic design and are worthwhile reading for practitioners who have little background in the subject.

The agile view of design (and other topics) for WebApps is presented by Wallace and his colleagues (*Extreme Programming for Web Projects,* Addison-Wesley, 2003). Conallen (*Building Web Applications with UML,* 2d ed., Addison-Wesley, 2002) and Rosenberg and Scott (*Applying Use-Case Driven Object Modeling with UML,* Addison-Wesley, 2001) present detailed examples of WebApps modeled using UML.

Design techniques are also mentioned within the context of books written about specific development environments. Interested readers should examine books on HTML, CSS, J2EE, Java, .NET, XML, Perl, Ruby on Rails, Ajax, and a variety of WebApp creation applications (*Dreamweaver, HomePage, Frontpage, GoLive, MacroMedia Flash,* etc.) for useful design tidbits.

A wide variety of information sources on design for WebApps is available on the Internet. An up-to-date list of World Wide Web references that are relevant to WebApp design can be found at the SEPA website: **www.mhhe.com/engcs/compsci/pressman/professional/olc/ser.htm**.

QUALITY MANAGEMENT

In this part of *Software Engineering: A Practitioner's Approach* you'll learn about the principles, concepts, and techniques that are applied to manage and control software quality. These questions are addressed in the chapters that follow:

- What are the generic characteristics of high-quality software?
- How do we review quality and how are effective reviews conducted?
- What is software quality assurance?
- What strategies are applicable for software testing?
- What methods are used to design effective test cases?
- Are there realistic methods that will ensure that software is correct?
- How can we manage and control changes that always occur as software is built?
- What measures and metrics can be used to assess the quality of requirements and design models, source code, and test cases?

Once these questions are answered you'll be better prepared to ensure that high-quality software has been produced.

14 QUALITY CONCEPTS

The drumbeat for improved software quality began in earnest as software became increasingly integrated in every facet of our lives. By the 1990s, major corporations recognized that billions of dollars each year were being wasted on software that didn't deliver the features and functionality that were promised. Worse, both government and industry became increasingly concerned that a major software fault might cripple important infrastructure, costing tens of billions more. By the turn of the century, *CIO Magazine* [Lev01] trumpeted the headline, "Let's Stop Wasting $78 Billion a Year," lamenting the fact that "American businesses spend billions for software that doesn't do what it's supposed to do." *InformationWeek* [Ric01] echoed the same concern:

> Despite good intentions, defective code remains the hobgoblin of the software industry, accounting for as much as 45% of computer-system downtime and costing U.S. companies about $100 billion last year in lost productivity and repairs, says the Standish Group, a market research firm. That doesn't include the cost of losing angry customers. Because IT shops write applications that rely on packaged infrastructure software, bad code can wreak havoc on custom apps as well. . . .
>
> Just how bad is bad software? Definitions vary, but experts say it takes only three or four defects per 1,000 lines of code to make a program perform poorly. Factor in that most programmers inject about one error for every 10 lines of code they write, multiply that by the millions of lines of code in many commercial products, then figure it costs software vendors at least half their development budgets to fix errors while testing. Get the picture?

QUICK LOOK

What is it? The answer isn't as easy as you might think. You know quality when you see it, and yet, it can be an elusive thing to define. But for computer software, quality is something that we must define, and that's what I'll do in this chapter.

Who does it? Everyone—software engineers, managers, all stakeholders—involved in the software process is responsible for quality.

Why is it important? You can do it right, or you can do it over again. If a software team stresses quality in all software engineering activities, it reduces the amount of rework that it must do. That results in lower costs, and more importantly, improved time-to-market.

What are the steps? To achieve high-quality software, four activities must occur: proven software engineering process and practice, solid project management, comprehensive quality control, and the presence of a quality assurance infrastructure.

What is the work product? Software that meets its customer's needs, performs accurately and reliably, and provides value to all who use it.

How do I ensure that I've done it right? Track quality by examining the results of all quality control activities, and measure quality by examining errors before delivery and defects released to the field.

In 2005, *ComputerWorld* [Hil05] lamented that "bad software plagues nearly every organization that uses computers, causing lost work hours during computer downtime, lost or corrupted data, missed sales opportunities, high IT support and maintenance costs, and low customer satisfaction. A year later, *InfoWorld* [Fos06] wrote about the "the sorry state of software quality" reporting that the quality problem had not gotten any better.

Today, software quality remains an issue, but who is to blame? Customers blame developers, arguing that sloppy practices lead to low-quality software. Developers blame customers (and other stakeholders), arguing that irrational delivery dates and a continuing stream of changes force them to deliver software before it has been fully validated. Who's right? *Both*—and that's the problem. In this chapter, I consider software quality as a concept and examine why it's worthy of serious consideration whenever software engineering practices are applied.

14.1 WHAT IS QUALITY?

In his mystical book, *Zen and the Art of Motorcycle Maintenance,* Robert Persig [Per74] commented on the thing we call *quality*:

> Quality . . . you know what it is, yet you don't know what it is. But that's self-contradictory. But some things are better than others; that is, they have more quality. But when you try to say what the quality is, apart from the things that have it, it all goes poof! There's nothing to talk about. But if you can't say what Quality is, how do you know what it is, or how do you know that it even exists? If no one knows what it is, then for all practical purposes it doesn't exist at all. But for all practical purposes it really does exist. What else are the grades based on? Why else would people pay fortunes for some things and throw others in the trash pile? Obviously some things are better than others . . . but what's the betterness? . . . So round and round you go, spinning mental wheels and nowhere finding any-place to get traction. What the hell is Quality? What is it?

Indeed—what is it?

What are the different ways in which quality can be viewed?

At a somewhat more pragmatic level, David Garvin [Gar84] of the Harvard Business School suggests that "quality is a complex and multifaceted concept" that can be described from five different points of view. The *transcendental view* argues (like Persig) that quality is something that you immediately recognize, but cannot explicitly define. The *user view* sees quality in terms of an end user's specific goals. If a product meets those goals, it exhibits quality. The *manufacturer's view* defines quality in terms of the original specification of the product. If the product conforms to the spec, it exhibits quality. The *product view* suggests that quality can be tied to inherent characteristics (e.g., functions and features) of a product. Finally, the *value-based view* measures quality based on how much a customer is willing to pay for a product. In reality, quality encompasses all of these views and more.

Quality of design refers to the characteristics that designers specify for a product. The grade of materials, tolerances, and performance specifications all contribute to the quality of design. As higher-grade materials are used, tighter tolerances and greater levels of performance are specified, the design quality of a product increases, if the product is manufactured according to specifications.

In software development, quality of design encompasses the degree to which the design meets the functions and features specified in the requirements model. *Quality of conformance* focuses on the degree to which the implementation follows the design and the resulting system meets its requirements and performance goals.

But are quality of design and quality of conformance the only issues that software engineers must consider? Robert Glass [Gla98] argues that a more "intuitive" relationship is in order:

user satisfaction = compliant product + good quality + delivery within budget and schedule

At the bottom line, Glass contends that quality is important, but if the user isn't satisfied, nothing else really matters. DeMarco [DeM98] reinforces this view when he states: "A product's quality is a function of how much it changes the world for the better." This view of quality contends that if a software product provides substantial benefit to its end users, they may be willing to tolerate occasional reliability or performance problems.

14.2   SOFTWARE QUALITY

Even the most jaded software developers will agree that high-quality software is an important goal. But how do we define *software* quality? In the most general sense, software quality can be defined[1] as: *An effective software process applied in a manner that creates a useful product that provides measurable value for those who produce it and those who use it.*

There is little question that the preceding definition could be modified or extended and debated endlessly. For the purposes of this book, the definition serves to emphasize three important points:

1. An *effective software process* establishes the infrastructure that supports any effort at building a high-quality software product. The management aspects of process create the checks and balances that help avoid project chaos—a key contributor to poor quality. Software engineering practices allow the developer to analyze the problem and design a solid solution—both critical to building high-quality software. Finally, umbrella activities such as change management and technical reviews have as much to do with quality as any other part of software engineering practice.

2. A *useful product* delivers the content, functions, and features that the end user desires, but as important, it delivers these assets in a reliable, error-free

---

1   This definition has been adapted from [Bes04] and replaces a more manufacturing-oriented view presented in earlier editions of this book.

way. A useful product always satisfies those requirements that have been explicitly stated by stakeholders. In addition, it satisfies a set of implicit requirements (e.g., ease of use) that are expected of all high-quality software.

3. By *adding value for both the producer and user* of a software product, high-quality software provides benefits for the software organization and the end-user community. The software organization gains added value because high-quality software requires less maintenance effort, fewer bug fixes, and reduced customer support. This enables software engineers to spend more time creating new applications and less on rework. The user community gains added value because the application provides a useful capability in a way that expedites some business process. The end result is (1) greater software product revenue, (2) better profitability when an application supports a business process, and/or (3) improved availability of information that is crucial for the business.

14.2.1 Garvin's Quality Dimensions

David Garvin [Gar87] suggests that quality should be considered by taking a multidimensional viewpoint that begins with an assessment of conformance and terminates with a transcendental (aesthetic) view. Although Garvin's eight dimensions of quality were not developed specifically for software, they can be applied when software quality is considered:

Performance quality. Does the software deliver all content, functions, and features that are specified as part of the requirements model in a way that provides value to the end user?

Feature quality. Does the software provide features that surprise and delight first-time end users?

Reliability. Does the software deliver all features and capability without failure? Is it available when it is needed? Does it deliver functionality that is error-free?

Conformance. Does the software conform to local and external software standards that are relevant to the application? Does it conform to de facto design and coding conventions? For example, does the user interface conform to accepted design rules for menu selection or data input?

Durability. Can the software be maintained (changed) or corrected (debugged) without the inadvertent generation of unintended side effects? Will changes cause the error rate or reliability to degrade with time?

Serviceability. Can the software be maintained (changed) or corrected (debugged) in an acceptably short time period? Can support staff acquire all information they need to make changes or correct defects? Douglas Adams [Ada93] makes a wry comment that seems appropriate here: "The difference between something that can go wrong and something that can't possibly go wrong is that when something that can't possibly go wrong goes wrong it usually turns out to be impossible to get at or repair."

Aesthetics. There's no question that each of us has a different and very subjective vision of what is aesthetic. And yet, most of us would agree that an aesthetic entity has a certain elegance, a unique flow, and an obvious "presence" that are hard to quantify but are evident nonetheless. Aesthetic software has these characteristics.

Perception. In some situations, you have a set of prejudices that will influence your perception of quality. For example, if you are introduced to a software product that was built by a vendor who has produced poor quality in the past, your guard will be raised and your perception of the current software product quality might be influenced negatively. Similarly, if a vendor has an excellent reputation, you may perceive quality, even when it does not really exist.

Garvin's quality dimensions provide you with a "soft" look at software quality. Many (but not all) of these dimensions can only be considered subjectively. For this reason, you also need a set of "hard" quality factors that can be categorized in two broad groups: (1) factors that can be directly measured (e.g., defects uncovered during testing) and (2) factors that can be measured only indirectly (e.g., usability or maintainability). In each case measurement must occur. You should compare the software to some datum and arrive at an indication of quality.

14.2.2 McCall's Quality Factors

McCall, Richards, and Walters [McC77] propose a useful categorization of factors that affect software quality. These software quality factors, shown in Figure 14.1, focus on three important aspects of a software product: its operational characteristics, its ability to undergo change, and its adaptability to new environments.

Referring to the factors noted in Figure 14.1, McCall and his colleagues provide the following descriptions:

Correctness. The extent to which a program satisfies its specification and fulfills the customer's mission objectives.

Reliability. The extent to which a program can be expected to perform its intended function with required precision. [It should be noted that other, more complete definitions of reliability have been proposed (see Chapter 25).]

Efficiency. The amount of computing resources and code required by a program to perform its function.

Integrity. Extent to which access to software or data by unauthorized persons can be controlled.

Usability. Effort required to learn, operate, prepare input for, and interpret output of a program.

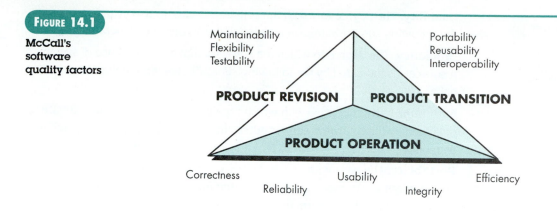

FIGURE 14.1

McCall's software quality factors

Maintainability. Effort required to locate and fix an error in a program. [This is a very limited definition.]

Flexibility. Effort required to modify an operational program.

Testability. Effort required to test a program to ensure that it performs its intended function.

Portability. Effort required to transfer the program from one hardware and/or software system environment to another.

Reusability. Extent to which a program [or parts of a program] can be reused in other applications—related to the packaging and scope of the functions that the program performs.

Interoperability. Effort required to couple one system to another.

It is difficult, and in some cases impossible, to develop direct measures[2] of these quality factors. In fact, many of the metrics defined by McCall et al. can be measured only indirectly. However, assessing the quality of an application using these factors will provide you with a solid indication of software quality.

14.2.3 ISO 9126 Quality Factors

The ISO 9126 standard was developed in an attempt to identify the key quality attributes for computer software. The standard identifies six key quality attributes:

Functionality. The degree to which the software satisfies stated needs as indicated by the following subattributes: suitability, accuracy, interoperability, compliance, and security.

Reliability. The amount of time that the software is available for use as indicated by the following subattributes: maturity, fault tolerance, recoverability.

---

2 A *direct measure* implies that there is a single countable value that provides a direct indication of the attribute being examined. For example, the "size" of a program can be measured directly by counting the number of lines of code.

Usability. The degree to which the software is easy to use as indicated by the following subattributes: understandability, learnability, operability.

Efficiency. The degree to which the software makes optimal use of system resources as indicated by the following subattributes: time behavior, resource behavior.

Maintainability. The ease with which repair may be made to the software as indicated by the following subattributes: analyzability, changeability, stability, testability.

Portability. The ease with which the software can be transposed from one environment to another as indicated by the following subattributes: adaptability, installability, conformance, replaceability.

Like other software quality factors discussed in the preceding subsections, the ISO 9126 factors do not necessarily lend themselves to direct measurement. However, they do provide a worthwhile basis for indirect measures and an excellent checklist for assessing the quality of a system.

14.2.4   Targeted Quality Factors

The quality dimensions and factors presented in Sections 14.2.1 and 14.2.2 focus on the software as a whole and can be used as a generic indication of the quality of an application. A software team can develop a set of quality characteristics and associated questions that would probe[3] the degree to which each factor has been satisfied. For example, McCall identifies *usability* as an important quality factor. If you were asked to review a user interface and assess its usability, how would you proceed? You might start with the subattributes suggested by McCall—understandability, learnability, and operability—but what do these mean in a pragmatic sense?

To conduct your assessment, you'll need to address specific, measurable (or at least, recognizable) attributes of the interface. For example [Bro03]:

Intuitiveness.   The degree to which the interface follows expected usage patterns so that even a novice can use it without significant training.

- Is the interface layout conducive to easy understanding?
- Are interface operations easy to locate and initiate?
- Does the interface use a recognizable metaphor?
- Is input specified to economize key strokes or mouse clicks?
- Does the interface follow the three golden rules? (Chapter 11)
- Do aesthetics aid in understanding and usage?

---

3   These characteristics and questions would be addressed as part of a software review (Chapter 15).

Efficiency.   The degree to which operations and information can be located or initiated.

- Does the interface layout and style allow a user to locate operations and information efficiently?
- Can a sequence of operations (or data input) be performed with an economy of motion?
- Are output data or content presented so that it is understood immediately?
- Have hierarchical operations been organized in a way that minimizes the depth to which a user must navigate to get something done?

Robustness.   The degree to which the software handles bad input data or inappropriate user interaction.

- Will the software recognize the error if data at or just outside prescribed boundaries is input? More importantly, will the software continue to operate without failure or degradation?
- Will the interface recognize common cognitive or manipulative mistakes and explicitly guide the user back on the right track?
- Does the interface provide useful diagnosis and guidance when an error condition (associated with software functionality) is uncovered?

Richness.   The degree to which the interface provides a rich feature set.

- Can the interface be customized to the specific needs of a user?
- Does the interface provide a macro capability that enables a user to identify a sequence of common operations with a single action or command?

As the interface design is developed, the software team would review the design prototype and ask the questions noted. If the answer to most of these questions is "yes," it is likely that the user interface exhibits high quality. A collection of questions similar to these would be developed for each quality factor to be assessed.

14.2.5   The Transition to a Quantitative View

In the preceding subsections, I have presented a variety of qualitative factors for the "measurement" of software quality. The software engineering community strives to develop precise measures for software quality and is sometimes frustrated by the subjective nature of the activity. Cavano and McCall [Cav78] discuss this situation:

> The determination of quality is a key factor in every day events—wine tasting contests, sporting events [e.g., gymnastics], talent contests, etc. In these situations, quality is judged in the most fundamental and direct manner: side by side comparison of objects under identical conditions and with predetermined concepts. The wine may be judged according to clarity, color, bouquet, taste, etc. However, this type of judgment is very subjective; to have any value at all, it must be made by an expert.

Subjectivity and specialization also apply to determining software quality. To help solve this problem, a more precise definition of software quality is needed as well as a way to derive quantitative measurements of software quality for objective analysis. . . . Since there is no such thing as absolute knowledge, one should not expect to measure software quality exactly, for every measurement is partially imperfect. Jacob Bronkowski described this paradox of knowledge in this way: "Year by year we devise more precise instruments with which to observe nature with more fineness. And when we look at the observations we are discomfited to see that they are still fuzzy, and we feel that they are as uncertain as ever."

In Chapter 23, I'll present a set of software metrics that can be applied to the quantitative assessment of software quality. In all cases, the metrics represent indirect measures; that is, we never really measure *quality* but rather some manifestation of quality. The complicating factor is the precise relationship between the variable that is measured and the quality of software.

14.3   THE SOFTWARE QUALITY DILEMMA

In an interview [Ven03] published on the Web, Bertrand Meyer discusses what I call the *quality dilemma:*

> If you produce a software system that has terrible quality, you lose because no one will want to buy it. If on the other hand you spend infinite time, extremely large effort, and huge sums of money to build the absolutely perfect piece of software, then it's going to take so long to complete and it will be so expensive to produce that you'll be out of business anyway. Either you missed the market window, or you simply exhausted all your resources. So people in industry try to get to that magical middle ground where the product is good enough not to be rejected right away, such as during evaluation, but also not the object of so much perfectionism and so much work that it would take too long or cost too much to complete.

It's fine to state that software engineers should strive to produce high-quality systems. It's even better to apply good practices in your attempt to do so. But the situation discussed by Meyer is real life and represents a dilemma for even the best software engineering organizations.

14.3.1   "Good Enough" Software

Stated bluntly, if we are to accept the argument made by Meyer, is it acceptable to produce "good enough" software? The answer to this question must be "yes," because major software companies do it every day. They create software with known bugs and deliver it to a broad population of end users. They recognize that some of the functions and features delivered in Version 1.0 may not be of the highest quality and plan for improvements in Version 2.0. They do this knowing that some customers will complain, but they recognize that time-to-market may trump better quality as long as the delivered product is "good enough."

Exactly what is "good enough"? Good enough software delivers high-quality functions and features that users desire, but at the same time it delivers other more obscure or specialized functions and features that contain known bugs. The software vendor hopes that the vast majority of end users will overlook the bugs because they are so happy with other application functionality.

This idea may resonate with many readers. If you're one of them, I can only ask you to consider some of the arguments against "good enough."

It is true that "good enough" may work in some application domains and for a few major software companies. After all, if a company has a large marketing budget and can convince enough people to buy version 1.0, it has succeeded in locking them in. As I noted earlier, it can argue that it will improve quality in subsequent versions. By delivering a good enough version 1.0, it has cornered the market.

If you work for a small company be wary of this philosophy. When you deliver a good enough (buggy) product, you risk permanent damage to your company's reputation. You may never get a chance to deliver version 2.0 because bad buzz may cause your sales to plummet and your company to fold.

If you work in certain application domains (e.g., real-time embedded software) or build application software that is integrated with hardware (e.g., automotive software, telecommunications software), delivering software with known bugs can be negligent and open your company to expensive litigation. In some cases, it can even be criminal. No one wants good enough aircraft avionics software!

So, proceed with caution if you believe that "good enough" is a short cut that can solve your software quality problems. It can work, but only for a few and only in a limited set of application domains.[4]

14.3.2 The Cost of Quality

The argument goes something like this—*we know that quality is important, but it costs us time and money—too much time and money to get the level of software quality we really want.* On its face, this argument seems reasonable (see Meyer's comments earlier in this section). There is no question that quality has a cost, but lack of quality also has a cost—not only to end users who must live with buggy software, but also to the software organization that has built and must maintain it. The real question is this: *which cost should we be worried about?* To answer this question, you must understand both the cost of achieving quality and the cost of low-quality software.

The *cost of quality* includes all costs incurred in the pursuit of quality or in performing quality-related activities and the downstream costs of lack of quality. To understand these costs, an organization must collect metrics to provide a baseline for the current cost of quality, identify opportunities for reducing these costs, and provide a normalized basis of comparison. The cost of quality can be divided into costs associated with prevention, appraisal, and failure.

---

4   A worthwhile discussion of the pros and cons of "good enough" software can be found in [Bre02].

Prevention costs include (1) the cost of management activities required to plan and coordinate all quality control and quality assurance activities, (2) the cost of added technical activities to develop complete requirements and design models, (3) test planning costs, and (4) the cost of all training associated with these activities.

Appraisal costs include activities to gain insight into product condition the "first time through" each process. Examples of appraisal costs include:

- Cost of conducting technical reviews (Chapter 15) for software engineering work products
- Cost of data collection and metrics evaluation (Chapter 23)
- Cost of testing and debugging (Chapters 18 through 21)

Failure costs are those that would disappear if no errors appeared before or after shipping a product to customers. Failure costs may be subdivided into internal failure costs and external failure costs. *Internal failure costs* are incurred when you detect an error in a product prior to shipment. Internal failure costs include

- Cost required to perform rework (repair) to correct an error
- Cost that occurs when rework inadvertently generates side effects that must be mitigated
- Costs associated with the collection of quality metrics that allow an organization to assess the modes of failure

External failure costs are associated with defects found after the product has been shipped to the customer. Examples of external failure costs are complaint resolution, product return and replacement, help line support, and labor costs associated with warranty work. A poor reputation and the resulting loss of business is another external failure cost that is difficult to quantify but nonetheless very real. Bad things happen when low-quality software is produced.

In an indictment of software developers who refuse to consider external failure costs, Cem Kaner [Kan95] states:

> Many of the external failure costs, such as goodwill, are difficult to quantify, and many companies therefore ignore them when calculating their cost-benefit tradeoffs. Other external failure costs can be reduced (e.g. by providing cheaper, lower-quality, post-sale support, or by charging customers for support) without increasing customer satisfaction. By ignoring the costs to our customers of bad products, quality engineers encourage quality-related decision-making that victimizes our customers, rather than delighting them.

As expected, the relative costs to find and repair an error or defect increase dramatically as we go from prevention to detection to internal failure to external failure costs. Figure 14.2, based on data collected by Boehm and Basili [Boe01b] and illustrated by Cigital Inc. [Cig07], illustrates this phenomenon.

The industry average cost to correct a defect during code generation is approximately $977 per error. The industry average cost to correct the same error if it is

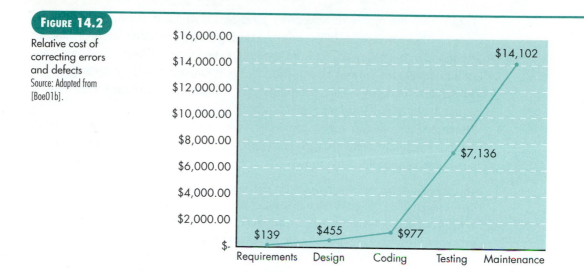

FIGURE 14.2

Relative cost of correcting errors and defects
Source: Adapted from [Boe01b].

discovered during system testing is $7,136 per error. Cigital Inc. [Cig07] considers a large application that has 200 errors introduced during coding.

> According to industry average data, the cost of finding and correcting defects during the coding phase is $977 per defect. Thus, the total cost for correcting the 200 "critical" defects during this phase (200 × $977) is approximately $195,400.
>
> Industry average data shows that the cost of finding and correcting defects during the system testing phase is $7,136 per defect. In this case, assuming that the system testing phase revealed approximately 50 critical defects (or only 25% of those found by Cigital in the coding phase), the cost of finding and fixing those defects (50 × $7,136) would have been approximately $356,800. This would also have resulted in 150 critical errors going undetected and uncorrected. The cost of finding and fixing these remaining 150 defects in the maintenance phase (150 × $14,102) would have been $2,115,300. Thus, the total cost of finding and fixing the 200 defects after the coding phase would have been $2,472,100 ($2,115,300 + $356,800).

Even if your software organization has costs that are half of the industry average (most have no idea what their costs are!), the cost savings associated with early quality control and assurance activities (conducted during requirements analysis and design) are compelling.

14.3.3 Risks

In Chapter 1 of this book, I wrote "people bet their jobs, their comforts, their safety, their entertainment, their decisions, and their very lives on computer software. It better be right." The implication is that low-quality software increases risks for both the developer and the end user. In the preceding subsection, I discussed one of these risks (cost). But the downside of poorly designed and implemented applications does not always stop with dollars and time. An extreme example [Gag04] might serve to illustrate.

Throughout the month of November 2000 at a hospital in Panama, 28 patients received massive overdoses of gamma rays during treatment for a variety of cancers. In the months that followed, 5 of these patients died from radiation poisoning and 15 others developed serious complications. What caused this tragedy? A software package, developed by a U.S. company, was modified by hospital technicians to compute doses of radiation for each patient.

The three Panamanian medical physicists, who "tweeked" the software to provide additional capability, were charged with second-degree murder. The U.S. company is faced with serious litigation in two countries. Gage and McCormick comment:

> This is not a cautionary tale for medical technicians, even though they can find themselves fighting to stay out of jail if they misunderstand or misuse technology. This also is not a tale of how human beings can be injured or worse by poorly designed or poorly explained software, although there are plenty of examples to make the point. This is a warning for any creator of computer programs: that software quality matters, that applications must be foolproof, and that—whether embedded in the engine of a car, a robotic arm in a factory or a healing device in a hospital—poorly deployed code can kill.

Poor quality leads to risks, some of them very serious.

14.3.4   Negligence and Liability

The story is all too common. A governmental or corporate entity hires a major software developer or consulting company to analyze requirements and then design and construct a software-based "system" to support some major activity. The system might support a major corporate function (e.g., pension management) or some governmental function (e.g., health care administration or homeland security).

Work begins with the best of intentions on both sides, but by the time the system is delivered, things have gone bad. The system is late, fails to deliver desired features and functions, is error-prone, and does not meet with customer approval. Litigation ensues.

In most cases, the customer claims that the developer has been negligent (in the manner in which it has applied software practices) and is therefore not entitled to payment. The developer often claims that the customer has repeatedly changed its requirements and has subverted the development partnership in other ways. In every case, the quality of the delivered system comes into question.

14.3.5   Quality and Security

As the criticality of Web-based systems and applications grows, application security has become increasingly important. Stated simply, software that does not exhibit high quality is easier to hack, and as a consequence, low-quality software can indirectly increase the security risk with all of its attendant costs and problems.

In an interview in *ComputerWorld,* author and security expert Gary McGraw comments [Wil05]:

> Software security relates entirely and completely to quality. You must think about security, reliability, availability, dependability—at the beginning, in the design, architecture, test, and coding phases, all through the software life cycle [process]. Even people aware

of the software security problem have focused on late life-cycle stuff. The earlier you find the software problem, the better. And there are two kinds of software problems. One is bugs, which are implementation problems. The other is software flaws—architectural problems in the design. People pay too much attention to bugs and not enough on flaws.

To build a secure system, you must focus on quality, and that focus must begin during design. The concepts and methods discussed in Part 2 of this book lead to a software architecture that reduces "flaws." By eliminating architectural flaws (thereby improving software quality), you will make it far more difficult to hack the software.

14.3.6   The Impact of Management Actions

Software quality is often influenced as much by management decisions as it is by technology decisions. Even the best software engineering practices can be subverted by poor business decisions and questionable project management actions.

In Part 4 of this book I discuss project management within the context of the software process. As each project task is initiated, a project leader will make decisions that can have a significant impact on product quality.

Estimation decisions.   As I note in Chapter 26, a software team is rarely given the luxury of providing an estimate for a project *before* delivery dates are established and an overall budget is specified. Instead, the team conducts a "sanity check" to ensure that delivery dates and milestones are rational. In many cases there is enormous time-to-market pressure that forces a team to accept unrealistic delivery dates. As a consequence, shortcuts are taken, activities that lead to higher-quality software may be skipped, and product quality suffers. If a delivery date is irrational, it is important to hold your ground. Explain why you need more time, or alternatively, suggest a subset of functionality that can be delivered (with high quality) in the time allotted.

Scheduling decisions.   When a software project schedule is established (Chapter 27), tasks are sequenced based on dependencies. For example, because component **A** depends on processing that occurs within components **B, C,** and **D,** component **A** cannot be scheduled for testing until components **B, C,** and **D** are fully tested. A project schedule would reflect this. But if time is very short, and **A** must be available for further critical testing, you might decide to test **A** without its subordinate components (which are running slightly behind schedule), so that you can make it available for other testing that must be done before delivery. After all, the deadline looms. As a consequence, **A** may have defects that are hidden, only to be discovered much later. Quality suffers.

Risk-oriented decisions.   Risk management (Chapter 28) is one of the key attributes of a successful software project. You really do need to know what might go wrong and establish a contingency plan if it does. Too many software teams prefer blind optimism, establishing a development schedule under the assumption that nothing will go wrong. Worse, they don't have a way of handling things that do go wrong. As a consequence, when a risk becomes a reality, chaos reigns, and as the degree of craziness rises, the level of quality invariably falls.

The software quality dilemma can best be summarized by stating Meskimen's Law—*There's never time to do it right, but always time to do it over again.* My advice: taking the time to do it right is almost never the wrong decision.

14.4 ACHIEVING SOFTWARE QUALITY

Software quality doesn't just appear. It is the result of good project management and solid software engineering practice. Management and practice are applied within the context of four broad activities that help a software team achieve high software quality: software engineering methods, project management techniques, quality control actions, and software quality assurance.

14.4.1 Software Engineering Methods

? What do I need to do to affect quality in a positive way?

If you expect to build high-quality software, you must understand the problem to be solved. You must also be capable of creating a design that conforms to the problem while at the same time exhibiting characteristics that lead to software that exhibits the quality dimensions and factors discussed in Section 14.2.

In Part 2 of this book, I presented a wide array of concepts and methods that can lead to a reasonably complete understanding of the problem and a comprehensive design that establishes a solid foundation for the construction activity. If you apply those concepts and adopt appropriate analysis and design methods, the likelihood of creating high-quality software will increase substantially.

14.4.2 Project Management Techniques

The impact of poor management decisions on software quality has been discussed in Section 14.3.6. The implications are clear: if (1) a project manager uses estimation to verify that delivery dates are achievable, (2) schedule dependencies are understood and the team resists the temptation to use short cuts, (3) risk planning is conducted so problems do not breed chaos, software quality will be affected in a positive way.

In addition, the project plan should include explicit techniques for quality and change management. Techniques that lead to good project management practices are discussed in Part 4 of this book.

14.4.3 Quality Control

? What is software quality control?

Quality control encompasses a set of software engineering actions that help to ensure that each work product meets its quality goals. Models are reviewed to ensure that they are complete and consistent. Code may be inspected in order to uncover and correct errors before testing commences. A series of testing steps is applied to uncover errors in processing logic, data manipulation, and interface communication. A combination of measurement and feedback allows a software team to tune the process when any of these work products fail to meet quality goals. Quality control activities are discussed in detail throughout the remainder of Part 3 of this book.

WebRef

Useful links to SQA resources can be found at **www.niwotridge .com/Resources/ PM- SWEResources/ SoftwareQuality Assurance.htm**

14.4.4   Quality Assurance

Quality assurance establishes the infrastructure that supports solid software engineering methods, rational project management, and quality control actions—all pivotal if you intend to build high-quality software. In addition, quality assurance consists of a set of auditing and reporting functions that assess the effectiveness and completeness of quality control actions. The goal of quality assurance is to provide management and technical staff with the data necessary to be informed about product quality, thereby gaining insight and confidence that actions to achieve product quality are working. Of course, if the data provided through quality assurance identifies problems, it is management's responsibility to address the problems and apply the necessary resources to resolve quality issues. Software quality assurance is discussed in detail in Chapter 16.

14.5   SUMMARY

Concern for the quality of the software-based systems has grown as software becomes integrated into every aspect of our daily lives. But it is difficult to develop a comprehensive description of software quality. In this chapter quality has been defined as an effective software process applied in a manner that creates a useful product that provides measurable value for those who produce it and those who use it.

A wide variety of software quality dimensions and factors have been proposed over the years. All try to define a set of characteristics that, if achieved, will lead to high software quality. McCall's and the ISO 9126 quality factors establish characteristics such as reliability, usability, maintainability, functionality, and portability as indicators that quality exists.

Every software organization is faced with the software quality dilemma. In essence, everyone wants to build high-quality systems, but the time and effort required to produce "perfect" software are simply unavailable in a market-driven world. The question becomes, should we build software that is "good enough"? Although many companies do just that, there is a significant downside that must be considered.

Regardless of the approach that is chosen, quality does have a cost that can be discussed in terms of prevention, appraisal, and failure. Prevention costs include all software engineering actions that are designed to prevent defects in the first place. Appraisal costs are associated with those actions that assess software work products to determine their quality. Failure costs encompass the internal price of failure and the external effects that poor quality precipitates.

Software quality is achieved through the application of software engineering methods, solid management practices, and comprehensive quality control—all supported by a software quality assurance infrastructure. In the chapters that follow, quality control and assurance are discussed in some detail.

PROBLEMS AND POINTS TO PONDER

14.1. Describe how you would assess the quality of a university before applying to it. What factors would be important? Which would be critical?

14.2. Garvin [Gar84] describes five different views of quality. Provide an example of each using one or more well-known electronic products with which you are familiar.

14.3. Using the definition of software quality proposed in Section 14.2, do you think it's possible to create a useful product that provides measurable value without using an effective process? Explain your answer.

14.4. Add two additional questions to each of Garvin's quality dimensions presented in Section 14.2.1.

14.5. McCall's quality factors were developed during the 1970s. Almost every aspect of computing has changed dramatically since the time that they were developed, and yet, McCall's factors continue to apply to modern software. Can you draw any conclusions based on this fact?

14.6. Using the subattributes noted for the ISO 9126 quality factor "maintainability" in Section 14.2.3, develop a set of questions that explore whether or not these attributes are present. Follow the example shown in Section 14.2.4.

14.7. Describe the software quality dilemma in your own words.

14.8. What is "good enough" software? Name a specific company and specific products that you believe were developed using the good enough philosophy.

14.9. Considering each of the four aspects of the cost of quality, which do you think is the most expensive and why?

14.10. Do a Web search and find three other examples of "risks" to the public that can be directly traced to poor software quality. Consider beginning your search at **http://catless.ncl.ac.uk/risks.**

14.11. Are *quality* and *security* the same thing? Explain.

14.12. Explain why it is that many of us continue to live by Meskimen's law. What is it about the software business that causes this?

FURTHER READINGS AND INFORMATION SOURCES

Basic software quality concepts are considered in books by Henry and Hanlon (*Software Quality Assurance,* Prentice-Hall, 2008), Khan and his colleagues (*Software Quality: Concepts and Practice,* Alpha Science International, Ltd., 2006), O'Regan (*A Practical Approach to Software Quality,* Springer, 2002), and Daughtrey (*Fundamental Concepts for the Software Quality Engineer,* ASQ Quality Press, 2001).

Duvall and his colleagues (*Continuous Integration: Improving Software Quality and Reducing Risk,* Addison-Wesley, 2007), Tian (*Software Quality Engineering,* Wiley-IEEE Computer Society Press, 2005), Kandt (*Software Engineering Quality Practices,* Auerbach, 2005), Godbole (*Software Quality Assurance: Principles and Practice,* Alpha Science International, Ltd., 2004), and Galin (*Software Quality Assurance: From Theory to Implementation,* Addison-Wesley, 2003) present detailed treatments of SQA. Quality assurance in the context of the agile process is considered by Stamelos and Sfetsos (*Agile Software Development Quality Assurance,* IGI Global, 2007).

Solid design leads to high software quality. Jayasawal and Patton (*Design for Trustworthy Software,* Prentice-Hall, 2006) and Ploesch (*Contracts, Scenarios and Prototypes,* Springer, 2004) discuss tools and techniques for developing "robust" software.

Measurement is an important component of software quality engineering. Ejiogu (*Software Metrics: The Discipline of Software Quality,* BookSurge Publishing, 2005), Kan (*Metrics and Models in Software Quality Engineering,* Addison-Wesley, 2002), and Nance and Arthur (*Managing Software Quality,* Springer, 2002) discuss important quality-related metrics and models. The team-oriented aspects of software quality are considered by Evans (*Achieving Software Quality through Teamwork,* Artech House Publishers, 2004).

A wide variety of information sources on software quality is available on the Internet. An up-to-date list of World Wide Web references relevant to software quality can be found at the SEPA website: **www.mhhe.com/engcs/compsci/pressman/professional/olc/ser.htm.**

15 REVIEW TECHNIQUES

Software reviews are a "filter" for the software process. That is, reviews are applied at various points during software engineering and serve to uncover errors and defects that can then be removed. Software reviews "purify" software engineering work products, including requirements and design models, code, and testing data. Freedman and Weinberg [Fre90] discuss the need for reviews this way:

Technical work needs reviewing for the same reason that pencils need erasers: *To err is human.* The second reason we need technical reviews is that although people are good at catching some of their own errors, large classes of errors escape the originator more easily than they escape anyone else. The review process is, therefore, the answer to the prayer of Robert Burns:

O wad some power the giftie give us

to see ourselves as other see us

A review—any review—is a way of using the diversity of a group of people to:

1. Point out needed improvements in the product of a single person or team;

QUICK LOOK

What is it? You'll make mistakes as you develop software engineering work products. There's no shame in that—as long as you try hard, very hard, to find and correct the mistakes before they are delivered to end users. Technical reviews are the most effective mechanism for finding mistakes early in the software process.

Who does it? Software engineers perform technical reviews, also called peer reviews, with their colleagues.

Why is it important? If you find an error early in the process, it is less expensive to correct. In addition, errors have a way of amplifying as the process proceeds. So a relatively minor error left untreated early in the process can be amplified into a major set of errors later in the project. Finally, reviews save time by reducing the amount of rework that will be required late in the project.

What are the steps? Your approach to reviews will vary depending on the degree of formality you select. In general, six steps are employed, although not all are used for every type of review: planning, preparation, structuring the meeting, noting errors, making corrections (done outside the review), and verifying that corrections have been performed properly.

What is the work product? The output of a review is a list of issues and/or errors that have been uncovered. In addition, the technical status of the work product is also indicated.

How do I ensure that I've done it right? First, select the type of review that is appropriate for your development culture. Follow the guidelines that lead to successful reviews. If the reviews that you conduct lead to higher-quality software, you've done it right.

Reviews are like a filter in the software process workflow. Too few, and the flow is "dirty." Too many, and the flow slows to a trickle. Use metrics to determine which reviews work and emphasize them. Remove ineffective reviews from the flow to accelerate the process.

2. Confirm those parts of a product in which improvement is either not desired or not needed;

3. Achieve technical work of more uniform, or at least more predictable, quality than can be achieved without reviews, in order to make technical work more manageable.

Many different types of reviews can be conducted as part of software engineering. Each has its place. An informal meeting around the coffee machine is a form of review, if technical problems are discussed. A formal presentation of software architecture to an audience of customers, management, and technical staff is also a form of review. In this book, however, I focus on *technical or peer reviews,* exemplified by *casual reviews, walkthroughs,* and *inspections.* A technical review (TR) is the most effective filter from a quality control standpoint. Conducted by software engineers (and others) for software engineers, the TR is an effective means for uncovering errors and improving software quality.

15.1 COST IMPACT OF SOFTWARE DEFECTS

Within the context of the software process, the terms *defect* and *fault* are synonymous. Both imply a quality problem that is discovered *after* the software has been released to end users (or to another framework activity in the software process). In earlier chapters, we used the term *error* to depict a quality problem that is discovered by software engineers (or others) *before* the software is released to the end user (or to another framework activity in the software process).

Bugs, Errors, and Defects

INFO

The goal of software quality control, and in a broader sense, quality management in general, is to remove quality problems in the software. These problems are referred to by various names—*bugs, faults, errors,* or *defects* to name a few. Are each of these terms synonymous, or are there subtle differences between them?

In this book I make a clear distinction between an *error* (a quality problem found *before* the software is released to end users) and a *defect* (a quality problem found only *after* the software has been released to end users[1]). I make this distinction because errors and defects have very different economic, business, psychological, and human impact. As

software engineers, we want to find and correct as many errors as possible before the customer and/or end user encounter them. We want to avoid defects—because defects (justifiably) make software people look bad.

It is important to note, however, that the temporal distinction made between errors and defects in this book is *not* mainstream thinking. The general consensus within the software engineering community is that defects and errors, faults, and bugs are synonymous. That is, the point in time that the problem was encountered has no bearing on the term used to describe the problem. Part of the argument in favor of this view is that it is sometimes difficult to make a

---

1 If software process improvement is considered, a quality problem that is propagated from one process framework activity (e.g., **modeling**) to another (e.g., **construction**) can also be called a "defect" (because the problem should have been found before a work product (e.g., a design model) was "released" to the next activity.

clear distinction between pre- and post-release (e.g., consider an incremental process used in agile development).

Regardless of how you choose to interpret these terms, recognize that the point in time at which a problem is discovered does matter and that software engineers should try hard—*very* hard—to find problems before their customers and end users encounter them. If you have further interest in this issue, a reasonably thorough discussion of the terminology surrounding "bugs" can be found at **www.softwaredevelopment.ca/bugs.shtml**.

The primary objective of technical reviews is to find errors during the process so that they do not become defects after release of the software. The obvious benefit of technical reviews is the early discovery of errors so that they do not propagate to the next step in the software process.

A number of industry studies indicate that design activities introduce between 50 and 65 percent of all errors (and ultimately, all defects) during the software process. However, review techniques have been shown to be up to 75 percent effective [Jon86] in uncovering design flaws. By detecting and removing a large percentage of these errors, the review process substantially reduces the cost of subsequent activities in the software process.

15.2 DEFECT AMPLIFICATION AND REMOVAL

A *defect amplification model* [IBM81] can be used to illustrate the generation and detection of errors during the design and code generation actions of a software process. The model is illustrated schematically in Figure 15.1. A box represents a software engineering action. During the action, errors may be inadvertently generated. Review may fail to uncover newly generated errors and errors from previous steps, resulting in some number of errors that are passed through. In some cases, errors passed through from previous steps are amplified (amplification factor, x) by current work. The box subdivisions represent each of these characteristics and the percent of efficiency for detecting errors, a function of the thoroughness of the review.

Figure 15.2 illustrates a hypothetical example of defect amplification for a software process in which no reviews are conducted. Referring to the figure, each test step is assumed to uncover and correct 50 percent of all incoming errors without introducing any new errors (an optimistic assumption). Ten preliminary design defects are amplified to 94 errors before testing commences. Twelve latent errors (defects) are released to the field. Figure 15.3 considers the same conditions except that design and code reviews are conducted as part of each software engineering action. In this case, 10 initial preliminary (architectural) design errors are amplified to 24 errors before testing commences. Only three latent errors exist. The relative costs associated with the discovery and correction of errors, overall cost (with and without review for our hypothetical example) can be established. The number of errors uncovered during each of the steps noted in Figures 15.2 and 15.3 is multiplied by the cost to remove an

FIGURE 15.1

Defect amplification model

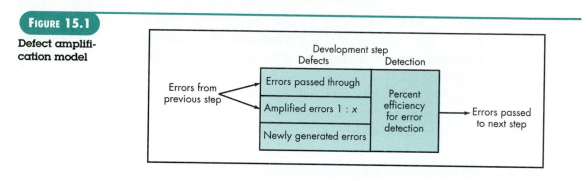

FIGURE 15.2

Defect amplification—no reviews

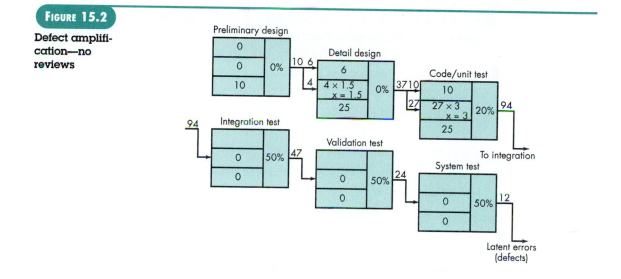

FIGURE 15.3

Defect amplification—reviews conducted

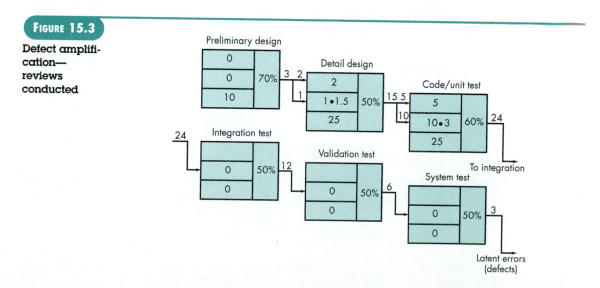

error (1.5 cost units for design, 6.5 cost units before test, 15 cost units during test, and 67 cost units after release).[2] Using these data, the total cost for development and maintenance when reviews are conducted is 783 cost units. When no reviews are conducted, total cost is 2177 units—nearly three times more costly.

To conduct reviews, you must expend time and effort, and your development organization must spend money. However, the results of the preceding example leave little doubt that you can pay now or pay much more later.

15.3   REVIEW METRICS AND THEIR USE

Technical reviews are one of many actions that are required as part of good software engineering practice. Each action requires dedicated human effort, Since available project effort is finite, it is important for a software engineering organization to understand the effectiveness of each action by defining a set of metrics (Chapter 23) that can be used to assess their efficacy.

Although many metrics can be defined for technical reviews, a relatively small subset can provide useful insight. The following review metrics can be collected for each review that is conducted:

- *Preparation effort, E_p*—the effort (in person-hours) required to review a work product prior to the actual review meeting
- *Assessment effort, E_a*—the effort (in person-hours) that is expended during the actual review
- *Rework effort, E_r*—the effort (in person-hours) that is dedicated to the correction of those errors uncovered during the review
- *Work product size, WPS*—a measure of the size of the work product that has been reviewed (e.g., the number of UML models, or the number of document pages, or the number of lines of code)
- *Minor errors found, Err_{minor}*—the number of errors found that can be categorized as minor (requiring less than some prespecified effort to correct)
- *Major errors found, Err_{major}*—the number of errors found that can be categorized as major (requiring more than some prespecified effort to correct)

These metrics can be further refined by associating the type of work product that was reviewed for the metrics collected.

15.3.1   Analyzing Metrics

Before analysis can begin, a few simple computations must occur. The total review effort and the total number of errors discovered are defined as:

$$E_{review} = E_p + E_a + E_r$$
$$Err_{tot} = Err_{minor} + Err_{major}$$

---

2   These multipliers are somewhat different than the data presented in Figure 14.2, which is more current. However, they serve to illustrate the costs of defect amplification nicely.

Error density represents the errors found per unit of work product reviewed.

$$\text{Error density} = \frac{\text{Err}_{\text{tot}}}{\text{WPS}}$$

For example, if a requirements model is reviewed to uncover errors, inconsistencies, and omissions, it would be possible to compute the error density in a number of different ways. The requirements model contains 18 UML diagrams as part of 32 overall pages of descriptive materials. The review uncovers 18 minor errors and 4 major errors. Therefore, $\text{Err}_{\text{tot}} = 22$. Error density is 1.2 errors per UML diagram or 0.68 errors per requirements model page.

If reviews are conducted for a number of different types of work products (e.g., requirements model, design model, code, test cases), the percentage of errors uncovered for each review can be computed against the total number of errors found for all reviews. In addition, the error density for each work product can be computed.

Once data are collected for many reviews conducted across many projects, average values for error density enable you to estimate the number of errors to be found in a new (as yet unreviewed document). For example, if the average error density for a requirements model is 0.6 errors per page, and a new requirement model is 32 pages long, a rough estimate suggests that your software team will find about 19 or 20 errors during the review of the document. If you find only 6 errors, you've done an extremely good job in developing the requirements model or your review approach was not thorough enough.

Once testing has been conducted (Chapters 17 through 20), it is possible to collect additional error data, including the effort required to find and correct errors uncovered during testing and the error density of the software. The costs associated with finding and correcting an error during testing can be compared to those for reviews. This is discussed in Section 15.3.2.

15.3.2   Cost Effectiveness of Reviews

It is difficult to measure the cost effectiveness of any technical review in real time. A software engineering organization can assess the effectiveness of reviews and their cost benefit only after reviews have been completed, review metrics have been collected, average data have been computed, and then the downstream quality of the software is measured (via testing).

Returning to the example presented in Section 15.3.1, the average error density for requirements models was determined to be 0.6 errors per page. The effort required to correct a minor model error (immediately after the review) was found to require 4 person-hours. The effort required for a major requirement error was found to be 18 person-hours. Examining the review data collected, you find that minor errors occur about 6 times more frequently than major errors. Therefore, you can estimate that the average effort to find and correct a requirements error during review is about 6 person-hours.

Requirements-related errors uncovered during testing require an average of 45 person-hours to find and correct (no data are available on the relative severity of the error). Using the averages noted, we get:

$$\text{Effort saved per error} = E_{testing} - E_{reviews}$$
$$45 - 6 = 30 \text{ person-hours/error}$$

Since 22 errors were found during the review of the requirements model, a saving of about 660 person-hours of testing effort would be achieved. And that's just for requirements-related errors. Errors associated with design and code would add to the overall benefit. The bottom line—effort saved leads to shorter delivery cycles and improved time to market.

In his book on peer reviews, Karl Wiegers [Wie02] discusses anecdotal data from major companies that have used *inspections* (a relatively formal type of technical review) as part of their software quality control activities. Hewlett Packard reported a 10 to 1 return on investment for inspections and noted that actual product delivery accelerated by an average of 1.8 calendar months. AT&T indicated that inspections reduced the overall cost of software errors by a factor of 10 and that quality improved by an order of magnitude and productivity increased by 14 percent. Others report similar benefits. Technical reviews (for design and other technical activities) provide a demonstrable cost benefit and actually save time.

But for many software people, this statement is counterintuitive. "Reviews take time," software people argue, "and we don't have the time to spare!" They argue that time is a precious commodity on every software project and the ability to review "every work product in detail" absorbs too much time.

The examples presented earlier in this section indicate otherwise. More importantly, industry data for software reviews has been collected for more than two decades and is summarized qualitatively using the graphs illustrated in Figure 15.4.

FIGURE 15.4

Effort expended with and without reviews
Source: Adapted from [Fag86].

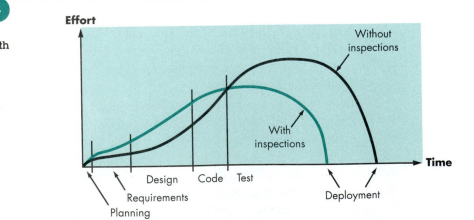

Referring to the figure, the effort expended when reviews are used does increase early in the development of a software increment, but this early investment for reviews pays dividends because testing and corrective effort is reduced. As important, the deployment date for development with reviews is sooner than the deployment date without reviews. Reviews don't take time, they save it!

15.4 REVIEWS: A FORMALITY SPECTRUM

Technical reviews should be applied with a level of formality that is appropriate for the product to be built, the project time line, and the people who are doing the work. Figure 15.5 depicts a reference model for technical reviews [Lai02] that identifies four characteristics that contribute to the formality with which a review is conducted.

Each of the reference model characteristics helps to define the level of review formality. The formality of a review increases when (1) distinct roles are explicitly defined for the reviewers, (2) there is a sufficient amount of planning and preparation for the review, (3) a distinct structure for the review (including tasks and internal work products) is defined, and (4) follow-up by the reviewers occurs for any corrections that are made.

To understand the reference model, let's assume that you've decided to review the interface design for **SafeHomeAssured.com**. You can do this in a variety of different ways that range from relatively casual to extremely rigorous. If you decide that the casual approach is most appropriate, you ask a few colleagues (peers) to examine the interface prototype in an effort to uncover potential problems. All of you decide that there will be no advance preparation, but that you will evaluate the prototype in a reasonably structured way—looking at layout first, aesthetics next, navigation options after that, and so on. As the designer, you decide to take a few notes, but nothing formal.

FIGURE 15.5

Reference model for technical reviews

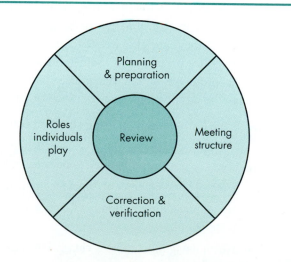

But what if the interface is pivotal to the success of the entire project? What if human lives depended on an interface that was ergonomically sound? You might decide that a more rigorous approach was necessary. A review team would be formed. Each person on the team would have a specific role to play—leading the team, recording findings, presenting the material, and so on. Each reviewer would be given access to the work product (in this case, the interface prototype) before the review and would spend time looking for errors, inconsistencies, and omissions. A set of specific tasks would be conducted based on an agenda that was developed before the review occurred. The results of the review would be formally recorded, and the team would decide on the status of the work product based on the outcome of the review. Members of the review team might also verify that the corrections made were done properly.

In this book I consider two broad categories of technical reviews: informal reviews and more formal technical reviews. Within each broad category, a number of different approaches can be chosen. These are presented in the sections that follow.

15.5   INFORMAL REVIEWS

Informal reviews include a simple desk check of a software engineering work product with a colleague, a casual meeting (involving more than two people) for the purpose of reviewing a work product, or the review-oriented aspects of pair programming (Chapter 3).

A simple *desk check* or a *casual meeting* conducted with a colleague is a review. However, because there is no advance planning or preparation, no agenda or meeting structure, and no follow-up on the errors that are uncovered, the effectiveness of such reviews is considerably lower than more formal approaches. But a simple desk check can and does uncover errors that might otherwise propagate further into the software process.

One way to improve the efficacy of a desk check review is to develop a set of simple review checklists for each major work product produced by the software team. The questions posed within the checklist are generic, but they will serve to guide the reviewers as they check the work product. For example, let's reexamine a desk check of the interface prototype for **SafeHomeAssured.com**. Rather than simply playing with the prototype at the designer's workstation, the designer and a colleague examine the prototype using a checklist for interfaces:

- Is the layout designed using standard conventions? Left to right? Top to bottom?
- Does the presentation need to be scrolled?
- Are color and placement, typeface, and size used effectively?
- Are all navigation options or functions represented at the same level of abstraction?
- Are all navigation choices clearly labeled?

and so on. Any errors or issues noted by the reviewers are recorded by the designer for resolution at a later time. Desk checks may be scheduled in an ad hoc manner, or they may be mandated as part of good software engineering practice. In general, the amount of material to be reviewed is relatively small and the overall time spent on a desk check spans little more than one or two hours.

In Chapter 3, I described *pair programming* in the following manner: "XP recommends that two people work together at one computer workstation to create code for a story. This provides a mechanism for real-time problem solving (two heads are often better than one) and real-time quality assurance."

Pair programming can be characterized as a continuous desk check. Rather than scheduling a review at some point in time, pair programming encourages continuous review as a work product (design or code) is created. The benefit is immediate discovery of errors and better work product quality as a consequence.

In their discussion of the efficacy of pair programming, Williams and Kessler [Wil00] state:

> Anecdotal and initial statistical evidence indicates that pair programming is a powerful technique for productively generating high quality software products. The pair works and shares ideas together to tackle the complexities of software development. They continuously perform inspections on each other's artifacts leading to the earliest, most efficient form of defect removal possible. In addition, they keep each other intently focused on the task at hand.

Some software engineers argue that the inherent redundancy built into pair programming is wasteful of resources. After all, why assign two people to a job that one person can accomplish? The answer to this question can be found in Section 15.3.2. If the quality of the work product produced as a consequence of pair programming is significantly better than the work of an individual, the quality-related savings can more than justify the "redundancy" implied by pair programming.

INFO

Review Checklists

Even when reviews are well organized and properly conducted, it's not a bad idea to provide reviewers with a "crib sheet." That is, it's worthwhile to have a checklist that provides each reviewer with the questions that should be asked about the specific work product that is undergoing review.

One of the most comprehensive collections of review checklists has been developed by NASA at the Goddard Space Flight Center and is available at **http://sw-assurance.gsfc.nasa.gov/disciplines/quality/index.php**

Other useful technical review checklists have also been proposed by:

Process Impact (**www.processimpact.com/pr_goodies.shtml**)

Software Dioxide (**www.softwaredioxide.com/Channels/ConView.asp?id=6309**)

Macadamian (**www.macadamian.com**)

The Open Group Architecture Review Checklist (**www.opengroup.org/architecture/togaf7-doc/arch/p4/comp/clists/syseng.htm**)

DFAS [downloadable] (**www.dfas.mil/technology/pal/ssps/docstds/spm036.doc**)

15.6   FORMAL TECHNICAL REVIEWS

A *formal technical review* (FTR) is a software quality control activity performed by software engineers (and others). The objectives of an FTR are: (1) to uncover errors in function, logic, or implementation for any representation of the software; (2) to verify that the software under review meets its requirements; (3) to ensure that the software has been represented according to predefined standards; (4) to achieve software that is developed in a uniform manner; and (5) to make projects more manageable. In addition, the FTR serves as a training ground, enabling junior engineers to observe different approaches to software analysis, design, and implementation. The FTR also serves to promote backup and continuity because a number of people become familiar with parts of the software that they may not have otherwise seen.

The FTR is actually a class of reviews that includes *walkthroughs* and *inspections.* Each FTR is conducted as a meeting and will be successful only if it is properly planned, controlled, and attended. In the sections that follow, guidelines similar to those for a walkthrough are presented as a representative formal technical review. If you have interest in software inspections, as well as additional information on walkthroughs, see [Rad02], [Wie02], or [Fre90].

15.6.1   The Review Meeting

Regardless of the FTR format that is chosen, every review meeting should abide by the following constraints:

- Between three and five people (typically) should be involved in the review.
- Advance preparation should occur but should require no more than two hours of work for each person.
- The duration of the review meeting should be less than two hours.

Given these constraints, it should be obvious that an FTR focuses on a specific (and small) part of the overall software. For example, rather than attempting to review an entire design, walkthroughs are conducted for each component or small group of components. By narrowing the focus, the FTR has a higher likelihood of uncovering errors.

The focus of the FTR is on a work product (e.g., a portion of a requirements model, a detailed component design, source code for a component). The individual who has developed the work product—the *producer*—informs the project leader that the work product is complete and that a review is required. The project leader contacts a *review leader,* who evaluates the product for readiness, generates copies of product materials, and distributes them to two or three *reviewers* for advance preparation. Each reviewer is expected to spend between one and two hours reviewing the product, making notes, and otherwise becoming familiar with the work. Concurrently, the review leader also reviews the product and establishes an agenda for the review meeting, which is typically scheduled for the next day.

Quote:

"There is no urge so great as for one man to edit another man's work."

Mark Twain

WebRef

The NASA SATC *Formal Inspection Guidebook* can be downloaded from **satc.gsfc.nasa .gov/Documents/ fi/gdb/fi.pdf**.

KEY POINT

An FTR focuses on a relatively small portion of a work product.

The review meeting is attended by the review leader, all reviewers, and the producer. One of the reviewers takes on the role of a *recorder,* that is, the individual who records (in writing) all important issues raised during the review. The FTR begins with an introduction of the agenda and a brief introduction by the producer. The producer then proceeds to "walk through" the work product, explaining the material, while reviewers raise issues based on their advance preparation. When valid problems or errors are discovered, the recorder notes each.

At the end of the review, all attendees of the FTR must decide whether to: (1) accept the product without further modification, (2) reject the product due to severe errors (once corrected, another review must be performed), or (3) accept the product provisionally (minor errors have been encountered and must be corrected, but no additional review will be required). After the decision is made, all FTR attendees complete a sign-off, indicating their participation in the review and their concurrence with the review team's findings.

15.6.2   Review Reporting and Record Keeping

During the FTR, a reviewer (the recorder) actively records all issues that have been raised. These are summarized at the end of the review meeting, and a *review issues list* is produced. In addition, a *formal technical review summary report* is completed. A review summary report answers three questions:

1. What was reviewed?
2. Who reviewed it?
3. What were the findings and conclusions?

The review summary report is a single page form (with possible attachments). It becomes part of the project historical record and may be distributed to the project leader and other interested parties.

The review issues list serves two purposes: (1) to identify problem areas within the product and (2) to serve as an action item checklist that guides the producer as corrections are made. An issues list is normally attached to the summary report.

You should establish a follow-up procedure to ensure that items on the issues list have been properly corrected. Unless this is done, it is possible that issues raised can "fall between the cracks." One approach is to assign the responsibility for follow-up to the review leader.

15.6.3   Review Guidelines

Guidelines for conducting formal technical reviews must be established in advance, distributed to all reviewers, agreed upon, and then followed. A review that is uncontrolled can often be worse than no review at all. The following represents a minimum set of guidelines for formal technical reviews:

1. *Review the product, not the producer.* An FTR involves people and egos. Conducted properly, the FTR should leave all participants with a warm feeling of

accomplishment. Conducted improperly, the FTR can take on the aura of an inquisition. Errors should be pointed out gently; the tone of the meeting should be loose and constructive; the intent should not be to embarrass or belittle. The review leader should conduct the review meeting to ensure that the proper tone and attitude are maintained and should immediately halt a review that has gotten out of control.

2. *Set an agenda and maintain it.* One of the key maladies of meetings of all types is drift. An FTR must be kept on track and on schedule. The review leader is chartered with the responsibility for maintaining the meeting schedule and should not be afraid to nudge people when drift sets in.

3. *Limit debate and rebuttal.* When an issue is raised by a reviewer, there may not be universal agreement on its impact. Rather than spending time debating the question, the issue should be recorded for further discussion off-line.

4. *Enunciate problem areas, but don't attempt to solve every problem noted.* A review is not a problem-solving session. The solution of a problem can often be accomplished by the producer alone or with the help of only one other individual. Problem solving should be postponed until after the review meeting.

5. *Take written notes.* It is sometimes a good idea for the recorder to make notes on a wall board, so that wording and priorities can be assessed by other reviewers as information is recorded. Alternatively, notes may be entered directly into a notebook computer.

6. *Limit the number of participants and insist upon advance preparation.* Two heads are better than one, but 14 are not necessarily better than 4. Keep the number of people involved to the necessary minimum. However, all review team members must prepare in advance. Written comments should be solicited by the review leader (providing an indication that the reviewer has reviewed the material).

7. *Develop a checklist for each product that is likely to be reviewed.* A checklist helps the review leader to structure the FTR meeting and helps each reviewer to focus on important issues. Checklists should be developed for analysis, design, code, and even testing work products.

8. *Allocate resources and schedule time for FTRs.* For reviews to be effective, they should be scheduled as tasks during the software process. In addition, time should be scheduled for the inevitable modifications that will occur as the result of an FTR.

9. *Conduct meaningful training for all reviewers.* To be effective all review participants should receive some formal training. The training should stress both process-related issues and the human psychological side of reviews. Freedman and Weinberg [Fre90] estimate a one-month learning curve for every 20 people who are to participate effectively in reviews.

uote:

"A meeting is too often an event in which minutes are taken and hours are wasted."

Author unknown

uote:

"It is one of the most beautiful compensations of life, that no man can sincerely try to help another without helping himself."

Ralph Waldo Emerson

10. *Review your early reviews.* Debriefing can be beneficial in uncovering problems with the review process itself. The very first product to be reviewed should be the review guidelines themselves.

Because many variables (e.g., number of participants, type of work products, timing and length, specific review approach) have an impact on a successful review, a software organization should experiment to determine what approach works best in a local context.

15.6.4   Sample-Driven Reviews

In an ideal setting, every software engineering work product would undergo a formal technical review. In the real word of software projects, resources are limited and time is short. As a consequence, reviews are often skipped, even though their value as a quality control mechanism is recognized.

Thelin and his colleagues [The01] suggest a sample-driven review process in which samples of all software engineering work products are inspected to determine which work products are most error prone. Full FTR resources are then focused only on those work products that are likely (based on data collected during sampling) to be error prone.

To be effective, the sample-driven review process must attempt to quantify those work products that are primary targets for full FTRs. To accomplish this, the following steps are suggested [The01]:

1. Inspect a fraction a_i of each software work product i. Record the number of faults f_i found within a_i.

2. Develop a gross estimate of the number of faults within work product i by multiplying f_i by $1/a_i$.

3. Sort the work products in descending order according to the gross estimate of the number of faults in each.

4. Focus available review resources on those work products that have the highest estimated number of faults.

The fraction of the work product that is sampled must be representative of the work product as a whole and large enough to be meaningful to the reviewers who do the sampling. As a_i increases, the likelihood that the sample is a valid representation of the work product also increases. However, the resources required to do sampling also increase. A software engineering team must establish the best value for a_i for the types of work products produced.[3]

---

3   Thelin and his colleagues have conducted a detailed simulation that can assist in making this determination. See [The01] for details.

SAFEHOME

Quality Issues

The scene: Doug Miller's office as the *SafeHome* software project begins.

The players: Doug Miller (manager of the *SafeHome* software engineering team) and other members of the product software engineering team.

The conversation:

Doug: I know we didn't spend time developing a quality plan for this project, but we're already into it and we have to consider quality … right?

Jamie: Sure. We've already decided that as we develop the requirements model [Chapters 6 and 7], Ed has committed to develop a testing procedure for each requirement.

Doug: That's really good, but we're not going to wait until testing to evaluate quality, are we?

Vinod: No! Of course not. We've got reviews scheduled into the project plan for this software increment. We'll begin quality control with the reviews.

Jamie: I'm a bit concerned that we won't have enough time to conduct all the reviews. In fact, I know we won't.

Doug: Hmmm. So what do you propose?

Jamie: I say we select those elements of the requirements and design model that are most critical to *SafeHome* and review them.

Vinod: But what if we miss something in a part of the model we don't review?

Shakira: I read something about a sampling technique [Section 15.6.4] that might help us target candidates for review. (Shakira explains the approach.)

Jamie: Maybe … but I'm not sure we even have time to sample every element of the models.

Vinod: What do you want us to do, Doug?

Doug: Let's steal something from Extreme Programming [Chapter 3]. We'll develop the elements of each model in pairs—two people—and conduct an informal review of each as we go. We'll then target "critical" elements for a more formal team review, but keep those reviews to a minimum. That way, everything gets looked at by more than one set of eyes, but we still maintain our delivery dates.

Jamie: That means we're going to have to revise the schedule.

Doug: So be it. Quality trumps schedule on this project.

15.7   SUMMARY

The intent of every technical review is to find errors and uncover issues that would have a negative impact on the software to be deployed. The sooner an error is uncovered and corrected, the less likely that error will propagate to other software engineering work products and amplify itself, resulting in significantly more effort to correct it.

To determine whether quality control activities are working, a set of metrics should be collected. Review metrics focus on the effort required to conduct the review and the types and severity of errors uncovered during the review. Once metrics data are collected, they can be used to assess the efficacy of the reviews you conduct. Industry data indicates that reviews provide a significant return on investment.

A reference model for review formality identifies the roles people play, planning and preparation, meeting structure, correction approach, and verification as the characteristics that indicate the degree of formality with which a review is conducted. Informal reviews are casual in nature, but can still be used effectively to uncover errors. Formal reviews are more structured and have the highest probability of leading to high-quality software.

Informal reviews are characterized by minimal planning and preparation and little record keeping. Desk checks and pair programming fall into the informal review category.

A formal technical review is a stylized meeting that has been shown to be extremely effective in uncovering errors. Walkthroughs and inspections establish defined roles for each reviewer, encourage planning and advance preparation, require the application of defined review guidelines, and mandate record keeping and status reporting. Sample-driven reviews can be used when it is not possible to conduct formal technical reviews for all work products.

PROBLEMS AND POINTS TO PONDER

15.1. Explain the difference between an *error* and a *defect*.

15.2. Why can't we just wait until testing to find and correct all software errors?

15.3. Assume that 10 errors have been introduced in the requirements model and that each error will be amplified by a factor of 2:1 into design and an addition 20 design errors are introduced and then amplified 1.5:1 into code where an additional 30 errors are introduced. Assume further that all unit testing will find 30 percent of all errors, integration will find 30 percent of the remaining errors, and validation tests will find 50 percent of the remaining errors. No reviews are conducted. How many errors will be released to the field.

15.4. Reconsider the situation described in Problem 15.3, but now assume that requirements, design, and code reviews are conducted and are 60 percent effective in uncovering all errors at that step. How many errors will be released to the field?

15.5. Reconsider the situation described in Problems 15.3 and 15.4. If each of the errors released to the field costs $4,800 to find and correct and each error found in review costs $240 to find and correct, how much money is saved by conducting reviews?

15.6. Describe the meaning of Figure 15.4 in your own words.

15.7. Which of the reference model characteristics do you think has the strongest bearing on review formality? Explain why.

15.8. Can you think of a few instances in which a desk check might create problems rather than provide benefits?

15.9. A formal technical review is effective only if everyone has prepared in advance. How do you recognize a review participant who has not prepared? What do you do if you're the review leader?

15.10. Considering all of the review guidelines presented in Section 15.6.3, which do you think is most important and why?

FURTHER READINGS AND INFORMATION SOURCES

There have been relatively few books written on software reviews. Recent editions that provide worthwhile guidance include books by Wong (*Modern Software Review,* IRM Press, 2006), Radice (*High Quality, Low Cost Software Inspections,* Paradoxicon Publishers, 2002), Wiegers (*Peer Reviews in Software: A Practical Guide,* Addison-Wesley, 2001), and Gilb and Graham (*Software Inspection,* Addison-Wesley, 1993). Freedman and Weinberg (*Handbook of Walkthroughs, Inspections and Technical Reviews,* Dorset House, 1990) remains a classic text and continues to provide worthwhile information about this important subject.

A wide variety of information sources on software reviews is available on the Internet. An up-to-date list of World Wide Web references relevant to software reviews can be found at the SEPA website: **www.mhhe.com/engcs/compsci/pressman/professional/olc/ser.htm**.

The software engineering approach described in this book works toward a single goal: to produce on-time, high-quality software. Yet many readers will be challenged by the question: "What is software quality?"
Philip Crosby [Cro79], in his landmark book on quality, provides a wry answer to this question:

The problem of quality management is not what people don't know about it. The problem is what they think they do know. . . .

In this regard, quality has much in common with sex. Everybody is for it. (Under certain conditions, of course.) Everyone feels they understand it. (Even though they wouldn't want to explain it.) Everyone thinks execution is only a matter of following natural inclinations. (After all, we do get along somehow.) And, of course, most people feel that problems in these areas are caused by other people. (If only they would take the time to do things right.)

QUICK LOOK

What is it? It's not enough to talk the talk by saying that software quality is important. You have to (1) explicitly define what is meant when you say "software quality," (2) create a set of activities that will help ensure that every software engineering work product exhibits high quality, (3) perform quality control and assurance activities on every software project, (4) use metrics to develop strategies for improving your software process and, as a consequence, the quality of the end product.

Who does it? Everyone involved in the software engineering process is responsible for quality.

Why is it important? You can do it right, or you can do it over again. If a software team stresses quality in all software engineering activities, it reduces the amount of rework that it must do. That results in lower costs, and more importantly, improved time-to-market.

What are the steps? Before software quality assurance (SQA) activities can be initiated, it is important to define *software quality* at a number of different levels of abstraction. Once you understand what quality is, a software team must identify a set of SQA activities that will filter errors out of work products before they are passed on.

What is the work product? A Software Quality Assurance Plan is created to define a software team's SQA strategy. During modeling and coding, the primary SQA work product is the output of technical reviews (Chapter 15). During testing (Chapters 17 through 20), test plans and procedures are produced. Other work products associated with process improvement may also be generated.

How do I ensure that I've done it right? Find errors before they become defects! That is, work to improve your defect removal efficiency (Chapter 23), thereby reducing the amount of rework that your software team has to perform.

Indeed, quality is a challenging concept—one that I addressed in some detail in Chapter 14.[1]

Some software developers continue to believe that software quality is something you begin to worry about after code has been generated. Nothing could be further from the truth! *Software quality assurance* (often called *quality management*) is an umbrella activity (Chapter 2) that is applied throughout the software process.

Software quality assurance (SQA) encompasses (1) an SQA process, (2) specific quality assurance and quality control tasks (including technical reviews and a multi-tiered testing strategy), (3) effective software engineering practice (methods and tools), (4) control of all software work products and the changes made to them (Chapter 22), (5) a procedure to ensure compliance with software development standards (when applicable), and (6) measurement and reporting mechanisms.

In this chapter, I focus on the management issues and the process-specific activities that enable a software organization to ensure that it does "the right things at the right time in the right way."

16.1 BACKGROUND ISSUES

Quality control and assurance are essential activities for any business that produces products to be used by others. Prior to the twentieth century, quality control was the sole responsibility of the craftsperson who built a product. As time passed and mass production techniques became commonplace, quality control became an activity performed by people other than the ones who built the product.

Quote:

"You made too many wrong mistakes."

Yogi Berra

The first formal quality assurance and control function was introduced at Bell Labs in 1916 and spread rapidly throughout the manufacturing world. During the 1940s, more formal approaches to quality control were suggested. These relied on measurement and continuous process improvement [Dem86] as key elements of quality management.

Today, every company has mechanisms to ensure quality in its products. In fact, explicit statements of a company's concern for quality have become a marketing ploy during the past few decades.

The history of quality assurance in software development parallels the history of quality in hardware manufacturing. During the early days of computing (1950s and 1960s), quality was the sole responsibility of the programmer. Standards for quality assurance for software were introduced in military contract software development during the 1970s and have spread rapidly into software development in the commercial world [IEE93]. Extending the definition presented earlier, software quality assurance is a "planned and systematic pattern of actions" [Sch98c] that are required to ensure high quality in software. The scope of quality assurance responsibility might best be characterized by paraphrasing a once-popular automobile commercial: "Quality Is Job #1." The implication for software is that many different constituencies

---

1   If you have not read Chapter 14, you should do so now.

have software quality assurance responsibility—software engineers, project managers, customers, salespeople, and the individuals who serve within an SQA group.

The SQA group serves as the customer's in-house representative. That is, the people who perform SQA must look at the software from the customer's point of view. Does the software adequately meet the quality factors noted in Chapter 14? Has software development been conducted according to preestablished standards? Have technical disciplines properly performed their roles as part of the SQA activity? The SQA group attempts to answer these and other questions to ensure that software quality is maintained.

16.2   ELEMENTS OF SOFTWARE QUALITY ASSURANCE

WebRef

An in-depth discussion of SQA, including a wide array of definitions, can be obtained at **www.swqual .com/newsletter/ vol2/no1/ vol2no1.html**.

Software quality assurance encompasses a broad range of concerns and activities that focus on the management of software quality. These can be summarized in the following manner [Hor03]:

Standards.   The IEEE, ISO, and other standards organizations have produced a broad array of software engineering standards and related documents. Standards may be adopted voluntarily by a software engineering organization or imposed by the customer or other stakeholders. The job of SQA is to ensure that standards that have been adopted are followed and that all work products conform to them.

Reviews and audits.   Technical reviews are a quality control activity performed by software engineers for software engineers (Chapter 15). Their intent is to uncover errors. Audits are a type of review performed by SQA personnel with the intent of ensuring that quality guidelines are being followed for software engineering work. For example, an audit of the review process might be conducted to ensure that reviews are being performed in a manner that will lead to the highest likelihood of uncovering errors.

Testing.   Software testing (Chapters 17 through 20) is a quality control function that has one primary goal—to find errors. The job of SQA is to ensure that testing is properly planned and efficiently conducted so that it has the highest likelihood of achieving its primary goal.

Error/defect collection and analysis.   The only way to improve is to measure how you're doing. SQA collects and analyzes error and defect data to better understand how errors are introduced and what software engineering activities are best suited to eliminating them.

Change management.   Change is one of the most disruptive aspects of any software project. If it is not properly managed, change can lead to confusion, and confusion almost always leads to poor quality. SQA ensures that adequate change management practices (Chapter 22) have been instituted.

Education.   Every software organization wants to improve its software engineering practices. A key contributor to improvement is education of software engineers, their managers, and other stakeholders. The SQA organization takes the lead in software process improvement (Chapter 30) and is a key proponent and sponsor of educational programs.

Vendor management.   Three categories of software are acquired from external software vendors—*shrink-wrapped packages* (e.g., Microsoft *Office*), a *tailored shell* [Hor03] that provides a basic skeletal structure that is custom tailored to the needs of a purchaser, and *contracted software* that is custom designed and constructed from specifications provided by the customer organization. The job of the SQA organization is to ensure that high-quality software results by suggesting specific quality practices that the vendor should follow (when possible), and incorporating quality mandates as part of any contract with an external vendor.

Security management.   With the increase in cyber crime and new government regulations regarding privacy, every software organization should institute policies that protect data at all levels, establish firewall protection for WebApps, and ensure that software has not been tampered with internally. SQA ensures that appropriate process and technology are used to achieve software security.

Safety.   Because software is almost always a pivotal component of human-rated systems (e.g., automotive or aircraft applications), the impact of hidden defects can be catastrophic. SQA may be responsible for assessing the impact of software failure and for initiating those steps required to reduce risk.

Risk management.   Although the analysis and mitigation of risk (Chapter 28) is the concern of software engineers, the SQA organization ensures that risk management activities are properly conducted and that risk-related contingency plans have been established.

In addition to each of these concerns and activities, SQA works to ensure that software support activities (e.g., maintenance, help lines, documentation, and manuals) are conducted or produced with quality as a dominant concern.

> uote:
>
> "Excellence is the unlimited ability to improve the quality of what you have to offer."
>
> **Rick Petin**

INFO

Quality Management Resources

There are dozens of quality management resources available on the Web, including professional societies, standards organizations, and general information sources. The sites that follow provide a good starting point:

American Society for Quality (ASQ) Software Division
   www.asq.org/software

Association for Computer Machinery **www.acm.org**
Data and Analysis Center for Software (DACS)
   www.dacs.dtic.mil/
International Organization for Standardization (ISO)
   www.iso.ch
ISO SPICE
   www.isospice.com

Malcolm Baldridge National Quality Award
  www.quality.nist.gov
Software Engineering Institute
  www.sei.cmu.edu/
Software Testing and Quality Engineering
  www.stickyminds.com
Six Sigma Resources
  www.isixsigma.com/
  www.asq.org/sixsigma/

TickIT International: Quality certification topics
  www.tickit.org/international.htm
Total Quality Management (TQM)
  General information:
    www.gslis.utexas.edu/~rpollock/tqm.html
  Articles: **www.work911.com/tqmarticles.htm**
  Glossary:
    www.quality.org/TQM-MSI/TQM-glossary
    .html

16.3 SQA Tasks, Goals, and Metrics

Software quality assurance is composed of a variety of tasks associated with two different constituencies—the software engineers who do technical work and an SQA group that has responsibility for quality assurance planning, oversight, record keeping, analysis, and reporting.

Software engineers address quality (and perform quality control activities) by applying solid technical methods and measures, conducting technical reviews, and performing well-planned software testing.

16.3.1 SQA Tasks

The charter of the SQA group is to assist the software team in achieving a high-quality end product. The Software Engineering Institute recommends a set of SQA actions that address quality assurance planning, oversight, record keeping, analysis, and reporting. These actions are performed (or facilitated) by an independent SQA group that:

? **What is the role of an SQA group?**

Prepares an SQA plan for a project. The plan is developed as part of project planning and is reviewed by all stakeholders. Quality assurance actions performed by the software engineering team and the SQA group are governed by the plan. The plan identifies evaluations to be performed, audits and reviews to be conducted, standards that are applicable to the project, procedures for error reporting and tracking, work products that are produced by the SQA group, and feedback that will be provided to the software team.

Participates in the development of the project's software process description. The software team selects a process for the work to be performed. The SQA group reviews the process description for compliance with organizational policy, internal software standards, externally imposed standards (e.g., ISO-9001), and other parts of the software project plan.

Reviews software engineering activities to verify compliance with the defined software process. The SQA group identifies, documents, and tracks deviations from the process and verifies that corrections have been made.

Audits designated software work products to verify compliance with those defined as part of the software process. The SQA group reviews selected work products; identifies, documents, and tracks deviations; verifies that corrections have been made; and periodically reports the results of its work to the project manager.

Ensures that deviations in software work and work products are documented and handled according to a documented procedure. Deviations may be encountered in the project plan, process description, applicable standards, or software engineering work products.

Records any noncompliance and reports to senior management. Noncompliance items are tracked until they are resolved.

In addition to these actions, the SQA group coordinates the control and management of change (Chapter 22) and helps to collect and analyze software metrics.

16.3.2 Goals, Attributes, and Metrics

The SQA actions described in the preceding section are performed to achieve a set of pragmatic goals:

Requirements quality. The correctness, completeness, and consistency of the requirements model will have a strong influence on the quality of all work products that follow. SQA must ensure that the software team has properly reviewed the requirements model to achieve a high level of quality.

Design quality. Every element of the design model should be assessed by the software team to ensure that it exhibits high quality and that the design itself conforms to requirements. SQA looks for attributes of the design that are indicators of quality.

Code quality. Source code and related work products (e.g., other descriptive information) must conform to local coding standards and exhibit characteristics that will facilitate maintainability. SQA should isolate those attributes that allow a reasonable analysis of the quality of code.

Quality control effectiveness. A software team should apply limited resources in a way that has the highest likelihood of achieving a high-quality result. SQA analyzes the allocation of resources for reviews and testing to assess whether they are being allocated in the most effective manner.

Figure 16.1 (adapted from [Hya96]) identifies the attributes that are indicators for the existence of quality for each of the goals discussed. Metrics that can be used to indicate the relative strength of an attribute are also shown.

FIGURE 16.1 Software quality goals, attributes, and metrics
Source: Adapted from [Hya96].

Goal	Attribute	Metric
Requirement quality	Ambiguity	Number of ambiguous modifiers (e.g., many, large, human-friendly)
	Completeness	Number of TBA, TBD
	Understandability	Number of sections/subsections
	Volatility	Number of changes per requirement
		Time (by activity) when change is requested
	Traceability	Number of requirements not traceable to design/code
	Model clarity	Number of UML models
		Number of descriptive pages per model
		Number of UML errors
Design quality	Architectural integrity	Existence of architectural model
	Component completeness	Number of components that trace to architectural model
		Complexity of procedural design
	Interface complexity	Average number of pick to get to a typical function or content
		Layout appropriateness
	Patterns	Number of patterns used
Code quality	Complexity	Cyclomatic complexity
	Maintainability	Design factors (Chapter 8)
	Understandability	Percent internal comments
		Variable naming conventions
	Reusability	Percent reused components
	Documentation	Readability index
QC effectiveness	Resource allocation	Staff hour percentage per activity
	Completion rate	Actual vs. budgeted completion time
	Review effectiveness	See review metrics (Chapter 14)
	Testing effectiveness	Number of errors found and criticality
		Effort required to correct an error
		Origin of error

16.4 FORMAL APPROACHES TO SQA

In the preceding sections, I have argued that software quality is everyone's job and that it can be achieved through competent software engineering practice as well as through the application of technical reviews, a multi-tiered testing strategy, better control of software work products and the changes made to them, and the application of accepted software engineering standards. In addition, quality can be defined

WebRef

Useful information on SQA and formal quality methods can be found at **www.gslis .utexas.edu/ ~rpollock/tqm .html**.

in terms of a broad array of quality attributes and measured (indirectly) using a variety of indices and metrics.

Over the past three decades, a small, but vocal, segment of the software engineering community has argued that a more formal approach to software quality assurance is required. It can be argued that a computer program is a mathematical object. A rigorous syntax and semantics can be defined for every programming language, and a rigorous approach to the specification of software requirements (Chapter 21) is available. If the requirements model (specification) and the programming language can be represented in a rigorous manner, it should be possible to apply mathematic proof of correctness to demonstrate that a program conforms exactly to its specifications.

Attempts to prove programs correct are not new. Dijkstra [Dij76a] and Linger, Mills, and Witt [Lin79], among others, advocated proofs of program correctness and tied these to the use of structured programming concepts (Chapter 10).

16.5   STATISTICAL SOFTWARE QUALITY ASSURANCE

Statistical quality assurance reflects a growing trend throughout industry to become more quantitative about quality. For software, statistical quality assurance implies the following steps:

What steps are required to perform statistical SQA?

1. Information about software errors and defects is collected and categorized.

2. An attempt is made to trace each error and defect to its underlying cause (e.g., nonconformance to specifications, design error, violation of standards, poor communication with the customer).

3. Using the Pareto principle (80 percent of the defects can be traced to 20 percent of all possible causes), isolate the 20 percent (the *vital few*).

4. Once the vital few causes have been identified, move to correct the problems that have caused the errors and defects.

This relatively simple concept represents an important step toward the creation of an adaptive software process in which changes are made to improve those elements of the process that introduce error.

16.5.1   A Generic Example

To illustrate the use of statistical methods for software engineering work, assume that a software engineering organization collects information on errors and defects for a period of one year. Some of the errors are uncovered as software is being developed. Others (defects) are encountered after the software has been released to its end users. Although hundreds of different problems are uncovered, all can be tracked to one (or more) of the following causes:

- Incomplete or erroneous specifications (IES)
- Misinterpretation of customer communication (MCC)

uote:

"A statistical analysis, properly conducted, is a delicate dissection of uncertainties, a surgery of suppositions."

M. J. Moroney

- Intentional deviation from specifications (IDS)
- Violation of programming standards (VPS)
- Error in data representation (EDR)
- Inconsistent component interface (ICI)
- Error in design logic (EDL)
- Incomplete or erroneous testing (IET)
- Inaccurate or incomplete documentation (IID)
- Error in programming language translation of design (PLT)
- Ambiguous or inconsistent human/computer interface (HCI)
- Miscellaneous (MIS)

To apply statistical SQA, the table in Figure 16.2 is built. The table indicates that IES, MCC, and EDR are the vital few causes that account for 53 percent of all errors. It should be noted, however, that IES, EDR, PLT, and EDL would be selected as the vital few causes if only serious errors are considered. Once the vital few causes are determined, the software engineering organization can begin corrective action. For example, to correct MCC, you might implement requirements gathering techniques (Chapter 5) to improve the quality of customer communication and specifications. To improve EDR, you might acquire tools for data modeling and perform more stringent data design reviews.

It is important to note that corrective action focuses primarily on the vital few. As the vital few causes are corrected, new candidates pop to the top of the stack.

Statistical quality assurance techniques for software have been shown to provide substantial quality improvement [Art97]. In some cases, software organizations

FIGURE 16.2

Data collection for statistical SQA

Error	Total No.	%	Serious No.	%	Moderate No.	%	Minor No.	%
IES	205	22%	34	27%	68	18%	103	24%
MCC	156	17%	12	9%	68	18%	76	17%
IDS	48	5%	1	1%	24	6%	23	5%
VPS	25	3%	0	0%	15	4%	10	2%
EDR	130	14%	26	20%	68	18%	36	8%
ICI	58	6%	9	7%	18	5%	31	7%
EDL	45	5%	14	11%	12	3%	19	4%
IET	95	10%	12	9%	35	9%	48	11%
IID	36	4%	2	2%	20	5%	14	3%
PLT	60	6%	15	12%	19	5%	26	6%
HCI	28	3%	3	2%	17	4%	8	2%
MIS	56	6%	0	0%	15	4%	41	9%
Totals	942	100%	128	100%	379	100%	435	100%

have achieved a 50 percent reduction per year in defects after applying these techniques.

The application of the statistical SQA and the Pareto principle can be summarized in a single sentence: *Spend your time focusing on things that really matter, but first be sure that you understand what really matters!*

16.5.2   Six Sigma for Software Engineering

Six Sigma is the most widely used strategy for statistical quality assurance in industry today. Originally popularized by Motorola in the 1980s, the Six Sigma strategy "is a rigorous and disciplined methodology that uses data and statistical analysis to measure and improve a company's operational performance by identifying and eliminating defects' in manufacturing and service-related processes" [ISI08]. The term Six Sigma is derived from six standard deviations—3.4 instances (defects) per million occurrences—implying an extremely high quality standard. The Six Sigma methodology defines three core steps:

> **? What are the core steps of the Six Sigma methodology?**

- *Define* customer requirements and deliverables and project goals via well-defined methods of customer communication.
- *Measure* the existing process and its output to determine current quality performance (collect defect metrics).
- *Analyze* defect metrics and determine the vital few causes.

If an existing software process is in place, but improvement is required, Six Sigma suggests two additional steps:

- *Improve* the process by eliminating the root causes of defects.
- *Control* the process to ensure that future work does not reintroduce the causes of defects.

These core and additional steps are sometimes referred to as the DMAIC (define, measure, analyze, improve, and control) method.

If an organization is developing a software process (rather than improving an existing process), the core steps are augmented as follows:

- *Design* the process to (1) avoid the root causes of defects and (2) to meet customer requirements.
- *Verify* that the process model will, in fact, avoid defects and meet customer requirements.

This variation is sometimes called the DMADV (define, measure, analyze, design, and verify) method.

A comprehensive discussion of Six Sigma is best left to resources dedicated to the subject. If you have further interest, see [ISI08], [Pyz03], and [Sne03].

16.6   SOFTWARE RELIABILITY

There is no doubt that the reliability of a computer program is an important element of its overall quality. If a program repeatedly and frequently fails to perform, it matters little whether other software quality factors are acceptable.

Software reliability, unlike many other quality factors, can be measured directly and estimated using historical and developmental data. *Software reliability* is defined in statistical terms as "the probability of failure-free operation of a computer program in a specified environment for a specified time" [Mus87]. To illustrate, program X is estimated to have a reliability of 0.999 over eight elapsed processing hours. In other words, if program X were to be executed 1000 times and require a total of eight hours of elapsed processing time (execution time), it is likely to operate correctly (without failure) 999 times.

Whenever software reliability is discussed, a pivotal question arises: What is meant by the term *failure*? In the context of any discussion of software quality and reliability, failure is nonconformance to software requirements. Yet, even within this definition, there are gradations. Failures can be only annoying or catastrophic. One failure can be corrected within seconds, while another requires weeks or even months to correct. Complicating the issue even further, the correction of one failure may in fact result in the introduction of other errors that ultimately result in other failures.

16.6.1   Measures of Reliability and Availability

KEY POINT

Software reliability problems can almost always be traced to defects in design or implementation.

Early work in software reliability attempted to extrapolate the mathematics of hardware reliability theory to the prediction of software reliability. Most hardware-related reliability models are predicated on failure due to wear rather than failure due to design defects. In hardware, failures due to physical wear (e.g., the effects of temperature, corrosion, shock) are more likely than a design-related failure. Unfortunately, the opposite is true for software. In fact, all software failures can be traced to design or implementation problems; wear (see Chapter 1) does not enter into the picture.

There has been an ongoing debate over the relationship between key concepts in hardware reliability and their applicability to software. Although an irrefutable link has yet to be established, it is worthwhile to consider a few simple concepts that apply to both system elements.

KEY POINT

It is important to note that MTBF and related measures are based on CPU time, not wall clock time.

If we consider a computer-based system, a simple measure of reliability is *mean-time-between-failure* (MTBF):

$$MTBF = MTTF + MTTR$$

where the acronyms MTTF and MTTR are *mean-time-to-failure* and *mean-time-to-repair*,[2] respectively.

---

2   Although debugging (and related corrections) may be required as a consequence of failure, in many cases the software will work properly after a restart with no other change.

Many researchers argue that MTBF is a far more useful measure than other quality-related software metrics discussed in Chapter 23. Stated simply, an end user is concerned with failures, not with the total defect count. Because each defect contained within a program does not have the same failure rate, the total defect count provides little indication of the reliability of a system. For example, consider a program that has been in operation for 3000 processor hours without failure. Many defects in this program may remain undetected for tens of thousand of hours before they are discovered. The MTBF of such obscure errors might be 30,000 or even 60,000 processor hours. Other defects, as yet undiscovered, might have a failure rate of 4000 or 5000 hours. Even if every one of the first category of errors (those with long MTBF) is removed, the impact on software reliability is negligible.

However, MTBF can be problematic for two reasons: (1) it projects a time span between failures, but does not provide us with a projected failure rate, and (2) MTBF can be misinterpreted to mean average life span even though this is *not* what it implies.

An alternative measure of reliability is *failures-in-time* (FIT)—a statistical measure of how many failures a component will have over one billion hours of operation. Therefore, 1 FIT is equivalent to one failure in every billion hours of operation.

In addition to a reliability measure, you should also develop a measure of availability. *Software availability* is the probability that a program is operating according to requirements at a given point in time and is defined as

ADVICE

Some aspects of availability (not discussed here) have nothing to do with failure. For example, scheduling downtime (for support functions) causes the software to be unavailable.

$$\text{Availability} = \frac{\text{MTTF}}{\text{MTTF} + \text{MTTR}} \times 100\%$$

The MTBF reliability measure is equally sensitive to MTTF and MTTR. The availability measure is somewhat more sensitive to MTTR, an indirect measure of the maintainability of software.

16.6.2 Software Safety

Quote:

"The safety of the people shall be the highest law."

Cicero

Software safety is a software quality assurance activity that focuses on the identification and assessment of potential hazards that may affect software negatively and cause an entire system to fail. If hazards can be identified early in the software process, software design features can be specified that will either eliminate or control potential hazards.

A modeling and analysis process is conducted as part of software safety. Initially, hazards are identified and categorized by criticality and risk. For example, some of the hazards associated with a computer-based cruise control for an automobile might be: (1) causes uncontrolled acceleration that cannot be stopped, (2) does not respond to depression of brake pedal (by turning off), (3) does not engage when switch is activated, and (4) slowly loses or gains speed. Once these system-level hazards are identified, analysis techniques are used to assign severity and probability of occurrence.[3] To be effective, software must be analyzed in the context of the entire

---

3 This approach is similar to the risk analysis methods described in Chapter 28. The primary difference is the emphasis on technology issues rather than project-related topics.

system. For example, a subtle user input error (people are system components) may be magnified by a software fault to produce control data that improperly positions a mechanical device. If and only if a set of external environmental conditions is met, the improper position of the mechanical device will cause a disastrous failure. Analysis techniques [Eri05] such as fault tree analysis, real-time logic, and Petri net models can be used to predict the chain of events that can cause hazards and the probability that each of the events will occur to create the chain.

Once hazards are identified and analyzed, safety-related requirements can be specified for the software. That is, the specification can contain a list of undesirable events and the desired system responses to these events. The role of software in managing undesirable events is then indicated.

Although software reliability and software safety are closely related to one another, it is important to understand the subtle difference between them. Software reliability uses statistical analysis to determine the likelihood that a software failure will occur. However, the occurrence of a failure does not necessarily result in a hazard or mishap. Software safety examines the ways in which failures result in conditions that can lead to a mishap. That is, failures are not considered in a vacuum, but are evaluated in the context of an entire computer-based system and its environment.

A comprehensive discussion of software safety is beyond the scope of this book. If you have further interest in software safety and related system issues, see [Smi05], [Dun02], and [Lev95].

16.7   THE ISO 9000 QUALITY STANDARDS[4]

A *quality assurance system* may be defined as the organizational structure, responsibilities, procedures, processes, and resources for implementing quality management [ANS87]. Quality assurance systems are created to help organizations ensure their products and services satisfy customer expectations by meeting their specifications. These systems cover a wide variety of activities encompassing a product's entire life cycle including planning, controlling, measuring, testing and reporting, and improving quality levels throughout the development and manufacturing process. ISO 9000 describes quality assurance elements in generic terms that can be applied to any business regardless of the products or services offered.

To become registered to one of the quality assurance system models contained in ISO 9000, a company's quality system and operations are scrutinized by third-party auditors for compliance to the standard and for effective operation. Upon successful registration, a company is issued a certificate from a registration body represented by the auditors. Semiannual surveillance audits ensure continued compliance to the standard.

---

4   This section, written by Michael Stovsky, has been adapted from "Fundamentals of ISO 9000," a workbook developed for *Essential Software Engineering,* a video curriculum developed by R. S. Pressman & Associates, Inc. Reprinted with permission.

WebRef

Extensive links to ISO 9000/9001 resources can be found at **www.tantara.ab .ca/info.htm**.

The requirements delineated by ISO 9001:2000 address topics such as management responsibility, quality system, contract review, design control, document and data control, product identification and traceability, process control, inspection and testing, corrective and preventive action, control of quality records, internal quality audits, training, servicing, and statistical techniques. In order for a software organization to become registered to ISO 9001:2000, it must establish policies and procedures to address each of the requirements just noted (and others) and then be able to demonstrate that these policies and procedures are being followed. If you desire further information on ISO 9001:2000, see [Ant06], [Mut03], or [Dob04].

INFO

The ISO 9001:2000 Standard

The following outline defines the basic elements of the ISO 9001:2000 standard. Comprehensive information on the standard can be obtained from the International Organization for Standardization (**www.iso.ch**) and other Internet sources (e.g., **www.praxiom.com**).

Establish the elements of a quality management system.
   Develop, implement, and improve the system.
   Define a policy that emphasizes the importance of the
     system.
Document the quality system.
   Describe the process.
   Produce an operational manual.
   Develop methods for controlling (updating) documents.
   Establish methods for record keeping.
Support quality control and assurance.
   Promote the importance of quality among all stakeholders.
   Focus on customer satisfaction.

Define a quality plan that addresses objectives, responsibilities, and authority.
   Define communication mechanisms among stakeholders.
Establish review mechanisms for the quality management
     system.
   Identify review methods and feedback mechanisms.
   Define follow-up procedures.
Identify quality resources including personnel, training,
     and infrastructure elements.
   Establish control mechanisms.
   For planning
   For customer requirements
   For technical activities (e.g., analysis, design, testing)
   For project monitoring and management
Define methods for remediation.
   Assess quality data and metrics.
   Define approach for continuous process and quality
     improvement.

16.8 THE SQA PLAN

The *SQA Plan* provides a road map for instituting software quality assurance. Developed by the SQA group (or by the software team if an SQA group does not exist), the plan serves as a template for SQA activities that are instituted for each software project.

A standard for SQA plans has been published by the IEEE [IEE93]. The standard recommends a structure that identifies: (1) the purpose and scope of the plan, (2) a description of all software engineering work products (e.g., models, documents, source code) that fall within the purview of SQA, (3) all applicable standards and practices that are applied during the software process, (4) SQA actions and tasks (including reviews and audits) and their placement throughout the software process, (5) the tools and methods that support SQA actions and tasks, (6) software configuration management (Chapter 22) procedures, (7) methods for assembling, safeguarding, and maintaining all SQA-related records, and (8) organizational roles and responsibilities relative to product quality.

SOFTWARE TOOLS

Software Quality Management

Objective: The objective of SQA tools is to assist a project team in assessing and improving the quality of software work product.

Mechanics: Tools mechanics vary. In general, the intent is to assess the quality of a specific work product. Note: A wide array of software testing tools (see Chapters 17 through 20) are often included within the SQA tools category.

Representative Tools:[5]
ARM, developed by NASA (**satc.gsfc.nasa.gov/tools/index.html**), provides measures that can be used to assess the quality of a software requirements document.

QPR ProcessGuide and Scorecard, developed by QPR Software (**www.qpronline.com**), provides support for Six Sigma and other quality management approaches.

Quality Tools and Templates, developed by iSixSigma (**www.isixsigma.com/tt/**), describes a wide array of useful tools and methods for quality management.

NASA Quality Resources, developed by the Goddard Space Flight Center (**sw-assurance.gsfc.nasa.gov/index.php**) provides useful forms, templates, checklists, and tools for SQA.

16.9 SUMMARY

Software quality assurance is a software engineering umbrella activity that is applied at each step in the software process. SQA encompasses procedures for the effective application of methods and tools, oversight of quality control activities such as technical reviews and software testing, procedures for change management, procedures for assuring compliance to standards, and measurement and reporting mechanisms.

To properly conduct software quality assurance, data about the software engineering process should be collected, evaluated, and disseminated. Statistical SQA helps to improve the quality of the product and the software process itself. Software reliability models extend measurements, enabling collected defect data to be extrapolated into projected failure rates and reliability predictions.

In summary, you should note the words of Dunn and Ullman [Dun82]: "Software quality assurance is the mapping of the managerial precepts and design disciplines of quality assurance onto the applicable managerial and technological space of software engineering." The ability to ensure quality is the measure of a mature engineering discipline. When the mapping is successfully accomplished, mature software engineering is the result.

---

5   Tools noted here do not represent an endorsement, but rather a sampling of tools in this category. In most cases, tool names are trademarked by their respective developers.

PROBLEMS AND POINTS TO PONDER

16.1. Some people say that "variation control is the heart of quality control." Since every program that is created is different from every other program, what are the variations that we look for and how do we control them?

16.2. Is it possible to assess the quality of software if the customer keeps changing what it is supposed to do?

16.3. Quality and reliability are related concepts but are fundamentally different in a number of ways. Discuss the differences.

16.4. Can a program be correct and still not be reliable? Explain.

16.5. Can a program be correct and still not exhibit good quality? Explain.

16.6. Why is there often tension between a software engineering group and an independent software quality assurance group? Is this healthy?

16.7. You have been given the responsibility for improving the quality of software across your organization. What is the first thing that you should do? What's next?

16.8. Besides counting errors and defects, are there other countable characteristics of software that imply quality? What are they and can they be measured directly?

16.9. The MTBF concept for software is open to criticism. Explain why?

16.10. Consider two safety-critical systems that are controlled by computer. List at least three hazards for each that can be directly linked to software failures.

16.11. Acquire a copy of ISO 9001:2000 and ISO 9000-3. Prepare a presentation that discusses three ISO 9001 requirements and how they apply in a software context.

FURTHER READINGS AND INFORMATION SOURCES

Books by Hoyle (*Quality Management Fundamentals,* Butterworth-Heinemann, 2007), Tian (*Software Quality Engineering,* Wiley-IEEE Computer Society Press, 2005), El Emam (*The ROI from Software Quality,* Auerbach, 2005), Horch (*Practical Guide to Software Quality Management,* Artech House, 2003), and Nance and Arthur (*Managing Software Quality,* Springer, 2002) are excellent management-level presentations on the benefits of formal quality assurance programs for computer software. Books by Deming [Dem86], Juran (*Juran on Quality by Design,* Free Press, 1992), and Crosby ([Cro79] and *Quality Is Still Free,* McGraw-Hill, 1995) do not focus on software, but are must reading for senior managers with software development responsibility. Gluckman and Roome (*Everyday Heroes of the Quality Movement,* Dorset House, 1993) humanizes quality issues by telling the story of the players in the quality process. Kan (*Metrics and Models in Software Quality Engineering,* Addison-Wesley, 1995) presents a quantitative view of software quality.

Books by Evans (*Total Quality: Management, Organization and Strategy,* 4th ed., South-Western College Publishing, 2004), Bru (*Six Sigma for Managers,* McGraw-Hill, 2005), and Dobb (*ISO 9001:2000 Quality Registration Step-by-Step,* 3d ed., Butterworth-Heinemann, 2004) are representative of the many books written on TQM, Six Sigma, and ISO 9001:2000, respectively.

Pham (*System Software Reliability,* Springer, 2006), Musa (*Software Reliability Engineering: More Reliable Software, Faster Development and Testing,* 2d ed., McGraw-Hill, 2004) and Peled (*Software Reliability Methods,* Springer, 2001) have written practical guides that describe methods for measuring and analyzing software reliability.

Vincoli (*Basic Guide to System Safety,* Wiley, 2006), Dhillon (*Engineering Safety,* World Scientific Publishing Co., Inc., 2003), Hermann (*Software Safety and Reliability,* Wiley-IEEE Computer Society Press, 2000), Storey (*Safety-Critical Computer Systems,* Addison-Wesley, 1996), and Leveson [Lev95] are the most comprehensive discussions of software and system safety published to date. In addition, van der Meulen (*Definitions for Hardware and Software Safety*

Engineers, Springer-Verlag, 2000) offers a complete compendium of important concepts and terms for reliability and safety; Gartner (*Testing Safety-Related Software,* Springer-Verlag, 1999) provides specialized guidance for testing safety critical systems; Friedman and Voas (*Software Assessment: Reliability Safety and Testability,* Wiley, 1995) provide useful models for assessing reliability and safety. Ericson (*Hazard Analysis Techniques for System Safety,* Wiley, 2005) addresses the increasingly important domain of hazard analysis.

A wide variety of information sources on software quality assurance and related topics is available on the Internet. An up-to-date list of World Wide Web references relevant to SQA can be found at the SEPA website **www.mhhe.com/engcs/compsci/pressman/professional/ olc/ser.htm**.

SOFTWARE TESTING STRATEGIES

17

A strategy for software testing provides a road map that describes the steps to be conducted as part of testing, when these steps are planned and then undertaken, and how much effort, time, and resources will be required. Therefore, any testing strategy must incorporate test planning, test case design, test execution, and resultant data collection and evaluation.

A software testing strategy should be flexible enough to promote a customized testing approach. At the same time, it must be rigid enough to encourage reasonable planning and management tracking as the project progresses. Shooman [Sho83] discusses these issues:

> In many ways, testing is an individualistic process, and the number of different types of tests varies as much as the different development approaches. For many years, our

QUICK LOOK

What is it? Software is tested to uncover errors that were made inadvertently as it was designed and constructed. But how do you conduct the tests? Should you develop a formal plan for your tests? Should you test the entire program as a whole or run tests only on a small part of it? Should you rerun tests you've already conducted as you add new components to a large system? When should you involve the customer? These and many other questions are answered when you develop a software testing strategy.

Who does it? A strategy for software testing is developed by the project manager, software engineers, and testing specialists.

Why is it important? Testing often accounts for more project effort than any other software engineering action. If it is conducted haphazardly, time is wasted, unnecessary effort is expended, and even worse, errors sneak through undetected. It would therefore seem reasonable to establish a systematic strategy for testing software.

What are the steps? Testing begins "in the small" and progresses "to the large." By this I mean that early testing focuses on a single component or a small group of related components and applies tests to uncover errors in the data and processing logic that have been encapsulated by the component(s). After components are tested they must be integrated until the complete system is constructed. At this point, a series of high-order tests are executed to uncover errors in meeting customer requirements. As errors are uncovered, they must be diagnosed and corrected using a process that is called debugging.

What is the work product? A *Test Specification* documents the software team's approach to testing by defining a plan that describes an overall strategy and a procedure that defines specific testing steps and the types of tests that will be conducted.

How do I ensure that I've done it right? By reviewing the *Test Specification* prior to testing, you can assess the completeness of test cases and testing tasks. An effective test plan and procedure will lead to the orderly construction of the software and the discovery of errors at each stage in the construction process.

only defense against programming errors was careful design and the native intelligence of the programmer. We are now in an era in which modern design techniques [and technical reviews] are helping us to reduce the number of initial errors that are inherent in the code. Similarly, different test methods are beginning to cluster themselves into several distinct approaches and philosophies.

These "approaches and philosophies" are what I call *strategy*—the topic to be presented in this chapter. In Chapters 18 through 20, the testing methods and techniques that implement the strategy are presented.

17.1   A STRATEGIC APPROACH TO SOFTWARE TESTING

Testing is a set of activities that can be planned in advance and conducted systematically. For this reason a template for software testing—a set of steps into which you can place specific test case design techniques and testing methods—should be defined for the software process.

A number of software testing strategies have been proposed in the literature. All provide you with a template for testing and all have the following generic characteristics:

- To perform effective testing, you should conduct effective technical reviews (Chapter 15). By doing this, many errors will be eliminated before testing commences.

- Testing begins at the component level and works "outward" toward the integration of the entire computer-based system.

- Different testing techniques are appropriate for different software engineering approaches and at different points in time.

- Testing is conducted by the developer of the software and (for large projects) an independent test group.

- Testing and debugging are different activities, but debugging must be accommodated in any testing strategy.

A strategy for software testing must accommodate low-level tests that are necessary to verify that a small source code segment has been correctly implemented as well as high-level tests that validate major system functions against customer requirements. A strategy should provide guidance for the practitioner and a set of milestones for the manager. Because the steps of the test strategy occur at a time when deadline pressure begins to rise, progress must be measurable and problems should surface as early as possible.

17.1.1   Verification and Validation

Software testing is one element of a broader topic that is often referred to as verification and validation (V&V). *Verification* refers to the set of tasks that ensure that software correctly implements a specific function. *Validation* refers to a different set of tasks that ensure that the software that has been built is traceable to customer requirements. Boehm [Boe81] states this another way:

Verification: "Are we building the product right?"

Validation: "Are we building the right product?"

The definition of V&V encompasses many software quality assurance activities (Chapter 16).[1]

Verification and validation includes a wide array of SQA activities: technical reviews, quality and configuration audits, performance monitoring, simulation, feasibility study, documentation review, database review, algorithm analysis, development testing, usability testing, qualification testing, acceptance testing, and installation testing. Although testing plays an extremely important role in V&V, many other activities are also necessary.

Testing does provide the last bastion from which quality can be assessed and, more pragmatically, errors can be uncovered. But testing should not be viewed as a safety net. As they say, "You can't test in quality. If it's not there before you begin testing, it won't be there when you're finished testing." Quality is incorporated into software throughout the process of software engineering. Proper application of methods and tools, effective technical reviews, and solid management and measurement all lead to quality that is confirmed during testing.

Miller [Mil77] relates software testing to quality assurance by stating that "the underlying motivation of program testing is to affirm software quality with methods that can be economically and effectively applied to both large-scale and small-scale systems."

17.1.2 Organizing for Software Testing

For every software project, there is an inherent conflict of interest that occurs as testing begins. The people who have built the software are now asked to test the software. This seems harmless in itself; after all, who knows the program better than its developers? Unfortunately, these same developers have a vested interest in demonstrating that the program is error-free, that it works according to customer requirements, and that it will be completed on schedule and within budget. Each of these interests mitigate against thorough testing.

From a psychological point of view, software analysis and design (along with coding) are constructive tasks. The software engineer analyzes, models, and then creates a computer program and its documentation. Like any builder, the software

---

1 It should be noted that there is a strong divergence of opinion about what types of testing constitute "validation." Some people believe that *all* testing is verification and that validation is conducted when requirements are reviewed and approved, and later, by the user when the system is operational. Other people view unit and integration testing (Sections 17.3.1 and 17.3.2) as verification and higher-order testing (Sections 17.6 and 17.7) as validation.

engineer is proud of the edifice that has been built and looks askance at anyone who attempts to tear it down. When testing commences, there is a subtle, yet definite, attempt to "break" the thing that the software engineer has built. From the point of view of the builder, testing can be considered to be (psychologically) destructive. So the builder treads lightly, designing and executing tests that will demonstrate that the program works, rather than uncovering errors. Unfortunately, errors will be present. And, if the software engineer doesn't find them, the customer will!

There are often a number of misconceptions that you might infer erroneously from the preceding discussion: (1) that the developer of software should do no testing at all, (2) that the software should be "tossed over the wall" to strangers who will test it mercilessly, (3) that testers get involved with the project only when the testing steps are about to begin. Each of these statements is incorrect.

The software developer is always responsible for testing the individual units (components) of the program, ensuring that each performs the function or exhibits the behavior for which it was designed. In many cases, the developer also conducts integration testing—a testing step that leads to the construction (and test) of the complete software architecture. Only after the software architecture is complete does an independent test group become involved.

KEY POINT

An independent test group does not have the "conflict of interest" that builders of the software might experience.

The role of an *independent test group* (ITG) is to remove the inherent problems associated with letting the builder test the thing that has been built. Independent testing removes the conflict of interest that may otherwise be present. After all, ITG personnel are paid to find errors.

However, you don't turn the program over to ITG and walk away. The developer and the ITG work closely throughout a software project to ensure that thorough tests will be conducted. While testing is conducted, the developer must be available to correct errors that are uncovered.

Quote:

"The first mistake that people make is thinking that the testing team is responsible for assuring quality."

Brian Marick

The ITG is part of the software development project team in the sense that it becomes involved during analysis and design and stays involved (planning and specifying test procedures) throughout a large project. However, in many cases the ITG reports to the software quality assurance organization, thereby achieving a degree of independence that might not be possible if it were a part of the software engineering organization.

17.1.3 Software Testing Strategy—The Big Picture

The software process may be viewed as the spiral illustrated in Figure 17.1. Initially, system engineering defines the role of software and leads to software requirements analysis, where the information domain, function, behavior, performance, constraints, and validation criteria for software are established. Moving inward along the spiral, you come to design and finally to coding. To develop computer software, you spiral inward (counterclockwise) along streamlines that decrease the level of abstraction on each turn.

FIGURE 17.1

Testing
strategy

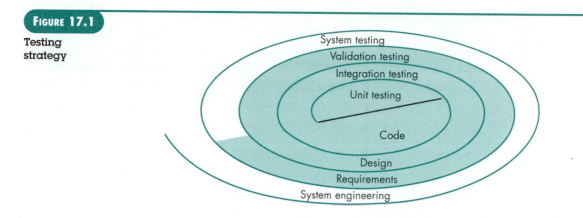

A strategy for software testing may also be viewed in the context of the spiral (Figure 17.1). *Unit testing* begins at the vortex of the spiral and concentrates on each unit (e.g., component, class, or WebApp content object) of the software as implemented in source code. Testing progresses by moving outward along the spiral to *integration testing,* where the focus is on design and the construction of the software architecture. Taking another turn outward on the spiral, you encounter *validation testing,* where requirements established as part of requirements modeling are validated against the software that has been constructed. Finally, you arrive at *system testing,* where the software and other system elements are tested as a whole. To test computer software, you spiral out in a clockwise direction along streamlines that broaden the scope of testing with each turn.

Considering the process from a procedural point of view, testing within the context of software engineering is actually a series of four steps that are implemented sequentially. The steps are shown in Figure 17.2. Initially, tests focus on each

? **What is the overall strategy for software testing?**

WebRef

Useful resources for software testers can be found at **www .SQAtester.com**.

FIGURE 17.2

Software
testing steps

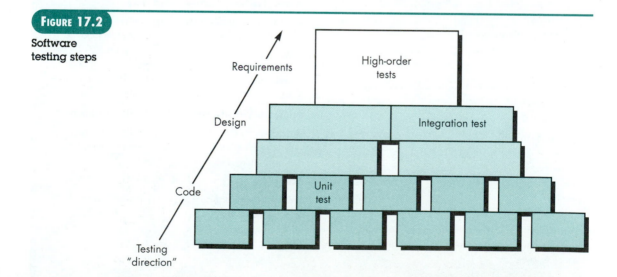

component individually, ensuring that it functions properly as a unit. Hence, the name *unit testing*. Unit testing makes heavy use of testing techniques that exercise specific paths in a component's control structure to ensure complete coverage and maximum error detection. Next, components must be assembled or integrated to form the complete software package. *Integration testing* addresses the issues associated with the dual problems of verification and program construction. Test case design techniques that focus on inputs and outputs are more prevalent during integration, although techniques that exercise specific program paths may be used to ensure coverage of major control paths. After the software has been integrated (constructed), a set of *high-order tests* is conducted. Validation criteria (established during requirements analysis) must be evaluated. *Validation testing* provides final assurance that software meets all informational, functional, behavioral, and performance requirements.

The last high-order testing step falls outside the boundary of software engineering and into the broader context of computer system engineering. Software, once validated, must be combined with other system elements (e.g., hardware, people, databases). *System testing* verifies that all elements mesh properly and that overall system function/performance is achieved.

17.1.4   Criteria for Completion of Testing

A classic question arises every time software testing is discussed: "When are we done testing—how do we know that we've tested enough?" Sadly, there is no definitive answer to this question, but there are a few pragmatic responses and early attempts at empirical guidance.

When are we finished testing?

One response to the question is: "You're never done testing; the burden simply shifts from you (the software engineer) to the end user." Every time the user executes a computer program, the program is being tested. This sobering fact underlines the importance of other software quality assurance activities. Another response (somewhat cynical but nonetheless accurate) is: "You're done testing when you run out of time or you run out of money."

Although few practitioners would argue with these responses, you need more rigorous criteria for determining when sufficient testing has been conducted. The *cleanroom software engineering* approach (Chapter 21) suggests statistical use techniques [Kel00] that execute a series of tests derived from a statistical sample of all possible program executions by all users from a targeted population. Others (e.g., [Sin99]) advocate using statistical modeling and software reliability theory to predict the completeness of testing.

WebRef

A comprehensive glossary of testing terms can be found at **www .testingstandards .co.uk/living_ glossary.htm**.

By collecting metrics during software testing and making use of existing software reliability models, it is possible to develop meaningful guidelines for answering the question: "When are we done testing?" There is little debate that further work remains to be done before quantitative rules for testing can be established, but the empirical approaches that currently exist are considerably better than raw intuition.

17.2   STRATEGIC ISSUES

Later in this chapter, I present a systematic strategy for software testing. But even the best strategy will fail if a series of overriding issues are not addressed. Tom Gilb [Gil95] argues that a software testing strategy will succeed when software testers:

What guidelines lead to a successful software testing strategy?

Specify product requirements in a quantifiable manner long before testing commences. Although the overriding objective of testing is to find errors, a good testing strategy also assesses other quality characteristics such as portability, maintainability, and usability (Chapter 14). These should be specified in a way that is measurable so that testing results are unambiguous.

State testing objectives explicitly. The specific objectives of testing should be stated in measurable terms. For example, test effectiveness, test coverage, mean-time-to-failure, the cost to find and fix defects, remaining defect density or frequency of occurrence, and test work-hours should be stated within the test plan.

WebRef

An excellent list of testing resources can be found at **www .io.com/~wazmo/ qa/**.

Understand the users of the software and develop a profile for each user category. Use cases that describe the interaction scenario for each class of user can reduce overall testing effort by focusing testing on actual use of the product.

Develop a testing plan that emphasizes "rapid cycle testing." Gilb [Gil95] recommends that a software team "learn to test in rapid cycles (2 percent of project effort) of customer-useful, at least field 'trialable,' increments of functionality and/or quality improvement." The feedback generated from these rapid cycle tests can be used to control quality levels and the corresponding test strategies.

Build "robust" software that is designed to test itself. Software should be designed in a manner that uses antibugging (Section 17.3.1) techniques. That is, software should be capable of diagnosing certain classes of errors. In addition, the design should accommodate automated testing and regression testing.

Use effective technical reviews as a filter prior to testing. Technical reviews (Chapter 15) can be as effective as testing in uncovering errors. For this reason, reviews can reduce the amount of testing effort that is required to produce high-quality software.

Conduct technical reviews to assess the test strategy and test cases themselves. Technical reviews can uncover inconsistencies, omissions, and outright errors in the testing approach. This saves time and also improves product quality.

Develop a continuous improvement approach for the testing process. The test strategy should be measured. The metrics collected during testing should be used as part of a statistical process control approach for software testing.

> **Quote:**
>
> "Testing only to end-user requirements is like inspecting a building based on the work done by the interior designer at the expense of the foundations, girders, and plumbing."
>
> **Boris Beizer**

17.3   TEST STRATEGIES FOR CONVENTIONAL SOFTWARE[2]

There are many strategies that can be used to test software. At one extreme, you can wait until the system is fully constructed and then conduct tests on the overall system in hopes of finding errors. This approach, although appealing, simply does not work. It will result in buggy software that disappoints all stakeholders. At the other extreme, you could conduct tests on a daily basis, whenever any part of the system is constructed. This approach, although less appealing to many, can be very effective. Unfortunately, some software developers hesitate to use it. What to do?

A testing strategy that is chosen by most software teams falls between the two extremes. It takes an incremental view of testing, beginning with the testing of individual program units, moving to tests designed to facilitate the integration of the units, and culminating with tests that exercise the constructed system. Each of these classes of tests is described in the sections that follow.

17.3.1   Unit Testing

Unit testing focuses verification effort on the smallest unit of software design—the software component or module. Using the component-level design description as a

---

2   Throughout this book, I use the terms *conventional software* or *traditional software* to refer to common hierarchical or call-and-return software architectures that are frequently encountered in a variety of application domains. Traditional software architectures are *not* object-oriented and do not encompass WebApps.

FIGURE 17.3

Unit test

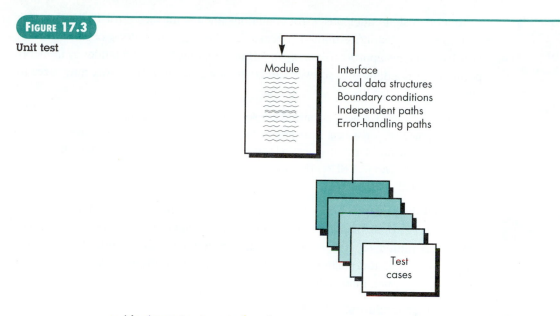

guide, important control paths are tested to uncover errors within the boundary of the module. The relative complexity of tests and the errors those tests uncover is limited by the constrained scope established for unit testing. The unit test focuses on the internal processing logic and data structures within the boundaries of a component. This type of testing can be conducted in parallel for multiple components.

Unit-test considerations.   Unit tests are illustrated schematically in Figure 17.3. The module interface is tested to ensure that information properly flows into and out of the program unit under test. Local data structures are examined to ensure that data stored temporarily maintains its integrity during all steps in an algorithm's execution. All independent paths through the control structure are exercised to ensure that all statements in a module have been executed at least once. Boundary conditions are tested to ensure that the module operates properly at boundaries established to limit or restrict processing. And finally, all error-handling paths are tested.

Data flow across a component interface is tested before any other testing is initiated. If data do not enter and exit properly, all other tests are moot. In addition, local data structures should be exercised and the local impact on global data should be ascertained (if possible) during unit testing.

Selective testing of execution paths is an essential task during the unit test. Test cases should be designed to uncover errors due to erroneous computations, incorrect comparisons, or improper control flow.

Boundary testing is one of the most important unit testing tasks. Software often fails at its boundaries. That is, errors often occur when the nth element of an n-dimensional array is processed, when the ith repetition of a loop with i passes is invoked, when the maximum or minimum allowable value is encountered. Test cases that exercise data structure, control flow, and data values just below, at, and just above maxima and minima are very likely to uncover errors.

It's not a bad idea to design unit test cases before you develop code for a component. It helps ensure that you'll develop code that will pass the tests.

? What errors are commonly found during unit testing?

A good design anticipates error conditions and establishes error-handling paths to reroute or cleanly terminate processing when an error does occur. Yourdon [You75] calls this approach *antibugging*. Unfortunately, there is a tendency to incorporate error handling into software and then never test it. A true story may serve to illustrate:

> A computer-aided design system was developed under contract. In one transaction processing module, a practical joker placed the following error handling message after a series of conditional tests that invoked various control flow branches: ERROR! THERE IS NO WAY YOU CAN GET HERE. This "error message" was uncovered by a customer during user training!

Among the potential errors that should be tested when error handling is evaluated are: (1) error description is unintelligible, (2) error noted does not correspond to error encountered, (3) error condition causes system intervention prior to error handling, (4) exception-condition processing is incorrect, or (5) error description does not provide enough information to assist in the location of the cause of the error.

Unit-test procedures.   Unit testing is normally considered as an adjunct to the coding step. The design of unit tests can occur before coding begins or after source code has been generated. A review of design information provides guidance for establishing test cases that are likely to uncover errors in each of the categories discussed earlier. Each test case should be coupled with a set of expected results.

Because a component is not a stand-alone program, driver and/or stub software must often be developed for each unit test. The unit test environment is illustrated in Figure 17.4. In most applications a *driver* is nothing more than a "main program" that accepts test case data, passes such data to the component (to be tested), and prints

---

FIGURE 17.4

Unit-test environment

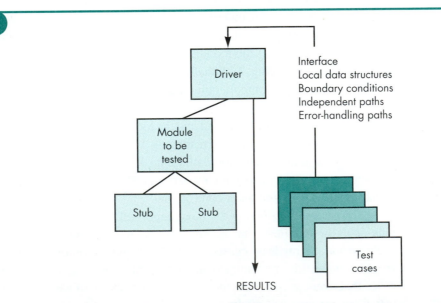

Driver

Interface
Local data structures
Boundary conditions
Independent paths
Error-handling paths

Module to be tested

Stub   Stub

Test cases

RESULTS

relevant results. *Stubs* serve to replace modules that are subordinate (invoked by) the component to be tested. A stub or "dummy subprogram" uses the subordinate module's interface, may do minimal data manipulation, prints verification of entry, and returns control to the module undergoing testing.

Drivers and stubs represent testing "overhead." That is, both are software that must be written (formal design is not commonly applied) but that is not delivered with the final software product. If drivers and stubs are kept simple, actual overhead is relatively low. Unfortunately, many components cannot be adequately unit tested with "simple" overhead software. In such cases, complete testing can be postponed until the integration test step (where drivers or stubs are also used).

Unit testing is simplified when a component with high cohesion is designed. When only one function is addressed by a component, the number of test cases is reduced and errors can be more easily predicted and uncovered.

17.3.2   Integration Testing

A neophyte in the software world might ask a seemingly legitimate question once all modules have been unit tested: "If they all work individually, why do you doubt that they'll work when we put them together?" The problem, of course, is "putting them together"—interfacing. Data can be lost across an interface; one component can have an inadvertent, adverse effect on another; subfunctions, when combined, may not produce the desired major function; individually acceptable imprecision may be magnified to unacceptable levels; global data structures can present problems. Sadly, the list goes on and on.

Integration testing is a systematic technique for constructing the software architecture while at the same time conducting tests to uncover errors associated with interfacing. The objective is to take unit-tested components and build a program structure that has been dictated by design.

There is often a tendency to attempt nonincremental integration; that is, to construct the program using a "big bang" approach. All components are combined in advance. The entire program is tested as a whole. And chaos usually results! A set of errors is encountered. Correction is difficult because isolation of causes is complicated by the vast expanse of the entire program. Once these errors are corrected, new ones appear and the process continues in a seemingly endless loop.

Incremental integration is the antithesis of the big bang approach. The program is constructed and tested in small increments, where errors are easier to isolate and correct; interfaces are more likely to be tested completely; and a systematic test approach may be applied. In the paragraphs that follow, a number of different incremental integration strategies are discussed.

Top-down integration.   *Top-down integration testing* is an incremental approach to construction of the software architecture. Modules are integrated by moving downward through the control hierarchy, beginning with the main control module

FIGURE 17.5

Top-down
integration

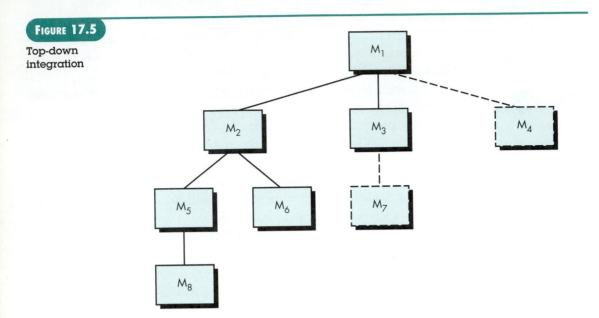

(main program). Modules subordinate (and ultimately subordinate) to the main control module are incorporated into the structure in either a depth-first or breadth-first manner.

Referring to Figure 17.5, *depth-first integration* integrates all components on a major control path of the program structure. Selection of a major path is somewhat arbitrary and depends on application-specific characteristics. For example, selecting the left-hand path, components M_1, M_2, M_5 would be integrated first. Next, M_8 or (if necessary for proper functioning of M_2) M_6 would be integrated. Then, the central and right-hand control paths are built. *Breadth-first integration* incorporates all components directly subordinate at each level, moving across the structure horizontally. From the figure, components M_2, M_3, and M_4 would be integrated first. The next control level, M_5, M_6, and so on, follows. The integration process is performed in a series of five steps:

? **What are the steps for top-down integration?**

1. The main control module is used as a test driver and stubs are substituted for all components directly subordinate to the main control module.

2. Depending on the integration approach selected (i.e., depth or breadth first), subordinate stubs are replaced one at a time with actual components.

3. Tests are conducted as each component is integrated.

4. On completion of each set of tests, another stub is replaced with the real component.

5. Regression testing (discussed later in this section) may be conducted to ensure that new errors have not been introduced.

The process continues from step 2 until the entire program structure is built.

The top-down integration strategy verifies major control or decision points early in the test process. In a "well-factored" program structure, decision making occurs at upper levels in the hierarchy and is therefore encountered first. If major control problems do exist, early recognition is essential. If depth-first integration is selected, a complete function of the software may be implemented and demonstrated. Early demonstration of functional capability is a confidence builder for all stakeholders.

What problems may be encountered when top-down integration is chosen?

Top-down strategy sounds relatively uncomplicated, but in practice, logistical problems can arise. The most common of these problems occurs when processing at low levels in the hierarchy is required to adequately test upper levels. Stubs replace low-level modules at the beginning of top-down testing; therefore, no significant data can flow upward in the program structure. As a tester, you are left with three choices: (1) delay many tests until stubs are replaced with actual modules, (2) develop stubs that perform limited functions that simulate the actual module, or (3) integrate the software from the bottom of the hierarchy upward.

The first approach (delay tests until stubs are replaced by actual modules) can cause you to lose some control over correspondence between specific tests and incorporation of specific modules. This can lead to difficulty in determining the cause of errors and tends to violate the highly constrained nature of the top-down approach. The second approach is workable but can lead to significant overhead, as stubs become more and more complex. The third approach, called bottom-up integration is discussed in the paragraphs that follow.

Bottom-up integration.   *Bottom-up integration testing,* as its name implies, begins construction and testing with *atomic modules* (i.e., components at the lowest levels in the program structure). Because components are integrated from the bottom up, the functionality provided by components subordinate to a given level is always available and the need for stubs is eliminated. A bottom-up integration strategy may be implemented with the following steps:

1. Low-level components are combined into clusters (sometimes called *builds*) that perform a specific software subfunction.

What are the steps for bottom-up integration?

2. A *driver* (a control program for testing) is written to coordinate test case input and output.

3. The cluster is tested.

4. Drivers are removed and clusters are combined moving upward in the program structure.

KEY POINT

Bottom-up integration eliminates the need for complex stubs.

Integration follows the pattern illustrated in Figure 17.6. Components are combined to form clusters 1, 2, and 3. Each of the clusters is tested using a driver (shown as a dashed block). Components in clusters 1 and 2 are subordinate to M_a. Drivers D_1 and D_2 are removed and the clusters are interfaced directly to M_a. Similarly, driver D_3 for cluster 3 is removed prior to integration with module M_b. Both M_a and M_b will ultimately be integrated with component M_c, and so forth.

FIGURE 17.6

Bottom-up
integration

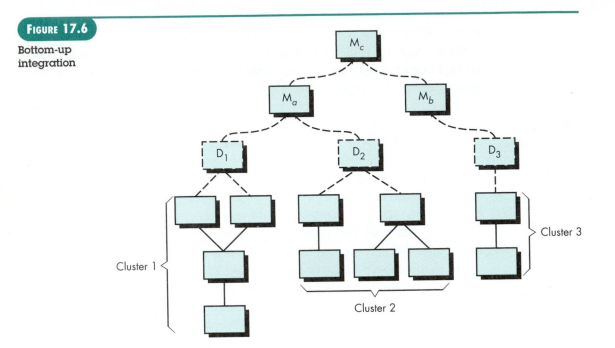

As integration moves upward, the need for separate test drivers lessens. In fact, if the top two levels of program structure are integrated top down, the number of drivers can be reduced substantially and integration of clusters is greatly simplified.

Regression testing.   Each time a new module is added as part of integration testing, the software changes. New data flow paths are established, new I/O may occur, and new control logic is invoked. These changes may cause problems with functions that previously worked flawlessly. In the context of an integration test strategy, *regression testing* is the reexecution of some subset of tests that have already been conducted to ensure that changes have not propagated unintended side effects.

In a broader context, successful tests (of any kind) result in the discovery of errors, and errors must be corrected. Whenever software is corrected, some aspect of the software configuration (the program, its documentation, or the data that support it) is changed. Regression testing helps to ensure that changes (due to testing or for other reasons) do not introduce unintended behavior or additional errors.

Regression testing may be conducted manually, by reexecuting a subset of all test cases or using automated capture/playback tools. *Capture/playback tools* enable the software engineer to capture test cases and results for subsequent playback and comparison. The *regression test suite* (the subset of tests to be executed) contains three different classes of test cases:

- A representative sample of tests that will exercise all software functions.
- Additional tests that focus on software functions that are likely to be affected by the change.
- Tests that focus on the software components that have been changed.

Regression testing is an important strategy for reducing "side effects." Run regression tests every time a major change is made to the software (including the integration of new components).

As integration testing proceeds, the number of regression tests can grow quite large. Therefore, the regression test suite should be designed to include only those tests that address one or more classes of errors in each of the major program functions. It is impractical and inefficient to reexecute every test for every program function once a change has occurred.

Smoke testing. *Smoke testing* is an integration testing approach that is commonly used when product software is developed. It is designed as a pacing mechanism for time-critical projects, allowing the software team to assess the project on a frequent basis. In essence, the smoke-testing approach encompasses the following activities:

1. Software components that have been translated into code are integrated into a *build.* A build includes all data files, libraries, reusable modules, and engineered components that are required to implement one or more product functions.

2. A series of tests is designed to expose errors that will keep the build from properly performing its function. The intent should be to uncover "show-stopper" errors that have the highest likelihood of throwing the software project behind schedule.

3. The build is integrated with other builds, and the entire product (in its current form) is smoke tested daily. The integration approach may be top down or bottom up.

The daily frequency of testing the entire product may surprise some readers. However, frequent tests give both managers and practitioners a realistic assessment of integration testing progress. McConnell [McC96] describes the smoke test in the following manner:

> The smoke test should exercise the entire system from end to end. It does not have to be exhaustive, but it should be capable of exposing major problems. The smoke test should be thorough enough that if the build passes, you can assume that it is stable enough to be tested more thoroughly.

Smoke testing provides a number of benefits when it is applied on complex, time-critical software projects:

- *Integration risk is minimized.* Because smoke tests are conducted daily, incompatibilities and other show-stopper errors are uncovered early, thereby reducing the likelihood of serious schedule impact when errors are uncovered.

- *The quality of the end product is improved.* Because the approach is construction (integration) oriented, smoke testing is likely to uncover functional errors as well as architectural and component-level design errors. If these errors are corrected early, better product quality will result.

- *Error diagnosis and correction are simplified.* Like all integration testing approaches, errors uncovered during smoke testing are likely to be associated with "new software increments"—that is, the software that has just been added to the build(s) is a probable cause of a newly discovered error.

- *Progress is easier to assess.* With each passing day, more of the software has been integrated and more has been demonstrated to work. This improves team morale and gives managers a good indication that progress is being made.

WebRef

Pointers to commentary on testing strategies can be found at **www.qalinks.com**.

Strategic options.   There has been much discussion (e.g., [Bei84]) about the relative advantages and disadvantages of top-down versus bottom-up integration testing. In general, the advantages of one strategy tend to result in disadvantages for the other strategy. The major disadvantage of the top-down approach is the need for stubs and the attendant testing difficulties that can be associated with them. Problems associated with stubs may be offset by the advantage of testing major control functions early. The major disadvantage of bottom-up integration is that "the program as an entity does not exist until the last module is added" [Mye79]. This drawback is tempered by easier test case design and a lack of stubs.

Selection of an integration strategy depends upon software characteristics and, sometimes, project schedule. In general, a combined approach (sometimes called *sandwich testing*) that uses top-down tests for upper levels of the program structure, coupled with bottom-up tests for subordinate levels may be the best compromise.

? What is a "critical module" and why should we identify it?

As integration testing is conducted, the tester should identify critical modules. A *critical module* has one or more of the following characteristics: (1) addresses several software requirements, (2) has a high level of control (resides relatively high in the program structure), (3) is complex or error prone, or (4) has definite performance requirements. Critical modules should be tested as early as is possible. In addition, regression tests should focus on critical module function.

Integration test work products.   An overall plan for integration of the software and a description of specific tests is documented in a *Test Specification*. This work product incorporates a test plan and a test procedure and becomes part of the software configuration. Testing is divided into phases and builds that address specific functional and behavioral characteristics of the software. For example, integration testing for the *SafeHome* security system might be divided into the following test phases:

- *User interaction* (command input and output, display representation, error processing and representation)

- *Sensor processing* (acquisition of sensor output, determination of sensor conditions, actions required as a consequence of conditions)

- *Communications functions* (ability to communicate with central monitoring station)

- *Alarm processing* (tests of software actions that occur when an alarm is encountered)

Each of these integration test phases delineates a broad functional category within the software and generally can be related to a specific domain within the software architecture. Therefore, program builds (groups of modules) are created to correspond to each phase. The following criteria and corresponding tests are applied for all test phases:

? **What criteria should be used to design integration tests?**

Interface integrity. Internal and external interfaces are tested as each module (or cluster) is incorporated into the structure.

Functional validity. Tests designed to uncover functional errors are conducted.

Information content. Tests designed to uncover errors associated with local or global data structures are conducted.

Performance. Tests designed to verify performance bounds established during software design are conducted.

A schedule for integration, the development of overhead software, and related topics are also discussed as part of the test plan. Start and end dates for each phase are established and "availability windows" for unit-tested modules are defined. A brief description of overhead software (stubs and drivers) concentrates on characteristics that might require special effort. Finally, test environment and resources are described. Unusual hardware configurations, exotic simulators, and special test tools or techniques are a few of many topics that may also be discussed.

The detailed testing procedure that is required to accomplish the test plan is described next. The order of integration and corresponding tests at each integration step are described. A listing of all test cases (annotated for subsequent reference) and expected results are also included.

A history of actual test results, problems, or peculiarities is recorded in a *Test Report* that can be appended to the *Test Specification,* if desired. Information contained in this section can be vital during software maintenance. Appropriate references and appendixes are also presented.

Like all other elements of a software configuration, the test specification format may be tailored to the local needs of a software engineering organization. It is important to note, however, that an integration strategy (contained in a test plan) and testing details (described in a test procedure) are essential ingredients and must appear.

17.4 TEST STRATEGIES FOR OBJECT-ORIENTED SOFTWARE[3]

The objective of testing, stated simply, is to find the greatest possible number of errors with a manageable amount of effort applied over a realistic time span. Although this fundamental objective remains unchanged for object-oriented software, the nature of object-oriented software changes both testing strategy and testing tactics (Chapter 19).

---

3 Basic object-oriented concepts are presented in Appendix 2.

17.4.1   Unit Testing in the OO Context

When object-oriented software is considered, the concept of the unit changes. Encapsulation drives the definition of classes and objects. This means that each class and each instance of a class packages attributes (data) and the operations that manipulate these data. An encapsulated class is usually the focus of unit testing. However, operations (methods) within the class are the smallest testable units. Because a class can contain a number of different operations, and a particular operation may exist as part of a number of different classes, the tactics applied to unit testing must change.

You can no longer test a single operation in isolation (the conventional view of unit testing) but rather as part of a class. To illustrate, consider a class hierarchy in which an operation X is defined for the superclass and is inherited by a number of subclasses. Each subclass uses operation X, but it is applied within the context of the private attributes and operations that have been defined for the subclass. Because the context in which operation X is used varies in subtle ways, it is necessary to test operation X in the context of each of the subclasses. This means that testing operation X in a stand-alone fashion (the conventional unit-testing approach) is usually ineffective in the object-oriented context.

Class testing for OO software is the equivalent of unit testing for conventional software. Unlike unit testing of conventional software, which tends to focus on the algorithmic detail of a module and the data that flow across the module interface, class testing for OO software is driven by the operations encapsulated by the class and the state behavior of the class.

17.4.2   Integration Testing in the OO Context

Because object-oriented software does not have an obvious hierarchical control structure, traditional top-down and bottom-up integration strategies (Section 17.3.2) have little meaning. In addition, integrating operations one at a time into a class (the conventional incremental integration approach) is often impossible because of the "direct and indirect interactions of the components that make up the class" [Ber93].

There are two different strategies for integration testing of OO systems [Bin94b]. The first, *thread-based testing*, integrates the set of classes required to respond to one input or event for the system. Each thread is integrated and tested individually. Regression testing is applied to ensure that no side effects occur. The second integration approach, *use-based testing*, begins the construction of the system by testing those classes (called *independent classes*) that use very few (if any) *server* classes. After the independent classes are tested, the next layer of classes, called *dependent classes*, that use the independent classes are tested. This sequence of testing layers of dependent classes continues until the entire system is constructed.

The use of drivers and stubs also changes when integration testing of OO systems is conducted. Drivers can be used to test operations at the lowest level and for the testing of whole groups of classes. A driver can also be used to replace the user interface so that tests of system functionality can be conducted prior to implementation of the interface. Stubs can be used in situations in which collaboration between classes is required but one or more of the collaborating classes has not yet been fully implemented.

Cluster testing is one step in the integration testing of OO software. Here, a cluster of collaborating classes (determined by examining the CRC and object-relationship model) is exercised by designing test cases that attempt to uncover errors in the collaborations.

17.5 TEST STRATEGIES FOR WEBAPPS

The strategy for WebApp testing adopts the basic principles for all software testing and applies a strategy and tactics that are used for object-oriented systems. The following steps summarize the approach:

1. The content model for the WebApp is reviewed to uncover errors.

2. The interface model is reviewed to ensure that all use cases can be accommodated.

3. The design model for the WebApp is reviewed to uncover navigation errors.

4. The user interface is tested to uncover errors in presentation and/or navigation mechanics.

5. Each functional component is unit tested.

6. Navigation throughout the architecture is tested.

7. The WebApp is implemented in a variety of different environmental configurations and is tested for compatibility with each configuration.

8. Security tests are conducted in an attempt to exploit vulnerabilities in the WebApp or within its environment.

9. Performance tests are conducted.

10. The WebApp is tested by a controlled and monitored population of end users. The results of their interaction with the system are evaluated for content and navigation errors, usability concerns, compatibility concerns, and WebApp reliability and performance.

Because many WebApps evolve continuously, the testing process is an ongoing activity, conducted by support staff who use regression tests derived from the tests developed when the WebApp was first engineered. Methods for WebApp testing are considered in Chapter 20.

17.6 VALIDATION TESTING

Validation testing begins at the culmination of integration testing, when individual components have been exercised, the software is completely assembled as a package, and interfacing errors have been uncovered and corrected. At the validation or system level, the distinction between conventional software, object-oriented software, and WebApps disappears. Testing focuses on user-visible actions and user-recognizable output from the system.

Validation can be defined in many ways, but a simple (albeit harsh) definition is that validation succeeds when software functions in a manner that can be reasonably expected by the customer. At this point a battle-hardened software developer might protest: "Who or what is the arbiter of reasonable expectations?" If a *Software Requirements Specification* has been developed, it describes all user-visible attributes of the software and contains a *Validation Criteria* section that forms the basis for a validation-testing approach.

17.6.1   Validation-Test Criteria

Software validation is achieved through a series of tests that demonstrate conformity with requirements. A test plan outlines the classes of tests to be conducted, and a test procedure defines specific test cases that are designed to ensure that all functional requirements are satisfied, all behavioral characteristics are achieved, all content is accurate and properly presented, all performance requirements are attained, documentation is correct, and usability and other requirements are met (e.g., transportability, compatibility, error recovery, maintainability).

After each validation test case has been conducted, one of two possible conditions exists: (1) The function or performance characteristic conforms to specification and is accepted or (2) a deviation from specification is uncovered and a deficiency list is created. Deviations or errors discovered at this stage in a project can rarely be corrected prior to scheduled delivery. It is often necessary to negotiate with the customer to establish a method for resolving deficiencies.

17.6.2   Configuration Review

An important element of the validation process is a *configuration review*. The intent of the review is to ensure that all elements of the software configuration have been properly developed, are cataloged, and have the necessary detail to bolster the support activities. The configuration review, sometimes called an audit, is discussed in more detail in Chapter 22.

17.6.3   Alpha and Beta Testing

It is virtually impossible for a software developer to foresee how the customer will really use a program. Instructions for use may be misinterpreted; strange combinations of data may be regularly used; output that seemed clear to the tester may be unintelligible to a user in the field.

When custom software is built for one customer, a series of acceptance tests are conducted to enable the customer to validate all requirements. Conducted by the end user rather than software engineers, an acceptance test can range from an informal "test drive" to a planned and systematically executed series of tests. In fact, acceptance testing can be conducted over a period of weeks or months, thereby uncovering cumulative errors that might degrade the system over time.

If software is developed as a product to be used by many customers, it is impractical to perform formal acceptance tests with each one. Most software product builders use a process called alpha and beta testing to uncover errors that only the end user seems able to find.

The *alpha test* is conducted at the developer's site by a representative group of end users. The software is used in a natural setting with the developer "looking over the shoulder" of the users and recording errors and usage problems. Alpha tests are conducted in a controlled environment.

The *beta test* is conducted at one or more end-user sites. Unlike alpha testing, the developer generally is not present. Therefore, the beta test is a "live" application of the software in an environment that cannot be controlled by the developer. The customer records all problems (real or imagined) that are encountered during beta testing and reports these to the developer at regular intervals. As a result of problems reported during beta tests, you make modifications and then prepare for release of the software product to the entire customer base.

A variation on beta testing, called *customer acceptance testing,* is sometimes performed when custom software is delivered to a customer under contract. The customer performs a series of specific tests in an attempt to uncover errors before accepting the software from the developer. In some cases (e.g., a major corporate or governmental system) acceptance testing can be very formal and encompass many days or even weeks of testing.

> **? What is the difference between an alpha test and a beta test?**

SafeHome

Preparing for Validation

The scene: Doug Miller's office, as component-level design continues and construction of certain components continues.

The players: Doug Miller, software engineering manager, Vinod, Jamie, Ed, and Shakira—members of the *SafeHome* software engineering team.

The conversation:

Doug: The first increment will be ready for validation in what . . . about three weeks?

Vinod: That's about right. Integration is going well. We're smoke testing daily, finding some bugs but nothing we can't handle. So far, so good.

Doug: Talk to me about validation.

Shakira: Well, we'll use all of the use cases as the basis for our test design. I haven't started yet, but I'll be developing tests for all of the use cases that I've been responsible for.

Ed: Same here.

Jamie: Me too, but we've got to get our act together for acceptance test and also for alpha and beta testing, no?

Doug: Yes. In fact I've been thinking; we could bring in an outside contractor to help us with validation. I have the money in the budget . . . and it'd give us a new point of view.

Vinod: I think we've got it under control.

Doug: I'm sure you do, but an ITG gives us an independent look at the software.

Jamie: We're tight on time here, Doug. I for one don't have the time to babysit anybody you bring in to do the job.

Doug: I know, I know. But if an ITG works from requirements and use cases, not too much babysitting will be required.

Vinod: I still think we've got it under control.

Doug: I hear you, Vinod, but I going to overrule on this one. Let's plan to meet with the ITG rep later this week. Get 'em started and see what they come up with.

Vinod: Okay, maybe it'll lighten the load a bit.

17.7   SYSTEM TESTING

At the beginning of this book, I stressed the fact that software is only one element of a larger computer-based system. Ultimately, software is incorporated with other system elements (e.g., hardware, people, information), and a series of system integration and validation tests are conducted. These tests fall outside the scope of the software process and are not conducted solely by software engineers. However, steps taken during software design and testing can greatly improve the probability of successful software integration in the larger system.

A classic system-testing problem is "finger pointing." This occurs when an error is uncovered, and the developers of different system elements blame each other for the problem. Rather than indulging in such nonsense, you should anticipate potential interfacing problems and (1) design error-handling paths that test all information coming from other elements of the system, (2) conduct a series of tests that simulate bad data or other potential errors at the software interface, (3) record the results of tests to use as "evidence" if finger pointing does occur, and (4) participate in planning and design of system tests to ensure that software is adequately tested.

System testing is actually a series of different tests whose primary purpose is to fully exercise the computer-based system. Although each test has a different purpose, all work to verify that system elements have been properly integrated and perform allocated functions. In the sections that follow, I discuss the types of system tests that are worthwhile for software-based systems.

17.7.1   Recovery Testing

Many computer-based systems must recover from faults and resume processing with little or no downtime. In some cases, a system must be fault tolerant; that is, processing faults must not cause overall system function to cease. In other cases, a system failure must be corrected within a specified period of time or severe economic damage will occur.

Recovery testing is a system test that forces the software to fail in a variety of ways and verifies that recovery is properly performed. If recovery is automatic (performed by the system itself), reinitialization, checkpointing mechanisms, data recovery, and restart are evaluated for correctness. If recovery requires human intervention, the mean-time-to-repair (MTTR) is evaluated to determine whether it is within acceptable limits.

17.7.2   Security Testing

Any computer-based system that manages sensitive information or causes actions that can improperly harm (or benefit) individuals is a target for improper or illegal penetration. Penetration spans a broad range of activities: hackers who attempt to penetrate systems for sport, disgruntled employees who attempt to penetrate for revenge, dishonest individuals who attempt to penetrate for illicit personal gain.

Security testing attempts to verify that protection mechanisms built into a system will, in fact, protect it from improper penetration. To quote Beizer [Bei84]: "The system's security must, of course, be tested for invulnerability from frontal attack—but must also be tested for invulnerability from flank or rear attack."

During security testing, the tester plays the role(s) of the individual who desires to penetrate the system. Anything goes! The tester may attempt to acquire passwords through external clerical means; may attack the system with custom software designed to break down any defenses that have been constructed; may overwhelm the system, thereby denying service to others; may purposely cause system errors, hoping to penetrate during recovery; may browse through insecure data, hoping to find the key to system entry.

Given enough time and resources, good security testing will ultimately penetrate a system. The role of the system designer is to make penetration cost more than the value of the information that will be obtained.

17.7.3   Stress Testing

Earlier software testing steps resulted in thorough evaluation of normal program functions and performance. Stress tests are designed to confront programs with abnormal situations. In essence, the tester who performs stress testing asks: "How high can we crank this up before it fails?"

Stress testing executes a system in a manner that demands resources in abnormal quantity, frequency, or volume. For example, (1) special tests may be designed that generate ten interrupts per second, when one or two is the average rate, (2) input data rates may be increased by an order of magnitude to determine how input functions will respond, (3) test cases that require maximum memory or other resources are executed, (4) test cases that may cause thrashing in a virtual operating system are designed, (5) test cases that may cause excessive hunting for disk-resident data are created. Essentially, the tester attempts to break the program.

A variation of stress testing is a technique called *sensitivity testing.* In some situations (the most common occur in mathematical algorithms), a very small range of data contained within the bounds of valid data for a program may cause extreme and even erroneous processing or profound performance degradation. Sensitivity testing attempts to uncover data combinations within valid input classes that may cause instability or improper processing.

uote:

"If you're trying to find true system bugs and you haven't subjected your software to a real stress test, then it's high time you started."

Boris Beizer

17.7.4   Performance Testing

For real-time and embedded systems, software that provides required function but does not conform to performance requirements is unacceptable. Performance testing is designed to test the run-time performance of software within the context of an integrated system. Performance testing occurs throughout all steps in the testing process. Even at the unit level, the performance of an individual module may be assessed as tests are conducted. However, it is not until all system elements are fully integrated that the true performance of a system can be ascertained.

Performance tests are often coupled with stress testing and usually require both hardware and software instrumentation. That is, it is often necessary to measure resource utilization (e.g., processor cycles) in an exacting fashion. External instrumentation can monitor execution intervals, log events (e.g., interrupts) as they occur, and sample machine states on a regular basis. By instrumenting a system, the tester can uncover situations that lead to degradation and possible system failure.

17.7.5 Deployment Testing

In many cases, software must execute on a variety of platforms and under more than one operating system environment. *Deployment testing,* sometimes called *configuration testing,* exercises the software in each environment in which it is to operate. In addition, deployment testing examines all installation procedures and specialized installation software (e.g., "installers") that will be used by customers, and all documentation that will be used to introduce the software to end users.

As an example, consider the Internet-accessible version of *SafeHome* software that would allow a customer to monitor the security system from remote locations. The *SafeHome* WebApp must be tested using all Web browsers that are likely to be encountered. A more thorough deployment test might encompass combinations of Web browsers with various operating systems (e.g., Linux, Mac OS, Windows). Because security is a major issue, a complete set of security tests would be integrated with the deployment test.

SOFTWARE TOOLS

Test Planning and Management

Objective: These tools assist a software team in planning the testing strategy that is chosen and managing the testing process as it is conducted.

Mechanics: Tools in this category address test planning, test storage, management and control, requirements traceability, integration, error tracking, and report generation. Project managers use them to supplement project scheduling tools. Testers use these tools to plan testing activities and to control the flow of information as the testing process proceeds.

Representative Tools:[4]

QaTraq Test Case Management Tool, developed by Traq Software (**www.testmanagement.com**), "encourages a structured approach to test management."

QADirector, developed by Compuware Corp. (**www.compuware.com/qacenter**), provides a single point of control for managing all phases of the testing process.

TestWorks, developed by Software Research, Inc. (**www.soft.com/Products/index.html**), contains a fully integrated suite of testing tools including tools for test management and reporting.

OpensourceTesting.org (**www.opensourcetesting.org/testmgt.php**) lists a variety of open-source test management and planning tools.

NI TestStand, developed by National Instruments Corp. (**www.ni.com**), allows you to "develop, manage, and execute test sequences written in any programming language."

---

4   Tools noted here do not represent an endorsement, but rather a sampling of tools in this category. In most cases, tool names are trademarked by their respective developers.

17.8 THE ART OF DEBUGGING

Software testing is a process that can be systematically planned and specified. Test-case design can be conducted, a strategy can be defined, and results can be evaluated against prescribed expectations.

Debugging occurs as a consequence of successful testing. That is, when a test case uncovers an error, debugging is the process that results in the removal of the error. Although debugging can and should be an orderly process, it is still very much an art. As a software engineer, you are often confronted with a "symptomatic" indication of a software problem as you evaluate the results of a test. That is, the external manifestation of the error and its internal cause may have no obvious relationship to one another. The poorly understood mental process that connects a symptom to a cause is debugging.

17.8.1 The Debugging Process

Debugging is not testing but often occurs as a consequence of testing.[5] Referring to Figure 17.7, the debugging process begins with the execution of a test case. Results are assessed and a lack of correspondence between expected and actual performance is encountered. In many cases, the noncorresponding data are a symptom of an underlying cause as yet hidden. The debugging process attempts to match symptom with cause, thereby leading to error correction.

Be certain to avoid a third outcome: The cause is found, but the "correction" does not solve the problem or introduces still another error.

The debugging process will usually have one of two outcomes: (1) the cause will be found and corrected or (2) the cause will not be found. In the latter case, the person performing debugging may suspect a cause, design a test case to help validate that suspicion, and work toward error correction in an iterative fashion.

Why is debugging so difficult? In all likelihood, human psychology (see Section 17.8.2) has more to do with an answer than software technology. However, a few characteristics of bugs provide some clues:

? **Why is debugging so difficult?**

1. The symptom and the cause may be geographically remote. That is, the symptom may appear in one part of a program, while the cause may actually be located at a site that is far removed. Highly coupled components (Chapter 8) exacerbate this situation.

2. The symptom may disappear (temporarily) when another error is corrected.

3. The symptom may actually be caused by nonerrors (e.g., round-off inaccuracies).

4. The symptom may be caused by human error that is not easily traced.

---

5 In making the statement, we take the broadest possible view of testing. Not only does the developer test software prior to release, but the customer/user tests software every time it is used!

FIGURE 17.7

The
debugging
process

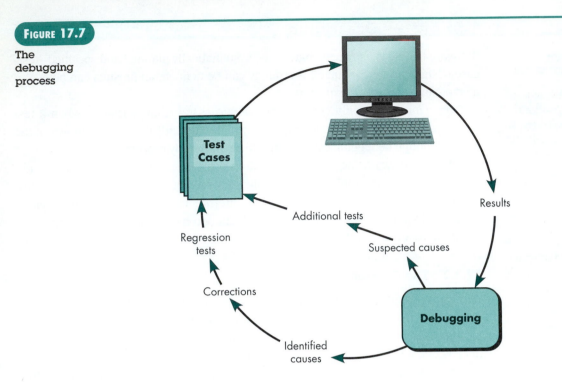

FIGURE 17.7

The
debugging
process

5. The symptom may be a result of timing problems, rather than processing problems.

6. It may be difficult to accurately reproduce input conditions (e.g., a real-time application in which input ordering is indeterminate).

7. The symptom may be intermittent. This is particularly common in embedded systems that couple hardware and software inextricably.

8. The symptom may be due to causes that are distributed across a number of tasks running on different processors.

During debugging, you'll encounter errors that range from mildly annoying (e.g., an incorrect output format) to catastrophic (e.g., the system fails, causing serious economic or physical damage). As the consequences of an error increase, the amount of pressure to find the cause also increases. Often, pressure forces some software developers to fix one error and at the same time introduce two more.

17.8.2 Psychological Considerations

Unfortunately, there appears to be some evidence that debugging prowess is an innate human trait. Some people are good at it and others aren't. Although experimental evidence on debugging is open to many interpretations, large variances in debugging ability have been reported for programmers with the same education and experience. Commenting on the human aspects of debugging, Shneiderman [Shn80] states:

> Debugging is one of the more frustrating parts of programming. It has elements of problem solving or brain teasers, coupled with the annoying recognition that you have made a mistake. Heightened anxiety and the unwillingness to accept the possibility of errors increases the task difficulty. Fortunately, there is a great sigh of relief and a lessening of tension when the bug is ultimately . . . corrected.

Although it may be difficult to "learn" debugging, a number of approaches to the problem can be proposed. I examine them in Section 17.8.3.

SafeHome

Debugging

The scene: Ed's cubical as code and unit testing is conducted.

The players: Ed and Shakira—members of the *SafeHome* software engineering team.

The conversation:

Shakira (looking in through the entrance to the cubical): Hey . . . where were you at lunchtime?

Ed: Right here . . . working.

Shakira: You look miserable . . . what's the matter?

Ed (sighing audibly): I've been working on this . . . bug since I discovered it at 9:30 this morning and it's what, 2:45 . . . I'm clueless.

Shakira: I thought we all agreed to spend no more than one hour debugging stuff on our own; then we get help, right?

Ed: Yeah, but . . .

Shakira (walking into the cubical): So what's the problem?

Ed: It's complicated, and besides, I've been looking at this for, what, 5 hours. You're not going to see it in 5 minutes.

Shakira: Indulge me . . . what's the problem?

[Ed explains the problem to Shakira, who looks at it for about 30 seconds without speaking, then . . .]

Shakira (a smile is gathering on her face): Uh, right there, the variable named *setAlarmCondition*. Shouldn't it be set to "false" before the loop gets started?

[Ed stares at the screen in disbelief, bends forward, and begins to bang his head gently against the monitor. Shakira, smiling broadly now, stands and walks out.]

17.8.3 Debugging Strategies

ADVICE

Set a time limit, say two hours, on the amount of time you spend trying to debug a problem on your own. After that, get help!

Regardless of the approach that is taken, debugging has one overriding objective—to find and correct the cause of a software error or defect. The objective is realized by a combination of systematic evaluation, intuition, and luck. Bradley [Bra85] describes the debugging approach in this way:

> Debugging is a straightforward application of the scientific method that has been developed over 2,500 years. The basis of debugging is to locate the problem's source [the cause] by binary partitioning, through working hypotheses that predict new values to be examined.
>
> Take a simple non-software example: A lamp in my house does not work. If nothing in the house works, the cause must be in the main circuit breaker or outside; I look around

to see whether the neighborhood is blacked out. I plug the suspect lamp into a working socket and a working appliance into the suspect circuit. So goes the alternation of hypothesis and test.

In general, three debugging strategies have been proposed [Mye79]: (1) brute force, (2) backtracking, and (3) cause elimination. Each of these strategies can be conducted manually, but modern debugging tools can make the process much more effective.

Debugging tactics.   The *brute force* category of debugging is probably the most common and least efficient method for isolating the cause of a software error. You apply brute force debugging methods when all else fails. Using a "let the computer find the error" philosophy, memory dumps are taken, run-time traces are invoked, and the program is loaded with output statements. You hope that somewhere in the morass of information that is produced you'll find a clue that can lead to the cause of an error. Although the mass of information produced may ultimately lead to success, it more frequently leads to wasted effort and time. Thought must be expended first!

Backtracking is a fairly common debugging approach that can be used successfully in small programs. Beginning at the site where a symptom has been uncovered, the source code is traced backward (manually) until the cause is found. Unfortunately, as the number of source lines increases, the number of potential backward paths may become unmanageably large.

The third approach to debugging—*cause elimination*—is manifested by induction or deduction and introduces the concept of binary partitioning. Data related to the error occurrence are organized to isolate potential causes. A "cause hypothesis" is devised and the aforementioned data are used to prove or disprove the hypothesis. Alternatively, a list of all possible causes is developed and tests are conducted to eliminate each. If initial tests indicate that a particular cause hypothesis shows promise, data are refined in an attempt to isolate the bug.

Automated debugging.   Each of these debugging approaches can be supplemented with debugging tools that can provide you with semiautomated support as debugging strategies are attempted. Hailpern and Santhanam [Hai02] summarize the state of these tools when they note, ". . . many new approaches have been proposed and many commercial debugging environments are available. Integrated development environments (IDEs) provide a way to capture some of the language-specific predetermined errors (e.g., missing end-of-statement characters, undefined variables, and so on) without requiring compilation." A wide variety of debugging compilers, dynamic debugging aids ("tracers"), automatic test-case generators, and cross-reference mapping tools are available. However, tools are not a substitute for careful evaluation based on a complete design model and clear source code.

Debugging

Objective: These tools provide automated assistance for those who must debug software problems. The intent is to provide insight that may be difficult to obtain if approaching the debugging process manually.

Mechanics: Most debugging tools are programming language and environment specific.

Representative Tools:[6]

Borland Gauntlet, distributed by Borland (**www.borland.com**), assists in both testing and debugging.

Coverty Prevent SQS, developed by Coverty (**www.coverty.com**), provides debugging assistance for both C++ and Java.

C++Test, developed by Parasoft (**www.parasoft.com**), is a unit-testing tool that supports a full range of tests on C and C++ code. Debugging features assist in the diagnosis of errors that are found.

CodeMedic, developed by NewPlanet Software (**www.newplanetsoftware.com/medic/**), provides a graphical interface for the standard UNIX debugger, *gdb,* and implements its most important features. *gdb* currently supports C/C++, Java, PalmOS, various embedded systems, assembly language, FORTRAN, and Modula-2.

GNATS, a freeware application (**www.gnu.org/software/gnats/**), is a set of tools for tracking bug reports.

The people factor. Any discussion of debugging approaches and tools is incomplete without mention of a powerful ally—other people! A fresh viewpoint, unclouded by hours of frustration, can do wonders.[7] A final maxim for debugging might be: "When all else fails, get help!"

17.8.4   Correcting the Error

Once a bug has been found, it must be corrected. But, as we have already noted, the correction of a bug can introduce other errors and therefore do more harm than good. Van Vleck [Van89] suggests three simple questions that you should ask before making the "correction" that removes the cause of a bug:

uote:

"The best tester isn't the one who finds the most bugs ... the best tester is the one who gets the most bugs fixed."

Cem Kaner et al.

1. *Is the cause of the bug reproduced in another part of the program?* In many situations, a program defect is caused by an erroneous pattern of logic that may be reproduced elsewhere. Explicit consideration of the logical pattern may result in the discovery of other errors.

2. *What "next bug" might be introduced by the fix I'm about to make?* Before the correction is made, the source code (or, better, the design) should be evaluated to assess coupling of logic and data structures. If the correction is to be made in a highly coupled section of the program, special care must be taken when any change is made.

---

6   Tools noted here do not represent an endorsement, but rather a sampling of tools in this category. In most cases, tool names are trademarked by their respective developers.

7   The concept of pair programming (recommended as part of the Extreme Programming model discussed in Chapter 3) provides a mechanism for "debugging" as the software is designed and coded.

3. *What could we have done to prevent this bug in the first place?* This question is the first step toward establishing a statistical software quality assurance approach (Chapter 16). If you correct the process as well as the product, the bug will be removed from the current program and may be eliminated from all future programs.

17.9   SUMMARY

Software testing accounts for the largest percentage of technical effort in the software process. Regardless of the type of software you build, a strategy for systematic test planning, execution, and control begins by considering small elements of the software and moves outward toward the program as a whole.

The objective of software testing is to uncover errors. For conventional software, this objective is achieved through a series of test steps. Unit and integration tests concentrate on functional verification of a component and incorporation of components into the software architecture. Validation testing demonstrates traceability to software requirements, and system testing validates software once it has been incorporated into a larger system. Each test step is accomplished through a series of systematic test techniques that assist in the design of test cases. With each testing step, the level of abstraction with which software is considered is broadened.

The strategy for testing object-oriented software begins with tests that exercise the operations within a class and then moves to thread-based testing for integration. Threads are sets of classes that respond to an input or event. Use-based tests focus on classes that do not collaborate heavily with other classes.

WebApps are tested in much the same way as OO systems. However, tests are designed to exercise content, functionality, the interface, navigation, and aspects of WebApp performance and security.

Unlike testing (a systematic, planned activity), debugging can be viewed as an art. Beginning with a symptomatic indication of a problem, the debugging activity must track down the cause of an error. Of the many resources available during debugging, the most valuable is the counsel of other members of the software engineering staff.

PROBLEMS AND POINTS TO PONDER

17.1. Using your own words, describe the difference between verification and validation. Do both make use of test-case design methods and testing strategies?

17.2. List some problems that might be associated with the creation of an independent test group. Are an ITG and an SQA group made up of the same people?

17.3. Is it always possible to develop a strategy for testing software that uses the sequence of testing steps described in Section 17.1.3? What possible complications might arise for embedded systems?

17.4. Why is a highly coupled module difficult to unit test?

17.5. The concept of "antibugging" (Section 17.2.1) is an extremely effective way to provide built-in debugging assistance when an error is uncovered:

    a. Develop a set of guidelines for antibugging.
    b. Discuss advantages of using the technique.
    c. Discuss disadvantages.

17.6. How can project scheduling affect integration testing?

17.7. Is unit testing possible or even desirable in all circumstances? Provide examples to justify your answer.

17.8. Who should perform the validation test—the software developer or the software user? Justify your answer.

17.9. Develop a complete test strategy for the *SafeHome* system discussed earlier in this book. Document it in a *Test Specification.*

17.10. As a class project, develop a *Debugging Guide* for your installation. The guide should provide language and system-oriented hints that have been learned through the school of hard knocks! Begin with an outline of topics that will be reviewed by the class and your instructor. Publish the guide for others in your local environment.

FURTHER READINGS AND INFORMATION SOURCES

Virtually every book on software testing discusses strategies along with methods for test-case design. Everett and Raymond (*Software Testing,* Wiley-IEEE Computer Society Press, 2007), Black (*Pragmatic Software Testing,* Wiley, 2007), Spiller and his colleagues (*Software Testing Process: Test Management,* Rocky Nook, 2007), Perry (*Effective Methods for Software Testing,* 3d ed., Wiley, 2005), Lewis (*Software Testing and Continuous Quality Improvement,* 2d ed., Auerbach, 2004), Loveland and his colleagues (*Software Testing Techniques,* Charles River Media, 2004), Burnstein (*Practical Software Testing,* Springer, 2003), Dustin (*Effective Software Testing,* Addison-Wesley, 2002), Craig and Kaskiel (*Systematic Software Testing,* Artech House, 2002), Tamres (*Introducing Software Testing,* Addison-Wesley, 2002), Whittaker (*How to Break Software,* Addison-Wesley, 2002), and Kaner and his colleagues (*Lessons Learned in Software Testing,* Wiley, 2001) are only a small sampling of many books that discuss testing principles, concepts, strategies, and methods.

For those readers with interest in agile software development methods, Crispin and House (*Testing Extreme Programming,* Addison-Wesley, 2002) and Beck (*Test Driven Development: By Example,* Addison-Wesley, 2002) present testing strategies and tactics for Extreme Programming. Kamer and his colleagues (*Lessons Learned in Software Testing,* Wiley, 2001) present a collection of over 300 pragmatic "lessons" (guidelines) that every software tester should learn. Watkins (*Testing IT: An Off-the-Shelf Testing Process,* Cambridge University Press, 2001) establishes an effective testing framework for all types of developed and acquired software. Manges and O'Brien (*Agile Testing with Ruby and Rails,* Apress, 2008) addresses testing strategies and techniques for the Ruby programming language and Web framework.

Sykes and McGregor (*Practical Guide to Testing Object-Oriented Software,* Addison-Wesley, 2001), Bashir and Goel (*Testing Object-Oriented Software,* Springer-Verlag, 2000), Binder (*Testing Object-Oriented Systems,* Addison-Wesley, 1999), Kung and his colleagues (*Testing Object-Oriented Software,* IEEE Computer Society Press, 1998), and Marick (*The Craft of Software Testing,* Prentice-Hall, 1997) present strategies and methods for testing OO systems.

Guidelines for debugging are contained in books by Grötker and his colleagues (*The Developer's Guide to Debugging,* Springer, 2008), Agans (*Debugging,* Amacon, 2006), Zeller (*Why Programs Fail: A Guide to Systematic Debugging,* Morgan Kaufmann, 2005), Tells and Hsieh (*The Science of Debugging,* The Coreolis Group, 2001), and Robbins (*Debugging Applications,* Microsoft Press, 2000). Kaspersky (*Hacker Debugging Uncovered,* A-List Publishing, 2005) addresses the technology of debugging tools. Younessi (*Object-Oriented Defect Management of Software,* Prentice-Hall, 2002) presents techniques for managing defects that are encountered in object-oriented systems. Beizer [Bei84] presents an interesting "taxonomy of bugs" that can lead to effective methods for test planning.

Books by Madisetti and Akgul (*Debugging Embedded Systems,* Springer, 2007), Robbins (*Debugging Microsoft .NET 2.0 Applications,* Microsoft Press, 2005), Best (*Linux Debugging and Performance Tuning,* Prentice-Hall, 2005), Ford and Teorey (*Practical Debugging in C++,* Prentice-Hall, 2002), Brown (*Debugging Perl,* McGraw-Hill, 2000), and Mitchell (*Debugging Java,* McGraw-Hill, 2000) address the special nature of debugging for the environments implied by their titles.

A wide variety of information sources on software testing strategies are available on the Internet. An up-to-date list of World Wide Web references that are relevant to software testing strategies can be found at the SEPA website: **www.mhhe.com/engcs/compsci/pressman/professional/olc/ser.htm**.

TESTING CONVENTIONAL APPLICATIONS

Testing presents an interesting anomaly for software engineers, who by their nature are constructive people. Testing requires that the developer discard preconceived notions of the "correctness" of software just developed and then work hard to design test cases to "break" the software. Beizer [Bei90] describes this situation effectively when he states:

> There's a myth that if we were really good at programming, there would be no bugs to catch. If only we could really concentrate, if only everyone used structured programming, top-down design, . . . then there would be no bugs. So goes the myth. There are bugs, the myth says, because we are bad at what we do; and if we are bad at it, we should feel guilty about it. Therefore, testing and test case design is an admission of failure, which instills a goodly dose of guilt. And the tedium of testing is just punishment for our errors. Punishment for what? For being human? Guilt for what? For failing to achieve inhuman perfection? For not distinguishing between what another programmer thinks and what he says? For failing to be telepathic? For not solving human communications problems that have been kicked around . . . for forty centuries?

Should testing instill guilt? Is testing really destructive? The answer to these questions is "No!"

In this chapter, I discuss techniques for software test-case design for conventional applications. Test-case design focuses on a set of techniques for the creation of test cases that meet overall testing objectives and the testing strategies discussed in Chapter 17.

QUICK LOOK

What is it? Once source code has been generated, software must be tested to uncover (and correct) as many errors as possible before delivery to your customer. Your goal is to design a series of test cases that have a high likelihood of finding errors—but how? That's where software testing techniques enter the picture. These techniques provide systematic guidance for designing tests that (1) exercise the internal logic and interfaces of every software component and (2) exercise the input and output domains of the program to uncover errors in program function, behavior, and performance.

Who does it? During early stages of testing, a software engineer performs all tests. However, as the testing process progresses, testing specialists may become involved.

Why is it important? Reviews and other SQA actions can and do uncover errors, but they are not sufficient. Every time the program is executed, the customer tests it! Therefore, you have to execute the program before it gets to the customer with the specific intent of finding and removing all errors. In order to find the highest possible number of errors, tests must be conducted systematically and test cases must be designed using disciplined techniques.

What are the steps? For conventional applications, software is tested from two different perspectives: (1) internal program logic is exercised using "white box" test-case design techniques and (2) software requirements are exercised using "black box" test-case design techniques. Use cases assist in the design of tests to uncover errors at the software validation level. In every case, the intent is to find the maximum number of errors with the minimum amount of effort and time.

What is the work product? A set of test cases designed to exercise both internal logic, interfaces, component collaborations, and external requirements is designed and documented, expected results are defined, and actual results are recorded.

How do I ensure that I've done it right? When you begin testing, change your point of view. Try hard to "break" the software! Design test cases in a disciplined fashion and review the test cases you do create for thoroughness. In addition, you can evaluate test coverage and track error detection activities.

18.1   SOFTWARE TESTING FUNDAMENTALS

? **What are the characteristics of testability?**

The goal of testing is to find errors, and a good test is one that has a high probability of finding an error. Therefore, you should design and implement a computer-based system or a product with "testability" in mind. At the same time, the tests themselves must exhibit a set of characteristics that achieve the goal of finding the most errors with a minimum of effort.

Testability.   James Bach[1] provides the following definition for testability: "*Software testability* is simply how easily [a computer program] can be tested." The following characteristics lead to testable software.

Operability. "The better it works, the more efficiently it can be tested." If a system is designed and implemented with quality in mind, relatively few bugs will block the execution of tests, allowing testing to progress without fits and starts.

Observability. "What you see is what you test." Inputs provided as part of testing produce distinct outputs. System states and variables are visible or queriable during execution. Incorrect output is easily identified. Internal errors are automatically detected and reported. Source code is accessible.

Controllability. "The better we can control the software, the more the testing can be automated and optimized." All possible outputs can be generated through some combination of input, and I/O formats are consistent and structured. All code is executable through some combination of input. Software and hardware states and

---

1   The paragraphs that follow are used with permission of James Bach (copyright 1994) and have been adapted from material that originally appeared in a posting in the newsgroup comp.software-eng.

variables can be controlled directly by the test engineer. Tests can be conveniently specified, automated, and reproduced.

Decomposability. "By controlling the scope of testing, we can more quickly isolate problems and perform smarter retesting." The software system is built from independent modules that can be tested independently.

Simplicity. "The less there is to test, the more quickly we can test it." The program should exhibit *functional simplicity* (e.g., the feature set is the minimum necessary to meet requirements); *structural simplicity* (e.g., architecture is modularized to limit the propagation of faults), and *code simplicity* (e.g., a coding standard is adopted for ease of inspection and maintenance).

Stability. "The fewer the changes, the fewer the disruptions to testing." Changes to the software are infrequent, controlled when they do occur, and do not invalidate existing tests. The software recovers well from failures.

Understandability. "The more information we have, the smarter we will test." The architectural design and the dependencies between internal, external, and shared components are well understood. Technical documentation is instantly accessible, well organized, specific and detailed, and accurate. Changes to the design are communicated to testers.

You can use the attributes suggested by Bach to develop a software configuration (i.e., programs, data, and documents) that is amenable to testing.

Test Characteristics. And what about the tests themselves? Kaner, Falk, and Nguyen [Kan93] suggest the following attributes of a "good" test:

A good test has a high probability of finding an error. To achieve this goal, the tester must understand the software and attempt to develop a mental picture of how the software might fail. Ideally, the classes of failure are probed. For example, one class of potential failure in a graphical user interface is the failure to recognize proper mouse position. A set of tests would be designed to exercise the mouse in an attempt to demonstrate an error in mouse position recognition.

A good test is not redundant. Testing time and resources are limited. There is no point in conducting a test that has the same purpose as another test. Every test should have a different purpose (even if it is subtly different).

A good test should be "best of breed" [Kan93]. In a group of tests that have a similar intent, time and resource limitations may mitigate toward the execution of only a subset of these tests. In such cases, the test that has the highest likelihood of uncovering a whole class of errors should be used.

A good test should be neither too simple nor too complex. Although it is sometimes possible to combine a series of tests into one test case, the possible side effects associated with this approach may mask errors. In general, each test should be executed separately.

What is a "good" test?

SafeHome

Designing Unique Tests

The scene: Vinod's cubical.

The players: Vinod and Ed—members of the *SafeHome* software engineering team.

The conversation:

Vinod: So these are the test cases you intend to run for the *passwordValidation* operation.

Ed: Yeah, they should cover pretty much all possibilities for the kinds of passwords a user might enter.

Vinod: So let's see . . . you note that the correct password will be 8080, right?

Ed: Uh huh.

Vinod: And you specify passwords 1234 and 6789 to test for error in recognizing invalid passwords?

Ed: Right, and I also test passwords that are close to the correct password, see . . . 8081 and 8180.

Vinod: Those are okay, but I don't see much point in running both the 1234 and 6789 inputs. They're redundant . . . test the same thing, don't they?

Ed: Well, they're different values.

Vinod: That's true, but if 1234 doesn't uncover an error . . . in other words . . . the *passwordValidation* operation notes that it's an invalid password, it's not likely that 6789 will show us anything new.

Ed: I see what you mean.

Vinod: I'm not trying to be picky here . . . it's just that we have limited time to do testing, so it's a good idea to run tests that have a high likelihood of finding new errors.

Ed: Not a problem . . . I'll give this a bit more thought.

18.2   INTERNAL AND EXTERNAL VIEWS OF TESTING

KEY POINT

White-box tests can be designed only after component-level design (or source code) exists. The logical details of the program must be available.

Any engineered product (and most other things) can be tested in one of two ways: (1) Knowing the specified function that a product has been designed to perform, tests can be conducted that demonstrate each function is fully operational while at the same time searching for errors in each function. (2) Knowing the internal workings of a product, tests can be conducted to ensure that "all gears mesh," that is, internal operations are performed according to specifications and all internal components have been adequately exercised. The first test approach takes an external view and is called black-box testing. The second requires an internal view and is termed white-box testing.[2]

Black-box testing alludes to tests that are conducted at the software interface. A black-box test examines some fundamental aspect of a system with little regard for the internal logical structure of the software. *White-box testing* of software is predicated on close examination of procedural detail. Logical paths through the software and collaborations between components are tested by exercising specific sets of conditions and/or loops.

At first glance it would seem that very thorough white-box testing would lead to "100 percent correct programs." All we need do is define all logical paths, develop test cases to exercise them, and evaluate results, that is, generate test cases to exercise program logic exhaustively. Unfortunately, exhaustive testing presents

---

2   The terms *functional testing* and *structural testing* are sometimes used in place of black-box and white-box testing, respectively.

certain logical problems. For even small programs, the number of possible logical paths can be very large. White-box testing should not, however, be dismissed as impractical. A limited number of important logical paths can be selected and exercised. Important data structures can be probed for validity.

INFO

Exhaustive Testing

Consider a 100-line program in the language C. After some basic data declaration, the program contains two nested loops that execute from 1 to 20 times each, depending on conditions specified at input. Inside the interior loop, four if-then-else constructs are required. There are approximately 10^{14} possible paths that may be executed in this program!

To put this number in perspective, we assume that a magic test processor ("magic" because no such processor exists) has been developed for exhaustive testing. The processor can develop a test case, execute it, and evaluate the results in one millisecond. Working 24 hours a day, 365 days a year, the processor would work for 3170 years to test the program. This would, undeniably, cause havoc in most development schedules.

Therefore, it is reasonable to assert that exhaustive testing is impossible for large software systems.

18.3   WHITE-BOX TESTING

> **Quote:**
>
> "Bugs lurk in corners and congregate at boundaries."
>
> **Boris Beizer**

White-box testing, sometimes called *glass-box testing,* is a test-case design philosophy that uses the control structure described as part of component-level design to derive test cases. Using white-box testing methods, you can derive test cases that (1) guarantee that all independent paths within a module have been exercised at least once, (2) exercise all logical decisions on their true and false sides, (3) execute all loops at their boundaries and within their operational bounds, and (4) exercise internal data structures to ensure their validity.

18.4   BASIS PATH TESTING

Basis path testing is a white-box testing technique first proposed by Tom McCabe [McC76]. The basis path method enables the test-case designer to derive a logical complexity measure of a procedural design and use this measure as a guide for defining a basis set of execution paths. Test cases derived to exercise the basis set are guaranteed to execute every statement in the program at least one time during testing.

18.4.1   Flow Graph Notation

Before we consider the basis path method, a simple notation for the representation of control flow, called a *flow graph* (or *program graph*) must be introduced.[3] The flow graph depicts logical control flow using the notation illustrated in Figure 18.1. Each structured construct (Chapter 10) has a corresponding flow graph symbol.

---

3   In actuality, the basis path method can be conducted without the use of flow graphs. However, they serve as a useful notation for understanding control flow and illustrating the approach.

FIGURE 18.1

Flow graph notation

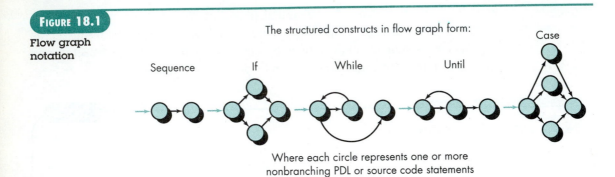

The structured constructs in flow graph form:

Sequence   If   While   Until   Case

Where each circle represents one or more
nonbranching PDL or source code statements

To illustrate the use of a flow graph, consider the procedural design representation in Figure 18.2a. Here, a flowchart is used to depict program control structure. Figure 18.2b maps the flowchart into a corresponding flow graph (assuming that no compound conditions are contained in the decision diamonds of the flowchart). Referring to Figure 18.2b, each circle, called a *flow graph node,* represents one or more procedural statements. A sequence of process boxes and a decision diamond can map into a single node. The arrows on the flow graph, called *edges* or *links,* represent flow of control and are analogous to flowchart arrows. An edge must terminate at a node, even if the node does not represent any procedural statements (e.g., see the flow graph symbol for the if-then-else construct). Areas bounded by edges and nodes are called *regions.* When counting regions, we include the area outside the graph as a region.[4]

ADVICE

A flow graph should be drawn only when the logical structure of a component is complex. The flow graph allows you to trace program paths more readily.

FIGURE 18.2   (a) Flowchart and (b) flow graph

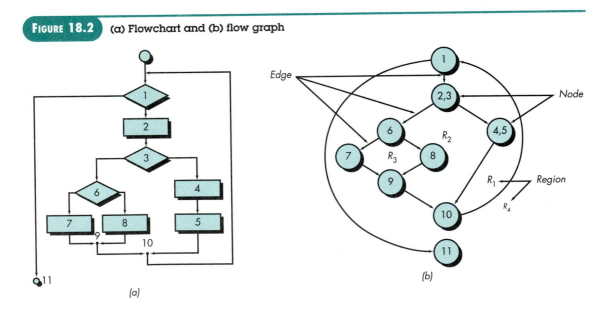

Edge

Node

R_2

R_3

R_1 Region

R_4

(a)

(b)

---

4   A more detailed discussion of graphs and their uses is presented in Section 18.6.1.

FIGURE 18.3

Compound
logic

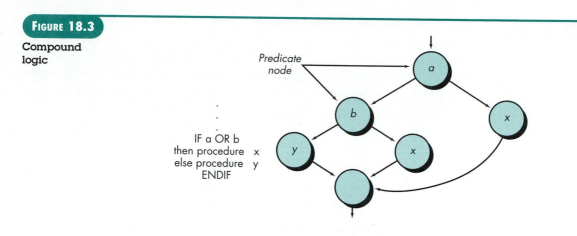

Predicate
node

IF a OR b
then procedure x
else procedure y
ENDIF

When compound conditions are encountered in a procedural design, the generation of a flow graph becomes slightly more complicated. A compound condition
occurs when one or more Boolean operators (logical OR, AND, NAND, NOR) is present in a conditional statement. Referring to Figure 18.3, the program design language
(PDL) segment translates into the flow graph shown. Note that a separate node is
created for each of the conditions *a* and *b* in the statement IF *a* OR *b*. Each node that
contains a condition is called a *predicate node* and is characterized by two or more
edges emanating from it.

18.4.2   Independent Program Paths

An *independent path* is any path through the program that introduces at least one
new set of processing statements or a new condition. When stated in terms of a flow
graph, an independent path must move along at least one edge that has not been
traversed before the path is defined. For example, a set of independent paths for the
flow graph illustrated in Figure 18.2b is

Path 1: 1-11

Path 2: 1-2-3-4-5-10-1-11

Path 3: 1-2-3-6-8-9-10-1-11

Path 4: 1-2-3-6-7-9-10-1-11

Note that each new path introduces a new edge. The path

1-2-3-4-5-10-1-2-3-6-8-9-10-1-11

is not considered to be an independent path because it is simply a combination of
already specified paths and does not traverse any new edges.

Paths 1 through 4 constitute a *basis set* for the flow graph in Figure 18.2b. That is,
if you can design tests to force execution of these paths (a basis set), every statement
in the program will have been guaranteed to be executed at least one time and every
condition will have been executed on its true and false sides. It should be noted that

the basis set is not unique. In fact, a number of different basis sets can be derived for a given procedural design.

How do you know how many paths to look for? The computation of cyclomatic complexity provides the answer. *Cyclomatic complexity* is a software metric that provides a quantitative measure of the logical complexity of a program. When used in the context of the basis path testing method, the value computed for cyclomatic complexity defines the number of independent paths in the basis set of a program and provides you with an upper bound for the number of tests that must be conducted to ensure that all statements have been executed at least once.

Cyclomatic complexity has a foundation in graph theory and provides you with an extremely useful software metric. Complexity is computed in one of three ways:

1. The number of regions of the flow graph corresponds to the cyclomatic complexity.

2. Cyclomatic complexity $V(G)$ for a flow graph G is defined as

    $V(G) = E - N + 2$

    where E is the number of flow graph edges and N is the number of flow graph nodes.

3. Cyclomatic complexity $V(G)$ for a flow graph G is also defined as

    $V(G) = P + 1$

    where P is the number of predicate nodes contained in the flow graph G.

Referring once more to the flow graph in Figure 18.2b, the cyclomatic complexity can be computed using each of the algorithms just noted:

1. The flow graph has four regions.

2. $V(G) = 11$ edges $- 9$ nodes $+ 2 = 4$.

3. $V(G) = 3$ predicate nodes $+ 1 = 4$.

Therefore, the cyclomatic complexity of the flow graph in Figure 18.2b is 4.

More important, the value for $V(G)$ provides you with an upper bound for the number of independent paths that form the basis set and, by implication, an upper bound on the number of tests that must be designed and executed to guarantee coverage of all program statements.

SAFEHOME

Using Cyclomatic Complexity

The scene: Shakira's cubicle.

The players: Vinod and Shakira—members of the *SafeHome* software engineering team who are working on test planning for the security function.

The conversation:

Shakira: Look . . . I know that we should unit-test all the components for the security function, but there are a lot of 'em and if you consider the number of operations that have to be exercised, I don't know . . . maybe we should forget white-box testing, integrate everything, and start running black-box tests.

Vinod: You figure we don't have enough time to do component tests, exercise the operations, and then integrate?

Shakira: The deadline for the first increment is getting closer than I'd like . . . yeah, I'm concerned.

Vinod: Why don't you at least run white-box tests on the operations that are likely to be the most error prone?

Shakira (exasperated): And exactly how do I know which are the most error prone?

Vinod: V of G.

Shakira: Huh?

Vinod: Cyclomatic complexity—V of G. Just compute V(G) for each of the operations within each of the

components and see which have the highest values for V(G). They're the ones that are most likely to be error prone.

Shakira: And how do I compute V of G?

Vinod: It's really easy. Here's a book that describes how to do it.

Shakira (leafing through the pages): Okay, it doesn't look hard. I'll give it a try. The ops with the highest V(G) will be the candidates for white-box tests.

Vinod: Just remember that there are no guarantees. A component with a low V(G) can still be error prone.

Shakira: Alright. But at least this'll help me to narrow down the number of components that have to undergo white-box testing.

18.4.3   Deriving Test Cases

The basis path testing method can be applied to a procedural design or to source code. In this section, I present basis path testing as a series of steps. The procedure *average,* depicted in PDL in Figure 18.4, will be used as an example to illustrate each step in the test-case design method. Note that *average,* although an extremely simple algorithm, contains compound conditions and loops. The following steps can be applied to derive the basis set:

1. **Using the design or code as a foundation, draw a corresponding flow graph.** A flow graph is created using the symbols and construction rules presented in Section 18.4.1. Referring to the PDL for *average* in Figure 18.4, a flow graph is created by numbering those PDL statements that will be mapped into corresponding flow graph nodes. The corresponding flow graph is shown in Figure 18.5.

2. **Determine the cyclomatic complexity of the resultant flow graph.** The cyclomatic complexity V(G) is determined by applying the algorithms described in Section 18.4.2. It should be noted that V(G) can be determined without developing a flow graph by counting all conditional statements in the PDL (for the procedure *average,* compound conditions count as two) and adding 1. Referring to Figure 18.5,

$V(G)$ = 6 regions
$V(G)$ = 17 edges − 13 nodes + 2 = 6
$V(G)$ = 5 predicate nodes + 1 = 6

FIGURE 18.4

PDL with
nodes
identified

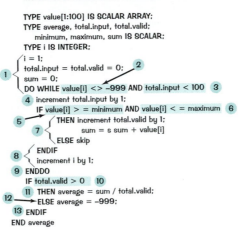

```
PROCEDURE average;

*   This procedure computes the average of 100 or fewer
    numbers that lie between bounding values; it also computes the
    sum and the total number valid.

INTERFACE RETURNS average, total.input, total.valid;
INTERFACE ACCEPTS value, minimum, maximum;

TYPE value[1:100] IS SCALAR ARRAY;
TYPE average, total.input, total.valid;
    minimum, maximum, sum IS SCALAR;
TYPE i IS INTEGER;
    i = 1;
    total.input = total.valid = 0;      2
1   sum = 0;
    DO WHILE value[i] <> –999 AND total.input < 100   3
    4   increment total.input by 1;
        IF value[i] > = minimum AND value[i] < = maximum   6
    5       THEN increment total.valid by 1;
        7       sum = s sum + value[i]
                ELSE skip
    8   ENDIF
        increment i by 1;
    9   ENDDO
        IF total.valid > 0   10
        11   THEN average = sum / total.valid;
    12   ELSE average = –999;
    13 ENDIF
END average
```

3. **Determine a basis set of linearly independent paths.** The value of $V(G)$
   provides the upper bound on the number of linearly independent paths
   through the program control structure. In the case of procedure *average*, we
   expect to specify six paths:

   Path 1: 1-2-10-11-13

   Path 2: 1-2-10-12-13

FIGURE 18.5

Flow graph for
the procedure
average

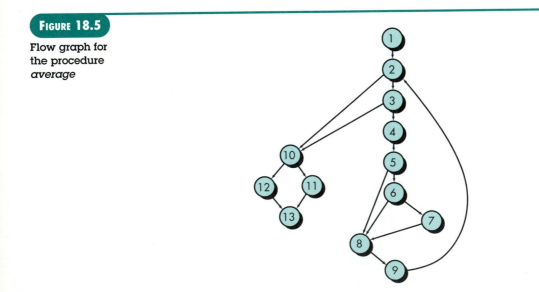

Path 3: 1-2-3-10-11-13

Path 4: 1-2-3-4-5-8-9-2-. . .

Path 5: 1-2-3-4-5-6-8-9-2-. . .

Path 6: 1-2-3-4-5-6-7-8-9-2-. . .

The ellipsis (. . .) following paths 4, 5, and 6 indicates that any path through the remainder of the control structure is acceptable. It is often worthwhile to identify predicate nodes as an aid in the derivation of test cases. In this case, nodes 2, 3, 5, 6, and 10 are predicate nodes.

4. **Prepare test cases that will force execution of each path in the basis set.** Data should be chosen so that conditions at the predicate nodes are appropriately set as each path is tested. Each test case is executed and compared to expected results. Once all test cases have been completed, the tester can be sure that all statements in the program have been executed at least once.

It is important to note that some independent paths (e.g., path 1 in our example) cannot be tested in stand-alone fashion. That is, the combination of data required to traverse the path cannot be achieved in the normal flow of the program. In such cases, these paths are tested as part of another path test.

18.4.4 Graph Matrices

The procedure for deriving the flow graph and even determining a set of basis paths is amenable to mechanization. A data structure, called a *graph matrix,* can be quite useful for developing a software tool that assists in basis path testing.

A graph matrix is a square matrix whose size (i.e., number of rows and columns) is equal to the number of nodes on the flow graph. Each row and column corresponds to an identified node, and matrix entries correspond to connections (an edge) between nodes. A simple example of a flow graph and its corresponding graph matrix [Bei90] is shown in Figure 18.6.

FIGURE 18.6

Graph matrix

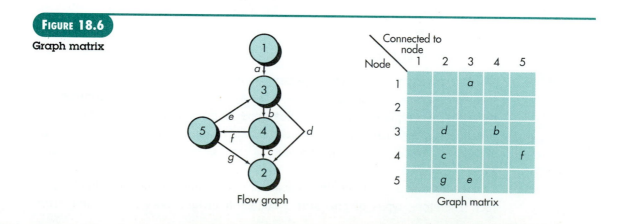

Flow graph

Graph matrix

Referring to the figure, each node on the flow graph is identified by numbers, while each edge is identified by letters. A letter entry is made in the matrix to correspond to a connection between two nodes. For example, node 3 is connected to node 4 by edge *b*.

? What is a graph matrix and how do I extend it for use in testing?

To this point, the graph matrix is nothing more than a tabular representation of a flow graph. However, by adding a *link weight* to each matrix entry, the graph matrix can become a powerful tool for evaluating program control structure during testing. The link weight provides additional information about control flow. In its simplest form, the link weight is 1 (a connection exists) or 0 (a connection does not exist). But link weights can be assigned other, more interesting properties:

- The probability that a link (edge) will be execute.
- The processing time expended during traversal of a link
- The memory required during traversal of a link
- The resources required during traversal of a link.

Beizer [Bei90] provides a thorough treatment of additional mathematical algorithms that can be applied to graph matrices. Using these techniques, the analysis required to design test cases can be partially or fully automated.

18.5   CONTROL STRUCTURE TESTING

Quote:

"Paying more attention to running tests than to designing them is a classic mistake."

Brian Marick

The basis path testing technique described in Section 18.4 is one of a number of techniques for control structure testing. Although basis path testing is simple and highly effective, it is not sufficient in itself. In this section, other variations on control structure testing are discussed. These broaden testing coverage and improve the quality of white-box testing.

18.5.1   Condition Testing

Condition testing [Tai89] is a test-case design method that exercises the logical conditions contained in a program module. A simple condition is a Boolean variable or a relational expression, possibly preceded with one NOT ($\neg$) operator. A relational expression takes the form

$$E_1 \text{ <relational-operator> } E_2$$

KEY POINT

Errors are much more common in the neighborhood of logical conditions than they are in the locus of sequential processing statements.

where E_1 and E_2 are arithmetic expressions and <relational-operator> is one of the following: $<$, $\leq$, $=$, $\neq$ (nonequality), $>$, or $\geq$. A *compound condition* is composed of two or more simple conditions, Boolean operators, and parentheses. We assume that Boolean operators allowed in a compound condition include OR ($|$), AND (&), and NOT ($\neg$). A condition without relational expressions is referred to as a Boolean expression.

If a condition is incorrect, then at least one component of the condition is incorrect. Therefore, types of errors in a condition include Boolean operator errors (incorrect/missing/extra Boolean operators), Boolean variable errors, Boolean parenthesis errors, relational operator errors, and arithmetic expression errors. The condition testing method focuses on testing each condition in the program to ensure that it does not contain errors.

18.5.2 Data Flow Testing

The data flow testing method [Fra93] selects test paths of a program according to the locations of definitions and uses of variables in the program. To illustrate the data flow testing approach, assume that each statement in a program is assigned a unique statement number and that each function does not modify its parameters or global variables. For a statement with S as its statement number,

$$\text{DEF}(S) = \{X \mid \text{statement } S \text{ contains a definition of } X\}$$
$$\text{USE}(S) = \{X \mid \text{statement } S \text{ contains a use of } X\}$$

If statement S is an *if* or *loop statement,* its DEF set is empty and its USE set is based on the condition of statement S. The definition of variable X at statement S is said to be *live* at statement S' if there exists a path from statement S to statement S' that contains no other definition of X.

A *definition-use (DU) chain* of variable X is of the form $[X, S, S']$, where S and S' are statement numbers, X is in DEF(S) and USE(S'), and the definition of X in statement S is live at statement S'.

One simple data flow testing strategy is to require that every DU chain be covered at least once. We refer to this strategy as the DU testing strategy. It has been shown that DU testing does not guarantee the coverage of all branches of a program. However, a branch is not guaranteed to be covered by DU testing only in rare situations such as if-then-else constructs in which the *then part* has no definition of any variable and the *else part* does not exist. In this situation, the else branch of the *if* statement is not necessarily covered by DU testing.

18.5.3 Loop Testing

Loops are the cornerstone for the vast majority of all algorithms implemented in software. And yet, we often pay them little heed while conducting software tests.

Loop testing is a white-box testing technique that focuses exclusively on the validity of loop constructs. Four different classes of loops [Bei90] can be defined: simple loops, concatenated loops, nested loops, and unstructured loops (Figure 18.7).

Simple loops. The following set of tests can be applied to simple loops, where n is the maximum number of allowable passes through the loop.

1. Skip the loop entirely.

2. Only one pass through the loop.

3. Two passes through the loop.

FIGURE 18.7

Classes of
Loops

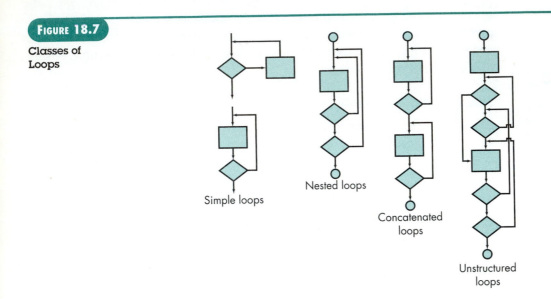

Simple loops

Nested loops

Concatenated
loops

Unstructured
loops

4. m passes through the loop where $m < n$.

5. $n - 1, n, n + 1$ passes through the loop.

Nested loops.   If we were to extend the test approach for simple loops to nested
loops, the number of possible tests would grow geometrically as the level of nesting
increases. This would result in an impractical number of tests. Beizer [Bei90] suggests an approach that will help to reduce the number of tests:

1. Start at the innermost loop. Set all other loops to minimum values.

2. Conduct simple loop tests for the innermost loop while holding the outer
    loops at their minimum iteration parameter (e.g., loop counter) values. Add
    other tests for out-of-range or excluded values.

3. Work outward, conducting tests for the next loop, but keeping all other outer
    loops at minimum values and other nested loops to "typical" values.

4. Continue until all loops have been tested.

You can't test unstruc-
tured loops effectively.
Refactor them.

Concatenated loops.   Concatenated loops can be tested using the approach
defined for simple loops, if each of the loops is independent of the other. However,
if two loops are concatenated and the loop counter for loop 1 is used as the initial
value for loop 2, then the loops are not independent. When the loops are not independent, the approach applied to nested loops is recommended.

Unstructured loops.   Whenever possible, this class of loops should be redesigned
to reflect the use of the structured programming constructs (Chapter 10).

18.6 BLACK-BOX TESTING

Black-box testing, also called *behavioral testing*, focuses on the functional requirements of the software. That is, black-box testing techniques enable you to derive sets of input conditions that will fully exercise all functional requirements for a program. Black-box testing is not an alternative to white-box techniques. Rather, it is a complementary approach that is likely to uncover a different class of errors than white-box methods.

Black-box testing attempts to find errors in the following categories: (1) incorrect or missing functions, (2) interface errors, (3) errors in data structures or external database access, (4) behavior or performance errors, and (5) initialization and termination errors.

Unlike white-box testing, which is performed early in the testing process, black-box testing tends to be applied during later stages of testing (see Chapter 17). Because black-box testing purposely disregards control structure, attention is focused on the information domain. Tests are designed to answer the following questions:

What questions do black-box tests answer?

- How is functional validity tested?
- How are system behavior and performance tested?
- What classes of input will make good test cases?
- Is the system particularly sensitive to certain input values?
- How are the boundaries of a data class isolated?
- What data rates and data volume can the system tolerate?
- What effect will specific combinations of data have on system operation?

By applying black-box techniques, you derive a set of test cases that satisfy the following criteria [Mye79]: (1) test cases that reduce, by a count that is greater than one, the number of additional test cases that must be designed to achieve reasonable testing, and (2) test cases that tell you something about the presence or absence of classes of errors, rather than an error associated only with the specific test at hand.

KEY POINT

A graph represents the relationships between data objects and program objects, enabling you to derive test cases that search for errors associated with these relationships.

18.6.1 Graph-Based Testing Methods

The first step in black-box testing is to understand the objects[5] that are modeled in software and the relationships that connect these objects. Once this has been accomplished, the next step is to define a series of tests that verify "all objects have the expected relationship to one another" [Bei95]. Stated in another way, software testing begins by creating a graph of important objects and their relationships and

---

5   In this context, you should consider the term *objects* in the broadest possible context. It encompasses data objects, traditional components (modules), and object-oriented elements of computer software.

FIGURE 18.8

(a) Graph
notation; (b)
simple
example

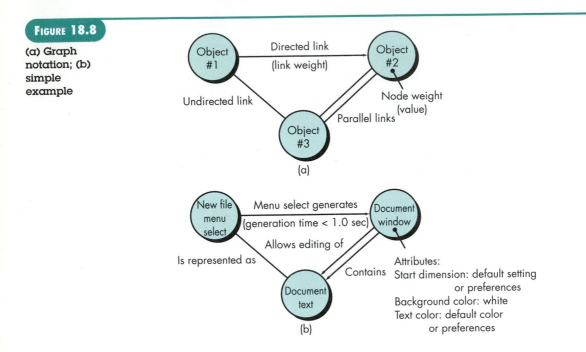

then devising a series of tests that will cover the graph so that each object and relationship is exercised and errors are uncovered.

To accomplish these steps, you begin by creating a *graph*—a collection of *nodes* that represent objects, *links* that represent the relationships between objects, *node weights* that describe the properties of a node (e.g., a specific data value or state behavior), and *link weights* that describe some characteristic of a link.

The symbolic representation of a graph is shown in Figure 18.8a. Nodes are represented as circles connected by links that take a number of different forms. A *directed link* (represented by an arrow) indicates that a relationship moves in only one direction. A *bidirectional link,* also called a *symmetric link,* implies that the relationship applies in both directions. *Parallel links* are used when a number of different relationships are established between graph nodes.

As a simple example, consider a portion of a graph for a word-processing application (Figure 18.8b) where

Object #1 = **newFile** (menu selection)

Object #2 = **documentWindow**

Object #3 = **documentText**

Referring to the figure, a menu select on **newFile** generates a document window. The node weight of **documentWindow** provides a list of the window attributes that are to be expected when the window is generated. The link weight indicates that the window must be generated in less than 1.0 second. An undirected link establishes a symmetric relationship between the **newFile** menu selection and **documentText,** and parallel links indicate relationships between **documentWindow** and **documentText.** In reality, a far more detailed graph would have to be generated as a precursor to test-case design. You can then derive test cases by traversing the graph and covering each of the relationships shown. These test cases are designed in an attempt to find errors in any of the relationships. Beizer [Bei95] describes a number of behavioral testing methods that can make use of graphs:

> **Transaction flow modeling.** The nodes represent steps in some transaction (e.g., the steps required to make an airline reservation using an online service), and the links represent the logical connection between steps (e.g., **flightInformationInput** is followed by *validationAvailabilityProcessing*). The data flow diagram (Chapter 7) can be used to assist in creating graphs of this type.

> **Finite state modeling.** The nodes represent different user-observable states of the software (e.g., each of the "screens" that appear as an order entry clerk takes a phone order), and the links represent the transitions that occur to move from state to state (e.g., **orderInformation** is verified during *inventoryAvailabilityLook-up* and is followed by **customerBillingInformation** input). The state diagram (Chapter 7) can be used to assist in creating graphs of this type.

> **Data flow modeling.** The nodes are data objects, and the links are the transformations that occur to translate one data object into another. For example, the node FICA tax withheld (**FTW**) is computed from gross wages (**GW**) using the relationship, **FTW = 0.62 × GW.**

> **Timing modeling.** The nodes are program objects, and the links are the sequential connections between those objects. Link weights are used to specify the required execution times as the program executes.

A detailed discussion of each of these graph-based testing methods is beyond the scope of this book. If you have further interest, see [Bei95] for a comprehensive coverage.

18.6.2 Equivalence Partitioning

Input classes are known relatively early in the software process. For this reason, begin thinking about equivalence partitioning as the design is created.

Equivalence partitioning is a black-box testing method that divides the input domain of a program into classes of data from which test cases can be derived. An ideal test case single-handedly uncovers a class of errors (e.g., incorrect processing of all character data) that might otherwise require many test cases to be executed before the general error is observed.

Test-case design for equivalence partitioning is based on an evaluation of *equivalence classes* for an input condition. Using concepts introduced in the preceding section, if a set of objects can be linked by relationships that are symmetric, transitive, and reflexive, an equivalence class is present [Bei95]. An equivalence class represents a set of valid or invalid states for input conditions. Typically, an input condition is either a specific numeric value, a range of values, a set of related values, or a Boolean condition. Equivalence classes may be defined according to the following guidelines:

How do I define equivalence classes for testing?

1. If an input condition specifies a range, one valid and two invalid equivalence classes are defined.

2. If an input condition requires a specific value, one valid and two invalid equivalence classes are defined.

3. If an input condition specifies a member of a set, one valid and one invalid equivalence class are defined.

4. If an input condition is Boolean, one valid and one invalid class are defined.

By applying the guidelines for the derivation of equivalence classes, test cases for each input domain data item can be developed and executed. Test cases are selected so that the largest number of attributes of an equivalence class are exercised at once.

18.6.3   Boundary Value Analysis

A greater number of errors occurs at the boundaries of the input domain rather than in the "center." It is for this reason that *boundary value analysis* (BVA) has been developed as a testing technique. Boundary value analysis leads to a selection of test cases that exercise bounding values.

Boundary value analysis is a test-case design technique that complements equivalence partitioning. Rather than selecting any element of an equivalence class, BVA leads to the selection of test cases at the "edges" of the class. Rather than focusing solely on input conditions, BVA derives test cases from the output domain as well [Mye79].

Guidelines for BVA are similar in many respects to those provided for equivalence partitioning:

1. If an input condition specifies a range bounded by values *a* and *b,* test cases should be designed with values *a* and *b* and just above and just below *a* and *b.*

2. If an input condition specifies a number of values, test cases should be developed that exercise the minimum and maximum numbers. Values just above and below minimum and maximum are also tested.

KEY POINT

BVA extends equivalence partitioning by focusing on data at the "edges" of an equivalence class.

3. Apply guidelines 1 and 2 to output conditions. For example, assume that a temperature versus pressure table is required as output from an engineering analysis program. Test cases should be designed to create an output report that produces the maximum (and minimum) allowable number of table entries.

4. If internal program data structures have prescribed boundaries (e.g., a table has a defined limit of 100 entries), be certain to design a test case to exercise the data structure at its boundary.

Most software engineers intuitively perform BVA to some degree. By applying these guidelines, boundary testing will be more complete, thereby having a higher likelihood for error detection.

18.6.4   Orthogonal Array Testing

There are many applications in which the input domain is relatively limited. That is, the number of input parameters is small and the values that each of the parameters may take are clearly bounded. When these numbers are very small (e.g., three input parameters taking on three discrete values each), it is possible to consider every input permutation and exhaustively test the input domain. However, as the number of input values grows and the number of discrete values for each data item increases, exhaustive testing becomes impractical or impossible.

Orthogonal array testing can be applied to problems in which the input domain is relatively small but too large to accommodate exhaustive testing. The orthogonal array testing method is particularly useful in finding *region faults*—an error category associated with faulty logic within a software component.

To illustrate the difference between orthogonal array testing and more conventional "one input item at a time" approaches, consider a system that has three input items, X, Y, and Z. Each of these input items has three discrete values associated with it. There are $3^3 = 27$ possible test cases. Phadke [Pha97] suggests a geometric view of the possible test cases associated with X, Y, and Z illustrated in Figure 18.9. Referring to the figure, one input item at a time may be varied in sequence along each input axis. This results in relatively limited coverage of the input domain (represented by the left-hand cube in the figure).

When orthogonal array testing occurs, an L9 *orthogonal array* of test cases is created. The L9 orthogonal array has a "balancing property" [Pha97]. That is, test cases (represented by dark dots in the figure) are "dispersed uniformly throughout the test domain," as illustrated in the right-hand cube in Figure 18.9. Test coverage across the input domain is more complete.

FIGURE 18.9

A geometric view of test cases
Source: [Pha97]

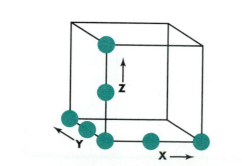

One input item at a time

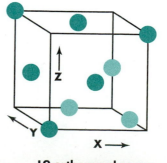

L9 orthogonal array

To illustrate the use of the L9 orthogonal array, consider the *send* function for a fax application. Four parameters, P1, P2, P3, and P4, are passed to the *send* function. Each takes on three discrete values. For example, P1 takes on values:

P1 = 1, send it now
P1 = 2, send it one hour later
P1 = 3, send it after midnight

P2, P3, and P4 would also take on values of 1, 2, and 3, signifying other send functions.

If a "one input item at a time" testing strategy were chosen, the following sequence of tests (P1, P2, P3, P4) would be specified: (1, 1, 1, 1), (2, 1, 1, 1), (3, 1, 1, 1), (1, 2, 1, 1), (1, 3, 1, 1), (1, 1, 2, 1), (1, 1, 3, 1), (1, 1, 1, 2), and (1, 1, 1, 3). Phadke [Pha97] assesses these test cases by stating:

> Such test cases are useful only when one is certain that these test parameters do not interact. They can detect logic faults where a single parameter value makes the software malfunction. These faults are called *single mode faults*. This method cannot detect logic faults that cause malfunction when two or more parameters simultaneously take certain values; that is, it cannot detect any interactions. Thus its ability to detect faults is limited.

Given the relatively small number of input parameters and discrete values, exhaustive testing is possible. The number of tests required is $3^4 = 81$, large but manageable. All faults associated with data item permutation would be found, but the effort required is relatively high.

The orthogonal array testing approach enables you to provide good test coverage with far fewer test cases than the exhaustive strategy. An L9 orthogonal array for the fax *send* function is illustrated in Figure 18.10.

FIGURE 18.10

An L9 orthogonal array

Test case	Test parameters			
	P1	P2	P3	P4
1	1	1	1	1
2	1	2	2	2
3	1	3	3	3
4	2	1	2	3
5	2	2	3	1
6	2	3	1	2
7	3	1	3	2
8	3	2	1	3
9	3	3	2	1

Phadke [Pha97] assesses the result of tests using the L9 orthogonal array in the following manner:

Detect and isolate all single mode faults. A single mode fault is a consistent problem with any level of any single parameter. For example, if all test cases of factor P1 = 1 cause an error condition, it is a single mode failure. In this example tests 1, 2 and 3 [Figure 18.10] will show errors. By analyzing the information about which tests show errors, one can identify which parameter values cause the fault. In this example, by noting that tests 1, 2, and 3 cause an error, one can isolate [logical processing associated with "send it now" (P1 = 1)] as the source of the error. Such an isolation of fault is important to fix the fault.

Detect all double mode faults. If there exists a consistent problem when specific levels of two parameters occur together, it is called a *double mode fault*. Indeed, a double mode fault is an indication of pairwise incompatibility or harmful interactions between two test parameters.

Multimode faults. Orthogonal arrays [of the type shown] can assure the detection of only single and double mode faults. However, many multimode faults are also detected by these tests.

You can find a detailed discussion of orthogonal array testing in [Pha89].

Test-Case Design

Objective: To assist the software team in developing a complete set of test cases for both black-box and white-box testing.

Mechanics: These tools fall into two broad categories: static testing tools and dynamic testing tools. Three different types of static testing tools are used in the industry: code-based testing tools, specialized testing languages, and requirements-based testing tools. Code-based testing tools accept source code as input and perform a number of analyses that result in the generation of test cases. Specialized testing languages (e.g., ATLAS) enable a software engineer to write detailed test specifications that describe each test case and the logistics for its execution. Requirements-based testing tools isolate specific user requirements and suggest test cases (or classes of tests) that will exercise the requirements. Dynamic testing tools interact with an executing program, checking path coverage, testing assertions about the value of specific variables, and otherwise instrumenting the execution flow of the program.

Representative Tools:[6]

McCabeTest, developed by McCabe & Associates (**www.mccabe.com**), implements a variety of path testing techniques derived from an assessment of cyclomatic complexity and other software metrics.

TestWorks, developed by Software Research, Inc. (**www.soft.com/Products**), is a complete set of automated testing tools that assists in the design of tests cases for software developed in C/C++ and Java and provides support for regression testing.

T-VEC Test Generation System, developed by T-VEC Technologies (**www.t-vec.com**), is a tool set that supports unit, integration, and validation testing by assisting in the design of test cases using information contained in an OO requirements specification.

e-TEST Suite, developed by Empirix, Inc. (**www.empirix .com**), encompasses a complete set of tools for testing WebApps, including tools that assist test-case design and test planning.

---

6   Tools noted here do not represent an endorsement, but rather a sampling of tools in this category. In most cases, tool names are trademarked by their respective developers.

18.7   MODEL-BASED TESTING

Model-based testing (MBT) is a black-box testing technique that uses information contained in the requirements model as the basis for the generation of test cases. In many cases, the model-based testing technique uses UML state diagrams, an element of the behavioral model (Chapter 7), as the basis for the design of test cases.[7] The MBT technique requires five steps:

1. **Analyze an existing behavioral model for the software or create one.** Recall that a *behavioral model* indicates how software will respond to external events or stimuli. To create the model, you should perform the steps discussed in Chapter 7: (1) evaluate all use cases to fully understand the sequence of interaction within the system, (2) identify events that drive the interaction sequence and understand how these events relate to specific objects, (3) create a sequence for each use case, (4) build a UML state diagram for the system (e.g., see Figure 7.6), and (5) review the behavioral model to verify accuracy and consistency.

2. **Traverse the behavioral model and specify the inputs that will force the software to make the transition from state to state.** The inputs will trigger events that will cause the transition to occur.

3. **Review the behavioral model and note the expected outputs as the software makes the transition from state to state.** Recall that each state transition is triggered by an event and that as a consequence of the transition, some function is invoked and outputs are created. For each set of inputs (test cases) you specified in step 2, specify the expected outputs as they are characterized in the behavioral model. "A fundamental assumption of this testing is that there is some mechanism, a *test oracle*, that will determine whether or not the results of a test execution are correct" [DAC03]. In essence, a test oracle establishes the basis for any determination of the correctness of the output. In most cases, the oracle is the requirements model, but it could also be another document or application, data recorded elsewhere, or even a human expert.

4. **Execute the test cases.** Tests can be executed manually or a test script can be created and executed using a testing tool.

5. **Compare actual and expected results and take corrective action as required.**

MBT helps to uncover errors in software behavior, and as a consequence, it is extremely useful when testing event-driven applications.

---

7   Model-based testing can also be used when software requirements are represented with decision tables, grammars, or Markov chains [DAC03].

18.8   TESTING FOR SPECIALIZED ENVIRONMENTS, ARCHITECTURES, AND APPLICATIONS

Unique guidelines and approaches to testing are sometimes warranted when specialized environments, architectures, and applications are considered. Although the testing techniques discussed earlier in this chapter and in Chapters 19 and 20 can often be adapted to specialized situations, it's worth considering their unique needs individually.

18.8.1   Testing GUIs

Graphical user interfaces (GUIs) will present you with interesting testing challenges. Because reusable components are now a common part of GUI development environments, the creation of the user interface has become less time consuming and more precise (Chapter 11). But, at the same time, the complexity of GUIs has grown, leading to more difficulty in the design and execution of test cases.

Because many modern GUIs have the same look and feel, a series of standard tests can be derived. Finite-state modeling graphs may be used to derive a series of tests that address specific data and program objects that are relevant to the GUI. This model-based testing technique was discussed in Section 18.7.

Because of the large number of permutations associated with GUI operations, GUI testing should be approached using automated tools. A wide array of GUI testing tools has appeared on the market over the past few years.[8]

18.8.2   Testing of Client-Server Architectures

The distributed nature of client-server environments, the performance issues associated with transaction processing, the potential presence of a number of different hardware platforms, the complexities of network communication, the need to service multiple clients from a centralized (or in some cases, distributed) database, and the coordination requirements imposed on the server all combine to make testing of client-server architectures and the software that resides within them considerably more difficult than stand-alone applications. In fact, recent industry studies indicate a significant increase in testing time and cost when client-server environments are developed.

In general, the testing of client-server software occurs at three different levels: (1) Individual client applications are tested in a "disconnected" mode; the operation of the server and the underlying network are not considered. (2) The client software and associated server applications are tested in concert, but network operations are not explicitly exercised. (3) The complete client-server architecture, including network operation and performance, is tested.

8   Hundreds, if not thousands, of GUI testing tool resources can be evaluated on the Web. A good starting point for open-source tools is **www.opensourcetesting.org/functional.php**.

Although many different types of tests are conducted at each of these levels of detail, the following testing approaches are commonly encountered for client-server applications:

What types of tests are conducted for client-server systems?

- **Application function tests.** The functionality of client applications is tested using the methods discussed earlier in this chapter and in Chapters 19 and 20. In essence, the application is tested in stand-alone fashion in an attempt to uncover errors in its operation.

- **Server tests.** The coordination and data management functions of the server are tested. Server performance (overall response time and data throughput) is also considered.

- **Database tests.** The accuracy and integrity of data stored by the server is tested. Transactions posted by client applications are examined to ensure that data are properly stored, updated, and retrieved. Archiving is also tested.

- **Transaction tests.** A series of tests are created to ensure that each class of transactions is processed according to requirements. Tests focus on the correctness of processing and also on performance issues (e.g., transaction processing times and transaction volume).

- **Network communication tests.** These tests verify that communication among the nodes of the network occurs correctly and that message passing, transactions, and related network traffic occur without error. Network security tests may also be conducted as part of these tests.

To accomplish these testing approaches, Musa [Mus93] recommends the development of *operational profiles* derived from client-server usage scenarios.[9] An operational profile indicates how different types of users interoperate with the client-server system. That is, the profiles provide a "pattern of usage" that can be applied when tests are designed and executed. For example, for a particular type of user, what percentage of transactions will be inquiries? updates? orders?

To develop the operational profile, it is necessary to derive a set of scenarios that are similar to use cases (Chapters 5 and 6). Each scenario addresses who, where, what, and why. That is, who the user is, where (in the physical client-server architecture) the system interaction occurs, what the transaction is, and why it has occurred. Scenarios can be derived using requirements elicitation techniques (Chapter 5) or through less formal discussions with end users. The result, however, should be the same. Each scenario should provide an indication of the system functions that will be required to service a particular user, the order in which those functions are required, the timing and response that is expected, and the frequency with which each function is used. These data are then combined (for all users) to create the operational profile. In general, testing effort and the number of test cases to be executed are

---

9   It should be noted that operational profiles can be used in testing for all types of system architectures, not just client-server architecture.

allocated to each usage scenario based on frequency of usage and criticality of the functions performed.

18.8.3 Testing Documentation and Help Facilities

The term *software testing* conjures images of large numbers of test cases prepared to exercise computer programs and the data that they manipulate. Recalling the definition of software presented in Chapter 1, it is important to note that testing must also extend to the third element of the software configuration—documentation.

Errors in documentation can be as devastating to the acceptance of the program as errors in data or source code. Nothing is more frustrating than following a user guide or an online help facility exactly and getting results or behaviors that do not coincide with those predicted by the documentation. It is for this reason that that documentation testing should be a meaningful part of every software test plan.

Documentation testing can be approached in two phases. The first phase, technical review (Chapter 15), examines the document for editorial clarity. The second phase, live test, uses the documentation in conjunction with the actual program.

Surprisingly, a live test for documentation can be approached using techniques that are analogous to many of the black-box testing methods discussed earlier. Graph-based testing can be used to describe the use of the program; equivalence partitioning and boundary value analysis can be used to define various classes of input and associated interactions. MBT can be used to ensure that documented behavior and actual behavior coincide. Program usage is then tracked through the documentation.

18.8.4 Testing for Real-Time Systems

The time-dependent, asynchronous nature of many real-time applications adds a new and potentially difficult element to the testing mix—time. Not only does the test-case designer have to consider conventional test cases but also event handling (i.e., interrupt processing), the timing of the data, and the parallelism of the tasks (processes) that handle the data. In many situations, test data provided when a real-time system is in one state will result in proper processing, while the same data provided when the system is in a different state may lead to error.

For example, the real-time software that controls a new photocopier accepts operator interrupts (i.e., the machine operator hits control keys such as RESET or DARKEN) with no error when the machine is making copies (in the "copying" state). These same operator interrupts, if input when the machine is in the "jammed" state, cause a display of the diagnostic code indicating the location of the jam to be lost (an error).

In addition, the intimate relationship that exists between real-time software and its hardware environment can also cause testing problems. Software tests must consider the impact of hardware faults on software processing. Such faults can be extremely difficult to simulate realistically.

Comprehensive test-case design methods for real-time systems continue to evolve. However, an overall four-step strategy can be proposed:

> **?** **What is an effective strategy for testing a real-time system?**

- **Task testing.** The first step in the testing of real-time software is to test each task independently. That is, conventional tests are designed for each task and executed independently during these tests. Task testing uncovers errors in logic and function but not timing or behavior.

- **Behavioral testing.** Using system models created with automated tools, it is possible to simulate the behavior of a real-time system and examine its behavior as a consequence of external events. These analysis activities can serve as the basis for the design of test cases that are conducted when the real-time software has been built. Using a technique that is similar to equivalence partitioning (Section 18.6.2), events (e.g., interrupts, control signals) are categorized for testing. For example, events for the photocopier might be user interrupts (e.g., reset counter), mechanical interrupts (e.g., paper jammed), system interrupts (e.g., toner low), and failure modes (e.g., roller overheated). Each of these events is tested individually, and the behavior of the executable system is examined to detect errors that occur as a consequence of processing associated with these events. The behavior of the system model (developed during the analysis activity) and the executable software can be compared for conformance. Once each class of events has been tested, events are presented to the system in random order and with random frequency. The behavior of the software is examined to detect behavior errors.

- **Intertask testing.** Once errors in individual tasks and in system behavior have been isolated, testing shifts to time-related errors. Asynchronous tasks that are known to communicate with one another are tested with different data rates and processing load to determine if intertask synchronization errors will occur. In addition, tasks that communicate via a message queue or data store are tested to uncover errors in the sizing of these data storage areas.

- **System testing.** Software and hardware are integrated, and a full range of system tests are conducted in an attempt to uncover errors at the software-hardware interface. Most real-time systems process interrupts. Therefore, testing the handling of these Boolean events is essential. Using the state diagram (Chapter 7), the tester develops a list of all possible interrupts and the processing that occurs as a consequence of the interrupts. Tests are then designed to assess the following system characteristics:

  - Are interrupt priorities properly assigned and properly handled?
  - Is processing for each interrupt handled correctly?
  - Does the performance (e.g., processing time) of each interrupt-handling procedure conform to requirements?
  - Does a high volume of interrupts arriving at critical times create problems in function or performance?

In addition, global data areas that are used to transfer information as part of interrupt processing should be tested to assess the potential for the generation of side effects.

18.9 PATTERNS FOR SOFTWARE TESTING

WebRef

A software testing patterns catalog can be found at **www.rbsc .com/pages/ TestPatternList.htm**.

The use of patterns as a mechanism for describing solutions to specific design problems was discussed in Chapter 12. But patterns can also be used to propose solutions to other software engineering situations—in this case, software testing. *Testing patterns* describe common testing problems and solutions that can assist you in dealing with them.

Not only do testing patterns provide you with useful guidance as testing activities commence, they also provide three additional benefits described by Marick [Mar02]:

1. They [patterns] provide a vocabulary for problem-solvers. "Hey, you know, we should use a Null Object."

2. They focus attention on the forces behind a problem. That allows [test case] designers to better understand when and why a solution applies.

3. They encourage iterative thinking. Each solution creates a new context in which new problems can be solved.

POINT

Testing patterns can help a software team communicate more effectively about testing and better understand the forces that lead to a specific testing approach.

Although these benefits are "soft," they should not be overlooked. Much of software testing, even during the past decade, has been an ad hoc activity. If testing patterns can help a software team to communicate about testing more effectively;

to understand the motivating forces that lead to a specific approach to testing, and to approach the design of tests as an evolutionary activity in which each iteration results in a more complete suite of test cases, then patterns have accomplished much.

Testing patterns are described in much the same way as design patterns (Chapter 12). Dozens of testing patterns have been proposed in the literature (e.g., [Mar02]). The following three testing patterns (presented in abstract form only) provide representative examples:

Pattern name: **PairTesting**

Abstract: A process-oriented pattern, **PairTesting** describes a technique that is analogous to pair programming (Chapter 3) in which two testers work together to design and execute a series of tests that can be applied to unit, integration or validation testing activities.

Pattern name: **SeparateTestInterface**

Abstract: There is a need to test every class in an object-oriented system, including "internal classes" (i.e., classes that do not expose any interface outside of the component that used them). The **SeparateTestInterface** pattern describes how to create "a test interface that can be used to describe specific tests on classes that are visible only internally to a component" [Lan01].

Pattern name: **ScenarioTesting**

Abstract: Once unit and integration tests have been conducted, there is a need to determine whether the software will perform in a manner that satisfies users. The **ScenarioTesting** pattern describes a technique for exercising the software from the user's point of view. A failure at this level indicates that the software has failed to meet a user visible requirement [Kan01].

A comprehensive discussion of testing patterns is beyond the scope of this book. If you have further interest, see [Bin99] and [Mar02] for additional information on this important topic.

18.10 SUMMARY

The primary objective for test-case design is to derive a set of tests that have the highest likelihood for uncovering errors in software. To accomplish this objective, two different categories of test-case design techniques are used: white-box testing and black-box testing.

White-box tests focus on the program control structure. Test cases are derived to ensure that all statements in the program have been executed at least once during testing and that all logical conditions have been exercised. Basis path testing, a white-box technique, makes use of program graphs (or graph matrices) to derive the set of linearly independent tests that will ensure statement coverage. Condition and data flow testing further exercise program logic, and loop testing complements other white-box techniques by providing a procedure for exercising loops of varying degrees of complexity.

Hetzel [Het84] describes white-box testing as "testing in the small." His implication is that the white-box tests that have been considered in this chapter are typically applied to small program components (e.g., modules or small groups of modules). Black-box testing, on the other hand, broadens your focus and might be called "testing in the large."

Black-box tests are designed to validate functional requirements without regard to the internal workings of a program. Black-box testing techniques focus on the information domain of the software, deriving test cases by partitioning the input and output domain of a program in a manner that provides thorough test coverage. Equivalence partitioning divides the input domain into classes of data that are likely to exercise a specific software function. Boundary value analysis probes the program's ability to handle data at the limits of acceptability. Orthogonal array testing provides an efficient, systematic method for testing systems with small numbers of input parameters. Model-based testing uses elements of the requirements model to test the behavior of an application.

Specialized testing methods encompass a broad array of software capabilities and application areas. Testing for graphical user interfaces, client-server architectures, documentation and help facilities, and real-time systems each require specialized guidelines and techniques.

Experienced software developers often say, "Testing never ends, it just gets transferred from you [the software engineer] to your customer. Every time your customer uses the program, a test is being conducted." By applying test-case design, you can achieve more complete testing and thereby uncover and correct the highest number of errors before the "customer's tests" begin.

PROBLEMS AND POINTS TO PONDER

18.1. Myers [Mye79] uses the following program as a self-assessment for your ability to specify adequate testing: A program reads three integer values. The three values are interpreted as representing the lengths of the sides of a triangle. The program prints a message that states whether the triangle is scalene, isosceles, or equilateral. Develop a set of test cases that you feel will adequately test this program.

18.2. Design and implement the program (with error handling where appropriate) specified in Problem 18.1. Derive a flow graph for the program and apply basis path testing to develop test cases that will guarantee that all statements in the program have been tested. Execute the cases and show your results.

18.3. Can you think of any additional testing objectives that are not discussed in Section 18.1.1?

18.4. Select a software component that you have designed and implemented recently. Design a set of test cases that will ensure that all statements have been executed using basis path testing.

18.5. Specify, design, and implement a software tool that will compute the cyclomatic complexity for the programming language of your choice. Use the graph matrix as the operative data structure in your design.

18.6. Read Beizer [Bei95] or a related Web-based source (e.g., **www.laynetworks.com/ Discrete%20Mathematics_1g.htm**) and determine how the program you have developed in Problem 18.5 can be extended to accommodate various link weights. Extend your tool to process execution probabilities or link processing times.

18.7. Design an automated tool that will recognize loops and categorize them as indicated in Section 18.5.3.

18.8. Extend the tool described in Problem 18.7 to generate test cases for each loop category, once encountered. It will be necessary to perform this function interactively with the tester.

18.9. Give at least three examples in which black-box testing might give the impression that "everything's OK," while white-box tests might uncover an error. Give at least three examples in which white-box testing might give the impression that "everything's OK," while black-box tests might uncover an error.

18.10. Will exhaustive testing (even if it is possible for very small programs) guarantee that the program is 100 percent correct?

18.11. Test a user manual (or help facility) for an application that you use frequently. Find at least one error in the documentation.

FURTHER READINGS AND INFORMATION SOURCES

Virtually all books dedicated to software testing consider both strategy and tactics. Therefore, further readings noted for Chapter 17 are equally applicable for this chapter. Everett and Raymond (*Software Testing,* Wiley-IEEE Computer Society Press, 2007), Black (*Pragmatic Software Testing,* Wiley, 2007), Spiller and his colleagues (*Software Testing Process: Test Management,* Rocky Nook, 2007), Perry (*Effective Methods for Software Testing,* 3d ed., Wiley, 2005), Lewis (*Software Testing and Continuous Quality Improvement,* 2d ed., Auerbach, 2004), Loveland and his colleagues (*Software Testing Techniques,* Charles River Media, 2004), Burnstein (*Practical Software Testing,* Springer, 2003), Dustin (*Effective Software Testing,* Addison-Wesley, 2002), Craig and Kaskiel (*Systematic Software Testing,* Artech House, 2002), Tamres (*Introducing Software Testing,* Addison-Wesley, 2002), and Whittaker (*How to Break Software,* Addison-Wesley, 2002) are only a small sampling of many books that discuss testing principles, concepts, strategies, and methods.

A second edition of Myers [Mye79] classic text has been produced by Myers and his colleagues (*The Art of Software Testing,* 2d ed., Wiley, 2004) and covers test-case design techniques in considerable detail. Pezze and Young (*Software Testing and Analysis,* Wiley, 2007), Perry (*Effective Methods for Software Testing,* 3d ed., Wiley, 2006), Copeland (*A Practitioner's Guide to Software Test Design,* Artech, 2003), Hutcheson (*Software Testing Fundamentals,* Wiley, 2003), Jorgensen (*Software Testing: A Craftsman's Approach,* 2d ed., CRC Press, 2002) each provide useful presentations of test-case design methods and techniques. Beizer's [Bei90] classic text provides comprehensive coverage of white-box techniques, introducing a level of mathematical rigor that has often been missing in other treatments of testing. His later book [Bei95] presents a concise treatment of important methods.

Software testing is a resource-intensive activity. It is for this reason that many organizations automate parts of the testing process. Books by Li and Wu (*Effective Software Test Automation,* Sybex, 2004); Mosely and Posey (*Just Enough Software Test Automation,* Prentice-Hall, 2002); Dustin, Rashka, and Poston (*Automated Software Testing: Introduction, Management, and Performance,* Addison-Wesley, 1999); Graham and her colleagues (*Software Test Automation,* Addison-Wesley, 1999); and Poston (*Automating Specification-Based Software Testing,* IEEE Computer Society, 1996) discuss tools, strategies, and methods for automated testing. Nquyen and his colleagues (*Global Software Test Automation,* Happy About Press, 2006) present an executive overview of testing automation.

Thomas and his colleagues (*Java Testing Patterns,* Wiley, 2004) and Binder [Bin99] describe testing patterns that cover testing of methods, classes/clusters, subsystems, reusable components, frameworks, and systems as well as test automation and specialized database testing.

A wide variety of information sources on test-case design methods is available on the Internet. An up-to-date list of World Wide Web references that are relevant to testing techniques can be found at the SEPA website: **www.mhhe.com/engcs/compsci/pressman/professional/ olc/ser.htm**.

TESTING OBJECT-ORIENTED APPLICATIONS

In Chapter 18, I noted that the objective of testing, stated simply, is to find the greatest possible number of errors with a manageable amount of effort applied over a realistic time span. Although this fundamental objective remains unchanged for object-oriented software, the nature of OO programs changes both testing strategy and testing tactics.

It could be argued that as reusable class libraries grow in size, greater reuse will mitigate the need for heavy testing of OO systems. Exactly the opposite is true. Binder [Bin94b] discusses this when he states:

> [E]ach reuse is a new context of usage and retesting is prudent. It seems likely that more, not less testing will be needed to obtain high reliability in object-oriented systems.

QUICK LOOK

What is it? The architecture of object-oriented (OO) software results in a series of layered subsystems that encapsulate collaborating classes. Each of these system elements (subsystems and classes) performs functions that help to achieve system requirements. It is necessary to test an OO system at a variety of different levels in an effort to uncover errors that may occur as classes collaborate with one another and subsystems communicate across architectural layers.

Who does it? Object-oriented testing is performed by software engineers and testing specialists.

Why is it important? You have to execute the program before it gets to the customer with the specific intent of removing all errors, so that the customer will not experience the frustration associated with a poor-quality product. In order to find the highest possible number of errors, tests must be conducted systematically and test cases must be designed using disciplined techniques.

What are the steps? OO testing is strategically analogous to the testing of conventional systems, but it is tactically different. Because the OO analysis and design models are similar in structure and content to the resultant OO program, "testing" is initiated with the review of these models. Once code has been generated, OO testing begins "in the small" with class testing. A series of tests are designed that exercise class operations and examine whether errors exist as one class collaborates with other classes. As classes are integrated to form a subsystem, thread-based, use-based, and cluster testing along with fault-based approaches are applied to fully exercise collaborating classes. Finally, use cases (developed as part of the requirements model) are used to uncover errors at the software validation level.

What is the work product? A set of test cases, designed to exercise classes, their collaborations, and behaviors is designed and documented; expected results are defined, and actual results are recorded.

How do I ensure that I've done it right? When you begin testing, change your point of view. Try hard to "break" the software! Design test cases in a disciplined fashion, and review the tests cases you do create for thoroughness.

To adequately test OO systems, three things must be done: (1) the definition of testing must be broadened to include error discovery techniques applied to object-oriented analysis and design models, (2) the strategy for unit and integration testing must change significantly, and (3) the design of test cases must account for the unique characteristics of OO software.

19.1   BROADENING THE VIEW OF TESTING

The construction of object-oriented software begins with the creation of requirements (analysis) and design models.[1] Because of the evolutionary nature of the OO software engineering paradigm, these models begin as relatively informal representations of system requirements and evolve into detailed models of classes, class relationships, system design and allocation, and object design (incorporating a model of object connectivity via messaging). At each stage, the models can be "tested" in an attempt to uncover errors prior to their propagation to the next iteration.

It can be argued that the review of OO analysis and design models is especially useful because the same semantic constructs (e.g., classes, attributes, operations, messages) appear at the analysis, design, and code levels. Therefore, a problem in the definition of class attributes that is uncovered during analysis will circumvent side effects that might occur if the problem were not discovered until design or code (or even the next iteration of analysis).

Although the review of the OO analysis and design models is an integral part of "testing" an OO application, recognize that it is not sufficient in and of itself. You must conduct executable tests as well.

For example, consider a class in which a number of attributes are defined during the first iteration of analysis. An extraneous attribute is appended to the class (due to a misunderstanding of the problem domain). Two operations are then specified to manipulate the attribute. A review is conducted and a domain expert points out the problem. By eliminating the extraneous attribute at this stage, the following problems and unnecessary effort may be avoided during analysis:

1. Special subclasses may have been generated to accommodate the unnecessary attribute or exceptions to it. Work involved in the creation of unnecessary subclasses has been avoided.

2. A misinterpretation of the class definition may lead to incorrect or extraneous class relationships.

3. The behavior of the system or its classes may be improperly characterized to accommodate the extraneous attribute.

If the problem is not uncovered during analysis and propagated further, the following problems could occur (and will have been avoided because of the earlier review) during design:

1. Improper allocation of the class to subsystem and/or tasks may occur during system design.

---

1   Analysis and design modeling techniques are presented in Part 2 of this book. Basic OO concepts are presented in Appendix 2.

2. Unnecessary design work may be expended to create the procedural design for the operations that address the extraneous attribute.

3. The messaging model will be incorrect (because messages must be designed for the operations that are extraneous).

If the problem remains undetected during design and passes into the coding activity, considerable effort will be expended to generate code that implements an unnecessary attribute, two unnecessary operations, messages that drive interobject communication, and many other related issues. In addition, testing of the class will absorb more time than necessary. Once the problem is finally uncovered, modification of the system must be carried out with the ever-present potential for side effects that are caused by change.

During latter stages of their development, object-oriented analysis (OOA) and design (OOD) models provide substantial information about the structure and behavior of the system. For this reason, these models should be subjected to rigorous review prior to the generation of code.

All object-oriented models should be tested (in this context, the term *testing* incorporates technical reviews) for correctness, completeness, and consistency within the context of the model's syntax, semantics, and pragmatics [Lin94a].

19.2   TESTING OOA AND OOD MODELS

Analysis and design models cannot be tested in the conventional sense, because they cannot be executed. However, technical reviews (Chapter 15) can be used to examine their correctness and consistency.

19.2.1   Correctness of OOA and OOD Models

The notation and syntax used to represent analysis and design models will be tied to the specific analysis and design methods that are chosen for the project. Hence syntactic correctness is judged on proper use of the symbology; each model is reviewed to ensure that proper modeling conventions have been maintained.

During analysis and design, you can assess semantic correctness based on the model's conformance to the real-world problem domain. If the model accurately reflects the real world (to a level of detail that is appropriate to the stage of development at which the model is reviewed), then it is semantically correct. To determine whether the model does, in fact, reflect real-world requirements, it should be presented to problem domain experts who will examine the class definitions and hierarchy for omissions and ambiguity. Class relationships (instance connections) are evaluated to determine whether they accurately reflect real-world object connections.[2]

---

2   Use cases can be invaluable in tracking analysis and design models against real-world usage scenarios for the OO system.

19.2.2   Consistency of Object-Oriented Models

The consistency of object-oriented models may be judged by "considering the relationships among entities in the model. An inconsistent analysis or design model has representations in one part that are not correctly reflected in other portions of the model" [McG94].

To assess consistency, you should examine each class and its connections to other classes. The class-responsibility-collaboration (CRC) model or an object-relationship diagram can be used to facilitate this activity. As you learned in Chapter 6, the CRC model is composed of CRC index cards. Each CRC card lists the class name, its responsibilities (operations), and its collaborators (other classes to which it sends messages and on which it depends for the accomplishment of its responsibilities). The collaborations imply a series of relationships (i.e., connections) between classes of the OO system. The object relationship model provides a graphic representation of the connections between classes. All of this information can be obtained from the analysis model (Chapters 6 and 7).

To evaluate the class model the following steps have been recommended [McG94]:

1. **Revisit the CRC model and the object-relationship model.** Cross-check to ensure that all collaborations implied by the requirements model are properly reflected in the both.

2. **Inspect the description of each CRC index card to determine if a delegated responsibility is part of the collaborator's definition.** For example, consider a class defined for a point-of-sale checkout system and called **CreditSale.** This class has a CRC index card as illustrated in Figure 19.1.

FIGURE 19.1

An example CRC index card used for review

class name: credit sale	
class type: transaction event	
class characteristics: nontangible, atomic, sequential, permanent, guarded	
responsibilities:	collaborators:
read credit card	credit card
get authorization	credit authority
post purchase amount	product ticket
	sales ledger
	audit file
generate bill	bill

For this collection of classes and collaborations, ask whether a responsibility (e.g., *read credit card*) is accomplished if delegated to the named collaborator (**CreditCard**). That is, does the class **CreditCard** have an operation that enables it to be read? In this case the answer is "yes." The object-relationship is traversed to ensure that all such connections are valid.

3. **Invert the connection to ensure that each collaborator that is asked for service is receiving requests from a reasonable source.** For example, if the **CreditCard** class receives a request for purchase amount from the **CreditSale** class, there would be a problem. **CreditCard** does not know the purchase amount.

4. **Using the inverted connections examined in step 3, determine whether other classes might be required or whether responsibilities are properly grouped among the classes.**

5. **Determine whether widely requested responsibilities might be combined into a single responsibility.** For example, *read credit card* and *get authorization* occur in every situation. They might be combined into a *validate credit request* responsibility that incorporates getting the credit card number and gaining authorization.

You should apply steps 1 through 5 iteratively to each class and through each evolution of the requirements model.

Once the design model (Chapters 9 through 11) is created, you should also conduct reviews of the system design and the object design. The system design depicts the overall product architecture, the subsystems that compose the product, the manner in which subsystems are allocated to processors, the allocation of classes to subsystems, and the design of the user interface. The object model presents the details of each class and the messaging activities that are necessary to implement collaborations between classes.

The system design is reviewed by examining the object-behavior model developed during object-oriented analysis and mapping required system behavior against the subsystems designed to accomplish this behavior. Concurrency and task allocation are also reviewed within the context of system behavior. The behavioral states of the system are evaluated to determine which exist concurrently. Use cases are used to exercise the user interface design.

The object model should be tested against the object-relationship network to ensure that all design objects contain the necessary attributes and operations to implement the collaborations defined for each CRC index card. In addition, the detailed specification of operation details (i.e., the algorithms that implement the operations) is reviewed.

19.3   OBJECT-ORIENTED TESTING STRATEGIES

As I noted in Chapter 18, the classical software testing strategy begins with "testing in the small" and works outward toward "testing in the large." Stated in the jargon of software testing (Chapter 18), you begin with *unit testing,* then progress toward *integration testing,* and culminate with *validation and system testing.* In conventional applications, unit testing focuses on the smallest compilable program unit—the subprogram (e.g., component, module, subroutine, procedure). Once each of these units has been testing individually, it is integrated into a program structure while a series of regression tests are run to uncover errors due to interfacing the modules and side effects that are caused by the addition of new units. Finally, the system as a whole is tested to ensure that errors in requirements are uncovered.

19.3.1   Unit Testing in the OO Context

POINT

The smallest testable "unit" in OO software is the class. Class testing is driven by the operations encapsulated by the class and the state behavior of the class.

When object-oriented software is considered, the concept of the unit changes. Encapsulation drives the definition of classes and objects. This means that each class and each instance of a class (object) packages attributes (data) and the operations (also known as methods or services) that manipulate these data. Rather than testing an individual module, the smallest testable unit is the encapsulated class. Because a class can contain a number of different operations and a particular operation may exist as part of a number of different classes, the meaning of unit testing changes dramatically.

We can no longer test a single operation in isolation (the conventional view of unit testing) but rather, as part of a class. To illustrate, consider a class hierarchy in which an operation $X()$ is defined for the superclass and is inherited by a number of subclasses. Each subclass uses operation $X()$, but it is applied within the context of the private attributes and operations that have been defined for each subclass. Because the context in which operation $X()$ is used varies in subtle ways, it is necessary to test operation $X()$ in the context of each of the subclasses. This means that testing operation $X()$ in a vacuum (the traditional unit-testing approach) is ineffective in the object-oriented context.

Class testing for OO software is the equivalent of unit testing for conventional software.[3] Unlike unit testing of conventional software, which tends to focus on the algorithmic detail of a module and the data that flows across the module interface, class testing for OO software is driven by the operations encapsulated by the class and the state behavior of the class.

19.3.2   Integration Testing in the OO Context

Because object-oriented software does not have a hierarchical control structure, conventional top-down and bottom-up integration strategies have little meaning.

---

3   Test-case design methods for OO classes are discussed in Sections 19.4 through 19.6.

In addition, integrating operations one at a time into a class (the conventional incremental integration approach) is often impossible because of the "direct and indirect interactions of the components that make up the class" [Ber93].

There are two different strategies for integration testing of OO systems [Bin94a]. The first, *thread-based testing,* integrates the set of classes required to respond to one input or event for the system. Each thread is integrated and tested individually. Regression testing is applied to ensure that no side effects occur. The second integration approach, *use-based testing,* begins the construction of the system by testing those classes (called *independent classes*) that use very few (if any) of server classes. After the independent classes are tested, the next layer of classes, called *dependent classes,* that use the independent classes are tested. This sequence of testing layers of dependent classes continues until the entire system is constructed. Unlike conventional integration, the use of driver and stubs (Chapter 18) as replacement operations is to be avoided, when possible.

Cluster testing [McG94] is one step in the integration testing of OO software. Here, a cluster of collaborating classes (determined by examining the CRC and object-relationship model) is exercised by designing test cases that attempt to uncover errors in the collaborations.

19.3.3 Validation Testing in an OO Context

At the validation or system level, the details of class connections disappear. Like conventional validation, the validation of OO software focuses on user-visible actions and user-recognizable outputs from the system. To assist in the derivation of validation tests, the tester should draw upon use cases (Chapters 5 and 6) that are part of the requirements model. The use case provides a scenario that has a high likelihood of uncovered errors in user-interaction requirements.

Conventional black-box testing methods (Chapter 18) can be used to drive validation tests. In addition, you may choose to derive test cases from the object-behavior model and from an event flow diagram created as part of OOA.

19.4   OBJECT-ORIENTED TESTING METHODS

The architecture of object-oriented software results in a series of layered subsystems that encapsulate collaborating classes. Each of these system elements (subsystems and classes) performs functions that help to achieve system requirements. It is necessary to test an OO system at a variety of different levels in an effort to uncover errors that may occur as classes collaborate with one another and subsystems communicate across architectural layers.

Test-case design methods for object-oriented software continue to evolve. However, an overall approach to OO test-case design has been suggested by Berard [Ber93]:

1. Each test case should be uniquely identified and explicitly associated with the class to be tested.

KEY POINT

Integration testing for OO software tests a set of classes that are required to respond to a given event.

Quote:

"I see testers as the bodyguards of the project. We defend our developer's flank from failure, while they focus on creating success."

James Bach

2. The purpose of the test should be stated.

3. A list of testing steps should be developed for each test and should contain:

   a. A list of specified states for the class that is to be tested

   b. A list of messages and operations that will be exercised as a consequence of the test

   c. A list of exceptions that may occur as the class is tested

   d. A list of external conditions (i.e., changes in the environment external to the software that must exist in order to properly conduct the test)

   e. Supplementary information that will aid in understanding or implementing the test

Unlike conventional test-case design, which is driven by an input-process-output view of software or the algorithmic detail of individual modules, object-oriented testing focuses on designing appropriate sequences of operations to exercise the states of a class.

19.4.1 The Test-Case Design Implications of OO Concepts

WebRef

An excellent collection of papers and resources on OO testing can be found at **www.rbsc.com**.

As a class evolves through the requirements and design models, it becomes a target for test-case design. Because attributes and operations are encapsulated, testing operations outside of the class is generally unproductive. Although encapsulation is an essential design concept for OO, it can create a minor obstacle when testing. As Binder [Bin94a] notes, "Testing requires reporting on the concrete and abstract state of an object." Yet, encapsulation can make this information somewhat difficult to obtain. Unless built-in operations are provided to report the values for class attributes, a snapshot of the state of an object may be difficult to acquire.

Inheritance may also present you with additional challenges during test-case design. I have already noted that each new usage context requires retesting, even though reuse has been achieved. In addition, multiple inheritance[4] complicates testing further by increasing the number of contexts for which testing is required [Bin94a]. If subclasses instantiated from a superclass are used within the same problem domain, it is likely that the set of test cases derived for the superclass can be used when testing the subclass. However, if the subclass is used in an entirely different context, the superclass test cases will have little applicability and a new set of tests must be designed.

19.4.2 Applicability of Conventional Test-Case Design Methods

The white-box testing methods described in Chapter 18 can be applied to the operations defined for a class. Basis path, loop testing, or data flow techniques can help to ensure that every statement in an operation has been tested. However, the concise

---

4 An OO concept that should be used with extreme care.

structure of many class operations causes some to argue that the effort applied to white-box testing might be better redirected to tests at a class level.

Black-box testing methods are as appropriate for OO systems as they are for systems developed using conventional software engineering methods. As I noted in Chapter 18, use cases can provide useful input in the design of black-box and state-based tests.

19.4.3   Fault-Based Testing[5]

The object of *fault-based testing* within an OO system is to design tests that have a high likelihood of uncovering plausible faults. Because the product or system must conform to customer requirements, preliminary planning required to perform fault-based testing begins with the analysis model. The tester looks for plausible faults (i.e., aspects of the implementation of the system that may result in defects). To determine whether these faults exist, test cases are designed to exercise the design or code.

Of course, the effectiveness of these techniques depends on how testers perceive a plausible fault. If real faults in an OO system are perceived to be implausible, then this approach is really no better than any random testing technique. However, if the analysis and design models can provide insight into what is likely to go wrong, then fault-based testing can find significant numbers of errors with relatively low expenditures of effort.

What types of faults are encountered in operation calls and message connections?

Integration testing looks for plausible faults in operation calls or message connections. Three types of faults are encountered in this context: unexpected result, wrong operation/message used, and incorrect invocation. To determine plausible faults as functions (operations) are invoked, the behavior of the operation must be examined.

Integration testing applies to attributes as well as to operations. The "behaviors" of an object are defined by the values that its attributes are assigned. Testing should exercise the attributes to determine whether proper values occur for distinct types of object behavior.

It is important to note that integration testing attempts to find errors in the client object, not the server. Stated in conventional terms, the focus of integration testing is to determine whether errors exist in the calling code, not the called code. The operation call is used as a clue, a way to find test requirements that exercise the calling code.

19.4.4   Test Cases and the Class Hierarchy

Inheritance does not obviate the need for thorough testing of all derived classes. In fact, it can actually complicate the testing process. Consider the following situation. A class **Base** contains operations *inherited()* and *redefined()*. A class **Derived** redefines *redefined()* to serve in a local context. There is little doubt that **Derived::redefined()**

---

5   Sections 19.4.3 through 19.4.6 have been adapted from an article by Brian Marick posted on the Internet newsgroup comp.testing. This adaptation is included with the permission of the author. For further information on these topics, see [Mar94]. It should be noted that the techniques discussed in Sections 19.4.3 through 19.4.6 are also applicable for conventional software.

has to be tested because it represents a new design and new code. But does **Derived::inherited()** have to be retested?

If **Derived::inherited()** calls *redefined()* and the behavior of *redefined()* has changed, **Derived::inherited()** may mishandle the new behavior. Therefore, it needs new tests even though the design and code have not changed. It is important to note, however, that only a subset of all tests for **Derived::inherited()** may have to be conducted. If part of the design and code for *inherited()* does not depend on *redefined()* (i.e., that does not call it nor call any code that indirectly calls it), that code need not be retested in the derived class.

Base::redefined() and **Derived::redefined()** are two different operations with different specifications and implementations. Each would have a set of test requirements derived from the specification and implementation. Those test requirements probe for plausible faults: integration faults, condition faults, boundary faults, and so forth. But the operations are likely to be similar. Their sets of test requirements will overlap. The better the OO design, the greater is the overlap. New tests need to be derived only for those **Derived::redefined()** requirements that are not satisfied by the **Base::redefined()** tests.

To summarize, the **Base::redefined()** tests are applied to objects of class **Derived.** Test inputs may be appropriate for both base and derived classes, but the expected results may differ in the derived class.

KEY POINT

Even though a base class has been thoroughly tested, you will still have to test all classes derived from it.

19.4.5 Scenario-Based Test Design

Fault-based testing misses two main types of errors: (1) incorrect specifications and (2) interactions among subsystems. When errors associated with an incorrect specification occur, the product doesn't do what the customer wants. It might do the wrong thing or omit important functionality. But in either circumstance, quality (conformance to requirements) suffers. Errors associated with subsystem interaction occur when the behavior of one subsystem creates circumstances (e.g., events, data flow) that cause another subsystem to fail.

KEY POINT

Scenario-based testing will uncover errors that occur when any actor interacts with the software.

Scenario-based testing concentrates on what the user does, not what the product does. This means capturing the tasks (via use cases) that the user has to perform and then applying them and their variants as tests.

Scenarios uncover interaction errors. But to accomplish this, test cases must be more complex and more realistic than fault-based tests. Scenario-based testing tends to exercise multiple subsystems in a single test (users do not limit themselves to the use of one subsystem at a time).

As an example, consider the design of scenario-based tests for a text editor by reviewing the use cases that follow:

Use Case: Fix the Final Draft

Background: It's not unusual to print the "final" draft, read it, and discover some annoying errors that weren't obvious from the on-screen image. This use case describes the sequence of events that occurs when this happens.

1. Print the entire document.

2. Move around in the document, changing certain pages.

3. As each page is changed, it's printed.

4. Sometimes a series of pages is printed.

This scenario describes two things: a test and specific user needs. The user needs are obvious: (1) a method for printing single pages and (2) a method for printing a range of pages. As far as testing goes, there is a need to test editing after printing (as well as the reverse). Therefore, you work to design tests that will uncover errors in the editing function that were caused by the printing function; that is, errors that will indicate that the two software functions are not properly independent.

Use Case: Print a New Copy

Background: Someone asks the user for a fresh copy of the document. It must be printed.

1. Open the document.

2. Print it.

3. Close the document.

Again, the testing approach is relatively obvious. Except that this document didn't appear out of nowhere. It was created in an earlier task. Does that task affect this one?

In many modern editors, documents remember how they were last printed. By default, they print the same way next time. After the **Fix the Final Draft** scenario, just selecting "Print" in the menu and clicking the Print button in the dialog box will cause the last corrected page to print again. So, according to the editor, the correct scenario should look like this:

Use Case: Print a New Copy

1. Open the document.

2. Select "Print" in the menu.

3. Check if you're printing a page range; if so, click to print the entire document.

4. Click on the Print button.

5. Close the document.

But this scenario indicates a potential specification error. The editor does not do what the user reasonably expects it to do. Customers will often overlook the check noted in step 3. They will then be annoyed when they trot off to the printer and find one page when they wanted 100. Annoyed customers signal specification bugs.

You might miss this dependency as you design tests, but it is likely that the problem would surface during testing. You would then have to contend with the probable response, "That's the way it's supposed to work!"

19.4.6   Testing Surface Structure and Deep Structure

Surface structure refers to the externally observable structure of an OO program. That is, the structure that is immediately obvious to an end user. Rather than performing functions, the users of many OO systems may be given objects to manipulate in some way. But whatever the interface, tests are still based on user tasks. Capturing these tasks involves understanding, watching, and talking with representative users (and as many nonrepresentative users as are worth considering).

There will surely be some difference in detail. For example, in a conventional system with a command-oriented interface, the user might use the list of all commands as a testing checklist. If no test scenarios existed to exercise a command, testing has likely overlooked some user tasks (or the interface has useless commands). In an object-based interface, the tester might use the list of all objects as a testing checklist.

The best tests are derived when the designer looks at the system in a new or unconventional way. For example, if the system or product has a command-based interface, more thorough tests will be derived if the test-case designer pretends that operations are independent of objects. Ask questions like, "Might the user want to use this operation—which applies only to the **Scanner** object—while working with the printer?" Whatever the interface style, test-case design that exercises the surface structure should use both objects and operations as clues leading to overlooked tasks.

Deep structure refers to the internal technical details of an OO program, that is, the structure that is understood by examining the design and/or code. Deep structure testing is designed to exercise dependencies, behaviors, and communication mechanisms that have been established as part of the design model for OO software.

The requirements and design models are used as the basis for deep structure testing. For example, the UML collaboration diagram or the deployment model depicts collaborations between objects and subsystems that may not be externally visible. The test-case design then asks: "Have we captured (as a test) some task that exercises the collaboration noted on the collaboration diagram? If not, why not?"

KEY POINT

Testing surface structure is analogous to black-box testing. Deep structure testing is similar to white-box testing.

Quote:

"Be not ashamed of mistakes and thus make them crimes."

Confucius

19.5   TESTING METHODS APPLICABLE AT THE CLASS LEVEL

ADVICE

The number of possible permutations for random testing can grow quite large. A strategy similar to orthogonal array testing can be used to improve testing efficiency.

Testing "in the small" focuses on a single class and the methods that are encapsulated by the class. Random testing and partitioning are methods that can be used to exercise a class during OO testing.

19.5.1   Random Testing for OO Classes

To provide brief illustrations of these methods, consider a banking application in which an **Account** class has the following operations: *open(), setup(), deposit(), withdraw(), balance(), summarize(), creditLimit(),* and *close()* [Kir94]. Each of these operations may be applied for **Account,** but certain constraints (e.g., the account must be opened before other operations can be applied and closed after all operations are completed) are implied by the nature of the problem. Even with these constraints, there are many permutations of the operations. The minimum behavioral life history of an instance of **Account** includes the following operations:

open • setup • deposit • withdraw • close

This represents the minimum test sequence for account. However, a wide variety of other behaviors may occur within this sequence:

open • setup • deposit • [deposit | withdraw | balance | summarize | creditLimit]^n • withdraw • close

A variety of different operation sequences can be generated randomly. For example:

Test case r_1: open • setup • deposit • deposit • balance • summarize • withdraw • close

Test case r_2: open • setup • deposit • withdraw • deposit • balance • creditLimit • withdraw • close

These and other random order tests are conducted to exercise different class instance life histories.

19.5.2   Partition Testing at the Class Level

What testing options are available at the class level?

Partition testing reduces the number of test cases required to exercise the class in much the same manner as equivalence partitioning (Chapter 18) for traditional software. Input and output are categorized and test cases are designed to exercise each category. But how are the partitioning categories derived?

State-based partitioning categorizes class operations based on their ability to change the state of the class. Again considering the **Account** class, state operations include *deposit()* and *withdraw()*, whereas nonstate operations include *balance()*, *summarize()*, and *creditLimit()*. Tests are designed in a way that exercises operations that change state and those that do not change state separately. Therefore,

> *Test case p_1:* open • setup • deposit • deposit • withdraw • withdraw • close
>
> *Test case p_2:* open • setup • deposit • summarize • creditLimit • withdraw • close

Test case p_1 changes state, while test case p_2 exercises operations that do not change state (other than those in the minimum test sequence).

Attribute-based partitioning categorizes class operations based on the attributes that they use. For the **Account** class, the attributes **balance** and **creditLimit** can be used to define partitions. Operations are divided into three partitions: (1) operations that use **creditLimit,** (2) operations that modify **creditLimit,** and (3) operations that do not use or modify **creditLimit.** Test sequences are then designed for each partition.

Category-based partitioning categorizes class operations based on the generic function that each performs. For example, operations in the **Account** class can be categorized in initialization operations (*open, setup*), computational operations (*deposit, withdraw*), queries (*balance, summarize, creditLimit*), and termination operations (*close*).

19.6   INTERCLASS TEST-CASE DESIGN

uote:

"The boundary that defines the scope of unit and integration testing is different for object-oriented development. Tests can be designed and exercised at many points in the process. Thus 'design a little, code a little' becomes 'design a little, code a little, test a little.'"

Robert Binder

Test-case design becomes more complicated as integration of the object-oriented system begins. It is at this stage that testing of collaborations between classes must begin. To illustrate "interclass test-case generation" [Kir94], we expand the banking example introduced in Section 19.5 to include the classes and collaborations noted in Figure 19.2. The direction of the arrows in the figure indicates the direction of messages, and the labeling indicates the operations that are invoked as a consequence of the collaborations implied by the messages.

Like the testing of individual classes, class collaboration testing can be accomplished by applying random and partitioning methods, as well as scenario-based testing and behavioral testing.

19.6.1 Multiple Class Testing

Kirani and Tsai [Kir94] suggest the following sequence of steps to generate multiple class random test cases:

1. For each client class, use the list of class operations to generate a series of random test sequences. The operations will send messages to other server classes.

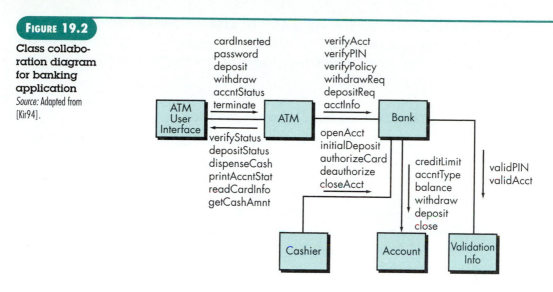

FIGURE 19.2

Class collaboration diagram for banking application

Source: Adapted from [Kir94].

2. For each message that is generated, determine the collaborator class and the corresponding operation in the server object.

3. For each operation in the server object (that has been invoked by messages sent from the client object), determine the messages that it transmits.

4. For each of the messages, determine the next level of operations that are invoked and incorporate these into the test sequence.

To illustrate [Kir94], consider a sequence of operations for the **Bank** class relative to an **ATM** class (Figure 19.2):

verifyAcct • verifyPIN • [[verifyPolicy • withdrawReq] | depositReq | acctInfoREQ]^n

A random test case for the **Bank** class might be

Test case r_3 = **verifyAcct • verifyPIN • depositReq**

In order to consider the collaborators involved in this test, the messages associated with each of the operations noted in test case r_3 are considered. **Bank** must collaborate with **ValidationInfo** to execute the *verifyAcct()* and *verifyPIN()*. **Bank** must collaborate with **Account** to execute *depositReq()*. Hence, a new test case that exercises these collaborations is

Test case r_4 = **verifyAcct [Bank:validAcctValidationInfo] • verifyPIN**
[Bank: validPinValidationInfo] • depositReq [Bank: depositaccount]

The approach for multiple class partition testing is similar to the approach used for partition testing of individual classes. A single class is partitioned as discussed in Section 19.5.2. However, the test sequence is expanded to include those operations that are invoked via messages to collaborating classes. An alternative approach partitions tests based on the interfaces to a particular class. Referring to Figure 19.2, the **Bank** class receives messages from the **ATM** and **Cashier** classes. The methods within **Bank** can therefore be tested by partitioning them into those that serve **ATM** and those that serve **Cashier.** State-based partitioning (Section 19.5.2) can be used to refine the partitions further.

19.6.2 Tests Derived from Behavior Models

The use of the state diagram as a model that represents the dynamic behavior of a class is discussed in Chapter 7. The state diagram for a class can be used to help derive a sequence of tests that will exercise the dynamic behavior of the class (and those classes that collaborate with it). Figure 19.3 [Kir94] illustrates a state diagram for the **Account** class discussed earlier. Referring to the figure, initial transitions move through the *empty acct* and *setup acct* states. The majority of all behavior for instances of the class occurs while in the *working acct* state. A final withdrawal and account closure cause the account class to make transitions to the *nonworking acct* and *dead acct* states, respectively.

The tests to be designed should achieve coverage of every state. That is, the operation sequences should cause the **Account** class to make transition through all allowable states:

Test case s_1: **open • setupAccnt • deposit (initial) • withdraw (final) • close**

It should be noted that this sequence is identical to the minimum test sequence discussed in Section 19.5.2. Adding additional test sequences to the minimum sequence,

Test case s_2: **open • setupAccnt • deposit(initial) • deposit • balance • credit • withdraw (final) • close**
Test case s_3: **open • setupAccnt • deposit(initial) • deposit • withdraw • accntInfo • withdraw (final) • close**

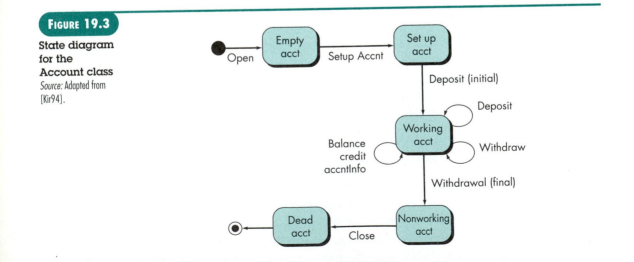

FIGURE 19.3

State diagram for the Account class
Source: Adapted from [Kir94].

Still more test cases could be derived to ensure that all behaviors for the class have been adequately exercised. In situations in which the class behavior results in a collaboration with one or more classes, multiple state diagrams are used to track the behavioral flow of the system.

The state model can be traversed in a "breadth-first" [McG94] manner. In this context, breadth-first implies that a test case exercises a single transition and that when a new transition is to be tested only previously tested transitions are used.

Consider a **CreditCard** object that is part of the banking system. The initial state of **CreditCard** is *undefined* (i.e., no credit card number has been provided). Upon reading the credit card during a sale, the object takes on a *defined* state; that is, the attributes card number and expiration date, along with bank-specific identifiers are defined. The credit card is *submitted* when it is sent for authorization, and it is *approved* when authorization is received. The transition of **CreditCard** from one state to another can be tested by deriving test cases that cause the transition to occur. A breadth-first approach to this type of testing would not exercise *submitted* before it exercised *undefined* and *defined*. If it did, it would make use of transitions that had not been previously tested and would therefore violate the breadth-first criterion.

19.7 SUMMARY

The overall objective of object-oriented testing—to find the maximum number of errors with a minimum amount of effort is identical to the objective of conventional software testing. But the strategy and tactics for OO testing differ significantly. The view of testing broadens to include the review of both the requirements and design model. In addition, the focus of testing moves away from the procedural component (the module) and toward the class.

Because the OO requirements and design models and the resulting source code are semantically coupled, testing (in the form of technical reviews) begins during the modeling activity. For this reason, the review of CRC, object-relationship, and object-behavior models can be viewed as first-stage testing.

Once code is available, unit testing is applied for each class. The design of tests for a class uses a variety of methods: fault-based testing, random testing, and partition testing. Each of these methods exercise the operations encapsulated by the class. Test sequences are designed to ensure that relevant operations are exercised. The state of the class, represented by the values of its attributes, is examined to determine if errors exist.

Integration testing can be accomplished using a thread-based or use-based strategy. Thread-based testing integrates the set of classes that collaborate to respond to one input or event. Use-based testing constructs the system in layers, beginning with those classes that do not make use of server classes. Integration test-case design methods can also make use of random and partition tests. In addition, scenario-based testing and tests derived from behavioral models can be used to test a class and its collaborators. A test sequence tracks the flow of operations across class collaborations.

OO system validation testing is black-box oriented and can be accomplished by applying the same black-box methods discussed for conventional software. However, scenario-based testing dominates the validation of OO systems, making the use case a primary driver for validation testing.

PROBLEMS AND POINTS TO PONDER

19.1. In your own words, describe why the class is the smallest reasonable unit for testing within an OO system.

19.2. Why do we have to retest subclasses that are instantiated from an existing class, if the existing class has already been thoroughly tested? Can we use the test-case design for the existing class?

19.3. Why should "testing" begin with object-oriented analysis and design?

19.4. Derive a set of CRC index cards for *SafeHome*, and conduct the steps noted in Section 19.2.2 to determine if inconsistencies exist.

19.5. What is the difference between thread-based and use-based strategies for integration testing? How does cluster testing fit in?

19.6. Apply random testing and partitioning to three classes defined in the design for the *SafeHome* system. Produce test cases that indicate the operation sequences that will be invoked.

19.7. Apply multiple class testing and tests derived from the behavioral model for the *SafeHome* design.

19.8. Derive four additional tests using random testing and partitioning methods as well as multiple class testing and tests derived from the behavioral model for the banking application presented in Sections 19.5 and 19.6.

FURTHER READINGS AND INFORMATION SOURCES

Many books on testing noted in the *Further Readings* sections of Chapters 17 and 18 discuss testing of OO systems to some extent. Schach (*Object-Oriented and Classical Software Engineering,* McGraw-Hill, 6th ed., 2004) considers OO testing within the context of broader software engineering practice. Sykes and McGregor (*Practical Guide to Testing Object-Oriented Software,* Addison-Wesley, 2001), Bashir and Goel (*Testing Object-Oriented Software,* Springer 2000), Binder (*Testing Object-Oriented Systems,* Addison-Wesley, 1999), and Kung and his colleagues (*Testing Object-Oriented Software,* Wiley-IEEE Computer Society Press, 1998) treat OO testing in significant detail.

A wide variety of information sources on object-oriented testing methods is available on the Internet. An up-to-date list of World Wide Web references that are relevant to testing techniques can be found at the SEPA website: **www.mhhe.com/engcs/compsci/pressman/professional/olc/ser.htm**.

There is an urgency that always pervades a WebApp project. Stakeholders—concerned about competition from other WebApps, coerced by customer demands, and worried that they'll miss a market window—press to get the WebApp online. As a consequence, technical activities that often occur late in the process, such as WebApp testing, are sometimes given short shrift. This can be a catastrophic mistake. To avoid it, you and other team members must ensure that each work product exhibits high quality. Wallace and his colleagues [Wal03] note this when they state:

Testing shouldn't wait until the project is finished. Start testing before you write one line of code. Test constantly and effectively, and you will develop a much more durable Web site.

Since requirements and design models cannot be tested in the classical sense, you and your team should conduct technical reviews (Chapter 15) as well as executable tests. The intent is to uncover and correct errors before the WebApp is made available to its end users.

QUICK LOOK

What is it? WebApp testing is a collection of related activities with a single goal: to uncover errors in WebApp content, function, usability, navigability, performance, capacity, and security. To accomplish this, a testing strategy that encompasses both reviews and executable testing is applied.

Who does it? Web engineers and other project stakeholders (managers, customers, end users) all participate in WebApp testing.

Why is it important? If end users encounter errors that shake their faith in the WebApp, they will go elsewhere for the content and function they need, and the WebApp will fail. For this reason, you must work to eliminate as many errors as possible before the WebApp goes online.

What are the steps? The WebApp testing process begins by focusing on user-visible aspects of the WebApp and proceeds to tests that exercise technology and infrastructure. Seven testing steps are performed: content testing, interface testing, navigation testing, component testing, configuration testing, performance testing, and security testing.

What is the work product? In some instances a WebApp test plan is produced. In every instance, a suite of test cases is developed for every testing step and an archive of test results is maintained for future use.

How do I ensure that I've done it right? Although you can never be sure that you've performed every test that is needed, you can be certain that testing has uncovered errors (and that those errors have been corrected). In addition, if you've established a test plan, you can check to ensure that all planned tests have been conducted.

20.1   TESTING CONCEPTS FOR WEBAPPS

Testing is the process of exercising software with the intent of finding (and ultimately correcting) errors. This fundamental philosophy, first presented in Chapter 17, does not change for WebApps. In fact, because Web-based systems and applications reside on a network and interoperate with many different operating systems, browsers (residing on a variety of devices), hardware platforms, communications protocols, and "backroom" applications, the search for errors represents a significant challenge.

To understand the objectives of testing within a Web engineering context, you should consider the many dimensions of WebApp quality.[1] In the context of this discussion, I consider quality dimensions that are particularly relevant in any discussion of WebApp testing. I also consider the nature of the errors that are encountered as a consequence of testing, and the testing strategy that is applied to uncover these errors.

20.1.1   Dimensions of Quality

Quality is incorporated into a Web application as a consequence of good design. It is evaluated by applying a series of technical reviews that assess various elements of the design model and by applying a testing process that is discussed throughout this chapter. Both reviews and testing examine one or more of the following quality dimensions [Mil00a]:

> **?** How do we assess quality within the context of a WebApp and its environment?

- *Content* is evaluated at both a syntactic and semantic level. At the syntactic level, spelling, punctuation, and grammar are assessed for text-based documents. At a semantic level, correctness (of information presented), consistency (across the entire content object and related objects), and lack of ambiguity are all assessed.

- *Function* is tested to uncover errors that indicate lack of conformance to customer requirements. Each WebApp function is assessed for correctness, instability, and general conformance to appropriate implementation standards (e.g., Java or AJAX language standards).

- *Structure* is assessed to ensure that it properly delivers WebApp content and function, that it is extensible, and that it can be supported as new content or functionality is added.

- *Usability* is tested to ensure that each category of user is supported by the interface and can learn and apply all required navigation syntax and semantics.

- *Navigability* is tested to ensure that all navigation syntax and semantics are exercised to uncover any navigation errors (e.g., dead links, improper links, erroneous links).

---

1   Generic software quality dimensions, equally applicable for WebApps, were discussed in Chapter 14.

- *Performance* is tested under a variety of operating conditions, configurations, and loading to ensure that the system is responsive to user interaction and handles extreme loading without unacceptable operational degradation.

- *Compatibility* is tested by executing the WebApp in a variety of different host configurations on both the client and server sides. The intent is to find errors that are specific to a unique host configuration.

- *Interoperability* is tested to ensure that the WebApp properly interfaces with other applications and/or databases.

- *Security* is tested by assessing potential vulnerabilities and attempting to exploit each. Any successful penetration attempt is deemed a security failure.

Strategy and tactics for WebApp testing have been developed to exercise each of these quality dimensions and are discussed later in this chapter.

20.1.2 Errors within a WebApp Environment

Errors encountered as a consequence of successful WebApp testing have a number of unique characteristics [Ngu00]:

1. Because many types of WebApp tests uncover problems that are first evidenced on the client side (i.e., via an interface implemented on a specific browser or a personal communication device), you often see a symptom of the error, not the error itself.

2. Because a WebApp is implemented in a number of different configurations and within different environments, it may be difficult or impossible to reproduce an error outside the environment in which the error was originally encountered.

3. Although some errors are the result of incorrect design or improper HTML (or other programming language) coding, many errors can be traced to the WebApp configuration.

4. Because WebApps reside within a client-server architecture, errors can be difficult to trace across three architectural layers: the client, the server, or the network itself.

5. Some errors are due to the *static operating environment* (i.e., the specific configuration in which testing is conducted), while others are attributable to the dynamic operating environment (i.e., instantaneous resource loading or time-related errors).

These five error attributes suggest that environment plays an important role in the diagnosis of all errors uncovered during the WebApp testing. In some situations (e.g., content testing), the site of the error is obvious, but in many other types of WebApp testing (e.g., navigation testing, performance testing, security testing) the underlying cause of the error may be considerably more difficult to determine.

20.1.3   Testing Strategy

The strategy for WebApp testing adopts the basic principles for all software testing (Chapter 17) and applies a strategy and tactics that have been recommended for object-oriented systems (Chapter 19). The following steps summarize the approach:

KEY POINT

The overall strategy for WebApp testing can be summarized in the 10 steps noted here.

1. The content model for the WebApp is reviewed to uncover errors.
2. The interface model is reviewed to ensure that all use cases can be accommodated.
3. The design model for the WebApp is reviewed to uncover navigation errors.
4. The user interface is tested to uncover errors in presentation and/or navigation mechanics.
5. Functional components are unit tested.
6. Navigation throughout the architecture is tested.
7. The WebApp is implemented in a variety of different environmental configurations and is tested for compatibility with each configuration.
8. Security tests are conducted in an attempt to exploit vulnerabilities in the WebApp or within its environment.
9. Performance tests are conducted.
10. The WebApp is tested by a controlled and monitored population of end users; the results of their interaction with the system are evaluated for content and navigation errors, usability concerns, compatibility concerns, and WebApp security, reliability, and performance.

WebRef

Excellent articles on WebApp testing can be found at **www.stickyminds.com/testing.asp**

Because many WebApps evolve continuously, the testing process is an ongoing activity, conducted by Web support staff who use regression tests derived from the tests developed when the WebApp was first engineered.

20.1.4   Test Planning

The use of the word *planning* (in any context) is anathema to some Web developers. These developers don't plan; they just start—hoping that a killer WebApp will emerge. A more disciplined approach recognizes that planning establishes a road map for all work that follows. It's worth the effort. In their book on WebApp testing, Splaine and Jaskiel [Spl01] state:

> Except for the simplest of Web sites, it quickly becomes apparent that some sort of test planning is needed. All too often, the initial number of bugs found from ad hoc testing is large enough that not all of them are fixed the first time they're detected. This puts an additional burden on people who test Web sites and applications. Not only must they conjure up imaginative new tests, but they must also remember how previous tests were executed in order to reliably re-test the Web site/application, and ensure that known bugs have been removed and that no new bugs have been introduced.

KEY POINT

The test plan identifies the testing task set, the work products to be developed, and the way in which results are to be evaluated, recorded, and reused.

The questions you should ask are: How do we "conjure up imaginative new tests," and what should those tests focus on? The answers to these questions are contained within a test plan.

A WebApp test plan identifies (1) the task set[2] to be applied as testing commences, (2) the work products to be produced as each testing task is executed, and (3) the manner in which the results of testing are evaluated, recorded, and reused when regression testing is conducted. In some cases, the test plan is integrated with the project plan. In others, the test plan is a separate document.

20.2 THE TESTING PROCESS—AN OVERVIEW

You begin the WebApp testing process with tests that exercise content and interface functionality that are immediately visible to end users. As testing proceeds, aspects of the design architecture and navigation are exercised. Finally, the focus shifts to tests that examine technological capabilities that are not always apparent to end users—WebApp infrastructure and installation/implementation issues.

Figure 20.1 juxtaposes the WebApp testing process with the design pyramid for WebApps (Chapter 13). Note that as the testing flow proceeds from left to right and

FIGURE 20.1

The testing process

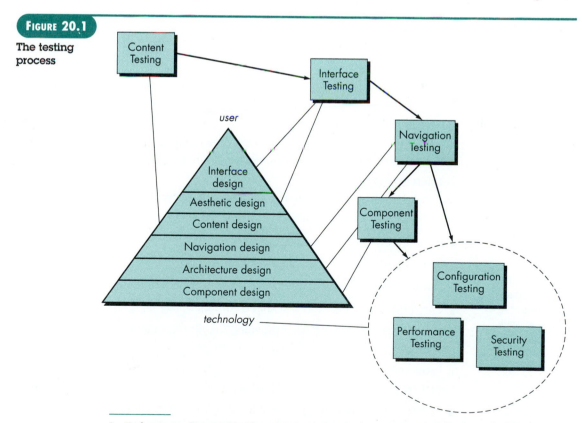

---

2   Task sets are discussed in Chapter 2. A related term—*workflow*—is also used to describe a series of tasks required to accomplish a software engineering activity.

top to bottom, user-visible elements of the WebApp design (top elements of the pyramid) are tested first, followed by infrastructure design elements.

20.3   CONTENT TESTING

Errors in WebApp content can be as trivial as minor typographical errors or as significant as incorrect information, improper organization, or violation of intellectual property laws. *Content testing* attempts to uncover these and many other problems before the user encounters them.

Content testing combines both reviews and the generation of executable test cases. Reviews are applied to uncover semantic errors in content (discussed in Section 20.3.1). Executable testing is used to uncover content errors that can be traced to dynamically derived content that is driven by data acquired from one or more databases.

20.3.1   Content Testing Objectives

Content testing objectives are: (1) to uncover syntactic errors in content, (2) to uncover semantic errors, and (3) to find structural errors.

Content testing has three important objectives: (1) to uncover syntactic errors (e.g., typos, grammar mistakes) in text-based documents, graphical representations, and other media; (2) to uncover semantic errors (i.e., errors in the accuracy or completeness of information) in any content object presented as navigation occurs, and (3) to find errors in the organization or structure of content that is presented to the end user.

To accomplish the first objective, automated spelling and grammar checkers may be used. However, many syntactic errors evade detection by such tools and must be discovered by a human reviewer (tester). In fact, a large website might enlist the services of a professional copy editor to uncover typographical errors, grammatical mistakes, errors in content consistency, errors in graphical representations, and cross-referencing errors.

Semantic testing focuses on the information presented within each content object. The reviewer (tester) must answer the following questions:

What questions should be asked and answered to uncover semantic errors in content?

- Is the information factually accurate?
- Is the information concise and to the point?
- Is the layout of the content object easy for the user to understand?
- Can information embedded within a content object be found easily?
- Have proper references been provided for all information derived from other sources?
- Is the information presented consistent internally and consistent with information presented in other content objects?
- Is the content offensive, misleading, or does it open the door to litigation?
- Does the content infringe on existing copyrights or trademarks?

- Does the content contain internal links that supplement existing content? Are the links correct?

- Does the aesthetic style of the content conflict with the aesthetic style of the interface?

Obtaining answers to each of these questions for a large WebApp (containing hundreds of content objects) can be a daunting task. However, failure to uncover semantic errors will shake the user's faith in the WebApp and can lead to failure of the Web-based application.

Content objects exist within an architecture that has a specific style (Chapter 13). During content testing, the structure and organization of the content architecture is tested to ensure that required content is presented to the end user in the proper order and relationships. For example, the **SafeHomeAssured.com** WebApp presents a variety of information about sensors that are used as part of security and surveillance products. Content objects provide descriptive information, technical specifications, a photographic representation, and related information. Tests of the **SafeHomeAssured.com** content architecture strive to uncover errors in the presentation of this information (e.g., a description of Sensor X is presented with a photo of Sensor Y).

20.3.2 Database Testing

Modern WebApps do much more than present static content objects. In many application domains, WebApps interface with sophisticated database management systems and build dynamic content objects that are created in real time using the data acquired from a database.

For example, a financial services WebApp can produce complex text-based, tabular, and graphical information about a specific equity (e.g., a stock or mutual fund). The composite content object that presents this information is created dynamically after the user has made a request for information about a specific equity. To accomplish this, the following steps are required: (1) a large equities database is queried, (2) relevant data are extracted from the database, (3) the extracted data must be organized as a content object, and (4) this content object (representing customized information requested by an end user) is transmitted to the client environment for display. Errors can and do occur as a consequence of each of these steps. The objective of database testing is to uncover these errors, but database testing is complicated by a variety of factors:

1. *The original client-side request for information is rarely presented in the form [e.g., structured query language (SQL)] that can be input to a database management system (DBMS).* Therefore, tests should be designed to uncover errors made in translating the user's request into a form that can be processed by the DBMS.

2. *The database may be remote to the server that houses the WebApp.* Therefore, tests that uncover errors in communication between the WebApp and the remote database must be developed.[3]

3. *Raw data acquired from the database must be transmitted to the WebApp server and properly formatted for subsequent transmittal to the client.* Therefore, tests that demonstrate the validity of the raw data received by the WebApp server must be developed, and additional tests that demonstrate the validity of the transformations applied to the raw data to create valid content objects must also be created.

4. *The dynamic content object(s) must be transmitted to the client in a form that can be displayed to the end user.* Therefore, a series of tests must be designed to (1) uncover errors in the content object format and (2) test compatibility with different client environment configurations.

Considering these four factors, test-case design methods should be applied for each of the "layers of interaction" [Ngu01] noted in Figure 20.2. Testing should ensure that (1) valid information is passed between the client and server from the interface layer, (2) the WebApp processes scripts correctly and properly extracts or formats user data, (3) user data are passed correctly to a server-side data transformation function that formats appropriate queries (e.g., SQL), (4) queries are passed to a data management

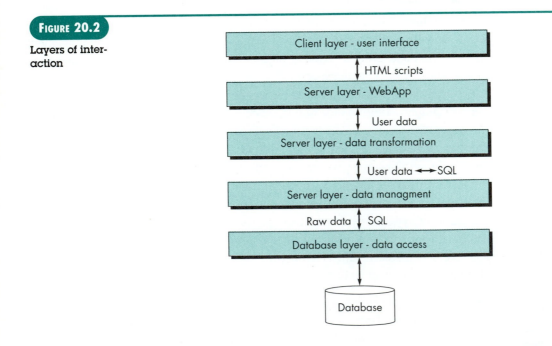

FIGURE 20.2

Layers of inter-action

layer[4] that communicates with database access routines (potentially located on another machine).

The data transformation, data management, and database access layers shown in Figure 20.2 are often constructed with reusable components that have been validated separately and as a package. If this is the case, WebApp testing focuses on the design of test cases to exercise the interactions between the client layer and the first two server layers (WebApp and data transformation) shown in the figure.

The user interface layer is tested to ensure that scripts are properly constructed for each user query and properly transmitted to the server side. The WebApp layer on the server side is tested to ensure that user data are properly extracted from scripts and properly transmitted to the data transformation layer on the server side. The data transformation functions are tested to ensure that the correct SQL is created and passed to appropriate data management components.

A detailed discussion of the underlying technology that must be understood to adequately design these database tests is beyond the scope of this book. If you have additional interest, see [Sce02], [Ngu01], and [Bro01].

Quote:

"... we are unlikely to have confidence in a Web site that suffers frequent downtime, hangs in the middle of a transaction, or has a poor sense of usability. Testing, therefore, has a crucial role in the overall development process."

Wing Lam

20.4   USER INTERFACE TESTING

Verification and validation of a WebApp user interface occurs at three distinct points. During requirements analysis, the interface model is reviewed to ensure that it conforms to stakeholder requirements and to other elements of the requirements model. During design the interface design model is reviewed to ensure that generic quality criteria established for all user interfaces (Chapter 11) have been achieved and that application-specific interface design issues have been properly addressed. During testing, the focus shifts to the execution of application-specific aspects of user interaction as they are manifested by interface syntax and semantics. In addition, testing provides a final assessment of usability.

ADVICE

With the exception of WebApp-oriented specifics, the interface strategy noted here is applicable to all types of client-server software.

20.4.1   Interface Testing Strategy

Interface testing exercises interaction mechanisms and validates aesthetic aspects of the user interface. The overall strategy for interface testing is to (1) uncover errors related to specific interface mechanisms (e.g., errors in the proper execution of a menu link or the way data are entered in a form) and (2) uncover errors in the way the interface implements the semantics of navigation, WebApp functionality, or content display. To accomplish this strategy, a number of tactical steps are initiated:

- *Interface features are tested to ensure that design rules, aesthetics, and related visual content are available for the user without error.* Features include type

---

4   The data management layer typically incorporates an SQL call-level interface (SQL-CLI) such as Microsoft OLE/ADO or Java Database Connectivity (JDBC).

fonts, the use of color, frames, images, borders, tables, and related interface features that are generated as WebApp execution proceeds.

- *Individual interface mechanisms are tested in a manner that is analogous to unit testing.* For example, tests are designed to exercise all forms, client-side scripting, dynamic HTML, scripts, streaming content, and application-specific interface mechanisms (e.g., a shopping cart for an e-commerce application). In many cases, testing can focus exclusively on one of these mechanisms (the "unit") to the exclusion of other interface features and functions.

- *Each interface mechanism is tested within the context of a use case or NSU* (Chapter 13) *for a specific user category.* This testing approach is analogous to integration testing in that tests are conducted as interface mechanisms are integrated to allow a use case or NSU to be executed.

- *The complete interface is tested against selected use cases and NSUs to uncover errors in the semantics of the interface.* This testing approach is analogous to validation testing because the purpose is to demonstrate conformance to specific use-case or NSU semantics. It is at this stage that a series of usability tests are conducted.

- *The interface is tested within a variety of environments (e.g., browsers) to ensure that it will be compatible.* In actuality, this series of tests can also be considered to be part of configuration testing.

20.4.2 Testing Interface Mechanisms

When a user interacts with a WebApp, the interaction occurs through one or more interface mechanisms. A brief overview of testing considerations for each interface mechanism is presented in the paragraphs that follow [Spl01].

External link testing should occur throughout the life of the WebApp. Part of a support strategy should be regularly scheduled link tests.

Links.   Each navigation link is tested to ensure that the proper content object or function is reached.[5] You build a list of all links associated with the interface layout (e.g., menu bars, index items) and then execute each individually. In addition, links within each content object must be exercised to uncover bad URLs or links to improper content objects or functions. Finally, links to external WebApps should be tested for accuracy and also evaluated to determine the risk that they will become invalid over time.

Forms.   At a macroscopic level, tests are performed to ensure that (1) labels correctly identify fields within the form and that mandatory fields are identified visually for the user, (2) the server receives all information contained within the form and that no data are lost in the transmission between client and server, (3) appropriate defaults are used when the user does not select from a pull-down menu or set of buttons, (4) browser functions (e.g., the "back" arrow) do not corrupt data entered in

---

5   These tests can be performed as part of either interface or navigation testing.

a form, and (5) scripts that perform error checking on data entered work properly and provide meaningful error messages.

At a more targeted level, tests should ensure that (1) form fields have proper width and data types, (2) the form establishes appropriate safeguards that preclude the user from entering text strings longer than some predefined maximum, (3) all appropriate options for pull-down menus are specified and ordered in a way that is meaningful to the end user, (4) browser "auto-fill" features do not lead to data input errors, and (5) tab key (or some other key) initiates proper movement between form fields.

Client-side scripting tests and tests associated with dynamic HTML should be repeated whenever a new version of a popular browser is released.

Client-side scripting. Black-box tests are conducted to uncover any errors in processing as the script is executed. These tests are often coupled with forms testing, because script input is often derived from data provided as part of forms processing. A compatibility test should be conducted to ensure that the scripting language that has been chosen will work properly in the environmental configurations that support the WebApp. In addition to testing the script itself, Splaine and Jaskiel [Spl01] suggest that "you should ensure that your company's [WebApp] standards state the preferred language and version of scripting language to be used for client-side (and server-side) scripting."

Dynamic HTML. Each Web page that contains dynamic HTML is executed to ensure that the dynamic display is correct. In addition, a compatibility test should be conducted to ensure that the dynamic HTML works properly in the environmental configurations that support the WebApp.

Pop-up windows. A series of tests ensure that (1) the pop-up is properly sized and positioned, (2) the pop-up does not cover the original WebApp window, (3) the aesthetic design of the pop-up is consistent with the aesthetic design of the interface, and (4) scroll bars and other control mechanisms appended to the pop-up are properly located and function as required.

CGI scripts. Black-box tests are conducted with an emphasis on data integrity (as data are passed to the CGI script) and script processing (once validated data have been received). In addition, performance testing can be conducted to ensure that the server-side configuration can accommodate the processing demands of multiple invocations of CGI scripts [Spl01].

Streaming content. Tests should demonstrate that streaming data are up-to-date, properly displayed, and can be suspended without error and restarted without difficulty.

Cookies. Both server-side and client-side testing are required. On the server side, tests should ensure that a cookie is properly constructed (contains correct data) and properly transmitted to the client side when specific content or functionality is requested. In addition, the proper persistence of the cookie is tested to ensure that its expiration date is correct. On the client side, tests determine whether the WebApp properly attaches existing cookies to a specific request (sent to the server).

Application-specific interface mechanisms. Tests conform to a checklist of functionality and features that are defined by the interface mechanism. For example, Splaine and Jaskiel [Spl01] suggest the following checklist for shopping cart functionality defined for an e-commerce application:

- Boundary-test (Chapter 18) the minimum and maximum number of items that can be placed in the shopping cart.
- Test a "check out" request for an empty shopping cart.
- Test proper deletion of an item from the shopping cart.
- Test to determine whether a purchase empties the cart of its contents.
- Test to determine the persistence of shopping cart contents (this should be specified as part of customer requirements).
- Test to determine whether the WebApp can recall shopping cart contents at some future date (assuming that no purchase was made).

20.4.3 Testing Interface Semantics

Once each interface mechanism has been "unit" tested, the focus of interface testing changes to a consideration of interface semantics. Interface semantics testing "evaluates how well the design takes care of users, offers clear direction, delivers feedback, and maintains consistency of language and approach" [Ngu00].

A thorough review of the interface design model can provide partial answers to the questions implied by the preceding paragraph. However, each use-case scenario (for each user category) should be tested once the WebApp has been implemented. In essence, a use case becomes the input for the design of a testing sequence. The intent of the testing sequence is to uncover errors that will preclude a user from achieving the objective associated with the use case.

As each use case is tested, it's a good idea to maintain a checklist to ensure that every menu item has been exercised at least one time and that every embedded link within a content object has been used. In addition, the test series should include improper menu selection and link usage. The intent is to determine whether the WebApp provides effective error handling and recovery.

20.4.4 Usability Tests

Usability testing is similar to interface semantics testing (Section 20.4.3) in the sense that it also evaluates the degree to which users can interact effectively with the WebApp and the degree to which the WebApp guides users' actions, provides meaningful feedback, and enforces a consistent interaction approach. Rather than focusing intently on the semantics of some interactive objective, usability reviews and tests are designed to determine the degree to which the WebApp interface makes the user's life easy.[6]

---

6 The term *user-friendliness* has been used in this context. The problem, of course, is that one user's perception of a "friendly" interface may be radically different from another's.

You will invariably contribute to the design of usability tests, but the tests themselves are conducted by end users. The following sequence of steps is applied [Spl01]:

1. Define a set of usability testing categories and identify goals for each.
2. Design tests that will enable each goal to be evaluated.
3. Select participants who will conduct the tests.
4. Instrument participants' interaction with the WebApp while testing is conducted.
5. Develop a mechanism for assessing the usability of the WebApp.

Usability testing can occur at a variety of different levels of abstraction: (1) the usability of a specific interface mechanism (e.g., a form) can be assessed, (2) the usability of a complete Web page (encompassing interface mechanisms, data objects, and related functions) can be evaluated, or (3) the usability of the complete WebApp can be considered.

The first step in usability testing is to identify a set of usability categories and establish testing objectives for each category. The following test categories and objectives (written in the form of a question) illustrate this approach:[7]

What characteristics of usability become the focus of testing and what specific objectives are addressed?

Interactivity—Are interaction mechanisms (e.g., pull-down menus, buttons, pointers) easy to understand and use?

Layout—Are navigation mechanisms, content, and functions placed in a manner that allows the user to find them quickly?

Readability—Is text well written and understandable?[8] Are graphic representations easy to understand?

Aesthetics—Do layout, color, typeface, and related characteristics lead to ease of use? Do users "feel comfortable" with the look and feel of the WebApp?

Display characteristics—Does the WebApp make optimal use of screen size and resolution?

Time sensitivity—Can important features, functions, and content be used or acquired in a timely manner?

Personalization—Does the WebApp tailor itself to the specific needs of different user categories or individual users?

Accessibility—Is the WebApp accessible to people who have disabilities?

A series of tests is designed within each of these categories. In some cases, the "test" may be a visual review of a Web page. In other cases interface semantics tests may be executed again, but in this instance usability concerns are paramount.

---

7 For additional information on usability, see Chapter 11.
8 The FOG Readability Index and others may be used to provide a quantitative assessment of readability See **http://developer.gnome.org/documents/usability/usability-readability.html** for more details.

FIGURE 20.3

Qualitative assessment of usability

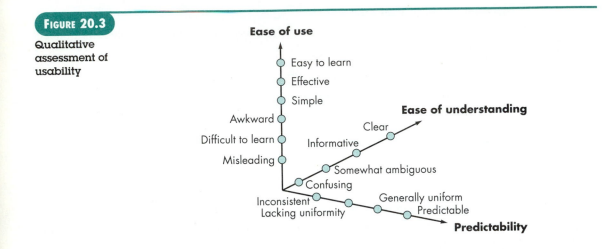

As an example, we consider usability assessment for interaction and interface mechanisms. Constantine and Lockwood [Con99] suggest that the following list of interface features should be reviewed and tested for usability: animation, buttons, color, control, dialogue, fields, forms, frames, graphics, labels, links, menus, messages, navigation, pages, selectors, text, and tool bars. As each feature is assessed, it is graded on a qualitative scale by the users who are doing the testing. Figure 20.3 depicts a possible set of assessment "grades" that can be selected by users. These grades are applied to each feature individually, to a complete Web page, or to the WebApp as a whole.

20.4.5 Compatibility Tests

Different computers, display devices, operating systems, browsers, and network connection speeds can have a significant influence on WebApp operation. Each computing configuration can result in differences in client-side processing speeds, display resolution, and connection speeds. Operating system vagaries may cause WebApp processing issues. Different browsers sometimes produce slightly different results, regardless of the degree of HTML standardization within the WebApp. Required plug-ins may or may not be readily available for a particular configuration.

In some cases, small compatibility issues present no significant problems, but in others, serious errors can be encountered. For example, download speeds may become unacceptable, lack of a required plug-in may make content unavailable, browser differences can change page layout dramatically, font styles may be altered and become illegible, or forms may be improperly organized. *Compatibility testing* strives to uncover these problems before the WebApp goes online.

The first step in compatibility testing is to define a set of "commonly encountered" client-side computing configurations and their variants. In essence, a tree structure is created, identifying each computing platform, typical display devices, the operating systems supported on the platform, the browsers available, likely Internet

POINT

WebApps execute within a variety of client-side environments. The objective of compatibility testing to uncover errors associated with a specific environment (e.g., browser).

connection speeds, and similar information. Next, a series of compatibility validation tests are derived, often adapted from existing interface tests, navigation tests, performance tests, and security tests. The intent of these tests is to uncover errors or execution problems that can be traced to configuration differences.

SafeHome

WebApp Testing

The scene: Doug Miller's office.

The players: Doug Miller (manager of the *SafeHome* software engineering group) and Vinod Raman (a member of the product software engineering team).

The conversation:

Doug: What do you think of the **SafeHomeAssured.com** e-commerce WebApp V0.0?

Vinod: The outsourcing vendor's done a good job. Sharon [development manager for the vendor] tells me they're testing as we speak.

Doug: I'd like you and the rest of the team to do a little informal testing on the e-commerce site.

Vinod (grimacing): I thought we were going to hire a third-party testing company to validate the WebApp. We're still killing ourselves trying to get the product software out the door.

Doug: We're going to hire a testing vendor for performance and security testing, and our outsourcing vendor is already testing. Just thought another point of view would be helpful, and besides, we'd like to keep costs in line, so . . .

Vinod (sighs): What are you looking for?

Doug: I want to be sure that the interface and all navigation are solid.

Vinod: I suppose we can start with the use cases for each of the major interface functions:

Learn about *SafeHome.*
Specify the *SafeHome* system you need.
Purchase a *SafeHome* system.
Get technical support.

Doug: Good. But take the navigation paths all the way to their conclusion.

Vinod (looking through a notebook of use cases): Yeah, when you select **Specify the SafeHome system you need,** that'll take you to:

Select SafeHome components.
Get *SafeHome* component recommendations.

We can exercise the semantics of each path.

Doug: While you're there, check out the content that appears at each navigation node.

Vinod: Of course . . . and the functional elements as well. Who's testing usability?

Doug: Oh . . . the testing vendor will coordinate usability testing. We've hired a market research firm to line up 20 typical users for the usability study, but if you guys uncover any usability issues . . .

Vinod: I know, pass them along.

Doug: Thanks, Vinod.

20.5 COMPONENT-LEVEL TESTING

Component-level testing, also called *function testing,* focuses on a set of tests that attempt to uncover errors in WebApp functions. Each WebApp function is a software component (implemented in one of a variety of programming or scripting languages) and can be tested using black-box (and in some cases, white-box) techniques as discussed in Chapter 18.

Component-level test cases are often driven by forms-level input. Once forms data are defined, the user selects a button or other control mechanism to initiate execution. The following test-case design methods (Chapter 18) are typical:

- *Equivalence partitioning*—The input domain of the function is divided into input categories or classes from which test cases are derived. The input form is assessed to determine what classes of data are relevant for the function. Test cases for each class of input are derived and executed, while other classes of input are held constant. For example, an e-commerce application may implement a function that computes shipping charges. Among a variety of shipping information provided via a form is the user's postal code. Test cases are designed in an attempt to uncover errors in postal code processing by specifying postal code values that might uncover different classes of errors (e.g., an incomplete postal code, a correct postal code, a nonexistent postal code, an erroneous postal code format).

- *Boundary value analysis*—Forms data are tested at their boundaries. For example, the shipping calculation function noted previously requests the maximum number of days required for product delivery. A minimum of 2 days and a maximum of 14 are noted on the form. However, boundary value tests might input values of 0, 1, 2, 13, 14, and 15 to determine how the function reacts to data at and outside the boundaries of valid input.[9]

- *Path testing*—If the logical complexity of the function is high,[10] path testing (a white-box test-case design method) can be used to ensure that every independent path in the program has been exercised.

In addition to these test-case design methods, a technique called *forced error testing* [Ngu01] is used to derive test cases that purposely drive the WebApp component into an error condition. The purpose is to uncover errors that occur during error handling (e.g., incorrect or nonexistent error messages, WebApp failure as a consequence of the error, erroneous output driven by erroneous input, side effects that are related to component processing).

Each component-level test case specifies all input values and the expected output to be provided by the component. The actual output produced as a consequence of the test is recorded for future reference during support and maintenance.

In many situations, the correct execution of a WebApp function is tied to proper interfacing with a database that may be external to the WebApp. Therefore, database testing becomes an integral part of the component-testing regime.

---

9 In this case, a better input design might eliminate potential errors. The maximum number of days could be selected from a pull-down menu, precluding the user from specifying out-of-bounds input.

10 Logical complexity can be determined by computing cyclomatic complexity of the algorithm. See Chapter 18 for additional details.

20.6 NAVIGATION TESTING

A user travels through a WebApp in much the same way as a visitor walks through a store or museum. There are many pathways that can be taken, many stops that can be made, many things to learn and look at, activities to initiate, and decisions to make. This navigation process is predictable in the sense that every visitor has a set of objectives when he arrives. At the same time, the navigation process can be unpredictable because the visitor, influenced by something he sees or learns, may choose a path or initiate an action that is not typical for the original objective. The job of navigation testing is (1) to ensure that the mechanisms that allow the WebApp user to travel through the WebApp are all functional and (2) to validate that each navigation semantic unit (NSU) can be achieved by the appropriate user category.

20.6.1 Testing Navigation Syntax

uote:

"We're not lost. We're locationally challenged."

John M. Ford

The first phase of navigation testing actually begins during interface testing. Navigation mechanisms are tested to ensure that each performs its intended function. Splaine and Jaskiel [Spl01] suggest that each of the following navigation mechanisms should be tested:

- *Navigation links*—these mechanisms include internal links within the WebApp, external links to other WebApps, and anchors within a specific Web page. Each link should be tested to ensure that proper content or functionality is reached when the link is chosen.

- *Redirects*—these links come into play when a user requests a nonexistent URL or selects a link whose content has been removed or whose name has changed. A message is displayed for the user and navigation is redirected to another page (e.g., the home page). Redirects should be tested by requesting incorrect internal links or external URLs and assessing how the WebApp handles these requests.

- *Bookmarks*—although bookmarks are a browser function, the WebApp should be tested to ensure that a meaningful page title can be extracted as the bookmark is created.

- *Frames and framesets*—each frame contains the content of a specific Web page, and a frameset contains multiple frames and enables the display of multiple Web pages at the same time. Because it is possible to nest frames and framesets within one another, these navigation and display mechanisms should be tested for correct content, proper layout and sizing, download performance, and browser compatibility.

- *Site maps*—a site map provides a complete table of contents for all Web pages. Each site map entry should be tested to ensure that the links take the user to the proper content or functionality.

- *Internal search engines*—complex WebApps often contain hundreds or even thousands of content objects. An internal search engine allows the user to perform a keyword search within the WebApp to find needed content. Search engine testing validates the accuracy and completeness of the search, the error-handling properties of the search engine, and advanced search features (e.g., the use of Boolean operators in the search field).

Some of the tests noted can be performed by automated tools (e.g., link checking), while others are designed and executed manually. The intent throughout is to ensure that errors in navigation mechanics are found before the WebApp goes online.

20.6.2   Testing Navigation Semantics

? What questions must be asked and answered as each NSU is tested?

In Chapter 13 a navigation semantic unit (NSU) is defined as "a set of information and related navigation structures that collaborate in the fulfillment of a subset of related user requirements" [Cac02]. Each NSU is defined by a set of navigation paths (called "ways of navigating") that connect navigation nodes (e.g., Web pages, content objects, or functionality). Taken as a whole, each NSU allows a user to achieve specific requirements defined by one or more use cases for a user category. Navigation testing exercises each NSU to ensure that these requirements can be achieved. You should answer the following questions as each NSU is tested:

- Is the NSU achieved in its entirety without error?
- Is every navigation node (defined for an NSU) reachable within the context of the navigation paths defined for the NSU?
- If the NSU can be achieved using more than one navigation path, has every relevant path been tested?
- If guidance is provided by the user interface to assist in navigation, are directions correct and understandable as navigation proceeds?
- Is there a mechanism (other than the browser "back" arrow) for returning to the preceding navigation node and to the beginning of the navigation path?
- Do mechanisms for navigation within a large navigation node (i.e., a long Web page) work properly?
- If a function is to be executed at a node and the user chooses not to provide input, can the remainder of the NSU be completed?
- If a function is executed at a node and an error in function processing occurs, can the NSU be completed?
- Is there a way to discontinue the navigation before all nodes have been reached, but then return to where the navigation was discontinued and proceed from there?
- Is every node reachable from the site map? Are node names meaningful to end users?

If NSUs have not been created as part of WebApp analysis or design, you can apply use cases for the design of navigation test cases. The same set of questions are asked and answered.

- If a node within an NSU is reached from some external source, is it possible to process to the next node on the navigation path? Is it possible to return to the previous node on the navigation path?

- Does the user understand his location within the content architecture as the NSU is executed?

Navigation testing, like interface and usability testing, should be conducted by as many different constituencies as possible. You have responsibility for early stages of navigation testing, but later stages should be conducted by other project stakeholders, an independent testing team, and ultimately, by nontechnical users. The intent is to exercise WebApp navigation thoroughly.

20.7 CONFIGURATION TESTING

Configuration variability and instability are important factors that make WebApp testing a challenge. Hardware, operating system(s), browsers, storage capacity, network communication speeds, and a variety of other client-side factors are difficult to predict for each user. In addition, the configuration for a given user can change [e.g., operating system (OS) updates, new ISP and connection speeds] on a regular basis. The result can be a client-side environment that is prone to errors that are both subtle and significant. One user's impression of the WebApp and the manner in which she interacts with it can differ significantly from another user's experience, if both users are not working within the same client-side configuration.

The job of configuration testing is not to exercise every possible client-side configuration. Rather, it is to test a set of probable client-side and server-side configurations to ensure that the user experience will be the same on all of them and to isolate errors that may be specific to a particular configuration.

20.7.1 Server-Side Issues

On the server side, configuration test cases are designed to verify that the projected server configuration [i.e., WebApp server, database server, operating system(s), firewall software, concurrent applications] can support the WebApp without error. In essence, the WebApp is installed within the server-side environment and tested to ensure that it operates without error.

As server-side configuration tests are designed, you should consider each component of the server configuration. Among the questions that need to be asked and answered during server-side configuration testing are:

> **?** **What questions must be asked and answered as server-side configuration testing is conducted?**

- Is the WebApp fully compatible with the server OS?

- Are system files, directories, and related system data created correctly when the WebApp is operational?

- Do system security measures (e.g., firewalls or encryption) allow the WebApp to execute and service users without interference or performance degradation?

- Has the WebApp been tested with the distributed server configuration[11] (if one exists) that has been chosen?
- Is the WebApp properly integrated with database software? Is the WebApp sensitive to different versions of database software?
- Do server-side WebApp scripts execute properly?
- Have system administrator errors been examined for their effect on WebApp operations?
- If proxy servers are used, have differences in their configuration been addressed with on-site testing?

20.7.2 Client-Side Issues

On the client side, configuration tests focus more heavily on WebApp compatibility with configurations that contain one or more permutations of the following components [Ngu01]:

- *Hardware*—CPU, memory, storage, and printing devices
- *Operating systems*—Linux, Macintosh OS, Microsoft Windows, a mobile-based OS
- *Browser software*—Firefox, Safari, Internet Explorer, Opera, Chrome, and others
- *User interface components*—Active X, Java applets, and others
- *Plug-ins*—QuickTime, RealPlayer, and many others
- *Connectivity*—cable, DSL, regular modem, T1, WiFi

In addition to these components, other variables include networking software, the vagaries of the ISP, and applications running concurrently.

To design client-side configuration tests, you must reduce the number of configuration variables to a manageable number.[12] To accomplish this, each user category is assessed to determine the likely configurations to be encountered within the category. In addition, industry market share data may be used to predict the most likely combinations of components. The WebApp is then tested within these environments.

20.8 SECURITY TESTING

WebApp security is a complex subject that must be fully understood before effective security testing can be accomplished.[13] WebApps and the client-side and server-side environments in which they are housed represent an attractive target for external hackers, disgruntled employees, dishonest competitors, and anyone else who

---

11 For example, a separate application server and database server may be used. Communication between the two machines occurs across a network connection.
12 Running tests on every possible combination of configuration components is far too time consuming.
13 Books by Cross and Fisher [Cro07], Andrews and Whittaker [And06], and Trivedi [Tri03] provide useful information about the subject.

wishes to steal sensitive information, maliciously modify content, degrade performance, disable functionality, or embarrass a person, organization, or business.

Security tests are designed to probe vulnerabilities of the client-side environment, the network communications that occur as data are passed from client to server and back again, and the server-side environment. Each of these domains can be attacked, and it is the job of the security tester to uncover weaknesses that can be exploited by those with the intent to do so.

On the client side, vulnerabilities can often be traced to preexisting bugs in browsers, e-mail programs, or communication software. Nguyen [Ngu01] describes a typical security hole:

> One of the commonly mentioned bugs is Buffer Overflow, which allows malicious code to be executed on the client machine. For example, entering a URL into a browser that is much longer than the buffer size allocated for the URL will cause a memory overwrite (buffer overflow) error if the browser does not have error detection code to validate the length of the input URL. A seasoned hacker can cleverly exploit this bug by writing a long URL with code to be executed that can cause the browser to crash or alter security settings (from high to low), or, at worst, to corrupt user data.

Another potential vulnerability on the client side is unauthorized access to cookies placed within the browser. Websites created with malicious intent can acquire information contained within legitimate cookies and use this information in ways that jeopardize the user's privacy, or worse, set the stage for identity theft.

Data communicated between the client and server are vulnerable to *spoofing*. Spoofing occurs when one end of the communication pathway is subverted by an entity with malicious intent. For example, a user can be spoofed by a malicious website that acts as if it is the legitimate WebApp server (identical look and feel). The intent is to steal passwords, proprietary information, or credit data.

On the server side, vulnerabilities include denial-of-service attacks and malicious scripts that can be passed along to the client side or used to disable server operations. In addition, server-side databases can be accessed without authorization (data theft).

To protect against these (and many other) vulnerabilities, one or more of the following security elements is implemented [Ngu01]:

- *Firewall*—a filtering mechanism that is a combination of hardware and software that examines each incoming packet of information to ensure that it is coming from a legitimate source, blocking any data that are suspect.

- *Authentication*—a verification mechanism that validates the identity of all clients and servers, allowing communication to occur only when both sides are verified.

- *Encryption*—an encoding mechanism that protects sensitive data by modifying it in a way that makes it impossible to read by those with malicious intent. Encryption is strengthened by using *digital certificates* that allow the client to verify the destination to which the data are transmitted.

- *Authorization*—a filtering mechanism that allows access to the client or server environment only by those individuals with appropriate authorization codes (e.g., userID and password).

Security tests should be designed to probe each of these security technologies in an effort to uncover security holes.

The actual design of security tests requires in-depth knowledge of the inner workings of each security element and a comprehensive understanding of a full range of networking technologies. In many cases, security testing is outsourced to firms that specialize in these technologies.

20.9   PERFORMANCE TESTING

Nothing is more frustrating than a WebApp that takes minutes to load content when competitive sites download similar content in seconds. Nothing is more aggravating than trying to log on to a WebApp and receiving a "server-busy" message, with the suggestion that you try again later. Nothing is more disconcerting than a WebApp that responds instantly in some situations, and then seems to go into an infinite wait state in other situations. All of these occurrences happen on the Web every day, and all of them are performance related.

Performance testing is used to uncover performance problems that can result from lack of server-side resources, inappropriate network bandwidth, inadequate database capabilities, faulty or weak operating system capabilities, poorly designed WebApp functionality, and other hardware or software issues that can lead to degraded client-server performance. The intent is twofold: (1) to understand how the system responds as *loading* (i.e., number of users, number of transactions, or overall data volume) increases and (2) to collect metrics that will lead to design modifications to improve performance.

20.9.1   Performance Testing Objectives

Some aspects of WebApp performance, at least as it is perceived by the end user, are difficult to test. Network loading, the vagaries of network interfacing hardware, and similar issues are not easily tested at the WebApp level.

Performance tests are designed to simulate real-world loading situations. As the number of simultaneous WebApp users grows, or the number of online transactions increases, or the amount of data (downloaded or uploaded) increases, performance testing will help answer the following questions:

- Does the server response time degrade to a point where it is noticeable and unacceptable?
- At what point (in terms of users, transactions, or data loading) does performance become unacceptable?
- What system components are responsible for performance degradation?
- What is the average response time for users under a variety of loading conditions?

- Does performance degradation have an impact on system security?
- Is WebApp reliability or accuracy affected as the load on the system grows?
- What happens when loads that are greater than maximum server capacity are applied?
- Does performance degradation have an impact on company revenues?

To develop answers to these questions, two different performance tests are conducted: (1) *load testing* examines real-world loading at a variety of load levels and in a variety of combinations, and (2) *stress testing* forces loading to be increased to the breaking point to determine how much capacity the WebApp environment can handle. Each of these testing strategies is considered in the sections that follow.

20.9.2 Load Testing

The intent of load testing is to determine how the WebApp and its server-side environment will respond to various loading conditions. As testing proceeds, permutations to the following variables define a set of test conditions:

N, number of concurrent users

T, number of online transactions per unit of time

D, data load processed by the server per transaction

In every case, these variables are defined within normal operating bounds of the system. As each test condition is run, one or more of the following measures are collected: average user response, average time to download a standardized unit of data, or average time to process a transaction. You should examine these measures to determine whether a precipitous decrease in performance can be traced to a specific combination of N, T, and D.

Load testing can also be used to assess recommended connection speeds for users of the WebApp. Overall throughput, P, is computed in the following manner:

$$P = N \times T \times D$$

As an example, consider a popular sports news site. At a given moment, 20,000 concurrent users submit a request (a transaction, T) once every 2 minutes on average. Each transaction requires the WebApp to download a new article that averages 3K bytes in length. Therefore, throughput can be calculated as:

$$P = [20,000 \times 0.5 \times 3Kb]/60 = 500 \text{ Kbytes/sec}$$
$$= 4 \text{ megabits per second}$$

The network connection for the server would therefore have to support this data rate and should be tested to ensure that it does.

20.9.3 Stress Testing

Stress testing is a continuation of load testing, but in this instance the variables, N, T, and D are forced to meet and then exceed operational limits. The intent of these tests is to answer each of the following questions:

- Does the system degrade "gently," or does the server shut down as capacity is exceeded?
- Does server software generate "server not available" messages? More generally, are users aware that they cannot reach the server?
- Does the server queue resource requests and empty the queue once capacity demands diminish?
- Are transactions lost as capacity is exceeded?
- Is data integrity affected as capacity is exceeded?
- What values of N, T, and D force the server environment to fail? How does failure manifest itself? Are automated notifications sent to technical support staff at the server site?
- If the system does fail, how long will it take to come back online?
- Are certain WebApp functions (e.g., compute intensive functionality, data streaming capabilities) discontinued as capacity reaches the 80 or 90 percent level?

A variation of stress testing is sometimes referred to as *spike/bounce testing* [Spl01]. In this testing regime, load is spiked to capacity, then lowered quickly to normal operating conditions, and then spiked again. By bouncing system loading, you can determine how well the server can marshal resources to meet very high demand and then release them when normal conditions reappear (so that they are ready for the next spike).

TOOLS

Tools Taxonomy for WebApp Testing

In his paper on the testing of e-commerce systems, Lam [Lam01] presents a useful taxonomy of automated tools that have direct applicability for testing in a Web engineering context. We have appended representative tools in each category.[14]

Configuration and content management tools manage version and change control of WebApp content objects and functional component.

Representative tool(s): Comprehensive list at **www.daveeaton.com/scm/CMTools.html**
Database performance tools measure database performance, such as the time to perform selected database queries. These tools facilitate database optimization.
Representative tool(s): BMC Software (**www.bmc.com**)

---

14 Tools noted here do not represent an endorsement, but rather a sampling of tools in this category. In addition, tool names are registered trademarks of the companies noted.

Debuggers are typical programming tools that find and resolve software defects in the code. They are part of most modern application development environments.
Representative tool(s):
Accelerated Technology
(**www.acceleratedtechnology.com**)
Apple Debugging Tools
(**developer.apple.com/tools/performance/**)
IBM VisualAge Environment (**www.ibm.com**)
Microsoft Debugging Tools (**www.microsoft.com**)

Defect management systems record defects and track their status and resolution. Some include reporting tools to provide management information on defect spread and defect resolution rates.
Representative tool(s):
EXCEL Quickbigs (**www.excelsoftware.com**)
ForeSoft BugTrack (**www.bugtrack.net**)
McCabe TRUETrack (**www.mccabe.com**)

Network monitoring tools watch the level of network traffic. They are useful for identifying network bottlenecks and testing the link between front- and back-end systems.
Representative tool(s):
Comprehensive list at
www.slac.stanford.edu/xorg/nmtf/nmtf-tools.html

Regression testing tools store test cases and test data and can reapply the test cases after successive software changes.
Representative tool(s):
Compuware QARun
(**www.compuware.com/products/qacenter/qarun**)
Rational VisualTest (**www.rational.com**)
Seque Software (**www.seque.com**)

Site monitoring tools monitor a site's performance, often from a user perspective. Use them to compile statistics such as end-to-end response time and throughput and to periodically check a site's availability.
Representative tool(s): Keynote Systems
(**www.keynote.com**)

Stress tools help developers explore system behavior under high levels of operational usage and find a system's breakpoints.
Representative tool(s):
Mercury Interactive (**www.merc-int.com**)
Open-source testing tools
(**www.opensourcetesting.org/performance.php**)
Web Performance Load Tester
(**www.webperformanceinc.com**)

System resource monitors are part of most OS server and Web server software; they monitor resources such as disk space, CPU usage, and memory.
Representative tool(s):
Successful Hosting.com
(**www.successfulhosting.com**)
Quest Software Foglight (**www.quest.com**)

Test data generation tools assist users in generating test data.
Representative tool(s):
Comprehensive list at
www.softwareqatest.com/qatweb1.html

Test result comparators help compare the results of one set of testing to that of another set. Use them to check that code changes have not introduced adverse changes in system behavior.
Representative tool(s):
Useful list at **www.aptest.com/resources.html**

Transaction monitors measure the performance of high-volume transaction processing systems.
Representative tool(s):
QuotiumPro (**www.quotium.com**)
Software Research eValid
(**www.soft.com/eValid/index.html**)

Website security tools help detect potential security problems. You can often set up security probing and monitoring tools to run on a scheduled basis.
Representative tool(s):
Comprehensive list at
www.timberlinetechnologies.com/products/www.html

20.10 SUMMARY

The goal of WebApp testing is to exercise each of the many dimensions of WebApp quality with the intent of finding errors or uncovering issues that may lead to quality failures. Testing focuses on content, function, structure, usability, navigability, performance, compatibility, interoperability, capacity, and security. It incorporates reviews that occur as the WebApp is designed, and tests that are conducted once the WebApp has been implemented.

The WebApp testing strategy exercises each quality dimension by initially examining "units" of content, functionality, or navigation. Once individual units have been validated, the focus shifts to tests that exercise the WebApp as a whole. To accomplish this, many tests are derived from the user's perspective and are driven by information contained in use cases. A WebApp test plan is developed and identifies testing steps, work products (e.g., test cases), and mechanisms for the evaluation of test results. The testing process encompasses seven different types of testing.

Content testing (and reviews) focus on various categories of content. The intent is to uncover both semantic and syntactic errors that affect the accuracy of content or the manner in which it is presented to the end user. Interface testing exercises the interaction mechanisms that enable a user to communicate with the WebApp and validates aesthetic aspects of the interface. The intent is to uncover errors that result from poorly implemented interaction mechanisms or from omissions, inconsistencies, or ambiguities in interface semantics.

Navigation testing applies use cases, derived as part of the modeling activity, in the design of test cases that exercise each usage scenario against the navigation design. Navigation mechanisms are tested to ensure that any errors impeding completion of a use case are identified and corrected. Component testing exercises content and functional units within the WebApp.

Configuration testing attempts to uncover errors and/or compatibility problems that are specific to a particular client or server environment. Tests are then conducted to uncover errors associated with each possible configuration. Security testing incorporates a series of tests designed to exploit vulnerabilities in the WebApp and its environment. The intent is to find security holes. Performance testing encompasses a series of tests that are designed to assess WebApp response time and reliability as demands on server-side resource capacity increase.

PROBLEMS AND POINTS TO PONDER

20.1. Are there any situations in which WebApp testing should be totally disregarded?

20.2. In your own words, discuss the objectives of testing in a WebApp context.

20.3. Compatibility is an important quality dimension. What must be tested to ensure that compatibility exists for a WebApp?

20.4. Which errors tend to be more serious—client-side errors or server-side errors? Why?

20.5. What elements of the WebApp can be "unit tested"? What types of tests must be conducted only after the WebApp elements are integrated?

20.6. Is it always necessary to develop a formal written test plan? Explain.

20.7. Is it fair to say that the overall WebApp testing strategy begins with user-visible elements and moves toward technology elements? Are there exceptions to this strategy?

20.8. Is content testing *really* testing in a conventional sense? Explain.

20.9. Describe the steps associated with database testing for a WebApp. Is database testing predominantly a client-side or server-side activity?

20.10. What is the difference between testing that is associated with interface mechanisms and testing that addresses interface semantics?

20.11. Assume that you are developing an online pharmacy **(YourCornerPharmacy.com)** that caters to senior citizens. The pharmacy provides typical functions, but also maintains a database for each customer so that it can provide drug information and warn of potential drug interactions. Discuss any special usability tests for this WebApp.

20.12. Assume that you have implemented a drug interaction checking function for **YourCornerPharmacy.com** (Problem 20.11). Discuss the types of component-level tests that would have to be conducted to ensure that this function works properly. [Note: A database would have to be used to implement this function.]

20.13. What is the difference between testing for navigation syntax and navigation semantics?

20.14. Is it possible to test every configuration that a WebApp is likely to encounter on the server side? On the client side? If it is not, how do you select a meaningful set of configuration tests?

20.15. What is the objective of security testing? Who performs this testing activity?

20.16. YourCornerPharmacy.com (Problem 20.11) has become wildly successful, and the number of users has increased dramatically in the first two months of operation. Draw a graph that depicts probable response time as a function of number of users for a fixed set of server-side resources. Label the graph to indicate points of interest on the "response curve."

20.17. In response to it success **YourCornerPharmacy.com** (Problem 20.11) has implemented a special server solely to handle prescription refills. On average, 1000 concurrent users submit a refill request once every two minutes. The WebApp downloads a 500-byte block of data in response. What is the approximate required throughput for this server in megabits per second?

20.18. What is the difference between load testing and stress testing?

FURTHER READINGS AND INFORMATION SOURCES

The literature for WebApp testing continues to evolve. Books by Andrews and Whittaker (*How to Break Web Software,* Addison-Wesley, 2006), Ash (*The Web Testing Companion,* Wiley, 2003), Nguyen and his colleagues (*Testing Applications for the Web,* 2d ed., Wiley, 2003), Dustin and his colleagues (*Quality Web Systems,* Addison-Wesley, 2002), and Splaine and Jaskiel [Spl01] are among the most complete treatments of the subject published to date. Mosley (*Client-Server Software Testing on the Desktop and the Web,* Prentice Hall, 1999) addresses both client-side and server-side testing issues.

Useful information on WebApp testing strategies and methods, as well as a worthwhile discussion of automated testing tools is presented by Stottlemeyer (*Automated Web Testing Toolkit,* Wiley, 2001). Graham and her colleagues (*Software Test Automation,* Addison-Wesley, 1999) present additional material on automated tools.

Microsoft (*Performance Testing Guidance for Web Applications,* Microsoft Press, 2008) and Subraya (*Integrated Approach to Web Performance Testing,* IRM Press, 2006) present detailed treatments of performance testing for WebApps. Chirillo (*Hack Attacks Revealed,* 2d ed., Wiley, 2003), Splaine (*Testing Web Security,* Wiley, 2002), Klevinsky and his colleagues (*Hack I.T.:*

Security through Penetration Testing, Addison-Wesley, 2002), and Skoudis (*Counter Hack,* Prentice Hall, 2001) provide much useful information for those who must design security tests. In addition, books that address security testing for software in general can provide important guidance for those who must test WebApps. Representative titles include: Basta and Halton (*Computer Security and Penetration Testing,* Thomson Delmar Learning, 2007), Wysopal and his colleagues (*The Art of Software Security Testing,* Addison-Wesley, 2006), and Gallagher and his colleagues (*Hunting Security Bugs,* Microsoft Press, 2006).

A wide variety of information sources on WebApp testing is available on the Internet. An up-to-date list of World Wide Web references relevant to WebApp testing can be found at the SEPA website: **www.mhhe.com/engcs/compsci/pressman/professional/olc/ser.htm**.

FORMAL MODELING AND VERIFICATION

Unlike reviews and testing that begin once software models and code have been developed, formal modeling and verification incorporate specialized modeling methods that are integrated with prescribed verification approaches. Without the appropriate modeling approach, verification cannot be accomplished.

In this chapter I discuss two formal modeling and verification methods—*cleanroom software engineering* and *formal methods*. Both demand a specialized specification approach and each applies a unique verification method. Both are quite rigorous and neither is used widely by the software engineering community. But if you intend to build bulletproof software, these methods can help you immeasurably. They're worth learning about.

QUICK LOOK

What is it? How many times have you heard someone say, "Do it right the first time"? If we achieved that in software, there'd be considerably less effort expended on unnecessary software rework. Two advanced software engineering methods—cleanroom software engineering and formal methods—help a software team to "do it right the first time" by providing a mathematically based approach to program modeling and the ability to verify that the model is correct. Cleanroom software engineering emphasizes mathematical verification of correctness before program construction commences and certification of software reliability as part of the testing activity. Formal methods use set theory and logic notation to create a clear statement of facts (requirements) that can be analyzed to improve (or even prove) correctness and consistency. The bottom line for both methods is the creation of software with extremely low failure rates.

Who does it? A specially trained software engineer.

Why is it important? Mistakes create rework. Rework takes time and increases costs. Wouldn't it be nice if you could dramatically reduce the number of mistakes (bugs) introduced as the

software is designed and built? That's the premise of formal modeling and verification.

What are the steps? Requirements and design models are created using specialized notation that is amenable to mathematical verification. Cleanroom software engineering uses box structure representation that encapsulates the system (or some aspect of the system) at a specific level of abstraction. Correctness verification is applied once the box structure design is complete. Once correctness has been verified for each box structure, statistical usage testing commences. Formal methods translate software requirements into a more formal representation by applying the notation and heuristics of sets to define the data invariant, states, and operations for a system function.

What is the work product? A specialized, formal model of requirements is developed. The results of correctness proofs and statistical use tests are recorded.

How do I ensure that I've done it right? Formal proof of correctness is applied to the requirements model. Statistical use testing exercises usage scenarios to ensure that errors in user functionality are uncovered and corrected.

Cleanroom software engineering is an approach that emphasizes the need to build correctness into software as it is being developed. Instead of the classic analysis, design, code, test, and debug cycle, the cleanroom approach suggests a different point of view [Lin94b]:

> The philosophy behind cleanroom software engineering is to avoid dependence on costly defect removal processes by writing code increments right the first time and verifying their correctness before testing. Its process model incorporates the statistical quality certification of code increments as they accumulate into a system.

In many ways, the cleanroom approach elevates software engineering to another level by emphasizing the need to *prove* correctness.

Models developed using *formal methods* are described using a formal syntax and semantics that specify system function and behavior. The specification is mathematical in form (e.g., predicate calculus can be used as the basis for a formal specification language). In his introduction to formal methods, Anthony Hall [Hal90] makes a comment that applies equally to cleanroom methods:

> Formal methods [and cleanroom software engineering] are controversial. Their advocates claim that they can revolutionize [software] development. Their detractors think they are impossibly difficult. Meanwhile, for most people, formal methods [and cleanroom software engineering] are so unfamiliar that it is difficult to judge the competing claims.

In this chapter, I explore formal modeling and verification methods and examine their potential impact on software engineering in the years to come.

21.1 THE CLEANROOM STRATEGY

Cleanroom software engineering makes use of a specialized version of the incremental software model introduced in Chapter 2. A "pipeline of software increments" [Lin94b] is developed by small independent software teams. As each increment is certified, it is integrated into the whole. Hence, functionality of the system grows with time.

The sequence of cleanroom tasks for each increment is illustrated in Figure 21.1. Within the pipeline for cleanroom increments, the following tasks occur:

Increment planning.   A project plan that adopts the incremental strategy is developed. The functionality of each increment, its projected size, and a cleanroom development schedule are created. Special care must be taken to ensure that certified increments will be integrated in a timely manner.

Requirements gathering.   Using techniques similar to those introduced in Chapter 5, a more-detailed description of customer-level requirements (for each increment) is developed.

Box structure specification.   A specification method that makes use of *box structures* is used to describe the functional specification. Box structures

FIGURE 21.1

The cleanroom
process model

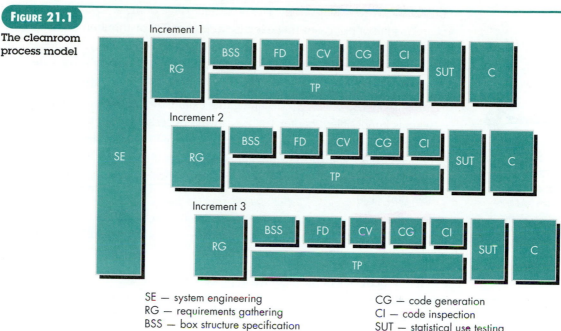

SE — system engineering
RG — requirements gathering
BSS — box structure specification
FD — formal design
CV — correctness verification

CG — code generation
CI — code inspection
SUT — statistical use testing
C — certification
TP — test planning

Quote:

"Cleanroom
software
engineering
achieves statistical
quality control
over software
development by
strictly separating
the design process
from the testing
process in a
pipeline of
incremental
software
development."

Harlan Mills

"isolate and separate the creative definition of behavior, data, and procedures at each level of refinement" [Hev93].

Formal design.   Using the box structure approach, cleanroom design is a natural and seamless extension of specification. Although it is possible to make a clear distinction between the two activities, specifications (called *black boxes*) are iteratively refined (within an increment) to become analogous to architectural and component-level designs (called *state boxes* and *clear boxes*, respectively).

Correctness verification.   The cleanroom team conducts a series of rigorous correctness verification activities on the design and then the code. Verification (Section 21.3.2) begins with the highest-level box structure (specification) and moves toward design detail and code. The first level of correctness verification occurs by applying a set of "correctness questions" [Lin88]. If these do not demonstrate that the specification is correct, more formal (mathematical) methods for verification are used.

Code generation, inspection, and verification.   The box structure specifications, represented in a specialized language, are translated into the appropriate programming language. Technical reviews (Chapter 15) are then used to ensure semantic conformance of the code and box structures and syntactic correctness of the code. Then correctness verification is conducted for the source code.

Statistical test planning.   The projected usage of the software is analyzed, and a suite of test cases that exercise a "probability distribution" of usage is planned and designed (Section 21.4). Referring to Figure 21.1, this cleanroom activity is conducted in parallel with specification, verification, and code generation.

Cleanroom emphasizes tests that exercise the way software is really used. Use cases provide input to the test planning process.

Statistical use testing.   Recalling that exhaustive testing of computer software is impossible (Chapter 18), it is always necessary to design a finite number of test cases. Statistical use techniques [Poo88] execute a series of tests derived from a statistical sample (the probability distribution noted earlier) of all possible program executions by all users from a targeted population (Section 21.4).

Certification.   Once verification, inspection, and usage testing have been completed (and all errors are corrected), the increment is certified as ready for integration.

The first four activities in the cleanroom process set the stage for the formal verification activities that follow. For this reason, I begin the discussion of the cleanroom approach with the modeling activities that are essential for formal verification to be applied.

21.2 FUNCTIONAL SPECIFICATION

Quote:

"It's a funny thing about life: If you refuse to accept anything but the best, you may very often get it."

W. Somerset Maugham

? **How is refinement accomplished as part of a box structure specification?**

The modeling approach in cleanroom software engineering uses a method called *box structure specification*. A "box" encapsulates the system (or some aspect of the system) at some level of detail. Through a process of elaboration or stepwise refinement, boxes are refined into a hierarchy where each box has referential transparency. That is, "the information content of each box specification is sufficient to define its refinement, without depending on the implementation of any other box" [Lin94b]. This enables the analyst to partition a system hierarchically, moving from essential representation at the top to implementation-specific detail at the bottom. Three types of boxes are used:

Black box.   The black box specifies the behavior of a system or a part of a system. The system (or part) responds to specific stimuli (events) by applying a set of transition rules that map the stimulus into a response.

State box.   The state box encapsulates state data and services (operations) in a manner that is analogous to objects. In this specification view, inputs to the state box (stimuli) and outputs (responses) are represented. The state box also represents the "stimulus history" of the black box, that is, the data encapsulated in the state box that must be retained between the transitions implied.

Clear box.   The transition functions that are implied by the state box are defined in the clear box. Stated simply, a clear box contains the procedural design for the state box.

FIGURE 21.2

FIGURE 21.2

Box structure
refinement

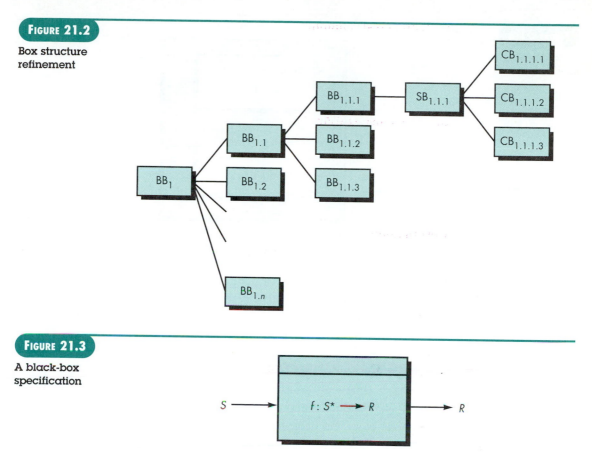

FIGURE 21.3

A black-box
specification

Figure 21.2 illustrates the refinement approach using box structure specification. A black box (BB_1) defines responses for a complete set of stimuli. BB_1 can be refined into a set of black boxes, $BB_{1.1}$ to $BB_{1.n}$, each of which addresses a class of behavior. Refinement continues until a cohesive class of behavior is identified (e.g., $BB_{1.1.1}$). A state box ($SB_{1.1.1}$) is then defined for the black box ($BB_{1.1.1}$). In this case, $SB_{1.1.1}$ contains all data and services required to implement the behavior defined by $BB_{1.1.1}$. Finally, $SB_{1.1.1}$ is refined into clear boxes ($CB_{1.1.1.n}$) and procedural design details are specified.

As each of these refinement steps occurs, verification of correctness also occurs. State-box specifications are verified to ensure that each conforms to the behavior defined by the parent black-box specification. Similarly, clear-box specifications are verified against the parent state box.

KEY POINT

Box structure
refinement and
correctness verification
occur simultaneously.

21.2.1 Black-Box Specification

A *black-box* specification describes an abstraction, stimuli, and response using the notation shown in Figure 21.3 [Mil88]. The function f is applied to a sequence S^* of inputs (stimuli) S and transforms them into an output (response) R. For simple software components, f may be a mathematical function, but in general, f is described using natural language (or a formal specification language).

FIGURE 21.4

A state-box
specification

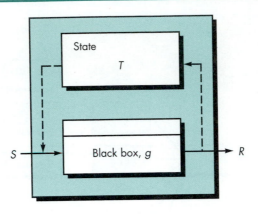

Many of the concepts introduced for object-oriented systems are also applicable for the black box. Data abstractions and the operations that manipulate those abstractions are encapsulated by the black box. Like a class hierarchy, the black-box specification can exhibit usage hierarchies in which low-level boxes inherit the properties of those boxes higher in the tree structure.

21.2.2 State-Box Specification

The *state box* is "a simple generalization of a state machine" [Mil88]. Recalling the discussion of behavioral modeling and state diagrams in Chapter 7, a state is some observable mode of system behavior. As processing occurs, a system responds to events (stimuli) by making a transition from the current state to some new state. As the transition is made, an action may occur. The state box uses a data abstraction to determine the transition to the next state and the action (response) that will occur as a consequence of the transition.

Referring to Figure 21.4 , the state box incorporates a black box *g*. The stimulus *S* that is input to the black box arrives from some external source and a set of internal system states *T*. Mills [Mil88] provides a mathematical description of the function *f* of the black box contained within the state box:

$$g : S^* \times T^* \rightarrow R \times T$$

where *g* is a subfunction that is tied to a specific state *t*. When considered collectively, the state-subfunction pairs (*t*, *g*) define the black-box function *f*.

21.2.3 Clear-Box Specification

The clear-box specification is closely aligned with procedural design and structured programming. In essence, the subfunction *g* within the state box is replaced by the structured programming constructs that implement *g*.

As an example, consider the clear box shown in Figure 21.5. The black box *g*, shown in Figure 21.3, is replaced by a sequence construct that incorporates a conditional.

FIGURE 21.5

A clear-box
specification

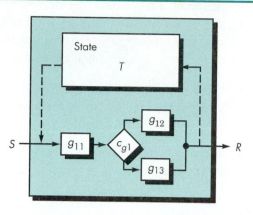

These, in turn, can be refined into lower-level clear boxes as stepwise refinement
proceeds.

It is important to note that the procedural specification described in the clear-box
hierarchy can be proved to be correct. This topic is considered in Section 21.3.

21.3   CLEANROOM DESIGN

Cleanroom software engineering makes heavy use of the structured programming
philosophy (Chapter 10). But in this case, structured programming is applied far more
rigorously.

Basic processing functions (described during earlier refinements of the specification) are refined using a "stepwise expansion of mathematical functions into
structures of logical connectives [e.g., if-then-else] and subfunctions, where the
expansion [is] carried out until all identified subfunctions could be directly stated in
the programming language used for implementation" [Dye92].

The structured programming approach can be used effectively to refine function,
but what about data design? Here a number of fundamental design concepts
(Chapter 8) come into play. Program data are encapsulated as a set of abstractions
that are serviced by subfunctions. The concepts of data encapsulation, information
hiding, and data typing are used to create the data design.

29.3.1   Design Refinement

Each clear-box specification represents the design of a procedure (subfunction)
required to accomplish a state-box transition. Within the clear box, structured programming constructs and stepwise refinement are used to represent procedural detail. For example, a program function f is refined into a sequence of subfunctions g
and h. These in turn are refined into conditional constructs (e.g., if-then-else and do-
while). Further refinement continues until there is enough procedural detail to create
the component in question.

At each level of refinement, the cleanroom team[1] performs a *formal correctness verification.* To accomplish this, a set of generic correctness conditions are attached to the structured programming constructs. If a function *f* is expanded into a sequence *g* and *h,* the correctness condition for all input to *f* is

? What conditions are applied to prove structured constructs correct?

- Does *g* followed by *h* do *f*?

When a function *p* is refined into a conditional of the form, if <*c*> then *q*, else *r*, the correctness condition for all input to *p* is

- Whenever condition <*c*> is true, does *q* do *p*; and whenever <*c*> is false, does *r* do *p*?

When function *m* is refined as a loop, the correctness conditions for all input to *m* are

- Is termination guaranteed?
- Whenever <*c*> is true, does *n* followed by *m* do *m*; and whenever <*c*> is false, does skipping the loop still do *m*?

Each time a clear box is refined to the next level of detail, these correctness conditions are applied.

21.3.2   Design Verification

If you limit yourself to just the structured constructs as you develop a procedural design, proof of correctness is straightforward. If you violate the constructs, correctness proofs are difficult or impossible.

You should note that the use of the structured programming constructs constrains the number of correctness tests that must be conducted. A single condition is checked for sequences; two conditions are tested for if-then-else, and three conditions are verified for loops.

To illustrate correctness verification for a procedural design, we use a simple example first introduced by Linger, Mills, and Witt [Lin79]. The intent is to design and verify a small program that finds the integer part *y* of a square root of a given integer *x*. The procedural design is represented using the flowchart in Figure 21.6.[2]

To verify the correctness of this design, entry and exit conditions are added as shown in Figure 21.6. The entry condition notes that *x* must be greater than or equal to 0. The exit condition requires that *x* remain unchanged and that *y* satisfy the expression noted in the figure. To prove the design to be correct, it is necessary to prove the conditions *init, loop, cont, yes,* and *exit* shown in Figure 21.6 are true in all cases. These are sometimes called *subproofs.*

1. The condition *init* demands that [$x \geq 0$ and $y = 0$]. Based on the requirements of the problem, the entry condition is assumed correct.[3] Therefore, the first part of the *init* condition, $x \geq 0$, is satisfied. Referring to the flowchart, the

---

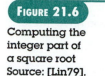

Computing the integer part of a square root
Source: [Lin79].

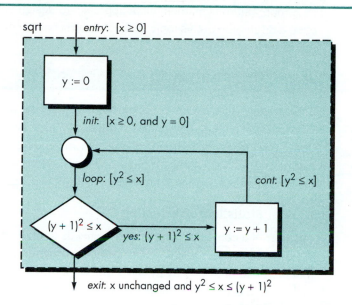

exit: x unchanged and $y^2 \le x \le (y + 1)^2$

statement immediately preceding the *init* condition, sets $y = 0$. Therefore, the second part of the *init* condition is also satisfied. Hence, *init* is true.

2. The *loop* condition may be encountered in one of two ways: (1) directly from *init* (in this case, the *loop* condition is satisfied directly) or via control flow that passes through the condition *cont*. Since the *cont* condition is identical to the *loop* condition, *loop* is true regardless of the flow path that leads to it.

3. The *cont* condition is encountered only after the value of y is incremented by 1. In addition, the control flow path that leads to *cont* can be invoked only if the *yes* condition is also true. Hence, if $(y + 1)^2 \le x$, it follows that $y^2 \le x$. The *cont* condition is satisfied.

4. The *yes* condition is tested in the conditional logic shown. Hence, the *yes* condition must be true when control flow moves along the path shown.

5. The *exit* condition first demands that x remain unchanged. An examination of the design indicates that x appears nowhere to the left of an assignment operator. There are no function calls that use x. Hence, it is unchanged. Since the conditional test $(y + 1)^2 \le x$ must fail to reach the *exit* condition, it follows that $(y + 1)^2 \le x$. In addition, the *loop* condition must still be true (i.e., $y^2 \le x$). Therefore, $(y + 1)^2 > x$ and $y^2 \le x$ can be combined to satisfy the exit condition.

To prove a design correct, you must first identify all conditions and then prove that each takes on the appropriate Boolean value. These are called *subproofs*.

You must further ensure that the loop terminates. An examination of the *loop* condition indicates that, because y is incremented and $x \ge 0$, the loop must eventually terminate.

The five steps just noted are a proof of the correctness of the design of the algorithm noted in Figure 21.6. You are now certain that the design will, in fact, compute the integer part of a square root.

A more rigorous mathematical approach to design verification is possible. However, a discussion of this topic is beyond the scope of this book. If you have interest, refer to [Lin79].

21.4   CLEANROOM TESTING

The strategy and tactics of cleanroom testing are fundamentally different from conventional testing approaches (Chapters 17 through 20). Conventional methods derive a set of test cases to uncover design and coding errors. The goal of cleanroom testing is to validate software requirements by demonstrating that a statistical sample of use cases (Chapter 5) have been executed successfully.

21.4.1   Statistical Use Testing

The user of a computer program rarely needs to understand the technical details of the design. The user-visible behavior of the program is driven by inputs and events that are often produced by the user. But in complex systems, the possible spectrum of input and events (i.e., the use cases) can be extremely broad. What subset of use cases will adequately verify the behavior of the program? This is the first question addressed by statistical use testing.

Statistical use testing "amounts to testing software the way users intend to use it" [Lin94b]. To accomplish this, cleanroom testing teams (also called *certification teams*) must determine a usage probability distribution for the software. The specification (black box) for each increment of the software is analyzed to define a set of stimuli (inputs or events) that cause the software to change its behavior. Based on interviews with potential users, the creation of usage scenarios, and a general understanding of the application domain, a probability of use is assigned to each stimuli.

Test cases are generated for each set of stimuli[4] according to the usage probability distribution. To illustrate, consider the *SafeHome* system discussed earlier in this book. Cleanroom software engineering is being used to develop a software increment that manages user interaction with the security system keypad. Five stimuli have been identified for this increment. Analysis indicates the percent probability distribution of each stimulus. To make selection of test cases easier, these probabilities are mapped into intervals numbered between 1 and 99 [Lin94] and illustrated in the following table:

Program Stimulus	Probability	Interval
Arm/disarm (AD)	50%	1–49
Zone set (ZS)	15%	50–63
Query (Q)	15%	64–78
Test (T)	15%	79–94
Panic alarm	5%	95–99

---

4   Automated tools may be used to accomplish this. For further information, see [Dye92].

To generate a sequence of usage test cases that conform to the usage probability distribution, random numbers between 1 and 99 are generated. Each random number corresponds to an interval on the preceding probability distribution. Hence, the sequence of usage test cases is defined randomly but corresponds to the appropriate probability of stimuli occurrence. For example, assume the following random-number sequences are generated:

13-94-22-24-45-56
81-19-31-69-45-9
38-21-52-84-86-4

Selecting the appropriate stimuli based on the distribution interval shown in the table, the following use cases are derived:

AD–T–AD–AD–AD–ZS
T–AD–AD–AD–Q–AD–AD
AD–AD–ZS–T–T–AD

The testing team executes these use cases and verifies software behavior against the specification for the system. Timing for tests is recorded so that interval times may be determined. Using interval times, the certification team can compute mean-time-to-failure. If a long sequence of tests is conducted without failure, the MTTF is low and software reliability may be assumed high.

21.4.2 Certification

The verification and testing techniques discussed earlier in this chapter lead to software components (and entire increments) that can be certified. Within the context of the cleanroom software engineering approach, *certification* implies that the reliability [measured by mean-time-to-failure (MTTF)] can be specified for each component.

The potential impact of certifiable software components goes far beyond a single cleanroom project. Reusable software components can be stored along with their usage scenarios, program stimuli, and probability distributions. Each component would have a certified reliability under the usage scenario and testing regime described. This information is invaluable to others who intend to use the components.

The certification approach involves five steps [Woh94]: (1) usage scenarios must be created, (2) a usage profile is specified, (3) test cases are generated from the profile, (4) tests are executed and failure data are recorded and analyzed, and (5) reliability is computed and certified. Steps 1 through 4 have been discussed in an earlier section. Certification for cleanroom software engineering requires the creation of three models [Poo93]:

> **Sampling model.** Software testing executes *m* random test cases and is certified if no failures or a specified numbers of failures occur. The value of *m* is derived mathematically to ensure that required reliability is achieved.

How do we certify a software component?

Component model. A system composed of *n* components is to be certified. The component model enables the analyst to determine the probability that component *i* will fail prior to completion.

Certification model. The overall reliability of the system is projected and certified.

At the completion of statistical use testing, the certification team has the information required to deliver software that has a certified MTTF computed using each of these models. If you have further interest, see [Cur86], [Mus87], or [Poo93] for additional detail.

21.5 FORMAL METHODS CONCEPTS

The Encyclopedia of Software Engineering [Mar01] defines formal methods in the following manner:

> Formal methods used in developing computer systems are mathematically based techniques for describing system properties. Such formal methods provide frameworks within which people can specify, develop, and verify systems in a systematic, rather than ad hoc manner.

The desired properties of a formal specification—consistency, completeness, and lack of ambiguity—are the objectives of all specification methods. However, the mathematically based specification language used for formal methods results in a much higher likelihood of achieving these properties. The formal syntax of a specification language (Section 21.7) enables requirements or design to be interpreted in only one way, eliminating ambiguity that often occurs when a natural language (e.g., English) or a graphical notation (e.g., UML) must be interpreted by a reader. The descriptive facilities of set theory and logic notation enable a clear statement of requirements. To be consistent, requirements stated in one place in a specification should not be contradicted in another place. Consistency is achieved[5] by mathematically proving that initial facts can be formally mapped (using inference rules) into later statements within the specification.

To introduce basic formal methods concepts, let's consider a few simple examples to illustrate the use of mathematical specification, without getting bogged down in too much mathematical detail.

Example 1: A symbol table. A program is used to maintain a symbol table. Such a table is used frequently in many different types of applications. It consists of a collection of items without any duplication. An example of a typical symbol table is

---

5   In reality, completeness is difficult to ensure, even when formal methods are used. Some aspects of a system may be left undefined as the specification is being created; other characteristics may be purposely omitted to allow designers some freedom in choosing an implementation approach; and finally, it is impossible to consider every operational scenario in a large, complex system. Things may simply be omitted by mistake.

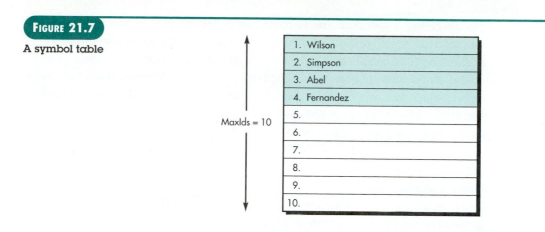

FIGURE 21.7

A symbol table

MaxIds = 10

| 1. Wilson |
| 2. Simpson |
| 3. Abel |
| 4. Fernandez |
| 5. |
| 6. |
| 7. |
| 8. |
| 9. |
| 10. |

shown in Figure 21.7. It represents the table used by an operating system to hold the names of the users of the system. Other examples of tables include the collection of names of staff in a payroll system, the collection of names of computers in a network communications system, and the collection of destinations in a system for producing transportation timetables.

Assume that the table presented in this example consists of no more than *MaxIds* names. This statement, which places a constraint on the table, is a component of a condition known as a *data invariant*. A data invariant is a condition that is true throughout the execution of the system that contains a collection of data. The data invariant that holds for the symbol table just discussed has two components: (1) that the table will contain no more than *MaxIds* names and (2) that there will be no duplicate names in the table. In the case of the symbol table program, this means that no matter when the symbol table is examined during execution of the system, it will always contain no more than *MaxIds* names and will contain no duplicates.

KEY POINT

A data invariant is a set of conditions that are true throughout the execution of the system that contains a collection of data.

Another important concept is that of a *state*. Many formal languages, such as OCL (Section 21.7.1), use the notion of states as they were discussed in Chapter 7; that is, a system can be in one of several states, each representing an externally observable mode of behavior. However, a different definition for the term *state* is used in the Z language (Section 21.7.2). In Z (and related languages), the state of a system is represented by the system's stored data (hence, Z suggests a much larger number of states, representing each possible configuration of the data). Using the latter definition in the example of the symbol table program, the state is the symbol table.

ADVICE

Another way of looking at the notion of the state is to say that data determines state. That is, you can examine data to see what state the system is in.

The final concept is that of an *operation*. This is an action that takes place within a system and reads or writes data. If the symbol table program is concerned with adding and removing names from the symbol table, then it will be associated with two operations: an operation to *add()* a specified name to the symbol table and an operation to *remove()* an existing name from the table.[6] If the program provides the facility to

---

6   It should be noted that adding a name cannot occur in the *full* state and deleting a name is impossible in the *empty* state.

check whether a specific name is contained in the table, then there would be an operation that would return some indication of whether the name is in the table.

Three types of conditions can be associated with operations: invariants, preconditions, and postconditions. An *invariant* defines what is guaranteed not to change. For example, the symbol table has an invariant that states that the number of elements is always less than or equal to *MaxIds*. A *precondition* defines the circumstances in which a particular operation is valid. For example, the precondition for an operation that adds a name to a staff identifier symbol table is valid only if the name that is to be added is not contained in the table and also if there are fewer than *MaxIds* staff identifiers in the table. The *postcondition* of an operation defines what is guaranteed to be true upon completion of an operation. This is defined by its effect on the data. For the *add()* operation, the postcondition would specify mathematically that the table has been augmented with the new identifier.

Example 2: A block handler. One of the more important parts of a simple operating system is the subsystem that maintains files created by users. Part of the filing subsystem is the *block handler*. Files in the file store are composed of blocks of storage that are held on a file storage device. During the operation of the computer, files will be created and deleted, requiring the acquisition and release of blocks of storage. In order to cope with this, the filing subsystem will maintain a reservoir of unused (free) blocks and keep track of blocks that are currently in use. When blocks are released from a deleted file, they are normally added to a queue of blocks waiting to be added to the reservoir of unused blocks. This is shown in Figure 21.8. In this figure, a number of components are shown: the reservoir of unused blocks, the blocks that currently make up the files administered by the operating system, and those blocks that are waiting to be added to the reservoir. The waiting blocks are held in a queue, with each element of the queue containing a set of blocks from a deleted file.

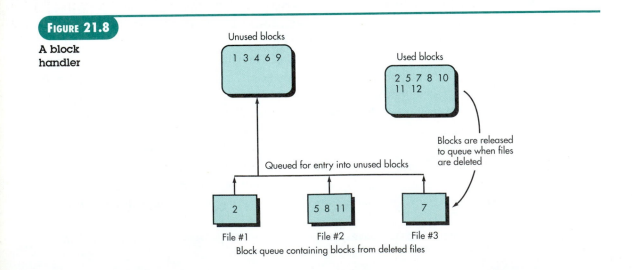

FIGURE 21.8

A block handler

Brain storming techniques can work well when you must develop a data invariant for a reasonably complex function. Have members of the software team write bounds, restrictions, and limitations for the function and then combine and edit.

For this subsystem the state is the collection of free blocks, the collection of used blocks, and the queue of returned blocks. The data invariant, expressed in natural language, is

- No block will be marked as both unused and used.
- All the sets of blocks held in the queue will be subsets of the collection of currently used blocks.
- No elements of the queue will contain the same block numbers.
- The collection of used blocks and blocks that are unused will be the total collection of blocks that make up files.
- The collection of unused blocks will have no duplicate block numbers.
- The collection of used blocks will have no duplicate block numbers.

Some of the operations associated with this data are: *add()* a collection of blocks to the end of the queue, *remove()* a collection of used blocks from the front of the queue and place them in the collection of unused blocks, and *check()* whether the queue of blocks is empty.

The precondition of *add()* is that the blocks to be added must be in the collection of used blocks. The postcondition is that the collection of blocks is now found at the end of the queue. The precondition of *remove()* is that the queue must have at least one item in it. The postcondition is that the blocks must be added to the collection of unused blocks. The *check()* operation has no precondition. This means that the operation is always defined, regardless of what value the state is. The postcondition delivers the value *true* if the queue is empty and *false* otherwise.

In the examples noted in this section, I introduce the key concepts of formal specification but without emphasizing the mathematics that are required to make the specification formal. In Section 21.6, I consider how mathematical notation can be used to formally specify some element of a system.

21.6 APPLYING MATHEMATICAL NOTATION[7] FOR FORMAL SPECIFICATION

To illustrate the use of mathematical notation in the formal specification of a software component, we revisit the block handler example presented in Section 21.5. To review, an important component of a computer's operating system maintains files that have been created by users. The block handler maintains a reservoir of unused blocks and will also keep track of blocks that are currently in use. When blocks are released from a deleted file, they are normally added to a queue of blocks waiting to

---

7   I have written this section making the assumption that you are familiar with the mathematical notation associated with sets and sequences and the logical notation used in predicate calculus. If you need a review, a brief overview is presented as a supplementary resource at the 7th edition website. For more detailed information, see [Jec06] or [Pot04].

be added to the reservoir of unused blocks. This has been depicted schematically in Figure 21.8.

How can I represent states and data invariants using a set and logic operators?

A set named *BLOCKS* will consist of every block number. *AllBlocks* is a set of blocks that lie between 1 and *MaxBlocks*. The state will be modeled by two sets and a sequence. The two sets are *used* and *free*. Both contain blocks—the *used* set contains the blocks that are currently used in files, and the *free* set contains blocks that are available for new files. The sequence will contain sets of blocks that are ready to be released from files that have been deleted. The state can be described as

$$used, free: \mathbb{P} \, BLOCKS$$
$$BlockQueue: seq \, \mathbb{P} \, BLOCKS$$

This is very much like the declaration of program variables. It states that *used* and *free* will be sets of blocks and that *BlockQueue* will be a sequence, each element of which will be a set of blocks. The data invariant can be written as

$$used \cap free = \varnothing \wedge$$
$$used \cup free = AllBlocks \wedge$$
$$\forall \, i: dom \, BlockQueue \bullet BlockQueue \, i \subseteq used \wedge$$
$$\forall \, i, j: dom \, BlockQueue \bullet i \neq j = BlockQueue \, i \cap BlockQueue \, j = \varnothing$$

WebRef

Extensive information of formal methods can be found at **www.afm.sbu .ac.uk**.

The mathematical components of the data invariant match four of the bulleted, natural-language components described earlier. The first line of the data invariant states that there will be no common blocks in the used collection and free collections of blocks. The second line states that the collection of used blocks and free blocks will always be equal to the whole collection of blocks in the system. The third line indicates the *i*th element in the block queue will always be a subset of the used blocks. The final line states that, for any two elements of the block queue that are not the same, there will be no common blocks in these two elements. The final two natural language components of the data invariant are implemented by virtue of the fact that *used* and *free* are sets and therefore will not contain duplicates.

The first operation to be defined is one that removes an element from the head of the block queue. The precondition is that there must be at least one item in the queue:

$$\#BlockQueue > 0,$$

The postcondition is that the head of the queue must be removed and placed in the collection of free blocks and the queue adjusted to show the removal:

$$used' = used \setminus head \, BlockQueue \wedge$$
$$free' = free \cup head \, BlockQueue \wedge$$
$$BlockQueue' = tail \, BlockQueue$$

A convention used in many formal methods is that the value of a variable after an operation is primed. Hence, the first component of the preceding expression states that the new used blocks (*used'*) will be equal to the old used blocks minus the blocks that have been removed. The second component states that the new free blocks (*free'*) will be the old free blocks with the head of the block queue added to it. The third component states that the new block queue will be equal to the tail of the old value of the block queue, that is, all elements in the queue apart from the first one. A second operation adds a collection of blocks, *Ablocks,* to the block queue. The precondition is that *Ablocks* is currently a set of used blocks:

? How do I represent pre- and postconditions?

$$Ablocks \subseteq used$$

The postcondition is that the set of blocks is added to the end of the block queue and the set of used and free blocks remains unchanged:

$$BlockQueue' = BlockQueue \frown \langle Ablocks \rangle \wedge$$
$$used' = used \wedge$$
$$free' = free$$

There is no question that the mathematical specification of the block queue is considerably more rigorous than a natural language narrative or a graphical model. The additional rigor requires effort, but the benefits gained from improved consistency and completeness can be justified for some application domains.

21.7 FORMAL SPECIFICATION LANGUAGES

A formal specification language is usually composed of three primary components: (1) a syntax that defines the specific notation with which the specification is represented, (2) semantics to help define a "universe of objects" [Win90] that will be used to describe the system, and (3) a set of relations that define the rules that indicate which objects properly satisfy the specification.

The syntactic domain of a formal specification language is often based on a syntax that is derived from standard set theory notation and predicate calculus. The *semantic domain* of a specification language indicates how the language represents system requirements.

It is possible to use different semantic abstractions to describe the same system in different ways. We did this in a less formal fashion in Chapters 6 and 7. Information, function, and behavior were each represented. Different modeling notation can be used to represent the same system. The semantics of each representation provides complementary views of the system. To illustrate this approach when formal methods are used, assume that a formal specification language is used to describe the set of events that cause a particular state to occur in a system. Another formal relation depicts all functions that occur within a given state. The intersection of these two relations provides an indication of the events that will cause specific functions to occur.

A variety of formal specification languages are in use today. OCL [OMG03b], Z [ISO02], LARCH [Gut93], and VDM [Jon91] are representative formal specification languages that exhibit the characteristics noted previously. In this chapter, I present a brief discussion of OCL and Z.

TABLE 21.1   SUMMARY OF KEY OCL NOTATION

x.y	Obtain the property y of object x. A property can be an attribute, the set of objects at the end of an association, the result of evaluating an operation, or other things depending on the type of UML diagram. If x is a Set, then y is applied to every element of x; the results are collected into a new Set.
c−>f()	Apply the built-in OCL operation f to Collection c itself (as opposed to each of the objects in c). Examples of built-in operations are listed below.
and, or, =, <>	Logical and, logical or, equals, not-equals.
p implies q	True if either q is true or p is false.

Sample of Operations on Collections (including Sets and Sequences)

C−>size()	The number of elements in Collection c.
C−>isEmpty()	True if c has no elements, false otherwise.
c1−>includesAll(c2)	True if every element of c2 is found in c1.
c1−>excludesAll(c2)	True if no element of c2 is found in c1.
C−>forAll(elem | boolexpr)	True if boolexpr is true when applied to every element of c. As an element is being evaluated, it is bound to the variable elem, which can be used in boolexpr. This implements universal quantification, discussed earlier.
C−>forAll(elem1, elem2 | boolexpr)	Same as above, except that boolexpr is evaluated for every possible *pair* of elements taken from c, including cases where the pair consists of the same element.
C−>isUnique(elem | expr)	True if expr evaluates to a different value when applied to every element of c.

Sample of Operations Specific to Sets

s1−>intersection(s2)	The set of those elements found s1 and also in s2.
s1−>union(s2)	The set of those elements found in either s1 or s2.
s1−>excluding(x)	The set s1 with object x omitted.

Sample Operation Specific to Sequences

Seq−>first()	The object that is the first element in the sequence seq.

21.7.1   Object Constraint Language (OCL)[8]

Object Constraint Language (OCL) is a formal notation developed so that users of UML can add more precision to their specifications. All of the power of logic and discrete mathematics is available in the language. However, the designers of OCL decided that only ASCII characters (rather than conventional mathematical notation) should

---

8   This section has been contributed by Professor Timothy Lethbridge of The University of Ottawa and is presented here with permission.

be used in OCL statements. This makes the language more friendly to people who are less mathematically inclined, and more easily processed by computer. But it also makes OCL a little wordy in places.

To use OCL, you start with one or more UML diagrams—most commonly class, state, or activity diagrams (Appendix 1). OCL expressions are added and state facts about elements of the diagrams. These expressions are called *constraints*; any implementation derived from the model must ensure each of the constraints always remains true.

Like an object-oriented programming language, an OCL expression involves operators operating on objects. However, the result of a complete expression must always be a Boolean, that is, true or false. The objects can be instances of the OCL **Collection** class, of which **Set** and **Sequence** are two subclasses.

The object **self** is the element of the UML diagram in the context of which the OCL expression is being evaluated. Other objects can be obtained by *navigating* using the . (dot) symbol from the **self** object. For example:

- If **self** is class **C**, with attribute **a**, then **self.a** evaluates to the object stored in **a**.
- If **C** has a one-to-many association called *assoc* to another class **D**, then **self.assoc** evaluates to a **Set** whose elements are of type **D**.
- Finally (and a little more subtly), if **D** has attribute **b**, then the expression **self.assoc.b** evaluates to the set of all the **b**'s belonging to all **D**'s.

OCL provides built-in operations implementing set and logic operators, constructive specification, and related mathematics. A small sample of these is presented in Table 21.1.

To illustrate the use of OCL in specification, we reexamine the block handler example, introduced in Section 21.5. The first step is to develop a UML model (Figure 21.9). This class diagram specifies many relationships among the objects involved. However, OCL expressions are added to allow implementers of the system to know more precisely what must remain true as the system runs.

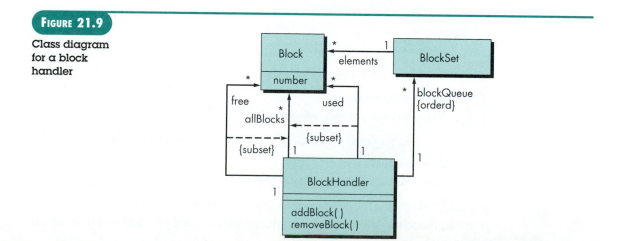

The OCL expressions that supplement the class diagram correspond to the six parts of the invariant discussed in Section 21.5. In the example that follows, the invariant is repeated in English and then the corresponding OCL expression is written. It is considered good practice to provide natural language text along with the formal logic; doing so helps you to understand the logic, and also helps reviewers to uncover mistakes, e.g., situations where English and the logic do not correspond.

1. *No block will be marked as both unused and used.*

   context BlockHandler inv:

       (self.used−>intersection(self.free)) −>isEmpty()

   Note that each expression starts with the key word ***context.*** This indicates the element of the UML diagram that the expression constrains. Alternatively, you could place the constraint directly on the UML diagram, surrounded by braces {}. The keyword **self** here refers to the instance of **BlockHandler;** in the following, as is permissible in OCL, we will omit the **self**.

2. *All the sets of blocks held in the queue will be subsets of the collection of currently used blocks.*

   context BlockHandler inv:

       blockQueue−>forAll(aBlockSet | used−>includesAll(aBlockSet))

3. *No elements of the queue will contain the same block numbers.*

   context BlockHandler inv:

       blockQueue−>forAll(blockSet1, blockSet2 |

           blockSet1 <> blockSet2 implies

           blockSet1.elements.number−>excludesAll(blockSet2elements.number))

   The expression before **implies** is needed to ensure we ignore pairs where both elements are the same block.

4. *The collection of used blocks and blocks that are unused will be the total collection of blocks that make up files.*

   context BlockHandler inv:

       allBlocks = used−>union(free)

5. *The collection of unused blocks will have no duplicate block numbers.*

   context BlockHandler inv:

       free−>isUnique(aBlock | aBlock.number)

6. *The collection of used blocks will have no duplicate block numbers.*

   context BlockHandler inv:

       used−>isUnique(aBlock | aBlock.number)

OCL can also be used to specify preconditions and postconditions of operations. For example, the following describes operations that remove and add sets of blocks to the queue. Note that the notation **x@pre** indicates the object **x** as it existed *prior* to the operation; this is opposite to mathematical notation discussed earlier, where it is the **x** *after* the operation that is specially designated (as **x'**).

```
context BlockHandler::removeBlocks()
    pre: blockQueue–>size() >0
    post: used = used@pre-blockQueue@pre–>first() and
        free = free@pre–>union(blockQueue@pre–>first()) and
        blockQueue = blockQueue@pre–>excluding(blockQueue@pre–>first)

context BlockHandler::addBlocks(aBlockSet :BlockSet)
    pre: used–>includesAll(aBlockSet.elements)
    post: (blockQueue.elements = blockQueue.elements@pre
        –> append (aBlockSet.elements) and
        used = used@pre and
        free = free@pre
```

OCL is a modeling language, but it has all of the attributes of a formal language. OCL allows the expression of various constraints, pre- and postconditions, guards, and other characteristics that relate to the objects represented in various UML models.

21.7.2 The Z Specification Language

Z (properly pronounced as "zed") is a specification language that is widely used within the formal methods community. The Z language applies typed sets, relations, and functions within the context of first-order predicate logic to build *schemas*—a means for structuring the formal specification.

WebRef

Detailed information about the Z language can be found at **www.users.cs .york.ac.uk/ ~susan/abs/ z.htm**.

Z specifications are organized as a set of schemas—a language structure that introduces variables and specifies the relationship between these variables. A schema is essentially the formal specification analog of the programming language component. Schemas are used to structure a formal specification in the same way that components are used to structure a system.

A schema describes the stored data that a system accesses and alters. In the context of Z, this is called the "state." This usage of the term *state* in Z is slightly different from the use of the word in the rest of this book.[9] In addition, the schema identifies the operations that are applied to change state and the relationships that occur within the system. The generic structure of a schema takes the form:

———— schemaName————————————————
    declarations
———————————————————————————————————
    invariant
———————————————————————————————————

———————

9 Recall that in other chapters *state* has been used to identify an externally observable mode of behavior for a system.

where declarations identify the variables that comprise the system state and the invariant imposes constraints on the manner in which the state can evolve. A summary of Z language notation is presented in Table 21.2.

TABLE 21.2   SUMMARY OF Z NOTATION

Z notation is based on typed set theory and first-order logic. Z provides a construct, called a schema, to describe a specification's state space and operations. A schema groups variable declarations with a list of predicates that constrain the possible value of a variable. In Z, the schema X is defined by the form

$$
\begin{array}{|l}
\hline
\quad X\text{---} \\
\text{declarations} \\
\hline
\text{predicates} \\
\hline
\end{array}
$$

Global functions and constants are defined by the form

$$
\begin{array}{|l}
\text{declarations} \\
\hline
\text{predicates} \\
\end{array}
$$

The declaration gives the type of the function or constant, while the predicate gives it value. Only an abbreviated set of Z symbols is presented in this table.

Sets:

$S : \mathbb{P}\, X$	S is declared as a set of Xs.
$X \in S$	x is a member of S.
$x \notin S$	x is not a member of S.
$S \subseteq T$	S is a subset of T: Every member of S is also in T.
$S \cup T$	The union of S and T: It contains every member of S or T or both.
$S \cap T$	The intersection of S and T: It contains every member of both S and T.
$S \setminus T$	The difference of S and T: It contains every member of S except those also in T.
$\varnothing$	Empty set: It contains no members.
$\{x\}$	Singleton set: It contains just x.
$\mathbb{N}$	The set of natural numbers 0, 1, 2, ….
$S : \mathbb{F}\, X$	S is declared as a finite set of Xs.
$\max\,(S)$	The maximum of the nonempty set of numbers S.

Functions:

$f{:}X \rightarrowtail Y$	f is declared as a partial injection from X to Y.
$\operatorname{dom} f$	The domain of f: the set of values x for which $f(x)$ is defined.
$\operatorname{ran} f$	The range of f: the set of values taken by $f(x)$ as x varies over the domain of f.
$f \oplus \{x \mapsto y\}$	A function that agrees with f except that x is mapped to y.
$\{x\} \lhd f$	A function like f, except that x is removed from its domain.

Logic:

$P \wedge Q$	P and Q: It is true if both P and Q are true.
$P \Rightarrow Q$	P implies Q: It is true if either Q is true or P is false.
$\theta\, S' = \theta\, S$	No components of schema S change in an operation.

The following example of a schema describes the state of the block handler and the data invariant:

──── BlockHandler ─────────────────────────
used, free : $\mathbb{P}$ *BLOCKS*
BlockQueue : seq $\mathbb{P}$ *BLOCKS*
used $\cap$ *free* = $\varnothing$ $\wedge$
used $\cup$ *free* = *AllBlocks* $\wedge$
$\forall i$: **dom** *BlockQueue* • *BlockQueue i* $\subseteq$ *used* $\wedge$
$\forall i, j$: dom *BlockQueue* • $i \neq j$ => *BlockQueue i* $\cap$ *BlockQueue j* = $\varnothing$
───

As we have noted, the schema consists of two parts. The part above the central line represents the variables of the state, while the part below the central line describes the data invariant. Whenever the schema specifies operations that change the state, it is preceded by the Δ symbol. The following example of a schema describes the operation that removes an element from the block queue:

──── RemoveBlocks ──────────────────
Δ *BlockHandler*
─────────────────────────────────
#BlockQueue > 0,
used' = *used* \ head *BlockQueue* $\wedge$
free' = *free* $\cup$ head *BlockQueue* $\wedge$
BlockQueue' = tail *BlockQueue*
─────────────────────────────────

The inclusion of Δ *BlockHandler* results in all variables that make up the state being available for the *RemoveBlocks* schema and ensures that the data invariant will hold before and after the operation has been executed.

The second operation, which adds a collection of blocks to the end of the queue, is represented as

---
────AddBlocks────────────────────
Δ *BlockHandler*
Ablocks? : BLOCKS
─────────────────────────────────
Ablocks? $\subseteq$ *used*
BlockQueue' = *BlockQueue* ⌢ ⟨Ablocks?⟩ $\wedge$
used' = *used* $\wedge$
free' = *free*
─────────────────────────────────

By convention in Z, an input variable that is read, but does not form part of the state, is terminated by a question mark. Thus, Ablocks?, which acts as an input parameter, is terminated by a question mark.

21.8 SUMMARY

Cleanroom software engineering is a formal approach to software development that can lead to software that has remarkably high quality. It uses box structure specification for analysis and design modeling and emphasizes correctness verification, rather than testing, as the primary mechanism for finding and removing errors. Statistical use testing is applied to develop the failure rate information necessary to certify the reliability of delivered software.

The cleanroom approach begins with analysis and design models that use a box structure representation. A "box" encapsulates the system (or some aspect of the system) at a specific level of abstraction. Black boxes are used to represent the externally observable behavior of a system. State boxes encapsulate state data and operations. A clear box is used to model the procedural design that is implied by the data and operations of a state box.

Correctness verification is applied once the box structure design is complete. The procedural design for a software component is partitioned into a series of subfunctions. To prove the correctness of the subfunctions, exit conditions are defined for each subfunction and a set of subproofs is applied. If each exit condition is satisfied, the design must be correct.

Once correctness verification is complete, statistical use testing commences. Unlike conventional testing, cleanroom software engineering does not emphasize unit or integration testing. Rather, the software is tested by defining a set of usage scenarios, determining the probability of use for each scenario, and then defining random tests that conform to the probabilities. The error records that result are

---

10 Tools noted here do not represent an endorsement, but rather a sampling of tools in this category. In most cases, tool names are trademarked by their respective developers.

combined with sampling, component, and certification models to enable mathematical computation of projected reliability for the software component.

Formal methods use the descriptive facilities of set theory and logic notation to enable a software engineer to create a clear statement of facts (requirements). The underlying concepts that govern formal methods are: (1) the data invariant, a condition true throughout the execution of the system that contains a collection of data; (2) the state, a representation of a system's externally observable mode of behavior, or (in Z and related languages) the stored data that a system accesses and alters; and (3) the operation, an action that takes place in a system and reads or writes data to a state. An operation is associated with two conditions: a precondition and a postcondition.

Will cleanroom software engineering or formal methods ever be widely used? The answer is "probably not." They are more difficult to learn than conventional software engineering methods and represent significant "culture shock" for some software practitioners. But the next time you hear someone lament, "Why can't we get this software right the first time?" you'll know that there are techniques that can help you to do exactly that.

PROBLEMS AND POINTS TO PONDER

21.1. If you had to pick one aspect of cleanroom software engineering that makes it radically different from conventional or object-oriented software engineering approaches, what would it be?

21.2. How do an incremental process model and certification work together to produce high-quality software?

21.3. Using box structure specification, develop "first-pass" analysis and design models for the *SafeHome* system.

21.4. A bubble-sort algorithm is defined in the following manner:

```
procedure bubblesort;
var i, t, integer;
begin
repeat until t=a[1]
        t:=a[1];
        for j:= 2 to n do
            if a[j-1] > a[j] then begin
                t:=a[j-1];
                a[j-1]:=a[j];
                a[j]:=t;
                end
    endrep
    end
```

Partition the design into subfunctions, and define a set of conditions that would enable you to prove that this algorithm is correct.

21.5. Document a correctness verification proof for the bubble sort discussed in Problem 21.4.

21.6. Select a program that you use regularly (e.g., an e-mail handler, a word processor, a spreadsheet program). Create a set of usage scenarios for the program. Define the probability of use for each scenario, and then develop a program stimuli and probability distribution table similar to the one shown in Section 21.4.1.

21.7. For the program stimuli and probability distribution table developed in Problem 21.6, use a random-number generator to develop a set of test cases for use in statistical use testing.

21.8. In your own words, describe the intent of certification in the cleanroom software engineering context.

21.9. You have been assigned to a team that is developing software for a fax modem. Your job is to develop the "phone book" portion of the application. The phone book function enables up to *MaxNames* people to be stored along with associated company names, fax numbers, and other related information. Using natural language, define

    a. The data invariant.
    b. The state.
    c. The operations that are likely.

21.10. You have been assigned to a software team that is developing software, called MemoryDoubler, that provides greater apparent memory for a PC than physical memory. This is accomplished by identifying, collecting, and reassigning blocks of memory that have been assigned to an existing application but are not being used. The unused blocks are reassigned to applications that require additional memory. Making appropriate assumptions and using natural language, define

    a. The data invariant.
    b. The state.
    c. The operations that are likely.

21.11. Using the OCL or Z notation presented in Table 21.1 or 21.2, select some part of the *SafeHome* security system described earlier in this book and attempt to specify it with OCL or Z.

21.12. Using one or more of the information sources noted in the references to this chapter or *Further Readings and Information Sources,* develop a half-hour presentation on the basic syntax and semantics of a formal specification language other than OCL or Z.

FURTHER READINGS AND INFORMATION SOURCES

Relatively few books on advanced specification and verification techniques have been published in recent years. However, some new additions to the literature are worth considering. A book edited by Gabbar (*Modern Formal Methods and Applications,* Springer, 2006) presents both fundamentals, new developments, and advanced applications. Jackson (*Software Abstractions,* The MIT Press, 2006) presents all of the basics and an approach that he calls "lightweight formal methods." Monin and Hinchey (*Understanding Formal Methods,* Springer, 2003) provide an excellent introduction to the subject. Butler and other editors (*Integrated Formal Methods,* Springer, 2002) present a variety of papers on formal methods topics.

In addition to books referenced in this chapter, Prowell and his colleagues (*Cleanroom Software Engineering: Technology and Process,* Addison-Wesley, 1999) provide an in-depth treatment of all important aspects of the cleanroom approach. Useful discussions of cleanroom topics have been edited by Poore and Trammell (*Cleanroom Software Engineering: A Reader,* Blackwell Publishing, 1996). Becker and Whittaker (*Cleanroom Software Engineering Practices,* Idea Group Publishing, 1996) present an excellent overview for those who are unfamiliar with cleanroom practices.

The Cleanroom Pamphlet (Software Technology Support Center, Hill AF Base, April 1995) contains reprints of a number of important articles. The Data and Analysis Center for Software (DACS) (**www.dacs.dtic.mil**) provides many useful papers, guidebooks, and other information sources on cleanroom software engineering.

Design verification via proof of correctness lies at the heart of the cleanroom approach. Books by Cupillari (*The Nuts and Bolts of Proofs,* 3d ed., Academic Press, 2005), Solow (*How to*

Read and Do Proofs, 4th ed., Wiley, 2004), Eccles (*An Introduction to Mathematical Reasoning,* Cambridge University Press, 1998), provide excellent introductions into the mathematical basics. Stavely (*Toward Zero-Defect Software,* Addison-Wesley, 1998), Baber (*Error-Free Software,* Wiley, 1991), and Schulmeyer (*Zero Defect Software,* McGraw-Hill, 1990) discuss proof of correctness in considerable detail.

In the formal methods domain, books by Casey (*A Programming Approach to Formal Methods,* McGraw-Hill, 2000), Hinchey and Bowan (*Industrial Strength Formal Methods,* Springer-Verlag, 1999), Hussmann (*Formal Foundations for Software Engineering Methods,* Springer-Verlag, 1997), and Sheppard (*An Introduction to Formal Specification with Z and VDM,* McGraw-Hill, 1995) provide useful guidance. In addition, language-specific books such as Warmer and Kleppe (*Object Constraint Language,* Addison-Wesley, 1998), Jacky (*The Way of Z: Practical Programming with Formal Methods,* Cambridge University Press, 1997), Harry (*Formal Methods Fact File: VDM and Z,* Wiley, 1997), and Cooper and Barden (*Z in Practice,* Prentice-Hall, 1995) provide useful introductions to formal methods as well as a variety of modeling languages.

A wide variety of information sources on cleanroom software engineering and formal methods is available on the Internet. An up-to-date list of World Wide Web references relevant to formal modeling and verification can be found at the SEPA website: **www.mhhe.com/engcs/ compsci/pressman/professional/olc/ser.htm**.

Change is inevitable when computer software is built. And change increases the level of confusion when you and other members of a software team are working on a project. Confusion arises when changes are not analyzed before they are made, recorded before they are implemented, reported to those with a need to know, or controlled in a manner that will improve quality and reduce error. Babich [Bab86] discusses this when he states:

> The art of coordinating software development to minimize . . . confusion is called configuration management. Configuration management is the art of identifying, organizing, and controlling modifications to the software being built by a programming team. The goal is to maximize productivity by minimizing mistakes.

Software configuration management (SCM) is an umbrella activity that is applied throughout the software process. Because change can occur at any time,

---

QUICK
LOOK

What is it? When you build computer software, change happens. And because it happens, you need to manage it effectively. Software configuration management (SCM), also called change management, is a set of activities designed to manage change by identifying the work products that are likely to change, establishing relationships among them, defining mechanisms for managing different versions of these work products, controlling the changes imposed, and auditing and reporting on the changes made.

Who does it? Everyone involved in the software process is involved with change management to some extent, but specialized support positions are sometimes created to manage the SCM process.

Why is it important? If you don't control change, it controls you. And that's never good. It's very easy for a stream of uncontrolled changes to turn a well-run software project into chaos. As a consequence, software quality suffers and delivery is delayed. For that reason,

change management is an essential part of quality management.

What are the steps? Because many work products are produced when software is built, each must be uniquely identified. Once this is accomplished, mechanisms for version and change control can be established. To ensure that quality is maintained as changes are made, the process is audited; and to ensure that those with a need to know are informed about changes, reporting is conducted.

What is the work product? A Software Configuration Management Plan defines the project strategy for change management. In addition, when formal SCM is invoked, the change control process produces software change requests, reports, and engineering change orders.

How do I ensure that I've done it right? When every work product can be accounted for, traced, and controlled; when every change can be tracked and analyzed; when everyone who needs to know about a change has been informed—you've done it right.

SCM activities are developed to (1) identify change, (2) control change, (3) ensure that change is being properly implemented, and (4) report changes to others who may have an interest.

It is important to make a clear distinction between software support and software configuration management. Support is a set of software engineering activities that occur after software has been delivered to the customer and put into operation. Software configuration management is a set of tracking and control activities that are initiated when a software engineering project begins and terminates only when the software is taken out of operation.

A primary goal of software engineering is to improve the ease with which changes can be accommodated and reduce the amount of effort expended when changes must be made. In this chapter, I discuss the specific activities that enable you to manage change.

22.1 SOFTWARE CONFIGURATION MANAGEMENT

The output of the software process is information that may be divided into three broad categories: (1) computer programs (both source level and executable forms), (2) work products that describe the computer programs (targeted at various stakeholders), and (3) data or content (contained within the program or external to it). The items that comprise all information produced as part of the software process are collectively called a *software configuration*.

> **uote:**
>
> "There is nothing permanent except change."
>
> **Heraclitus,
> 500 B.C.**

As software engineering work progresses, a hierarchy of *software configuration items* (SCIs)—a named element of information that can be as small as a single UML diagram or as large as the complete design document—is created. If each SCI simply led to other SCIs, little confusion would result. Unfortunately, another variable enters the process—*change*. Change may occur at any time, for any reason. In fact, the *First Law of System Engineering* [Ber80] states: "No matter where you are in the system life cycle, the system will change, and the desire to change it will persist throughout the life cycle."

What is the origin of these changes? The answer to this question is as varied as the changes themselves. However, there are four fundamental sources of change:

> **?** **What is the origin of changes that are requested for software?**

- New business or market conditions dictate changes in product requirements or business rules.

- New stakeholder needs demand modification of data produced by information systems, functionality delivered by products, or services delivered by a computer-based system.

- Reorganization or business growth/downsizing causes changes in project priorities or software engineering team structure.

- Budgetary or scheduling constraints cause a redefinition of the system or product.

Software configuration management is a set of activities that have been developed to manage change throughout the life cycle of computer software. SCM can be viewed as a software quality assurance activity that is applied throughout the software process. In the sections that follow, I describe major SCM tasks and important concepts that can help you to manage change.

22.1.1   An SCM Scenario[1]

A typical CM operational scenario involves a project manager who is in charge of a software group, a configuration manager who is in charge of the CM procedures and policies, the software engineers who are responsible for developing and maintaining the software product, and the customer who uses the product. In the scenario, assume that the product is a small one involving about 15,000 lines of code being developed by a team of six people. (Note that other scenarios of smaller or larger teams are possible, but, in essence, there are generic issues that each of these projects face concerning CM.)

What are the goals of and the activities performed by each of the constituencies involved in change management?

At the operational level, the scenario involves various roles and tasks. For the project manager, the goal is to ensure that the product is developed within a certain time frame. Hence, the manager monitors the progress of development and recognizes and reacts to problems. This is done by generating and analyzing reports about the status of the software system and by performing reviews on the system.

The goals of the configuration manager are to ensure that procedures and policies for creating, changing, and testing of code are followed, as well as to make information about the project accessible. To implement techniques for maintaining control over code changes, this manager introduces mechanisms for making official requests for changes, for evaluating them (via a Change Control Board that is responsible for approving changes to the software system), and for authorizing changes. The manager creates and disseminates task lists for the engineers and basically creates the project context. Also, the manager collects statistics about components in the software system, such as information determining which components in the system are problematic.

KEY POINT

There must be a mechanism to ensure that simultaneous changes to the same component are properly tracked, managed, and executed.

For the software engineers, the goal is to work effectively. This means engineers do not unnecessarily interfere with each other in the creation and testing of code and in the production of supporting work products. But, at the same time, they try to communicate and coordinate efficiently. Specifically, engineers use tools that help build a consistent software product. They communicate and coordinate by notifying one another about tasks required and tasks completed. Changes are propagated across each other's work by merging files. Mechanisms exist to ensure that, for components that undergo simultaneous changes, there is some way of resolving conflicts and

---

1   This section is extracted from [Dar01]. Special permission to reproduce "Spectrum of Functionality in CM System" by Susan Dart [Dar01], © 2001 by Carnegie Mellon University is granted by the Software Engineering Institute.

merging changes. A history is kept of the evolution of all components of the system along with a log with reasons for changes and a record of what actually changed. The engineers have their own workspace for creating, changing, testing, and integrating code. At a certain point, the code is made into a baseline from which further development continues and from which variants for other target machines are made.

The customer uses the product. Since the product is under CM control, the customer follows formal procedures for requesting changes and for indicating bugs in the product.

Ideally, a CM system used in this scenario should support all these roles and tasks; that is, the roles determine the functionality required of a CM system. The project manager sees CM as an auditing mechanism; the configuration manager sees it as a controlling, tracking, and policy making mechanism; the software engineer sees it as a changing, building, and access control mechanism; and the customer sees it as a quality assurance mechanism.

22.1.2   Elements of a Configuration Management System

In her comprehensive white paper on software configuration management, Susan Dart [Dar01] identifies four important elements that should exist when a configuration management system is developed:

- *Component elements*—a set of tools coupled within a file management system (e.g., a database) that enables access to and management of each software configuration item.

- *Process elements*—a collection of actions and tasks that define an effective approach to change management (and related activities) for all constituencies involved in the management, engineering, and use of computer software.

- *Construction elements*—a set of tools that automate the construction of software by ensuring that the proper set of validated components (i.e., the correct version) have been assembled.

- *Human elements*—a set of tools and process features (encompassing other CM elements) used by the software team to implement effective SCM.

These elements (to be discussed in more detail in later sections) are not mutually exclusive. For example, component elements work in conjunction with construction elements as the software process evolves. Process elements guide many human activities that are related to SCM and might therefore be considered human elements as well.

22.1.3   Baselines

Change is a fact of life in software development. Customers want to modify requirements. Developers want to modify the technical approach. Managers want to modify the project strategy. Why all this modification? The answer is really quite simple.

As time passes, all constituencies know more (about what they need, which approach would be best, and how to get it done and still make money). This additional knowledge is the driving force behind most changes and leads to a statement of fact that is difficult for many software engineering practitioners to accept: *Most changes are justified!*

A *baseline* is a software configuration management concept that helps you to control change without seriously impeding justifiable change. The IEEE (IEEE Std. No. 610.12-1990) defines a baseline as:

> A specification or product that has been formally reviewed and agreed upon, that thereafter serves as the basis for further development, and that can be changed only through formal change control procedures.

Before a software configuration item becomes a baseline, changes may be made quickly and informally. However, once a baseline is established, changes can be made, but a specific, formal procedure must be applied to evaluate and verify each change.

In the context of software engineering, a baseline is a milestone in the development of software. A baseline is marked by the delivery of one or more software configuration items that have been approved as a consequence of a technical review (Chapter 15). For example, the elements of a design model have been documented and reviewed. Errors are found and corrected. Once all parts of the model have been reviewed, corrected, and then approved, the design model becomes a baseline. Further changes to the program architecture (documented in the design model) can be made only after each has been evaluated and approved. Although baselines can be defined at any level of detail, the most common software baselines are shown in Figure 22.1.

FIGURE 22.1

Baselined SCIs and the project database

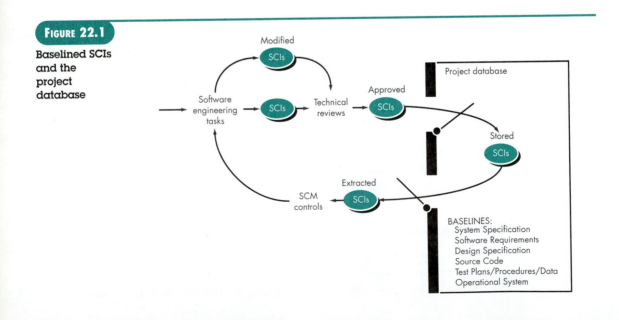

The progression of events that lead to a baseline is also illustrated in Figure 22.1. Software engineering tasks produce one or more SCIs. After SCIs are reviewed and approved, they are placed in a *project database* (also called a *project library* or *software repository* and discussed in Section 22.2). When a member of a software engineering team wants to make a modification to a baselined SCI, it is copied from the project database into the engineer's private workspace. However, this extracted SCI can be modified only if SCM controls (discussed later in this chapter) are followed. The arrows in Figure 22.1 illustrate the modification path for a baselined SCI.

22.1.4 Software Configuration Items

I have already defined a software configuration item as information that is created as part of the software engineering process. In the extreme, a SCI could be considered to be a single section of a large specification or one test case in a large suite of tests. More realistically, an SCI is all or part of a work product (e.g., a document, an entire suite of test cases, or a named program component).

In addition to the SCIs that are derived from software work products, many software engineering organizations also place software tools under configuration control. That is, specific versions of editors, compilers, browsers, and other automated tools are "frozen" as part of the software configuration. Because these tools were used to produce documentation, source code, and data, they must be available when changes to the software configuration are to be made. Although problems are rare, it is possible that a new version of a tool (e.g., a compiler) might produce different results than the original version. For this reason, tools, like the software that they help to produce, can be baselined as part of a comprehensive configuration management process.

In reality, SCIs are organized to form configuration objects that may be cataloged in the project database with a single name. A *configuration object* has a name, attributes, and is "connected" to other objects by relationships. Referring to Figure 22.2, the configuration objects, **DesignSpecification, DataModel, ComponentN, SourceCode,** and **TestSpecification** are each defined separately. However, each of the objects is related to the others as shown by the arrows. A curved arrow indicates a compositional relation. That is, **DataModel** and **ComponentN** are part of the object **DesignSpecification.** A double-headed straight arrow indicates an interrelationship. If a change were made to the **SourceCode** object, the interrelationships enable you to determine what other objects (and SCIs) might be affected.[2]

---

2   These relationships are defined within the database. The structure of the database (repository) is discussed in greater detail in Section 22.2.

FIGURE 22.2

Configuration
objects

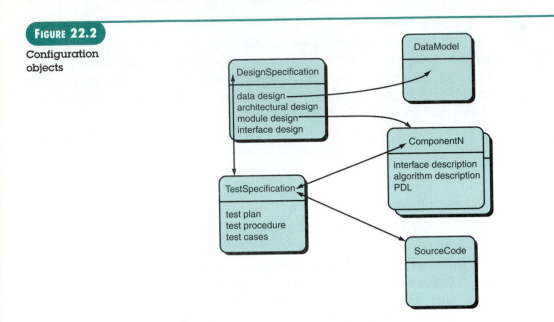

22.2   THE SCM REPOSITORY

In the early days of software engineering, software configuration items were maintained as paper documents (or punched computer cards!), placed in file folders or three-ring binders, and stored in metal cabinets. This approach was problematic for many reasons: (1) finding a configuration item when it was needed was often difficult, (2) determining which items were changed, when and by whom was often challenging, (3) constructing a new version of an existing program was time consuming and error prone, and (4) describing detailed or complex relationships between configuration items was virtually impossible.

Today, SCIs are maintained in a project database or repository. *Webster's Dictionary* defines the word *repository* as "any thing or person thought of as a center of accumulation or storage." During the early history of software engineering, the repository was indeed a person—the programmer who had to remember the location of all information relevant to a software project, who had to recall information that was never written down and reconstruct information that had been lost. Sadly, using a person as "the center for accumulation and storage" (although it conforms to Webster's definition) does not work very well. Today, the repository is a "thing"—a database that acts as the center for both accumulation and storage of software engineering information. The role of the person (the software engineer) is to interact with the repository using tools that are integrated with it.

22.2.1   The Role of the Repository

The SCM repository is the set of mechanisms and data structures that allow a software team to manage change in an effective manner. It provides the obvious functions of a modern database management system by ensuring data integrity, sharing, and integration. In addition, the SCM repository provides a hub for the integration of software tools, is central to the flow of the software process, and can enforce uniform structure and format for software engineering work products.

To achieve these capabilities, the repository is defined in terms of a meta-model. The *meta-model* determines how information is stored in the repository, how data can be accessed by tools and viewed by software engineers, how well data security and integrity can be maintained, and how easily the existing model can be extended to accommodate new needs.

22.2.2   General Features and Content

The features and content of the repository are best understood by looking at it from two perspectives: what is to be stored in the repository and what specific services are provided by the repository. A detailed breakdown of types of representations, documents, and other work products that are stored in the repository is presented in Figure 22.3.

A robust repository provides two different classes of services: (1) the same types of services that might be expected from any sophisticated database management system and (2) services that are specific to the software engineering environment.

A repository that serves a software engineering team should also (1) integrate with or directly support process management functions, (2) support specific rules that govern the SCM function and the data maintained within the repository, (3) provide an interface to other software engineering tools, and (4) accommodate storage of sophisticated data objects (e.g., text, graphics, video, audio).

WebRef

An example of a commercially available repository can be obtained at **www.oracle.com/ technology/ products/ repository/index .html**.

FIGURE 22.3

Content of the repository

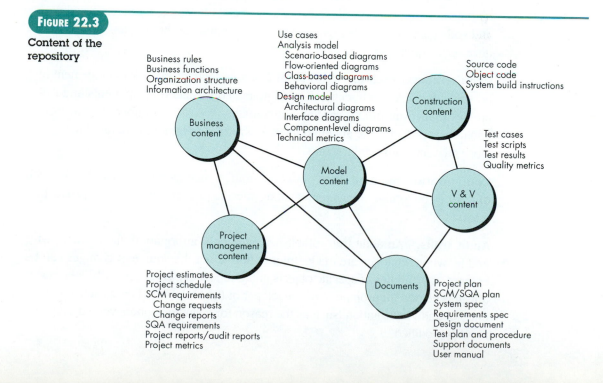

22.2.3 SCM Features

To support SCM, the repository must have a tool set that provides support for the following features:

Versioning.   As a project progresses, many versions (Section 22.3.2) of individual work products will be created. The repository must be able to save all of these versions to enable effective management of product releases and to permit developers to go back to previous versions during testing and debugging.

The repository must be able to control a wide variety of object types, including text, graphics, bit maps, complex documents, and unique objects like screen and report definitions, object files, test data, and results. A mature repository tracks versions of objects with arbitrary levels of granularity; for example, a single data definition or a cluster of modules can be tracked.

Dependency tracking and change management.   The repository manages a wide variety of relationships among the data elements stored in it. These include relationships between enterprise entities and processes, among the parts of an application design, between design components and the enterprise information architecture, between design elements and deliverables, and so on. Some of these relationships are merely associations, and some are dependencies or mandatory relationships.

The ability to keep track of all of these relationships is crucial to the integrity of the information stored in the repository and to the generation of deliverables based on it, and it is one of the most important contributions of the repository concept to the improvement of the software process. For example, if a UML class diagram is modified, the repository can detect whether related classes, interface descriptions, and code components also require modification and can bring affected SCIs to the developer's attention.

Requirements tracing.   This special function depends on link management and provides the ability to track all the design and construction components and deliverables that result from a specific requirements specification (forward tracing). In addition, it provides the ability to identify which requirement generated any given work product (backward tracing).

Configuration management.   A configuration management facility keeps track of a series of configurations representing specific project milestones or production releases.

Audit trails.   An audit trail establishes additional information about when, why, and by whom changes are made. Information about the source of changes can be entered as attributes of specific objects in the repository. A repository trigger mechanism is helpful for prompting the developer or the tool that is being used to initiate entry of audit information (such as the reason for a change) whenever a design element is modified.

22.3 THE SCM PROCESS

The software configuration management process defines a series of tasks that have four primary objectives: (1) to identify all items that collectively define the software configuration, (2) to manage changes to one or more of these items, (3) to facilitate the construction of different versions of an application, and (4) to ensure that software quality is maintained as the configuration evolves over time.

A process that achieves these objectives need not be bureaucratic or ponderous, but it must be characterized in a manner that enables a software team to develop answers to a set of complex questions:

? **What questions should the SCM process be designed to answer?**

- How does a software team identify the discrete elements of a software configuration?

- How does an organization manage the many existing versions of a program (and its documentation) in a manner that will enable change to be accommodated efficiently?

- How does an organization control changes before and after software is released to a customer?

- Who has responsibility for approving and ranking requested changes?

- How can we ensure that changes have been made properly?

- What mechanism is used to apprise others of changes that are made?

These questions lead to the definition of five SCM tasks—identification, version control, change control, configuration auditing, and reporting—illustrated in Figure 22.4.

Referring to the figure, SCM tasks can viewed as concentric layers. SCIs flow outward through these layers throughout their useful life, ultimately becoming part

FIGURE 22.4

Layers of the SCM process

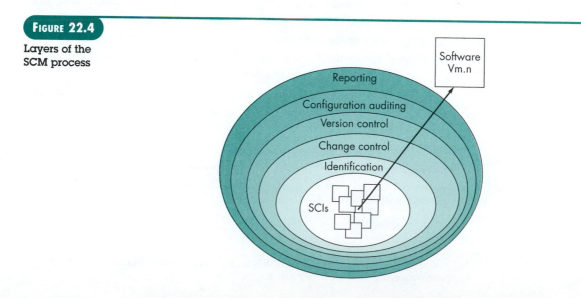

of the software configuration of one or more versions of an application or system. As an SCI moves through a layer, the actions implied by each SCM task may or may not be applicable. For example, when a new SCI is created, it must be identified. However, if no changes are requested for the SCI, the change control layer does not apply. The SCI is assigned to a specific version of the software (version control mechanisms come into play). A record of the SCI (its name, creation date, version designation, etc.) is maintained for configuration auditing purposes and reported to those with a need to know. In the sections that follow, we examine each of these SCM process layers in more detail.

22.3.1   Identification of Objects in the Software Configuration

To control and manage software configuration items, each should be separately named and then organized using an object-oriented approach. Two types of objects can be identified [Cho89]: basic objects and aggregate objects.[3] A *basic object* is a unit of information that you create during analysis, design, code, or test. For example, a basic object might be a section of a requirements specification, part of a design model, source code for a component, or a suite of test cases that are used to exercise the code. An *aggregate object* is a collection of basic objects and other aggregate objects. For example, a **DesignSpecification** is an aggregate object. Conceptually, it can be viewed as a named (identified) list of pointers that specify aggregate objects such as **ArchitecturalModel** and **DataModel,** and *basic objects* such as **ComponentN** and **UMLClassDiagramN**.

KEY POINT

The interrelationships established for configuration objects allow you to assess the impact of change.

Each object has a set of distinct features that identify it uniquely: a name, a description, a list of resources, and a "realization." The object name is a character string that identifies the object unambiguously. The object description is a list of data items that identify the SCI type (e.g., model element, program, data) represented by the object, a project identifier, and change and/or version information. Resources are "entities that are provided, processed, referenced or otherwise required by the object" [Cho89]. For example, data types, specific functions, or even variable names may be considered to be object resources. The realization is a pointer to the "unit of text" for a basic object and null for an aggregate object.

Configuration object identification can also consider the relationships that exist between named objects. For example, using the simple notation

Class diagram <part-of> requirements model;

Requirements model <part-of> requirements specification;

you can create a hierarchy of SCIs.

---

3   The concept of an aggregate object [Gus89] has been proposed as a mechanism for representing a complete version of a software configuration.

In many cases, objects are interrelated across branches of the object hierarchy. These cross-structural relationships can be represented in the following manner:

> DataModel <interrelated> DataFlowModel
>
> DataModel <interrelated> TestCaseClassM

In the first case, the interrelationship is between a composite object, while the second relationship is between an aggregate object (**DataModel**) and a basic object (**TestCaseClassM**).

The identification scheme for software objects must recognize that objects evolve throughout the software process. Before an object is baselined, it may change many times, and even after a baseline has been established, changes may be quite frequent.

22.3.2   Version Control

Version control combines procedures and tools to manage different versions of configuration objects that are created during the software process. A version control system implements or is directly integrated with four major capabilities: (1) a project database (repository) that stores all relevant configuration objects, (2) a *version management* capability that stores all versions of a configuration object (or enables any version to be constructed using differences from past versions), (3) a *make facility* that enables you to collect all relevant configuration objects and construct a specific version of the software. In addition, version control and change control systems often implement an *issues tracking* (also called *bug tracking*) capability that enables the team to record and track the status of all outstanding issues associated with each configuration object.

A number of version control systems establish a *change set*—a collection of all changes (to some baseline configuration) that are required to create a specific version of the software. Dart [Dar91] notes that a change set "captures all changes to all files in the configuration along with the reason for changes and details of who made the changes and when."

A number of named change sets can be identified for an application or system. This enables you to construct a version of the software by specifying the change sets (by name) that must be applied to the baseline configuration. To accomplish this, a *system modeling* approach is applied. The system model contains: (1) a *template* that includes a component hierarchy and a "build order" for the components that describes how the system must be constructed, (2) construction rules, and (3) verification rules.[4]

A number of different automated approaches to version control have been proposed over the last few decades. The primary difference in approaches is the sophistication of the attributes that are used to construct specific versions and variants of a system and the mechanics of the process for construction.

---

4   It is also possible to query the system model to assess how a change in one component will impact other components.

The Concurrent Versions System (CVS)

The use of tools to achieve version control is essential for effective change management. The *Concurrent Versions System* (CVS) is a widely used tool for version control. Originally designed for source code, but useful for any text-based file, the CVS system (1) establishes a simple repository, (2) maintains all versions of a file in a single named file by storing only the differences between progressive versions of the original file, and (3) protects against simultaneous changes to a file by establishing different directories for each developer, thus insulating one from another. CVS merges changes when each developer completes her work.

It is important to note that CVS is not a "build" system; that is, it does not construct a specific version of the software. Other tools (e.g., *Makefile*) must be integrated with CVS to accomplish this. CVS does not implement a change control process (e.g., change requests, change reports, bug tracking).

Even with these limitations, CVS "is a dominant open-source network-transparent version control system [that] is useful for everyone from individual developers to large, distributed teams" [CVS07]. Its client-server architecture allows users to access files via Internet connections, and its open-source philosophy makes it available on most popular platforms.

CVS is available at no cost for Windows, Mac OS, LINUX, and UNIX environments. See [CVS07] for further details.

22.3.3 Change Control

The reality of change control in a modern software engineering context has been summed up beautifully by James Bach [Bac98]:

> Change control is vital. But the forces that make it necessary also make it annoying. We worry about change because a tiny perturbation in the code can create a big failure in the product. But it can also fix a big failure or enable wonderful new capabilities. We worry about change because a single rogue developer could sink the project; yet brilliant ideas originate in the minds of those rogues, and a burdensome change control process could effectively discourage them from doing creative work.

Bach recognizes that we face a balancing act. Too much change control and we create problems. Too little, and we create other problems.

For a large software project, uncontrolled change rapidly leads to chaos. For such projects, change control combines human procedures and automated tools to provide a mechanism for the control of change. The change control process is illustrated schematically in Figure 22.5. A *change request* is submitted and evaluated to assess technical merit, potential side effects, overall impact on other configuration objects and system functions, and the projected cost of the change. The results of the evaluation are presented as a *change report,* which is used by a *change control authority* (CCA)—a person or group that makes a final decision on the status and priority of the change. An *engineering change order* (ECO) is generated for each approved change. The ECO describes the change to be made, the constraints that must be respected, and the criteria for review and audit.

The object(s) to be changed can be placed in a directory that is controlled solely by the software engineer making the change. A version control system (see the CVS sidebar) updates the original file once the change has been made. As an alternative,

Quote:

"The art of progress is to preserve order amid change and to preserve change amid order."

Alfred North Whitehead

KEY POINT

It should be noted that a number of change requests may be combined to result in a single ECO and that ECOs typically result in changes to multiple configuration objects.

FIGURE 22.5

**The change
control process**

Need for change is recognized

↓

Change request from user

↓

Developer evaluates

↓

Change report is generated

↓

Change control authority decides

↙   ↘

Request is queued for action, ECO generated   Change request is denied

↓   ↓

Assign individuals to configuration objects   User is informed

↓

"Check out" configuration objects (items)

↓

Make the change

↓

Review (audit) the change

↓

"Check in" the configuration items that have been changed

↓

Establish a baseline for testing

↓

Perform quality assurance and testing activities

↓

"Promote" changes for inclusion in next release (revision)

↓

Rebuild appropriate version of software

↓

Review (audit) the change to all configuration items

↓

Include changes in new version

↓

Distribute the new version

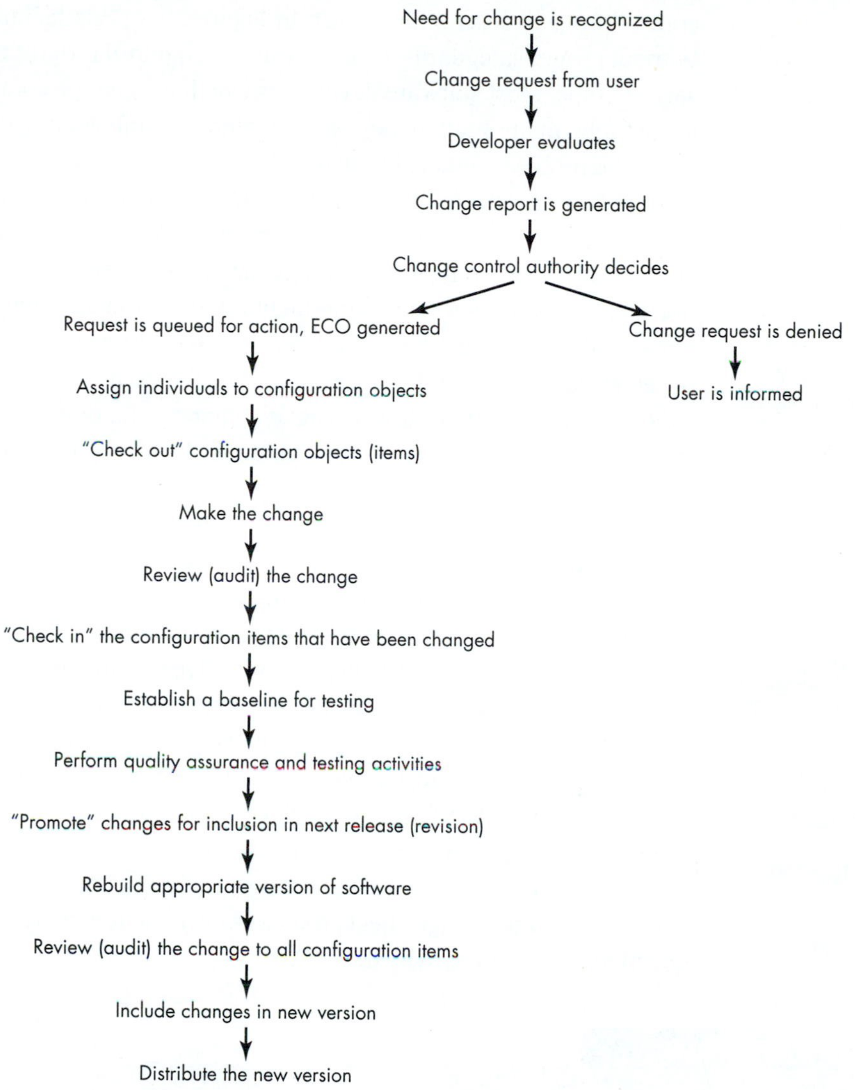

the object(s) to be changed can be "checked out" of the project database (repository), the change is made, and appropriate SQA activities are applied. The object(s) is (are) then "checked in" to the database and appropriate version control mechanisms (Section 22.3.2) are used to create the next version of the software.

These version control mechanisms, integrated within the change control process, implement two important elements of change management—access control and synchronization control. *Access control* governs which software engineers have the authority to access and modify a particular configuration object. *Synchronization control* helps to ensure that parallel changes, performed by two different people, don't overwrite one another.

You may feel uncomfortable with the level of bureaucracy implied by the change control process description shown in Figure 22.5. This feeling is not uncommon. Without proper safeguards, change control can retard progress and create unnecessary red tape. Most software developers who have change control mechanisms (unfortunately, many have none) have created a number of layers of control to help avoid the problems alluded to here.

Opt for a bit more change control than you think you'll need. It's likely that too much will be the right amount.

Prior to an SCI becoming a baseline, only *informal change control* need be applied. The developer of the configuration object (SCI) in question may make whatever changes are justified by project and technical requirements (as long as changes do not affect broader system requirements that lie outside the developer's scope of work). Once the object has undergone technical review and has been approved, a baseline can be created.[5] Once an SCI becomes a baseline, *project level change control* is implemented. Now, to make a change, the developer must gain approval from the project manager (if the change is "local") or from the CCA if the change affects other SCIs. In some cases, formal generation of change requests, change reports, and ECOs is dispensed with. However, assessment of each change is conducted and all changes are tracked and reviewed.

When the software product is released to customers, *formal change control* is instituted. The formal change control procedure has been outlined in Figure 22.5.

uote:

"Change is inevitable, except for vending machines."

Bumper sticker

The change control authority plays an active role in the second and third layers of control. Depending on the size and character of a software project, the CCA may be composed of one person—the project manager—or a number of people (e.g., representatives from software, hardware, database engineering, support, marketing). The role of the CCA is to take a global view, that is, to assess the impact of change beyond the SCI in question. How will the change affect hardware? How will the change affect performance? How will the change modify customers' perception of the product? How will the change affect product quality and reliability? These and many other questions are addressed by the CCA.

SAFEHOME

SCM Issues

The scene: Doug Miller's office as the *SafeHome* software project begins.

The players: Doug Miller (manager of the *SafeHome* software engineering team) and Vinod Raman, Jamie Lazar, and other members of the product software engineering team.

The conversation:

Doug: I know it's early, but we've got to talk about change management.

Vinod (laughing): Hardly. Marketing called this morning with a few "second thoughts." Nothing major, but it's just the beginning.

---

5   A baseline can be created for other reasons as well. For example, when "daily builds" are created, all components checked in by a given time become the baseline for the next day's work.

Jamie: We've been pretty informal about change management on past projects.

Doug: I know, but this is bigger and more visible, and as I recall . . .

Vinod (nodding): We got killed by uncontrolled changes on the home lighting control project . . . remember the delays that . . .

Doug (frowning): A nightmare that I'd prefer not to relive.

Jamie: So what do we do?

Doug: As I see it, three things. First we have to develop—or borrow—a change control process.

Jamie: You mean how people request changes?

Vinod: Yeah, but also how we evaluate the change, decide when to do it (if that's what we decide), and how we keep records of what's affected by the change.

Doug: Second, we've got to get a really good SCM tool for change and version control.

Jamie: We can build a database for all of our work products.

Vinod: They're called SCIs in this context, and most good tools provide some support for that.

Doug: That's a good start, now we have to . . .

Jamie: Uh, Doug, you said there were three things . . .

Doug (smiling): Third—we've all got to commit to follow the change management process and use the tools—no matter what, okay?

22.3.4   Configuration Audit

Identification, version control, and change control help you to maintain order in what would otherwise be a chaotic and fluid situation. However, even the most successful control mechanisms track a change only until an ECO is generated. How can a software team ensure that the change has been properly implemented? The answer is twofold: (1) technical reviews and (2) the software configuration audit.

The technical review (Chapter 15) focuses on the technical correctness of the configuration object that has been modified. The reviewers assess the SCI to determine consistency with other SCIs, omissions, or potential side effects. A technical review should be conducted for all but the most trivial changes.

A *software configuration audit* complements the technical review by assessing a configuration object for characteristics that are generally not considered during review. The audit asks and answers the following questions:

? **What are the primary questions that we ask during a configuration audit?**

1. Has the change specified in the ECO been made? Have any additional modifications been incorporated?

2. Has a technical review been conducted to assess technical correctness?

3. Has the software process been followed and have software engineering standards been properly applied?

4. Has the change been "highlighted" in the SCI? Have the change date and change author been specified? Do the attributes of the configuration object reflect the change?

5. Have SCM procedures for noting the change, recording it, and reporting it been followed?

6. Have all related SCIs been properly updated?

In some cases, the audit questions are asked as part of a technical review. However, when SCM is a formal activity, the configuration audit is conducted separately by the quality assurance group. Such formal configuration audits also ensure that the correct SCIs (by version) have been incorporated into a specific build and that all documentation is up-to-date and consistent with the version that has been built.

22.3.5 Status Reporting

Configuration status reporting (sometimes called *status accounting*) is an SCM task that answers the following questions: (1) What happened? (2) Who did it? (3) When did it happen? (4) What else will be affected?

Develop a "need to know" list for every configuration object and keep it up-to-date. When a change is made, be sure that everyone on the list is notified.

The flow of information for configuration status reporting (CSR) is illustrated in Figure 22.5. Each time an SCI is assigned new or updated identification, a CSR entry is made. Each time a change is approved by the CCA (i.e., an ECO is issued), a CSR entry is made. Each time a configuration audit is conducted, the results are reported as part of the CSR task. Output from CSR may be placed in an online database or website, so that software developers or support staff can access change information by keyword category. In addition, a CSR report is generated on a regular basis and is intended to keep management and practitioners appraised of important changes.

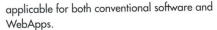

---

6   Tools noted here do not represent an endorsement, but rather a sampling of tools in this category. In most cases, tool names are trademarked by their respective developers.

22.4 CONFIGURATION MANAGEMENT FOR WEBAPPS

Earlier in this book, I discussed the special nature of Web applications and the specialized methods (called *Web engineering* methods[7]) that are required to build them. Among the many characteristics that differentiate WebApps from traditional software is the ubiquitous nature of change.

WebApp developers often use an iterative, incremental process model that applies many principles derived from agile software development (Chapter 3). Using this approach, an engineering team often develops a WebApp increment in a very short time period using a customer-driven approach. Subsequent increments add additional content and functionality, and each is likely to implement changes that lead to enhanced content, better usability, improved aesthetics, better navigation, enhanced performance, and stronger security. Therefore, in the agile world of WebApps, change is viewed somewhat differently.

> **What impact does uncontrolled change have on a WebApp?**

If you're a member of a WebApp team, you must embrace change. And yet, a typical agile team eschews all things that appear to be process-heavy, bureaucratic, and formal. Software configuration management is often viewed (albeit incorrectly) to have these characteristics. This seeming contradiction is remedied not by rejecting SCM principles, practices, and tools, but rather, by molding them to meet the special needs of WebApp projects.

22.4.1 Dominant Issues

As WebApps become increasing important to business survival and growth, the need for configuration management grows. Why? Because without effective controls, improper changes to a WebApp (recall that immediacy and continuous evolution are the dominant attributes of many WebApps) can lead to: unauthorized posting of new product information, erroneous or poorly tested functionality that frustrates visitors to a website, security holes that jeopardize internal company systems, and other economically unpleasant or even disastrous consequences.

The general strategies for software configuration management (SCM) described in this chapter are applicable, but tactics and tools must be adapted to conform to the unique nature of WebApps. Four issues [Dar99] should be considered when developing tactics for WebApp configuration management.

Content. A typical WebApp contains a vast array of content—text, graphics, applets, scripts, audio/video files, forms, active page elements, tables, streaming data, and many others. The challenge is to organize this sea of content into a rational set of configuration objects (Section 22.1.4) and then establish appropriate configuration control mechanisms for these objects. One approach is to model the WebApp content using conventional data modeling techniques (Chapter 6), attaching a set of

---

7 See [Pre08] for a comprehensive discussion of Web engineering methods.

specialized properties to each object. The static/dynamic nature of each object and its projected longevity (e.g., temporary, fixed existence, or permanent object) are examples of properties that are required to establish an effective SCM approach. For example, if a content item is changed hourly, it has temporary longevity. The control mechanisms for this item would be different (less formal) than those applied for a forms component that is a permanent object.

People.   Because a significant percentage of WebApp development continues to be conducted in an ad hoc manner, any person involved in the WebApp can (and often does) create content. Many content creators have no software engineering background and are completely unaware of the need for configuration management. As a consequence, the application grows and changes in an uncontrolled fashion.

Scalability.   The techniques and controls applied to a small WebApp do not scale upward well. It is not uncommon for a simple WebApp to grow significantly as interconnections with existing information systems, databases, data warehouses, and portal gateways are implemented. As size and complexity grow, small changes can have far-reaching and unintended effects that can be problematic. Therefore, the rigor of configuration control mechanisms should be directly proportional to application scale.

Politics.   Who "owns" a WebApp? This question is argued in companies large and small, and its answer has a significant impact on the management and control activities. In some instances Web developers are housed outside the IT organization, creating potential communication difficulties. Dart [Dar99] suggests the following questions to help understand the politics associated with Web engineering:

> **How do I determine who has responsibility for WebApp CM?**

- Who assumes responsibility for the accuracy of the information on the website?
- Who ensures that quality control processes have been followed before information is published to the site?
- Who is responsible for making changes?
- Who assumes the cost of change?

The answers to these questions help determine the people within an organization who must adopt a configuration management process for WebApps.

Configuration management for WebApps continues to evolve (e.g., [Ngu06]). A conventional SCM process may be too cumbersome, but a new generation of *content management tools* that are specifically designed for Web engineering has emerged over the past few years. These tools establish a process that acquires existing information (from a broad array of WebApp objects), manages changes to the objects, structures it in a way that enables it to be presented to an end user, and then provides it to the client-side environment for display.

22.4.2   WebApp Configuration Objects

WebApps encompass a broad range of configuration objects—content objects (e.g., text, graphics, images, video, audio), functional components (e.g., scripts, applets), and interface objects (e.g., COM or CORBA). WebApp objects can be identified (assigned file names) in any manner that is appropriate for the organization. However, the following conventions are recommended to ensure that cross-platform compatibility is maintained: filenames should be limited to 32 characters in length, mixed-case or all-caps names should be avoided, and the use of underscores in file names should be avoided. In addition, URL references (links) within a configuration object should always use relative paths (e.g., ../products/alarmsensors.html).

All WebApp content has format and structure. Internal file formats are dictated by the computing environment in which the content is stored. However, *rendering format* (often called *display format*) is defined by the aesthetic style and design rules established for the WebApp. *Content structure* defines a content architecture; that is, it defines the way in which content objects are assembled to present meaningful information to an end user. Boiko [Boi04] defines structure as "maps that you lay over a set of content chunks [objects] to organize them and make them accessible to the people who need them."

22.4.3   Content Management

Content management is related to configuration management in the sense that a content management system (CMS) establishes a process (supported by appropriate tools) that acquires existing content (from a broad array of WebApp configuration objects), structures it in a way that enables it to be presented to an end user, and then provides it to the client-side environment for display.

The most common use of a content management system occurs when a dynamic WebApp is built. Dynamic WebApps create Web pages "on-the-fly." That is, the user typically queries the WebApp requesting specific information. The WebApp queries a database, formats the information accordingly, and presents it to the user. For example, a music company provides a library of CDs for sale. When a user requests a CD or its e-music equivalent, a database is queried and a variety of information about the artist, the CD (e.g., its cover image or graphics), the musical content, and sample audio are all downloaded and configured into a standard content template. The resultant Web page is built on the server side and passed to the client-side browser for examination by the end user. A generic representation of this is shown in Figure 22.6.

In the most general sense, a CMS "configures" content for the end user by invoking three integrated subsystems: a collection subsystem, a management subsystem, and a publishing subsystem [Boi04].

The collection subsystem.   Content is derived from data and information that must be created or acquired by a content developer. The *collection subsystem* encompasses all actions required to create and/or acquire content, and the technical

FIGURE 22.6

Content
management
system

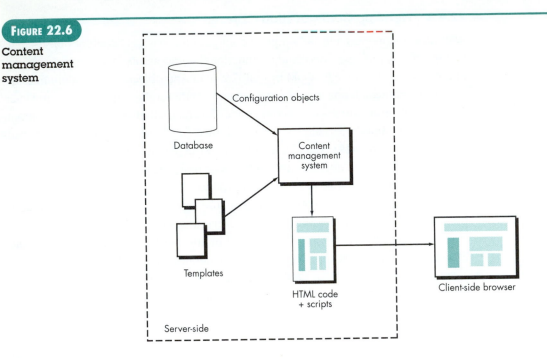

functions that are necessary to (1) convert content into a form that can be represented by a mark-up language (e.g., HTML, XML), and (2) organize content into packets that can be displayed effectively on the client side.

Content creation and acquisition (often called *authoring*) commonly occurs in parallel with other WebApp development activities and is often conducted by nontechnical content developers. This activity combines elements of creativity and research and is supported by tools that enable the content author to characterize content in a manner that can be standardized for use within the WebApp.

Once content exists, it must be converted to conform to the requirements of a CMS. This implies stripping raw content of any unnecessary information (e.g., redundant graphical representations), formatting the content to conform to the requirements of the CMS, and mapping the results into an information structure that will enable it to be managed and published.

The management subsystem.   Once content exists, it must be stored in a repository, cataloged for subsequent acquisition and use, and labeled to define (1) current status (e.g., is the content object complete or in development?), (2) the appropriate version of the content object, and (3) related content objects. Therefore, the *management subsystem* implements a repository that encompasses the following elements:

- *Content database*—the information structure that has been established to store all content objects
- *Database capabilities*—functions that enable the CMS to search for specific content objects (or categories of objects), store and retrieve

objects, and manage the file structure that has been established for the content

- *Configuration management functions*—the functional elements and associated workflow that support content object identification, version control, change management, change auditing, and reporting

In addition to these elements, the management subsystem implements an administration function that encompasses the metadata and rules that control the overall structure of the content and the manner in which it is supported.

The publishing subsystem.   Content must be extracted from the repository, converted to a form that is amenable to publication, and formatted so that it can be transmitted to client-side browsers. The publishing subsystem accomplishes these tasks using a series of templates. Each *template* is a function that builds a publication using one of three different components [Boi04]:

> The publishing subsystem extracts content from the repository and delivers it to client-side browsers.

- *Static elements*—text, graphics, media, and scripts that require no further processing are transmitted directly to the client side.

- *Publication services*—function calls to specific retrieval and formatting services that personalize content (using predefined rules), perform data conversion, and build appropriate navigation links.

- *External services*—access to external corporate information infrastructure such as enterprise data or "back-room" applications.

A content management system that encompasses each of these subsystems is applicable for major WebApp projects. However, the basic philosophy and functionality associated with a CMS are applicable to all dynamic WebApps.

---

8   Tools noted here do not represent an endorsement, but rather a sampling of tools in this category. In most cases, tool names are trademarked by their respective developers.

authorized content providers to develop controlled updates to specified WebApp content.

Additional information on SCM and content management tools for Web engineering can be found at one or more of the following websites: *Web Developer's Virtual* *Encyclopedia* (**www.wdlv.com**), *WebDeveloper* (**www.webdeveloper.com**), *Developer Shed* (www.devshed.com), *webknowhow.net* (**www.webknowhow.net**), or *WebReference* (**www.webreference.com**).

22.4.4 Change Management

The workflow associated with change control for conventional software (Section 22.3.3) is generally too ponderous for WebApp development. It is unlikely that the change request, change report, and engineering change order sequence can be achieved in an agile manner that is acceptable for most WebApp development projects. How then do we manage a continuous stream of changes requested for WebApp content and functionality?

To implement effective change management within the "code and go" philosophy that continues to dominate WebApp development, the conventional change control process must be modified. Each change should be categorized into one of four classes:

Class 1— a content or function change that corrects an error or enhances local content or functionality

Class 2—a content or function change that has an impact on other content objects or functional components

Class 3—a content or function change that has a broad impact across a WebApp (e.g., major extension of functionality, significant enhancement or reduction in content, major required changes in navigation)

Class 4—a major design change (e.g., a change in interface design or navigation approach) that will be immediately noticeable to one or more categories of user

Once the requested change has been categorized, it can be processed according to the algorithm shown in Figure 22.7.

Referring to the figure, class 1 and 2 changes are treated informally and are handled in an agile manner. For a class 1 change, you would evaluate the impact of the change, but no external review or documentation is required. As the change is made, standard check-in and check-out procedures are enforced by configuration repository tools. For class 2 changes, you should review the impact of the change on related objects (or ask other developers responsible for those objects to do so). If the

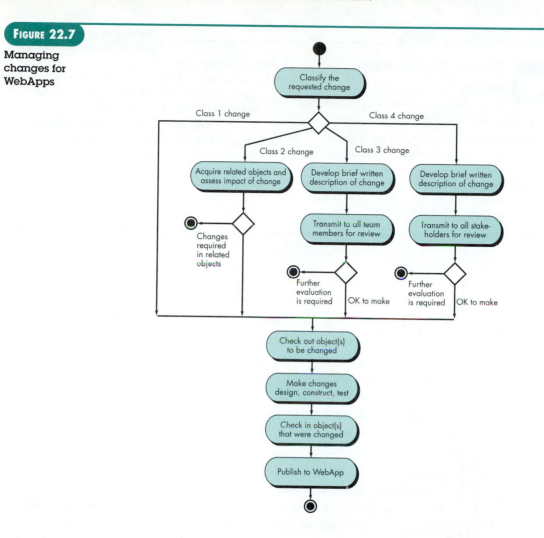

FIGURE 22.7

Managing changes for WebApps

change can be made without requiring significant changes to other objects, modification occurs without additional review or documentation. If substantive changes are required, further evaluation and planning are necessary.

Class 3 and 4 changes are also treated in an agile manner, but some descriptive documentation and more formal review procedures are required. A *change description*—describing the change and providing a brief assessment of the impact of the change—is developed for class 3 changes. The description is distributed to all members of the team who review it to better assess its impact. A change description is also developed for class 4 changes, but in this case, the review is conducted by all stakeholders.

SOFTWARE TOOLS

Change Management

Objective: To assist Web engineers and content developers in managing changes as they are made to WebApp configuration objects.

Mechanics: Tools in this category were originally developed for conventional software, but can be adapted for use by Web engineers and content developers to make controlled changes to WebApps. They support automated check-in and check-out, version control and rollback, reporting, and other SCM functions.

Representative Tools:[9]

ChangeMan WCM, developed by Serena (**www.serena.com**), is one of a suite of change management tools that provide complete SCM capabilities.

ClearCase, developed by Rational (**www-306.ibm.com/software/rational/sw-atoz/indexC.html**), is a suite of tools that provide full configuration management capabilities for WebApps.

Source Integrity, developed by mks (**www.mks.com**), is a SCM tool that can be integrated with selected development environments.

22.4.5   Version Control

As a WebApp evolves through a series of increments, a number of different versions may exist at the same time. One version (the current operational WebApp) is available via the Internet for end users; another version (the next WebApp increment) may be in the final stages of testing prior to deployment; a third version is in development and represents a major update in content, interface aesthetics, and functionality. Configuration objects must be clearly defined so that each can be associated with the appropriate version. In addition, control mechanisms must be established. Dreilinger [Dre99] discusses the importance of version (and change) control when he writes:

> In an *uncontrolled* site where multiple authors have access to edit and contribute, the potential for conflict and problems arises—more so when these authors work from different offices at different times of day and night. You may spend the day improving the file *index.html* for a customer. After you've made your changes, another developer who works at home after hours, or in another office, may spend the night uploading their own newly revised version of the file *index.html*, completely overwriting your work with no way to get it back!

It's likely that you've experienced a similar situation. To avoid it, a version control process is required.

1. *A central repository for the WebApp project should be established.* The repository will hold current versions of all WebApp configuration objects (content, functional components, and others).

2. *Each Web engineer creates his or her own working folder.* The folder contains those objects that are being created or changed at any given time.

---

9   Tools noted here do not represent an endorsement, but rather a sampling of tools in this category. In most cases, tool names are trademarked by their respective developers.

3. *The clocks on all developer workstations should be synchronized.* This is done to avoid overwriting conflicts when two developers make updates that are very close to one another in time.

4. *As new configuration objects are developed or existing objects are changed, they are imported into the central repository.* The version control tool (see discussion of CVS in the sidebar) will manage all check-in and check-out functions from the working folders of each WebApp developer. The tool will also provide automatic e-mail updates to all interested parties when changes to the repository are made.

5. *As objects are imported or exported from the repository, an automatic, time-stamped log message is made.* This provides useful information for auditing and can become part of an effective reporting scheme.

The version control tool maintains different versions of the WebApp and can revert to an older version if required.

22.4.6 Auditing and Reporting

In the interest of agility, the auditing and reporting functions are deemphasized in Web engineering work.[10] However, they are not eliminated altogether. All objects that are checked into or out of the repository are recorded in a log that can be reviewed at any point in time. A complete log report can be created so that all members of the WebApp team have a chronology of changes over a defined period of time. In addition, an automated e-mail notification (addressed to those developers and stakeholders who have interest) can be sent every time an object is checked in or out of the repository.

INFO

SCM Standards

The following list of SCM standards (extracted in part from www.12207.com) is reasonably comprehensive:

IEEE Standards	**standards.ieee.org/ catalog/olis/**
IEEE 828	Software Configuration Management Plans
IEEE 1042	Software Configuration Management

ISO Standards	**www.iso.ch/iso/en/ ISOOnline.frontpage**
ISO 10007-1995	Quality Management, Guidance for CM
ISO/IEC 12207	Information Technology-Software Life Cycle Processes
ISO/IEC TR 15271	Guide for ISO/IEC 12207

---

10 This is beginning to change. There is an increasing emphasis on SCM as one element of WebApp security [Sar06]. By providing a mechanism for tracking and reporting every change made to every WebApp object, a change management tool can provide valuable protection against malicious changes.

ISO/IEC TR 15846	Software Engineering-Software Life Cycle Process-Configuration Management for Software Order	DoD MIL STD-973 MIL-HDBK-61	Configuration Management Configuration Management Guidance
EIA Standards	**www.eia.org/**	**Other Standards**	
EIA 649	National Consensus Standard for Configuration Management	DO-178B	Guidelines for the Development of Aviation Software
EIA CMB4-1A	Configuration Management Definitions for Digital Computer Programs	ESA PSS-05-09	Guide to Software Configuration Management
EIA CMB4-2	Configuration Identification for Digital Computer Programs	AECL CE-1001-STD rev.1	Standard for Software Engineering of Safety Critical Software
EIA CMB4-3	Computer Software Libraries	DOE SCM checklist:	http://cio.doe.gov/ITReform/ sqse/download/cmcklst.doc
EIA CMB4-4	Configuration Change Control for Digital Computer Programs	BS-6488	British Std., Configuration Management of Computer-Based Systems
EIA CMB6-1C	Configuration and Data Management References Order		
EIA CMB6-3	Configuration Identification	Best Practice—UK	Office of Government Commerce: **www.ogc.gov.uk**
EIA CMB6-4	Configuration Control	CMII	Institute of CM Best Practices: **www.icmhq.com**
EIA CMB6-5	Textbook for Configuration Status Accounting		
EIA CMB7-1	Electronic Interchange of Configuration Management Data		
U.S. Military Standards	**Information of MIL standards: www-library.itsi.disa.mil**		

A *Configuration Management Resource Guide* provides complementary information for those interested in CM processes and practice. It is available at **www.quality.org/config/cm-guide.html**.

22.5 SUMMARY

Software configuration management is an umbrella activity that is applied throughout the software process. SCM identifies, controls, audits, and reports modifications that invariably occur while software is being developed and after it has been released to a customer. All work products created as part of software engineering become part of a software configuration. The configuration is organized in a manner that enables orderly control of change.

The software configuration is composed of a set of interrelated objects, also called software configuration items, that are produced as a result of some software engineering activity. In addition to documents, programs, and data, the development environment that is used to create software can also be placed under configuration control. All SCIs are stored within a repository that implements a set of mechanisms and data structures to ensure data integrity, provide integration support for other software tools, support information sharing among all members of the software team, and implement functions in support of version and change control.

Once a configuration object has been developed and reviewed, it becomes a baseline. Changes to a baselined object result in the creation of a new version of that object. The evolution of a program can be tracked by examining the revision history of all configuration objects. Version control is the set of procedures and tools for managing the use of these objects.

Change control is a procedural activity that ensures quality and consistency as changes are made to a configuration object. The change control process begins with a change request, leads to a decision to make or reject the request for change, and culminates with a controlled update of the SCI that is to be changed.

The configuration audit is an SQA activity that helps to ensure that quality is maintained as changes are made. Status reporting provides information about each change to those with a need to know.

Configuration management for WebApps is similar in most respects to SCM for conventional software. However, each of the core SCM tasks should be streamlined to make it as lean as possible, and special provisions for content management must be implemented.

PROBLEMS AND POINTS TO PONDER

22.1. Why is the First Law of System Engineering true? Provide specific examples for each of the four fundamental reasons for change.

22.2. What are the four elements that exist when an effective SCM system is implemented? Discuss each briefly.

22.3. Discuss the reasons for baselines in your own words.

22.4. Assume that you're the manager of a small project. What baselines would you define for the project and how would you control them?

22.5. Design a project database (repository) system that would enable a software engineer to store, cross reference, trace, update, and change all important software configuration items. How would the database handle different versions of the same program? Would source code be handled differently than documentation? How will two developers be precluded from making different changes to the same SCI at the same time?

22.6. Research an existing SCM tool and describe how it implements control for versions, variants, and configuration objects in general.

22.7. The relations <part-of> and <interrelated> represent simple relationships between configuration objects. Describe five additional relationships that might be useful in the context of an SCM repository.

22.8. Research an existing SCM tool and describe how it implements the mechanics of version control. Alternatively, read two or three papers on SCM and describe the different data structures and referencing mechanisms that are used for version control.

22.9. Develop a checklist for use during configuration audits.

22.10. What is the difference between an SCM audit and a technical review? Can their function be folded into one review? What are the pros and cons?

22.11. Briefly describe the differences between SCM for conventional software and SCM for WebApps.

22.12. What is content management? Use the Web to research the features of a content management tool and provide a brief summary.

FURTHER READINGS AND INFORMATION SOURCES

Among the more recent SCM offerings are Leon (*Software Configuration Management Handbook,* 2d ed., Artech House Publishers, 2005), Maraia (*The Build Master: Microsoft's Software Configuration Management Best Practices,* Addison-Wesley, 2005), Keyes (*Software Configuration Management,* Auerbach, 2004), and Hass (*Configuration Management Principles and Practice,* Addison-Wesley, 2002). Each of these books presents the entire SCM process in substantial detail. Maraia (*Software Configuration Management Implementation Roadmap,* Wiley, 2004) presents a unique how-to guide for those who must implement SCM within an organization. Lyon (*Practical CM,* Raven Publishing, 2003, available at **www.configuration.org**) has written a comprehensive guide for the CM professional that includes pragmatic guidelines for implementing every aspect of a configuration management system (updated yearly). White and Clemm (*Software Configuration Management Strategies and Rational ClearCase,* Addison-Wesley, 2000) present SCM within the context of one of the more popular SCM tools.

Berczuk and Appleton (*Software Configuration Management Patterns,* Addison-Wesley, 2002) present a variety of useful patterns that assist in understanding SCM and implementing effective SCM systems. Brown et al. (*Anti-Patterns and Patterns in Software Configuration Management,* Wiley, 1999) discuss the things not to do (anti-patterns) when implementing an SCM process and then consider their remedies. Bays (*Software Release Methodology,* Prentice Hall, 1999) focuses on the mechanics of "successful product release," an important complement to effective SCM.

As WebApps have become more dynamic, content management has become an essential topic for Web engineers. Books by White (*The Content Management Handbook,* Curtin University Books, 2005), Jenkins and his colleagues (*Enterprise Content Management Methods,* Open Text Corporation, 2005), Boiko [Boi04], Mauthe and Thomas (*Professional Content Management Systems,* Wiley, 2004), Addey and his colleagues (*Content Management Systems,* Glasshaus, 2003), Rockley (*Managing Enterprise Content,* New Riders Press, 2002), Hackos (*Content Management for Dynamic Web Delivery,* Wiley, 2002), and Nakano (*Web Content Management,* Addison-Wesley, 2001) present worthwhile treatments of the subject.

In addition to generic discussions of the topic, Lim and his colleagues (*Enhancing Microsoft Content Management Server with ASP.NET 2.0,* Packt Publishing, 2006), Ferguson (*Creating Content Management Systems in Java,* Charles River Media, 2006), IBM Redbooks (*IBM Workplace Web Content Management for Portal 5.1 and IBM Workplace Web Content Management 2.5,* Vivante, 2006), Fritz and his colleagues (*Typo3: Enterprise Content Management,* Packt Publishing, 2005), and Forta (*Reality ColdFusion: Intranets and Content Management,* Pearson Education, 2002) present content management within the context of specific tools and languages.

A wide variety of information sources on software configuration management and content management is available on the Internet. An up-to-date list of World Wide Web references relevant to software configuration management can be found at the SEPA website: **www.mhhe.com/engcs/compsci/pressman/professional/olc/ser.htm**.

A key element of any engineering process is measurement. You can use measures to better understand the attributes of the models that you create and to assess the quality of the engineered products or systems that you build. But unlike other engineering disciplines, software engineering is not grounded in the basic quantitative laws of physics. Direct measures, such as voltage, mass, velocity, or temperature, are uncommon in the software world. Because software measures and metrics are often indirect, they are open to debate. Fenton [Fen91] addresses this issue when he states:

Measurement is the process by which numbers or symbols are assigned to the attributes of entities in the real world in such a way as to define them according to clearly defined rules. . . . In the physical sciences, medicine, economics, and more recently the social sciences, we are now able to measure attributes that were previously thought to

QUICK LOOK

What is it? By its nature, engineering is a quantitative discipline. Product metrics help software engineers gain insight into the design and construction of the software they build by focusing on specific, measurable attributes of software engineering work products.

Who does it? Software engineers use product metrics to help them build higher-quality software.

Why is it important? There will always be a qualitative element to the creation of computer software. The problem is that qualitative assessment may not be enough. You need objective criteria to help guide the design of data, architecture, interfaces, and components. When testing, you need quantitative guidance that will help in the selection of test cases and their targets. Product metrics provide a basis from which analysis, design, coding, and testing can be conducted more objectively and assessed more quantitatively.

What are the steps? The first step in the measurement process is to derive the software measures and metrics that are appropriate for

the representation of software that is being considered. Next, data required to derive the formulated metrics are collected. Once computed, appropriate metrics are analyzed based on preestablished guidelines and past data. The results of the analysis are interpreted to gain insight into the quality of the software, and the results of the interpretation lead to modification of requirements and design models, source code, or test cases. In some instances, it may also lead to modification of the software process itself.

What is the work product? Product metrics that are computed from data collected from the requirements and design models, source code, and test cases.

How do I ensure that I've done it right? You should establish the objectives of measurement before data collection begins, defining each product metric in an unambiguous manner. Define only a few metrics and then use them to gain insight into the quality of a software engineering work product.

be unmeasurable. . . . Of course, such measurements are not as refined as many measurements in the physical sciences . . . , but they exist [and important decisions are made
based on them]. We feel that the obligation to attempt to "measure the unmeasurable" in
order to improve our understanding of particular entities is as powerful in software engineering as in any discipline.

But some members of the software community continue to argue that software is
"unmeasurable" or that attempts at measurement should be postponed until we better understand software and the attributes that should be used to describe it. This is
a mistake.

Although product metrics for computer software are imperfect, they can provide
you with a systematic way to assess quality based on a set of clearly defined rules.
They also provide you with on-the-spot, rather than after-the-fact, insight. This
enables you to discover and correct potential problems before they become catastrophic defects.

In this chapter, I present measures that can be used to assess the quality of the
product as it is being engineered. These measures of internal product attributes provide you with a real-time indication of the efficacy of the requirements, design, and
code models; the effectiveness of test cases; and the overall quality of the software
to be built.

23.1   A FRAMEWORK FOR PRODUCT METRICS

As I noted in the introduction, measurement assigns numbers or symbols to attributes
of entities in the real word. To accomplish this, a measurement model encompassing a
consistent set of rules is required. Although the theory of measurement (e.g., [Kyb84])
and its application to computer software (e.g., [Zus97]) are topics that are beyond the
scope of this book, it is worthwhile to establish a fundamental framework and a set of
basic principles that guide the definition of product metrics for software.

What's the
difference
between a
measure and
a metric?

23.1.1   Measures, Metrics, and Indicators

Although the terms *measure, measurement,* and *metrics* are often used interchangeably,
it is important to note the subtle differences between them. Because *measure* can be
used either as a noun or a verb, definitions of the term can become confusing. Within
the software engineering context, a *measure* provides a quantitative indication of the
extent, amount, dimension, capacity, or size of some attribute of a product or process.
Measurement is the act of determining a measure. The *IEEE Standard Glossary of Software Engineering Terminology* [IEE93b] defines *metric* as "a quantitative measure of the
degree to which a system, component, or process possesses a given attribute."

When a single data point has been collected (e.g., the number of errors uncovered
within a single software component), a measure has been established. Measurement
occurs as the result of the collection of one or more data points (e.g., a number of
component reviews and unit tests are investigated to collect measures of the number

of errors for each). A software metric relates the individual measures in some way (e.g., the average number of errors found per review or the average number of errors found per unit test).

A software engineer collects measures and develops metrics so that indicators will be obtained. An *indicator* is a metric or combination of metrics that provides insight into the software process, a software project, or the product itself. An indicator provides insight that enables the project manager or software engineers to adjust the process, the project, or the product to make things better.

23.1.2 The Challenge of Product Metrics

Over the past four decades, many researchers have attempted to develop a single metric that provides a comprehensive measure of software complexity. Fenton [Fen94] characterizes this research as a search for "the impossible holy grail." Although dozens of complexity measures have been proposed [Zus90], each takes a somewhat different view of what complexity is and what attributes of a system lead to complexity. By analogy, consider a metric for evaluating an attractive car. Some observers might emphasize body design; others might consider mechanical characteristics; still others might tout cost, or performance, or the use of alternative fuels, or the ability to recycle when the car is junked. Since any one of these characteristics may be at odds with others, it is difficult to derive a single value for "attractiveness." The same problem occurs with computer software.

Yet there is a need to measure and control software complexity. And if a single value of this quality metric is difficult to derive, it should be possible to develop measures of different internal program attributes (e.g., effective modularity, functional independence, and other attributes discussed in Chapter 8). These measures and the metrics derived from them can be used as independent indicators of the quality of requirements and design models. But here again, problems arise. Fenton [Fen94] notes this when he states: "The danger of attempting to find measures which characterize so many different attributes is that inevitably the measures have to satisfy conflicting aims. This is counter to the representational theory of measurement." Although Fenton's statement is correct, many people argue that product measurement conducted during the early stages of the software process provides software engineers with a consistent and objective mechanism for assessing quality.

It is fair to ask, however, just how valid product metrics are. That is, how closely aligned are product metrics to the long-term reliability and quality of a computer-based system? Fenton [Fen91] addresses this question in the following way:

> In spite of the intuitive connections between the internal structure of software products [product metrics] and its external product and process attributes, there have actually been very few scientific attempts to establish specific relationships. There are a number of reasons why this is so; the most commonly cited is the impracticality of conducting relevant experiments.

Each of the "challenges" noted here is a cause for caution, but it is no reason to dismiss product metrics.[1] Measurement is essential if quality is to be achieved.

23.1.3   Measurement Principles

Before I introduce a series of product metrics that (1) assist in the evaluation of the analysis and design models, (2) provide an indication of the complexity of procedural designs and source code, and (3) facilitate the design of more effective testing, it is important for you to understand basic measurement principles. Roche [Roc94] suggests a measurement process that can be characterized by five activities:

What are the steps of an effective measurement process?

- *Formulation.* The derivation of software measures and metrics appropriate for the representation of the software that is being considered.

- *Collection.* The mechanism used to accumulate data required to derive the formulated metrics.

- *Analysis.* The computation of metrics and the application of mathematical tools.

- *Interpretation.* The evaluation of metrics resulting in insight into the quality of the representation.

- *Feedback.* Recommendations derived from the interpretation of product metrics transmitted to the software team.

Software metrics will be useful only if they are characterized effectively and validated so that their worth is proven. The following principles [Let03b] are representative of many that can be proposed for metrics characterization and validation:

ADVICE

In reality, many product metrics in use today do not conform to these principles as well as they should. But that doesn't mean that they have no value—just be careful when you use them, understanding that they are intended to provide insight, not hard scientific verification.

- *A metric should have desirable mathematical properties.* That is, the metric's value should be in a meaningful range (e.g., 0 to 1, where 0 truly means absence, 1 indicates the maximum value, and 0.5 represents the "halfway point"). Also, a metric that purports to be on a rational scale should not be composed of components that are only measured on an ordinal scale.

- *When a metric represents a software characteristic that increases when positive traits occur or decreases when undesirable traits are encountered, the value of the metric should increase or decrease in the same manner.*

- *Each metric should be validated empirically in a wide variety of contexts before being published or used to make decisions.* A metric should measure the factor of interest, independently of other factors. It should "scale up" to large systems and work in a variety of programming languages and system domains.

---

1   Although criticism of specific metrics is common in the literature, many critiques focus on esoteric issues and miss the primary objective of metrics in the real world: to help the software engineer establish a systematic and objective way to gain insight into his or her work and to improve product quality as a result.

Although formulation, characterization, and validation are critical, collection and analysis are the activities that drive the measurement process. Roche [Roc94] suggests the following principles for these activities: (1) whenever possible, data collection and analysis should be automated; (2) valid statistical techniques should be applied to establish relationships between internal product attributes and external quality characteristics (e.g., whether the level of architectural complexity correlates with the number of defects reported in production use); and (3) interpretative guidelines and recommendations should be established for each metric.

23.1.4 Goal-Oriented Software Measurement

WebRef

A useful discussion of GQM can be found at **www.thedacs.com /GoldPractices/ practices/gqma .html**.

The *Goal/Question/Metric* (GQM) paradigm has been developed by Basili and Weiss [Bas84] as a technique for identifying meaningful metrics for any part of the software process. GQM emphasizes the need to (1) establish an explicit measurement *goal* that is specific to the process activity or product characteristic that is to be assessed, (2) define a set of *questions* that must be answered in order to achieve the goal, and (3) identify well-formulated *metrics* that help to answer these questions.

A *goal definition template* [Bas94] can be used to define each measurement goal. The template takes the form:

Analyze {the name of activity or attribute to be measured} **for the purpose of** {the over-all objective of the analysis[2]} **with respect to** {the aspect of the activity or attribute that is considered} **from the viewpoint of** {the people who have an interest in the measurement} **in the context of** {the environment in which the measurement takes place}.

As an example, consider a goal definition template for *SafeHome*:

Analyze the *SafeHome* software architecture **for the purpose of** evaluating architectural components **with respect to** the ability to make *SafeHome* more extensible **from the viewpoint of** the software engineers performing the work **in the context of** product enhancement over the next three years.

With a measurement goal explicitly defined, a set of questions is developed. Answers to these questions help the software team (or other stakeholders) to determine whether the measurement goal has been achieved. Among the questions that might be asked are:

Q_1:   Are architectural components characterized in a manner that compartmentalizes function and related data?

Q_2:   Is the complexity of each component within bounds that will facilitate modification and extension?

Each of these questions should be answered quantitatively, using one or more measures and metrics. For example, a metric that provides an indication of the cohesion

---

2   van Solingen and Berghout [Sol99] suggest that the objective is almost always "understanding, controlling or improving" the process activity or product attribute.

(Chapter 8) of an architectural component might be useful in answering Q_1. Metrics discussed later in this chapter might provide insight for Q_2. In every case, the metrics that are chosen (or derived) should conform to the measurement principles discussed in Section 23.1.3 and the measurement attributes discussed in Section 23.1.5.

23.1.5   The Attributes of Effective Software Metrics

Hundreds of metrics have been proposed for computer software, but not all provide practical support to the software engineer. Some demand measurement that is too complex, others are so esoteric that few real-world professionals have any hope of understanding them, and others violate the basic intuitive notions of what high-quality software really is.

Ejiogu [Eji91] defines a set of attributes that should be encompassed by effective software metrics. The derived metric and the measures that lead to it should be:

How should we assess the quality of a proposed software metric?

- *Simple and computable.* It should be relatively easy to learn how to derive the metric, and its computation should not demand inordinate effort or time.
- *Empirically and intuitively persuasive.* The metric should satisfy the engineer's intuitive notions about the product attribute under consideration (e.g., a metric that measures module cohesion should increase in value as the level of cohesion increases).
- *Consistent and objective.* The metric should always yield results that are unambiguous. An independent third party should be able to derive the same metric value using the same information about the software.
- *Consistent in its use of units and dimensions.* The mathematical computation of the metric should use measures that do not lead to bizarre combinations of units. For example, multiplying people on the project teams by programming language variables in the program results in a suspicious mix of units that are not intuitively persuasive.
- *Programming language independent.* Metrics should be based on the requirements model, the design model, or the structure of the program itself. They should not be dependent on the vagaries of programming language syntax or semantics.
- *An effective mechanism for high-quality feedback.* That is, the metric should provide you with information that can lead to a higher-quality end product.

ADVICE

Experience indicates that a product metric will be used only if it is intuitive and easy to compute. If dozens of "counts" have to be made, and complex computations are required, it is unlikely that the metric will be widely adopted.

Although most software metrics satisfy these attributes, some commonly used metrics may fail to satisfy one or two of them. An example is the function point (discussed in Section 23.2.1)—a measure of the "functionality" delivered by the software. It can be argued[3] that the consistent and objective attribute fails because an independent third party may not be able to derive the same function point value as a colleague

---

3   An equally vigorous counterargument can be made. Such is the nature of software metrics.

using the same information about the software. Should we therefore reject the FP measure? The answer is "Of course not!" FP provides useful insight and therefore provides distinct value, even if it fails to satisfy one attribute perfectly.

23.2   METRICS FOR THE REQUIREMENTS MODEL

Technical work in software engineering begins with the creation of the requirements model. It is at this stage that requirements are derived and a foundation for design is established. Therefore, product metrics that provide insight into the quality of the analysis model are desirable.

Although relatively few analysis and specification metrics have appeared in the literature, it is possible to adapt metrics that are often used for project estimation and apply them in this context. These metrics examine the requirements model with the intent of predicting the "size" of the resultant system. Size is sometimes (but not always) an indicator of design complexity and is almost always an indicator of increased coding, integration, and testing effort.

23.2.1   Function-Based Metrics

The *function point* (FP) *metric* can be used effectively as a means for measuring the functionality delivered by a system.[4] Using historical data, the FP metric can then be used to (1) estimate the cost or effort required to design, code, and test the software; (2) predict the number of errors that will be encountered during testing; and (3) forecast the number of components and/or the number of projected source lines in the implemented system.

Function points are derived using an empirical relationship based on countable (direct) measures of software's information domain and qualitative assessments of software complexity. Information domain values are defined in the following manner:[5]

Number of external inputs (EIs). Each *external input* originates from a user or is transmitted from another application and provides distinct application-oriented data or control information. Inputs are often used to update *internal logical files* (ILFs). Inputs should be distinguished from inquiries, which are counted separately.

Number of external outputs (EOs). Each *external output* is derived data within the application that provides information to the user. In this context external output refers to reports, screens, error messages, etc. Individual data items within a report are not counted separately.

Number of external inquiries (EQs). An *external inquiry* is defined as an online input that results in the generation of some immediate software response in the form of an online output (often retrieved from an ILF).

Number of internal logical files (ILFs). Each *internal logical file* is a logical grouping of data that resides within the application's boundary and is maintained via external inputs.

Number of external interface files (EIFs). Each *external interface file* is a logical grouping of data that resides external to the application but provides information that may be of use to the application.

Once these data have been collected, the table in Figure 23.1 is completed and a complexity value is associated with each count. Organizations that use function point methods develop criteria for determining whether a particular entry is simple, average, or complex. Nonetheless, the determination of complexity is somewhat subjective.

To compute function points (FP), the following relationship is used:

$$FP = \text{count total} \times [0.65 + 0.01 \times \Sigma\ (F_i)] \tag{23.1}$$

where count total is the sum of all FP entries obtained from Figure 23.1.

---

4   Hundreds of books, papers, and articles have been written on FP metrics. A worthwhile bibliography can be found at [IFP05].

5   In actuality, the definition of information domain values and the manner in which they are counted are a bit more complex. The interested reader should see [IFP01] for more details.

FIGURE 23.1

Computing
function points

Information Domain Value	Count	Weighting factor		
		Simple	Average	Complex
External Inputs (EIs)	[ ] ×	3	4	6 = [ ]
External Outputs (EOs)	[ ] ×	4	5	7 = [ ]
External Inquiries (EQs)	[ ] ×	3	4	6 = [ ]
Internal Logical Files (ILFs)	[ ] ×	7	10	15 = [ ]
External Interface Files (EIFs)	[ ] ×	5	7	10 = [ ]
Count total	⟶			[ ]

KEY POINT

Value adjustment
factors are used to
provide an indication
of problem complexity.

The F_i (i = 1 to 14) are *value adjustment factors* (VAF) based on responses to the following questions [Lon02]:

1. Does the system require reliable backup and recovery?

2. Are specialized data communications required to transfer information to or from the application?

3. Are there distributed processing functions?

4. Is performance critical?

5. Will the system run in an existing, heavily utilized operational environment?

6. Does the system require online data entry?

7. Does the online data entry require the input transaction to be built over multiple screens or operations?

8. Are the ILFs updated online?

9. Are the inputs, outputs, files, or inquiries complex?

10. Is the internal processing complex?

11. Is the code designed to be reusable?

12. Are conversion and installation included in the design?

13. Is the system designed for multiple installations in different organizations?

14. Is the application designed to facilitate change and ease of use by the user?

WebRef

An online FP calculator
can be found at
irb.cs.uni-
magdeburg.de/
sw-eng/us/
java/fp/.

Each of these questions is answered using a scale that ranges from 0 (not important or applicable) to 5 (absolutely essential). The constant values in Equation (23.1) and the weighting factors that are applied to information domain counts are determined empirically.

To illustrate the use of the FP metric in this context, we consider a simple analysis model representation, illustrated in Figure 23.2. Referring to the figure, a data flow diagram (Chapter 7) for a function within the *SafeHome* software is represented.

FIGURE 23.2

A data flow
model for
SafeHome
software

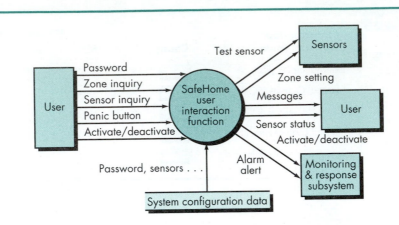

The function manages user interaction, accepting a user password to activate or deactivate the system, and allows inquiries on the status of security zones and various security sensors. The function displays a series of prompting messages and sends appropriate control signals to various components of the security system.

The data flow diagram is evaluated to determine a set of key information domain measures required for computation of the function point metric. Three external inputs—**password, panic button**, and **activate/deactivate**—are shown in the figure along with two external inquiries—**zone inquiry** and **sensor inquiry**. One ILF (**system configuration file**) is shown. Two external outputs (**messages** and **sensor status**) and four EIFs (**test sensor, zone setting, activate/deactivate, and alarm alert**) are also present. These data, along with the appropriate complexity, are shown in Figure 23.3.

The count total shown in Figure 23.3 must be adjusted using Equation (23.1). For the purposes of this example, we assume that $\Sigma(F_i)$ is 46 (a moderately complex product). Therefore,

$$FP = 50 \times [0.65 + (0.01 \times 46)] = 56$$

Based on the projected FP value derived from the requirements model, the project team can estimate the overall implemented size of the *SafeHome* user interaction

FIGURE 23.3

Computing
function points

Information Domain Value	Count		Weighting factor				
			Simple	Average	Complex		
External Inputs (EIs)	3	×	(3)	4	6	=	9
External Outputs (EOs)	2	×	(4)	5	7	=	8
External Inquiries (EQs)	2	×	(3)	4	6	=	6
Internal Logical Files (ILFs)	1	×	(7)	10	15	=	7
External Interface Files (EIFs)	4	×	(5)	7	10	=	20
Count total							50

function. Assume that past data indicates that one FP translates into 60 lines of code (an object-oriented language is to be used) and that 12 FPs are produced for each person-month of effort. These historical data provide the project manager with important planning information that is based on the requirements model rather than preliminary estimates. Assume further that past projects have found an average of three errors per function point during requirements and design reviews and four errors per function point during unit and integration testing. These data can ultimately help you assess the completeness of your review and testing activities.

Uemura and his colleagues [Uem99] suggest that function points can also be computed from UML class and sequence diagrams. If you have further interest, see [Uem99] for details.

23.2.2 Metrics for Specification Quality

Davis and his colleagues [Dav93] propose a list of characteristics that can be used to assess the quality of the requirements model and the corresponding requirements specification: *specificity* (lack of ambiguity), *completeness, correctness, understandability, verifiability, internal and external consistency, achievability, concision, traceability, modifiability, precision,* and *reusability.* In addition, the authors note that high-quality specifications are electronically stored; executable or at least interpretable; annotated by relative importance; and stable, versioned, organized, cross-referenced, and specified at the right level of detail.

Although many of these characteristics appear to be qualitative in nature, Davis et al. [Dav93] suggest that each can be represented using one or more metrics. For example, we assume that there are n_r requirements in a specification, such that

$$n_r = n_f + n_{nf}$$

where n_f is the number of functional requirements and n_{nf} is the number of non-functional (e.g., performance) requirements.

KEY POINT

By measuring characteristics of the specification, it is possible to gain quantitative insight into specificity and completeness.

To determine the *specificity* (lack of ambiguity) of requirements, Davis et al. suggest a metric that is based on the consistency of the reviewers' interpretation of each requirement:

$$Q_1 = \frac{n_{ui}}{n_r}$$

where n_{ui} is the number of requirements for which all reviewers had identical interpretations. The closer the value of Q to 1, the lower is the ambiguity of the specification.

The *completeness* of functional requirements can be determined by computing the ratio

$$Q_2 = \frac{n_u}{n_i \times n_s}$$

where n_u is the number of unique functional requirements, n_i is the number of inputs (stimuli) defined or implied by the specification, and n_s is the number of states specified. The Q_2 ratio measures the percentage of necessary functions that have been specified for a system. However, it does not address nonfunctional require-ments. To incorporate these into an overall metric for completeness, you must con-sider the degree to which requirements have been validated:

$$Q_3 = \frac{n_c}{n_c + n_{nv}}$$

where n_c is the number of requirements that have been validated as correct and n_{nv} is the number of requirements that have not yet been validated.

23.3   METRICS FOR THE DESIGN MODEL

It is inconceivable that the design of a new aircraft, a new computer chip, or a new office building would be conducted without defining design measures, determining metrics for various aspects of design quality, and using them as indicators to guide the manner in which the design evolves. And yet, the design of complex software-based systems often proceeds with virtually no measurement. The irony of this is that design metrics for software are available, but the vast majority of software engineers continue to be unaware of their existence.

Design metrics for computer software, like all other software metrics, are not per-fect. Debate continues over their efficacy and the manner in which they should be applied. Many experts argue that further experimentation is required before design measures can be used. And yet, design without measurement is an unacceptable alternative.

In the sections that follow, I examine some of the more common design metrics for computer software. Each can provide you with improved insight, and all can help the design to evolve to a higher level of quality.

23.3.1   Architectural Design Metrics

Architectural design metrics focus on characteristics of the program architecture (Chapter 9) with an emphasis on the architectural structure and the effectiveness of modules or components within the architecture. These metrics are "black box" in the sense that they do not require any knowledge of the inner workings of a particular software component.

Card and Glass [Car90] define three software design complexity measures: struc-tural complexity, data complexity, and system complexity.

For hierarchical architectures (e.g., call-and-return architectures), *structural complexity* of a module i is defined in the following manner:

$$S(i) = f^2_{out}(i)$$

where $f_{out}(i)$ is the fan-out[6] of module i.

---

6   *Fan-out* is defined as the number of modules immediately subordinate to module i; that is, the number of modules that are directly invoked by module i.

Data complexity provides an indication of the complexity in the internal interface for a module *i* and is defined as

$$D(i) = \frac{v(i)}{f_{out}(i) + 1}$$

where $v(i)$ is the number of input and output variables that are passed to and from module *i*.

Finally, *system complexity* is defined as the sum of structural and data complexity, specified as

$$C(i) = S(i) + D(i)$$

As each of these complexity values increases, the overall architectural complexity of the system also increases. This leads to a greater likelihood that integration and testing effort will also increase.

Fenton [Fen91] suggests a number of simple morphology (i.e., shape) metrics that enable different program architectures to be compared using a set of straightforward dimensions. Referring to the call-and-return architecture in Figure 23.4, the following metrics can be defined:

$$\text{Size} = n + a$$

where *n* is the number of nodes and *a* is the number of arcs. For the architecture shown in Figure 23.4,

> Size = 17 + 18 = 35
>
> Depth = longest path from the root (top) node to a leaf node. For the architecture shown in Figure 23.4, depth = 4.
>
> Width = maximum number of nodes at any one level of the architecture. For the architecture shown in Figure 23.4, width = 6.

The arc-to-node ratio, $r = a/n$, measures the connectivity density of the architecture and may provide a simple indication of the coupling of the architecture. For the architecture shown in Figure 23.4, $r = 18/17 = 1.06$.

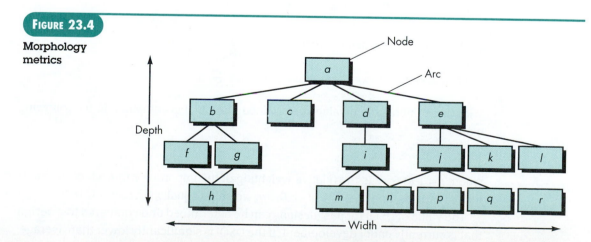

FIGURE 23.4

Morphology metrics

The U.S. Air Force Systems Command [USA87] has developed a number of software quality indicators that are based on measurable design characteristics of a computer program. Using concepts similar to those proposed in IEEE Std. 982.1-1988 [IEE94], the Air Force uses information obtained from data and architectural design to derive a *design structure quality index* (DSQI) that ranges from 0 to 1. The following values must be ascertained to compute the DSQI [Cha89]:

S_1 = total number of modules defined in the program architecture

S_2 = number of modules whose correct function depends on the source of data input or that produce data to be used elsewhere (in general, control modules, among others, would not be counted as part of S_2)

S_3 = number of modules whose correct function depends on prior processing

S_4 = number of database items (includes data objects and all attributes that define objects)

S_5 = total number of unique database items

S_6 = number of database segments (different records or individual objects)

S_7 = number of modules with a single entry and exit (exception processing is not considered to be a multiple exit)

Once values S_1 through S_7 are determined for a computer program, the following intermediate values can be computed:

Program structure: D_1, where D_1 is defined as follows: If the architectural design was developed using a distinct method (e.g., data flow-oriented design or object-oriented design), then $D_1 = 1$, otherwise $D_1 = 0$.

Module independence: $D_2 = 1 - \dfrac{S_2}{S_1}$

Modules not dependent on prior processing: $D_3 = 1 - \dfrac{S_3}{S_1}$

Database size: $D_4 = 1 - \dfrac{S_5}{S_4}$

Database compartmentalization: $D_5 = 1 - \dfrac{S_6}{S_4}$

Module entrance/exit characteristic: $D_6 = 1 - \dfrac{S_7}{S_1}$

With these intermediate values determined, the DSQI is computed in the following manner:

$$\text{DSQI} = \Sigma \, w_i D_i$$

where $i = 1$ to 6, w_i is the relative weighting of the importance of each of the intermediate values, and $\Sigma \, w_i = 1$ (if all D_i are weighted equally, then $w_i = 0.167$).

The value of DSQI for past designs can be determined and compared to a design that is currently under development. If the DSQI is significantly lower than average, further design work and review are indicated. Similarly, if major changes are to be made to an existing design, the effect of those changes on DSQI can be calculated.

23.3.2   Metrics for Object-Oriented Design

There is much about object-oriented design that is subjective—an experienced designer "knows" how to characterize an OO system so that it will effectively implement customer requirements. But, as an OO design model grows in size and complexity, a more objective view of the characteristics of the design can benefit both the experienced designer (who gains additional insight) and the novice (who obtains an indication of quality that would otherwise be unavailable).

In a detailed treatment of software metrics for OO systems, Whitmire [Whi97] describes nine distinct and measurable characteristics of an OO design:

? **What character- istics can be measured when we assess an OO design?**

Size. Size is defined in terms of four views: population, volume, length, and functionality. *Population* is measured by taking a static count of OO entities such as classes or operations. *Volume* measures are identical to population measures but are collected dynamically—at a given instant of time. *Length* is a measure of a chain of interconnected design elements (e.g., the depth of an inheritance tree is a measure of length). *Functionality* metrics provide an indirect indication of the value delivered to the customer by an OO application.

Complexity. Like size, there are many differing views of software complexity [Zus97]. Whitmire views complexity in terms of structural characteristics by examining how classes of an OO design are interrelated to one another.

Coupling. The physical connections between elements of the OO design (e.g., the number of collaborations between classes or the number of messages passed between objects) represent coupling within an OO system.

uote:

"Many of the decisions for which I had to rely on folklore and myth can now be made using quantitative data."

Scott Whitmire

Sufficiency. Whitmire defines *sufficiency* as "the degree to which an abstraction possesses the features required of it, or the degree to which a design component possesses features in its abstraction, from the point of view of the current application." Stated another way, we ask: "What properties does this abstraction (class) need to possess to be useful to me?" [Whi97]. In essence, a design component (e.g., a class) is *sufficient* if it fully reflects all properties of the application domain object that it is modeling—that is, that the abstraction (class) possesses the features required of it.

Completeness. The only difference between completeness and sufficiency is "the feature set against which we compare the abstraction or design component" [Whi97]. Sufficiency compares the abstraction from the point of view of the current application. *Completeness* considers multiple points of view, asking the question: "What properties are required to fully represent the problem domain object?" Because the criterion for completeness considers different points of view, it has an indirect implication about the degree to which the abstraction or design component can be reused.

Cohesion. Like its counterpart in conventional software, an OO component should be designed in a manner that has all operations working together to achieve a single, well-defined purpose. The cohesiveness of a class is determined by examining the degree to which "the set of properties it possesses is part of the problem or design domain" [Whi97].

Primitiveness. A characteristic that is similar to simplicity, primitiveness (applied to both operations and classes) is the degree to which an operation is atomic—that is, the operation cannot be constructed out of a sequence of other operations contained within a class. A class that exhibits a high degree of primitiveness encapsulates only primitive operations.

Similarity. The degree to which two or more classes are similar in terms of their structure, function, behavior, or purpose is indicated by this measure.

Volatility. As I have noted many times throughout this book, design changes can occur when requirements are modified or when modifications occur in other parts of an application, resulting in mandatory adaptation of the design component in question. Volatility of an OO design component measures the likelihood that a change will occur.

In reality, product metrics for OO systems can be applied not only to the design model, but also the requirements model. In the sections that follow, I discuss metrics that provide an indication of quality at the OO class level and the operation level. In addition, metrics applicable for project management and testing are also explored.

23.3.3 Class-Oriented Metrics—The CK Metrics Suite

The class is the fundamental unit of an OO system. Therefore, measures and metrics for an individual class, the class hierarchy, and class collaborations will be invaluable when you are required to assess OO design quality. A class encapsulates data and the function that manipulate the data. It is often the "parent" for subclasses (sometimes called children) that inherit its attributes and operations. It often collaborates with other classes. Each of these characteristics can be used as the basis for measurement.[7]

Chidamber and Kemerer have proposed one of the most widely referenced sets of OO software metrics [Chi94]. Often referred to as the *CK metrics suite,* the authors have proposed six class-based design metrics for OO systems.[8]

Weighted methods per class (WMC). Assume that n methods of complexity c_1, $c_2, \ldots, c_n$ are defined for a class **C**. The specific complexity metric that is chosen

---

7   It should be noted that the validity of some of the metrics discussed in this chapter is currently debated in the technical literature. Those who champion measurement theory demand a degree of formalism that some OO metrics do not provide. However, it is reasonable to state that the metrics noted provide useful insight for the software engineer.

8   Chidamber, Darcy, and Kemerer use the term *methods* rather than *operations.* Their usage of the term is reflected in this section.

(e.g., cyclomatic complexity) should be normalized so that nominal complexity for a method takes on a value of 1.0.

$$WMC = \Sigma c_i$$

for $i = 1$ to n. The number of methods and their complexity are reasonable indicators of the amount of effort required to implement and test a class. In addition, the larger the number of methods, the more complex is the inheritance tree (all subclasses inherit the methods of their parents). Finally, as the number of methods grows for a given class, it is likely to become more and more application specific, thereby limiting potential reuse. For all of these reasons, WMC should be kept as low as is reasonable.

Although it would seem relatively straightforward to develop a count for the number of methods in a class, the problem is actually more complex than it seems. A consistent counting approach [Chu95] should be developed.

Depth of the inheritance tree (DIT). This metric is "the maximum length from the node to the root of the tree" [Chi94]. Referring to Figure 23.5, the value of DIT for the class hierarchy shown is 4. As DIT grows, it is likely that lower-level classes will inherit many methods. This leads to potential difficulties when attempting to predict the behavior of a class. A deep class hierarchy (DIT is large) also leads to greater design complexity. On the positive side, large DIT values imply that many methods may be reused.

Number of children (NOC). The subclasses that are immediately subordinate to a class in the class hierarchy are termed its children. Referring to Figure 23.5, class C_2 has three children—subclasses C_{21}, C_{22}, and C_{23}. As the number of children grows, reuse increases, but also, as NOC increases, the abstraction represented by the parent class can be diluted if some of the children are not appropriate members of the parent class. As NOC increases, the amount of testing (required to exercise each child in its operational context) will also increase.

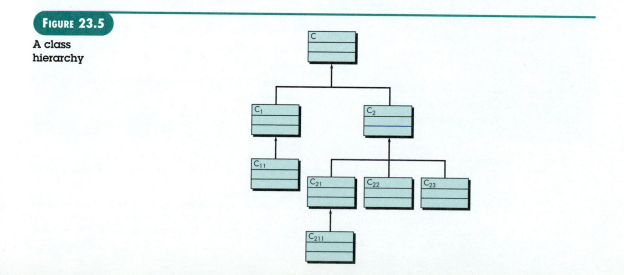

FIGURE 23.5

A class hierarchy

The concepts of coupling and cohesion apply to both conventional and OO software. Keep class coupling low and class and operation cohesion high.

Coupling between object classes (CBO).   The CRC model (Chapter 6) may be used to determine the value for CBO. In essence, CBO is the number of collaborations listed for a class on its CRC index card.[9] As CBO increases, it is likely that the reusability of a class will decrease. High values of CBO also complicate modifications and the testing that ensues when modifications are made. In general, the CBO values for each class should be kept as low as is reasonable. This is consistent with the general guideline to reduce coupling in conventional software.

Response for a class (RFC).   The response set of a class is "a set of methods that can potentially be executed in response to a message received by an object of that class" [Chi94]. RFC is the number of methods in the response set. As RFC increases, the effort required for testing also increases because the test sequence (Chapter 19) grows. It also follows that, as RFC increases, the overall design complexity of the class increases.

Lack of cohesion in methods (LCOM).   Each method within a class **C** accesses one or more attributes (also called instance variables). LCOM is the number of methods that access one or more of the same attributes.[10] If no methods access the same attributes, then LCOM = 0. To illustrate the case where LCOM ≠ 0, consider a class with six methods. Four of the methods have one or more attributes in common (i.e., they access common attributes). Therefore, LCOM = 4. If LCOM is high, methods may be coupled to one another via attributes. This increases the complexity of the class design. Although there are cases in which a high value for LCOM is justifiable, it is desirable to keep cohesion high; that is, keep LCOM low.[11]

SAFEHOME

Applying CK Metrics

The scene: Vinod's cubicle.

The players: Vinod, Jamie, Shakira, and Ed—members of the *SafeHome* software engineering team who are continuing to work on component-level design and test-case design.

The conversation:

Vinod: Did you guys get a chance to read the description of the CK metrics suite I sent you on Wednesday and make those measurements?

Shakira: Wasn't too complicated. I went back to my UML class and sequence diagrams, like you suggested, and got rough counts for DIT, RFC, and LCOM. I couldn't find the CRC model, so I didn't count CBO.

Jamie (smiling): You couldn't find the CRC model because I had it.

Shakira: That's what I love about this team, superb communication.

9   If CRC index cards are developed manually, completeness and consistency must be assessed before CBO can be determined reliably.

10   The formal definition is a bit more complex. See [Chi94] for details.

11   The LCOM metric provides useful insight in some situations, but it can be misleading in others. For example, keeping coupling encapsulated within a class increases the cohesion of the system as a whole. Therefore in at least one important sense, higher LCOM actually suggests that a class may have higher cohesion, not lower.

Vinod: I did my counts . . . did you guys develop numbers for the CK metrics?

[Jamie and Ed nod in the affirmative.]

Jamie: Since I had the CRC cards, I took a look at CBO and it looked pretty uniform across most of the classes. There was one exception, which I noted.

Ed: There are a few classes where RFC is pretty high, compared with the averages . . . maybe we should take a look at simplifying them.

Jamie: Maybe yes, maybe no. I'm still concerned about time, and I don't want to fix stuff that isn't really broken.

Vinod: I agree with that. Maybe we should look for classes that have bad numbers in at least two or more

of the CK metrics. Kind of two strikes and you're modified.

Shakira (looking over Ed's list of classes with high RFC): Look, see this class, it's got a high LCOM as well as a high RFC. Two strikes?

Vinod: Yeah I think so . . . it'll be difficult to implement because of complexity and difficult to test for the same reason. Probably worth designing two separate classes to achieve the same behavior.

Jamie: You think modifying it'll save us time?

Vinod: Over the long haul, yes.

23.3.4 Class-Oriented Metrics—The MOOD Metrics Suite

Harrison, Counsell, and Nithi [Har98b] propose a set of metrics for object-oriented design that provide quantitative indicators for OO design characteristics. A sampling of MOOD metrics follows.

Method inheritance factor (MIF). The degree to which the class architecture of an OO system makes use of inheritance for both methods (operations) and attributes is defined as

$$\text{MIF} = \frac{\Sigma M_i\,(C_i\,)}{\Sigma M_a\,(C_i\,)}$$

where the summation occurs over $i = 1$ to TC. TC is defined as the total number of classes in the architecture, C_i is a class within the architecture, and

$$M_a(C_i) = M_d(C_i) + M_i(C_i)$$

where

$M_a(C_i)$ = number of methods that can be invoked in association with C_i
$M_d(C_i)$ = number of methods declared in the class C_i
$M_i(C_i)$ = number of methods inherited (and not overridden) in C_i

The value of MIF [the attribute inheritance factor (AIF) is defined in an analogous manner] provides an indication of the impact of inheritance on the OO software.

Coupling factor (CF). Earlier in this chapter I noted that coupling is an indication of the connections between elements of the OO design. The MOOD metrics suite defines coupling in the following way:

$$\text{CF} = \Sigma_i\,\Sigma_j\,is\_client\,\frac{(C_i,\,C_j)}{T_c^2 - T_c}$$

where the summations occur over $i = 1$ to T_c and $j = 1$ to T_c. The function is_client = 1, if and only if a relationship exists between the client class C_c and the server class C_s, and $C_c \neq C_s$

= 0, otherwise

Although many factors affect software complexity, understandability, and maintainability, it is reasonable to conclude that as the value for CF increases, the complexity of the OO software will also increase and understandability, maintainability, and the potential for reuse may suffer as a result.

Harrison and her colleagues [Har98b] present a detailed analysis of MIF and CF along with other metrics and examine their validity for use in the assessment of design quality.

23.3.5   OO Metrics Proposed by Lorenz and Kidd

In their book on OO metrics, Lorenz and Kidd [Lor94] divide class-based metrics into four broad categories that each have a bearing on component-level design: size, inheritance, internals, and externals. Size-oriented metrics for an OO design class focus on counts of attributes and operations for an individual class and average values for the OO system as a whole. Inheritance-based metrics focus on the manner in which operations are reused through the class hierarchy. Metrics for class internals look at cohesion (Section 23.3.3) and code-oriented issues, and external metrics examine coupling and reuse. One example of the metrics proposed by Lorenz and Kidd is:

Class size (CS).   The overall size of a class can be determined using the following measures:

During review of the analysis model, CRC index cards will provide a reasonable indication of expected values for CS. If you encounter a class with a large number of responsibilities, consider partitioning it.

- The total number of operations (both inherited and private instance operations) that are encapsulated within the class
- The number of attributes (both inherited and private instance attributes) that are encapsulated by the class

The WMC metric proposed by Chidamber and Kemerer (Section 23.3.3) is also a weighted measure of class size. As I noted earlier, large values for CS indicate that a class may have too much responsibility. This will reduce the reusability of the class and complicate implementation and testing. In general, inherited or public operations and attributes should be weighted more heavily in determining class size [Lor94]. Private operations and attributes enable specialization and are more localized in the design. Averages for the number of class attributes and operations may also be computed. The lower the average values for size, the more likely that classes within the system can be reused widely.

23.3.6   Component-Level Design Metrics

Component-level design metrics for conventional software components focus on internal characteristics of a software component and include measures of the "three Cs"—module cohesion, coupling, and complexity. These measures can help you judge the quality of a component-level design.

Component-level design metrics may be applied once a procedural design has been developed and are "glass box" in the sense that they require knowledge of the inner workings of the module under consideration. Alternatively, they may be delayed until source code is available.

Cohesion metrics.   Bieman and Ott [Bie94] define a collection of metrics that provide an indication of the cohesiveness (Chapter 8) of a module. The metrics are defined in terms of five concepts and measures:

Data slice. Stated simply, a data slice is a backward walk through a module that looks for data values that affect the module location at which the walk began. It should be noted that both program slices (which focus on statements and conditions) and data slices can be defined.

Data tokens. The variables defined for a module can be defined as data tokens for the module.

Glue tokens. This set of data tokens lies on one or more data slice.

Superglue tokens. These data tokens are common to every data slice in a module.

Stickiness. The relative stickiness of a glue token is directly proportional to the number of data slices that it binds.

Bieman and Ott develop metrics for *strong functional cohesion* (SFC), *weak functional cohesion* (WFC), and *adhesiveness* (the relative degree to which glue tokens bind data slices together). A detailed discussion of the Bieman and Ott metrics is best left to the authors [Bie94].

Coupling metrics.   Module coupling provides an indication of the "connectedness" of a module to other modules, global data, and the outside environment. In Chapter 9, coupling was discussed in qualitative terms.

Dhama [Dha95] has proposed a metric for module coupling that encompasses data and control flow coupling, global coupling, and environmental coupling. The measures required to compute module coupling are defined in terms of each of the three coupling types noted previously.

For data and control flow coupling,

d_i = number of input data parameters
c_i = number of input control parameters
d_o = number of output data parameters
c_o = number of output control parameters

For global coupling,

g_d = number of global variables used as data
g_c = number of global variables used as control

For environmental coupling,

> w = number of modules called (fan-out)
>
> r = number of modules calling the module under consideration (fan-in)

Using these measures, a module coupling indicator m_c is defined in the following way:

$$m_c = \frac{k}{M}$$

where k is a proportionality constant and

$$M = d_i + (a \times c_i) + d_o + (b \times c_o) + g_d + (c \times g_c) + w + r$$

Values for k, a, b, and c must be derived empirically.

As the value for m_c increases, the overall module coupling decreases. In order to have the coupling metric move upward as the degree of coupling increases, a revised coupling metric may be defined as

$$C = 1 - m_c$$

where the degree of coupling increases as the value of M increases.

Complexity metrics.   A variety of software metrics can be computed to determine the complexity of program control flow. Many of these are based on the flow graph. A graph (Chapter 18) is a representation composed of nodes and links (also called edges). When the links (edges) are directed, the flow graph is a directed graph.

McCabe and Watson [McC94] identify a number of important uses for complexity metrics:

> Complexity metrics can be used to predict critical information about reliability and maintainability of software systems from automatic analysis of source code [or procedural design information]. Complexity metrics also provide feedback during the software project to help control the [design activity]. During testing and maintenance, they provide detailed information about software modules to help pinpoint areas of potential instability.

The most widely used (and debated) complexity metric for computer software is cyclomatic complexity, originally developed by Thomas McCabe [McC76] and discussed in detail in Chapter 18.

Zuse ([Zus90], [Zus97]) presents an encyclopedic discussion of no fewer than 18 different categories of software complexity metrics. The author presents the basic definitions for metrics in each category (e.g., there are a number of variations on the cyclomatic complexity metric) and then analyzes and critiques each. Zuse's work is the most comprehensive published to date.

KEY POINT

Cyclomatic complexity is only one of a large number of complexity metrics.

23.3.7   Operation-Oriented Metrics

Because the class is the dominant unit in OO systems, fewer metrics have been proposed for operations that reside within a class. Churcher and Shepperd [Chu95] discuss this when they state: "Results of recent studies indicate that methods tend to be small, both in terms of number of statements and in logical complexity [Wil93], suggesting that connectivity structure of a system may be more important than the content of individual modules." However, some insights can be gained by examining average characteristics for methods (operations). Three simple metrics, proposed by Lorenz and Kidd [Lor94], are appropriate:

Average operation size (OS_{avg}). Size can be determined by counting the number of lines of code or the number of messages sent by the operation. As the number of messages sent by a single operation increases, it is likely that responsibilities have not been well allocated within a class.

Operation complexity (OC). The complexity of an operation can be computed using any of the complexity metrics proposed for conventional software [Zus90]. Because operations should be limited to a specific responsibility, the designer should strive to keep OC as low as possible.

Average number of parameters per operation (NP_{avg}). The larger the number of operation parameters, the more complex the collaboration between objects. In general, NP_{avg} should be kept as low as possible.

23.3.8 User Interface Design Metrics

Although there is significant literature on the design of human/computer interfaces (Chapter 11), relatively little information has been published on metrics that would provide insight into the quality and usability of the interface.

Sears [Sea93] suggests that *layout appropriateness* (LA) is a worthwhile design metric for human/computer interfaces. A typical GUI uses layout entities—graphic icons, text, menus, windows, and the like—to assist the user in completing tasks. To accomplish a given task using a GUI, the user must move from one layout entity to the next. The absolute and relative position of each layout entity, the frequency with which it is used, and the "cost" of the transition from one layout entity to the next all contribute to the appropriateness of the interface.

A study of Web page metrics [Ivo01] indicates that simple characteristics of the elements of the layout can also have a significant impact on the perceived quality of the GUI design. The number of words, links, graphics, colors, and fonts (among other characteristics) contained within a Web page affect the perceived complexity and quality of that page.

It is important to note that the selection of a GUI design can be guided with metrics such as LA, but the final arbiter should be user input based on GUI prototypes. Nielsen and Levy [Nie94] report that "one has a reasonably large chance of success if one chooses between interface [designs] based solely on users' opinions. Users' average task performance and their subjective satisfaction with a GUI are highly correlated."

uote:

"You can learn at least one principle of user interface design by loading a dishwasher. If you crowd a lot in there, nothing gets very clean."

Author unknown

23.4 DESIGN METRICS FOR WEBAPPS

A useful set of measures and metrics for WebApps provides quantitative answers to the following questions:

- Does the user interface promote usability?
- Are the aesthetics of the WebApp appropriate for the application domain and pleasing to the user?
- Is the content designed in a manner that imparts the most information with the least effort?
- Is navigation efficient and straightforward?
- Has the WebApp architecture been designed to accommodate the special goals and objectives of WebApp users, the structure of content and functionality, and the flow of navigation required to use the system effectively?
- Are components designed in a manner that reduces procedural complexity and enhances correctness, reliability, and performance?

ADVICE

Many of these metrics are applicable to all user interfaces and should be considered in conjunction with those presented in Section 23.3.8.

Today, each of these questions can be addressed only qualitatively because a validated suite of metrics that would provide quantitative answers does not yet exist.

In the paragraphs that follow, I present a representative sampling of WebApp design metrics that have been proposed in the literature. It is important to note that many of these metrics have not as yet been validated and should be used judiciously.

Interface metrics. For WebApps, the following interface measures can be considered:

Suggested Metric	*Description*
Layout appropriateness	See Section 23.3.8.
Layout complexity	Number of distinct regions[12] defined for an interface
Layout region complexity	Average number of distinct links per region
Recognition complexity	Average number of distinct items the user must look at before making a navigation or data input decision
Recognition time	Average time (in seconds) that it takes a user to select the appropriate action for a given task
Typing effort	Average number of key strokes required for a specific function
Mouse pick effort	Average number of mouse picks per function
Selection complexity	Average number of links that can be selected per page
Content acquisition time	Average number of words of text per Web page
Memory load	Average number of distinct data items that the user must remember to achieve a specific objective

---

12 A distinct region is an area within the layout display that accomplishes some specific set of related functions (e.g., a menu bar, a static graphical display, a content area, an animated display).

Aesthetic (graphic design) metrics. By its nature, aesthetic design relies on qualitative judgment and is not generally amenable to measurement and metrics. However, Ivory and her colleagues [Ivo01] propose a set of measures that may be useful in assessing the impact of aesthetic design:

Suggested Metric	Description
Word count	Total number of words that appear on a page
Body text percentage	Percentage of words that are body versus display text (i.e., headers)
Emphasized body text %	Portion of body text that is emphasized (e.g., bold, capitalized)
Text positioning count	Changes in text position from flush left
Text cluster count	Text areas highlighted with color, bordered regions, rules, or lists
Link count	Total links on a page
Page size	Total bytes for the page as well as elements, graphics, and style sheets
Graphic percentage	Percentage of page bytes that are for graphics
Graphics count	Total graphics on a page (not including graphics specified in scripts, applets, and objects)
Color count	Total colors employed
Font count	Total fonts employed (i.e., face + size + bold + italic)

Content metrics. Metrics in this category focus on content complexity and on clusters of content objects that are organized into pages [Men01].

Suggested Metric	Description
Page wait	Average time required for a page to download at different connection speeds
Page complexity	Average number of different types of media used on page, not including text
Graphic complexity	Average number of graphics media per page
Audio complexity	Average number of audio media per page
Video complexity	Average number of video media per page
Animation complexity	Average number of animations per page
Scanned image complexity	Average number of scanned images per page

Navigation metrics. Metrics in this category address the complexity of the navigational flow [Men01]. In general, they are applicable only for static Web applications, which don't include dynamically generated links and pages.

Suggested Metric	Description
Page-linking complexity	Number of links per page
Connectivity	Total number of internal links, not including dynamically generated links
Connectivity density	Connectivity divided by page count

Using a subset of the metrics suggested, it may be possible to derive empirical relations that allow a WebApp development team to assess technical quality and predict effort based on projected estimates of complexity. Further work remains to be accomplished in this area.

23.5   METRICS FOR SOURCE CODE

Halstead's theory of "software science" [Hal77] proposed the first analytical "laws" for computer software.[14] Halstead assigned quantitative laws to the development of computer software, using a set of primitive measures that may be derived after code is generated or estimated once design is complete. The measures are:

n_1 = number of distinct operators that appear in a program
n_2 = number of distinct operands that appear in a program
N_1 = total number of operator occurrences
N_2 = total number of operand occurrences

Halstead uses these primitive measures to develop expressions for the overall program length, potential minimum volume for an algorithm, the actual volume (number of bits required to specify a program), the program level (a measure of software complexity), the language level (a constant for a given language), and other features such as development effort, development time, and even the projected number of faults in the software.

---

13 Tools noted here do not represent an endorsement, but rather a sampling of tools in this category.
14 It should be noted that Halstead's "laws" have generated substantial controversy, and many believe that the underlying theory has flaws. However, experimental verification for selected programming languages has been performed (e.g., [Fel89]).

Halstead shows that length N can be estimated

$$N = n_1 \log_2 n_1 + n_2 \log_2 n_2$$

and program volume may be defined

$$V = N \log_2 (n_1 + n_2)$$

It should be noted that V will vary with programming language and represents the volume of information (in bits) required to specify a program.

Theoretically, a minimum volume must exist for a particular algorithm. Halstead defines a volume ratio L as the ratio of volume of the most compact form of a program to the volume of the actual program. In actuality, L must always be less than 1. In terms of primitive measures, the volume ratio may be expressed as

$$L = \frac{2}{n_1} \times \frac{n_2}{N_2}$$

Halstead's work is amenable to experimental verification and a large body of research has been conducted to investigate software science. A discussion of this work is beyond the scope of this book. For further information, see [Zus90], [Fen91], and [Zus97].

23.6 METRICS FOR TESTING

Testing metrics fall into two broad categories: (1) metrics that attempt to predict the likely number of tests required at various testing levels, and (2) metrics that focus on test coverage for a given component.

Although much has been written on software metrics for testing (e.g., [Het93]), the majority of metrics proposed focus on the process of testing, not the technical characteristics of the tests themselves. In general, testers must rely on analysis, design, and code metrics to guide them in the design and execution of test cases.

Architectural design metrics provide information on the ease or difficulty associated with integration testing (Section 23.3) and the need for specialized testing software (e.g., stubs and drivers). Cyclomatic complexity (a component-level design metric) lies at the core of basis path testing, a test-case design method presented in Chapter 18. In addition, cyclomatic complexity can be used to target modules as candidates for extensive unit testing. Modules with high cyclomatic complexity are more likely to be error prone than modules whose cyclomatic complexity is lower. For this reason, you should expend above average effort to uncover errors in such modules before they are integrated in a system.

23.6.1 Halstead Metrics Applied to Testing

Testing effort can be estimated using metrics derived from Halstead measures (Section 23.5). Using the definitions for program volume V and program level PL, Halstead effort e can be computed as

$$PL = \frac{1}{(n_1/2) \times (N_2/n_2)} \tag{23.2a}$$

$$e = \frac{V}{PL} \tag{23.2b}$$

The percentage of overall testing effort to be allocated to a module k can be estimated using the following relationship:

$$\text{Percentage of testing effort } (k) = \frac{e(k)}{\Sigma e(i)} \qquad (23.3)$$

where $e(k)$ is computed for module k using Equations (23.2) and the summation in the denominator of Equation (23.3) is the sum of Halstead effort across all modules of the system.

23.6.2   Metrics for Object-Oriented Testing

The OO design metrics noted in Section 23.3 provide an indication of design quality. They also provide a general indication of the amount of testing effort required to exercise an OO system. Binder [Bin94b] suggests a broad array of design metrics that have a direct influence on the "testability" of an OO system. The metrics consider aspects of encapsulation and inheritance.

Lack of cohesion in methods (LCOM).[15] The higher the value of LCOM, the more states must be tested to ensure that methods do not generate side effects.

Percent public and protected (PAP). Public attributes are inherited from other classes and therefore are visible to those classes. Protected attributes are accessible to methods in subclasses. This metric indicates the percentage of class attributes that are public or protected. High values for PAP increase the likelihood of side effects among classes because public and protected attributes lead to high potential for coupling.[16] Tests must be designed to ensure that such side effects are uncovered.

Public access to data members (PAD). This metric indicates the number of classes (or methods) that can access another class's attributes, a violation of encapsulation. High values for PAD lead to the potential for side effects among classes. Tests must be designed to ensure that such side effects are uncovered.

Number of root classes (NOR). This metric is a count of the distinct class hierarchies that are described in the design model. Test suites for each root class and the corresponding class hierarchy must be developed. As NOR increases, testing effort also increases.

Fan-in (FIN). When used in the OO context, fan-in in the inheritance hierarchy is an indication of multiple inheritance. FIN > 1 indicates that a class inherits its attributes and operations from more than one root class. FIN > 1 should be avoided when possible.

Number of children (NOC) and depth of the inheritance tree (DIT).[17] As I mentioned in Chapter 19, superclass methods will have to be retested for each subclass.

OO testing can be quite complex. Metrics can assist you in targeting testing resources at threads, scenarios, and packages of classes that are "suspect" based on measured characteristics. Use them.

---

15 See Section 23.3.3 for a description of LCOM.
16 Some people promote designs with none of the attributes being public or private, that is, PAP = 0. This implies that all attributes must be accessed in other classes via methods.
17 See Section 23.3.3 for a description of NOC and DIT.

23.7   METRICS FOR MAINTENANCE

All of the software metrics introduced in this chapter can be used for the development of new software and the maintenance of existing software. However, metrics designed explicitly for maintenance activities have been proposed.

IEEE Std. 982.1-1988 [IEE93] suggests a *software maturity index* (SMI) that provides an indication of the stability of a software product (based on changes that occur for each release of the product). The following information is determined:

M_T = number of modules in the current release
F_c = number of modules in the current release that have been changed
F_a = number of modules in the current release that have been added
F_d = number of modules from the preceding release that were deleted in the current release

The software maturity index is computed in the following manner:

$$\text{SMI} = \frac{M_T - (F_a + F_c + F_d)}{M_T}$$

As SMI approaches 1.0, the product begins to stabilize. SMI may also be used as a metric for planning software maintenance activities. The mean time to produce a release of a software product can be correlated with SMI, and empirical models for maintenance effort can be developed.

SOFTWARE TOOLS

Product Metrics

Objective: To assist software engineers in developing meaningful metrics that assess the work products produced during analysis and design modeling, source code generation, and testing.

Mechanics: Tools in this category span a broad array of metrics and are implemented either as a stand-alone application or (more commonly) as functionality that exists within tools for analysis and design, coding, or testing. In most cases, the metrics tool analyzes a representation of the software (e.g., a UML model or source code) and develops one or more metrics as a result.

Representative Tools:[18] *Krakatau Metrics,* developed by Power Software (**www.powersoftware.com/products**), computes complexity, Halstead, and related metrics for C/C++ and Java.

Metrics4C—developed by +1 Software Engineering (**www.plus-one.com/Metrics4C_fact_sheet.html**), computes a variety of architectural, design, and code-oriented metrics as well as project-oriented metrics.

Rational Rose, distributed by IBM (**www-304.ibm.com/jct03001c/software/awdtools/developer/rose/**), is a comprehensive tool set for UML modeling that incorporates a number of metrics analysis features.

RSM, developed by M-Squared Technologies (**msquaredtechnologies.com/m2rsm/index.html**), computes a wide variety of code-oriented metrics for C, C++, and Java.

Understand, developed by Scientific Toolworks, Inc. (**www.scitools.com**), calculates code-oriented metrics for a variety of programming languages.

---

18 Tools noted here do not represent an endorsement, but rather a sampling of tools in this category. In most cases, tool names are trademarked by their respective developers.

23.8   SUMMARY

Software metrics provide a quantitative way to assess the quality of internal product attributes, thereby enabling you to assess quality before the product is built. Metrics provide the insight necessary to create effective requirements and design models, solid code, and thorough tests.

To be useful in a real-world context, a software metric must be simple and computable, persuasive, consistent, and objective. It should be programming language independent and provide you with effective feedback.

Metrics for the requirements model focus on function, data, and behavior—the three components of the model. Metrics for design consider architecture, component-level design, and interface design issues. Architectural design metrics consider the structural aspects of the design model. Component-level design metrics provide an indication of module quality by establishing indirect measures for cohesion, coupling, and complexity. User interface design metrics provide an indication of the ease with which a GUI can be used. WebApp metrics consider aspects of the user interface as well as WebApp aesthetics, content, and navigation.

Metrics for OO systems focus on measurement that can be applied to the class and the design characteristics—localization, encapsulation, information hiding, inheritance, and object abstraction techniques—that make the class unique. The CK metrics suite defines six class-oriented software metrics that focus on the class and the class hierarchy. The metrics suite also develops metrics to assess the collaborations between classes and the cohesion of methods that reside within a class. At a class-oriented level, the CK metrics suite can be augmented with metrics proposed by Lorenz and Kidd and the MOOD metrics suite.

Halstead provides an intriguing set of metrics at the source code level. Using the number of operators and operands present in the code, software science provides a variety of metrics that can be used to assess program quality.

Few product metrics have been proposed for direct use in software testing and maintenance. However, many other product metrics can be used to guide the testing process and as a mechanism for assessing the maintainability of a computer program. A wide variety of OO metrics have been proposed to assess the testability of an OO system.

PROBLEMS AND POINTS TO PONDER

23.1. Measurement theory is an advanced topic that has a strong bearing on software metrics. Using [Zus97], [Fen91], [Zus90], or Web-based sources, write a brief paper that outlines the main tenets of measurement theory. Individual project: Develop a presentation on the subject and present it to your class.

23.2. Why is it that a single, all-encompassing metric cannot be developed for program complexity or program quality? Try to come up with a measure or metric from everyday life that violates the attributes of effective software metrics defined in Section 23.1.5.

23.3. A system has 12 external inputs, 24 external outputs, fields 30 different external queries, manages 4 internal logical files, and interfaces with 6 different legacy systems (6 EIFs). All of these data are of average complexity and the overall system is relatively simple. Compute FP for the system.

23.4. Software for System X has 24 individual functional requirements and 14 nonfunctional requirements. What is the specificity of the requirements? The completeness?

23.5. A major information system has 1140 modules. There are 96 modules that perform control and coordination functions and 490 modules whose function depends on prior processing. The system processes approximately 220 data objects that each have an average of three attributes. There are 140 unique database items and 90 different database segments. Finally, 600 modules have single entry and exit points. Compute the DSQI for this system.

23.6. A class **X** has 12 operations. Cyclomatic complexity has been computed for all operations in the OO system, and the average value of module complexity is 4. For class **X**, the complexity for operations 1 to 12 is 5, 4, 3, 3, 6, 8, 2, 2, 5, 5, 4, 4, respectively. Compute the weighted methods per class.

23.7. Develop a software tool that will compute cyclomatic complexity for a programming language module. You may choose the language.

23.8. Develop a small software tool that will perform a Halstead analysis on programming language source code of your choosing.

23.9. A legacy system has 940 modules. The latest release required that 90 of these modules be changed. In addition, 40 new modules were added and 12 old modules were removed. Compute the software maturity index for the system.

FURTHER READINGS AND INFORMATION SOURCES

There is a surprisingly large number of books that are dedicated to software metrics, although the majority focus on process and project metrics to the exclusion of product metrics. Lanza and her colleagues (*Object-Oriented Metrics in Practice,* Springer, 2006) discuss OO metrics and their use for assessing the quality of a design. Genero (*Metrics for Software Conceptual Models,* Imperial College Press, 2005) and Ejiogu (*Software Metrics,* BookSurge Publishing, 2005) present a wide variety of technical metrics for use cases, UML models, and other modeling representations. Hutcheson (*Software Testing Fundamentals: Methods and Metrics,* Wiley, 2003) presents a set of metrics for testing. Kan (*Metrics and Models in Software Quality Engineering,* Addison-Wesley, 2d ed., 2002), Fenton and Pfleeger (*Software Metrics: A Rigorous and Practical Approach,* Brooks-Cole Publishing, 1998), and Zuse [Zus97] have written thorough treatments of product metrics.

Books by Card and Glass [Car90], Zuse [Zus90], Fenton [Fen91], Ejiogu [Eji91], Moeller and Paulish (*Software Metrics,* Chapman and Hall, 1993), and Hetzel [Het93] all address product metrics in some detail. Oman and Pfleeger (*Applying Software Metrics,* IEEE Computer Society Press, 1997) have edited an anthology of important papers on software metrics.

Methods for establishing a metrics program and the underlying principles for software measurement are considered by Ebert and his colleagues (*Best Practices in Software Measurement,* Springer, 2004). Shepperd (*Foundations of Software Measurement,* Prentice-Hall, 1996) also addresses measurement theory in some detail. Current research is presented in the *Proceedings of the Symposium on Software Metrics* (IEEE, published annually).

A comprehensive summary of dozens of useful software metrics is presented in [IEE93]. In general, a discussion of each metric has been distilled to the essential "primitives" (measures) required to compute the metric and the appropriate relationships to effect the computation. An appendix provides discussion and many references.

Whitmire [Whi97] presents a comprehensive and mathematically sophisticated treatment of OO metrics. Lorenz and Kidd [Lor94] and Hendersen-Sellers (*Object-Oriented Metrics: Measures of Complexity,* Prentice-Hall, 1996) provide treatments that are dedicated to OO metrics.

A wide variety of information sources on software metrics is available on the Internet. An up-to-date list of World Wide Web references that are relevant to software metrics can be found at the SEPA website: **www.mhhe.com/engcs/compsci/pressman/professional/olc/ser.htm.**

Four

MANAGING SOFTWARE PROJECTS

In this part of *Software Engineering: A Practitioner's Approach* you'll learn the management techniques required to plan, organize, monitor, and control software projects. These questions are addressed in the chapters that follow:

- How must people, process, and problem be managed during a software project?

- How can software metrics be used to manage a software project and the software process?

- How does a software team generate reliable estimates of effort, cost, and project duration?

- What techniques can be used to assess the risks that can have an impact on project success?

- How does a software project manager select a set of software engineering work tasks?

- How is a project schedule created?

- Why are maintenance and reengineering so important for both software engineering managers and practitioners?

Once these questions are answered, you'll be better prepared to manage software projects in a way that will lead to timely delivery of a high-quality product.

24
PROJECT MANAGEMENT CONCEPTS

In the preface to his book on software project management, Meiler Page-Jones [Pag85] makes a statement that can be echoed by many software engineering consultants:

> I've visited dozens of commercial shops, both good and bad, and I've observed scores of data processing managers, again, both good and bad. Too often, I've watched in horror as these managers futilely struggled through nightmarish projects, squirmed under impossible deadlines, or delivered systems that outraged their users and went on to devour huge chunks of maintenance time.

What Page-Jones describes are symptoms that result from an array of management and technical problems. However, if a post mortem were to be conducted

QUICK LOOK

What is it? Although many of us (in our darker moments) take Dilbert's view of "management," it remains a very necessary activity when computer-based systems and products are built. Project management involves the planning, monitoring, and control of the people, process, and events that occur as software evolves from a preliminary concept to full operational deployment.

Who does it? Everyone "manages" to some extent, but the scope of management activities varies among people involved in a software project. A software engineer manages her day-to-day activities, planning, monitoring, and controlling technical tasks. Project managers plan, monitor, and control the work of a team of software engineers. Senior managers coordinate the interface between the business and software professionals.

Why is it important? Building computer software is a complex undertaking, particularly if it involves many people working over a relatively long time. That's why software projects need to be managed.

What are the steps? Understand the four P's—people, product, process, and project. People must be organized to perform software work effectively. Communication with the customer and other stakeholders must occur so that product scope and requirements are understood. A process that is appropriate for the people and the product should be selected. The project must be planned by estimating effort and calendar time to accomplish work tasks: defining work products, establishing quality checkpoints, and identifying mechanisms to monitor and control work defined by the plan.

What is the work product? A project plan is produced as management activities commence. The plan defines the process and tasks to be conducted, the people who will do the work, and the mechanisms for assessing risks, controlling change, and evaluating quality.

How do I ensure that I've done it right? You're never completely sure that the project plan is right until you've delivered a high-quality product on time and within budget. However, a project manager does it right when he encourages software people to work together as an effective team, focusing their attention on customer needs and product quality.

for every project, it is very likely that a consistent theme would be encountered: project management was weak.

In this chapter and Chapters 25 through 29, I'll present the key concepts that lead to effective software project management. This chapter considers basic software project management concepts and principles. Chapter 25 presents process and project metrics, the basis for effective management decision making. The techniques that are used to estimate cost are discussed in Chapter 26. Chapter 27 will help you to define a realistic project schedule. The management activities that lead to effective risk monitoring, mitigation, and management are presented in Chapter 28. Finally, Chapter 29 considers maintenance and reengineering and discusses the management issues that you'll encounter when you must deal with legacy systems.

24.1 THE MANAGEMENT SPECTRUM

Effective software project management focuses on the four P's: people, product, process, and project. The order is not arbitrary. The manager who forgets that software engineering work is an intensely human endeavor will never have success in project management. A manager who fails to encourage comprehensive stakeholder communication early in the evolution of a product risks building an elegant solution for the wrong problem. The manager who pays little attention to the process runs the risk of inserting competent technical methods and tools into a vacuum. The manager who embarks without a solid project plan jeopardizes the success of the project.

24.1.1 The People

The cultivation of motivated, highly skilled software people has been discussed since the 1960s. In fact, the "people factor" is so important that the Software Engineering Institute has developed a *People Capability Maturity Model* (People-CMM), in recognition of the fact that "every organization needs to continually improve its ability to attract, develop, motivate, organize, and retain the workforce needed to accomplish its strategic business objectives" [Cur01].

The people capability maturity model defines the following key practice areas for software people: staffing, communication and coordination, work environment, performance management, training, compensation, competency analysis and development, career development, workgroup development, team/culture development, and others. Organizations that achieve high levels of People-CMM maturity have a higher likelihood of implementing effective software project management practices.

The People-CMM is a companion to the *Software Capability Maturity Model–Integration* (Chapter 30) that guides organizations in the creation of a mature software process. Issues associated with people management and structure for software projects are considered later in this chapter.

24.1.2 The Product

Before a project can be planned, product objectives and scope should be established, alternative solutions should be considered, and technical and management constraints should be identified. Without this information, it is impossible to define reasonable (and accurate) estimates of the cost, an effective assessment of risk, a realistic breakdown of project tasks, or a manageable project schedule that provides a meaningful indication of progress.

As a software developer, you and other stakeholders must meet to define product objectives and scope. In many cases, this activity begins as part of the system engineering or business process engineering and continues as the first step in software requirements engineering (Chapter 5). Objectives identify the overall goals for the product (from the stakeholders' points of view) without considering how these goals will be achieved. Scope identifies the primary data, functions, and behaviors that characterize the product, and more important, attempts to bound these characteristics in a quantitative manner.

Once the product objectives and scope are understood, alternative solutions are considered. Although very little detail is discussed, the alternatives enable managers and practitioners to select a "best" approach, given the constraints imposed by delivery deadlines, budgetary restrictions, personnel availability, technical interfaces, and myriad other factors.

24.1.3 The Process

Those who adhere to the agile process philosophy (Chapter 3) argue that their process is leaner than others. That may be true, but they still have a process, and agile software engineering still requires discipline.

A software process (Chapters 2 and 3) provides the framework from which a comprehensive plan for software development can be established. A small number of framework activities are applicable to all software projects, regardless of their size or complexity. A number of different task sets—tasks, milestones, work products, and quality assurance points—enable the framework activities to be adapted to the characteristics of the software project and the requirements of the project team. Finally, umbrella activities—such as software quality assurance, software configuration management, and measurement—overlay the process model. Umbrella activities are independent of any one framework activity and occur throughout the process.

24.1.4 The Project

We conduct planned and controlled software projects for one primary reason—it is the only known way to manage complexity. And yet, software teams still struggle. In a study of 250 large software projects between 1998 and 2004, Capers Jones [Jon04] found that "about 25 were deemed successful in that they achieved their schedule, cost, and quality objectives. About 50 had delays or overruns below

35 percent, while about 175 experienced major delays and overruns, or were terminated without completion." Although the success rate for present-day software projects may have improved somewhat, our project failure rate remains much higher than it should be.[1]

To avoid project failure, a software project manager and the software engineers who build the product must avoid a set of common warning signs, understand the critical success factors that lead to good project management, and develop a commonsense approach for planning, monitoring, and controlling the project. Each of these issues is discussed in Section 24.5 and in the chapters that follow.

24.2   PEOPLE

In a study published by the IEEE [Cur88], the engineering vice presidents of three major technology companies were asked what was the most important contributor to a successful software project. They answered in the following way:

VP 1: I guess if you had to pick one thing out that is most important in our environment, I'd say it's not the tools that we use, it's the people.

VP 2: The most important ingredient that was successful on this project was having smart people . . . very little else matters in my opinion. . . . The most important thing you do for a project is selecting the staff. . . . The success of the software development organization is very, very much associated with the ability to recruit good people.

VP 3: The only rule I have in management is to ensure I have good people—real good people—and that I grow good people—and that I provide an environment in which good people can produce.

Indeed, this is a compelling testimonial on the importance of people in the software engineering process. And yet, all of us, from senior engineering vice presidents to the lowliest practitioner, often take people for granted. Managers argue (as the preceding group had) that people are primary, but their actions sometimes belie their words. In this section I examine the stakeholders who participate in the software process and the manner in which they are organized to perform effective software engineering.

24.2.1   The Stakeholders

The software process (and every software project) is populated by stakeholders who can be categorized into one of five constituencies:

1. *Senior managers* who define the business issues that often have a significant influence on the project.

---

1   Given these statistics, it's reasonable to ask how the impact of computers continues to grow exponentially. Part of the answer, I think, is that a substantial number of these "failed" projects are ill conceived in the first place. Customers lose interest quickly (because what they've requested wasn't really as important as they first thought), and the projects are cancelled.

2. *Project (technical) managers* who must plan, motivate, organize, and control the practitioners who do software work.

3. *Practitioners* who deliver the technical skills that are necessary to engineer a product or application.

4. *Customers* who specify the requirements for the software to be engineered and other stakeholders who have a peripheral interest in the outcome.

5. *End users* who interact with the software once it is released for production use.

Every software project is populated by people who fall within this taxonomy.[2] To be effective, the project team must be organized in a way that maximizes each person's skills and abilities. And that's the job of the team leader.

24.2.2   Team Leaders

Project management is a people-intensive activity, and for this reason, competent practitioners often make poor team leaders. They simply don't have the right mix of people skills. And yet, as Edgemon states: "Unfortunately and all too frequently it seems, individuals just fall into a project manager role and become accidental project managers" [Edg95].

In an excellent book of technical leadership, Jerry Weinberg [Wei86] suggests an MOI model of leadership:

What do we look for when choosing someone to lead a software project?

Motivation. The ability to encourage (by "push or pull") technical people to produce to their best ability.

Organization. The ability to mold existing processes (or invent new ones) that will enable the initial concept to be translated into a final product.

Ideas or innovation. The ability to encourage people to create and feel creative even when they must work within bounds established for a particular software product or application.

Weinberg suggests that successful project leaders apply a problem-solving management style. That is, a software project manager should concentrate on understanding the problem to be solved, managing the flow of ideas, and at the same time, letting everyone on the team know (by words and, far more important, by actions) that quality counts and that it will not be compromised.

Another view [Edg95] of the characteristics that define an effective project manager emphasizes four key traits:

Quote:

"In simplest terms, a leader is one who knows where he wants to go, and gets up, and goes."

John Erskine

Problem solving. An effective software project manager can diagnose the technical and organizational issues that are most relevant, systematically structure a solution or properly motivate other practitioners to develop the solution, apply lessons learned from past projects to new situations, and

---

2   When WebApps are developed, other nontechnical people may be involved in content creation.

remain flexible enough to change direction if initial attempts at problem solution are fruitless.

Managerial identity. A good project manager must take charge of the project. She must have the confidence to assume control when necessary and the assurance to allow good technical people to follow their instincts.

Achievement. A competent manager must reward initiative and accomplishment to optimize the productivity of a project team. She must demonstrate through her own actions that controlled risk taking will not be punished.

Influence and team building. An effective project manager must be able to "read" people; she must be able to understand verbal and nonverbal signals and react to the needs of the people sending these signals. The manager must remain under control in high-stress situations.

24.2.3 The Software Team

uote:

"Not every group is a team, and not every team is effective."

Glenn Parker

There are almost as many human organizational structures for software development as there are organizations that develop software. For better or worse, organizational structure cannot be easily modified. Concern with the practical and political consequences of organizational change are not within the software project manager's scope of responsibility. However, the organization of the people directly involved in a new software project is within the project manager's purview.

The "best" team structure depends on the management style of your organization, the number of people who will populate the team and their skill levels, and the overall problem difficulty. Mantei [Man81] describes seven project factors that should be considered when planning the structure of software engineering teams:

What factors should be considered when the structure of a software team is chosen?

- Difficulty of the problem to be solved
- "Size" of the resultant program(s) in lines of code or function points
- Time that the team will stay together (team lifetime)
- Degree to which the problem can be modularized
- Required quality and reliability of the system to be built
- Rigidity of the delivery date
- Degree of sociability (communication) required for the project

Constantine [Con93] suggests four "organizational paradigms" for software engineering teams:

What options do we have when defining the structure of a software team?

1. A *closed paradigm* structures a team along a traditional hierarchy of authority. Such teams can work well when producing software that is quite similar to past efforts, but they will be less likely to be innovative when working within the closed paradigm.

2. A *random paradigm* structures a team loosely and depends on individual initiative of the team members. When innovation or technological breakthrough is required, teams following the random paradigm will excel. But such teams may struggle when "orderly performance" is required.

3. An *open paradigm* attempts to structure a team in a manner that achieves some of the controls associated with the closed paradigm but also much of the innovation that occurs when using the random paradigm. Work is performed collaboratively, with heavy communication and consensus-based decision making the trademarks of open paradigm teams. Open paradigm team structures are well suited to the solution of complex problems but may not perform as efficiently as other teams.

4. A *synchronous paradigm* relies on the natural compartmentalization of a problem and organizes team members to work on pieces of the problem with little active communication among themselves.

As an historical footnote, one of the earliest software team organizations was a closed paradigm structure originally called the *chief programmer team.* This structure was first proposed by Harlan Mills and described by Baker [Bak72]. The nucleus of the team was composed of a *senior engineer* (the chief programmer), who plans, coordinates, and reviews all technical activities of the team; *technical staff* (normally two to five people), who conduct analysis and development activities; and a *backup engineer,* who supports the senior engineer in his or her activities and can replace the senior engineer with minimum loss in project continuity. The chief programmer may be served by one or more specialists (e.g., telecommunications expert, database designer), support staff (e.g., technical writers, clerical personnel), and a software librarian.

As a counterpoint to the chief programmer team structure, Constantine's random paradigm [Con93] suggests a software team with creative independence whose approach to work might best be termed *innovative anarchy.* Although the free-spirited approach to software work has appeal, channeling creative energy into a high-performance team must be a central goal of a software engineering organization. To achieve a high-performance team:

• Team members must have trust in one another.

• The distribution of skills must be appropriate to the problem.

• Mavericks may have to be excluded from the team, if team cohesiveness is to be maintained.

Regardless of team organization, the objective for every project manager is to help create a team that exhibits cohesiveness. In their book, *Peopleware,* DeMarco and Lister [DeM98] discuss this issue:

We tend to use the word team fairly loosely in the business world, calling any group of people assigned to work together a "team." But many of these groups just don't seem like

? **What is a "jelled" team?**

teams. They don't have a common definition of success or any identifiable team spirit. What is missing is a phenomenon that we call *jell.*

A jelled team is a group of people so strongly knit that the whole is greater than the sum of the parts. . . .

Once a team begins to jell, the probability of success goes way up. The team can become unstoppable, a juggernaut for success. . . . They don't need to be managed in the traditional way, and they certainly don't need to be motivated. They've got momentum.

DeMarco and Lister contend that members of jelled teams are significantly more productive and more motivated than average. They share a common goal, a common culture, and in many cases, a "sense of eliteness" that makes them unique.

? **Why is it that teams fail to jell?**

But not all teams jell. In fact, many teams suffer from what Jackman [Jac98] calls "team toxicity." She defines five factors that "foster a potentially toxic team environment": (1) a frenzied work atmosphere, (2) high frustration that causes friction among team members, (3) a "fragmented or poorly coordinated" software process, (4) an unclear definition of roles on the software team, and (5) "continuous and repeated exposure to failure."

Quote:

"Do or do not. There is no try."

Yoda from *Star Wars*

To avoid a frenzied work environment, the project manager should be certain that the team has access to all information required to do the job and that major goals and objectives, once defined, should not be modified unless absolutely necessary. A software team can avoid frustration if it is given as much responsibility for decision making as possible. An inappropriate process (e.g., unnecessary or burdensome work tasks or poorly chosen work products) can be avoided by understanding the product to be built, the people doing the work, and by allowing the team to select the process model. The team itself should establish its own mechanisms for accountability (technical reviews[3] are an excellent way to accomplish this) and define a series of corrective approaches when a member of the team fails to perform. And finally, the key to avoiding an atmosphere of failure is to establish team-based techniques for feedback and problem solving.

In addition to the five toxins described by Jackman, a software team often struggles with the differing human traits of its members. Some team members are extroverts; others are introverts. Some people gather information intuitively, distilling broad concepts from disparate facts. Others process information linearly, collecting and organizing minute details from the data provided. Some team members are comfortable making decisions only when a logical, orderly argument is presented. Others are intuitive, willing to make a decision based on "feel." Some practitioners want a detailed schedule populated by organized tasks that enable them to achieve closure for some element of a project. Others prefer a more spontaneous environment in which open issues are okay. Some work hard to get things done long before a milestone date, thereby avoiding stress as the date approaches, while others are

---

3   Technical reviews are discussed in detail in Chapter 15.

energized by the rush to make a last-minute deadline. A detailed discussion of the psychology of these traits and the ways in which a skilled team leader can help people with opposing traits to work together is beyond the scope of this book.[4] However, it is important to note that recognition of human differences is the first step toward creating teams that jell.

24.2.4   Agile Teams

Over the past decade, agile software development (Chapter 3) has been suggested as an antidote to many of the problems that have plagued software project work. To review, the agile philosophy encourages customer satisfaction and early incremental delivery of software, small highly motivated project teams, informal methods, minimal software engineering work products, and overall development simplicity.

The small, highly motivated project team, also called an *agile team,* adopts many of the characteristics of successful software project teams discussed in the preceding section and avoids many of the toxins that create problems. However, the agile philosophy stresses individual (team member) competency coupled with group collaboration as critical success factors for the team. Cockburn and Highsmith [Coc01a] note this when they write:

> If the people on the project are good enough, they can use almost any process and accomplish their assignment. If they are not good enough, no process will repair their inadequacy—"people trump process" is one way to say this. However, lack of user and executive support can kill a project—"politics trump people." Inadequate support can keep even good people from accomplishing the job.

KEY POINT

An agile team is a self-organizing team that has autonomy to plan and make technical decisions.

To make effective use of the competencies of each team member and to foster effective collaboration through a software project, agile teams are *self-organizing.* A self-organizing team does not necessarily maintain a single team structure but instead uses elements of Constantine's random, open, and synchronous paradigms discussed in Section 24.2.3.

Many agile process models (e.g., Scrum) give the agile team significant autonomy to make the project management and technical decisions required to get the job done. Planning is kept to a minimum, and the team is allowed to select its own approach (e.g., process, methods, tools), constrained only by business requirements and organizational standards. As the project proceeds, the team self-organizes to focus individual competency in a way that is most beneficial to the project at a given point in time. To accomplish this, an agile team might conduct daily team meetings to coordinate and synchronize the work that must be accomplished for that day.

Based on information obtained during these meetings, the team adapts its approach in a way that accomplishes an increment of work. As each day passes, continual self-organization and collaboration move the team toward a completed software increment.

---

4   An excellent introduction to these issues as they relate to software project teams can be found in [Fer98].

24.2.5 Coordination and Communication Issues

There are many reasons that software projects get into trouble. The scale of many development efforts is large, leading to complexity, confusion, and significant difficulties in coordinating team members. Uncertainty is common, resulting in a continuing stream of changes that ratchets the project team. Interoperability has become a key characteristic of many systems. New software must communicate with existing software and conform to predefined constraints imposed by the system or product.

These characteristics of modern software—scale, uncertainty, and interoperability—are facts of life. To deal with them effectively, you must establish effective methods for coordinating the people who do the work. To accomplish this, mechanisms for formal and informal communication among team members and between multiple teams must be established. Formal communication is accomplished through "writing, structured meetings, and other relatively non-interactive and impersonal communication channels" [Kra95]. Informal communication is more personal. Members of a software team share ideas on an ad hoc basis, ask for help as problems arise, and interact with one another on a daily basis.

SAFEHOME

Team Structure

The scene: Doug Miller's office prior to the initiation of the *SafeHome* software project.

The players: Doug Miller (manager of the *SafeHome* software engineering team) and Vinod Raman, Jamie Lazar, and other members of the product software engineering team.

The conversation:

Doug: Have you guys had a chance to look over the preliminary info on *SafeHome* that marketing has prepared?

Vinod (nodding and looking at his teammates): Yes. But we have a bunch of questions.

Doug: Let's hold on that for a moment. I'd like to talk about how we're going to structure the team, who's responsible for what . . .

Jamie: I'm really into the agile philosophy, Doug. I think we should be a self-organizing team.

Vinod: I agree. Given the tight time line and some of the uncertainty, and that fact that we're all really competent [laughs], that seems like the right way to go.

Doug: That's okay with me, but you guys know the drill.

Jamie (smiling and talking as if she was reciting something): "We make tactical decisions, about who does what and when, but it's our responsibility to get product out the door on time.

Vinod: And with quality.

Doug: Exactly. But remember there are constraints. Marketing defines the software increments to be produced—in consultation with us, of course.

Jamie: And?

Doug: And, we're going to use UML as our modeling approach.

Vinod: But keep extraneous documentation to an absolute minimum.

Doug: Who is the liaison with me?

Jamie: We decided that Vinod will be the tech lead—he's got the most experience, so Vinod is your liaison, but feel free to talk to any of us.

Doug (laughing): Don't worry, I will.

24.3   THE PRODUCT

A software project manager is confronted with a dilemma at the very beginning of a software project. Quantitative estimates and an organized plan are required, but solid information is unavailable. A detailed analysis of software requirements would provide necessary information for estimates, but analysis often takes weeks or even months to complete. Worse, requirements may be fluid, changing regularly as the project proceeds. Yet, a plan is needed "now!"

Like it or not, you must examine the product and the problem it is intended to solve at the very beginning of the project. At a minimum, the scope of the product must be established and bounded.

24.3.1   Software Scope

The first software project management activity is the determination of *software scope.* Scope is defined by answering the following questions:

If you can't bound a characteristic of the software you intend to build, list the characteristic as a project risk (Chapter 25).

> **Context.** How does the software to be built fit into a larger system, product, or business context, and what constraints are imposed as a result of the context?
>
> **Information objectives.** What customer-visible data objects are produced as output from the software? What data objects are required for input?
>
> **Function and performance.** What function does the software perform to transform input data into output? Are any special performance characteristics to be addressed?

Software project scope must be unambiguous and understandable at the management and technical levels. A statement of software scope must be bounded. That is, quantitative data (e.g., number of simultaneous users, target environment, maximum allowable response time) are stated explicitly, constraints and/or limitations (e.g., product cost restricts memory size) are noted, and mitigating factors (e.g., desired algorithms are well understood and available in Java) are described.

24.3.2   Problem Decomposition

Problem decomposition, sometimes called *partitioning* or *problem elaboration,* is an activity that sits at the core of software requirements analysis (Chapters 6 and 7). During the scoping activity no attempt is made to fully decompose the problem. Rather, decomposition is applied in two major areas: (1) the functionality and content (information) that must be delivered and (2) the process that will be used to deliver it.

In order to develop a reasonable project plan, you must decompose the problem. This can be accomplished using a list of functions or with use cases.

Human beings tend to apply a divide-and-conquer strategy when they are confronted with a complex problem. Stated simply, a complex problem is partitioned into smaller problems that are more manageable. This is the strategy that applies as project planning begins. Software functions, described in the statement of scope, are evaluated and refined to provide more detail prior to the beginning of estimation (Chapter 26). Because both cost and schedule estimates are functionally oriented, some degree of decomposition is often useful. Similarly, major content or data objects are decomposed into their constituent parts, providing a reasonable understanding of the information to be produced by the software.

As an example, consider a project that will build a new word-processing product. Among the unique features of the product are continuous voice as well as virtual keyboard input via a multitouch screen, extremely sophisticated "automatic copy edit" features, page layout capability, automatic indexing and table of contents, and others. The project manager must first establish a statement of scope that bounds these features (as well as other more mundane functions such as editing, file management, and document production). For example, will continuous voice input require that the product be "trained" by the user? Specifically, what capabilities will the copy edit feature provide? Just how sophisticated will the page layout capability be and will it encompass the capabilities implied by a multitouch screen?

As the statement of scope evolves, a first level of partitioning naturally occurs. The project team learns that the marketing department has talked with potential customers and found that the following functions should be part of automatic copy editing: (1) spell checking, (2) sentence grammar checking, (3) reference checking for large documents (e.g., Is a reference to a bibliography entry found in the list of entries in the bibliography?), (4) the implementation of a style sheet feature that imposed consistency across a document, and (5) section and chapter reference validation for large documents. Each of these features represents a subfunction to be implemented in software. Each can be further refined if the decomposition will make planning easier.

24.4 THE PROCESS

The framework activities (Chapter 2) that characterize the software process are applicable to all software projects. The problem is to select the process model that is appropriate for the software to be engineered by your project team.

Your team must decide which process model is most appropriate for (1) the customers who have requested the product and the people who will do the work, (2) the characteristics of the product itself, and (3) the project environment in which the software team works. When a process model has been selected, the team then defines a preliminary project plan based on the set of process framework activities. Once the preliminary plan is established, process decomposition begins. That is, a complete plan, reflecting the work tasks required to populate the framework activities must be created. We explore these activities briefly in the sections that follow and present a more detailed view in Chapter 26.

24.4.1 Melding the Product and the Process

Project planning begins with the melding of the product and the process. Each function to be engineered by your team must pass through the set of framework activities that have been defined for your software organization.

FIGURE 24.1

Melding the problem and the process

COMMON PROCESS FRAMEWORK ACTIVITIES	communication	planning	modeling	construction	deployment
Software Engineering Tasks					
Product Functions					
Text input					
Editing and formatting					
Automatic copy edit					
Page layout capability					
Automatic indexing and TOC					
File management					
Document production					

Assume that the organization has adopted the generic framework activities—**communication, planning, modeling, construction,** and **deployment**—discussed in Chapter 2. The team members who work on a product function will apply each of the framework activities to it. In essence, a matrix similar to the one shown in Figure 24.1 is created. Each major product function (the figure notes functions for the word-processing software discussed earlier) is listed in the left-hand column. Framework activities are listed in the top row. Software engineering work tasks (for each framework activity) would be entered in the following row.[5] The job of the project manager (and other team members) is to estimate resource requirements for each matrix cell, start and end dates for the tasks associated with each cell, and work products to be produced as a consequence of each task. These activities are considered in Chapter 26.

24.4.2 Process Decomposition

KEY POINT

The process framework establishes a skeleton for project planning. It is adapted by allocating a task set that is appropriate to the project.

A software team should have a significant degree of flexibility in choosing the software process model that is best for the project and the software engineering tasks that populate the process model once it is chosen. A relatively small project that is similar to past efforts might be best accomplished using the linear sequential approach. If the deadline is so tight that full functionality cannot reasonably be delivered, an incremental strategy might be best. Similarly, projects with other characteristics (e.g., uncertain requirements, breakthrough technology, difficult customers, significant reuse potential) will lead to the selection of other process models.[6]

---

5   It should be noted that work tasks must be adapted to the specific needs of the project based on a number of adaptation criteria.

6   Recall that project characteristics also have a strong bearing on the structure of the software team (Section 24.2.3).

Once the process model has been chosen, the process framework is adapted to it. In every case, the generic process framework discussed earlier can be used. It will work for linear models, for iterative and incremental models, for evolutionary models, and even for concurrent or component assembly models. The process framework is invariant and serves as the basis for all work performed by a software organization.

But actual work tasks do vary. Process decomposition commences when the project manager asks, "How do we accomplish this framework activity?" For example, a small, relatively simple project might require the following work tasks for the communication activity:

1. Develop list of clarification issues.

2. Meet with stakeholders to address clarification issues.

3. Jointly develop a statement of scope.

4. Review the statement of scope with all concerned.

5. Modify the statement of scope as required.

These events might occur over a period of less than 48 hours. They represent a process decomposition that is appropriate for the small, relatively simple project.

Now, consider a more complex project, which has a broader scope and more significant business impact. Such a project might require the following work tasks for the **communication**:

1. Review the customer request.

2. Plan and schedule a formal, facilitated meeting with all stakeholders.

3. Conduct research to specify the proposed solution and existing approaches.

4. Prepare a "working document" and an agenda for the formal meeting.

5. Conduct the meeting.

6. Jointly develop mini-specs that reflect data, functional, and behavioral features of the software. Alternatively, develop use cases that describe the software from the user's point of view.

7. Review each mini-spec or use case for correctness, consistency, and lack of ambiguity.

8. Assemble the mini-specs into a scoping document.

9. Review the scoping document or collection of use cases with all concerned.

10. Modify the scoping document or use cases as required.

Both projects perform the framework activity that we call **communication**, but the first project team performs half as many software engineering work tasks as the second.

24.5 THE PROJECT

In order to manage a successful software project, you have to understand what can go wrong so that problems can be avoided. In an excellent paper on software projects, John Reel [Ree99] defines 10 signs that indicate that an information systems project is in jeopardy:

What are the signs that a software project is in jeopardy?

1. Software people don't understand their customer's needs.
2. The product scope is poorly defined.
3. Changes are managed poorly.
4. The chosen technology changes.
5. Business needs change [or are ill defined].
6. Deadlines are unrealistic.
7. Users are resistant.
8. Sponsorship is lost [or was never properly obtained].
9. The project team lacks people with appropriate skills.
10. Managers [and practitioners] avoid best practices and lessons learned.

Jaded industry professionals often refer to the 90–90 rule when discussing particularly difficult software projects: The first 90 percent of a system absorbs 90 percent of the allotted effort and time. The last 10 percent takes another 90 percent of the allotted effort and time [Zah94]. The seeds that lead to the 90–90 rule are contained in the signs noted in the preceding list.

But enough negativity! How does a manager act to avoid the problems just noted? Reel [Ree99] suggests a five-part commonsense approach to software projects:

> **Quote:**
>
> "We don't have time to stop for gas, we're already late."
>
> **M. Cleron**

1. *Start on the right foot.* This is accomplished by working hard (very hard) to understand the problem that is to be solved and then setting realistic objectives and expectations for everyone who will be involved in the project. It is reinforced by building the right team (Section 24.2.3) and giving the team the autonomy, authority, and technology needed to do the job.

2. *Maintain momentum.* Many projects get off to a good start and then slowly disintegrate. To maintain momentum, the project manager must provide incentives to keep turnover of personnel to an absolute minimum, the team should emphasize quality in every task it performs, and senior management should do everything possible to stay out of the team's way.[7]

---

7 The implication of this statement is that bureaucracy is reduced to a minimum, extraneous meetings are eliminated, and dogmatic adherence to process and project rules is deemphasized. The team should be self-organizing and autonomous.

3. *Track progress.* For a software project, progress is tracked as work products (e.g., models, source code, sets of test cases) are produced and approved (using technical reviews) as part of a quality assurance activity. In addition, software process and project measures (Chapter 25) can be collected and used to assess progress against averages developed for the software development organization.

4. *Make smart decisions.* In essence, the decisions of the project manager and the software team should be to "keep it simple." Whenever possible, decide to use commercial off-the-shelf software or existing software components or patterns, decide to avoid custom interfaces when standard approaches are available, decide to identify and then avoid obvious risks, and decide to allocate more time than you think is needed to complex or risky tasks (you'll need every minute).

5. *Conduct a postmortem analysis.* Establish a consistent mechanism for extracting lessons learned for each project. Evaluate the planned and actual schedules, collect and analyze software project metrics, get feedback from team members and customers, and record findings in written form.

24.6   THE W⁵HH PRINCIPLE

In an excellent paper on software process and projects, Barry Boehm [Boe96] states: "you need an organizing principle that scales down to provide simple [project] plans for simple projects." Boehm suggests an approach that addresses project objectives, milestones and schedules, responsibilities, management and technical approaches, and required resources. He calls it the *W⁵HH Principle,* after a series of questions that lead to a definition of key project characteristics and the resultant project plan:

How do we define key project characteristics?

Why is the system being developed? All stakeholders should assess the validity of business reasons for the software work. Does the business purpose justify the expenditure of people, time, and money?

What will be done? The task set required for the project is defined.

When will it be done? The team establishes a project schedule by identifying when project tasks are to be conducted and when milestones are to be reached.

Who is responsible for a function? The role and responsibility of each member of the software team is defined.

Where are they located organizationally? Not all roles and responsibilities reside within software practitioners. The customer, users, and other stakeholders also have responsibilities.

How will the job be done technically and managerially? Once product scope is established, a management and technical strategy for the project must be defined.

How much of each resource is needed? The answer to this question is derived by developing estimates (Chapter 26) based on answers to earlier questions.

Boehm's W^5HH Principle is applicable regardless of the size or complexity of a software project. The questions noted provide you and your team with an excellent planning outline.

24.7   CRITICAL PRACTICES

The Airlie Council[8] has developed a list of "critical software practices for performance-based management." These practices are "consistently used by, and considered critical by, highly successful software projects and organizations whose 'bottom line' performance is consistently much better than industry averages" [Air99].

Critical practices[9] include: metric-based project management (Chapter 25), empirical cost and schedule estimation (Chapters 26 and 27), earned value tracking (Chapter 27), defect tracking against quality targets (Chapters 14 though 16), and people aware management (Section 24.2). Each of these critical practices is addressed throughout Parts 3 and 4 of this book.

SOFTWARE TOOLS

Software Tools for Project Managers

The "tools" listed here are generic and apply to a broad range of activities performed by project managers. Specific project management tools (e.g., scheduling tools, estimating tools, risk analysis tools) are considered in later chapters.

Representative Tools:[10]

The Software Program Manager's Network (**www.spmn.com**) has developed a simple tool called *Project Control Panel,* which provides project managers with an direct indication of project status.

The tool has "gauges" much like a dashboard and is implemented with Microsoft Excel. It is available for download at **www.spmn.com/products_software.html**.

Ganthead.com (**www.gantthead.com/**) has developed a set of useful *checklists for project managers.*

Ittoolkit.com (**www.ittoolkit.com**) provides "a collection of planning guides, process templates and smart worksheets" available on CD-ROM.

24.8 SUMMARY

Software project management is an umbrella activity within software engineering. It begins before any technical activity is initiated and continues throughout the modeling, construction, and deployment of computer software.

Four P's have a substantial influence on software project management—people, product, process, and project. People must be organized into effective teams, motivated to do high-quality software work, and coordinated to achieve effective communication. Product requirements must be communicated from customer to developer, partitioned (decomposed) into their constituent parts, and positioned for work by the software team. The process must be adapted to the people and the product. A common process framework is selected, an appropriate software engineering paradigm is applied, and a set of work tasks is chosen to get the job done. Finally, the project must be organized in a manner that enables the software team to succeed.

The pivotal element in all software projects is people. Software engineers can be organized in a number of different team structures that range from traditional control hierarchies to "open paradigm" teams. A variety of coordination and communication techniques can be applied to support the work of the team. In general, technical reviews and informal person-to-person communication have the most value for practitioners.

The project management activity encompasses measurement and metrics, estimation and scheduling, risk analysis, tracking, and control. Each of these topics is considered in the chapters that follow.

PROBLEMS AND POINTS TO PONDER

24.1. Based on information contained in this chapter and your own experience, develop "ten commandments" for empowering software engineers. That is, make a list of 10 guidelines that will lead to software people who work to their full potential.

24.2. The Software Engineering Institute's People Capability Maturity Model (People-CMM) takes an organized look at "key practice areas" that cultivate good software people. Your instructor will assign you one KPA for analysis and summary.

24.3. Describe three real-life situations in which the customer and the end user are the same. Describe three situations in which they are different.

24.4. The decisions made by senior management can have a significant impact on the effectiveness of a software engineering team. Provide five examples to illustrate that this is true.

24.5. Review a copy of Weinberg's book [Wei86], and write a two- or three-page summary of the issues that should be considered in applying the MOI model.

24.6. You have been appointed a project manager within an information systems organization. Your job is to build an application that is quite similar to others your team has built, although this one is larger and more complex. Requirements have been thoroughly documented by the customer. What team structure would you choose and why? What software process model(s) would you choose and why?

24.7. You have been appointed a project manager for a small software products company. Your job is to build a breakthrough product that combines virtual reality hardware with state-of-the-art software. Because competition for the home entertainment market is intense, there is significant pressure to get the job done. What team structure would you choose and why? What software process model(s) would you choose and why?

24.8. You have been appointed a project manager for a major software products company. Your job is to manage the development of the next-generation version of its widely used word-processing software. Because competition is intense, tight deadlines have been established and announced. What team structure would you choose and why? What software process model(s) would you choose and why?

24.9. You have been appointed a software project manager for a company that services the genetic engineering world. Your job is to manage the development of a new software product that will accelerate the pace of gene typing. The work is R&D oriented, but the goal is to produce a product within the next year. What team structure would you choose and why? What software process model(s) would you choose and why?

24.10. You have been asked to develop a small application that analyzes each course offered by a university and reports the average grade obtained in the course (for a given term). Write a statement of scope that bounds this problem.

24.11. Do a first-level functional decomposition of the page layout function discussed briefly in Section 24.3.2.

FURTHER READINGS AND INFORMATION SOURCES

The Project Management Institute (*Guide to the Project Management Body of Knowledge,* PMI, 2001) covers all important aspects of project management. Bechtold (*Essentials of Software Project Management,* 2d ed., Management Concepts, 2007), Wysocki (*Effective Software Project Management,* Wiley, 2006), Stellman and Greene (*Applied Software Project Management,* O'Reilly, 2005), and Berkun (*The Art of Project Management,* O'Reilly, 2005) teach basic skills and provide detailed guidance for all software project management tasks. McConnell (*Professional Software Development,* Addison-Wesley, 2004) offers pragmatic advice for achieving "shorter schedules, higher quality products, and more successful projects." Henry (*Software Project Management,* Addison-Wesley, 2003) offers real-world advice that is useful for all project managers.

Tom DeMarco and his colleagues (*Adrenaline Junkies and Template Zombies,* Dorset House, 2008) have written an insightful treatment of the human patterns that are encountered in every software project. An excellent four-volume series written by Weinberg (*Quality Software Management,* Dorset House, 1992, 1993, 1994, 1996) introduces basic systems thinking and management concepts, explains how to use measurements effectively, and addresses "congruent action," the ability to establish "fit" between the manager's needs, the needs of technical staff, and the needs of the business. It will provide both new and experienced managers with useful information. Futrell and his colleagues (*Quality Software Project Management,* Prentice-Hall, 2002) present a voluminous treatment of project management. Brown and his colleagues (*Antipatterns in Project Management,* Wiley, 2000) discuss what not to do during the management of a software project.

Brooks (*The Mythical Man-Month,* Anniversary Edition, Addison-Wesley, 1995) has updated his classic book to provide new insight into software project and management issues. McConnell (*Software Project Survival Guide,* Microsoft Press, 1997) presents excellent pragmatic guidance for those who must manage software projects. Purba and Shah (*How to Manage a Successful Software Project,* 2d ed., Wiley, 2000) present a number of case studies that indicate why some projects succeed and others fail. Bennatan (*On Time Within Budget,* 3d ed., Wiley, 2000) presents useful tips and guidelines for software project managers. Weigers (*Practical Project Initiation,* Microsoft Press, 2007) provides practical guidelines for getting a software project off the ground successfully.

It can be argued that the most important aspect of software project management is people management. Cockburn (*Agile Software Development,* Addison-Wesley, 2002) presents one of the best discussions of software people written to date. DeMarco and Lister [DeM98] have written the definitive book on software people and software projects. In addition, the following books on this subject have been published in recent years and are worth examining:

Cantor, M., *Software Leadership: A Guide to Successful Software Development*, Addison-Wesley, 2001.

Carmel, E., *Global Software Teams: Collaborating Across Borders and Time Zones*, Prentice Hall, 1999.

Constantine, L., *Peopleware Papers: Notes on the Human Side of Software*, Prentice Hall, 2001.

Garton, C., and K. Wegryn, *Managing Without Walls*, McPress, 2006.

Humphrey, W. S., *Managing Technical People: Innovation, Teamwork, and the Software Process*, Addison-Wesley, 1997.

Humphrey, W. S., *TSP-Coaching Development Teams*, Addison-Wesley, 2006.

Jones, P. H., *Handbook of Team Design: A Practitioner's Guide to Team Systems Development*, McGraw-Hill, 1997.

Karolak, D. S., *Global Software Development: Managing Virtual Teams and Environments*, IEEE Computer Society, 1998.

Peters, L., *Getting Results from Software Development Teams*, Microsoft Press, 2008.

Whitehead, R., *Leading a Software Development Team*, Addison-Wesley, 2001.

Even though they do not relate specifically to the software world and sometimes suffer from oversimplification and broad generalization, best-selling "management" books by Kanter (*Confidence*, Three Rivers Press, 2006), Covy (*The 8th Habit*, Free Press, 2004), Bossidy (*Execution: The Discipline of Getting Things Done*, Crown Publishing, 2002), Drucker (*Management Challenges for the 21st Century*, Harper Business, 1999), Buckingham and Coffman (*First, Break All the Rules: What the World's Greatest Managers Do Differently*, Simon and Schuster, 1999), and Christensen (*The Innovator's Dilemma*, Harvard Business School Press, 1997) emphasize "new rules" defined by a rapidly changing economy. Older titles such as *Who Moved My Cheese?*, *The One-Minute Manager*, and *In Search of Excellence* continue to provide valuable insights that can help you to manage people and projects more effectively.

A wide variety of information sources on the software project management are available on the Internet. An up-to-date list of World Wide Web references relevant to software project management can be found at the SEPA website: **www.mhhe.com/engcs/compsci/pressman/professional/olc/ser.htm**.

25

PROCESS AND PROJECT METRICS

Measurement enables us to gain insight into the process and the project by providing a mechanism for objective evaluation. Lord Kelvin once said:

> When you can measure what you are speaking about and express it in numbers, you know something about it; but when you cannot measure, when you cannot express it in numbers, your knowledge is of a meager and unsatisfactory kind: it may be the beginning of knowledge, but you have scarcely, in your thoughts, advanced to the stage of a science.

The software engineering community has taken Lord Kelvin's words to heart. But not without frustration and more than a little controversy!

Measurement can be applied to the software process with the intent of improving it on a continuous basis. Measurement can be used throughout a software project to assist in estimation, quality control, productivity assessment, and project control. Finally, measurement can be used by software engineers to help assess the quality of work products and to assist in tactical decision making as a project proceeds (Chapter 23).

QUICK LOOK

What is it? Software process and project metrics are quantitative measures that enable you to gain insight into the efficacy of the software process and the projects that are conducted using the process as a framework. Basic quality and productivity data are collected. These data are then analyzed, compared against past averages, and assessed to determine whether quality and productivity improvements have occurred. Metrics are also used to pinpoint problem areas so that remedies can be developed and the software process can be improved.

Who does it? Software metrics are analyzed and assessed by software managers. Measures are often collected by software engineers.

Why is it important? If you don't measure, judgment can be based only on subjective evaluation. With measurement, trends (either good or bad) can be spotted, better estimates can be made, and true improvement can be accomplished over time.

What are the steps? Begin by defining a limited set of process, project, and product measures that are easy to collect. These measures are often normalized using either size- or function-oriented metrics. The result is analyzed and compared to past averages for similar projects performed within the organization. Trends are assessed and conclusions are generated.

What is the work product? A set of software metrics that provide insight into the process and understanding of the project.

How do I ensure that I've done it right? By applying a consistent, yet simple measurement scheme that is never to be used to assess, reward, or punish individual performance.

Within the context of the software process and the projects that are conducted using the process, a software team is concerned primarily with productivity and quality metrics—measures of software development "output" as a function of effort and time applied and measures of the "fitness for use" of the work products that are produced. For planning and estimating purposes, your interest is historical. What was software development productivity on past projects? What was the quality of the software that was produced? How can past productivity and quality data be extrapolated to the present? How can it help you plan and estimate more accurately?

In their guidebook on software measurement, Park, Goethert, and Florac [Par96b] note the reasons that we measure: (1) to *characterize* in an effort to gain an understanding "of processes, products, resources, and environments, and to establish baselines for comparisons with future assessments"; (2) to *evaluate* "to determine status with respect to plans"; (3) to *predict* by "gaining understandings of relationships among processes and products and building models of these relationships"; and (4) to *improve* by "identify[ing] roadblocks, root causes, inefficiencies, and other opportunities for improving product quality and process performance."

Measurement is a management tool. If conducted properly, it provides a project manager with insight. And as a result, it assists the project manager and the software team in making decisions that will lead to a successful project.

25.1 METRICS IN THE PROCESS AND PROJECT DOMAINS

Process metrics have long-term impact. Their intent is to improve the process itself. Project metrics often contribute to the development of process metrics.

Process metrics are collected across all projects and over long periods of time. Their intent is to provide a set of process indicators that lead to long-term software process improvement. *Project metrics* enable a software project manager to (1) assess the status of an ongoing project, (2) track potential risks, (3) uncover problem areas before they go "critical," (4) adjust work flow or tasks, and (5) evaluate the project team's ability to control quality of software work products.

Measures that are collected by a project team and converted into metrics for use during a project can also be transmitted to those with responsibility for software process improvement (Chapter 30). For this reason, many of the same metrics are used in both the process and project domains.

25.1.1 Process Metrics and Software Process Improvement

The only rational way to improve any process is to measure specific attributes of the process, develop a set of meaningful metrics based on these attributes, and then use the metrics to provide indicators that will lead to a strategy for improvement (Chapter 30). But before I discuss software metrics and their impact on software process improvement, it is important to note that process is only one of a number of "controllable factors in improving software quality and organizational performance" [Pau94].

Referring to Figure 25.1, process sits at the center of a triangle connecting three factors that have a profound influence on software quality and organizational

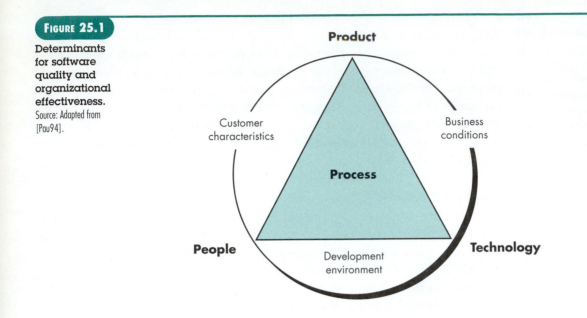

performance. The skill and motivation of people has been shown [Boe81] to be the single most influential factor in quality and performance. The complexity of the product can have a substantial impact on quality and team performance. The technology (i.e., the software engineering methods and tools) that populates the process also has an impact.

In addition, the process triangle exists within a circle of environmental conditions that include the development environment (e.g., integrated software tools), business conditions (e.g., deadlines, business rules), and customer characteristics (e.g., ease of communication and collaboration).

You can only measure the efficacy of a software process indirectly. That is, you derive a set of metrics based on the outcomes that can be derived from the process. Outcomes include measures of errors uncovered before release of the software, defects delivered to and reported by end users, work products delivered (productivity), human effort expended, calendar time expended, schedule conformance, and other measures. You can also derive process metrics by measuring the characteristics of specific software engineering tasks. For example, you might measure the effort and time spent performing the umbrella activities and the generic software engineering activities described in Chapter 2.

Grady [Gra92] argues that there are "private and public" uses for different types of process data. Because it is natural that individual software engineers might be sensitive to the use of metrics collected on an individual basis, these data should be private to the individual and serve as an indicator for the individual only. Examples of *private metrics* include defect rates (by individual), defect rates (by component), and errors found during development.

? **What is the difference between private and public uses for software metrics?**

The "private process data" philosophy conforms well with the Personal Software Process approach (Chapter 2) proposed by Humphrey [Hum97]. Humphrey recognizes that software process improvement can and should begin at the individual level. Private process data can serve as an important driver as you work to improve your software engineering approach.

Some process metrics are private to the software project team but public to all team members. Examples include defects reported for major software functions (that have been developed by a number of practitioners), errors found during technical reviews, and lines of code or function points per component or function.[1] The team reviews these data to uncover indicators that can improve team performance.

Public metrics generally assimilate information that originally was private to individuals and teams. Project-level defect rates (absolutely not attributed to an individual), effort, calendar times, and related data are collected and evaluated in an attempt to uncover indicators that can improve organizational process performance.

Software process metrics can provide significant benefit as an organization works to improve its overall level of process maturity. However, like all metrics, these can be misused, creating more problems than they solve. Grady [Gra92] suggests a "software metrics etiquette" that is appropriate for both managers and practitioners as they institute a process metrics program:

? **What guidelines should be applied when we collect software metrics?**

- Use common sense and organizational sensitivity when interpreting metrics data.

- Provide regular feedback to the individuals and teams who collect measures and metrics.

- Don't use metrics to appraise individuals.

- Work with practitioners and teams to set clear goals and metrics that will be used to achieve them.

- Never use metrics to threaten individuals or teams.

- Metrics data that indicate a problem area should not be considered "negative." These data are merely an indicator for process improvement.

- Don't obsess on a single metric to the exclusion of other important metrics.

As an organization becomes more comfortable with the collection and use of process metrics, the derivation of simple indicators gives way to a more rigorous approach called *statistical software process improvement* (SSPI). In essence, SSPI uses software failure analysis to collect information about all errors and defects[2] encountered as an application, system, or product is developed and used.

---

1   Lines of code and function point metrics are discussed in Sections 25.2.1 and 25.2.2.

2   In this book, an *error* is defined as some flaw in a software engineering work product that is uncovered *before* the software is delivered to the end user. A *defect* is a flaw that is uncovered *after* delivery to the end user. It should be noted that others do not make this distinction.

25.1.2   Project Metrics

Unlike software process metrics that are used for strategic purposes, software project measures are tactical. That is, project metrics and the indicators derived from them are used by a project manager and a software team to adapt project workflow and technical activities.

The first application of project metrics on most software projects occurs during estimation. Metrics collected from past projects are used as a basis from which effort and time estimates are made for current software work. As a project proceeds, measures of effort and calendar time expended are compared to original estimates (and the project schedule). The project manager uses these data to monitor and control progress.

As technical work commences, other project metrics begin to have significance. Production rates represented in terms of models created, review hours, function points, and delivered source lines are measured. In addition, errors uncovered during each software engineering task are tracked. As the software evolves from requirements into design, technical metrics (Chapter 23) are collected to assess design quality and to provide indicators that will influence the approach taken to code generation and testing.

The intent of project metrics is twofold. First, these metrics are used to minimize the development schedule by making the adjustments necessary to avoid delays and mitigate potential problems and risks. Second, project metrics are used to assess product quality on an ongoing basis and, when necessary, modify the technical approach to improve quality.

As quality improves, defects are minimized, and as the defect count goes down, the amount of rework required during the project is also reduced. This leads to a reduction in overall project cost.

? How should we use metrics during the project itself?

SafeHome

Establishing a Metrics Approach

The scene: Doug Miller's office as the *SafeHome* software project is about to begin.

The players: Doug Miller (manager of the *SafeHome* software engineering team) and Vinod Raman and Jamie Lazar, members of the product software engineering team.

The conversation:

Doug: Before we start work on this project, I'd like you guys to define and collect a set of simple metrics. To start, you'll have to define your goals.

Vinod (frowning): We've never done that before, and . . .

Jamie (interrupting): And based on the time line management has been talking about, we'll never have the time. What good are metrics anyway?

Doug (raising his hand to stop the onslaught): Slow down and take a breath, guys. The fact that we've never done it before is all the more reason to start now, and the metrics work I'm talking about shouldn't take much time at all . . . in fact, it just might save us time.

Vinod: How?

Doug: Look, we're going to be doing a lot more in-house software engineering as our products get more intelligent, become Web enabled, all that . . . and we need to understand the process we use to build software . . . and improve it so we can build software better. The only way to do that is to measure.

Jamie: But we're under time pressure, Doug. I'm not in favor of more paper pushing . . . we need the time to do our work, not collect data.

Doug (calmly): Jamie, an engineer's work involves collecting data, evaluating it, and using the results to improve the product and the process. Am I wrong?

Jamie: No, but . . .

Doug: What if we hold the number of measures we collect to no more than five or six and focus on quality?

Vinod: No one can argue against high quality . . .

Jamie: True . . . but, I don't know. I still think this isn't necessary.

Doug: I'm going to ask you to humor me on this one. How much do you guys know about software metrics?

Jamie (looking at Vinod): Not much.

Doug: Here are some Web refs . . . spend a few hours getting up to speed.

Jamie (smiling): I thought you said this wouldn't take any time.

Doug: Time you spend learning is never wasted . . . go do it and then we'll establish some goals, ask a few questions, and define the metrics we need to collect.

25.2 SOFTWARE MEASUREMENT

In Chapter 23, I noted that measurements in the physical world can be categorized in two ways: direct measures (e.g., the length of a bolt) and indirect measures (e.g., the "quality" of bolts produced, measured by counting rejects). Software metrics can be categorized similarly.

> **Quote:**
>
> "Not everything that can be counted counts, and not everything that counts can be counted."
>
> **Albert Einstein**

Direct measures of the software process include cost and effort applied. Direct measures of the product include lines of code (LOC) produced, execution speed, memory size, and defects reported over some set period of time. Indirect measures of the product include functionality, quality, complexity, efficiency, reliability, maintainability, and many other "–abilities" that are discussed in Chapter 14.

The cost and effort required to build software, the number of lines of code produced, and other direct measures are relatively easy to collect, as long as specific conventions for measurement are established in advance. However, the quality and functionality of software or its efficiency or maintainability are more difficult to assess and can be measured only indirectly.

Because many factors affect software work, don't use metrics to compare individuals or teams.

I have partitioned the software metrics domain into process, project, and product metrics and noted that product metrics that are private to an individual are often combined to develop project metrics that are public to a software team. Project metrics are then consolidated to create process metrics that are public to the software organization as a whole. But how does an organization combine metrics that come from different individuals or projects?

To illustrate, consider a simple example. Individuals on two different project teams record and categorize all errors that they find during the software process. Individual measures are then combined to develop team measures. Team A found 342 errors during the software process prior to release. Team B found 184 errors. All other things being equal, which team is more effective in uncovering errors throughout the process? Because you do not know the size or complexity of the projects, you cannot answer this question. However, if the measures are normalized, it is

Project	LOC	Effort	$(000)	Pp. doc.	Errors	Defects	People
alpha	12,100	24	168	365	134	29	3
beta	27,200	62	440	1224	321	86	5
gamma	20,200	43	314	1050	256	64	6

possible to create software metrics that enable comparison to broader organizational averages.

25.2.1   Size-Oriented Metrics

Size-oriented software metrics are derived by normalizing quality and/or productivity measures by considering the *size* of the software that has been produced. If a software organization maintains simple records, a table of size-oriented measures, such as the one shown in Figure 25.2, can be created. The table lists each software development project that has been completed over the past few years and corresponding measures for that project. Referring to the table entry (Figure 25.2) for project alpha: 12,100 lines of code were developed with 24 person-months of effort at a cost of $168,000. It should be noted that the effort and cost recorded in the table represent all software engineering activities (analysis, design, code, and test), not just coding. Further information for project alpha indicates that 365 pages of documentation were developed, 134 errors were recorded before the software was released, and 29 defects were encountered after release to the customer within the first year of operation. Three people worked on the development of software for project alpha.

In order to develop metrics that can be assimilated with similar metrics from other projects, you can choose lines of code as a normalization value. From the rudimentary data contained in the table, a set of simple size-oriented metrics can be developed for each project:

- Errors per KLOC (thousand lines of code)
- Defects per KLOC
- $ per KLOC
- Pages of documentation per KLOC

In addition, other interesting metrics can be computed:

- Errors per person-month
- KLOC per person-month
- $ per page of documentation

Size-oriented metrics are not universally accepted as the best way to measure the software process. Most of the controversy swirls around the use of lines of code as a key measure. Proponents of the LOC measure claim that LOC is an "artifact" of all software development projects that can be easily counted, that many existing software estimation models use LOC or KLOC as a key input, and that a large body of literature and data predicated on LOC already exists. On the other hand, opponents argue that LOC measures are programming language dependent, that when productivity is considered, they penalize well-designed but shorter programs; that they cannot easily accommodate nonprocedural languages; and that their use in estimation requires a level of detail that may be difficult to achieve (i.e., the planner must estimate the LOC to be produced long before analysis and design have been completed).

25.2.2   Function-Oriented Metrics

Function-oriented software metrics use a measure of the functionality delivered by the application as a normalization value. The most widely used function-oriented metric is the function point (FP). Computation of the function point is based on characteristics of the software's information domain and complexity. The mechanics of FP computation have been discussed in Chapter 23.[3]

The function point, like the LOC measure, is controversial. Proponents claim that FP is programming language independent, making it ideal for applications using conventional and nonprocedural languages, and that it is based on data that are more likely to be known early in the evolution of a project, making FP more attractive as an estimation approach. Opponents claim that the method requires some "sleight of hand" in that computation is based on subjective rather than objective data, that counts of the information domain (and other dimensions) can be difficult to collect after the fact, and that FP has no direct physical meaning—it's just a number.

25.2.3   Reconciling LOC and FP Metrics

The relationship between lines of code and function points depends upon the programming language that is used to implement the software and the quality of the design. A number of studies have attempted to relate FP and LOC measures. The following table[4] [QSM02] provides rough estimates of the average number of lines of code required to build one function point in various programming languages:

---

3   See Section 23.2.1 for a detailed discussion of FP computation.

4   Used with permission of Quantitative Software Management (www.qsm.com), copyright 2002.

Programming Language	LOC per Function Point			
	Average	**Median**	**Low**	**High**
Access	35	38	15	47
Ada	154	—	104	205
APS	86	83	20	184
ASP 69	62	—	32	127
Assembler	337	315	91	694
C	162	109	33	704
C++	66	53	29	178
Clipper	38	39	27	70
COBOL	77	77	14	400
Cool:Gen/IEF	38	31	10	180
Culprit	51	—	—	—
DBase IV	52	—	—	—
Easytrieve+	33	34	25	41
Excel47	46	—	31	63
Focus	43	42	32	56
FORTRAN	—	—	—	—
FoxPro	32	35	25	35
Ideal	66	52	34	203
IEF/Cool:Gen	38	31	10	180
Informix	42	31	24	57
Java	63	53	77	—
JavaScript	58	63	42	75
JCL	91	123	26	150
JSP	59	—	—	—
Lotus Notes	21	22	15	25
Mantis	71	27	22	250
Mapper	118	81	16	245
Natural	60	52	22	141
Oracle	30	35	4	217
PeopleSoft	33	32	30	40
Perl	60	—	—	—
PL/1	78	67	22	263
Powerbuilder	32	31	11	105
REXX	67	—	—	—
RPG II/III	61	49	24	155
SAS	40	41	33	49
Smalltalk	26	19	10	55
SQL	40	37	7	110
VBScript36	34	27	50	—
Visual Basic	47	42	16	158

A review of these data indicates that one LOC of C++ provides approximately 2.4 times the "functionality" (on average) as one LOC of C. Furthermore, one LOC of Smalltalk provides at least four times the functionality of an LOC for a conventional programming language such as Ada, COBOL, or C. Using the information contained in the table, it is possible to "backfire" [Jon98] existing software to estimate the number of function points, once the total number of programming language statements are known.

LOC and FP measures are often used to derive productivity metrics. This invariably leads to a debate about the use of such data. Should the LOC/person-month (or FP/person-month) of one group be compared to similar data from another? Should managers appraise the performance of individuals by using these metrics? The answer to these questions is an emphatic "No!" The reason for this response is that many factors influence productivity, making for "apples and oranges" comparisons that can be easily misinterpreted.

Function points and LOC-based metrics have been found to be relatively accurate predictors of software development effort and cost. However, in order to use LOC and FP for estimation (Chapter 26), an historical baseline of information must be established.

Within the context of process and project metrics, you should be concerned primarily with productivity and quality—measures of software development "output" as a function of effort and time applied and measures of the "fitness for use" of the work products that are produced. For process improvement and project planning purposes, your interest is historical. What was software development productivity on past projects? What was the quality of the software that was produced? How can past productivity and quality data be extrapolated to the present? How can it help us improve the process and plan new projects more accurately?

25.2.4 Object-Oriented Metrics

Conventional software project metrics (LOC or FP) can be used to estimate object-oriented software projects. However, these metrics do not provide enough granularity for the schedule and effort adjustments that are required as you iterate through an evolutionary or incremental process. Lorenz and Kidd [Lor94] suggest the following set of metrics for OO projects:

Number of scenario scripts. A scenario script (analogous to use cases discussed throughout Part 2 of this book) is a detailed sequence of steps that describe the interaction between the user and the application. Each script is organized into triplets of the form

> {**initiator,** *action,* **participant**}

where **initiator** is the object that requests some service (that initiates a message), *action* is the result of the request, and **participant** is the server object that satisfies the request. The number of scenario scripts is directly correlated to the size of the application and to the number of test cases that must be developed to exercise the system once it is constructed.

Number of key classes.   *Key classes* are the "highly independent components" [Lor94] that are defined early in object-oriented analysis (Chapter 6).[5] Because key classes are central to the problem domain, the number of such classes is an indication of the amount of effort required to develop the software and also an indication of the potential amount of reuse to be applied during system development.

Number of support classes.   *Support classes* are required to implement the system but are not immediately related to the problem domain. Examples might be user interface (GUI) classes, database access and manipulation classes, and computation classes. In addition, support classes can be developed for each of the key classes. Support classes are defined iteratively throughout an evolutionary process. The number of support classes is an indication of the amount of effort required to develop the software and also an indication of the potential amount of reuse to be applied during system development.

Average number of support classes per key class.   In general, key classes are known early in the project. Support classes are defined throughout. If the average number of support classes per key class were known for a given problem domain, estimating (based on total number of classes) would be greatly simplified. Lorenz and Kidd suggest that applications with a GUI have between two and three times the number of support classes as key classes. Non-GUI applications have between one and two times the number of support classes as key classes.

Number of subsystems.   A *subsystem* is an aggregation of classes that support a function that is visible to the end user of a system. Once subsystems are identified, it is easier to lay out a reasonable schedule in which work on subsystems is partitioned among project staff.

To be used effectively in an object-oriented software engineering environment, metrics similar to those noted above should be collected along with project measures such as effort expended, errors and defects uncovered, and models or documentation pages produced. As the database grows (after a number of projects have been completed), relationships between the object-oriented measures and project measures will provide metrics that can aid in project estimation.

25.2.5   Use-Case–Oriented Metrics

Use cases[6] are used widely as a method for describing customer-level or business domain requirements that imply software features and functions. It would seem reasonable to use the use case as a normalization measure similar to LOC or FP.

It is not uncommon for multiple-scenario scripts to mention the same functionality or data objects. Therefore, be careful when using script counts. Many scripts can sometimes be reduced to a single class or set of code.

ADVICE

Classes can vary in size and complexity. Therefore, it's worth considering classifying class counts by size and complexity.

---

5   We referred to key classes as *analysis classes* in Part 2 of this book.
6   Use cases are introduced in Chapters 5 and 6.

Like FP, the use case is defined early in the software process, allowing it to be used for estimation before significant modeling and construction activities are initiated. Use cases describe (indirectly, at least) user-visible functions and features that are basic requirements for a system. The use case is independent of programming language. In addition, the number of use cases is directly proportional to the size of the application in LOC and to the number of test cases that will have to be designed to fully exercise the application.

Because use cases can be created at vastly different levels of abstraction, there is no standard "size" for a use case. Without a standard measure of what a use case is, its application as a normalization measure (e.g., effort expended per use case) is suspect.

Researchers have suggested *use-case points* (UCPs) as a mechanism for estimating project effort and other characteristics. The UCP is a function of the number of actors and transactions implied by the use-case models and is analogous to the FP in some ways. If you have further interest, see [Cle06].

25.2.6   WebApp Project Metrics

The objective of all WebApp projects is to deliver a combination of content and functionality to the end user. Measures and metrics used for traditional software engineering projects are difficult to translate directly to WebApps. Yet, it is possible to develop a database that allows access to internal productivity and quality measures derived over a number of projects. Among the measures that can be collected are:

Number of static Web pages. Web pages with static content (i.e., the end user has no control over the content displayed on the page) are the most common of all WebApp features. These pages represent low relative complexity and generally require less effort to construct than dynamic pages. This measure provides an indication of the overall size of the application and the effort required to develop it.

Number of dynamic Web pages. Web pages with dynamic content (i.e., end-user actions or other external factors result in customized content displayed on the page) are essential in all e-commerce applications, search engines, financial applications, and many other WebApp categories. These pages represent higher relative complexity and require more effort to construct than static pages. This measure provides an indication of the overall size of the application and the effort required to develop it.

Number of internal page links. Internal page links are pointers that provide a hyperlink to some other Web page within the WebApp. This measure provides an indication of the degree of architectural coupling within the WebApp. As the number of page links increases, the effort expended on navigational design and construction also increases.

Number of persistent data objects. One or more persistent data objects (e.g., a database or data file) may be accessed by a WebApp. As the number of persistent data objects grows, the complexity of the WebApp also grows and the effort to implement it increases proportionally.

Number of external systems interfaced. WebApps must often interface with "backroom" business applications. As the requirement for interfacing grows, system complexity and development effort also increase.

Number of static content objects. Static content objects encompass static text-based, graphical, video, animation, and audio information that are incorporated within the WebApp. Multiple content objects may appear on a single Web page.

Number of dynamic content objects. Dynamic content objects are generated based on end-user actions and encompass internally generated text-based, graphical, video, animation, and audio information that are incorporated within the WebApp. Multiple content objects may appear on a single Web page.

Number of executable functions. An executable function (e.g., a script or applet) provides some computational service to the end user. As the number of executable functions increases, modeling and construction effort also increase.

Each of the preceding measures can be determined at a relatively early stage. For example, you can define a metric that reflects the degree of end-user customization that is required for the WebApp and correlate it to the effort expended on the project and/or the errors uncovered as reviews and testing are conducted. To accomplish this, you define

N_{sp} = number of Static Web pages
N_{dp} = number of Dynamic Web pages

Then,

$$\text{Customization index, } C = \frac{N_{dp}}{N_{dp} + N_{sp}}$$

The value of C ranges from 0 to 1. As C grows larger, the level of WebApp customization becomes a significant technical issue.

Similar WebApp metrics can be computed and correlated with project measures such as effort expended, errors and defects uncovered, and models or documentation pages produced. As the database grows (after a number of projects have been completed), relationships between the WebApp measures and project measures will provide indicators that can aid in project estimation.

SOFTWARE TOOLS

Project and Process Metrics

Objective: To assist in the definition, collection, evaluation, and reporting of software measures and metrics.

Mechanics: Each tool varies in its application, but all provide mechanisms for collecting and evaluating data that lead to the computation of software metrics.

Representative Tools: [7]

Function Point WORKBENCH, developed by Charismatek (**www.charismatek.com.au**), offers a wide array of FP-oriented metrics.

MetricCenter, developed by Distributive Software (**www.distributive.com**), supports automating data collection, analysis, chart formatting, report generation, and other measurement tasks.

PSM Insight, developed by Practical Software and Systems Measurement (**www.psmsc.com**), assists in the creation and subsequent analysis of a project measurement database.

SLIM tool set, developed by QSM (**www.qsm.com**), provides a comprehensive set of metrics and estimation tools.

SPR tool set, developed by Software Productivity Research (**www.spr.com**), offers a comprehensive collection of FP-oriented tools.

TychoMetrics, developed by Predicate Logic, Inc. (**www.predicate.com**), is a tool suite for management metrics collection and reporting.

25.3 METRICS FOR SOFTWARE QUALITY

Software is a complex entity. Therefore, errors are to be expected as work products are developed. Process metrics are intended to improve the software process so that errors are uncovered in the most effective manner.

The overriding goal of software engineering is to produce a high-quality system, application, or product within a time frame that satisfies a market need. To achieve this goal, you must apply effective methods coupled with modern tools within the context of a mature software process. In addition, a good software engineer (and good software engineering managers) must measure if high quality is to be realized.

The quality of a system, application, or product is only as good as the requirements that describe the problem, the design that models the solution, the code that leads to an executable program, and the tests that exercise the software to uncover errors. You can use measurement to assess the quality of the requirements and design models, the source code, and the test cases that have been created as the software is engineered. To accomplish this real-time assessment, you apply product metrics (Chapter 23) to evaluate the quality of software engineering work products in objective, rather than subjective ways.

A project manager must also evaluate quality as the project progresses. Private metrics collected by individual software engineers are combined to provide project-level results. Although many quality measures can be collected, the primary thrust at the project level is to measure errors and defects. Metrics derived from these measures provide an indication of the effectiveness of individual and group software quality assurance and control activities.

---

7   Tools noted here do not represent an endorsement, but rather a sampling of tools in this category. In most cases, tool names are trademarked by their respective developers.

Metrics such as work product errors per function point, errors uncovered per review hour, and errors uncovered per testing hour provide insight into the efficacy of each of the activities implied by the metric. Error data can also be used to compute the *defect removal efficiency* (DRE) for each process framework activity. DRE is discussed in Section 25.3.3.

25.3.1   Measuring Quality

Although there are many measures of software quality,[8] correctness, maintainability, integrity, and usability provide useful indicators for the project team. Gilb [Gil88] suggests definitions and measures for each.

Correctness. A program must operate correctly or it provides little value to its users. Correctness is the degree to which the software performs its required function. The most common measure for correctness is defects per KLOC, where a defect is defined as a verified lack of conformance to requirements. When considering the overall quality of a software product, defects are those problems reported by a user of the program after the program has been released for general use. For quality assessment purposes, defects are counted over a standard period of time, typically one year.

Maintainability. Software maintenance and support accounts for more effort than any other software engineering activity. Maintainability is the ease with which a program can be corrected if an error is encountered, adapted if its environment changes, or enhanced if the customer desires a change in requirements. There is no way to measure maintainability directly; therefore, you must use indirect measures. A simple time-oriented metric is *mean-time-to-change* (MTTC), the time it takes to analyze the change request, design an appropriate modification, implement the change, test it, and distribute the change to all users. On average, programs that are maintainable will have a lower MTTC (for equivalent types of changes) than programs that are not maintainable.

Integrity. Software integrity has become increasingly important in the age of cyber terrorists and hackers. This attribute measures a system's ability to withstand attacks (both accidental and intentional) to its security. Attacks can be made on all three components of software: programs, data, and documentation.

To measure integrity, two additional attributes must be defined: threat and security. *Threat* is the probability (which can be estimated or derived from empirical evidence) that an attack of a specific type will occur within a given time. *Security* is the probability (which can be estimated or derived from

---

8   A detailed discussion of the factors that influence software quality and the metrics that can be used to assess software quality has been presented in Chapter 23.

empirical evidence) that the attack of a specific type will be repelled. The integrity of a system can then be defined as:

Integrity = Σ [1 − (threat × (1 − security))]

For example, if threat (the probability that an attack will occur) is 0.25 and security (the likelihood of repelling an attack) is 0.95, the integrity of the system is 0.99 (very high). If, on the other hand, the threat probability is 0.50 and the likelihood of repelling an attack is only 0.25, the integrity of the system is 0.63 (unacceptably low).

Usability. If a program is not easy to use, it is often doomed to failure, even if the functions that it performs are valuable. Usability is an attempt to quantify ease of use and can be measured in terms of the characteristics presented in Chapter 11.

The four factors just described are only a sampling of those that have been proposed as measures for software quality. Chapter 23 considers this topic in additional detail.

25.3.2 Defect Removal Efficiency

A quality metric that provides benefit at both the project and process level is *defect removal efficiency* (DRE). In essence, DRE is a measure of the filtering ability of quality assurance and control actions as they are applied throughout all process framework activities.

When considered for a project as a whole, DRE is defined in the following manner:

$$\text{DRE} = \frac{E}{E + D}$$

ADVICE

If DRE is low as you move through analysis and design, spend some time improving the way you conduct technical reviews.

where E is the number of errors found before delivery of the software to the end user and D is the number of defects found after delivery.

The ideal value for DRE is 1. That is, no defects are found in the software. Realistically, D will be greater than 0, but the value of DRE can still approach 1 as E increases for a given value of D. In fact, as E increases, it is likely that the final value of D will decrease (errors are filtered out before they become defects). If used as a metric that provides an indicator of the filtering ability of quality control and assurance activities, DRE encourages a software project team to institute techniques for finding as many errors as possible before delivery.

DRE can also be used within the project to assess a team's ability to find errors before they are passed to the next framework activity or software engineering action. For example, requirements analysis produces a requirements model that can be reviewed to find and correct errors. Those errors that are not found during the review of the requirements model are passed on to design (where they may or may not be found). When used in this context, we redefine DRE as

$$\text{DRE}_i = \frac{E_i}{E_i + E_{i+1}}$$

where E_i is the number of errors found during software engineering action i and E_{i+1} is the number of errors found during software engineering action $i + 1$ that are traceable to errors that were not discovered in software engineering action i.

A quality objective for a software team (or an individual software engineer) is to achieve DRE_i that approaches 1. That is, errors should be filtered out before they are passed on to the next activity or action.

SAFEHOME

Establishing a Metrics Approach

The scene: Doug Miller's office two days after initial meeting on software metrics.

The players: Doug Miller (manager of the *SafeHome* software engineering team) and Vinod Raman and Jamie Lazar, members of the product software engineering team.

The conversation:

Doug: You both had a chance to learn a little about process and project metrics?

Vinod and Jamie: [Both nod.]

Doug: It's always a good idea to establish goals when you adopt any metrics. What are yours?

Vinod: Our metrics should focus on quality. In fact, our overall goal is to keep the number of errors we pass on from one software engineering activity to the next to an absolute minimum.

Doug: And be very sure you keep the number of defects released with the product to as close to zero as possible.

Vinod (nodding): Of course.

Jamie: I like DRE as a metric, and I think we can use it for the entire project, but also as we move from one framework activity to the next. It'll encourage us to find errors at each step.

Vinod: I'd also like to collect the number of hours we spend on reviews.

Jamie: And the overall effort we spend on each software engineering task.

Doug: You can compute a review-to-development ratio . . . might be interesting.

Jamie: I'd like to track some use-case data as well. Like the amount of effort required to develop a use case, the amount of effort required to build software to implement a use case, and . . .

Doug (smiling): I thought we were going to keep this simple.

Vinod: We should, but once you get into this metrics stuff, there's a lot of interesting things to look at.

Doug: I agree, but let's walk before we run and stick to our goal. Limit data to be collected to five or six items, and we're ready to go.

25.4   INTEGRATING METRICS WITHIN THE SOFTWARE PROCESS

The majority of software developers still do not measure, and sadly, most have little desire to begin. As I noted earlier in this chapter, the problem is cultural. Attempting to collect measures where none have been collected in the past often precipitates resistance. "Why do we need to do this?" asks a harried project manager. "I don't see the point," complains an overworked practitioner.

In this section, I consider some arguments for software metrics and present an approach for instituting a metrics collection program within a software engineering organization. But before I begin, some words of wisdom (now more than two decades old) are suggested by Grady and Caswell [Gra87]:

Some of the things we describe here will sound quite easy. Realistically, though, establishing a successful company-wide software metrics program is hard work. When we say that you must wait at least three years before broad organizational trends are available, you get some idea of the scope of such an effort.

The caveat suggested by the authors is well worth heeding, but the benefits of measurement are so compelling that the hard work is worth it.

25.4.1   Arguments for Software Metrics

Why is it so important to measure the process of software engineering and the product (software) that it produces? The answer is relatively obvious. If you do not measure, there no real way of determining whether you are improving. And if you are not improving, you are lost.

By requesting and evaluating productivity and quality measures, a software team (and its management) can establish meaningful goals for improvement of the software process. Early in this book, I noted that software is a strategic business issue for many companies. If the process through which it is developed can be improved, a direct impact on the bottom line can result. But to establish goals for improvement, the current status of software development must be understood. Hence, measurement is used to establish a process baseline from which improvements can be assessed.

The day-to-day rigors of software project work leave little time for strategic thinking. Software project managers are concerned with more mundane (but equally important) issues: developing meaningful project estimates, producing higher-quality systems, getting product out the door on time. By using measurement to establish a project baseline, each of these issues becomes more manageable. I have already noted that the baseline serves as a basis for estimation. Additionally, the collection of quality metrics enables an organization to "tune" its software process to remove the "vital few" causes of defects that have the greatest impact on software development.[9]

25.4.2   Establishing a Baseline

By establishing a metrics baseline, benefits can be obtained at the process, project, and product (technical) levels. Yet the information that is collected need not be fundamentally different. The same metrics can serve many masters. The metrics baseline consists of data collected from past software development projects and can be as simple as the table presented in Figure 25.2 or as complex as a comprehensive database containing dozens of project measures and the metrics derived from them.

To be an effective aid in process improvement and/or cost and effort estimation, baseline data must have the following attributes: (1) data must be reasonably accurate—"guestimates" about past projects are to be avoided, (2) data should be collected for as many projects as possible, (3) measures must be consistent (for example, a line of code must be interpreted consistently across all projects for which

---

9   These ideas have been formalized into an approach called *statistical software quality assurance*.

FIGURE 25.3

Software
metrics collec-
tion process

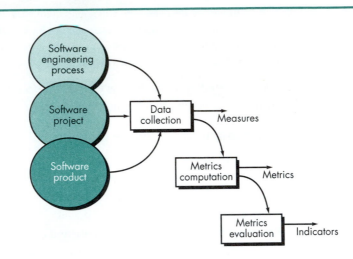

data are collected), (4) applications should be similar to work that is to be estimated—it makes little sense to use a baseline for batch information systems work to estimate a real-time, embedded application.

25.4.3 Metrics Collection, Computation, and Evaluation

KEY POINT

Baseline metrics data should be collected from a large representative sampling of past software projects.

The process for establishing a metrics baseline is illustrated in Figure 25.3. Ideally, data needed to establish a baseline have been collected in an ongoing manner. Sadly, this is rarely the case. Therefore, data collection requires an historical investigation of past projects to reconstruct required data. Once measures have been collected (unquestionably the most difficult step), metrics computation is possible. Depending on the breadth of measures collected, metrics can span a broad range of application-oriented metrics (e.g., LOC, FP, object-oriented, WebApp) as well as other quality- and project-oriented metrics. Finally, metrics must be evaluated and applied during estimation, technical work, project control, and process improvement. Metrics evaluation focuses on the underlying reasons for the results obtained and produces a set of indicators that guide the project or process.

25.5 METRICS FOR SMALL ORGANIZATIONS

ADVICE

If you're just starting to collect metrics data, remember to keep it simple. If you bury yourself with data, your metrics effort will fail.

The vast majority of software development organizations have fewer than 20 software people. It is unreasonable, and in most cases unrealistic, to expect that such organizations will develop comprehensive software metrics programs. However, it is reasonable to suggest that software organizations of all sizes measure and then use the resultant metrics to help improve their local software process and the quality and timeliness of the products they produce.

A commonsense approach to the implementation of any software process-related activity is: keep it simple, customize to meet local needs, and be sure it adds value.

In the paragraphs that follow, I examine how these guidelines relate to metrics for small shops.[10]

? How should
we derive a
set of "simple"
software metrics.

"Keep it simple" is a guideline that works reasonably well in many activities. But how should you derive a "simple" set of software metrics that still provides value, and how can you be sure that these simple metrics will meet the specific needs of your software organization? You can begin by focusing not on measurement but rather on results. The software group is polled to define a single objective that requires improvement. For example, "reduce the time to evaluate and implement change requests." A small organization might select the following set of easily collected measures:

- Time (hours or days) elapsed from the time a request is made until evaluation is complete, t_{queue}.

- Effort (person-hours) to perform the evaluation, W_{eval}.

- Time (hours or days) elapsed from completion of evaluation to assignment of change order to personnel, t_{eval}.

- Effort (person-hours) required to make the change, W_{change}.

- Time required (hours or days) to make the change, t_{change}.

- Errors uncovered during work to make change, E_{change}.

- Defects uncovered after change is released to the customer base, D_{change}.

Once these measures have been collected for a number of change requests, it is possible to compute the total elapsed time from change request to implementation of the change and the percentage of elapsed time absorbed by initial queuing, evaluation and change assignment, and change implementation. Similarly, the percentage of effort required for evaluation and implementation can be determined. These metrics can be assessed in the context of quality data, E_{change} and D_{change}. The percentages provide insight into where the change request process slows down and may lead to process improvement steps to reduce t_{queue}, W_{eval}, t_{eval}, W_{change}, and/or E_{change}. In addition, the defect removal efficiency can be computed as

$$DRE = \frac{E_{change}}{E_{change} + D_{change}}$$

DRE can be compared to elapsed time and total effort to determine the impact of quality assurance activities on the time and effort required to make a change.

For small groups, the cost of collecting measures and computing metrics ranges from 3 to 8 percent of project budget during the learning phase and then drops to less than 1 percent of project budget after software engineers and project managers have become familiar with the metrics program [Gra99]. These costs can show a

---

10 This discussion is equally relevant to software teams that have adopted an agile software development process (Chapter 3).

substantial return on investment if the insights derived from metrics data lead to meaningful process improvement for the software organization.

25.6   ESTABLISHING A SOFTWARE METRICS PROGRAM

The Software Engineering Institute has developed a comprehensive guidebook [Par96b] for establishing a "goal-driven" software metrics program. The guidebook suggests the following steps:

WebRef

A Guidebook for Goal Driven Software Measurement can be downloaded from www.sei.cmu.edu.

1. Identify your business goals.

2. Identify what you want to know or learn.

3. Identify your subgoals.

4. Identify the entities and attributes related to your subgoals.

5. Formalize your measurement goals.

6. Identify quantifiable questions and the related indicators that you will use to help you achieve your measurement goals.

7. Identify the data elements that you will collect to construct the indicators that help answer your questions.

8. Define the measures to be used, and make these definitions operational.

9. Identify the actions that you will take to implement the measures.

10. Prepare a plan for implementing the measures.

A detailed discussion of these steps is best left to the SEI's guidebook. However, a brief overview of key points is worthwhile.

Because software supports business functions, differentiates computer-based systems or products, or acts as a product in itself, goals defined for the business can almost always be traced downward to specific goals at the software engineering level. For example, consider the *SafeHome* product. Working as a team, software engineering and business managers develop a list of prioritized business goals:

KEY POINT

The software metrics you choose should be driven by the business and technical goals you wish to accomplish.

1. Improve our customers' satisfaction with our products.

2. Make our products easier to use.

3. Reduce the time it takes us to get a new product to market.

4. Make support for our products easier.

5. Improve our overall profitability.

The software organization examines each business goal and asks: "What activities do we manage, execute, or support and what do we want to improve within these activities?" To answer these questions the SEI recommends the creation of an "entity-question list" in which all things (entities) within the software process that are managed or influenced by the software organization are noted. Examples of entities include development resources, work products, source code, test cases, change requests, software engineering tasks, and schedules. For each entity listed, software people develop a set of questions that assess quantitative characteristics of the entity (e.g., size, cost, time to develop). The questions derived as a consequence of the creation of an entity-question list lead to the derivation of a set of subgoals that relate directly to the entities created and the activities performed as part of the software process.

Consider the fourth goal: "Make support for our products easier." The following list of questions might be derived for this goal [Par96b]:

- Do customer change requests contain the information we require to adequately evaluate the change and then implement it in a timely manner?
- How large is the change request backlog?
- Is our response time for fixing bugs acceptable based on customer need?
- Is our change control process (Chapter 22) followed?
- Are high-priority changes implemented in a timely manner?

Based on these questions, the software organization can derive the following subgoal: *Improve the performance of the change management process.* The software process entities and attributes that are relevant to the subgoal are identified, and the measurement goals associated with them are delineated.

The SEI [Par96b] provides detailed guidance for steps 6 through 10 of its goal-driven measurement approach. In essence, you refine measurement goals into questions that are further refined into entities and attributes that are then refined into metrics.

INFO

Establishing a Metrics Program

The Software Productivity Center (**www.spc.ca**) suggests an eight-step approach for establishing a metrics program within a software organization that can be used as an alternative to the SEI approach described in Section 25.6. Their approach is summarized in this sidebar.

1. Understand the existing software process.
   Framework activities (Chapter 2) are identified.
   Input information for each activity is described.
   Tasks associated with each activity are defined.
   Quality assurance functions are noted.
   Work products that are produced are listed.
2. Define the goals to be achieved by establishing a metrics program
   Examples: improve accuracy of estimation, improve product quality.

3. Identify metrics required to achieve goals.
   Questions to be answered are defined; for example, *How many errors found in one framework activity can be traced to the preceding framework activity?*
   Create measures and metrics that will help answer these questions.
4. Identify the measures and metrics to be collected and computed.
5. Establish a measurement collection process by answering these questions:
   What is the source of the measurements?
   Can tools be used to collect the data?
   Who is responsible for collecting the data?
   When are data collected and recorded?
   How are data stored?

What validation mechanisms are used to ensure that the data are correct?

6. Acquire appropriate tools to assist in collection and assessment.

7. Establish a metrics database.

The relative sophistication of the database is established.

Use of related tools (e.g., an SCM repository, Chapter 26) is explored.

Existing database products are evaluated.

8. Define appropriate feedback mechanisms.

Who requires ongoing metrics information?

How is the information to be delivered?

What is the format of the information?

A considerably more detailed description of these eight steps can be downloaded from **www.spc.ca/resources/ metrics/**.

25.7 SUMMARY

Measurement enables managers and practitioners to improve the software process; assist in the planning, tracking, and control of software projects; and assess the quality of the product (software) that is produced. Measures of specific attributes of the process, project, and product are used to compute software metrics. These metrics can be analyzed to provide indicators that guide management and technical actions.

Process metrics enable an organization to take a strategic view by providing insight into the effectiveness of a software process. Project metrics are tactical. They enable a project manager to adapt project workflow and technical approach in a real-time manner.

Both size- and function-oriented metrics are used throughout the industry. Size-oriented metrics use the line of code as a normalizing factor for other measures such as person-months or defects. The function point is derived from measures of the information domain and a subjective assessment of problem complexity. In addition, object-oriented metrics and Web application metrics can be used.

Software quality metrics, like productivity metrics, focus on the process, the project, and the product. By developing and analyzing a metrics baseline for quality, an organization can correct those areas of the software process that are the cause of software defects.

Measurement results in cultural change. Data collection, metrics computation, and metrics analysis are the three steps that must be implemented to begin a metrics program. In general, a goal-driven approach helps an organization focus on the right metrics for its business. By creating a metrics baseline—a database containing process and product measurements—software engineers and their managers can gain better insight into the work that they do and the product that they produce.

PROBLEMS AND POINTS TO PONDER

25.1. Describe the difference between process and project metrics in your own words.

25.2. Why should some software metrics be kept "private"? Provide examples of three metrics that should be private. Provide examples of three metrics that should be public.

25.3. What is an indirect measure, and why are such measures common in software metrics work?

25.4. Grady suggests an etiquette for software metrics. Can you add three more rules to those noted in Section 25.1.1?

25.5. Team A found 342 errors during the software engineering process prior to release. Team B found 184 errors. What additional measures would have to be made for projects A and B to determine which of the teams eliminated errors more efficiently? What metrics would you propose to help in making the determination? What historical data might be useful?

25.6. Present an argument against lines of code as a measure for software productivity. Will your case hold up when dozens or hundreds of projects are considered?

25.7. Compute the function point value for a project with the following information domain characteristics:

> Number of user inputs: 32
> Number of user outputs: 60
> Number of user inquiries: 24
> Number of files: 8
> Number of external interfaces: 2

Assume that all complexity adjustment values are average. Use the algorithm noted in Chapter 23.

25.8. Using the table presented in Section 25.2.3, make an argument against the use of assembler language based on the functionality delivered per statement of code. Again referring to the table, discuss why C++ would present a better alternative than C.

25.9. The software used to control a photocopier requires 32,000 lines of C and 4,200 lines of Smalltalk. Estimate the number of function points for the software inside the copier.

25.10. A Web engineering team has built an e-commerce WebApp that contains 145 individual pages. Of these pages, 65 are dynamic; that is, they are internally generated based on end-user input. What is the customization index for this application?

25.11. A WebApp and its support environment have not been fully fortified against attack. Web engineers estimate that the likelihood of repelling an attack is only 30 percent. The system does not contain sensitive or controversial information, so the threat probability is 25 percent. What is the integrity of the WebApp?

25.12. At the conclusion of a project, it has been determined that 30 errors were found during the modeling activity and 12 errors were found during the construction activity that were traceable to errors that were not discovered in the modeling activity. What is the DRE for the modeling activity?

25.13. A software team delivers a software increment to end users. The users uncover eight defects during the first month of use. Prior to delivery, the software team found 242 errors during formal technical reviews and all testing tasks. What is the overall DRE for the project after one month's usage?

FURTHER READINGS AND INFORMATION SOURCES

Software process improvement (SPI) has received a significant amount of attention over the past two decades. Since measurement and software metrics are key to successfully improving the software process, many books on SPI also discuss metrics. Rico (*ROI of Software Process Improvement,* J. Ross Publishing, 2004) provides an in-depth discussion of SPI and the metrics that can help an organization achieve it. Ebert and his colleagues (*Best Practices in Software Measurement,* Springer, 2004) address the use of measurement within the context of ISO and CMMI standards. Kan (*Metrics and Models in Software Quality Engineering,* 2d ed., Addison-Wesley, 2002) presents a collection of relevant metrics.

Ebert and Dumke (*Software Measurement,* Springer, 2007) provide a useful treatment of measurement and metrics as they should be applied for IT projects. McGarry and his colleagues (*Practical Software Measurement,* Addison-Wesley, 2001) present in-depth advice for assessing the software process. A worthwhile collection of papers has been edited by Haug and his colleagues (*Software Process Improvement: Metrics, Measurement, and Process Modeling,* Springer-Verlag, 2001). Florac and Carlton (*Measuring the Software Process,* Addison-Wesley, 1999) and Fenton and Pfleeger (*Software Metrics: A Rigorous and Practical Approach,* Revised, Brooks/Cole Publishers, 1998) discuss how software metrics can be used to provide the indicators necessary to improve the software process.

Laird and Brennan (*Software Measurement and Estimation,* Wiley-IEEE Computer Society Press, 2006) and Goodman (*Software Metrics: Best Practices for Successful IT Management,* Rothstein Associates, Inc., 2004) discuss the use of software metrics for project management and estimation. Putnam and Myers (*Five Core Metrics,* Dorset House, 2003) draw on a database of more the 6000 software projects to demonstrate how five core metrics—time, effort, size, reliability, and process productivity—can be used to control software projects. Maxwell (*Applied Statistics for Software Managers,* Prentice-Hall, 2003) presents techniques for analyzing software project data. Munson (*Software Engineering Measurement,* Auerbach, 2003) discusses a broad array of software engineering measurement issues. Jones (*Software Assessments, Benchmarks and Best Practices,* Addison-Wesley, 2000) describes both quantitative measurement and qualitative factors that help an organization assess its software process and practices.

Function point measurement has become a widely used technique in many areas of software engineering work. Parthasarathy (*Practical Software Estimation: Function Point Methods for Insourced and Outsourced Projects,* Addison-Wesley, 2007) provide a comprehensive guide. Garmus and Herron (*Function Point Analysis: Measurement Practices for Successful Software Projects,* Addison-Wesley, 2000) discuss process metrics with an emphasis on function point analysis.

Relatively little has been published on metrics for Web engineering work, However, Kaushik (*Web Analytics: An Hour a Day,* Sybex, 2007), Stern (*Web Metrics: Proven Methods for Measuring Web Site Success,* Wiley, 2002), Inan and Kean (*Measuring the Success of Your Website,* Longman, 2002), and Nobles and Grady (*Web Site Analysis and Reporting,* Premier Press, 2001) address Web metrics from a business and marketing perspective.

The latest research in the metrics area is summarized by the IEEE (*Symposium on Software Metrics,* published yearly). A wide variety of information sources on the process and project metrics is available on the Internet. An up-to-date list of World Wide Web references relevant to process and project metrics can be found at the SEPA website: **www.mhhe.com/engcs/ compsci/pressman/professional/olc/ser.htm**.

ESTIMATION FOR SOFTWARE PROJECTS

Software project management begins with a set of activities that are collectively called *project planning*. Before the project can begin, the software team should estimate the work to be done, the resources that will be required, and the time that will elapse from start to finish. Once these activities are accomplished, the software team should establish a project schedule that defines software engineering tasks and milestones, identifies who is responsible for conducting each task, and specifies the intertask dependencies that may have a strong bearing on progress.

In an excellent guide to "software project survival," Steve McConnell [McC98] presents a real-world view of project planning:

> Many technical workers would rather do technical work than spend time planning. Many technical managers do not have sufficient training in technical management to

QUICK LOOK

What is it? A real need for software has been established; stakeholders are onboard, software engineers are ready to start, and the project is about to begin. But how do you proceed? Software project planning encompasses five major activities—estimation, scheduling, risk analysis, quality management planning, and change management planning. In the context of this chapter, we consider only estimation—your attempt to determine how much money, effort, resources, and time it will take to build a specific software-based system or product.

Who does it? Software project managers—using information solicited from project stakeholders and software metrics data collected from past projects.

Why is it important? Would you build a house without knowing how much you were about to spend, the tasks that you need to perform, and the time line for the work to be conducted? Of course not, and since most computer-based systems and products cost considerably more to build than a large house, it would seem

reasonable to develop an estimate before you start creating the software.

What are the steps? Estimation begins with a description of the scope of the problem. The problem is then decomposed into a set of smaller problems, and each of these is estimated using historical data and experience as guides. Problem complexity and risk are considered before a final estimate is made.

What is the work product? A simple table delineating the tasks to be performed, the functions to be implemented, and the cost, effort, and time involved for each is generated.

How do I ensure that I've done it right? That's hard, because you won't really know until the project has been completed. However, if you have experience and follow a systematic approach, generate estimates using solid historical data, create estimation data points using at least two different methods, establish a realistic schedule, and continually adapt it as the project moves forward, you can feel confident that you've given it your best shot.

feel confident that their planning will improve a project's outcome. Since neither party wants to do planning, it often doesn't get done.

But failure to plan is one of the most critical mistakes a project can make . . . effective planning is needed to resolve problems upstream [early in the project] at low cost, rather than downstream [late in the project] at high cost. The average project spends *80 percent* of its time on rework—fixing mistakes that were made earlier in the project.

McConnell argues that every team can find the time to plan (and to adapt the plan throughout the project) simply by taking a small percentage of the time that would have been spent on rework that occurs because planning was not conducted.

26.1   OBSERVATIONS ON ESTIMATION

Planning requires you to make an initial commitment, even though it's likely that this "commitment" will be proven wrong. Whenever estimates are made, you look into the future and accept some degree of uncertainty as a matter of course. To quote Frederick Brooks [Bro95]:

> . . . our techniques of estimating are poorly developed. More seriously, they reflect an unvoiced assumption that is quite untrue, i.e., that all will go well. . . . because we are uncertain of our estimates, software managers often lack the courteous stubbornness to make people wait for a good product.

Although estimating is as much art as it is science, this important action need not be conducted in a haphazard manner. Useful techniques for time and effort estimation do exist. Process and project metrics can provide historical perspective and powerful input for the generation of quantitative estimates. Past experience (of all people involved) can aid immeasurably as estimates are developed and reviewed. Because estimation lays a foundation for all other project planning actions, and project planning provides the road map for successful software engineering, we would be ill advised to embark without it.

uote:

"Good estimating approaches and solid historical data offer the best hope that reality will win out over impossible demands."

Caper Jones

Estimation of resources, cost, and schedule for a software engineering effort requires experience, access to good historical information (metrics), and the courage to commit to quantitative predictions when qualitative information is all that exists. Estimation carries inherent risk,[1] and this risk leads to uncertainty.

Project complexity has a strong effect on the uncertainty inherent in planning. Complexity, however, is a relative measure that is affected by familiarity with past effort. The first-time developer of a sophisticated e-commerce application might consider it to be exceedingly complex. However, a Web engineering team developing its tenth e-commerce WebApp would consider such work run-of-the-mill. A number of quantitative software complexity measures have been proposed [Zus97]. Such measures are applied at the design or code level and are therefore difficult to use during

---

1   Systematic techniques for risk analysis are presented in Chapter 28.

software planning (before a design and code exist). However, other, more subjective assessments of complexity (e.g., function point complexity adjustment factors described in Chapter 23) can be established early in the planning process.

Project size is another important factor that can affect the accuracy and efficacy of estimates. As size increases, the interdependency among various elements of the software grows rapidly.[2] Problem decomposition, an important approach to estimating, becomes more difficult because the refinement of problem elements may still be formidable. To paraphrase Murphy's law: "What can go wrong will go wrong"—and if there are more things that can fail, more things will fail.

The *degree of structural uncertainty* also has an effect on estimation risk. In this context, structure refers to the degree to which requirements have been solidified, the ease with which functions can be compartmentalized, and the hierarchical nature of the information that must be processed.

The availability of historical information has a strong influence on estimation risk. By looking back, you can emulate things that worked and improve areas where problems arose. When comprehensive software metrics (Chapter 25) are available for past projects, estimates can be made with greater assurance, schedules can be established to avoid past difficulties, and overall risk is reduced.

Estimation risk is measured by the degree of uncertainty in the quantitative estimates established for resources, cost, and schedule. If project scope is poorly understood or project requirements are subject to change, uncertainty and estimation risk become dangerously high. As a planner, you and the customer should recognize that variability in software requirements means instability in cost and schedule.

However, you should not become obsessive about estimation. Modern software engineering approaches (e.g., evolutionary process models) take an iterative view of development. In such approaches, it is possible—although not always politically acceptable—to revisit the estimate (as more information is known) and revise it when the customer makes changes to requirements.

26.2 THE PROJECT PLANNING PROCESS

The objective of software project planning is to provide a framework that enables the manager to make reasonable estimates of resources, cost, and schedule. In addition, estimates should attempt to define best-case and worst-case scenarios so that project outcomes can be bounded. Although there is an inherent degree of uncertainty, the software team embarks on a plan that has been established as a consequence of these tasks. Therefore, the plan must be adapted and updated as the project proceeds. In the following sections, each of the actions associated with software project planning is discussed.

---

2   Size often increases due to "scope creep" that occurs when problem requirements change. Increases in project size can have a geometric impact on project cost and schedule (Michael Mah, personal communication).

Task Set for Project Planning

1. Establish project scope.
2. Determine feasibility.
3. Analyze risks (Chapter 28).
4. Define required resources.
   a. Determine required human resources.
   b. Define reusable software resources.
   c. Identify environmental resources.
5. Estimate cost and effort.
   a. Decompose the problem.

   b. Develop two or more estimates using size, function points, process tasks, or use cases.
   c. Reconcile the estimates.
6. Develop a project schedule (Chapter 27).
   a. Establish a meaningful task set.
   b. Define a task network.
   c. Use scheduling tools to develop a time-line chart.
   d. Define schedule tracking mechanisms.

26.3 SOFTWARE SCOPE AND FEASIBILITY

Software scope describes the functions and features that are to be delivered to end users; the data that are input and output; the "content" that is presented to users as a consequence of using the software; and the performance, constraints, interfaces, and reliability that *bound* the system. Scope is defined using one of two techniques:

1. A narrative description of software scope is developed after communication with all stakeholders.

2. A set of use cases[3] is developed by end users.

Project feasibility is important, but a consideration of business need is even more important. It does no good to build a high-tech system or product that no one wants.

Functions described in the statement of scope (or within the use cases) are evaluated and in some cases refined to provide more detail prior to the beginning of estimation. Because both cost and schedule estimates are functionally oriented, some degree of decomposition is often useful. Performance considerations encompass processing and response time requirements. Constraints identify limits placed on the software by external hardware, available memory, or other existing systems.

Once scope has been identified (with the concurrence of the customer), it is reasonable to ask: "Can we build software to meet this scope? Is the project feasible?" All too often, software engineers rush past these questions (or are pushed past them by impatient managers or other stakeholders), only to become mired in a project that is doomed from the onset. Putnam and Myers [Put97a] address this issue when they write:

> [N]ot everything imaginable is feasible, not even in software, evanescent as it may appear to outsiders. On the contrary, software feasibility has four solid dimensions: *Technology—* Is a project technically feasible? Is it within the state of the art? Can defects be reduced to a level matching the application's needs? *Finance—*Is it financially feasible? Can development be completed at a cost the software organization, its client, or the market can

---

3   Use cases have been discussed in detail throughout Part 2 of this book. A use case is a scenario-based description of the user's interaction with the software from the user's point of view.

afford? *Time*—Will the project's time-to-market beat the competition? *Resources*—Does the organization have the resources needed to succeed?

Putnam and Myers correctly suggest that scoping is not enough. Once scope is understood, you must work to determine if it can be done within the dimensions just noted. This is a crucial, although often overlooked, part of the estimation process.

26.4 RESOURCES

The second planning task is estimation of the resources required to accomplish the software development effort. Figure 26.1 depicts the three major categories of software engineering resources—people, reusable software components, and the development environment (hardware and software tools). Each resource is specified with four characteristics: description of the resource, a statement of availability, time when the resource will be required, and duration of time that the resource will be applied. The last two characteristics can be viewed as a *time window*. Availability of the resource for a specified window must be established at the earliest practical time.

26.4.1 Human Resources

The planner begins by evaluating software scope and selecting the skills required to complete development. Both organizational position (e.g., manager, senior software engineer) and specialty (e.g., telecommunications, database, client-server) are

FIGURE 26.1

Project resources

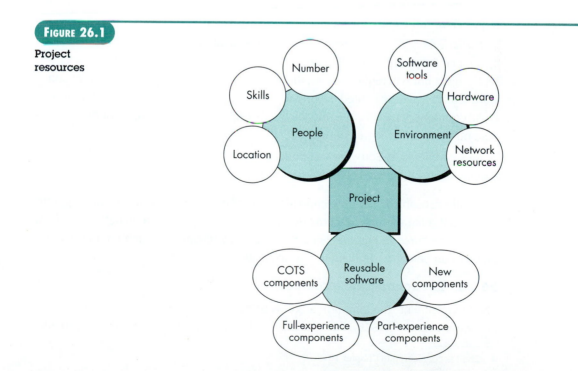

specified. For relatively small projects (a few person-months), a single individual may perform all software engineering tasks, consulting with specialists as required. For larger projects, the software team may be geographically dispersed across a number of different locations. Hence, the location of each human resource is specified.

The number of people required for a software project can be determined only after an estimate of development effort (e.g., person-months) is made. Techniques for estimating effort are discussed later in this chapter.

26.4.2   Reusable Software Resources

Component-based software engineering (CBSE)[4] emphasizes reusability—that is, the creation and reuse of software building blocks. Such building blocks, often called *components,* must be cataloged for easy reference, standardized for easy application, and validated for easy integration. Bennatan [Ben00] suggests four software resource categories that should be considered as planning proceeds:

Never forget that integrating a variety of reusable components can be a significant challenge. Worse, the integration problem resurfaces as various components are upgraded.

Off-the-shelf components. Existing software that can be acquired from a third party or from a past project. COTS (commercial off-the-shelf) components are purchased from a third party, are ready for use on the current project, and have been fully validated.

Full-experience components. Existing specifications, designs, code, or test data developed for past projects that are similar to the software to be built for the current project. Members of the current software team have had full experience in the application area represented by these components. Therefore, modifications required for full-experience components will be relatively low risk.

Partial-experience components. Existing specifications, designs, code, or test data developed for past projects that are related to the software to be built for the current project but will require substantial modification. Members of the current software team have only limited experience in the application area represented by these components. Therefore, modifications required for partial-experience components have a fair degree of risk.

New components. Software components must be built by the software team specifically for the needs of the current project.

Ironically, reusable software components are often neglected during planning, only to become a paramount concern later in the software process. It is better to specify software resource requirements early. In this way technical evaluation of the alternatives can be conducted and timely acquisition can occur.

26.4.3   Environmental Resources

The environment that supports a software project, often called the *software engineering environment* (SEE), incorporates hardware and software. Hardware provides

---

4   CBSE is considered in Chapter 10.

a platform that supports the tools (software) required to produce the work products that are an outcome of good software engineering practice.[5] Because most software organizations have multiple constituencies that require access to the SEE, you must prescribe the time window required for hardware and software and verify that these resources will be available.

When a computer-based system (incorporating specialized hardware and software) is to be engineered, the software team may require access to hardware elements being developed by other engineering teams. For example, software for a robotic device used within a manufacturing cell may require a specific robot (e.g., a robotic welder) as part of the validation test step; a software project for advanced page layout may need a high-speed digital printing system at some point during development. Each hardware element must be specified as part of planning.

26.5 SOFTWARE PROJECT ESTIMATION

Quote:

"In an age of outsourcing and increased competition, the ability to estimate more accurately . . . has emerged as a critical success factor for many IT groups."

Rob Thomsett

Software cost and effort estimation will never be an exact science. Too many variables—human, technical, environmental, political—can affect the ultimate cost of software and effort applied to develop it. However, software project estimation can be transformed from a black art to a series of systematic steps that provide estimates with acceptable risk. To achieve reliable cost and effort estimates, a number of options arise:

1. Delay estimation until late in the project (obviously, we can achieve 100 percent accurate estimates after the project is complete!).

2. Base estimates on similar projects that have already been completed.

3. Use relatively simple decomposition techniques to generate project cost and effort estimates.

4. Use one or more empirical models for software cost and effort estimation.

Unfortunately, the first option, however attractive, is not practical. Cost estimates must be provided up-front. However, you should recognize that the longer you wait, the more you know, and the more you know, the less likely you are to make serious errors in your estimates.

The second option can work reasonably well, if the current project is quite similar to past efforts and other project influences (e.g., the customer, business conditions, the software engineering environment, deadlines) are roughly equivalent. Unfortunately, past experience has not always been a good indicator of future results.

The remaining options are viable approaches to software project estimation. Ideally, the techniques noted for each option should be applied in tandem; each used as a cross-check for the other. Decomposition techniques take a divide-and-conquer

---

5   Other hardware—the *target environment*—is the computer on which the software will execute when it has been released to the end user.

approach to software project estimation. By decomposing a project into major functions and related software engineering activities, cost and effort estimation can be performed in a stepwise fashion. Empirical estimation models can be used to complement decomposition techniques and offer a potentially valuable estimation approach in their own right. A model is based on experience (historical data) and takes the form

$$d = f(v_i)$$

where d is one of a number of estimated values (e.g., effort, cost, project duration) and v_i are selected independent parameters (e.g., estimated LOC or FP).

Automated estimation tools implement one or more decomposition techniques or empirical models and provide an attractive option for estimating. In such systems, the characteristics of the development organization (e.g., experience, environment) and the software to be developed are described. Cost and effort estimates are derived from these data.

Each of the viable software cost estimation options is only as good as the historical data used to seed the estimate. If no historical data exist, costing rests on a very shaky foundation. In Chapter 25, we examined the characteristics of some of the software metrics that provide the basis for historical estimation data.

26.6   DECOMPOSITION TECHNIQUES

Software project estimation is a form of problem solving, and in most cases, the problem to be solved (i.e., developing a cost and effort estimate for a software project) is too complex to be considered in one piece. For this reason, you should decompose the problem, recharacterizing it as a set of smaller (and hopefully, more manageable) problems.

In Chapter 24, the decomposition approach was discussed from two different points of view: decomposition of the problem and decomposition of the process. Estimation uses one or both forms of partitioning. But before an estimate can be made, you must understand the scope of the software to be built and generate an estimate of its "size."

26.6.1   Software Sizing

KEY POINT

The "size" of software to be built can be estimated using a direct measure, LOC, or an indirect measure, FP.

The accuracy of a software project estimate is predicated on a number of things: (1) the degree to which you have properly estimated the size of the product to be built; (2) the ability to translate the size estimate into human effort, calendar time, and dollars (a function of the availability of reliable software metrics from past projects); (3) the degree to which the project plan reflects the abilities of the software team; and (4) the stability of product requirements and the environment that supports the software engineering effort.

In this section, I consider the *software sizing* problem. Because a project estimate is only as good as the estimate of the size of the work to be accomplished, sizing represents your first major challenge as a planner. In the context of project planning, size refers to a quantifiable outcome of the software project. If a direct approach is taken, size can be measured in lines of code (LOC). If an indirect approach is chosen, size is represented as function points (FP).

Putnam and Myers [Put92] suggest four different approaches to the sizing problem:

? **How do we size the software that we're planning to build?**

- *"Fuzzy logic" sizing.* This approach uses the approximate reasoning techniques that are the cornerstone of fuzzy logic. To apply this approach, the planner must identify the type of application, establish its magnitude on a qualitative scale, and then refine the magnitude within the original range.

- *Function point sizing.* The planner develops estimates of the information domain characteristics discussed in Chapter 23.

- *Standard component sizing.* Software is composed of a number of different "standard components" that are generic to a particular application area. For example, the standard components for an information system are subsystems, modules, screens, reports, interactive programs, batch programs, files, LOC, and object-level instructions. The project planner estimates the number of occurrences of each standard component and then uses historical project data to estimate the delivered size per standard component.

- *Change sizing.* This approach is used when a project encompasses the use of existing software that must be modified in some way as part of a project. The planner estimates the number and type (e.g., reuse, adding code, changing code, deleting code) of modifications that must be accomplished.

Putnam and Myers suggest that the results of each of these sizing approaches be combined statistically to create a *three-point* or *expected-value* estimate. This is accomplished by developing optimistic (low), most likely, and pessimistic (high) values for size and combining them using Equation (26.1), described in Section 26.6.2.

26.6.2 Problem-Based Estimation

In Chapter 25, lines of code and function points were described as measures from which productivity metrics can be computed. LOC and FP data are used in two ways during software project estimation: (1) as estimation variables to "size" each element of the software and (2) as baseline metrics collected from past projects and used in conjunction with estimation variables to develop cost and effort projections.

? **What do LOC- and FP-based estimation have in common?**

LOC and FP estimation are distinct estimation techniques. Yet both have a number of characteristics in common. You begin with a bounded statement of software scope and from this statement attempt to decompose the statement of scope into problem functions that can each be estimated individually. LOC or FP (the estimation variable) is then estimated for each function. Alternatively, you may choose another component for sizing, such as classes or objects, changes, or business processes affected.

Baseline productivity metrics (e.g., LOC/pm or FP/pm[6]) are then applied to the appropriate estimation variable, and cost or effort for the function is derived. Function estimates are combined to produce an overall estimate for the entire project.

It is important to note, however, that there is often substantial scatter in productivity metrics for an organization, making the use of a single-baseline productivity metric suspect. In general, LOC/pm or FP/pm averages should be computed by project domain. That is, projects should be grouped by team size, application area, complexity, and other relevant parameters. Local domain averages should then be computed. When a new project is estimated, it should first be allocated to a domain, and then the appropriate domain average for past productivity should be used in generating the estimate.

The LOC and FP estimation techniques differ in the level of detail required for decomposition and the target of the partitioning. When LOC is used as the estimation variable, decomposition is absolutely essential and is often taken to considerable levels of detail. The greater the degree of partitioning, the more likely reasonably accurate estimates of LOC can be developed.

For FP estimates, decomposition works differently. Rather than focusing on function, each of the information domain characteristics—inputs, outputs, data files, inquiries, and external interfaces—as well as the 14 complexity adjustment values discussed in Chapter 23 are estimated. The resultant estimates can then be used to derive an FP value that can be tied to past data and used to generate an estimate.

Regardless of the estimation variable that is used, you should begin by estimating a range of values for each function or information domain value. Using historical data or (when all else fails) intuition, estimate an optimistic, most likely, and pessimistic size value for each function or count for each information domain value. An implicit indication of the degree of uncertainty is provided when a range of values is specified.

A three-point or expected value can then be computed. The *expected value* for the estimation variable (size) S can be computed as a weighted average of the optimistic (S_{opt}), most likely (S_m), and pessimistic (S_{pess}) estimates. For example,

$$S = \frac{S_{opt} + 4S_m + S_{pess}}{6} \tag{26.1}$$

gives heaviest credence to the "most likely" estimate and follows a beta probability distribution. We assume that there is a very small probability the actual size result will fall outside the optimistic or pessimistic values.

Once the expected value for the estimation variable has been determined, historical LOC or FP productivity data are applied. Are the estimates correct? The only reasonable answer to this question is: "You can't be sure." Any estimation technique, no matter how sophisticated, must be cross-checked with another approach. Even then, common sense and experience must prevail.

How do we compute the "expected value" for software size?

---

6   The acronym *pm* means person-month of effort.

26.6.3 An Example of LOC-Based Estimation

As an example of LOC and FP problem-based estimation techniques, I consider a software package to be developed for a computer-aided design application for mechanical components. The software is to execute on an engineering workstation and must interface with various computer graphics peripherals including a mouse, digitizer, high-resolution color display, and laser printer. A preliminary statement of software scope can be developed:

> The mechanical CAD software will accept two- and three-dimensional geometric data from an engineer. The engineer will interact and control the CAD system through a user interface that will exhibit characteristics of good human/machine interface design. All geometric data and other supporting information will be maintained in a CAD database. Design analysis modules will be developed to produce the required output, which will be displayed on a variety of graphics devices. The software will be designed to control and interact with peripheral devices that include a mouse, digitizer, laser printer, and plotter.

ADVICE

Many modern applications reside on a network or are part of a client-server architecture. Therefore, be sure that your estimates include the effort required to develop "infrastructure" software.

This statement of scope is preliminary—it is not bounded. Every sentence would have to be expanded to provide concrete detail and quantitative bounding. For example, before estimation can begin, the planner must determine what "characteristics of good human/machine interface design" means or what the size and sophistication of the "CAD database" are to be.

For our purposes, assume that further refinement has occurred and that the major software functions listed in Figure 26.2 are identified. Following the decomposition technique for LOC, an estimation table (Figure 26.2) is developed. A range of LOC estimates is developed for each function. For example, the range of LOC estimates for the 3D geometric analysis function is optimistic, 4600 LOC; most likely, 6900 LOC; and pessimistic, 8600 LOC. Applying Equation 26.1, the expected value for the 3D geometric analysis function is 6800 LOC. Other estimates are derived in a similar

FIGURE 26.2

Estimation table for the LOC methods

Function	Estimated LOC
User interface and control facilities (UICF)	2,300
Two-dimensional geometric analysis (2DGA)	5,300
Three-dimensional geometric analysis (3DGA)	6,800
Database management (DBM)	3,350
Computer graphics display facilities (CGDF)	4,950
Peripheral control function (PCF)	2,100
Design analysis modules (DAM)	8,400
Estimated lines of code	33,200

ADVICE

Do not succumb to the temptation to use this result as your project estimate. You should derive another result using a different approach.

fashion. By summing vertically in the estimated LOC column, an estimate of 33,200 lines of code is established for the CAD system.

A review of historical data indicates that the organizational average productivity for systems of this type is 620 LOC/pm. Based on a burdened labor rate of $8000 per month, the cost per line of code is approximately $13. Based on the LOC estimate and the historical productivity data, the total estimated project cost is $431,000 and the estimated effort is 54 person-months.[7]

SAFEHOME

Estimating

The scene: Doug Miller's office as project planning begins.

The players: Doug Miller (manager of the *SafeHome* software engineering team) and Vinod Raman, Jamie Lazar, and other members of the product software engineering team.

The conversation:

Doug: We need to develop an effort estimate for the project and then we've got to define a micro schedule for the first increment and a macro schedule for the remaining increments.

Vinod (nodding): Okay, but we haven't defined any increments yet.

Doug: True, but that's why we need to estimate.

Jamie (frowning): You want to know how long it's going to take us?

Doug: Here's what I need. First, we need to functionally decompose the *SafeHome* software ... at a high level ... then we've got to estimate the number of lines of code that each function will take ... then ...

Jamie: Whoa! How are we supposed to do that?

Vinod: I've done it on past projects. You begin with use cases, determine the functionality required to implement each, guesstimate the LOC count for each piece of the function. The best approach is to have everyone do it independently and then compare results.

Doug: Or you can do a functional decomposition for the entire project.

Jamie: But that'll take forever and we've got to get started.

Vinod: No ... it can be done in a few hours ... this morning, in fact.

Doug: I agree ... we can't expect exactitude, just a ballpark idea of what the size of *SafeHome* will be.

Jamie: I think we should just estimate effort ... that's all.

Doug: We'll do that too. Then use both estimates as a cross-check.

Vinod: Let's go do it ...

26.6.4   An Example of FP-Based Estimation

Decomposition for FP-based estimation focuses on information domain values rather than software functions. Referring to the table presented in Figure 26.3, you would estimate inputs, outputs, inquiries, files, and external interfaces for the CAD software. An FP value is computed using the technique discussed in Chapter 23. For the purposes of this estimate, the complexity weighting factor is assumed to be average. Figure 26.3 presents the results of this estimate.

---

7   Estimates are rounded to the nearest $1000 and person-month. Further precision is unnecessary and unrealistic, given the limitations of estimation accuracy.

FIGURE 26.3

Estimating
information
domain values

Information domain value	Opt.	Likely	Pess.	Est. count	Weight	FP count
Number of external inputs	20	24	30	24	4	97
Number of external outputs	12	15	22	16	5	78
Number of external inquiries	16	22	28	22	5	88
Number of internal logical files	4	4	5	4	10	42
Number of external interface files	2	2	3	2	7	15
Count total						320

Each of the complexity weighting factors is estimated, and the value adjustment factor is computed as described in Chapter 23:

Factor	Value
Backup and recovery	4
Data communications	2
Distributed processing	0
Performance critical	4
Existing operating environment	3
Online data entry	4
Input transaction over multiple screens	5
Master files updated online	3
Information domain values complex	5
Internal processing complex	5
Code designed for reuse	4
Conversion/installation in design	3
Multiple installations	5
Application designed for change	5
Value adjustment factor	**1.17**

Finally, the estimated number of FP is derived:

$$FP_{estimated} = \text{count total} \times [0.65 + 0.01 \times \Sigma(F_i)] = 375$$

The organizational average productivity for systems of this type is 6.5 FP/pm. Based on a burdened labor rate of $8000 per month, the cost per FP is approximately $1230. Based on the FP estimate and the historical productivity data, the total estimated project cost is $461,000 and the estimated effort is 58 person-months.

26.6.5   Process-Based Estimation

The most common technique for estimating a project is to base the estimate on the process that will be used. That is, the process is decomposed into a relatively small set of tasks and the effort required to accomplish each task is estimated.

FIGURE 26.4

Process-based estimation table

Activity →	CC	Planning	Risk analysis	Engineering		Construction release		CE	Totals
Task →				Analysis	Design	Code	Test		
Function ↓									
UICF				0.50	2.50	0.40	5.00	n/a	8.40
2DGA				0.75	4.00	0.60	2.00	n/a	7.35
3DGA				0.50	4.00	1.00	3.00	n/a	8.50
CGDF				0.50	3.00	1.00	1.50	n/a	6.00
DBM				0.50	3.00	0.75	1.50	n/a	5.75
PCF				0.25	2.00	0.50	1.50	n/a	4.25
DAM				0.50	2.00	0.50	2.00	n/a	5.00
Totals	0.25	0.25	0.25	3.50	20.50	4.50	16.50		46.00
% effort	1%	1%	1%	8%	45%	10%	36%		

CC = customer communication   CE = customer evaluation

Like the problem-based techniques, process-based estimation begins with a delineation of software functions obtained from the project scope. A series of framework activities must be performed for each function. Functions and related framework activities[8] may be represented as part of a table similar to the one presented in Figure 26.4.

Once problem functions and process activities are melded, you estimate the effort (e.g., person-months) that will be required to accomplish each software process activity for each software function. These data constitute the central matrix of the table in Figure 26.4. Average labor rates (i.e., cost/unit effort) are then applied to the effort estimated for each process activity. It is very likely the labor rate will vary for each task. Senior staff are heavily involved in early framework activities and are generally more expensive than junior staff involved in construction and release.

Costs and effort for each function and framework activity are computed as the last step. If process-based estimation is performed independently of LOC or FP estimation, we now have two or three estimates for cost and effort that may be compared and reconciled. If both sets of estimates show reasonable agreement, there is good reason to believe that the estimates are reliable. If, on the other hand, the results of these decomposition techniques show little agreement, further investigation and analysis must be conducted.

ADVICE

If time permits, use finer granularity when specifying tasks in Figure 26.4. For example, break analysis into its major tasks and estimate each separately.

26.6.6   An Example of Process-Based Estimation

To illustrate the use of process-based estimation, consider the CAD software introduced in Section 26.6.3. The system configuration and all software functions remain unchanged and are indicated by project scope.

---

8   The framework activities chosen for this project differ somewhat from the generic activities discussed in Chapter 2. They are: customer communication (CC), planning, risk analysis, engineering, and construction/release.

Referring to the completed process-based table shown in Figure 26.4, estimates of effort (in person-months) for each software engineering activity are provided for each CAD software function (abbreviated for brevity). The engineering and construction release activities are subdivided into the major software engineering tasks shown. Gross estimates of effort are provided for customer communication, planning, and risk analysis. These are noted in the total row at the bottom of the table. Horizontal and vertical totals provide an indication of estimated effort required for analysis, design, code, and test. It should be noted that 53 percent of all effort is expended on front-end engineering tasks (requirements analysis and design), indicating the relative importance of this work.

Based on an average burdened labor rate of $8000 per month, the total estimated project cost is $368,000 and the estimated effort is 46 person-months. If desired, labor rates could be associated with each framework activity or software engineering task and computed separately.

26.6.7 Estimation with Use Cases

As I have noted throughout Part 2 of this book, use cases provide a software team with insight into software scope and requirements. However, developing an estimation approach with use cases is problematic for the following reasons [Smi99]:

Why is it difficult to develop an estimation technique using use cases?

- Use cases are described using many different formats and styles—there is no standard form.

- Use cases represent an external view (the user's view) of the software and can therefore be written at many different levels of abstraction.

- Use cases do not address the complexity of the functions and features that are described.

- Use cases can describe complex behavior (e.g., interactions) that involve many functions and features.

Unlike an LOC or a function point, one person's "use case" may require months of effort while another person's use case may be implemented in a day or two.

Although a number of investigators have considered use cases as an estimation input, no proven estimation method has emerged to date.[9] Smith [Smi99] suggests that use cases can be used for estimation, but only if they are considered within the context of the "structural hierarchy" that they are used to describe.

Smith argues that any level of this structural hierarchy can be described by no more than 10 use cases. Each of these use cases would encompass no more than 30 distinct scenarios. Obviously, use cases that describe a large system are written at a much higher level of abstraction (and represent considerably more development effort) than use cases that are written to describe a single subsystem. Therefore,

---

9 Recent work in the derivation of *use-case points* [Cle06] may ultimately lead to a workable estimation approach using use cases.

before use cases can be used for estimation, the level within the structural hierarchy is established, the average length (in pages) of each use case is determined, the type of software (e.g., real-time, business, engineering/scientific, WebApp, embedded) is defined, and a rough architecture for the system is considered. Once these characteristics are established, empirical data may be used to establish the estimated number of LOC or FP per use case (for each level of the hierarchy). Historical data are then used to compute the effort required to develop the system.

To illustrate how this computation might be made, consider the following relationship:[10]

$$\text{LOC estimate} = N \times \text{LOC}_{avg} + [(S_a/S_h - 1) + (P_a/P_h - 1)] \times \text{LOC}_{adjust} \qquad (26.2)$$

where

N	= actual number of use cases
LOC_{avg}	= historical average LOC per use case for this type of subsystem
LOC_{adjust}	= represents an adjustment based on n percent of LOC_{avg} where n is defined locally and represents the difference between this project and "average" projects
S_a	= actual scenarios per use case
S_h	= average scenarios per use case for this type of subsystem
P_a	= actual pages per use case
P_h	= average pages per use case for this type of subsystem

Expression (26.2) could be used to develop a rough estimate of the number of LOC based on the actual number of use cases adjusted by the number of scenarios and the page length of the use cases. The adjustment represents up to n percent of the historical average LOC per use case.

26.6.8   An Example of Use-Case–Based Estimation

The CAD software introduced in Section 26.6.3 is composed of three subsystem groups: user interface subsystem (includes UICF), engineering subsystem group (includes the 2DGA, 3DGA, and DAM subsystems), and infrastructure subsystem group (includes CGDF and PCF subsystems). Six use cases describe the user interface subsystem. Each use case is described by no more than 10 scenarios and has an average length of six pages. The engineering subsystem group is described by 10 use cases (these are considered to be at a higher level of the structural hierarchy). Each of these use cases has no more than 20 scenarios associated with it and has an average length of eight pages. Finally, the infrastructure subsystem group is described by five use cases with an average of only six scenarios and an average length of five pages.

---

10 It is important to note that Expression (26.2) is used for illustrative purposes only. Like all estimation models, it must be validated locally before it can be used with confidence.

FIGURE 26.5

Use-case estimation

	use cases	scenarios	pages	scenarios	pages	LOC	LOC estimate
User interface subsystem	6	10	6	12	5	560	3,366
Engineering subsystem group	10	20	8	16	8	3100	31,233
Infrastructure subsystem group	5	6	5	10	6	1650	7,970
Total LOC estimate							42,568

Using the relationship noted in Expression (26.2) with n = 30 percent, the table shown in Figure 26.5 is developed. Considering the first row of the table, historical data indicate that UI software requires an average of 800 LOC per use case when the use case has no more than 12 scenarios and is described in less than five pages. These data conform reasonably well for the CAD system. Hence the LOC estimate for the user interface subsystem is computed using expression (26.2). Using the same approach, estimates are made for both the engineering and infrastructure subsystem groups. Figure 26.5 summarizes the estimates and indicates that the overall size of the CAD is estimated at 42,500 LOC.

Using 620 LOC/pm as the average productivity for systems of this type and a burdened labor rate of $8000 per month, the cost per line of code is approximately $13. Based on the use-case estimate and the historical productivity data, the total estimated project cost is $552,000 and the estimated effort is 68 person-months.

26.6.9 Reconciling Estimates

> **Quote:**
>
> "Complicated methods might not yield a more accurate estimate, particularly when developers can incorporate their own intuition into the estimate."
>
> **Philip Johnson et al.**

The estimation techniques discussed in the preceding sections result in multiple estimates that must be reconciled to produce a single estimate of effort, project duration, or cost. To illustrate this reconciliation procedure, I again consider the CAD software introduced in Section 26.6.3.

The total estimated effort for the CAD software ranges from a low of 46 person-months (derived using a process-based estimation approach) to a high of 68 person-months (derived with use-case estimation). The average estimate (using all four approaches) is 56 person-months. The variation from the average estimate is approximately 18 percent on the low side and 21 percent on the high side.

What happens when agreement between estimates is poor? The answer to this question requires a reevaluation of information used to make the estimates. Widely divergent estimates can often be traced to one of two causes: (1) the scope of the project is not adequately understood or has been misinterpreted by the planner, or (2) productivity data used for problem-based estimation techniques is inappropriate for the application, obsolete (in that it no longer accurately reflects the software engineering organization), or has been misapplied. You should determine the cause of divergence and then reconcile the estimates.

Automated Estimation Techniques for Software Projects

Automated estimation tools allow the planner to estimate cost and effort and to perform what-if analyses for important project variables such as delivery date or staffing. Although many automated estimation tools exist (see sidebar later in this chapter), all exhibit the same general characteristics and all perform the following six generic functions [Jon96]:

1. *Sizing of project deliverables.* The "size" of one or more software work products is estimated. Work products include the external representation of software (e.g., screen, reports), the software itself (e.g., KLOC), functionality delivered (e.g., function points), and descriptive information (e.g., documents).

2. *Selecting project activities.* The appropriate process framework is selected, and the software engineering task set is specified.

3. *Predicting staffing levels.* The number of people who will be available to do the work is specified. Because the relationship between people available and work (predicted effort) is highly nonlinear, this is an important input.

4. *Predicting software effort.* Estimation tools use one or more models (Section 26.7) that relate the size of the project deliverables to the effort required to produce them.

5. *Predicting software cost.* Given the results of step 4, costs can be computed by allocating labor rates to the project activities noted in step 2.

6. *Predicting software schedules.* When effort, staffing level, and project activities are known, a draft schedule can be produced by allocating labor across software engineering activities based on recommended models for effort distribution discussed later in this chapter.

When different estimation tools are applied to the same project data, a relatively large variation in estimated results can be encountered. More important, predicted values sometimes are significantly different than actual values. This reinforces the notion that the output of estimation tools should be used as one "data point" from which estimates are derived—not as the only source for an estimate.

26.7   EMPIRICAL ESTIMATION MODELS

An estimation model for computer software uses empirically derived formulas to predict effort as a function of LOC or FP.[11] Values for LOC or FP are estimated using the approach described in Sections 26.6.3 and 26.6.4. But instead of using the tables described in those sections, the resultant values for LOC or FP are plugged into the estimation model.

The empirical data that support most estimation models are derived from a limited sample of projects. For this reason, no estimation model is appropriate for all classes of software and in all development environments. Therefore, you should use the results obtained from such models judiciously.

An estimation model should be calibrated to reflect local conditions. The model should be tested by applying data collected from completed projects, plugging the data into the model, and then comparing actual to predicted results. If agreement is poor, the model must be tuned and retested before it can be used.

> **KEY POINT**
>
> An estimation model reflects the population of projects from which it has been derived. Therefore, the model is domain sensitive.

---

11 An empirical model using use cases as the independent variable is suggested in Section 26.6.6. However, relatively few have appeared in the literature to date.

26.7.1   The Structure of Estimation Models

A typical estimation model is derived using regression analysis on data collected from past software projects. The overall structure of such models takes the form [Mat94]

$$E = A + B \times (e_v)^C \qquad \qquad (26.3)$$

where *A, B,* and *C* are empirically derived constants, *E* is effort in person-months, and e_v is the estimation variable (either LOC or FP). In addition to the relationship noted in Equation (26.3), the majority of estimation models have some form of project adjustment component that enables *E* to be adjusted by other project characteristics (e.g., problem complexity, staff experience, development environment). Among the many LOC-oriented estimation models proposed in the literature are

None of these models should be used without careful calibration to your environment.

$E = 5.2 \times (KLOC)^{0.91}$	Walston-Felix model
$E = 5.5 + 0.73 \times (KLOC)^{1.16}$	Bailey-Basili model
$E = 3.2 \times (KLOC)^{1.05}$	Boehm simple model
$E = 5.288 \times (KLOC)^{1.047}$	Doty model for KLOC > 9

FP-oriented models have also been proposed. These include

$E = -91.4 + 0.355 \, FP$	Albrecht and Gaffney model
$E = -37 + 0.96 \, FP$	Kemerer model
$E = -12.88 + 0.405 \, FP$	Small project regression model

A quick examination of these models indicates that each will yield a different result for the same values of LOC or FP. The implication is clear. Estimation models must be calibrated for local needs!

26.7.2   The COCOMO II Model

WebRef

Detailed information on COCOMO II, including downloadable software, can be obtained at **sunset.usc.edu/ research/ COCOMOII/ cocomo_main.html.**

In his classic book on "software engineering economics," Barry Boehm [Boe81] introduced a hierarchy of software estimation models bearing the name COCOMO, for *COnstructive COst MOdel.* The original COCOMO model became one of the most widely used and discussed software cost estimation models in the industry. It has evolved into a more comprehensive estimation model, called COCOMO II [Boe00]. Like its predecessor, COCOMO II is actually a hierarchy of estimation models that address the following areas:

- *Application composition model.* Used during the early stages of software engineering, when prototyping of user interfaces, consideration of software and system interaction, assessment of performance, and evaluation of technology maturity are paramount.

- *Early design stage model.* Used once requirements have been stabilized and basic software architecture has been established.

- *Post-architecture-stage model.* Used during the construction of the software.

Like all estimation models for software, the COCOMO II models require sizing information. Three different sizing options are available as part of the model hierarchy: object points, function points, and lines of source code.

FIGURE 26.6

Complexity
weighting for
object types.
Source: [Boe96].

Object type	Complexity weight		
	Simple	Medium	Difficult
Screen	1	2	3
Report	2	5	8
3GL component			10

The COCOMO II application composition model uses object points and is illustrated in the following paragraphs. It should be noted that other, more sophisticated estimation models (using FP and KLOC) are also available as part of COCOMO II.

What is an object point?

Like function points, the *object point* is an indirect software measure that is computed using counts of the number of (1) screens (at the user interface), (2) reports, and (3) components likely to be required to build the application. Each object instance (e.g., a screen or report) is classified into one of three complexity levels (i.e., simple, medium, or difficult) using criteria suggested by Boehm [Boe96]. In essence, complexity is a function of the number and source of the client and server data tables that are required to generate the screen or report and the number of views or sections presented as part of the screen or report.

Once complexity is determined, the number of screens, reports, and components are weighted according to the table illustrated in Figure 26.6. The object point count is then determined by multiplying the original number of object instances by the weighting factor in the figure and summing to obtain a total object point count. When component-based development or general software reuse is to be applied, the percent of reuse (%reuse) is estimated and the object point count is adjusted:

$$NOP = (\text{object points}) \times [(100 - \%reuse)/100]$$

where NOP is defined as new object points.

To derive an estimate of effort based on the computed NOP value, a "productivity rate" must be derived. Figure 26.7 presents the productivity rate

$$PROD = \frac{NOP}{\text{person-month}}$$

for different levels of developer experience and development environment maturity.

Once the productivity rate has been determined, an estimate of project effort is computed using

$$\text{Estimated effort} = \frac{NOP}{PROD}$$

In more advanced COCOMO II models,[12] a variety of scale factors, cost drivers, and adjustment procedures are required. A complete discussion of these is beyond

---

12 As noted earlier, these models use FP and KLOC counts for the size variable.

| FIGURE 26.7 | Productivity rate for object points. |
| Source: [Boe96]. |

Developer's experience/capability	Very low	Low	Nominal	High	Very high
Environment maturity/capability	Very low	Low	Nominal	High	Very high
PROD	4	7	13	25	50

the scope of this book. If you have further interest, see [Boe00] or visit the COCOMO II website.

26.7.3   The Software Equation

The *software equation* [Put92] is a dynamic multivariable model that assumes a specific distribution of effort over the life of a software development project. The model has been derived from productivity data collected for over 4000 contemporary software projects. Based on these data, we derive an estimation model of the form

$$E = \frac{LOC \times B^{0.333}}{P^3} \times \frac{1}{t^4} \tag{26.4}$$

where

E = effort in person-months or person-years

t = project duration in months or years

B = "special skills factor"[13]

P = "productivity parameter" that reflects: overall process maturity and management practices, the extent to which good software engineering practices are used, the level of programming languages used, the state of the software environment, the skills and experience of the software team, and the complexity of the application

WebRef

Information on software cost estimation tools that have evolved from the software equation can be found at **www.qsm.com**.

Typical values might be $P = 2000$ for development of real-time embedded software, $P = 10{,}000$ for telecommunication and systems software, and $P = 28{,}000$ for business systems applications. The productivity parameter can be derived for local conditions using historical data collected from past development efforts.

You should note that the software equation has two independent parameters: (1) an estimate of size (in LOC) and (2) an indication of project duration in calendar months or years.

---

13 B increases slowly as "the need for integration, testing, quality assurance, documentation, and management skills grows" [Put92]. For small programs (KLOC = 5 to 15), $B = 0.16$. For programs greater than 70 KLOC, $B = 0.39$.

To simplify the estimation process and use a more common form for their estimation model, Putnam and Myers [Put92] suggest a set of equations derived from the software equation. Minimum development time is defined as

$$t_{min} = 8.14 \frac{LOC}{P^{0.43}} \text{ in months for } t_{min} > 6 \text{ months} \qquad (26.5a)$$

$$E = 180 \, Bt^3 \text{ in person-months for } E \geq 20 \text{ person-months} \qquad (26.5b)$$

Note that t in Equation (26.5b) is represented in years.

Using Equation (26.5) with $P = 12,000$ (the recommended value for scientific software) for the CAD software discussed earlier in this chapter,

$$t_{min} = 8.14 \times \frac{33,200}{12,000^{0.43}} = 12.6 \text{ calendar months}$$

$$E = 180 \times 0.28 \times (1.05)^3 = 58 \text{ person-months}$$

The results of the software equation correspond favorably with the estimates developed in Section 26.6. Like the COCOMO model noted in Section 26.7.2, the software equation continues to evolve. Further discussion of an extended version of this estimation approach can be found in [Put97b].

26.8 ESTIMATION FOR OBJECT-ORIENTED PROJECTS

It is worthwhile to supplement conventional software cost estimation methods with a technique that has been designed explicitly for OO software. Lorenz and Kidd [Lor94] suggest the following approach:

1. Develop estimates using effort decomposition, FP analysis, and any other method that is applicable for conventional applications.

2. Using the requirements model (Chapter 6), develop use cases and determine a count. Recognize that the number of use cases may change as the project progresses.

3. From the requirements model, determine the number of key classes (called analysis classes in Chapter 6).

4. Categorize the type of interface for the application and develop a multiplier for support classes:

Interface Type	Multiplier
No GUI	2.0
Text-based user interface	2.25
GUI	2.5
Complex GUI	3.0

Multiply the number of key classes (step 3) by the multiplier to obtain an estimate for the number of support classes.

5. Multiply the total number of classes (key + support) by the average number of work units per class. Lorenz and Kidd suggest 15 to 20 person-days per class.

6. Cross-check the class-based estimate by multiplying the average number of work units per use case.

26.9   SPECIALIZED ESTIMATION TECHNIQUES

The estimation techniques discussed in Sections 26.6 through 26.8 can be used for any software project. However, when a software team encounters an extremely short project duration (weeks rather than months) that is likely to have a continuing stream of changes, project planning in general and estimation in particular should be abbreviated.[14] In the sections that follow, I examine two specialized estimation techniques.

26.9.1   Estimation for Agile Development

Because the requirements for an agile project (Chapter 3) are defined by a set of user scenarios (e.g., "stories" in Extreme Programming), it is possible to develop an estimation approach that is informal, reasonably disciplined, and meaningful within the context of project planning for each software increment. Estimation for agile projects uses a decomposition approach that encompasses the following steps:

? How are estimates developed when an agile process is applied?

1. Each user scenario (the equivalent of a mini use case created at the very start of a project by end users or other stakeholders) is considered separately for estimation purposes.

2. The scenario is decomposed into the set of software engineering tasks that will be required to develop it.

KEY POINT

In the context of estimation for agile projects, "volume" is an estimate of the overall size of a user scenario in LOC or FP.

3a. The effort required for each task is estimated separately. Note: Estimation can be based on historical data, an empirical model, or "experience."

3b. Alternatively, the "volume" of the scenario can be estimated in LOC, FP, or some other volume-oriented measure (e.g., use-case count).

4a. Estimates for each task are summed to create an estimate for the scenario.

4b. Alternatively, the volume estimate for the scenario is translated into effort using historical data.

5. The effort estimates for all scenarios that are to be implemented for a given software increment are summed to develop the effort estimate for the increment.

Because the project duration required for the development of a software increment is quite short (typically three to six weeks), this estimation approach serves two purposes: (1) to be certain that the number of scenarios to be included in the increment conforms to the available resources, and (2) to establish a basis for allocating effort as the increment is developed.

---

14 "Abbreviated" does *not* mean eliminated. Even short-duration projects must be planned, and estimation is the foundation of solid planning.

26.9.2   Estimation for WebApp Projects

WebApp projects often adopt the agile process model. A modified function point measure, coupled with the steps outlined in Section 26.9.1, can be used to develop an estimate for the WebApp. Roetzheim [Roe00] suggests the following approach when adapting function points for WebApp estimation:

- *Inputs* are each input screen or form (for example, CGI or Java), each maintenance screen, and if you use a tab notebook metaphor anywhere, each tab.
- *Outputs* are each static Web page, each dynamic Web page script (for example, ASP, ISAPI, or other DHTML script), and each report (whether Web based or administrative in nature).
- *Tables* are each logical table in the database plus, if you are using XML to store data in a file, each XML object (or collection of XML attributes).
- *Interfaces* retain their definition as logical files (for example, unique record formats) into our out-of-the-system boundaries.
- *Queries* are each externally published or use a message-oriented interface. A typical example is DCOM or COM external references.

Function points (interpreted in the manner noted) are a reasonable indicator of volume for a WebApp.

Mendes and her colleagues [Men01] suggest that the volume of a WebApp is best determined by collecting measures (called "predictor variables") associated with the application (e.g., page count, media count, function count), its Web page characteristics (e.g., page complexity, linking complexity, graphic complexity), media characteristics (e.g., media duration), and functional characteristics (e.g., code length, reused code length). These measures can be used to develop empirical estimation models for total project effort, page authoring effort, media authoring effort, and scripting effort. However, further work remains to be done before such models can be used with confidence.

SOFTWARE TOOLS

Effort and Cost Estimation

Objective: The objective of effort and cost estimation tools is to provide a project team with estimates of effort required, project duration, and cost in a manner that addresses the specific characteristics of the project at hand and the environment in which the project is to be built.

Mechanics: In general, cost estimation tools make use of an historical database derived from local projects and data collected across the industry, and an empirical model (e.g., COCOMO II) that is used to derive effort, duration, and cost estimates. Characteristics of the project and the development environment are input and the tool provides a range of estimation outputs.

Representative Tools:[15]
Costar, developed by Softstar Systems (**www.softstarsystems.com**), uses the COCOMO II model to develop software estimates.

---

15 Tools noted here do not represent an endorsement, but rather a sampling of tools in this category. In most cases, tool names are trademarked by their respective developers.

Cost Xpert, developed by Cost Xpert Group, Inc.
(**www.costxpert.com**), integrates multiple
estimation models and an historical project database.

Estimate Professional, developed by the Software
Productivity Centre, Inc. (**www.spc.com**), is based
on COCOMO II and the SLIM Model.

Knowledge Plan, developed by Software Productivity
Research (**www.spr.com**), uses function point input as
the primary driver for a complete estimation package.

Price S, developed by Price Systems
(**www.pricesystems.com**), is one of the oldest

and most widely used estimating tools for large-scale
software development projects.

SEER/SEM, developed by Galorath, Inc.
(**www.galorath.com**), provides comprehensive
estimation capability, sensitivity analysis, risk
assessment, and other features.

SLIM-Estimate, developed by QSM (**www.qsm.com**),
draws on comprehensive "industry knowledge bases"
to provide a "sanity check" for estimates derived using
local data.

26.10   THE MAKE/BUY DECISION

In many software application areas, it is often more cost effective to acquire rather than
develop computer software. Software engineering managers are faced with a make/
buy decision that can be further complicated by a number of acquisition options:
(1) software may be purchased (or licensed) off-the-shelf, (2) "full-experience" or
"partial-experience" software components (see Section 26.4.2) may be acquired and
then modified and integrated to meet specific needs, or (3) software may be custom
built by an outside contractor to meet the purchaser's specifications.

The steps involved in the acquisition of software are defined by the criticality of the
software to be purchased and the end cost. In some cases (e.g., low-cost PC software),
it is less expensive to purchase and experiment than to conduct a lengthy evaluation
of potential software packages. In the final analysis, the make/buy decision is made
based on the following conditions: (1) Will the delivery date of the software product be
sooner than that for internally developed software? (2) Will the cost of acquisition plus
the cost of customization be less than the cost of developing the software internally?
(3) Will the cost of outside support (e.g., a maintenance contract) be less than the cost
of internal support? These conditions apply for each of the acquisition options.

26.10.1   Creating a Decision Tree

? **Is there a
systematic
way to sort
through the
options associated
with the make/
buy decision?**

The steps just described can be augmented using statistical techniques such as decision tree analysis.[16] For example, Figure 26.8 depicts a decision tree for a software-
based system X. In this case, the software engineering organization can (1) build
system X from scratch, (2) reuse existing partial-experience components to construct
the system, (3) buy an available software product and modify it to meet local needs,
or (4) contract the software development to an outside vendor.

---

16 A worthwhile introduction to decision tree analysis can be found at **http://en.wikipedia.org/
wiki/Decision_tree**.

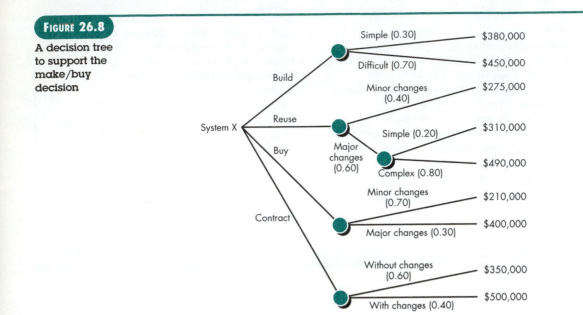

FIGURE 26.8

A decision tree to support the make/buy decision

If the system is to be built from scratch, there is a 70 percent probability that the job will be difficult. Using the estimation techniques discussed earlier in this chapter, the project planner estimates that a difficult development effort will cost $450,000. A "simple" development effort is estimated to cost $380,000. The expected value for cost, computed along any branch of the decision tree, is

$$\text{Expected cost} = \Sigma \text{ (path probability)}_i \times \text{(estimated path cost)}_i$$

where i is the decision tree path. For the build path,

$$\text{Expected cost}_{build} = 0.30 \ (\$380K) + 0.70 \ (\$450K) = \$429K$$

Following other paths of the decision tree, the projected costs for reuse, purchase, and contract, under a variety of circumstances, are also shown. The expected costs for these paths are

$$\text{Expected cost}_{reuse} = 0.40 \ (\$275K) + 0.60 \ [0.20 \ (\$310K) + 0.80 \ (\$490K)] = \$382K$$
$$\text{Expected cost}_{buy} = 0.70 \ (\$210K) + 0.30 \ (\$400K) = \$267K$$
$$\text{Expected cost}_{contract} = 0.60 \ (\$350K) + 0.40 \ (\$500K) = \$410K$$

Based on the probability and projected costs that have been noted in Figure 26.8, the lowest expected cost is the "buy" option.

It is important to note, however, that many criteria—not just cost—must be considered during the decision-making process. Availability, experience of the developer/ vendor/contractor, conformance to requirements, local "politics," and the likelihood of change are but a few of the criteria that may affect the ultimate decision to build, reuse, buy, or contract.

26.10.2 Outsourcing

Sooner or later, every company that develops computer software asks a fundamental question: "Is there a way that we can get the software and systems we need at a lower price?" The answer to this question is not a simple one, and the emotional discussions that occur in response to the question always lead to a single word: *outsourcing*.

In concept, outsourcing is extremely simple. Software engineering activities are contracted to a third party who does the work at lower cost and, hopefully, higher quality. Software work conducted within a company is reduced to a contract management activity.[17]

The decision to outsource can be either strategic or tactical. At the strategic level, business managers consider whether a significant portion of all software work can be contracted to others. At the tactical level, a project manager determines whether part or all of a project can be best accomplished by subcontracting the software work.

Regardless of the breadth of focus, the outsourcing decision is often a financial one. A detailed discussion of the financial analysis for outsourcing is beyond the scope of this book and is best left to others (e.g., [Min95]). However, a brief review of the pros and cons of the decision is worthwhile.

On the positive side, cost savings can usually be achieved by reducing the number of software people and the facilities (e.g., computers, infrastructure) that support them. On the negative side, a company loses some control over the software that it needs. Since software is a technology that differentiates its systems, services, and products, a company runs the risk of putting the fate of its competitiveness into the hands of a third party.

The trend toward outsourcing will undoubtedly continue. The only way to blunt the trend is to recognize that software work is extremely competitive at all levels. The only way to survive is to become as competitive as the outsourcing vendors themselves.

SAFEHOME

Outsourcing

The scene: Meeting room at CPI Corporation early in the project.

The players: Mal Golden, senior manager, product development; Lee Warren, engineering manager; Joe Camalleri, executive VP, business development; and Doug Miller, project manager, software engineering.

The conversation:

Joe: We're considering outsourcing the *SafeHome* software engineering portion of the product.

Doug (shocked): When did this happen?

Lee: We got a quote from an offshore developer. It comes in at 30 percent below what your group seems to believe it will cost. Here. [Hands the quote to Doug who reads it.]

Mal: As you know, Doug, we're trying to keep costs down and 30 percent is 30 percent. Besides, these people come highly recommended.

---

17 Outsourcing can be viewed more generally as any activity that leads to the acquisition of software or software components from a source outside the software engineering organization.

Doug (taking a breath and trying to remain calm): You guys caught me by surprise here, but before you make a final decision a few comments?

Joe (nodding): Sure, go ahead.

Doug: We haven't worked with this outsourcing company before, right?

Mal: Right, but . . .

Doug: And they note that any changes to spec will be billed at an additional rate, right?

Joe (frowning): True, but we expect that things will be reasonably stable.

Doug: A bad assumption, Joe.

Joe: Well, . . .

Doug: It's likely that we'll release new versions of this product over the next few years. And it's reasonable to assume that software will provide many of the new features, right?
[All nod.]

Doug: Have we ever coordinated an international project before?

Lee (looking concerned): No, but I'm told . . .

Doug (trying to suppress his anger): So what you're telling me is: (1) we're about to work with an unknown vendor, (2) the costs to do this are not as low as they seem, (3) we're de facto committing to work with them over many product releases, no matter what they do on the first one, and (4) we're going to learn on-the-job relative to an international project.
[All remain silent.]

Doug: Guys . . . I think this is a mistake, and I'd like you to take a day to reconsider. We'll have far more control if we do the work in-house. We have the expertise, and I can guarantee that it won't cost us much more . . . the risk will be lower, and I know you're all risk averse, as I am.

Joe (frowning): You've made a few good points, but you have a vested interest in keeping this project in-house.

Doug: That's true, but it doesn't change the facts.

Joe (with a sigh): Okay, let's table this for a day or two, give it some more thought, and meet again for a final decision. Doug, can I speak with you privately?

Doug: Sure . . . I really do want to be sure we do the right thing.

26.11 SUMMARY

A software project planner must estimate three things before a project begins: how long it will take, how much effort will be required, and how many people will be involved. In addition, the planner must predict the resources (hardware and software) that will be required and the risk involved.

The statement of scope helps the planner to develop estimates using one or more techniques that fall into two broad categories: decomposition and empirical modeling. Decomposition techniques require a delineation of major software functions, followed by estimates of either (1) the number of LOC, (2) selected values within the information domain, (3) the number of use cases, (4) the number of person-months required to implement each function, or (5) the number of person-months required for each software engineering activity. Empirical techniques use empirically derived expressions for effort and time to predict these project quantities. Automated tools can be used to implement a specific empirical model.

Accurate project estimates generally use at least two of the three techniques just noted. By comparing and reconciling estimates developed using different techniques, the planner is more likely to derive an accurate estimate. Software project estimation can never be an exact science, but a combination of good historical data and systematic techniques can improve estimation accuracy.

PROBLEMS AND POINTS TO PONDER

26.1. Assume that you are the project manager for a company that builds software for household robots. You have been contracted to build the software for a robot that mows the lawn for a homeowner. Write a statement of scope that describes the software. Be sure your statement of scope is bounded. If you're unfamiliar with robots, do a bit of research before you begin writing. Also, state your assumptions about the hardware that will be required. Alternate: Replace the lawn mowing robot with another problem that is of interest to you.

26.2. Software project complexity is discussed briefly in Section 26.1. Develop a list of software characteristics (e.g., concurrent operation, graphical output) that affect the complexity of a project. Prioritize the list.

26.3. Performance is an important consideration during planning. Discuss how performance can be interpreted differently depending upon the software application area.

26.4. Do a functional decomposition of the robot software you described in Problem 26.1. Estimate the size of each function in LOC. Assuming that your organization produces 450 LOC/pm with a burdened labor rate of $7000 per person-month, estimate the effort and cost required to build the software using the LOC-based estimation technique described in this chapter.

26.5. Use the COCOMO II model to estimate the effort required to build software for a simple ATM that produces 12 screens, 10 reports, and will require approximately 80 software components. Assume average complexity and average developer/environment maturity. Use the application composition model with object points.

26.6. Use the software equation to estimate the lawn mowing robot software. Assume that Equation (26.4) is applicable and that $P = 8000$.

26.7. Compare the effort estimates derived in Problems 26.4 and 26.6. What is the standard deviation, and how does it affect your degree of certainty about the estimate?

26.8. Using the results obtained in Problem 26.7, determine whether it's reasonable to expect that the software can be built within the next six months and how many people would have to be used to get the job done.

26.9. Develop a spreadsheet model that implements one or more of the estimation techniques described in this chapter. Alternatively, acquire one or more online models for estimation from Web-based sources.

26.10. For a project team: Develop a software tool that implements each of the estimation techniques developed in this chapter.

26.11. It seems odd that cost and schedule estimates are developed during software project planning—before detailed software requirements analysis or design has been conducted. Why do you think this is done? Are there circumstances when it should not be done?

26.12. Recompute the expected values noted for the decision tree in Figure 26.8 assuming that every branch has a 50–50 probability. Would this change your final decision?

FURTHER READINGS AND INFORMATION SOURCES

Most software project management books contain discussions of project estimation. The Project Management Institute (*PMBOK Guide*, PMI, 2001), Wysoki and his colleagues (*Effective Project Management*, Wiley, 2000), Lewis (*Project Planning Scheduling and Control*, 3d ed., McGraw-Hill, 2000), Bennatan (*On Time, Within Budget: Software Project Management Practices and Techniques*, 3d ed., Wiley, 2000), and Phillips [Phi98] provide useful estimation guidelines.

McConnell (*Software Estimation: Demystifying the Black Art*, Microsoft Press, 2006) has written a pragmatic guide that provides worthwhile guidance for anyone who must estimate the cost of software. Parthasarathy (*Practical Software Estimation*, Addison-Wesley, 2007) emphasizes function points as an estimation metric. Laird and Brennan (*Software Measurement and Estimation: A Practical Approach,* Wiley-IEEE Computer Society Press, 2006) addresses measurement and its use in software estimation. Pfleeger (*Software Cost Estimation and Sizing Methods, Issues, and Guidelines,* RAND Corporation, 2005) has developed an abbreviated guidebook that addresses many estimation fundamentals. Jones (*Estimating Software Costs,* 2d ed., McGraw-Hill, 2007) has written one of the most comprehensive treatments of models and data that are applicable to software estimating in every application domain. Coombs (*IT Project Estimation,* Cambridge University Press, 2002 and Roetzheim and Beasley (*Software Project Cost and Schedule Estimating: Best Practices,* Prentice-Hall, 1997) present many useful models and suggest step-by-step guidelines for generating the best possible estimates.

A wide variety of information sources on software estimation is available on the Internet. An up-to-date list of World Wide Web references relevant to software estimating can be found at the SEPA website: **www.mhhe.com/engcs/compsci/pressman/professional/olc/ser.htm**.

In the late 1960s, a bright-eyed young engineer was chosen to "write" a computer program for an automated manufacturing application. The reason for his selection was simple. He was the only person in his technical group who had attended a computer programming seminar. He knew the ins and outs of assembly language and FORTRAN but nothing about software engineering and even less about project scheduling and tracking.

His boss gave him the appropriate manuals and a verbal description of what had to be done. He was informed that the project must be completed in two months.

He read the manuals, considered his approach, and began writing code. After two weeks, the boss called him into his office and asked how things were going.

"Really great," said the young engineer with youthful enthusiasm. "This was much simpler than I thought. I'm probably close to 75 percent finished."

QUICK
LOOK

What is it? You've selected an appropriate process model, you've identified the software engineering tasks that have to be performed, you estimated the amount of work and the number of people, you know the deadline, you've even considered the risks. Now it's time to connect the dots. That is, you have to create a network of software engineering tasks that will enable you to get the job done on time. Once the network is created, you have to assign responsibility for each task, make sure it gets done, and adapt the network as risks become reality. In a nutshell, that's software project scheduling and tracking.

Who does it? At the project level, software project managers using information solicited from software engineers. At an individual level, software engineers themselves.

Why is it important? In order to build a complex system, many software engineering tasks occur in parallel, and the result of work performed during one task may have a profound effect on work to be conducted in another task. These interdependencies are very difficult to understand without a schedule. It's also virtually impossible to assess progress on a moderate or large software project without a detailed schedule.

What are the steps? The software engineering tasks dictated by the software process model are refined for the functionality to be built. Effort and duration are allocated to each task and a task network (also called an "activity network") is created in a manner that enables the software team to meet the delivery deadline established.

What is the work product? The project schedule and related information are produced.

How do I ensure that I've done it right? Proper scheduling requires that: (1) all tasks appear in the network, (2) effort and timing are intelligently allocated to each task, (3) interdependencies between tasks are properly indicated, (4) resources are allocated for the work to be done, and (5) closely spaced milestones are provided so that progress can be tracked.

The boss smiled and encouraged the young engineer to keep up the good work. They planned to meet again in a week's time.

A week later the boss called the engineer into his office and asked, "Where are we?"

"Everything's going well," said the youngster, "but I've run into a few small snags. I'll get them ironed out and be back on track soon."

"How does the deadline look?" the boss asked.

"No problem," said the engineer. "I'm close to 90 percent complete."

If you've been working in the software world for more than a few years, you can finish the story. It'll come as no surprise that the young engineer[1] stayed 90 percent complete for the entire project duration and finished (with the help of others) only one month late.

This story has been repeated tens of thousands of times by software developers during the past five decades. The big question is why?

27.1 BASIC CONCEPTS

Although there are many reasons why software is delivered late, most can be traced to one or more of the following root causes:

- An unrealistic deadline established by someone outside the software team and forced on managers and practitioners.
- Changing customer requirements that are not reflected in schedule changes.
- An honest underestimate of the amount of effort and/or the number of resources that will be required to do the job.
- Predictable and/or unpredictable risks that were not considered when the project commenced.
- Technical difficulties that could not have been foreseen in advance.
- Human difficulties that could not have been foreseen in advance.
- Miscommunication among project staff that results in delays.
- A failure by project management to recognize that the project is falling behind schedule and a lack of action to correct the problem.

uote:

"Excessive or irrational schedules are probably the single most destructive influence in all of software."

Capers Jones

Aggressive (read "unrealistic") deadlines are a fact of life in the software business. Sometimes such deadlines are demanded for reasons that are legitimate, from the point of view of the person who sets the deadline. But common sense says that legitimacy must also be perceived by the people doing the work.

Napoleon once said: "Any commander-in-chief who undertakes to carry out a plan which he considers defective is at fault; he must put forth his reasons, insist on the plan being changed, and finally tender his resignation rather than be the instrument of his army's downfall." These are strong words that many software project managers should ponder.

---

1   In case you were wondering, this story is autobiographical.

The estimation activities discussed in Chapter 26 and the scheduling techniques described in this chapter are often implemented under the constraint of a defined deadline. If best estimates indicate that the deadline is unrealistic, a competent project manager should "protect his or her team from undue [schedule] pressure . . . [and] reflect the pressure back to its originators" [Pag85].

To illustrate, assume that your software team has been asked to build a real-time controller for a medical diagnostic instrument that is to be introduced to the market in nine months. After careful estimation and risk analysis (Chapter 28), you come to the conclusion that the software, as requested, will require 14 calendar months to create with available staff. How should you proceed?

It is unrealistic to march into the customer's office (in this case the likely customer is marketing/sales) and demand that the delivery date be changed. External market pressures have dictated the date, and the product must be released. It is equally foolhardy to refuse to undertake the work (from a career standpoint). So, what to do? I recommend the following steps in this situation:

1. Perform a detailed estimate using historical data from past projects. Determine the estimated effort and duration for the project.

2. Using an incremental process model (Chapter 2), develop a software engineering strategy that will deliver critical functionality by the imposed deadline, but delay other functionality until later. Document the plan.

? What should you do when management demands a deadline that is impossible?

3. Meet with the customer and (using the detailed estimate), explain why the imposed deadline is unrealistic. Be certain to note that all estimates are based on performance on past projects. Also be certain to indicate the percent improvement that would be required to achieve the deadline as it currently exists.[2] The following comment is appropriate:

> I think we may have a problem with the delivery date for the XYZ controller software. I've given each of you an abbreviated breakdown of development rates for past software projects and an estimate that we've done a number of different ways. You'll note that I've assumed a 20 percent improvement in past development rates, but we still get a delivery date that's 14 calendar months rather than 9 months away.

4. Offer the incremental development strategy as an alternative:

> We have a few options, and I'd like you to make a decision based on them. First, we can increase the budget and bring on additional resources so that we'll have a shot at getting this job done in nine months. But understand that this will increase the risk of poor quality due to the tight time line.[3] Second, we can remove a number of the software functions and capabilities that you're requesting. This will make the preliminary

---

2 If the required improvement is 10 to 25 percent, it may actually be possible to get the job done. But, more likely, the required improvement in team performance will be greater than 50 percent. This is an unrealistic expectation.

3 You might also add that increasing the number of people does not reduce calendar time proportionally.

version of the product somewhat less functional, but we can announce all functionality and then deliver over the 14-month period. Third, we can dispense with reality and wish the project complete in nine months. We'll wind up with nothing that can be delivered to a customer. The third option, I hope you'll agree, is unacceptable. Past history and our best estimates say that it is unrealistic and a recipe for disaster.

There will be some grumbling, but if a solid estimate based on good historical data is presented, it's likely that negotiated versions of option 1 or 2 will be chosen. The unrealistic deadline evaporates.

27.2   PROJECT SCHEDULING

Fred Brooks was once asked how software projects fall behind schedule. His response was as simple as it was profound: "One day at a time."

The reality of a technical project (whether it involves building a hydroelectric plant or developing an operating system) is that hundreds of small tasks must occur to accomplish a larger goal. Some of these tasks lie outside the mainstream and may be completed without worry about impact on project completion date. Other tasks lie on the "critical path." If these "critical" tasks fall behind schedule, the completion date of the entire project is put into jeopardy.

As a project manager, your objective is to define all project tasks, build a network that depicts their interdependencies, identify the tasks that are critical within the network, and then track their progress to ensure that delay is recognized "one day at a time." To accomplish this, you must have a schedule that has been defined at a degree of resolution that allows progress to be monitored and the project to be controlled.

Software project scheduling is an action that distributes estimated effort across the planned project duration by allocating the effort to specific software engineering tasks. It is important to note, however, that the schedule evolves over time. During early stages of project planning, a macroscopic schedule is developed. This type of schedule identifies all major process framework activities and the product functions to which they are applied. As the project gets under way, each entry on the macroscopic schedule is refined into a detailed schedule. Here, specific software actions and tasks (required to accomplish an activity) are identified and scheduled.

Scheduling for software engineering projects can be viewed from two rather different perspectives. In the first, an end date for release of a computer-based system has already (and irrevocably) been established. The software organization is constrained to distribute effort within the prescribed time frame. The second view of software scheduling assumes that rough chronological bounds have been discussed but that the end date is set by the software engineering organization. Effort is distributed to make best use of resources, and an end date is defined after careful analysis of the software. Unfortunately, the first situation is encountered far more frequently than the second.

ADVICE

The tasks required to achieve a project manager's objective should not be performed manually. There are many excellent scheduling tools. Use them.

uote:

"Overly optimistic scheduling doesn't result in shorter actual schedules, it results in longer ones."

Steve McConnell

27.2.1 Basic Principles

Like all other areas of software engineering, a number of basic principles guide software project scheduling:

Compartmentalization. The project must be compartmentalized into a number of manageable activities and tasks. To accomplish compartmentalization, both the product and the process are refined.

Interdependency. The interdependency of each compartmentalized activity or task must be determined. Some tasks must occur in sequence, while others can occur in parallel. Some activities cannot commence until the work product produced by another is available. Other activities can occur independently.

Time allocation. Each task to be scheduled must be allocated some number of work units (e.g., person-days of effort). In addition, each task must be assigned a start date and a completion date that are a function of the interdependencies and whether work will be conducted on a full-time or part-time basis.

Effort validation. Every project has a defined number of people on the software team. As time allocation occurs, you must ensure that no more than the allocated number of people has been scheduled at any given time. For example, consider a project that has three assigned software engineers (e.g., three person-days are available per day of assigned effort[4]). On a given day, seven concurrent tasks must be accomplished. Each task requires 0.50 person-days of effort. More effort has been allocated than there are people to do the work.

Defined responsibilities. Every task that is scheduled should be assigned to a specific team member.

Defined outcomes. Every task that is scheduled should have a defined outcome. For software projects, the outcome is normally a work product (e.g., the design of a component) or a part of a work product. Work products are often combined in deliverables.

Defined milestones. Every task or group of tasks should be associated with a project milestone. A milestone is accomplished when one or more work products has been reviewed for quality (Chapter 15) and has been approved.

Each of these principles is applied as the project schedule evolves.

27.2.2 The Relationship Between People and Effort

In a small software development project a single person can analyze requirements, perform design, generate code, and conduct tests. As the size of a project increases, more people must become involved. (We can rarely afford the luxury of approaching a 10 person-year effort with one person working for 10 years!)

----

4   In reality, less than three person-days of effort are available because of unrelated meetings, sickness, vacation, and a variety of other reasons. For our purposes, however, we assume 100 percent availability.

FIGURE 27.1

The relationship between effort and delivery time

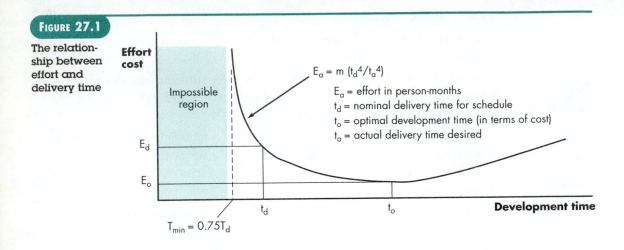

$$E_a = m \, (t_d^4/t_a^4)$$

E_a = effort in person-months
t_d = nominal delivery time for schedule
t_o = optimal development time (in terms of cost)
t_a = actual delivery time desired

$T_{min} = 0.75T_d$

If you must add people to a late project, be sure that you've assigned them work that is highly compartmentalized.

There is a common myth that is still believed by many managers who are responsible for software development projects: "If we fall behind schedule, we can always add more programmers and catch up later in the project." Unfortunately, adding people late in a project often has a disruptive effect on the project, causing schedules to slip even further. The people who are added must learn the system, and the people who teach them are the same people who were doing the work. While teaching, no work is done, and the project falls further behind.

In addition to the time it takes to learn the system, more people increase the number of communication paths and the complexity of communication throughout a project. Although communication is absolutely essential to successful software development, every new communication path requires additional effort and therefore additional time.

Over the years, empirical data and theoretical analysis have demonstrated that project schedules are elastic. That is, it is possible to compress a desired project completion date (by adding additional resources) to some extent. It is also possible to extend a completion date (by reducing the number of resources).

The *Putnam-Norden-Rayleigh (PNR) Curve*[5] provides an indication of the relationship between effort applied and delivery time for a software project. A version of the curve, representing project effort as a function of delivery time, is shown in Figure 27.1. The curve indicates a minimum value t_o that indicates the least cost for delivery (i.e., the delivery time that will result in the least effort expended). As we move left of t_o (i.e., as we try to accelerate delivery), the curve rises nonlinearly.

If delivery can be delayed, the PNR curve indicates that project costs can be reduced substantially.

As an example, we assume that a project team has estimated a level of effort E_d will be required to achieve a nominal delivery time t_d that is optimal in terms of

---

5   Original research can be found in [Nor70] and [Put78].

schedule and available resources. Although it is possible to accelerate delivery, the curve rises very sharply to the left of t_d. In fact, the PNR curve indicates that the project delivery time cannot be compressed much beyond $0.75t_d$. If we attempt further compression, the project moves into "the impossible region" and risk of failure becomes very high. The PNR curve also indicates that the lowest cost delivery option, $t_o = 2t_d$. The implication here is that delaying project delivery can reduce costs significantly. Of course, this must be weighed against the business cost associated with the delay.

The software equation [Put92] introduced in Chapter 26 is derived from the PNR curve and demonstrates the highly nonlinear relationship between chronological time to complete a project and human effort applied to the project. The number of delivered lines of code (source statements), L, is related to effort and development time by the equation:

$$L = P \times E^{1/3}t^{4/3}$$

where E is development effort in person-months, P is a productivity parameter that reflects a variety of factors that lead to high-quality software engineering work (typical values for P range between 2000 and 12,000), and t is the project duration in calendar months.

Rearranging this software equation, we can arrive at an expression for development effort E:

$$E = \frac{L^3}{P^3t^4} \tag{27.1}$$

where E is the effort expended (in person-years) over the entire life cycle for software development and maintenance and t is the development time in years. The equation for development effort can be related to development cost by the inclusion of a burdened labor rate factor ($/person-year).

This leads to some interesting results. Consider a complex, real-time software project estimated at 33,000 LOC, 12 person-years of effort. If eight people are assigned to the project team, the project can be completed in approximately 1.3 years. If, however, we extend the end date to 1.75 years, the highly nonlinear nature of the model described in Equation (27.1) yields:

$$E = \frac{L^3}{P^3t^4} \sim 3.8 \text{ person-years}$$

This implies that, by extending the end date by six months, we can reduce the number of people from eight to four! The validity of such results is open to debate, but the implication is clear: benefit can be gained by using fewer people over a somewhat longer time span to accomplish the same objective.

27.2.3   Effort Distribution

Each of the software project estimation techniques discussed in Chapter 26 leads to estimates of work units (e.g., person-months) required to complete software development. A recommended distribution of effort across the software process is often referred to as the *40–20–40 rule.* Forty percent of all effort is allocated to front-end analysis and design. A similar percentage is applied to back-end testing. You can correctly infer that coding (20 percent of effort) is deemphasized.

? **How should effort be distributed across the software process workflow?**

This effort distribution should be used as a guideline only.[6] The characteristics of each project dictate the distribution of effort. Work expended on project planning rarely accounts for more than 2 to 3 percent of effort, unless the plan commits an organization to large expenditures with high risk. Customer communication and requirements analysis may comprise 10 to 25 percent of project effort. Effort expended on analysis or prototyping should increase in direct proportion with project size and complexity. A range of 20 to 25 percent of effort is normally applied to software design. Time expended for design review and subsequent iteration must also be considered.

Because of the effort applied to software design, code should follow with relatively little difficulty. A range of 15 to 20 percent of overall effort can be achieved. Testing and subsequent debugging can account for 30 to 40 percent of software development effort. The criticality of the software often dictates the amount of testing that is required. If software is human rated (i.e., software failure can result in loss of life), even higher percentages are typical.

27.3   DEFINING A TASK SET FOR THE SOFTWARE PROJECT

Regardless of the process model that is chosen, the work that a software team performs is achieved through a set of tasks that enable you to define, develop, and ultimately support computer software. No single task set is appropriate for all projects. The set of tasks that would be appropriate for a large, complex system would likely be perceived as overkill for a small, relatively simple software product. Therefore, an effective software process should define a collection of task sets, each designed to meet the needs of different types of projects.

As I noted in Chapter 2, a task set is a collection of software engineering work tasks, milestones, work products, and quality assurance filters that must be accomplished to complete a particular project. The task set must provide enough discipline to achieve high software quality. But, at the same time, it must not burden the project team with unnecessary work.

In order to develop a project schedule, a task set must be distributed on the project time line. The task set will vary depending upon the project type and the degree of rigor with which the software team decides to do its work. Although it is difficult

---

6   Today, the 40-20-40 rule is under attack. Some believe that more than 40 percent of overall effort should be expended during analysis and design. On the other hand, some proponents of agile development (Chapter 3) argue that less time should be expended "up front" and that a team should move quickly to construction.

to develop a comprehensive taxonomy of software project types, most software organizations encounter the following projects:

WebRef

An adaptable process model (APM) has been developed to assist in defining task sets for various software projects. A complete description of the APM can be found at **www .rspa.com/apm**.

1. *Concept development projects* that are initiated to explore some new business concept or application of some new technology.

2. *New application development* projects that are undertaken as a consequence of a specific customer request.

3. *Application enhancement* projects that occur when existing software undergoes major modifications to function, performance, or interfaces that are observable by the end user.

4. *Application maintenance projects* that correct, adapt, or extend existing software in ways that may not be immediately obvious to the end user.

5. *Reengineering projects* that are undertaken with the intent of rebuilding an existing (legacy) system in whole or in part.

Even within a single project type, many factors influence the task set to be chosen. These include [Pre05]: size of the project, number of potential users, mission criticality, application longevity, stability of requirements, ease of customer/developer communication, maturity of applicable technology, performance constraints, embedded and nonembedded characteristics, project staff, and reengineering factors. When taken in combination, these factors provide an indication of the *degree of rigor* with which the software process should be applied.

27.3.1   A Task Set Example

Concept development projects are initiated when the potential for some new technology must be explored. There is no certainty that the technology will be applicable, but a customer (e.g., marketing) believes that potential benefit exists. Concept development projects are approached by applying the following actions:

1.1   **Concept scoping** determines the overall scope of the project.

1.2   **Preliminary concept planning** establishes the organization's ability to undertake the work implied by the project scope.

1.3   **Technology risk assessment** evaluates the risk associated with the technology to be implemented as part of the project scope.

1.4   **Proof of concept** demonstrates the viability of a new technology in the software context.

1.5   **Concept implementation** implements the concept representation in a manner that can be reviewed by a customer and is used for "marketing" purposes when a concept must be sold to other customers or management.

1.6   **Customer reaction** to the concept solicits feedback on a new technology concept and targets specific customer applications.

A quick scan of these actions should yield few surprises. In fact, the software engineering flow for concept development projects (and for all other types of projects as well) is little more than common sense.

27.3.2 Refinement of Software Engineering Actions

The software engineering actions described in the preceding section may be used to define a macroscopic schedule for a project. However, the macroscopic schedule must be refined to create a detailed project schedule. Refinement begins by taking each action and decomposing it into a set of tasks (with related work products and milestones).

As an example of task decomposition, consider Action 1.1, Concept Scoping. Task refinement can be accomplished using an outline format, but in this book, a process design language approach is used to illustrate the flow of the concept scoping action:

> Task definition: Action 1.1 Concept Scoping
> 1.1.1   Identify need, benefits and potential customers;
> 1.1.2   Define desired output/control and input events that drive the application;
> Begin Task 1.1.2
> 1.1.2.1 TR: Review written description of need[7]
> 1.1.2.2 Derive a list of customer visible outputs/inputs
> 1.1.2.3 TR: Review outputs/inputs with customer and revise as required; endtask
> Task 1.1.2
> 1.1.3   Define the functionality/behavior for each major function;
> Begin Task 1.1.3
> 1.1.3.1 TR: Review output and input data objects derived in task 1.1.2;
> 1.1.3.2 Derive a model of functions/behaviors;
> 1.1.3.3 TR: Review functions/behaviors with customer and revise as required;
> endtask Task 1.1.3
> 1.1.4   Isolate those elements of the technology to be implemented in software;
> 1.1.5   Research availability of existing software;
> 1.1.6   Define technical feasibility;
> 1.1.7   Make quick estimate of size;
> 1.1.8   Create a scope definition;
> endtask definition: Action 1.1

The tasks and subtasks noted in the process design language refinement form the basis for a detailed schedule for the concept scoping action.

---

7 TR indicates that a technical review (Chapter 15) is to be conducted.

27.4 DEFINING A TASK NETWORK

KEY POINT

The task network is a useful mechanism for depicting intertask dependencies and determining the critical path.

Individual tasks and subtasks have interdependencies based on their sequence. In addition, when more than one person is involved in a software engineering project, it is likely that development activities and tasks will be performed in parallel. When this occurs, concurrent tasks must be coordinated so that they will be complete when later tasks require their work product(s).

A *task network,* also called an *activity network,* is a graphic representation of the task flow for a project. It is sometimes used as the mechanism through which task sequence and dependencies are input to an automated project scheduling tool. In its simplest form (used when creating a macroscopic schedule), the task network depicts major software engineering actions. Figure 27.2 shows a schematic task network for a concept development project.

The concurrent nature of software engineering actions leads to a number of important scheduling requirements. Because parallel tasks occur asynchronously, you should determine intertask dependencies to ensure continuous progress toward completion. In addition, you should be aware of those tasks that lie on the *critical path.* That is, tasks that must be completed on schedule if the project as a whole is to be completed on schedule. These issues are discussed in more detail later in this chapter.

It is important to note that the task network shown in Figure 27.2 is macroscopic. In a detailed task network (a precursor to a detailed schedule), each action shown in the figure would be expanded. For example, Task 1.1 would be expanded to show all tasks detailed in the refinement of Actions 1.1 shown in Section 27.3.2.

FIGURE 27.2 A task network for concept development

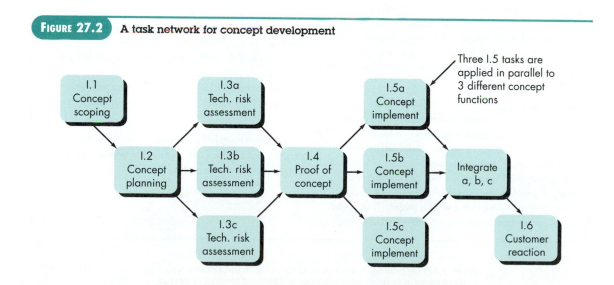

27.5 SCHEDULING

Scheduling of a software project does not differ greatly from scheduling of any multitask engineering effort. Therefore, generalized project scheduling tools and techniques can be applied with little modification for software projects.

Program evaluation and review technique (PERT) and the *critical path method* (CPM) are two project scheduling methods that can be applied to software development. Both techniques are driven by information already developed in earlier project planning activities: estimates of effort, a decomposition of the product function, the selection of the appropriate process model and task set, and decomposition of the tasks that are selected.

Interdependencies among tasks may be defined using a task network. Tasks, sometimes called the project *work breakdown structure* (WBS), are defined for the product as a whole or for individual functions.

Both PERT and CPM provide quantitative tools that allow you to (1) determine the critical path—the chain of tasks that determines the duration of the project, (2) establish "most likely" time estimates for individual tasks by applying statistical models, and (3) calculate "boundary times" that define a time "window" for a particular task.

27.5.1   Time-Line Charts

When creating a software project schedule, you begin with a set of tasks (the work breakdown structure). If automated tools are used, the work breakdown is input as

---

SOFTWARE TOOLS

Project Scheduling

Objective: The objective of project scheduling tools is to enable a project manager to define work tasks; establish their dependencies; assign human resources to tasks; and develop a variety of graphs, charts, and tables that aid in tracking and control of the software project.

Mechanics: In general, project scheduling tools require the specification of a work breakdown structure of tasks or the generation of a task network. Once the task breakdown (an outline) or network is defined, start and end dates, human resources, hard deadlines, and other data are attached to each. The tool then generates a variety of time-line charts and other tables that enable a manager to assess the task flow of a project. These data can be updated continually as the project is under way.

Representative Tools:[8]

AMS Realtime, developed by Advanced Management Systems (**www.amsusa.com**), provides scheduling capabilities for projects of all sizes and types.

Microsoft Project, developed by Microsoft (**www.microsoft.com**), is the most widely used PC-based project scheduling tool.

4C, developed by *4C Systems* (**www.4csys.com**), supports all aspects of project planning including scheduling.

A comprehensive list of project management software vendors and products can be found at **www.infogoal .com/pmc/pmcswr.htm**.

---

8   Tools noted here do not represent an endorsement, but rather a sampling of tools in this category. In most cases, tool names are trademarked by their respective developers.

a task network or task outline. Effort, duration, and start date are then input for each task. In addition, tasks may be assigned to specific individuals.

As a consequence of this input, a *time-line chart,* also called a *Gantt chart,* is generated. A time-line chart can be developed for the entire project. Alternatively, separate charts can be developed for each project function or for each individual working on the project.

Figure 27.3 illustrates the format of a time-line chart. It depicts a part of a software project schedule that emphasizes the concept scoping task for a word-processing (WP) software product. All project tasks (for concept scoping) are listed in the left-hand column. The horizontal bars indicate the duration of each task. When multiple bars occur at the same time on the calendar, task concurrency is implied. The diamonds indicate milestones.

Once the information necessary for the generation of a time-line chart has been input, the majority of software project scheduling tools produce *project tables*—a tabular listing of all project tasks, their planned and actual start and end dates, and a variety of related information (Figure 27.4). Used in conjunction with the time-line chart, project tables enable you to track progress.

KEY POINT

A time-line chart enables you to determine what tasks will be conducted at a given point in time.

FIGURE 27.3   An example time-line chart

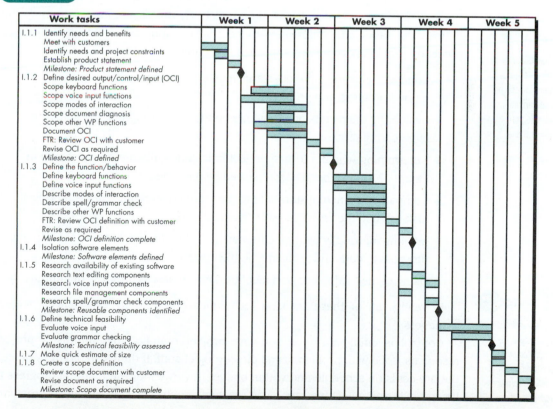

FIGURE 27.4   An example project table

Work tasks	Planned start	Actual start	Planned complete	Actual complete	Assigned person	Effort allocated	Notes
I.1.1 Identify needs and benefits							Scoping will require more effort/time
Meet with customers	wk1, d1	wk1, d1	wk1, d2	wk1, d2	BLS	2 p-d	
Identify needs and project constraints	wk1, d2	wk1, d2	wk1, d2	wk1, d2	JPP	1 p-d	
Establish product statement	wk1, d3	wk1, d3	wk1, d3	wk1, d3	BLS/JPP	1 p-d	
Milestone: Product statement defined	wk1, d3	wk1, d3	wk1, d3	wk1, d3			
I.1.2 Define desired output/control/input (OCI)							
Scope keyboard functions	wk1, d4	wk1, d4	wk2, d2		BLS	1.5 p-d	
Scope voice input functions	wk1, d3	wk1, d3	wk2, d2		JPP	2 p-d	
Scope modes of interaction	wk2, d1		wk2, d3		MLL	1 p-d	
Scope document diagnostics	wk2, d1		wk2, d2		BLS	1.5 p-d	
Scope other WP functions	wk1, d4	wk1, d4	wk2, d3		JPP	2 p-d	
Document OCI	wk2, d1		wk2, d3		MLL	3 p-d	
FTR: Review OCI with customer	wk2, d3		wk2, d3		all	3 p-d	
Revise OCI as required	wk2, d4		wk2, d4		all	3 p-d	
Milestone: OCI defined	wk2, d5		wk2, d5				
I.1.3 Define the function/behavior							

27.5.2   Tracking the Schedule

If it has been properly developed, the project schedule becomes a road map that defines the tasks and milestones to be tracked and controlled as the project proceeds. Tracking can be accomplished in a number of different ways:

- Conducting periodic project status meetings in which each team member reports progress and problems
- Evaluating the results of all reviews conducted throughout the software engineering process
- Determining whether formal project milestones (the diamonds shown in Figure 27.3) have been accomplished by the scheduled date
- Comparing the actual start date to the planned start date for each project task listed in the resource table (Figure 27.4)
- Meeting informally with practitioners to obtain their subjective assessment of progress to date and problems on the horizon
- Using earned value analysis (Section 27.6) to assess progress quantitatively

In reality, all of these tracking techniques are used by experienced project managers.

Control is employed by a software project manager to administer project resources, cope with problems, and direct project staff. If things are going well (i.e., the project is on schedule and within budget, reviews indicate that real progress is being made and milestones are being reached), control is light. But when problems occur, you must exercise control to reconcile them as quickly as possible. After a problem has been diagnosed, additional resources may be focused on the problem area: staff may be redeployed or the project schedule can be redefined.

When faced with severe deadline pressure, experienced project managers sometimes use a project scheduling and control technique called *time-boxing* [Jal04]. The time-boxing strategy recognizes that the complete product may not be deliverable by the predefined deadline. Therefore, an incremental software paradigm (Chapter 2) is chosen, and a schedule is derived for each incremental delivery.

The tasks associated with each increment are then time-boxed. This means that the schedule for each task is adjusted by working backward from the delivery date for the increment. A "box" is put around each task. When a task hits the boundary of its time box (plus or minus 10 percent), work stops and the next task begins.

The initial reaction to the time-boxing approach is often negative: "If the work isn't finished, how can we proceed?" The answer lies in the way work is accomplished. By the time the time-box boundary is encountered, it is likely that 90 percent of the task has been completed.[9] The remaining 10 percent, although important, can (1) be delayed until the next increment or (2) be completed later if required. Rather than becoming "stuck" on a task, the project proceeds toward the delivery date.

27.5.3 Tracking Progress for an OO Project

Although an iterative model is the best framework for an OO project, task parallelism makes project tracking difficult. You may have difficulty establishing meaningful milestones for an OO project because a number of different things are happening at once. In general, the following major milestones can be considered "completed" when the criteria noted have been met.

Technical milestone: OO analysis completed

- All classes and the class hierarchy have been defined and reviewed.
- Class attributes and operations associated with a class have been defined and reviewed.
- Class relationships (Chapter 6) have been established and reviewed.
- A behavioral model (Chapter 7) has been created and reviewed.
- Reusable classes have been noted.

Technical milestone: OO design completed

- The set of subsystems has been defined and reviewed.
- Classes are allocated to subsystems and reviewed.
- Task allocation has been established and reviewed.

---

9 A cynic might recall the saying: "The first 90 percent of the system takes 90 percent of the time; the remaining 10 percent of the system takes 90 percent of the time."

- Responsibilities and collaborations have been identified.
- Attributes and operations have been designed and reviewed.
- The communication model has been created and reviewed.

Technical milestone: OO programming completed

- Each new class has been implemented in code from the design model.
- Extracted classes (from a reuse library) have been implemented.
- Prototype or increment has been built.

Technical milestone: OO testing

Debugging and testing occur in concert with one another. The status of debugging is often assessed by considering the type and number of "open" errors (bugs).

- The correctness and completeness of OO analysis and design models has been reviewed.
- A class-responsibility-collaboration network (Chapter 6) has been developed and reviewed.
- Test cases are designed, and class-level tests (Chapter 19) have been conducted for each class.
- Test cases are designed, and cluster testing (Chapter 19) is completed and the classes are integrated.
- System-level tests have been completed.

Recalling that the OO process model is iterative, each of these milestones may be revisited as different increments are delivered to the customer.

27.5.4 Scheduling for WebApp Projects

WebApp project scheduling distributes estimated effort across the planned time line (duration) for building each WebApp increment. This is accomplished by allocating the effort to specific tasks. It is important to note, however, that the overall WebApp schedule evolves over time. During the first iteration, a macroscopic schedule is developed. This type of schedule identifies all WebApp increments and projects the dates on which each will be deployed. As the development of an increment gets under way, the entry for the increment on the macroscopic schedule is refined into a detailed schedule. Here, specific development tasks (required to accomplish an activity) are identified and scheduled.

As an example of macroscopic scheduling, consider the **SafeHomeAssured.com** WebApp. Recalling earlier discussions of **SafeHomeAssured.com**, seven increments can be identified for the Web-based component of the project:

Increment 1: Basic company and product information

Increment 2: Detailed product information and downloads

Increment 3: Product quotes and processing product orders

Increment 4: Space layout and security system design

FIGURE 27.5   Time line for macroscopic project schedule

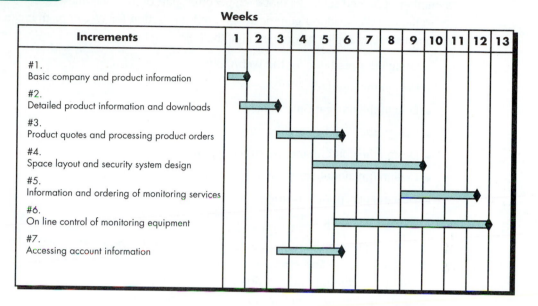

Increment 5: Information and ordering of monitoring services

Increment 6: Online control of monitoring equipment

Increment 7: Accessing account information

The team consults and negotiates with stakeholders and develops a *preliminary* deployment schedule for all seven increments. A time-line chart for this schedule is illustrated in Figure 27.5.

It is important to note that the deployment dates (represented by diamonds on the time-line chart) are preliminary and may change as more detailed scheduling of the increments occurs. However, this macroscopic schedule provides management with an indication of when content and functionality will be available and when the entire project will be completed. As a preliminary estimate, the team will work to deploy all increments with a 12-week time line. It's also worth noting that some of the increments will be developed in parallel (e.g., increments 3, 4, 6 and 7). This assumes that the team will have sufficient people to do this parallel work.

Once the macroscopic schedule has been developed, the team is ready to schedule work tasks for a specific increment. To accomplish this, you can use a generic process framework that is applicable for all WebApp increments. A *task list* is created by using the generic tasks derived as part of the framework as a starting point and then adapting these by considering the content and functions to be derived for a specific WebApp increment.

Each framework action (and its related tasks) can be adapted in one of four ways: (1) a task is applied as is, (2) a task is eliminated because it is not necessary for the increment, (3) a new (custom) task is added, and (4) a task is refined (elaborated) into a number of named subtasks that each becomes part of the schedule.

To illustrate, consider a generic *design modeling* action for WebApps that can be accomplished by applying some or all of the following tasks:

- Design the aesthetic for the WebApp.
- Design the interface.
- Design the navigation scheme.
- Design the WebApp architecture.
- Design the content and the structure that supports it.
- Design functional components.
- Design appropriate security and privacy mechanisms.
- Review the design.

As an example, consider the generic task *Design the Interface* as it is applied to the fourth increment of **SafeHomeAssured.com**. Recall that the fourth increment implements the content and function for describing the living or business space to be secured by the *SafeHome* security system. Referring to Figure 27.5, the fourth increment commences at the beginning of the fifth week and terminates at the end of the ninth week.

There is little question that the *Design the Interface* task must be conducted. The team recognizes that the interface design is pivotal to the success of the increment and decides to refine (elaborate) the task. The following subtasks are derived for the *Design the Interface* task for the fourth increment:

- Develop a sketch of the page layout for the space design page.
- Review layout with stakeholders.
- Design space layout navigation mechanisms.
- Design "drawing board" layout.[10]
- Develop procedural details for the graphical wall layout function.
- Develop procedural details for the wall length computation and display function.
- Develop procedural details for the graphical window layout function.
- Develop procedural details for the graphical door layout function.
- Design mechanisms for selecting security system components (sensors, cameras, microphones, etc.).

---

10 At this stage, the team envisions creating the space by literally drawing the walls, windows, and doors using graphical functions. Wall lines will "snap" onto grip points. Dimensions of the wall will be displayed automatically. Windows and doors will be positioned graphically. The end user can also select specific sensors, cameras, etc., and position them once the space has been defined.

- Develop procedural details for the graphical layout of security system components.

- Conduct pair walkthroughs as required.

These tasks become part of the increment schedule for the fourth WebApp increment and are allocated over the increment development schedule. They can be input to scheduling software and used for tracking and control.

SafeHome

Tracking the Schedule

The scene: Doug Miller's office prior to the initiation of the *SafeHome* software project.

The players: Doug Miller (manager of the *SafeHome* software engineering team) and Vinod Raman, Jamie Lazar, and other members of the product software engineering team.

The conversation:

Doug (glancing at a PowerPoint slide): The schedule for the first *SafeHome* increment seems reasonable, but we're going to have trouble tracking progress.

Vinod (a concerned look on his face): Why? We have tasks scheduled on a daily basis, plenty of work products, and we've been sure that we're not overallocating resources.

Doug: All good, but how do we know when the requirements model for the first increment is complete?

Jamie: Things are iterative, so that's difficult.

Doug: I understand that, but . . . well, for instance, take "analysis classes defined." You indicated that as a milestone.

Vinod: We have.

Doug: Who makes that determination?

Jamie (aggravated): They're done when they're done.

Doug: That's not good enough, Jamie. We have to schedule TRs [technical reviews, Chapter 15], and you haven't done that. The successful completion of a review on the analysis model, for instance, is a reasonable milestone. Understand?

Jamie (frowning): Okay, back to the drawing board.

Doug: It shouldn't take more than an hour to make the corrections . . . everyone else can get started now.

27.6 EARNED VALUE ANALYSIS

KEY POINT

Earned value provides a quantitative indication of progress.

In Section 27.5, I discussed a number of qualitative approaches to project tracking. Each provides the project manager with an indication of progress, but an assessment of the information provided is somewhat subjective. It is reasonable to ask whether there is a quantitative technique for assessing progress as the software team progresses through the work tasks allocated to the project schedule. In fact, a technique for performing quantitative analysis of progress does exist. It is called *earned value analysis* (EVA). Humphrey [Hum95] discusses earned value in the following manner:

> The earned value system provides a common value scale for every [software project] task, regardless of the type of work being performed. The total hours to do the whole project are estimated, and every task is given an earned value based on its estimated percentage of the total.

Stated even more simply, earned value is a measure of progress. It enables you to assess the "percent of completeness" of a project using quantitative analysis rather than rely on a gut feeling. In fact, Fleming and Koppleman [Fle98] argue that earned value analysis "provides accurate and reliable readings of performance from as early as 15 percent into the project." To determine the earned value, the following steps are performed:

How do I compute earned value and use it to assess progress?

1. The *budgeted cost of work scheduled* (BCWS) is determined for each work task represented in the schedule. During estimation, the work (in person-hours or person-days) of each software engineering task is planned. Hence, $BCWS_i$ is the effort planned for work task i. To determine progress at a given point along the project schedule, the value of BCWS is the sum of the $BCWS_i$ values for all work tasks that should have been completed by that point in time on the project schedule.

2. The BCWS values for all work tasks are summed to derive the *budget at completion* (BAC). Hence,

   $BAC = \Sigma\ (BCWS_k)$ for all tasks k

3. Next, the value for *budgeted cost of work performed* (BCWP) is computed. The value for BCWP is the sum of the BCWS values for all work tasks that have actually been completed by a point in time on the project schedule.

Wilkens [Wil99] notes that "the distinction between the BCWS and the BCWP is that the former represents the budget of the activities that were planned to be completed and the latter represents the budget of the activities that actually were completed." Given values for BCWS, BAC, and BCWP, important progress indicators can be computed:

$$\text{Schedule performance index, SPI} = \frac{BCWP}{BCWS}$$

$$\text{Schedule variance, SV} = BCWP - BCWS$$

WebRef

A wide array of earned value analysis resources can be found at **www.acq.osd.mil/pm/**.

SPI is an indication of the efficiency with which the project is utilizing scheduled resources. An SPI value close to 1.0 indicates efficient execution of the project schedule. SV is simply an absolute indication of variance from the planned schedule.

$$\text{Percent scheduled for completion} = \frac{BCWS}{BAC}$$

provides an indication of the percentage of work that should have been completed by time t.

$$\text{Percent complete} = \frac{BCWP}{BAC}$$

provides a quantitative indication of the percent of completeness of the project at a given point in time t.

It is also possible to compute the *actual cost of work performed* (ACWP). The value for ACWP is the sum of the effort actually expended on work tasks that have been completed by a point in time on the project schedule. It is then possible to compute

$$\text{Cost performance index, } CPI = \frac{BCWP}{ACWP}$$

$$\text{Cost variance, } CV = BCWP - ACWP$$

A CPI value close to 1.0 provides a strong indication that the project is within its defined budget. CV is an absolute indication of cost savings (against planned costs) or shortfall at a particular stage of a project.

Like over-the-horizon radar, earned value analysis illuminates scheduling difficulties before they might otherwise be apparent. This enables you to take corrective action before a project crisis develops.

27.7   SUMMARY

Scheduling is the culmination of a planning activity that is a primary component of software project management. When combined with estimation methods and risk analysis, scheduling establishes a road map for the project manager.

Scheduling begins with process decomposition. The characteristics of the project are used to adapt an appropriate task set for the work to be done. A task network depicts each engineering task, its dependency on other tasks, and its projected duration. The task network is used to compute the critical path, a time-line chart, and a variety of project information. Using the schedule as a guide, you can track and control each step in the software process.

PROBLEMS AND POINTS TO PONDER

27.1. "Unreasonable" deadlines are a fact of life in the software business. How should you proceed if you're faced with one?

27.2. What is the difference between a macroscopic schedule and a detailed schedule? Is it possible to manage a project if only a macroscopic schedule is developed? Why?

27.3. Is there ever a case where a software project milestone is not tied to a review? If so, provide one or more examples.

27.4. "Communication overhead" can occur when multiple people work on a software project. The time spent communicating with others reduces individual productively (LOC/month), and the result can be less productivity for the team. Illustrate (quantitatively) how engineers who are well versed in good software engineering practices and use technical reviews can increase the production rate of a team (when compared to the sum of individual production rates). Hint: You can assume that reviews reduce rework and that rework can account for 20 to 40 percent of a person's time.

27.5. Although adding people to a late software project can make it later, there are circumstances in which this is not true. Describe them.

27.6. The relationship between people and time is highly nonlinear. Using Putnam's software equation (described in Section 27.2.2), develop a table that relates number of people to project duration for a software project requiring 50,000 LOC and 15 person-years of effort (the productivity parameter is 5000 and $B = 0.37$). Assume that the software must be delivered in 24 months plus or minus 12 months.

27.7. Assume that you have been contracted by a university to develop an online course registration system (OLCRS). First, act as the customer (if you're a student, that should be easy!) and specify the characteristics of a good system. (Alternatively, your instructor will provide you with a set of preliminary requirements for the system.) Using the estimation methods discussed in Chapter 26, develop an effort and duration estimate for OLCRS. Suggest how you would:

a. Define parallel work activities during the OLCRS project.

b. Distribute effort throughout the project.

c. Establish milestones for the project.

27.8. Select an appropriate task set for the OLCRS project.

27.9. Define a task network for OLCRS described in Problem 27.7, or alternatively, for another software project that interests you. Be sure to show tasks and milestones and to attach effort and duration estimates to each task. If possible, use an automated scheduling tool to perform this work.

27.10. If an automated scheduling tool is available, determine the critical path for the network defined in Problem 27.9.

27.11. Using a scheduling tool (if available) or paper and pencil (if necessary), develop a timeline chart for the OLCRS project.

27.12. Assume you are a software project manager and that you've been asked to compute earned value statistics for a small software project. The project has 56 planned work tasks that are estimated to require 582 person-days to complete. At the time that you've been asked to do the earned value analysis, 12 tasks have been completed. However the project schedule indicates that 15 tasks should have been completed. The following scheduling data (in person-days) are available:

Task	Planned Effort	Actual Effort
1	12.0	12.5
2	15.0	11.0
3	13.0	17.0
4	8.0	9.5
5	9.5	9.0
6	18.0	19.0
7	10.0	10.0
8	4.0	4.5
9	12.0	10.0
10	6.0	6.5
11	5.0	4.0
12	14.0	14.5
13	16.0	—
14	6.0	—
15	8.0	—

Compute the SPI, schedule variance, percent scheduled for completion, percent complete, CPI, and cost variance for the project.

FURTHER READINGS AND INFORMATION SOURCES

Virtually every book written on software project management contains a discussion of scheduling. Wysoki (*Effective Project Management,* Wiley, 2006), Lewis (*Project Planning Scheduling and Control,* 4th ed., McGraw-Hill, 2006), Luckey and Phillips (*Software Project Management for Dummies,* For Dummies, 2006), Kerzner (*Project Management: A Systems Approach to Planning, Scheduling, and Controlling,* 9th ed., Wiley, 2005), Hughes (*Software Project Management,* McGraw-Hill, 2005), The Project Management Institute (*PMBOK Guide,* 3d ed., PMI, 2004), Lewin (*Better Software Project Management,* Wiley, 2001), and Bennatan (*On Time, Within Budget: Software Project Management Practices and Techniques,* 3d ed., Wiley, 2000) contain worthwhile discussions of the subject. Although application specific, Harris (*Planning and Scheduling Using Microsoft Office Project 2007,* Eastwood Harris Pty Ltd., 2007) provides a useful discussion of how scheduling tools can be used to successfully track and control a software project.

Fleming and Koppelman (*Earned Value Project Management,* 3d ed., Project Management Institute Publications, 2006), Budd (*A Practical Guide to Earned Value Project Management,* Management Concepts, 2005), and Webb and Wake (*Using Earned Value: A Project Manager's Guide,* Ashgate Publishing, 2003) discuss the use of earned value techniques for project planning, tracking, and control in considerable detail.

A wide variety of information sources on software project scheduling is available on the Internet. An up-to-date list of World Wide Web references relevant to software project scheduling can be found at the SEPA website: **www.mhhe.com/engcs/compsci/pressman/professional/olc/ser.htm**.

28

RISK MANAGEMENT

In his book on risk analysis and management, Robert Charette [Cha89] presents a conceptual definition of risk:

> First, risk concerns future happenings. Today and yesterday are beyond active concern, as we are already reaping what was previously sowed by our past actions. The question is, can we, therefore, by changing our actions today, create an opportunity for a different and hopefully better situation for ourselves tomorrow. This means, second, that risk involves change, such as in changes of mind, opinion, actions, or places. . . . [Third,] risk involves choice, and the uncertainty that choice itself entails. Thus paradoxically, risk, like death and taxes, is one of the few certainties of life.

When you consider risk in the context of software engineering, Charette's three conceptual underpinnings are always in evidence. The future is your

---

QUICK LOOK

What is it? Risk analysis and management are actions that help a software team to understand and manage uncertainty. Many problems can plague a software project. A risk is a potential problem—it might happen, it might not. But, regardless of the outcome, it's a really good idea to identify it, assess its probability of occurrence, estimate its impact, and establish a contingency plan should the problem actually occur.

Who does it? Everyone involved in the software process—managers, software engineers, and other stakeholders—participate in risk analysis and management.

Why is it important? Think about the Boy Scout motto: "Be prepared." Software is a difficult undertaking. Lots of things can go wrong, and frankly, many often do. It's for this reason that being prepared—understanding the risks and taking proactive measures to avoid or manage them—is a key element of good software project management.

What are the steps? Recognizing what can go wrong is the first step, called "risk identification." Next, each risk is analyzed to determine the likelihood that it will occur and the damage that it will do if it does occur. Once this information is established, risks are ranked, by probability and impact. Finally, a plan is developed to manage those risks that have high probability and high impact.

What is the work product? A risk mitigation, monitoring, and management (RMMM) plan or a set of risk information sheets is produced.

How do I ensure that I've done it right? The risks that are analyzed and managed should be derived from thorough study of the people, the product, the process, and the project. The RMMM should be revisited as the project proceeds to ensure that risks are kept up to date. Contingency plans for risk management should be realistic.

concern—what risks might cause the software project to go awry? Change is your concern—how will changes in customer requirements, development technologies, target environments, and all other entities connected to the project affect timeliness and overall success? Last, you must grapple with choices—what methods and tools should you use, how many people should be involved, how much emphasis on quality is "enough"?

Peter Drucker [Dru75] once said, "While it is futile to try to eliminate risk, and questionable to try to minimize it, it is essential that the risks taken be the right risks." Before you can identify the "right risks" to be taken during a software project, it is important to identify all risks that are obvious to both managers and practitioners.

28.1 REACTIVE VERSUS PROACTIVE RISK STRATEGIES

uote:

"If you don't actively attack the risks, they will actively attack you."

Tom Gilb

Reactive risk strategies have been laughingly called the "Indiana Jones school of risk management" [Tho92]. In the movies that carried his name, Indiana Jones, when faced with overwhelming difficulty, would invariably say, "Don't worry, I'll think of something!" Never worrying about problems until they happened, Indy would react in some heroic way.

Sadly, the average software project manager is not Indiana Jones and the members of the software project team are not his trusty sidekicks. Yet, the majority of software teams rely solely on reactive risk strategies. At best, a reactive strategy monitors the project for likely risks. Resources are set aside to deal with them, should they become actual problems. More commonly, the software team does nothing about risks until something goes wrong. Then, the team flies into action in an attempt to correct the problem rapidly. This is often called a *fire-fighting mode*. When this fails, "crisis management" [Cha92] takes over and the project is in real jeopardy.

A considerably more intelligent strategy for risk management is to be proactive. A *proactive* strategy begins long before technical work is initiated. Potential risks are identified, their probability and impact are assessed, and they are ranked by importance. Then, the software team establishes a plan for managing risk. The primary objective is to avoid risk, but because not all risks can be avoided, the team works to develop a contingency plan that will enable it to respond in a controlled and effective manner. Throughout the remainder of this chapter, I discuss a proactive strategy for risk management.

28.2 SOFTWARE RISKS

Although there has been considerable debate about the proper definition for software risk, there is general agreement that risk always involves two characteristics: *uncertainty*—the risk may or may not happen; that is, there are no 100 percent probable risks[1]—and *loss*—if the risk becomes a reality, unwanted consequences or losses will occur [Hig95]. When risks are analyzed, it is important to quantify the level of uncertainty and the degree of loss associated with each risk. To accomplish this, different categories of risks are considered.

Project risks threaten the project plan. That is, if project risks become real, it is likely that the project schedule will slip and that costs will increase. Project risks identify potential budgetary, schedule, personnel (staffing and organization), resource, stakeholder, and requirements problems and their impact on a software project. In Chapter 26, project complexity, size, and the degree of structural uncertainty were also defined as project (and estimation) risk factors.

Technical risks threaten the quality and timeliness of the software to be produced. If a technical risk becomes a reality, implementation may become difficult or impossible. Technical risks identify potential design, implementation, interface, verification, and maintenance problems. In addition, specification ambiguity, technical uncertainty, technical obsolescence, and "leading-edge" technology are also risk factors. Technical risks occur because the problem is harder to solve than you thought it would be.

Business risks threaten the viability of the software to be built and often jeopardize the project or the product. Candidates for the top five business risks are (1) building an excellent product or system that no one really wants (market risk), (2) building a product that no longer fits into the overall business strategy for the company (strategic risk), (3) building a product that the sales force doesn't understand how to sell (sales risk), (4) losing the support of senior management due to a change in focus or a change in people (management risk), and (5) losing budgetary or personnel commitment (budget risks).

It is extremely important to note that simple risk categorization won't always work. Some risks are simply unpredictable in advance.

Another general categorization of risks has been proposed by Charette [Cha89]. *Known risks* are those that can be uncovered after careful evaluation of the project plan, the business and technical environment in which the project is being developed, and other reliable information sources (e.g., unrealistic delivery date, lack of documented requirements or software scope, poor development environment). *Predictable risks* are extrapolated from past project experience (e.g., staff turnover, poor communication with the customer, dilution of staff effort as ongoing maintenance requests are serviced). *Unpredictable risks* are the joker in the deck. They can and do occur, but they are extremely difficult to identify in advance.

What types of risks are you likely to encounter as software is built?

Quote:

"Projects with no real risks are losers. They are almost always devoid of benefit; that's why they weren't done years ago."

Tom DeMarco and Tim Lister

---

1   A risk that is 100 percent probable is a constraint on the software project.

Seven Principles of Risk Management

The Software Engineering Institute (SEI) (**www.sei.cmu.edu**) identifies seven principles that "provide a framework to accomplish effective risk management." They are:

Maintain a global perspective—view software risks within the context of a system in which it is a component and the business problem that it is intended to solve

Take a forward-looking view—think about the risks that may arise in the future (e.g., due to changes in the software); establish contingency plans so that future events are manageable.

Encourage open communication—if someone states a potential risk, don't discount it. If a risk is proposed in an informal manner, consider it. Encourage all stakeholders and users to suggest risks at any time.

Integrate—a consideration of risk must be integrated into the software process.

Emphasize a continuous process—the team must be vigilant throughout the software process, modifying identified risks as more information is known and adding new ones as better insight is achieved.

Develop a shared product vision—if all stakeholders share the same vision of the software, it is likely that better risk identification and assessment will occur.

Encourage teamwork—the talents, skills, and knowledge of all stakeholders should be pooled when risk management activities are conducted.

28.3   RISK IDENTIFICATION

Risk identification is a systematic attempt to specify threats to the project plan (estimates, schedule, resource loading, etc.). By identifying known and predictable risks, the project manager takes a first step toward avoiding them when possible and controlling them when necessary.

Although generic risks are important to consider, it's the product-specific risks that cause the most headaches. Be certain to spend the time to identify as many product-specific risks as possible.

There are two distinct types of risks for each of the categories that have been presented in Section 28.2: generic risks and product-specific risks. *Generic risks* are a potential threat to every software project. *Product-specific risks* can be identified only by those with a clear understanding of the technology, the people, and the environment that is specific to the software that is to be built. To identify product-specific risks, the project plan and the software statement of scope are examined, and an answer to the following question is developed: "What special characteristics of this product may threaten our project plan?"

One method for identifying risks is to create a risk item checklist. The checklist can be used for risk identification and focuses on some subset of known and predictable risks in the following generic subcategories:

- *Product size*—risks associated with the overall size of the software to be built or modified.

- *Business impact*—risks associated with constraints imposed by management or the marketplace.

- *Stakeholder characteristics*—risks associated with the sophistication of the stakeholders and the developer's ability to communicate with stakeholders in a timely manner.

- *Process definition*—risks associated with the degree to which the software process has been defined and is followed by the development organization.

- *Development environment*—risks associated with the availability and quality of the tools to be used to build the product.

- *Technology to be built*—risks associated with the complexity of the system to be built and the "newness" of the technology that is packaged by the system.

- *Staff size and experience*—risks associated with the overall technical and project experience of the software engineers who will do the work.

The risk item checklist can be organized in different ways. Questions relevant to each of the topics can be answered for each software project. The answers to these questions allow you to estimate the impact of risk. A different risk item checklist format simply lists characteristics that are relevant to each generic subcategory. Finally, a set of "risk components and drivers" [AFC88] are listed along with their probability of occurrence. Drivers for performance, support, cost, and schedule are discussed in answer to later questions.

A number of comprehensive checklists for software project risk are available on the Web (e.g., [Baa07], [NAS07], [Wor04]). You can use these checklists to gain insight into generic risks for software projects.

28.3.1 Assessing Overall Project Risk

The following questions have been derived from risk data obtained by surveying experienced software project managers in different parts of the world [Kei98]. The questions are ordered by their relative importance to the success of a project.

Is the software project we're working on at serious risk?

1. Have top software and customer managers formally committed to support the project?

2. Are end users enthusiastically committed to the project and the system/product to be built?

3. Are requirements fully understood by the software engineering team and its customers?

4. Have customers been involved fully in the definition of requirements?

5. Do end users have realistic expectations?

6. Is the project scope stable?

7. Does the software engineering team have the right mix of skills?

8. Are project requirements stable?

9. Does the project team have experience with the technology to be implemented?

10. Is the number of people on the project team adequate to do the job?

11. Do all customer/user constituencies agree on the importance of the project and on the requirements for the system/product to be built?

If any one of these questions is answered negatively, mitigation, monitoring, and management steps should be instituted without fail. The degree to which the project is at risk is directly proportional to the number of negative responses to these questions.

28.3.2   Risk Components and Drivers

The U.S. Air Force [AFC88] has published a pamphlet that contains excellent guidelines for software risk identification and abatement. The Air Force approach requires that the project manager identify the risk drivers that affect software risk components—performance, cost, support, and schedule. In the context of this discussion, the risk components are defined in the following manner:

uote:

"Risk management is project management for adults."

Tim Lister

- *Performance risk*—the degree of uncertainty that the product will meet its requirements and be fit for its intended use.

- *Cost risk*—the degree of uncertainty that the project budget will be maintained.

- *Support risk*—the degree of uncertainty that the resultant software will be easy to correct, adapt, and enhance.

- *Schedule risk*—the degree of uncertainty that the project schedule will be maintained and that the product will be delivered on time.

The impact of each risk driver on the risk component is divided into one of four impact categories—negligible, marginal, critical, or catastrophic. Referring to Figure 28.1 [Boe89], a characterization of the potential consequences of errors (rows labeled 1) or a failure to achieve a desired outcome (rows labeled 2) are described. The impact category is chosen based on the characterization that best fits the description in the table.

28.4   RISK PROJECTION

Risk projection, also called *risk estimation,* attempts to rate each risk in two ways—(1) the likelihood or probability that the risk is real and (2) the consequences of the problems associated with the risk, should it occur. You work along with other managers and technical staff to perform four risk projection steps:

1. Establish a scale that reflects the perceived likelihood of a risk.

2. Delineate the consequences of the risk.

3. Estimate the impact of the risk on the project and the product.

4. Assess the overall accuracy of the risk projection so that there will be no misunderstandings.

FIGURE 28.1

Impact
assessment.
Source: [Boe89].

Components / Category		Performance	Support	Cost	Schedule
Catastrophic	1	Failure to meet the requirement would result in mission failure		Failure results in increased costs and schedule delays with expected values in excess of $500K	
	2	Significant degradation to nonachievement of technical performance	Nonresponsive or unsupportable software	Significant financial shortages, budget overrun likely	Unachievable IOC
Critical	1	Failure to meet the requirement would degrade system performance to a point where mission success is questionable		Failure results in operational delays and/or increased costs with expected value of $100K to $500K	
	2	Some reduction in technical performance	Minor delays in software modifications	Some shortage of financial resources, possible overruns	Possible slippage in IOC
Marginal	1	Failure to meet the requirement would result in degradation of secondary mission		Costs, impacts, and/or recoverable schedule slips with expected value of $1K to $100K	
	2	Minimal to small reduction in technical performance	Responsive software support	Sufficient financial resources	Realistic, achievable schedule
Negligible	1	Failure to meet the requirement would create inconvenience or nonoperational impact		Error results in minor cost and/or schedule impact with expected value of less than $1K	
	2	No reduction in technical performance	Easily supportable software	Possible budget underrun	Early achievable IOC

Note: (1) The potential consequence of undetected software errors or faults.
         (2) The potential consequence if the desired outcome is not achieved.

The intent of these steps is to consider risks in a manner that leads to prioritization. No software team has the resources to address every possible risk with the same degree of rigor. By prioritizing risks, you can allocate resources where they will have the most impact.

Think hard about the software you're about to build and ask yourself, "what can go wrong?" Create your own list and ask other members of the team to do the same.

28.4.1   Developing a Risk Table

A risk table provides you with a simple technique for risk projection.[2] A sample risk table is illustrated in Figure 28.2.

You begin by listing all risks (no matter how remote) in the first column of the table. This can be accomplished with the help of the risk item checklists referenced in Section 28.3. Each risk is categorized in the second column (e.g., PS implies a

---

2   The risk table can be implemented as a spreadsheet model. This enables easy manipulation and sorting of the entries.

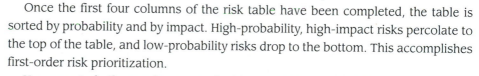

FIGURE 28.2

Sample risk table prior to sorting

Risks	Category	Probability	Impact	RMMM
Size estimate may be significantly low	PS	60%	2	
Larger number of users than planned	PS	30%	3	
Less reuse than planned	PS	70%	2	
End-users resist system	BU	40%	3	
Delivery deadline will be tightened	BU	50%	2	
Funding will be lost	CU	40%	1	
Customer will change requirements	PS	80%	2	
Technology will not meet expectations	TE	30%	1	
Lack of training on tools	DE	80%	3	
Staff inexperienced	ST	30%	2	
Staff turnover will be high	ST	60%	2	
Σ				
Σ				
Σ				

Impact values:
   1—catastrophic
   2—critical
   3—marginal
   4—negligible

project size risk, BU implies a business risk). The probability of occurrence of each risk is entered in the next column of the table. The probability value for each risk can be estimated by team members individually. One way to accomplish this is to poll individual team members in round-robin fashion until their collective assessment of risk probability begins to converge.

Next, the impact of each risk is assessed. Each risk component is assessed using the characterization presented in Figure 28.1, and an impact category is determined. The categories for each of the four risk components—performance, support, cost, and schedule—are averaged[3] to determine an overall impact value.

KEY POINT

A risk table is sorted by probability and impact to rank risks.

Once the first four columns of the risk table have been completed, the table is sorted by probability and by impact. High-probability, high-impact risks percolate to the top of the table, and low-probability risks drop to the bottom. This accomplishes first-order risk prioritization.

You can study the resultant sorted table and define a cutoff line. The *cutoff line* (drawn horizontally at some point in the table) implies that only risks that lie above the line will be given further attention. Risks that fall below the line are reevaluated to accomplish second-order prioritization. Referring to Figure 28.3, risk impact and

---

3 A weighted average can be used if one risk component has more significance for a project.

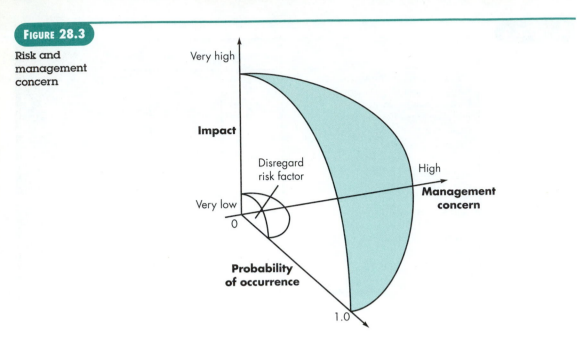

probability have a distinct influence on management concern. A risk factor that has a high impact but a very low probability of occurrence should not absorb a significant amount of management time. However, high-impact risks with moderate to high probability and low-impact risks with high probability should be carried forward into the risk analysis steps that follow.

All risks that lie above the cutoff line should be managed. The column labeled RMMM contains a pointer into a *risk mitigation, monitoring, and management plan* or, alternatively, a collection of risk information sheets developed for all risks that lie above the cutoff. The RMMM plan and risk information sheets are discussed in Sections 28.5 and 28.6.

Risk probability can be determined by making individual estimates and then developing a single consensus value. Although that approach is workable, more sophisticated techniques for determining risk probability have been developed [AFC88]. Risk drivers can be assessed on a qualitative probability scale that has the following values: impossible, improbable, probable, and frequent. Mathematical probability can then be associated with each qualitative value (e.g., a probability of 0.7 to 0.99 implies a highly probable risk).

28.4.2   Assessing Risk Impact

Three factors affect the consequences that are likely if a risk does occur: its nature, its scope, and its timing. The nature of the risk indicates the problems that are likely if it occurs. For example, a poorly defined external interface to customer hardware (a technical risk) will preclude early design and testing and will likely lead to system integration problems late in a project. The scope of a risk combines the severity (just how serious is it?) with its overall distribution (how much of the project will be affected or how many stakeholders are harmed?). Finally, the timing of a risk considers when and for how long the impact will be felt. In most cases, you want the "bad news" to occur as soon as possible, but in some cases, the longer the delay, the better.

? How do we assess the consequences of a risk?

Returning once more to the risk analysis approach proposed by the U.S. Air Force [AFC88], you can apply the following steps to determine the overall consequences of a risk: (1) determine the average probability of occurrence value for each risk component; (2) using Figure 28.1, determine the impact for each component based on the criteria shown, and (3) complete the risk table and analyze the results as described in the preceding sections.

The overall *risk exposure* RE is determined using the following relationship [Hal98]:

$$\text{RE} = P \times C$$

where P is the probability of occurrence for a risk, and C is the cost to the project should the risk occur.

For example, assume that the software team defines a project risk in the following manner:

Risk identification. Only 70 percent of the software components scheduled for reuse will, in fact, be integrated into the application. The remaining functionality will have to be custom developed.

Risk probability. 80 percent (likely).

Risk impact. Sixty reusable software components were planned. If only 70 percent can be used, 18 components would have to be developed from scratch (in addition to other custom software that has been scheduled for development). Since the average component is 100 LOC and local data indicate that the software engineering cost for each LOC is $14.00, the overall cost (impact) to develop the components would be $18 \times 100 \times 14 = \$25,200$.

Risk exposure. RE = 0.80 × 25,200 ~ $20,200.

Compare RE for all risks to the cost estimate for the project. If RE is greater than 50 percent of the project cost, the viability of the project must be evaluated.

Risk exposure can be computed for each risk in the risk table, once an estimate of the cost of the risk is made. The total risk exposure for all risks (above the cutoff in the risk table) can provide a means for adjusting the final cost estimate for a project. It can also be used to predict the probable increase in staff resources required at various points during the project schedule.

The risk projection and analysis techniques described in Sections 28.4.1 and 28.4.2 are applied iteratively as the software project proceeds. The project team should revisit the risk table at regular intervals, reevaluating each risk to determine when new circumstances cause its probability and impact to change. As a consequence of this activity, it may be necessary to add new risks to the table, remove some risks that are no longer relevant, and change the relative positions of still others.

SAFEHOME

Risk Analysis

The scene: Doug Miller's office prior to the initiation of the *SafeHome* software project.

The players: Doug Miller (manager of the *SafeHome* software engineering team) and Vinod Raman, Jamie Lazar, and other members of the product software engineering team.

The conversation:

Doug: I'd like to spend some time brainstorming risks for the *SafeHome* project.

Jamie: As in what can go wrong?

Doug: Yep. Here are a few categories where things can go wrong. [He shows everyone the categories noted in the introduction to Section 28.3.]

Vinod: Umm . . . do you want us to just call them out, or . . .

Doug: No here's what I thought we'd do. Everyone make a list of risks . . . right now . . ."

[Ten minutes pass, everyone is writing.]

Doug: Okay, stop.

Jamie: But I'm not done!

Doug: That's okay. We'll revisit the list again. Now, for each item on your list, assign a percent likelihood that the risk will occur. Then, assign an impact to the project on a scale of 1 (minor) to 5 (catastrophic).

Vinod: So if I think that the risk is a coin flip, I specify a 50 percent likelihood, and if I think it'll have a moderate project impact, I specify a 3, right?

Doug: Exactly.

[Five minutes pass, everyone is writing.]

Doug: Okay, stop. Now we'll make a group list on the white board. I'll do the writing; we'll call out one entry from your list in round-robin format.

[Fifteen minutes pass; the list is created.]

Jamie (pointing at the board and laughing): Vinod, that risk (pointing toward an entry on the board) is ridiculous. There's a higher likelihood that we'll all get hit by lightning. We should remove it.

Doug: No, let's leave it for now. We consider all risks, no matter how weird. Later we'll winnow the list.

Jamie: But we already have over 40 risks . . . how on earth can we manage them all?

Doug: We can't. That's why we'll define a cut-off after we sort these guys. I'll do that off-line and we'll meet again tomorrow. For now, get back to work . . . and in your spare time, think about any risks that we've missed.

28.5   RISK REFINEMENT

During early stages of project planning, a risk may be stated quite generally. As time passes and more is learned about the project and the risk, it may be possible to refine the risk into a set of more detailed risks, each somewhat easier to mitigate, monitor, and manage.

? **What's a good way to describe a risk?**

One way to do this is to represent the risk in *condition-transition-consequence* (CTC) format [Glu94]. That is, the risk is stated in the following form:

Given that <condition> then there is concern that (possibly) <consequence>.

Using the CTC format for the reuse risk noted in Section 28.4.2, you could write:

> Given that all reusable software components must conform to specific design standards and that some do not conform, then there is concern that (possibly) only 70 percent of the planned reusable modules may actually be integrated into the as-built system, resulting in the need to custom engineer the remaining 30 percent of components.

This general condition can be refined in the following manner:

> **Subcondition 1.** Certain reusable components were developed by a third party with no knowledge of internal design standards.
>
> **Subcondition 2.** The design standard for component interfaces has not been solidified and may not conform to certain existing reusable components.
>
> **Subcondition 3.** Certain reusable components have been implemented in a language that is not supported on the target environment.

The consequences associated with these refined subconditions remain the same (i.e., 30 percent of software components must be custom engineered), but the refinement helps to isolate the underlying risks and might lead to easier analysis and response.

28.6   RISK MITIGATION, MONITORING, AND MANAGEMENT

All of the risk analysis activities presented to this point have a single goal—to assist the project team in developing a strategy for dealing with risk. An effective strategy must consider three issues: risk avoidance, risk monitoring, and risk management and contingency planning.

If a software team adopts a proactive approach to risk, avoidance is always the best strategy. This is achieved by developing a plan for *risk mitigation.* For example, assume that high staff turnover is noted as a project risk r_1. Based on past history and management intuition, the likelihood l_1 of high turnover is estimated to be 0.70 (70 percent, rather high) and the impact x_1 is projected as critical. That is, high turnover will have a critical impact on project cost and schedule.

To mitigate this risk, you would develop a strategy for reducing turnover. Among the possible steps to be taken are:

What can we do to mitigate a risk?

- Meet with current staff to determine causes for turnover (e.g., poor working conditions, low pay, competitive job market).
- Mitigate those causes that are under your control before the project starts.
- Once the project commences, assume turnover will occur and develop techniques to ensure continuity when people leave.
- Organize project teams so that information about each development activity is widely dispersed.

- Define work product standards and establish mechanisms to be sure that all models and documents are developed in a timely manner.
- Conduct peer reviews of all work (so that more than one person is "up to speed").
- Assign a backup staff member for every critical technologist.

As the project proceeds, *risk-monitoring* activities commence. The project manager monitors factors that may provide an indication of whether the risk is becoming more or less likely. In the case of high staff turnover, the general attitude of team members based on project pressures, the degree to which the team has jelled, interpersonal relationships among team members, potential problems with compensation and benefits, and the availability of jobs within the company and outside it are all monitored.

In addition to monitoring these factors, a project manager should monitor the effectiveness of risk mitigation steps. For example, a risk mitigation step noted here called for the definition of work product standards and mechanisms to be sure that work products are developed in a timely manner. This is one mechanism for ensuring continuity, should a critical individual leave the project. The project manager should monitor work products carefully to ensure that each can stand on its own and that each imparts information that would be necessary if a newcomer were forced to join the software team somewhere in the middle of the project.

Risk management and contingency planning assumes that mitigation efforts have failed and that the risk has become a reality. Continuing the example, the project is well under way and a number of people announce that they will be leaving. If the mitigation strategy has been followed, backup is available, information is documented, and knowledge has been dispersed across the team. In addition, you can temporarily refocus resources (and readjust the project schedule) to those functions that are fully staffed, enabling newcomers who must be added to the team to "get up to speed." Those individuals who are leaving are asked to stop all work and spend their last weeks in "knowledge transfer mode." This might include video-based knowledge capture, the development of "commentary documents or Wikis," and/or meeting with other team members who will remain on the project.

If RE for a specific risk is less than the cost of risk mitigation, don't try to mitigate the risk but continue to monitor it.

It is important to note that risk mitigation, monitoring, and management (RMMM) steps incur additional project cost. For example, spending the time to back up every critical technologist costs money. Part of risk management, therefore, is to evaluate when the benefits accrued by the RMMM steps are outweighed by the costs associated with implementing them. In essence, you perform a classic cost-benefit analysis. If risk aversion steps for high turnover will increase both project cost and duration by an estimated 15 percent, but the predominant cost factor is "backup," management may decide not to implement this step. On the other hand, if the risk aversion steps are projected to increase costs by 5 percent and duration by only 3 percent, management will likely put all into place.

For a large project, 30 or 40 risks may be identified. If between three and seven risk management steps are identified for each, risk management may become a project in itself! For this reason, you should adapt the Pareto 80–20 rule to software risk. Experience indicates that 80 percent of the overall project risk (i.e., 80 percent of the potential for project failure) can be accounted for by only 20 percent of the identified risks. The work performed during earlier risk analysis steps will help you to determine which of the risks reside in that 20 percent (e.g., risks that lead to the highest risk exposure). For this reason, some of the risks identified, assessed, and projected may not make it into the RMMM plan—they don't fall into the critical 20 percent (the risks with highest project priority).

Risk is not limited to the software project itself. Risks can occur after the software has been successfully developed and delivered to the customer. These risks are typically associated with the consequences of software failure in the field.

Software safety and hazard analysis (e.g., [Dun02], [Her00], [Lev95]) are software quality assurance activities (Chapter 16) that focus on the identification and assessment of potential hazards that may affect software negatively and cause an entire system to fail. If hazards can be identified early in the software engineering process, software design features can be specified that will either eliminate or control potential hazards.

28.7 THE RMMM PLAN

A risk management strategy can be included in the software project plan, or the risk management steps can be organized into a separate *risk mitigation, monitoring, and management plan* (RMMM). The RMMM plan documents all work performed as part of risk analysis and is used by the project manager as part of the overall project plan.

Some software teams do not develop a formal RMMM document. Rather, each risk is documented individually using a *risk information sheet* (RIS) [Wil97]. In most cases, the RIS is maintained using a database system so that creation and information entry, priority ordering, searches, and other analysis may be accomplished easily. The format of the RIS is illustrated in Figure 28.4.

Once RMMM has been documented and the project has begun, risk mitigation and monitoring steps commence. As I have already discussed, risk mitigation is a problem avoidance activity. Risk monitoring is a project tracking activity with three primary objectives: (1) to assess whether predicted risks do, in fact, occur; (2) to ensure that risk aversion steps defined for the risk are being properly applied; and (3) to collect information that can be used for future risk analysis. In many cases, the problems that occur during a project can be traced to more than one risk. Another job of risk monitoring is to attempt to allocate origin [what risk(s) caused which problems throughout the project].

FIGURE 28.4

Risk informa-
tion sheet.
Source: [Wil97].

Risk information sheet			
Risk ID: P02-4-32	Date: 5/9/09	Prob: 80%	Impact: high

Description:
Only 70 percent of the software components scheduled for reuse will, in fact, be integrated into the application. The remaining functionality will have to be custom developed.

Refinement/context:
Subcondition 1: Certain reusable components were developed by a third party with no knowledge of internal design standards.
Subcondition 2: The design standard for component interfaces has not been solidified and may not conform to certain existing reusable components.
Subcondition 3: Certain reusable components have been implemented in a language that is not supported on the target environment.

Mitigation/monitoring:
1. Contact third party to determine conformance with design standards.
2. Press for interface standards completion; consider component structure when deciding on interface protocol.
3. Check to determine number of components in subcondition 3 category; check to determine if language support can be acquired.

Management/contingency plan/trigger:
RE computed to be $20,200. Allocate this amount within project contingency cost. Develop revised schedule assuming that 18 additional components will have to be custom built; allocate staff accordingly.
Trigger: Mitigation steps unproductive as of 7/1/09.

Current status:
5/12/09: Mitigation steps initiated.

Originator: D. Gagne	Assigned: B. Laster

SOFTWARE TOOLS

Risk Management

Objective: The objective of risk management tools is to assist a project team in defining risks, assessing their impact and probability, and tracking risks throughout a software project.

Mechanics: In general, risk management tools assist in generic risk identification by providing a list of typical project and business risks, provide checklists or other "interview" techniques that assist in identifying project specific risks, assign probability and impact to each risk, support risk mitigation strategies, and generate many different risk-related reports.

Representative Tools:[4]

@*risk,* developed by Palisade Corporation (**www .palisade.com**), is a generic risk analysis tool that uses Monte Carlo simulation to drive its analytical engine.

Riskman, distributed by ABS Consulting (**www.absconsulting.com/riskmansoftware/ index.html**), is a risk evaluation expert system that identifies project-related risks.

Risk Radar, developed by SPMN (**www.spmn.com**), assists project managers in identifying and managing project risks.

---

4 Tools noted here do not represent an endorsement, but rather a sampling of tools in this category. In most cases, tool names are trademarked by their respective developers.

Risk+, developed by Deltek (**www.deltek.com**), integrates with Microsoft Project to quantify cost and schedule uncertainty.

X:PRIMER, developed by GrafP Technologies (**www.grafp.com**) is a generic Web-based tool that

predicts what can go wrong on a project and identifies root causes for potential failures and effective countermeasures.

28.8 SUMMARY

Whenever a lot is riding on a software project, common sense dictates risk analysis. And yet, most software project managers do it informally and superficially, if they do it at all. The time spent identifying, analyzing, and managing risk pays itself back in many ways—less upheaval during the project, a greater ability to track and control a project, and the confidence that comes with planning for problems before they occur.

Risk analysis can absorb a significant amount of project planning effort. Identification, projection, assessment, management, and monitoring all take time. But the effort is worth it. To quote Sun Tzu, a Chinese general who lived 2500 years ago, "If you know the enemy and know yourself, you need not fear the result of a hundred battles." For the software project manager, the enemy is risk.

PROBLEMS AND POINTS TO PONDER

28.1. Provide five examples from other fields that illustrate the problems associated with a reactive risk strategy.

28.2. Describe the difference between "known risks" and "predictable risks."

28.3. Add three additional questions or topics to each of the risk item checklists presented at the SEPA website.

28.4. You've been asked to build software to support a low-cost video editing system. The system accepts digital video as input, stores the video on disk, and then allows the user to do a wide range of edits to the digitized video. The result can then be output to DVD or other media. Do a small amount of research on systems of this type and then make a list of technology risks that you would face as you begin a project of this type.

28.5. You're the project manager for a major software company. You've been asked to lead a team that's developing "next generation" word-processing software. Create a risk table for the project.

28.6. Describe the difference between risk components and risk drivers.

28.7. Develop a risk mitigation strategy and specific risk mitigation activities for three of the risks noted in Figure 28.2.

28.8. Develop a risk monitoring strategy and specific risk monitoring activities for three of the risks noted in Figure 28.2. Be sure to identify the factors that you'll be monitoring to determine whether the risk is becoming more or less likely.

28.9. Develop a risk management strategy and specific risk management activities for three of the risks noted in Figure 28.2.

28.10. Attempt to refine three of the risks noted in Figure 28.2, and then create risk information sheets for each.

28.11. Represent three of the risks noted in Figure 28.2 using a CTC format.

28.12. Recompute the risk exposure discussed in Section 28.4.2 when cost/LOC is $16 and the probability is 60 percent.

28.13. Can you think of a situation in which a high-probability, high-impact risk would not be considered as part of your RMMM plan?

28.14. Describe five software application areas in which software safety and hazard analysis would be a major concern.

FURTHER READINGS AND INFORMATION SOURCES

The software risk management literature has expanded significantly over the past few decades. Vun (*Modeling Risk,* Wiley, 2006) presents a detailed mathematical treatment of risk analysis that can be applied to software projects. Crohy and his colleagues (*The Essentials of Risk Management,* McGraw-Hill, 2006), Mulcahy (*Risk Management, Tricks of the Trade for Project Managers,* RMC Publications, Inc., 2003), Kendrick (*Identifying and Managing Project Risk,* American Management Association, 2003), and Marrison (*The Fundamentals of Risk Measurement,* McGraw-Hill, 2002) present useful methods and tools that every project manager can use.

DeMarco and Lister (*Dancing with Bears,* Dorset House, 2003) have written an entertaining and insightful book that guides software managers and practitioners through risk management. Moynihan (*Coping with IT/IS Risk Management,* Springer-Verlag, 2002) presents pragmatic advice from project managers who deal with risk on a continuing basis. Royer (*Project Risk Management,* Management Concepts, 2002) and Smith and Merritt (*Proactive Risk Management,* Productivity Press, 2002) suggest a proactive process for risk management. Karolak (*Software Engineering Risk Management,* Wiley, 2002) has written a guidebook that introduces an easy-to-use risk analysis model with worthwhile checklists and questionnaires supported by a software package.

Capers Jones (*Assessment and Control of Software Risks,* Prentice Hall, 1994) presents a detailed discussion of software risks that includes data collected from hundreds of software projects. Jones defines 60 risk factors that can affect the outcome of software projects. Boehm [Boe89] suggests excellent questionnaire and checklist formats that can prove invaluable in identifying risk. Charette [Cha89] presents a detailed treatment of the mechanics of risk analysis, calling on probability theory and statistical techniques to analyze risks. In a companion volume, Charette (*Application Strategies for Risk Analysis,* McGraw-Hill, 1990) discusses risk in the context of both system and software engineering and suggests pragmatic strategies for risk management. Gilb (*Principles of Software Engineering Management,* Addison-Wesley, 1988) presents a set of "principles" (which are often amusing and sometimes profound) that can serve as a worthwhile guide for risk management.

Ewusi-Mensah (*Software Development Failures: Anatomy of Abandoned Projects,* MIT Press, 2003) and Yourdon (*Death March,* Prentice Hall, 1997) discuss what happens when risks overwhelm a software project team. Bernstein (*Against the Gods,* Wiley, 1998) presents an entertaining history of risk that goes back to ancient times.

The Software Engineering Institute has published many detailed reports and guidebooks on risk analysis and management. The Air Force Systems Command pamphlet AFSCP 800-45 [AFC88] describes risk identification and reduction techniques. Every issue of the *ACM Software Engineering Notes* has a section entitled "Risks to the Public" (editor, P. G. Neumann). If you want the latest and best software horror stories, this is the place to go.

A wide variety of information sources on software risk management is available on the Internet. An up-to-date list of World Wide Web references relevant to risk management can be found at the SEPA website: **www.mhhe.com/engcs/compsci/pressman/professional/olc/ser.htm**.

MAINTENANCE AND REENGINEERING

Regardless of its application domain, its size, or its complexity, computer software will evolve over time. Change drives this process. For computer software, change occurs when errors are corrected, when the software is adapted to a new environment, when the customer requests new features or functions, and when the application is reengineered to provide benefit in a modern context. Over the past 30 years, Manny Lehman [e.g., Leh97a] and his colleagues have performed detailed analyses of industry-grade software and

---

QUICK LOOK

What is it? Consider any technology product that has served you well. You use it regularly, but it's getting old. It breaks too often, takes longer to repair than you'd like, and no longer represents the newest technology. What to do? For a time, you try to fix it, patch it, even extend its functionality. That's called maintenance. But maintenance becomes increasingly difficult as the years pass. There comes a time when you'll need to rebuild it. You'll create a product with added functionality, better performance and reliability, and improved maintainability. That's what we call reengineering.

Who does it? At an organizational level, maintenance is performed by support staff that are part of the software engineering organization. Reengineering is performed by business specialists (often consulting companies), and at the software level, reengineering is performed by software engineers.

Why is it important? We live in a rapidly changing world. The demands on business functions and the information technology that supports them are changing at a pace that puts enormous competitive pressure on every commercial organization. That's why software must be maintained continually, and at the appropriate time, reengineered to keep pace.

What are the steps? Maintenance corrects defects, adapts the software to meet a changing environment, and enhances functionality to meet the evolving needs of customers. At a strategic level, business process reengineering (BPR) defines business goals, identifies and evaluates existing business processes, and creates revised business processes that better meet current goals. Software reengineering encompasses inventory analysis, document restructuring, reverse engineering, program and data restructuring, and forward engineering. The intent of these activities is to create versions of existing programs that exhibit higher quality and better maintainability.

What is the work product? A variety of maintenance and reengineering work products (e.g., use cases, analysis and design models, test procedures) are produced. The final output is upgraded software.

How do I ensure that I've done it right? Use the same SQA practices that are applied in every software engineering process—technical reviews assess the analysis and design models; specialized reviews consider business applicability and compatibility; and testing is applied to uncover errors in content, functionality, and interoperability.

? How do
legacy
systems evolve as
time passes?

systems in an effort to develop a *unified theory for software evolution*. The details of this work are beyond the scope of this book, but the underlying laws that have been derived are worthy of note [Leh97b]:

The Law of Continuing Change (1974): Software that has been implemented in a real-world computing context and will therefore evolve over time (called *E-type systems*) must be continually adapted else they become progressively less satisfactory.

The Law of Increasing Complexity (1974): As an E-type system evolves its complexity increases unless work is done to maintain or reduce it.

The Law of Self Regulation (1974): The E-type system evolution process is self-regulating with distribution of product and process measures close to normal.

The Law of Conservation of Organizational Stability (1980): The average effective global activity rate in an evolving E-type system is invariant over product lifetime.

The Law of Conservation of Familiarity (1980): As an E-type system evolves all associated with it, developers, sales personnel, users, for example, must maintain mastery of its content and behavior to achieve satisfactory evolution. Excessive growth diminishes that mastery. Hence the average incremental growth remains invariant as the system evolves.

The Law of Continuing Growth (1980): The functional content of E-type systems must be continually increased to maintain user satisfaction over their lifetime.

The Law of Declining Quality (1996): The quality of E-type systems will appear to be declining unless they are rigorously maintained and adapted to operational environment changes.

The Feedback System Law (1996): E-type evolution processes constitute multi-level, multi-loop, multi-agent feedback systems and must be treated as such to achieve significant improvement over any reasonable base.

The laws that Lehman and his colleagues have defined are an inherent part of a software engineer's reality. In this chapter, I'll discuss the challenge of software maintenance and the reengineering activities that are required to extend the effective life of legacy systems.

29.1 SOFTWARE MAINTENANCE

It begins almost immediately. Software is released to end users, and within days, bug reports filter back to the software engineering organization. Within weeks, one class of users indicates that the software must be changed so that it can accommodate the special needs of their environment. And within months, another corporate group who wanted nothing to do with the software when it was released now recognizes that it may provide them with unexpected benefit. They'll need a few enhancements to make it work in their world.

The challenge of software maintenance has begun. You're faced with a growing queue of bug fixes, adaptation requests, and outright enhancements that must be planned, scheduled, and ultimately accomplished. Before long, the queue has grown long and the work it implies threatens to overwhelm the available resources. As time passes, your organization finds that it's spending more money and time maintaining existing programs than it is engineering new applications. In fact, it's not unusual for a software organization to expend as much as 60 to 70 percent of all resources on software maintenance.

You may ask why so much maintenance is required and why so much effort is expended. Osborne and Chikofsky [Osb90] provide a partial answer:

> Much of the software we depend on today is on average 10 to 15 years old. Even when these programs were created using the best design and coding techniques known at the time [and most were not], they were created when program size and storage space were principle concerns. They were then migrated to new platforms, adjusted for changes in machine and operating system technology and enhanced to meet new user needs—all without enough regard to overall architecture. The result is the poorly designed structures, poor coding, poor logic, and poor documentation of the software systems we are now called on to keep running . . .

Another reason for the software maintenance problem is the mobility of software people. It is likely that the software team (or person) that did the original work is no longer around. Worse, other generations of software people have modified the system and moved on. And today, there may be no one left who has any direct knowledge of the legacy system.

As I noted in Chapter 22, the ubiquitous nature of change underlies all software work. Change is inevitable when computer-based systems are built; therefore, you must develop mechanisms for evaluating, controlling, and making modifications.

Throughout this book, I've emphasized the importance of understanding the problem (analysis) and developing a well-structured solution (design). In fact, Part 2 of the book is dedicated to the mechanics of these software engineering actions, and Part 3 focuses on the techniques required to be sure you've done them correctly. Both analysis and design lead to an important software characteristic that we call maintainability. In essence, *maintainability* is a qualitative indication[1] of the ease with which existing software can be corrected, adapted, or enhanced. Much of what software engineering is about is building systems that exhibit high maintainability.

But what is maintainability? Maintainable software exhibits effective modularity (Chapter 8). It makes use of design patterns (Chapter 12) that allow ease of understanding. It has been constructed using well-defined coding standards and conventions, leading to source code that is self-documenting and understandable. It has undergone a variety of quality assurance techniques (Part 3 of this book) that have uncovered potential maintenance problems before the software is released. It has been created by software engineers who recognize that they may not be around

uote:

"Program maintainability and program understandability are parallel concepts: the more difficult a program is to understand, the more difficult it is to maintain.

Gerald Berns

---

1   There are some quantitative measures that provide an indirect indication of maintainability (e.g., [Sch99], [SEI02]).

when changes must be made. Therefore, the design and implementation of the software must "assist" the person who is making the change.

29.2   SOFTWARE SUPPORTABILITY

In order to effectively support industry-grade software, your organization (or its designee) must be capable of making the corrections, adaptations, and enhancements that are part of the maintenance activity. But in addition, the organization must provide other important support activities that include ongoing operational support, end-user support, and reengineering activities over the complete life cycle of the software. A reasonable definition of *software supportability* is

> . . . the capability of supporting a software system over its whole product life. This implies satisfying any necessary needs or requirements, but also the provision of equipment, support infrastructure, additional software, facilities, manpower, or any other resource required to maintain the software operational and capable of satisfying its function [SSO08].

In essence, supportability is one of many quality factors that should be considered during the analysis and design actions that are part of the software process. It should be addressed as part of the requirements model (or specification) and considered as the design evolves and construction commences.

WebRef

A wide array of downloadable documents on software supportability can be found at **www.software-supportability.org/ Downloads.html**.

For example, the need to "antibug" software at the component and code level has been discussed earlier in the book. The software should contain facilities to assist support personnel when a defect is encountered in the operational environment (and make no mistake, defects *will* be encountered). In addition, support personnel should have access to a database that contains records of all defects that have already been encountered—their characteristics, cause, and cure. This will enable support personnel to examine "similar" defects and may provide a means for more rapid diagnosis and correction.

Although defects encountered in an application are a critical support issue, supportability also demands that resources be provided to support day-to-day end-user issues. The job of end-user support personnel is to answer user queries about the installation, operation, and use of the application.

29.3   REENGINEERING

In a seminal article written for the *Harvard Business Review,* Michael Hammer [Ham90] laid the foundation for a revolution in management thinking about business processes and computing:

> It is time to stop paving the cow paths. Instead of embedding outdated processes in silicon and software, we should obliterate them and start over. We should "reengineer" our businesses: use the power of modern information technology to radically redesign our business processes in order to achieve dramatic improvements in their performance.

> Every company operates according to a great many unarticulated rules. . . . Reengineering strives to break away from the old rules about how we organize and conduct our business.

Like all revolutions, Hammer's call to arms resulted in both positive and negative changes. During the 1990s, some companies made a legitimate effort to reengineer, and the results led to improved competitiveness. Others relied solely on downsizing and outsourcing (instead of reengineering) to improve their bottom line. "Mean" organizations with little potential for future growth often resulted [DeM95a].

By the end of the first decade of the twenty-first century, the hype associated with reengineering waned, but the process itself continues in companies large and small. The nexus between business reengineering and software engineering lies in a "system view."

Software is often the realization of the business rules that Hammer discusses. Today, major companies have tens of thousands of computer programs that support the "old business rules." As managers work to modify the rules to achieve greater effectiveness and competitiveness, software must keep pace. In some cases, this means the creation of major new computer-based systems.[2] But in many others, it means the modification or rebuilding of existing applications.

In the sections that follow, I examine reengineering in a top-down manner, beginning with a brief overview of business process reengineering and proceeding to a more detailed discussion of the technical activities that occur when software is reengineered.

29.4 BUSINESS PROCESS REENGINEERING

Business process reengineering (BPR) extends far beyond the scope of information technologies and software engineering. Among the many definitions (most somewhat abstract) that have been suggested for BPR is one published in *Fortune Magazine* [Ste93]: "the search for, and the implementation of, radical change in business process to achieve breakthrough results." But how is the search conducted, and how is the implementation achieved? More important, how can we ensure that the "radical change" suggested will in fact lead to "breakthrough results" instead of organizational chaos?

29.4.1 Business Processes

A business process is "a set of logically related tasks performed to achieve a defined business outcome" [Dav90]. Within the business process, people, equipment, material resources, and business procedures are combined to produce a specified result. Examples of business processes include designing a new product, purchasing services and supplies, hiring a new employee, and paying suppliers. Each demands a set of tasks, and each draws on diverse resources within the business.

---

2   The explosion of Web-based applications and systems is indicative of this trend.

As a software
engineer, your work
occurs at the bottom
of this hierarchy. Be
sure, however, that
someone has given
serious thought to the
levels above. If this
hasn't been done, your
work is at risk.

Every business process has a defined customer—a person or group that receives the outcome (e.g., an idea, a report, a design, a service, a product). In addition, business processes cross organizational boundaries. They require that different organizational groups participate in the "logically related tasks" that define the process.

Every system is actually a hierarchy of subsystems. A business is no exception. The overall business is segmented in the following manner:

The business → business systems → business processes → business subprocesses

Each business system (also called *business function*) is composed of one or more business processes, and each business process is defined by a set of subprocesses.

BPR can be applied at any level of the hierarchy, but as the scope of BPR broadens (i.e., as we move upward in the hierarchy), the risks associated with BPR grow dramatically. For this reason, most BPR efforts focus on individual processes or subprocesses.

29.4.2   A BPR Model

Like most engineering activities, business process reengineering is iterative. Business goals and the processes that achieve them must be adapted to a changing business environment. For this reason, there is no start and end to BPR—it is an evolutionary process. A model for business process reengineering is depicted in Figure 29.1. The model defines six activities:

Business definition. Business goals are identified within the context of four key drivers: cost reduction, time reduction, quality improvement, and personnel

FIGURE 29.1

A BPR model

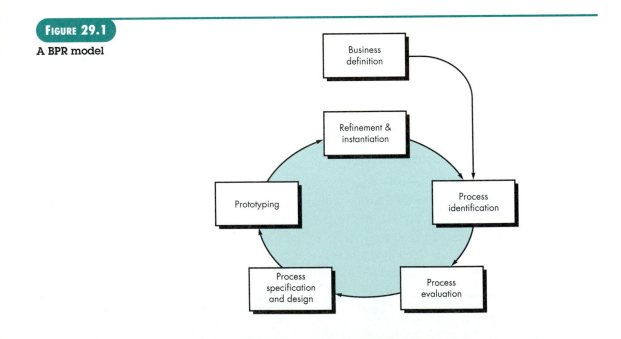

development and empowerment. Goals may be defined at the business level or for a specific component of the business.

Process identification. Processes that are critical to achieving the goals defined in the business definition are identified. They may then be ranked by importance, by need for change, or in any other way that is appropriate for the reengineering activity.

Process evaluation. The existing process is thoroughly analyzed and measured. Process tasks are identified; the costs and time consumed by process tasks are noted; and quality/performance problems are isolated.

Process specification and design. Based on information obtained during the first three BPR activities, use cases (Chapters 5 and 6) are prepared for each process that is to be redesigned. Within the context of BPR, use cases identify a scenario that delivers some outcome to a customer. With the use case as the specification of the process, a new set of tasks are designed for the process.

Prototyping. A redesigned business process must be prototyped before it is fully integrated into the business. This activity "tests" the process so that refinements can be made.

Refinement and instantiation. Based on feedback from the prototype, the business process is refined and then instantiated within a business system.

These BPR activities are sometimes used in conjunction with workflow analysis tools. The intent of these tools is to build a model of existing workflow in an effort to better analyze existing processes.

SOFTWARE TOOLS

Business Process Reengineering (BPR)

Objective: The objective of BPR tools is to support the analysis and assessment of existing business processes and the specification and design of new ones.

Mechanics: Tools mechanics vary. In general, BPR tools allow a business analyst to model existing business processes in an effort to assess workflow inefficiencies or functional problems. Once existing problems are identified, tools allow the analysis to prototype and/or simulate revised business processes.

Representative Tools:[3]

Extend, developed by ImagineThat, Inc. (**www.imaginethatinc.com**), is a simulation tool for modeling existing processes and exploring new ones. Extend provides comprehensive what-if capability that enables a business analysis to explore different process scenarios.

e-Work, developed by Metastorm (**www.metastorm.com**), provides business process management support for both manual and automated processes.

---

3   Tools noted here do not represent an endorsement, but rather a sampling of tools in this category. In most cases, tool names are trademarked by their respective developers.

IceTools, developed by Blue Ice (**www.blueice.com**), is a collection of BPR templates for Microsoft Office and Microsoft Project.

SpeeDev, developed by SpeeDev Inc. (**www.speedev.com**), is one of many tools that enable an organization to model process workflow (in this case, IT workflow).

Workflow tool suite, developed by MetaSoftware (**www.metasoftware.com**), incorporates a suite of tools for workflow modeling, simulation, and scheduling. A useful list of BPR tool links can be found at **www.opfro.org/index.html?Components/ Producers/Tools/BusinessProcessReengineering Tools.html~Contents**.

29.5 SOFTWARE REENGINEERING

The scenario is all too common: An application has served the business needs of a company for 10 or 15 years. During that time it has been corrected, adapted, and enhanced many times. People approached this work with the best intentions, but good software engineering practices were always shunted to the side (due to the press of other matters). Now the application is unstable. It still works, but every time a change is attempted, unexpected and serious side effects occur. Yet the application must continue to evolve. What to do?

Unmaintainable software is not a new problem. In fact, the broadening emphasis on software reengineering has been spawned by software maintenance problems that have been building for more than four decades.

29.5.1 A Software Reengineering Process Model

Reengineering takes time, it costs significant amounts of money, and it absorbs resources that might be otherwise occupied on immediate concerns. For all of these reasons, reengineering is not accomplished in a few months or even a few years. Reengineering of information systems is an activity that will absorb information technology resources for many years. That's why every organization needs a pragmatic strategy for software reengineering.

A workable strategy is encompassed in a reengineering process model. I'll discuss the model later in this section, but first, some basic principles.

Reengineering is a rebuilding activity. To better understand it, consider an analogous activity: the rebuilding of a house. Consider the following situation. You've purchased a house in another state. You've never actually seen the property, but you acquired it at an amazingly low price, with the warning that it might have to be completely rebuilt. How would you proceed?

- Before you can start rebuilding, it would seem reasonable to inspect the house. To determine whether it is in need of rebuilding, you (or a professional inspector) would create a list of criteria so that your inspection would be systematic.

WebRef

An excellent source of information on software reengineering can be found at **reengineer.org**.

- Before you tear down and rebuild the entire house, be sure that the structure is weak. If the house is structurally sound, it may be possible to "remodel" without rebuilding (at much lower cost and in much less time).

- Before you start rebuilding be sure you understand how the original was built. Take a peek behind the walls. Understand the wiring, the plumbing, and the structural internals. Even if you trash them all, the insight you'll gain will serve you well when you start construction.

- If you begin to rebuild, use only the most modern, long-lasting materials. This may cost a bit more now, but it will help you to avoid expensive and time-consuming maintenance later.

- If you decide to rebuild, be disciplined about it. Use practices that will result in high quality—today and in the future.

Although these principles focus on the rebuilding of a house, they apply equally well to the reengineering of computer-based systems and applications.

To implement these principles, you can use a software reengineering process model that defines six activities, shown in Figure 29.2. In some cases, these activities occur in a linear sequence, but this is not always the case. For example, it may be that reverse engineering (understanding the internal workings of a program) may have to occur before document restructuring can commence.

FIGURE 29.2

A software reengineering process model

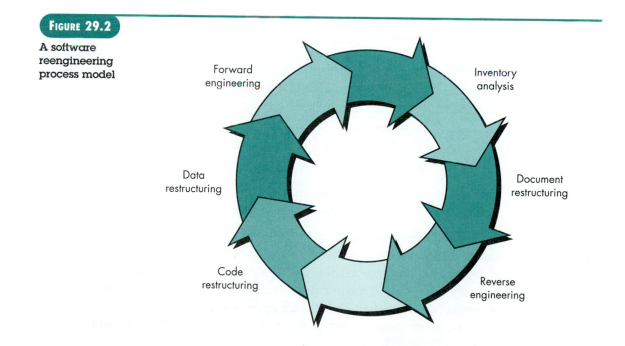

Forward engineering

Inventory analysis

Data restructuring

Document restructuring

Code restructuring

Reverse engineering

29.5.2   Software Reengineering Activities

The reengineering paradigm shown in Figure 29.2 is a cyclical model. This means that each of the activities presented as a part of the paradigm may be revisited. For any particular cycle, the process can terminate after any one of these activities.

Inventory analysis. Every software organization should have an inventory of all applications. The inventory can be nothing more than a spreadsheet model containing information that provides a detailed description (e.g., size, age, business criticality) of every active application. By sorting this information according to business criticality, longevity, current maintainability and supportability, and other locally important criteria, candidates for reengineering appear. Resources can then be allocated to candidate applications for reengineering work.

It is important to note that the inventory should be revisited on a regular cycle. The status of applications (e.g., business criticality) can change as a function of time, and as a result, priorities for reengineering will shift.

Document restructuring. Weak documentation is the trademark of many legacy systems. But what can you do about it? What are your options?

1. *Creating documentation is far too time consuming.* If the system works, you may choose to live with what you have. In some cases, this is the correct approach. It is not possible to re-create documentation for hundreds of computer programs. If a program is relatively static, is coming to the end of its useful life, and is unlikely to undergo significant change, let it be!

2. *Documentation must be updated, but your organization has limited resources.* You'll use a "document when touched" approach. It may not be necessary to fully redocument an application. Rather, those portions of the system that are currently undergoing change are fully documented. Over time, a collection of useful and relevant documentation will evolve.

3. *The system is business critical and must be fully redocumented.* Even in this case, an intelligent approach is to pare documentation to an essential minimum.

Each of these options is viable. Your software organization must choose the one that is most appropriate for each case.

Reverse engineering. The term *reverse engineering* has its origins in the hardware world. A company disassembles a competitive hardware product in an effort to understand its competitor's design and manufacturing "secrets." These secrets could be easily understood if the competitor's design and manufacturing specifications were obtained. But these documents are proprietary and unavailable to the company doing the reverse engineering. In essence, successful reverse engineering derives one or more design and manufacturing specifications for a product by examining actual specimens of the product.

WebRef

An array of resources for the reengineering community can be obtained at **www.comp.lancs .ac.uk/projects/ RenaissanceWeb/**.

Reverse engineering for software is quite similar. In most cases, however, the program to be reverse engineered is not a competitor's. Rather, it is the company's own work (often done many years earlier). The "secrets" to be understood are obscure because no specification was ever developed. Therefore, reverse engineering for software is the process of analyzing a program in an effort to create a representation of the program at a higher level of abstraction than source code. Reverse engineering is a process of *design recovery*. Reverse engineering tools extract data, architectural, and procedural design information from an existing program.

Code restructuring. The most common type of reengineering (actually, the use of the term reengineering is questionable in this case) is *code restructuring*.[4] Some legacy systems have a relatively solid program architecture, but individual modules were coded in a way that makes them difficult to understand, test, and maintain. In such cases, the code within the suspect modules can be restructured.

To accomplish this activity, the source code is analyzed using a restructuring tool. Violations of structured programming constructs are noted and code is then restructured (this can be done automatically) or even rewritten in a more modern programming language. The resultant restructured code is reviewed and tested to ensure that no anomalies have been introduced. Internal code documentation is updated.

Data restructuring. A program with weak data architecture will be difficult to adapt and enhance. In fact, for many applications, information architecture has more to do with the long-term viability of a program than the source code itself.

Unlike code restructuring, which occurs at a relatively low level of abstraction, data restructuring is a full-scale reengineering activity. In most cases, data restructuring begins with a reverse engineering activity. Current data architecture is dissected, and necessary data models are defined (Chapters 6 and 9). Data objects and attributes are identified, and existing data structures are reviewed for quality.

When data structure is weak (e.g., flat files are currently implemented, when a relational approach would greatly simplify processing), the data are reengineered.

Because data architecture has a strong influence on program architecture and the algorithms that populate it, changes to the data will invariably result in either architectural or code-level changes.

Forward engineering. In an ideal world, applications would be rebuilt using an automated "reengineering engine." The old program would be fed into the engine, analyzed, restructured, and then regenerated in a form that exhibited the best

---

4   Code restructuring has some of the elements of "refactoring," a redesign concept introduced in Chapter 8 and discussed elsewhere in this book.

aspects of software quality. In the short term, it is unlikely that such an "engine" will appear, but vendors have introduced tools that provide a limited subset of these capabilities that addresses specific application domains (e.g., applications that are implemented using a specific database system). More important, these reengineering tools are becoming increasingly more sophisticated.

Forward engineering not only recovers design information from existing software but uses this information to alter or reconstitute the existing system in an effort to improve its overall quality. In most cases, reengineered software reimplements the function of the existing system and also adds new functions and/or improves overall performance.

29.6   REVERSE ENGINEERING

Reverse engineering conjures an image of the "magic slot." You feed a haphazardly designed, undocumented source file into the slot and out the other end comes a complete design description (and full documentation) for the computer program. Unfortunately, the magic slot doesn't exist. Reverse engineering can extract design information from source code, but the abstraction level, the completeness of the documentation, the degree to which tools and a human analyst work together, and the directionality of the process are highly variable.

The *abstraction level* of a reverse engineering process and the tools used to effect it refers to the sophistication of the design information that can be extracted from source code. Ideally, the abstraction level should be as high as possible. That is, the reverse engineering process should be capable of deriving procedural design representations (a low-level abstraction), program and data structure information (a somewhat higher level of abstraction), object models, data and/or control flow models (a relatively high level of abstraction), and entity relationship models (a high level of abstraction). As the abstraction level increases, you are provided with information that will allow easier understanding of the program.

The *completeness* of a reverse engineering process refers to the level of detail that is provided at an abstraction level. In most cases, the completeness decreases as the abstraction level increases. For example, given a source code listing, it is relatively easy to develop a complete procedural design representation. Simple architectural design representations may also be derived, but it is far more difficult to develop a complete set of UML diagrams or models.

Completeness improves in direct proportion to the amount of analysis performed by the person doing reverse engineering. *Interactivity* refers to the degree to which the human is "integrated" with automated tools to create an effective reverse engineering process. In most cases, as the abstraction level increases, interactivity must increase or completeness will suffer.

If the *directionality* of the reverse engineering process is one-way, all information extracted from the source code is provided to the software engineer who can

The reverse engineering process

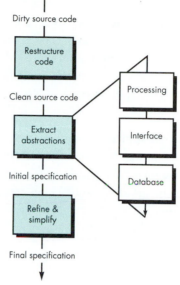

Dirty source code

Restructure code

Clean source code

Processing

Extract abstractions

Interface

Initial specification

Database

Refine & simplify

Final specification

then use it during any maintenance activity. If directionality is two-way, the information is fed to a reengineering tool that attempts to restructure or regenerate the old program.

WebRef

Useful resources for "design recovery and program understanding" can be found at **wwwsel.iit.nrc.ca/ projects/dr/ dr.html**.

The reverse engineering process is represented in Figure 29.3. Before reverse engineering activities can commence, unstructured ("dirty") source code is restructured (Section 29.5.1) so that it contains only the structured programming constructs.[5] This makes the source code easier to read and provides the basis for all the subsequent reverse engineering activities.

The core of reverse engineering is an activity called *extract abstractions*. You must evaluate the old program and from the (often undocumented) source code, develop a meaningful specification of the processing that is performed, the user interface that is applied, and the program data structures or database that is used.

29.6.1   Reverse Engineering to Understand Data

In some cases, the first reengineering activity attempts to construct a UML class diagram.

Reverse engineering of data occurs at different levels of abstraction and is often the first reengineering task. At the program level, internal program data structures must often be reverse engineered as part of an overall reengineering effort. At the system level, global data structures (e.g., files, databases) are often reengineered to accommodate new database management paradigms (e.g., the move from flat file to relational or object-oriented database systems). Reverse engineering of the

---

5   Code can be restructured using a *restructuring engine*—a tool that restructures source code.

ADVICE

The approach to reverse engineering for data for conventional software follows an analogous path: (1) build a data model, (2) identify attributes of data objects, and (3) define relationships.

current global data structures sets the stage for the introduction of a new systemwide database.

Internal data structures. Reverse engineering techniques for internal program data focus on the definition of classes of objects. This is accomplished by examining the program code with the intent of grouping related program variables. In many cases, the data organization within the code identifies abstract data types. For example, record structures, files, lists, and other data structures often provide an initial indicator of classes.

Database structure. Regardless of its logical organization and physical structure, a database allows the definition of data objects and supports some method for establishing relationships among the objects. Therefore, reengineering one database schema into another requires an understanding of existing objects and their relationships.

The following steps [Pre94] may be used to define the existing data model as a precursor to reengineering a new database model: (1) build an initial object model, (2) determine candidate keys (the attributes are examined to determine whether they are used to point to another record or table; those that serve as pointers become candidate keys), (3) refine the tentative classes, (4) define generalizations, and (5) discover associations using techniques that are analogous to the CRC approach. Once information defined in the preceding steps is known, a series of transformations [Pre94] can be applied to map the old database structure into a new database structure.

29.6.2   Reverse Engineering to Understand Processing

Reverse engineering to understand processing begins with an attempt to understand and then extract procedural abstractions represented by the source code. To understand procedural abstractions, the code is analyzed at varying levels of abstraction: system, program, component, pattern, and statement.

The overall functionality of the entire application system must be understood before more detailed reverse engineering work occurs. This establishes a context for further analysis and provides insight into interoperability issues among applications within the system. Each of the programs that make up the application system represents a functional abstraction at a high level of detail. A block diagram, representing the interaction between these functional abstractions, is created. Each component performs some subfunction and represents a defined procedural abstraction. A processing narrative for each component is developed. In some situations, system, program, and component specifications already exist. When this is the case, the specifications are reviewed for conformance to existing code.[6]

Quote:

"There exists a passion for comprehension, just as there exists a passion for music. That passion is rather common in children, but gets lost in most people later on."

Albert Einstein

---

6   Often, specifications written early in the life history of a program are never updated. As changes are made, the code no longer conforms to the specification.

Things become more complex when the code inside a component is considered. You should look for sections of code that represent generic procedural patterns. In almost every component, a section of code prepares data for processing (within the module), a different section of code does the processing, and another section of code prepares the results of processing for export from the component. Within each of these sections, you can encounter smaller patterns; for example, data validation and bounds checking often occur within the section of code that prepares data for processing.

For large systems, reverse engineering is generally accomplished using a semiautomated approach. Automated tools can be used to help you understand the semantics of existing code. The output of this process is then passed to restructuring and forward engineering tools to complete the reengineering process.

29.6.3 Reverse Engineering User Interfaces

Sophisticated GUIs have become de rigueur for computer-based products and systems of every type. Therefore, the redevelopment of user interfaces has become one of the most common types of reengineering activity. But before a user interface can be rebuilt, reverse engineering should occur.

To fully understand an existing user interface, the structure and behavior of the interface must be specified. Merlo and his colleagues [Mer93] suggest three basic questions that must be answered as reverse engineering of the UI commences:

? How do I understand the workings of an existing user interface?

- What are the basic actions (e.g., keystrokes and mouse clicks) that the interface must process?

- What is a compact description of the behavioral response of the system to these actions?

- What is meant by a "replacement," or more precisely, what concept of equivalence of interfaces is relevant here?

Behavioral modeling notation (Chapter 7) can provide a means for developing answers to the first two questions. Much of the information necessary to create a behavioral model can be obtained by observing the external manifestation of the existing interface. But additional information necessary to create the behavioral model must be extracted from the code.

It is important to note that a replacement GUI may not mirror the old interface exactly (in fact, it may be radically different). It is often worthwhile to develop a new interaction metaphor. For example, an old UI requests that a user provide a scale factor (ranging from 1 to 10) to shrink or magnify a graphical image. A reengineered GUI might use a slide-bar and mouse to accomplish the same function.

Reverse Engineering

Objective: To help software engineers understand the internal design structure of complex programs.

Mechanics: In most cases, reverse engineering tools accept source code as input and produce a variety of structural, procedural, data, and behavioral design representations.

Representative Tools:[7]

Imagix 4D, developed by Imagix (**www.imagix.com**), "helps software developers understand complex or

legacy C and C++ software" by reverse engineering and documenting source code.

Understand, developed by Scientific Toolworks, Inc. (**www.scitools.com**), parses Ada, Fortran, C, C++, and Java "to reverse engineer, automatically document, calculate code metrics, and help you understand, navigate and maintain source code."

A comprehensive listing of reverse engineering tools can be found at **http://scgwiki.iam.unibe.ch:8080/ SCG/370**.

29.7 RESTRUCTURING

Software restructuring modifies source code and/or data in an effort to make it amenable to future changes. In general, restructuring does not modify the overall program architecture. It tends to focus on the design details of individual modules and on local data structures defined within modules. If the restructuring effort extends beyond module boundaries and encompasses the software architecture, restructuring becomes forward engineering (Section 29.7).

Restructuring occurs when the basic architecture of an application is solid, even though technical internals need work. It is initiated when major parts of the software are serviceable and only a subset of all modules and data need extensive modification.[8]

Although code restructuring can alleviate immediate problems associated with debugging or small changes, it is not reengineering. Real benefit is achieved only when data and architecture are restructured.

29.7.1 Code Restructuring

Code restructuring is performed to yield a design that produces the same function but with higher quality than the original program. In general, code restructuring techniques (e.g., Warnier's logical simplification techniques [War74]) model program logic using Boolean algebra and then apply a series of transformation rules that yield restructured logic. The objective is to take "spaghetti-bowl" code and derive a procedural design that conforms to the structured programming philosophy (Chapter 10).

Other restructuring techniques have also been proposed for use with reengineering tools. A resource exchange diagram maps each program module and the resources (data types, procedures and variables) that are exchanged between it and

---

7 Tools noted here do not represent an endorsement, but rather a sampling of tools in this category. In most cases, tool names are trademarked by their respective developers.

8 It is sometimes difficult to make a distinction between extensive restructuring and redevelopment. Both are reengineering.

other modules. By creating representations of resource flow, the program architecture can be restructured to achieve minimum coupling among modules.

29.7.2 Data Restructuring

Before data restructuring can begin, a reverse engineering activity called *analysis of source code* should be conducted. All programming language statements that contain data definitions, file descriptions, I/O, and interface descriptions are evaluated. The intent is to extract data items and objects, to get information on data flow, and to understand the existing data structures that have been implemented. This activity is sometimes called *data analysis*.

Once data analysis has been completed, *data redesign* commences. In its simplest form, a *data record standardization* step clarifies data definitions to achieve consistency among data item names or physical record formats within an existing data structure or file format. Another form of redesign, called *data name rationalization*, ensures that all data naming conventions conform to local standards and that aliases are eliminated as data flow through the system.

When restructuring moves beyond standardization and rationalization, physical modifications to existing data structures are made to make the data design more effective. This may mean a translation from one file format to another, or in some cases, translation from one type of database to another.

SOFTWARE TOOLS

Software Restructuring

Objective: The objective of restructuring tools is to transform older unstructured computer software into modern programming languages and design structures.

Mechanics: In general, source code is input and transformed into a better structured program. In some cases, the transformation occurs within the same programming language. In other cases, an older programming language is transformed into a more modern language.

Representative Tools:[9]

DMS Software Reengineering Toolkit, developed by Semantic Design (**www.semdesigns.com**), provides a variety of restructuring capabilities for COBOL, C/C++, Java, Fortran 90, and VHDL.

Clone Doctor, developed by Semantic Designs, Inc. (**www.semdesigns.com**), analyzes and transforms programs written in C, C++, Java, or COBOL or any other text-based computer language.

plusFORT, developed by Polyhedron (**www.polyhedron.com**) is a suite of FORTRAN tools that contains capabilities for restructuring poorly designed FORTRAN programs into the modern FORTRAN or C standard.

Pointers to a variety of reengineering and reverse engineering tools can be found at **www.csse .monash.edu/~ipeake/reeng/free-swre-tools .html** and **www.cs.ualberta.ca/~kenw/toolsdir/ all.html**.

---

9   Tools noted here do not represent an endorsement, but rather a sampling of tools in this category. In most cases, tool names are trademarked by their respective developers.

29.8   FORWARD ENGINEERING

A program with control flow that is the graphic equivalent of a bowl of spaghetti, with "modules" that are 2000 statements long, with few meaningful comment lines in 290,000 source statements and no other documentation must be modified to accommodate changing user requirements. You have the following options:

1. You can struggle through modification after modification, fighting the ad hoc design and tangled source code to implement the necessary changes.

2. You can attempt to understand the broader inner workings of the program in an effort to make modifications more effectively.

3. You can redesign, recode, and test those portions of the software that require modification, applying a software engineering approach to all revised segments.

4. You can completely redesign, recode, and test the program, using reengineering tools to assist you in understanding the current design.

There is no single "correct" option. Circumstances may dictate the first option even if the others are more desirable.

Reengineering is a lot like getting your teeth cleaned. You can think of a thousand reasons to delay it, and you'll get away with procrastinating for quite a while. But eventually, your delaying tactics will come back to cause pain.

Rather than waiting until a maintenance request is received, the development or support organization uses the results of inventory analysis to select a program that (1) will remain in use for a preselected number of years, (2) is currently being used successfully, and (3) is likely to undergo major modification or enhancement in the near future. Then, option 2, 3, or 4 is applied.

At first glance, the suggestion that you redevelop a large program when a working version already exists may seem quite extravagant. Before passing judgment, consider the following points:

1. The cost to maintain one line of source code may be 20 to 40 times the cost of initial development of that line.

2. Redesign of the software architecture (program and/or data structure), using modern design concepts, can greatly facilitate future maintenance.

3. Because a prototype of the software already exists, development productivity should be much higher than average.

4. The user now has experience with the software. Therefore, new requirements and the direction of change can be ascertained with greater ease.

5. Automated tools for reengineering will facilitate some parts of the job.

6. A complete software configuration (documents, programs, and data) will exist upon completion of preventive maintenance.

A large in-house software developer (e.g., a business systems software development group for a large consumer products company) may have 500 to 2000 production programs within its domain of responsibility. These programs can be ranked by importance and then reviewed as candidates for forward engineering.

The forward engineering process applies software engineering principles, concepts, and methods to re-create an existing application. In most cases, forward engineering does not simply create a modern equivalent of an older program. Rather, new user and technology requirements are integrated into the reengineering effort. The redeveloped program extends the capabilities of the older application.

29.8.1 Forward Engineering for Client-Server Architectures

Over the past few decades, many mainframe applications have been reengineered to accommodate client-server architectures (including WebApps). In essence, centralized computing resources (including software) are distributed among many client platforms. Although a variety of different distributed environments can be designed, the typical mainframe application that is reengineered into a client-server architecture has the following features:

- Application functionality migrates to each client computer.
- New GUI interfaces are implemented at the client sites.
- Database functions are allocated to the server.
- Specialized functionality (e.g., compute-intensive analysis) may remain at the server site.
- New communications, security, archiving, and control requirements must be established at both the client and server sites.

It is important to note that the migration from mainframe to client-server computing requires both business and software reengineering. In addition, an "enterprise network infrastructure" [Jay94] should be established.

In some cases, migration to a client-server architecture should be approached not as reengineering, but as a new development effort. Reengineering enters the picture only when specific functionality from the old system is to be integrated into the new architecture.

Reengineering for client-server applications begins with a thorough analysis of the business environment that encompasses the existing mainframe. Three layers of abstraction can be identified. The *database sits* at the foundation of a client-server architecture and manages transactions and queries from server applications. Yet these transactions and queries must be controlled within the context of a set of business rules (defined by an existing or reengineered business process). Client applications provide targeted functionality to the user community.

The functions of the existing database management system and the data architecture of the existing database must be reverse engineered as a precursor to the redesign of the database foundation layer. In some cases a new data model (Chapter 6) is created. In every case, the client-server database is reengineered to ensure that transactions are executed in a consistent manner, that all updates are performed only by authorized users, that core business rules are enforced (e.g., before a vendor record is deleted, the server ensures that no related accounts payable, contracts, or communications exist for that vendor), that queries can be accommodated efficiently, and that full archiving capability has been established.

The business rules layer represents software resident at both the client and the server. This software performs control and coordination tasks to ensure that transactions and queries between the client application and the database conform to the established business process.

The client applications layer implements business functions that are required by specific groups of end users. In many instances, a mainframe application is segmented into a number of smaller, reengineered desktop applications. Communication among the desktop applications (when necessary) is controlled by the business rules layer.

A comprehensive discussion of client-server software design and reengineering is best left to books dedicated to the subject. If you have further interest, see [Van02], [Cou00], or [Orf99].

29.8.2   Forward Engineering for Object-Oriented Architectures

Object-oriented software engineering has become the development paradigm of choice for many software organizations. But what about existing applications that were developed using conventional methods? In some cases, the answer is to leave such applications "as is." In others, older applications must be reengineered so that they can be easily integrated into large, object-oriented systems.

Reengineering conventional software into an object-oriented implementation uses many of the same techniques discussed in Part 2 of this book. First, the existing software is reverse engineered so that appropriate data, functional, and behavioral models can be created. If the reengineered system extends the functionality or behavior of the original application, use cases (Chapters 5 and 6) are created. The data models created during reverse engineering are then used in conjunction with CRC modeling (Chapter 6) to establish the basis for the definition of classes. Class hierarchies, object-relationship models, object-behavior models, and subsystems are defined, and object-oriented design commences.

As object-oriented forward engineering progresses from analysis to design, a CBSE process model (Chapter 10) can be invoked. If the existing application resides within a domain that is already populated by many object-oriented applications, it is likely that a robust component library exists and can be used during forward engineering.

For those classes that must be engineered from scratch, it may be possible to reuse algorithms and data structures from the existing conventional application. However, these must be redesigned to conform to the object-oriented architecture.

29.9   THE ECONOMICS OF REENGINEERING

In a perfect world, every unmaintainable program would be retired immediately, to be replaced by high-quality, reengineered applications developed using modern software engineering practices. But we live in a world of limited resources. Reengineering drains resources that can be used for other business purposes. Therefore, before an organization attempts to reengineer an existing application, it should perform a cost-benefit analysis.

A cost-benefit analysis model for reengineering has been proposed by Sneed [Sne95]. Nine parameters are defined:

P_1 = current annual maintenance cost for an application
P_2 = current annual operations cost for an application
P_3 = current annual business value of an application
P_4 = predicted annual maintenance cost after reengineering
P_5 = predicted annual operations cost after reengineering
P_6 = predicted annual business value after reengineering
P_7 = estimated reengineering costs
P_8 = estimated reengineering calendar time
P_9 = reengineering risk factor (P_9 = 1.0 is nominal)
L = expected life of the system

The cost associated with continuing maintenance of a candidate application (i.e., reengineering is not performed) can be defined as

$$C_{maint} = [P_3 - (P_1 + P_2)] \times L \tag{29.1}$$

The costs associated with reengineering are defined using the following relationship:

$$C_{reeng} = P_6 - (P_4 + P_5) \times (L - P_8) - (P_7 \times P_9) \tag{29.2}$$

Using the costs presented in Equations (29.1) and (29.2), the overall benefit of reengineering can be computed as

$$\text{Cost benefit} = C_{reeng} - C_{maint} \tag{29.3}$$

The cost-benefit analysis presented in these equations can be performed for all high-priority applications identified during inventory analysis (Section 29.4.2). Those applications that show the highest cost-benefit can be targeted for reengineering, while work on others can be postponed until resources are available.

29.10 SUMMARY

Software maintenance and support are ongoing activities that occur throughout the life cycle of an application. During these activities, defects are corrected, applications are adapted to a changing operational or business environment, enhancements are implemented at the request of stakeholders, and users are supported as they integrate an application into their personal or business workflow.

Reengineering occurs at two different levels of abstraction. At the business level, reengineering focuses on the business process with the intent of making changes to improve competitiveness in some area of the business. At the software level, reengineering examines information systems and applications with the intent of restructuring or reconstructing them so that they exhibit higher quality.

Business process reengineering defines business goals; identifies and evaluates existing business processes (in the context of defined goals); specifies and designs revised processes; and prototypes, refines, and instantiates them within a business. BPR has a focus that extends beyond software. The result of BPR is often the definition of ways in which information technologies can better support the business.

Software reengineering encompasses a series of activities that include inventory analysis, document restructuring, reverse engineering, program and data restructuring, and forward engineering. The intent of these activities is to create versions of existing programs that exhibit higher quality and better maintainability—programs that will be viable well into the twenty-first century.

The cost-benefit of reengineering can be determined quantitatively. The cost of the status quo, that is, the cost associated with ongoing support and maintenance of an existing application, is compared to the projected costs of reengineering and the resultant reduction in maintenance and support costs. In almost every case in which a program has a long life and currently exhibits poor maintainability or supportability, reengineering represents a cost-effective business strategy.

PROBLEMS AND POINTS TO PONDER

29.1. Consider any job that you've held in the last five years. Describe the business process in which you played a part. Use the BPR model described in Section 29.4.2 to recommend changes to the process in an effort to make it more efficient.

29.2. Do some research on the efficacy of business process reengineering. Present pro and con arguments for this approach.

29.3. Your instructor will select one of the programs that everyone in the class has developed during this course. Exchange your program randomly with someone else in the class. Do not explain or walk through the program. Now, implement an enhancement (specified by your instructor) in the program you have received.

    a. Perform all software engineering tasks including a brief walkthrough (but not with the author of the program).
    b. Keep careful track of all errors encountered during testing.
    c. Discuss your experiences in class.

29.4. Explore the inventory analysis checklist presented at the SEPA website and attempt to develop a quantitative software rating system that could be applied to existing programs in an effort to pick candidate programs for reengineering. Your system should extend beyond the economic analysis presented in Section 29.9.

29.5. Suggest alternatives to paper and ink or conventional electronic documentation that could serve as the basis for document restructuring. (Hint: Think of new descriptive technologies that could be used to communicate the intent of the software.)

29.6. Some people believe that artificial intelligence technology will increase the abstraction level of the reverse engineering process. Do some research on this subject (i.e., the use of AI for reverse engineering), and write a brief paper that takes a stand on this point.

29.7. Why is completeness difficult to achieve as abstraction level increases?

29.8. Why must interactivity increase if completeness is to increase?

29.9. Using information obtained via the Web, present characteristics of three reverse engineering tools to your class.

29.10. There is a subtle difference between restructuring and forward engineering. What is it?

29.11. Research the literature and/or Internet sources to find one or more papers that discuss case studies of mainframe to client-server reengineering. Present a summary.

29.12. How would you determine P_4 through P_7 in the cost-benefit model presented in Section 29.9?

FURTHER READINGS AND INFORMATION SOURCES

It is ironic that software maintenance and support represent the most costly activities in the life of an application, and yet, fewer books have been written about maintenance and support than any other major software engineering topics. Among recent additions to the literature are books by Jarzabek (*Effective Software Maintenance and Evolution,* Auerbach, 2007), Grubb and Takang (*Software Maintenance: Concepts and Practice,* World Scientific Publishing Co., 2d ed., 2003), and Pigoski (*Practical Software Maintenance,* Wiley, 1996). These books cover basic maintenance and support practices and present useful management guidance. Maintenance techniques that focus on client-server environments are discussed by Schneberger (*Client/Server Software Maintenance,* McGraw-Hill, 1997). Current research in "software evolution" is presented in an anthology edited by Mens and Demeyer (*Software Evolution,* Springer, 2008).

Like many hot topics in the business community, the hype surrounding business process reengineering has given way to a more pragmatic view of the subject. Hammer and Champy (*Reengineering the Corporation,* HarperBusiness, revised edition, 2003) precipitated early interest with their best-selling book. Other books by Smith and Fingar [*Business Process Management (BPM): The Third Wave,* Meghan-Kiffer Press, 2003], Jacka and Keller (*Business Process Mapping: Improving Customer Satisfaction,* Wiley, 2001), Sharp and McDermott (*Workflow Modeling,* Artech House, 2001), Andersen (*Business Process Improvement Toolbox,* American Society for Quality, 1999), and Harrington et al. (*Business Process Improvement Workbook,* McGraw-Hill, 1997) present case studies and detailed guidelines for BPR.

Fong (*Information Systems Reengineering and Integration,* Springer, 2006) describes database conversion techniques, reverse engineering, and forward engineering as they are applied for major information systems. Demeyer and his colleagues (*Object Oriented Reengineering Patterns,* Morgan Kaufmann, 2002) provides a patterns-based view of how to refactor and/or reengineer OO systems. Secord and his colleagues (*Modernizing Legacy Systems,* Addison-Wesley, 2003), Ulrich (*Legacy Systems: Transformation Strategies,* Prentice Hall, 2002), Valenti (*Successful Software Reengineering,* IRM Press, 2002), and Rada (*Reengineering Software: How to Reuse Programming to Build New, State-of-the-Art Software,* Fitzroy Dearborn Publishers, 1999) focus on strategies and practices for reengineering at a technical level. Miller (*Reengineering Legacy Software Systems,* Digital Press, 1998) "provides a framework for keeping application systems synchronized with business strategies and technology changes."

Cameron (*Reengineering Business for Success in the Internet Age,* Computer Technology Research, 2000) and Umar [*Application (Re)Engineering: Building Web-Based Applications and Dealing with Legacies,* Prentice Hall, 1997] provide worthwhile guidance for organizations that want to transform legacy systems into a Web-based environment. Cook (*Building Enterprise Information Architectures: Reengineering Information Systems,* Prentice Hall, 1996) discusses the bridge between BPR and information technology. Aiken (*Data Reverse Engineering,* McGraw-Hill, 1996) discusses how to reclaim, reorganize, and reuse organizational data. Arnold (*Software Reengineering,* IEEE Computer Society Press, 1993) has put together an excellent anthology of early papers that focus on software reengineering technologies.

A wide variety of information sources on software reengineering is available on the Internet. An up-to-date list of World Wide Web references relevant to software maintenance and reengineering can be found at the SEPA website: **www.mhhe.com/engcs/compsci/pressman/ professional/olc/ser.htm**.

In this part of *Software Engineering: A Practitioner's Approach*, we consider a number of advanced topics that will extend your understanding of software engineering. The following questions are addressed in the chapters that follow:

- What is software process improvement and how can it be used to improve the state of software engineering practice?

- What emerging trends can be expected to have a significant influence on software engineering practice in the next decade?

- What is the road ahead for software engineers?

Once these questions are answered, you'll understand topics that may have a profound impact on software engineering in the years to come.

Long before the phrase "software process improvement" was widely used, I worked with major corporations in an attempt to improve the state of their software engineering practices. As a consequence of my experiences, I wrote a book entitled *Making Software Engineering Happen* [Pre88]. In the preface of that book I made the following comment:

> For the past ten years I have had the opportunity to help a number of large companies implement software engineering practices. The job is difficult and rarely goes as smoothly as one might like—but when it succeeds, the results are profound. Software projects are more likely to be completed on time. Communication between all constituencies involved in software development is improved. The level of confusion and chaos that is often prevalent for large software projects is reduced substantially. The number of errors encountered by the customer drops substantially. The credibility of the software organization increases. And management has one less problem to worry about.
>
> But all is not sweetness and light. Many companies attempt to implement software engineering practice and give up in frustration. Others do it half-way and never see the benefits noted above. Still others do it in a heavy-handed fashion that results in open rebellion among technical staff and managers and subsequent loss of morale.

QUICK LOOK

What is it? Software process improvement encompasses a set of activities that will lead to a better software process and, as a consequence, higher-quality software delivered in a more timely manner.

Who does it? The people who champion SPI come from three groups: technical managers, software engineers, and individuals who have quality assurance responsibility.

Why is it important? Some software organizations have little more than an ad hoc software process. As they work to improve their software engineering practices, they must address weaknesses in their existing process and try to improve their approach to software work.

What are the steps? The approach to SPI is iterative and continuous, but it can be viewed in five steps: (1) assessment of the current software process, (2) education and training of practitioners and managers, (3) selection and justification of process elements, software engineering methods, and tools, (4) implementation of the SPI plan, and (5) evaluation and tuning based on the results of the plan.

What is the work product? Although there are many intermediate SPI work products, the end result is an improved software process that leads to higher-quality software.

How do I ensure that I've done it right? The software your organization produces will be delivered with fewer defects, rework at each stage of the software process will be reduced, and on-time delivery will become much more likely.

Although those words were written more than 20 years ago, they remain equally true today.

As we move into the second decade of the twenty-first century, most major software engineering organizations have attempted to "make software engineering happen." Some have implemented individual practices that have helped to improve the quality of the product they build and the timeliness of their delivery. Others have established a "mature" software process that guides their technical and project management activities. But others continue to struggle. Their practices are hit-and-miss, and their process is ad hoc. Occasionally, their work is spectacular, but in the main, each project is an adventure, and no one knows whether it will end badly or well.

So, which of these two cohorts needs software process improvement? The answer (which may surprise you) is *both*. Those that have succeeded in making software engineering happen cannot become complacent. They must work continually to improve their approach to software engineering. And those that struggle must begin their journey down the road toward improvement.

30.1   WHAT IS SPI?

KEY POINT

SPI implies a defined software process, an organizational approach, and a strategy for improvement.

The term *software process improvement* (SPI) implies many things. First, it implies that elements of an effective software process can be defined in an effective manner; second, that an existing organizational approach to software development can be assessed against those elements; and third, that a meaningful strategy for improvement can be defined. The SPI strategy transforms the existing approach to software development into something that is more focused, more repeatable, and more reliable (in terms of the quality of the product produced and the timeliness of delivery).

Because SPI is not free, it must deliver a return on investment. The effort and time that is required to implement an SPI strategy must pay for itself in some measurable way. To do this, the results of improved process and practice must lead to a reduction in software "problems" that cost time and money. It must reduce the number of defects that are delivered to end users, reduce the amount of rework due to quality problems, reduce the costs associated with software maintenance and support (Chapter 29), and reduce the indirect costs that occur when software is delivered late.

30.1.1   Approaches to SPI

Although an organization can choose a relatively informal approach to SPI, the vast majority choose one of a number of SPI frameworks. An *SPI framework* defines (1) a set of characteristics that must be present if an effective software process is to be achieved, (2) a method for assessing whether those characteristics are present, (3) a mechanism for summarizing the results of any assessment, and (4) a strategy for assisting a software organization in implementing those process characteristics that have been found to be weak or missing.

Quote:

"Much of the software crisis is self-inflicted, as when a CIO says, 'I'd rather have it wrong than have it late. We can always fix it later.'"

Mark Paulk

FIGURE 30.1

Elements of an SPI framework.
Source: Adapted from [Rou02].

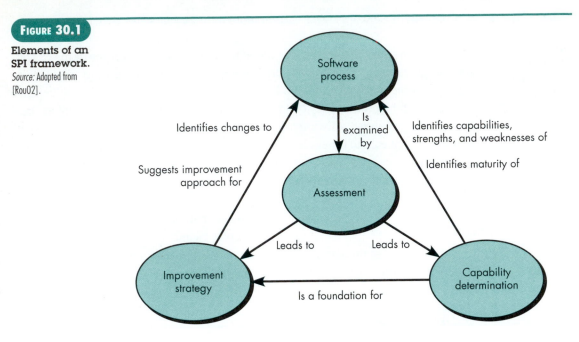

An SPI framework assesses the "maturity" of an organization's software process and provides a qualitative indication of a maturity level. In fact, the term "maturity model" (Section 30.1.2) is often applied. In essence, the SPI framework encompasses a maturity model that in turn incorporates a set of process quality indicators that provide an overall measure of the process quality that will lead to product quality.

Figure 30.1 provides an overview of a typical SPI framework. The key elements of the framework and their relationship to one another are shown.

You should note that there is no universal SPI framework. In fact, the SPI framework that is chosen by an organization reflects the constituency that is championing the SPI effort. Conradi [Con96] defines six different SPI support constituencies:

? **What groups champion an SPI effort?**

> **Quality certifiers.** Process improvement efforts championed by this group focus on the following relationship:
>
> **Quality**(*Process*) ⇒ **Quality**(*Product*)
>
> Their approach is to emphasize assessment methods and to examine a well-defined set of characteristics that allow them to determine whether the process exhibits quality. They are most likely to adopt a process framework such as the CMM, SPICE, TickIT, or Bootstrap.[1]
>
> **Formalists.** This group wants to understand (and when possible, optimize) process workflow. To accomplish this, they use process modeling languages

---

1   Each of these SPI frameworks is discussed later in this chapter.

(PMLs) to create a model of the existing process and then design extensions or modifications that will make the process more effective.

? *"What are the different constituencies that support SPI?"*

Tool advocates. This group insists on a tool-assisted approach to SPI that models workflow and other process characteristics in a manner that can be analyzed for improvement.

Practitioners. This constituency uses a pragmatic approach, "emphasizing mainstream project-, quality- and product management, applying project-level planning and metrics, but with little formal process modeling or enactment support" [Con96].

Reformers. The goal of this group is organizational change that might lead to a better software process. They tend to focus more on human issues (Section 30.5) and emphasize measures of human capability and structure.

Ideologists. This group focuses on the suitability of a particular process model for a specific application domain or organizational structure. Rather than typical software process models (e.g., iterative models), ideologists would have a greater interest in a process that would, say, support reuse or reengineering.

As an SPI framework is applied, the sponsoring constituency (regardless of its overall focus) must establish mechanisms to: (1) support technology transition, (2) determine the degree to which an organization is ready to absorb process changes that are proposed, and (3) measure the degree to which changes have been adopted.

30.1.2   Maturity Models

A *maturity model* is applied within the context of an SPI framework. The intent of the maturity model is to provide an overall indication of the "process maturity" exhibited by a software organization. That is, an indication of the quality of the software process, the degree to which practitioner's understand and apply the process, and the general state of software engineering practice. This is accomplished using some type of ordinal scale.

KEY POINT

A maturity model defines levels of software process competence and implementation.

For example, the Software Engineering Institute's *Capability Maturity Model* (Section 30.4) suggests five levels of maturity [Sch96]:

Level 5, Optimized—The organization has quantitative feedback systems in place to identify process weaknesses and strengthen them pro-actively. Project teams analyze defects to determine their causes; software processes are evaluated and updated to prevent known types of defects from recurring.

Level 4, Managed—Detailed software process and product quality metrics establish the quantitative evaluation foundation. Meaningful variations in process performance can be distinguished from random noise, and trends in process and product qualities can be predicted.

Level 3, Defined—Processes for management and engineering are documented, standardized, and integrated into a standard software process for the organization.

All projects use an approved, tailored version of the organization's standard software process for developing software.

Level 2, Repeatable—Basic project management processes are established to track cost, schedule, and functionality. Planning and managing new products is based on experience with similar projects.

Level 1, Initial—Few processes are defined, and success depends more on individual heroic efforts than on following a process and using a synergistic team effort.

The CMM maturity scale goes no further, but experience indicates that many organizations exhibit levels of "process immaturity" [Sch96] that undermine any rational attempt at improving software engineering practices. Schorsch [Sch06] suggests four levels of immaturity that are often encountered in the real world of software development organizations:

"How do you recognize an organization that will resist SPI efforts?"

Level 0, Negligent—Failure to allow successful development process to succeed. All problems are perceived to be technical problems. Managerial and quality assurance activities are deemed to be overhead and superfluous to the task of software development process. Reliance on silver pellets.

Level –1, Obstructive—Counterproductive processes are imposed. Processes are rigidly defined and adherence to the form is stressed. Ritualistic ceremonies abound. Collective management precludes assigning responsibility. Status quo über alles.

Level –2, Contemptuous—Disregard for good software engineering institutionalized. Complete schism between software development activities and software process improvement activities. Complete lack of a training program.

Level –3, Undermining—Total neglect of own charter, conscious discrediting of peer organization's software process improvement efforts. Rewarding failure and poor performance.

Schorsch's immaturity levels are toxic for any software organization. If you encounter any one of them, attempts at SPI are doomed to failure.

The overriding question is whether maturity scales, such as the one proposed as part of the CMM, provide any real benefit. I think that they do. A maturity scale provides an easily understood snapshot of process quality that can be used by practitioners and managers as a benchmark from which improvement strategies can be planned.

30.1.3   Is SPI for Everyone?

For many years, SPI was viewed as a "corporate" activity—a euphemism for something that only large companies perform. But today, a significant percentage of all software development is being performed by companies that employ fewer than 100 people. Can a small company initiate SPI activities and do it successfully?

ADVICE

If a specific process model or SPI approach feels like overkill for your organization, it probably is.

There are substantial cultural differences between large software development organizations and small ones. It should come as no surprise that small organizations are more informal, apply fewer standard practices, and tend to be self-organizing. They also tend to pride themselves on the "creativity" of individual members of the software organization, and initially view an SPI framework as overly bureaucratic and ponderous. Yet, process improvement is as important for a small organization as it is for a large one.

Within small organizations the implementation of an SPI framework requires resources that may be in short supply. Managers must allocate people and money to make software engineering happen. Therefore, regardless of the size of the software organization, it's reasonable to consider the business motivation for SPI.

SPI will be approved and implemented only after its proponents demonstrate financial leverage [Bir98]. Financial leverage is demonstrated by examining technical benefits (e.g., fewer defects delivered to the field, reduced rework, lower maintenance costs, or more rapid time-to-market) and translating them into dollars. In essence, you must show a realistic return on investment (Section 30.7) for SPI costs.

30.2 THE SPI PROCESS

The hard part of SPI isn't the definition of characteristics that define a high-quality software process or the creation of a process maturity model. Those things are relatively easy. Rather, the hard part is establishing a consensus for initiating SPI and defining an ongoing strategy for implementing it across a software organization.

The Software Engineering Institute has developed IDEAL—"an organizational improvement model that serves as a roadmap for initiating, planning, and implementing improvement actions" [SEI08]. IDEAL is representative of many process models for SPI, defining five distinct activities—initiating, diagnosing, establishing, acting, and learning—that guide an organization through SPI activities.

In this book, I present a somewhat different road map for SPI, based on the process model for SPI originally proposed in [Pre88]. It applies a commonsense philosophy that requires an organization to (1) look in the mirror, (2) then get smarter so it can make intelligent choices, (3) select the process model (and related technology elements) that best meets its needs, (4) instantiate the model into its operating environment and its culture, and (5) evaluate what has been done. These five activities (discussed in the subsections[2] that follow) are applied in an iterative (cyclical) manner in an effort to foster continuous process improvement.

30.2.1 Assessment and Gap Analysis

Any attempt to improve your current software process without first assessing the efficacy of current framework activities and associated software engineering practices would be like starting on a long journey to a new location with no idea where you are starting from. You'd depart with great flourish, wander around trying to get your bearings, expend lots of energy and endure large doses of frustration, and likely,

---

2 Some of the content in these sections has been adapted from [Pre88] with permission.

Be sure to understand
your strengths as well
as your weaknesses. If
you're smart, you'll
build on the strengths.

decide you really didn't want to travel anyway. Stated simply, before you begin any journey, it's a good idea to know precisely where you are.

The first road-map activity, called *assessment,* allows you to get your bearings. The intent of assessment is to uncover both strengths and weaknesses in the way your organization applies the existing software process and the software engineering practices that populate the process.

Assessment examines a wide range of actions and tasks that will lead to a high-quality process. For example, regardless of the process model that is chosen, the software organization must establish generic mechanisms such as: defined approaches for customer communication; established methods for representing user requirements; defining a project management framework that includes scoping, estimation, scheduling, and project tracking; risk analysis methods; change management procedures; quality assurance and control activities including reviews; and many others. Each is considered within the context of the framework and umbrella activities (Chapter 2) that have been established and is assessed to determine whether each of the following questions has been addressed:

- Is the objective of the action clearly defined?
- Are work products required as input and produced as output identified and described?
- Are the work tasks to be performed clearly described?
- Are the people who must perform the action identified by role?
- Have entry and exit criteria been established?
- Have metrics for the action been established?
- Are tools available to support the action?
- Is there an explicit training program that addresses the action?
- Is the action performed uniformly for all projects?

Although the questions noted imply a *yes* or *no* answer, the role of assessment is to look behind the answer to determine whether the action in question is being performed in a manner that would conform to best practice.

As the process assessment is conducted, you (or those who have been hired to perform the assessment) should also focus on the following attributes:

? "What
   generic
attributes do you
look for during
assessment?"

Consistency. Are important activities, actions, and tasks applied consistently across all software projects and by all software teams?

Sophistication. Are management and technical actions performed with a level of sophistication that implies a thorough understanding of best practice?

Acceptance. Is the software process and software engineering practice widely accepted by management and technical staff?

Commitment. Has management committed the resources required to achieve consistency, sophistication, and acceptance?

The difference between local application and best practice represents a "gap" that offers opportunities for improvement. The degree to which consistency, sophistication, acceptance, and commitment are achieved indicates the amount of cultural change that will be required to achieve meaningful improvement.

30.2.2   Education and Training

Although few software people question the benefit of an agile, organized software process or solid software engineering practices, many practitioners and managers do not know enough about either subject.[3] As a consequence, inaccurate perceptions of process and practice lead to inappropriate decisions when an SPI framework is introduced. It follows that a key element of any SPI strategy is education and training for practitioners, technical managers and more senior managers who have direct contact with the software organization. Three types of education and training should be conducted:

Try to provide "just-in-time" training targeted to the real needs of a software team.

Generic concepts and methods. Directed toward both managers and practitioners, this category stresses both process and practice. The intent is to provide professionals with the intellectual tools they need to apply the software process effectively and to make rational decisions about improvements to the process.

Specific technology and tools. Directed primarily toward practitioners, this category stresses technologies and tools that have been adopted for local use. For example, if UML has been chosen for analysis and design modeling, a training curriculum for software engineering using UML would be established.

Business communication and quality-related topics. Directed toward all stakeholders, this category focuses on "soft" topics that help enable better communication among stakeholders and foster a greater quality focus.

In a modern context, education and training can be delivered in a variety of different ways. Everything from podcasts, to Internet-based training (e.g., [QAI08]), to DVDs, to classroom courses can be offered as part of an SPI strategy.

As you make your choices, be sure to consider the culture of your organization and the level of acceptance that each choice will likely elicit.

30.2.3   Selection and Justification

Once the initial assessment activity[4] has been completed and education has begun, a software organization should begin to make choices. These choices occur during a *selection and justification activity* in which process characteristics and specific software engineering methods and tools are chosen to populate the software process.

First, you should choose the process model (Chapters 2 and 3) that best fits your organization, its stakeholders, and the software that you build. You should decide

---

3   If you've spent time reading this book, you won't be one of them!

4   In actuality, assessment is an ongoing activity. It is conducted periodically in an effort to determine whether the SPI strategy has achieved its immediate goals and to set the stage for future improvement.

which of the set of framework activities will be applied, the major work products that will be produced, and the quality assurance checkpoints that will enable your team to assess progress. If the SPI assessment activity indicates specific weaknesses (e.g., no formal SQA functions), you should focus attention on process characteristics that will address these weaknesses directly.

Next, develop a work breakdown for each framework activity (e.g., modeling), defining the task set that would be applied for a typical project. You should also consider the software engineering methods that can be applied to achieve these tasks. As choices are made, education and training should be coordinated to ensure that understanding is reinforced.

Ideally, everyone works together to select various process and technology elements and moves smoothly toward the installation or migration activity (Section 30.2.4). In reality, selection can be a rocky road. It is often difficult to achieve consensus among different constituencies. If the criteria for selection are established by committee, people may argue endlessly about whether the criteria are appropriate and whether a choice truly meets the criteria that have been established.

It is true that a bad choice can do more harm than good, but "paralysis by analysis" means that little if any progress occurs and process problems remain. As long as the process characteristic or technology element has a good chance at meeting an organization's needs, it's sometimes better to pull the trigger and make a choice, rather than waiting for the optimal solution.

Once a choice is made, time and money must be expended to instantiate it within an organization, and these resource expenditures should be justified. A discussion of cost justification and return on investment for SPI is presented in Section 30.7.

30.2.4   Installation/Migration

Installation is the first point at which a software organization feels the effects of changes implemented as a consequence of the SPI road map. In some cases, an entirely new process is recommended for an organization. Framework activities, software engineering actions, and individual work tasks must be defined and installed as part of a new software engineering culture. Such changes represent a substantial organizational and technological transition and must be managed very carefully.

In other cases, changes associated with SPI are relatively minor, representing small, but meaningful modifications to an existing process model. Such changes are often referred to as *process migration*. Today, many software organizations have a "process" in place. The problem is that it doesn't work in an effective manner. Therefore, an incremental *migration* from one process (that doesn't work as well as desired) to another process is a more effective strategy.

Installation and migration are actually *software process redesign* (SPR) activities. Scacchi [Sca00] states that "SPR is concerned with identification, application, and refinement of new ways to dramatically improve and transform software processes." When a formal approach to SPR is initiated, three different process models are considered: (1) the existing ("as is") process, (2) a transitional ("here to there") process, and (3) the target ("to be") process. If the target process is significantly different from the existing process, the only rational approach to installation is an incremental strategy in which the transitional process is implemented in steps. The transitional process provides a series of way-points that enable the software organization's culture to adapt to small changes over a period of time.

30.2.5   Evaluation

Although it is listed as the last activity in the SPI road map, *evaluation* occurs throughout SPI. The evaluation activity assesses the degree to which changes have been instantiated and adopted, the degree to which such changes result in better software quality or other tangible process benefits, and the overall status of the process and the organizational culture as SPI activities proceed.

Both qualitative factors and quantitative metrics are considered during the evaluation activity. From a qualitative point of view, past management and practitioner attitudes about the software process can be compared to attitudes polled after installation of process changes. Quantitative metrics (Chapter 25) are collected from projects that have used the transitional or "to be" process and compared with similar metrics that were collected for projects that were conducted under the "as is" process.

30.2.6   Risk Management for SPI

KEY POINT

SPI often fails because risks were not properly considered and no contingency planning occurred.

SPI is a risky undertaking. In fact, more than half of all SPI efforts end in failure. The reasons for failure vary greatly and are organizationally specific. Among the most common risks are: a lack of management support, cultural resistance by technical staff, a poorly planned SPI strategy, an overly formal approach to SPI, selection of an inappropriate process, a lack of buy-in by key stakeholders, an inadequate budget, a lack of staff training, organizational instability, and a myriad of other factors. The role of those chartered with the responsibility for SPI is to analyze likely risks and develop an internal strategy for mitigating them.

A software organization should manage risk at three key points in the SPI process [Sta97b]: prior to the initiation of the SPI road map, during the execution of SPI activities (assessment, education, selection, installation), and during the evaluation activity that follows the instantiation of some process characteristic. In general, the following categories [Sta97b] can be identified for SPI risk factors: budget and cost, content and deliverables, culture, maintenance of SPI deliverables, mission and goals, organizational management, organizational stability, process stakeholders, schedule for SPI development, SPI development environment, SPI development process, SPI project management, and SPI staff.

Within each category, a number of generic risk factors can be identified. For example, the organizational culture has a strong bearing on risk. The following generic risk factors[5] can be defined for the culture category [Sta97b]:

- Attitude toward change, based on prior efforts to change
- Experience with quality programs, level of success
- Action orientation for solving problems versus political struggles
- Use of facts to manage the organization and business
- Patience with change; ability to spend time socializing
- Tools orientation—expectation that tools can solve the problems
- Level of "planfulness"—ability of organization to plan
- Ability of organization members to participate with various levels of organization openly at meetings
- Ability of organization members to manage meetings effectively
- Level of experience in organization with defined processes

Using the risk factors and generic attributes as a guide, risk exposure is computed in the following manner:

$$\text{Exposure} = (\text{risk probability}) \times (\text{estimated loss})$$

A risk table (Chapter 28) can be developed to isolate those risks that warrant further management attention.

30.2.7   Critical Success Factors

In Section 30.2.6, I noted that SPI is a risky endeavor and that the failure rate for companies that try to improve their process is distressingly high. Organizational risks, people risks, and project management risks present challenges for those who lead any SPI effort. Although risk management is important, it's equally important to recognize those critical factors that lead to success.

After examining 56 software organizations and their SPI efforts, Stelzer and Mellis [Ste99] identify a set of critical success factors (CSFs) that must be present if SPI is to succeed. The top five CSFs are presented in this section.

> **? What critical success factors are crucial for successful SPI?**

Management commitment and support. Like most activities that precipitate organizational and cultural change, SPI will succeed only if management is actively involved. Senior business managers should recognize the importance of software to their company and be active sponsors of the SPI effort. Technical managers should be heavily involved in the development of the local SPI strategy. As the authors of the study note: "Software process improvement is not feasible without investing time, money, and effort" [Ste99]. Management commitment and support are essential to sustain that investment.

---

5   Risk factors for each of the risk categories noted in this section can be found in [Sta97b].

Staff involvement. SPI cannot be imposed top down, nor can it be imposed from the outside. If SPI efforts are to succeed, improvement must be organic—sponsored by technical managers and senior technologists, and adopted by local practitioners.

Process integration and understanding. The software process does not exist in an organizational vacuum. It must be characterized in a manner that is integrated with other business processes and requirements. To accomplish this, those responsible for the SPI effort must have an intimate knowledge and understanding of other business processes. In addition, they must understand the "as is" software process and appreciate how much transitional change is tolerable within the local culture.

A customized SPI strategy. There is no cookie-cutter SPI strategy. As I noted earlier in this chapter, the SPI road map must be adapted to the local environment—team culture, product mix, and local strengths and weaknesses must all be considered.

Solid management of the SPI project. SPI is a project like any other. It involves coordination, scheduling, parallel tasks, deliverables, adaptation (when risks become realities), politics, budget control, and much more. Without active and effective management, an SPI project is doomed to failure.

30.3 THE CMMI

WebRef

Complete information on the CMMI can be obtained at **www.sei.cmu .edu/cmmi/**.

The original CMM was developed and upgraded by the Software Engineering Institute throughout the 1990s as a complete SPI framework. Today, it has evolved into the *Capability Maturity Model Integration* (CMMI) [CMM07], a comprehensive process meta-model that is predicated on a set of system and software engineering capabilities that should be present as organizations reach different levels of process capability and maturity.

The CMMI represents a process meta-model in two different ways: (1) as a "continuous" model and (2) as a "staged" model. The continuous CMMI meta-model describes a process in two dimensions as illustrated in Figure 30.2. Each process area (e.g., project planning or requirements management) is formally assessed against specific goals and practices and is rated according to the following capability levels:

Level 0: *Incomplete*—the process area (e.g., requirements management) is either not performed or does not achieve all goals and objectives defined by the CMMI for level 1 capability for the process area.

Level 1: *Performed*—all of the specific goals of the process area (as defined by the CMMI) have been satisfied. Work tasks required to produce defined work products are being conducted.

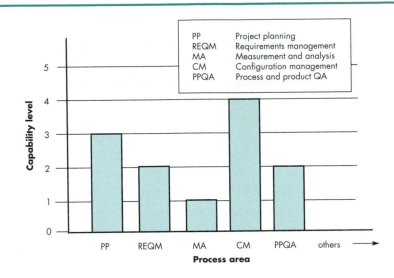

FIGURE 30.2

CMMI process area capability profile.
Source: [Phi02].

Level 2: *Managed*—all capability level 1 criteria have been satisfied. In addition, all work associated with the process area conforms to an organizationally defined policy; all people doing the work have access to adequate resources to get the job done; stakeholders are actively involved in the process area as required; all work tasks and work products are "monitored, controlled, and reviewed; and are evaluated for adherence to the process description" [CMM07].

Level 3: *Defined*—all capability level 2 criteria have been achieved. In addition, the process is "tailored from the organization's set of standard processes according to the organization's tailoring guidelines, and contributes work products, measures, and other process-improvement information to the organizational process assets" [CMM07].

Level 4: *Quantitatively managed*—all capability level 3 criteria have been achieved. In addition, the process area is controlled and improved using measurement and quantitative assessment. "Quantitative objectives for quality and process performance are established and used as criteria in managing the process" [CMM07].

Level 5: *Optimized*—all capability level 4 criteria have been achieved. In addition, the process area is adapted and optimized using quantitative (statistical) means to meet changing customer needs and to continually improve the efficacy of the process area under consideration.

The CMMI defines each process area in terms of "specific goals" and the "specific practices" required to achieve these goals. *Specific goals* establish the characteristics that must exist if the activities implied by a process area are to be effective. *Specific practices* refine a goal into a set of process-related activities.

For example, **project planning** is one of eight process areas defined by the CMMI for "project management" category.[6] The specific goals (SG) and the associated specific practices (SP) defined for **project planning** are [CMM07]:

SG 1 Establish Estimates

WebRef

Complete information as well as a downloadable version of the CMMI can be obtained at **www.sei.cmu.edu/cmmi/**.

SP 1.1-1 Estimate the Scope of the Project

SP 1.2-1 Establish Estimates of Work Product and Task Attributes

SP 1.3-1 Define Project Life Cycle

SP 1.4-1 Determine Estimates of Effort and Cost

SG 2 Develop a Project Plan

SP 2.1-1 Establish the Budget and Schedule

SP 2.2-1 Identify Project Risks

SP 2.3-1 Plan for Data Management

SP 2.4-1 Plan for Project Resources

SP 2.5-1 Plan for Needed Knowledge and Skills

SP 2.6-1 Plan Stakeholder Involvement

SP 2.7-1 Establish the Project Plan

SG 3 Obtain Commitment to the Plan

SP 3.1-1 Review Plans That Affect the Project

SP 3.2-1 Reconcile Work and Resource Levels

SP 3.3-1 Obtain Plan Commitment

In addition to specific goals and practices, the CMMI also defines a set of five generic goals and related practices for each process area. Each of the five generic goals corresponds to one of the five capability levels. Hence, to achieve a particular capability level, the generic goal for that level and the generic practices that correspond to that goal must be achieved. To illustrate, the generic goals (GG) and practices (GP) for the **project planning** process area are [CMM07]:

GG 1 Achieve Specific Goals

GP 1.1 Perform Base Practices

GG 2 Institutionalize a Managed Process

GP 2.1 Establish an Organizational Policy

GP 2.2 Plan the Process

GP 2.3 Provide Resources

GP 2.4 Assign Responsibility

GP 2.5 Train People

---

6 Other process areas defined for "project management" include: project monitoring and control, supplier agreement management, integrated project management for IPPD, risk management, integrated teaming, integrated supplier management, and quantitative project management.

GP 2.6 Manage Configurations

GP 2.7 Identify and Involve Relevant Stakeholders

GP 2.8 Monitor and Control the Process

GP 2.9 Objectively Evaluate Adherence

GP 2.10 Review Status with Higher-Level Management

GG 3 Institutionalize a Defined Process

GP 3.1 Establish a Defined Process

GP 3.2 Collect Improvement Information

GG 4 Institutionalize a Quantitatively Managed Process

GP 4.1 Establish Quantitative Objectives for the Process

GP 4.2 Stabilize Subprocess Performance

GG 5 Institutionalize an Optimizing Process

GP 5.1 Ensure Continuous Process Improvement

GP 5.2 Correct Root Causes of Problems

The staged CMMI model defines the same process areas, goals, and practices as the continuous model. The primary difference is that the staged model defines five maturity levels, rather than five capability levels. To achieve a maturity level, the specific goals and practices associated with a set of process areas must be achieved. The relationship between maturity levels and process areas is shown in Figure 30.3.

INFO

The CMMI—Should We or Shouldn't We?

The CMMI is a process meta-model. It defines (in 700+ pages) the process characteristics that should exist if an organization wants to establish a software process that is complete. The question that has been debated for well over a decade is: "Is the CMMI overkill?" Like most things in life (and in software), the answer is not a simple "yes" or "no."

The spirit of the CMMI should always be adopted. At the risk of oversimplification, it argues that software development must be taken seriously—it must be planned thoroughly, it must be controlled uniformly, it must be tracked accurately, and it must be conducted professionally. It must focus on the needs of project stakeholders, the skills of the software engineers, and the quality of the end product. No one would argue with these ideas.

The detailed requirements of the CMMI should be seriously considered if an organization builds large complex systems that involve dozens or hundreds of

people over many months or years. It may be that the CMMI is "just right" in such situations, if the organizational culture is amenable to standard process models and management is committed to making it a success. However, in other situations, the CMMI may simply be too much for an organization to successfully assimilate. Does this mean that the CMMI is "bad" or "overly bureaucratic" or "old fashioned?" No . . . it does not. It simply means that what is right for one organizational culture may not be right for another.

The CMMI is a significant achievement in software engineering. It provides a comprehensive discussion of the activities and actions that should be present when an organization builds computer software. Even if a software organization chooses not to adopt its details, every software team should embrace its spirit and gain insight from its discussion of software engineering process and practice.

FIGURE 30.3

Process areas
required to
achieve a
maturity level.
Source: [Phi02].

Level	Focus	Process Areas
Optimizing	*Continuous process improvement*	Organizational innovation and deployment Causal analysis and resolution
Quantitatively managed	*Quantitative management*	Organizational process performance Quantitative project management
Defined	*Process standardization*	Requirements development Technical solution Product integration Verification Validation Organizational process focus Organizational process definition Organizational training Integrated project management Integrated supplier management Risk management Decision analysis and resolution Organizational environment for integration Integrated teaming
Managed	*Basic project management*	Requirements management Project planning Project monitoring and control Supplier agreement management Measurement and analysis Process and product quality assurance Configuration management
Performed		

30.4   THE PEOPLE CMM

The People CMM
suggests practices that
improve the workforce
competence and
culture.

A software process, no matter how well conceived, will not succeed without talented, motivated software people. The *People Capability Maturity Model* "is a roadmap for implementing workforce practices that continuously improve the capability of an organization's workforce" [Cur02]. Developed in the mid-1990s and refined over the intervening years, the goal of the People CMM is to encourage continuous improvement of generic workforce knowledge (called "core competencies"), specific software engineering and project management skills (called "workforce competencies"), and process-related abilities.

Like the CMM, CMMI, and related SPI frameworks, the People CMM defines a set of five organizational maturity levels that provide an indication of the relative sophistication of workforce practices and processes. These maturity levels [CMM08] are tied to the existence (within an organization) of a set of key process areas (KPAs). An overview of organizational levels and related KPAs is shown in Figure 30.4.

Level	Focus	Process Areas
Optimized	*Continuous improvement*	**Continuous workforce innovation** **Organizational performance alignment** **Continuous capability improvement**
Predictable	*Quantifies and manages knowledge, skills, and abilities*	**Mentoring** **Organizational capability management** **Quantitative performance management** **Competency-based assets** **Empowered workgroups** **Competency integration**
Defined	*Identifies and develops knowledge, skills, and abilities*	**Participatory culture** **Workgroup development** **Competency-based practices** **Career development** **Competency development** **Workforce planning** **Competency analysis**
Managed	*Repeatable, basic people management practices*	**Compensation** **Training and development** **Performance management** **Work environment** **Communication and co-ordination** **Staffing**
Initial	*Inconsistent practices*	

The People CMM complements any SPI framework by encouraging an organization to nurture and improve its most important asset—its people. As important, it establishes a workforce atmosphere that enables a software organization to "attract, develop, and retain outstanding talent" [CMM08].

30.5 OTHER SPI FRAMEWORKS

Although the SEI's CMM and CMMI are the most widely applied SPI frameworks, a number of alternatives[7] have been proposed and are in use. Among the most widely used of these alternatives are:

- **SPICE**—an international initiative to support ISO's process assessment and life cycle process standards [SPI99]
- **ISO/IEC 15504** for (Software) Process Assessment [ISO08]

---

7 It's reasonable to argue that some of these frameworks are not so much "alternatives" as they are complementary approaches to SPI. A comprehensive table of many more SPI frameworks can be found at **www.geocities.com/lbu_measure/spi/spi.htm#p2**.

- **Bootstrap**—an SPI framework for small and medium-sized organizations that conforms to SPICE [Boo06]
- **PSP and TSP**—individual and team-specific SPI frameworks ([Hum97], [Hum00]) that focus on process in-the-small, a more rigorous approach to software development coupled with measurement
- **TickIT**—an auditing method [Tic05] that assesses an organization's compliance to ISO Standard 9001:2000

A brief overview of each of these SPI frameworks is presented in the paragraphs that follow. If you have further interest, a wide array of print and Web-based resources is available for each.

In addition to the CMM, are there other SPI frameworks that we might consider?

SPICE. The SPICE (*Software Process Improvement and Capability dEtermination*) model provides an SPI assessment framework that is compliant with ISO 15504:2003 and ISO 12207. The SPICE document suite [SDS08] presents a complete SPI framework including a model for process management, guidelines for conducting an assessment and rating the process under consideration, construction, selection, and use of assessment instruments and tools, and training for assessors.

Bootstrap. The *Bootstrap* SPI framework "has been developed to ensure conformance with the emerging ISO standard for software process assessment and improvement (SPICE) and to align the methodology with ISO 12207" [Boo06]. The objective of Bootstrap is to evaluate a software process using a set of software engineering best practices as a basis for assessment. Like the CMMI, Bootstrap provides a process maturity level using the results of questionnaires that gather information about the "as is" software process and software projects. SPI guidelines are based on maturity level and organizational goals.

PSP and TSP. Although SPI is generally characterized as an organizational activity, there is no reason why process improvement cannot be conducted at an individual or team level. Both PSP and TSP (Chapter 2) emphasize the need to continuously collect data about the work that is being performed and to use that data to develop strategies for improvement. Watts Humphrey [Hum97], the developer of both methods, comments:

> The PSP [and TSP] will show you how to plan and track your work and how to consistently produce high quality software. Using PSP [and TSP] will give you the data that show the effectiveness of your work and identify your strengths and weaknesses. . . . To have a successful and rewarding career, you need to know your skills and abilities, strive to improve them, and capitalize on your unique talents in the work you do.

TickIT. The Ticket auditing method ensures compliance with *ISO 9001:2000 for Software*—a generic standard that applies to any organization that wants to improve the overall quality of the products, systems, or services that it provides. Therefore, the standard is directly applicable to software organizations and companies.

uote:

"Software organizations have exhibited significant shortcomings in their ability to capitalize on the experiences gained from completed projects."

NASA

The underlying strategy suggested by ISO 9001:2000 is described in the following manner [ISO01]:

ISO 9001:2000 stresses the importance for an organization to identify, implement, manage and continually improve the effectiveness of the processes that are necessary for the quality management system, and to manage the interactions of these processes in order to achieve the organization's objectives. . . . Process effectiveness and efficiency can be assessed through internal or external review processes and be evaluated on a maturity scale.

WebRef

An excellent summary of ISO 9001: 2000 can be found at **http://praxiom .com/iso-9001 .htm**.

ISO 9001:2000 has adopted a "plan-do-check-act" cycle that is applied to the quality management elements of a software project. Within a software context, "plan" establishes the process objectives, activities, and tasks necessary to achieve high-quality software and resultant customer satisfaction. "Do" implements the software process (including both framework and umbrella activities). "Check" monitors and measures the process to ensure that all requirements established for quality management have been achieved. "Act" initiates software process improvement activities that continually work to improve the process. TickIt can be used throughout the "plan-do-check-act" cycle to ensure that SPI progress is being made. TickIT auditors assess the application of the cycle as a precursor to ISO 9001:2000 certification. For a detailed discussion of ISO 9001:2000 and TickIT you should examine [Ant06], [Tri05], or [Sch03].

30.6 SPI Return on Investment

SPI is hard work and requires substantial investment of dollars and people. Managers who approve the budget and resources for SPI will invariably ask the question: "How do I know that we'll achieve a reasonable return for the money we're spending?"

At a qualitative level, proponents of SPI argue that an improved software process will lead to improved software quality. They contend that improved process will result in the implementation of better quality filters (resulting in fewer propagated defects), better control of change (resulting in less project chaos), and less technical rework (resulting in lower cost and better time-to-market). But can these qualitative benefits be translated into quantitative results? The classic return on investment (ROI) equation is:

$$\text{ROI} = \left[\frac{\Sigma(benefits) - \Sigma(costs)}{\Sigma(costs)} \right] \times 100\%$$

where

benefits include the cost savings associated with higher product quality (fewer defects), less rework, reduced effort associated with changes, and the income that accrues from shorter time-to-market.

costs include both direct SPI costs (e.g., training, measurement) and indirect costs associated with greater emphasis on quality control and change management activities and more rigorous application of software engineering methods (e.g., the creation of a design model).

In the real world, these quantitative benefits and costs are sometimes difficult to measure with accuracy, and all are open to interpretation. But that doesn't mean that a software organization should conduct an SPI program without careful analysis of the costs and benefits that accrue. A comprehensive treatment of ROI for SPI can be found in a unique book by David Rico [Ric04].

30.7 SPI TRENDS

Over the past two decades, many companies have attempted to improve their software engineering practices by applying an SPI framework to effect organizational change and technology transition. As I noted earlier in this chapter, over half fail in this endeavor. Regardless of success or failure, all spend significant amounts of money. David Rico [Ric04] reports that a typical application of an SPI framework such as the SEI CMM can cost between $25,000 and $70,000 per person and take years to complete! It should come as no surprise that the future of SPI should emphasize a less costly and time-consuming approach.

To be effective in the twenty-first century world of software development, future SPI frameworks must become significantly more agile. Rather than an organizational focus (which can take years to complete successfully), contemporary SPI efforts should focus on the project level, working to improve a team process in weeks, not months or years. To achieve meaningful results (even at the project level) in a short time frame, complex framework models may give way to simpler models. Rather than dozens of key practices and hundreds of supplementary practices, an agile SPI framework should emphasize only a few pivotal practices (e.g., analogous to the framework activities discussed throughout this book).

Any attempt at SPI demands a knowledgeable workforce, but education and training expenses can be expensive and should be minimized (and streamlined). Rather than classroom courses (expensive and time consuming), future SPI efforts should rely on Web-based training that is targeted at pivotal practices. Rather than far-reaching attempts to change organizational culture (with all of the political perils that ensue), cultural change should occur as it does in the real world, one small group at a time until a tipping point is reached.

The SPI work of the past two decades has significant merit. The frameworks and models that have been developed represent substantial intellectual assets for the software engineering community. But like all things, these assets guide future attempts at SPI not by becoming a recurring dogma, but by serving as the basis for better, simpler, and more agile SPI models.

30.8   SUMMARY

A software process improvement framework defines the characteristics that must be present if an effective software process is to be achieved, an assessment method that helps determine whether those characteristics are present, and a strategy for assisting a software organization in implementing those process characteristics that have been found to be weak or missing. Regardless of the constituency that sponsors SPI, the goal is to improve process quality and, as a consequence, improve software quality and timeliness.

A process maturity model provides an overall indication of the "process maturity" exhibited by a software organization. It provides a qualitative feel for the relative effectiveness of the software process that is currently being used.

The SPI road map begins with assessment—a series of evaluation activities that uncover both strengths and weaknesses in the way your organization applies the existing software process and the software engineering practices that populate the process. As a consequence of assessment, a software organization can develop an overall SPI plan.

One of the key elements of any SPI plan is education and training, an activity that focuses on improving the knowledge level of managers and practitioners. Once staff becomes well versed in current software technologies, selection and justification commence. These tasks lead to choices about the architecture of the software process, the methods that populate it, and the tools that support it. Installation and evaluation are SPI activities that instantiate process changes and assess their efficacy and impact.

To successfully improve its software process, an organization must exhibit the following characteristics: management commitment and support for SPI, staff involvement throughout the SPI process, process integration into the overall organizational culture, an SPI strategy that has been customized for local needs, and solid management of the SPI project.

A number of SPI frameworks are in use today. The SEI's CMM and CMMI are widely used. The People CMM has been customized to assess the quality of the organizational culture and the people who populate it. SPICE, Bootstrap, PSP, TSP, and TickIT are additional frameworks that can lead to effective SPI.

SPI is hard work that requires substantial investment of dollars and people. To ensure that a reasonable return on investment is achieved, an organization must measure the costs associated with SPI and the benefits that can be directly attributed to it.

PROBLEMS AND POINTS TO PONDER

30.1. Why is it that software organizations often struggle when they embark on an effort to improve local software process?

30.2. Describe the concept of "process maturity" in your own words.

30.3. Do some research (check the SEI website) and determine the process maturity distribution for software organizations in the United States and worldwide.

30.4. You work for a very small software organization—only 11 people are involved in developing software. Is SPI for you? Explain your answer.

30.5. Assessment is analogous to an annual physical exam. Using a physical exam as a metaphor, describe the SPI assessment activity.

30.6. What is the difference between an "as is" process, a "here to there" process, and a "to be" process?

30.7. How is risk management applied within the context of SPI?

30.8. Select one of the critical success factors noted in Section 30.2.7. Do some research and write a brief paper on how it can be achieved.

30.9. Do some research and explain how the CMMI differs from its predecessor, the CMM.

30.10. Select one of the SPI frameworks discussed in Section 30.5, and write a brief paper describing it in more detail.

FURTHER READINGS AND INFORMATION SOURCES

One of the most readily accessible and comprehensive resources for information on SPI has been developed by the Software Engineering Institute and is available at **www.sei.cmu.edu**. The SEI website contains hundreds of papers, studies, and detailed SPI framework descriptions.

Over the past few years, a number of worthwhile books have been added to a broad literature developed during the past two decades. Land (*Jumpstart CMM/CMMI Software Process Improvements,* Wiley-IEEE Computer Society, 2007) melds the requirements defined as part of the SEI CMM and CMMI with IEEE software engineering standards with an emphasis on the intersection of process and practice. Mutafelija and Stromberg (*Systematic Process Improvement Using ISO 9001:2000 and CMMI,* Artech House Publishers, 2007) discuss both the ISO 9001:2000 and CMMI SPI frameworks and the "synergy" between them. Conradi and his colleagues (*Software Process Improvement: Results and Experience from the Field,* Springer, 2006) presents the results of a series of case studies and experiments related to SPI. Van Loon (*Process Assessment and Improvement: A Practical Guide for Managers, Quality Professionals and Assessors,* Springer, 2006) discusses SPI within the context of ISO/IEC 15504. Watts Humphrey (*PSP,* Addison-Wesley, 2005, and *TSP,* Addison-Wesley, 2005) addresses his Personal Team Process SPI framework and his Team Software Process SPI framework in two separate books. Fantina (*Practical Software Process Improvement,* Artech House Publishers, 2004) provides pragmatic how-to guidance with an emphasis on CMMI/CMM.

A wide variety of information sources on software process improvement is available on the Internet. An up-to-date list of World Wide Web references relevant to SPI can be found at the SEPA website: **www.mhhe.com/engcs/compsci/pressman/professional/olc/ser.htm**.

Throughout the relatively brief history of software engineering, practitioners and researchers have developed an array of process models, technical methods, and automated tools in an effort to foster fundamental change in the way we build computer software. Even though past experience indicates otherwise, there is a tacit desire to find the "silver bullet"—the magic process or transcendent technology that will allow us to build large, complex, software-based systems easily, without confusion, without mistakes, without delay—without the many problems that continue to plague software work.

But history indicates that our quest for the silver bullet appears doomed to failure. New technologies are introduced regularly, hyped as a "solution" to many of the problems software engineers face, and incorporated into projects large and small. Industry pundits stress the importance of these "new" software technologies, the cognoscenti of the software community adopt them with enthusiasm, and ultimately, they do play a role in the software engineering world. But they tend not to meet their promise, and as a consequence, the quest continues.

QUICK LOOK

What is it? No one can predict the future with absolute certainty. But it is possible to assess trends in the software engineering area and from those trends to suggest possible directions for the technology. That's what I attempt to do in this chapter.

Who does it? Anyone who is willing to spend the time to stay abreast of software engineering issues can try to predict the future direction of the technology.

Why is it important? Why did ancient kings hire soothsayers? Why do major multinational corporations hire consulting firms and think tanks to prepare forecasts? Why does a substantial percentage of the public read horoscopes? We want to know what's coming so we can ready ourselves.

What are the steps? There is no formula for predicting the road ahead. We attempt to do this by collecting data, organizing it to provide useful information, examining subtle associations to extract knowledge, and from this knowledge suggest probable trends that predict how things will be at some future time.

What is the work product? A view of the near-term future that may or may not be correct.

How do I ensure that I've done it right? Predicting the road ahead is an art, not a science. In fact, it's quite rare when a serious prediction about the future is absolutely right or unequivocally wrong (with the exception, thankfully, of predictions of the end of the world). We look for trends and try to extrapolate them. We can assess the correctness of the extrapolation only as time passes.

? **What are the "big questions" when we consider technology evolution?**

Mili and Cowan [Mil00b] comment on the challenges we face when trying to isolate meaningful technology trends:

> **What Factors Determine the Success of a Trend?** What characterizes successful technological trends: Their technical merit? Their ability to open new markets? Their ability to alter the economics of existing markets?

> **What Lifecycle Does a Trend Follow?** Whereas the traditional view is that trends evolve along a well defined, predictable lifecycle that proceeds from a research idea to a finished product through a transfer process, we find that many current trends have either short circuited this cycle or followed another one.

> **How Early Can a Successful Trend Be Identified?** If we know how to identify success factors, and/or we understand the lifecycle of a trend, then we seek to identify early signs of success of a trend. Rhetorically, we seek the ability to recognize the next trend ahead of everybody else.

> **What Aspects of Evolution Are Controllable?** Can corporations use their market clout to impose trends? Can the government use its resources to impose trends? What role do standards play in defining trends? The careful analysis of Ada vs. Java, for example, should be enlightening in this regard.

There are no easy answers to these questions, and there can be no debate that past attempts at identifying meaningful technologies are mediocre at best.

In past editions of this book (over the past 30 years), I have discussed emerging technologies and their projected impact on software engineering. Some have been widely adopted, but others never reached their potential. My conclusion: technologies come and go; the real trends you and I should explore are softer. By this I mean that progress in software engineering will be guided by business, organizational, market, and cultural trends. Those trends lead to technology innovation.

In this chapter, we'll look at a few software engineering technology trends, but my primary emphasis will be on some of the business, organizational, market, and cultural trends that may have an important influence on software engineering technology over the next 10 or 20 years.

31.1   TECHNOLOGY EVOLUTION

In a fascinating book that provides a compelling look at how computing (and other related) technologies will evolve, Ray Kurzweil [Kur05] argues that technological evolution is similar to biological evolution, but occurs at a rate that is orders of magnitude faster. Evolution (whether biological or technological) occurs as a result of positive feedback—"the more capable methods resulting from one stage of evolutionary progress are used to create the next stage" [Kur06].

The big questions for the twenty-first century are: (1) How rapidly does a technology evolve? (2) How significant are the effects of positive feedback. (3) How profound will the resultant changes be?

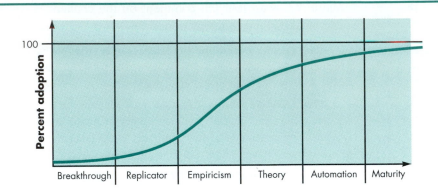

When a successful new technology is introduced, the initial concept moves
through a reasonably predictable "innovation life cycle" [Gai95] illustrated in
Figure 31.1. In the *breakthrough* phase, a problem is recognized and repeated
attempts at a viable solution are attempted. At some point, a solution shows
promise. The initial breakthrough work is reproduced in the *replicator* phase and
gains wider usage. *Empiricism* leads to the creation of empirical rules that govern the
use of the technology, and repeated success leads to a broader *theory* of usage that
is followed by the creation of automated tools during the *automation* phase. Finally,
the technology matures and is used widely.

You should note that many research and technology trends never reach maturity.
In fact, the vast majority of "promising" technologies in the software engineering
domain receive widespread interest for a few years and then fall into niche usage by
a dedicated band of adherents. This is not to say that these technologies lack merit,
but rather to emphasize that the journey through the innovation life cycle is long
and hard.

Kurzweil [Kur05] agrees that computing technologies evolve through an "S-curve"
that exhibits relatively slow growth during the technology's formative years, rapid
acceleration during its growth period, and then a leveling-off period as the technology reaches its limits. But computing and other related technologies have exhibited
explosive (exponential) growth during the central stages shown in Figure 31.1 and
will continue to do so. In addition, as one S-curve ends, another replaces it with even
more explosive growth during its growth period.[1] Today, we are at the knee of the
S-curve for modern computing technologies—at the transition between early growth
and the explosive growth that is to follow. The implication is that over the next 20 to
40 years, we will see dramatic (even mind-boggling) changes in computing capability.
The coming decades will result in order-of-magnitude changes in computing speed,
size, capacity, and energy consumption (to name only a few characteristics).

---

1   For example, the limits of integrated circuits may be reached within the next decade, but that tech-
    nology may be replaced by molecular computing technologies and another accelerated S-curve.

Kurzweil [Kur05] suggests that within 20 years, technology evolution will accelerate at an increasingly rapid pace, ultimately leading to an era of nonbiological intelligence that will merge with and extend human intelligence in ways that are fascinating to contemplate.

And all of this, no matter how it evolves, will require software and systems that make our current efforts look infantile by comparison. By the year 2040, a combination of extreme computation, nanotechnology, massively high bandwidth ubiquitous networks, and robotics will lead us into a different world.[2] Software, possibly in forms we cannot yet comprehend, will continue to reside at the core of this new world. Software engineering will not go away.

31.2   OBSERVING SOFTWARE ENGINEERING TRENDS

Section 31.1 briefly considered the fascinating possibilities that may accrue from long-term trends in computing and related technologies. But what of the near term?

Barry Boehm [Boe08] suggests that "software engineers [will] face the often formidable challenges of dealing with rapid change, uncertainty and emergence, dependability, diversity, and interdependence, but they also have opportunities to make significant contributions that will make a difference for the better." But what are the trends that will enable you to face these challenges in the years ahead?

In the introduction to this chapter, I noted that "soft trends" have a significant impact on the overall direction of software engineering. But other ("harder") research- and technology-oriented trends remain important. Research trends "are driven by general perceptions of the state of the art and the state of the practice, by researcher perceptions of practitioner needs, by national funding programs that rally around specific strategic goals, and by sheer technical interest" [Mil00a]. Technology trends occur when research trends are extrapolated to meet industry needs and are shaped by market-driven demand.

KEY POINT

The "hype cycle" presents a realistic view of short-term technology integration. The long-term trend, however, is exponential.

In Section 31.1, I discussed the S-curve model for technology evolution. The S-curve is appropriate for considering the long-term effects of core technologies as they evolve. But what of more modest, short-term innovations, tools, and methods? The Gartner Group [Gar08]—a consultancy that studies technology trends across many industries—has developed a *hype cycle for emerging technologies,* represented in Figure 31.2. The Gartner Group cycle exhibits five phases:

- *Technology trigger*—a research breakthrough or launch of an innovative new product that leads to media coverage and public enthusiasm.

- *Peak of inflated expectations*—overenthusiasm and overly optimistic projections of impact based on limited, but well-publicized successes.

---

2   Kurzweil [Kur05] presents a reasoned technical argument that predicts a strong artificial intelligence (that will pass the Turing Test) by 2029 and suggests that the evolution of humans and machines will begin to merge by 2045. The vast majority of readers of this book will live to see whether this, in fact, comes to pass.

FIGURE 31.2

The Gartner Group's hype cycle for emerging technologies.
Source: [Gar08].

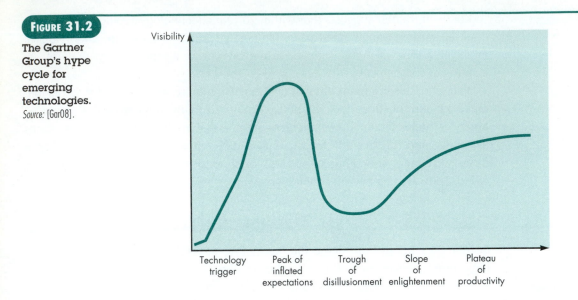

- *Disillusionment*—overly optimistic projections of impact are not met and critics begin the drumbeat; the technology becomes unfashionable among the cognoscenti.
- *Slope of enlightenment*—growing usage by a wide variety of companies leads to a better understanding of the technology's true potential; off-the-shelf methods and tools emerge to support the technology.
- *Plateau of productivity*—real-world benefits are now obvious, and usage penetrates a significant percentage of the potential market.

Not every software engineering technology makes it all the way through the hype cycle. In some cases, disillusionment is justified and the technology is relegated to obscurity.

31.3   IDENTIFYING "SOFT TRENDS"

Quote:

"640K ought to be enough for anybody."

Bill Gates, chairman of Microsoft, 1981

Each nation with a substantial IT industry has a set of unique characteristics that define the manner in which business is conducted, the organizational dynamics that arise within a company, the distinct marketing issues that apply to local customers, and the overriding culture that dictates all human interaction. However, some trends in each of these areas are universal and have as much to do with sociology, anthropology, and group psychology (often referred to as the "soft sciences") as they do with academic or industrial research.

Connectivity and collaboration (enabled by high-bandwidth communication) has already led to software teams that do not occupy the same physical space (telecommuting and part-time employment in a local context). One team collaborates with other teams that are separated by time zones, primary language, and culture.

? **What soft trends will impact technologies related to software engineering?**

Software engineering must respond with an overarching process model for "distributed teams" that is agile enough to meet the demands of immediacy but disciplined enough to coordinate disparate groups.

Globalization leads to a diverse workforce (in terms of language, culture, problem resolution, management philosophy, communication priorities, and person-to-person interaction). This, in turn, demands a flexible organizational structure. Different teams (in different countries) must respond to engineering problems in a way that best accommodates their unique needs, while at the same time fostering a level of uniformity that allows a global project to proceed. This type of organization suggests fewer levels of management and a greater emphasis on team-level decision making. It can lead to greater agility, but only if communication mechanisms have been established so that every team can understand project and technical status (via networked groupware) at any time. Software engineering methods and tools can help achieve some level of uniformity (teams speak the same "language" implemented through specific methods and tools). Software process can provide the framework for the instantiation of these methods and tools.

In some world regions (the United States and Europe are examples), the population is aging. This undeniable demographic (and cultural trend) implies that many experienced software engineers and managers will be leaving the field over the coming decade. The software engineering community must respond with viable mechanisms that capture the knowledge of these aging managers and technologists [e.g., the use of *patterns* (Chapter 12) is a step in the right direction], so that it will be available to future generations of software workers. In other regions of the world, the number of young people available to the software industry is exploding. This provides an opportunity to mold a software engineering culture without the burden of 50 years of "old-school" prejudices.

It is estimated that over one billion new consumers will enter the worldwide marketplace over the next decade. Consumer spending in "emerging economies will double to well over $9 trillion" [Pet06]. There is little doubt that a nontrivial percentage of this spending will be applied to products and services that have a digital component—that are software based or software driven. The implication—an increasing demand for new software. The question then is, "Can new software engineering technologies be developed to meet this worldwide demand?" Modern market trends are often driven by the supply side.[3] In other cases, demand-side requirements drive the market. In either case, a cycle of innovation and demand progresses in a way that sometimes makes it difficult to determine which came first!

Finally, human culture itself will impact the direction of software engineering. Every generation establishes its own imprint on local culture, and yours will be no different. Faith Popcorn [Pop08], a well-known consultant who specializes in

---

3   Supply side adopts a "build it and they will come" approach to markets. Unique technologies are created, and consumers flock to adopt them—sometimes!

cultural trends, characterizes them in the following manner: "Our Trends are not fads. Our Trends endure. Our Trends evolve. They represent underlying forces, first causes, basic human needs, attitudes, aspirations. They help us navigate the world, understand what's happening and why, and prepare for what is yet to come." A detailed discussion of how modern cultural trends will have an impact on software engineering is best left to those who specialize in the "soft sciences."

31.3.1   Managing Complexity

When the first edition of this book was written (1982), digital consumer products as we now know them today didn't exist, and mainframe-based systems containing a million lines of source code (LOC) were considered to be quite large. Today, it is not uncommon for small digital devices to encompass between 60,000 to 200,000 lines of custom software, coupled with a few million LOC for operating system features. Modern computer-based systems containing 10 to 50 million lines of code are not uncommon.[4] In the relatively near future, systems[5] requiring over 1 billion LOC will begin to emerge.[6]

Think about that for a moment!

Consider the interfaces for a billion LOC system, both to the outside world, to other interoperable systems, to the Internet (or its successor), and to the millions of internal components that must all work together to make this computing monster operate successfully. Is there a reliable way to ensure that all of these connections will allow information to flow properly?

Consider the project itself. How do we manage the workflow and track progress? Will conventional approaches scale upward by orders of magnitude?

Consider the number of people (and their locations) who will be doing the work, the coordination of people and technology, the unrelenting flow of changes, the likelihood of a multiplatform, multioperating system environment. Is there a way to manage and coordinate people who are working on a monster project?

Consider the engineering challenge. How can we analyze tens of thousands of requirements, constraints, and restrictions in a way that ensures that inconsistency and ambiguity, omissions, and outright errors are uncovered and corrected? How can we create a design architecture that is robust enough to handle a system of this size? How can software engineers establish a change management system that will have to handle hundreds of thousands of changes?

Consider the challenge of quality assurance. How can we perform verification and validation in a meaningful way? How do you test a 1 billion LOC system?

uote:

"There is no reason anyone would want a computer in their home."

Ken Olson, President, Chairman, and Founder of Digital Equipment Corp., 1977

---

4   For example, modern PC operating systems (e.g., Linux, MacOS, and Windows) have between 30 and 60 million LOC. Operating system software for mobile devices can exceed 2 million LOC.

5   In reality, this "system" will actually be a system of systems—hundreds of interoperable applications working together to achieve some overall objective.

6   Not all complex systems are large. A relatively small application (say, less than 100,000 LOC can still be exceedingly complex.

In the early days, software engineers attempted to manage complexity in what can only be described as an ad hoc fashion. Today, we use process, methods, and tools to keep complexity under control. But tomorrow? Is our current approach up to the task?

31.3.2   Open-World Software

Concepts such as ambient intelligence,[7] context-aware applications, and pervasive/ ubiquitous computing—all focus on integrating software-based systems into an environment far broader that a PC, a mobile computing device, or any other digital device. These separate visions of the near-term future of computing collectively suggest "open-world software"—software that is designed to adapt to a continually changing environment "by self-organizing its structure and self-adapting its behavior" [Bar06].

KEY POINT

Open-world software encompasses ambient intelligence, context-aware apps, and pervasive computing.

To help illustrate the challenges that software engineers will face in the foreseeable future, consider the notion of *ambient intelligence* (amI). Ducatel [Duc01] defines amI in the following way: "People are surrounded by intelligent, intuitive interfaces that are embedded in all kinds of objects. The ambient intelligence environment is capable of recognizing and responding to the presence of different individuals [while working] in a seamless, unobstrusive way."

Let's examine a vision of the near future in which amI has become ubiquitous. You've just purchased a personal communicator (called a P-com, a pocket-sized mobile device) and have spent the last few weeks creating[8] your "image"—everything from your daily schedule, to-do list, address book, medical records, business-related information, travel documents, wish list (things you're looking for, e.g., a specific book, a bottle of hard-to-find wine, a local course in glass blowing), and "Digital-Me" (D-Me) that describes you at a level of detail that allows a digital introduction to others (sort of a *MySpace* or *FaceBook* that moves with you). The P-com contains a personal identifier called a "key of keys"—a multifunctional personal identifier that would provide access to and enable queries from a wide range of amI devices and systems.

It should be obvious that significant privacy and security issues come into play. A "trust management system" [Duc01] will be an integral part of amI and will manage privileges that enable communication with networks, health, entertainment, financial, employment, and personal systems.

New amI-capable systems will be added to the network constantly, each providing useful capabilities and demanding access to your P-com. Therefore, the P-com software must be designed so that it can adapt to the requirements that emerge as some new amI systems go online. There are many ways to accomplish this, but the bottom line is this: the P-com software must be flexible and robust in ways that conventional software can't match.

---

7   A worthwhile and quite detailed introduction to ambient intelligence can be found at **www.emergingcommunication.com/volume6.html**. More information can be obtained at **www.ambientintelligence.org/**.

8   All interaction with the P-com occurs via continuous voice recognition commands and statements, which has evolved to become 99 percent accurate.

31.3.3   Emergent Requirements

At the beginning of a software project, there's a truism that applies equally to every stakeholder involved: "You don't know what you don't know." That means that customers rarely define "stable" requirements. It also means that software engineers cannot always foresee where ambiguities and inconsistencies lie. Requirements change—but that's nothing new.

As systems become more complex, it follows that even a rudimentary attempt to state comprehensive requirements is doomed to failure. A statement of overall goals may be possible, delineation of intermediate objectives can be accomplished, but stable requirements—not a chance! Requirements will emerge as everyone involved in the engineering and construction of a complex system learns more about it, the environment in which it is to reside, and the users who will interact with it.

This reality implies a number of software engineering trends. First, process models must be designed to embrace change and adopt the basic tenets of the agile philosophy (Chapter 3). Next, methods that yield engineering models (e.g., requirements and design models) must be used judiciously because those models will change repeatedly as more knowledge about the system is acquired. Finally, tools that support both process and methods must make adaptation and change easy.

But there is another aspect to emergent requirements. The vast majority of software developed to date assumes that the boundary between the software-based system and its external environment is stable. The boundary may change, but it will do so in a controlled manner, allowing the software to be adapted as part of a regular software maintenance cycle. This assumption is beginning to change. Open-world software (Section 31.2.2) demands that computer-based systems "adapt and react to changes dynamically, even if they're unanticipated" [Bar06].

By their nature, emergent requirements lead to change. How do we control the evolution of a widely used application or system over its lifetime, and what effect does this have on the way we design software?

As the number of changes grows, the likelihood of unintended side effects also grows. This should be a cause for concern as complex systems with emergent requirements become the norm. The software engineering community must develop methods that help software teams predict the impact of change across an entire system, thereby mitigating unintended side effects. Today, our ability to accomplish this is severely limited.

31.3.4   The Talent Mix

As software-based systems become more complex, as communication and collaboration among global teams becomes commonplace, as emergent requirements (with the resultant flow of changes) become the norm, the very nature of a software engineering team may change. Each software team must bring a variety of creative talent and technical skills to its part of a complex system, and the overall process must allow the output of these islands of talent to merge effectively.

Alexandra Weber Morales [Mor05] suggests the talent mix of a "software dream team." The *Brain* is a chief architect who is able to navigate the demands of stakeholders and map them into a technology framework that is both extensible and implementable. The *Data Grrl* is a database and data structures guru who "blasts through rows and columns with profound understanding of predicate logic and set theory as it pertains to the relational model." The *Blocker* is a technical leader (manager) who allows the team to work free of interference from other teams while at the same time ensuring that collaboration is occurring. The *Hacker* is a consummate programmer who is at home with patterns and languages and can use both effectively. The *Gatherer* "deftly discovers system requirements with . . . anthropological insight" and accurately expresses them with clarity.

31.3.5 Software Building Blocks

uote:

"The proper artistic response to digital technology is to embrace it as a new window on everything that's eternally human, and to use it with passion, wisdom, fearlessness and joy."

Ralph Lombreglia

All of us who have fostered a software engineering philosophy have emphasized the need for reuse—of source code, object-oriented classes, components, patterns, and COTS software. Although the software engineering community has made progress as it attempts to capture past knowledge and reuse proven solutions, a significant percentage of the software that is built today continues to be built "from scratch." Part of the reason for this is a continuing desire (by stakeholders and software engineering practitioners) for "unique solutions."

In the hardware world, original equipment manufacturers (OEMs) of digital devices use application-specific standard products (ASSPs) produced by silicon vendors almost exclusively. This "merchant hardware" provides the building blocks necessary to implement everything from a mobile phone to an HD-DVD player. Increasingly, the same OEMs are using "merchant software"—software building blocks designed specifically for a unique application domain [e.g., VoIP devices]. Michael Ward [War07] comments:

> One advantage of the use of software components is that the OEM can leverage the functionality provided by the software without having to develop in-house expertise in the specific functions or invest developer time on the effort to implement and validate the components. Other advantages include the ability to acquire and deploy only the specific set of functionalities that are needed for the system, as well as the ability to integrate these components into an already-existing architecture.
>
> However, the software component approach does have a disadvantage in that there is a given level of effort required to integrate the individual components into the overall product. This integration challenge may be further complicated if the components are sourced from a variety of vendors, each with its own interface methodologies. As additional sources of components are used, the effort required to manage various vendors increases, and there is a greater risk of encountering problems related to the interaction across components from different sources.

In addition to components packaged as merchant software, there is an increasing tendency to adopt *software platform solutions* that "incorporate collections of related functionalities, typically provided within an integrated software framework" [War07]. A software platform frees an OEM from the work associated with developing base functionality and instead allows the OEM to dedicate software effort on those features that differentiate its product.

31.3.6   Changing Perceptions of "Value"

During the last quarter of the twentieth century, the operative question that businesspeople asked when discussing software was: "Why does it cost so much?" That question is rarely asked today and has been replaced by "Why can't we get it (software and/or the software-based product) sooner?"

When computer software is considered, the modern perception of value is changing from business value (cost and profitability) to customer values that include: speed of delivery, richness of functionality, and overall product quality.

31.3.7   Open Source

Who owns the software you or your organization uses? Increasingly, the answer is "everyone." The "open source" movement has been described in the following manner [OSO08]: "Open source is a development method for software that harnesses the power of distributed peer review and transparency of process. The promise of open source is better quality, higher reliability, more flexibility, lower cost, and an end to predatory vendor lock-in." The term *open source* when applied to computer software, implies that software engineering work products (models, source code, test suites) are open to the public and can be reviewed and extended (with controls) by anyone with interest and permission.

An open-source "team" may have a number of full-time "dream team" members (Section 31.3.4), but the number of people working on the software expands and contracts as interest in the application strengthens or weakens. The power of the open-source team is derived from constant peer review and design/code refactoring that results in a slow progression toward an optimal solution.

If you have further interest, Weber [Web05] provides a worthwhile introduction, and Feller and his colleagues [Fel07] have edited a comprehensive and objective anthology that considers the benefits and problems associated with open source.

INFO

Technologies to Watch

Many emerging technologies are likely to have a significant impact on the types of computer-based systems that evolve. These technologies add to the challenges confronting software engineers. The following technologies are worthy of note:

Grid computing—this technology (available today) creates a network that taps the billions of unused CPU cycles from every machine on the network and allows exceedingly complex computing jobs to be completed without a dedicated supercomputer. For a real-life example encompassing over 4.5 million computers, visit http://setiathome.berkeley.edu/.

Open-world computing—"It's ambient, implicit, invisible, and adaptive. It's when network devices embedded in the environment provide unobtrusive connectivity and services all the time" [McC05].

Microcommerce—a new branch of e-commerce that charges very small amounts for access to or purchase of various forms of intellectual property. Apple iTunes is a widely used example.

Cognitive machines—the "holy grail" in the robotics field is to develop machines that are aware of their environment, that can "pick up on cues, respond to ever-changing situations, and interact with people naturally" [PCM03]. Cognitive machines are still in the early stages of development, but the potential is enormous.

OLED displays—an OLED "uses a carbon-based designer molecule that emits light when an electric current passes through it. Piece lots of molecules

together and you've got a superthin display of stunning quality—no power-draining backlight required" [PCM03]. The result—ultrathin displays that can be rolled up or folded, sprayed onto a curved surface, or otherwise adapted to a specific environment.

RFIDs—radio frequency identification brings open-world computing to an industrial base and the consumer products industry. Everything from tubes of toothpaste to automobile engines will be identifiable as it moves through the supply chain to its ultimate destination.

Web 2.0—one of a broad array of Web services that will lead to even greater integration of the Web into both commerce and personal computing.

For further discussion of technologies to watch, presented in a unique combination of video and print, visit the Consumer Electronics Association website at **www.ce.org/Press/CEA_Pubs/135.asp**.

31.4   TECHNOLOGY DIRECTIONS

uote:

"But what is it good for?"

Engineer at the Advanced Computing Systems Division of IBM, 1968, commenting on the microchip

We always seem to think that software engineering will change more rapidly than it does. A new "hype" technology (it could be a new process, a unique method, or an exciting tool) is introduced, and pundits suggest that "everything" will change. But software engineering is about far more than technology—it's about people and their ability to communicate their needs and innovate to make those needs a reality. Whenever people are involved, change occurs slowly in fits and starts. It's only when a "tipping point" [Gla02] is reached, that a technology cascades across the software engineering community and broad-based change truly does occur.

In this section I'll examine a few trends in process, methods, and tools that are likely to have some influence on software engineering over the next decade. Will they lead to a tipping point? We'll just have to wait and see.

31.4.1   Process Trends

It can be argued that all of the business, organizational, and cultural trends discussed in Section 31.3 reinforce the need for process. But do the frameworks discussed in Chapter 30 provide a road map into the future? Will process frameworks evolve to find a better balance between discipline and creativity? Will the software process adapt to the differing needs of stakeholders who procure software, those who build it, and those who use it? Can it provide a means for reducing risk for all three constituencies at the same time?

These and many other questions remain open. However, some trends are beginning to emerge. Conradi and Fuggetta [Con02] suggest six "theses on how to enhance and better apply SPI frameworks." They begin their discussion with the following statement:

> A software procurer's goal is to select the best contractor objectively and rationally. A software company's goal is to survive and grow in a competitive market. An end user's goal is to acquire the software product that can solve the right problem, at the right time, at an acceptable price. We cannot expect the same SPI approach and consequent effort to accommodate all these viewpoints.

In the paragraphs that follow, I have adapted the theses proposed by Conradi and Fuggetta [Con02] to suggest possible process trends over the next decade.

? **What process trends are likely over the next decade?**

1. *As SPI frameworks evolve, they will emphasize "strategies that focus on goal orientation and product innovation"* [Con02]. In the fast-paced world of software development, long-term SPI strategies rarely survive in a dynamic business environment. Too much changes too quickly. This means that a stable, step-by-step road map for SPI may have to be replaced with a framework that emphasizes short-term goals that have a product orientation. If the requirements for a new software-based product line will emerge over a series of incremental product releases (to be delivered to end users via the Web) the software organization may recognize the need to improve its ability to manage change. Process improvements associated with change management must be coordinated with the release cycle of the product in a way that will improve change management while at the same time not being disruptive.

2. *Because software engineers have a good sense of where the process is weak, process changes should generally be driven by their needs and should start form the bottom up.* Conradi and Fuggetta [Con02] suggest that future SPI activities should "use a simple and focused scorecard to start with, not a large assessment." By focusing SPI efforts narrowly and working from the bottom up, practitioners will begin to see substantive changes early—changes that make a real difference in the way that software engineering work is conducted.

3. *Automated software process technology (SPT) will move away from global process management (broad-based support of the entire software process) to focus on those aspects of the software process that can best benefit from automation.* No one is against tools and automation, but in many instances, SPT has not met its promise (see Section 31.2). To be most effective, it should focus on umbrella activities (Chapter 2)—the most stable elements of the software process.

4. *Greater emphasis will be placed on the return on investment of SPI activities.* In Chapter 30, you learned that return on investment (ROI) can be defined as:

$$\text{ROI} = \frac{\Sigma(benefits) - \Sigma(costs)}{\Sigma(costs)} \times 100\%$$

To date, software organizations have struggled to clearly delineate "benefits" in a quantitative manner. It can be argued [Con02] that "we therefore need a standardized market-value model, such as the one employed in Cocomo II (see Chapter 26) to account for software improvement initiatives."

5. *As time passes, the software community may come to understand that expertise in sociology and anthropology may have as much or more to do with successful SPI as other, more technical disciplines.* Above all else, SPI changes organizational culture, and cultural change involves individuals and groups of people. Conradi and Fuggetta [Con02] correctly note that "software developers are knowledge workers. They tend to respond negatively to top-level dictates on how to do work or change processes." Much can be learned by examining the sociology of groups to better understand effective ways to introduce change.

6. *New modes of learning may facilitate the transition to a more effective software process.* In this context, "learning" implies learning from successes and mistakes. A software organization that collects metrics (Chapters 23 and 25) allows itself to understand how elements of a process affect the quality of the end product.

31.4.2   The Grand Challenge

There is one trend that is undeniable—software-based systems will undoubtedly become bigger and more complex as time passes. It is the engineering of these large, complex systems, regardless of delivery platform or application domain, that poses the "grand challenge" [Bro06] for software engineers. Manfred Broy [Bro06] suggests that software engineers can meet "the daunting challenge of complex software systems development" by creating new approaches to understanding system models and using those models as a basis for the construction of high-quality next-generation software.

As the software engineering community develops new model-driven approaches (discussed later in this section) to the representation of system requirements and design, the following characteristics [Bro06] must be addressed:

? **What system character-istics must analysts and designers consider for future apps?**

- *Multifunctionality*—as digital devices evolve into their second and third generation, they have begun to deliver a rich set of sometimes unrelated functions. The mobile phone, once considered a communication device, is now used for taking photos, keeping a calendar, navigating a journey, and as a music player. If open-world interfaces come to pass, these mobile devices will be used for much more over the coming years. As Broy [Bro06] notes, "engineers must describe the detailed context in which the functions will be delivered and, most important, must identify the potentially harmful interactions between the system's different features."

- *Reactivity and timeliness*—digital devices increasingly interact with the real world and must react to external stimuli in a timely manner. They must interface with a broad array of sensors and must respond in a time frame that is appropriate to the task at hand. New methods must be developed that (1) help software engineers predict the timing of various reactive features and (2) implement those features in a way that makes the feature less machine dependent and more portable.

- *New modes of user interaction*—the keyboard and mouse work well in a PC environment, but open-world trends for software mean that new modes of interaction must be modeled and implemented. Whether these new approaches use multitouch interfaces, voice recognition, or direct mind interfaces,[9] new generations of software for digital devices must model these new human-computer interfaces.

- *Complex architectures*—a luxury automobile has over 2000 functions controlled by software that resides within a complex hardware architecture that includes multiple CPUs, a sophisticated bus structure, actuators, sensors, an increasingly sophisticated human interface, and many safety-rated components. Even more complex systems are on the immediate horizon, presenting significant challenges for software designers.

- *Heterogeneous, distributed systems*—the real-time components of any modern embedded system can be connected via an internal bus, a wireless network, or across the Internet (or all three).

- *Criticality*—software has become the pivotal component in virtually all business-critical systems and in most safety-critical systems. Yet, the software engineering community has only begun to apply even the most basic principles of software safety.

- *Maintenance variability*—the life of software within a digital device rarely lasts beyond 3 to 5 years, but the complex avionics systems within an aircraft has a useful life of at least 20 years. Automobile software falls somewhere in between. Should this have an impact on design?

Broy [Bro06] argues that these and other software characteristics can be managed only if the software engineering community develops a more effective distributed and collaborative software engineering philosophy, better requirements engineering approaches, a more robust approach to model-driven development, and better software tools. In the sections that follow I'll explore each of these areas briefly.

31.4.3 Collaborative Development

It seems almost too obvious to state, but I'll do so anyway: *software engineering is an information technology.* From the onset of any software project, every stakeholder

---

9   A brief discussion of direct mind interfaces can be found at **http://en.wikipedia.org/wiki/ Brain-computer_interface**, and a commercial example is described at **http://au.gamespot .com/news/6166959.html**.

KEY POINT

Collaboration involves the timely dissemination of information and an effective process for communication and decision making.

must share information—about basic business goals and objectives, about specific system requirements, about architectural design issues, about almost every aspect of the software to be built.

Today, software engineers collaborate across time zones and international boundaries, and every one of them must share information. The same holds for open-source projects in which hundreds or thousands of software developers work to build an open-source app. Again, information must be disseminated so that open collaboration can occur.

The challenge over the next decade is to develop methods and tools that facilitate that collaboration. Today, we continue to struggle to make collaboration easy. Eugene Kim [Kim04] comments:

> Consider a basic collaborative task: document-sharing. A number of applications (both commercial and open source) claim to solve the document-sharing problem, and yet, the predominant method for sharing files is to email them back and forth. This is the computational equivalent of sneakernet. If the tools that purport to solve this problem are good, why aren't we using them?
>
> We see similar problems in other basic areas. I can walk into any meeting anywhere in the world with a piece of paper in hand, and I can be sure that people will be able to read it, mark it up, pass it around, and file it away. I can't say the same for electronic documents. I can't annotate a Web page or use the same filing system for both my email and my Word documents, at least not in a way that is guaranteed to be interoperable with applications on my own machine and on others. Why not?
>
> . . . In order to make a real impact in the collaborative space, tools must not only be good, they must be interoperable.

But a lack of comprehensive collaborative tools is only one part of the challenge faced by those who must develop software collaboratively.

Today, a significant percentage[10] of IT projects are outsourced internationally, and the number will grow substantially over the next decade. Not surprisingly, Bhat and his colleagues [Bha06] contend that requirements engineering is the crucial activity in an outsourcing project. They identify a number of success factors that lead to successful collaborative efforts:

- *Shared goals*—project goals must be clearly enunciated, and all stakeholders must understand them and agree with their intent.

- *Shared culture*—cultural differences should be clearly defined, and an educational approach (that will help to mitigate those differences) and a communication approach (that will facilitate knowledge transfer) should be developed.

---

10 Approximately 20 percent of a typical IT budget for large companies is currently dedicated to outsourcing, and the percentage is growing every year. (Source: www.logicacmg.com/page/400002849.)

- *Shared process*—in some ways, process serves as the skeleton of a collaborative project, providing a uniform means for assessing progress and direction and introducing a common technical "language" for all team members.

- *Shared responsibility*—every team member must recognize the importance of requirements engineering and work to provide the best possible definition of the system.

When combined, these success factors lead to "trust"—a global team that can rely on disparate groups to accomplish the job they are assigned.

31.4.4   Requirements Engineering

Basic requirements engineering actions—elicitation, elaboration, negotiation, specification, and validation—were presented in Chapters 5 through 7. The success or failure of these actions has a very strong influence on the success or failure of the entire software engineering process. And yet, requirements engineering (RE) has been compared to "trying to put a hose clamp around jello" [Gon04]. As I've noted in many places throughout this book, software requirements have a tendency to keep changing, and with the advent of open-world systems, emergent requirements (and near-continuous change) may become the norm.

Today, most "informal" requirements engineering approaches begin with the creation of user scenarios (e.g., use cases). More formal approaches create one or more requirements models and use these as a basis for design. Formal methods enable a software engineer to represent requirements using a verifiable mathematical notation. All can work reasonably well when requirements are stable, but do not readily solve the problem of dynamic or emergent requirements.

There are a number of distinct requirements engineering research directions including natural language processing from translated textual descriptions into more structured representations (e.g., analysis classes), greater reliance on databases for structuring and understanding software requirements, the use of RE patterns to describe typical problems and solutions when requirements engineering tasks are conducted, and goal-oriented requirements engineering. However, at the industry level, RE actions remain relatively informal and surprisingly basic. To improve the manner in which requirements are defined, the software engineering community will likely implement three distinct subprocesses as RE is conducted [Gli07]: (1) improved knowledge acquisition and knowledge sharing that allows more complete understanding of application domain constraints and stakeholder needs, (2) greater emphasis on iteration as requirements are defined, and (3) more effective communication and coordination tools that enable all stakeholders to collaborate effectively.

KEY POINT

"New RE subprocesses include: (1) improved knowledge acquisition, (2) even more iteration, and (3) more effective communication and coordination tools."

The RE subprocesses noted in the preceding paragraph will only succeed if they are properly integrated into an evolving approach to software engineering. As pattern-based problem solving and component-based solutions begin to dominate many application domains, RE must accommodate the desire for agility (rapid incremental delivery) and the inherent emergent requirements that result. The con-current nature of many software engineering process models means that RE will be integrated with design and construction activities. As a consequence, the notion of a static "software specification" is beginning to disappear, to be replaced by "value-driven requirements" [Som05] derived as stakeholders respond to features and func-tions delivered in early software increments.

31.4.5   Model-Driven Software Development

KEY POINT

Model-driven approaches address a continuing challenge for all software developers—how to represent software at a higher level of abstraction than code.

Software engineers grapple with abstraction at virtually every step in the software engineering process. As design commences, architectural and component-level abstractions are represented and assessed. They must then be translated into a pro-gramming language representation that transforms the design (a relatively high level of abstraction) into an operable system with a specific computing environment (a low level of abstraction). *Model-driven software development*[11] couples domain-specific modeling languages with transformation engines and generators in a way that facilitates the representation of abstraction at high levels and then transforms it into lower levels [Sch06].

Domain-specific modeling languages (DSMLs) represent "application structure, behavior and requirements within particular application domains" and are described with meta-models that "define the relationships among concepts in the domain and precisely specify the key semantics and constraints associated with these domain concepts" [Sch06]. The key difference between a DSML and a general-purpose mod-eling language such as UML (Appendix 1) is that the DSML is tuned to design con-cepts inherent in the application domain and can therefore represent relationships and constraints among design elements in an efficient manner.

31.4.6   Postmodern Design

In an interesting article on software design in the "postmodern era," Philippe Kruchten [Kru05] makes the following observation:

> Computer science hasn't achieved the grand narrative that explains it all, the *big picture*— we haven't found the fundamental laws of software that would play the role that the fun-damental laws of physics play in other engineering disciplines. We still live with the bitter aftertaste of the Internet bubble burst and the Y2K doomsday. So, in this postmodern era, where it seems that everything matters a bit yet not much really matters, what are the next directions for software design?

Part of any attempt to understand trends in software design is to establish bound-aries for design. Where does requirements engineering stop and design begin? Where does design stop and code generation begin? The answers to these questions are not as easy as they might first appear. Even though the requirements model should focus on "what," not "how," every analyst does a bit of design and almost all

11 The term *model-driven engineering* (MDE) is also used.

designers do a bit of analysis. Similarly, as the design of software components moves closer to algorithmic detail, a designer begins to represent the component at a level of abstraction that is close to code.

Postmodern design will continue to emphasize the importance of software architecture (Chapter 9). A designer must state an architectural issue, make a decision that addresses the issue, and then clearly define the assumptions, constraints, and implications that the decision places on the software as a whole. But is there a framework in which the issues can be described and the architecture can be defined? Aspect-oriented software development (Chapter 2) or model-driven software development (Section 31.4.4) may become important design approaches in the years ahead, but it's still too soon to tell. It may be that breakthroughs in component-based development (Chapter 10) may lead to a design philosophy that emphasizes the assembly of existing components. If the past is prologue, it's highly likely that many "new" design methods will emerge, but few will ride the hype curve (Figure 31.2) much beyond the "trough of disillusionment."

31.4.7   Test-Driven Development

Requirements drive design, and design establishes a foundation for construction. This simple software engineering reality works reasonably well and is essential as a software architecture is created. However, a subtle change can provide significant benefit when component-level design and construction are considered.

In *test-driven development* (TDD), requirements for a software component serve as the basis for the creation of a series of test cases that exercise the interface and attempt to find errors in the data structures and functionality delivered by the component. TDD is not really a new technology but rather a trend that emphasizes the design of test cases *before* the creation of source code.[12]

The TDD process follows the simple procedural flow illustrated in Figure 31.3. Before the first small segment of code is created, a software engineer creates a test to exercise the code (to try to make the code fail). The code is then written to satisfy the test. If it passes, a new test is created for the next segment of code to be developed. The process continues until the component is fully coded and all tests execute without error. However, if any test succeeds in finding an error, the existing code is refactored (corrected) and all tests created to that point are reexecuted. This iterative flow continues until there are no tests left to be created, implying that the component meets all requirements defined for it.

During TDD, code is developed in very small increments (one subfunction at a time), and no code is written until a test exists to exercise it. You should note that each iteration results in one or more new tests that are added to a regression test suite that is run with every change. This is done to ensure that the new code has not generated side effects that cause errors in the older code.

KEY POINT

"TDD is a trend that emphasizes the design of test cases *before* the creation of source code."

---

12 Recall that Extreme Programming (Chapter 3) emphasizes this approach as part of its agile process model.

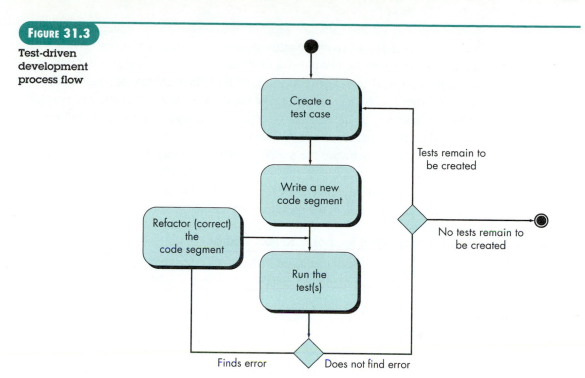

Figure 31.3

Test-driven development process flow

Create a test case

Write a new code segment

Refactor (correct) the code segment

Run the test(s)

Tests remain to be created

No tests remain to be created

Finds error

Does not find error

In TDD, tests drive the detailed component design and the resultant source code. The results of these tests cause immediate modifications to the component design (via the code), and more important, the resultant component (when completed) has been verified in stand-alone fashion. If you have further interest in TDD, see [Bec04b] or [Ast04].

31.5   TOOLS-RELATED TRENDS

Hundreds of industry-grade software engineering tools are introduced each year. The majority are provided by tools vendors who claim that their tool will improve project management, or requirements analysis, or design modeling, or code generation, or testing, or change management, or any of the many software engineering activities, actions, and tasks discussed throughout this book. Other tools have been developed as open-source offerings. The majority of open-source tools focus on "programming" activities with a specific emphasis on the construction activity (particularly code generation). Still other tools grow out of research efforts at universities and government labs. Although they have appeal in very limited applications, the majority are not ready for broad industry application.

At the industry level, the most comprehensive tools packages form *software engineering environments* (SEE)[13] that integrate a collection of individual tools around a central database (repository). When considered as a whole, an SEE integrates

---

13 The term *integrated development environment* (IDE) is also used.

information across the software process and assists in the collaboration that is required for many large, complex software-based systems. But current environments are not easily extensible (it's difficult to integrate a COTS tool that is not part of the package) and tend to be general purpose (i.e., they are not application domain specific). There is also a substantial time lag between the introduction of new technology solutions (e.g., model-driven software development) and the availability of viable SEEs that support the new technology.

Future trends in software tools will follow two distinct paths—a *human-focused path* that responds to some of the "soft trends" discussed in Section 31.3, and a technology-centered path that addresses new technologies (Section 31.4) as they are introduced and adopted. In the sections that follow, I'll examine each path briefly.

31.5.1   Tools That Respond to Soft Trends

The soft trends discussed in Section 31.3—the need to manage complexity, accommodate emergent requirements, establish process models that embrace change, coordinate global teams with a changing talent mix, among others—suggest a new era in which tools support for stakeholder collaboration will become as important as tools support for technology. But what kind of tool set supports these soft trends?

One example of research in this area is GENESIS—a generalized, open-source environment designed to support collaborative software engineering work [Ave04]. The GENESIS environment may or may not gain widespread usage, but its basic elements are representative of the direction of collaborative SEEs that will evolve to support the soft trends noted in this chapter.

A collaborative SEE "supports co-operation and communication among software engineers belonging to distributed development teams involved in modeling, controlling, and measuring software development and maintenance processes. Moreover, it includes an artifact management function that stores and manages software artifacts (work products) produced by different teams in the course of their work" [Bol02].

Figure 31.4 illustrates an architecture for a collaborative SEE. The architecture, based on the GENESIS environment [Ave04], is constructed of subsystems that are integrated within a common Web client and is complemented by server-based components that provide support for all clients. Each development organization has its own client-side subsystems that communicate to other clients. Referring to Figure 31.4, a *resource management subsystem* manages the allocation of human resources to different projects or subprojects; a *work product management system* is "responsible for the creation, modification, deletion," indexing, searching, and storage of all software engineering work products [Ave04]; a *workflow management subsystem* coordinates the definition, instantiation, and implementation of software process activities, actions, and tasks; an *event engine* "collects events" that occur during the software process (e.g., a successful review of a work product, the completion of unit testing of a component) and notifies others; a *communication system* supports both synchronous and asynchronous communication among the distributed teams.

FIGURE 31.4

Collaborative SEE architecture.
Source: Adapted from [Ave04].

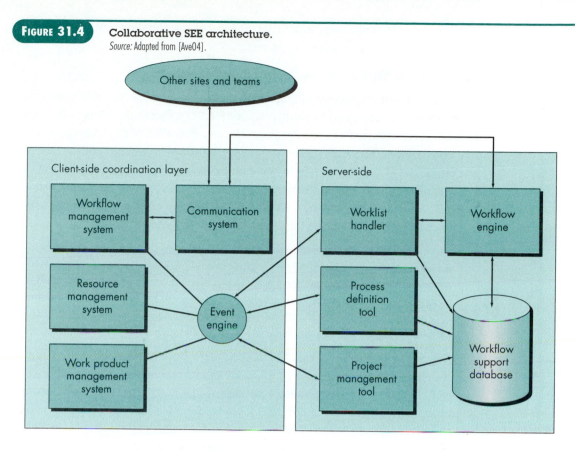

On the server side, four components share a workflow support database. The components implement the following functions:

- *Process definition*—a tool set that enables a team to define new process activities, actions, or tasks and defines the rules that govern how these process elements interact with one another and the work products they produce.

- *Project management*—a tool set that allows the team to build a project plan and coordinate the plan with other teams or projects.

- *Workflow engine*—"interacts with the event engine to propagate events that are relevant for the execution of cooperating processes executed on other sites" [Ave04].

- *Worklist handler*—interacts with the server-side database to provide a software engineer with information about the task currently under way or any future task that is derived from work that is currently being performed.

Although the architecture of a collaborative SEE may vary considerably from the one discussed in this section, the basic functional elements (management systems and components) will appear to achieve the level of coordination that is required for a distributed software engineering project.

31.5.2   Tools That Address Technology Trends

Agility in software engineering (Chapter 3) is achieved when stakeholders work as a team. Therefore, the trend toward collaborative SEEs (Section 31.5.1) will provide benefits even when software is developed locally. But what of the technology tools that complement the system and components that empower better collaboration?

One of the dominant trends in technology tools is the creation of a tool set that supports model-driven development (Section 31.4.4) with an emphasis on architecture-driven design. Oren Novotny [Nov04] suggests that the model rather than the source code becomes the central software engineering focus:

> Platform independent models are created in UML and then undergo various levels of transformation to eventually wind up as source code for a specific platform. It stands to reason then, that the model, not the file, should become the new unit of output. A model has many different views at different levels of abstraction. At the highest level, platform independent components can be specified in analysis; at the lowest level there is a platform specific implementation that reduces to a set of classes in code.

Novotny argues that a new generation of tools will work in conjunction with a repository to create models at all necessary levels of abstraction, establish relationships between the various models, translate models at one level of abstraction to another level (e.g., translate a design model into source code), manage changes and versions, and coordinate quality control and assurance actions against the software models.

In addition to complete software engineering environments, point-solution tools that address everything from requirements gathering to design/code refactoring to testing will continue to evolve and become more functionally capable. In some instances, modeling and testing tools targeted at a specific application domain will provide enhanced benefit when compared to their generic equivalents.

31.6   SUMMARY

The trends that have an effect on software engineering technology often come from the business, organizational, market, and cultural arenas. These "soft trends" can guide the direction of research and the technology that is derived as a consequence of research.

As a new technology is introduced, it moves through a life cycle that does not always lead to widespread adoption, even though original expectations are high. The degree to which any software engineering technology gains widespread adoption is tied to its ability to address the problems posed by both soft and hard trends.

Soft trends—the growing need for connectivity and collaboration, global projects, knowledge transfer, the impact of emerging economies, and the influence of human culture itself, lead to a set of challenges that span managing complexity and emergent requirements to juggling an ever-changing talent mix among geographically dispersed software teams.

Hard trends—the ever-accelerating pace of technology change—flow out of soft trends and affect the structure of the software and scope of the process and the manner in which a process framework is characterized. Collaborative development, new forms of requirements engineering, model-based and test-driven development, and postmodern design will change the methods landscape. Tools environments will respond to a growing need for communication and collaboration and at the same time integrate domain-specific point solutions that may change the nature of current software engineering tasks.

PROBLEMS AND POINTS TO PONDER

31.1. Get a copy of the best-selling book *The Tipping Point* by Malcolm Gladwell (available via Google Book Search), and discuss how his theories apply to the adoption of new software engineering technologies.

31.2. Why does open-world software present a challenge to conventional software engineering approaches?

31.3. Review the Gartner Group's *hype cycle for emerging technologies*. Select a well-known technology product and present a brief history that illustrates how it traveled along the curve. Select another well-known technology product that did not follow the path suggested by the hype curve.

31.4. What is a "soft trend"?

31.5. You're faced with an extremely complex problem that will require a lengthy solution. How would you go about addressed the complexity and crafting a solution?

31.6. What are "emergent requirements" and why do they present a challenge to software engineers?

31.7. Select an open-source development effort (other than Linux), and present a brief history of its evolution and relative success.

31.8. Describe how you think the software process will change over the next decade.

31.9. You're based in Los Angeles and are working on a global software engineering team. You and colleagues in London, Mumbai, Hong Kong, and Sydney must edit a 245-page requirements specification for a large system. The first editing pass must be completed in three days. Describe the ideal online tool set that would enable you to collaborate effectively.

31.10. Describe model-driven software development in your own words. Do the same for test-driven development.

FURTHER READINGS AND INFORMATION SOURCES

Books that discuss the road ahead for software and computing span a vast array of technical, scientific, economic, political, and social issues. Kurweil (*The Singularity Is Near,* Penguin Books, 2005) presents a compelling look at a world that will change in truly profound ways by the middle of this century. Sterling (*Tomorrow Now,* Random House, 2002) reminds us that real progress is rarely orderly and efficient. Teich (*Technology and the Future,* Wadworth, 2002) presents thoughtful essays on the societal impact of technology and how changing culture shapes technology. Naisbitt, Philips, and Naisbitt (*High Tech/High Touch,* Nicholas Brealey, 2001) note that many of us have become "intoxicated" with high technology and that the "great irony of the high-tech age is that we've become enslaved to devices that were supposed to give us freedom." Zey (*The Future Factor,* McGraw-Hill, 2000) discusses five forces that will shape human destiny during this century. Negroponte's *(Being Digital,* Alfred A. Knopf, 1995) was a best seller in the mid-1990s and continues to provide an insightful view of computing and its overall impact.

As software becomes part of the fabric of virtually every facet of our lives, "cyberethics" has evolved as an important topic of discussion. Books by Spinello (*Cyberethics: Morality and Law in Cyberspace,* Jones & Bartlett Publishers, 2002), Halbert and Ingulli (*Cyberethics,* South-Western College Publishers, 2001), and Baird and his colleagues (*Cyberethics: Social and Moral Issues in the Computer Age,* Prometheus Books, 2000) consider the topic in detail. The U.S Government has published a voluminous report on CD-ROM (*21st Century Guide to Cybercrime,* Progressive Management, 2003) that considers all aspects of computer crime, intellectual property issues, and the National Infrastructure Protection Center (NIPC).

A wide variety of information sources on future directions in software-related technologies and software engineering is available on the Internet. An up-to-date list of World Wide Web references relevant to future trends in software engineering can be found at the SEPA website: **www.mhhe.com/engcs/compsci/pressman/professional/olc/ser.htm**.

CONCLUDING COMMENTS

In the 31 chapters that have preceded this one, I've explored a process for software engineering that encompasses management procedures and technical methods, basic concepts and principles, specialized techniques, people-oriented activities and tasks that are amenable to automation, paper-and-pencil notation, and software tools. I have argued that measurement, discipline, and an overriding focus on agility and quality will result in software that meets the customer's needs, software that is reliable, software that is maintainable, software that is better. Yet, I have never promised that software engineering is a panacea.

As we move into the second decade of this new century, software and systems technologies remain a challenge for every software professional and every company that builds computer-based systems. Although he wrote these words with a twentieth century outlook, Max Hopper [Hop90] accurately describes the current state of affairs:

> Because changes in information technology are becoming so rapid and unforgiving, and the consequences of falling behind are so irreversible, companies will either master the technology or die. . . . Think of it as a technology treadmill. Companies will have to run harder and harder just to stay in place.

Changes in software engineering technology are indeed "rapid and unforgiving," but at the same time progress is often quite slow. By the time a decision is made to adopt a new process, method, or tool; conduct the training necessary to understand its application; and introduce the technology into the software development culture, something newer (and even better) has come along, and the process begins anew.

QUICK LOOK

What is it? As we come to the end of a relatively long journey through software engineering, it's time to put things into perspective and make a few concluding comments.

Who does it? Authors like me. When you come to the end of a long and challenging book, it's nice to wrap things up in a meaningful way.

Why is it important? It's always worthwhile to remember where we've been and to consider where we're going.

What are the steps? I'll consider where we've been and address some of the core issues and some directions for the future.

What is the work product? A discussion that will help you understand the big picture.

How do I ensure that I've done it right? That's difficult to accomplish in real time. It's only after a number of years that either you or I can tell whether the software engineering concepts, principles, methods, and techniques discussed in this book have helped you to become a better software engineer.

One thing I've learned over my years in this field is that software engineering practitioners are "fashion conscious." The road ahead will be littered with the carcasses of exciting new technologies (the latest fashion) that never really made it (despite the hype). It will be shaped by more modest technologies that somehow modify the direction and width of the thoroughfare. I discussed a few of those in Chapter 31.

In this concluding chapter I'll take a broader view and consider where we've been and where we're going from a more philosophical perspective.

32.1   THE IMPORTANCE OF SOFTWARE—REVISITED

The importance of computer software can be stated in many ways. In Chapter 1, software was characterized as a differentiator. The function delivered by software differentiates products, systems, and services and provides competitive advantage in the marketplace. But software is more than a differentiator. When taken as a whole, software engineering work products generate the most important commodity that any individual, business, or government can acquire—information.

In Chapter 31, I briefly discussed open-world computing—ambient intelligence, context-aware applications, and pervasive/ubiquitous computing—a direction that will fundamentally change our perception of computers, the things that we do with them (and they do for us), and our perception of information as a guide, a commodity, and a necessity. I also noted that software required to support open-world computing will present dramatic new challenges for software engineers. But far more important, the coming pervasiveness of computer software will present even more dramatic challenges for society as a whole. Whenever a technology has a broad impact—an impact that can save lives or endanger them, build businesses or destroy them, inform government leaders or mislead them—it must be "handled with care."

32.2   PEOPLE AND THE WAY THEY BUILD SYSTEMS

The software required for high-technology systems becomes more and more complex with each passing year, and the size of resultant programs increases proportionally. The rapid growth in the size of the "average" program would present us with few problems if it wasn't for one simple fact: As program size increases, the number of people who must work on the program must also increase.

Experience indicates that as the number of people on a software project team increases, the overall productivity of the group may suffer. One way around this problem is to create a number of software engineering teams, thereby compartmentalizing people into individual working groups. However, as the number of software engineering teams grows, communication between them becomes as difficult and time consuming as communication between individuals. Worse, communication (between individuals or teams) tends to be inefficient—that is, too much time is spent transferring too little information content, and all too often, important information "falls into the cracks."

If the software engineering community is to deal effectively with the communication dilemma, the road ahead for software engineers must include radical changes in the way individuals and teams communicate with one another. In Chapter 31, I discussed collaborative environments that may provide dramatic improvements in the ways teams communicate.

In the final analysis, communication is the transfer of knowledge, and the acquisition (and transfer) of knowledge is changing in profound ways. As search engines become increasingly sophisticated and Web 2.0 applications provide better synergy, the world's largest library of research papers and reports, tutorials, commentary, and references becomes readily accessible and usable.

If past history is any indication, it is fair to say that people themselves will not change. However, the ways in which they communicate, the environment in which they work, the manner in which they acquire knowledge, the methods and tools that they use, the discipline that they apply, and therefore, the overall culture for software development will change in significant and even profound ways.

32.3 NEW MODES FOR REPRESENTING INFORMATION

Over the history of computing, a subtle transition has occurred in the terminology that is used to describe software development work performed for the business community. Forty years ago, the term *data processing* was the operative phrase for describing the use of computers in a business context. Today, data processing has given way to another phrase—*information technology*—that implies the same thing but presents a subtle shift in focus. The emphasis is not merely to process large quantities of data but rather to extract meaningful information from this data. Obviously, this was always the intent, but the shift in terminology reflects a far more important shift in management philosophy.

When software applications are discussed today, the words *data, information*, and *content* occur repeatedly. We encounter the word *knowledge* in some artificial intelligence applications, but its use is relatively rare. Virtually no one discusses *wisdom* in the context of software applications.

Data is raw information—collections of facts that must be processed to be meaningful. Information is derived by associating facts within a given context. Knowledge associates information obtained in one context with other information obtained in a different context. Finally, wisdom occurs when generalized principles are derived from disparate knowledge. Each of these four views of "information" is represented schematically in Figure 32.1.

To date, the vast majority of all software has been built to process data or information. Software engineers are now equally concerned with systems that process

FIGURE 32.1

An "information" spectrum

Data:
no associativity

Information:
associativity within
one context

Knowledge:
associativity within
multiple contexts

Wisdom:
creation of generalized
principles based on
existing knowledge
from different sources

Quote:

"Wisdom is the power that enables us to use knowledge for the benefit of ourselves and others."

Thomas J. Watson

knowledge.[1] Knowledge is two dimensional. Information collected on a variety of related and unrelated topics is connected to form a body of fact that we call *knowledge*. The key is our ability to associate information from a variety of different sources that may not have any obvious connection and combine it in a way that provides us with some distinct benefit.[2]

To illustrate the progression from data to knowledge, consider census data indicating that the birthrate in 1996 in the United States was 4.9 million. This number represents a data value. Relating this piece of data with birthrates for the preceding 40 years, we can derive a useful piece of information—aging baby boomers of the 1950s and early 1960s made a last-gasp effort to have children prior to the end of their child-bearing years. In addition, gen-Xers began their childbearing years. The census data can then be connected to other seemingly unrelated pieces of information. For example, the current number of elementary school teachers who will retire during the next decade, the number of college students graduating with degrees in primary and secondary education, the pressure on politicians to hold down taxes and therefore limit pay increases for teachers. All of these pieces of information can be combined to formulate a representation of knowledge—there will be significant pressure on the education system in the United States in the early twenty-first century, and this pressure will continue for a number of decades. Using this knowledge, a business opportunity may emerge. There may be significant opportunity to develop new modes of learning that are more effective and less costly than current approaches.

---

1   The rapid growth of data mining and data warehousing technologies reflect this growing trend.
2   The semantic Web (Web 2.0) allows the creation of "mashups" that may provide a facile mechanism for achieving this.

The road ahead for software leads to systems that process knowledge. We have been processing data using computers for over 50 years and extracting information for more than three decades. One of the most significant challenges facing the software engineering community is to build systems that take the next step along the spectrum—systems that extract knowledge from data and information in a way that is practical and beneficial.

32.4 THE LONG VIEW

In Section 32.3, I suggested that the road ahead leads to systems that "process knowledge." But the future of computing in general and software-based systems in particular may lead to events that are considerably more profound.

In a fascinating book that is must reading for every person involved in computing technologies, Ray Kurzweil [Kur05] suggests that we have reached a time when "the pace of technological change will be so rapid, its impact so deep, that human life will be irreversibly transformed." Kurzweil[3] makes a compelling argument that we are currently at the "knee" of an exponential growth curve that will lead to enormous increases in computing capacity over the next two decades. When coupled with equivalent advances in nanotechnology, genetics, and robotics, we may approach a time in the middle part of this century when the distinction between humans (as we know them today) and machines begins to blur—a time when human evolution accelerates in ways that are both frightening (to some) and spectacular (to others).

By sometime in the 2030s, Kurzweil argues that computing capacity and the requisite software will be sufficient to model every aspect of the human brain—all of the physical connections, analog processes, and chemical overlays. When this occurs, human beings will have achieved "strong AI (artificial intelligence)," and as a consequence, machines that truly do think (using today's conventional use of the word). But there will be a fundamental difference. Human brain processes are exceedingly complex and only loosely connected to external informal sources. They are also computationally slow, even in comparison to today's computing technology. When full human brain emulation occurs, "thought" will occur at speeds thousands of times more rapid than its human counterpart with intimate connections to a sea of information (think of the present-day Web as a primitive example). The result is . . . well . . . so fantastical that it's best left to Kurzweil to describe.

It's important to note that not everyone believes that the future Kurzweil describes is a good thing. In a now famous essay entitled "The Future Doesn't Need Us," Bill Joy [Joy00], one of the founders of Sun Microsystems, argues that "robotics, genetic

---

3 It's important to note that Kurzweil is not a run-of-the mill science fiction writer or a futurist without portfolio. He is a serious technologist who (from Wikipedia) "has been a pioneer in the fields of optical character recognition (OCR), text-to-speech synthesis, speech recognition technology, and electronic keyboard instruments."

engineering, and nanotech are threatening to make humans an endangered species." His arguments predicting a technology dystopia represent a counterpoint to Kurzweil's predicted utopian future. Both should be seriously considered as software engineers take one of the lead roles in defining the long view for the human race.

32.5   THE SOFTWARE ENGINEER'S RESPONSIBILITY

Software engineering has evolved into a respected, worldwide profession. As professionals, software engineers should abide by a code of ethics that guides the work that they do and the products that they produce. An ACM/IEEE-CS Joint Task Force has produced a *Software Engineering Code of Ethics and Professional Practices* (Version 5.1). The code [ACM98] states:

> Software engineers shall commit themselves to making the analysis, specification, design, development, testing and maintenance of software a beneficial and respected profession. In accordance with their commitment to the health, safety and welfare of the public, software engineers shall adhere to the following Eight Principles:
>
> 1. PUBLIC—Software engineers shall act consistently with the public interest.
> 2. CLIENT AND EMPLOYER—Software engineers shall act in a manner that is in the best interests of their client and employer consistent with the public interest.
> 3. PRODUCT—Software engineers shall ensure that their products and related modifications meet the highest professional standards possible.
> 4. JUDGMENT—Software engineers shall maintain integrity and independence in their professional judgment.
> 5. MANAGEMENT—Software engineering managers and leaders shall subscribe to and promote an ethical approach to the management of software development and maintenance.
> 6. PROFESSION—Software engineers shall advance the integrity and reputation of the profession consistent with the public interest.
> 7. COLLEAGUES—Software engineers shall be fair to and supportive of their colleagues.
> 8. SELF—Software engineers shall participate in lifelong learning regarding the practice of their profession and shall promote an ethical approach to the practice of the profession.

WebRef

A complete discussion of the ACM/IEEE code of ethics can be found at **seeri.etsu.edu/ Codes/default .shtm.**

Although each of these eight principles is equally important, an overriding theme appears: a software engineer should work in the public interest. On a personal level, a software engineer should abide by the following rules:

- Never steal data for personal gain.
- Never distribute or sell proprietary information obtained as part of your work on a software project.

- Never maliciously destroy or modify another person's programs, files, or data.
- Never violate the privacy of an individual, a group, or an organization.
- Never hack into a system for sport or profit.
- Never create or promulgate a computer virus or worm.
- Never use computing technology to facilitate discrimination or harassment.

Over the past decade, certain members of the software industry have lobbied for protective legislation that [SEE03]: (1) allows companies to release software without disclosing known defects, (2) exempts developers from liability for any damages resulting from these known defects, (3) constrains others from disclosing defects without permission from the original developer, (4) allows the incorporation of "self-help" software within a product that can disable (via remote command) the operation of the product, and (5) exempts developers of software with "self-help" from damages should the software be disabled by a third party.

Like all legislation, debate often centers on issues that are political, not technological. However, many people (including me) feel that protective legislation, if improperly drafted, conflicts with the software engineering code of ethics by indirectly exempting software engineers from their responsibility to produce high-quality software.

32.6 A Final Comment

It has been 30 years since I began work on the first edition of this book. I can still recall sitting at my desk as a young professor, writing the manuscript for a book on a subject that few people cared about and even fewer really understood. I remember the rejection letters from publishers, who argued (politely, but firmly) that there would never be a market for a book on "software engineering." Luckily, McGraw-Hill decided to give it a try,[4] and the rest, as they say, is history.

Over the past 30 years, this book has changed dramatically—in scope, in size, in style, and in content. Like software engineering, it has grown and (I hope) matured over the years.

An engineering approach to the development of computer software is now conventional wisdom. Although debate continues on the "right paradigm," the importance of agility, the degree of automation, and the most effective methods, the underlying principles of software engineering are now accepted throughout the industry. Why, then, have we seen their broad adoption only recently?

The answer, I think, lies in the difficulty of technology transition and the cultural change that accompanies it. Even though most of us appreciate the need for an

---

4   Actually, credit should go to Peter Freeman and Eric Munson, who convinced McGraw-Hill that it was worth a shot. Over a million copies later, it's fair to say they made a good decision.

engineering discipline for software, we struggle against the inertia of past practice and face new application domains (and the developers who work in them) that appear ready to repeat the mistakes of the past. To ease the transition we need many things—an agile, adaptable, and sensible software process; more effective methods; more powerful tools; better acceptance by practitioners and support from managers; and no small dose of education.

You may not agree with every approach described in this book. Some of the techniques and opinions are controversial; others must be tuned to work well in different software development environments. It is my sincere hope, however, that *Software Engineering: A Practitioner's Approach* has delineated the problems we face, demonstrated the strength of software engineering concepts, and provided a framework of methods and tools.

As we move further into the twenty-first century, software continues to be the most important product and the most important industry on the world stage. Its impact and importance have come a long, long way. And yet, a new generation of software developers must meet many of the same challenges that faced earlier generations. Let us hope that the people who meet the challenge—software engineers—will have the wisdom to develop systems that improve the human condition.

AN INTRODUCTION TO UML[1]

The *Unified Modeling Language* (UML) is "a standard language for writing software blueprints. UML may be used to visualize, specify, construct, and document the artifacts of a software-intensive system" [Boo05]. In other words, just as building architects create blueprints to be used by a construction company, software architects create UML diagrams to help software developers build the software. If you understand the vocabulary of UML (the diagrams' pictorial elements and their meanings), you can much more easily understand and specify a system and explain the design of that system to others.

Grady Booch, Jim Rumbaugh, and Ivar Jacobson developed UML in the mid-1990s with much feedback from the software development community. UML merged a number of competing modeling notations that were in use by the software industry at the time. In 1997, UML 1.0 was submitted to the Object Management Group, a nonprofit consortium involved in maintaining specifications for use by the computer industry. UML 1.0 was revised to UML 1.1 and adopted later that year. The current standard is UML 2.0 and is now an ISO standard. Because this standard is so new, many older references, such as [Gam95] do not use UML notation.

UML 2.0 provides 13 different diagrams for use in software modeling. In this appendix, I will discuss only *class, deployment, use case, sequence, communication, activity,* and *state* diagrams. These diagrams are used in this edition of *Software Engineering: A Practitioner's Approach.*

You should note that there are many optional features in UML diagrams. The UML language provides these (sometimes arcane) options so that you can express all the important aspects of a system. At the same time, you have the flexibility to suppress those parts of the diagram that are not relevant to the aspect being modeled in order to avoid cluttering the diagram with irrelevant details. Therefore, the omission of a particular feature does not mean that the feature is absent; it may mean that the feature was suppressed. In this appendix, exhaustive coverage of all the features of the UML diagrams is *not* presented. Instead, I will focus on the standard options, especially those options that have been used in this book.

---

1 This appendix has been contributed by Dale Skrien and has been adapted from his book, *An Introduction to Object-Oriented Design and Design Patterns in Java* (McGraw-Hill, 2008). All content is used with permission.

CLASS DIAGRAMS

To model classes, including their attributes, operations, and their relationships and associations with other classes,[2] UML provides a *class diagram*. A class diagram provides a static or structural view of a system. It does not show the dynamic nature of the communications between the objects of the classes in the diagram.

The main elements of a class diagram are boxes, which are the icons used to represent classes and interfaces. Each box is divided into horizontal parts. The top part contains the name of the class. The middle section lists the attributes of the class. An *attribute* refers to something that an object of that class knows or can provide all the time. Attributes are usually implemented as fields of the class, but they need not be. They could be values that the class can compute from its instance variables or values that the class can get from other objects of which it is composed. For example, an object might always know the current time and be able to return it to you whenever you ask. Therefore, it would be appropriate to list the current time as an attribute of that class of objects. However, the object would most likely not have that time stored in one of its instance variables, because it would need to continually update that field. Instead, the object would likely compute the current time (e.g., through consultation with objects of other classes) at the moment when the time is requested. The third section of the class diagram contains the operations or behaviors of the class. An *operation* refers to what objects of the class can do. It is usually implemented as a method of the class.

Figure A1.1 presents a simple example of a **Thoroughbred** class that models thoroughbred horses. It has three attributes displayed—mother, father, and birthyear. The diagram also shows three operations: *getCurrentAge(), getFather(),* and *getMother().* There may be other suppressed attributes and operations not shown in the diagram.

Each attribute can have a name, a type, and a level of visibility. The type and visibility are optional. The type follows the name and is separated from the name by a

FIGURE A1.1

A class diagram for a Thoroughbred class

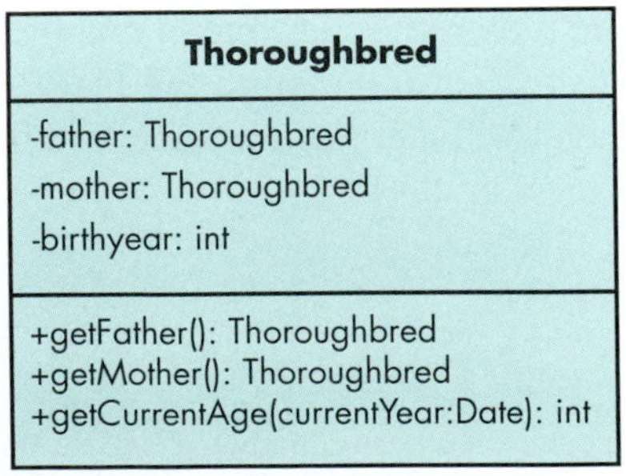

Thoroughbred
-father: Thoroughbred   -mother: Thoroughbred   -birthyear: int
+getFather(): Thoroughbred   +getMother(): Thoroughbred   +getCurrentAge(currentYear:Date): int

---

2   If you are unfamiliar with object-oriented concepts, a brief introduction is presented in Appendix 2.

colon. The visibility is indicated by a preceding –, #, ~, or +, indicating, respectively, *private, protected, package,* or *public* visibility. In Figure A1.1, all attributes have private visibility, as indicated by the leading minus sign (–). You can also specify that an attribute is a static or class attribute by underlining it. Each operation can also be displayed with a level of visibility, parameters with names and types, and a return type.

An abstract class or abstract method is indicated by the use of italics for the name in the class diagram. See the **Horse** class in Figure A1.2 for an example. An interface is indicated by adding the phrase "«interface»" (called a *stereotype*) above the name. See the **OwnedObject** interface in Figure A1.2. An interface can also be represented graphically by a hollow circle.

It is worth mentioning that the icon representing a class can have other optional parts. For example, a fourth section at the bottom of the class box can be used to list the responsibilities of the class. This section is particularly useful when transitioning from CRC cards (Chapter 6) to class diagrams in that the responsibilities listed on the CRC cards can be added to this fourth section in the class box in the UML diagram before creating the attributes and operations that carry out these responsibilities. This fourth section is not shown in any of the figures in this appendix.

Class diagrams can also show relationships between classes. A class that is a subclass of another class is connected to it by an arrow with a solid line for its shaft and with a triangular hollow arrowhead. The arrow points from the subclass to the superclass. In UML, such a relationship is called a *generalization*. For example, in Figure A1.2, the **Thoroughbred** and **QuarterHorse** classes are shown to be subclasses of the **Horse** abstract class. An arrow with a dashed line for the arrow shaft indicates implementation of an interface. In UML, such a relationship is called a *realization*. For example, in Figure A1.2, the **Horse** class implements or realizes the **OwnedObject** interface.

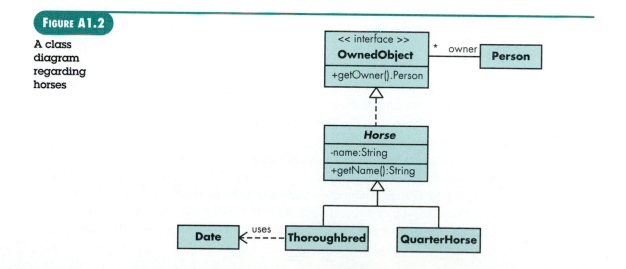

FIGURE A1.2

A class diagram regarding horses

An *association* between two classes means that there is a structural relationship between them. Associations are represented by solid lines. An association has many optional parts. It can be labeled, as can each of its ends, to indicate the role of each class in the association. For example, in Figure A1.2, there is an association between **OwnedObject** and **Person** in which the **Person** plays the role of owner. Arrows on either or both ends of an association line indicate navigability. Also, each end of the association line can have a multiplicity value displayed. Navigability and multiplicity are explained in more detail later in this section. An association might also connect a class with itself, using a loop. Such an association indicates the connection of an object of the class with other objects of the same class.

An association with an arrow at one end indicates one-way navigability. The arrow means that from one class you can easily access the second associated class to which the association points, but from the second class, you cannot necessarily easily access the first class. Another way to think about this is that the first class is aware of the second class, but the second class object is not necessarily directly aware of the first class. An association with no arrows usually indicates a two-way association, which is what was intended in Figure A1.2, but it could also just mean that the navigability is not important and so was left off.

It should be noted that an attribute of a class is very much the same thing as an association of the class with the class type of the attribute. That is, to indicate that a class has a property called "name" of type String, one could display that property as an attribute, as in the **Horse** class in Figure A1.2. Alternatively, one could create a one-way association from the **Horse** class to the **String** class with the role of the **String** class being "name." The attribute approach is better for primitive data types, whereas the association approach is often better if the property's class plays a major role in the design, in which case it is valuable to have a class box for that type.

A *dependency* relationship represents another connection between classes and is indicated by a dashed line (with optional arrows at the ends and with optional labels). One class depends on another if changes to the second class might require changes to the first class. An association from one class to another automatically indicates a dependency. No dashed line is needed between classes if there is already an association between them. However, for a transient relationship (i.e., a class that does not maintain any long-term connection to another class but does use that class occasionally) we should draw a dashed line from the first class to the second. For example, in Figure A1.2, the **Thoroughbred** class uses the **Date** class whenever its *getCurrentAge()* method is invoked, and so the dependency is labeled "uses."

The *multiplicity* of one end of an association means the number of objects of that class associated with the other class. A multiplicity is specified by a nonnegative integer or by a range of integers. A multiplicity specified by "0..1" means that there are 0 or 1 objects on that end of the association. For example, each person in the world has either a Social Security number or no such number (especially if they are not U.S.

citizens), and so a multiplicity of 0..1 could be used in an association between a **Person** class and a **SocialSecurityNumber** class in a class diagram. A multiplicity specified by "1..*" means one or more, and a multiplicity specified by "0..*" or just "*" means zero or more. An * was used as the multiplicity on the **OwnedObject** end of the association with class **Person** in Figure A1.2 because a **Person** can own zero or more objects.

If one end of an association has multiplicity greater than 1, then the objects of the class referred to at that end of the association are probably stored in a collection, such as a set or ordered list. One could also include that collection class itself in the UML diagram, but such a class is usually left out and is implicitly assumed to be there due to the multiplicity of the association.

An *aggregation* is a special kind of association indicated by a hollow diamond on one end of the icon. It indicates a "whole/part" relationship, in that the class to which the arrow points is considered a "part" of the class at the diamond end of the association. A *composition* is an aggregation indicating strong ownership of the parts. In a composition, the parts live and die with the owner because they have no role in the software system independent of the owner. See Figure A1.3 for examples of aggregation and composition.

A **College** has an aggregation of **Building** objects, which represent the buildings making up the campus. The college also has a collection of courses. If the college were to fold, the buildings would still exist (assuming the college wasn't physically destroyed) and could be used for other things, but a **Course** object has no use outside of the college at which it is being offered. If the college were to cease to exist as a business entity, the **Course** object would no longer be useful and so it would also cease to exist.

Another common element of a class diagram is a *note*, which is represented by a box with a dog-eared corner and is connected to other icons by a dashed line. It can have arbitrary content (text and graphics) and is similar to comments in programming languages. It might contain comments about the role of a class or constraints that all objects of that class must satisfy. If the contents are a constraint, braces surround the contents. Note the constraint attached to the **Course** class in Figure A1.3.

FIGURE A1.3

The relationship between Colleges, Courses, and Buildings

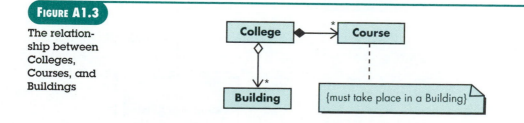

DEPLOYMENT DIAGRAMS

A UML *deployment diagram* focuses on the structure of a software system and is useful for showing the physical distribution of a software system among hardware platforms and execution environments. Suppose, for example, you are developing a Web-based graphics-rendering package. Users of your package will use their Web browser to go to your website and enter rendering information. Your website would render a graphical image according to the user's specification and send it back to the user. Because graphics rendering can be computationally expensive, you decide to move the rendering itself off the Web server and onto a separate platform. Therefore, there will be three hardware devices involved in your system: the Web client (the users' computer running a browser), the computer hosting the Web server, and the computer hosting the rendering engine.

Figure A1.4 shows the deployment diagram for such a package. In such a diagram, hardware components are drawn in boxes labeled with "«device»". Communication paths between hardware components are drawn with lines with optional labels. In Figure A1.4, the paths are labeled with the communication protocol and the type of network used to connect the devices.

Each node in a deployment diagram can also be annotated with details about the device. For example, in Figure A1.4, the browser client is depicted to show that it contains an artifact consisting of the Web browser software. An artifact is typically a file containing software running on a device. You can also specify tagged values, as is shown in Figure A1.4 in the Web server node. These values define the vendor of the Web server and the operating system used by the server.

Deployment diagrams can also display execution environment nodes, which are drawn as boxes containing the label "«execution environment»". These nodes represent systems, such as operating systems, that can host other software.

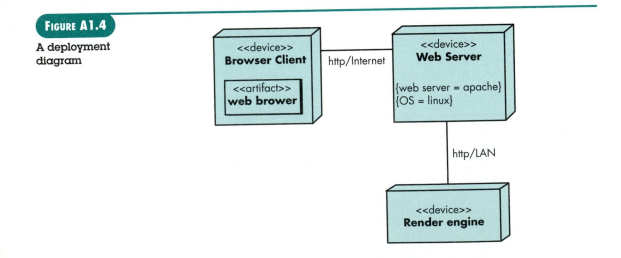

FIGURE A1.4

A deployment diagram

USE-CASE DIAGRAMS

Use cases (Chapters 5 and 6) and the UML *use-case diagram* help you determine the functionality and features of the software from the user's perspective. To give you a feeling for how use cases and use-case diagrams work, I'll create some for a software application for managing digital music files, similar to Apple's iTunes software. Some of the things the software might do include:

- Download an MP3 music file and store it in the application's library.
- Capture streaming music and store it in the application's library.
- Manage the application's library (e.g., delete songs or organize them in playlists).
- Burn a list of the songs in the library onto a CD.
- Load a list of the songs in the library onto an iPod or MP3 player.
- Convert a song from MP3 format to AAC format and vice versa.

This is not an exhaustive list, but it is sufficient to understand the role of use cases and use-case diagrams.

A *use case* describes how a user interacts with the system by defining the steps required to accomplish a specific goal (e.g., burning a list of songs onto a CD). Variations in the sequence of steps describe various scenarios (e.g., what if all the songs in the list don't fit on one CD?).

A UML use-case diagram is an overview of all the use cases and how they are related. It provides a big picture of the functionality of the system. A use-case diagram for the digital music application is shown in Figure A1.5.

In this diagram, the stick figure represents an *actor* (Chapter 5) that is associated with one category of user (or other interaction element). Complex systems typically have more than one actor. For example, a vending machine application might have three actors representing customers, repair personnel, and vendors who refill the machine.

In the use-case diagram, the use cases are displayed as ovals. The actors are connected by lines to the use cases that they carry out. Note that none of the details of the use cases are included in the diagram and instead need to be stored separately. Note also that the use cases are placed in a rectangle but the actors are not. This rectangle is a visual reminder of the system boundaries and that the actors are outside the system.

Some use cases in a system might be related to each other. For example, there are similar steps in burning a list of songs to a CD and in loading a list of songs to an iPod. In both cases, the user first creates an empty list and then adds songs from the library to the list. To avoid duplication in use cases, it is usually better to create a new use case representing the duplicated activity, and then let the other uses cases include this new use case as one of their steps. Such inclusion is indicated in

FIGURE A1.5

**A use-case
diagram for
the music
system**

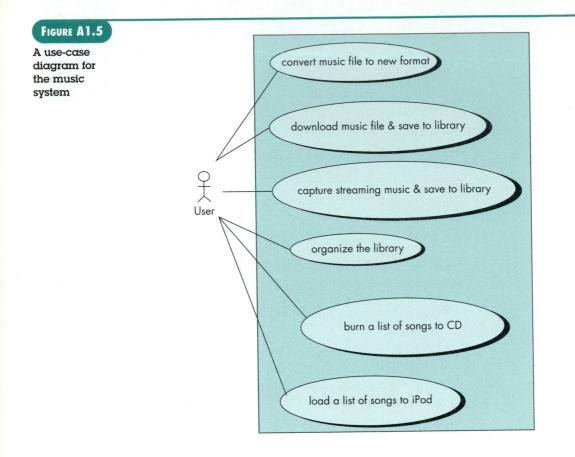

use-case diagrams, as in Figure A1.6, by means of a dashed arrow labeled «include» connecting a use case with an included use case.

A use-case diagram, because it displays all use cases, is a helpful aid for ensuring that you have covered all the functionality of the system. In the digital music organizer, you would surely want more use cases, such as a use case for playing a song in the library. But keep in mind that the most valuable contribution of use cases to the software development process is the textual description of each use case, not the overall use-case diagram. [Fow04b]. It is through the descriptions that you are able to form a clear understanding of the goals of the system you are developing.

SEQUENCE DIAGRAMS

In contrast to class diagrams and deployment diagrams, which show the static structure of a software component, a *sequence diagram* is used to show the dynamic communications between objects during execution of a task. It shows the temporal order in which messages are sent between the objects to accomplish that task. One might use a sequence diagram to show the interactions in one use case or in one scenario of a software system.

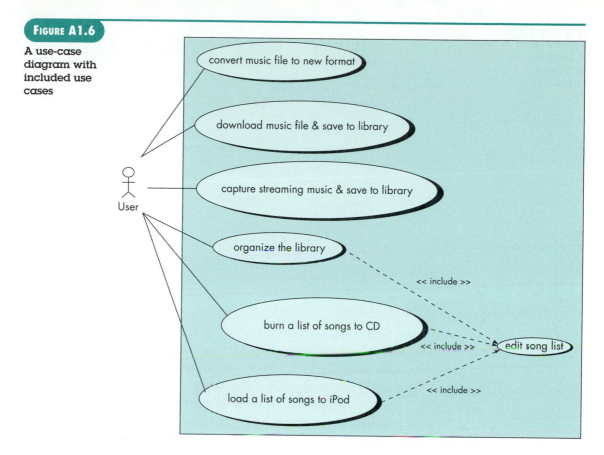

FIGURE A1.6

A use-case diagram with included use cases

In Figure A1.7, you see a sequence diagram for a drawing program. The diagram shows the steps involved in highlighting a figure in a drawing when it has been clicked. Each box in the row at the top of the diagram usually corresponds to an object, although it is possible to have the boxes model other things, such as classes. If the box represents an object (as is the case in all our examples), then inside the box you can optionally state the type of the object preceded by the colon. You can also precede the colon and type by a name for the object, as shown in the third box in Figure A1.7. Below each box there is a dashed line called the *lifeline* of the object. The vertical axis in the sequence diagram corresponds to time, with time increasing as you move downward.

A sequence diagram shows method calls using horizontal arrows from the *caller* to the *callee*, labeled with the method name and optionally including its parameters, their types, and the return type. For example, in Figure A1.7, the **MouseListener** calls the **Drawing**'s *getFigureAt()* method. When an object is executing a method (that is, when it has an activation frame on the stack), you can optionally display a white bar, called an *activation bar*, down the object's lifeline. In Figure A1.7, activation bars are drawn for all method calls. The diagram can also optionally show the return from a method call with a dashed arrow and an optional label. In Figure A1.7,

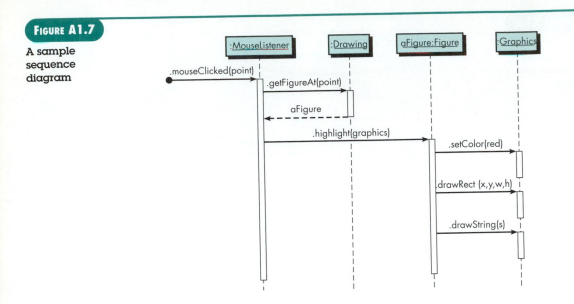

the *getFigureAt()* method call's return is shown labeled with the name of the object that was returned. A common practice, as we have done in Figure A1.7, is to leave off the return arrow when a void method has been called, since it clutters up the diagram while providing little information of importance. A black circle with an arrow coming from it indicates a *found message* whose source is unknown or irrelevant.

You should now be able to understand the task that Figure A1.7 is displaying. An unknown source calls the *mouseClicked()* method of a **MouseListener**, passing in the point where the click occurred as the argument. The **MouseListener** in turn calls the *getFigureAt()* method of a **Drawing**, which returns a **Figure.** The **MouseListener** then calls the highlight method of **Figure**, passing in a **Graphics** object as an argument. In response, **Figure** calls three methods of the **Graphics** object to draw the figure in red.

The diagram in Figure A1.7 is very straightforward and contains no conditionals or loops. If logical control structures are required, it is probably best to draw a separate sequence diagram for each case. That is, if the message flow can take two different paths depending on a condition, then draw two separate sequence diagrams, one for each possibility.

If you insist on including loops, conditionals, and other control structures in a sequence diagram, you can use *interaction frames*, which are rectangles that surround parts of the diagram and that are labeled with the type of control structures they represent. Figure A1.8 illustrates this, showing the process involved in highlighting all figures inside a given rectangle. The **MouseListener** is sent the **rectDragged** message. The **MouseListener** then tells the drawing to highlight all figures in the rectangle by called the method *highlightFigures()*, passing the rectangle as the argument. The method loops through all **Figure** objects in the **Drawing** object and, if the

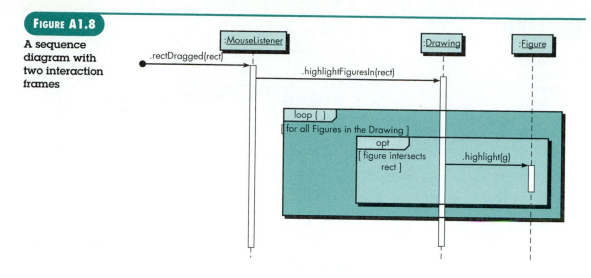

FIGURE A1.8

A sequence diagram with two interaction frames

Figure intersects the rectangle, the **Figure** is asked to highlight itself. The phrases in square brackets are called *guards*, which are Boolean conditions that must be true if the action inside the interaction frame is to continue.

There are many other special features that can be included in a sequence diagram. For example:

1. You can distinguish between synchronous and asynchronous messages. Synchronous messages are shown with solid arrowheads while asynchronous messages are shown with stick arrowheads.

2. You can show an object sending itself a message with an arrow going out from the object, turning downward, and then pointing back to the same object.

3. You can show object creation by drawing an arrow appropriately labeled (for example, with a «create» label) to an object's box. In this case, the box will appear lower in the diagram than the boxes corresponding to objects already in existence when the action begins.

4. You can show object destruction by a big X at the end of the object's lifeline. Other objects can destroy an object, in which case an arrow points from the other object to the X. An X is also useful for indicating that an object is no longer usable and so is ready for garbage collection.

The last three features are all shown in the sequence diagram in Figure A1.9.

COMMUNICATION DIAGRAMS

The UML *communication diagram* (called a "collaboration diagram" in UML 1.X) provides another indication of the temporal order of the communications but emphasizes the relationships among the objects and classes instead of the temporal order.

Creation,
destruction,
and loops in
sequence
diagrams

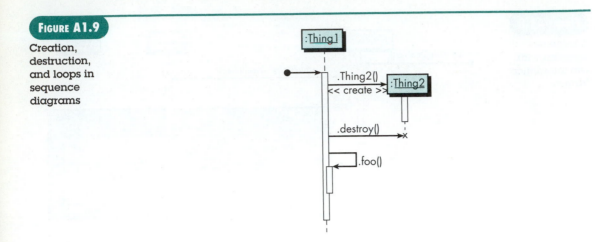

A UML
communica-
tion diagram

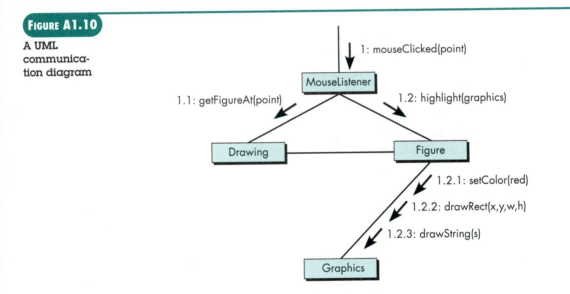

A communication diagram, illustrated in Figure A1.10, displays the same actions shown in the sequence diagram in Figure A1.7.

In a communication diagram the interacting objects are represented by rectangles. Associations between objects are represented by lines connecting the rectangles. There is typically an incoming arrow to one object in the diagram that starts the sequence of message passing. That arrow is labeled with a number and a message name. If the incoming message is labeled with the number 1 and if it causes the receiving object to invoke other messages on other objects, then those messages are represented by arrows from the sender to the receiver along an association line and are given numbers 1.1, 1.2, and so forth, in the order they are called. If those messages in turn invoke other messages, another decimal point and number are added to the number labeling these messages, to indicate further nesting of the message passing.

In Figure A1.10, you see that the **mouseClicked** message invokes the methods *getFigureAt()* and then *highlight()*. The *highlight()* message invokes three other messages: *setColor(), drawRect(),* and *drawstring().* The numbering in each label shows the nesting as well as the sequential nature of each message.

There are many optional features that can be added to the arrow labels. For example, you can precede the number with a letter. An incoming arrow could be labeled **A1: mouseClicked(point)**. indicating an execution thread, A. If other messages are executed in other threads, their label would be preceded by a different letter. For example, if the *mouseClicked()* method is executed in thread A but it creates a new thread B and invokes *highlight()* in that thread, then the arrow from **MouseListener** to **Figure** would be labeled **1.B2: highlight(graphics)**.

If you are interested in showing the relationships among the objects in addition to the messages being sent between them, the communication diagram is probably a better option than the sequence diagram. If you are more interested in the temporal order of the message passing, then a sequence diagram is probably better.

ACTIVITY DIAGRAMS

A UML *activity diagram* depicts the dynamic behavior of a system or part of a system through the flow of control between actions that the system performs. It is similar to a flowchart except that an activity diagram can show concurrent flows.

The main component of an activity diagram is an *action* node, represented by a rounded rectangle, which corresponds to a task performed by the software system. Arrows from one action node to another indicate the flow of control. That is, an arrow between two action nodes means that after the first action is complete the second action begins. A solid black dot forms the *initial node* that indicates the starting point of the activity. A black dot surrounded by a black circle is the *final node* indicating the end of the activity.

A *fork* represents the separation of activities into two or more concurrent activities. It is drawn as a horizontal black bar with one arrow pointing to it and two or more arrows pointing out from it. Each outgoing arrow represents a flow of control that can be executed concurrently with the flows corresponding to the other outgoing arrows. These concurrent activities can be performed on a computer using different threads or even using different computers.

Figure A1.11 shows a sample activity diagram involving baking a cake. The first step is finding the recipe. Once the recipe has been found, the dry ingredients and wet ingredients can be measured and mixed and the oven can be preheated. The mixing of the dry ingredients can be done in parallel with the mixing of the wet ingredients and the preheating of the oven.

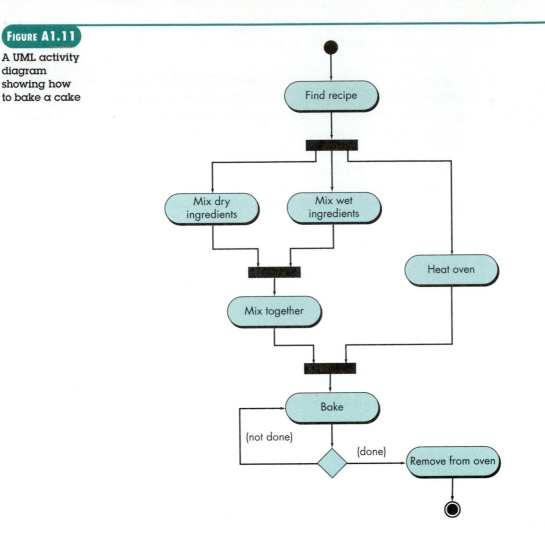

A *join* is a way of synchronizing concurrent flows of control. It is represented by a horizontal black bar with two or more incoming arrows and one outgoing arrow. The flow of control represented by the outgoing arrow cannot begin execution until all flows represented by incoming arrows have been completed. In Figure A1.11, we have a join before the action of mixing together the wet and dry ingredients. This join indicates that all dry ingredients must be mixed and all wet ingredients must be mixed before the two mixtures can be combined. The second join in the figure indicates that, before the baking of the cake can begin, all ingredients must be mixed together and the oven must be at the right temperature.

A *decision* node corresponds to a branch in the flow of control based on a condition. Such a node is displayed as a white triangle with an incoming arrow and two or more outgoing arrows. Each outgoing arrow is labeled with a guard (a condition inside square brackets). The flow of control follows the outgoing arrow whose guard is true. It is advisable to make sure that the conditions cover all possibilities so that exactly one of them is true every time a decision node is reached. Figure A1.11 shows a decision node following the baking of the cake. If the cake is done, then it is removed from the oven. Otherwise, it is baked for a while longer.

One of the things the activity diagram in Figure A1.11 does not tell you is who or what does each of the actions. Often, the exact division of labor does not matter. But if you do want to indicate how the actions are divided among the participants, you can decorate the activity diagram with swimlanes, as shown in Figure A1.12. *Swimlanes*, as the name implies, are formed by dividing the diagram into strips or "lanes," each of which corresponds to one of the participants. All actions in one lane are done by the corresponding participant. In Figure A1.12, Evan is responsible for mixing the dry

FIGURE A1.12

The cake-baking activity diagram with swimlanes added

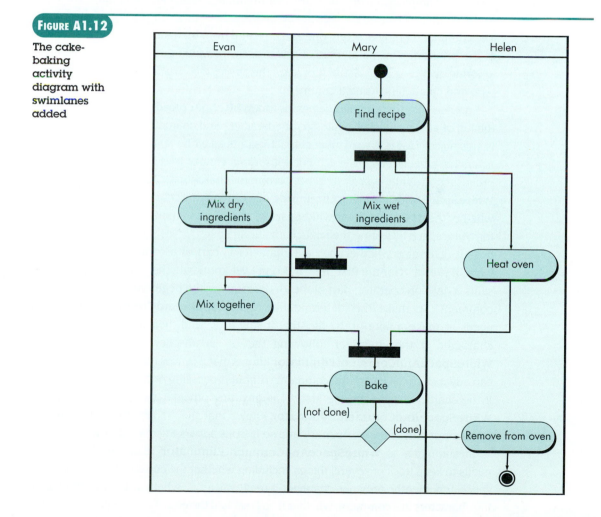

ingredients and then mixing the dry and wet ingredients together, Helen is responsible for heating the oven and taking the cake out, and Mary is responsible for everything else.

STATE DIAGRAMS

The behavior of an object at a particular point in time often depends on the state of the object, that is, the values of its variables at that time. As a trivial example, consider an object with a Boolean instance variable. When asked to perform an operation, the object might do one thing if that variable is *true* and do something else if it is *false.*

A UML *state diagram* models an object's states, the actions that are performed depending on those states, and the transitions between the states of the object.

As an example, consider the state diagram for a part of a Java compiler. The input to the compiler is a text file, which can be thought of as a long string of characters. The compiler reads characters one at a time and from them determines the structure of the program. One small part of this process of reading the characters involves ignoring "white-space" characters (e.g., the *space, tab, newline,* and *return* characters) and characters inside a comment.

Suppose that the compiler delegates to a **WhiteSpaceAndCommentEliminator** the job of advancing over white-space characters and characters in comments. That is, this object's job is to read input characters until all white-space and comment characters have been read, at which point it returns control to the compiler to read and process non-white-space and noncomment characters. Think about how the **WhiteSpaceAndCommentEliminator** object reads in characters and determines whether the next character is white space or part of a comment. The object can check for white space by testing the next character against " ", "\t", "\n", and "\r". But how does it determine whether the next character is part of a comment? For example, when it sees a"/"for the first time, it doesn't yet know whether that character represents a division operator, part of the /= operator, or the beginning of a line or block comment. To make this determination, **WhiteSpaceAndCommentEliminator** needs to make a note of the fact that it saw a "/" and then move on to the next character. If the character following the "/" is another "/" or an "*", then **WhiteSpaceAndCommentEliminator** knows that it is now reading a comment and can advance to the end of the comment without processing or saving any characters. If the character following the first "/" is anything other than a "/" or an "*", then **WhiteSpaceAndCommentEliminator** knows that the "/" represents the division operator or part of the /= operator and so it stops advancing over characters.

In summary, as **WhiteSpaceAndCommentEliminator** reads in characters, it needs to keep track of several things, including whether the current character is white space, whether the previous character it read was a "/", whether it is currently reading characters in a comment, whether it has reached the end of comment, and so forth.

These all correspond to different states of the **WhiteSpaceAndCommentEliminator** object. In each of these states, **WhiteSpaceAndCommentEliminator** behaves differently with regard to the next character read in.

To help you visualize all the states of this object and how it changes state, you can use a UML state diagram as shown in Figure A1.13. A state diagram displays states using rounded rectangles, each of which has a name in its upper half. There is also a black circle called the "initial pseudostate," which isn't really a state and instead just points to the initial state. In Figure A1.13, the **start** state is the initial state. Arrows from one state to another state indicate transitions or changes in the state of the object. Each transition is labeled with a trigger event, a slash (/), and an activity. All parts of the transition labels are optional in state diagrams. If the object is in one state and the trigger event for one of its transitions occurs, then that transition's activity is performed and the object takes on the new state indicated by the transition. For example, in Figure A1.13, if the **WhiteSpaceAndCommentEliminator** object is in the **start** state and the next character is "/", then **WhiteSpaceAndCommentEliminator** advances past that character and changes to the **saw '/'** state. If the character after the "/" is another "/", then the object advances to the **line comment** state and stays there until it reads

---

FIGURE A1.13   A state diagram for advancing past white space and comments in Java

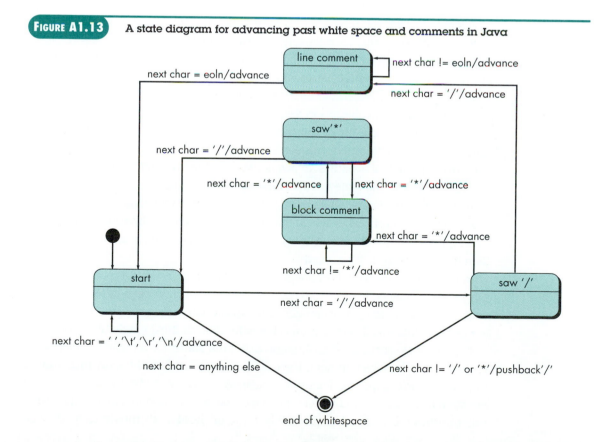

an end-of-line character. If instead the next character after the "/" is a "*", then the object advances to the **block comment** state and stays there until it sees another "*" followed by a "/", which indicates the end of the block comment. Study the diagram to make sure you understand it. Note that, after advancing past white space or a comment, **WhiteSpaceAndCommentEliminator** goes back to the **start** state and starts over. That behavior is necessary since there might be several successive comments or white-space characters before any other characters in the Java source code.

An object may transition to a final state, indicated by a black circle with a white circle around it, which indicates there are no more transitions. In Figure A1.13, the **WhiteSpaceAndCommentEliminator** object is finished when the next character is not white space or part of a comment. Note that all transitions except the two transitions leading to the final state have activities consisting of advancing to the next character. The two transitions to the final state do not advance over the next character because the next character is part of a word or symbol of interest to the compiler. Note that if the object is in the **saw '/'** state but the next character is not "/" or "*", then the "/" is a division operator or part of the /= operator and so we don't want to advance. In fact, we want to back up one character to make the "/" into the next character, so that the "/" can be used by the compiler. In Figure A1.13, this activity of backing up is labeled as pushback '/'.

A state diagram will help you to uncover missed or unexpected situations. That is, with a state diagram, it is relatively easy to ensure that all possible trigger events for all possible states have been accounted for. For example, in Figure A1.13, you can easily verify that every state has included transitions for all possible characters.

UML state diagrams can contain many other features not included in Figure A1.13. For example, when an object is in a state, it usually does nothing but sit and wait for a trigger event to occur. However, there is a special kind of state, called an *activity state*, in which the object performs some activity, called a *do-activity*, while it is in that state. To indicate that a state is an activity state in the state diagram, you include in the bottom half of the state's rounded rectangle the phrase "do/" followed by the activity that is to be done while in that state. The do-activity may finish before any state transitions occur, after which the activity state behaves like a normal waiting state. If a transition out of the activity state occurs before the do-activity is finished, then the do-activity is interrupted.

Because a trigger event is optional when a transition occurs, it is possible that no trigger event may be listed as part of a transition's label. In such cases for normal waiting states, the object will immediately transition from that state to the new state. For activity states, such a transition is taken as soon as the do-activity finishes.

Figure A1.14 illustrates this situation using the states for a business telephone. When a caller is placed on hold, the call goes into the **on hold with music** state (soothing music is played for 10 seconds). After 10 seconds, the do-activity of the state is completed and the state behaves like a normal nonactivity state. If the caller pushes the # key when the call is in the **on hold with music** state, the call

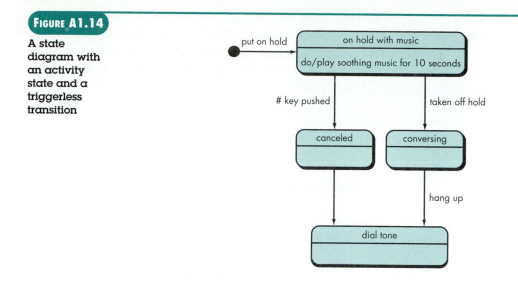

FIGURE A1.14

A state diagram with an activity state and a triggerless transition

transitions to the **canceled** state and then transitions immediately to the **dial tone** state. If the # key is pushed before the 10 seconds of soothing music has completed, the do-activity is interrupted and the music stops immediately.

OBJECT CONSTRAINT LANGUAGE—AN OVERVIEW

The wide variety of diagrams available as part of UML provide you with a rich set of representational forms for the design model. However, graphical representations are often not enough. You may need a mechanism for explicitly and formally representing information that constrains some element of the design model. It is possible, of course, to describe constraints in a natural language such as English, but this approach invariably leads to inconsistency and ambiguity. For this reason, a more formal language—one that draws on set theory and formal specification languages (see Chapter 21) but has the somewhat less mathematical syntax of a programming language—seems appropriate.

The *Object Constraint Language* (OCL) complements UML by allowing you to use a formal grammar and syntax to construct unambiguous statements about various design model elements (e.g., classes and objects, events, messages, interfaces). The simplest OCL statements are constructed in four parts: (1) a *context* that defines the limited situation in which the statement is valid, (2) a *property* that represents some characteristics of the context (e.g., if the context is a class, a property might be an attribute), (3) an *operation* (e.g., arithmetic, set-oriented) that manipulates or qualifies a property, and (4) keywords (e.g., **if, then, else, and, or, not, implies**) that are used to specify conditional expressions.

As a simple example of an OCL expression, consider the printing system discussed in Chapter 10. The guard condition placed on the **jobCostAccepted** event that causes a transition between the states *computingJobCost* and *formingJob* within the statechart diagram for the **PrintJob** object (Figure 10.9). In the diagram (Figure 10.9), the guard condition is expressed in natural language and implies that authorization can only occur if the customer is authorized to approve the cost of the job. In OCL, the expression may take the form:

```
customer
    self.authorizationAuthority = 'yes'
```

where a Boolean attribute, **authorizationAuthority,** of the class (actually a specific instance of the class) named **Customer** must be set to "yes" for the guard condition to be satisfied.

As the design model is created, there are often instances in which pre- or post-conditions must be satisfied prior to completion of some action specified by the design. OCL provides a powerful tool for specifying pre- and postconditions in a formal manner. As an example, consider an extension to the print shop system (discussed as an example in Chapter 10) in which the customer provides an upper cost bound for the print job and a "drop-dead" delivery date at the same time as other print job characteristics are specified. If cost and delivery estimates exceed these bounds, the job is not submitted and the customer must be notified. In OCL, a set of pre- and postconditions may be specified in the following manner:

```
context PrintJob::validate(upperCostBound : Integer, custDeliveryReq :
    Integer)
pre: upperCostBound > 0
    and custDeliveryReq > 0
    and self.jobAuthorization = 'no'
post: if self.totalJobCost <= upperCostBound
        and self.deliveryDate <= custDeliveryReq
    then
        self.jobAuthorization = 'yes'
    endif
```

This OCL statement defines an invariant **(inv)**—conditions that must exist prior to (pre) and after (post) some behavior. Initially, a precondition establishes that bounding cost and delivery date must be specified by the customer, and authorization must be set to "no." After costs and delivery are determined, the postcondition specified is applied. It should also be noted that the expression:

```
self.jobAuthorization = 'yes'
```

is not assigning the value "yes" but is declaring that the **jobAuthorization** must have been set to "yes" by the time the operation finishes. A complete description of OCL is beyond the scope of this appendix. The complete OCL specification can be obtained at **www.omg.org/technology/documents/formal/ocl.htm**.

FURTHER READINGS AND INFORMATION SOURCES

Dozens of books discuss UML. Those that address the latest version include: Miles and Hamilton (*Learning UML 2.0,* O'Reilly Media, Inc., 2006); Booch, Rumbaugh, and Jacobson (*Unified Modeling Language User Guide,* 2d ed., Addison-Wesley, 2005), Ambler (*The Elements of UML 2.0 Style,* Cambridge University Press, 2005), and Pilone and Pitman (*UML 2.0 in a Nutshell,* O'Reilly Media, Inc., 2005).

A wide variety of information sources on the use of UML in the software engineering modeling is available on the Internet. An up-to-date list of World Wide Web references can be found under "analysis" and "design" at the SEPA website: **www.mhhe.com/engcs/compsci/ pressman/professional/olc/ser.htm**.

OBJECT-ORIENTED CONCEPTS

What is an object-oriented (OO) viewpoint? Why is a method considered to be object oriented? What is an object? As OO concepts gained widespread adherents during the 1980s and 1990s, there were many different opinions about the correct answers to these questions, but today a coherent view of OO concepts has emerged. This appendix is designed to provide you with a brief overview of this important topic and to introduce basic concepts and terminology.

To understand the object-oriented point of view, consider an example of a real-world object—the thing you are sitting in right now—a chair. **Chair** is a subclass of a much larger class that we can call **PieceOfFurniture.** Individual chairs are members (usually called instances) of the class **Chair**. A set of generic attributes can be associated with every object in the class **PieceOfFurniture**. For example, all furniture has a cost, dimensions, weight, location, and color, among many possible attributes. These apply whether we are talking about a table or a chair, a sofa or an armoire. Because **Chair** is a member of **PieceOfFurniture**, **Chair** inherits all attributes defined for the class.

We have attempted an anecdotal definition of a class by describing its attributes, but something is missing. Every object in the class **PieceOfFurniture** can be manipulated in a variety of ways. It can be bought and sold, physically modified (e.g., you can saw off a leg or paint the object purple), or moved from one place to another. Each of these *operations* (other terms are *services* or *methods*) will modify one or more attributes of the object. For example, if the attribute location is a composite data item defined as

location = building + floor + room

then an operation named *move()* would modify one or more of the data items (**building**, **floor**, or **room**) that form the attribute location. To do this, *move()* must have "knowledge" of these data items. The operation *move()* could be used for a chair or a table, as long as both are instances of the class **PieceOfFurniture**. Valid operations for the class **PieceOfFurniture**—*buy(), sell(), weigh()*—are specified as part of the class definition and are inherited by all instances of the class.

The class **Chair** (and all objects in general) encapsulates data (the attribute values that define the chair), operations (the actions that are applied to change the attributes of chair), other objects, constants (set values), and other related information. *Encapsulation* means that all of this information is packaged under one name and can be reused as one specification or program component.

Now that I have introduced a few basic concepts, a more formal definition of *object oriented* will prove more meaningful. Coad and Yourdon [Coa91] define the term this way:

Object oriented = objects + classification + inheritance + communication

Three of these concepts have already been introduced. Communication is discussed later in this appendix.

CLASSES AND OBJECTS

A class is an OO concept that encapsulates the data and procedural abstractions required to describe the content and behavior of some real-world entity. Data abstractions that describe the class are enclosed by a "wall" of procedural abstractions [Tay90] (represented in Figure A2.1) that are capable of manipulating the data in some way. In a well-designed class, the only way to reach the attributes (and operate on them) is to go through one of the methods that form the "wall" illustrated in the figure. Therefore, the class encapsulates data (inside the wall) and the processing that manipulates the data (the methods that make up the wall). This achieves information hiding (Chapter 8) and reduces the impact of side effects associated with change. Since the methods tend to manipulate a limited number of attributes, their cohesion is improved, and because communication occurs only through the methods that make up the "wall," the class tends to be less strongly coupled from other elements of a system.[1]

FIGURE A2.1

A schematic representation of a class

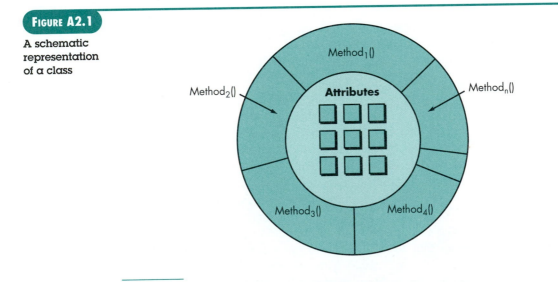

---

[1]   It should be noted, however, that coupling can become a serious problem in OO systems. It arises when classes from various parts of the system are used as the data types of attributes, and arguments to methods. Even though access to the objects may only be through procedure calls, this does not mean that coupling is necessarily low, just lower than if direct access to the internals of objects were allowed.

Stated another way, a class is a generalized description (e.g., a template or blueprint) that describes a collection of similar objects. By definition, objects are instances of a specific class and inherit its attributes and the operations that are available to manipulate the attributes. A *superclass* (often called a *base class*) is a generalization of a set of classes that are related to it. A *subclass* is a specialization of the superclass. For example, the superclass **MotorVehicle** is a generalization of the classes **Truck, SUV, Automobile,** and **Van.** The subclass **Automobile** inherits all attributes of **MotorVehicle,** but in addition, incorporates additional attributes that are specific only to automobiles.

These definitions imply the existence of a class hierarchy in which the attributes and operations of the superclass are inherited by subclasses that may each add additional "private" attributes and methods. For example, the operations *sitOn()* and *turn()* might be private to the **Chair** subclass.

ATTRIBUTES

You have learned that attributes are attached to classes and that they describe the class in some way. An attribute can take on a value defined by an enumerated *domain*. In most cases, a domain is simply a set of specific values. For example, assume that a class **Automobile** has an attribute color. The domain of values for color is {**white, black, silver, gray, blue, red, yellow, green**}. In more complex situations, the domain can be a class. Continuing the example, the class **Automobile** also has an attribute powerTrain that is itself a class. The class **PowerTrain** would contain attributes that describe the specific engine and transmission for the car.

The *features* (values of the domain) can be augmented by assigning a default value (feature) to an attribute. For example, the color attribute defaults to **white**. It may also be useful to associate a probability with a particular feature by assigning {value, probability} pairs. Consider the color attribute for automobile. In some applications (e.g., manufacturing planning) it might be necessary to assign a probability to each of the colors (e.g., white and black are highly probable as automobile colors).

OPERATIONS, METHODS, AND SERVICES

An object encapsulates data (represented as a collection of attributes) and the algorithms that process the data. These algorithms are called *operations, methods,* or *services*[2] and can be viewed as processing components.

Each of the operations that is encapsulated by an object provides a representation of one of the behaviors of the object. For example, the operation *GetColor()* for the object **Automobile** will extract the color stored in the color attribute. The implication of the existence of this operation is that the class **Automobile** has been designed to

---

2   In the context of this discussion, the term *operations* is used, but the terms *methods* and *services* are equally popular.

receive a stimulus (we call the stimulus a *message*) that requests the color of the particular instance of a class. Whenever an object receives a stimulus, it initiates some behavior. This can be as simple as retrieving the color of automobile or as complex as the initiation of a chain of stimuli that are passed among a variety of different objects. In the latter case, consider an example in which the initial stimulus received by **Object 1** results in the generation of two other stimuli that are sent to **Object 2** and **Object 3**. Operations encapsulated by the second and third objects act on the stimuli, returning necessary information to the first object. **Object 1** then uses the returned information to satisfy the behavior demanded by the initial stimulus.

OBJECT-ORIENTED ANALYSIS AND DESIGN CONCEPTS

Requirements modeling (also called analysis modeling) focuses primarily on classes that are extracted directly from the statement of the problem. These *entity classes* typically represent things that are to be stored in a database and persist throughout the duration of the application (unless they are specifically deleted).

Design refines and extends the set of entity classes. Boundary and controller classes are developed and/or refined during design. *Boundary classes* create the interface (e.g., interactive screen and printed reports) that the user sees and interacts with as the software is used. Boundary classes are designed with the responsibility of managing the way entity objects are represented to users.

Controller classes are designed to manage (1) the creation or update of entity objects, (2) the instantiation of boundary objects as they obtain information from entity objects, (3) complex communication between sets of objects, and (4) validation of data communicated between objects or between the user and the application.

The concepts discussed in the paragraphs that follow can be useful in analysis and design work.

Inheritance. Inheritance is one of the key differentiators between conventional and object-oriented systems. A subclass **Y** inherits all of the attributes and operations associated with its superclass **X**. This means that all data structures and algorithms originally designed and implemented for **X** are immediately available for **Y**—no further work need be done. Reuse has been accomplished directly.

Any change to the attributes or operations contained within a superclass is immediately inherited by all subclasses. Therefore, the class hierarchy becomes a mechanism through which changes (at high levels) can be immediately propagated through a system.

It is important to note that at each level of the class hierarchy new attributes and operations may be added to those that have been inherited from higher levels in the hierarchy. In fact, whenever a new class is to be created, you have a number of options:

- The class can be designed and built from scratch. That is, inheritance is not used.

- The class hierarchy can be searched to determine if a class higher in the hierarchy contains most of the required attributes and operations. The new class inherits from the higher class and additions may then be added, as required.

- The class hierarchy can be restructured so that the required attributes and operations can be inherited by the new class.

- Characteristics of an existing class can be overridden, and different versions of attributes or operations are implemented for the new class.

Like all fundamental design concepts, inheritance can provide significant benefit for the design, but if it is used inappropriately,[3] it can complicate a design unnecessarily and lead to error-prone software that is difficult to maintain.

Messages. Classes must interact with one another to achieve design goals. A message stimulates some behavior to occur in the receiving object. The behavior is accomplished when an operation is executed.

The interaction between objects is illustrated schematically in Figure A2.2. An operation within **SenderObject** generates a message of the form *message* (<parameters>) where the parameters identify **ReceiverObject** as the object to be stimulated by the message, the operation within **ReceiverObject** that is to receive the message, and the data items that provide information that is required for the operation to be successful. The collaboration defined between classes as part of the requirements model provides useful guidance in the design of messages.

Cox [Cox86] describes the interchange between classes in the following manner:

> An object [class] is requested to perform one of its operations by sending it a message telling the object what to do. The receiver [object] responds to the message by first choosing the operation that implements the message name, executing this operation, and then returning control to the caller. Messaging ties an object-oriented system together. Messages provide insight into the behavior of individual objects and the OO system as a whole.

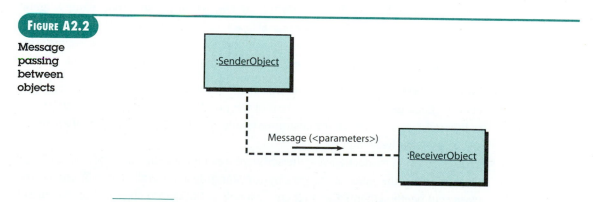

FIGURE A2.2

Message passing between objects

---

3   For example, designing a subclass that inherits attributes and operations from more than one superclass (sometimes called "multiple inheritance") is frowned upon by most designers.

Polymorphism. *Polymorphism* is a characteristic that greatly reduces the effort required to extend the design of an existing object-oriented system. To understand polymorphism, consider a conventional application that must draw four different types of graphs: line graphs, pie charts, histograms, and Kiviat diagrams. Ideally, once data are collected for a particular type of graph, the graph should draw itself. To accomplish this in a conventional application (and maintain module cohesion), it would be necessary to develop drawing modules for each type of graph. Then, within the design, control logic similar to the following would have to be embedded:

```
case of graphtype:
    if graphtype = linegraph then DrawLineGraph (data);
    if graphtype = piechart then DrawPieChart (data);
    if graphtype = histogram then DrawHisto (data);
    if graphtype = kiviat then DrawKiviat (data);
end case;
```

Although this design is reasonably straightforward, adding new graph types could be tricky. A new drawing module would have to be created for each graph type and then the control logic would have to be updated to reflect the new graph type.

To solve this problem in an object-oriented system, all of the graphs become sub-classes of a general class called **Graph**. Using a concept called *overloading* [Tay90], each subclass defines an operation called *draw*. An object can send a *draw* message to any one of the objects instantiated from any one of the subclasses. The object receiving the message will invoke its own *draw* operation to create the appropriate graph. Therefore, the design is reduced to

```
draw <graphtype>
```

When a new graph type is to be added to the system, a subclass is created with its own *draw* operation. But no changes are required within any object that wants a graph drawn because the message **draw <graphtype>** remains unchanged. To summarize, polymorphism enables a number of different operations to have the same name. This in turn decouples objects from one another, making each more independent.

Design classes. The requirements model defines a complete set of analysis classes. Each describes some element of the problem domain, focusing on aspects of the problem that are user or customer visible. The level of abstraction of an analysis class is relatively high.

As the design model evolves, the software team must define a set of *design classes* that (1) refine the analysis classes by providing design detail that will enable the classes to be implemented and (2) create a new set of design classes that implement a software infrastructure that supports the business solution. Five different types of design classes, each representing a different layer of the design architecture are suggested [Amb01]:

- *User interface classes* define all abstractions that are necessary for human-computer interaction (HCI).

- *Business domain classes* are often refinements of the analysis classes defined earlier. The classes identify the attributes and operations (methods) that are required to implement some element of the business domain.

- *Process classes* implement lower-level business abstractions required to fully manage the business domain classes.

- *Persistent classes* represent data stores (e.g., a database) that will persist beyond the execution of the software.

- *System classes* implement software management and control functions that enable the system to operate and communicate within its computing environment and with the outside world.

As the architectural design evolves, the software team should develop a complete set of attributes and operations for each design class. The level of abstraction is reduced as each analysis class is transformed into a design representation. That is, analysis classes represent objects (and associated methods that are applied to them) using the jargon of the business domain. Design classes present significantly more technical detail as a guide for implementation.

Arlow and Neustadt [Arl02] suggest that each design class be reviewed to ensure that it is "well formed." They define four characteristics of a well-formed design class:

Complete and sufficient. A design class should be the complete encapsulation of all attributes and methods that can reasonably be expected (based on a knowledgeable interpretation of the class name) to exist for the class. For example, the class **Scene** defined for video-editing software is complete only if it contains all attributes and methods that can reasonably be associated with the creation of a video scene. Sufficiency ensures that the design class contains only those methods that are sufficient to achieve the intent of the class, no more and no less.

Primitiveness. Methods associated with a design class should be focused on accomplishing one specific function for the class. Once the function has been implemented with a method, the class should not provide another way to accomplish the same thing. For example, the class **VideoClip** of the video editing software might have attributes start-point and end-point to indicate the start and end points of the clip (note that the raw video loaded into the system may be longer than the clip that is used). The methods, *setStartPoint()* and *setEndPoint()* provide the only means for establishing start and end points for the clip.

High cohesion. A cohesive design class is single minded. That is, it has a small, focused set of responsibilities and single-mindedly applies attributes and methods to implement those responsibilities. For example, the class **VideoClip** of the video-editing software might contain a set of methods for editing the video clip. As long as each method focuses solely on attributes associated with the video clip, cohesion is maintained.

Low coupling. Within the design model, it is necessary for design classes to collaborate with one another. However, collaboration should be kept to an acceptable minimum. If a design model is highly coupled (all design classes collaborate with all other design classes), the system is difficult to implement, test, and maintain over time. In general, design classes within a subsystem should have only limited knowledge of other classes. This restriction, called the *Law of Demeter* [Lie03], suggests that a method should only send messages to methods in neighboring classes.[4]

FURTHER READINGS AND INFORMATION SOURCES

Over the past three decades hundreds of books have been written on object-oriented programming, analysis, and design. Weisfeld (*The Object-Oriented Thought Process*, 2d ed., Sams Publishing, 2003) presents a worthwhile treatment of general OO concepts and principles. McLaughlin and his colleagues (*Head First Object-Oriented Analysis and Design: A Brain Friendly Guide to OOA&D*, O'Reilly Media, Inc., 2006) provide an accessible and enjoyable treatment of OO analysis and design approaches. A more in-depth treatment of OO analysis and design is presented by Booch and his colleagues (*Object-Oriented Analysis and Design with Applications*, 3d ed., Addison-Wesley, 2007). Wu (*An Introduction to Object-Oriented Programming with Java*, McGraw-Hill, 2005) has written a comprehensive book on OO programming that is typical of dozens written for many different programming languages.

A wide variety of information sources on object-oriented technologies is available on the Internet. An up-to-date list of World Wide Web references can be found under "analysis" and "design" at the SEPA website: **www.mhhe.com/engcs/compsci/pressman/professional/olc/ser.htm**.

---

4   A less formal way of stating the Law of Demeter is, "Each unit should only talk to its friends; don't talk to strangers."

REFERENCES

[Abb83] Abbott, R., "Program Design by Informal English Descriptions," *CACM*, vol. 26, no. 11, November 1983, pp. 892–894.

[ACM98] ACM/IEEE-CS Joint Task Force, *Software Engineering Code of Ethics and Professional Practice*, 1998, available at www.acm.org/serving/se/code.htm.

[Ada93] Adams, D., *Mostly Harmless*, Macmillan, 1993.

[AFC88] *Software Risk Abatement*, AFCS/AFLC Pamphlet 800-45, U.S. Air Force, September 30, 1988.

[Agi03] The Agile Alliance Home Page, www.agilealliance.org/home.

[Air99] Airlie Council, "Performance Based Management: The Program Manager's Guide Based on the 16-Point Plan and Related Metrics," Draft Report, March 8, 1999.

[Aka04] Akao, Y., *Quality Function Deployment*, Productivity Press, 2004.

[Ale77] Alexander, C., *A Pattern Language*, Oxford University Press, 1977.

[Ale79] Alexander, C., *The Timeless Way of Building*, Oxford University Press, 1979.

[Amb95] Ambler, S., "Using Use-Cases," *Software Development*, July 1995, pp. 53–61.

[Amb98] Ambler, S., *Process Patterns: Building Large-Scale Systems Using Object Technology*, Cambridge University Press/SIGS Books, 1998.

[Amb01] Ambler, S., *The Object Primer*, 2d ed., Cambridge University Press, 2001.

[Amb02a] Ambler, S., "What Is Agile Modeling (AM)?" 2002, www.agilemodeling.com/index.htm.

[Amb02b] Ambler, S., and R. Jeffries, *Agile Modeling*, Wiley, 2002.

[Amb02c] Ambler, S., "UML Component Diagramming Guidelines," available at www.modelingstyle.info/, 2002.

[Amb04] Ambler, S., *"Examining the Cost of Change Curve,"* in *The Object Primer*, 3d ed., Cambridge University Press, 2004.

[Amb06] Ambler, S., "The Agile Unified Process (AUP), 2006, available at www.ambysoft.com/unifiedprocess/agileUP.html.

[And06] Andrews, M., and J. Whittaker, *How to Break Web Software: Functional and Security Testing of Web Applications and Web Services*, Addison-Wesley, 2006.

[ANS87] ANSI/ASQC A3-1987, *Quality Systems Terminology*, 1987.

[Ant06] Anton, D., and C. Anton, *ISO 9001 Survival Guide*, 3d ed., AEM Consulting Group, 2006.

[AOS07] AOSD.net (Aspect-Oriented Software Development), glossary, available at http://aosd.net/wiki/index.php?title=Glossary.

[App00] Appleton, B., "Patterns and Software: Essential Concepts and Terminology," February 2000, available at www.cmcrossroads.com/bradapp/docs/patterns-intro.html.

[App08] Apple Computer, *Accessibility*, 2008, available at www.apple.com/disability/.

[Arl02] Arlow, J., and I. Neustadt, *UML and the Unified Process*, Addison-Wesley, 2002.

[Arn89] Arnold, R. S., "Software Restructuring," *Proc. IEEE*, vol. 77, no. 4, April 1989, pp. 607–617.

[Art97] Arthur, L. J., "Quantum Improvements in Software System Quality," *CACM*, vol. 40, no. 6, June 1997, pp. 47–52.

[Ast04] Astels, D., *Test Driven Development: A Practical Guide*, Prentice Hall, 2004.

[Ave04] Aversan, L., et al., "Managing Coordination and Cooperation in Distributed Software Processes: The GENESIS Environment," *Software Process Improvement and Practice*, vol. 9, Wiley Interscience, 2004, pp. 239–263.

[Baa07] de Baar, B., "Project Risk Checklist," 2007, available at www.softwareprojects.org/project_riskmanagement_starting62.htm.

[Bab86] Babich, W. A., *Software Configuration Management*, Addison-Wesley, 1986.

[Bac97] Bach, J., "'Good Enough Quality: Beyond the Buzzword," *IEEE Computer*, vol. 30, no. 8, August 1997, pp. 96–98.

[Bac98] Bach, J., "The Highs and Lows of Change Control," *Computer*, vol. 31, no. 8, August 1998, pp. 113–115.

[Bae98] Baetjer, Jr., H., *Software as Capital*, IEEE Computer Society Press, 1998, p. 85.

[Bak72] Baker, F. T., "Chief Programmer Team Management of Production Programming," *IBM Systems Journal.*, vol. 11, no. 1, 1972, pp. 56–73.

[Ban06] Baniassad, E., et al., "Discovering Early Aspects," *IEEE Software*, vol. 23, no. 1, January–February, 2006, pp. 61–69.

[Bar06] Baresi, L., E. DiNitto, and C. Ghezzi, "Toward Open-World Software: Issues and Challenges," *IEEE Computer*, vol. 39, no. 10, October 2006, pp. 36–43.

[Bas84] Basili, V. R., and D. M. Weiss, "A Methodology for Collecting Valid Software Engineering Data," *IEEE Trans. Software Engineering*, vol. SE-10, 1984, pp. 728–738.

[Bas03] Bass, L., P. Clements, and R. Kazman, *Software Architecture in Practice*, 2d ed., Addison-Wesley, 2003.

[Bec00] Beck, K., *Extreme Programming Explained: Embrace Change*, Addison-Wesley, 1999.

[Bec01a] Beck, K., et al., "Manifesto for Agile Software Development," www.agilemanifesto.org/.

[Bec04a] Beck, K., *Extreme Programming Explained: Embrace Change*, 2d ed., Addison-Wesley, 2004.

[Bec04b] Beck, K., *Test-Driven Development: By Example*, 2d ed., Addison-Wesley, 2002.

[Bee99] Beedle, M., et al., "SCRUM: An Extension Pattern Language for Hyperproductive Software Development," included in: *Pattern Languages of Program Design 4*, Addison-Wesley Longman, Reading MA, 1999, downloadable from http://jeffsutherland.com/scrum/scrum_plop.pdf.

[Bei84] Beizer, B., *Software System Testing and Quality Assurance*, Van Nostrand-Reinhold, 1984.

[Bei90] Beizer, B., *Software Testing Techniques*, 2d ed., Van Nostrand-Reinhold, 1990.

[Bei95] Beizer, B., *Black-Box Testing*, Wiley, 1995.

[Bel81] Belady, L., Foreword to *Software Design: Methods and Techniques* (L. J. Peters, author), Yourdon Press, 1981.

[Bel95] Bellinzona R., M. G. Gugini, and B. Pernici, "Reusing Specifications in OO Applications," *IEEE Software*, March 1995, pp. 65–75.

[Ben99] Bentley, J., *Programming Pearls*, 2d ed., Addison-Wesley, 1999.

[Ben00] Bennatan, E. M., *Software Project Management: A Practitioner's Approach*, 3d ed., McGraw-Hill, 2000.

[Ben02] Bennett, S., S. McRobb, and R. Farmer, *Object-Oriented Analysis and Design*, 2d ed., McGraw-Hill, 2002.

[Ber80] Bersoff, E. H., V. D. Henderson, and S. G. Siegel, *Software Configuration Management*, Prentice Hall, 1980.

[Ber93] Berard, E., *Essays on Object-Oriented Software Engineering*, vol. 1, Addison-Wesley, 1993.

[Bes04] Bessin, J., "The Business Value of Quality," IBM developerWorks, June 15, 2004, available at www-128.ibm.com/developerworks/rational/library/4995.html.

[Bha06] Bhat, J., M. Gupta, and S. Murthy, "Lessons from Offshore Outsourcing," *IEEE Software*, vol. 23, no. 5, September–October 2006.

[Bie94] Bieman, J. M., and L. M. Ott, "Measuring Functional Cohesion," *IEEE Trans. Software Engineering*, vol. SE-20, no. 8, August 1994, pp. 308–320.

[Bin93] Binder, R., "Design for Reuse Is for Real," *American Programmer*, vol. 6, no. 8, August 1993, pp. 30–37.

[Bin94a] Binder, R., "Testing Object-Oriented Systems: A Status Report," *American Programmer*, vol. 7, no. 4, April 1994, pp. 23–28.

[Bin94b] Binder, R. V., "Object-Oriented Software Testing," *Communications of the ACM*, vol. 37, no. 9, September 1994, p. 29.

[Bin99] Binder, R., *Testing Object-Oriented Systems: Models, Patterns, and Tools*, Addison-Wesley, 1999.

[Bir98] Biró, M., and T. Remzsö, "Business Motivations for Software Process Improvement," ERCIM News No. 32, January 1998, available at www.ercim.org/publication/Ercim_News/enw32/biro.html.

[Boe81] Boehm, B., *Software Engineering Economics*, Prentice Hall, 1981.

[Boe88] Boehm, B., "A Spiral Model for Software Development and Enhancement," *Computer*, vol. 21, no. 5, May 1988, pp. 61–72.

[Boe89] Boehm, B. W., *Software Risk Management*, IEEE Computer Society Press, 1989.

[Boe96] Boehm, B., "Anchoring the Software Process," *IEEE Software*, vol. 13, no. 4, July 1996, pp. 73–82.

[Boe98] Boehm, B., "Using the WINWIN Spiral Model: A Case Study," *Computer*, vol. 31, no. 7, July 1998, pp. 33–44.

[Boe00] Boehm, B., et al., *Software Cost Estimation in COCOMO II*, Prentice Hall, 2000.

[Boe01a] Boehm, B., "The Spiral Model as a Tool for Evolutionary Software Acquisition," *CrossTalk*, May 2001, available at www.stsc.hill.af.mil/crosstalk/2001/05/boehm.html.

[Boe01b] Boehm, B., and V. Basili, "Software Defect Reduction Top 10 List," *IEEE Computer*, vol. 34, no. 1, January 2001, pp. 135–137.

[Boe08] Boehm, B., "Making a Difference in the Software Century," *IEEE Computer*, vol. 41, no. 3, March 2008, pp. 32–38.

[Boh66] Bohm, C., and G. Jacopini, "Flow Diagrams, Turing Machines and Languages with Only Two Formation Rules," *CACM*, vol. 9, no. 5, May 1966, pp. 366–371.

[Boh00] Bohl, M., and M. Rynn, *Tools for Structured Design: An Introduction to Programming Logic*, 5th ed., Prentice Hall, 2000.

[Boi04] Boiko, B., *Content Management Bible*, 2d ed., Wiley, 2004.

[Bol02] Boldyreff, C., et al., "Environments to Support Collaborative Software Engineering," 2002, downloadable from www.cs.put.poznan.pl/dweiss/site/publications/download/csmre-paper.pdf.

[Boo94] Booch, G., *Object-Oriented Analysis and Design*, 2d ed., Benjamin Cummings, 1994.

[Boo05] Booch, G., J. Rumbaugh, and I. Jacobsen, *The Unified Modeling Language User Guide*. 2d ed., Addison-Wesley, 2005.

[Boo06] Bootstrap-institute.com, 2006, www.cse.dcu.ie/espinode/directory/directory.html.

[Boo08] Booch, G., *Handbook of Software Architecture*, 2008, available at www.booch.com/architecture/systems.jsp.

[Bor01] Borchers, J., *A Pattern Approach to Interaction Design*, Wiley, 2001.

[Bos00] Bosch, J., *Design & Use of Software Architectures*, Addison-Wesley, 2000.

[Bra85] Bradley, J. H., "The Science and Art of Debugging," *Computerworld*, August 19, 1985, pp. 35–38.

[Bra94] Bradac, M., D. Perry, and L. Votta, "Prototyping a Process Monitoring Experiment," *IEEE Trans. Software Engineering*, vol. 20, no. 10, October 1994, pp. 774–784.

[Bre02] Breen, P., "Exposing the Fallacy of 'Good Enough' Software," informit.com, February 1, 2002, available at www.informit.com/articles/article.asp?p=25141&rl=1.

[Bro95] Brooks, F., *The Mythical Man-Month*, Silver Anniversary edition, Addison-Wesley, 1995.

[Bro96] Brown, A. W., and K. C. Wallnau, "Engineering of Component Based Systems," *Component-Based Software Engineering*, IEEE Computer Society Press, 1996, pp. 7–15.

[Bro01] Brown, B., *Oracle9i Web Development*, 2d ed., McGraw-Hill, 2001.

[Bro03] Brooks, F, "Three Great Challenges for Half-Century-Old Computer Science," *JACM*, vol. 50, no. 1, January 2003, pp. 25–26.

[Bro06] Broy, M., "The 'Grand Challenge' in Informatics: Engineering Software Intensive Systems," *IEEE Computer*, vol. 39, no. 10, October 2006, pp. 72–80.

[Buc99] Bucanac, C., "The V-Model," University of Karlskrona/Ronneby, January 1999, downloadable from www.bucanac.com/documents/The_V-Model.pdf.

[Bud96] Budd, T., *An Introduction to Object-Oriented Programming*, 2d ed., Addison-Wesley, 1996.

[Bus96] Buschmann, F., et al., *Pattern-Oriented Software Architecture*, Wiley, 1996.

[Bus07] Buschmann, F., et al., *Pattern-Oriented Software Architecture, A System of Patterns*, Wiley, 2007.

[Cac02] Cachero, C., et al., "Conceptual Navigation Analysis: A Device and Platform Independent Navigation Specification," *Proc. 2nd Intl. Workshop on Web-Oriented Technology*, June 2002, downloadable from www.dsic.upv.es/~west/iwwost02/papers/cachero.pdf.

[Cai03] Caine, Frarber, and Gordon, Inc., *PDL/81*, 2003, available at www.cfg.com/pdl81/lpd.html.

[Car90] Card, D. N., and R. L. Glass, *Measuring Software Design Quality*, Prentice Hall, 1990.

[Cas89] Cashman, M., "Object Oriented Domain Analysis," *ACM Software Engineering Notes*, vol. 14, no. 6, October 1989, p. 67.

[Cav78] Cavano, J. P., and J. A. McCall, "A Framework for the Measurement of Software Quality," *Proc. ACM Software Quality Assurance Workshop*, November 1978, pp. 133–139.

[CCS02] CS3 Consulting Services, 2002, www.cs3inc.com/DSDM.htm.

[Cec06] Cechich, A., et al., "Trends on COTS Component Identification," *Proc. Fifth Intl. Conf. on COTS-Based Software Systems*, IEEE, 2006.

[Cha89] Charette, R. N., *Software Engineering Risk Analysis and Management*, McGraw-Hill/ Intertext, 1989.

[Cha92] Charette, R. N., "Building Bridges over Intelligent Rivers," *American Programmer*, vol. 5, no. 7, September 1992, pp. 2–9.

[Cha93] de Champeaux, D., D. Lea, and P. Faure, *Object-Oriented System Development*, Addison-Wesley, 1993.

[Cha03] Chakravarti, A., "Online Software Design Pattern Links," 2003, available at www .anupriyo.com/oopfm.shtml.

[Che77] Chen, P., *The Entity-Relationship Approach to Logical Database Design*, QED Information Systems, 1977.

[Chi94] Chidamber, S. R., and C. F. Kemerer, "A Metrics Suite for Object-Oriented Design," *IEEE Trans. Software Engineering*, vol. SE-20, no. 6, June 1994, pp. 476–493.

[Cho89] Choi, S. C., and W. Scacchi, "Assuring the Correctness of a Configured Software Description," *Proc. 2nd Intl. Workshop on Software Configuration Management*, ACM, Princeton, NJ, October 1989, pp. 66–75.

[Chu95] Churcher, N. I., and M. J. Shepperd, "Towards a Conceptual Framework for Object-Oriented Metrics," *ACM Software Engineering Notes*, vol. 20, no. 2, April 1995, pp. 69–76.

[Cig07] Cigital, Inc., "Case Study: Finding Defects Earlier Yields Enormous Savings," 2007, available at www.cigital.com/solutions/roi-cs2.php.

[Cla05] Clark, S., and E. Baniasaad, *Aspect-Oriented Analysis and Design*, Addison-Wesley, 2005.

[Cle95] Clements, P., "From Subroutines to Subsystems: Component Based Software Development," *American Programmer*, vol. 8, no. 11, November 1995.

[Cle03] Clements, P., R. Kazman, and M. Klein, *Evaluating Software Architectures: Methods and Case Studies*, Addison-Wesley, 2003.

[Cle06] Clemmons, R., "Project Estimation with Use Case Points," *CrossTalk*, February 2006, p. 18–222, downloadable from www.stsc.hill.af.mil/crosstalk/2006/02/0602Clemmons.pdf.

[CMM07] *Capability Maturity Model Integration (CMMI)*, Software Engineering Institute, 2007, available at www.sei.cmu.edu/cmmi/.

[CMM08] *People Capability Maturity Model Integration (People CMM)*, Software Engineering Institute, 2008, available at www.sei.cmu.edu/cmm-p/.

[Coa91] Coad, P., and E. Yourdon, *Object-Oriented Analysis*, 2d ed., Prentice Hall, 1991.

[Coa99] Coad, P., E. Lefebvre, and J. DeLuca, *Java Modeling in Color with UML*, Prentice Hall, 1999.

[Coc01a] Cockburn, A., and J. Highsmith, "Agile Software Development: The People Factor," *IEEE Computer*, vol. 34, no. 11, November 2001, pp. 131–133.

[Coc01b] Cockburn, A., *Writing Effective Use-Cases*, Addison-Wesley, 2001.

[Coc02] Cockburn, A., *Agile Software Development*, Addison-Wesley, 2002.

[Coc04] Cockburn, A., "What the Agile Toolbox Contains," *CrossTalk*, November 2004, available at www.stsc.hill.af.mil/crosstalk/2004/11/0411Cockburn.html.

[Coc05] Cockburn, A., *Crystal Clear*, Addison-Wesley, 2005.

[Con96] Conradi, R., "Software Process Improvement: Why We Need SPIQ," NTNU, October 1996, downloadable from www.idi.ntnu.no/grupper/su/publ/pdf/nik96-spiq.pdf.

[Con02] Conradi, R., and A. Fuggetta, "Improving Software Process Improvement," *IEEE Software*, July–August 2002, pp. 2–9, downloadable from http://citeseer.ist.psu.edu/ conradi02improving.html.

[Con93] Constantine, L., "Work Organization: Paradigms for Project Management and Organization, *CACM*, vol. 36, no. 10, October 1993, pp. 34–43.

[Con95] Constantine, L, "What DO Users Want? Engineering Usability in Software," *Windows Tech Journal*, December 1995, available from www.forUse.com.

[Con03] Constantine, L., and L. Lockwood, *Software for Use*, Addison-Wesley, 1999; see also www.foruse.com/.

[Cop05] Coplien, J., "Software Patterns," 2005, available at http://hillside.net/patterns/ definition.html.

[Cor98] Corfman, R., "An Overview of Patterns," in *The Patterns Handbook*, SIGS Books, 1998.

[Cou00] Coulouris, G., J. Dollimore, and T. Kindberg, *Distributed Systems: Concepts and Design*, 3d ed., Addison-Wesley, 2000.

[Cox86] Cox, Brad, *Object-Oriented Programming*, Addison-Wesley, 1986.

[Cri92] Christel, M. G., and K. C. Kang, "Issues in Requirements Elicitation," Software Engineering Institute, CMU/SEI-92-TR-12 7, September 1992.

[Cro79] Crosby, P., *Quality Is Free*, McGraw-Hill, 1979.

[Cro07] Cross, M., and M. Fisher, *Developer's Guide to Web Application Security*, Syngress Publishing, 2007.

[Cur86] Curritt, P. A., M. Dyer, and H. D. Mills, "Certifying the Reliability of Software," *IEEE Trans, Software Engineering*, vol. SE-12, no. 1, January 1994.

[Cur88] Curtis, B., et al., "A Field Study of the Software Design Process for Large Systems," *IEEE Trans. Software Engineering*, vol. SE-31, no. 11, November 1988, pp. 1268–1287.

[Cur01] Curtis, B., W. Hefley, and S. Miller, *People Capability Maturity Model*, Addison-Wesley, 2001.

[CVS07] Concurrent Versions System, Ximbiot, http://ximbiot.com/cvs/wiki/index.php?title=Main_Page, 2007.

[DAC03} "An Overview of Model-Based Testing for Software," Data and Analysis Center for Software, CR/TA 12, June 2003, downloadable from www.goldpractices.com/dwnload/practice/pdf/Model_Based_Testing.pdf.

[Dah72] Dahl, O., E. Dijkstra, and C. Hoare, *Structured Programming*, Academic Press, 1972.

[Dar91] Dart, S., "Concepts in Configuration Management Systems," *Proc. Third International Workshop on Software Configuration Management*, ACM SIGSOFT, 1991, downloadable from www.sei.cmu.edu/legacy/scm/abstracts/abscm_concepts.html.

[Dar99] Dart, S., "Change Management: Containing the Web Crisis," *Proc. Software Configuration Management Symposium*, Toulouse, France, 1999, available at www.perforce.com/perforce/conf99/dart.html.

[Dar01] Dart, S., *Spectrum of Functionality in Configuration Management Systems*, Software Engineering Institute, 2001, available at www.sei.cmu.edu/legacy/scm/tech_rep/TR11_90/TOC_TR11_90.html.

[Das05] Dasari, R., "Lean Software Development," a white paper, downloadable from www.projectperfect.com.au/downloads/Info/info_lean_development.pdf, 2005.

[Dav90] Davenport, T. H., and J. E. Young, "The New Industrial Engineering: Information Technology and Business Process Redesign," *Sloan Management Review*, Summer 1990, pp. 11–27.

[Dav93] Davis, A., et al., "Identifying and Measuring Quality in a Software Requirements Specification," *Proc. First Intl. Software Metrics Symposium*, IEEE, Baltimore, MD, May 1993, pp. 141–152.

[Dav95a] Davis, M., "Process and Product: Dichotomy or Duality," *Software Engineering Notes*, ACM Press, vol. 20, no. 2, April, 1995, pp. 17–18.

[Dav95b] Davis, A., *201 Principles of Software Development*, McGraw-Hill, 1995.

[Day99] Dayani-Fard, H., et al., "Legacy Software Systems: Issues, Progress, and Challenges," IBM Technical Report: TR-74.165-k, April 1999, available at www.cas.ibm.com/toronto/publications/TR-74.165/k/legacy.html.

[Dem86] Deming, W. E., *Out of the Crisis*, MIT Press, 1986.

[DeM79] DeMarco, T., *Structured Analysis and System Specification*, Prentice Hall, 1979.

[DeM95] DeMarco, T., *Why Does Software Cost So Much?* Dorset House, 1995.

[DeM95a] DeMarco, T., "Lean and Mean," *IEEE Software*, November 1995, pp. 101–102.

[DeM98] DeMarco, T., and T. Lister, *Peopleware*, 2d ed., Dorset House, 1998.

[DeM02] DeMarco, T., and B. Boehm, "The Agile Methods Fray," IEEE Computer, vol. 35, no. 6, June 2002, pp. 90–92.

[Den73] Dennis, J., "Modularity," in *Advanced Course on Software Engineering* (F. L. Bauer, ed.), Springer-Verlag, 1973, pp. 128–182.

[Dev01] Devedzik, V., "Software Patterns," in *Handbook of Software Engineering and Knowledge Engineering*, World Scientific Publishing Co., 2001.

[Dha95] Dhama, H., "Quantitative Metrics for Cohesion and Coupling in Software," *Journal of Systems and Software*, vol. 29, no. 4, April 1995.

[Dij65] Dijkstra, E., "Programming Considered as a Human Activity," in *Proc. 1965 IFIP Congress*, North-Holland Publishing Co., 1965.

[Dij72] Dijkstra, E., "The Humble Programmer," 1972 ACM Turing Award Lecture, *CACM*, vol. 15, no. 10, October 1972, pp. 859–866.

[Dij76a] Dijkstra, E., "Structured Programming," in *Software Engineering, Concepts and Techniques*, (J. Buxton et al., eds.), Van Nostrand-Reinhold, 1976.

[Dij76b] Dijkstra, E., *A Discipline of Programming*, Prentice Hall, 1976.

[Dij82] Dijksta, E., "On the Role of Scientific Thought," *Selected Writings on Computing: A Personal Perspective*, Springer-Verlag, 1982.

[Dix99] Dix, A., "Design of User Interfaces for the Web," *Proc. User Interfaces to Data Systems Conference*, September 1999, downloadable from www.comp.lancs.ac.uk/computing/users/dixa/topics/webarch/.

[Dob04] Dobb, F., *ISO 9001:2000 Quality Registration Step-by-Step*, 3d ed., Butterworth-Heinemann, 2004.

[Don99] Donahue, G., S. Weinschenck, and J. Nowicki, "Usability Is Good Business," Compuware Corp., July 1999, available from www.compuware.com.

[Dre99] Dreilinger, S., "CVS Version Control for Web Site Projects," 1999, available at www.durak.org/cvswebsites/howto-cvs/howto-cvs.html.

[Dru75] Drucker, P., *Management*, W. H. Heinemann, 1975.

[Duc01] Ducatel, K., et al., *Scenarios for Ambient Intelligence in 2010*, ISTAG-European Commission, 2001, downloadable from ftp://ftp.cordis.europa.eu/pub/ist/docs/istagscenarios2010.pdf.

[Dun82] Dunn, R., and R. Ullman, *Quality Assurance for Computer Software*, McGraw-Hill, 1982.

[Dun01] Dunaway, D., and S. Masters, *CMM-Based Appraisal for Internal Process Improvement (CBA IPI Version 1,2 Method Description)*, Software Engineering Institute, 2001, downloadable from www.sei.cmu.edu/publications/documents/01.reports/01tr033.html.

[Dun02] Dunn, W., *Practical Design of Safety-Critical Computer Systems*, William Dunn, 2002.

[Duy02] VanDuyne, D., J. Landay, and J. Hong, *The Design of Sites*, Addison-Wesley, 2002.

[Dye92] Dyer, M., *The Cleanroom Approach to Quality Software Development*, Wiley, 1992.

[Edg95] Edgemon, J., "Right Stuff: How to Recognize It When Selecting a Project Manager," *Application Development Trends*, vol. 2, no. 5, May 1995, pp. 37–42.

[Eji91] Ejiogu, L., *Software Engineering with Formal Metrics*, QED Publishing, 1991.

[Elr01] Elrad, T., R. Filman, and A. Bader (eds.), "Aspect Oriented Programming," *Comm. ACM*, vol. 44, no. 10, October 2001, special issue.

[Eri05] Ericson, C., *Hazard Analysis Techniques for System Safety*, Wiley-Interscience, 2005.

[Eri08] Erickson, T., *The Interaction Design Patterns Page*, May 2008, available at www.visi.com/~snowfall/InteractionPatterns.html.

[Eva04] Evans, E., *Domain Driven Design*, Addison-Wesley, 2003.

[Fag86] Fagan, M., "Advances in Software Inspections," *IEEE Trans. Software Engineering*, vol. 12, no. 6, July 1986.

[Fel89] Felican, L., and G. Zalateu, "Validating Halstead's Theory for Pascal Programs," *IEEE Trans. Software Engineering*, vol. SE-15, no. 2, December 1989, pp. 1630–1632.

[Fel07] Feller, J., et al. (eds.), *Perspectives on Free and Open Source Software*, The MIT Press, 2007.

[Fen91] Fenton, N., *Software Metrics*, Chapman and Hall, 1991.

[Fen94] Fenton, N., "Software Measurement: A Necessary Scientific Basis," *IEEE Trans. Software Engineering*, vol. SE-20, no. 3, March 1994, pp. 199–206.

[Fer97] Ferguson, P., et al., "Results of Applying the Personal Software Process," *IEEE Computer*, vol. 30, no. 5, May 1997, pp. 24–31.

[Fer98] Ferdinandi, P. L., "Facilitating Communication," *IEEE Software*, September 1998, pp. 92–96.

[Fer00] Fernandez, E. B., and X. Yuan, "Semantic Analysis Patterns," *Proceedings of the 19th Int. Conf. on Conceptual Modeling, ER2000*, Lecture Notes in Computer Science 1920, Springer, 2000, pp. 183–195. Also available from www.cse.fau.edu/~ed/SAPpaper2.pdf.

[Fir93] Firesmith, D. G., *Object-Oriented Requirements Analysis and Logical Design*, Wiley, 1993.

[Fis06] Fisher, R., and D. Shapiro, *Beyond Reason: Using Emotions as You Negotiate*, Penguin, 2006.

[Fit54] Fitts, P., "The Information Capacity of the Human Motor System in Controlling the Amplitude of Movement," *Journal of Experimental Psychology*, vol. 47, 1954, pp. 381–391.

[Fle98] Fleming, Q. W., and J. M. Koppelman, "Earned Value Project Management," *CrossTalk*, vol. 11, no. 7, July 1998, p. 19.

[Fos06] Foster, E., "Quality Culprits," InfoWorld Grip Line Weblog, May 2, 2006, available at http://weblog.infoworld.com/gripeline/2006/05/02_a395.html.

[Fow97] Fowler, M., *Analysis Patterns: Reusable Object Models*, Addison-Wesley, 1997.

[Fow00] Fowler, M., et al., *Refactoring: Improving the Design of Existing Code*, Addison-Wesley, 2000.

[Fow01] Fowler, M., and J. Highsmith, "The Agile Manifesto," *Software Development Magazine*, August 2001, www.sdmagazine.com/documents/s=844/sdm0108a/0108a.htm.

[Fow02] Fowler. M., "The New Methodology," June 2002, www.martinfowler.com/articles/newMethodology.html#N8B.

[Fow03] Fowler, M., et al., *Patterns of Enterprise Application Architecture*, Addison-Wesley, 2003.

[Fow04] Fowler, M., *UML Distilled*, 3d ed., Addison-Wesley, 2004.

[Fra93] Frankl, P. G., and S. Weiss, "An Experimental Comparison of the Effectiveness of Branch Testing and Data Flow," *IEEE Trans. Software Engineering*, vol. SE-19, no. 8, August 1993, pp. 770–787.

[Fra03] Francois, A., "Software Architecture for Immersipresence," IMSC Technical Report IMSC-03-001, University of Southern California, December 2003, available at http://iris.usc.edu/~afrancoi/pdf/sai-tr.pdf.

[Fre80] Freeman, P., "The Context of Design," in *Software Design Techniques*, 3d ed. (P. Freeman and A. Wasserman, eds.), IEEE Computer Society Press, 1980, pp. 2–4.

[Fre90] Freedman, D. P., and G. M. Weinberg, *Handbook of Walkthroughs, Inspections and Technical Reviews*, 3d ed., Dorset House, 1990.

[Gag04] Gage, D., and J. McCormick, "We Did Nothing Wrong," *Baseline Magazine*, March 4, 2004, available at www.baselinemag.com/article2/0,1397,1544403,00.asp.

[Gai95] Gaines, B., "Modeling and Forecasting the Information Sciences," Technical Report, University of Calgary, Calgary, Alberta, September 1995.

[Gam95] Gamma, E., et al., *Design Patterns: Elements of Reusable Object-Oriented Software*, Addison-Wesley, 1995.

[Gar84] Garvin, D., "What Does 'Product Quality' Really Mean?" *Sloan Management Review*, Fall 1984, pp. 25–45.

[Gar87] Garvin D., *"Competing on the Eight Dimensions of Quality,"* Harvard Business Review, November 1987, pp. 101–109. A summary is available at www.acm.org/crossroads/xrds6-4/software.html.

[Gar95] Garlan, D., and M. Shaw, "An Introduction to Software Architecture," *Advances in Software Engineering and Knowledge Engineering*, vol. I (V. Ambriola and G. Tortora, eds.), World Scientific Publishing Company, 1995.

[Gar08] GartnerGroup, "Understanding Hype Cycles," 2008, available at www.gartner.com/pages/story.php.id.8795.s.8.jsp.

[Gau89] Gause, D. C., and G. M. Weinberg, *Exploring Requirements: Quality Before Design*, Dorset House, 1989.

[Gey01] Geyer-Schulz, A., and M. Hahsler, "Software Engineering with Analysis Patterns," Technical Report 01/2001, Institut für Informationsverarbeitung und -wirtschaft, Wirschaftsuniversität Wien, November 2001, downloadable from wwwai.wu-wien.ac.at/~hahsler/research/virlib_working2001/virlib/.

[Gil88] Gilb, T., *Principles of Software Project Management*, Addison-Wesley, 1988.

[Gil95] Gilb, T., "What We Fail to Do in Our Current Testing Culture," *Testing Techniques Newsletter* (online edition, ttn@soft.com), Software Research, January 1995.

[Gil06] Gillis, D., "Pattern-Based Design," tehan + lax blog, September 14, 2006, available at www.teehanlax.com/blog/?p=96.

[Gla98] Glass, R., "Defining Quality Intuitively," *IEEE Software*, May 1998, pp. 103–104, 107.

[Gla00] Gladwell, M., *The Tipping Point*, Back Bay Books, 2002.

[Gli07] Glinz, M., and R. Wieringa, "Stakeholders in Requirements Engineering," *IEEE Software*, vol. 24, no. 2, March–April 2007, pp. 18–20.

[Glu94] Gluch, D., "A Construct for Describing Software Development Risks," CMU/SEI-94-TR-14, Software Engineering Institute, 1994.

[Gna99] Gnaho, C., and F. Larcher, "A User-Centered Methodology for Complex and Customizable Web Engineering," *Proc. 1st ICSE Workshop on Web Engineering*, ACM, Los Angeles, May 1999.

[Gon04] Gonzales, R., "Requirements Engineering," Sandia National Laboratories, a slide presentation, available at www.incose.org/enchantment/docs/04AprRequirementsEngineering.pdf.

[Gor02] Gordon, B., and M. Gordon, *The Complete Guide to Digital Graphic Design*, Watson-Guptill, 2002.

[Gor06] Gorton, I., *Essential Software Architecture*, Springer, 2006.

[Gra87] Grady, R. B., and D. L. Caswell, *Software Metrics: Establishing a Company-Wide Program*, Prentice Hall, 1987.

[Gra92] Grady, R. B., *Practical Software Metrics for Project Management and Process Improvement*, Prentice Hall, 1992.

[Gra99] Grable, R., et al., "Metrics for Small Projects: Experiences at SED," *IEEE Software*, March 1999, pp. 21–29.

[Gra03] Gradecki, J., and N. Lesiecki, *Mastering AspectJ: Aspect-Oriented Programming in Java*, Wiley, 2003.

[Gru02] Grundy, J., "Aspect-Oriented Component Engineering," 2002, www.cs.auckland.ac.nz/~john-g/aspects.html.

[Gus89] Gustavsson, A., "Maintaining the Evolution of Software Objects in an Integrated Environment," *Proc. 2nd Intl. Workshop on Software Configuration Management*, ACM, Princeton, NJ, October 1989, pp. 114–117.

[Gut93] Guttag, J. V., and J. J. Horning, *Larch: Languages and Tools for Formal Specification*, Springer-Verlag, 1993.

[Hac98] Hackos, J., and J. Redish, *User and Task Analysis for Interface Design*, Wiley, 1998.

[Hai02] Hailpern, B., and P. Santhanam, "Software Debugging, Testing and Verification," *IBM Systems Journal*, vol. 41, no. 1, 2002, available at www.research.ibm.com/journal/sj/411/hailpern.html.

[Hal77] Halstead, M., *Elements of Software Science*, North-Holland, 1977.

[Hal90] Hall, A., "Seven Myths of Formal Methods," *IEEE Software*, September 1990, pp. 11–20.

[Hal98] Hall, E. M., *Managing Risk: Methods for Software Systems Development*, Addison-Wesley, 1998.

[Ham90] Hammer, M., "Reengineer Work: Don't Automate, Obliterate," *Harvard Business Review*, July–August 1990, pp. 104–112.

[Han95] Hanna, M., "Farewell to Waterfalls," *Software Magazine*, May 1995, pp. 38–46.

[Har98a] Harmon, P., "Navigating the Distributed Components Landscape," *Cutter IT Journal.*, vol. 11, no. 2, December 1998, pp. 4–11.

[Har98b] Harrison, R., S. J. Counsell, and R. V. Nithi, "An Evaluation of the MOOD Set of Object-Oriented Software Metrics," *IEEE Trans. Software Engineering*, vol. SE-24, no. 6, June 1998, pp. 491–496.

[Her00] Herrmann, D., *Software Safety and Reliability*, Wiley-IEEE Computer Society Press, 2000.

[Het84] Hetzel, W., *The Complete Guide to Software Testing*, QED Information Sciences, 1984.

[Het93] Hetzel, W., *Making Software Measurement Work*, QED Publishing, 1993.

[Hev93] Hevner, A. R., and H. D. Mills, "Box Structure Methods for System Development with Objects," *IBM Systems Journal*, vol. 31, no. 2, February 1993, pp. 232–251.

[Hig95] Higuera, R. P., "Team Risk Management," *CrossTalk*, U.S. Dept. of Defense, January 1995, pp. 2–4.

[Hig00] Highsmith, J., *Adaptive Software Development: An Evolutionary Approach to Managing Complex Systems*, Dorset House Publishing, 2000.

[Hig01] Highsmith, J. (ed.), "The Great Methodologies Debate: Part 1," *Cutter IT Journal.*, vol. 14, no. 12, December 2001.

[Hig02a] Highsmith, J. (ed.), "The Great Methodologies Debate: Part 2," *Cutter IT Journal.*, vol. 15, no. 1, January 2002.

[Hig02b] Highsmith, J., *Agile Software Development Ecosystems*, Addison-Wesley, 2002.

[Hil05] Hildreth, S., "Buggy Software: Up from a Low Quality Quagmire," *Computerworld*, July 25, 2005, available at www.computerworld.com/developmenttopics/development/story/ 0,10801,103378,00.html.

[Hil08] Hillside.net, *Patterns Catalog*, 2008, available at http://hillside.net/patterns/ onlinepatterncatalog.htm.

[Hob06] Hoberman, S., *Data Modeling Made Simple*, Technics Publications, 2006.

[Hof00] Hofmeister, C., R. Nord, and D. Soni, *Applied Software Architecture*, Addison-Wesley, 2000.

[Hof01] Hofmann, C., et al., "Approaches to Software Architecture," 2001, downloadable from http://citeseer.nj.nec.com/84015.html.

[Hol06] Holzner, S., *Design Patterns for Dummies*, For Dummies Publishers, 2006.

[Hoo96] Hooker, D., "Seven Principles of Software Development," September 1996, available at http://c2.com/cgi/wikiSevenPrinciplesOfSoftwareDevelopment.

[Hop90] Hopper, M. D., "Rattling SABRE, New Ways to Compete on Information," *Harvard Business Review*, May–June 1990.

[Hor03] Horch, J., *Practical Guide to Software Quality Management*, 2d ed., Artech House, 2003.

[HPR02] Hypermedia Design Patterns Repository, 2002, available at www.designpattern .lu.unisi.ch/index.htm.

[Hum95] Humphrey, W., *A Discipline for Software Engineering*, Addison-Wesley, 1995.

[Hum96] Humphrey, W., "Using a Defined and Measured Personal Software Process," *IEEE Software*, vol. 13, no. 3, May–June 1996, pp. 77–88.

[Hum97] Humphrey, W., *Introduction to the Personal Software Process*, Addison-Wesley, 1997.

[Hum98] Humphrey, W., "The Three Dimensions of Process Improvement, Part III: The Team Process," *CrossTalk*, April 1998, available at www.stsc.hill.af.mil/crosstalk/1998/apr/ dimensions.asp.

[Hum00] Humphrey, W., *Introduction to the Team Software Process*, Addison-Wesley, 2000.

[Hun99] Hunt, A., D. Thomas, and W. Cunningham, *The Pragmatic Programmer*, Addison-Wesley, 1999.

[Hur83] Hurley, R. B., *Decision Tables in Software Engineering*, Van Nostrand-Reinhold, 1983.

[Hya96] Hyatt, L., and L. Rosenberg, "A Software Quality Model and Metrics for Identifying Project Risks and Assessing Software Quality," NASA SATC, 1996, available at http://satc .gsfc.nasa.gov/support/STC_APR96/qualtiy/stc_qual.html.

[IBM81] "Implementing Software Inspections," course notes, IBM Systems Sciences Institute, IBM Corporation, 1981.

[IBM03] IBM, *Web Services Globalization Model*, 2003, available at www.ibm.com/ developerworks/webservices/library/ws-global/.

[IEE93a] *IEEE Standards Collection: Software Engineering*, IEEE Standard 610.12-1990, IEEE, 1993.

[IEE93b] *IEEE Standard Glossary of Software Engineering Terminology*, IEEE, 1993.

[IEE00] IEEE Standard Association, IEEE-Std-1471-2000, *Recommended Practice for Architectural Description of Software-Intensive Systems*, 2000, available at http://standards.ieee.org/ reading/ieee/std_public/description/se/1471-2000_desc.html.

[IFP01] *Function Point Counting Practices Manual*, Release 4.1.1, International Function Point Users Group, 2001, available from www.ifpug.org/publications/manual.htm.

[IFP05] Function Point Bibliography/Reference Library, International Function Point Users Group, 2005, available from www.ifpug.org/about/bibliography.htm.

[ISI08] iSixSigma, LLC, "New to Six Sigma: A Guide for Both Novice and Experiences Quality Practitioners," 2008, available at www.isixsigma.com/library/content/six-sigma-newbie.asp.

[ISO00] ISO 9001: 2000 Document Set, International Organization for Standards, 2000, www.iso .ch/iso/en/iso9000-14000/iso9000/iso9000index.html.

[ISO02] *Z Formal Specification Notation—Syntax, Type System and Semantics*, ISO/IEC 13568:2002, Intl. Standards Organization, 2002.

[ISO08] ISO SPICE, 2008, www.isospice.com/categories/SPICE-Project/.

[Ivo01] Ivory, M., R. Sinha, and M. Hearst, " Empirically Validated Web Page Design Metrics," ACM *SIGCHI'01*, March 31–April 4, 2001, available at http://webtango.berkeley.edu/papers/ chi2001/.

[Jac75] Jackson, M. A., *Principles of Program Design*, Academic Press, 1975.

[Jac92] Jacobson, I., *Object-Oriented Software Engineering*, Addison-Wesley, 1992.

[Jac98] Jackman, M., "Homeopathic Remedies for Team Toxicity," *IEEE Software*, July 1998, pp. 43-45.

[Jac99] Jacobson, I., G. Booch, and J. Rumbaugh, *The Unified Software Development Process*, Addison-Wesley, 1999.

[Jac02a] Jacobson, I., "A Resounding 'Yes' to Agile Processes—But Also More," *Cutter IT Journal*, vol. 15, no. 1, January 2002, pp. 18–24.

[Jac02b] Jacyntho, D., D. Schwabe, and G. Rossi, "An Architecture for Structuring Complex Web Applications," 2002, available at www2002.org/CDROM/alternate/478/.

[Jac04] Jacobson, I., and P. Ng, *Aspect-Oriented Software Development*, Addison-Wesley, 2004.

[Jal04] Jalote, P., et al., "Timeboxing: A Process Model for Iterative Software Development," *Journal of Systems and Software,*vol. 70, issue 2, 2004, pp. 117–127. Available at www.cse.iitk.ac.in/users/jalote/papers/Timeboxing.pdf.

[Jay94] Jaychandra, Y., *Re-engineering the Networked Enterprise*, McGraw-Hill, 1994.

[Jec06] Jech, T., *Set Theory*, 3d ed., Springer, 2006.

[Jon86] Jones, C., *Programming Productivity*, McGraw-Hill, 1986.

[Jon91] Jones, C., *Systematic Software Development Using VDM*, 2d ed., Prentice Hall, 1991.

[Jon96] Jones, C., "How Software Estimation Tools Work," *American Programmer*, vol. 9, no. 7, July 1996, pp. 19–27.

[Jon98] Jones, C., *Estimating Software Costs*, McGraw-Hill, 1998.

[Jon04] Jones, C., "Software Project Management Practices: Failure Versus Success," *CrossTalk*, October 2004. Available at www.stsc.hill.af.mil/crossTalk/2004/10/0410Jones.html.

[Joy00] Joy, B., "The Future Doesn't Need Us," *Wired*, vol. 8, no. 4, April 2000.

[Kai02] Kaiser, J., "Elements of Effective Web Design," About, Inc., 2002, available at http://webdesign.about.com/library/weekly/aa091998.htm.

[Kal03] Kalman, S., *Web Security Field Guide*, Cisco Press, 2003.

[Kan93] Kaner, C., J. Falk, and H. Q. Nguyen, *Testing Computer Software*, 2d ed., Van Nostrand-Reinhold, 1993.

[Kan95] Kaner, C., "Lawyers, Lawsuits, and Quality Related Costs, 1995, available at www.badsoftware.com/plaintif.htm.

[Kan01] Kaner, C., "Pattern: Scenario Testing" (draft), 2001, available at www.testing.com/test-patterns/patterns/pattern-scenario-testing-kaner.html.

[Kar94] Karten, N., *Managing Expectations*, Dorset House, 1994.

[Kau95] Kauffman, S., *At Home in the Universe*, Oxford, 1995.

[Kaz98] Kazman, R., et al., *The Architectural Tradeoff Analysis Method*, Software Engineering Institute, CMU/SEI-98-TR-008, July 1998.

[Kaz03] Kazman, R., and A. Eden, "Defining the Terms Architecture, Design, and Implementation," *news@sei interactive*, Software Engineering Institute, vol. 6, no. 1, 2003, available at www.sei.cmu.edu/news-at-sei/columns/the_architect/2003/1q03/architect-1q03.htm.

[Kei98] Keil, M., et al., "A Framework for Identifying Software Project Risks," *CACM*, vol. 41, no. 11, November 1998, pp. 76–83.

[Kel00] Kelly, D., and R. Oshana, "Improving Software Quality Using Statistical Techniques, Information and Software Technology," Elsevier, vol. 42, August 2000, pp. 801–807, available at www.eng.auburn.edu/~kchang/comp6710/readings/Improving_Quality_with_Statistical_Testing_InfoSoftTech_August2000.pdf.

[Ker78] Kernighan, B., and P. Plauger, *The Elements of Programming Style*, 2d ed., McGraw-Hill, 1978.

[Ker05] Kerievsky, J., *Industrial XP: Making XP Work in Large Organizations*, Cutter Consortium, Executive Report, vol. 6., no. 2, 2005, available at www.cutter.com/content-and-analysis/resource-centers/agile-project-management/sample-our-research/apmr0502.html.

[Kim04] Kim, E., "A Manifesto for Collaborative Tools," *Dr. Dobb's Journal*, May 2004, available at www.blueoxen.com/papers/0000D/.

[Kir94] Kirani, S., and W. T. Tsai, "Specification and Verification of Object-Oriented Programs," Technical Report TR 94-64, Computer Science Department, University of Minnesota, December 1994.

[Kiz05] Kizza, J., *Computer Network Security*, Springer, 2005.

[Knu98] Knuth, D., *The Art of Computer Programming*, three volumes, Addison-Wesley, 1998.

[Kon02] Konrad, S., and B. Cheng, "Requirements Patterns for Embedded Systems," *Proceedings of the 10th Anniversary IEEE Joint International Conference on Requirements Engineering*, IEEE, September 2002, pp. 127–136, downloadable from http://citeseer.ist.psu.edu/669258.html.

[Kra88] Krasner, G., and S. Pope, "A Cookbook for Using the Model-View-Controller User Interface Paradigm in Smalltalk-80," *Journal of Object-Oriented Programming*, vol. 1, no. 3, August–September 1988, pp. 26–49.

[Kra95] Kraul, R., and L. Streeter, "Coordination in Software Development," *CACM*, vol. 38, no. 3, March 1995, pp. 69–81.

[Kru05] Krutchen, P., "Software Design in a Postmodern Era," *IEEE Software*, vol. 22, no. 2, March–April, 2005, pp. 16–18.

[Kru06] Kruchten, P., H. Obbink, and J. Stafford (eds.), "Software Architectural" (special issue), *IEEE Software*, vol. 23, no. 2, March–April, 2006.

[Kur05] Kurzweil, R., *The Singularity Is Near*, Penguin Books, 2005.

[Kyb84] Kyburg, H. E., *Theory and Measurement*, Cambridge University Press, 1984.

[Laa00] Laakso, S., et al., "Improved Scroll Bars," *CHI 2000 Conf. Proc.*, ACM, 2000, pp. 97–98, available at www.cs.helsinki.fi/u/salaakso/patterns/.

[Lai02] Laitenberger, A., "A Survey of Software Inspection Technologies," in *Handbook on Software Engineering and Knowledge Engineering*, World Scientific Publishing Company, 2002.

[Lam01] Lam, W., "Testing E-Commerce Systems: A Practical Guide," *IEEE IT Pro*, March–April 2001, pp. 19–28.

[Lan01] Lange, M., "It's Testing Time! Patterns for Testing Software, June 2001, downloadable from www.testing.com/test-patterns/patterns/index.html.

[Lan02] Land, R., "A Brief Survey of Software Architecture," Technical Report, Dept. of Computer Engineering, Mälardalen University, Sweden, February 2002.

[Leh97a] Lehman, M., and L. Belady, *Program Evolution: Processes of Software Change*, Academic Press, 1997.

[Leh97b] Lehman, M., et al., "Metrics and Laws of Software Evolution—The Nineties View," *Proceedings of the 4th International Software Metrics Symposium (METRICS '97)*, IEEE, 1997, downloadable from www.ece.utexas.edu/~perry/work/papers/feast1.pdf.

[Let01] Lethbridge, T., and R. Laganiere, *Object-Oriented Software Engineering: Practical Software Development Using UML and Java*, McGraw-Hill, 2001.

[Let03a] Lethbridge, T., Personal communication on domain analysis, May 2003.

[Let03b] Lethbridge, T., Personal communication on software metrics, June 2003.

[Lev95] Leveson, N. G., *Safeware: System Safety and Computers*, Addison-Wesley, 1995.

[Lev01] Levinson, M., "Let's Stop Wasting $78 billion a Year," *CIO Magazine*, October 15, 2001, available at www.cio.com/archive/101501/wasting.html.

[Lew06] Lewicki, R., B. Barry, and D. Saunders, *Essentials of Negotiation*, McGraw-Hill, 2006.

[Lie03] Lieberherr, K., "Demeter: Aspect-Oriented Programming," May 2003, available at www.ccs.neu.edu/home/lieber/LoD.html.

[Lin79] Linger, R., H. Mills, and B. Witt, *Structured Programming*, Addison-Wesley, 1979.

[Lin88] Linger, R. M., and H. D. Mills, "A Case Study in Cleanroom Software Engineering: The IBM COBOL Structuring Facility," *Proc. COMPSAC '88*, Chicago, October 1988.

[Lin94] Linger, R., "Cleanroom Process Model," *IEEE Software*, vol. 11, no. 2, March 1994, pp. 50–58.

[Lis88] Liskov, B., "Data Abstraction and Hierarchy," *SIGPLAN Notices*, vol. 23, no. 5, May 1988.

[Liu98] Liu, K., et al., "Report on the First SEBPC Workshop on Legacy Systems," Durham University, February 1998, available at www.dur.ac.uk/CSM/SABA/legacy-wksp1/report.html.

[Lon02] Longstreet, D., "Fundamental of Function Point Analysis," Longstreet Consulting, Inc., 2002, available at www.ifpug.com/fpafund.htm.

[Lor94] Lorenz, M., and J. Kidd, *Object-Oriented Software Metrics*, Prentice Hall, 1994.

[Maa07] Maassen, O., and S. Stelting, "Creational Patterns: Creating Objects in an OO System," 2007, available at www.informit.com/articles/article.asp?p=26452&rl=1.

[Man81] Mantai, M., "The Effect of Programming Team Structures on Programming Tasks," *CACM*, vol. 24, no. 3, March 1981, pp. 106–113.

[Man97] Mandel, T., *The Elements of User Interface Design*, Wiley, 1997.

[Mar94] Marick, B., *The Craft of Software Testing*, Prentice Hall, 1994.

[Mar00] Martin, R., "Design Principles and Design Patterns," downloadable from www.objectmentor.com, 2000.

[Mar01] Marciniak, J. J. (ed.), *Encyclopedia of Software Engineering*, 2d ed., Wiley, 2001.

[Mar02] Marick, B., "Software Testing Patterns," 2002, www.testing.com/test-patterns/index.html.

[McC76] McCabe, T., "A Software Complexity Measure," *IEEE Trans. Software Engineering*, vol. SE-2, December 1976, pp. 308–320.

[McC77] McCall, J., P. Richards, and G. Walters, "Factors in Software Quality," three volumes, NTIS AD-A049-014, 015, 055, November 1977.

[McC94] McCabe, T. J., and A. H. Watson, "Software Complexity," *CrossTalk*, vol. 7, no. 12, December 1994, pp. 5–9.

[McC96] McConnell, S., "Best Practices: Daily Build and Smoke Test", *IEEE Software*, vol. 13, no. 4, July 1996, pp. 143–144.

[McC98] McConnell, S., *Software Project Survival Guide*, Microsoft Press, 1998.

[McC99] McConnell, S., "Software Engineering Principles," *IEEE Software*, vol. 16, no. 2, March–April 1999, available at www.stevemcconnell.com/ieeesoftware/eic04.htm.

[McC04] McConnell, S., *Code Complete*, Microsoft Press, 2004.

[McC05] McCrory, A., "Ten Technologies to Watch in 2006," SeachCIO.com, October 27, 2005, available at http://searchcio.techtarget.com/originalContent/0,289142,sid19_gci1137889,00.html.

[McDE93] McDermid, J., and P. Rook, "Software Development Process Models," in *Software Engineer's Reference Book*, CRC Press, 1993, pp. 15/26–15/28.

[McG91] McGlaughlin, R., "Some Notes on Program Design," *Software Engineering Notes*, vol. 16, no. 4, October 1991, pp. 53–54.

[McG94] McGregor, J. D., and T. D. Korson, "Integrated Object-Oriented Testing and Development Processes," *Communications of the ACM*, vol. 37, no. 9, September, 1994, pp. 59–77.

[Men01] Mendes, E., N. Mosley, and S. Counsell, "Estimating Design and Authoring Effort," *IEEE Multimedia*, vol. 8, no. 1, January–March 2001, pp. 50–57.

[Mer93] Merlo, E., et al., "Reengineering User Interfaces," *IEEE Software*, January 1993, pp. 64–73.

[Mic08] *Microsoft Accessibility Technology for Everyone*, 2008, available at www.microsoft.com/enable/.

[Mic04] Microsoft, "Prescriptive Architecture: Integration and Patterns," *MSDN*, May 2004, available at http://msdn2.microsoft.com/en-us/library/ms978700.aspx.

[Mic07] Microsoft, "Patterns and Practices," *MSDN*, 2007, available at http://msdn2.microsoft.com/en-us/library/ms998478.aspx.

[Mil72] Mills, H. D., "Mathematical Foundations for Structured Programming," Technical Report FSC 71-6012, IBM Corp., Federal Systems Division, Gaithersburg, MD, 1972.

[Mil77] Miller, E., "The Philosophy of Testing," in *Program Testing Techniques*, IEEE Computer Society Press, 1977, pp. 1–3.

[Mil87] Mills, H. D., M. Dyer, and R. Linger, "Cleanroom Software Engineering," *IEEE Software*, September 1987, pp. 19–25.

[Mil88] Mills, H. D., "Stepwise Refinement and Verification in Box Structured Systems," *Computer*, vol. 21, no. 6, June 1988, pp. 23–35.

[Mil00a] Miller, E., "WebSite Testing," 2000, available at www.soft.com/eValid/Technology/White.Papers/website.testing.html.

[Mil00b] Mili, A., and R, Cowan, "Software Engineering Technology Watch," April 6, 2000, available at www.serc.net/projects/TechWatch/NSF%20TechWatch%20Proposal.htm.

[Min95] Minoli, D., *Analyzing Outsourcing*, McGraw-Hill, 1995.

[Mon84] Monk, A. (ed.), *Fundamentals of Human-Computer Interaction*, Academic Press, 1984.

[Mor81] Moran, T. P., "The Command Language Grammar: A Representation for the User Interface of Interactive Computer Systems," *Intl. Journal of Man-Machine Studies*, vol. 15, pp. 3–50.

[Mor05] Morales, A., "The Dream Team," *Dr. Dobbs Portal*, March 3, 2005, available at www.ddj.com/dept/global/184415303.

[Mus87] Musa, J. D., A. Iannino, and K. Okumoto, *Engineering and Managing Software with Reliability Measures*, McGraw-Hill, 1987.

[Mus93] Musa, J., "Operational Profiles in Software Reliability Engineering," *IEEE Software*, March 1993, pp. 14–32.

[Mut03] Mutafelija, B., and H. Stromberg, *Systematic Process Improvement Using ISO 9001:2000 and CMMI*, Artech, 2003.

[Mye78] Myers, G., *Composite Structured Design*, Van Nostrand, 1978.

[Mye79] Myers, G., *The Art of Software Testing*, Wiley, 1979.

[NAS07] NASA, *Software Risk Checklist*, Form LeR-F0510.051, March 2007, downloadable from http://osat-ext.grc.nasa.gov/rmo/spa/SoftwareRiskChecklist.doc.

[Nau69] Naur, P., and B. Randall (eds.), *Software Engineering: A Report on a Conference Sponsored by the NATO Science Committee*, NATO, 1969.

[Ngu00] Nguyen, H., "Testing Web-Based Applications," *Software Testing and Quality Engineering*, May–June 2000, available at www.stqemagazine.com.

[Ngu01] Nguyen, H., *Testing Applications on the Web*, Wiley, 2001.

[Ngu06] Nguyen, T., "Model-Based Version and Configuration Management for a Web Engineering Lifecycle," *Proc. 15th Intl. World Wide Web Conf.*, Edinburg, Scotland, 2006, download from www2006.org/programme/item.php?id=4552.

[Nie92] Nierstrasz, O., S. Gibbs, and D. Tsichritzis, "Component-Oriented Software Development," *CACM*, vol. 35, no. 9, September 1992, pp. 160–165.

[Nie94] Nielsen, J., and J. Levy, "Measuring Usability: Preference vs. Performance," *CACM*, vol. 37, no. 4, April 1994, pp. 65–75.

[Nie96] Nielsen, J., and A. Wagner, "User Interface Design for the WWW," *Proc. CHI '96 Conf. on Human Factors in Computing Systems*, ACM Press, 1996, pp. 330–331.

[Nie00] Nielsen, J., *Designing Web Usability*, New Riders Publishing, 2000.

[Nog00] Nogueira, J., C. Jones, and Luqi, "Surfing the Edge of Chaos: Applications to Software Engineering," Command and Control Research and Technology Symposium, Naval Post Graduate School, Monterey, CA, June 2000, downloadable from www.dodccrp.org/2000CCRTS/cd/html/pdf_papers/Track_4/075.pdf.

[Nor70] Norden, P., "Useful Tools for Project Management" in *Management of Production*, M. K. Starr (ed.), Penguin Books, 1970.

[Nor86] Norman, D. A., "Cognitive Engineering," in *User Centered Systems Design*, Lawrence Earlbaum Associates, 1986.

[Nor88] Norman, D., *The Design of Everyday Things*, Doubleday, 1988.

[Nov04] Novotny, O., "Next Generation Tools for Object-Oriented Development," *The Architecture Journal*, January 2005, available at http://msdn2.microsoft.com/en-us/library/aa480062.aspx.

[Noy02] Noyes, B., "Rugby, Anyone?" *Managing Development* (an online publication of Fawcette Technical Publications), June 2002, www.fawcette.com/resources/managingdev/methodologies/scrum/.

[Off02] Offutt, J., "Quality Attributes of Web Software Applications," *IEEE Software*, March–April 2002, pp. 25–32.

[Ols99] Olsina, L., et al., "Specifying Quality Characteristics and Attributes for Web Sites," *Proc. 1st ICSE Workshop on Web Engineering*, ACM, Los Angeles, May 1999.

[Ols06] Olsen, G., "From COM to Common," *Component Technologies*, ACM, vol. 4, no. 5, June 2006, available at http://acmqueue.com/modules.php?name=Content&pa=showpage&pid=394.

[OMG03a] Object Management Group, *OMG Unified Modeling Language Specification*, version 1.5, March 2003, available from www.rational.com/uml/resources/documentation/.

[OMG03b] "Object Constraint Language Specification," in *Unified Modeling Language*, v2.0, Object Management Group, September 2003, downloadable from www.omg.org.

[Orf99] Orfali, R., D. Harkey, and J. Edwards, *Client/Server Survival Guide*, 3d ed., Wiley, 1999.

[Osb90] Osborne, W. M., and E. J. Chikofsky, "Fitting Pieces to the Maintenance Puzzle," *IEEE Software*, January 1990, pp. 10–11.

[OSO08] OpenSource.org, 2008, available at www.opensource.org/.

[Pag85] Page-Jones, M., *Practical Project Management*, Dorset House, 1985, p. vii.

[Pal02] Palmer, S., and J. Felsing, *A Practical Guide to Feature Driven Development*, Prentice Hall, 2002.

[Par72] Parnas, D. L., "On Criteria to Be Used in Decomposing Systems into Modules," *CACM*, vol. 14, no. 1, April 1972, pp. 221–227.

[Par96a] Pardee, W., *To Satisfy and Delight Your Customer*, Dorset House, 1996.

[Par96b] Park, R. E., W. B. Goethert, and W. A. Florac, *Goal Driven Software Measurement— A Guidebook*, CMU/SEI-96-BH-002, Software Engineering Institute, Carnegie Mellon University, August 1996.

[Pat07] Patton, J., "Understanding User Centricity," *IEEE Software*, vol. 24, no. 6, November–December, 2007, pp. 9–11.

[Pau94] Paulish, D., and A. Carleton, "Case Studies of Software Process Improvement Measurement," *Computer*, vol. 27, no. 9, September 1994, pp. 50–57.

[PCM03] "Technologies to Watch," *PC Magazine*, July 2003, available at www.pcmag.com/ article2/0,4149,1130591,00.asp.

[Per74] Persig, R., *Zen and the Art of Motorcycle Maintenance*, Bantam Books, 1974.

[Pet06] Pethokoukis, J., "Small Biz Watch: Future Business Trends," *U.S. News & World Report*, January 20, 2006, available at www.usnews.com/usnews/biztech/articles/060120/ 20sbw.htm.

[Pha89] Phadke, M. S., *Quality Engineering Using Robust Design*, Prentice Hall, 1989.

[Pha97] Phadke, M. S., "Planning Efficient Software Tests," *CrossTalk*, vol. 10, no. 10, October 1997, pp. 11–15.

[Phi98] Phillips, D., *The Software Project Manager's Handbook*, IEEE Computer Society Press, 1998.

[Phi02] Phillips, M., "CMMI V1.1 Tutorial.," April 2002, available at www.sei.cmu.edu/cmmi/.

[Pol45] Polya, G., *How to Solve It*, Princeton University Press, 1945.

[Poo88] Poore, J. H., and H. D. Mills, "Bringing Software Under Statistical Quality Control," *Quality Progress*, November 1988, pp. 52–55.

[Poo93] Poore, J. H., H. D. Mills, and D. Mutchler, "Planning and Certifying Software System Reliability," *IEEE Software*, vol. 10, no. 1, January 1993, pp. 88–99.

[Pop03] Poppendieck, M., and T. Poppendieck, *Lean Software Development*, Addison-Wesley, 2003.

[Pop06a] Poppendeick, LLC, *Lean Software Development*, available at www.poppendieck.com/.

[Pop06b] Poppendieck, M., and T. Poppendieck, *Implementing Lean Software Development*, Addison-Wesley, 2006.

[Pop08] Popcorn, F., *Faith Popcorn's Brain Reserve*, 2008, available at www.faithpopcorn.com/.

[Pot04] Potter, M., *Set Theory and Its Philosophy: A Critical Introduction*, Oxford University Press, 2004.

[Pow98] Powell, T., *Web Site Engineering*, Prentice Hall, 1998.

[Pow02] Powell, T., *Web Design*, 2d ed., McGraw-Hill/Osborne, 2002.

[Pre94] Premerlani, W., and M. Blaha, "An Approach for Reverse Engineering of Relational Databases," *CACM*, vol. 37, no. 5, May 1994, pp. 42–49.

[Pre88] Pressman, R., *Making Software Engineering Happen*, Prentice Hall, 1988.

[Pre05] Pressman, R., *Adaptable Process Model*, revision 2.0, R. S. Pressman & Associates, 2005, available at www.rspa.com/apm/index.html.

[Pre08] Pressman, R., and D. Lowe, *Web Engineering: A Practitioner's Approach*, McGraw-Hill, 2008.

[Put78] Putnam, L., "A General Empirical Solution to the Macro Software Sizing and Estimation Problem," *IEEE Trans. Software Engineering*, vol. SE-4, no. 4, July 1978, pp. 345–361.

[Put92] Putnam, L., and W. Myers, *Measures for Excellence*, Yourdon Press, 1992.

[Put97a] Putnam, L., and W. Myers, "How Solved Is the Cost Estimation Problem?" *IEEE Software*, November 1997, pp. 105–107.

[Put97b] Putnam, L., and W. Myers, *Industrial Strength Software: Effective Management Using Measurement*, IEEE Computer Society Press, 1997.

[Pyz03] Pyzdek, T., *The Six Sigma Handbook*, McGraw-Hill, 2003.

[QAI08] *A Software Engineering Curriculum*, QAI, 2008, information can be obtained at www .qaieschool.com/innerpages/offer.asp.

[QSM02] "QSM Function Point Language Gearing Factors," Version 2.0, Quantitative Software Management, 2002, www.qsm.com/FPGearing.html.

[Rad02] Radice, R., *High-Quality Low Cost Software Inspections*, Paradoxicon Publishing, 2002.

[Rai06] Raiffa, H., *The Art and Science of Negotiation*, Belknap Press, 2005.

[Ree99] Reel, J. S., "Critical Success Factors in Software Projects," *IEEE Software*, May 1999, pp. 18–23.

[Ric01] Ricadel, A., "The State of Software Quality," *InformationWeek*, May 21, 2001, available at www.informationweek.com/838/quality.htm.

[Ric04] Rico, D., *ROI of Software Process Improvement*, J. Ross Publishing, 2004. A summary article can be found at http://davidfrico.com/rico03a.pdf.

[Roc94] Roche, J. M., "Software Metrics and Measurement Principles," *Software Engineering Notes*, ACM, vol. 19, no. 1, January 1994, pp. 76–85.

[Roc06] *Graphic Design That Works*, Rockport Publishers, 2006.

[Roe00] Roetzheim, W., "Estimating Internet Development," *Software Development*, August 2000, available at www.sdmagazine.com/documents/s=741/sdm0008d/0008d.htm.

[Roo96] Roos, J., "The Poised Organization: Navigating Effectively on Knowledge Landscapes," 1996, available at www.imd.ch/fac/roos/paper_po.html.

[Ros75] Ross, D., J. Goodenough, and C. Irvine, "Software Engineering: Process, Principles and Goals," *IEEE Computer*, vol. 8, no. 5, May 1975.

[Ros04] Rosenhainer, L., "Identifying Crosscutting Concerns in Requirements Specifications," 2004, available at http://trese.cs.utwente.nl/workshops/oopsla-early-aspects-2004/Papers/Rosenhainer.pdf.

[Rou02] Rout, T (project manager), *SPICE: Software Process Assessment—Part 1: Concepts and Introductory Guide*, 2002, downloadable from www.sqi.gu.edu.au/spice/suite/download.html.

[Roy70] Royce, W. W., "Managing the Development of Large Software Systems: Concepts and Techniques," *Proc. WESCON*, August 1970.

[Roz05] Rozanski, N., and E. Woods, *Software Systems Architecture*, Addison-Wesley, 2005.

[Rub88] Rubin, T., *User Interface Design for Computer Systems*, Halstead Press (Wiley), 1988.

[Rum91] Rumbaugh, J., et al., *Object-Oriented Modeling and Design*, Prentice Hall, 1991.

[Sar06] Sarwate, A., "Hot or Not: Web Application Vulnerabilities," *SC Magazine*, December 27, 2006, available at http://scmagazine.com/us/news/article/623765/hot-not-web-application-vulnerabilities.

[Sca00] Scacchi, W., "Understanding Software Process Redesign Using Modeling, Analysis, and Simulation," *Software Process Improvement and Practice*, Wiley, 2000, pp. 185–195, downloadable at www.ics.uci.edu/~wscacchi/Papers/Software_Process_Redesign/SPIP-ProSim99.pdf.

[Sce02] Sceppa, D., *Microsoft ADO.NET*, Microsoft Press, 2002.

[Sch95] Schwabe, D., and G. Rossi, "The Object-Oriented Hypermedia Design Model," *CACM*, vol. 38, no. 8, August 1995, pp. 45–46.

[Sch96] Schorsch, T., "The Capability Im-Maturity Model," *CrossTalk*, November 1996, available at www.stsc.hill.af.mil/crosstalk/1996/11/xt96d11h.asp.

[Sch98a] Schneider, G., and J. Winters, *Applying Use Cases*, Addison-Wesley, 1998.

[Sch98b] Schwabe, D., and G. Rossi, "Developing Hypermedia Applications Using OOHDM," *Proc. Workshop on Hypermedia Development Process, Methods and Models, Hypertext '98*, 1998, downloadable from http://citeseer.nj.nec.com/schwabe98developing.html.

[Sch98c] Schulmeyer, G. C., and J. I. McManus (eds.), *Handbook of Software Quality Assurance*, 3d ed., Prentice Hall, 1998.

[Sch99] Schneidewind, N., "Measuring and Evaluating Maintenance Process Using Reliability, Risk, and Test Metrics," *IEEE Trans. SE*, vol. 25, no. 6, November–December 1999, pp. 768–781, downloadable from www.dacs.dtic.mil/topics/reliability/IEEETrans.pdf.

[Sch01a] Schwabe, D., G. Rossi, and Barbosa, S., "Systematic Hypermedia Application Design Using OOHDM," 2001, available at www-di.inf.puc-rio.br/~schwabe/HT96WWW/section1.html.

[Sch01b] Schwaber, K., and M. Beedle, *Agile Software Development with SCRUM*, Prentice Hall, 2001.

[Sch02] Schwaber, K., "Agile Processes and Self-Organization," Agile Alliance, 2002, www.aanpo.org/articles/index.

[Sch03] Schlickman, J., *ISO 9001: 2000 Quality Management System Design*, Artech House Publishers, 2003.

[Sch06] Schmidt, D., "Model-Driven Engineering," *IEEE Computer*, vol. 39, no. 2, February 2006, pp. 25–31.

[SDS08] Spice Document Suite, "The SPICE and ISO Document Suite," ISO-Spice, 2008, available at www.isospice.com/articles/9/1/SPICE-Project/Page1.html.

[Sea93] Sears, A., "Layout Appropriateness: A Metric for Evaluating User Interface Widget Layout, *IEEE Trans. Software Engineering*, vol. SE-19, no. 7, July 1993, pp. 707–719.

[SEE03] The Software Engineering Ethics Research Institute, "UCITA Updates," 2003, available at http://seeri.etsu.edu/default.htm.

[SEI00] *SCAMPI, V1.0 Standard CMMI ®Assessment Method for Process Improvement: Method Description*, Software Engineering Institute, Technical Report CMU/SEI-2000-TR-009, downloadable from www.sei.cmu.edu/publications/documents/00.reports/00tr009.html.

[SEI02] "Maintainability Index Technique for Measuring Program Maintainability," SEI, 2002, available at www.sei.cmu.edu/str/descriptions/mitmpm_body.html.

[SEI08] "The Ideal Model," Software Engineering Institute, 2008, available at www.sei.cmu.edu/ideal/.

[Sha95a] Shaw, M., and D. Garlan, "Formulations and Formalisms in Software Architecture," *Volume 1000—Lecture Notes in Computer Science*, Springer-Verlag, 1995.

[Sha95b] Shaw, M., et al., "Abstractions for Software Architecture and Tools to Support Them," *IEEE Trans. Software Engineering*, vol. SE-21, no. 4, April 1995, pp. 314–335.

[Sha96] Shaw, M., and D. Garlan, *Software Architecture*, Prentice Hall, 1996.

[Sha05] Shalloway, A., and J. Trott, *Design Patterns Explained*, 2d ed., Addison-Wesley, 2005.

[Shn80] Shneiderman, B., *Software Psychology*, Winthrop Publishers, 1980, p. 28.

[Shn04] Shneiderman, B., and C. Plaisant, *Designing the User Interface*, 4th ed., Addison-Wesley, 2004.

[Sho83] Shooman, M. L., *Software Engineering*, McGraw-Hill, 1983.

[Sim05] Simsion, G., and G. Witt, *Data Modeling Essentials*, 3d ed., Morgan Kaufman, 2005.

[Sin99] Singpurwalla, N., and S. Wilson, *Statistical Methods in Software Engineering: Reliability and Risk*, Springer-Verlag, 1999.

[Smi99] Smith, J., "The Estimation of Effort Based on Use Cases," Rational Software Corp., 1999, downloadable from www.rational.com/media/whitepapers/finalTP171.PDF.

[Smi05] Smith, D, *Reliability, Maintainability and Risk*, 7th ed., Butterworth-Heinemann, 2005.

[Sne95] Sneed, H., "Planning the Reengineering of Legacy Systems," *IEEE Software*, January 1995, pp. 24–25.

[Sne03] Snee, R., and R. Hoerl, *Leading Six Sigma*, Prentice Hall, 2003.

[Sol99] van Solingen, R., and E. Berghout, *The Goal/Question/Metric Method*, McGraw-Hill, 1999.

[Som97] Somerville, I., and P. Sawyer, *Requirements Engineering*, Wiley, 1997.

[Som05] Somerville, I., "Integrating Requirements Engineering: A Tutorial," *IEEE Software*, vol. 22, no. 1, January–February 2005, pp. 16–23.

[SPI99] "SPICE: Software Process Assessment, Part 1: Concepts and Introduction," Version 1.0, ISO/IEC JTC1, 1999.

[Spl01] Splaine, S., and S. Jaskiel, *The Web Testing Handbook*, STQE Publishing, 2001.

[Spo02] Spolsky, J, "The Law of Leaky Abstractions," November 2002, available at www.joelonsoftware.com/articles/LeakyAbstractions.html.

[Sri01] Sridhar, M., and N. Mandyam, "Effective Use of Data Models in Building Web Applications," 2001, available at www2002.org/CDROM/alternate/698/.

[SSO08] Software-Supportability.org, www.software-supportability.org/, 2008.

[Sta97] Stapleton, J., *DSDM—Dynamic System Development Method: The Method in Practice*, Addison-Wesley, 1997.

[Sta97b] Statz, J., D. Oxley, and P. O'Toole, "Identifying and Managing Risks for Software Process Improvement," *CrossTalk*, April 1997, available at www.stsc.hill.af.mil/crosstalk/1997/04/identifying.asp.

[Ste74] Stevens, W., G. Myers, and L. Constantine, "Structured Design," *IBM Systems Journal*, vol. 13, no. 2, 1974, pp. 115–139.

[Ste93] Stewart, T. A., "Reengineering: The Hot New Managing Tool," *Fortune*, August 23, 1993, pp. 41–48.

[Ste99] Stelzer, D., and W. Mellis, "Success Factors of Organizational Change in Software Process Improvement," *Software Process Improvement and Practice*, vol. 4, no. 4, Wiley, 1999, downloadable from www.systementwicklung.uni-koeln.de/forschung/artikel/dokumente/successfactors.pdf.

[Ste03] Stephens, M., and D. Rosenberg, *Extreme Programming Refactored*, Apress, 2003.

[Sto05] Stone, D., et al., *User Interface Design and Evaluation*, Morgan Kaufman, 2005.

[Tai89] Tai, K. C., "What to Do Beyond Branch Testing," *ACM Software Engineering Notes*, vol. 14, no. 2, April 1989, pp. 58–61.

[Tay90] Taylor, D., *Object-Oriented Technology: A Manager's Guide*, Addison-Wesley, 1990.

[Tha97] Thayer, R. H., and M. Dorfman, *Software Requirements Engineering*, 2d ed., IEEE Computer Society Press, 1997.

[The01] Thelin, T., H. Petersson, and C. Wohlin, "Sample Driven Inspections," *Proc. of Workshop on Inspection in Software Engineering (WISE'01)*, Paris, France, July 2001, pp. 81–91, downloadable from http://www.cas.mcmaster.ca/wise/wise01/ThelinPeterssonWohlin.pdf.

[Tho92] Thomsett, R., "The Indiana Jones School of Risk Management," *American Programmer*, vol. 5, no. 7, September 1992, pp. 10–18.

[Tic05] *TickIT*, 2005, www.tickit.org/.

[Tid02] Tidwell, J., "IU Patterns and Techniques," May 2002, available at http://time-tripper.com/uipatterns/index.html.

[Til93] Tillmann, G., *A Practical Guide to Logical Data Modeling*, McGraw-Hill, 1993.

[Til00] Tillman, H., "Evaluating Quality on the Net," Babson College, May 30, 2000, available at www.hopetillman.com/findqual.html#2.

[Tog01] Tognozzi, B., "First Principles," *askTOG*, 2001, available at www.asktog.com/basics/firstPrinciples.html.

[Tra95] Tracz, W., "Third International Conference on Software Reuse—Summary," *ACM Software Engineering Notes*, vol. 20, no. 2, April 1995, pp. 21–22.

[Tre03] Trivedi, R, *Professional Web Services Security*, Wrox Press, 2003.

[Tri05] Tricker, R., and B. Sherring-Lucas, *ISO 9001: 2000 In Brief*, 2d ed., Butterworth-Heinemann, 2005.

[Tyr05] Tyree, J., and A. Akerman, "Architectural Decisions: Demystifying Architecture," *IEEE Software*, vol. 22, no. 2, March–April, 2005.

[Uem99] Uemura, T., S. Kusumoto, and K. Inoue: "A Function Point Measurement Tool for UML Design Specifications,'" *Proc. of Sixth International Symposium on Software Metrics*, IEEE, November 1999, pp. 62–69

[Ull97] Ullman, E., *Close to the Machine: Technophilia and Its Discontents*, City Lights Books, 2002.

[UML03] The UML Café, "Customers Don't Print Themselves," May 2003, available at www.theumlcafe.com/a0079.htm.

[Uni03] Unicode, Inc., *The Unicode Home Page*, 2003, available at www.unicode.org/.

[USA87] *Management Quality Insight*, AFCSP 800-14 (U.S. Air Force), January 20, 1987.

[Vac06] Vacca, J., *Practical Internet Security*, Springer, 2006.

[Van89] Van Vleck, T., "Three Questions About Each Bug You Find," *ACM Software Engineering Notes*, vol. 14, no. 5, July 1989, pp. 62–63.

[Van02] Van Steen, M., and A. Tanenbaum, *Distributed Systems: Principles and Paradigms*, Prentice Hall, 2002.

[Ven03] Venners, B., "Design by Contract: A Conversation with Bertrand Meyer," *Artima Developer*, December 8, 2003, available at www.artima.com/intv/contracts.html.

[Wal03] Wallace, D., I. Raggett, and J. Aufgang, *Extreme Programming for Web Projects*, Addison-Wesley, 2003.

[War74] Warnier, J. D., *Logical Construction of Programs*, Van Nostrand-Reinhold, 1974.

[War07] Ward, M., "Using VoIP Software Building zBlocks—A Look at the Choices," TMNNet, 2007, available at www.tmcnet.com/voip/0605/featurearticle-using-voip-software-building-blocks.htm.

[Web05] Weber, S., *The Success of Open Source*, Harvard University Press, 2005.

[Wei86] Weinberg, G., *On Becoming a Technical Leader*, Dorset House, 1986.

[Wel99] Wells, D., "XP—Unit Tests," 1999, available at www.extremeprogramming.org/rules/unittests.html.

[Wel01] vanWelie, M., "Interaction Design Patterns," 2001, available at www.welie.com/patterns/.

[Whi95] Whittle, B., "Models and Languages for Component Description and Reuse," *ACM Software Engineering Notes*, vol. 20, no. 2, April 1995, pp. 76–89.

[Whi97] Whitmire, S., *Object-Oriented Design Measurement*, Wiley, 1997.

[Wie02] Wiegers, K., *Peer Reviews in Software*, Addison-Wesley, 2002.

[Wie03] Wiegers, K., *Software Requirements*, 2d ed., Microsoft Press, 2003.

[Wil93] Wilde, N., and R. Huitt, "Maintaining Object-Oriented Software," *IEEE Software*, January 1993, pp. 75–80.

[Wil97] Williams, R. C, J. A. Walker, and A. J. Dorofee, "Putting Risk Management into Practice," *IEEE Software*, May 1997, pp. 75–81.

[Wil99] Wilkens, T. T., "Earned Value, Clear and Simple," Primavera Systems, April 1, 1999, p. 2.

[Wil00] Williams, L., and R. Kessler, "All I Really Need to Know about Pair Programming I Learned in Kindergarten," *CACM*, vol. 43, no. 5, May 2000, available at http://collaboration.csc.ncsu.edu/laurie/Papers/Kindergarten.PDF.

[Wil05] Willoughby, M., "Q&A: Quality Software Means More Secure Software," *Computerworld*, March 21, 2005, available at www.computerworld.com/securitytopics/security/story/0,10801,91316,00.html.

[Win90] Wing, J. M., "A Specifier's Introduction to Formal Methods," *IEEE Computer*, vol. 23, no. 9, September 1990, pp. 8–24.

[Wir71] Wirth, N., "Program Development by Stepwise Refinement," *CACM*, vol. 14, no. 4, 1971, pp. 221–227.

[Wir90] Wirfs-Brock, R., B. Wilkerson, and L. Weiner, *Designing Object-Oriented Software*, Prentice Hall, 1990.

[WMT02] Web Mapping Testbed Tutorial., 2002, available at www.webmapping.org/vcgdocuments/vcgTutorial/.

[Woh94] Wohlin, C., and P. Runeson, "Certification of Software Components," *IEEE Trans. Software Engineering*, vol. SE-20, no. 6, June 1994, pp. 494–499.

[Wor04] World Bank, *Digital Technology Risk Checklist*, 2004, downloadable from www.moonv6.org/lists/att-0223/WWBANK_Technology_Risk_Checklist_Ver_6point1.pdf.

[W3C03] World Wide Web Consortium, *Web Content Accessibility Guidelines*, 2003, available at www.w3.org/TR/2003/WD-WCAG20-20030624/.

[Yac03] Yacoub, S., et al., *Pattern-Oriented Analysis and Design*, Addison-Wesley, 2003.

[You75] Yourdon, E., *Techniques of Program Structure and Design*, Prentice Hall, 1975.

[You79] Yourdon, E., and L. Constantine, *Structured Design*, Prentice Hall, 1979.

[You95] Yourdon, E., "When Good Enough Is Best," *IEEE Software*, vol. 12, no. 3, May 1995, pp. 79–81.

[You01] Young, R., *Effective Requirements Practices*, Addison-Wesley, 2001.

[Zah90] Zahniser, R. A., "Building Software in Groups," *American Programmer*, vol. 3, nos. 7–8, July–August 1990.

[Zah94] Zahniser, R., "Timeboxing for Top Team Performance," *Software Development*, March 1994, pp. 35–38.

[Zha98] Zhao, J, "On Assessing the Complexity of Software Architectures," *Proc. Intl. Software Architecture Workshop*, ACM, Orlando, FL, 1998, pp. 163–167.

[Zha02] Zhao, H., "Fitt's Law: Modeling Movement Time in HCI," *Theories in Computer Human Interaction*, University of Maryland, October 2002, available at www.cs.umd.edu/class/fall2002/cmsc838s/tichi/fitts.html.

[Zul92] Zultner, R., "Quality Function Deployment for Software: Satisfying Customers," *American Programmer*, February 1992, pp. 28–41.

[Zus90] Zuse, H., *Software Complexity: Measures and Methods*, DeGruyter, 1990.

[Zus97] Zuse, H., *A Framework of Software Measurement*, DeGruyter, 1997.